2000

BROOKMAN

UNITED STATES, UNITED NATIONS & CANADA

STAMPS & POSTAL COLLECTIBLES

FEATURING
SPECIALIZED LISTINGS
OF

STATE DUCK & INDIAN RESERVATION STAMPS
PLATE NO. COILS & UNEXPLODED BOOKLETS
U.S. SOUVENIR CARDS • PAGES • PANELS

UNITED STATES FIRST DAY COVERS

Plus

Confederate States
U.S. Possessions
U.S. Trust Territories
Canadian Provinces
U.N. First Day Covers

ILLUSTRATED/GRADING GUIDE

SUBJECT INDEX, IDENTIFIER & BIBLIOGRAPHY

1999
BROOKMAN

TERMS AND INFORMATION

CONDITION - We price United States stamps issued prior to 1890 in two grades - Average and Fine. From 1890 to present we list a price for F-VF and VF quality. **FOR INFORMATION ON GRADING SEE PAGE vii.**

GUM AND HINGING

Original Gum (O.G.)
    Prior to 1882, Unused stamps may have partial or no gum. If you require o.g., add the percentage indicated in ( ). **Example** (OG + 25%). From 1882 to present, o.g. can be expected, but stamps may have been hinged or have hinge remnants.

Never Hinged
    Most issues are priced in F-VF, Never Hinged condition. Premiums for Average, NH usually run about half the F-VF premium. Prices for Never Hinged stamps on issues prior to1882 will be quoted upon request.

SPECIAL PRICING INSTRUCTIONS

Average - From 1890-1934 **Average hinged perforated** stamps, when available, will be priced at 60-70% of the F-VF Hinged price depending upon the general quality of the issue.

    Average hinged imperforate stamps, when available, will be priced at 70-75% of the F-VF Hinged price depending upon the general quality of the issue.

    From 1935 to present, average quality, when available, will be priced at 20% below the F-VF price.

Very Fine NH, 1935-Date
    VF NH singles, plate blocks, line pairs, etc. are available (unless specifically priced at the following premiums: Add 10¢ to any item priced under 50¢. Add 20% to any item priced at 50¢ and up. Unless priced as Very Fine, sets are not available Very Fine and stamps should be listed individually with appropriate premium.

Very Fine Unused O.G. Plate Blocks & Line Pairs
    Very Fine Unused Plate Blocks and Line Pairs prior to #749 & 723 (and selected Back-of-the-Book Issues) are generally available at the respective F-VF NH price.

Very Fine Used
    From 1847-1934, Very Fine Used stamps, when available, are priced by adding the % indicated to the appropriate Fine or F-VF price. **Example** (VF + 50%).
    From 1935 to date, the premiums are the same as for VF NH copies.

MINIMUM ORDER OF $20 - Present day costs force us to require that mail orders total a minimum of $20.00. Send payment with order.

PRICES - Every effort will be made to maintain these prices throughout the life of this edition. However, prices are subject to change if market conditions require. We are not responsible for typographical errors.

BROOKMAN/BARRETT & WORTHEN
10 Chestnut Drive
Bedford, NH 03110
Phone (603) 472-5575
Fax (603) 472-8795
PRINTED IN USA

Edited By David S. Macdonald
First Day Covers Contributing Editors
Robert G. Driscoll
James McCusker

Front & Back Cover Photos Courtesy of Dale Enterprises, Inc. and Brookman/Barrett & Worthen

TABLE OF CONTENTS

STAMPS

TERMS AND INFORMATION..ii.
INDEX TO ADVERTISERS...iii.
GRADING GUIDE ....iv.
INTRODUCTION...v-vi.
COMMEMORATIVE IDENTIFIER................................vii-x.
DEFINITIVE IDENTIFIER ....xi-xvii.
SELECTED BIBLIOGRAPHY .... xx.

UNITED STATES
Air Mails 92-96
Autopost & Variable Rate 101
Certified Mail 97
Christmas Seal First Day Covers 173
Coil Plate Numbers Strips....................................102-104
Coil Plate Number First Day Covers.......................164-165
Commemorative Panels 185-186
Commemorative Year Sets 90
Errors 110-111
First Day Covers..139-174
Hunting Permit Stamps (Federal) 122
Hunting Permit Stamps (State) 125-127
Inauguration Covers..175
Indian Reservation Stamps 132
Mint Sheets 19-84,89-93
Offices in China...100
Officials 99-100
Parcel Post & Parcel Post Dues 100
Plate Number Blocks 6-84, 92-97
Postage 1-84
Postage Dues 98
Postal Stationery - Mint 112-115
Registration 97
Revenues 116-121
Savings Stamps 101
Self-Adhesive Coils, Panes and Booklets 106
Souvenir Cards 176-180
Souvenir Pages 181-184
Special Delivery 97
Special Handling...100
Test Coils 101
Unexploded Booklets 107-109
U.S.P.S. Mint Sets 90
World War II Patriotic Covers 174

U.S. RELATED AREAS
Canal Zone 187-189
Confederate States...187
Cuba..189
Guam..190
Hawaii..190
Marshall Islands 191-195
Micronesia..196-197
Palau 199-201
Philippines 191
Puerto Rico..191

UNITED NATIONS
U.N. New York 203-209
U.N. Geneva 211-213
U.N. Vienna 215-217
U.N. First Day Covers 219-224
U.N. Souvenir Cards 218
Postal Stationery - Mint 209,213,214,216

CANADA & PROVINCES
British Columbia...258
Canada 225-252
Canada Hunting Permit Stamps...............................253
Canada Year Sets 248
New Brunswick 258
Newfoundland 254-57
Nova Scotia 258
Prince Edward Island 258

DISCOUNT COUPONS 261
ORDER FORMS AND ADS..262-282

INDEX TO ADVERTISERS

Page #	Advertiser	Page #	Advertiser
89	American Topical Association	270	Linn's Stamp News
133	American First Day Cover Soc.	141	James T. McCusker, Inc.
105	American Philatelic Society	xxi	Mekeel's & Stamps Magazine
153	Artmaster Incorporated	2	Alan Miller Stamps
13	Brooklyn Gallery	15	Miller's Stamp Shop
105,137-8,162,167,272-75	Brookman/Barrett & Worthen	87	Plate Block Stamp Company
75	Brookman Stamp Company	xxii	Gary Posner, Inc.
81,260	Brookman Times	269	Regency Stamps, Ltd.
225	Champion Stamp Co., Inc.	210	Scottonline.com
91, 92	Dale Enterprises, Inc.	249	Scott Stamp Monthly
279	D&N Petro	276	Stamp Finder
121	Eric Jackson	270	Stampsites.com
9	Henry Gitner Philatelist, Inc.	xxi	U.S. Stamp News
91	Global Stamp News	282	Vidiforms Co., Inc.
123	Michael Jaffe Stamps	42c	World Stamp Expo
271	Krause Publications	5, 259	2000 Giveaway Contest

Postal Reply Cards, Covers and Color Inserts

42a	American Stamp Dealers Association
42d	Brookman/Barrett & Worthen
10a	Dale Enterprises, Inc.
10a, 10c	Linn's Stamp News
10d, 42a	Kenmore Stamp Co.
10a	American Philatelic Society
42a, Inside Front Cover	Stamp Collector
Inside Back Cover	Vidiforms

Featured Articles

v-vi	Welcome to Stamp Collecting by The American Philatelic Society
xviii-xix	Adventures in Topicals by George Griffenhagen, Editor Topical Times
120	The Beginning of State Duck Stamps by Michael Jaffe, Michael Jaffe Stamps
129-130	Welcome To First Day Cover Collecting by Barry Newton, Editor First Days
131-132	Fascinating Firsts - First Cachets by Marjory J. Sente

We wish to thank the advertisers who help keep the Brookman Price Guide available at the lowest possible price. We urge you to support our advertisers and let them know their ads were helpful to you.

BROOKMAN GRADING GUIDE

The following guide is a simplified approach to stamp grading designed to help you better understand the quality you can expect to receive when you order a specific grade. All grades listed below are for undamaged stamps free of faults such as tears, thin spots, creases, straight edges, scrapes, etc. Stamps with those defects are considered "seconds" and sell for prices below those listed. The stamps you receive may not always match the criteria given since each stamp must be judged on its own special merits such as freshness, color, cancellation, etc. For example: a well centered stamp may be graded only as "Average" because of a very heavy cancellation. Grading stamps is an art, not a science, and frequently the cliche "beauty is in the eye of the beholder" applies. Stamps offered throughout this price list fall into the "Group A" category unless the heading contains a (B) or (C).

GROUP A - WELL CENTERED ISSUES

| Average | Average | Average | Average |

| F-VF | F-VF | F-VF | F-VF |

| Very Fine | Very Fine | Very Fine | Very Fine |

GROUP A	AVERAGE	F-VF	VERY FINE
PERFORATED STAMPS	Perforations touch or barely clear of design on one or two sides.	Perforations well clear of design on all sides.	Design very well centered within perforations.
IMPERFORATE STAMPS	One edge may touch design.	All four edges are clear of design.	Four edges are well clear of and well centered around design.
COILS AND BOOKLET PANES	Perforated and imperforate edge may touch design on one or two edges.	Perforated and imperforate edges are clear of the design.	Design very well centered within perforated and imperf. edges.

NOTE: Stamps of poorer centering than "Average" grade are considered seconds.

"EXTREMELY FINE" is a grading term used to describe stamps that are almost "Perfect" in centering, color, freshness, cancellations, etc. This grade, when available, is priced substantially higher than Very Fine quality.

GROUP B - MEDIAN CENTERED ISSUES

| Average | Average | Average | Average | Average |

| F-VF | F-VF | Very Fine | Very Fine | Very Fine |

GROUP B	AVERAGE	F-VF	VERY FINE
PERFORATED STAMPS	Perforations touch or barely cut into design on one or two sides.	Perforations clear of design on all four sides.	Design well centered within perforations.
IMPERFORATE STAMPS	One or two edges may touch or barely cut into design.	All four edges are clear of design as in "A".	Four edges are well clear of and well centered around design as in "A".
COILS AND BOOKLET PANES	Perforated and imperforate edge may touch or barely cut into design.	Perforated and imperforate edges are clear of design as in "A".	Design well centered within perforated and imperforated edges.

GROUP C - POORLY CENTERED ISSUES

| Average | Average | Average | Average | Average |

| Fine | Fine | Very Fine | Very Fine | Very Fine |

GROUP C	AVERAGE	FINE	VERY FINE
PERFORATED STAMPS	Perforations may cut into design on one or more sides.	Perforations touch or just clear of design on or more sides.	Perforations will clear design on all four sides.
IMPERFORATE STAMPS	One or more edges may cut into design.	One or more edges touch the design.	All four edges clear of the design.
COILS AND BOOKLET PANES	Perforated and imp. edge may cut into design on one or more sides.	Perforated and imperforate edges may touch or just clear design.	Perforated & imperforated edges well clear of design on all four sides.

Welcome to Stamp Collecting!

Challenge...information...friendships... and just plain fun are part of "the World's Most Popular Hobby," stamp collecting! For more than 150 years, stamp collecting has been the hobby choice of royalty, movie stars, sports celebrities, and hundreds of thousands of other people. Why do so many different types of people like stamps? One reason is, the hobby of stamp collecting suits almost anybody -- it's very personal. You fit the hobby to yourself, instead of forcing yourself to fit rules, as with many hobbies. There's not much free choice about how to play golf or softball or square dance -- there are many rules.

But stamp collecting can be done in a very simple way using stamps you find on your everyday mail and place on plain paper in a three-ring binder. Or you can give a "want list" to a stamp dealer. He will pull the stamps you want from his stock, and you mount them in the correct spaces in a custom-made album that you bought.

Or you can go to stamp shows or stamp shops and spend hours looking through boxes of stamps and envelopes in search of a particular stamp with a certain postal marking or a special first-day cover that has a meaning to suit your own interests.

Stamp collecting is a special mix of the structured and the unstructured, and you can make it a personal hobby that will not be like anyone else's. It's a world all its own, and anyone can find a comfortable place in it.

"Stamp Collector" or "Philatelist"?

Some people think that a "philatelist" (fi-LAT-uh-list) means someone who is more expert or serious than someone who is a "stamp collector." That's not true! But one advantage of using the word "philately" (fi-LAT-uh-lee) is that it includes all areas of the hobby -- not just stamps -- such as postal markings, postal history, postal stationery, and the postal items from the time before there were stamps, such as folded letters.

Finding Material for Your Collection

You can easily find everything for your stamp hobby by mail. Stamps, other philatelic material, catalogues, albums, and so on are easy to get by mail order. The philatelic press carries advertising for all of these hobby needs, and stamp shows in your area also will have dealers there. If you are lucky, you also may have a retail stamp store nearby.

Stamp shows may be small one- or two-day events in your local area, or very large events in big-city convention halls lasting several days and featuring hundreds of dealers and thousands of pages of stamp exhibits to see. Stamp shows also provide chances to meet other collectors, some of whom you may have "met" only by mail before.

How to Learn About Your New Hobby

Organizations, publications, and other collectors can help you grow in the hobby. The hobbies/recreation section of your local library may have basic books about stamp collecting, and the reference department may have a set of catalogs.

If your local library has no books on stamp collecting, you can borrow some from the huge collection of the American Philatelic Research Library through interlibrary loan or by becoming a member of the American Philatelic Society.

The APS/APRL are the largest stamp club and library in the United States and offer many services to collectors, including a 100-page monthly magazine, insurance for stamp collections, and a Sales Division through which members can buy and sell stamps by mail among themselves. The APS/APRL are at P.O. Box 8000, State College, PA 16803, or call (814) 237-3803.

There also are many newspapers and magazines in the stamp hobby, including Linn's Stamp News, Stamp Collector, Scott Monthly Journal, Mekeel's, Global Stamp News, and Stamps. Some can be found on large newsstands.

Taking Care of Your Collection

Paper is very fragile and must be handled with care. Stamp collectors use special tools and

materials to protect their collectibles. Stamp tongs may look like cosmetic tweezers, but they have special tips that will not damage stamps, so be sure to buy your tongs from a stamp dealer and not in the beauty section at the drugstore!

Stamp albums and other storage methods (temporary file folders and boxes, envelopes, etc.) should be of archival-quality acid-free paper, and any plastic used on or near stamps and covers (postally-used envelopes of philatelic interest) also should be archival -- as used for safe storage by museums. Plastic that is not archivally safe has oil-based softeners that can leach out and do much damage to stamps. In recent years philatelic manufacturers have become more careful about their products, and it is easy now to find safe paper and plastic for hobby use.

Never use cellophane or other tapes around your stamps. Even so-called "magic" tape will cause damage that cannot be undone. Stamps should be put on pages either with hinges (small rectangles of special gummed paper) or with mounts (little self-adhesive plastic envelopes in many sizes to fit stamps and covers). Mounts keep stamps in the condition in which you bought them. Also available are pages with strips of plastic attached to them; these are "self-mounting" pages, meaning all you have to do is slip your stamp into the plastic strip.

Other hobby tools include gauges, for measuring the perforations on stamps, and watermark fluid, which makes the special marks in some stamp papers visible momentarily. "Perfs" and watermarks are important if you decide to do some types of specialized collecting.

A Stamp Is a Stamp?

Not really -- a stamp can be many things: a feast for the eye with beautiful design and color and printing technique...a study in history as you find out about the person, place, or event behind the stamp...a mystery story, as you try to find out how and why this stamp and envelope traveled and received certain postal markings. Collectors who enjoy postal history always want the stamp with its envelope, which is one reason why you should not be quick to soak stamps off their covers. If you find an old hoard of

envelopes, get some advice before you take the stamps off!

Some collectors enjoy the "scientific" side of the hobby, studying production methods and paper and ink types. This also might include collecting stamps in which something went wrong in production: errors, freaks, and oddities. Studying watermarks takes special fluids and lighting equipment, also needed to study the luminescent inks used on modern stamps to trigger high-tech canceling equipment in the post office.

Other branches of collecting include first-day covers (FDCs), which carry a stamp on the first day it was sold with that day's postmark. Some FDCs have a cachet (ca-SHAY), which is a design on the envelope that relates to the stamp and adds an attractive quality to the cover. Some clubs, catalogues, and dealers specialize in FDCs.

Clubs, etc.

It is possible to collect for a lifetime and never leave home -- get everything you need by mail -- but a lot of enjoyment can be added if you join a club or go to stamp shows and exhibitions, and meet other collectors like yourself. Local clubs usually have a general focus, have meetings, and may organize stamp shows as part of their activities. Specialty-collecting groups, which may focus on stamps of one country or one type of stamp, will have a publication as the main service to members, but may have other activities and occasional meetings at large stamp shows. The American Philatelic Society, "America's Stamp Club," is the oldest and largest stamp organization in the United States and has served hundreds of thousands of collectors since 1886.

Again, Welcome to Stamp Collecting!

The more you know about it, the more you will like it -- Happy Collecting!

This introduction was prepared by the American Philatelic Society, the oldest and largest national stamp organization in the United States. Information on membership benefits and services is available from APS, P.O. Box 8000, State College, PA 16803; telephone 237-3803.

COMMEMORATIVE, SPECIAL ISSUE & AIR MAIL IDENTIFIER

A

Abbott & Costello 2566
Acadia 746,762
Accounting, Certified Public 2361
Acheson, Dean 2755
Adams, Abigail 2146
Adams, John 2216b
Adams, John Q 2216f
Addams, Jane 878
African Elephant Herd 1388
Agave 1943
Aging Together 2011
AIDS Awareness 2806,2806b
Aircraft, American 3142
Air Force, U.S. C49
Air Force, 50th Anniv. 3167
Air Mail, 50th Anniversary C74
Airlift 1341
Alabama Statehood 1375
Alamo, The 776, 778d
Alaska Statehood 2066,C53
Alaska Territory 800,C131
Alaska Highway 2635
Alaska Purchase C70
Alaska-Yukon Expo 370-371
Alaskan Brown Bear 2310
Albania, Flag 918
Alcoholism 1927
Alcott, Louisa May 862
Alexandria, Virginia C40
Alger, Horatio 2010
Alliance for Progress 1234
Allied Nations 907
Alligator 1428
Alpine Skiing 3180
Alta California 1725
Amateur Radio 1260
America 2426,2512,C121,C131
Amer. Bankers Association 987
American Aircraft 3142
American Arts 1484-87,1553-55
American Automobile Assoc 1007
American Bald Eagle 1387
American Bankers Association 987
American Bar Association 1022
American Bicentennial 1456-59, 1476-79,1480-83,1543-46,1559-68, 1629-31,1686-94,1704,1716-20, 1722,1726,1728,1753,1937-38,2052
American Buffalo 1392
American Chemical Soc 1002,1685
American Dolls 3151
American Elk 2328
American Folklore 1317,1330, 1357,1370,1470,1548
American Indian 1364
American Indian Dances 3072-3076
American Inst. of Architects 1089
American Legion 1369
American Lobster 2304
American Music 1252
American Philatelic Society 750
American Revolution Bicentennial 1432
AMERIPEX '86 2145,2216-2219
Annapolis Tercentenary 984
Antarctic Treaty 1431,C130
Anthony, Susan B 784
Anti-aircraft Gun 900
Antillean Euphonia 3222
Anti-Pollution 1410-1413
Apollo 8 1371
Apollo-Soyuz 1569-1570
Appleseed, Johnny 1317
Appomattox Surrender 1182
Apprenticeship 1201
Arbor Day 717
Architecture, American 1779-1782, 1838-1841,1928-1931,2019-2022
Arctic Animals 3288-92
Arctic Explorations 1128
Arctic Fox 3289
Arctic Hare 3288
Arizona Statehood 1192
Arkansas River Navigation 1358
Arkansas Statehood 782,2167
Arlen, Harold 3100
Armadillo 2296
Armed Forces Reserve 1067
Armstrong, Edwin 2056
Armstrong, Louis 2982,2983
Army 785-789,934
Army, Continental 1565
Art, American 3236
Art Deco Style 3184j
Arthur, Chester A 2218c
Articles of Confederation 1726
Artists 884-888
Atlanta Olympics 3068
Atlantic Cable 1112
Atomic Energy Act 1200
Atoms for Peace 1070
Audubon, John J 874, 1241, 3236e, C71
Australia Bicentennial 2370
Austria, Flag 919
Authors 859-863
Automat, The 3184n
Automated Post Office 1164
Automobile, Electric 296
Automobiles 2385a
Automobiles, Antique 3019-23
Avant-Garde Art 3183d

B

Badger 2312
Bailey, Mildred 2860
Bailey, Liberty Hyde 1100
Balboa, Vasco Nunez de 397,401
Bald Eagle 771,940,1387,1831,2309
Ballet 1749,3237
Balloons 2032-2035,2530
Balloon - Jupiter C54
Baltimore & Ohio Railroad 1006
Banking and Commerce 1577-1578
Banneker, Benjamin 1804
Bara, Theda 2872
Barber, Samuel 3162
Barn Swallow 2286
Barrel Cactus 1942
Barry, John 790
Barrymore, John/Ethel/Lionel 2012
Bartholdi, Frederic Auguste 2147
Barton, Clara 967,2975c
Baseball 855,1370,1381,2016, 2046,2089,2097,2417,2619
Baseball World Series 3182n
Basketball - Naismith 1189,2560
Bass, Largemouth 2207
Beaut. of America 1318,1365-1368
Beach Umbrella 2443
Beau Geste 2447
Beaver 2316
Beavertail Cactus 1944
Beckwourth, Jim 2869q,2870q
Belgium, Flag 914
Bell, Alexander Graham 893, 1683
Benet, StephenVincent 3221
Benny, Jack 2564
Bergen & McCarthy 2563
Berlin Airlift 3211
Bethune, Mary McLeod 2137
Bierstadt, Albert 3236m
Big Band Leaders 3096-3099
Big Brothers/Big Sisters 2162
Bighorn Sheep 1467,2288
Biglin Brothers 1335
Bill of Rights 1312,2421
Bill, Pecos 3086
Bingham, George Caleb 3236f
Birds 1953-2002,2439,2646a
Birth of Liberty 618
Bison 2320
Bissell, Emily 1823
Black Bear 2299
Black Heritage 1744,1771 1804,1875,2016,2044,2073,2137,2203 2249,2371,2402,2442,567,2617,2746, 2816,2956,3058,3121,3181,3273
Black-footed Ferret 2333
Blacksmith 1718
Black-tailed Jack Rabbit 2305
Black-tailed Prairie Dog 2325
Blair, Montgomery C66
Blake, Eubie 2988
Blood Donor 1425
Blue Jay 2318
Blue Paloverde 3194
Blues Artists 2854-2861
Boar, Year of the 2876
Bobcat 2332
Bobwhite 2301
Bogart, Humphrey 3152
Bolivar, Simon 1110-1111
Boone, Daniel 1357
Boston Tea Party 1480-1483
Botanical Congress 1376-1379
Boulder Dam 774
Bow, Clara 2820
Boxing, Ash Can School 3182h
Box Turtle 2326
Boy Scouts 995,1145,2161,3183j
Boys' Clubs of America 1163
Braddock's Field 688
Breast Cancer Awareness 3081
Breast Cancer Research B1
Brice, Fanny 2565
Bridge at Niagara Falls 297
Bridge, Mississippi River 293,3209i
Bridger, Jim 2869c,2870c
Bright Eyes 3230-34
Broad-tailed Hummingbird 2289
Broadway Musicals 2770a
Brooklyn Bridge 2041
Brooklyn, Battle of 1003
Brown Pelican 1466
Brussels International Exhib 1104
Bryant, Bear 3143, 3148
Buchanan, James 2217f
Buffalo Soldiers 2818
Bugs Bunny 3137-38c
Bunker Hill, Battle of 1564
Bunyan, Paul 3084
Burbank, Luther 876
Bureau of Engraving & Printing 2875
Burgoyne 644,1728
Butterflies 1712-1715
Byrd Antarctic 733,753,768,2388

C

Cabrillo, Juan Rodriguez 2704
Cadillac, Landing of 1000
Calder, Alexander 3198-3202
California Gold Centennial 954
California Sea Lion 2329
California Settlement 1373
California Statehood 997
California-Pacific Exposition 773,778b
Cambridge 617
Camellia 1877
Camp Fire Girls 1167
Camp Fire, Inc 2163
Canada Centenary 1324
Canada Goose 2334
Canada-U.S. Friendship 961
Canal Locks, Sault Ste. Marie 298
Cancer 1263,1754
Cape Hatteras 1448-1451
CAPEX '78 1757
Cardinal 1465
Cardinal Honeyeater 3225
CARE 1439
Caribbean Coast C127
Carmichael, Hoagy 3103
Carnegie, Andrew 1171
Carolina Charter 1230
Carolina-Charleston 683
Carousel Animals 2390-2393
Carousel Horses 2976-2979
Carson, Kit 2869n,2870n
Carter Family, The 2773,2776
Caruso, Enrico 2250
Carver, George Washington 953,3183c
Cashman, Nellie 2869k,2870k
Cassatt, Mary 1322,3236o
Catfish 2209
Cather, Willa 1487
Catlin, George 3236k
Cats 2372-2375,3232
Catt, Carrie Chapman 959
Cattle 1504
Celebrate the Century 3182-91
Century of Progress 728-731,766-767,C18
Certified Public Accounting 2361
Champions of Liberty 1096,1110-11, 1117-18,1125-26,1136-37,1147-48, 1159-60,1165-66,1168-69,1174-75
Chancellorsville, Battle of 2975p
Chaney, Lon 2822, 3168
Chaney Jr., Lon 3172
Chanute, Octave C93-C94
Chaplains, Four 956
Chaplin, Charlie 2821,3183a
Charleston, SC 683
Chautauqua 1505
Chemical Society, American 1002
Chemistry 1685
Cherokee Strip 1360,2754
Chesnut, Mary 2975o
Chief Joseph 1364,2869f,2870f
Child Labor Reform 3183o
Children Learn, Helping 3125
Children's Classics 2785-88
Children's Friendship 1085
China Clipper C20-C22
China, Republic of 1188
Chinese New Year 2720,2817, 2876,3060,3120, 3179,3272
Chinese Resistance 906
Christmas 1205,1240, 1254-7,1276,1321,1336,1363,1384, 1414-18,1444-45,1471-72,1507-08, 1550-52,1579-80,1701-03,1729-30, 1768-69,1799-1800,1842-43,1939-0, 2025-30,2063-64,2107-08,2165-66, 2244-45,2367-68,2399-2400,2427-29, 2514-15,2578-85b,2710-19, 2789-2803a,2871-74a,3003-18, 3107-17, 3176-77,3244-52
Church, Frederic Edwin 3236n
Churchill, Winston S 1264
Cinco de Mayo 3203,3309
CIPEX 948
Circus, American 1309,2750-53
City Mail Delivery 1238
City of Refuge, Hawaii C84
Civil Service 2053
Civil War 2975
Civil War Centennial 1178-1182
Civilian-Conservation Corps 2037
Clark, George Rogers 651
Classic Books 2785-88
Classic Films 2445-48
Clemens, Samuel L 863
Clemente, Roberto 2097
Cleveland, Grover 2218d
Cline, Patsy 2772,2777
Coast and Geodetic Survey 1088
Coast Guard 936
Cochran, Jacqueline 3066
Cod, Atlantic 2206
Cody, Buffalo Bill 2869b,2870b
Cohan, George M 1756
Cole, Nat "King" 2852
Coleman, Bessie 2956
Collective Bargaining 1558
Colonial Communications 1476-1479
Colonial Craftsmen 1456-59
Colorado Statehood 1001,1711
Coltrane, John 2991
Columbia University 1029
Columbus, C. 230-45,2616,2620-29
Columbus-Puerto Rico 2805
Comedians 2566a
Comic Strips 3000
Commercial Aviation 1684
Common Dolphin 2511
Communications for Peace 1173
Communicaton, Pioneers of 3061-3064
Compact, Signing of the 550
Composers 879-883
Composers, Conducters & 3158-65
Computer Technology 3106
Comstock, Henry 1130
Concord 1683 2040
Condor, California 1430
Conductors & Composers 3158-65
Confederate Veterans, United 998
Confederation, Articles of 1726
Connecticut Statehood 2340
Connecticut Tercentenary 772,778a
Conservation 2074
Constitution Bicent 2412-2415
Constitution Drafting 2359a
Constitution Ratification 835,2336-48
Constitution Signing 798,2360
Constitution, U.S. Frigate 951
Construction Toys 3183n
Consumer Education 2005
Continental Army 1565
Continental Congress 1543-1546
Continental Marines 1567
Continental Navy 1566
Contrib. to the Cause 1559-1562
Cook, Capt. James 1732-1733
Coolidge, Calvin 2219b
Cooper, James Fenimore 860
Copernicus, Nicolaus 1488
Copley, John Singleton 1273
Coral Reefs 1827-1830
Cord (automobile) 2383
Coronado Expedition 898
Corregidor 925
Cottontail 2290
Count Basie 3096
Country Music 2771-74,2778a
CPA 2361
Cranes 2867-2868
Crater Lake 745,761
Crayola Crayons 3182d
Credit Union Act 2075
Credoes, American 1139-1144
Crested Honeycreeper 3224
Crime Prevention 2102
Crippled, Hope for 1385
Crockett, Davy 1330
Crosby, Bing 2850
Crossword Puzzle 3183l
Curtiss, Glenn C100
Curtiss, Jenny C1-C3, C74
Cutler, Manasseh 795
Cycling 3119
Czechoslovakia, Flag 910

D

Daffy Duck 3306-7
Dahlia 1878
Dance, American 1749-1752
Dante 1268
Dare, Virginia 796
Dartmouth College Case 1380
Davis, Benjamin O 3121
Davis, Dr. Allison 2816
Davis, Jefferson 2975f
Davis Sr., Benjamin O. 3121
Deaf Communication 2783-84
Dean, James 3082
Decatur, Stephen 791
Decl. of Indep 627,1687,1691-94
Deer Mouse 2324
Defense, National 899-901
de Grasse, Gen 703
Delaware 2336
Dempsey, Jack 3183m
Denmark, Flag 920
Dental Health 1135
Depression, America Survives 3185m
Desert Plants 1942-1945
Desert Shield, Storm 2551-52
Devils Tower 1084
Dickinson, Emily 1436
Dickson, William 3064
Dinosaurs 1390,2422-25
Dinosaurs, World of 3136
Dirksen, Everett 1874
Disabled 1925
Disabled Veterans 1421
Discobolus 3087
Disney, Walt 1355
District of Columbia 2561
Doctors 949
Dog, Year of the 2817
Dogs 1787,2098-2101,3230
Dolls, American 3151
Dorsey, Tommy & Jimmy 3097
Douglass, Frederick 1290,2975h
Dracula 3169
Drug Abuse, Prevent 1438
DuBois, W.E.B. 2617,3182l
Du Sable, Jean Baptiste Pointe 2249

Duck Decoys 2138-2141
Duesenberg 2385
Dulles, John Foster 1172
Dunbar, Paul Laurence 1554
Durand, Asher B. 3236g

E

Eagan, Eddie 2499
Eakins, Thomas 1335
Earhart, Amelia C68
Earp, Wyatt 2869j,2870j
Earth Days 2951-2954
Eastern Chipmunk 2297
Eastman, George 1062
Echo I 1173
Edison, Thomas A 654-656,945
Education 1833
Educators 869-873
Einstein, Albert 1774
Eisenhower, D.D 1383,2219g,2513
Electric Auto 296
Electric Light 654-656
Electric Train Toys 3184d
Electronics 1500-1502,C86
Eliot, Charles W 871
Eliot, T.S 2239
Elks, B.P.O 1342
Ellington, "Duke" 2211
Ellsworth, Lincoln 2389
Emancipation Proclamation 1233
Emerson, Ralph Waldo 861
Emigration, Hardships of 290,3209f
Empire State Building 3185b
Empire State Express 295
Employ the Handicapped 1155
Endangered Flora 1783-1786
Endangered Species 3105
Energy 1723-1724,2006-2009
Energy Conservation 1547
Engineers, Am. Soc. of Civil 1012
Ericsson, John, Statue of 628
Erie Canal 1325
Erikson, Leif 1359
Everglades National Park 952
Ewry, Ray 2497
Executive Branch of Gov't 2414
Explorers 2024,2093,2220-23,2386-89
EXPO '74, Spokane 1527

F

Fairbanks, Douglas 2088
Fallen Timbers, Battle of 680
Family Planning 1455
Family Unity 2104
Farming in the West 286,3209i
Farnsworth, Philo T 2058
Farragut, David 792,2975g
Faulkner, William 2350
Federal Deposit Insurance Corp 2071
Federal Reserve System 3183b
Fiedler, Arthur 3159
Fields, Dorothy 3102
Fields, W.C. 1803
Fillmore, Millard 2217d
Fine Arts 1259
Finnish Independence 1334
FIPEX 1075-1076
First Supersonic Flight 3173
Fish 2209a,3231
Fishing Flies 2549a
Fitzgerald, F. Scott 3104
Flag, Foreign 909-921
Flag, U.S. 1094,1132,1153
Flags, Historic U.S. 1345-1354
Flags, 50 States 1633-1682
Flappers, The Charleston 3184h
Florida Settlement 1271
Florida Statehood 927,2950
Flowering Trees 3193-97
Flowers 1876-79,1953-2002, 2076-79,2647-96
Flushing Remonstrance 1099
Folk Art, American 1706-1709 1745-1748,1775-1778,1834-1837, 2138-2141, 2240-2243,2351-2354,2390-2393
Folk Dance 1751
Folk Heroes 3083-3086
Folk Musicians 3212-15
Fontaine, Lynn 3287
Food for Peace 1231
Football Coaches 3143-50
Football, Intercollegiate 1382
Forest Conservation 1122
Forestry Congress, 5th World 1156
Fort Bliss 976
Fort Dearborn 728,730,766
Fort Duquesne 1123
Fort Harrod 1542
Fort Kearny 970
Fort Orange, Landing at 615
Fort Snelling 1409
Fort Sumter 1178
Fort Ticonderoga 1071
Foster, John 3236a
Foster, Stephen Collins 879
Four Chaplains 956
Four Freedoms 908,2840
Four-H Clubs (4-H) 1005
Four Horsemen of Notre Dame 3184l
France, Flag 915
Francis of Assisi 2023
Francisco, Peter 1562
Frankenstein 3170
Franklin, Benjamin 947,948,1073,1140,1690,2036,3139
Freedom from Hunger 1231
Freedom of the Press 1119
Fremont, John C. 2869i,2870i
Fremont on the Rocky Mtns 288,3209d
French Alliance 1753
French Revolution C120
French, Daniel Chester 887
Frost, Robert 1526
Fulbright Scholarships 3065
Fulton, Robert 1270
Fur Seal 1464
Future Farmers 1024

G

Gadsden Purchase 1028
Galvez, Gen. Bernardo de 1826
Gandhi, Mahatma 1174-1175
Garden Flowers2764a,2833a, 2997a,3029a
Gardening - Horticulture 1100
Garfield, James A 2218b
Garibaldi, Guiseppe 1168-1169
Garner, Errol 2992
Gatsby Style 3184b
Gehrig, Lou 2417
George, Walter F 1170
Georgia Bicentennial 726
Georgia Statehood 2339
German Immigration 2040
Geronimo 2869m,2870m
Gershwin, George 1484
Gettysburg, Battle of 1180,2975t
Gettysburg Address 978
Gibson Girl 3182m
Gilbert, John 2823
Girl Scouts 974,1199,2251,3183j
Giving and Sharing 3243
Glacier 748,764
Goddard, Robert H C69
Goethols, George W. 856
Gold Star Mothers 969
Golden Gate 399,403
Golden Gate Bridge 3185l
Golden Gate Exposition 852
Gompers, Samuel 988
Gone With The Wind 2446,3185i
Goodman, Benny 3099
Goodnight, Charles 2869l,2870l
Gospel Singers 3216-19
Gootscholt, Louise Moreau 3165
Grafe, Ferde 3163
Grand Army of the Republic 985
Grand Canyon 741,757,2512,3183h
Grand Coulee Dam 1009
Grange 1323
Grant, U.S. 787,2217i,2975d
Gray Squirrel 2295
Gray Wolf 2322,3292
Great Lakes Lighthouses 2973a
Great River Road 1319
Great Smoky Mountains 749,765,797
Great Train Robbery, The 3182c
Greece, Flag 916
Greeley, Horace 1177
Greely, Aldolphus W 2221
Greene, Nathaniel 785
Green-throated Carib 3223
Griffith, D.W 1555
Gunston Hall 1108
Gutenberg Bible 1014
Guthrie, Woody 3213

H

Habitats, Wildlife 1921-1924
Haida Canoe 1389
Halas, George 3146, 3150
Haley, Bill 2725,2732
Half Moon and Steamship 372-373
Hamilton, Alexander 1086
Hammarskjold, Dag 1203-1204
Hamster 3234
Hancock, Winfield 2975n
Handicapped 1155
Handy, W.C. 1372
Hanson, John 1941
Hanukkah 3118
Harding, Warren G 610-613,2219a
Harnett, William M 1386,3236i
Harris, Joel Chandler 980
Harrison, Benjamin 2218e
Harrison, William H 996,2216i
Hawaii C46
Hawaii Sesquicentennial 647-648
Hawaii Statehood 2080,C55
Hawaii Territory 799
Hawkins, Coleman 2984
Hawthorne, Nathaniel 2047
Hayes, Rutheford B 2218a
Health Research 2087
HemisFair '68 1340
Hemingway, Ernest M 2418
Henry, John 3085
Henry, Patrick 1144
Henson, M. & Peary, R.E. 2223
Herbert, Victor 881
Herkimer at Oriskany 1722
Hermitage, The 786,1037
Hickok, Wild Bill 2869o,2870o
Higher Education 1206
Hispanic Americans 2103
Historic Preservation 1440-1443
Hitchcock, Alfred 3226
Hoban, James 1935-1936
Holiday, Billie 2856
Holly, Buddy 2729,2736
Homemakers 1253
Homer, Winslow 1207,3236j
Homestead Act 1198
Hoover, Herbert C. 1269,2219c
Hopkins, Mark 870
Hopper, Edward 3236p
Horse Racing 1528
Horses 2155-2158
Horses, Sporting 2756-59
Horticulture 1100
Hospice Care 3276
Hospitals, Public 2210
Household Conveniences 3185g
House of Reps., U.S. 2412
Houston, Sam 1242
Howe, Elias 892
Huckleberry Finn 2787
Hudson-Fulton Celeb 372-373
Hughes, Charles Evans 1195
Huguenot-Walloon Tercn 614-616
Hull, Cordell 1235
Humane Treatment of Animals 1307
Hummingbirds 2646a
Hunger, Help End 2164
Hunt's Remedy Stamp 3182f

I

Idaho Statehood 896,2439
Iiwi 2311
Illinois Statehood 1339
Immigrants Arrive 3182i
Indep. Spirit, Rise of 1476-79
Indep., Skilled Hands for 1717-20
Indian Headdresses 2505a
Indian Hunting Buffalo 287,3209c
Indian Masks, Pac. NW 1834-1837
Indian Territory Centenary 972
Indiana Statehood 1308
Indiana Territory 996
Int'l. Aeronautics Conf 649-650
International Cooperation Year 1266
International Geophysical Year 1107
International Peace Garden 2014
International Philatelic Exhibition 630,778,948,1075-1076,1310-1311,1632, 1757,2145,2216-19
Int'l. Telecommun. Union 1274
International Women's Year 1571
International Year of the Child 1772
Intern'l. Year of the Disabled 1925
Intern'l. Youth Year 2160-2163
Interphil '76 1632
Inventors 889-893,2055-2058
Iowa Statehood 942,3088-89
Iowa Territory 838
Irish Immigration 3286
Irving, Washington 859
Ives, Frederic E. 3063
Ives, Charles 3164
Iwo Jima 929

J

Jackson, Andrew 786,941,2261g
Jackson, Mahalia 3216
Jackson, "Stonewall" 788,2975s
Jamestown Exposition 328-330
Jamestown Festival 1091
Jamestown, Founding of 329
Japan, Opening of 1021,1158
Jazz Artists 2854-2861
Jazz Flourishes 3184k
Jazz Musicians 2983-2992
Jeffers, Robinson 1485
Jefferson, Thomas 324,1141,2216c
Johnson, Andrew 2217h
Johnson, James P. 2985
Johnson, James Weldon 2371
Johnson, Joshua 3236h
Johnson, Lyndon B 1503,2219i
Johnson, Robert 2857
Johnston, Joseph E. 2975m
Jolson, Al 2849
Jones, Casey 993
Jones, John Paul 790,1789
Jones, Robert Tyre (Bobby) 1933,3185n
Joplin, Scott 2044
Joseph, Chief 1364
Julian, Percy Lavon 2746
Jupiter Balloon C54
Just, Ernest E. 3058

K

Kane, Elisha Kent 2220
Kansas City, Missouri 994
Kansas Statehood 1183
Kansas Territory 1061
Karloff, Boris 3170-71
Kearny Expedition 944
Keaton, Buster 2828
Keller, Helen & Anne Sullivan 1824
Kelly, Grace 2749
Kennedy, John F 1246,2219h
Kennedy, Robert F 1770
Kentucky Settlement 1542
Kentucky Statehood 904,2636
Kern, Jerome 2110
Key, Francis Scott 962,1142
Keystone Cops 2826
Kids Care 2951-2954
Killer Whales 2508
King, Jr., Dr. Martin Luther 1771
King Salmon 1079
Kline,Franz 3236s
Klondike Goldrush 3235
Knoxville World's Fair 2006-2009
Korea, Flag 921
Kosciuszko, Gen. Tadeusz 734
Kossuth, Lajos 1117-1118
Kwanzaa 3175

L

Labor Day 1082
Lacemaking 2351-2354
Ladybug 2315
Lafayette, Marquis de 1010,1097,1716
Lake Placid, NY 716
Land-Grant Colleges 1065,1206
Langley, Samuel P C118
Lanier, Sidney 1446
Laurel & Hardy 2562
Law and Order 1343
Learning Never Ends 1833
Leatherworker 1720
Ledbetter, Huddie "Leadbelly" 3212
Lee, Jason 964
Lee, Robert E. 788,982,2975b
Legend of Sleepy Hollow 1548
Legends of the West 2869,2870
Leon, Ponce de 2024
Letter Carriers 2420
Lewis and Clark Expedition 1063
Lexington-Concord 617-619,1563
Liberty Bell 627,C57,C62
Libraries, America's 2015
Library of Congress 2004
Life Magazine 3185c
Lighthouses 2474a
Lighthouses, Great Lakes 2973a
Lily 1879
Limner, The Freake 3236b
Lincoln, Abraham 367-369,906,978, 1113-1116,1143, 2081, 2217g,2433,2975j,C59
Lincoln-Douglas Debates 1115
Lindbergh Flight 1710,3184m,C10
Lions International 1326
Little House on the Prairie 2786
Little Women 2788
Livingston, Robert R. 323
Lloyd, Harold 2825
Locomobile 2381
Locomotives 2366a,2719,2847a
Lombardi, Vince 3145-3147
Long, Dr. Crawford W 875
Longfellow, Henry W 864
Louisiana Purchase 1020
Louisiana Purchase Expo 323-327
Louisiana Purchase, Map of 327
Louisiana Statehood 1197
Louisiana World Exposition 2086
Louis, Joe 2766
Love 1475,1951,2072,2143,2202, 2248,2378-79,2440-41,2535-37,2618, 2813-15,2948-49,2957-60a,3030a, 3123-24,3274-75
Low, Juliette Gordon 974
Lowell, James Russell 866
Ludington, Sybil 1559
Lugosi, Bela 3169
Luna Moth 2293
Lunt, Alfred 3287
Luther, Martin 2065
Luxembourg, Flag 912

M

Maass, Clara 1699
MacArthur, Gen. Douglas 1424
MacDonough, Thomas 791
MacDowell, Edward A. 882
Mackinac Bridge 1109
Madison, Dolley 1822
Madison, Helene 2500
Madison, James A. 2216d,2875,75a
Magna Carta 1265
Magsaysay, Ramon 1096
Mail Delivery, Tradit 2434-37,38
Mail Delivery, Future C122-125,26
Mail Order Business 1468
Mail Transport - ZIP CODE 1511
Mail Wagon 1903
Maine, Remember the 3192
Maine Statehood 1391
Malaria 1194
Mann, Horace 869
Mannerheim, Baron Gustaf Emil 1165-66
Marathon 3067
Marine Corps Reserve 1315
Mariner 10 1557
Marines, Continental 1567
Marines, World War II 929
Marquette on the Mississippi 285,3209a
Marquette, Jacques 1356
Marshall, George C. 3141
Marshall Is. & Micronesia 2506-07

Marshall, John 2415
Martin, Roberta 3217
Maryland Statehood 2342
Maryland Tercentenary 736
Masaryk, Thomas G 1147,1148
Massachusetts Bay Colony 682
Massachusetts Statehood 2341
Masters, Edgar Lee 1405
Masterson, Bat 2869h,2870h
Matzeliger, Jan 2567
Mayflower 548
Mayo, Drs. William & Charles 1251
Mazzei, Phillip C98
McCormack, John 2090
McCormick, Cyrus Hall 891
McDowell, Dr. Ephraim 1138
McKinley, William 326,2218f
McLoughlin, John 964
McMahon, Brien 1200
McPhatter, Clyde 2726,2733
Mead, Margaret 3184g
Meany, George 2848
Medal of Honor 2045
Mellon, Andrew W 1072
Melville, Herman 2094
Mercer, Johnny 3101
Merchant Marine 939
Mergenthaler, Ottmar 3062
Merman, Ethel 2853
Mesa Verde 743,759
Metropolitan Opera 2054
Mexican Independence 1157
MIA,POW & 2966
Michael, Moina 977
Michigan Centenary 775,778c
Michigan State College 1065
Michigan Statehood 2246
Micronesia & Marshall Is 2506-07
Mighty Casey 3083
Migratory Bird Treaty 1306
Military Services Bicent 1565-1568
Military Uniforms 1565-1568
Militia, American 1568
Millay, Edna St. Vincent 1926
Miller, Glenn 3098
Minerals 1538-1541,2700-03
Mingus, Charles 2989
Mining Prospector 291,3209g
Minnesota Statehood 1106
Minnesota Territory 981
Minute Man, The 619
Mississipi Statehood 1337
Mississippi Territory 955
Missouri Statehood 1426
Mobile, Battle of 1826
Mockingbird 2330
Model T Ford 3182a
Modern Dance 1752
Monarch Butterfly 2287
Monitor & Virginia 2975a
Monk, Thelonious 2990
Monmouth, Battle of 646
Monopoly Game 3185o
Monroe, James 325,1105,2216e
Monroe, Marilyn 2967
Montana Statehood 858,2401
Moon Landing 2419,2841,2842,C76
Moore, Marianne 2449
Moose 2298
Moran, Thomas 3236l
Morocco-U.S. Diplomacy 2349
Morse, Samuel F.B. 890
Morton, Jelly Roll 2986
Moses, (Grandma) 1370
Moses, Horace 2095
Mothers of America 737-738,54
Motion Pictures 926,2445-48
Mott, Lucretia 959
Mount McKinley 1454
Mount Rainier 742,750,758,770
Mount Rushmore 1011,C88
Mount Vernon 785
Mountain Goat 2323
Mountain Lion 2292
Movie Monsters 3168-72
Muir, John 1245,3182j
Mule Deer 2294
Mummy, The 3171
Murrow, Edward R. 2812
Muybridge, Edweard 3061
My Fair Lady 2770

N

Naismith - Basketball 1189
Nassau Hall 1083
Nation of Readers 2106
National Academy of Science 1237
National Archives 2081
National Capitol Sesqui 989-992
National Defense 899-901
National Grange 1323
National Guard 1017
Nation'l Letter Writing Week 1805-1810
National Park Service 1314
National Parks 740-49,750-751, 756-65,769-770,1448-1454,2081,C84
National Recovery Act 732
National Stamp Exhibition 735
NATO 1008,1127
Natural History Museum 1387-1390
Navajo Blankets 2235-2238
Naval Academy 794,3001
Naval Aviation 1185
Naval Review 1091
Navigation, Lake 294
Navigation, Ocean 299
Navy, Continental 1566
Navy, U.S. 790-794,935
Nebraska Statehood 1328
Nebraska Territory 1060
Netherlands 2003
Netherlands, Flag 913
Nevada Settlement 999
Nevada Statehood 1248
Nevin, Ethelbert 883
New Deal, FDR's 3185e
New Hampshire 1068
New Hampshire Statehood 2344
New Jersey Statehood 2338
New Jersey Tercentenary 1247
New Mexico Statehood 1191
New Netherlands 614
New Orleans, Battle of 1261
New Sweden, Settlement C117
New York City 1027,C38
New York Coliseum 1076
NY Skyline & Statue of Liberty C35
New York Statehood 2346
New York World's Fair 853,1244
Newburgh, New York 727,752
Newspaper Boys 1015
Niagara Falls 297,568,699
19th Amendment -Women Voting 3184e
Nixon, Richard M. 2955
Norris, George W. 1184
Norse-American 620,621
North Carolina Statehood 2347
North Dakota Statehood 858,2403
Northern Marianas 2804
Northern Sea Lion 2509
Northwest Ordinance 795
Northwest Territory 837
Norway, Flag 911
Numismatics 2558
Nursing 1190

O

Oakley, Annie 2869d,2870d
Ochs, Adolph S 1700
Oglethorpe, Gen. James E 726
Ohio River Canalization 681
Ohio Statehood 1018
O'Keeffe, Georgia 3069
Oklahoma! 2722,2769
Oklahoma Statehood 1092
Old Faithful, Yellowstone 1453
Old Man of the Mountains 1068
Olympians 2496-2500
Olympics 716,718-19,1146,1460-62, 1695-98,1790-98,2048-51,2067-70, 2082-85,2369,2380,2496-2500,2528, 2539,2553-57,2611-15,2619,2637-41, 2807-11,3068,3087,C85,C97, C101-12
Opera Singers 3154-57
Orchids 2076-2079
Ordinance of 1787 795
Oregon Statehood 1124
Oregon Territory 783,964
Oregon Trail 2747
Organ & Tissue Donation 3227
Organized Labor 1831
Oriskany, Battle of 644,1722
Ormandy, Eugene 3161
Osprey 2291
Osteopathic Medicine 1469
Ouimet, Francis 2377
Overland Mail 1120,2869t,2870t
Overrun Countries 909-21
Owens, Jesse 2496,3185j
Owls, American 1760-1763
Ox, Year of the 3120

P

Pacific '97 3130-31,3139-40
Pacific Dogwood 3197
Pacific Nwest Indian Masks 1834-37
Packard 2384
Paderewski, Ignacy Jan 1159-1160
Palau, Republic of 2999
Palmer, Nathaniel 2386
Palomar Observatory 966
Pan American Games 2247,C56
Pan American Union 895,C34
Pan-American Exposition 294-299
Panama Canal 398,402,856,3183f
Panama-Pacific Exposition 397-404
Papanicolaou, Dr. George 1754
Parakeet 3233
Parent Teacher Association 1463
Parker, Charlie 2987
Parker, Dorothy 2698
Patton, Gen. George S., Jr 1026
Peace Bridge 1721
Peace Corps 1447
Peace of 1783 727,752
Peale, Rembrandt 3236d
Peary, R. & M. Henson 2223
Pember, Phoebe 2975r
Penn, William 724
Pennsylvania Academy 1064
Pennsylvania State University 1065
Pennsylvania Statehood 2337
Pennsylvania Toleware 1775-1778
Performing Arts 1755-1756,1801, 1803, 2012,2088,2090,2110,2211,2250,2411
Perkins, Frances 1821
Perry, Commodore Matthew C. 1021
Petroleum Industry 1134
Phantom of the Opera 3168
Pharmacy 1473
Phillips, Ammi 3236c
Photography 1758
Physical Fitness 2043
Physical Fitness-Sokols 1262
Pickett, Bill 2869g,2870g
Pierce, Franklin 2217e
Pierce-Arrow 2382
Pika 2319
Pilgrim Tercentenary 548-550
Pilgrims, Landing of the 549,1420
Pioneer 10 1556
Piper, William C129,C132
Pitcher, Molly 646
Pitts, Zasu 2824
Pocahontas 330
Poe, Edgar Allan 986
Poets 864-868
Poland, Flag 909
Polar Bear 1429,3291
Polio 1087
Polish Millenium 1313
Polk, James K. 2217b,2587
Pons, Lily 3154
Ponselle, Rosa 3157
Pony Express 894,1154
Poor, Salem 1560
Poppy, Memorial 977
Popular Singers 2849-2853
Porgy & Bess 2768
Porter, Cole 2550
Porter, David D. 792
Post, Emily 3184f
Post, Wiley C95-C96
Postal Museum,National 2779-82
Postal Service Bicent 1572-1575
Postal Service Employees 1489-1498
Poultry Industry 968
POW & MIA 2966
Powell, John Wesley 1374
Powered Flight C47
Prairie Crab Apple 3196
Prehistoric Animals 2422-2425,3077-3080
Preserving Wetlands 2092
Presidents of the U.S. 2216-2219
Presley, Elvis 2721,2724,2731
Priestley, Joseph 2038
Printing Tercentenary 857
Printing Press, Early American 1593
Professional Management 1920
Prohibition Enforced 3184c
Project Mercury 1193
Pronghorn 2313
Pronghorn Antelope 1078
PTA 1463
Public Education 2159
Pueblo Pottery 1706-1709
Puerto Rico Elections 983
Puerto Rico Territory 801
Pulaski, Gen. Casimir 690
Pulitzer, Joseph 946
Pure Food and Drug Laws 1080
Putnam, Rufus 795

Q

Quilts 1745-1748
Quimby, Harriet C128

R

Rabbit, Year of the 3272
Raccoon 2331
Racing Car 2262
Radio Entertains America 3184i
Railroad Engineers 993
Railroad, Streamliner 3185k
Railroad, Transcontinental 922
Rainey, "Ma" 2859
Rand, Ayn 3308
Randolph, Asa Philip 2402
Range Conservation 1176
Rat, Year of the 3272
Rayburn, Sam 1202
Readers, Nation of 2106
Rebecca of Sunnybrook Farm 2785
Recreational Sports 2961-2965
Red Cross 702,967,1016,1239,1910
Redding, Otis 2728,2735
Red Fox 2335
Red-winged Blackbird 2303
Reed, Dr. Walter 877
Register and Vote 1249,1344
Religious Freedom 1099
Remember the Maine 3192
Remington, Frederic 888,1187,1934
Reptiles, Age of 1390
Retarded Children 1549
Reuter, Ernst 1136-1137
Rhode Island Tercentenary 777
Ribault, Jan, Monument to 616
Rickenbacker, Eddie 2998
Riley, James Whitcomb 868
Ringtail 2302
Rise of Spirit of Indep 1476-1479
Riverboats 3091-3095
River Otter 2314
Roanoke Voyages 2093
Robie House, F.L.Wright 3182o
Robinson, Jackie 2016
Rochambeau, Gen 703
Rockne, Knute 2376
Rock 'n Roll 2724-30,2737a-b
Rockwell, Norman 2839-2840
Rodgers, Jimmie 1755
Rogers, Will 975,1801
Roosevelt, Eleanor 1236,2105,3185d
Roosevelt, Franklin 930-933,1950,2219d,3185a
Roosevelt, Theodore 856,2218g3182b
Rooster, Year of the 2720
Roseate Spoonbill 2308
Roses 1876,2014,2378-2379
Ross, Betsy 1004
Rotary International 1066
Rothko, Mark 3236t
Rough Riders 973
Rural America 1504-1506
Rural Electrification Admin 2144
Rural Free Delivery 3090
Rushing, Jimmy 2858
Russell, Charles M 1243
Ruth, Babe (George Herman) . 2046,3184a

S

Sacagawea 2869s,2870s
Sagamore Hill 1023
Saguaro 1845
Saint-Gaudens, Augustus 886
St. Lawrence Seaway 1131,2091
St. Louis Worlds Fair 3182e
Salomon, Haym 1561
Salvation Army 1267
Sampson, William T. 793
San Francisco Bay 400-400A,404
San Fran.-Oakland Bay Bridge C36
San Jacinto 2204
San Juan 1437
San Martin, Jose de 1125-1126
Sandburg, Carl 1731
Saratoga 644
Saratoga, Surrender at 1728
Sargent, Winthrop 955
Saroyan, William 2538
Save Our Air,Cities,Soil,Water 1410-13
Savings & Loan 1911
Savings Bonds 2534
Savings Bonds-Servicemen 1320
Sawyer, Tom 1470
Scarlet Tanager 2306
Science & Industry 2031
Science, National Academy of 1237
Scientists 874-878
Scott, Blanche Stuart C99
Scott, Winfield 786
Sea Creatures 2508-11
Sea Otter 2510
Sea, Wonders of the 2863-2866
Seamstress 1717
Search for Peace 1326
SEATO 1151
Seattle World's Fair 1196
Seeing Eye Dogs 1787
Semmes, Raphael 2975i
Senate, U.S. 2413
Serra, Father Junipero C116
Service Women 1013
Servicemen, Honoring U.S. 1422
Servicemen-Savings Bonds 1320
Sesquicentennial Exposition 627
Sevier, John 941
Seward, William H 372-373
Shakespeare, William 1250
Sheeler, Charles 3236r
Sheridan, Philip H. 787
Sherman, William T. 787,2975q
Shield & Eagle 771
Shiloh, Battle of 1179,2975e
Shipbuilding 1095
Showboat 2767
Sikorsky, Igor C119
Silent Screen Stars 2819-2828
Silver Centennial 1130
SIPEX 1310-1311
Skiing 3180
Skilled Hands for Indep 1717-1720
Skylab 1529
Sleepy Hollow, Legend of 1548
Sleigh 1900
Sloan, John 1433
Sloop Restauration 620
Smith Alfred E. 937
Smith, Bessie 2854
Smith, Capt. John 328
Smithsonian Institution 943,3059
Smokey Bear 2096

Snow White and the Seven Dwarfs.. 3185h
Snowy Egret ... 2321
Snowy Owl ... 3290
Soccer, World Cup ... 2834-2837
Social Security Act ... 2153
Society of Philatelic American ... 797
Soil Conservation ... 1133
Sokol - Physical Fitness ... 1262
Solo Trans-Atlantic Flight ... 1710
Songwriters ... 3100-3103
Sonoran Desert ... 3293
Soo Locks ... 1069
Sound Recording ... 1705
Sousa, John Philip ... 880
South Carolina Statehood ... 2343
South Carolina Tercentenary ... 1407
South Dakota Statehood ... 858,2416
Southern Magnolia ... 3193
Space Achievements ... 1331-1332, 1434-1435,1556-1557,1759,1912-19, 2577a,2631-34
Space Discovery ... 3238-42
Space Fantasy ... 2745a
Space Shuttles ... 2543-2544A
Spanish Settlement in the Southwest . 3220
Special Occasions ... 2274a,2395-98
Special Olympics ... 1788,2142
Sperry, Lawrence and Elmer ... C114
Spirit of '76 ... 1629-1631
Spirit of St. Louis ... 1710,C10
Stagecoach ... 2448
Stamp Centenary ... 947,948
Stamp Collecting ... 1474,2201a
Stanton, Elizabeth ... 959
Stars and Stripes Forever ... 3153
State Birds and Flowers ... 1953-2002
State Flags ... 1633-1682
Statehood: ND,SD,MT,WA ... 858
Statue of Liberty ... 899,1075,2147, 2224,C35,C58,C63,C80,C87
Statue of Liberty & NY Skyline ... C35
Steamboats ... 2409a
Steamship "Savannah" ... 923
Steel Industry ... 1090
Stefansson, Vilhjalmur ... 2222
Steinbeck, John ... 1773
Steinmetz, Charles ... 2055
Steuben, Baron Friedrich von ... 689
Stevenson, Adlai E ... 1275
Stock Exchange, NY ... 2630
Stock Market Crash ... 3184o
Stokowski, leopold ... 3158
Stone Mountain Memorial ... 1408
Stone, Harlan Fiske ... 965
Stratford Hall ... 788
Streetcars ... 2059-2062
Stuart, Gilbert Charles ... 884
Stuyvesant, Peter ... 971
Sullivan, Anne & Helen Keller ... 1824
Sullivan, Maj. Gen. John ... 657
Sun Yat-sen ... 906,1188
Superman Arrives ... 3185f
Supersonic Flight, First ... 3173
Supreme Court Building ... 991
Sweden-U.S. Treaty ... 2036
Swedish Pioneers ... 958
Swedish-Finnish Tercentenary ... 836
Switzerland ... 2532
Sylvester & Tweety ... 3204-5
Szell, George ... 3160

T

Taft, Robert A ... 1161
Taft, William H ... 2218h
Talking Pictures ... 1727
Tanner, Henry Ossawa ... 1486
Taylor, Zachary ... 2217c
Teachers ... 1093
Teddy Bear Created ... 3182k
Telegraph Centenary ... 924
Telephone Centenary ... 1683
Tennessee Statehood ... 941,3070-71
Tennessee Valley Authority ... 2042
Terry, Sonny ... 3214
Tesla, Nikola ... 2057
Texas Independence ... 776, 778d
Texas Republic ... 2204
Texas Statehood ... 938,2968
Tharpe, Sister Rosetta ... 3219
Theater ... 1750
Third International Philatelic Exh. ... 778
Thirteenth Amendment ... 902
Thoreau, Henry David ... 1327
Thorpe, Jim ... 2089,3183g
Thurber, James ... 2862
Tibbett, Lawrence ... 3156
Tiger Swallowtail ... 2300
Tiger, Year of the ... 3179
Tilghman, Bill ... 2869r,2870r
TIPEX Souvenir Sheet ... 778
Torch ... 901
Toscanini, Arturo ... 2411
Touro Synagogue ... 2017
Traffic Safety ... 1272
Trans-Atlantic Airmail ... C24
Trans-continental Telephone Line ... 3183e
Trans-Mississippi Expo.. 285-293,3209-10
Trans-Miss. Philatelic Expo ... 751
Trans-Pacific Airmail ... C20-22,C115
Treaty of Paris ... 2052
Trees, American ... 1764-1767
Troops Guarding Train ... 289,3209e
Tropical Birds ... 3222-25
Tropical Flowers ... 3310-13
Trout ... 1427
Trucking Industry ... 1025
Truman, Harry S ... 1499,2219f
Trumbull, John ... 1361
Truth, Sojourner ... 2203
Tubman, Harriet ... 1744,2975k
Tucher, Richard ... 3155
Turners, American Society of ... 979
Twain, Mark ... 863
Tyler, John ... 2217a

U

U.S.-Canada Friendship ... 961
U.S.-Canada Peace Bridge ... 1721
U.S. Capitol Building ... 992
U.S.-Japan Treaty ... 1158
U.S.-Morocco Diplomacy ... 2349
U.S.-Netherlands Diplomacy ... 2003
U.S. Supreme Court ... 2415
U.S.-Sweden Treaty ... 2036
United Confederate Veterans ... 998
United Nations ... 1419,2974
United Nations Conference ... 928
United Way ... 2275
Univ. Postal Congress... 2434-38, C122-26
Univ.Postal Union ... 1530-1537, C42-C44
Urban Planning ... 1333
USPS Emblem ... 1396
Utah Settlement ... 950
Utah Statehood ... 3024

V

Valens, Ritchie ... 2727,2734
Valentino, Rudolph ... 2819
Valley Forge ... 645,1729
Van Buren, Martin ... 2216h
Varela, Padre Felix ... 3166
Vermont Sesquicentennial ... 643
Vermont Statehood ... 903,2533
Verrazano-Narrows Bridge ... 1258
Verville, Alfred V ... C113
Veterans Administration ... 1825
Veterans of Foreign Wars ... 1525
Veterans, Korean War ... 2152
Veterans, Viet Nam War ... 1802
Veterans, World War I ... 2154
Veterans, World War II ... 940
Victorian Love ... 3274-75
Victory ... 537
Vietnam Veterans' Memorial ... 2109
Viking Mission to Mars ... 1759
Viking Ship ... 621
Virgin Islands Territory ... 802
Virginia Capes, Battle of ... 1938
Virginia Statehood ... 2345
Voice of America ... 1329
Voluntarism ... 2039
Volunteer Firemen ... 971
von Karman, Dr. Theodore ... 2699

W

Walker, Dr. Mary E ... 2013
Walker, Madam C.J ... 3181
Wallenberg, Raoul ... 3135
Ward, Clara ... 3218
Warner, Pop ... 3144, 3149
Washington and Lee University ... 982
Washington at Cambridge ... 617
Washington Crossing Delaware ... 1696
Washington, Dinah ... 2730,2737
Washington Reviewing Army at Valley Forge ... 1697
Washington Statehood ... 858,2404
Washington Territory ... 1019
Washington, Booker T ... 873,1074
Washington, D.C. ... 989-992,2561
Washington, George ... 704-715, 785,854,947-48,982,1003, 1139,1686,1688-89,1704, 1729,1952,2081,2216a,3140
Water Conservation ... 1150
Waterfowl Conservation ... 1362
Waterfowl Preservation Act ... 2092
Waters, Ethel ... 2851
Waters, Muddy ... 2855
Watie, Stand ... 2975l
Wayne, Gen. Anthony ... 680
Webster, Daniel ... 725,1380
Webster, Noah ... 1121
Wells, Ida B ... 2442
West Point ... 789
West Virginia Statehood ... 1232
West, Benjamin ... 1553
Western Cattle in Storm... 292,3209h,3210
Wharton, Edith ... 1832
Wharton, Joseph ... 1920
Wheat Fields ... 1506
Wheatland ... 1081
Wheelwright ... 1719
Wheels of Freedom ... 1162
Whistler, James A. McNeill ... 885
White House ... 990,2219e
White, Josh ... 3215
White Plains, Battle of ... 629-630
White, William Allen ... 960
White-tailed Deer ... 2317
Whitman, Walt ... 867
Whitney, Eli ... 889
Whittier, John Greenleaf ... 865
Whooping Crane ... 1098
Wightman, Hazel ... 2498
Wilder, Thornton ... 3134
Wild Animals ... 2709a
Wilderness, Battle of the ... 1181
Wildflowers ... 2647-96
Wildlife ... 1757,1921-24, 2286-2335,2709a
Wildlife Conservation ... 1077-79,1098, 1392,1427-30,1464-67
Wild Turkey ... 1077
Wiley, Harvey W ... 1080
Wilkes, Lt. Charles ... 2387
Willard, Frances E ... 872
Williams, Hank ... 2723,2771
Williams, Roger ... 777
Williams, Tennessee ... 3002
Wills, Bob ... 2774,2778
Wilson, Woodrow ... 2218i,3183k
Win the War ... 905
Wisconsin Statehood ... 957,3206
Wisconsin Tercentenary ... 739,755
Wizard of Oz ... 2445
Wolf, "Howlin" ... 2861
Wolf Trap Farm Park ... 1452,2018
Wolverine ... 2327
Wolfman, The ... 3172
Woman Suffrage ... 1406,2980
Woman, American ... 1152
Women, Armed Services ... 1013
Women in the Military ... 3174
Women, Progress of ... 959
Women's Clubs ... 1316
Wood Carvings ... 2240-2243
Woodchuck ... 2307
Wood, Grant ... 3236q
Woodson, Carter G ... 2073
Wool Industry ... 1423
Workman's Compensation ... 1186
World Columbian Expo ... 2586, 2616
World Peace Through Law ... 1576
World Peace / World Trade ... 1129
World Refugee Year ... 1149
World Stamp Expo '89 ... 2410,2433
World's Fair ... 323-327,853, 1196,1244,2006-2009,2086
World University Games ... 2748
World War I, U.S. Enters ... 3183i
World War II .. 2559,2697,2765,2838,2981
Wright Brothers ... 3182g,C45,C91-C92
Wyoming Statehood ... 897,2444

XYZ

X, Malcolm ... 3273
Yat-sen, Sun ... 906
Yellow Poplar ... 3195
Yellowstone ... 744,760
YMCA Youth Camping ... 2160
Yorktown, Battle of ... 703,1686,1937
Yosemite ... 740,751,756,769
Young, Whitney Moore ... 1875
Youth Camping ... 2160
Youth Month ... 963
Youth, Support Our ... 1342
Yugoslavia Flag ... 917
Zaharias, Mildred Didrikson ... 1932
Zeppelin, Graf ... C13-C15,C18
Zion ... 747,763

DEFINITIVE ISSUE IDENTIFIER

The purpose of these listings is to aid the novice and intermediate collector in identifying U.S. definitive issues.
The first step in identification should be to note the stamp's denomination, color, and subject and then locate it on the list below. If that step does not provide you with a definitive Scott No., you will have to do some additional work.
If the identification can only be made by determining the stamp's "type", grill size or press from which the stamp was printed, it will be necessary to check the appropriate pages of the Brookman or Scott catalogs for this information.
If the identification can only be made by determining the stamp's perf measurements or watermark. If you do not own these "tools," contact your favorite dealer and/or watermark detector. If you do not own these "tools," contact your favorite dealer.
* With few exceptions, this list features major Scott Nos. and omits Reprints, Re-issues and Special Printings.
* Watermark and Press notations are not listed when they do not contribute to the stamp's identification.
* Scott nos. followed by "**" were also issued Bullseye Perf. 11.2
* Scott nos. followed by a "*" were issued both Untagged and Tagged.
* All bklt. singles are perforated on two or three sides only.

| | 803 | 1030 | 5/40 | 63/92 | 134/206 |
| | Prexie Issue | Liberty Issue | | | |

Den.	Color	Subject	Type / Comment	Press	Perf.	Wmk.	Scott #
½¢	olive brn	N. Hale		F	11		551
½¢	olive brn	N. Hale		R	11x10.5		653
½¢	dp orng	B. Franklin	1938 Prexie Issue		11x10.5		803
½¢	rd orng	B. Franklin	1954 Liberty Issue		11x10.5		1030
1¢	blue	B. Franklin	Ty I		Imperf		5
1¢	blue	B. Franklin	Ty Ib		Imperf		5A
1¢	blue	B. Franklin	Ty Ia		Imperf		6
1¢	blue	B. Franklin	Ty II		Imperf		7
1¢	blue	B. Franklin	Ty III		Imperf		8
1¢	blue	B. Franklin	Ty IIIa		Imperf		8A
1¢	blue	B. Franklin	Ty IV		Imperf		9
1¢	blue	B. Franklin	Ty I		15		18
1¢	brt. bl	B. Franklin	Ty I, reprint, w/o gum		12		40
1¢	blue	B. Franklin	Ty Ia		15		19
1¢	blue	B. Franklin	Ty II		15		20
1¢	blue	B. Franklin	Ty III		15		21
1¢	blue	B. Franklin	Ty IIIa		15		22
1¢	blue	B. Franklin	Ty IV		15		23
1¢	blue	B. Franklin	Ty V		15		24
1¢	blue	B. Franklin			12		63
1¢	blue	B. Franklin	"Z" Grill		12		85A
1¢	blue	B. Franklin	"E" Grill		12		86
1¢	blue	B. Franklin	"F" Grill		12		92
1¢	buff	B. Franklin	Issue of 1869 "G grill"		12		112
1¢	buff	B. Franklin	w/o grill, original gum		12		112b
1¢	buff	B. Franklin	Re-iss/wht crackly gum		12		123
1¢	buff	B. Franklin	Same, soft porous paper		12		133
1¢	brn. orng.	B. Franklin	Same, w/o gum		12		133a
1¢	ultra	B. Franklin	hard paper, w/grill		12		134
1¢	ultra	B. Franklin	Same, w/o grill		12		145
1¢	ultra	B. Franklin	Same, w/Secret mark		12		156
1¢	dk. ultra	B. Franklin	Soft porous paper		12		182
1¢	gray bl.	B. Franklin	Same, re-engraved		12		206
1¢	ultra	B. Franklin			12		212
1¢	dull bl.	B. Franklin	w/o Triangles		12		219
1¢	ultra	B. Franklin	w/ Tri. in Top corners		12	NW	246
1¢	blue	B. Franklin	w/ Tri. in Top corners		12	NW	247
1¢	blue	B. Franklin	w/ Tri. in Top corners		12	DL	264
1¢	dp. grn	B. Franklin	w/ Tri. in Top corners		12	DL	279
1¢	blue grn	B. Franklin	"Series 1902"		12	DL	300
1¢	blue grn	B. Franklin	"Series 1902"		Imperf	DL	314
1¢	blue grn	B. Franklin	"Series 1902" B. Pn./6		12	DL	300b
1¢	blue grn	B. Franklin	"Series 1902" Coil		12 Hz	DL	316
1¢	blue grn	B. Franklin	"Series 1902" Coil		12 Vert	DL	318
1¢	green	B. Franklin			12	DL	331
1¢	green	B. Franklin	Blue Paper		12	DL	357
1¢	green	B. Franklin			12	SL	374
1¢	green	B. Franklin			Imperf	DL	343
1¢	green	B. Franklin			Imperf	SL	383
1¢	green	B. Franklin	Bklt. Pn. of 6		12	DL	331a
1¢	green	B. Franklin	Bklt. Pn. of 6		12	SL	374a
1¢	green	B. Franklin	Coil		12 Hz	DL	348
1¢	green	B. Franklin	Coil		12 Hz	SL	385
1¢	green	B. Franklin	Coil		12 Vert	DL	352
1¢	green	B. Franklin	Coil		12 Vert	SL	387
1¢	green	B. Franklin	Coil		8.5 Hz	SL	390
1¢	green	B. Franklin	Coil		8.5 Vert	SL	392
1¢	green	Washington			12	SL	405
1¢	green	Washington			10	SL	424
1¢	green	Washington		F	10	NW	462
1¢	green	Washington		R	10	NW	543
1¢	green	Washington		F	11	NW	498
1¢	gray grn	Washington	Offset	F	11	NW	525
1¢	green	Washington	19mm x 22.5mm	R	11	NW	544
1¢	green	Washington	19.5-20mm x 22mm	R	11	NW	545
1¢	gray grn	Washington	Rossbach Press		12.5	NW	536
1¢	green	Washington		R	11x10	NW	538
1¢	green	Washington		R	10x11	NW	542
1¢	green	Washington			Imperf	SL	408
1¢	green	Washington			Imperf	NW	481
1¢	green	Washington	Offset		Imperf	NW	531
1¢	green	Washington	Bklt. Pn. of 6		12	SL	405b

Den.	Color	Subject	Type / Comment	Press	Perf.	Wmk.	Scott #
1¢	green	Washington	Bklt. Pn. of 6		10	SL	424d
1¢	green	Washington	Bklt. Pn. of 6		10	NW	462a
1¢	green	Washington	Bklt. Pn. of 6		11	NW	498e
1¢	green	Washington	Bklt. Pn. of 30		11	NW	498f
1¢	green	Washington	Coil		8.5 Hz	SL	410
1¢	green	Washington	Coil		8.5 Vert	SL	412
1¢	green	Washington	Coil	F	10 Hz	SL	441
1¢	green	Washington	Coil	R	10 Hz	SL	448
1¢	green	Washington	Coil	R	10 Hz	SL	441
1¢	green	Washington	Coil	R	10 Hz	NW	486
1¢	green	Washington	Coil	F	10 Vert	SL	443
1¢	green	Washington	Coil	R	10 Vert	SL	452
1¢	green	Washington	Coil	R	10 Vert	NW	490
1¢	deep grn	B. Franklin		F	11		552
1¢	green	B. Franklin	19¾ x 22¼mm	R	11		594
1¢	green	B. Franklin	19¼ x 22¾mm	R	11		596
1¢	green	B. Franklin		R	11x10		578
1¢	green	B. Franklin		R	10		581
1¢	green	B. Franklin		R	11x10.5		632
1¢	green	B. Franklin		F	Imperf		575
1¢	deep grn	B. Franklin	Bklt. Pn. of 6	F	11		552a
1¢	green	B. Franklin	Bklt. Pn. of 6	R	11x10.5		632a
1¢	green	B. Franklin	Coil	R	10 Vert		597
1¢	yel. grn.	B. Franklin	Coil	R	10 Hz		604
1¢	green	B. Franklin	Kansas Ovpt.		11x10.5		658
1¢	green	B. Franklin	Nebraska Ovpt.		11x10.5		669
1¢	green	Washington	1938 Prexie Issue		11x10.5		804
1¢	green	Washington	Bklt. Pn. of 6		11x10.5		804b
1¢	green	Washington	Coil		10 Vert		839
1¢	green	Washington	Coil		10 Hz		848
1¢	dk green	Washington	1954 Liberty Issue		11x10.5		1031
1¢	dk green	Washington	Coil		10 Vert		1054
1¢	green	A. Jackson			11x10.5		1209*
1¢	green	A. Jackson	Coil		10 Vert		1225*
1¢	green	T. Jefferson			11x10.5		1278
1¢	green	T. Jefferson	Bklt. Pn. of 8		11x10.5		1278a
1¢	green	T. Jefferson	B.Pn./4 + 2 labels		11x10.5		1278b
1¢	green	T. Jefferson	Coil		10 Vert		1299
1¢	dk blue	Inkwell & Quill			11x10.5		1581
1¢	dk blue	Inkwell & Quill	Coil		10 Vert		1811
1¢	black	Dorothea Dix			11		1844**
1¢	violet	Omnibus	Coil		10 Vert		1897
1¢	violet	Omnibus	Coil, re-engraved		10 Vert	B	2225
1¢	brnish verm	Margaret Mitchell			11		2168
1¢	multi	Kestrel	No "¢" Sign		11		2476
1¢	multi	Kestrel	'¢' sign added		11		2477
1¢	multi	Kestrel	Coil		10 Vert		3044
1¼¢	turquoise	Palace of Governors			10.5x11		1031A
1¼¢	turquoise	Palace of Governors	Coil		10 Hz		1054A
1¼¢	lt. grn	Albert Gallatin			11x10.5		1279
1½¢	yel brn	W.G. Harding		F	11		553
1½¢	yel brn	W.G. Harding		R	10		582
1½¢	yel brn	W.G. Harding		R	11x10.5		633
1½¢	brown	W.G. Harding	"Full Face"	R	11x10.5		684
1½¢	yel brn	W.G. Harding		F	Imperf		576
1½¢	yel brn	W.G. Harding		R	Imperf		631
1½¢	brown	W.G. Harding	Coil		10 Vert		598
1½¢	yel brn	W.G. Harding	Coil		10 Hz		605
1½¢	brown	W.G. Harding	"Full Face," Coil		10 Vert		686
1½¢	brown	W.G. Harding	Kansas Ovpt.		11x10.5		659
1½¢	brown	W.G. Harding	Nebraska Ovpt.		11x10.5		670
1½¢	bstr brn	M. Washington			11x10.5		805
1½¢	bstr brn	M. Washington	Coil		10 Vert		840
1½¢	bstr brn	M. Washington	Coil		10 Hz		849
1½¢	brn carm	Mount Vernon			10.5x11		1032
2¢	black	A. Jackson			12		73
2¢	black	A. Jackson	"D" Grill		12		84
2¢	black	A. Jackson	"Z" Grill		12		85B
2¢	black	A. Jackson	"E" Grill		12		87
2¢	black	A. Jackson	"F" Grill		12		93
2¢	brown	Horse & Rider	Issue of 1869 "G grill"		12		113
2¢	brown	Horse & Rider	w/o grill, original gum		12		113b
2¢	brown	Horse & Rider	Re-iss/wht crackly gum		12		124
2¢	red brown	A. Jackson	Hard paper, w/grill		12		135
2¢	red brown	A. Jackson	Hard paper,w/o grill		12		146
2¢	brown	A. Jackson	Same, w/secret mark		12		157
2¢	vermillion	A. Jackson	Yellowish wove (hard)		12		178
2¢	vermillion	A. Jackson	Soft porous paper		12		183
2¢	red brown	Washington			12		210
2¢	pl rd brn	Washington	Special Printing		12		211B
2¢	green	Washington			12		213
2¢	lake	Washington	w/o Triangles		12		219D
2¢	carmine	Washington	w/o Tri.		12		220

DEFINITIVE ISSUE IDENTIFIER

Den.	Color	Subject	Type / Comment	Press	Perf.	Wmk.	Scott #
2¢	pink	Washington	Ty I Tri. in Top corners		12	NW	248
2¢	carm. lake	Washington	Ty I Tri. "		12	NW	249
2¢	carmine	Washington	Ty I Tri. "		12	NW	250
2¢	carmine	Washington	Ty I Tri. "		12	DL	265
2¢	carmine	Washington	Ty II Tri. "		12	NW	251
2¢	carmine	Washington	Ty II Tri. "		12	DL	266
2¢	carmine	Washington	Ty III Tri. "		12	NW	252
2¢	carmine	Washington	Ty III Tri. "		12	DL	267
2¢	red	Washington	Ty III Tri. "		12	DL	279B
2¢	carm rose	Washington	Ty III Tri. "		12	DL	279Bc

319/322 "Shield" | 332/393 "TWO" Cents | 406/546 "2" Cents | 554/671

Den.	Color	Subject	Type / Comment	Press	Perf.	Wmk.	Scott #
2¢	red	Washington	Bklt. Pn. of 6		12	DL	279Be
2¢	carmine	Washington	"Series 1902"		12	DL	301
2¢	carmine	Washington	"Series 1902" B.Pn./6		12	DL	301c
2¢	carmine	Washington	"Shield" Design, Die I		12	DL	319
2¢	carmine	Washington	"Shield", Die II		12	DL	319i
2¢	carmine	Washington	"Shield", B.Pn./6, Die I		12	DL	319g
2¢	carmine	Washington	"Shield", B.Pn./6, Die II		12	DL	319h
2¢	lake	Washington	"Shield", B.Pn./6, Die II		12	DL	319q
2¢	carmine	Washington	"Shield" Design		Imperf	DL	320
2¢	lake	Washington	"Shield" Design		Imperf	DL	320a
2¢	carmine	Washington	"Shield" Coil		12 Hz	DL	321
2¢	carmine	Washington	"Shield" Coil		12 Vert	DL	322
2¢	carmine	Washington	"TWO CENTS" Design		12	DL	332
2¢	carmine	Washington	"TWO..." Blue Paper		12	DL	358
2¢	carmine	Washington	"TWO..."		12	SL	375
2¢	lake	Washington	"TWO..."		12	SL	375v
2¢	carmine	Washington	"TWO..."	F	11	DL	519
2¢	carmine	Washington	"TWO..."		Imperf	DL	344
2¢	carmine	Washington	"TWO..."		Imperf	SL	384
2¢	dark carm	Washington	"TWO..."		Imperf	SL	384v
2¢	carmine	Washington	"TWO..." Bklt. Pn. of 6		12	DL	332a
2¢	carmine	Washington	"TWO..." Bklt. Pn. of 6		12	SL	375a
2¢	carmine	Washington	"TWO..." Coil		12 Hz	DL	349
2¢	carmine	Washington	"TWO..." Coil		12 Hz	SL	386
2¢	carmine	Washington	"TWO..." Coil		12 Vert	DL	353
2¢	carmine	Washington	"TWO..." Coil		12 Vert	SL	388
2¢	carmine	Washington	"TWO..." Coil		8.5 Hz	SL	391
2¢	carmine	Washington	"TWO..." Coil		8.5 Vert	SL	393
2¢	carmine	Washington	"2 CENTS" Design		12	SL	406
2¢	lake	Washington	"2..."		12	SL	406v
2¢	carmine	Washington	"2..."		10	SL	425
2¢	carmine	Washington	"2..."		10	NW	463
2¢	pf carm rd	Washington	"2..."		11	SL	461
2¢	carmine	Washington	"2..." Ty I	F	11	NW	499
2¢	carmine	Washington	"2..." Ty Ia	F	11	NW	500
2¢	carmine	Washington	"2..." Offset Ty. IV		11	NW	526
2¢	carmine	Washington	"2..." Offset Ty. V		11	NW	527
2¢	carmine	Washington	"2..." Offset Ty. Va		11	NW	528
2¢	carmine	Washington	"2..." Offset Ty. VI		11	NW	528A
2¢	carmine	Washington	"2..." Offset Ty. VII		11	NW	528B
2¢	carm rose	Washington	"2..." Coil Waste:				
2¢	carm rose	Washington	Ty III	R	11	NW	546
2¢	carm rose	Washington	Ty II	R	11x10	NW	539
2¢	carm rose	Washington	Ty III	R	11x10	NW	540
2¢	carmine	Washington	"2 CENTS"	F	Imperf	SL	409
2¢	carmine	Washington	"2..."	F	Imperf	NW	482
2¢	carm rose	Washington	"2..." Offset Ty IV		Imperf	NW	532
2¢	carmine	Washington	"2..." Offset Ty V		Imperf	NW	533
2¢	carmine	Washington	"2..." Offset Ty Va		Imperf	NW	534
2¢	carmine	Washington	"2..." Offset Ty VI		Imperf	NW	534A
2¢	carmine	Washington	"2..." Offset Ty VII		Imperf	NW	534B
2¢	carmine	Washington	"2..." Bklt. Pn. of 6		12	SL	406a
2¢	carmine	Washington	"2..." Bklt. Pn. of 6		10	SL	425e
2¢	carmine	Washington	"2..." Bklt. Pn. of 6		10	NW	463a
2¢	carmine	Washington	"2..." Bklt. Pn. of 6	F	11	NW	499e
2¢	carmine	Washington	"2..." Bklt. Pn. of 30	F	11	NW	499f
2¢	carmine	Washington	"2 CENTS" Coil		8.5 Hz	SL	411
2¢	carmine	Washington	"2..." Coil		8.5 Vert	SL	413
2¢	carmine	Washington	"2..." Coil Ty I	F	10 Hz	SL	442
2¢	red	Washington	"2..." Coil Ty I	R	10 Hz	SL	449
2¢	carmine	Washington	"2..." Coil Ty II	R	10 Hz	NW	487
2¢	carmine	Washington	"2..." Coil Ty III	R	10 Hz	SL	450
2¢	carmine	Washington	"2..." Coil Ty III	R	10 Hz	NW	488
2¢	carmine	Washington	"2..." Coil Ty I	F	10 Vert	SL	444
2¢	carm red	Washington	"2..." Coil Ty I	R	10 Vert	SL	453
2¢	red	Washington	"2..." Coil Ty II	R	10 Vert	SL	454
2¢	carmine	Washington	"2..." Coil Ty II	R	10 Vert	NW	491
2¢	carmine	Washington	"2..." Coil Ty III	R	10 Vert	SL	455
2¢	carmine	Washington	"2..." Coil Ty III	R	10 Vert	NW	492
2¢	carmine	Washington	"2..." Hz Coil Ty I	R	Imperf	SL	459
2¢	deep rose	Washington	"2..." Hz Coil Ty Ia/ Shermack Ty III Perfs	F	*	NW	482A
2¢	carmine	Washington		F	11		554
2¢	carmine	Washington	19¾ x 22¼ mm	R	11		595

Den.	Color	Subject	Type / Comment	Press	Perf.	Wmk.	Scott #
2¢	carmine	Washington	19¾ x 22¼ mm	R	11x10		579
2¢	carmine	Washington	Die I	R	11x10.5		634
2¢	carmine	Washington	Die II	R	11x10.5		634A
2¢	carmine	Washington		R	10		583
2¢	carmine	Washington		F	Imperf		577
2¢	carmine	Washington	Bklt. Pn. of 6	F	11		554c
2¢	carmine	Washington	Bklt. Pn. of 6	R	10		583a
2¢	carmine	Washington	Bklt. Pn. of 6	R	11x10.5		634d
2¢	carmine	Washington	Coil		10 Vert		599
2¢	carmine	Washington	Coil Die II		10 Vert		599A
2¢	carmine	Washington	Coil		10 Hz		606
2¢	carmine	Washington	Kansas Ovpt.		11x10.5		660
2¢	carmine	Washington	Nebraska Ovpt.		11x10.5		671
2¢	rose carm	J. Adams			11x10.5		806
2¢	rose carm	J. Adams	Bklt. Pn. of 6		11x10.5		806b
2¢	rose carm	J. Adams	Coil		10 Vert		841
2¢	rose carm	J. Adams	Coil		10 Hz		850
2¢	carm rose	T. Jefferson			11x10.5		1033
2¢	carm rose	T. Jefferson	Coil		10 Vert		1055*
2¢	dk bl gray	Frank Lloyd Wright			11x10.5		1280
2¢	dk bl gray	Frank Lloyd Wright	B. Pn. of 5 + Label		11x10.5		1280a
2¢	dk bl gray	Frank Lloyd Wright	Booklet Pn. of 6		11x10.5		1280c
2¢	red brn	Speaker's Stand			11x10.5		1582
2¢	brn black	Igor Stravinsky			10.5x11		1845
2¢	black	Locomotive	Coil		10 Vert		1897A
2¢	black	Locomotive	Coil, "Re-engraved"		10 Vert	B	2226
2¢	brt blue	Mary Lyon			11		2169
2¢	multi	Red-headed Woodpecker			11.1		3032
2.5¢	gray bl	Bunker Hill			11x10.5		1034
2.5¢	gray bl	Bunker Hill	Coil		10 Vert		1056

10/26a | 64/94 | 136/214 | 221 | 253/268

Den.	Color	Subject	Type / Comment	Press	Perf.	Wmk.	Scott #
3¢	orng brn	Washington	Ty I		Imperf		10
3¢	dull red	Washington	Ty I		Imperf		11
3¢	rose	Washington	Ty I		15		25
3¢	dull red	Washington	Ty II		15		26
3¢	dull red	Washington	Ty IIa		15		26a
3¢	pink	Washington			12		64
3¢	pgn bld pink	Washington			12		64a
3¢	rose pink	Washington			12		64b
3¢	rose	Washington			12		65
3¢	lake	Washington			12		66
3¢	scarlet	Washington			12		74
3¢	rose	Washington	"A" Grill		12		79
3¢	rose	Washington	"B" Grill		12		82
3¢	rose	Washington	"C" Grill		12		83
3¢	rose	Washington	"D" Grill		12		85
3¢	rose	Washington	"Z" Grill		12		85C
3¢	rose	Washington	"E" Grill		12		88
3¢	rose	Washington	"F" Grill		12		94
3¢	ultra	Locomotive	"G grill"		12		114
3¢	ultra	Locomotive	w/o grill, Original gum		12		114a
3¢	green	Washington	Hard paper, w/grill		12		136
3¢	green	Washington	Same, w/o grill		12		147
3¢	green	Washington	Same, w/secret mark		12		158
3¢	green	Washington	Same, Soft porous paper		12		184
3¢	blue grn	Washington	Same, re-engraved		12		207
3¢	vermillion	Washington			12		214

302 | 333/541 | 720/722 | 12/30A | 67/95

Den.	Color	Subject	Type / Comment	Press	Perf.	Wmk.	Scott #
3¢	purple	A. Jackson	w/o Triangles		12		221
3¢	purple	A. Jackson	w/ Tri. in Top corners		12	NW	253
3¢	purple	A Jackson	w/ Tri. in Top corners		12	DL	268
3¢	violet	A. Jackson	"Series 1902"		12	DL	302
3¢	dp violet	Washington		F	12	DL	333
3¢	dp violet	Washington	Blue paper	F	12	DL	359
3¢	dp violet	Washington		F	12	SL	376
3¢	dp violet	Washington		F	10	SL	426
3¢	violet	Washington		F	10	NW	464
3¢	lt violet	Washington	Ty I	F	11	NW	501
3¢	dk violet	Washington	Ty II	F	11	NW	502
3¢	violet	Washington	Ty III Offset		11	NW	529
3¢	purple	Washington	Ty IV Offset		11	NW	530
3¢	violet	Washington	Ty II Coil Waste	R	11x10	NW	541
3¢	dp violet	Washington		F	Imperf	DL	345
3¢	violet	Washington	Ty I	F	Imperf	NW	483

Den.	Color	Subject	Type / Comment	Press	Perf.	Wmk.	Scott #
3¢	violet	Washington	Ty II	F	Imperf	NW	484
3¢	violet	Washington	Ty IV Offset		Imperf	NW	535
3¢	lt violet	Washington	B. Pn. of 6, Ty I	F	11	NW	501b
3¢	dk violet	Washington	B. Pn. of 6, Ty II	F	11	NW	502b
3¢	dp violet	Washington	Coil "Orangeburg"	F	12 Vert	SL	389
3¢	dp violet	Washington	Coil	F	8.5 Vert	SL	394
3¢	violet	Washington	Coil, Ty I	F	10 Vert	SL	445
3¢	violet	Washington	Coil, Ty I	R	10 Vert	SL	456
3¢	violet	Washington	Coil, Ty I	R	10 Hz	NW	489
3¢	dp violet	Washington	Coil, Ty I	R	10 Vert	NW	493
3¢	dull violet	Washington	Coil, Ty II	R	10 Vert	NW	494
3¢	violet	A. Lincoln		F	11		555
3¢	violet	A. Lincoln		R	10		584
3¢	violet	A. Lincoln		R	11x10.5		635
3¢	violet	A. Lincoln	Coil		10 Vert		600
3¢	violet	A. Lincoln	Kansas Ovpt.		11x10.5		661
3¢	violet	A. Lincoln	Nebraska Ovpt.		11x10.5		672
3¢	dp violet	Washington	Stuart Portrait		11x10.5		720
3¢	dp violet	Washington	Stuart B. Pn. of 6		11x10.5		720b
3¢	dp violet	Washington	Stuart Coil		10 Vert		721
3¢	dp violet	Washington	Stuart Coil		10 Hz		722
3¢	dp violet	T. Jefferson			11x10.5		807
3¢	dp violet	T. Jefferson	Bklt. Pn. of 6		11x10.5		807a
3¢	dp violet	T. Jefferson	Coil		10 Vert		842
3¢	dp violet	T. Jefferson	Coil		10 Hz		851
3¢	dp violet	Statue of Liberty			11x10.5		1035*
3¢	dp violet	Liberty	Bklt. Pn. of 6		11x10.5		1035a
3¢	dp violet	Liberty	Coil		10 Vert		1057*
3¢	violet	F. Parkman			10.5x11		1281
3¢	violet	F. Parkman	Coil		10 Vert		1297
3¢	olive	Early Ballot Box			11x10.5		1584
3¢	olive grn	Henry Clay			11x10.5		1846
3¢	dark grn	Handcar	Coil		10 Vert		1898
3¢	brt blue	Paul D. White MD			11		2170
3¢	claret	Conestoga Wagon	Coil		10 Vert		2252
3¢	multi	Bluebird			11		2478
3¢	multi	Eastern Bluebird			11.1		3033
(3¢)	multi	Dove	ABN		11x10.8		2877
(3¢)	multi	Dove	SVS		10.8x10.9		2878
3.1¢	brn (yel)	Guitar	Coil		10 Vert		1613
3.4¢	dk blsh grn	School Bus	Coil		10 Vert		2123
3.5¢	prpl (yel)	Weaver Violins	Coil		10 Vert		1813
4¢	**blue grn**	**A. Jackson**			**12**		**211**
4¢	carmine	A. Jackson			12		215
4¢	dk brn	A. Lincoln	w/ Triangles		12		222
4¢	dk brn	A. Lincoln	w/ Tri. in Top corners		12	NW	254
4¢	dk brn	A. Lincoln	w/ Tri. in Top corners		12	DL	269
4¢	rose brn	A. Lincoln	w/ Tri. in Top corners		12	DL	280
4¢	brown	U.S. Grant	"Series 1902"		12	DL	303
4¢	brown	U.S. Grant	Coil, Shermack Ty III		*	DL	314A
4¢	orng brn	Washington		F	12	DL	334
4¢	orng brn	Washington	Blue Paper	F	12	DL	360
4¢	brown	Washington		F	12	SL	377
4¢	brown	Washington		F	10	SL	427
4¢	orng brn	Washington		F	10	NW	465
4¢	brown	Washington		F	11	NW	503
4¢	orng brn	Washington		F	Imperf	DL	346
4¢	orng brn	Washington	Coil	F	12 Hz	DL	350
4¢	orng brn	Washington	Coil	F	12 Vert	DL	354
4¢	brown	Washington	Coil	F	8.5 Vert	SL	395
4¢	brown	Washington	Coil	F	10 Vert	SL	446
4¢	brown	Washington	Coil	R	10 Vert	SL	457
4¢	orng brn	Washington	Coil	R	10 Vert	NW	495
4¢	yel brn	M. Washington		F	11		556
4¢	yel brn	M. Washington		R	10		585
4¢	yel brn	M. Washington		R	11x10.5		636
4¢	yel brn	M. Washington	Coil		10 Vert		601
4¢	yel brn	M. Washington	Kansas Ovpt.		11x10.5		662
4¢	yel brn	M. Washington	Nebraska Ovpt.		11x10.5		673
4¢	brown	W.H. Taft			11x10.5		685
4¢	brown	W.H. Taft	Coil		10 Vert		687
4¢	red violet	J. Madison			11x10.5		808
4¢	red violet	J. Madison	Coil		10 Vert		843
4¢	red violet	A. Lincoln			11x10.5		1036*
4¢	red violet	A. Lincoln	Bklt. Pn. of 6		11x10.5		1036a
4¢	red violet	A. Lincoln	Coil		10 Vert		1058
4¢	black	A. Lincoln			11x10.5		1282*
4¢	black	A. Lincoln	Coil		10 Vert		1303
4¢	rose mag	"Books, etc."			11x10.5		1585
4¢	violet	Carl Schurz			10.5x11		1847
4¢	rdsh brn	Stagecoach	Coil		10 Vert		1898A
4¢	rdsh brn	Stagecoach	Coil, re-engr.	B	10 Vert		2228
4¢	bl violet	Father Flanagan			11		2171
4¢	claret	Steam Carriage	Coil		10		2451
4½¢	**dark gray**	**White House**			**11x10.5**		**809**
4½¢	dark gray	White House	Coil		10 Vert		844
4½¢	blue grn	The Hermitage			10.5x11		1037
4½¢	blue grn	The Hermitage	Coil		10 Hz		1059
4.9¢	brn blk	Buckboard	Coil		10 Vert		2124
5¢	**rd brn**	**B. Franklin**			**Imperf**		**1**
5¢	rd brn	B. Franklin	Bluish paper (reprint)		Imperf		3
5¢	rd brn	T. Jefferson			Imperf		12
5¢	brick red	T. Jefferson	Ty I		15		27
5¢	rd brn	T. Jefferson	Ty I		15		28
5¢	brt rd brn	T. Jefferson	Ty I		15		28b
5¢	Indian red	T. Jefferson	Ty I		15		28A
5¢	brown	T. Jefferson	Ty I		15		29

Den.	Color	Subject	Type / Comment	Press	Perf.	Wmk.	Scott #
5¢	orng brn	T. Jefferson	Ty II		15		30
5¢	brown	T. Jefferson	Ty II		15		30A
5¢	buff	T. Jefferson			12		67
5¢	red brn	T. Jefferson			12		75
5¢	brown	T. Jefferson			12		76
5¢	brown	T. Jefferson	"A" Grill		12		80
5¢	brown	T. Jefferson	"F" Grill		12		95
5¢	blue	Z. Taylor	Yellowish wove (hard)		12		179
5¢	blue	Z. Taylor	Soft Porous Paper		12		185
5¢	yel brn	J. Garfield			12		205
5¢	indigo	J. Garfield			12		216
5¢	choc	U.S. Grant	w/o Triangles		12		223
5¢	choc	U.S. Grant	w/ Tri. in Top corners		12	NW	255
5¢	choc	U.S. Grant	w/ Tri. in Top corners		12	DL	270
5¢	dk blue	U.S. Grant	w/ Tri. in Top corners		12	DL	281
5¢	blue	A. Lincoln	"Series 1902"		12	DL	304
5¢	blue	A. Lincoln	"Series 1902"		Imperf	DL	315
5¢	blue	Washington			12	DL	335
5¢	blue	Washington	Blue Paper		12	DL	361
5¢	blue	Washington			12	SL	378
5¢	blue	Washington			10	SL	428
5¢	blue	Washington			10	NW	466
5¢	blue	Washington			11	NW	504
5¢	blue	Washington			Imperf	DL	347
5¢	blue	Washington	Coil		12 Hz	DL	351
5¢	blue	Washington	Coil		12 Vert	DL	355
5¢	blue	Washington	Coil		8.5 Vert	SL	396
5¢	blue	Washington	Coil	F	10 Vert	SL	447
5¢	blue	Washington	Coil	R	10 Vert	SL	458
5¢	blue	Washington	Coil	R	10 Vert	NW	496
5¢	carmine	Washington	Error of Color		10	NW	467
5¢	rose	Washington	Error of Color		11	NW	505
5¢	carmine	Washington	Error of Color		Imperf	NW	485
5¢	dk blue	T. Roosevelt		F	11		557
5¢	blue	T. Roosevelt		R	10		586
5¢	dk blue	T. Roosevelt	Coil	R	10 Vert		602
5¢	dk blue	T. Roosevelt			11x10.5		637
5¢	dp blue	T. Roosevelt	Kansas Ovpt.		11x10.5		663
5¢	dp blue	T. Roosevelt	Nebraska Ovpt.		11x10.5		674
5¢	brt blue	J. Monroe			11x10.5		810
5¢	brt blue	J. Monroe	Coil		10 Vert		845
5¢	blue	J. Monroe			11x10.5		1038
5¢	dk bl gray	Washington			11x10.5		1213*
5¢	dk bl gray	Washington	Bklt. Pn. of 5 + "Mailman" Label		11x10.5		1213a
			"Use Zone Nos." Label		11x10.5		1213a*
			"Use Zip Code" Label		11x10.5		1213a*
5¢	dk bl gray	Washington	Coil		10 Vert		1229*
5¢	blue	Washington			11x10.5		1283*
5¢	blue	Washington	Re-engr. (clean face)		11x10.5		1283B
5¢	blue	Washington	Coil		10 Vert		1304
5¢	henna brn	Pearl Buck			10.5x11		1848
5¢	gray grn	Motorcycle	Coil		10 Vert		1899
5¢	dk olv grn	Hugo Black			11		2172
5¢	carmine	Luis Munoz Marin			11		2173*
5¢	black	Milk Wagon	Coil		10 Vert		2253
5¢	red	Circus Wagon	Coil Engraved		10 Vert		2452
5¢	carmine	Circus Wagon	Coil Gravure		10 Vert		2452B
5¢	brown	Canoe	Coil Engraved		10 Vert		2453
5¢	red	Canoe	Coil Gravure		10 Vert		2454
5.2¢	carmine	Sleigh	Coil		10 Vert		1900
5.3¢	black	Elevator	Coil		10 Vert		2254
5.5¢	dp mag	Star Rt Truck	Coil		10 Vert		2125
5.9¢	blue	Bicycle	Coil		10 Vert		1901
6¢	**ultra**	**Washington**	**"G" Grill**		**12**		**115**
6¢	carmine	A. Lincoln	hard wh paper, w/grill		12		137
6¢	carmine	A. Lincoln	Same, w/o grill		12		148
6¢	dull pink	A. Lincoln	Same, secret mark		12		159
6¢	pink	A. Lincoln	Same, sft porous pap		12		186
6¢	rose	A. Lincoln	Same, re-engraved		12		208
6¢	brn red	A. Lincoln	Same, re-engraved		12		208a
6¢	brn red	J. Garfield	w/o Triangles		12		224
6¢	dull brn	J. Garfield	w/ Tri. in Top corners		12	NW	256
6¢	dull brn	J. Garfield	w/ Tri. in Top corners		12	DL	271
6¢	dull brn	J. Garfield	w/ Tri. in Top corners		12	USIR	271a
6¢	lake	J. Garfield	w/ Tri. in Top corners		12	DL	282
6¢	claret	J. Garfield	"Series 1902"		12	DL	305
6¢	rd orng	Washington			12	DL	336
6¢	rd orng	Washington	Blue paper		12	DL	362
6¢	rd orng	Washington			12	SL	379
6¢	rd orng	Washington			10	SL	429
6¢	rd orng	Washington			10	NW	468
6¢	rd orng	Washington			11	NW	506
6¢	rd orng	J. Garfield		F	11		558
6¢	rd orng	J. Garfield		R	10		587
6¢	rd orng	J. Garfield		R	11x10.5		638
6¢	rd orng	J. Garfield	Kansas Ovpt.		11x10.5		664
6¢	rd orng	J. Garfield	Nebraska Ovpt.		11x10.5		675
6¢	dp orng	J. Garfield	Coil		10 Vert		723
6¢	red orng	J.Q. Adams			11x10.5		811
6¢	red orng	J.Q. Adams	Coil		10 Vert		846
6¢	carmine	T. Roosevelt			11x10.5		1039
6¢	gray brn	F.D. Roosevelt			10.5x11		1284*
6¢	gray brn	F.D. Roosevelt	Bklt. Pn. of 8		11x10.5		1284b
6¢	gray brn	F.D. Roosevelt	Bklt. Pn. of 5 + Label		11x10.5		1284c
6¢	gray brn	F.D. Roosevelt	Coil		10 Hz		1298
6¢	gray brn	F.D. Roosevelt	Coil		10 Vert		1305
6¢	dk bl,rd & grn	Flag & White House			11		1338

DEFINITIVE ISSUE IDENTIFIER

Den.	Color	Subject	Type / Comment	Press	Perf.	Wmk.	Scott #
6¢	dk bl,rd & grn	Flag & White House			11x10.5		1338D
6¢	dk bl,rd & grn	Flag & White House Coil			10 Vert		1338A
6¢	dk bl gray	D.D. Eisenhower			11x10.5		1393
6¢	dk bl gray	Eisenhower	Bklt. Pn of 8		11x10.5		1393a
6¢	dk bl gray	Eisenhower	Bklt. Pn of 5 + Label		11x10.5		1393b
6¢	dk bl gray	Eisenhower	Coil		10 Vert		1401
6¢	orng verm	Walter Lippmann			11		1849
6¢	multi	Circle of Stars	Bklt. Single		11		1892
6¢	red brn	Tricycle	Coil		10 Vert		2126
6.3¢	brick red	Liberty Bell	Coil		10 Vert		1518
7¢	**vermilion**	**E.M. Stanton**	**Hard wh paper, w/grill**		**12**		**138**
7¢	vermilion	E.M. Stanton	Same, w/o grill		12		149
7¢	orng verm	E.M. Stanton	Same, w/secret mark		12		160
7¢	black	Washington			12	SL	407
7¢	black	Washington			10	SL	430
7¢	black	Washington			10	NW	469
7¢	black	Washington			11	NW	507
7¢	black	Wm. McKinley		F	11		559
7¢	black	Wm. McKinley		R	10		588
7¢	black	Wm. McKinley		R	11x10.5		639
7¢	black	Wm. McKinley	Kansas Ovpt.		11x10.5		665
7¢	black	Wm. McKinley	Nebraska Ovpt.		11x10.5		676
7¢	sepia	A. Jackson			11x10.5		812
7¢	rose carm	W. Wilson			11x10.5		1040
7¢	brt blue	B. Franklin			10.5x11		1393D
7¢	brt carm	Abraham Baldwin			10.5x11		1850
7.1¢	lake	Tractor	Coil		10 Vert		2127
7.4¢	brown	Baby Buggy	Coil		10 Vert		1902
7.6¢	brown	Carreta	Coil		10 Vert		2255
7.7¢	brn (brt yl)	Saxhorns	Coil		10 Vert		1614
7.9¢	carm (yl)	Drum	Coil		10 Vert		1615
8¢	**lilac**	**W.T. Sherman w/o Triangles**			**12**		**225**
8¢	violet brn	W.T. Sherman	w/ Tri. in Top corners		12	NW	257
8¢	violet brn	W.T. Sherman	w/ Tri. in Top corners		12	DL	272
8¢	violet brn	W.T. Sherman	w/ Tri. in Top corners		12	USIR	272a
8¢	violet blk	M. Washington	"Series 1902"		12	DL	306
8¢	olive grn	Washington			12	DL	337
8¢	olive grn	Washington	Blue Paper		12	DL	363
8¢	olive grn	Washington			12	SL	380
8¢	pl olv grn	B. Franklin			12	SL	414
8¢	pl olv grn	B. Franklin			10	SL	431
8¢	olv grn	B. Franklin			10	NW	470
8¢	olv grn	B. Franklin			11	NW	508
8¢	olv grn	U.S. Grant		F	11		560
8¢	olv grn	U.S. Grant		R	10		589
8¢	olv grn	U.S. Grant		R	11x10.5		640
8¢	olv grn	U.S. Grant	Kansas Ovpt.		11x10.5		666
8¢	olv grn	U.S. Grant	Nebraska Ovpt.		11x10.5		677
8¢	olv grn	M. Van Buren			11x10.5		813
8¢	dk viol bl & carm	Statue of Liberty		Flat	11		1041
		Statue of Liberty		Rotary	11		1041B
		Statue of Liberty Redrawn		Giori	11		1042
8¢	brown	Gen. J.J. Pershing		R	11x10.5		1042A
8¢	violet	Albert Einstein			11x10.5		1285*
8¢	multi	Flag & Wh House			11x10.5		1338F
8¢	multi	Flag & Wh House Coil			10 Vert		1338G
8¢	blk,rd & bl gry	Eisenhower			11		1394
8¢	dp claret	Eisenhower	Bklt. sgl./B.Pn. of 8		11x10.5		1395a
8¢	dp claret	Eisenhower	Bklt. Pn. of 6		11x10.5		1395b
8¢	dp claret	Eisenhower	Bklt. Pn. of 4 + 2 Labels		11x10.5		1395c
8¢	dp claret	Eisenhower	Bklt. Pn. of 7 + Label		11x10.5		1395d
8¢	multi	Postal Service Emblem			11x10.5		1396
8¢	dp claret	Eisenhower	Coil		10 Vert		1402
8¢	olive blk	Henry Knox			10.5x11		1851
8.3¢	green	Ambulance	Coil		10 Vert		2128
8.3¢	green	Ambulance	Coil Precan.	B	10 Vert		2231
8.4¢	dk bl (yel)	Grand Piano	Coil		10 Vert		1615C
8.4¢	dp claret	Wheel Chair	Coil		10 Vert		2256
8.5¢	dk pris grn	Tow Truck	Coil		10 Vert		2129
9¢	**salmn rd**	**B. Franklin**			**12**	**SL**	**415**
9¢	salmn rd	B. Franklin			10	SL	432
9¢	salmn rd	B. Franklin			10	NW	471
9¢	salmn rd	B. Franklin			11	NW	509
9¢	rose	T. Jefferson		F	11		561
9¢	rose	T. Jefferson		R	10		590
9¢	orng red	T. Jefferson		R	11x10.5		641
9¢	lt rose	T. Jefferson	Kansas Ovpt.		11x10.5		667
9¢	lt rose	T. Jefferson	Nebraska Ovpt.		11x10.5		678
9¢	rose pink	W.H. Harrison			11x10.5		814
9¢	rose lilac	Alamo			10.5x11		1043
9¢	slate grn	Capitol Dome			11x10.5		1591
9¢	slate grn	Capitol Dome	Bklt. Single		11x10.5		1590
9¢	slate grn	Capitol Dome	Bklt. Single		10		1590a
9¢	slate grn	Capitol Dome	Coil		10 Vert		1616
9¢	dark grn	Sylvanus Thayer			10.5x11		1852
9.3¢	carm rose	Mail Wagon	Coil		10 Vert		1903
10¢	**black**	**Washington**			**Imperf**		**2**
10¢	black	Washington	Bluish paper (reprint)		Imperf		4
10¢	green	Washington	Ty I		Imperf		13
10¢	green	Washington	Ty II		Imperf		14
10¢	green	Washington	Ty III		Imperf		15
10¢	green	Washington	Ty IV		Imperf		16
10¢	green	Washington	Ty I		15		31

13/35 62B/96 17/36b 69/97

Den.	Color	Subject	Type / Comment	Press	Perf.	Wmk.	Scott #
10¢	green	Washington	Ty II		15		32
10¢	green	Washington	Ty III		15		33
10¢	green	Washington	Ty IV		15		34
10¢	green	Washington	Ty V		15		35
10¢	dark grn	Washington	Premier Gravure, Ty I		12		62B
10¢	yel grn	Washington	Ty II		12		68
10¢	green	Washington	"Z" Grill		12		85D
10¢	green	Washington	"E" Grill		12		89
10¢	yel grn	Washington	"F" Grill		12		96
10¢	yellow	Eagle & Shield	"G" Grill		12		116
10¢	brown	T. Jefferson	w/grill, Hard wh paper		12		139
10¢	brown	T. Jefferson	Same, w/o grill		12		150
10¢	brown	T. Jefferson	Same, w/secret mark		12		161
10¢	brown	T. Jefferson	Soft porous paper:				
		w/o secret mark			12		187
		w/secret mark			12		188
10¢	brown	T. Jefferson	Soft paper, re-engr.		12		209
10¢	green	D. Webster	w/o Triangles		12		226
10¢	dark grn	D. Webster	w/ Tri. in Top corners		12	NW	258
10¢	dark grn	D. Webster	w/ Tri. in Top corners		12	DL	273
10¢	brown	D. Webster	Ty I "		12	DL	282C
10¢	orng brn/brn	D. Webster	Ty II "		12	DL	283
10¢	pl rd brn	D. Webster	"Series 1902"		12	DL	307
10¢	yellow	Washington			12	DL	338
10¢	yellow	Washington	Blue Paper		12	DL	364
10¢	yellow	Washington			12	SL	381
10¢	yellow	Washington	Coil		12 Vert	DL	356
10¢	orng yel	B. Franklin			12	SL	416
10¢	orng yel	B. Franklin			10	SL	433
10¢	orng yel	B. Franklin			10	NW	472
10¢	orng yel	B. Franklin			11	NW	510
10¢	orng yel	B. Franklin	Coil	R	10 Vert	NW	497
10¢	yel orng	J. Monroe		F	11	NW	562
10¢	yel orng	J. Monroe		R	10	NW	591
10¢	orange	J. Monroe		R	11x10.5	NW	642
10¢	orange	J. Monroe	Coil	R	10 Vert	NW	603
10¢	orng yel	J. Monroe	Kansas Ovpt.		11x10.5	NW	668
10¢	orng yel	J. Monroe	Nebraska Ovpt.		11x10.5	NW	679
10¢	brn red	J. Tyler			11x10.5		815
10¢	brn red	J. Tyler	Coil		10 Vert		847
10¢	rose lake	Indep. Hall			10.5x11		1044*
10¢	lilac	A. Jackson			11x10.5		1286*
10¢	red & bl	Crossed Flags			11x10.5		1509
10¢	red & bl	Crossed Flags	Coil		10 Vert		1519
10¢	blue	Jefferson Mem.			11x10.5		1510
10¢	blue	Jefferson Mem.	Bklt. Pn. of 5 + Label		11x10.5		1510b
10¢	blue	Jefferson Mem.	Bklt. Pn. of 8		11x10.5		1510c
10¢	blue	Jefferson Mem.	Bklt. Pn. of 6		11x10.5		1510d
10¢	blue	Jefferson Mem.	Coil		10 Vert		1520
10¢	multi	"Zip Code"			11x10.5		1511
10¢	violet	Justice			11x10.5		1592
10¢	violet	Justice	Coil		10 Vert		1617
10¢	prus bl	Richard Russell			10.5x11		1853
10¢	lake	Red Cloud			11		2175
10¢	sky blue	Canal Boat	Coil		10 Vert		2257
10¢	green	Tractor Trailer	Coil Intaglio		10 Vert		2457
10¢	green	Tractor Trailer	Coil Gravure		10 Vert		2458
10.1¢	slate blue	Oil Wagon	Coil		10 Vert		2130
10.9¢	purple	Hansom Cab	Coil		10 Vert		1904
11	**dark grn**	**B. Franklin**			**10**	**SL**	**434**
11¢	dark grn	B. Franklin			10	NW	473
11¢	light grn	B. Franklin			11	NW	511
11¢	lt bl/bl grn	R.B. Hayes		F	11		563
11¢	light blue	R.B. Hayes		R	11x10.5		692
11¢	ultra	J.K. Polk			11x10.5		816
11¢	carm & dk viol bl	Statue of Liberty			11		1044A*
11¢	orange	Printing Press			11x10.5		1593
11¢	dk blue	Alden Partridge			11		1854
11¢	red	RR Caboose	Coil		10 Vert		1905
11¢	dk green	Stutz Bearcat	Coil		10 Vert		2131
12¢	**black**	**Washington**			**Imperf**		**17**
12¢	black	Washington	Plate 1		15		36
12¢	black	Washington	Plate 3		15		36b
12¢	black	Washington			12		69
12¢	black	Washington	"Z" Grill		12		85E
12¢	black	Washington	"E" Grill		12		90
12¢	black	Washington	"F" Grill		12		97
12¢	green	S.S. Adriatic	"G grill"		12		117
12¢	dull violet	H. Clay	Hard wh paper, w/grill		12		140
12¢	dull violet	H. Clay	Same, w/o grill		12		151
12¢	blksh viol	H. Clay	Same, w/secret mark		12		162
12¢	claret brn	B. Franklin			12	SL	417
12¢	claret brn	B. Franklin			10	SL	435

DEFINITIVE ISSUE IDENTIFIER

Den.	Color	Subject	Type / Comment	Press	Perf.	Wmk.	Scott #
12¢	copper rd	B. Franklin			10	SL	435a
12¢	claret brn	B. Franklin			10	NW	474
12¢	claret brn	B. Franklin			11	NW	512
12¢	brn carm	B. Franklin			11	NW	512a
12¢	brn violet	G. Cleveland		F	11		564
12¢	brn violet	G. Cleveland		R	11x10.5		693
12¢	bright viol	Z. Taylor			11x10.5		817
12¢	red	B. Harrison			11x10.5		1045*
12¢	black	Henry Ford			10.5x11		1286A*
12¢	rd brn (bge)	Liberty Torch	Coil		10 Vert		1816
12¢	dk blue	Stanley Stmr	Ty I Coil		10 Vert		2132
12¢	dk blue	Stanley Stmr	Ty II Coil, precanc.		10 Vert		2132b
12.5¢	olive grn	Pushcart	Coil		10 Vert		2133
13¢	purp blk	B. Harrison	"Series 1902"		12	DL	308
13¢	blue grn	Washington			12	DL	339
13¢	blue grn	Washington	Blue Paper		12	DL	365
13¢	apple grn	B. Franklin			11	NW	513
13¢	green	B. Harrison		F	11		622
13¢	yel grn	B. Harrison		R	11x10.5		694
13¢	bue grn	M. Fillmore			11x10.5		818
13¢	brown	J.F. Kennedy			11x10.5		1287*
13¢	brown	Liberty Bell			11x10.5		1595
13¢	brown	Liberty Bell	Bklt. Pn. of 6		11x10.5		1595a
13¢	brown	Liberty Brll	Bklt. Pn. of 7 + Label		11x10.5		1595b
13¢	brown	Liberty Bell	Bklt. Pn. of 8		11x10.5		1595c
13¢	brown	Liberty Bell	Bklt. Pn of 5 + Label		11x10.5		1595d
13¢	brown	Liberty Bell	Coil		10 Vert		1618
13¢	multi	Eagle & Shield	Bullseye Perfs		11x10.5		1596
13¢	multi	Eagle & Shield	Line Perfs		11		1596d
13¢	dk bl & rd	Flag Over Indep. Hall			11x10.5		1622
13¢	dk. bl & rd	Flag Over Indep. Hall			11		1622c
13¢	dk bl & rd	Flag Over Indep. Hall	Coil		10 Vert		1625
13¢	bl & rd	Flag Over Captl	Bklt. Single		11x10.5		1623
13¢	bl & rd	Flag Over Captl	Bklt. Single		10		1623b
13¢	bl & rd	Flag Over Captl	B. Pn. of 8 (7 #1623 (13¢) + 1 # 1590 (9¢))		11X10.5		1623a
13¢	bl & rd	Flag Over Capt	B. Pn. of 8 (7 #1623b (13¢) + 1 #1590a (9¢))		10		1623c
13¢	brn & bl (grn bistr)	Indian Head Penny			11		1734
13¢	lt maroon	Crazy Horse			10.5x11		1855
13¢	black	Patrol Wagon	Coil		10 Vert		2258
13.2¢	slate grn	Coal Car	Coil		10 Vert		2259
14¢	blue	American Indian		F	11		565
14¢	dk blue	American Indian		R	11x10.5		695
14¢	blue	F. Pierce			11x10.5		819
14¢	gray brn	Fiorello LaGuardia			11x10.5		1397
14¢	slate grn	Sinclair Lewis			11		1856
14¢	sky blue	Iceboat	Coil, overall tag		10 Vert		2134
14¢	sky blue	Iceboat, Ty II	Coil, block tag	B	10 Vert		2134b
14¢	crimson	Julia Ward Howe			11		2176
15¢	black	A. Lincoln			12		77
15¢	black	A. Lincoln	"Z" Grill		12		85F
15¢	black	A. Lincoln	"E" Grill		12		91
15¢	black	A. Lincoln	"F" Gril		12		98
15¢	brn & bl	Landing of Columbus:					
			Ty I Frame, "G grill"		12		118
			Same, w/o grill, o.g.		12		118a
			Ty II Frame, "G grill"		12		119
			Ty III, wh crackly gum		12		129
15¢	orange	D. Webster	Hard wh paper, w/grill		12		141
15¢	brt orng	D. Webster	Same, w/o grill		12		152
15¢	yel orng	D. Webster	Same, w/secret mark		12		163
15¢	red orng	D. Webster	Soft porous paper		12		189
15¢	indigo	H. Clay	w/o Triangles		12		227
15¢	dk blue	H. Clay	w/ Tri. in Top corners		12	NW	259
15¢	dk blue	H. Clay	w/ Tri. in Top corners		12	DL	274
15¢	olive grn	H. Clay	w/ Tri. in Top corners		12	DL	284
15¢	olive grn	H. Clay	"Series 1902"		12	DL	309
15¢	pl ultra	Washington			12	DL	340
15¢	pl ultra	Washington	Blue Paper		12	DL	366
15¢	pl ultra	Washington			12	SL	382
15¢	gray	B. Franklin			12	SL	418
15¢	gray	B. Franklin			10	SL	437
15¢	gray	B. Franklin			10	NW	475
15¢	gray	B. Franklin			11	NW	514
15¢	gray	Statue of Liberty		F	11		566
15¢	gray	Statue of Liberty		R	11x10.5		696
15¢	blue gray	J. Buchanan			11x10.5		820
15¢	rose lake	John Jay			11x10.5		1046*
15¢	maroon	O.W. Holmes			11x10.5		1288
15¢	dk rse clrt	O.W. Holmes	Type II		11x10.5		1288d
15¢	dk rse clrt	O.W. Holmes	Bklt. sgl./B.Pn. of 8		10		1288Bc
15¢	gray, dk bl & red	Ft McHenry Flag			11		1597
15¢		Ft McHenry Flag	Bklt. sgl./B. Pn. of 8		11x10.5		1598a
15¢		Ft McHenry Flag	Coil		10 Vert		1618C
15¢	multi	Roses	Bklt. sgl./B. Pn. of 8		10		1737a
15¢	sepia (yel)	Windmills	Bklt. Pn. of 10		11		1742a
15¢	rd brn & sepia	Dolley Madison			11		1822
15¢	claret	Buffalo Bill Cody			11		2177
15¢	violet	Tugboat	Coil		10 Vert		2260
15¢	multi	Beach Umbrella	Bklt. sgl./B. Pn. of 10		11.5x11		2443a
16¢	black	A. Lincoln			11x10.5		821
16¢	brown	Ernie Pyle			11x10.5		1398
16¢	blue	Statue of Liberty			11x10.5		1599
16¢	blue	Statue of Liberty	Coil		10 Vert		1619
16.7¢	rose	Popcorn Wagon	Coil		10 Vert		2261
17¢	black	W. Wilson		F	11		623
17¢	black	W. Wilson		R	10.5x11		697
17¢	rose red	A. Johnson			11x10.5		822
17¢	green	Rachel Carson			10.5x11		1857
17¢	ultra	Electric Auto	Coil		10 Vert		1906
17¢	sky blue	Dog Sled	Coil		10 Vert		2135
17¢	dk bl grn	Belva Ann Lockwood			11		2178
17.5¢	dk violet	Racing Car	Coil		10 Vert		2262
18¢	brn carm	U.S. Grant			11x10.5		823
18¢	violet	Dr. Elizabeth Blackwell			11x10.5		1399
18¢	dark bl	George Mason			10.5x11		1858
18¢	dark brn	Wildlife Animals	Bklt. Pn. of 10		11		1889a
18¢	multi	Flag/Amber Waves...			11		1890
18¢	multi	Flag/Sea to...Sea	Coil		10 Vert		1891
18¢	multi	Flag/Purple Mtns...Bklt. Single			11		1893
18¢	multi	Flag/Purple Mnts...Bklt. Pn. of 8 (7 #1893 (18¢) + 1 #1892 (6¢))			11		1893a
18¢	dk brn	Surrey	Coil		10 Vert		1907
18¢	multi	Washington & Monument	Coil		10 Vert		2149
19¢	brt violet	R.B. Hayes			11x10.5		824
19¢	brown	Sequoyah			10.5x11		1859
19¢	multi	Fawn			11.5x11		2479
19¢	multi	Fishing Boat	Coil Type I		10 Vert		2529
19¢	multi	Fishing Boat	Coil Type III		9.8 Vert		2529C
19¢	multi	Balloon	Bklt. sgl./B. Pn. of 10		10		2530,a
20¢	ultra	B. Franklin			12	SL	419
20¢	ultra	B. Franklin			10	SL	438
20¢	lt. ultra	B. Franklin			10	NW	476
20¢	lt. ultra	B. Franklin			11	NW	515
20¢	carm rse	Golden Rose		F	11		567
20¢	carm rse	Golden Gate		R	10.5x11		698
20¢	brt bl grn	J. Garfield			11x10.5		825
20¢	ultra	Monticello			10.5x11		1047
20¢	dp olive	George C. Marshall			11x10.5		1289*
20¢	claret	Ralph Bunche			10.5x11		1860
20¢	green	Thomas H. Gallaudet			10.5x11		1861
20¢	black	Harry S. Truman			11		1862**
20¢	blk, dk bl & red	Flag/Supreme Court			11		1894
20¢		Flag/Sup. Ct.	Coil		10 Vert		1895
20¢		Flag/Sup. Ct.	Bklt. sgl./Pns. of 6 & 10		11x10.5		1896,a,b
20¢	vermilion	Fire Pumper	Coil		10 Vert		1908
20¢	dk blue	Rocky Mtn. Bighorn	Bklt. sgl./Pn. of 10		11		1949a
20¢	sky blue	Consumer Ed.	Coil		10 Vert		2005
20¢	bl violet	Cable Car	Coil		10 Vert		2263
20¢	red brown	Virginia Agpar			11.1x11		2179
20¢	green	Cog Railway	Coil		10 Vert		2463
20¢	multi	Blue Jay	Bklt. Sgl./B. Pn. of 10		11x10		2483,a
20¢	multi	Blue Jay	Self-adhesive		Die-Cut		3048
20¢	multi	Blue Jay	Coil		11.6 Vert		3053
20.5¢	rose	Fire Engine	Coil		10 Vert		2264
21¢	dull blue	Chester A. Arthur			11x10.5		826
21¢	green	Amadeo Giannini			11x10.5		1400
21¢	bl violet	Chester Carlson			11		2181
21¢	olive grn	RR Mail Car	Coil		10 Vert		2265
21.1¢	multi	Envelopes	Coil		10 Vert		2150
22¢	vermilion	G. Cleveland			11x10.5		827
22¢	dk chlky bl	John J. Audubon			11		1863**
22¢	bl rd blk	Flag/Capitol			11		2114
22¢	bl rd blk	Flag/Capitol	Coil		10 Vert		2115
22¢	bl rd blk	Flag/Capitol/"of the People"	Bklt. Sgl.		10 Hz		2116
22¢	bl rd blk	Flag/Capitol/"of the People"	B. Pn. of 5		10 Hz		2116a
22¢	blk & brn	Seashells	Bklt. Pn. of 10		10		2121a
22¢	multi	Fish	Bklt. Pn. of 5		10 Hz		2209a
22¢	multi	Flag & Fireworks			11		2276
22¢	multi	Flag & Fireworks	Bklt. Pn. of 20		11		2276a
23¢	purple	Mary Cassatt			11		2181
23¢	dk blue	Lunch Wagon	Coil		10 Vert		2464
23¢	multi	Flag & Presorted First Class	Coil		10 Vert		2605
23¢	multi	USA & Flag Presort First Cl	Coil		10 Vert	ABNC	2606
23¢	multi	USA & Flag Presort First Cl	Coil		10 Vert	BEP	2607
23¢	multi	USA & Flag Presort First Cl	Coil		10 Vert	SVS	2608
24¢	gray lilac	Washington	"Twenty Four Cents"		15		37
24¢	red lilac	Washington	"24 Cents"		12		70
24¢	brn lilac	Washington			12		70a
24¢	steel blue	Washington			12		70b
24¢	violet	Washington			12		70c
24¢	grayish lil	Washington			12		70d
24¢	lilac	Washington			12		78
24¢	grayish lil	Washington			12		78a
24¢	gray	Washington			12		78b
24¢	blkish viol	Washington			12		78c
24¢	gray lilac	Washington	"F" Grill		12		99
24¢	grn & viol	Decl. of Indep.	"G grill"		12		120
24¢	grn & viol	Decl. of Indep.	w/o grill, original gum		12		120a
24¢	purple	Gen'l. W. Scott	Hard wh paper, w/grill		12		142
24¢	purple	Gen'l. W. Scott	Same, w/o grill		12		153
24¢	gray blk	B. Harrison			11x10.5		828
24¢	red (blue)	Old North Church			11x10.5		1603
24.1¢	dp ultra	Tandem Bicycle	Coil		10 Vert		2266
25¢	yel grn	Niagara Falls		F	11		568
25¢	blue grn	Niagara Falls		R	10.5x11		699
25¢	dp rd lil	Wm. McKinley			11x10.5		829
25¢	green	Paul Revere			11x10.5		1048
25¢	green	Paul Revere	Coil		10 Vert		1059A*
25¢	rose	Frederick Douglass			11x10.5		1290*
25¢	orng brn	Bread Wagon	Coil		10 Vert		2136
25¢	blue	Jack London			11		2182
25¢	blue	Jack London	Bklt. Pn. of 10		11		2182a
25¢	blue	Jack London	Bklt. Sgl./B. Pn. of 6		10		2197,a
25¢	multi	Flag & Clouds			11		2278
25¢	multi	Flag & Clouds	Bklt. Sgl./B. Pn. of 6		10		2285Ac
25¢	multi	Flag/Yosemite	Coil		10 Vert		2280

DEFINITIVE ISSUE IDENTIFIER

Den.	Color	Subject	Type / Comment	Press	Perf.	Wmk.	Scott #
25¢	multi	Honeybee	Coil		10 Vert		2281
25¢	multi	Pheasant	Bklt. Sgl./B. Pn. of 10		11		2283,a
25¢	multi	Pheasant	Same, w/o red in sky		11		2283b,c
25¢	multi	Grossbeak	Bklt. Single		10		2284
25¢	multi	Owl	Bklt. Single		10		2285
25¢	multi	Grossbk & Owl	Bklt. Pn. of 10 (5 ea.)		10		2285b
25¢	multi	Eagle & Shield	Self-adhesive		Die cut		2431
25¢	dk rd & bl	Flag	Self-adhesive		Die cut		2475
28¢	brn (bl)	Ft. Nisqually			11x10.5		1604
28¢	myrtle grn	Sitting Bull			11		2183
29¢	blue (bl)	Sandy Hook Lighthouse			11x10.5		1605
29¢	blue	Earl Warren			11		2184
29¢	dk violet	T. Jefferson			11		2185
29¢	multi	Red Squirrel	Self-adhesive		Die cut		2489
29¢	multi	Rose	Self-adhesive		Die cut		2490
29¢	multi	Pine Cone	Self-adhesive		Die cut		2491
29¢	blk & multi	Wood Duck	Bklt. sgl./B. Pn. of 10		10		2484,a
29¢	red & multi	Wood Duck	Bklt. sgl./B. Pn. of 10		11		2485,c
29¢	multi	African Violet	Bklt. sgl./B. Pn. of 10		10x11		2486,a
29¢	bl,rd,clear	Flag/Rushmore	Coil, Engraved		10		2523
29¢	bl,rd,brn	Flag/Rushmore	Coil, Gravure		10		2523A
29¢	multi	Tulip			11		2524
29¢	multi	Tulip			12.5x13		2524a
29¢	multi	Tulip	Coil	Roulette	10 Vert		2525
29¢	multi	Tulip	Coil		10 Vert		2526
29¢	multi	Tulip	Bklt. sgl./B. Pn. of 10		11		2527,a
29¢	multi	Flag/Rings	Bklt. sgl./B. Pn. of 10		11		2528
29¢	multi	Flags on Parade			11		2531
29¢	blk,gld,grn	Liberty/Torch	Self-adhesive		Die cut		2531A
29¢	multi	Flag & Pledge	blk. denom Bklt. sgl., Bklt. Pn. of 10		10		2593,a
29¢	multi	Flag & Pledge	red denom., Bklt. sgl., Bklt. Pn. of 10		10		2594,a
29¢	brn,multi	Eagle & Shield	Self-adhesive		Die cut		2595
29¢	grn,multi	Eagle & Shield	Self-adhesive		Die cut		2596
29¢	red,multi	Eagle & Shield	Self-adhesive		Die cut		2597
29¢	multi	Eagle	Self-adhesive		Die cut		2598
29¢	blue,red	Flag/White House	Coil		10 Vert		2609
29¢	multi	Liberty	Self-adhesive		Die cut		2599
30¢	orange	B. Franklin	Numeral at bottom	15			38
30¢	orange	B. Franklin	Numerals at Top	12			71
30¢	orange	B. Franklin	"A" Grill	12			81
30¢	orange	B. Franklin	"F" Grill	12			100
30¢	bl & carm	Eagle, Shield & Flags, "G" Grill		12			121
			w/o grill, original gum	12			121a
30¢	black	A. Hamilton	Hard wh paper, w/grill	12			143
30¢	black	A. Hamilton	Same, w/o grill	12			154
30¢	gray blk	A. Hamilton	Same	12			165
30¢	full blk./grnish	A. Hamilton	Soft porous paper	12			190
30¢	orng brn	A. Hamilton		12			217
30¢	black	T. Jefferson		12			228
30¢	orng red	B. Franklin		12		SL	420
30¢	orng red	B. Franklin		10		SL	439
30¢	orng red	B. Franklin		10		NW	476A
30¢	orng red	B. Franklin		11		NW	516
30¢	olive brn	Buffalo		F	11		569
30¢	brown	Buffalo		R	10.5x11		700
30¢	dp ultra	T. Roosevelt			11x10.5		830
30¢	blue	T. Roosevelt			11x10.5		830 var
30¢	dp blue	T. Roosevelt			11x10.5		830 var
30¢	black	R.E. Lee			11x10.5		1049
30¢	red lilac	John Dewey			10.5x11		1291*
30¢	green	Morris School			11x10.5		1606
30¢	olv gray	Frank C. Laubach			11		1864**
30¢	multi	Cardinal			11		2480
32¢	blue	Ferryboat	Coil		10 Vert		2466
32¢	multi	Peach	Booklet Single		10x11		2487
32¢	multi	Peach	Self-adhesive		Die cut		2493
32¢	multi	Peach	Self-adhesive Coil		Die cut		2495
32¢	multi	Pear	Booklet Single		10x11		2488
32¢	multi	Pear	Self-adhesive		Die Cut		2494
32¢	multi	Pear	Self-adhesive Coil		Die cut		2495A
32¢	multi	Peach & Pear	Bklt. Pane of 10		10x11		2488a
32¢	multi	Peach & Pear	Self-adhesive Pane		Die cut		2494A
32¢	multi	Peach & Pear	Self-adhesive Coil		Die-cut		2495-95A
32¢	multi	Pink Rose	Self-adhesive		Die cut		2492
32¢	red-brown	James K. Polk			11.2		2587
32¢	multi	Flag over Porch			10.04		2897
32¢	multi	Flag over Porch	Coil	BEP	9.9 Vert		2913
32¢	multi	Flag over Porch	Coil	SVS	9.9 Vert		2914
32¢	multi	Flag over Porch	Self-adhesive Coil		Die cut 8.7		2915
32¢	multi	Flag over Porch	Self-adhesive Coil		Die cut 9.7		2915A
32¢	multi	Flag over Porch	Self-adhesive Coil		Die cut 11.5		2915B
32¢	multi	Flag over Porch	Self-adhesive Coil		Die cut 10.9		2915C
32¢	multi	Flag over Porch	Self-adhesive Coil		Die cut 9.8		2915D
32¢	multi	Flag over Porch	Bklt. Sgle./P.Pn. of 10		11x10		2916a
32¢	multi	Flag over Porch	Self-adhesive		Die-cut 8.8		2920,20b
32¢	multi	Flag over Porch	Self-adhesive		Die-cut 11.3		2920d
32¢	multi	Flag over Porch	Self-adhesive		Die-cut 9.8		2921a
32¢	multi	Flag over Porch	Linerless SA Coil		Die-cut		3133
32¢	multi	Flag over Field	Self-adhesive		Die cut		2919
32¢		Henry R. Luce			11		2935
32¢		Lila & DeWitt Wallace			11		2936
32¢	brown	Milton S. Hershey			11		2933
32¢		Cal Farley			11		2934
32¢	multi	Yellow Rose	Self-adhesive		Die-cut		3049

Den.	Color	Subject	Type / Comment	Press	Perf.	Wmk.	Scott#
32¢	multi	Yellow Rose	Self-adhesive Coil		Die-cut 9.8 Vert.		3054
32¢	multi	Statue of Liberty			Die-cut 11		3122
32¢	multi	Statue of Liberty			Die-cut 11.5x11.8		3122E
32¢	multi	Citron, Moth	Self-adhesive		Die-cut		3126,28a
32¢	multi	Flowering Pineapple, Cockroaches	Self-adhesive		Die-cut		3127,29a
35¢	gray	Charles R. Drew M.D.			10.5x11		1865
35¢	black	Dennis Chavez			11		2186
37¢	blue	Robert Millikan			10.5x11		1866
39¢	rose lilac	Grenville Clark			11		1867**
40¢	brn red	J. Marshall			11x10.5		1050
40¢	bl black	Thomas Paine			11x10.5		1292*
40¢	dk grn	Lillian M. Gilbreth			11		1868**
40¢	dk blue	Claire Chennault			11		2187
45¢	brt blue	Harvey Cushing, MD			11		2188
45¢	multi	Pumpkinseed Fish			11		2481
46¢	carmine	Ruth Benedict			11		2938
50¢	orange	T. Jefferson	w/ Tri. in Top corners	12		NW	260
50¢	orange	T. Jefferson	w/ Tri. in Top corners	12		DL	275
50¢	orange	T. Jefferson	"Series 1902"	12		DL	310
50¢	violet	Washington		12		DL	341
50¢	violet	B. Franklin		12		SL	421
50¢	violet	B. Franklin		12		DL	422
50¢	violet	B. Franklin		10		SL	440
50¢	lt violet	B. Franklin		10		NW	477
50¢	rd violet	B. Franklin		11		NW	517
50¢	lilac	Arlington Amph		F	11		570
50¢	lilac	Arlington Amph		R	10.5x11		701
50¢	lt rd viol	W.H. Taft			11x10.5		831
50¢	brt prpl	S.B. Anthony			11x10.5		1051
50¢	rose mag	Lucy Stone			11x10.5		1293*
50¢	blk & orng	Iron "Betty" Lamp			11		1608
50¢	brown	Chester W. Nimitz			11		1869**
52¢	purple	Hubert Humphrey			11		2189
55¢	green	Alice Hamilton			11		2940
56¢	scarlet	John Harvard			11		2190
65¢	dk blue	"Hap" Arnold			11		2191
75¢	dp mag	Wendell Wilkie			11		2192
78¢	purple	Alice Paul			11.2		2943
90¢	blue	Washington	"Ninety Cents"	15			39
90¢	blue	Washington	"90 Cents"	12			72
90¢	blue	Washington	Same, "F" Grill	12			101
90¢	carm & blk	A. Lincoln	"G grill"	12			122
90¢	carm & blk	A. Lincoln	w/o grill, o.g.	12			122a
90¢	carmine	Com. Perry	Hard wh paper, w/grill	12			144
90¢	carmine	Com. Perry	Same, w/o grill	12			155
90¢	rose carm	Com. Perry	Same	12			166
90¢	carmine	Com. Perry	Soft porous paper	12			191
90¢	purple	Com. Perry	Soft porous paper	12			218
90¢	orange	Com. Perry		12			229
$1.00	black	Com. Perry	Ty I	12		NW	261
$1.00	black	Com. Perry	Ty I	12		DL	276
$1.00	black	Com. Perry	Ty II	12		NW	261A
$1.00	black	Com. Perry	Ty II	12		DL	276A
$1.00	black	D.G. Farragut		12		DL	311
$1.00	violet brn	Washington		12		DL	342
$1.00	violet brn	B. Franklin		10		DL	423
$1.00	violet blk	B. Franklin		10		NW	460
$1.00	violet blk	B. Franklin		10		NW	478
$1.00	violet brn	B. Franklin		11		NW	518
$1.00	deep brn	B. Franklin		11		NW	518b
$1.00	violet blk	Lincoln Memorial			11		571
$1.00	prpl & blk	W. Wilson			11		832
$1.00	prpl & blk	W. Wilson			11	USIR	832b
$1.00	rd viol & blk	W. Wilson	Dry Print, smooth gum		11		832c
$1.00	purple	P. Henry			11x10.5		1052
$1.00	dl purple	Eugene O'Neill			11x10.5		1294*
$1.00	dl purple	Eugene O'Neill	Coil		10 Vert		1305
$1.00	brn,orng&yel (tan)	Rush Lamp & Candle Holder			11		1610
$1.00	dk prus grn	Bernard Revel			11		2193
$1.00	dk blue	Johns Hopkins			11		2194
$1.00	bl & scar	Seaplane	Coil		10 Vert		2468
$1.00	gold,multi	Eagle & Olympic Rings			11		2539
$1.00	blue	Burgoyne			11.5		2590
$2.00	brt blue	J. Madison	w/ Tri. in Top corners	12		NW	262
$2.00	brt blue	J. Madison	w/ Tri. in Top corners	12		DL	277
$2.00	dk blue	J. Madison	"Series 1902"	12		DL	312
$2.00	dk blue	J. Madison	"Series 1902"	10		NW	479
$2.00	orng rd & blk	B. Franklin		11			523
$2.00	carm & blk	B. Franklin		11			547
$2.00	dp blue	U.S. Capitol		11			572
$2.00	yel grn&blk	W.G. Harding		11			833
$2.00	dk grn&rd (tan)	Kerosene Table Lamp		11			1611
$2.00	brt viol	William Jennings Bryan		11			2195
$2.00	multi	Bobcat		11			2482
$2.90	multi	Eagle		11			2540
$2.90	multi	Space Shuttle		11x10½			2543
$3.00	multi	Challenger Shuttle		11.2			2544, 2544v
$3.00	multi	Mars Pathfinder		Souv. Sheet			3178
$5.00	dk green	J. Marshall	w/ Tri. in Top corners	12		NW	263
$5.00	dk green	J. Marshall	w/ Tri. in Top corners	12		DL	278
$5.00	dk green	J. Marshall	"Series 1902"	12		DL	313

Den.	Color	Subject	Type / Comment	Press	Perf.	Wmk.	Scott#
$5.00	lt green	J. Marshall	"Series 1902"		10	NW	480
$5.00	dp grn & blk	B. Franklin			11		524
$5.00	carm & bl	Freedom Statue/Capitol			11		573
$5.00	carm & blk	C. Coolidge			11		834
$5.00	rd brn & blk	C. Coolidge			11		834a
$5.00	black	A. Hamilton			11		1053
$5.00	gray blk	John Bassett Moore			11x10.5		1295*
$5.00	rd brn,yel&orng (tan)	RR Conductors Lantern			11		1612
$5.00	copper rd	Bret Harte			11		2196
$5.00	slate grn	Washington & Jackson			11.5		2592
$8.75	**multi**	**Eagle & Moon**			**11**		**2394**
$9.35	multi	Eagle & Moon	Bklt. sgl./B. Pn. of 3		10 Vert		1909,a
$9.95	**multi**	**Eagle**			**11**		**2541**
$9.95	multi	Moon Landing			10.7x11.1		2842
$10.75	multi	Eagle & Moon	Bklt. sgl./B. Pn. of 3		10 Vert		2122,a
$10.75	multi	Endeavor Shuttle			11		2544A
$14.00	**multi**	**Spread winged Eagle**			**11**		**2542**
* (4¢)	gold,carm	Text only	Make-up rate		11		2521
(5¢)	multi	Butte	Coil		9.8 Vert		2902
(5¢)	multi	Butte	Self-adhesive Coil		Die-cut 11.5		2902B
(5¢)	multi	Mountain	Coil	BEP	9.8 Vert		2903
(5¢)	multi	Mountain	Coil	SVS	9.8 Vert		2904
(5¢)	multi	Mountain	Self-adhesive Coil		Die-cut 11.5		2904A
(5¢)	multi	Mountain	Self-adhesive Coil		Die-cut 9.8		2904B
(10¢)	multi	Automobile	Coil		9.8 Vert		2905
(10¢)	multi	Automobile	Self-adhesive Coil		Die-cut 11.5		2907
(10¢)	multi	Eagle & Shield	Coil "Bulk Rate, USA"			10 Vert	2602
(10¢)	multi	Eagle & Shield	Coil "USA Bulk Rate"		10 Vert	BEP	2603
(10¢)	multi	Eagle & Shield	Coil "USA Bulk Rate"		10 Vert	SVS	2604
(10¢)	multi	Eagle & Shield	Self-adhesive Coil		Die-cut 11.5		2906
A (15¢)	**orange**	**Eagle**			**11**		**1735**
A	orange	Eagle	Bklt. Sgl./Pn. of 8		11x10.5		1736,a
A	orange	Eagle	Coil		10 Vert		1743
(15¢)	multi	Auto Tail Fin	Coil	BEP	9.8 Vert		2908
(15¢)	multi	Auto Tail Fin	Coil	SVS	9.8 Vert		2909
(15¢)	multi	Auto Tail Fin	Self-adhesive Coil		Die-cut 11.5		2910
B (18¢)	**violet**	**Eagle**			**11x10.5**		**1818**
B	violet	Eagle	Bklt. sgl./Pn of 8		10		1819,a
B	violet	Eagle	Coil		10 Vert		1820
C (20¢)	**brown**	**Eagle**			**11x10.5**		**1946**
C	brown	Eagle	Coil		10 Vert		1947
C	brown	Eagle	Bklt. sgl./Pn. of 10		11x10.5		1948,a
D (22¢)	**green**	**Eagle**			**11**		**2111**
D	green	Eagle	Coil		10 Vert		2112
D	green	Eagle	Bklt. sgl./Pn. of 10		11		2113,a
E (25¢)	**multi**	**Earth**			**11**		**2277**
E	multi	Earth	Coil		10 Vert		2279
E	multi	Earth	Bklt. sgl./Pn. of 10		10		2282a
(25¢)	multi	Juke Box	Coil	BEP	9.8 Vert		2911
(25¢)	multi	Juke Box	Coil	SVS	9.8 Vert		2912
(25¢)	multi	Juke Box	Self-adhesive Coil		Die-cut 11.5		2912A
(25¢)	multi	Juke Box	Self-adhesive Coil		Die-cut 9.8		2912B
(25¢)	multi	Juke Box	Linerless SA Coil		Die-cut		3132
F (29¢)	**multi**	**Tulip**			**13**		**2517**
F	multi	Tulip	Coil		10		2518
F	multi	Tulip	Bklt. Stamp	BEP	11 bullseye		2519
F	multi	Tulip	Bklt. Stamp	KCS	11		2520
F	blk,dk bl,red	Flag	Self-adhesive		Die cut		2522
G (20¢)	**multi**	**FlagBlack "G"**		**BEP**	**11.2x11.1**		**2879**
G (20¢)	multi	Flag Red "G"		SVS	11x10.9		2880
G (25¢)	multi	Flag, Black "G"	Coil	SVS	9.8 vert.		2888
G (32¢)	multi	Flag, Black "G"		BEP	11.2x11.1		2881
G (32¢)	multi	Flag, Red "G"		SVS	11x10.9		2882
G (32¢)	multi	Flag, Black "G"	Bklt. Stamp	BEP	10x9.9		2883
G (32¢)	multi	Flag, Blue "G"	Bklt. Stamp	ABN	10.9		2884
G (32¢)	multi	Flag, Red "G"	Bklt. Stamp	SVS	11x10.9		2885
G (32¢)	multi	Flag	Self-adhesive		Die cut		2886,87
G (32¢)	multi	Flag, Black "G"	Coil	BEP	9.8 vert.		2889
G (32¢)	multi	Flag, Blue "G"	Coil	ABN	9.8 vert.		2890
G (32¢)	multi	Flag, Red "G"	Coil	SVS	9.8 vert.		2891
G (32¢)	multi	Flag, Red "G"	Coil	Roulette	9.8 vert.		2892

Adventures in Topicals

By George Griffenhagen
Editor of *Topical Time*

There is much more to topical stamp collecting than accumulating postage stamps picturing something or someone associated with a theme. To experience the adventure of topical collecting, you need to expand your horizons by including a variety of philatelic elements in your collection. As promised in the last installment of this series, we will review the variety of philatelic elements that awaits your discovery.

To most people, a postage stamp is something they stick on an envelope to mail a letter. However, stamp collectors know that postage stamps come in a variety of forms. There are Definitives (most 19th century stamps were definitives); Commemoratives (they made their appearance at the close of the 19th century); Semi-Postals (also called charity stamps); Provisionals (to fill and urgent need); and Locals (for use in a limited geographical area). The stamp design is generally limited to a single stamp, but Composites are those in which the design extends over two or more stamps have become popular. Se-tenants consist of two or more adjacent stamps differing in design or denomination, while Tete-beche is a term describing adjacent stamps, one of which is inverted.

Any of the above stamps can include Surcharges (inscriptions that change the face value) or Overprints (inscriptions that change the purpose of a stamp); a classical example of the latter is the 1928 U.S. George Washington stamp with an overprint for MOLLY PITCHER, Revolutionary War heroine.

Perfins and Watermarks offer interesting philatelic elements. Among the thousands of Perfins (named for PERforated INSignia), topical collectors can find designs for anchors, bells, coffee grinders, dancers, eagles, fish, flags, spinning wheels, swans, and windmills. Watermarks (patterns impressed into the paper during manufacture) also come in a variety of images including anchors, birds, coats-of-arms, flowers, lions, moons, posthorns, pyramids, stars, swans, and trees.

Marginal inscriptions frequently include more than plate numbers or other post office inscriptions. Designs on tabs and margins (selvage) of stamps and souvenir sheets often supplement a theme as much as the design of the stamp itself. Equally interesting are the tabs and marginal advertisements attached to postage stamps.

The introduction of postage stamp booklets in 1895 offered opportunities for governmental promotional messages and commercial advertising on covers, interleaves, and labels required to make the total face value of the booklet a convenient multiple of the local currency. Commercial advertising was introduced into the stamp booklets during the first decade of the 19th century. By the 1920s, entire stamp booklets were devoted to advertisements of a single firm.

There are, of course, many stamps that are not postage stamps. Revenues (also called fiscals or tax stamps) are stamps indicating the payment of a fee or collection of a tax. They predate postage stamps by several centuries, having been used in The Netherlands as early as 1627 and in Spain as early as 1637. Even though revenues are not postage stamps, they lay claim to being the "most historic stamps of all time." It was a 1765 revenue stamp imposing a tax on legal documents in the British colonies in America which ignited the American Revolutionary War. Cinderellas are virtually any item that looks like a postage stamp but is not a postage stamp. They include such material as advertising seals, bogus stamps, charity seals,

fantasy stamps, food rationing stamps, political seals, poster stamps, and propaganda seals. There are even Test Stamps issued by various postal administrations for use in developing stamp vending machines.

Covers (envelopes that have passed through the mail bearing appropriate postal markings) were used centuries before the introduction of the postage stamp. Today they are classified either as Commercial or Philatelic. Many adventures lies ahead for the collector who searches for a particular stamp that belongs in a topical collection. By the second half of the 19th century, envelopes were imprinted with a wide range of colorful advertisements (called Corner Cards referring to the return address). Patriotic Cover became popular during the American Civil War, and Mourning Covers (with their black borders) were widely used during the Victorian era. Other interesting covers include Balloon Mail (which preceeded First Flight Covers), Paquebots (mail posted on ther high seas), Crash/Wreck Covers, Free Frank Covers, and Censored Covers. First Day Covers (FDCs) comprise the major portion of philatelic covers.

Postal Stationery includes all forms of stationery bearing a printed stamp (indicium). Pre-stamped letter sheets were used as early as the 17th century, but it was the British Mulready which was introduced in 1840 that popularized postal stationery. The first Postal Card bearing an indicium was issued in Austria in 1869, and the Aerogramme (air letter) led to the subsequent use of the British Airgraph and the American V-Mail during World War II.

Cancellations (called postmarks when they include date and place of posting) come in a variety of forms. The most desirable for the topical collector are Fancy Cancels applied by obliterators made of cork or wood. The rarest were produced in Waterbury, Connecticut, from 1865 to 1869. With the introduction of rapid cancelling machines, Slogan Cancels, Pictorial Cancels, and First Day of Issue cancels were created. The introduction of the postage meter in the early 20th century also led to a variety of advertising slogans.

Other philatelic elements of interest to the topical collector are Maximum Cards (introduced around 1900); Autographs on stamps and covers; and the Telephone Card (which was used as early as the 1880s to prepay telephone calls). The scope of material for the topical collector is limited only by one's imagination.

SELECTED and ANNOTATED BIBLIOGRAPHY

The volumes listed below are recommended for the library of any collector who wishes to gain more knowledge in the areas covered by the *1996 Brookman*. While the main emphasis is on stamps, many of these volumes contain good postal history information. Check with your favorite dealer for availability and price. (To conserve space, some bibliographic notations have been abbreviated).

19th & 20th Century

Cummings, William W., ed., *Scott 1995 Specialized Catalogue of U.S. Stamps*
This annual publication offers a treasure trove of information on virtually every area of the postage and revenue stamps of the US, UN & US Possesstions. A "must have."

Sloane, George B., *Sloane's Column,* arr. by George Turner, 1961, (BIA 1980)
A subject by subject arrangement of Sloane's 1350 columns which appeared in "STAMPS" magazine from1932-1958 covering virtually every facet of U.S. philately.

White, Roy, *Encyclopedia of the Colors of U.S. Postage Stamps,* Vol 1-5, 1981, 86.
The first four volumes cover US stamps from 1847-1918 plus a few selected issues. Volume five covers the US Postage Dues from1879-1916. They are the finest available works for classifying the colors of U.S. postage stamps.

19th Century
General

Brookman, Lester G., *The United States Postage Stamps of the 19th Century,* 3 vol., 1966. (Reprinted in 1989 by D.G.Phillipps Co.)
This is the finest and most informative work on 19th Century issues. Each stamp, from the 5¢ Franklin of 1847 thru the $2 Trans-Mississippi of 1898, is given separate, and often in-depth treatment. This is a must for any collector.

Luff, John N., *The Postage Stamps of the United States,* 1902.
While much of Luff's information has been superseded by Brookman, his treatment of Postmaster Provisionals and several Back-of-the-book sections make this a worthwhile volume. (The "Gossip Reprint", 1937, is more useful and recommended.)

Perry, Elliot, *Pat Paragraphs,* arr by George Turner & Thomas Stanton, BIA, 1981.
A subject by subject arrangement of Perry's 58 pamphlets which were published from 1931-1958. The emphasis is on the 19th century classics as well as carriers & locals.

Baker, Hugh J. and J. David, *Bakers' U.S. Classics,* 1985
An annotated compilation of the Bakers' columns from "STAMPS" magazine which appeared from 1962-1969. This major work provides extensive coverage of nearly all aspects of U.S. and Confederate philately.

By Issue or Subject

Ashbrook, Stanley B., *The United States One Cent Stamp of 1851-57,* 2 vol, 1938.
Although most of stamp and plating information in Volume 1 has been superseded by Mortimer Neinken's great work, Vol. 2 features an indispensible amount of information on the postal history of the period.

Neinken, Mortimer L., *The United States One Cent Stamp of 1851 to 1861,* 1972.
United States, The 1851-57 Twelve Cent Stamp, 1964.
The One cent book supplements and updates, but does not replace, Ashbrook's study. The Twelve cent booklet deals almost exclusively with the plating of this issue. Both are fundamental works.

Chase, Dr. Carroll, *The 3¢ Stamp of the U.S. 1851-57 Issue,* Rev. ed., 1942.
This outstanding work provides the most comprehensive information available in one place on this popular issue. (The Quarterman reprint, 1975, contains a new forward, corrections, additions and a selected bibliography of articles.)

Hill, Henry W., *The United States Five Cent Stamps of 1856-1861,* 1955.
This extensively illustrated volume is the only work dealing exclusively with this issue. It includes studies on stamps, plating, cancels, and postal history.

Neinken, Mortimer L., *The United States Ten Cent Stamps of 1855-1859,* 1960.
This work not only provides an indispensable amount of stamp and plating information, but it also reprints Chapters 50-53 from Ashbrook Vol. 2 dealing with California, Ocean and Western Mails.

Cole, Maurice F., *The Black Jacks of 1863-1867,* 1950.
A superb study of the issue with major emphasis on postal history.

Lane, Maryette B., *The Harry F. Allen Collection of Black Jacks, A Study of the Stamp and it's Use,* 1969
The title says it all. This book beautifully complements, but does not replace, Cole.

Ashbrook, Stanley B., *The U.S. Issues of 1869, Preceded by Some Additional Notes on "The premieres Gravures of 1861",* 1943
This work concentrates on the design sources and production of the 1869 issue. Ashbrook concludes with his "Addendum" attacking Scott for listing the Premieres.

Willard, Edward L., *The U.S. Two Cent Red Brown of 1883-1887,* 2 vol., 1970.
Volume I deals with the background, production and varieties of the stamp. Vol. II deals exclusively with the cancellations found on the stamp. A good Banknote intro.

20th Century
General

King, Beverly S. and Johl, Max G. *The United States Postages Stamps of the Twentieth Century,* Vol. 1 revised, Vol. 2-4, 1934-38.
These volumes are still the standard work on 20th Century U.S. postage stamps from 1901 to 1937. (The 1976 Quarterman reprint contains only the regular issue, air mail and Parcel Post sections from the original volumes. It is highly recommended.

By Issue or Subject

Armstrong, Martin A., *Washington-Franklins, 1908-1921,* 2nd Edition, 1979.
Armstrong, Martin A., *US Definitive Series, 1922-1938,* 2nd Edition, 1980.
Armstrong, Martin A., *United States Coil Issues, 1906-38,* 1977
Each of these volumes not only supplements the information found in Johl, but expands each area to include studies of essays, proofs, booklet panes, private perfs, Offices in China and the Canal Zone. One major plus is the wealth of illustrations, many of rare and unusual items, which were not included in Johl's work due to laws restricting the publication of stamp pictures prior to 1938.

20th Century
By Issue or Subject (cont.)

Schoen, DeVoss & Harvey, *Counterfeit Kansas-Nebraska Overprints on 1922-34 Issue plus First Day Covers of the Kansas-Nebraska Overprints,* 1973.
A fine pamphlet covering K-N varieties, errors and First Day covers, plus important information pointing out the differences between genuine and fake overprints.

Datz, Stephen, *U.S. Errors: Inverts, Imperforates, Colors Omitted,* 1992 Ed., 1991.
This volume does a superb job covering the subjects listed in its title, It is extensively illustrated and provides price, quantity and historical information.

Air Mail & Back-of-the-Book

Amercian Air Mail Society, *American Air Mail Catalog,* Fifth Ed., 5 vols + 1990 Pricing Supplement, 1974-1990.
Virtually everything there is to know about air mail stamps and postal history.

Arfken, George B., *Postage Due, The United States Large Numeral Postage Due Stamps, 1879-1894,* 1991.
A Comprehensive study of virtually every aspect of these interesting stamps. Additionally, about half the book is devoted to their extensive usage which helps to clarify some of the more complex markings and routings found on "Due" covers.

Gobie, Henry M. *The Speedy, A History of the U.S. Special Delivery Service,* 1976
Gobie, Henry M., *U.S. Parcel Post, A Postal History,* 1979.
Each of these volumes includes information on the stamps, but their main thrust is on the postal history of the respective services. Official documents and Postal Laws & Regulations have been extensively reproduced and numerous covers illustrating the various aspects of the services are pictured.

Markovits, Robert L., *United States, The 10¢ Registry Stamp of 1911,* 1973.
This pamphlet provides a superb blueprint for the formation of specialized collection around a single stamp. It is extensively illustrated and concludes with an extensive bibliography which touches upon a multitude of additional subjects.

McGovern, Edmund C., ed, *Catalog of the 19th Century Stamped Envelopes and Wrappers of the United States,* USPSS 1984

Haller, Austin P., ed., *Catalog of the 20th Century Stamped Envelopes and Wrappers of the United States,* USPSS 1990

Beachboard, John H., ed., *United States Postal Card Catalog,* USPSS 1990
Each of the three previous volumes contains the finest available information in their respective fields. They are indispensable to the postal stationery collector.

First Day Covers & Related Collectibles

Planty, Dr. Earl & Mellone, Michael, *Planty's Photo Encyclopedia of Cacheted FDCs,* 1923-1939, Vol. 1-10, 1976-1984

Mellone, Mike, *Specialized Catalog of First Day Covers of the 1940's (2nd ed.),* 1950's and 1960's, 2 vol., 2 vol., 3 vol. respectively, 1983-1985.

Pelcyger, Dr. Scott, *Mellone's Specialized Catalog of First Day Ceremony Programs & Events,* 1989
Each of these volumes illustrates virtually every known cachet and ceremony program for the stamps listed within. They each provide an invaluable resource.

Radford, Dr. Curtis D., *The Souvenir Card Collectors Society Numbering System for Forerunner and Modern Day Souvenir Card,* 1989.
The most informative work on this popular collecting area.

Revenues

Toppan, Deats and Holland, *'An Historical Reference List of the Revenue Stamps of the United States...",* 1899.
The information in this volume, while almost 100 years old, still provides the collector with much of the basic knowledge available today on US Revenues and "Match and Medicines" from 1862-1898. (The "Gossip" reprint is recommended.)

Confederate States

Dietz, August, *The Postal Service of the Confederate States of America,* 1929
This monumental work has been the "Bible" for Confederate collectors. Covering virtually every aspect of Confederate philately, its content remains useful, even after 60+ years. (A 1989 reprint makes this work more affordable for the average collector.)

Skinner, Gunter and Sanders, *The New Dietz Confederate States Catalog and Handbook,* 1986.
This volume makes an effort to cover every phase of Confederate philately and postal history. Despite the presence of some flaws, it is highly recommended.

Possessions

Plass, Brewster and Salz, *Canal Zone Stamps,* 1986.
Published by the Canal Zone Study Group, this outstanding well written and extensively illustrated volume, is now the "bible" for these fascinating issues.

Meyer, Harris, et. at, *Hawaii, Its Stamps and Postal History,* 1948.
After 45 years, this volume, which deals with virtually every facet of Hawaiian stamps and postal history, remains the finest work written on the subject.

Palmer, Maj. F.L., *The Postal Issues of the Philippines,* 1912
An ancient, but still useful study, with interesting information on the U.S. overprints.

British North America

Boggs, Winthrop S., *The Postage Stamps and Postal History of Canada,* 2 vol., 1945. (Quarterman reprint, One vol., 1975)
For almost 50 years the standard work on Canadian stamps and postal history. One of the "must have" books. (The reprint omits most of the Vol. 2 appendices.)

Lowe, Robson, *The Encyclopedia of British Empire Postage Stamps,* Vol. 5, North America, 1973
This work continues the fine tradition of Robson Lowe's earlier volumes dealing with the British Empire. Covering all of BNA, it is an essential tool for the collector.

1847 General Issue, Imperforate VF + 50% (C)

1,3,948a   2,4,948b

Scott's No.		Unused Fine	Ave.	Used Fine	Ave.
1	5¢ Franklin, Red Brown	3750.00	2250.00	475.00	300.00
1	5¢ Red Brown, Pen Cancel	...	...	250.00	175.00
2	10¢ Washington, Black	...	13000.00	1100.00	675.00
2	10¢ Black, Pen Cancel	...	...	600.00	425.00
3	5¢ Red Brown, 1875 Repro	750.00	550.00	...	...
4	10¢ Black, 1875 Reproduction	900.00	675.00	...	...

NOTE: SEE #948 FOR 5¢ BLUE AND 10¢ BROWN ORANGE.

1851-1856 Issue, Imperf "U.S. Postage" at Top (VF, OG+150%, VF+75% OG+75%) (C)

5A-9   10-11   12   13-16   17

No.	Description	Unused Fine	Ave.	Used Fine	Ave.
5A	1¢ Franklin, Blue, Type Ib	...	...	3500.00	2000.00
6	1¢ Blue, Type Ia	...	...	6500.00	3750.00
7	1¢ Blue, Type I	400.00	250.00	110.00	65.00
8	1¢ Blue, Type III	...	...	1600.00	975.00
8A	1¢ Blue, Type IIIa	2000.00	1200.00	675.00	400.00
9	1¢ Blue, Type IV	400.00	240.00	95.00	57.50
10	3¢ Wash., Orange Brown, Ty. I	1500.00	900.00	60.00	35.00
11	3¢ Dull Red, Type I	120.00	70.00	7.50	4.50
12	5¢ Jefferson, Red Brown, Ty. I	...	...	850.00	500.00
13	10¢ Wash., Green, Type I	...	...	600.00	350.00
14	10¢ Green, Type II	1600.00	975.00	190.00	135.00
15	10¢ Green, Type III	1600.00	975.00	190.00	135.00
16	10¢ Green, Type IV	...	...	1200.00	700.00
17	12¢ Washington, Black	...	1500.00	250.00	150.00

1857-61 Same Design as Above but Perf. 15 (VF,OG+200%, VF+100% OG+75%) (C)

18-24   25-26   37   38   39

No.	Description	Unused Fine	Ave.	Used Fine	Ave.
18	1¢ Franklin, Blue, Type I	700.00	425.00	350.00	200.00
19	1¢ Blue, Type Ia	...	...	3250.00	2000.00
20	1¢ Blue, Type II	425.00	250.00	160.00	95.00
21	1¢ Blue, Type III (Plate 4)	...	3500.00	1200.00	700.00
22	1¢ Blue, Type IIIa	675.00	400.00	300.00	175.00
23	1¢ Blue, Type IV	2500.00	1500.00	400.00	225.00
24	1¢ Blue, Type V	80.00	50.00	27.50	16.00
25	3¢ Washington, Rose, Type I	1000.00	600.00	45.00	27.50
26	3¢ Dull Red, Type II	45.00	25.00	4.25	2.50
27	5¢ Jefferson, Brick Red, Type I	...	5500.00	650.00	400.00
28	5¢ Red Brown, Type I	1500.00	900.00	300.00	170.00
28A	5¢ Indian Red, Type I	...	...	1650.00	1050.00
29	5¢ Brown, Type I	...	850.00	200.00	120.00
30	5¢ Orange Brown, Type II	...	525.00	750.00	450.00
30A	5¢ Brown, Type II	...	750.00	180.00	110.00
31	10¢ Wash., Green, Type I	...	4000.00	500.00	290.00
32	10¢ Green, Type II	2275.00	1300.00	180.00	110.00
33	10¢ Green, Type III	2275.00	1300.00	180.00	110.00
34	10¢ Green, Type IV	...	...	1475.00	795.00
35	10¢ Green, Type V	140.00	80.00	52.50	32.50
36	12¢ Wash., Black, Plate I	500.00	275.00	130.00	77.50
36b	12¢ Black, Plate III	375.00	200.00	120.00	67.50
37	24¢ Washington, Gray Lilac	550.00	325.00	210.00	120.00
38	30¢ Franklin, Orange	750.00	435.00	275.00	160.00
39	90¢ Washington, Blue	1200.00	750.00	...	...

NOTE: #5A THROUGH 38 WITH PEN CANCELS USUALLY SELL FOR 50-60% OF LISTED
USED PRICES. USED EXAMPLES OF #39 SHOULD ONLY BE PURCHASED WITH, OR
SUBJECT TO, A CERTIFICATE OF AUTHENTICITY.

#40-47 ARE 1875 REPRINTS OF THE 1857-60 ISSUE.

1861 New Designs, Perf.12, Thin Paper (VF,OG+150%, VF+75% OG+75%) (C)

Scott's No.		Unused Fine	Ave.	Used Fine	Ave.
62B	10¢ Wash., Dark Green	...	...	450.00	250.00

1861-62 Modified Designs, Perf. 12 (VF,OG+200%, VF+100% OG+75%) (C)

63   73   65   67,75-76   68

69   77   70,78   71   72

No.	Description	Unused Fine	Ave.	Used Fine	Ave.
63	1¢ Franklin, Blue	110.00	65.00	18.50	11.00
64	3¢ Washington, Pink	2200.00	425.00	250.00	...
64b	3¢ Rose Pink	210.00	125.00	80.00	45.00
65	3¢ Rose	70.00	40.00	1.85	1.15
67	5¢ Jefferson, Buff	5000.00	450.00	260.00	...
	10¢ Wash., Yellow Green	200.00	115.00	33.50	19.75
69	12¢ Washington, Black	475.00	275.00	60.00	33.75
70	24¢ Wash., Red Lilac	650.00	400.00	90.00	50.00
70b	24¢ Steel Blue	3000.00	300.00	160.00	...
70c	24¢ Violet, Thin Paper	3500.00	600.00	350.00	...
71	30¢ Franklin, Orange	525.00	300.00	85.00	50.00
72	90¢ Washington, Blue	1200.00	700.00	250.00	140.00

1861-66 New Vals. or Designs, Perf. 12 (VF,OG+200%, VF+100% OG+75%) (C)

No.	Description	Unused Fine	Ave.	Used Fine	Ave.
73	2¢ Jackson, Black	135.00	70.00	30.00	16.50
75	5¢ Jefferson, Red Brn.	1800.00	1075.00	290.00	170.00
76	5¢ Brown	375.00	235.00	70.00	42.50
77	15¢ Lincoln, Black	550.00	325.00	85.00	50.00
78	24¢ Washington, Lilac/Gray Lilac	375.00	215.00	60.00	35.00

1867 Designs of 1861-66 with Grills of Var. Sizes (VF,OG+200%, VF+100%OG+75%) (C)

Grills consist of small pyramids impressed on the stamp and are classified by area, shape of points and number of rows of points. On Grilled-All-Over and "C" Grills, points thrust upward on FACE of stamp; on all other grills points thrust upward on BACK of stamp. Points of "Z" grill show horizontal ridges (-); other grills from "D" through "I" show vertical (l) ridges or come to a point. It is important to see a Scott catalog for details of these interesting stamps.

1867 "A" Grill (Grill All Over)
79	3¢ Washington, Rose	...	1500.00	550.00	325.00

1867 "C" Grill 13 x 16mm Points Up
83	3¢ Washington, Rose	2500.00	1475.00	550.00	315.00

1867 "D" Grill 12 x 14mm Points Down
84	2¢ Jackson, Black	4500.00	...	1375.00	800.00
85	3¢ Washington, Rose	2250.00	1300.00	525.00	300.00

1867 "Z" Grill 11 x 14mm
85B	2¢ Jackson, Black	2850.00	1650.00	500.00	290.00
85C	3¢ Washington, Rose	...	3000.00	1350.00	800.00
85E	12¢ Washington, Black	4000.00	2350.00	675.00	400.00

1867 "E" Grill 11 x 13mm
86	1¢ Franklin, Blue	1000.00	625.00	280.00	170.00
87	2¢ Jackson, Black	400.00	250.00	67.50	37.50
88	3¢ Washington, Rose	300.00	165.00	12.00	6.95
89	10¢ Washington, Green	1700.00	1000.00	190.00	110.00
90	12¢ Washington, Black	1600.00	950.00	200.00	115.00
91	15¢ Lincoln, Black	3000.00	1600.00	395.00	225.00

1867 "F" Grill 9 x 13mm
92	1¢ Franklin, Blue	400.00	250.00	100.00	55.00
93	2¢ Jackson, Black	160.00	90.00	25.00	13.50
94	3¢ Washington, Red	140.00	80.00	3.50	1.95
95	5¢ Jefferson, Brown	1200.00	675.00	375.00	250.00
96	10¢ Wash., Yellow Green	1000.00	575.00	120.00	70.00
97	12¢ Washington, Black	1275.00	700.00	140.00	85.00
98	15¢ Lincoln, Black	1350.00	750.00	180.00	110.00
99	24¢ Washington, Gray Lilac	2000.00	1100.00	425.00	260.00
100	30¢ Franklin, Orange	2250.00	1300.00	400.00	250.00
101	90¢ Washington, Blue	3750.00	2000.00	835.00	475.00

#102-11 ARE 1875 RE-ISSUES OF THE 1861-66 ISSUE.

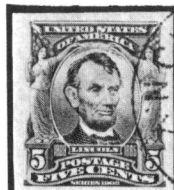

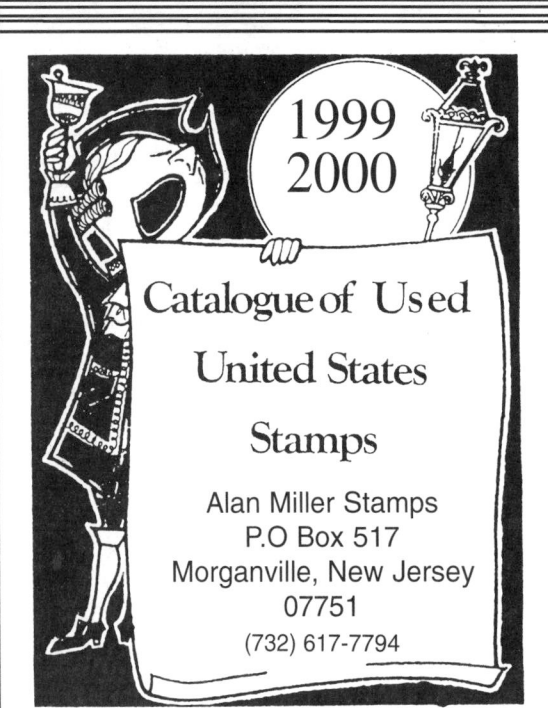

1869 Pictorial Issues-"G" Grill 9½ mm. (VF,OG+150%, VF+75%, OG+50%) (C)

| 112,123,133 | 113,124 | 114 | 115 | 116 |

| 117 | 119 | 120 | 121 | 122 |

Scott's No.		Unused Fine	Ave.	Used Fine	Ave.
112	1¢ Franklin, Buff	250.00	140.00	75.00	42.50
113	2¢ Horse & Rider, Brown	210.00	125.00	30.00	17.00
114	3¢ Locomotive, Ultramarine	120.00	70.00	10.75	6.50
115	6¢ Washington, Ultramarine	800.00	475.00	120.00	70.00
116	10¢ Shield & Eagle, Yellow	800.00	475.00	90.00	55.00
117	12¢ "S.S. Adriatic", Green	800.00	475.00	95.00	55.00
118	15¢ Columbus, Brn & Blue,Ty.I	2750.00	1600.00	375.00	220.00
119	15¢ Brown & Blue, Type II	1000.00	575.00	150.00	85.00
120	24¢ Decl. of Indep., Grn & Vio	2500.00	1400.00	450.00	260.00
121	30¢ Shield, Eagle & Flags	2650.00	1500.00	325.00	185.00
122	90¢ Lincoln, Carm. & Black	4000.00	2300.00	1250.00	775.00

1875 and 1880 Re-issues, without Grill (VF,OG+150%, VF+75%, OG+50%) (C)

123	1¢ Buff, Hard White Paper	250.00	140.00	200.00	115.00
124	2¢ Brown, Hard White Paper	325.00	175.00	295.00	165.00
133	1¢ Buff, Soft Porous Paper (1880)	125.00	75.00	140.00	77.50
133a	1¢ Brown Orange, w/o gum	160.00	110.00	125.00	70.00

#126-32 ARE 1875 RE-ISSUES OF THE 1869 ISSUE.

1870-71 Nat'l Print-Grilled-Hard Paper (VF,OG+150%, VF+75%, OG+50%) (C)

| 134/206 | 135/183 | 136/214 | 179,185 | 137/208 |

| 138,149,160 | 139/209 | 141/189 | 143/217 | 144/218 |

134	1¢ Franklin, Ultramarine	675.00	400.00	65.00	36.50
135	2¢ Jackson, Red Brown	385.00	210.00	40.00	22.50
136	3¢ Washington, Green	275.00	150.00	12.50	7.00
137	6¢ Lincoln, Carmine	1600.00	900.00	300.00	180.00
138	7¢ Stanton, Vermilion	1100.00	650.00	250.00	150.00
139	10¢ Jefferson, Brown	1800.00	1100.00	425.00	250.00
140	12¢ Clay, Dull Violet	...	...	1750.00	1200.00
141	15¢ Webster, Orange	2250.00	1300.00	650.00	375.00
143	30¢ Hamilton, Black		3000.00	1000.00	575.00
144	90¢ Perry, Carmine	...	3500.00	875.00	500.00

1870-71 Same as above but without Grill (VF,OG+150%, VF+75% OG+50%) (C)

145	1¢ Franklin, Ultramarine	170.00	100.00	8.00	4.75
146	2¢ Jackson, Red Brown	130.00	75.00	5.00	3.00
147	3¢ Washington, Green	130.00	75.00	1.00	.60
148	6¢ Lincoln, Carmine	250.00	145.00	14.00	8.25
149	7¢ Stanton, Vermilion	300.00	175.00	60.00	35.00
150	10¢ Jefferson, Brown	275.00	160.00	13.50	8.00
151	12¢ Clay, Dull Violet	675.00	375.00	75.00	42.50
152	15¢ Webster, Bright Orange	650.00	365.00	80.00	47.50
153	24¢ Scott, Purple	650.00	365.00	90.00	52.50
154	30¢ Hamilton, Black	1600.00	900.00	100.00	60.00
155	90¢ Perry, Carmine	1600.00	900.00	165.00	95.00

PRIOR TO 1882, UNUSED PRICES ARE FOR STAMPS WITH PARTIAL OR NO GUM, FOR ORIGINAL GUM, ADD % PREMIUM INDICATED IN ( ).

1870-71 National Print - Without Secret Marks

| 1¢ | 2¢ | 3¢ | 6¢ | 7¢ | 10¢ | 12¢ |

Arrows point to distinguishing characteristics: 1¢ ball is clear; 2¢ no spot of color; 3¢ light shading; 6¢ normal vertical lines; 7¢ no arcs of color cut around lines; 10¢ ball is clear; 12¢ normal 2.

1873 Continental Print-White Hard Paper (VF,OG+150%,VF+75%OG+50%)(C)
Same designs as preceding issue but with secret marks as shown below.

Arrows point to distinguishing characteristics: 1¢ dash in ball; 2¢ spot of color where lines join in scroll ornaments; 3¢ under part of ribbon heavily shaded; 6¢ first four vertical lines strengthened; 7¢ arcs of color cut around lines; 10¢ a crescent in the ball; 12¢ ball of 2 is crescent shaped.

Scott's No.		Unused Fine	Ave.	Used Fine	Ave.
156	1¢ Franklin, Ultramarine	100.00	62.50	2.00	1.15
157	2¢ Jackson, Brown	185.00	105.00	10.75	6.25
158	3¢ Washington, Green	55.00	30.00	.35	.25
159	6¢ Lincoln, Dull Pink	200.00	110.00	11.75	6.75
160	7¢ Stanton, Org. Vermilion	425.00	235.00	50.00	27.50
161	10¢ Jefferson, Brown	285.00	170.00	12.00	7.25
162	12¢ Clay, Blackish Violet	675.00	375.00	65.00	37.50
163	15¢ Webster, Yellow Orange	725.00	400.00	62.50	35.00
165	30¢ Hamilton, Gray Black	775.00	450.00	60.00	32.50
166	90¢ Perry, Rose Carmine	1200.00	700.00	160.00	95.00

1875-Continental Print-Yellowish Hard Paper (VF,OG+150%, VF+75% OG+50%)(C)

178	2¢ Jackson, Vermilion	160.00	95.00	6.00	3.65
179	5¢ Taylor, Blue	195.00	120.00	10.00	5.50

1879 American Prtg. - Continental Design, Soft Porous Paper (VF,OG+150%, VF + 75% OG + 50%) (C)

Soft porous paper is less transparent than hard paper. When held to the light it usually appears mottled, somewhat like newsprint.

182	1¢ Franklin, Dark Ultramarine	120.00	70.00	1.60	.95
183	2¢ Jackson, Vermilion	60.00	33.50	1.60	.95
184	3¢ Washington, Green	50.00	30.00	.30	.20
185	5¢ Taylor, Blue	240.00	130.00	8.75	5.00
186	6¢ Lincoln, Pink	400.00	225.00	12.50	7.50
187	10¢ Brown (no secret mark)	800.00	435.00	17.50	10.75
188	10¢ Brown (secret mark)	600.00	350.00	17.50	10.75
189	15¢ Webster, Red Orange	170.00	95.00	16.50	10.00
190	30¢ Hamilton, Full Black	450.00	250.00	37.50	21.75
191	90¢ Perry, Carmine	1000.00	575.00	165.00	95.00

#166-77,180-81,192-204 ARE 1875-80 RE-ISSUES.

| 212 | 210,213 | 211,215 | 205,216 |

1882 New Design (VF NH+75%, VF OG & Used+50%) (C)

Scott's No.		NH Fine	Unused,OG Fine	Ave.	Used Fine	Ave.
205	5¢ Garfield, Yel. Brn.	250.00	140.00	80.00	4.75	2.75

1881-82 Re-engraved Designs (VF NH+75%, VF OG & Used+60%) (C)

206	1¢ Franklin, Gray Blue	70.00	40.00	22.50	.50	.30
207	3¢ Washington, Blue Grn	75.00	42.50	25.00	.35	.22
208	6¢ Lincoln, Rose (1882)	525.00	300.00	165.00	45.00	25.00
208a	6¢ Brown Red (1883)	425.00	250.00	140.00	60.00	35.00
209	10¢ Jefferson, Brown (1882)	150.00	85.00	50.00	2.50	1.40
209b	10¢ Black Brown	350.00	195.00	115.00	16.50	9.75

1883-88 New Designs or Colors (VF NH+75%, VF OG & Used + 60%) (C)

210	2¢ Washington Red Brn	57.50	32.50	19.00	.25	.17
211	4¢ Jackson, Blue Green	260.00	150.00	85.00	7.50	4.25
212	1¢ Franklin, Ultramarine (1887)	110.00	65.00	35.00	.80	.50
213	2¢ Washington, Green (1887)	42.50	25.00	14.50	.30	.20
214	3¢ Wash., Vermilion (1887)	80.00	47.50	25.00	35.00	21.00
215	4¢ Jackson, Carmine (1888)	230.00	135.00	70.00	11.50	7.00
216	5¢ Garfield, Indigo (1888)	230.00	135.00	70.00	6.50	3.75
217	30¢ Hamilton, Orange Brn('88)	565.00	325.00	195.00	65.00	35.00
218	90¢ Perry, Purple (1888)	1200.00	725.00	425.00	140.00	80.00

#205C, 211B and 211D are Special Printings
NOTE: Deduct 30% for unused, without gum on #205-218.

219   219D,220   221   222   223

224   225   226   227   228

Scott's No.	VF	NH F-VF	Unused VF	F-VF	Used FVF
219	1¢ Franklin, Dull Blue 42.50	27.50	25.00	16.50	.25
219D	2¢ Washington, Lake 325.00	210.00	190.00	125.00	.55
220	2¢ Carmine 35.00	22.00	19.50	13.00	.25
220a	2¢ Cap on left "2" 115.00	70.00	65.00	42.50	1.75
220c	2¢ Cap on both "2's" 335.00	210.00	190.00	125.00	11.00
221	3¢ Jackson, Purple 120.00	75.00	67.50	45.00	5.25
222	4¢ Lincoln, Dark Brn 120.00	75.00	67.50	45.00	2.00
223	5¢ Grant, Chocolate 120.00	75.00	67.50	45.00	2.00
224	6¢ Garfield, Brn Red 130.00	78.50	72.50	47.50	16.00
225	8¢ Sherman, Lilac (1893) 95.00	57.50	55.00	35.00	9.50
226	10¢ Webster, Green 250.00	150.00	140.00	90.00	2.40
227	15¢ Clay, Indigo 350.00	215.00	200.00	130.00	16.50
228	30¢ Jefferson, Black 550.00	325.00	315.00	200.00	18.50
229	90¢ Perry, Orange 775.00	500.00	450.00	300.00	90.00

1893 Columbian Issue (VF Used + 50%) (B)

230   231   232

237   239   245

230	1¢ Blue 47.50	29.50	27.50	17.50	.40
231	2¢ Violet 42.50	26.50	24.00	15.75	.20
231v	2¢ Violet, "Broken Hat" 3rd person to left of Columbus has a triangular "cut" in his hat 130.00	75.00	70.00	45.00	.80
232	3¢ Green 110.00	66.50	65.00	40.00	11.75
233	4¢ Ultramarine 160.00	95.00	95.00	57.50	5.50
234	5¢ Chocolate 165.00	100.00	95.00	60.00	6.00
235	6¢ Purple 160.00	95.00	95.00	57.50	17.00
236	8¢ Magenta 145.00	92.50	85.00	55.00	8.25
237	10¢ Black Brown 260.00	150.00	150.00	92.50	6.50
238	15¢ Dark Gree 435.00	270.00	250.00	160.00	47.50
239	30¢ Orange Brown 550.00	350.00	325.00	215.00	65.00
240	50¢ Slate Blue 1050.00	650.00	600.00	400.00	120.00
241	$1 Salmo 2700.00	1650.00	1600.00	1000.00	465.00
242	$2 Brown Red 2850.00	1750.00	1650.00	1050.00	435.00
243	$3 Yellow Green 4400.00	2750.00	2500.00	1675.00	775.00
244	$4 Crimson Lake 6000.00	3750.00	3500.00	2250.00	975.00
245	$5 Black 7000.00	4500.00	4000.00	2650.00	1200.00

1894 Issue - Triangles - No Watermark (VF Used + 75%) (C)

246/279   252/279B   253,268   254,269,280   255,270,281

256,271,282   258/283   259,274,284   261,276   262,277

Scott's No.	NH VF	F-VF	Unused VF	F-VF	Used F-VF
246	1¢ Franklin, Ultramarine 47.50	30.00	27.50	18.00	3.50
247	1¢ Blue 110.00	75.00	67.50	45.00	1.75
248	2¢ Wash., Pink, Tri. A 42.50	27.50	25.00	16.50	2.50
249	2¢ Carmine Lake, Tri. A 235.00	150.00	135.00	90.00	1.75
250	2¢ Carmine, Triangle A 47.50	30.00	28.00	18.50	.40
251	2¢ Carmine, Triangle B 360.00	230.00	210.00	140.00	2.75
252	2¢ Carmine, TriC, Type III 200.00	125.00	115.00	75.00	3.00
253	3¢ Jackson, Purple 175.00	110.00	100.00	65.00	7.00
254	4¢ Lincoln, Dark Brown 210.00	130.00	120.00	80.00	3.25
255	5¢ Grant, Chocolate 160.00	100.00	90.00	60.00	4.00
256	6¢ Garfield, Dull Brown 260.00	165.00	150.00	100.00	16.50
257	8¢ Sherman, Violet Brn 225.00	145.00	130.00	87.50	11.00
258	10¢ Webster, Dark Grn 360.00	230.00	210.00	140.00	8.75
259	15¢ Clay, Dark Blue 465.00	290.00	275.00	175.00	35.00
260	50¢ Jefferson, Orange 700.00	430.00	400.00	260.00	70.00
261	$1 Perry, Black, Type I 1425.00	900.00	825.00	550.00	200.00
261A	$1 Black, Type II 3500.00	2200.00	1950.00	1275.00	475.00
262	$2 Madison, Bright Blue 4700.00	3000.00	2700.00	1800.00	625.00
263	$5 Marshall, Dark Green 6850.00	4400.00	4000.00	2650.00	1250.00

Triangle Varieties on the 2¢ Stamps

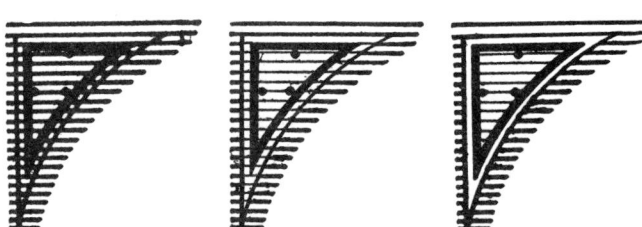

Triangle A   Triangle B   Triangle C

TRIANGLE A - The horizontal background lines run across the triangle and are of the same thickness within the triangle as the background lines.
TRIANGLE B - Horizontal lines cross the triangle but are thinner within the triangle than the background lines.
TRIANGLE C - The horizontal lines do not cross the triangle and the lines within the triangle are as thin as in Triangle B.

Circle Varieties on the $1 Stamps

Type I   Type II

Types of $1.00 stamps. Type I, the circles enclosing "$1" are broken where they meet the curved lines below "One Dollar." Type II, the circles are complete.

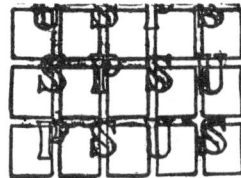

This illustration shows a block of 15 with the Double Line watermark. Since only 90 letters were used per 100 stamps, they appear in various positions on the stamps.

1895 Same Designs - Double Line Wmk. (VF Used + 50%) (C)

264	1¢ Franklin, Blue 11.50	7.25	7.00	4.25	.25
265	2¢ Wash., Carmine, Tri .A 55.00	35.00	31.50	21.00	.70
266	2¢ Carmine, Triangle B 57.50	36.50	33.50	22.00	2.50
267	2¢ Carmine, Triangle C Type III 9.00	6.00	5.75	3.75	.25
268	3¢ Jackson, Purple 65.00	41.75	38.50	25.75	.90
269	4¢ Lincoln, Dark Brown 65.00	40.00	38.00	25.00	1.25
270	5¢ Grant, Chocolate 65.00	41.75	38.50	25.75	1.50
271	6¢ Garfield, Dull Brown 140.00	87.50	80.00	52.50	3.75
272	8¢ Sherman, Violet Brn 100.00	62.50	57.50	37.50	1.00
273	10¢ Webster, Dark Green 130.00	85.00	75.00	50.00	1.30
274	15¢ Clay, Dark Blue 360.00	225.00	210.00	140.00	7.50
275	50¢ Jefferson, Orange 465.00	300.00	275.00	185.00	17.50
276	$1 Perry, Black, Type I 1100.00	700.00	635.00	425.00	52.50
276A	$1 Black, Type II 2150.00	1400.00	1250.00	850.00	120.00
277	$2 Madison, Bright Blue 1700.00	1100.00	1000.00	650.00	250.00
278	$5 Marshall, Dark Green 3800.00	2500.00	2250.00	1500.00	350.00

WIN $2000 WORTH OF FREE COVERS and/or STAMPS

In honor of the 2000 Edition of the Brookman Price Guide we will be giving away $2000 in Stamps and/or Covers to the person who in 25 words or less best describes his or her choice for the BEST UNITED STATES stamp issued in the 20th Century. Five renowned Philatelic personalities have accepted the huge undertaking of judging.

Our Judges are:

Robert Lamb, A.P.S. Executive Director

Michael Laurance, Editor & Publisher–Linn's Stamp News

Joseph B. Savarese, Executive Vice-President, ASDA

Betsy Towle – Exec. Director – Postal History Foundation

Les Winick – Prolific Stamp Journalist

The winner will have the option of choosing stamps and/or covers featured on price lists from **2 MAJOR NATIONAL PHILATELIC COMPANIES..... DALE ENTERPRISES, INC**. of Emmaus, Pa. And **BROOKMAN/BARRETT & WORTHEN** of Bedford, NH.

1897-1903 NEW Colors - Double Line Wmk. (VF Used + 50%) (C)

Scott's No.		VF	NH F-VF	Unused VF	F-VF	Used F-VF
279	1¢ Franklin, Green (1898)	17.50	11.50	10.50	7.00	.25
279B	2¢ Wash., Red Tri C, Ty IV	17.50	11.50	10.50	7.00	.25
279Be	2¢ Bklt. Pane of 6, TriC, Ty. IV	725.00	475.00	475.00	315.00	...
280	4¢ Lincoln, Rose Brown (1898)	57.50	35.00	32.50	21.75	.80
281	5¢ Grant, Dark Blue (1898)	65.00	40.00	38.00	25.00	.70
282	6¢ Garfield, Lake (1898)	80.00	52.50	48.50	32.50	2.00
282a	6¢ Purplish Lake	110.00	67.50	60.00	40.00	3.00
282C	10¢ Webster, Brn., Ty. I (1898)	330.00	200.00	190.00	125.00	2.00
283	10¢ Orange Brn., Type II (1898)	200.00	125.00	115.00	75.00	1.65
284	15¢ Clay, Olive Green (1898)	265.00	170.00	150.00	100.00	6.50

1898 Trans-Mississippi Issue (VF Used + 50%) (B)

285   286   288

290   292   293

285	1¢ Marquette, Green	50.00	32.50	29.50	19.50	4.65
286	2¢ Farming, Copper Red	45.00	29.50	27.00	18.00	1.15
287	4¢ Indian, Orange	250.00	165.00	150.00	100.00	17.50
288	5¢ Fremont, Dull Blue	240.00	150.00	140.00	90.00	16.50
289	8¢ Wagon Train, Vio. Brn.	315.00	210.00	185.00	125.00	30.00
290	10¢ Emigration, Gray Vio.	330.00	220.00	195.00	130.00	17.50
291	50¢ Mining, Sage Green	1050.00	675.00	600.00	400.00	130.00
292	$1 Cattle in Storm, Black	2250.00	1500.00	1350.00	900.00	375.00
293	$2 Bridge, Orange Brn.	3700.00	2400.00	2200.00	1450.00	650.00

Note: See # 3209-3210 for multi-color issues

1901 Pan-American Issue VF Used + 50% (B)

294   295   297   299

294-99	Set of 6	870.00	575.00	525.00	350.00	85.00
294	1¢ Steamship, Grn. & Blk.	35.00	22.50	21.00	14.00	2.50
295	2¢ Train, Carmine & Blk.	32.50	21.50	20.00	13.50	.80
296	4¢ Auto, Choc. & Black	150.00	97.50	90.00	60.00	13.00
297	5¢ Bridge, Ultra & Black	165.00	110.00	100.00	65.00	12.00
298	8¢ Canal, Brn. Vio & Blk.	210.00	140.00	130.00	85.00	40.00
299	10¢ Steamship, Brn. & Blk.	325.00	215.00	200.00	130.00	20.00

1902-03 Issue Perf. 12 VF Used + 50% (C)

300   301   302   304   306
308   310   312,479   313,480   319

300	1¢ Franklin, Blue Green	14.50	9.50	8.75	6.00	.20
300b	1¢ Booklet Pane of 6	975.00	650.00	625.00	425.00	...
301	2¢ Washington, Carmine	20.00	13.00	12.50	8.25	.20
301c	2¢ Booklet Pane of 6	850.00	575.00	550.00	375.00	...
302	3¢ Jackson, Bright Violet	87.50	56.50	55.00	35.00	2.25
303	4¢ Grant, Brown	95.00	60.00	57.50	37.50	1.00
304	5¢ Lincoln, Blue	95.00	60.00	57.50	37.50	1.15
305	6¢ Garfield, Claret	115.00	72.50	67.50	45.00	1.00

1902-03 Issue Perf. 12 VF Used + 50% (C)

Scott's No.		VF	NH F-VF	Unused VF	F-VF	Used F-VF
306	8¢ M. Wash., Violet Black	65.00	42.50	38.50	26.50	1.60
307	10¢ Webster, Red Brown	97.50	65.00	60.00	40.00	1.15
308	13¢ B. Harrison, Purp. Black	67.50	45.00	42.50	28.50	6.50
309	15¢ Clay, Olive Green	240.00	160.00	150.00	100.00	4.00
310	50¢ Jefferson, Orange	675.00	440.00	415.00	275.00	18.50
311	$1 Farragut, Black	1200.00	800.00	750.00	500.00	45.00
312	$2 Madison, Dark Blue	1700.00	1125.00	1050.00	700.00	140.00
313	$5 Marshall, Dark Green	4500.00	3000.00	2800.00	1850.00	525.00

1906-08 Same Designs, Imperforate VF Used + 30% (B)

314	1¢ Franklin, Blue Green	37.00	27.00	23.00	17.00	14.50
315	5¢ Lincoln, Blue	625.00	450.00	435.00	300.00	400.00

* Genuinely used examples of #315 are rare. Copies should have contemporary cancels and be purchased with, or subject to, a certificate of authenticity.

1903 Shield Issue, Perforated 12 VF Used + 50% (C)

319	2¢ Carmine, Die I	9.00	6.00	5.50	3.75	.20
319g	2¢ Booklet Pane of 6, D.I.	225.00	145.00	150.00	95.00	...
319f	2¢ Lake, Die II	17.50	11.00	10.50	7.00	.50
319h	2¢ Booklet Pane of 6, D.II.	370.00	250.00	240.00	160.00	...

1906 Shield Issue, Imperforate VF Used + 30% (B)

320	2¢ Carmine, Die I	38.50	28.00	24.00	18.00	13.50
320a	2¢ Lake, Die II	110.00	70.00	65.00	47.50	35.00

1904 Louisiana Purchase Issue VF Used + 50% (B)

323   325   327

323-27	Set of 5	665.00	445.00	415.00	275.00	65.00
323	1¢ Livingston, Green	48.50	32.00	30.00	20.00	3.25
324	2¢ Jefferson, Carmine	45.00	30.00	27.50	18.50	1.25
325	3¢ Monroe, Violet	145.00	97.50	90.00	60.00	25.00
326	5¢ McKinley, Blue	165.00	105.00	100.00	65.00	16.50
327	10¢ Map, Brown	300.00	200.00	185.00	125.00	22.50

1907 Jamestown Issue VF Used + 75% (C)

328   329   330

328-30	Set of 3	315.00	195.00	195.00	120.00	27.50
328	1¢ John Smith, Green	48.50	28.00	30.00	17.50	3.00
329	2¢ Jamestown, Carmine	60.00	36.50	37.50	22.50	2.75
330	5¢ Pocahontas, Blue	225.00	135.00	140.00	85.00	22.50

PLATE BLOCKS				ARROW BLOCKS			
	NH		Unused		NH		Unused
Scott #	VF	F-VF	F-VF	Scott #	VF	F-VF	F-VF
285	415.00	275.00	165.00	285	220.00	145.00	87.50
286	335.00	225.00	135.00	286	190.00	125.00	77.50
294 (6)	435.00	290.00	180.00	294	165.00	110.00	67.50
295 (6)	435.00	290.00	180.00	295	165.00	110.00	67.50
300 (6)	260.00	170.00	110.00	314	180.00	130.00	80.00
301 (6)	300.00	200.00	125.00	320	180.00	130.00	80.00
314	275.00	200.00	125.00	323	220.00	145.00	90.00
319 (6)	145.00	95.00	60.00	324	195.00	130.00	80.00
320 (6)	340.00	260.00	170.00	328	200.00	120.00	75.00
323	270.00	180.00	115.00	329	260.00	160.00	97.50
324	285.00	190.00	120.00	CENTER LINE BLOCKS			
328 (6)	400.00	250.00	160.00	314	300.00	225.00	140.00
329 (6)	575.00	350.00	225.00	320	280.00	215.00	135.00

1908-09 Wash-Franklins Double Line Wmk. - Perf. 12 VF Used + 50% (B)

331,357,374   332/519   333/541   338/381   342

1908-09 Wash-Franklins Double Line Wmk. - Perf. 12 VF Used + 50% (B)

Scott's No.			NH VF	NH F-VF	Unused VF	Unused F-VF	Used F-VF
331	1¢	Franklin, Green	12.50	8.00	7.50	5.00	.15
331a	1¢	Booklet Pane of 6	295.00	195.00	195.00	130.00	...
332	2¢	Washington, Carmine	12.50	8.00	7.75	5.00	.15
332a	2¢	Booklet Pane of 6	260.00	175.00	170.00	115.00	...
333	3¢	Deep Violet	56.50	37.50	35.00	23.50	2.15
334	4¢	Orange Brown	70.00	45.00	42.50	27.50	.90
335	5¢	Blue	83.50	55.00	51.50	35.00	1.75
336	6¢	Red Orange	100.00	67.50	62.50	42.50	4.00
337	8¢	Olive Green	77.50	52.50	48.50	32.50	2.00
338	10¢	Yellow	120.00	80.00	73.50	49.50	1.25
339	13¢	Blue Green	77.50	50.00	46.50	31.00	17.00
340	15¢	Ultramarine	110.00	73.50	67.50	45.00	5.00
341	50¢	Violet	525.00	370.00	325.00	225.00	15.00
342	$1	Violet Brown	850.00	565.00	525.00	350.00	65.00

1908-09 Series, Double Line Wmk. - Imperf. VF Used + 30% (B)

			NH VF	NH F-VF	Unused VF	Unused F-VF	Used F-VF
343	1¢	Franklin, Green	10.00	7.50	6.75	5.00	3.50
344	2¢	Washington, Carmine	14.00	10.50	9.50	7.00	2.50
345	3¢	Deep Violet	33.00	24.00	22.00	16.50	17.00
346	4¢	Orange Brown	43.50	32.50	30.00	22.50	18.00
347	5¢	Blue	72.50	57.50	51.50	38.50	27.50

PLATE BLOCKS

Scott #	NH VF	NH F-VF	Unused F-VF	Scott #	NH VF	NH F-VF	Unused F-VF
331 (6)	110.00	70.00	45.00	343 (6)	85.00	65.00	45.00
332 (6)	110.00	70.00	45.00	344 (6)	150.00	110.00	75.00
333 (6)	485.00	325.00	210.00	345 (6)	235.00	215.00	160.00

ARROW BLOCKS

Scott #	NH VF	NH F-VF	Unused F-VF
343	53.50	40.00	27.50
344	63.50	47.50	32.50
345	130.00	100.00	70.00
346	225.00	165.00	110.00
347	350.00	260.00	175.00

CENTER LINE BLOCKS

Scott #	NH VF	NH F-VF	Unused F-VF
343	53.50	42.50	32.50
344	62.50	47.50	37.50
345	140.00	110.00	80.00
346	225.00	165.00	130.00
347	375.00	295.00	225.00

1908-10 Coils, Double Line Wmk. - Perf. 12 Horiz. VF Used + 50% (C)

			NH VF	NH F-VF	Unused VF	Unused F-VF	Used F-VF
348	1¢	Franklin, Green	47.50	31.50	30.00	20.00	12.00
349	2¢	Washington, Carmine	85.00	58.50	52.50	35.00	7.00
350	4¢	Orange Brown	195.00	130.00	125.00	80.00	70.00
351	5¢	Blue	215.00	145.00	135.00	90.00	95.00

1909 Coils, Double Line Wmk. - Perf. 12 Vert. VF Used + 50% (C)

			NH VF	NH F-VF	Unused VF	Unused F-VF	Used F-VF
352	1¢	Franklin, Green	107.50	70.00	67.50	45.00	27.50
353	2¢	Washington, Carmine	105.00	67.50	65.00	42.50	7.50
354	4¢	Orange Brown	240.00	160.00	150.00	100.00	57.50
355	5¢	Blue	260.00	175.00	165.00	110.00	65.00
356	10¢	Yellow	3650.00	2350.00	2250.00	1500.00	875.00

(#348-56, should be purchased with, or subject to, a certificate of authenticity.)

1909 "Blue Papers", Double Line Wmk., Perf. 12 VF Used + 60% (B)

	COIL LINE PAIRS NH VF	NH F-VF	Unused F-VF		UNUSED COIL PAIRS NH VF	NH F-VF	Unused F-VF
Scott #							
348	335.00	220.00	150.00		130.00	85.00	57.50
349	525.00	365.00	260.00		230.00	165.00	100.00
352	675.00	465.00	325.00		295.00	195.00	125.00
353	675.00	465.00	325.00		290.00	190.00	120.00

			NH VF	NH F-VF	Unused VF	Unused F-VF	Used F-VF
357	1¢	Franklin, Green	190.00	115.00	110.00	70.00	75.00
358	2¢	Washington, Carmine	180.00	110.00	115.00	70.00	65.00
359	3¢	Deep Violet	...	2350.00	2300.00	1450.00	...
361	5¢	Blue	...	5500.00	...	3350.00	...
362	6¢	Red Orange	...	1750.00	1850.00	1075.00	1200.00
364	10¢	Yellow	...	1900.00	2150.00	1250.00	1350.00
365	13¢	Blue Green	...	3300.00	...	2150.00	1700.00
366	15¢	Pale Ultramarine	...	1600.00	1700.00	1000.00	1200.00

* Blue Papers, which were printed on experimental paper with approximately 35% rag content, actually have a grayish appearance which can best be observed by looking at the stamps from the gum side. Additionally, the watermark is more clearly visible than on the stamps printed on regular paper (#331-340). The stamps are also noted for having carbon specks imbedded in the texture of the paper.

* Blue Papers should be purchased with, or subject to, a certificate of authenticity. Genuinely used Blue Papers, other than the 1¢, 2¢ & 13¢ values, are extremely rare. Examples should have contemporary cancels.

NOTE: PLATE BLOCKS, AND OTHER BLOCKS, ARE ALL BLOCKS OF 4 UNLESS OTHERWISE INDICATED IN ( ).
NOTE: VF UNUSED PLATE BLOCKS AND LINE PAIRS ARE GENERALLY AVAILABLE AT THE RESPECTIVE F-VF NH PRICE.

1909 Commems. (Used) Perf. VF + 40% - Imperf. VF + 30% (B)

367,369   370   372

Scott's No.			NH VF	NH F-VF	Unused VF	Unused F-VF	Used F-VF
367	2¢	Lincoln, Perf. 12	8.75	6.00	5.75	4.00	1.50
368	2¢	Lincoln, Imperf.	45.00	32.50	30.00	22.50	17.50
369	2¢	Bluish Paper, Perf. 12	395.00	260.00	265.00	175.00	195.00
370	2¢	Alaska-Yukon, Perf. 12	16.50	10.75	10.75	7.00	1.50
371	2¢	Alaska-Yukon, Imperf.	57.50	43.50	39.50	29.50	19.50
372	2¢	Hudson-Fulton, Perf. 12	21.00	15.00	13.50	10.00	3.50
373	2¢	Hudson-Fulton, Imperf.	67.50	47.50	45.00	32.50	21.50

PLATE BLOCKS / ARROW BLOCKS

Scott #	NH VF	NH F-VF	Unused F-VF	Scott #	NH VF	NH F-VF	Unused F-VF
367 (6)	220.00	150.00	100.00	368	195.00	145.00	100.00
368 (6)	325.00	249.00	160.00	371	275.00	200.00	130.00
370 (6)	365.00	250.00	165.00	373	300.00	225.00	145.00
371 (6)	485.00	335.00	225.00	**CENTER LINE BLOCKS**			
372 (6)	490.00	335.00	225.00	368	250.00	190.00	130.00
373 (6)	550.00	375.00	250.00	371	300.00	230.00	160.00
				373	390.00	300.00	210.00

1910-11 Single Line Wmk. Perf 12 VF Used + 50% (B)

(Same designs as 1908-1909 Series)
This illustration shows a block of 15 stamps with the Single Line Watermark. The watermark appears in various positions on the stamps.

			NH VF	NH F-VF	Unused VF	Unused F-VF	Used F-VF
374	1¢	Franklin, Green	12.75	8.25	8.25	5.50	.20
374a	1¢	Booklet Pane of 6	250.00	165.00	165.00	110.00	...
375	2¢	Washington, Carmine	11.75	7.75	7.50	5.25	.20
375a	2¢	Booklet Pane of 6	215.00	140.00	140.00	95.00	...
376	3¢	Deep Violet	31.50	21.50	20.00	13.75	1.25
377	4¢	Brown	47.50	31.50	30.00	20.00	.45
378	5¢	Blue	47.50	31.50	30.00	20.00	.45
379	6¢	Red Orange	62.50	39.50	39.50	26.50	.60
380	8¢	Olive Green	200.00	130.00	130.00	85.00	10.00
381	10¢	Yellow	195.00	120.00	130.00	80.00	3.00
382	15¢	Pale Ultramarine	460.00	300.00	300.00	200.00	12.00

1911 Single Line Wmk., Imperf. VF Used + 30% (B)

			NH VF	NH F-VF	Unused VF	Unused F-VF	Used F-VF
383	1¢	Franklin, Green	4.50	3.25	3.00	2.25	1.85
384	2¢	Washington, Carmine	9.50	7.25	6.50	4.95	2.25

PLATE BLOCKS / ARROW BLOCKS

Scott #	NH VF	NH F-VF	Unused F-VF	Scott #	NH VF	NH F-VF	Unused F-VF
374 (6)	135.00	90.00	60.00	383	23.75	16.50	11.50
375 (6)	135.00	90.00	60.00	384	47.50	35.00	25.00
376 (6)	295.00	200.00	130.00	**CENTER LINE BLOCKS**			
377 (6)	365.00	240.00	160.00	383	40.00	30.00	20.00
378 (6)	400.00	270.00	175.00	384	85.00	65.00	45.00
383 (6)	75.00	55.00	40.00				
384 (6)	210.00	160.00	110.00				

1910 Coils S. Line Wmk. - Perf. 12 Horiz. VF Used + 50% (C)

			NH VF	NH F-VF	Unused VF	Unused F-VF	Used F-VF
385	1¢	Franklin, Green	45.00	30.00	29.50	19.50	12.00
386	2¢	Washington, Carmine	89.50	60.00	60.00	40.00	14.50

1910-11 Coils S. Line Wmk. - Perf. 12 Vert. VF Used + 50% (C)

			NH VF	NH F-VF	Unused VF	Unused F-VF	Used F-VF
387	1¢	Franklin, Green	200.00	140.00	135.00	90.00	36.50
388	2¢	Washington, Carmine	1300.00	850.00	850.00	550.00	225.00
389	3¢	Washington, Deep Violet	...	USED FINE			6750.00

(Examples of #388 and 389 must be purchased with, or subject to, a certificate.)

1910 Coils S. Line Wmk. - Perf. 8½ Horizontally VF Used + 50% (B)

			NH VF	NH F-VF	Unused VF	Unused F-VF	Used F-VF
390	1¢	Franklin, Green	8.25	5.65	5.50	3.75	4.00
391	2¢	Washington, Carmine	57.50	38.75	39.50	26.50	9.50

1910-13 Coils S. Line Wmk. - Perf. 8½ Vertically VF Used + 50% (B)

			NH VF	NH F-VF	Unused VF	Unused F-VF	Used F-VF
392	1¢	Franklin, Green	40.00	27.50	26.50	17.50	16.50
393	2¢	Washington, Carmine	72.50	48.50	47.50	31.50	7.50
394	3¢	Deep Violet	87.50	60.00	57.50	40.00	40.00
395	4¢	Brown	87.50	60.00	57.50	40.00	35.00
396	5¢	Blue	87.50	60.00	57.50	40.00	35.00

	COIL LINE PAIRS			UNUSED COIL PAIRS		
		NH	Unused		NH	Unused
Scott #	VF	F-VF	F-VF	VF	F-VF	F-VF
385	550.00	375.00	250.00	130.00	85.00	55.00
386	1050.00	700.00	475.00	295.00	195.00	130.00
387	875.00	600.00	400.00	525.00	350.00	225.00
390	65.00	44.00	30.00	20.00	13.00	8.75
391	335.00	225.00	150.00	140.00	95.00	65.00
392	235.00	160.00	110.00	100.00	70.00	43.50
393	365.00	250.00	165.00	190.00	130.00	87.50
394	525.00	370.00	250.00	220.00	150.00	100.00
395	525.00	370.00	250.00	220.00	150.00	100.00
396	525.00	370.00	250.00	220.00	150.00	100.00

1913 Panama-Pacific, Perf. 12 VF Used + 50% (B)

397,401   398,402   399,403   400,400A,404

Scott's No.		NH	Unused		Used
	VF	F-VF	VF	F-VF	F-VF
397-400A	Set of 5 .... 750.00	510.00	490.00	330.00	37.50
397	1¢ Balboa, Green........................30.00	20.00	20.00	13.50	1.25
398	2¢ Panama Canal, Carmine....32.50	21.00	21.00	14.00	.45
399	5¢ Golden Gate, Blue 125.00	82.50	82.50	55.00	8.00
400	10¢ San Fran., Orange Yel...235.00	160.00	150.00	100.00	17.00
400A	10¢ Orange.................................365.00	250.00	240.00	165.00	14.00

1914-15 Panama-Pacific, Perf. 10 VF Used + 50% (B)

401-04	Set of 4 .... 2050.00	1350.00	1300.00	925.00	65.00
401	1¢ Balboa, Green........................45.00	30.00	30.00	20.00	4.50
402	2¢ Panama, Carmine (1915)....130.00	87.50	85.00	57.50	1.25
403	5¢ Golden Gate, Blue(1915)....280.00	190.00	180.00	120.00	12.00
404	10¢ San Fran.,Orange(1915).....1650.00	1100.00	1075.00	750.00	50.00

1912-14 Single Line Wmk. - Perf. 12 VF Used + 50% (B)

405/545   406/546   337/380   419/515   423/518

NOTE: THE 1¢ TO 7¢ STAMPS FROM 1912-21 PICTURE WASHINGTON. THE 8¢ TO $5 STAMPS PICTURE FRANKLIN.

405	1¢ Washington, Green 10.50	6.75	6.75	4.50	.18
405b	1¢ Booklet Pane of 6 ....135.00	87.50	90.00	60.00	...
406	2¢ Carmine....................................9.75	6.25	6.00	4.00	.18
406a	2¢ Booklet Pane of 6 ....135.00	87.50	90.00	60.00	...
407	7¢ Black (1914) 135.00	90.00	90.00	60.00	8.50

1912 Single Line Wmk. - Imperf. VF Used + 30% (B)

408	1¢ Washington, Green 2.10	1.60	1.30	1.00	.50
409	2¢ Carmine.....................................2.25	1.70	1.50	1.15	.55

PLATE BLOCKS				ARROW BLOCKS			
		NH	Unused			NH	Unused
Scott #	VF	F-VF	F-VF	Scott #	VF	F-VF	F-VF
397 (6)	260.00	175.00	120.00	408	9.25	6.75	4.50
398 (6)	425.00	285.00	195.00	409	10.00	7.50	5.25
401 (6)	525.00	350.00	235.00		CENTER LINE BLOCKS		
405 (6)	110.00	75.00	50.00				
406 (6)	150.00	100.00	65.00	408	16.50	12.50	8.50
408 (6)	30.00	22.50	15.75	409	19.00	14.50	10.00
409 (6)	50.00	39.50	27.50				

1912 Coils Single Line Wmk. - Perf. 8½ Horiz. VF Used + 50% (B)

410	1¢ Washington, Green 12.00	8.00	7.75	5.25	3.75
411	2¢ Carmine....................................16.00	10.75	10.50	7.00	3.50

1912 Coils Single Line Wmk. - Perf. 8½ Vert. VF Used + 50% (B)

412	1¢ Washington, Green 45.00	29.50	29.50	20.00	4.50
413	2¢ Carmine....................................75.00	50.00	48.50	32.50	.90

	COIL LINE PAIRS			UNUSED COIL PAIRS		
		NH	Unused		NH	Unused
Scott #	VF	F-VF	F-VF	VF	F-VF	F-VF
410	75.00	50.00	32.50	30.00	20.00	13.00
411	85.00	57.50	37.50	40.00	27.50	17.50
412	175.00	120.00	75.00	110.00	72.50	50.00
413	360.00	240.00	165.00	185.00	125.00	80.00

1912-14 Franklin Design. Single Line Wmk. - Perf. 12 VF Used + 50% (B)

Scott's No.		NH	Unused		Used
	VF	F-VF	VF	F-VF	F-VF
414	8¢ Franklin, Olive Green 75.00	50.00	49.00	32.50	1.00
415	9¢ Salmon Red (1914).................95.00	62.50	60.00	40.00	10.75
416	10¢ Orange Yellow 80.00	53.50	52.50	35.00	.35
417	12¢ Claret Brown (1914)............85.00	56.50	55.00	36.50	3.50
418	15¢ Gray 150.00	100.00	95.00	65.00	3.00
419	20¢ Ultramarine 350.00	230.00	225.00	150.00	13.00
420	30¢ Orange Red (1914) 240.00	160.00	150.00	100.00	13.00
421	50¢ Violet (1914) 750.00	500.00	485.00	325.00	15.00

* #421 usually shows an offset on the back; #422 usually does not.

1912 Franklin Design. Double Line Wmk. - Perf. 12 VF Used + 50% (B)

422	50¢ Franklin, Violet 525.00	350.00	315.00	210.00	14.00
423	$1 Violet Brown........................950.00	625.00	600.00	400.00	50.00

1914-15 Flat Press Single Line Wmk., Perf. 10 VF Used + 50% (B)

424	1¢ Washington, Green....................5.00	3.15	3.15	2.10	.18
424d	1¢ Booklet Pane of 6 ....8.75	6.00	6.00	4.00	...
425	2¢ Rose Red 5.00	3.00	3.00	2.00	.18
425e	2¢ Booklet Pane of 6 ....45.00	30.00	29.50	20.00	...
426	3¢ Deep Violet 27.50	17.50	17.50	11.50	1.00
427	4¢ Brown 70.00	46.50	45.00	30.00	.45
428	5¢ Blue 65.00	42.50	41.50	27.50	.45
429	6¢ Red Orange 100.00	65.00	62.50	42.50	1.30
430	7¢ Black 160.00	105.00	100.00	67.50	3.35
431	8¢ Franklin, Olive Green 75.00	48.00	46.50	31.50	1.65
432	9¢ Salmon Red 95.00	60.00	57.50	38.50	7.75
433	10¢ Orange Yellow 95.00	60.00	58.00	39.00	.40
434	11¢ Dark Green (1915) 50.00	32.50	32.50	21.50	6.50
435	12¢ Claret Brown 52.50	32.50	32.50	21.50	3.50
435a	12¢ Copper Red 57.50	37.50	37.50	25.00	4.75
437	15¢ Gray 230.00	150.00	145.00	97.50	6.00
438	20¢ Ultramarine 400.00	260.00	250.00	165.00	3.50
439	30¢ Orange Red 500.00	330.00	325.00	210.00	13.75
440	50¢ Violet (1915) 1150.00	775.00	750.00	495.00	15.00

PLATE BLOCKS

		NH	Unused			Unused	
Scott #	VF	F-VF	F-VF	Scott #	VF	F-VF	F-VF
424 (6)	70.00	45.00	30.00	428 (6)	675.00	450.00	300.00
425 (6)	47.50	30.00	20.00	429 (6)	735.00	485.00	325.00
"COIL STAMPS" Impt. & Pl.# Blk. / 10				431 (6)	850.00	565.00	375.00
424 CS (10)	225.00	160.00	110.00	434 (6)	385.00	260.00	180.00
425 CS (10)	260.00	180.00	125.00	435 (6)	485.00	325.00	215.00
426 (6)	325.00	215.00	140.00	435a (6)	550.00	375.00	250.00
427 (6)	900.00	600.00	400.00				

1914 Coils Flat Press S.L. Wmk. - Perf. 10 Horiz. VF Used + 50% (B)

441	1¢ Washington, Green...................2.10	1.45	1.40	.95	.95
442	2¢ Carmine....................................18.00	12.50	11.50	8.00	5.75

1914 Coils Flat Press S.L. Wmk. - Perf. 10 Vert. VF Used + 50% (B)

443	1¢ Washington, Green...................44.50	29.50	29.00	19.50	4.75
444	2¢ Carmine....................................65.00	43.50	42.50	28.50	1.20
445	3¢ Violet 465.00	310.00	300.00	200.00	110.00
446	4¢ Brown 250.00	170.00	160.00	110.00	39.50
447	5¢ Blue 95.00	65.00	62.50	42.50	25.00

	COIL LINE PAIRS			UNUSED COIL PAIRS		
		NH	Unused		NH	Unused
Scott #	VF	F-VF	F-VF	VF	F-VF	F-VF
441	13.50	9.00	6.00	5.25	3.50	2.35
442	90.00	60.00	40.00	45.00	31.50	19.75
443	260.00	170.00	115.00	120.00	77.50	50.00
444	365.00	240.00	155.00	175.00	120.00	80.00
447	425.00	280.00	185.00	250.00	165.00	105.00

The two top stamps are Rotary Press While the underneath stamps are Flat Press. Note that the designs of the Rotary Press stamps are a little longer or Wider than Flat Press stamps. Flat Press Stamps usually show spots of color Back.

Perf. Horizontally   Perf. Vertically

1915 Coils Rotary S.L. Wmk. - Perf. 10 Horiz. VF Used + 50% (B)

448	1¢ Washington, Green.................14.00	9.00	9.00	6.00	3.25
449	2¢ Red, Type I	...	3000.00	1800.00	350.00
450	2¢ Carmine, Type III 19.50	13.00	12.75	8.50	3.25

1914-16 Coils Rotary S.L. Wmk. - Perf. 10 Vert. VF Used + 50% (B)

452	1¢ Washington, Green.................25.00	16.50	16.50	11.00	1.75
453	2¢ Carm. Rose, Type I 220.00	150.00	140.00	95.00	3.75
454	2¢ Red, Type II (1915) 210.00	140.00	135.00	90.00	8.75
455	2¢ Carmine, Type III (1915)........18.00	11.50	12.00	8.00	.85
456	3¢ Violet (1916) 500.00	330.00	325.00	210.00	85.00
457	4¢ Brown (1916) 57.50	37.50	37.50	25.00	16.75
458	5¢ Blue (1916) 65.00	43.50	42.50	28.50	16.75

United States & United Nations

...as well as Europe, Asia & Worldwide!

Save 10% on complete Country runs!

U.S. NH Year Sets 1940-1997 commemoratives, retail $1043.25 with 10% discount **$939.00**
(Year sets include all comm., airmails and major S/S.)
1954-1996 definitives, retail $462.35 with 10% discount
(includes all major Scott numbers) **$416.00**

U.N NH Year Sets
1951-1998 with #38 sheet & 6 booklets, retail $1246.75
with 10% discount **$1122.000**
1951-1998 without #38 and with 1995, '97 & '98 booklets,
retail $1097.50 with 10% discount **$987.75**
(U.N. year sets include commemoratives, definitives, airmails and flags. Geneva issues begin in 1969 and Vienna issues begin in 1979.)

Henry Gitner is your reliable and knowledgable supplier! We maintain one of the largest stocks in America of US, UN and Foreign stamps and covers.

Free Price Lists!

Free Topical & Worldwide Price Lists

Fair Prices!

We Buy!

Satisfaction Guaranteed!

UNITED STATES PRICE LIST: Sets, Year Sets, Definitive Sets, Booklet Panes - includes U.S. Trust Territories. Our extensive stock includes Plate Blocks, coils, FDC's, Back-of-the-Book material and a wealth of classics! **Also ask for our free price lists of Duck Stamps .**

UNITED NATIONS PRICE LIST: New York, Geneva & Vienna, 1951-date. Sets, Year Sets, Miniature Sheets, Souvenir Cards, Postal Stationery and Specialized Material including printings, varieties and errors.

See our Web site for a complete UN SPECIALIZED list including photos!

COUNTRY & TOPICAL PRICE LISTS: Austria • Belgium Parcel Posts • China • France • FSAT • Germany • Guyana • Israel • Palestine • Liechtenstein • Saudi Arabia • Switzerland • Trieste-Zone A • Vatican • Worldwide Year Sets 1958-Date • Artist Die Proofs • Austrian Black Prints • Belgium Imperfs & Proofs • Birds • Butterflies & Insects • Europa • French Imperfs • U.S. Photo Essays & Autographed Plate Blocks • Zeppelins & Aerophilately --- **We also have a large stock of Specialized Disney - please call, write or fax with your want list today!**

Not only do our prices reflect fair market prices but we offer a 10% savings under our **Monthly Purchase Plan.** Call or write for a free brochure!

Top Prices Paid for all U.S., U.N. Asia & Worldwide stamps and covers. Good collections, dealer's stock and better individual items are of special interest.

We pride ourselves on the quality of the stamps we sell, as well as the service we provide. Write, call or fax today!

Henry Gitner Philatelists, Inc.

Philately - The Quiet Excitement!

See our Web site!

P.O. Box 3077, Middletown, NY 10940
Tel: 914-343-5151   Fax: 914-343-0068
Email: hgitner@hgitner.com

Toll Free: 1-800-947-8267

http://www.hgitner.com

	COIL LINE PAIRS		UNUSED COIL PAIRS			
	NH		Unused	NH		Unused
Scott #	VF	F-VF	F-VF	VF	F-VF	F-VF
448	80.00	52.50	35.00	35.00	22.50	15.00
450	110.00	75.00	50.00	50.00	32.50	21.50
452	125.00	85.00	57.50	60.00	40.00	27.50
453	1000.00	675.00	450.00	565.00	375.00	235.00
454	850.00	575.00	375.00	500.00	335.00	215.00
455	100.00	67.50	45.00	47.50	30.00	20.00
457	265.00	175.00	120.00	140.00	95.00	62.50
458	315.00	210.00	140.00	160.00	110.00	70.00

	COIL LINE PAIRS		UNUSED COIL PAIRS			
	NH		Unused	NH		Unused
Scott #	VF	F-VF	F-VF	VF	F-VF	F-VF
486	9.00	6.25	4.25	3.35	2.50	1.65
487	210.00	140.00	95.00	67.50	45.00	30.75
488	37.50	25.00	17.50	12.00	8.25	5.75
489	60.00	40.00	27.50	20.00	13.50	9.00
490	8.00	5.50	3.75	2.70	1.80	1.20
492	100.00	72.50	47.50	40.00	27.00	18.00
493	175.00	130.00	95.00	67.50	47.50	32.50
494	110.00	80.00	55.00	42.50	29.00	21.00
495	120.00	90.00	65.00	46.00	31.00	22.75
496	46.50	33.50	23.50	14.50	10.00	7.25
497	215.00	155.00	110.00	82.50	55.00	38.75

1914 Imperf. Coil Rotary Press S.L. Wmk. - VF Used + 30% (B)

Scott's No.		NH VF	F-VF	Unused VF	F-VF	Used F-VF
459	2¢ Washington, Carmine	650.00	500.00	450.00	350.00	700.00

* Genuinely used examples of #459 are rare. Copies should have contemporary cancels and be purchased with, or subject to, a certificate of authenticity.

1915 Flat Press Double Line Wmk. - Perf. 10 VF Used + 75% (B)

460	$1 Franklin, Violet Black	1350.00	975.00	975.00	675.00	75.00

1915 Flat Press S. Line Wmk. - Perf. 11 VF Used + 100% (B)

461	2¢ Pale Carmine Red	250.00	135.00	165.00	90.00	195.00

(Counterfeits of #461 are common. Purchase with, or subject to, a certificate.)

1916-17 Flat Press, No Wmk. - Perf. 10 (VF Used + 50%) (B)

		NH VF	F-VF	Unused VF	F-VF	Used F-VF
462	1¢ Washington, Green	13.00	8.25	8.25	5.50	.30
462a	1¢ Booklet Pane of 6	20.00	12.50	13.50	9.00	...
463	2¢ Carmine	9.00	5.50	5.65	3.75	.25
463a	2¢ Booklet Pane of 6	160.00	110.00	100.00	75.00	...
464	3¢ Violet	150.00	90.00	90.00	60.00	11.50
465	4¢ Orange Brown	90.00	57.50	55.00	37.50	1.50
466	5¢ Blue	150.00	95.00	90.00	60.00	1.50
467	5¢ Carmine ERROR	1150.00	750.00	750.00	500.00	600.00
467	5¢ Single in Block of 9	1600.00	1150.00	1100.00	750.00	...
467	5¢ Pair in Block of 12	2700.00	2000.00	1850.00	1375.00	...
468	6¢ Red Orange	175.00	110.00	110.00	72.50	6.50
469	7¢ Black	215.00	135.00	135.00	90.00	9.00
470	8¢ Franklin, Olive Green	100.00	65.00	65.00	42.50	5.00
471	9¢ Salmon Red	110.00	70.00	67.50	45.00	11.50
472	10¢ Orange Yellow	200.00	125.00	125.00	82.50	1.00
473	11¢ Dark Green	77.50	50.00	50.00	32.50	15.00
474	12¢ Claret Brown	90.00	58.50	57.50	38.50	4.50
475	15¢ Gray	350.00	235.00	220.00	150.00	8.75
476	20¢ Ultramarine	450.00	290.00	275.00	190.00	10.75
477	50¢ Light Violet (1917)	1800.00	1200.00	1200.00	795.00	50.00
478	$1 Violet Black	1300.00	900.00	850.00	575.00	14.00

1917 Flat Press, No Wmk.-Perf. 10, Designs of 1902-3 VF used 35% (B)

479	$2 Madison, Dark Blue	675.00	425.00	425.00	275.00	35.00
480	$5 Marshall, Light Green	500.00	365.00	325.00	225.00	36.50

NOTE: #479 & 480 have the same designs as #312 & 313.

1916-17 Flat Press, No Wmk. - Imperforate VF Used + 30% (B)

481	1¢ Washington, Green	1.60	1.30	1.10	.90	.70
482	2¢ Carmine, Type I	2.65	2.00	1.80	1.40	1.00
483	3¢ Violet, Type I (1917)	24.00	18.00	17.50	13.00	6.50
484	3¢ Violet, Type II (1917)	19.50	14.50	13.50	10.00	4.35

*3¢ Type I, the 5th line from the left of the toga rope is broken or missing; 3¢ Type II, the 5th line is complete. See Scott for more details.

	PLATE BLOCKS				ARROW BLOCKS		
	NH		Unused		NH		Unused
Scott #	VF	F-VF	F-VF	Scott #	VF	F-VF	F-VF
462 (6)	270.00	180.00	120.00	481	8.00	6.50	4.25
463 (6)	225.00	150.00	100.00	482	12.75	10.00	6.75
473 (6)	650.00	450.00	300.00	483	110.00	85.00	60.00
474 (6)	1025.00	700.00	475.00	484	90.00	65.00	45.00
481 (6)	21.00	16.75	11.50		CENTER LINE BLOCKS		
482 (6)	38.50	30.00	22.50	481	13.50	10.00	7.00
483 (6)	200.00	160.00	115.00	482	16.75	13.00	8.75
484 (6)	165.00	130.00	90.00	483	130.00	100.00	70.00
				484	110.00	85.00	60.00

1916-19 Coils Rotary, No Wmk. - Perf. 10 Horiz. VF Used + 40% (B)

486	1¢ Washington, Green (1918)	1.50	1.10	1.00	.75	.20
487	2¢ Carmine, Type II	29.50	20.00	19.50	13.75	3.25
488	2¢ Carmine, Type III (1919)	5.25	3.50	3.50	2.40	1.50
489	3¢ Violet, Type I (1917)	9.00	6.00	5.50	4.00	1.35

1916-22 Coils, Rotary, No Wmk. - Perf. 10 Vert. VF Used + 40% (B)

490	1¢ Washington, Green	1.10	.75	.70	.50	.20
491	2¢ Carmine, Type II	...	...	2300.00	1500.00	500.00
492	2¢ Carmine, Type III	18.00	12.00	11.50	8.00	.20
493	3¢ Violet, Type I (1917)	30.00	21.50	20.00	14.50	2.50
494	3¢ Violet, Type II (1918)	18.00	13.00	12.50	9.00	.90
495	4¢ Orange Brown (1917)	19.50	14.00	13.50	9.50	3.50
496	5¢ Blue (1919)	7.00	4.75	4.50	3.25	.90
497	10¢ Franklin, Orng.Yel.(1922)	35.00	25.00	24.50	17.50	9.50

1917-19 Flat Press, No Watermark - Perf. 11 VF Used + 50% (B)

Scott's No.		NH VF	F-VF	Unused VF	F-VF	Used F-VF
498	1¢ Washington, Green	.90	.60	.65	.45	.20
498e	1¢ Booklet Pane of 6	5.25	3.50	3.75	2.50	...
499	2¢ Carmine, Ty. I	.80	.55	.55	.40	.20
499e	2¢ Booklet Pane of 6	9.75	6.50	6.50	4.35	...
500	2¢ Deep Rose, Ty. Ia	450.00	325.00	300.00	210.00	160.00
501	3¢ Light Violet, Type I	22.00	14.50	15.00	10.00	.20
501b	3¢ Booklet Pane of 6	120.00	80.00	82.50	55.00	...
502	3¢ Dark Violet, Type II	29.00	19.00	19.50	13.00	.50
502b	3¢ Booklet Pane of 6 (1918)	95.00	65.00	62.50	45.00	...
503	4¢ Brown	20.00	13.50	13.50	9.00	.25
504	5¢ Blue	17.50	12.00	12.00	8.25	.25
505	5¢ Rose ERROR	800.00	575.00	525.00	375.00	450.00
505	5¢ ERROR in Block of 9	1100.00	800.00	800.00	550.00	...
505	5¢ Pair in Block of 12	1800.00	1300.00	1250.00	900.00	...
506	6¢ Red Orange	23.50	15.75	15.00	10.00	.30
507	7¢ Black	52.50	35.00	35.00	23.50	.90
508	8¢ Franklin, Olive Bistre	24.00	16.00	16.00	11.00	.65
509	9¢ Salmon Red	27.50	18.00	18.50	12.50	1.75
510	10¢ Orange Yellow	35.00	23.00	24.00	15.75	.18
511	11¢ Light Green	18.00	12.00	11.00	8.25	2.25
512	12¢ Claret Brown	18.00	12.00	11.00	8.25	.40
513	13¢ Apple Green (1919)	21.50	14.50	14.75	9.75	5.00
514	15¢ Gray	72.50	45.00	47.50	32.50	.90
515	20¢ Light Ultramarine	95.00	62.50	65.00	42.50	.30
516	30¢ Orange Red	77.50	50.00	50.00	33.50	.90
517	50¢ Red Violet	125.00	85.00	87.50	60.00	.60
518	$1 Violet Brown	110.00	72.50	75.00	50.00	1.30
518b	$1 Deep Brown	...	1700.00	1600.00	1100.00	725.00

PLATE BLOCKS

	NH		Unused	Scott #	VF	F-VF	F-VF
Scott #	VF	F-VF	F-VF				
498 (6)	28.50	19.00	13.50	509 (6)	240.00	170.00	120.00
499 (6)	28.50	19.00	13.50	510 (6)	310.00	210.00	150.00
501 (6)	165.00	110.00	75.00	511 (6)	195.00	135.00	100.00
502 (6)	230.00	155.00	110.00	512 (6)	195.00	135.00	100.00
503 (6)	230.00	155.00	110.00	513 (6)	215.00	150.00	110.00
504 (6)	210.00	140.00	100.00	514 (6)	825.00	575.00	425.00
506 (6)	275.00	190.00	135.00	515 (6)	950.00	650.00	475.00
507 (6)	400.00	280.00	200.00	516 (6)	950.00	650.00	475.00
508 (6)	250.00	170.00	120.00				
	NH		Unused				

1917 Same Design as #332, D.L. Wmk. - Perf. 11 VF Used + 100% (C)

519	2¢ Washington, Carmine	575.00	350.00	385.00	250.00	475.00

(* Mint and used copies of #519 have been extensively counterfeited. Examples of either should be purchased with, or subject to, a certificate of authenticity.)

523,547	524	537

1918 Flat Press, No Watermark, Perf. 11 VF Used + 40% (B)

523	$2 Franklin,Orng. Red & Blk.	1250.00	900.00	850.00	600.00	190.00
524	$5 Deep Green & Black	465.00	330.00	295.00	210.00	29.50

1918-20 Offset Printing, Perforated 11 VF Used + 40% (B)

525	1¢ Washington, Gray Grn.	4.25	3.00	2.75	2.00	.65
526	2¢ Carmine, Type IV (1920)	47.50	35.00	30.00	22.50	3.75
527	2¢ Carmine, Type V (1920)	32.50	23.50	20.00	15.00	1.10
528	2¢ Carmine, Type Va (1920)	17.00	12.00	11.50	8.00	.50
528A	2¢ Carmine, Type VI (1920)	80.00	60.00	57.50	40.00	1.65
528B	2¢ Carmine, Type VII (1920)	38.75	27.00	25.00	17.50	.45
529	3¢ Violet, Type III	6.00	4.25	4.00	2.75	.30
530	3¢ Purple, Type IV	3.15	2.25	2.10	1.50	.25

1918-20 Offset Printing, Imperforate VF Used + 30% (B)

531	1¢ Washington, Green (1919)	16.50	12.75	11.00	8.50	7.50
532	2¢ Carmine Rose, Type IV (20)	65.00	47.50	42.50	32.50	27.50
533	2¢ Carmine, Type V (1920)	350.00	260.00	230.00	175.00	75.00
534	2¢ Carmine, Type Va (1920)	21.00	16.00	14.00	10.50	6.00
534A	2¢ Carmine, Type VI (1920)	70.00	52.50	45.00	35.00	25.00
534B	2¢ Carmine, Type VII (1920)	...	2000.00	1650.00	1350.00	625.00
535	3¢ Violet, Type IV	15.75	12.00	10.00	8.00	4.75

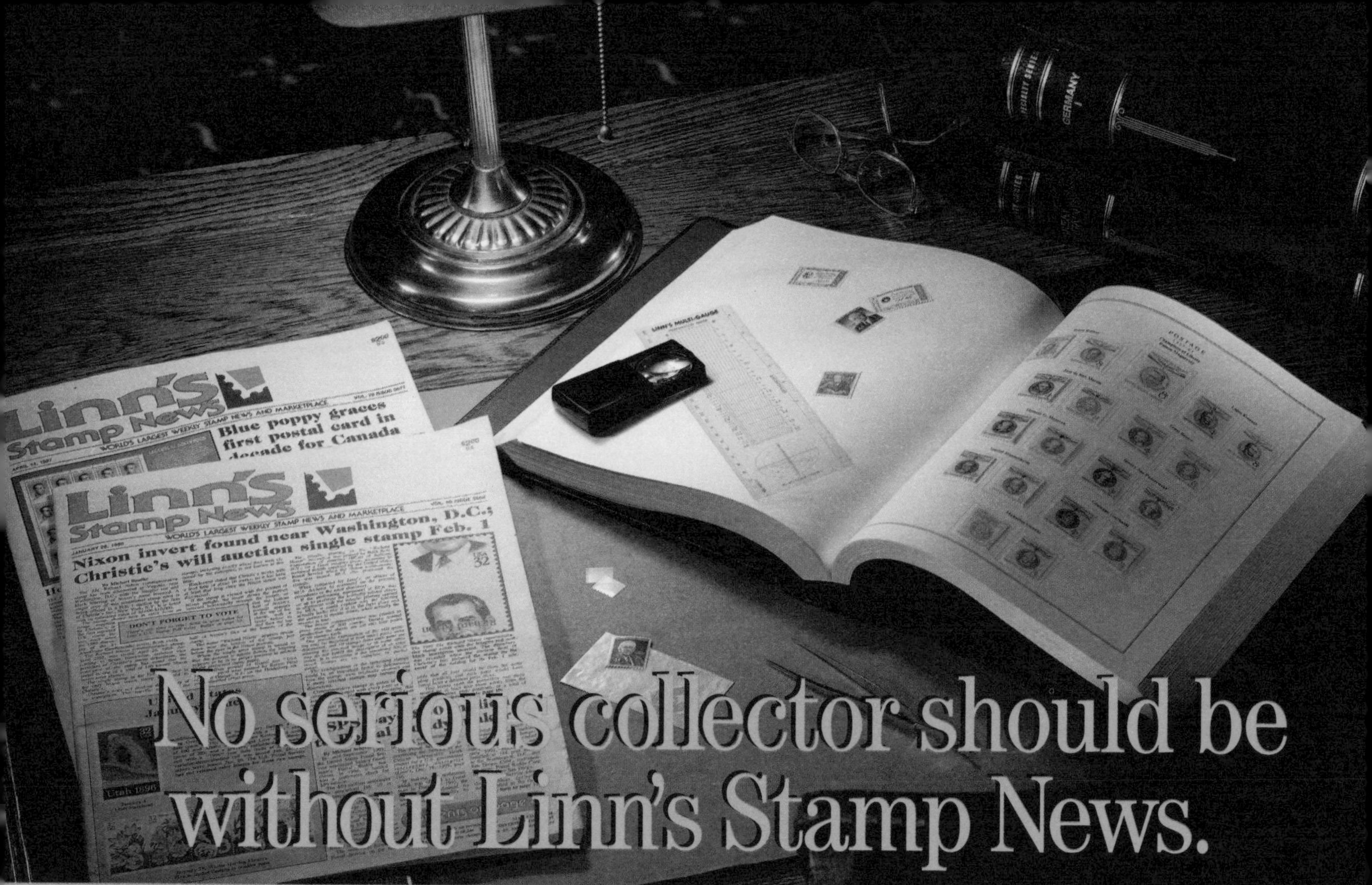

No serious collector should be without Linn's Stamp News.

Miss an issue of Linn's and you miss plenty:

- All the latest-breaking news from Linn's exclusive national and international sources.

- In-depth analysis from top authors on all aspects of collecting, including pricing trends, values, news issues, forgeries, security and more.

- Regular features you can't afford to miss — *Stamp Market Index, Stamp Market Tips and Tip of the Week, Collectors' Forum, Editor's Choice, Readers' Opinions, Postmark Pursuit, Collectors' Workshop, Refresher Course* and much more

- The world's largest stamp marketplace. Listings of events, auctions and sales. Classified ads and readers' notices for buying, selling and trading.

Right now you can receive Linn's at the special introductory rate of only $19.95... plus get a bonus refresher manual to help jump start your own collection. *Linn's Stamp Collecting Made Easy...* is yours FREE with your paid, introductory subscription.

Your FREE refresher course will take you on a simplified tour of the techniques, terms and intricacies of stamp collecting. We'll show you how to buy stamps, how to sort, soak, catalog, store and mount them.

We'll explain terms like roulette, souvenir sheet, overprint and surcharge. You'll learn the right way to use a perforation gauge.

Linn's is researched, written and published by stamp collectors like you. And we understand you want to get the most fun and satisfaction from your collecting.

Mail the card on the left and receive the special introductory rate of 26 issues for $19.95. You'll save over 60% off the regular price plus get our money back guarantee. We'll also send you FREE, Linn's 96-page, all illustrated: *STAMP COLLECTING MADE EASY* with your paid order.

P.O. Box 29, Sidney, OH 45365

Guarantee: Receive a complete refund if you are not completely satisfied at any time.

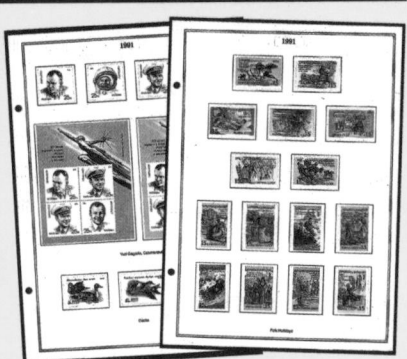

1919 Offset Printing, Perforated 12½ VF Used + 75% (B)

Scott's No.		NH VF	NH F-VF	Unused VF	Unused F-VF	Used F-VF
536	1¢ Washington, Gray Grn	39.50	23.50	24.75	15.00	17.00

PLATE BLOCKS

Scott #	NH VF	NH F-VF	Unused F-VF
525 (6)	39.50	30.00	20.00
526 (6)	365.00	260.00	185.00
527 (6)	280.00	200.00	130.00
528 (6)	140.00	100.00	70.00
528A (6)	650.00	475.00	325.00
528B (6)	275.00	200.00	135.00
529 (6)	90.00	65.00	45.00
530 (6)	35.00	25.00	17.00
531 (6)	130.00	100.00	70.00
532 (6)	525.00	390.00	265.00
534 (6)	155.00	120.00	85.00
534A (6)	525.00	400.00	275.00
535 (6)	115.00	90.00	62.50
536 (6)	300.00	195.00	135.00

ARROW BLOCKS

Scott #	NH VF	NH F-VF	Unused F-VF
531	75.00	56.50	37.50
532	275.00	210.00	140.00
534	85.00	65.00	48.50
534A	290.00	225.00	150.00
535	72.50	56.50	37.50

CENTER LINE BLOCKS

Scott #	NH VF	NH F-VF	Unused F-VF
531	100.00	77.50	52.50
532	335.00	240.00	160.00
534	97.50	75.00	55.00
534A	325.00	260.00	170.00
535	80.00	65.00	42.50

1919 Victory Issue VF Used + 50% (B)

			NH VF	NH F-VF	Unused VF	Unused F-VF	Used F-VF
537	3¢ Violet		17.50	11.50	11.50	7.50	2.75
537a	3¢ Deep Red Violet		875.00	575.00	600.00	395.00	135.00
537c	3¢ Red Violet		85.00	57.50	55.00	37.50	10.75

1919-21 Rotary Press Printing - Various Perfs. VF Used + 75% (C)

538	1¢ Wash. Perf. 11x10	21.00	12.00	13.50	8.00	7.50
538a	1¢ Vert. Pr. Imperf. Horiz.	95.00	65.00	67.50	45.00	100.00
539	2¢ Car. Rose, Ty. II, Pf. 11x10	...	...	...	2500.00	...
540	2¢ Car. Rose,T.III, Pf.11x10	25.00	14.00	15.00	9.00	7.50
540a	2¢ Vert. Pr., Imperf. Horiz.	95.00	65.00	67.50	45.00	100.00
541	3¢ Violet, Perf. 11x10	72.50	42.50	47.50	27.50	25.00
542	1¢ Green, Perf. 10x11 (1920)	25.00	15.00	16.00	9.50	.95
543	1¢ Green, Perf. 10 (1921)	1.40	.90	.95	.60	.20
544	1¢ Perf. 11 (19x22½ mm) (1922)	...	...	...	...	2400.00
545	1¢ Pf.11 (19½x22 mm) (21)	295.00	165.00	185.00	110.00	125.00
546	2¢ Carmine Rose, Pf.11 (21)	195.00	115.00	125.00	75.00	120.00

1920 Flat Press, No Watermark, Perf. 11 VF Used + 40% (B)

547	$2 Franklin, Carm. & Blk.	395.00	270.00	250.00	175.00	35.00

1920 Pilgrim Issue VF Used + 40% (B)

548	549	550

548-50	Set of 3	85.00	61.50	61.50	42.75	12.95
548	1¢ Mayflower, Green	7.00	5.00	4.85	3.50	1.95
549	2¢ Landing, Car. Rose	10.75	7.75	7.50	5.25	1.50
550	5¢ Compact, Deep Blue	70.00	50.00	50.00	35.00	10.00

PLATE BLOCKS

Scott #	NH VF	NH F-VF	Unused F-VF	Scott #	NH VF	NH F-VF	Unused F-VF
537 (6)	180.00	115.00	75.00	542 (6)	285.00	185.00	120.00
538	165.00	100.00	67.50	543 (4)	27.00	16.50	11.00
538a	1400.00	1000.00	700.00	543 (6)	65.00	41.50	27.50
540	175.00	105.00	70.00	548 (6)	67.50	47.50	35.00
540a	1200.00	850.00	600.00	549 (6)	85.00	62.50	45.00
541	500.00	350.00	235.00	550 (6)	675.00	515.00	365.00

1922-25 Regular Issue, Flat Press, Perf. 11 VF Used + 40% (B)

551,653	553/633	556/636	562/642	566,696

567,698	570,701	572	573

1922-25 Regular Issue, Flat Press, Perf. 11 VF Used + 40% (B)

Scott's No.		VF	NH F-VF	Unused VF	Unused F-VF	Used F-VF
551	½¢ Hale, Olive Brn ('25)	.35	.25	.30	.20	.15
552	1¢ Franklin, Green ('23)	2.70	2.00	1.90	1.35	.15
552a	1¢ Booklet Pane of 6	16.00	11.00	10.50	7.50	...
553	1½¢ Harding, Yel. Brn ('25)	5.50	3.85	3.50	2.50	.20
554	2¢ Wash. Carmine ('23)	3.65	2.50	2.40	1.70	.15
554c	2¢ Booklet Pane of 6	18.75	13.50	12.50	8.75	...
555	3¢ Lincoln, Violet ('23)	33.50	24.75	22.75	16.50	1.00
556	4¢ M. Wash., Yel. Brn. ('23)	33.50	24.75	22.75	16.50	.25
557	5¢ T. Roosevelt, Dk. Blue	33.50	24.75	22.75	16.50	.18
558	6¢ Garfield, Red Orange	62.50	45.00	41.50	30.00	.75
559	7¢ McKinley, Black ('23)	15.00	11.00	10.50	7.50	.60
560	8¢ Grant, Ol.Grn. ('23)	77.50	57.50	50.00	37.50	.60
561	9¢ Jefferson, Rose ('23)	28.75	20.00	18.75	13.50	1.00
562	10¢ Monroe, Orange ('23)	35.00	25.00	23.75	17.00	.20
563	11¢ Hayes, Greenish Blue	2.70	2.00	1.90	1.35	.45
564	12¢ Cleveland, Br. Vio. ('23)	14.00	10.00	9.00	6.50	.20
565	14¢ Indian, Blue ('23)	9.50	6.50	6.00	4.25	.70
566	15¢ Liberty, Gray	45.00	32.50	29.75	21.75	.20
567	20¢ Golden Gate,C.Rose ('23)	45.00	32.50	29.75	21.75	.20
568	25¢ Niagara Falls, Yel. Grn.	37.50	26.50	25.00	17.50	.55
569	30¢ Buffalo, Ol Brown ('23)	65.00	45.00	42.50	30.00	.40
570	50¢ Amphitheater, Lilac	105.00	75.00	70.00	50.00	.20
571	$1 Lincoln, Vio. Blk. (1923)	87.50	65.00	56.50	42.50	.50
572	$2 Capitol, Blue (1923)	185.00	130.00	125.00	87.50	8.00
573	$5 Carmine & Blue (1923)	350.00	250.00	240.00	170.00	12.50

1923-25 Flat Press - Imperforate VF Used + 25% (B)

PLATE BLOCKS

Scott #	NH VF	NH F-VF	Unused F-VF	Scott #	NH VF	NH F-VF	Unused F-VF
551 (6)	8.75	6.25	4.50	563 (6)	46.50	32.50	22.50
552 (6)	37.50	26.50	18.00	564 (6)	150.00	110.00	75.00
553 (6)	45.00	32.50	22.50	565 (6)	90.00	65.00	45.00
554 (6)	31.00	22.50	16.50	566 (6)	375.00	290.00	200.00
555 (6)	260.00	180.00	120.00	567 (6)	375.00	290.00	200.00
556 (6)	260.00	180.00	120.00	568 (6)	365.00	260.00	175.00
557 (6)	280.00	200.00	135.00	569 (6)	425.00	300.00	200.00
558 (6)	625.00	450.00	300.00	571 (6)	700.00	485.00	335.00
559 (6)	100.00	75.00	50.00				
560 (6)	900.00	650.00	450.00		**ARROW BLOCKS**		
561 (6)	250.00	175.00	120.00	571	385.00	275.00	185.00
562 (6)	300.00	220.00	150.00	572	825.00	575.00	375.00

575	1¢ Franklin, Green	13.00	10.00	9.00	7.00	4.00
576	1½¢ Harding, Yel. Brn. (1925)	2.80	2.20	1.90	1.50	1.30
577	2¢ Washington, Carmine	3.50	2.60	2.40	1.80	1.30

1923 Rotary Press, Perforated 11 x 10 VF Used + 75% (C)

578	1¢ Franklin, Green	170.00	100.00	110.00	65.00	110.00
579	2¢ Washington, Carmine	150.00	87.50	97.50	57.50	100.00

1923-26 Rotary Press, Perforated 10 VF Used + 50% (B)

581-91	Set of 11	300.00	210.00	200.00	137.50	17.85
581	1¢ Franklin, Green	18.00	12.00	12.00	8.00	.80
582	1½¢ Harding, Brown (1925)	9.00	6.00	6.00	4.00	.80
583	2¢ Wash., Carmine (1924)	3.95	2.65	2.60	1.75	.30
583a	2¢ Booklet Pane of 6	140.00	100.00	95.00	65.00	...
584	3¢ Lincoln, Violet (1925)	50.00	32.50	32.50	21.50	2.25
585	4¢ M. Wash., Yel Brn (1925)	31.50	20.75	21.00	14.00	.70
586	5¢ T. Roos., Blue (1925)	31.50	20.75	21.00	14.00	.35
587	6¢ Garfield, Red Or. (1925)	8.75	6.25	8.50	5.75	.55
588	7¢ McKinley, Blk. (1926)	19.00	13.00	12.75	8.50	6.50
589	8¢ Grant, Ol. (1926)	42.50	28.00	27.50	18.50	3.85
590	9¢ Jefferson, Rose (1926)	9.50	6.75	6.50	4.50	2.25
591	10¢ Monroe, Orange (1925)	100.00	68.50	65.00	45.00	.50

1923 Rotary Press, Perforated 11 VF Used + 100% (C)

594	1¢ Franklin, Green		...	FINE	USED	3850.00
595	2¢ Washington, Carmine	500.00	275.00	325.00	175.00	250.00

PLATE BLOCKS

Scott #	NH VF	NH F-VF	Unused F-VF	Scott #	NH VF	NH F-VF	Unused F-VF
575 (6)	125.00	95.00	65.00	589	325.00	220.00	150.00
576 (6)	32.50	25.00	17.50	590	77.50	52.50	35.00
577 (6)	50.00	39.50	27.50	591	800.00	550.00	375.00
579	950.00	550.00	375.00		**ARROW BLOCKS**		
581	175.00	120.00	80.00	575	60.00	42.50	30.00
582	65.00	45.00	30.00	576	12.50	9.75	6.75
583	42.50	29.00	19.50	577	15.00	11.50	8.00
584	350.00	240.00	165.00		**CENTER LINE BLOCKS**		
585	325.00	220.00	150.00	575	70.00	50.00	35.00
586	315.00	210.00	145.00	576	19.00	15.00	11.00
587	120.00	82.50	55.00	577	22.50	17.00	12.00
588	150.00	105.00	70.00				

NOTE: VF UNUSED PLATE BLOCKS AND LINE PAIRS ARE GENERALLY AVAILABLE AT THE RESPECTIVE F-VF NH PRICE.

Scott's No.	VF	NH F-VF	Unused VF	F-VF	Used F-VF
597-99,600-06 Set of 10	26.00	18.95	18.50	13.85	1.75

Perforated 10 Vertically

597	1¢ Franklin, Green	.55	.40	.40	.30	.20
598	1½¢ Harding, Brown (1925)	1.20	.90	.95	.70	.20
599	2¢ Washington, Car. Type I	.65	.50	.45	.35	.20
599A	2¢ Carmine, Type II (1929)	250.00	150.00	160.00	100.00	9.75
599A	2¢ Average Quality		90.00	...	60.00	6.75
600	3¢ Lincoln, Violet (1924)	9.50	7.00	6.50	5.00	.20
601	4¢ M. Washington, Yel. Brn.	7.00	5.00	4.75	3.50	.35
602	5¢ T. Roos., Dk. Blue (1924)	2.80	2.15	2.00	1.50	.20
603	10¢ Monroe, Orange (1924)	5.65	4.25	4.00	3.00	.20

Perforated 10 Horizontally

604	1¢ Franklin, Green (1924)	.45	.35	.35	.25	.20
605	1½¢ Harding, Yel. Brn. (1925)	.45	.35	.35	.25	.20
606	2¢ Washington, Carmine	.45	.35	.35	.25	.20

NOTE: Type I, #599, 634 - No heavy hair lines at top center of head.
Type II, #599A, 634A - Three heavy hair lines at top center of head.

NOTE: From 1923 to date, Unused Coil Pairs are usually available at double the single stamp price.

LINE PAIRS

Scott #	NH VF	NH F-VF	Unused F-VF	Scott #	NH VF	NH F-VF	Unused F-VF
597	3.00	2.25	1.80	601	52.50	40.00	27.50
598	8.75	6.50	4.50	602	17.75	12.95	9.75
599	2.75	2.00	1.60	603	35.00	26.00	18.50
599A	1200.00	750.00	500.00	604	5.00	3.75	2.80
599,599A	1400.00	900.00	600.00	605	4.25	3.25	2.50
600	47.50	35.00	25.00	606	3.50	2.60	2.00

1923 Harding Memorial (#610 VF Used + 30%, #612 VF Used + 50%)
Imperf. VF Used + 20% (B)

610-612 614 616

610-12	Set of 3	38.50	27.50	27.50	19.50	5.65
610	2¢ Black, Flat Press, Perf. 11	.95	.75	.70	.55	.20
611	2¢ Black, Flat Press Imperf.	10.75	8.50	7.75	5.75	3.95
612	2¢ Black, Rotary, Perf. 10	28.50	19.50	20.00	14.50	1.75

1924 Huguenot - Walloon Issue VF Used + 30% (B)

614-16	Set of 3	63.50	48.50	44.50	33.50	15.95
614	1¢ "New Netherlands"	5.00	3.65	3.65	2.75	2.75
615	2¢ Fort Orange	9.00	6.85	6.65	5.00	1.85
616	5¢ Ribault Monument	52.50	39.50	36.50	27.00	11.75

617 618 619

1925 Lexington - Concord Issue VF Used + 30% (B)

617-19	Set of 3	56.50	42.50	41.00	31.00	15.75
617	1¢ Cambridge	5.15	3.75	3.65	2.75	2.25
618	2¢ "Birth of Liberty"	9.00	6.85	6.65	5.00	3.50
619	5¢ "Minute Man"	45.00	33.50	32.50	24.50	11.00

PLATE BLOCKS				PLATE BLOCKS			
Scott #	VF	NH F-VF	Unused F-VF	Scott #	VF	NH F-VF	Unused F-VF
610 (6)	29.50	22.50	16.50	618 (6)	105.00	80.00	60.00
611 (6)	135.00	110.00	80.00	619 (6)	400.00	300.00	225.00
612	425.00	290.00	200.00	**ARROW BLOCKS**			
614 (6)	52.50	38.50	28.50	611	48.50	36.50	25.00
615 (6)	95.00	70.00	52.50	**CENTER LINE BLOCKS**			
616 (6)	450.00	335.00	250.00	611	95.00	72.50	50.00
617 (6)	65.00	50.00	37.50				

NOTE: PRIOR TO 1935, TO DETERMINE VERY FINE USED PRICE, ADD VF% AT BEGINNING OF EACH SET TO THE APPROPRIATE FINE PRICE.
MINIMUM 10¢ PER STAMP

620 621 622,694 623,697

1925 Norse American VF Used + 30% (B)

Scott's No.	VF	NH F-VF	Unused VF	F-VF	Used F-VF
620-21	Set of 2	29.75	22.50	22.50	17.00	11.75
620	2¢ Sloop, Carmine & Blk.	7.50	5.50	5.35	4.00	2.75
621	5¢ Viking Ship, Blue & Black	23.75	17.50	17.50	13.50	9.50

1925-26 Designs of 1922-25, Flat Press, Perf. 11 VF Used + 40% (B)

622	13¢ Harrison, Green (1926)	22.50	16.50	17.00	12.00	.55
623	17¢ Wilson, Black	29.50	21.00	20.00	15.00	.30

627 628 629,630

1926 Commemoratives VF Used + 30% (B)

627	2¢ Sesquicentennial	4.25	3.25	3.25	2.50	.50
628	5¢ Ericsson Memorial	10.50	8.00	8.00	5.75	2.50
629	2¢ Battle of White Plains	3.35	2.50	2.40	1.75	1.40
630	2¢ White Plains, Phil. Exhib. Souvenir Sheet of 25	625.00	525.00	500.00	400.00	425.00
630v	2¢ "Dot over S" Var. Sheet	650.00	550.00	525.00	425.00	450.00

1926 Rotary Press, Imperforate VF Used + 20% (B)

631	1½¢ Harding, Brown	3.25	2.50	2.35	1.85	1.65
631v	1½¢ Vert. Pair, Horiz. Gutter	8.50	7.00	6.50	5.50	...
631h	1½¢ Horiz. Pair, Vert. Gutter	8.50	7.00	6.50	5.50	...

PLATE BLOCKS				ARROW BLOCKS			
Scott #	VF	NH F-VF	Unused F-VF	Scott #	VF	NH F-VF	Unused F-VF
620 (8)	300.00	230.00	180.00	620	32.50	23.50	18.00
621 (8)	975.00	750.00	550.00	621	130.00	100.00	75.00
622 (6)	240.00	170.00	120.00	631	16.50	12.50	9.50
623 (6)	280.00	210.00	150.00	**CENTER LINE BLOCKS**			
627 (6)	60.00	47.50	35.00	620	40.00	32.50	24.00
628 (6)	125.00	95.00	70.00	621	145.00	115.00	85.00
629 (6)	53.50	42.50	32.50	631	32.50	25.00	18.00
631	85.00	72.50	52.50				

1926-1928 Rotary. Pf. 11x10½, Same as 1922-25 VF Used +30%
(634A VF Used +75%)

632-34,635-42	Set of 11	30.00	22.50	23.50	18.00	1.60
632	1¢ Franklin, Green (1927)	.35	.25	.30	.30	.15
632a	1¢ Booklet Pane of 6	9.75	7.00	7.50	5.50	...
633	1½¢ Harding, Yel. Brn. (1927)	3.00	2.30	2.25	1.75	.20
634	2¢ Wash., Carmine, Ty. I	.35	.25	.30	.20	.15
634d	2¢ Booklet Pane of 6 (1927)	2.95	2.10	2.30	1.65	...
634A	2¢ Carmine, Type II (1928)	575.00	350.00	325.00	200.00	12.50
635	3¢ Lincoln, Violet (1927)	.70	.55	.55	.45	.18
636	4¢ M. Wash., Yel. Brn. (1927)	4.00	3.00	3.00	2.25	.18
637	5¢ T. Roos., Dk. Blue (1927)	3.50	2.50	2.70	2.00	.18
638	6¢ Garfield, Red Or. (1927)	3.50	2.50	2.70	2.00	.18
639	7¢ McKinley, Black (1927)	3.50	2.50	2.70	2.00	.18
640	8¢ Grant, Ol. Green (1927)	3.50	2.50	2.70	2.00	.18
641	9¢ Jefferson, Or. Red (1927)	3.50	2.50	2.70	2.00	.18
642	10¢ Monroe, Or. (1927)	6.50	4.75	5.00	3.75	.20

PLATE BLOCKS

Scott #	VF	NH F-VF	Unused F-VF	Scott #	VF	NH F-VF	Unused F-VF
632	3.00	2.25	1.75	637	26.50	20.00	15.00
633	120.00	90.00	65.00	638	26.50	20.00	15.00
634 (4)	2.75	2.25	1.75	639	26.50	20.00	15.00
634 EE (10)	7.50	5.75	4.50	640	26.50	20.00	15.00
635	14.50	11.00	8.00	641	26.50	20.00	15.00
636	120.00	90.00	67.50	642	42.50	31.50	25.00

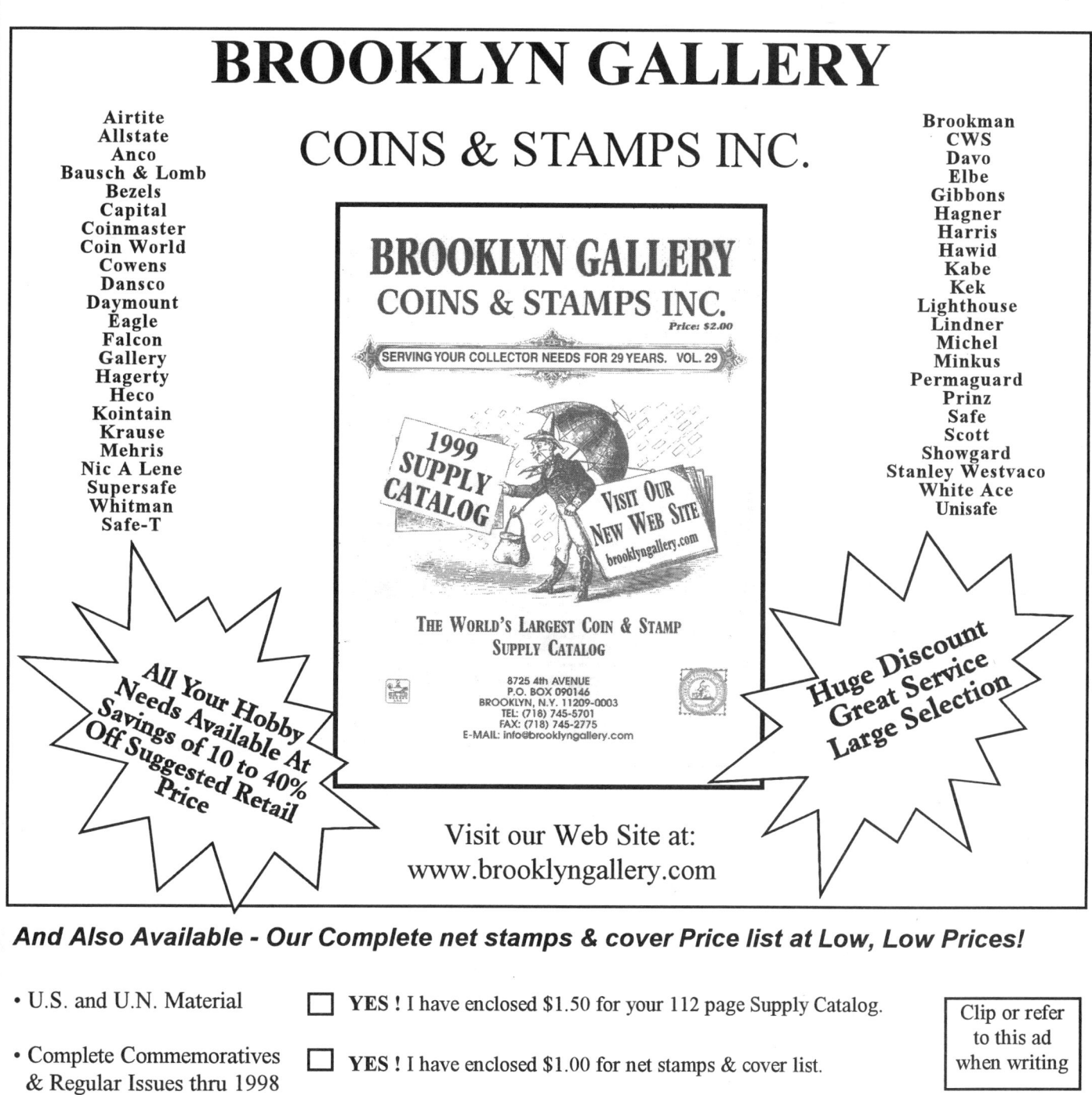

U.S. MINT SHEETS, F-VF, NH							
Scott No. (Size)	F-VF NH	Scott No. (Size)	F-VF NH	Scott No. (Size)	F-VF NH	Scott No. (Size)	F-VF NH
610 (100)	95.00	620 (100)	675.00	633 (100)	275.00	638 (100)	275.00
614 (50)	210.00	627 (50)	195.00	634 (100)	19.50	639 (100)	275.00
615 (50)	385.00	628 (50)	525.00	635 (100)	60.00	640 (100)	275.00
617 (50)	225.00	629 (100)	275.00	636 (100)	350.00	641 (100)	275.00
618 (50)	395.00	632 (100)	19.50	637 (100)	275.00	642 (100)	485.00

1927-28 Commemoratives VF Used + 30% (B) (#646-648 VF Used + 50%)

643   644   645   649

Scott's No.		NH		Unused		Used
		VF	F-VF	VF	F-VF	F-VF
643	2¢ Vermont Sesqui..........................	2.00	1.60	1.50	1.20	.80
644	2¢ Burgoyne Campaign	6.25	4.65	4.50	3.50	1.80
645	2¢ Valley Forge (1928).................	1.65	1.30	1.25	1.00	.50
646	2¢ "Molly Pitcher" ovpt (on #634) .	2.00	1.35	1.50	1.00	1.00
647	2¢ "Hawaii" ovpt (on #634)...........	9.00	6.25	6.75	4.50	4.00
648	5¢ "Hawaii" ovpt (on #637)..........	25.00	16.50	18.50	12.50	12.00
649	2¢ Aeronautics (1928).................	1.95	1.50	1.45	1.10	.75
650	5¢ Aeronautics (1928).................	8.50	6.50	6.50	5.00	2.75

651   654-656   657   663

1929 Commemorative VF Used + 30% (B)

651	2¢ George Rogers Clark...................	.90	.70	.70	.55	.50

1929 Rotary, Perf. 11x10½, Design of #551 VF Used + 30% (B)

653	½¢ Hale, Olive Brown	.35	.25	.30	.20	.15

1929 Commemoratives VF Used + 30% (B)

654	2¢ Edison, Flat, Perf. 11	1.20	.90	.90	.70	.65
655	2¢ Edison, Rtry, Perf. 11x10½	1.20	.85	.90	.65	.25
656	2¢ Edison Coil, Perf. 10 Vert	22.50	16.50	16.50	12.50	1.50
657	2¢ Sullivan Expedition	1.20	.90	.90	.70	.60

	PLATE BLOCKS				PLATE BLOCKS		
		NH	Unused			NH	Unused
Scott #	VF	F-VF	F-VF	Scott #	VF	F-VF	F-VF
643 (6)	58.50	45.00	37.50	653	2.50	1.85	1.35
644 (6)	60.00	46.50	37.50	654 (6)	42.75	33.50	25.75
645 (6)	46.50	35.00	25.00	655	60.00	45.00	32.50
646	47.50	33.50	25.00	657 (6)	38.75	30.00	23.50
647	200.00	135.00	95.00		ARROW BLOCKS		
648	400.00	270.00	200.00	651	4.15	3.15	2.50
649 (6)	20.00	16.00	12.00		COIL LINE PAIRS		
650 (6)	95.00	72.50	52.50	656	100.00	75.00	57.50
651 (6)	15.75	12.50	9.50				

KANSAS - NEBRASKA ISSUES

1929 "Kans." Overprints on Stamps #632-42 VF Used + 60% (C)

658-68	Set of 11	450.00	275.00	310.00	195.00	145.00
658	1¢ Franklin, Green	4.75	3.00	3.50	2.25	1.60
659	1½¢ Harding, Brown	6.50	4.00	4.75	3.00	2.25
660	2¢ Washington, Carmine	6.75	4.50	5.00	3.25	.90
661	3¢ Lincoln, Violet	35.00	22.50	25.00	16.00	12.00
662	4¢ M. Washington, Yel. Brn	35.00	22.50	25.00	16.00	8.00
663	5¢ T. Roosevelt, Deep Blue	25.00	16.00	18.00	11.00	8.75
664	6¢ Garfield, Red Orange	55.00	35.00	39.00	25.00	15.00
665	7¢ McKinley, Black	53.00	33.50	37.50	24.00	22.50
666	8¢ Grant, Olive Green	190.00	110.00	120.00	75.00	60.00
667	9¢ Jefferson, Light Rose	26.50	18.50	20.00	13.00	10.00
668	10¢ Monroe, Orng. Yel	41.50	26.50	28.50	18.00	10.00

NOTE: STAMP ILLUSTRATIONS INDICATE DESIGNS, PERFORATIONS AND TYPES MAY VARY

1929 "Nebr." Overprints on Stamps #632-42 VF Used + 60% (C)

Scott's No.		NH		Unused		Used
	VF	F-VF	VF	F-VF		F-VF
669-79	Set of 11 .... 560.00	350.00	395.00	250.00		130.00
669	1¢ Franklin, Green...................... 6.50	4.15	4.65	2.95		1.85
670	1½¢ Harding, Brown.................... 6.00	3.85	4.25	2.75		2.00
671	2¢ Washington, Carmine 6.00	3.85	4.25	2.75		1.25
672	3¢ Lincoln, Violet....................... 24.00	15.50	17.00	11.00		9.75
673	4¢ M. Washington, Yel. Brn........ 37.50	23.00	26.50	16.50		13.50
674	5¢ T. Roosevelt, Deep Blue......... 32.50	21.50	23.50	15.00		13.50
675	6¢ Garfield, Red Orange.............. 77.50	49.50	55.00	35.00		20.00
676	7¢ McKinley, Black 46.50	30.00	33.00	21.00		16.00
677	8¢ Grant, Olive Green 60.00	39.00	43.50	27.50		21.75
678	9¢ Jefferson, Light Rose 80.00	46.50	50.00	32.50		22.50
679	10¢ Monroe, Orng. Yel 225.00	140.00	160.00	100.00		18.50

NOTE: IN 1929, SOME 1¢-10¢ STAMPS WERE OVERPRINTED "Kans." AND "Nebr." AS A MEASURE OF PREVENTION AGAINST POST OFFICE ROBBERIES IN THOSE STATES, THEY WERE USED ABOUT ONE YEAR, THEN DISCONTINUED.
Genuine unused, o.g. K-N's have either a single horiz. gum breaker ridge or two widely spaced horiz. ridges (21 mm apart). Unused, o.g. stamps with two horiz. ridges spaced 10 mm apart have counterfeit ovpts. Unused stamps without ridges are regummed and/or have a fake ovpt.

PLATE BLOCKS							
	NH		Unused		NH		Unused
Scott #	VF	F-VF	F-VF	Scott #	VF	F-VF	F-VF
658	70.00	45.00	32.50	669	72.50	47.50	35.00
659	90.00	57.50	40.00	670	85.00	55.00	40.00
660	82.50	52.50	37.50	671	70.00	45.00	32.50
661	360.00	235.00	160.00	672	285.00	180.00	130.00
662	360.00	235.00	160.00	673	385.00	250.00	175.00
663	260.00	170.00	120.00	674	435.00	280.00	200.00
664	800.00	500.00	350.00	675	800.00	525.00	375.00
665	800.00	525.00	375.00	676	500.00	315.00	225.00
666	1400.00	900.00	650.00	677	700.00	450.00	325.00
667	335.00	210.00	150.00	678	900.00	575.00	400.00
668	550.00	350.00	250.00	679	1700.00	1100.00	800.00

1929-1930 Commemoratives VF Used + 30% (B)

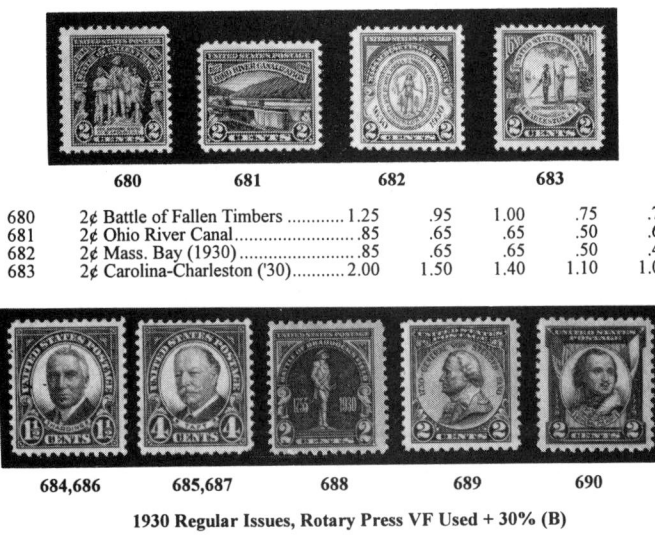

680   681   682   683

680	2¢ Battle of Fallen Timbers 1.25	.95	1.00	.75	.70
681	2¢ Ohio River Canal........................ .85	.65	.65	.50	.60
682	2¢ Mass. Bay (1930)........................ .85	.65	.65	.50	.45
683	2¢ Carolina-Charleston ('30)........... 2.00	1.50	1.40	1.10	1.00

684,686   685,687   688   689   690

1930 Regular Issues, Rotary Press VF Used + 30% (B)

684	1½¢ Harding, Brn., Pf. 11x10½........ .45	.35	.35	.25	.15
685	4¢ Taft, Brn., Pf. 11x10½............... 1.30	1.00	1.00	.80	.15
686	1½¢ Brown, Coil, Pf. 10 Vert........ 2.50	1.95	1.95	1.50	.20
687	4¢ Brown, Coil, Pf. 10 Vert......... 4.75	3.50	3.25	2.50	.55

1930-31 Commemoratives VF Used + 30% (B)

688	2¢ Braddock's Field........................ 1.60	1.20	1.25	.90	.85
689	2¢ Baron Von Steuben .... .80	.60	.60	.45	.45
690	2¢ General Pulaski (1931) .... .38	.28	.32	.22	.20

PLATE BLOCKS & LINE PAIRS							
	NH		Unused		NH		Unused
Scott #	VF	F-VF	F-VF	Scott #	VF	F-VF	F-VF
680 (6)	39.50	29.00	22.00	688 (6)	52.50	40.00	30.00
681 (6)	26.50	20.00	15.00	689 (6)	32.50	25.00	20.00
682 (6)	40.00	30.00	23.00	690 (6)	16.75	13.00	10.00
683 (6)	67.50	52.50	40.00	LINE PAIRS			
684	3.75	2.75	2.10	686	13.50	9.50	7.00
685	17.50	12.50	10.00	687	25.00	19.00	14.50

U.S. MINT SHEETS, F-VF, NH

Scott No. (Size)	F-VF NH	Scott No. (Size)	F-VF NH	Scott No. (Size)	F-VF NH	Scott No. (Size)	F-VF NH
643 (100)	215.00	649 (50)	82.50	655 (100)	135.00	683 (100)	175.00
644 (50)	260.00	650 (50)	385.00	657 (100)	130.00	684 (100)	35.00
645 (100)	165.00	651 (100)	45.00	680 (100)	140.00	685 (100)	110.00
646 (100)	150.00	653 (100)	17.50	681 (100)	95.00	688 (100)	150.00
647 (100)	675.00	654 (100)	125.00	682 (100)	120.00	689 (100)	75.00
						690 (100)	40.00

1931 Rotary Press, Pf. 11x10½ or 10½x11 VF Used + 30% (B)
Designs of #563-70, 622-23

Scott's No.		VF	NH F-VF	Unused VF	F-VF	Used F-VF
692-701	Set of ten	160.00	120.00	125.00	95.00	2.00
692	11¢ Hayes, Light Blue	4.50	3.35	3.35	2.50	.18
693	12¢ Cleveland, Brown Violet	9.00	6.50	6.50	5.00	.18
694	13¢ Harrison, Yel. Grn	3.50	2.60	2.65	2.00	.20
695	14¢ Indian, Dark Blue	5.75	4.25	4.25	3.25	.45
696	15¢ Liberty, Gray	13.00	9.50	10.00	7.50	.20
697	17¢ Wilson, Black	8.00	6.00	5.95	4.50	.25
698	20¢ Golden Gate, Car. Rose	16.00	11.75	12.00	9.00	.20
699	25¢ Niagara Falls, Blue Green	17.50	12.75	13.00	10.00	.20
700	30¢ Buffalo, Brown	26.50	20.00	21.00	16.00	.20
701	50¢ Amphitheater, Lilac	67.50	50.00	52.50	39.50	.20

PLATE BLOCKS

Scott #	NH VF	F-VF	Unused F-VF	Scott #	NH VF	F-VF	Unused F-VF
692	20.00	15.00	12.00	697	45.00	33.50	25.75
693	45.00	33.75	26.50	698	75.00	57.50	45.00
694	21.00	16.00	12.50	699	77.50	60.00	47.50
695	31.75	23.75	18.50	700	110.00	85.00	67.50
696	62.50	45.00	36.50	701	325.00	240.00	190.00

702   703   704   705

706   707   708   709   710

711   712   713   714   715

1931 Commemoratives VF Used + 30% (B)

702	2¢ Red Cross	.35	.25	.30	.20	.18
703	2¢ Battle of Yorktown	.55	.45	.45	.35	.30

1932 Washington Bicentennial VF Used + 40% (B)

704-15	Set of 12	42.50	32.75	31.95	23.95	2.25
704	½¢ Olive Brown	.35	.25	.30	.20	.15
705	1¢ Green	.35	.25	.30	.20	.15
706	1½¢ Brown	.70	.50	.55	.40	.18
707	2¢ Carmine Rose	.35	.25	.30	.20	.15
708	3¢ Deep Violet	.90	.65	.70	.50	.18
709	4¢ Light Brown	.50	.40	.40	.30	.18
710	5¢ Blue	2.65	2.00	2.10	1.60	.18
711	6¢ Red Orange	6.25	4.50	4.50	3.35	.18
712	7¢ Black	.50	.40	.40	.30	.18
713	8¢ Olive Bistre	5.00	3.75	4.00	3.00	.70
714	9¢ Pale Red	4.85	3.30	3.50	2.50	.20
715	10¢ Orange Yellow	22.00	16.00	16.50	12.50	.18

NOTE: VF USED STAMPS ARE PRICED AT A MINIMUM OF 10¢ PER STAMP MORE THAN THE F-VF PRICE.

PLATE BLOCKS

Scott #	VF	NH F-VF	Unused F-VF	Scott #	VF	NH F-VF	Unused F-VF
702	3.75	2.75	2.25	711	100.00	75.00	60.00
703 (4)	4.25	3.25	2.50	712	13.50	9.75	7.75
703 (6)	5.75	4.50	3.50	713	100.00	75.00	60.00
704-15	575.00	435.00	340.00	714	80.00	57.50	45.00
704	7.00	5.00	4.00	715	200.00	150.00	120.00
705	7.75	5.50	4.25		ARROW BLOCKS		
706	35.00	25.00	19.00	702	1.50	1.10	.85
707	3.75	2.75	2.00	703	2.95	2.25	1.75
708	27.50	20.00	16.00		CENTER LINE BLOCKS		
709	12.50	9.00	7.00	703	3.25	2.50	1.95
710	31.50	23.00	18.50				
PLATE BLOCKS							

U.S. MINT SHEETS, F-VF, NH

Scott No. (Size)	F-VF NH	Scott No. (Size)	F-VF NH	Scott No. (Size)	F-VF NH	Scott No. (Size)	F-VF NH
692 (100)	335.00	697 (100)	600.00	706 (100)	70.00	711 (100)	500.00
693 (100)	650.00	702 (100)	22.50	707 (100)	17.50	712 (100)	47.50
694 (100)	265.00	703 (50)	25.00	708 (100)	80.00	713 (100)	425.00
695 (100)	435.00	704 (100)	19.50	709 (100)	47.50	714 (100)	350.00
696 (100)	975.00	705 (100)	22.50	710 (100)	210.00	715 (100)	1650.00

716   717   718   719

720   721   722   723

1932 Commemoratives VF Used + 30% (B)

Scott's No.		VF	NH F-VF	Unused VF	F-VF	Used F-VF
716	2¢ Winter Olym., Lake Placid	.65	.50	.50	.40	.20
717	2¢ Arbor Day	.35	.25	.30	.20	.15
718	3¢ Summer Olympics	2.50	1.90	1.95	1.50	.18
719	5¢ Summer Olympics	3.50	2.75	2.80	2.15	.25

1932 Regular Issues, Rotary Press VF Used + 30% (B)

720	3¢ Washington, D. Violet	.35	.25	.30	.20	.15
720b	3¢ Booklet Pane of 6	65.00	47.50	45.00	32.50	...
721	3¢ D. Violet, Coil, Pf. 10 Vert.	3.75	2.75	2.70	2.00	.20
722	3¢ D. Violet, Coil, Pf. 10 Hor.	1.70	1.30	1.30	1.00	.50
723	6¢ Garfield, Orange, Coil, Perf. 10 Vertically	15.00	12.00	11.75	9.00	.30

724   725   726   727,752

1932 Commemoratives VF Used + 30% (B)

724	3¢ William Penn	.45	.35	.35	.25	.20
725	3¢ Daniel Webster	.55	.40	.40	.30	.30

1933 Commemoratives VF Used + 30% (B)

726	3¢ Georgia, Oglethorpe	.45	.35	.35	.25	.20
727	3¢ Peace, Newburgh	.35	.25	.30	.20	.15

PLATE BLOCKS & LINE PAIRS

Scott #	VF	NH F-VF	Unused F-VF	Scott #	VF	NH F-VF	Unused F-VF
716 (6)	20.00	15.00	11.50	726 (6)	22.50	18.00	13.50
717	12.50	9.50	7.50	726 (10)"cs"	27.50	22.50	17.50
718	28.00	21.75	16.00	727	8.25	6.50	5.00
719	47.50	36.50	28.50		LINE PAIRS		
720	2.35	1.75	1.35	721	9.75	7.50	6.00
724 (6)	18.00	14.50	10.50	722	7.00	5.25	3.95
725 (6)	32.50	25.00	20.00	723	72.50	55.00	40.00

1933 Commemoratives VF Used + 30% (B)

728,730a, 766a   729,731a, 767a   732   733,735a, 753   734

730,766

731,767

Scott's No. VF		NH VF	F-VF	Unused VF	F-VF	Used F-
728	1¢ Chicago, Ft. Dearborn 35	.25	.30	.20	.15
729	3¢ Chicago, Fed. Bldg. 35	.25	.30	.20	.15
1933 Chicago Souvenir Sheets						
730	1¢ Chicago, Imperf S/S of 25	...	...	32.50	32.50
730a	1¢ Single Stamp from sheet	...	...	.70	.60	.55
731	3¢ Chicago, Imperf. S/S of 25	...	...	30.00	27.50
731a	3¢ Single Stamp from Sheet	...	.65	.55	.50
1933 Commemoratives (continued)						
732	3¢ Natl. Recovery Act 35	.25	.30	.20	.15
733	3¢ Byrd. Antarctic Exp....................80	.65	.65	.50	.55
734	5¢ Gen. Kosciuszko 90	.70	.70	.55	.25
1934 Byrd Antarctic Souvenir Sheet						

735,768

735	3¢ Byrd, Imperf S/S of 6	...	...	16.00	15.00
735a	3¢ Single Stamp from sheet	...	2.75	2.50	2.25

NOTE: #730, 731 AND 735 WERE ISSUED WITHOUT GUM.

1934 Commemoratives VF Used + 30% (B)

736   737,738,754   739,755

Scott's No. VF		NH VF	F-VF	Unused VF	F-VF	Used F-
736	3¢ Maryland Tercentary 35	.25	.30	.20	.18
737	3¢ Mother's Day, Rotary, Perf. 11x10½................35	.25	.30	.20	.15
738	3¢ Mother's Day, Flat Press, Perf. 11................35	.25	.30	.20	.20
739	3¢ Wisconsin Tercentenary.................35	.25	.30	.20	.15

PLATE BLOCKS

Scott #	NH VF	F-VF	Unused F-VF	Scott #	NH VF	F-VF	Unused F-VF
728	3.80	2.90	2.35	734 (6)	52.50	42.50	35.00
729	5.00	4.00	3.00	736 (6)	16.00	12.50	10.00
732	2.50	2.00	1.60	737	1.85	1.50	1.25
733 (6)	21.75	17.50	14.50	738 (6)	7.50	6.00	5.00
				739 (6)	5.75	4.50	3.50

U.S. MINT SHEETS, F-VF, NH

Scott No. (Size)	F-VF NH	Scott No. (Size)	F-VF NH	Scott No. (Size)	F-VF NH	Scott No. (Size)	F-VF NH
716 (100)	65.00	724 (100)	45.00	729 (100)	22.50	737 (50)	10.00
717 (100)	29.50	725 (100)	65.00	732 (100)	20.00	738 (50)	18.00
718 (100)	210.00	726 (100)	50.00	733 (50)	50.00	739 (50)	18.00
719 (100)	295.00	727 (100)	22.50	734 (100)	100.00		
720 (100)	25.00	728 (100)	18.00	736 (100)	32.50		

1934 National Parks Issue - Perf. 11 VF Used + 30% (B)

740,751,756   744,760   747,763   749,765

741,757   742,750,758   743,759

745,761   746,762   748,764

		NH VF	F-VF	Unused VF	F-VF	Used F-
740-49	Set of 10......................14.50	11.95	12.50	9.50	6.25
740	1¢ Yosemite, Green..........................35	.25	.30	.20	.15
741	2¢ Grand Canyon, Red 35	.25	.30	.20	.15
742	3¢ Mt. Rainier, Violet.......................35	.25	.30	.20	.15
743	4¢ Mesa Verde, Brown......................65	.50	.50	.40	.45
744	5¢ Yellowstone, Blue 1.35	1.10	1.10	.90	.70
745	6¢ Crater Lake, Dk. Blue.................1.95	1.50	1.60	1.25	.90
746	7¢ Acadia, Black 1.15	.90	.90	.70	.70
747	8¢ Zion, Sage Green.......................2.85	2.25	2.25	1.80	1.50
748	9¢ Glacier, Red Orange...................2.75	2.15	2.15	1.75	.65
749	10¢ Great Smoky, Gray Blk 4.95	3.95	3.95	3.25	1.10

NOTE: PRICES THROUGHOUT THIS LIST ARE SUBJECT TO CHANGE WITHOUT NOTICE IF MARKET CONDITIONS REQUIRE. MINIMUM MAIL ORDER MUST TOTAL AT LEAST $20.00.

NATIONAL PARKS PLATE BLOCKS

Scott #	NH VF	NH F-VF	Unused F-VF	Scott #	NH VF	NH F-VF	Unused F-VF
740-49	170.00	130.00	110.00	745 (6)	28.75	22.50	18.00
740 (6)	2.10	1.65	1.35	746 (6)	18.00	14.50	11.50
741 (6)	2.40	1.95	1.50	747 (6)	28.75	22.50	18.00
742 (6)	3.00	2.50	2.00	748 (6)	28.75	22.50	18.00
743 (6)	13.00	10.00	8.00	749 (6)	45.00	35.00	27.50
744 (6)	14.50	11.00	8.50				

U.S. MINT SHEETS, F-VF, NH

Scott No. (Size)	F-VF NH	Scott No. (Size)	F-VF NH	Scott No. (Size)	F-VF NH	Scott No. (Size)	F-VF NH
740-49	650.00	742 (50)	13.50	745 (50)	100.00	748 (50)	115.00
740 (50)	9.75	743 (50)	37.50	746 (50)	55.00	749 (50)	210.00
741 (50)	11.00	744 (50)	57.50	747 (50)	120.00		

1934 National Parks Souvenir Sheets

750,770

751,769

Scott's No.		VF	NH VF	NH F-VF	Unused VF	Unused F-VF	Used F-
750	3¢ Parks, Imperf. Sheet of 6		42.50	...	35.00	32.50
750a	3¢ Single Stamp from Sheet...........	5.25	4.75	4.50	4.00	3.75
751	1¢ Parks, Imperf. Sheet of 6		15.00	...	12.50	12.00
751a	1¢ Single Stamp from Sheet...........	2.25	1.90	1.80	1.60	1.50

Horizontal Pairs Vertical Gutters   **Vertical Pair Horizontal Line**

Cross Gutter Block   **Arrow Block**

1935 Farley Special Printing Issue

These stamps were issued imperforate (except #752 & 753) and without gum. For average quality on #752 and 753, deduct 20%. Horiz. and Vert. Gutter or Line Blocks are available at double the pair price.

NOTE: #752, 766A-70A HAVE GUTTERS INSTEAD OF LINES.

Scott's No.		F-VF Plate Blocks	Hz. Pair Vert.Line	Vert. Pr. Hz.Line	Singles Unused	Singles Used
752-71	Set of 20.......................... (15)	380.00	125.00	82.50	27.50	26.00
752	3¢ Newburgh, Pf.10½x11	16.50	7.00	3.50	.20	.18
753	3¢ Byrd, Perf. 11 ....(6)	17.50	39.50	1.95	.50	.50
754	3¢ Mother's Day, Imperf....(6)	17.50	1.85	2.10	.55	.55
755	3¢ Wisconsin, Imperf.........(6)	17.50	1.85	2.10	.55	.55

National Parks, Imperforate

756-65	Set of 10...................... (6)	265.00	39.00	37.50	13.95	13.95
756	1¢ Yosemite ....(6)	5.95	.50	.45	.20	.20
757	2¢ Grand Canyon ....(6)	6.50	.50	.60	.20	.25
758	3¢ Mt. Rainier ....(6)	15.00	1.25	1.30	.50	.50
759	4¢ Mesa Verde ....(6)	21.50	2.50	2.50	1.10	1.10
760	5¢ Yellowstone................(6)	25.00	4.75	4.25	1.75	1.75
761	6¢ Crater Lake.................(6)	37.50	5.50	6.00	2.25	2.10
762	7¢ Acadia ....(6)	36.50	4.25	5.00	1.80	1.75
763	8¢ Zion ....(6)	42.50	5.75	5.00	2.00	1.80
764	9¢ Glacier ....(6)	45.00	5.00	5.25	2.00	1.85
765	10¢ Great Smoky...............(6)	50.00	12.00	10.00	3.85	3.75

Singles And Pairs From Souvenir Sheets, Imperforate

766a-70a	Set of 5	...	38.75	34.75	10.75	8.95
766a	1¢ Chicago	...	7.50	6.00	1.10	.70
767a	3¢ Chicago.	...	9.00	6.50	1.10	.70
768a	3¢ Byrd	...	8.50	7.50	3.00	2.75
769a	1¢ Park	...	4.75	4.25	1.85	1.80
770a	3¢ Park	...	11.00	12.50	4.25	3.75

Airmail Special Delivery, Imperforate (Design of CE1)

771	16¢ Dark Blue ....(6)	65.00	6.00	7.75	2.50	2.40

FARLEY SPECIAL PRINTING POSITION BLOCKS
All stamps are F-VF and without gum as issued

Scott's No.	Center Line Block	T or B Arrow Block	L or R Arrow Block	Scott's No.	Center Line Block	T or B Arrow Block	L or R Arrow Block
752-71	440.00	...	...	762	17.00	9.50	11.50
752	46.50	15.00	7.50	763	22.50	13.00	11.50
753	90.00	85.00	4.25	764	18.00	11.50	12.00
754	9.00	4.00	4.50	765	32.50	26.00	22.00
755	9.00	4.00	4.50	766a-70a	85.00	...	...
756-65	150.00	88.50	100.00	766a	17.50	...	...
756	3.75	1.15	1.00	767a	20.00	...	...
757	5.00	1.25	1.40	768a	18.50	...	...
758	6.75	2.90	3.25	769a	10.75	...	...
759	11.00	5.50	5.75	770a	26.50	...	...
760	18.00	10.50	9.50	771	70.00	13.00	16.75
761	20.00	12.50	13.50				

FARLEY UNCUT SHEETS, F-VF, NH

Scott No. (Size)	F-VF NH	Scott No. (Size)	F-VF NH	Scott No. (Size)	F-VF NH
752 (400)	375.00	759 (200)	265.00	767 (9 ss)	400.00
753 (200)	575.00	760 (200)	450.00	768 (25ss)	450.00
754 (200)	175.00	761 (200)	550.00	769 (20ss)	225.00
755 (200)	175.00	762 (200)	450.00	770 (20ss)	650.00
756-65	3500.00	763 (200)	525.00	771 (200)	725.00
756 (200)	60.00	764 (200)	535.00		
757 (200)	70.00	765 (200)	850.00		
758 (200)	150.00	766 (9 ss)	375.00		

VERY FINE COPIES OF #752 TO THE PRESENT ARE
AVAILABLE FOR THE FOLLOWING PREMIUMS:
ADD 10¢ TO ANY ITEM PRICED UNDER 50¢. ADD 20% TO ANY ITEM PRICED AT 50¢ &
UP. UNLESS PRICED AS VERY FINE, SETS ARE NOT AVAILABLE VERY FINE AND
STAMPS SHOULD BE LISTED INDIVIDUALLY WITH APPROPRIATE PREMIUM.

772   773   775

774   784   777

778

776   782   783

1935 Commemoratives

Scott's No.		Mint Sheet	Plate Block	F-VF NH	F-VF Used
772-75	Set of 4	...	...	.65	.55
772	3¢ Connecticut	9.95	1.90	.20	.15
773	3¢ California-Pacific	9.00	1.40	.20	.15
774	3¢ Boulder Dam	9.00 (6)	1.95	.20	.15
775	3¢ Michigan Centenary	9.00	1.40	.20	.15

1936 Commemoratives

776-78,782-84	Set of 6	...	...	3.35	2.85
776	3¢ Texas Centennial	8.75	1.50	.20	.15
777	3¢ Rhode Island............................	9.00	1.40	.20	.15
778	3¢ TIPEX Souv. Sht. of 4	...	...	2.65	2.25
778a	3¢ Conn., Imperforate	...	...	.65	.50
778b	3¢ Calif., Imperforate	...	...	.65	.50
778c	3¢ Mich., Imperforate	...	...	.65	.50
778d	3¢ Texas, Imperforate	...	...	.65	.50
782	3¢ Arkansas Cent	8.75	1.40	.20	.15
783	3¢ Oregon Territory	8.75	1.40	.20	.15
784	3¢ Susan B. Anthony ....(100)	17.50	1.00	.20	.15

1936-1937 Army - Navy Series

785   786   787

788   789

1936-1937 Army - Navy Series

790   791   792

793   794

Scott's No.		Mint Sheet	Plate Block	F-VF NH	F-VF Used
785-94	Set of 10.........................	190.00	47.50	3.65	1.60
785-94	Very Fine Set of 10	...	56.50	4.75	2.40
785	1¢ Army-Wash. & Greene	5.75	1.10	.20	.15
786	2¢ Army-Jackson & Scott (1937)......	6.50	1.10	.20	.15
787	3¢ Army-Sherman,Grant,Sheridan (37)	15.00	1.60	.30	.15
788	4¢ Army-Lee & Jackson (1937)........	35.00	11.00	.50	.25
789	5¢ Army-West Point (1937)..............	45.00	11.00	.80	.30
790	1¢ Navy-Jones & Barry	5.75	1.10	.25	.15
791	2¢ Navy-Decatur & MacDonough (37)	7.00	1.10	.20	.15
792	3¢ Navy-Farragut & Porter (1937)	14.50	1.50	.25	.15
793	4¢ Navy-Sampson, Dewey, Schley (37)	27.50	11.50	.40	.25
794	5¢ Navy-U.S. Naval Academy (37)	45.00	12.00	.80	.30

1937 Commemoratives

795   796   798   799

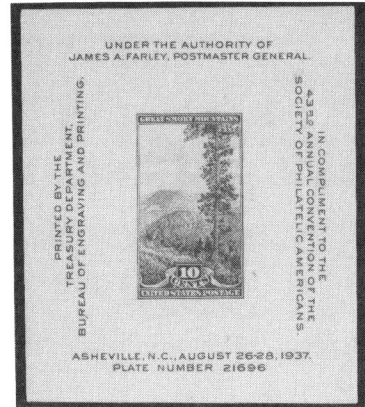

797

800   801   802

795-802	Set of 8.........................	...	...	2.00	1.50
795	3¢ Ordinance of 1787	8.00	1.20	.20	.15
796	5¢ Virginia Dare ....(48)	17.50 (6)	8.25	.25	.20
797	10¢ SPA Souvenir Sheet...................	...	...	.75	.65
798	3¢ Constitution Signing....................	9.75	1.50	.20	.15
799-802	Territorials Set of 4	33.75	5.75	.75	.50
799	3¢ Hawaii Territory	8.75	1.50	.20	.15
800	3¢ Alaska Territory	8.75	1.50	.20	.15
801	3¢ Puerto Rico Territory	8.75	1.50	.20	.15
802	3¢ Virgin Is. Territory	8.75	1.50	.20	.15

NOTE: FROM 1935 TO DATE, WITH FEW LISTED EXCEPTIONS, UNUSED PRICES ARE FOR NEVER HINGED STAMPS. HINGED STAMPS, WHEN AVAILABLE, ARE PRICED AT APPROXIMATELY 15% BELOW THE NEVER HINGED PRICE.

1938 Presidential Series

803

804,839,848   805,840,849   806,841,850   807,842,851

808,843   809,844   810,845   811,846   812

813   814   815,847   816   817

818   819   820   821   822

823   824   825   826   827

828   829   830   831

832   833   834

Scott's No.		Mint Sheet	Plate Block	F-VF NH	F-VF Used
803-34	Set of 32	...	795.00	175.00	12.50
803-34	Very Fine Set of 32	...	960.00	210.00	17.50
803-31	Set of 29 (½¢-50¢)	...	165.00	35.00	5.25
803-31	Very Fine Set of 29	...	210.00	42.00	7.75
803	½¢ Franklin ....(100)	5.00	.45	.20	.15
804	1¢ Washington ....(100)	7.00	.45	.20	.15
804b	1¢ Booklet Pane of 6, 2½ mm (1942)	...	...	2.00	...
804bv	Same, 3 mm Gutter (1939)	...	...	6.50	...
805	1½¢ Martha Washington ....(100)	7.00	.45	.20	.15
806	2¢ John Adams ....(100)	11.50	.45	.20	.15
806	2¢ Electric Eye Plate	...	(10) 7.50	...	...
806b	2¢ Booklet Pane of 6, 2½ mm (1942)	...	5.75	...	...
806bv	Same, 3 mm Gutter (1939)	...	...	8.95	...
807	3¢ Jefferson ....(100)	12.00	.45	.20	.15
807	3¢ Electric Eye Plate	...	(10) 25.00	...	...
807a	3¢ Booklet Pane of 6, 2½ mm (1942)	...	8.25	...	...
807av	Same, 3 mm Gutter (1939)	...	...	14.95	...
808	4¢ Madison ....(100)	110.00	4.50	1.00	.15
809	4½¢ White House ....(100)	25.00	1.30	.22	.15
810	5¢ Monroe ....(100)	28.00	1.20	.25	.15
811	6¢ John Quincy Adams ....(100)	35.00	1.40	.30	.15
812	7¢ Jackson ....(100)	40.00	1.65	.35	.15
813	8¢ Van Buren ....(100)	45.00	2.00	.40	.15

Scott's No.		Mint Sheet	Plate Block	F-VF NH	F-VF Used
814	9¢ William H. Harrison ....(100)	55.00	2.10	.45	.15
815	10¢ Tyler ....(100)	50.00	1.75	.40	.15
816	11¢ Polk ....(100)	62.50	3.75	.65	.15
817	12¢ Taylor ....(100)	120.00	6.00	1.25	.18
818	13¢ Fillmore ....(100)	180.00	8.50	1.85	.18
819	14¢ Pierce ....(100)	105.00	5.75	1.10	.18
820	15¢ Buchanan ....(100)	62.50	2.25	.50	.15
821	16¢ Lincoln ....(100)	110.00	6.00	1.20	.55
822	17¢ Andrew Johnson ....(100)	115.00	6.00	1.20	.18
823	18¢ Grant ....(100)	210.00	9.50	2.10	.22
824	19¢ Hayes ....(100)	160.00	7.95	1.70	.60
825	20¢ Garfield ....(100)	100.00	4.50	.95	.15
826	21¢ Arthur ....(100)	210.00	9.50	2.10	.20
827	22¢ Cleveland ....(100)	150.00	12.50	1.50	.75
828	24¢ Benjamin Harrison ....(100)	425.00	18.50	4.25	.35
829	25¢ McKinley ....(100)	95.00	4.25	.95	.15
830	30¢ Theodore Roosevelt ....(100)	550.00	24.00	5.50	.18
831	50¢ Taft	...	35.00	8.00	.18
832	$1 Wilson, Purple. & Black	...	45.00	10.00	.20
832b	$1 Wtmk. "USIR" (1951)	...	1750.00	300.00	65.00
832c	$1 Dry Printing,Red Vlt/Blk(1954)	...	40.00	9.00	.20
833	$2 Harding	...	125.00	25.00	3.75
834	$5 Coolidge	...	500.00	115.00	3.50

	ARROW BLOCKS				CENTER LINE BLOCKS		
Scott #	NH VF	NH F-VF	Unused F-VF	Scott #	NH VF	NH F-VF	Unused F-VF
832	52.50	45.00	...	832	57.50	50.00	...
833	140.00	115.00	...	833	150.00	120.00	...
834	600.00	500.00	...	834	685.00	575.00	...

1938 Commemoratives

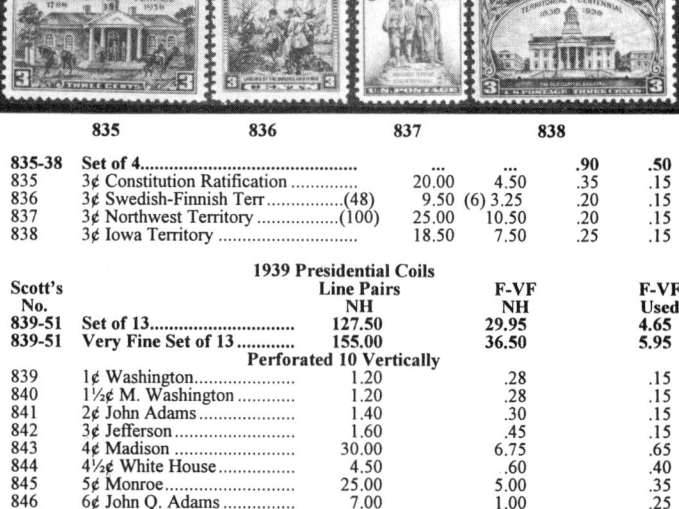

835   836   837   838

Scott's No.		Mint Sheet	Plate Block	F-VF NH	F-VF Used
835-38	Set of 4	...	...	.90	.50
835	3¢ Constitution Ratification	20.00	4.50	.35	.15
836	3¢ Swedish-Finnish Terr ....(48)	9.50	(6) 3.25	.20	.15
837	3¢ Northwest Territory ....(100)	25.00	10.50	.20	.15
838	3¢ Iowa Territory	18.50	7.50	.25	.15

1939 Presidential Coils

Scott's No.		Line Pairs NH	F-VF NH	F-VF Used
839-51	Set of 13	127.50	29.95	4.65
839-51	Very Fine Set of 13	155.00	36.50	5.95

Perforated 10 Vertically

839	1¢ Washington....................	1.20	.28	.15
840	1½¢ M. Washington	1.20	.28	.15
841	2¢ John Adams...................	1.40	.30	.15
842	3¢ Jefferson	1.60	.45	.15
843	4¢ Madison	30.00	6.75	.65
844	4½¢ White House	4.50	.60	.40
845	5¢ Monroe........................	25.00	5.00	.35
846	6¢ John Q. Adams...............	7.00	1.00	.25
847	10¢ Tyler..........................	46.50	11.00	.70

Perforated 10 Horizontally

848	1¢ Washington....................	2.10	.70	.20
849	1½¢ M. Washington	4.00	1.10	.50
850	2¢ John Adams...................	6.00	2.40	.70
851	3¢ Jefferson	5.50	2.10	.70

1939 Commemoratives

852   853   854   857

855   856   858

1939 Commemoratives (Continued)

Scott's No.		Mint Sheet	Plate Block	F-VF NH	F-VF Used
852-58	Set of 7..............................	...	...	3.95	.95
852	3¢ Golden Gate Expo	10.00	1.50	.20	.15
853	3¢ N.Y. World's Fair	10.50	2.10	.20	.15
854	3¢ Washington Inaugural	42.50	(6) 5.50	.85	.18
855	3¢ Baseball Centennial	110.00	11.00	2.25	.20
856	3¢ Panama Canal....................	19.50	(6) 4.00	.35	.18
857	3¢ Printing	9.00	1.40	.20	.15
858	3¢ 4 States to Statehood	9.00	1.40	.20	.15

1940 Famous Americans Series

863   868   873   878

883   888   893

859-93	Set of 35..............................	2375.00	385.00	29.75	16.95
859-93	Very Fine Set of 35	...	460.00	36.50	20.95
859/91	1¢,2¢,3¢ Values (21)	...	29.75	2.95	2.50
	Authors				
859	1¢ Washington Irving ....(70)	8.75	1.25	.20	.15
860	2¢ James F. Cooper ....(70)	10.00	1.25	.20	.15
861	3¢ Ralph W. Emerson..............(70)	10.50	1.40	.20	.15
862	5¢ Louisa M. Alcott................(70)	35.00	10.75	.35	.30
863	10¢ Samuel L. Clemens..........(70)	175.00	41.50	2.10	1.75
	Poets				
864	1¢ Henry W. Longfellow ....(70)	8.75	1.80	.20	.15
865	2¢ John G. Whittier ....(70)	10.75	1.85	.20	.15
866	3¢ James R. Lowell ....(70)	14.50	2.65	.20	.15
867	5¢ Walt Whitman ....(70)	37.50	12.00	.40	.25
868	10¢ James W. Riley.................(70)	185.00	49.50	2.10	1.90
	Educators				
869	1¢ Horace Mann.....................(70)	15.00	2.25	.20	.15
870	2¢ Mark Hopkins.....................(70)	8.75	1.40	.20	.15
871	3¢ Charles W. Eliot.................(70)	16.50	2.50	.22	.15
872	5¢ Frances E. Willard ....(70)	40.00	12.00	.40	.30
873	10¢ Booker T. Washington............(70)	150.00	39.50	2.00	1.65
	Scientists				
874	1¢ John James Audubon ....(70)	7.75	1.20	.20	.15
875	2¢ Dr. Crawford W. Long ....(70)	9.50	1.10	.20	.15
876	3¢ Luther Burbank ....(70)	10.50	1.30	.20	.15
877	5¢ Dr. Walter Reed ....(70)	27.50	7.75	.35	.20
878	10¢ Jane Addams ....(70)	115.00	27.50	1.65	1.50
	Composers				
879	1¢ Stephen C. Foster ....(70)	6.50	1.10	.20	.15
880	2¢ John Philip Sousa...............(70)	11.00	1.20	.20	.15
881	3¢ Victor Herbert ....(70)	10.75	1.40	.20	.15
882	5¢ Edward A. MacDowell ....(70)	46.50	12.50	.55	.30
883	10¢ Ethelbert Nevin ....(70)	295.00	47.50	4.25	2.00
	Artists				
884	1¢ Gilbert C. Stuart ....(70)	6.00	1.10	.20	.15
885	2¢ James A. Whistler...............(70)	7.00	1.00	.20	.15
886	3¢ Augustus Saint-Gaudens............(70)	9.50	1.10	.20	.15
887	5¢ Daniel Chester French ....(70)	45.00	10.75	.60	.30
888	10¢ Frederic Remington............(70)	165.00	35.00	1.95	1.65
	Inventors				
889	1¢ Eli Whitney ....(70)	11.00	2.25	.20	.15
890	2¢ Samuel F.B. Morse ....(70)	9.00	1.15	.20	.15
891	3¢ Cyrus H. McCormick ....(70)	17.75	2.00	.25	.15
892	5¢ Elias Howe ....(70)	105.00	16.50	1.25	.40
893	10¢ Alexander Graham Bell..........(70)	900.00	85.00	13.00	3.25

1940 Commemoratives

894   895   896   897

1940 Commemoratives (cont.)

898   899   900   901   902

Scott's No.		Mint Sheet	Plate Block	F-VF NH	F-VF Used
894-902	Set of 9	...	...	1.75	1.30
894	3¢ Pony Express	17.50	3.25	.30	.18
895	3¢ Pan American Union	16.00	3.25	.25	.18
896	3¢ Idaho Statehood	12.00	2.15	.20	.15
897	3¢ Wyoming Statehood	11.50	1.95	.20	.15
898	3¢ Coronado Expedition	10.75	1.75	.20	.15
899	1¢ Defense, Liberty ....(100)	8.75	.55	.20	.15
900	2¢ Defense, Anti-Aircraft ...(100)	8.75	.55	.20	.15
901	3¢ Defense, Torch.............(100)	15.00	.75	.20	.15
902	3¢ Thirteenth Amendment	17.00	3.85	.30	.20

1941-1943 Commemoratives

903   904   905

906   907   908

903-08	Set of 6............................	...	...	2.15	.90
903	3¢ Vermont Statehood	13.75	2.10	.20	.15
904	3¢ Kentucky (1942)	10.00	1.40	.20	.15
905	3¢ Win the War (1942) ....(100)	17.50	.60	.20	.15
906	5¢ China (1942)....................	75.00	17.50	1.35	.28
907	2¢ United Nations (1943).........(100)	6.75	.50	.20	.15
908	1¢ Four Freedoms (1943)..........(100)	6.75	.55	.20	.15

1943-44 Overrun Nations (Flags)

909   910   911

912   913   914

909-21	Set of 13	165.00	62.50	2.85	2.40
909-21	Very Fine Set of 13	...	72.50	3.75	3.25
909	5¢ Poland............................	13.00	7.25	.20	.18
910	5¢ Czechoslovakia..................	12.50	3.50	.20	.18
911	5¢ Norway...........................	8.00	1.60	.20	.15
912	5¢ Luxembourg......................	8.00	1.60	.20	.15
913	5¢ Netherlands......................	8.00	1.60	.20	.15
914	5¢ Belgium	8.00	1.60	.20	.15
915	5¢ France	8.00	1.60	.20	.15
916	5¢ Greece	27.50	15.00	.45	.35
917	5¢ Yugoslavia	22.50	7.50	.30	.22
918	5¢ Albania	22.50	7.50	.25	.22
919	5¢ Austria	19.75	5.00	.25	.22
920	5¢ Denmark	16.50	6.25	.25	.22
921	5¢ Korea (1944)	13.00	5.75	.20	.22
921v	5¢ "KORPA" Variety (1 per sheet) ..	45.00	...	25.00	...

(On #909-21, the country name rather than a plate number appears in the margin.)

1944 Commemoratives

922 923 924

925 926

Scott's No.		Mint Sheet	Plate Block	F-VF NH	F-VF Used
922-26	Set of 5	...	...	.85	.60
922	3¢ Transcontinental Railroad...........	13.50	1.65	.25	.15
923	3¢ Steamship "Savannah"	8.00	1.70	.20	.15
924	3¢ Telegraph	7.00	1.00	.20	.15
925	3¢ Corregidor, Philippines.............	8.50	1.10	.20	.15
926	3¢ Motion Pictures	9.50	1.10	.20	.15

1945 Commemoratives

927 928 929

930 931 932

933 934 935

936 937 938

927-38	Set of 12	...	...	1.60	1.25
927	3¢ Florida Statehood	6.50	.65	.20	.15
928	5¢ United Nations Conference..........	8.00	.65	.20	.15
929	3¢ Iwo Jima (Marines)	9.00	.75	.20	.15
930-33	Set of 4.................................	21.00	1.95	.70	.50
930	1¢ Roosevelt, Hyde Park...............	2.50	.40	.20	.15
931	2¢ Roosevelt, Warm Springs..........	4.50	.40	.20	.15
932	3¢ Roosevelt, White House	5.75	.50	.20	.15
933	5¢ Roosevelt, Map (1946)...............	9.00	.80	.20	.15
934	3¢ Army	6.50	.60	.20	.15
935	3¢ Navy	6.50	.60	.20	.15
936	3¢ Coast Guard	6.00	.55	.20	.15
937	3¢ Alfred E. Smith......................(100)	11.00	.50	.20	.15
938	3¢ Texas Statehood	5.50	.50	.20	.15

1946 Commemoratives

939 940 941

942 943 944

Scott's No.		Mint Sheet	Plate Block	F-VF NH	F-VF Used
939-44	Set of 6	...	...	.75	.65
939	3¢ Merchant Marine........................	5.85	.50	.20	.15
940	3¢ Honorable Discharge..............(100)	11.00	.50	.20	.15
941	3¢ Tennessee Statehood	5.50	.50	.20	.15
942	3¢ Iowa Centennial	5.50	.50	.20	.15
943	3¢ Smithsonian Institution	5.50	.50	.20	.15
944	3¢ Santa Fe, Kearny Expedition.	5.50	.50	.20	.15

1947 Commemoratives

945 946 947

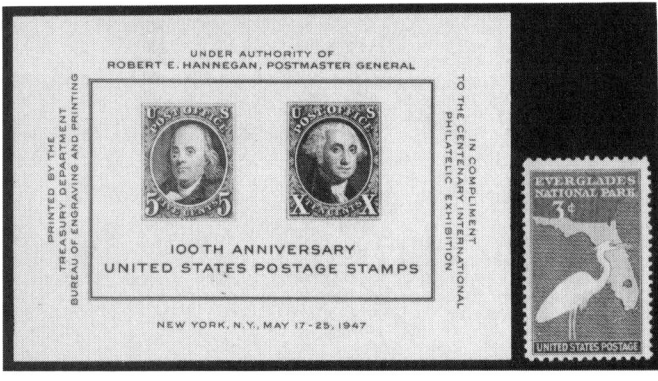 

948 952

949 950 951

945-52	Set of 8	...	...	1.75	1.35
945	3¢ Thomas A. Edison...................(70)	7.50	.50	.20	.15
946	3¢ Joseph Pulitzer	5.50	.50	.20	.15
947	3¢ Postage Centenary....................	5.50	.50	.20	.15
948	5¢ & 10¢ CIPEX Souv. Sheet	...	...	.90	.80
948a	5¢ Franklin, Blue	...	...	.40	.30
948b	10¢ Wash., Brown Orange	...	...	.50	.40
949	3¢ Doctors	6.25	.70	.20	.15
950	3¢ Utah Settlement Centennial	5.75	.60	.20	.15
951	3¢ Frigate Constitution	5.50	.50	.20	.15
952	3¢ Everglades Park	5.50	.50	.20	.15

NOTE: FROM 1935 TO DATE, WITH FEW LISTED EXCEPTIONS, UNUSED PRICES ARE FOR NEVER HINGED STAMPS. HINGED STAMPS, WHEN AVAILABLE, ARE PRICED AT APPROXIMATELY 15% BELOW THE NEVER HINGED PRICE.

953   954   955

956   957   958

959   960   961

962   963   964

965   966   967   969

968   970   971

972   973   974

975   976   977

978   979   980

Scott's No.		Mint Sheet	Plate Block	F-VF NH	F-VF Used
953-80	Set of 28............................	...	...	3.25	2.75
953	3¢ George W. Carver.................. (70)	7.50	.50	.20	.15
954	3¢ California Gold Rush	5.50	.50	.20	.15
955	3¢ Mississippi Territory	5.50	.50	.20	.15
956	3¢ Four Chaplains	5.50	.50	.20	.15
957	3¢ Wisconsin Centennial..................	5.50	.50	.20	.15
958	5¢ Swedish Pioneers	7.50	.65	.20	.15
959	3¢ Progress of Women	5.50	.50	.20	.15
960	3¢ William A. White .... (70)	7.50	.55	.20	.15
961	3¢ U.S. - Canada Friendship	5.50	.50	.20	.15
962	3¢ Francis Scott Key.......................	5.50	.50	.20	.15
963	3¢ American Youth	5.50	.50	.20	.15
964	3¢ Oregon Territory	5.50	.50	.20	.15
965	3¢ Harlan F. Stone .... (70)	7.50	.75	.20	.15
966	3¢ Palomar Observatory .... (70)	7.50	1.20	.20	.15
967	3¢ Clara Barton, Red Cross	5.50	.55	.20	.15
968	3¢ Poultry Industry	5.50	.55	.20	.15
969	3¢ Gold Star Mothers	5.50	.55	.20	.15
970	3¢ Fort Kearny, Nebraska	5.50	.55	.20	.15
971	3¢ Volunteer Firemen	5.50	.55	.20	.15
972	3¢ Indian Centennial	5.50	.55	.20	.15
973	3¢ Rough Riders	5.50	.55	.20	.15
974	3¢ Juliette Low, Girl Scouts.............	5.50	.55	.20	.15
975	3¢ Will Rogers, Humorist .... (70)	7.50	.55	.20	.15
976	3¢ Fort Bliss, Texas .... (70)	8.50	1.30	.20	.15
977	3¢ Moina Michael, Educator.............	5.50	.50	.20	.15
978	3¢ Gettysburg Address.....................	8.00	.70	.20	.15
979	3¢ Turners Society	5.50	.50	.20	.15
980	3¢ Joel Chandler Harris .... (70)	7.50	.60	.20	.15

1949 Commemoratives

981   982   983

984   985   986

981-86	Set of 6.................................	...	...	.75	.60
981	3¢ Minnesota Territory	5.50	.50	.20	.15
982	3¢ Washington & Lee University	5.50	.50	.20	.15
983	3¢ Puerto Rico Election	5.50	.50	.20	.15
984	3¢ Annapolis Tercentenary	5.50	.50	.20	.15
985	3¢ Grand Army of the Republic	5.50	.50	.20	.15
986	3¢ Edgar Allan Poe, Writer .... (70)	7.50	.60	.20	.15

NOTE: WE HAVE ESTABLISHED A MINIMUM PRICE OF .20 FOR UNUSED STAMPS AND .15 PER USED STAMP. THIS INCLUDES THE VALUE OF THE STAMP PLUS THE COST INVOLVED IN PROCESSING. YOU CAN USUALLY SAVE SUBSTANTIALLY WHEN PURCHASING COMPLETE SETS.

NOTE: PRICES THROUGHOUT THIS LIST ARE SUBJECT TO CHANGE WITHOUT NOTICE IF MARKET CONDITIONS REQUIRE. MINIMUM MAIL ORDER MUST TOTAL AT LEAST $20.00.

1950 Commemoratives

987   988   990

991   989   992

993   994   995

996   997

Scott's No.		Mint Sheet	Plate Block	F-VF NH	F-VF Used
987-97	**Set of 11**	...	...	1.50	1.15
987	3¢ Bankers Association....................	5.50	.50	.20	.15
988	3¢ Samuel Gompers, Labor...........(70)	7.25	.50	.20	.15
989-92	National Capitol, Set of 4	27.50	2.40	.60	.45
989	3¢ Freedom Statue, Capitol	6.00	.55	.20	.15
990	3¢ Executive Mansion.....................	7.50	.65	.20	.15
991	3¢ Supreme Court	6.50	.60	.20	.15
992	3¢ U.S. Capitol	9.00	.65	.20	.15
993	3¢ Railroad Engineers	6.50	.60	.20	.15
994	3¢ Kansas City Centenary	5.50	.50	.20	.15
995	3¢ Boy Scouts	6.00	.60	.20	.15
996	3¢ Indiana Territory	5.50	.50	.20	.15
997	3¢ California Statehood....................	5.75	.50	.20	.15

1951 Commemoratives

998   999   1000

1001   1002   1003

Scott's No.		Mint Sheet	Plate Block	F-VF NH	F-VF Used
998-1003	**Set of 6**	...	...	.70	.55
998	3¢ Confederate Veterans	6.75	.60	.20	.15
999	3¢ Nevada Settlement Centennial..5.50	.50	.20	.15	
1000	3¢ Landing of Cadillac, Detroit	5.50	.50	.20	.15
1001	3¢ Colorado Statehood.....................	5.50	.50	.20	.15
1002	3¢ Chemical Society	5.50	.50	.20	.15
1003	3¢ Battle of Brooklyn	5.50	.55	.20	.15

VERY FINE COPIES OF #752-DATE ARE AVAILABLE FOR THE FOLLOWING PREMIUMS:
ADD 10¢ TO ANY ITEM PRICED UNDER 50¢. ADD 20% TO ANY ITEM PRICED AT 50¢ & UP.
UNLESS PRICED AS VERY FINE, SETS ARE NOT AVAILABLE VERY FINE AND STAMPS
SHOULD BE LISTED INDIVIDUALLY WITH APPROPRIATE PREMIUM.

1952 Commemoratives

1004   1005   1006

1007   1008   1009   1011

1010   1012   1013

1014   1015   1016

Scott's No.		Mint Sheet	Plate Block	F-VF NH	F-VF Used
1004-16	**Set of 13**	...	...	1.60	1.25
1004	3¢ Betsy Ross	5.50	.55	.20	.15
1005	3¢ 4-H Clubs	5.50	.50	.20	.15
1006	3¢ B & O Railroad	5.50	.55	.20	.15
1007	3¢ Amer. Automobile Assoc.............	5.50	.50	.20	.15
1008	3¢ N.A.T.O. ....(100)	10.50	.50	.20	.15
1009	3¢ Grand Coulee Dam	5.50	.50	.20	.15
1010	3¢ Marquis de Lafayette..................	5.50	.50	.20	.15
1011	3¢ Mt. Rushmore Memorial	5.50	.55	.20	.15
1012	3¢ Civil Engineers Society...............	5.50	.50	.20	.15
1013	3¢ Service Women	5.50	.55	.20	.15
1014	3¢ Gutenberg Bible	5.50	.50	.20	.15
1015	3¢ Newspaper Boys	5.50	.50	.20	.15
1016	3¢ Int'l. Red Cross.........................	5.50	.50	.20	.15

1953 Commemoratives

1017   1018   1019

1020   1021   1022

Scott's No.		Mint Sheet	Plate Block	F-VF NH	F-VF Used
1017-28	**Set of 12**	...	...	1.50	1.25
1017	3¢ National Guard...........................	5.50	.50	.20	.15
1018	3¢ Ohio Statehood ....(70)	7.25	.50	.20	.15
1019	3¢ Washington Territory..................	5.50	.50	.20	.15
1020	3¢ Louisiana Purchase	5.50	.50	.20	.15
1021	5¢ Opening of Japan, Perry	7.50	.80	.20	.15
1022	3¢ American Bar Association	5.75	.70	.20	.15

1953 Commemoratives (cont.)

1023 1024 1025

1026 1027 1028

Scott's No.		Mint Sheet	Plate Block	F-VF NH	F-VF Used
1023	3¢ Sagamore Hill, T. Roosevelt	5.50	.50	.20	.15
1024	3¢ Future Farmers	5.50	.50	.20	.15
1025	3¢ Trucking Industry	5.50	.50	.20	.15
1026	3¢ General George S. Patton.............	7.50	.60	.20	.15
1027	3¢ New York City	5.50	.50	.20	.15
1028	3¢ Gadsden Purchase.......................	5.50	.50	.20	.15

1954 Commemoratives

1029 1060 1061

1062 1063

1029,1060-63	Set of 5	...	...	.65	.50
1029	3¢ Columbia University	5.50	.50	.20	.15

1954-1968 Liberty Series (B)
(Sheets of 100)

1030 1031,1054 1031A,1054A 1032 1033,1055

1034,1056 1035,1057 1036,1058 1037,1059 1038

1039 1040 1041,1041B 1042 1042A

		Mint Sheet	Plate Block	F-VF NH	F-VF Used
1030-53	Set of 28	...	497.50	115.00	11.50
1030-53	Very Fine Set of 28	...	600.00	140.00	14.00
1030-51	½¢-50¢ Values only (26)		56.50	12.75	2.40
1030	½¢ Franklin, Wet ('55)	5.00	.40	.20	.15
1030a	½¢ Dry Printing ('58)	6.00	.75	.20	.15
1031	1¢ Washington, Dry ('56)	4.50	.40	.20	.15

1954-1968 Liberty Series (B)
(Sheets of 100)

Scott's No.		Mint Sheet	Plate Block	F-VF NH	F-VF Used
1031b	1¢ Wet Printing ('54)......................	7.50	.70	.20	.15
1031A	1¼¢ Palace of Governors ('60)..........	5.50	.55	.20	.15
1032	1½¢ Mount Vernon (1956)	7.75	1.75	.20	.15
1033	2¢ Jefferson................................	7.00	.40	.20	.15
1034	2½¢ Bunker Hill (1959)	9.00	.60	.20	.15
1035	3¢ Statue of Liberty, Dry	10.00	.50	.20	.15
1035f	3¢ Booklet Pane of 6, Dry Printing....	...	...	6.50	3.50
1035b	3¢ Tagged, Dry Printing (1966)	37.50	7.75	.30	.30
1035e	3¢ Wet Printing..........................	19.50	1.10	.25	.18
1035a	3¢ Booklet Pane of 6, Wet Printing	...	...	5.95	...
1036	4¢ Abraham Lincoln, Dry	11.50	.50	.20	.15
1036a	4¢ Booklet Pane of 6 (1958)	...	...	2.75	2.25
1036b	4¢ Tagged, Dry Printing (1963)	80.00	11.95	.70	.65
1036c	4¢ Wet Printing..........................	12.75	.75	.20	.20
1037	4½¢ The Hermitage (1959)	13.00	.70	.20	.15
1038	5¢ James Monroe..........................	15.00	.60	.20	.15
1039	6¢ T. Roosevelt, Dry (1955)	37.50	1.65	.40	.15
1039a	6¢ Wet Printing..........................	50.00	2.25	.50	.18
1040	7¢ Woodrow Wilson (1956)	32.50	1.50	.35	.15
1041	8¢ St. of Liberty, Original, Flat	33.50	2.75	.35	.15
1041B	8¢ Liberty, Original, Rotary	38.50	3.75	.40	.15
1042	8¢ St. Lib., Redrawn (1958)	31.50	1.35	.32	.15

#1041,1041B: Torch Flame between "U.S." and "POSTAGE".
#1042: Torch Flame goes under "P" of "POSTAGE".

1042A	8¢ J.J. Pershing ('61)	32.50	1.50	.33	.15

1043 1044 1044A 1045 1046

1047 1048,1059A 1049 1050 1051

1052 1053

		Mint Sheet	Plate Block	F-VF NH	F-VF Used
1043	9¢ The Alamo ('56)	42.50	1.90	.40	.15
1044	10¢ Indep. Hall ('56)	37.50	1.35	.35	.15
1044b	10¢ Tagged (1966).........................	...	45.00	3.75	3.00
1044A	11¢ St. of Liberty ('61)	40.00	1.75	.40	.15
1044Ac	11¢ Tagged (1967)........................	...	47.50	2.25	2.15
1045	12¢ Ben. Harrison ('59)	55.00	2.25	.50	.15
1045a	12¢ Tagged (1968).........................	65.00	5.00	.65	.35
1046	15¢ John Jay ('58)	95.00	4.25	.95	.15
1046a	15¢ Tagged (1966).........................	...	11.75	1.50	.75
1047	20¢ Monticello ('56).......................	70.00	3.25	.70	.15
1048	25¢ Paul Revere ('58)	150.00	6.75	1.50	.15
1049	30¢ Robert E. Lee, Dry (1957)	150.00	7.00	1.50	.15
1049a	30¢ Wet Printing (1955)	...	11.50	2.75	1.75
1050	40¢ John Marshall, Dry (1958)	250.00	11.75	2.50	.15
1050a	40¢ Wet Printing (1955)	...	17.50	3.75	2.75
1051	50¢ S.B. Anthony, Dry (1958)	195.00	8.25	1.80	.15
1051a	50¢ Wet Printing (1955)	...	14.75	2.50	1.75
1052	$1 Patrick Henry, Dry (1958)	575.00	25.00	5.50	.15
1052a	$1 Wet Printing (1955)	...	36.50	8.50	3.95
1053	$5 Alex Hamilton ('56)	...	450.00	100.00	8.50

NOTE: USED STAMPS ARE OUR CHOICE OF WET OR DRY, TAGGED OR UNTAGGED.

1954-80 Liberty Series Coil Stamps, Perf. 10 (B)

		Line Pairs	F-VF NH	F-VF Used
1054-59A	**Set of 8 ....**	**24.75**	**2.85**	**2.25**
1054-59A	**Very Fine Set of 8 ....**	**31.75**	**3.60**	**3.00**

#1054A and #1059 are Perforated Horizontally.

1054	1¢ Washington, Dry, Large Holes ('57)	5.00	2.25	.75
1054s	1¢ Dry, Small Holes (1960)	1.10	.25	.15
1054c	1¢ Wet Printing (1954)	3.75	.60	.30
1054A	1¼¢ Pal. of Governors, Sm.Holes ('60) .	2.25	.20	.15
1054Al	1¼¢ Large Holes	325.00	22.50	1.00
1055	2¢ Jefferson, Dry, Large Holes (1957)	1.25	.30	.25
1055s	2¢ Dry, Small Holes (1961)	27.50	10.00	1.00
1055a	2¢ Tagged, Shiny Gum (1968)	.40	.20	.15
1055av	2¢ Tagged, Dull Gum	2.25	.35	...
1055d	2¢ Wet Printing, Yellow Gum (1954).......	4.50	.75	.50
1055dw	2¢ Wet Printing, White Gum	32.50	4.25	...

NOTE: SETS INCLUDE OUR CHOICE OF LARGE OR SMALL HOLES.

1954-80 Liberty Coils (cont.)

Scott's No.		Line Pairs	F-VF NH	F-VF Used
1056	2½¢ Bunker Hills, Large Holes ('59)........	3.25	.22	.20
1057	3¢ Liberty, Dry, Large Holes (1956)........	2.75	.45	.30
1057s	3¢ Dry Printing, Small Holes (1958)........	.60	.20	.15
1057b	3¢ Tagged, Small Holes (1967)........	37.50	2.00	1.75
1057c	3¢ Wet Printing,Large Holes (1954)........	3.50	.70	.50
1058	4¢ Lincoln, Dry, Large Holes (1958)........	5.00	1.00	.40
1058s	4¢ Dry Printing, Small Holes	.65	.20	.15
1059	4½¢ Hermitage, Large Holes (1959)	12.50	1.35	1.10
1059s	4½¢ Small Holes	475.00	22.50	...
1059A	25¢ Paul Revere (1965)	2.50	.75	.30
1059Ab	25¢ Tagged, Shiny Gum (1973)........	3.25	1.00	.50
1059Ad	25¢ Tagged, Dull Gum (1980)........	5.50	1.50	...

1954 Commemoratives (see also No.1029)

Scott's No.		Mint Sheet	Plate Block	F-VF NH	F-VF Used
1060	3¢ Nebraska Territory	5.50	.50	.20	.15
1061	3¢ Kansas Territory	5.50	.50	.20	.15
1062	3¢ George Eastman........(70)	7.50	.50	.20	.15
1063	3¢ Lewis & Clark Expedition	5.50	.50	.20	.15

1955 Commemoratives

1064   1065   1068

1066   1067   1069

1070   1071   1072

Scott's No.				F-VF NH	F-VF Used
1064-72	Set of 9	...	...	1.25	.95
1064	3¢ Penn. Academy of Fine Arts	5.50	.55	.20	.15
1065	3¢ Land Grant Colleges	5.50	.55	.20	.15
1066	8¢ Rotary International	12.50	1.40	.25	.15
1067	3¢ Armed Forces Reserves	5.50	.55	.20	.15
1068	3¢ Old Man of the Mtns, NH	5.75	.55	.20	.15
1069	3¢ Soo Locks Centennial	5.50	.55	.20	.15
1070	3¢ Atoms for Peace	5.75	.55	.20	.15
1071	3¢ Fort Ticonderoga, NY	5.75	.55	.20	.15
1072	3¢ Andrew Mellon........(70)	7.25	.55	.20	.15

1956 Commemoratives

1075

1956 Commemoratives (cont.)

1073   1074   1076

Scott's No.		Mint Sheet	Plate Block	F-VF NH	F-VF Used
1073-85	Set of 13	...	...	3.65	3.25
1073	3¢ Franklin 250th Anniv	5.75	.55	.20	.15
1074	3¢ Booker T. Washington	5.50	.55	.20	.15
1075	3¢ & 8¢ FIPEX Souv. Sheet	...	...	2.25	2.15
1075a	3¢ Liberty Single	...	...	1.00	.90
1075b	8¢ Liberty Single	...	...	1.25	1.15
1076	3¢ FIPEX Stamp	5.50	.55	.20	.15

1077   1078   1079

1080   1081   1082

1083   1084   1085

1077	3¢ Wildlife - Wild Turkey	5.50	.55	.20	.15
1078	3¢ Wildlife - Antelope	5.50	.55	.20	.15
1079	3¢ Wildlife - King Salmon	5.50	.55	.20	.15
1080	3¢ Pure Food & Drug Act	5.50	.55	.20	.15
1081	3¢ Wheatland, Buchanan	5.50	.50	.20	.15
1082	3¢ Labor Day	5.50	.50	.20	.15
1083	3¢ Nassau Hall, Princeton	5.50	.50	.20	.15
1084	3¢ Devils Tower, Wyoming	5.50	.55	.20	.15
1085	3¢ Children's Issue	5.50	.50	.20	.15

1957 Commemoratives

1086   1087   1088

1089   1090   1091

1092

1093

1094

1095   **1096**   **1097**

1098   **1099**

Scott's No.		Mint Sheet	Plate Block	F-VF NH	F-VF Used
1086-99	Set of 14	...	...	1.75	1.35
1086	3¢ Alexander Hamilton	5.50	.50	.20	.15
1087	3¢ Polio, March of Dimes	5.50	.50	.20	.15
1088	3¢ Coast & Geodetic Society	5.50	.50	.20	.15
1089	3¢ Architects Institute	5.50	.50	.20	.15
1090	3¢ Steel Industry	5.50	.50	.20	.15
1091	3¢ Naval Review, Jamestown	5.75	.50	.20	.15
1092	3¢ Oklahoma Statehood	5.50	.50	.20	.15
1093	3¢ School Teachers	7.50	.60	.20	.15
1094	4¢ 48-Star U.S. Flag	6.50	.55	.20	.15
1095	3¢ Shipbuilding Anniv .... (70)	7.50	.50	.20	.15
1096	8¢ Ramon Magsaysay .... (48)	10.75	1.10	.24	.15
1097	3¢ Birth of Lafayette	6.00	.50	.20	.15
1098	3¢ Wildlife - Whooping Crane	5.50	.50	.20	.15
1099	3¢ Religious Freedom	5.50	.50	.20	.15

1958 Commemoratives

1100

1104

1105

1106

1107

1108

1100,1104-1123	Set of 21	...	...	2.75	1.95
1100	3¢ Gardening-Horticulture	5.50	.50	.20	.15
1104	3¢ Brussels World Fair	5.50	.50	.20	.15
1105	3¢ James Monroe .... (70)	7.50	.50	.20	.15
1106	3¢ Minnesota Centennial..................	5.50	.50	.20	.15
1107	3¢ Geophysical Year........................	5.50	.50	.20	.15
1108	3¢ Gunston Hall, Virginia	5.50	.50	.20	.15

1109   **1110**   **1112**

Scott's No.		Mint Sheet	Plate Block	F-VF NH	F-VF Used
1109	3¢ Mackinac Bridge, MI.................	5.50	.50	.20	.15
1110	4¢ Simon Bolivar..........................(70)	8.50	.60	.20	.15
1111	8¢ Simon Bolivar..........................(72)	17.50	1.50	.25	.15
1112	4¢ Atlantic Cable Centennial	6.25	.55	.20	.15

1113   **1114**   **1115**

1116   **1118**   **1119**

1120   **1121**

1122   **1123**

1958-59 Lincoln Commemoratives

1113-16	Set of 4	29.00	2.60	.70	.50
1113	1¢ Beardless Lincoln ('59)	2.50	.40	.20	.15
1114	3¢ Bust of Lincoln ('59)	6.25	.55	.20	.15
1115	4¢ Lincoln-Douglas Debates.............	8.50	.85	.20	.15
1116	4¢ Statue of Lincoln ('59)	13.00	1.20	.25	.15

1958 Commemoratives (continued)

1117	4¢ Lajos Kossuth..........................(70)	8.50	.60	.20	.15
1118	8¢ Lajos Kossuth..........................(72)	17.50	1.20	.25	.15
1119	4¢ Freedom of Press	6.75	.55	.20	.15
1120	4¢ Overland Mail	6.50	.55	.20	.15
1121	4¢ Noah Webster ....(70)	8.50	.55	.20	.15
1122	4¢ Forest Conservation	6.25	.55	.20	.15
1123	4¢ Fort Duquesne, Pittsburgh............	6.25	.55	.20	.15

1959 Commemoratives

1124	1126	1127	1134

1128	1129	1130

1131	1132	1133

1135	1136	1137	1138

Scott's No.		Mint Sheet	Plate Block	F-VF NH	F-VF Used
1124-38	Set of 15..........................	...	...	1.95	1.60
1124	4¢ Oregon Statehood	6.25	.55	.20	.15
1125	4¢ Jose San Martin ....(70)	8.75	.55	.20	.15
1126	8¢ Jose San Martin ....(72)	16.50	1.10	.25	.15
1127	4¢ 10th Anniv. N.A.T.O. ....(70)	8.75	.55	.20	.15
1128	4¢ Arctic Explorations....................	6.25	.55	.20	.15
1129	8¢ World Peace & Trade	11.50	1.00	.25	.15
1130	4¢ Silver Discovery.......................	6.25	.60	.20	.15
1131	4¢ St. Lawrence Seaway..................	6.25	.55	.20	.15
1132	4¢ 49-Star Flag	6.25	.55	.20	.15
1133	4¢ Soil Conservation	6.25	.55	.20	.15
1134	4¢ Petroleum Industry....................	6.25	.55	.20	.15
1135	4¢ Dental Health...........................	10.00	.85	.22	.15
1136	4¢ Ernst Reuter........................(70)	8.50	.55	.20	.15
1137	8¢ Ernst Reuter........................(72)	16.50	1.10	.25	.15
1138	4¢ Dr. Ephraim McDowell ....(70)	8.75	.65	.20	.15

1960 Commemoratives

1139	1140	1141

1142	1143	1144

Scott's No.		Mint Sheet	Plate Block	F-VF NH	F-VF Used
1139-73	**Set of 35.........................**	...	...	4.95	3.75
1139-44	Set of 6............................	43.50	3.95	1.00	.65
1139	4¢ Washington Credo	6.50	.65	.20	.15
1140	4¢ Franklin Credo	6.50	.65	.20	.15
1141	4¢ Jefferson Credo	6.50	.65	.20	.15
1142	4¢ F.S. Key Credo........................	6.50	.65	.20	.15
1143	4¢ Lincoln Credo..........................	9.50	.85	.20	.15
1144	4¢ Henry Credo (1961)...................	9.50	.85	.20	.15

1960 Commemoratives (cont.)

1145	1146	1147	1151

1149	1150	1152

1153	1154	1155

Scott's No.		Mint Sheet	Plate Block	F-VF NH	F-VF Used
1145	4¢ Boy Scout Jubilee	8.75	.90	.20	.15
1146	4¢ Winter Olympics........................	6.75	.55	.20	.15
1147	4¢ Thomas G. Masaryk ....(70)	8.50	.55	.20	.15
1148	8¢ Thomas G. Masaryk ....(72)	16.50	1.10	.25	.15
1149	4¢ World Refugee Year	6.25	.55	.20	.15
1150	4¢ Water Conservation	6.25	.55	.20	.15
1151	4¢ Southeast Asia Treaty ....(70)	8.50	.55	.20	.15
1152	4¢ American Woman	6.25	.55	.20	.15
1153	4¢ 50-Star Flag	6.25	.55	.20	.15
1154	4¢ Pony Express Centennial..............	6.50	.65	.20	.15
1155	4¢ Employ the Handicapped	6.25	.55	.20	.15

1156	1157	1158	1159

1161	1162	1163	1167

1156	4¢ World Forestry Congress	6.25	.55	.20	.15
1157	4¢ Mexican Independence	6.25	.55	.20	.15
1158	4¢ U.S. - Japan Treaty	6.50	.55	.20	.15
1159	4¢ Ignacy J. Paderewski ....(70)	8.50	.55	.20	.15
1160	8¢ Ignacy J. Paderewski ....(72)	16.50	1.10	.25	.15
1161	4¢ Robert A. Taft ....(70)	8.50	.55	.20	.15
1162	4¢ Wheels of Freedom	6.25	.55	.20	.15
1163	4¢ Boys' Club of America	6.25	.55	.20	.15
1164	4¢ Automated Post Office................	6.25	.55	.20	.15

1960 Commemoratives (continued)

1164

1165

1169

1170

1171

1172

1173

Scott's No.		Mint Sheet	Plate Block	F-VF NH	F-VF Used
1165	4¢ Gustaf Mannerheim ....(70)	8.50	.55	.20	.15
1166	8¢ Gustaf Mannerheim ....(72)	16.50	1.10	.25	.15
1167	4¢ Camp Fire Girls	6.25	.55	.20	.15
1168	4¢ Guiseppe Garibaldi ....(70)	8.50	.55	.20	.15
1169	8¢ Guiseppe Garibaldi ....(72)	16.50	1.10	.25	.15
1170	4¢ Walter F. George ....(70)	8.50	.55	.20	.15
1171	4¢ Andrew Carnegie ....(70)	8.50	.55	.20	.15
1172	4¢ John Foster Dulles ....(70)	8.50	.55	.20	.15
1173	4¢ "Echo I" Satellite	11.50	1.00	.24	.15

1961 Commemoratives

1174

1175

1176

1177

1178   1179   1180

1181   1182   1183

1174-1190	Set of 17....................................	...	...	3.95	1.75
1174	4¢ Mahatma Gandhi ....(70)	8.50	.55	.20	.15
1175	8¢ Mahatma Gandhi ....(72)	16.50	1.20	.25	.15
1176	4¢ Range Conservation...................	6.50	.55	.20	.15
1177	4¢ Horace Greeley.......................(70)	8.50	.55	.20	.15

1961-1965 Civil War Centennial

1178-82	Set of 5	87.50	8.75	1.70	.55
1178	4¢ Fort Sumter (1961)	15.75	1.50	.30	.15
1179	4¢ Battle of Shiloh (1962)..............	11.50	1.10	.24	.15
1180	5¢ Gettysburg (1963).....................	16.00	1.75	.30	.15
1181	5¢ Wilderness (1964)	16.00	1.50	.35	.15
1182	5¢ Appomattox (1965).....................	31.75	3.25	.65	.15

1961 Commemoratives (cont.)

1184   1185   1186

1187

1188

1189

1190

Scott's No.		Mint Sheet	Plate Block	F-VF NH	F-VF Used
1183	4¢ Kansas Statehood........................	6.50	.55	.20	.15
1184	4¢ George W. Norris	6.25	.55	.20	.15
1185	4¢ Naval Aviation	6.75	.65	.20	.15
1186	4¢ Workmen's Compensation............	6.25	.55	.20	.15
1186v	Plate Number Inverted	6.75	.75	...	...
1187	4¢ Frederic Remington	6.50	.65	.20	.15
1188	4¢ Republic of China, Sun Yat-sen	9.50	8.50	.75	.15
1189	4¢ Basketball - James Naismith	12.00	1.00	.25	.15
1190	4¢ Nursing	13.75	1.15	.28	.15

1962 Commemoratives (See also 1179)

1191   1192   1193

1195   1194   1196

1197   1198   1199

1191-1207	Set of 17	...	...	2.35	1.85
1191	4¢ New Mexico Statehood................	6.25	.55	.20	.15
1192	4¢ Arizona Statehood.......................	6.50	.55	.20	.15
1193	4¢ Project Mercury.........................	6.75	.70	.20	.15
1194	4¢ Malaria Eradication.....................	6.25	.55	.20	.15
1195	4¢ Charles Evans Hughes.................	6.25	.55	.20	.15
1196	4¢ Seattle World's Fair...................	6.25	.55	.20	.15
1197	4¢ Louisiana Statehood...................	6.25	.55	.20	.15
1198	4¢ Homestead Act	6.25	.55	.20	.15
1199	4¢ Girl Scouts 50th Anniversary	6.50	.55	.20	.15

1962 Commemoratives (cont.)

1200

1201

1202

1203

1205

1206

1207

Scott's No.		Mint Sheet	Plate Block	F-VF NH	F-VF Used
1200	4¢ Brien McMahon	6.25	.55	.20	.15
1201	4¢ Apprenticeship Act	6.25	.55	.20	.15
1202	4¢ Sam Rayburn	6.25	.55	.20	.15
1203	4¢ Dag Hammarskjold	6.25	.55	.20	.15
1204	4¢ Hammarskjold "Error"	7.00	1.35	.20	.15

Note: The yellow background is inverted on #1204

1205	4¢ Christmas Wreath ....(100)	12.50	.55	.20	.15
1206	4¢ Higher Education	6.50	.65	.20	.15
1207	4¢ Winslow Homer Seascape	6.75	.55	.20	.15

1962-1963 Regular Issues

1208

1209,1225

1213,1229

		Mint Sheet	Plate Block	F-VF NH	F-VF Used
1208	5¢ Flag & Wh. Hse. ('63)...........(100)	14.50	.65	.20	.15
1208a	5¢ Flag Tagged (1966) ....(100)	28.50	2.00	.30	.20
1209	1¢ Andrew Jackson (1963)...........(100)	4.75	.40	.20	.15
1209a	1¢ Tagged (1966) ....(100)	7.50	.45	.20	.18
1213	5¢ George Washington ....(100)	14.50	.65	.20	.15
1213a	5¢ Pane of 5 "Mailman", Slog.I	...	...	5.75	4.75
1213a	5¢ Pane of 5 "Use Zone", Slog. II	...	...	25.75	12.50
1213a	5¢ Pane of 5 "Use Zip Code", Slog. III	...	...	3.00	2.25
1213b	5¢ Tagged (1963) ....(100)	32.50	8.00	.65	.50
1213c	5¢ Pane of 5 "Zone" Tagged, Slog. II	...	...	90.00	...
1213c	5¢ Pane of 5 "Zip" Tagged, Slog. III	...	...	1.35	...
1225	1¢ Jackson Coil	Line Pr.	2.50	.20	.15
1225a	1¢ Coil, Tagged (1966)	Line Pr.	.65	.20	.18
1229	5¢ Washington Coil	Line Pr.	2.95	.95	.15
1229a	5¢ Coil, Tagged (1963)	Line Pr.	8.95	1.50	.25

1963 Commemoratives (See also 1180)

1230

1231

1232

1230-41	Set of 12	...	...	1.80	1.20
1230	5¢ Carolina Charter	7.00	.65	.20	.15
1231	5¢ Food for Peace	7.00	.65	.20	.15
1232	5¢ West Virginia Statehood	7.00	.65	.20	.15

1963 Commemoratives (cont.)

1233

1234

1235

1236

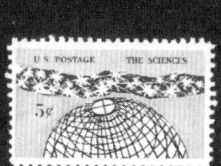
1237

1238

1239

1240

1241

Scott's No.		Mint Sheet	Plate Block	F-VF NH	F-VF Used
1233	5¢ Emancipation Proclamation	8.00	.85	.20	.15
1234	5¢ Alliance for Progress	7.00	.65	.20	.15
1235	5¢ Cordell Hull	7.00	.65	.20	.15
1236	5¢ Eleanor Roosevelt	7.00	.65	.20	.15
1237	5¢ The Sciences	7.00	.65	.20	.15
1238	5¢ City Mail Delivery	7.00	.65	.20	.15
1239	5¢ Int'l. Red Cross Centenary	7.00	.65	.20	.15
1240	5¢ Christmas Tree ....(100)	14.00	.65	.20	.15
1240a	5¢ Tagged...........(100)	62.50	7.50	.60	.50
1241	5¢ Audubon-Columbia Jays	7.75	.70	.20	.15

1964 Commemoratives (See also 1181)

1243

1242

1244

1245

1246

1247

1242-60	Set of 19	...	...	3.95	1.85
1242	5¢ Sam Houston	7.50	.65	.20	.15
1243	5¢ Charles M. Russell	7.50	.65	.20	.15
1244	5¢ N.Y. World's Fair	7.50	.65	.20	.15
1245	5¢ John Muir, Naturalist	7.50	.65	.20	.15
1246	5¢ John F. Kennedy Memorial	16.50	1.50	.35	.15
1247	5¢ New Jersey Tercentenary	7.50	.65	.20	.15

FOR INFORMATION CONCERNING VERY FINE SEE PAGE II

1964 Commemoratives (cont.)

1248   1249   1250   1251

1252   1254 1255   1256 1257   1253

1258   1259   1260

Scott's No.		Mint Sheet	Plate Block	F-VF NH	F-VF Used
1248	5¢ Nevada Statehood	7.00	.65	.20	.15
1249	5¢ Register and Vote	7.00	.65	.20	.15
1250	5¢ William Shakespeare	7.00	.65	.20	.15
1251	5¢ Doctors Mayo	14.50	1.25	.30	.15
1252	5¢ American Music	7.25	.65	.20	.15
1253	5¢ Homemakers, Sampler	7.25	.65	.20	.15
1254-7	5¢ Christmas, attached ....(100)	27.50	1.35	1.10	1.10
1254-7	5¢ Set of 4 Singles	...	...	1.00	.60
1254-7a	5¢ Christmas Tagged, attd .....(100)	75.00	8.75	3.00	2.95
1254-7a	5¢ Set of 4 Singles	...	...	2.65	2.40
1258	5¢ Verrazano-Narrows Bdg	7.00	.65	.20	.15
1259	5¢ Fine Arts - Stuart Davis	7.00	.65	.20	.15
1260	5¢ Amateur Radio	14.00	1.25	.30	.15

1965 Commemoratives

1262   1261   1263

1265   1264   1266

1261-76	Set of 16	...	...	2.75	2.00
1261	5¢ Battle of New Orleans	7.00	.65	.20	.15
1262	5¢ Physical Fitness - Sokol	7.00	.65	.20	.15
1263	5¢ Crusade Against Cancer	7.00	.65	.20	.15
1264	5¢ Churchill Memorial	7.50	.65	.20	.15
1265	5¢ Magna Carta	7.00	.65	.20	.15
1266	5¢ Int'l. Cooperation Year, U.N.	7.00	.65	.20	.15

1965 Commemoratives (cont.)

1267   1268   1269   1270

1271   1272   1273

1274   1276   1275

Scott's No.		Mint Sheet	Plate Block	F-VF NH	F-VF Used
1267	5¢ Salvation Army	7.00	.65	.20	.15
1268	5¢ Dante Alighieri	7.00	.65	.20	.15
1269	5¢ Herbert Hoover	7.00	.65	.20	.15
1270	5¢ Robert Fulton	7.00	.65	.20	.15
1271	5¢ 400th Anniv. of Florida	7.00	.65	.20	.15
1272	5¢ Traffic Safety	7.00	.65	.20	.15
1273	5¢ John S. Copley Painting	7.00	.65	.20	.15
1274	11¢ Telecommunication Union	25.00	5.50	.45	.30
1275	5¢ Adlai Stevenson	7.00	.65	.20	.15
1276	5¢ Christmas Angel ....(100)	13.50	.65	.20	.15
1276a	5¢ Christmas, Tagged ....(100)	65.00	8.75	.65	.35

1965-79 Prominent Americans Series
(Sheets of 100)

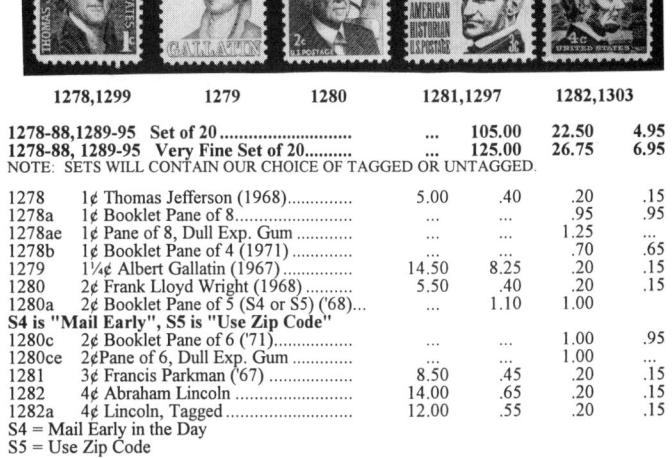

1278,1299   1279   1280   1281,1297   1282,1303

1278-88,1289-95	Set of 20	...	105.00	22.50	4.95
1278-88, 1289-95	Very Fine Set of 20	...	125.00	26.75	6.95

NOTE: SETS WILL CONTAIN OUR CHOICE OF TAGGED OR UNTAGGED.

1278	1¢ Thomas Jefferson (1968)	5.00	.40	.20	.15
1278a	1¢ Booklet Pane of 8	...	...	.95	.95
1278ae	1¢ Pane of 8, Dull Exp. Gum	...	...	1.25	...
1278b	1¢ Booklet Pane of 4 (1971)	...	...	.70	.65
1279	1¼¢ Albert Gallatin (1967)	14.50	8.25	.20	.15
1280	2¢ Frank Lloyd Wright (1968)	5.50	.40	.20	.15
1280a	2¢ Booklet Pane of 5 (S4 or S5) ('68)	...	1.10	1.00	

S4 is "Mail Early", S5 is "Use Zip Code"

1280c	2¢ Booklet Pane of 6 ('71)	...	...	1.00	.95
1280ce	2¢Pane of 6, Dull Exp. Gum	...	...	1.00	...
1281	3¢ Francis Parkman ('67)	8.50	.45	.20	.15
1282	4¢ Abraham Lincoln	14.00	.65	.20	.15
1282a	4¢ Lincoln, Tagged	12.00	.55	.20	.15

S4 = Mail Early in the Day
S5 = Use Zip Code

1283,1304   1283B,1304C   1284,1298   1285   1286

Scott's No.		Mint Sheet	Plate Block	F-VF NH	F-VF Used
1283	5¢ Washington, Dirty Face ('66)......	18.75	.75	.22	.15
1283a	5¢ Washington, Tagged	15.00	.65	.20	.15
1283B	5¢ Washington, Clean Face ('67).....	13.50	.70	.20	.15
1283Bv	5¢ Clean Face, Dull Gum..............	39.50	3.25	.40	...
1284	6¢ F.D.Roosevelt (1966)...............	23.00	.95	.24	.15
1284a	6¢ F.D.R., Tagged	20.00	.75	.20	.15
1284b	6¢ Booklet Pane of 8 (1967)	...	...	1.60	1.50
1284c	6¢ Pane of 5 (S4 or S5) (1968)...	...	...	1.50	1.35
1285	8¢ Albert Einstein (1966).............	28.50	1.40	.30	.15
1285a	8¢ Einstein, Tagged	22.50	1.15	.25	.20
1286	10¢ Andrew Jackson (1967)	26.50	1.25	.30	.15

| 1286A | 1287 | 1288/1305E | 1289 | 1290 |

| 1291 | 1292 | 1293 | 1294,1305C | 1295 |

1286A	12¢ Henry Ford (1968).................	32.50	1.40	.35	.15
1287	13¢ John F. Kennedy (1967)............	55.00	2.50	.60	.15
1288	15¢ O.W. Holmes, Die I (1968).......	36.50	1.75	.40	.15
1288d	15¢ Holmes, Die II (1979)	95.00	13.50	1.00	.20
1288B	15¢ Bklt. Single, Pf. 10 Die III........	...	...	.45	.15
1288Bc	15¢ Bk. Pane of 8, Die III (1978)......	...	...	3.25	3.25
1289	20¢ George C. Marshall (1967)	72.50	3.25	.75	.15
1289a	20¢ Marshall, Tagged (1973)	57.50	2.50	.60	.30
1289ad	20¢ Dull Gum	140.00	7.50	1.50	...
1290	25¢ Frederick Douglass (1967)	97.50	4.25	1.10	.15
1290a	25¢ Douglass, Tagged (1973)	85.00	3.50	.85	.15
1290ad	25¢ Dull Gum	115.00	6.75	1.20	...
1291	30¢ John Dewey (1968).................	100.00	4.65	1.05	.15
1291a	30¢ Dewey, Tagged(1973)...............	80.00	3.75	.85	.15
1292	40¢ Thomas Paine (1968)	125.00	5.95	1.35	.15
1292a	40¢ Paine, Tagged (1973)	100.00	4.75	1.10	.25
1292ad	40¢ Dull Gum	130.00	6.75	1.35	...
1293	50¢ Lucy Stone (1968).................	165.00	7.50	1.75	.15
1293a	50¢ Stone, Tagged (1973)	140.00	6.25	1.50	.25
1294	$1 Eugene O'Neill (1967).............	325.00	14.50	3.50	.15
1294a	$1 O'Neill, Tagged (1973)	275.00	12.50	3.00	.15
1295	$5 John B. Moore (1966).............	...	72.50	16.50	2.95
1295a	$5 Moore, Tagged (1973)..............	...	57.50	13.00	2.75

#1288 and 1305E: Die I top bar of "5" is horiz., tie touches lapel.
#1288d and 1305Ei: Die II top bar of "5" slopes down to right, tie does not touch lapel.
#1288B and 1288Bc: Die III booklets only, design shorter than Die I or II.

| 1305 | 1306 | 1307 |

1966-81 Prominent Americans, Coils, Perf. 10

Scott's No.		Line Pair	F-VF NH	F-VF Used
1297-1305C	**Prominent Am. Coils (9) ....**	12.95	4.65	1.90
1297-1305C	**Very Fine Set of 9 ....**	15.75	5.60	2.70
1297	3¢ Parkman (1975)	.50	.20	.15
1297b	3¢ Bureau Precancel	2.95	.40	.25
1297d	3¢ Dull Gum	5.00	.35	...
1298	6¢ F.D. Roosevelt, Pf. Hz. ('67).......	1.30	.20	.15
1299	1¢ Jefferson (1968)	.40	.20	.15
1299a	1¢ Bureau Precancel	250.00	19.50	1.00
1303	4¢ Lincoln	.60	.20	.15
1303a	4¢ Bureau Precancel	160.00	10.00	1.00
1304	5¢ Washington, Original	.50	.20	.15
1304a	5¢ Bureau Precancel	175.00	10.75	1.00
1304d	5¢ Dull Gum	8.50	1.10	...
1304C	5¢ Redrawn ('81)	1.80	.20	.15
1305	6¢ F.D.Roosevelt, Pf. Vert. ('68).......	.65	.22	.15
1305b	6¢ Bureau Precancel	300.00	16.00	1.50
1305E	15¢ Holmes, Die I (1978)	1.10	.45	.15
1305Ed	15¢ Die I, Dull Gum	6.50	1.60	...
1305Ef	15¢ Bureau Precancel	...	37.50	3.95
1305Ei	15¢ Holmes, Die II (1979)	1.65	.60	.25
1305C	$1 O'Neill (1973)	6.75	3.00	.95
1305Cd	$1 Dull Gum	7.75	3.50	...

NOTE: F.VF, NH Bureau Precancels have full original gum and have never been used.

Scott's No.		Mint Sheet	Plate Block	F-VF NH	F-VF Used
1306-22	Set of 17..........................	...	...	2.75	1.85
1306	5¢ Migratory Bird Treaty	7.50	.65	.20	.15
1307	5¢ Humane Treatment Animals	7.00	.65	.20	.15

| `1308 | 1309 | 1310 | 1312 |

| 1313 | 1314 | 1315 |

| 1316 | 1317 | 1318 |

| 1319 | 1320 | 1321 | 1322 |

1308	5¢ Indiana Statehood	7.00	.65	.20	.15
1309	5¢ American Circus (Clown)	8.75	.90	.20	.15
1310	5¢ SIPEX Stamp	7.00	.65	.20	.15
1311	5¢ SIPEX Souvenir Sheet	...	...	.20	.18
1312	5¢ Bill of Rights	7.50	.65	.20	.15
1313	5¢ Polish Millenium......................	7.00	.65	.20	.15
1314	5¢ National Park Service	7.75	.70	.20	.15
1314a	5¢ Parks, Tagged	16.50	2.00	.35	.30
1315	5¢ Marine Corps Reserve	7.00	.65	.20	.15
1315a	5¢ Marines, Tagged	16.50	2.00	.35	.30
1316	5¢ Fed. of Women's Clubs	7.00	.65	.20	.15
1316a	5¢ Women's Clubs, Tagged	16.50	2.00	.35	.30
1317	5¢ Johnny Appleseed	7.00	.65	.20	.15
1317a	5¢ Appleseed, Tagged	16.50	2.00	.35	..30
1318	5¢ Beautification of America	7.50	.65	.20	.15
1318a	5¢ Beautification, Tagged	16.50	2.00	.50	.30
1319	5¢ Great River Road......................	7.50	.65	.20	.15
1319a	5¢ Great River, Tagged	16.50	2.00	.35	.30
1320	5¢ Savings Bond - Servicemen.........	7.50	.65	.20	.15
1320a	5¢ Savings Bonds, Tagged	16.50	2.00	.35	.30
1321	5¢ Christmas, Madonna and Child by Hemming ....(100)	13.50	.65	.20	.15
1321a	5¢ Christmas, Tagged ....(100)	32.50	1.90	.35	.30
1322	5¢ Mary Cassatt Painting	8.00	.75	.20	.15
1322a	5¢ Cassatt, Tagged	16.50	2.00	.35	.30

1967 Commemoratives

1323   1324   1325

1326   1327   1328

1329   1330   1333   1334

1331   1332   1338/13386

1335   1336   1337

Scott's No.		Mint Sheet	Plate Block	F-VF NH	F-VF Used
1323-37	Set of 15.............................	...	...	3.95	1.65
1323	5¢ National Grange..................	8.00	.75	.20	.15
1324	5¢ Canada Centenary......................	7.00	.65	.20	.15
1325	5¢ Erie Canal...........................	7.00	.65	.20	.15
1326	5¢ Search for Peace - Lions	7.50	.80	.20	.15
1327	5¢ Henry David Thoreau....................	7.50	.65	.20	.15
1328	5¢ Nebraska Statehood....................	7.50	.65	.20	.15
1329	5¢ Voice of America......................	7.00	.65	.20	.15
1330	5¢ Davy Crockett.........................	7.50	.75	.20	.15
1331-2	5¢ Space Twins, Attached	44.75	4.50	1.95	1.50
1331-2	Set of 2 Singles	...	...	1.10	.35
1333	5¢ Urban Planning	7.00	.65	.20	.15
1334	5¢ Finnish Independence	7.00	.65	.20	.15
1335	5¢ Thomas Eakins Painting...............	7.00	.65	.20	.15
1336	5¢ Christmas, Madonna	7.00	.65	.20	.15
1337	5¢ Mississippi Statehood	7.75	.75	.20	.15

1968-71 Regular Issues

1338	6¢ Flag & White House ....(100)	16.50	.75	.20	.15
1338D	6¢ Same, Huck Press ('70)............(100)	17.00	(20)3.50	.20	.15
1338F	8¢ Flag & White House ('71) ....(100)	21.50	(20) 4.50	.24	.15
1338A	6¢ Flag & W.H.-Huck Coil ('69).......Full Line Pr.	2.50		.20	.15
1338A	6¢ Flag & W.H.-Huck Coil ('69).......Partial Line Pr.	1.00		...	...
1338G	8¢ Flag & W.H.-Huck Coil ('71).......Partial Line Pr.	2.10		.24	.15

NOTE: #1338 is 19mm x 22mm, #1338D is 18¼mm x 21 mm.

NOTE: FROM #752 TO DATE, AVERAGE QUALITY STAMPS, WHEN AVAILABLE, WILL BE PRICED AT APPROX. 20% BELOW THE APPROPRIATE FINE QUALITY PRICE. VERY FINE COPIES OF #752-DATE ARE AVAILABLE FOR THE FOLLOWING PREMIUMS: ADD 10¢ TO ANY ITEM PRICED UNDER 50¢. ADD 20% TO ANY ITEM PRICED AT 50¢ & UP. UNLESS PRICED AT VERY FINE, SETS ARE NOT AVAILABLE VERY FINE STAMPS SHOULD BE LISTED INDIVIDUALLY WITH APPROPRIATE PREMIUM.

1968 Commemoratives

1339   1341   1340

Scott's No.		Mint Sheet	Plate Block	F-VF NH	F-VF Used
1339-40,42-64	Set of 25.............................	...	...	6.65	4.50
1339	6¢ Illinois Statehood	7.75	.70	.20	.15
1340	6¢ Hemis Fair '68, San Antonio.........	7.75	.70	.20	.15

1968 Airlift to Servicemen

1341	$1 Eagle Holding Pennant	150.00	12.75	3.00	1.95

1968 Commemoratives (cont.)

1342   1343   1344

1345   1346   1347

1348   1349   1350

1351   1352   1353

1354   1355   1356

1342	6¢ Support Our Youth - Elks.............	7.75	.70	.20	.15
1343	6¢ Law and Order	14.75	1.60	.32	.15
1344	6¢ Register and Vote	7.75	.70	.20	.15

1968 Historic American Flags

1345-54	Hist. Flag, Strip/10	17.95	(20)7.95	3.75	3.50
1345-46	Plate Blk. of 4	...	1.40		
1345-54	Set of 10 Singles	...	...	3.00	2.75
1345	6¢ Fort Moultrie..........................	...	...	.40	.30
1346	6¢ Fort McHenry..........................	...	...	.40	.30
1347	6¢ Washington Cruisers	...	...	.35	.30
1348	6¢ Bennington..............................	...	...	.35	.30

Scott's No.		Mint Sheet	Plate Block	F-VF NH	F-VF Used
1349	6¢ Rhode Island	...	...	.35	.30
1350	6¢ First Stars & Stripes	...	...	.35	.30
1351	6¢ Bunker Hill........................	...	...	.35	.30
1352	6¢ Grand Union	...	...	.35	.30
1353	6¢ Philadelphia Light Horse	...	...	.35	.30
1354	6¢ First Navy Jack........................	...	...	.35	.30

1968 Commemoratives (continued)

1355	6¢ Walt Disney	22.50	2.10	.50	.15
1356	6¢ Father Marquette	7.75	.70	.20	.15

1357   1358   1359

1360   1361   1362

1363   1364

1357	6¢ Daniel Boone.........................	7.75	.70	.20	.15
1358	6¢ Arkansas River Navigation	7.75	.70	.20	.15
1359	6¢ Leif Erikson.............................	7.75	.70	.20	.15
1360	6¢ Cherokee Strip	9.00	.95	.20	.15
1361	6¢ John Trumbull Painting.............	9.50	.90	.20	.15
1362	6¢ Waterfowl Conservation..............	11.75	1.10	.25	.15
1363	6¢ Christmas, Angel Gabriel............	8.75 (10)	1.75	.20	.15
1363a	6¢ Christmas, Untagged................	21.50 (10)	4.50	.45	.25
1364	6¢ American Indian - Joseph	11.75	1.10	.25	.15

1969 Commemoratives

1365   1366
1367   1368

1369   1370   1371   1373

1372   1374   1375

1376   1377
1378   1379

1381   1380   1382

1383   1385   1386

1384   1384 Precancel

Scott's No.		Mint Sheet	Plate Block	F-VF NH	F-VF Used
1365-86	**Set of 22 (no precancels)**................	...	...	**7.85**	**2.95**
1365-8	6¢ Beautification, attached................	22.75	2.40	2.10	1.95
1365-8	Set of 4 Singles........................	...	...	1.65	.65
1369	6¢ American Legion	7.25	.70	.20	.15
1370	6¢ Grandma Moses Painting.............	7.50	.70	.20	.15
1371	6¢ Apollo 8 Mission	12.75	1.20	.27	.15
1372	6¢ W.C. Handy	8.25	.80	.20	.15
1373	6¢ California Settlement	7.50	.70	.20	.15
1374	6¢ John Wesley Powell......................	7.50	.70	.20	.15
1375	6¢ Alabama Statehood......................	7.50	.70	.20	.15
1376-9	6¢ Botanical Congress, att'd..............	28.75	2.95	2.65	2.50
1376-9	Set of Singles............................	...	...	2.20	.80
1380	6¢ Dartmouth College......................	7.50	.70	.20	.15
1381	6¢ Professional Baseball...................	55.00	4.95	1.20	.20
1382	6¢ College Football	16.50	1.40	.35	.15
1383	6¢ D.D. Eisenhower Memorial ......(32)	5.25	.75	.20	.15
1384	6¢ Christmas, Winter Sunday	8.25 (10)	1.75	.20	.15
1384a	6¢ Precancelled (Set of 4 Cities).......	200.00 (10)	110.00	2.65	2.00
1385	6¢ Crippled Children	7.50	.70	.20	.15
1386	6¢ William M. Harnett Painting ......(32)	5.25	.70	.20	.15

NOTE: #1384A EXISTS WITH "ATLANTA, GA", "BALTIMORE, MD", MEMPHIS, TN"
AND "NEW HAVEN, CT" PRECANCELS.

NOTE: UNUSED YEAR SETS HAVE SE-TENANTS ATTACHED, USED SETS HAVE SINGLES.

NOTE: PRICES THROUGHOUT THIS LIST ARE SUBJECT TO CHANGE WITHOUT NOTICE IF
MARKET CONDITIONS REQUIRE. MINIMUM MAIL ORDER MUST TOTAL AT LEAST $20.00.

1970 Commemoratives

1387 1389
1388 1390

1391 1392

Scott's No.		Mint Sheet	Plate Block	F-VF NH	F-VF Used
1387-92,1405-22	Set of 24 (no prec.)...........	...	...	6.75	2.80
1387-90	6¢ Natural History, attached......... (32)	7.25	1.00	.90	.90
1387-90	Set of 4 Singles	...	...	.85	.60
1391	6¢ Maine Statehood	8.25	.75	.20	.15
1392	6¢ Wildlife Conserv. - Buffalo	8.25	.75	.20	.15

1970-74 Regular Issue

1393,1401   1393D   1394/1402   1396

Ernie Pyle Journalist

1397   1398   1399   1400

1393-94,1396-1400	Set of 8	...	...	2.75	.95
1393	6¢ Eisenhower .... (100)	15.00	.75	.20	.15
1393v	6¢ Dull Gum .... (100)	39.50	4.00	.40	...
1393a	6¢ Booklet Pane of 8	...	...	1.75	1.50
1393ae	6¢ Pane of 8, Dull Exper. Gum.........	...	...	1.40	...
1393b	6¢ Bklt. Pane of 5, (S4 or S5) ('71)	...	1.50	1.25	1.20
1393D	7¢ Benjamin Franklin ('72)........... (100)	18.50	.85	.20	.15
1393Dv	7¢ Dull Gum .... (100)	39.50	2.75	.40	...
1394	8¢ Ike, Multicolored ('71)............ (100)	21.50	.90	.24	.15
1395	8¢ Ike, Deep Claret, Bklt. Single......	...	...	.25	.15
1395v	8¢ Booklet Single, Dull Gum	...	...	.25	...
1395a	Booklet Pane of 8 (1971)	...	...	2.15	2.10
1395b	Booklet Pane of 6 (1971)	...	...	1.70	1.65
1395c	Booklet Pane of 4 Dull('72)	...	...	1.60	1.50
1395d	Booklet Pane of 7, Dull (S4) (1972) .	...	...	3.25	2.75
1395d	Booklet Pane of 7, Dull (S5) (1972) .	...	...	1.85	1.75
S4 is "Mail Early", S5 is "Use Zip Code"					
1396	8¢ U.S. Postal Service ('71).......... (100)	21.50 (12)	3.00	.24	.15
1396	8¢ U.S. Postal Service....................	...	(20) 4.75	...	...
1397	14¢ Fiorello La Guardia ('72) .... (100)	35.00	1.60	.40	.15
1398	16¢ Ernie Pyle ('71).................... (100)	42.50	1.85	.45	.15
1399	18¢ Dr. Eliz. Blackwell ('74) .... (100)	52.50	2.25	.55	.15
1400	21¢ Amadeo P. Giannini ('73) .... (100)	57.50	2.50	.60	.25

1970-71 Dwight D. Eisenhower, Coils, Perf. 10 Vert

Scott's No.		Line Pair	F-VF NH	F-VF Used
1401	6¢ Gray.....................................	.50	.20	.15
1401a	6¢ Bureau Precancel	150.00	9.50	1.25
1401d	6¢ Dull Gum	2.25	.40	...
1402	8¢ Deep Claret ('71)	.60	.25	.15
1402b	8¢ Bureau Precancel	110.00	6.50	1.25

NOTE: #1395 ONLY EXISTS WITH ONE OR MORE STRAIGHT EDGES SINCE IT COMES FROM BOOKLET PANES.

1970 Commemoratives (continued)

1405   1406   1407

1408   1409   1419

1410   1411
1412   1413

1414   1414a   1420

1415   1416   1421   1422
1417   1418

Scott's No.		Mint Sheet	Plate Block	F-VF NH	F-VF Used
1405	6¢ Edgar Lee Masters - Poet	8.25	.75	.20	.15
1406	6¢ Women Suffrage......................	8.25	.75	.20	.15
1407	6¢ South Carolina Founding	8.25	.75	.20	.15
1408	6¢ Stone Mountain Memorial	12.00	1.10	.25	.15
1409	6¢ Fort Snelling, Minnesota............	8.25	.75	.20	.15
1410-13	6¢ Anti-Pollution, Attached	14.50 (10)	3.50	1.35	1.35
1410-13	Set of 4 Singles	...	...	1.20	.65
1414	6¢ Christmas, Nativity, Ty. I	8.25 (8)	1.50	.20	.15
1414a	6¢ Christmas, Nativity, Precncl	9.50 (8)	2.50	.20	.15
1414d	6¢ Type II, Horiz. Gum Breakers	45.00 (8)	10.75	.95	.30
1414e	6¢ Type II, Precancelled	52.50 (8)	12.50	1.10	.35
Type I - blurry impression, snowflakes in sky, no gum breakers					
Type II – sharper impression, no snowflakes in sky, with gum breakers					
1415-18	6¢ Christmas Toys, attd..................	25.00 (8)	5.00	2.35	2.25
1415-18	Set of 4 Singles	...	...	1.75	.60
1415a-18a	6¢ Toys, Precan., attached	37.50 (8)	7.50	3.50	3.50
1415a-18a	Set of 4 Singles	...	...	2.75	1.00
1419	6¢ United Nations 25th Anniv	8.25	.75	.20	.15
1420	6¢ Landing of the Pilgrims	8.25	.75	.20	.15
1421-22	6¢ DAV - Servicemen, attd	8.25	1.30	.42	.40
1421-22	Set of 2 Singles	...	...	.40	.30

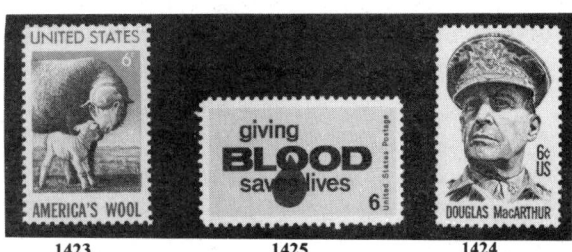

1423   1425   1424

1427   1428
1429   1430

1426   1432   1431

1433   1434   1435

1436   1437   1438   1439

1440   1441
1442   1443

1444   1445   1446   1447

Scott's No.		Mint Sheet	Plate Block	F-VF NH	F-VF Used
1423-45	**Set of 23**	...	...	**5.50**	**2.85**
1423	6¢ American Wool Industry	8.25	.75	.20	.15
1424	6¢ Gen. Douglas MacArthur	8.25	.75	.20	.15
1425	6¢ Blood Donor	8.25	.75	.20	.15
1426	8¢ Missouri Sesquicentennial	10.75 (12)	2.75	.24	.15
1427-30	8¢ Wildlife, attached (32)	8.75	1.20	1.10	1.00
1427-30	Set of 4 Singles	...	...	1.00	.70
1431	8¢ Antarctic Treaty	10.75	1.00	.24	.15
1432	8¢ Bicentennial Emblem	11.00	1.10	.24	.15
1433	8¢ John Sloan Painting	10.75	1.00	.24	.15
1434-5	8¢ Space Achievement, attd	12.75	1.15	.55	.50
1434-5	Set of 2 Singles	...	...	.50	.30
1436	8¢ Emily Dickinson	10.75	1.00	.24	.15
1437	8¢ San Juan, Puerto Rico	10.75	1.00	.24	.15
1438	8¢ Prevent Drug Abuse	10.75 (6)	1.50	.24	.15
1439	8¢ CARE	10.75 (8)	1.95	.24	.15
1440-3	8¢ Historic Preservation, attd (32)	8.75	1.20	1.10	.95
1440-3	Set of 4 Singles	...	...	1.00	.70
1444	8¢ Christmas, Adoration	10.75 (12)	2.75	.24	.15
1445	8¢ Christmas, Partridge	10.75 (12)	2.75	.24	.15

1972 Commemoratives

1448   1449   1454
1450   1451   1452   1453

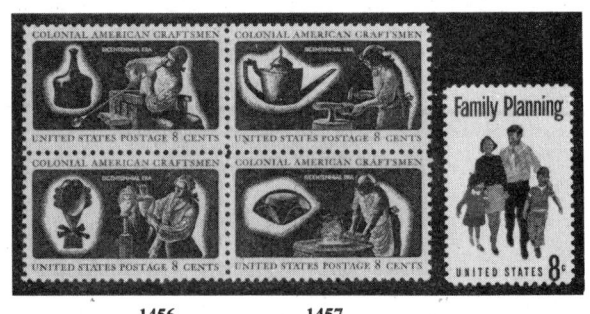

1456   1457
1458   1459   1455

		Mint Sheet	Plate Block	F-VF NH	F-VF Used
1446-74	**Set of 29**	...	...	**6.75**	**3.75**
1446	8¢ Sidney Lanier	10.75	1.00	.24	.15
1447	8¢ Peace Corps	11.75 (6)	1.60	.25	.15
1448-54,C84	Parks Set of 8	57.50	5.35	1.40	1.10
1448-51	2¢ Cape Hatteras, attached (100)	6.75	.60	.45	.45
1448-51	Set of 4 Singles	...	...	.44	.44
1452	6¢ Wolf Trap Farm	8.25	.75	.20	.15
1453	8¢ Old Faithful (32)	7.50	1.00	.24	.15
1454	15¢ Mt. McKinley	20.00	1.75	.45	.25
	See #C84 for 11¢ City of Refuge National Park Issue				
1455	8¢ Family Planning	10.75	1.10	.24	.15
1456-9	8¢ Colonial Craftsmen, attd	11.50	1.10	1.00	.85
1456-9	Set of 4 Singles	...	...	.90	.60

1460

1461

1462

1463　　**1464**
　　　　　　1466
　　　　　　1465
　　　　　　1467

1469　　**1468**　　**1470**

1471　　**1472**　　**1473**　　**1474**

Scott's No.		Mint Sheet	Plate Block	F-VF NH	F-VF Used
1460-62,C85	Olympics Set of 4	52.50	11.75	1.25	.70
1460	6¢ Olympics - Bicycling	8.50 (10)	1.85	.20	.15
1461	8¢ Olympics - Bobsledding	10.75 (10)	2.50	.24	.15
1462	15¢ Olympics - Running	21.00 (10)	4.50	.45	.35
	See #C85 for 11¢ Olympics				
1463	8¢ Parent Teacher Assn	10.75	1.00	.24	.15
1463r	8¢ P.T.A. Error Plate # Reversed	11.00	1.10	...	...
1464-7	8¢ Wildlife Conserv., attd (32)	7.50	1.10	1.00	.90
1464-7	Set of 4 Singles	...	...	.90	.70
1468	8¢ Mail Order Business	10.75 (12)	2.80	.24	.15
1469	8¢ Osteopathic Medicine	10.75 (6)	1.60	.25	.15
1470	8¢ Tom Sawyer	10.75	1.10	.25	.15
1471	8¢ Christmas Angel	10.75 (12)	2.80	.24	.15
1472	8¢ Christmas, Santa Claus	10.75 (12)	2.80	.24	.15
1473	8¢ Pharmacy	18.75	1.75	.38	.24
1474	8¢ Stamp Collecting (40)	8.50	1.00	.24	.15

1973 Commemoratives

1475

1476

1477

1475-1508	Set of 34	...	...	8.25	4.25
1475	8¢ Love	10.75 (6)	1.50	.24	.15
1476-79	Communications in Colonial America(4)	39.75	3.85	.95	.50
1476	8¢ Printers and Patriots	10.75	1.00	.24	.15
1477	8¢ Posting a Broadside	10.75	1.00	.24	.15

1478　　**1479**　　**1488**

1480　**1481**　　**1484**
1482　**1483**

1485　　**1486**　　**1487**

1489　**1490**　**1491**　**1492**　**1493**

1494　**1495**　**1496**　**1497**　**1498**

Scott's No.		Mint Sheet	Plate Block	F-VF NH	F-VF Used
1478	8¢ Postrider	10.75	1.00	.24	.15
1479	8¢ Drummer	10.75	1.00	.24	.15
1480-83	8¢ Boston Tea Party, attd	12.00	1.15	1.00	.90
1480-83	Set of 4 Singles	...	...	.90	.60
1484-87	Arts Set of 4	32.75	11.95	.95	.50
1484	8¢ Arts - George Gershwin (40)	9.00 (12)	3.25	.25	.15
1485	8¢ Arts - Robinson Jeffers (40)	9.00 (12)	3.25	.25	.15
1486	8¢ Arts - Henry Tanner (40)	8.50 (12)	3.00	.24	.15
1487	8¢ Arts - Willa Cather (40)	8.50 (12)	3.00	.24	.15
1488	8¢ Nicolaus Copernicus	11.50	1.10	.25	.15

1973 Postal Service Employees

1489-98	8¢ Postal Employees, strip, attd	13.00 (20)	5.50	2.50	2.50
1489-98	8¢ Set of 10 Singles	...	...	2.40	1.80

VERY FINE COPIES OF #752-DATE ARE AVAILABLE FOR THE FOLLOWING PREMIUMS:
ADD 10¢ TO ANY ITEM PRICED UNDER 50¢. ADD 20% TO ANY ITEM PRICED AT 50¢ & UP.

1500 1499 1501

1502 1503 1504

1505 1506 1507 1508

Scott's No.		Mint Sheet	Plate Block	F-VF NH	F-VF Used
1499	8¢ Harry S Truman ....(32)	7.25	1.00	.25	.15
1500-2,C86	Electronics Set of 4	52.50	4.95	1.15	.70
1500	6¢ Electronics - Marconi.....................	8.25	.85	.20	.15
1501	8¢ Electronics - Transistors	10.75	1.00	.24	.15
1502	15¢ Electronics - Inventions...............	21.75	1.85	.45	.35
See #C86 for 11¢ Electronics					
1503	8¢ Lyndon B. Johnson ....(32)	7.75 (12)	3.25	.25	.15
1504	8¢ Rural America - Cattle	10.75	1.00	.24	.15
1505	10¢ Rural America - Tent ('74)	13.50	1.30	.30	.15
1506	10¢ Rural America - Wheat ('74)	13.50	1.30	.30	.15
1507	8¢ Christmas, Madonna	10.75 (12)	3.00	.24	.15
1508	8¢ Christmas, Needlepoint.................	10.75 (12)	3.00	.24	.15

1509,1519 1510,1520 1511 1518

1973-1974 Regular Issues

1509	10¢ Crossed Flags ....(100)	28.50 (20)	6.50	.30	.15
1510	10¢ Jefferson Memorial ....(100)	28.50	1.35	.30	.15
1510b	Booklet Pane of 5	...	...	1.75	1.65
1510c	Booklet Pane of 8	...	...	2.25	2.00
1510d	Booklet Pane of 6 (1974)...................	...	...	6.50	5.00
1511	10¢ Zip Code (1974) ....(100)	28.00 (8)	2.50	.30	.15

1973-74 Regular Issue Coils, Perf. 10 Vert.

Scott's No.		Line Pair	F-VF NH	F-VF Used
1518	6.3¢ Liberty Bell Coil ('74)	.60	.20	.15
1518a	6.3¢ Bureau Precancel	1.50	.30	.20
1519	10¢ Crossed Flags Coil .... Full 5.75	Part 1.75	.35	.15
1520	10¢ Jeff. Memorial Coil	.70	.30	.15
1520a	10¢ Bureau Precancel	110.00	5.50	1.00

1525 1526 1527

1528 1529

1530 1531 1532 1533
1534 1535 1536 1537

1538 1540 1542
1539 1541

Scott's No.		Mint Sheet	Plate Block	F-VF NH	F-VF Used
1525-52	**Set of 28**..	...	...	**8.50**	**3.95**
1525	10¢ Veterans of Foreign Wars	13.50	1.30	.30	.15
1526	10¢ Robert Frost.................................	13.50	1.30	.30	.15
1527	10¢ Expo '74, Spokane ....(40)	11.00 (12)	3.75	.30	.15
1528	10¢ Horse Racing	13.50 (12)	3.75	.30	.15
1529	10¢ Skylab I	13.50	1.30	.30	.15
1530-37	10¢ U.P.U. Centenary blk, attd ....(32)	11.50 (10)	3.50	2.75	2.50
1530-37	Strip of 8	...	...	2.75	2.50
1530-37	Plate Block of 16	...	(16)	5.95	
1530-37	Set of 8 Singles	...	...	2.65	2.00
1538-41	10¢ Mineral Heritage blk, attd..........(48)	14.00	1.30	1.20	1.00
1538-41	Strip of 4	...	...	1.20	1.00
1538-41	Set of 4 Singles	...	...	1.10	.60
1542	10¢ Kentucky Settlement	13.50	1.30	.30	.15

1974 Commemoratives (cont.)

1543
1545

1544
1546

1547   1548   1549

1551   1550   1552

Scott's No.		Mint Sheet	Plate Block	F-VF NH	F-VF Used
1543-46	10¢ First Continental Congress, attd	15.00	1.40	1.30	1.10
1543-46	Set of 4 Singles	...	...	1.20	.60
1547	10¢ Energy Conservation	13.50	1.30	.30	.15
1548	10¢ Sleepy Hollow	13.50	1.30	.30	.15
1549	10¢ Retarded Children	13.50	1.30	.30	.15
1550	10¢ Christmas, Angel	13.50 (10)	3.25	.30	.15
1551	10¢ Christmas, Currier & Ives	13.50 (12)	3.75	.30	.15
1552	10¢ Christmas, Peace on Earth, Self-adhesive	16.00 (20)	7.25	.35	.25
1552	10¢ Same - Plate Block of 12	... (12)	4.50	...	...

NOTE: MOST COPIES OF #1552 ARE DISCOLORED FROM THE ADHESIVE. PRICE IS FOR DISCOLORED COPIES.

1975 Commemoratives

1553   1555   1554

1556   1557   1558

1553-80	Set of 28	...	...	7.95	3.75
1553-55	American Arts Issue				
1553	10¢ Benjamin West Portrait	13.50 (10)	3.25	.30	.15
1554	10¢ Paul Laurence Dunbar - Poet	13.50 (10)	3.25	.30	.15
1555	10¢ D.W. Griffith	14.00	1.30	.30	.15
1556	10¢ Space Pioneer - Jupiter	14.00	1.30	.30	.15
1557	10¢ Space Mariner 10	14.00	1.30	.30	.15
1558	10¢ Collective Bargaining	13.50 (8)	2.50	.30	.15

1975 Commemoratives (cont.)

1559   1560   1561

1562   1563   1564

1565   1566   1569
1567   1568   1570

Scott's No.		Mint Sheet	Plate Block	F-VF NH	F-VF Used
1559-62	Contributors to the Cause (4)	59.75	14.50	1.30	.75
1559	8¢ Sybil Ludington	10.75 (10)	2.50	.24	.20
1560	10¢ Salem Poor	13.50 (10)	3.25	.30	.15
1561	10¢ Haym Salomon	13.50 (10)	3.25	.30	.15
1562	18¢ Peter Francisco	25.00 (10)	6.25	.55	.35
1563	10¢ Lexington-Concord	11.00 (40)	3.75	.30	.15
1564	10¢ Battle of Bunker Hill	11.00 (40)	3.75	.30	.15
1565-68	10¢ Military Uniforms, attd	14.50 (12)	4.25	1.30	1.10
1565-68	Set of 4 Singles	...	...	1.20	.60
1569-70	10¢ Apollo Soyuz, attd	7.25 (24) (12)	4.00	.65	.50
1569-70	Set of 2 Singles	...	...	.60	.30

1571   1572   1573
               1574   1575

1571	10¢ Int'l. Women's Year	13.50 (6)	1.90	.30	.15
1572-75	10¢ Postal Service Bicent., attd	14.50 (12)	4.25	1.30	1.10
1572-75	Set of 4 Singles	...	...	1.20	.60

NOTE: UNUSED YEAR SETS HAVE SE-TENANTS ATTACHED, USED YEAR SETS HAVE SINGLES.

1975 Commemoratives (cont.)

| 1576 | 1577 | 1578 |

| 1579 | 1580 |

Scott's No.		Mint Sheet	Plate Block	F-VF NH	F-VF Used
1576	10¢ World Peace through Law	14.50	1.30	.30	.15
1577-78	10¢ Banking Commerce, attd. ....(40)	12.00	1.50	.65	.50
1577-78	Set of 2 Singles	...	...	.60	.30
1579	10¢ Christmas, Madonna and				
	Child by Ghirlandaio	13.50 (12)	3.75	.30	.15
1580	10¢ Christmas Card, Perf. 11.2	17.50 (12)	5.00	.40	.20
1580v	10¢ Christmas, Perf. 10.9	13.50 (12)	3.75	.30	.15
1580b	10¢ Christmas (P. 10½ x 11)	45.00 (12)	14.50	.85	.75

1975-1981 Americana Issue (Perf. 11 x 10½)

| 1581,1811 | 1582 | 1584 | 1585 |

| 1590/1616 | 1592,1617 | 1593 | 1594,1816 |

| 1595,1618 | 1596 | 1597/1618C | 1599,1619 |

| 1603 | 1604 | 1605 | 1606 |

| 1608 | 1610 | 1611 | 1612 |

1581-85,91-94,96-97,99-1612 Set of 19		...	130.00	27.50	5.50
1581	1¢ Ability to Write (1977)	5.00	.50	.20	.15
1581v	1¢ Dry Gum	7.00	1.25	.20	...
1582	2¢ Freedom/Speak Out ('77)	6.75	.50	.20	.15
1582v	2¢ Dry Gum, white paper	29.50	2.50	.30	...
1582b	2¢ Dry Gum, cream paper (1981)	18.50	2.75	.25	.20
1584	3¢ Cast a Free Ballot ('77)	11.00	.50	.20	.15
1584v	3¢ Dry Gum	19.50	1.30	.25	...
1585	4¢ Public That Reads ('77)	12.50	.60	.20	.15
1585v	4¢ Dry Gum	23.75	1.50	.25	...

1975-1981 Americana Issue (continued)
(Sheets of 100)

Scott's No.		Mint Sheet	Plate Block	F-VF NH	F-VF Used
1590	9¢ Assem., Bklt.Sngl Pf.11x10½ ('77)	...	...	.50	.45
1590 & 1623 attached Pair (from 1623a)		...	...	.80	.95
1590a	9¢ Booklet Single, Perf. 10	...	...	25.00	22.50
1590a & 1623b attd. Pair (from 1623c)		...	...	27.00	...
1591	9¢ Assemble, Large Size	25.00	1.25	.27	.15
1591v	9¢ Dry Gum	97.50	8.95	1.00	...
1592	10¢ Right to Petition ('77)	28.50	1.40	.30	.15
1592v	10¢ Dry Gum	67.50	3.75	.70	...
1593	11¢ Freedom of Press	29.00	1.35	.30	.15
1594	12¢ Freedom of Conscience ('81)	33.50	1.85	.35	.15
1595	13¢ Liberty Bell, Bklt. Single...........	...	...	.40	.15
1595a	13¢ Booklet Pane of 6	...	...	2.35	2.00
1595b	13¢ Booklet Pane of 7	...	...	2.50	2.25
1595c	13¢ Booklet Pane of 8	...	...	2.75	2.65
1595d	13¢ Booklet Pane of 5 (1976)	...	...	2.10	2.00
1596	13¢ Eagle & Shield, Bullseye Perfs.38.50 (12)		5.00	.40	.15
1596v	13¢ Line Perfs *	...(12)	595.00	40.00	...
1597	15¢ McHenry Flag, Pf. 11 ('78)..........	42.50 (20)	9.50	.45	.15
1598	15¢ McHenry Flag, Bklt. Sgl. ('78)	...	...	.60	.15
1598a	15¢ Booklet Pane of 8	...	...	4.75	2.75
1599	16¢ Statue of Liberty (1978)	47.50	2.25	.50	.20
1603	24¢ Old North Church	65.00	3.25	.70	.20
1604	28¢ Fort Nisqually (1978)	75.00	3.75	.80	.20
1604v	28¢ Dry Gum	160.00	13.50	1.70	...
1605	29¢ Lighthouse (1978)	75.00	3.75	.80	.65
1605v	29¢ Dry Gum	190.00	17.50	2.00	...
1606	30¢ Schoolhouse (1979)	80.00	3.75	.85	.15
1608	50¢ Iron "Betty" (1979)	130.00	6.00	1.40	.25
1610	$1 Rush Lamp (1979)	275.00	12.00	2.75	.25
1611	$2 Kerosene Table Lamp ('78)	535.00	23.00	5.50	.75
1612	$5 Railroad Lantern (1979)	1300.00	60.00	13.75	2.50

* #1596 Bullseye Perforations line up perfectly where horiz. and vertical rows
meet. Pf 11.2 #1596d Line Perfs. do not meet evenly. Perforated 11:
Note: #1608-1612 are Perforated 11.

1975-79 Americana Coil Issues - Perf. 10 Vert.

| 1613 | 1614 | 1615 | 1615C |

Scott's No.		Line Pair	F-VF NH	F-VF Used
1613-19,1811-16 Americana Coils (12) ....(11)		10.95	3.25	1.95
1613	3.1¢ Guitar (1979)	.70	.20	.18
1613a	3.1¢ Bureau Precancel, Lines Only	5.50	.30	.25
1614	7.7¢ Saxhorns (1976)	1.10	.25	.25
1614a	7.7¢ Bureau Precancel	3.75	.70	.45
1615	7.9¢ Drum Shiny Gum (1976)	.75	.25	.20
1615a	7.9¢ Bureau Precancel Shiny Gum	3.25	.35	.25
1615v	7.9¢ Dry Gum	3.50	.40	...
1615va	7.9¢ Bureau Precancel, Dry Gum	4.75	.50	...
1615C	8.4¢ Steinway Grand Piano Shiny Gum (1978) ..	2.25	.28	.20
1615Cd	8.4¢ Bureau Precancel, Shiny Gum ...	6.75	.55	.30
1615Cdv	8.4¢ Precancel, Dry Gum	3.75	.50	...
1616	9¢ Right to Assemble (1976)	.70	.28	.20
1616b	9¢ Bureau Precancel, Shiny Gum ...	7.95	1.50	.50
1616bv	9¢ Bureau Precancel, Dry Gum	2.50	.60	...
1617	10¢ Right to Petition, Shiny Gum (1977)	.95	.30	.15
1617a	10¢ Bureau Precancel, Dry Gum	37.50	1.75	.25
1617v	10¢ Dry Gum	1.50	.33	...
1618	13¢ Liberty Bell, Shiny Gum	.95	.35	.15
1618a	13¢ Bureau Precancel	79.50	9.50	1.00
1618v	13¢ Dry Gum	1.50	.55	...
1618va	13¢ Bureau Precancel, Dry Gum	19.50	1.40	...
1618C	15¢ Fort McHenry Flag (1978)	...	.45	.15
1619	16¢ Statue of Liberty Overall Tagging (1978)	1.40	.50	.35
1619a	16¢ Block Tagging (No Lines)..........	...	.90	.75

Note: Also see #1811-1816 for 1980-81 issues.

1975-77 Regular Issue

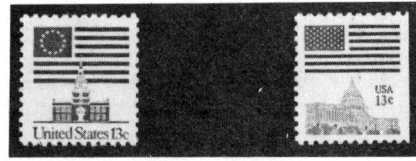

| 1622,1625 | 1623 |

1975-77 Regular Issues

Scott's No.		Mint Sheet	Plate Block	F-VF NH	F-VF Used
1622	13¢ Flag/Ind. Hall, Pf. 11x10½ ....(100)	35.00 (20)	8.25	.38	.15
1622c	13¢ Perf. 11 (1981) ....(100)	175.00 (20)	90.00	1.10	.95
* Plate Blocks of #1622 have Pl. #'s at Top or Bottom.					
* Plate Blocks of #1622c have Pl. #'s at Left or Right.					
1623	13¢ Flag over Capitol, Bklt. Sgl.				
	Pf. 11 x 10½ (1977)	...	...	.38	.20
1623a	13¢ & 9¢ Bklt. Pn./8 (7#1623,1#1590)	...	...	2.75	2.75
1623b	13¢ B. Sgl., Pf. 10 (1977)	...	...	.60	.55
1623c	13¢ & 9¢ B.P./8 (7#1623b,1#1590a)	...	28.75	18.50	...
1625	13¢ Flag over Ind. Hall, Coil.............(Partial Line)	3.75	.40	.15

1976 Commemoratives

| | 1629 | 1630 | 1631 | | 1632 | | |

Scott's No.		Mint Sheet	Plate Block	F-VF NH	F-VF Used
1629-32,83-85,90-1703 Set of 21		...	...	8.95	2.95
1629-31	13¢ Spirit of '76, attd	18.50 (12)	5.00	1.20	.90
1629-31	Set of 3 Singles	...	...	1.10	.50
1632	13¢ Interphil '76, Philadelphia.............	17.50	1.60	.38	.15

| | 1633 | | 1635 | | 1654 | |

1976 State Flags Issue

		Mint Sheet	Plate Block	F-VF NH	F-VF Used
1633-82	13¢ State Flags attd	19.50 (12)	4.75	...	...
1633-82	Set of 50 Singles	...	...	19.50	14.50
1633-82	13¢ Individual Singles.......................	...	...	.55	.35

1633	DE	1646	VT	1659	FL	1671	ND
1634	PA	1647	KY	1660	TX	1672	SD
1635	NJ	1648	TN	1661	IA	1673	MT
1636	GA	1649	OH	1662	WI	1674	WA
1637	CT	1650	LA	1663	CA	1675	ID
1638	MA	1651	IN	1664	MN	1676	WY
1639	MD	1652	MS	1665	OR	1677	UT
1640	SC	1653	IL	1666	KS	1678	OK
1641	NH	1654	AL	1667	WV	1679	NM
1642	VA	1655	ME	1668	NV	1680	AZ
1643	NY	1656	MO	1669	NE	1681	AK
1644	NC	1657	AR	1670	CO	1682	HI
1645	RI	1658	MI				

1976 Commemoratives (continued)

| | 1683 | | 1684 | | 1685 | |

1686-89 Example

1976 Commemoratives (continued)

Scott's No.		Mint Sheet	Plate Block	F-VF NH	F-VF Used
1683	13¢ Telephone Centennial..................	17.50	1.60	.38	.15
1684	13¢ Commercial Aviation	17.50 (10)	4.35	.38	.15
1685	13¢ Chemistry	17.50 (12)	4.70	.38	.15

1976 American Bicentennial Souvenir Sheets

		Mint Sheet	Plate Block	F-VF NH	F-VF Used
1686-89	Set of Four Souvenir Sheets..............	...	...	26.50	25.00
1686a-89e	Set of 20 Singles..............................	...	...	25.75	23.75
1686	13¢ Surrender of Cornwallis	...	...	4.25	4.00
1686a-e	Any Single..	...	...	.95	.90
1687	18¢ Decl. of Independence..................	...	...	6.00	5.75
1687a-e	Any Single..	...	...	1.35	1.30
1688	24¢ Washington Crossing Delaware ...	...	...	8.25	8.00
1688a-e	Any Single..	...	...	1.80	1.70
1689	31¢ Washington at Valley Forge	...	...	10.75	10.50
1689a-e	Any Single..	...	...	2.25	2.15

1976 Commemoratives (continued)

| | 1691 | 1692 | 1693 | 1694 | |

| | 1699 | | 1690 | | 1700 | |

| | 1697 | 1698 | |
| | 1695 | 1696 | |

1701

1702

1690	13¢ Ben Franklin and Map..................	17.50	1.60	.38	.15
1691-94	13¢ Dec. of Independence, attd...........	24.50 (16)	11.00	2.50	1.25
1691-94	Set of 4 Singles	...	...	2.40	.70
1695-98	13¢ Winter Olym. Games, attd............	22.50 (12)	6.50	1.90	1.80
1695-98	Set of 4 Singles	...	...	1.80	.70
1699	13¢ Clara Mass.........................(40)	15.75 (12)	5.35	.38	.15
1700	13¢ Adolph S. Ochs...................(32)	11.00	1.60	.38	.15
1701	13¢ Christmas, Nativity	17.50 (12)	4.75	.38	.15
1702	13¢ Christmas Winter Pastime, Andriotti Press..................................	17.50 (10)	3.95	.38	.15
1703	13¢ Same, Gravure-Intaglio	17.50 (20)	7.75	.38	.15

#1702: Andriotti Press, lettering at Base is Black, No Snowflakes in Sky.
#1703: Intaglio-Gravure, lettering at Base is Gray Black, Snowflakes in Sky.

NOTE: PRICES THROUGHOUT THIS LIST ARE SUBJECT TO CHANGE WITHOUT NOTICE IF MARKET CONDITIONS REQUIRE. MIN. MAIL ORDER MUST TOTAL AT LEAST $20.00.

1704   **1706**   **1707**
              1708   **1709**

1705   **1710**   **1711**

1712   **1713**   **1716**
1714   **1715**

1717   **1718**   **1721**
1719   **1720**

Scott's No.		Mint Sheet	Plate Block	F-VF NH	F-VF Used
1704-1730	**Set of 27**	...	...	**10.00**	**3.35**
1704	13¢ Washington at Princeton .... (40)	14.00 (10)	3.95	.38	.15
1705	13¢ Sound Recording	17.50	1.60	.38	.15
1706-09	13¢ Pueblo Art, block, attd .... (40)	15.75 (10)	4.50	1.65	1.25
1706-09	Strip of 4	...	...	1.65	1.25
1706-09	Set of 4 Singles..............................	...	...	1.50	.70
1710	13¢ Lindbergh's Flight	17.50 (12)	4.75	.38	.15
1711	13¢ Colorado Sthd., Line Perfs	17.50 (12)	4.75	.38	.15
1711c	Bullseye Perfs	57.50 (12)	19.50	1.15	.95
#1711 Perforated 11, #1711c Perf. 11.2					
1712-15	13¢ American Butterflies, attd	18.50 (12)	5.50	1.65	1.25
1712-15	Set of 4 Singles..............................	...	...	1.50	.70
1716	13¢ Lafayette's Landing .... (40)	14.00	1.60	.38	.15
1717-20	13¢ Revolutionary War Civilian Skills, attd	18.50 (12)	5.50	1.65	1.25
1717-20	Set of 4 Singles..............................	...	...	1.50	.70
1721	13¢ Peace Bridge 50th Ann.	17.50		1.60	.38	.15

1725

US Bicentennial 13 cents

1722   **1723**   **1726**
           1724

1727   **1728**   **1729**   **1730**

Scott's No.		Mint Sheet	Plate Block	F-VF NH	F-VF Used
1722	13¢ Herkimer at Oriskany .... (40)	14.00 (10)	3.95	.38	.15
1723-24	13¢ Energy Conservation, attd........ (40)	15.00 (12)	5.00	.80	.60
1723-24	Set of 2 Singles	...	...	.75	.30
1725	13¢ Alta California Settlement.............	17.50	1.60	.38	.15
1726	13¢ Articles of Confederation.............	17.50	1.60	.38	.15
1727	13¢ Talking Pictures..........................	17.50	1.60	.38	.15
1728	13¢ Surrender at Saratoga .... (40)	14.00 (10)	4.00	.38	.15
1729	13¢ Christmas, Washington at Valley Forge............................. (100)	34.50 (20)	8.00	.38	.15
1730	13¢ Christmas - Mailbox .... (100)	33.50 (10)	4.00	.38	.15

1731   **1732**   **1734**   **1735**
           1733

1737   **1738**   **1739**   **1740**   **1741**   **1742**

1978 Commemoratives

1731-33,44-69	**Set of 29**	...	...	**13.95**	**6.00**
1731	13¢ Carl Sandburg, Poet.....................	17.50	1.60	.38	.15
1732-33	Captain Cook, attached	17.50 (20)	8.50	.85	.75
1732	13¢ Captain Cook Portrait..................	...	1.50	.35	.15
1733	13¢ Hawaii Seascape..........................	...	1.50	.35	.15

1978-80 Regular Issues

1734	13¢ Indian Head Penny .... (150)	55.00	1.70	.38	.15
1735	(15¢) "A" & Eagle, Perf. 11 .... (100)	42.50	1.90	.45	.15
1735c	(15¢) Bullseye Perf. 11.2 .... (100)	52.50	2.75	.55	.35
1736	(15¢) "A" & Eagle, Perf. 11x10½ Booklet Single	...	...	.42	.15
1736a	15¢ Booklet Pane of 8	...	...	2.95	2.75
1737	15¢ Roses, Perf. 10, Bklt. Single	...	...	.45	.15
1737a	15¢ Booklet Pane of 8	...	...	3.25	3.00
1738-42	15¢ Windmills, Strip of 5 (1980)	...	...	2.35	2.25
1738-42	15¢ Set of 5 Singles..........................	...	...	2.25	.90
1742a	15¢ Booklet Pane of 10 (2 ea. #1738-42) (1980)	...	...	4.50	4.25
1743	(15¢) "A" & Eagle, Coil, Pf. Vert. ...... Line Pr.	1.00		.45	.15

NOTE: MODERN BOOKLET PANES ARE GLUED INTO BOOKLETS AND PRICES LISTED ARE FOR PANES WITHOUT SELVEDGE AND, USUALLY, FOLDED. LIMITED QUANTITIES EXIST UNFOLDED WITH FULL SELVEDGE—THESE ARE USUALLY PRICED ANYWHERE FROM 1½ TO 4 TIMES THESE PRICES WHEN AVAILABLE.

SPECIAL
STAMP COLLECTOR®
OFFER

Established 1914

Professionals Serving
Philately Since 1914

For information please contact us:

American Stamp Dealers Association, Inc.
3 School Street, Suite 205
Glen Cover, NY 11542-2548
Phone: 516-759-7000
Fax: 516-759-7014
E-mail: asda@erols.com

- ☐ Membership Application/Information
- ☐ Information on all "Mega Events".
- ☐ A list of stamp dealers in my area.
- ☐ A list of dealers specializing in my area.
- ☐ Brochure on how to sell a stamp collection.

Name:_____

Address:_____

City:_____

State:_____ Zip:_____

Speciality Area:_____

THE UNITED STATES POSTAL SERVICE
INVITES YOU TO

VOUS ÊTES INVITÉ
USTED ESTA INVITADO
VOI SIETE INVITATI
VOCÊ ESTÁ CONVIDADO
SIE SIND EINGELADEN
U BENT UITGENODIGD
INVITATION TIL
INVITASJON TIL

OLET TERVETULLUT
PAŃSTVO JEST ZAPROSZONE
DU INBJUDS HÄRMĒD
ВЫ ПРИГЛАШЕНЫ
ΕΙΣΤΑΙ ΚΑΛΕΣΜΕΝΒΙ
אתה מוזמן
أنت مدعو للحضور
我們誠意邀請您
조정합니다
ご招待

FOR ADDITIONAL
INFORMATION CONTACT:
WORLD STAMP EXPOSITION
P.O. BOX 44403
WASHINGTON, D.C. 20076-4403
FAX: 202-268-3710

WORLD

STAMP

EXPO
2000

U S A

SPONSORED BY

UNITED STATES
POSTAL SERVICE™

ANAHEIM CONVENTION CENTER
JULY 7-16 2000 • ANAHEIM, CALIFORNIA

Order Your Copy Today Of Brookman's

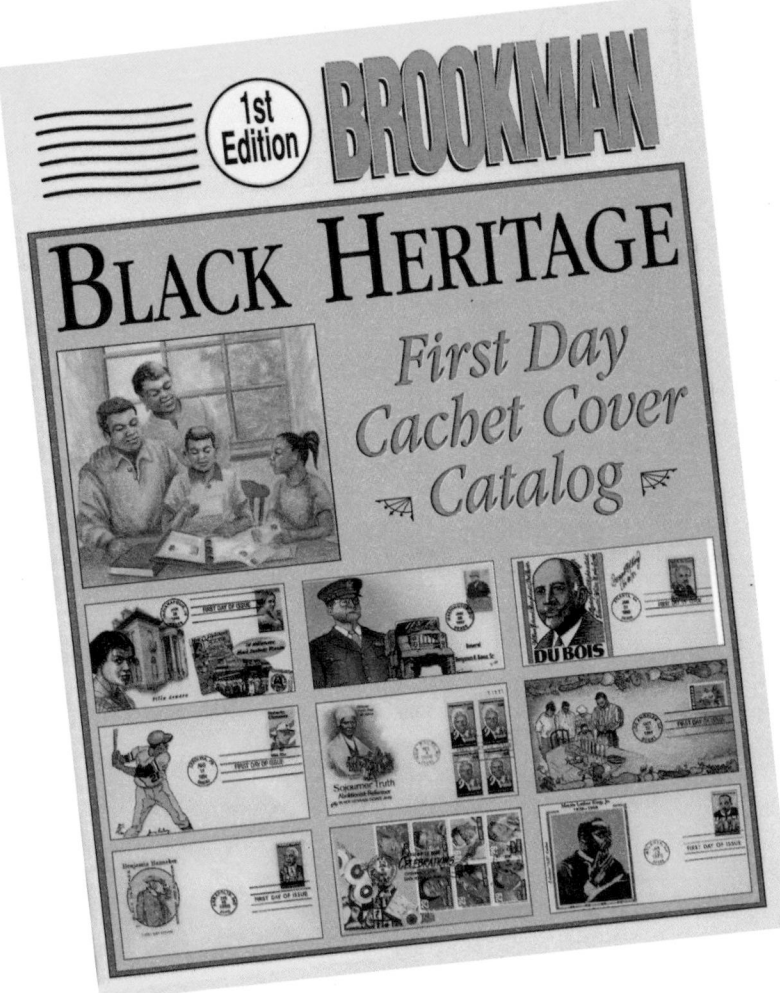

This catalog contains over 170 pages of photos of the many different cachets available for the Black Heritage cover series.

The ONLY catalog of this important and popular topic

1978 Commemoratives (continued)

1744   1745   1746
         1747   1748

1749   1750
1751   1752   1753

1754   1755   1756

1757

Scott's No.		Mint Sheet	Plate Block	F-VF NH	F-VF Used
1744	13¢ Harriet Tubman..........................	21.50 (12)	5.75	.45	.15
1745-48	13¢ Quilts, attd ....(48)	19.00 (12)	5.50	1.65	1.25
1745-48	Set of 4 Singles................................	...	...	1.50	.70
1749-52	13¢ American Dance, attd.................(48)	19.00 (12)	5.50	1.65	1.25
1749-52	Set of 4 Singles................................	...	...	1.50	.70
1753	13¢ French Alliance ....(40)	14.00	1.60	.38	.15
1754	13¢ Cancer Detection, Pap Test	18.50	1.75	.40	.15
#1755-56 Performing Arts					
1755	13¢ Jimmie Rodgers	17.50 (12)	5.00	.38	.15
1756	15¢ George M. Cohan	21.50 (12)	5.75	.45	.15

1978 CAPEX Souvenir Sheet

Scott's No.		Mint Sheet	Plate Block	F-VF NH	F-VF Used
1757	13¢x8 ($1.04) CAPEX				
	Souvenir Sheet.................................(6)	16.00	...	2.75	2.50
1757	S.Sh. with Plate No	...	2.95		
1757a-h	Set of 8 Singles	...	...	2.65	1.70
	Strip of Four (a-d)	...	...	1.40	1.25
	Strip of Four (e-h)	...	...	1.40	1.25
	Block of 8, attached	...	...	3.50	3.25

1978 Commemoratives (continued)

1758   1759   1760   1761
                         1762   1763

1764   1765   1768   1769
1766   1767

		Mint Sheet	Plate Block	F-VF NH	F-VF Used
1758	15¢ Photography ....(40)	15.75 (12)	5.75	.45	.15
1759	15¢ Viking Mission to Mars	18.50	2.10	.45	.15
1760-63	15¢ American Owls, attd...................	21.00	2.00	1.80	1.65
1760-63	Set of 4 Singles	...	...	1.70	.70
1764-67	15¢ American Trees, attd ....(40)	17.50 (12)	6.00	1.80	1.65
1764-67	Set of 4 Singles	...	...	1.70	.70
1768	15¢ Christmas Madonna ....(100)	39.50 (12)	5.50	.42	.15
1769	15¢ Christmas Hobbyhorse ....(100)	39.50 (12)	5.50	.42	.15

1979 Commemoratives

1770   1771   1772

1770-1802	Set of 33	...	...	14.85	4.95
1770	15¢ R.F. Kennedy ....(48)	18.50	1.80	.42	.15
1771	15¢ Martin Luther King, Jr................	20.00 (12)	6.25	.50	.15
1772	15¢ Int'l. Year of the Child	19.50	1.80	.42	.15

NOTE: PRICES THROUGHOUT THIS LIST ARE SUBJECT TO CHANGE WITHOUT NOTICE IF MARKET CONDITIONS REQUIRE. MINIMUM ORDER MUST TOTAL AT LEAST $20.00.

1774   1775   1776   1773
1777   1778

1779   1780   1783   1784
1781   1782   1785   1786

Scott's No.		Mint Sheet	Plate Block	F-VF NH	F-VF Used
1773	15¢ John Steinbeck	19.00	1.80	.42	.15
1774	15¢ Albert Einstein	19.00	1.80	.42	.15
1775-78	15¢ PA Toleware, attd ....(40)	18.00 (10)	5.00	1.90	1.50
1775-78	Set of 4 Singles	...	...	1.80	.80
1779-82	15¢ Architecture, attd ....(48)	22.50	2.50	2.00	1.75
1779-82	Set of 4 Singles	...	...	1.90	.80
1783-86	15¢ Endangered Flowers, attd	22.75 (12)	6.50	1.90	1.50
1783-86	Set of 4 Singles	...	...	1.80	.80

1787   1788   1789

1790   1791-94

1795   1796   1800
1797   1798   1799

1801   1802

Scott's No.		Mint Sheet	Plate Block	F-VF NH	F-VF Used
1787	15¢ Seeing Eye Dog	19.50 (20)	9.00	.42	.15
1788	15¢ Special Olympics	19.50 (10)	4.50	.42	.15
1789	15¢ John P. Jones, Perf. 11x12	19.50 (10)	4.50	.42	.15
1789a	15¢ Perf. 11	32.50 (10)	7.25	.65	.25
1790	10¢ Olympics - Decathalon	14.50 (12)	4.50	.32	.20
1791-94	15¢ Summer Olympics, attd	21.00 (12)	6.50	2.10	1.75
1791-94	Set of 4 Singles	...	...	1.95	.80
1795-98	15¢ Winter Olympics, Perf. 11 x 10½, attd. (1980)	21.00 (12)	6.50	2.10	1.50
1795-98	Set of 4 Singles	...	...	1.95	.80
1795-98a	15¢ Perf. 11 attd	47.50 (12)	14.00	4.00	3.95
1795-98a	Set of 4 Singles	...	...	3.75	3.60
1799	15¢ Christmas Madonna ....(100)	39.50 (12)	5.50	.42	.15
1800	15¢ Christmas Ornament..........(100)	39.50 (12)	5.50	.42	.15
1801	15¢ Will Rogers	21.00 (12)	6.00	.45	.15
1802	15¢ Vietnam Veterans	26.50 (10)	5.95	.55	.15

1980 Commemoratives (See also 1795-98)

1803   1804

1805   1807   1809
1806   1808   1810

				F-VF NH	F-VF Used
1803-10,21-43	Set of 31	...	...	14.65	4.65
1803	15¢ W.C. Fields	21.00 (12)	6.00	.45	.15
1804	15¢ Benjamin Banneker	19.50 (12)	5.50	.42	.15
1805-10	15¢ Letter Writing, attd.......(60)	29.50(36)	19.50	2.95	2.75
1805-10	Set of 6 Singles	...	...	2.75	1.20

1813   **1816**   **1818/1820**

1980-81 Americana Coils, Perf. 10 Vert.

Scott's No.		Line Pair	F-VF NH	F-VF Used
1811	1¢ Inkwell & Quill, Shiny Gum	.40	.20	.15
1811v	1¢ Dry Gum	.65	.20	...
1813	3.5¢ Two Violins, Coil	.95	.20	.15
1813a	3.5¢ Bureau Precancel	...	.30	.25
1816	12¢ Conscience, Coil (1981)	1.95	.35	.20
1816a	12¢ Bureau Precancel	39.50	1.50	.95

1981 "B" Eagle Regular Issue

Scott's No.		Mint Sheet	Plate Block	F-VF NH	F-VF Used
1818	(18¢) Perf. 11x10½..................(100)	47.50	2.25	.50	.15
1819	(18¢) Perf. 10, Booklet Single	...	...	.55	.15
1819a	(18¢) Booklet Pane of 8....................	...	...	3.95	3.75
1820	(18¢) Coil ....Line Pr.	1.50		.55	.15

1980 Commemoratives (continued)

1821   **1822**   **1823**

1824   **1825**   **1826**

1827   **1828**   **1834**   **1835**
1829   **1830**   **1836**   **1837**

1831   **1832**   **1833**   **1842**

1980 Commemoratives (continued)

1838   **1837**   **1843**
1840   **1841**

Scott's No.		Mint Sheet	Plate Block	F-VF NH	F-VF Used
1821	15¢ Frances Perkins..........................	21.00	1.95	.45	.15
1822	15¢ Dolley Madison ....(150)	57.50	1.80	.42	.15
1823	15¢ Emily Bissell..............................	19.50	1.80	.42	.15
1824	15¢ H. Keller/A. Sullivan..................	19.50	1.80	.42	.15
1825	15¢ Veterans Administration..............	19.50	1.80	.42	.15
1826	15¢ Gen. Bernardo de Galvez............	19.50	1.80	.42	.15
1827-30	15¢ Coral Reefs, attd................	20.50 (12)	6.00	1.85	1.35
1827-30	Set of 4 Singles...........................	...	...	1.70	.80
1831	15¢ Organized Labor	19.50 (12)	5.50	.42	.15
1832	15¢ Edith Wharton..........................	21.75	2.00	.45	.15
1833	15¢ Education in America..................	26.00 (6)	3.25	.55	.15
1834-37	15¢ Pacific Northwest Indian Masks, attd ....(40)	23.50 (10)	7.00	2.20	1.50
1834-37	Set of 4 Singles...........................	...	...	2.00	.80
1838-41	15¢ Am. Architecture, attd..............(40)	22.50	2.50	2.25	1.95
1838-41	Set of 4 Singles...........................	...	...	2.00	.80
1842	15¢ Christmas Madonna	19.50 (12)	5.50	.42	.15
1843	15¢ Christmas Toys..........................	21.50 (20)	10.00	.45	.15

ZIP, MAIL EARLY & COPYRIGHT BLOCKS

Due to space limitations, we do not list individual prices for Zip Code, Mail Early, Copyright and other inscription blocks. With the exception of those items listed below, these are priced at the total price for the single stamps plus one additional stamp. For example, if the single stamp retailed for 45¢, a zip block of 4 would retail for $2.25 (5x.45). Se-tenants should be based on the attached price plus 25%. (blocks of 6 would be 75% over attached block prices)

Scott's No.		Copyright Block	Mail Early Block	Zip Code Block
1274	1965 11¢ Telecommunication	...	...	3.75
1284	1966 6¢ F. D. Roosevelt......	...	4.50	3.75
1284a	Same, tagged	...	2.25	1.75
1347-49	1968, 6¢ Historic Flags........	...	2.35	...
1353-54	1968, 6¢ Historic Flags........	...	...	1.70
C72	1968, 10¢ 50 State Runway ...	5.50	4.50	...
C95-96	1979, 25¢ Wiley Post	7.50	...	7.50

1980-85 Great Americans Series,
Perf. 11 x 10½ (Sheets of 100)

| 1844 | 1845 | 1846 | 1847 |

| 1848 | 1849 | 1850 | 1851 |

| 1852 | 1853 | 1854 | 1855 |

| 1856 | 1857 | 1858 | 1859 |

| 1860 | 1861 | 1862 | 1863 |

| 1864 | 1865 | 1866 | 1867 |

| 1868 | 1869 |

Scott's No.		Mint Sheet	Plate Block	F-VF NH	F-VF Used
1844-69	Set of 26................................	...	...	12.75	3.75
1844	1¢ Dix, Bullseye Perfs. Pf.11.2 ('83)...	8.75 (20)	2.75	.20	.15
1844c	1¢ Dix, Line Pfs. Pf. 10.8 (1983)........	6.75 (20)	2.00	.20	.15
1845	2¢ Igor Stravinsky (1982)..................	6.75	.50	.20	.15
1846	3¢ Henry Clay (1983)	9.75	.65	.20	.15
1847	4¢ Carl Schurz (1983)	12.50	.65	.20	.15
1848	5¢ Pearl Buck (1983)........................	13.50	.70	.20	.15
1849	6¢ Walter Lippmann Perf. 11 (1985) ..	18.00 (20)	4.15	.20	.15
1850	7¢ Abraham Baldwin Perf. 11 (1985) .	20.00 (20)	4.50	.22	.15
1851	8¢ Gen. Henry Knox Perf. 11 (1985)...	21.50	1.25	.24	.15
1852	9¢ Sylvanus Thayer Perf. 11 (1985)....	25.00 (20)	6.00	.27	.15
1853	10¢ R. Russell Perf. 11 (1984)............	28.50 (20)	7.25	.30	.15
1854	11¢ Alden Partridge Perf. 11 (1985)....	30.00	1.60	.32	.15
1855	13¢ Crazy Horse (1982)	42.00	2.10	.45	.15
1856	14¢ Sinclair Lewis Perf. 11 (1985)	42.00 (10)	9.75	.45	.15
1857	17¢ Rachel Carson (1981).................	47.50	2.15	.50	.15
1858	18¢ George Mason (1981).................	47.50	2.50	.50	.20
1859	19¢ Sequoyah	55.00	2.65	.60	.18
1860	20¢ Dr. Ralph Bunche (1982)............	65.00	3.50	.70	.15
1861	20¢ Thomas Gallaudet (1983)	65.00	3.50	.70	.15
1862	20¢ Truman Perf. 11 Line Pfs. (1984)..	62.50 (20)	13.00	.65	.15
1862a	20¢ Truman, Perf 11.2, Lg.Block Tag..	67.50 (4)	4.50	.70	.30
1862b	20¢ Pf. 11.2, Overall Tagging (1990)..	72.50	5.75	.75	.50
1862d	20¢ Pf. 11.2, Shiny Gum	77.50	5.50	.80	...

1980-85 Great Americans Series, (cont.)
Perf. 11 x 10½ II (Sheets of 100)

Scott's No.		Mint Sheet	Plate Block	F-VF NH	F-VF Used
1863	22¢ Audubon, Perf 11 Line Pfs. ('85) ..	72.50 (20)	16.50	.75	.15
1863d	22¢ Bullseye Perfs, Perf. 11.2.............	72.50 (4)	5.75	.75	.20
1864	30¢ F.C. Laubach, Perf. 11Line Pfs. ('84)	85.00 (20)	19.75	.90	.15
1864a	30¢ Perf. 11.2, Large Block Tag...........	87.50	5.75	.90	.15
1864b	30¢ Perf. 11.2, Overall Tagging	...	39.50	2.50	2.00
1865	35¢ Dr. Charles Drew ('81)................	100.00	5.00	1.10	.20
1866	37¢ R. Millikan ('82)	100.00	4.75	1.10	.20
1867	39¢ Gren Clark, Perf 11 Line Pfs. ('85)	100.00 (20)	24.50	1.10	.20
1867c	39¢ Bullseye Perfs, Perf 11.2...............	100.00 (4)	6.75	1.10	.20
1868	40¢ L. Gilbreth, Pref. 11 Line Pfs. ('84)	110.00 (20)	25.00	1.20	.20
1868a	40¢ Bullseye Perfs, Perf 11.2...............	110.00	6.75	1.20	.20
1869	50¢ Nimitz, Perf. 11 Line Pfs. ('85).....	160.00 (4)	10.00	1.50	.20
1869a	50¢ Perf. 11.2, Block Tagging	150.00	8.25	1.60	.25
1869d	50¢ Perf.11.2, Overall Tag. Dull Gum .	195.00	12.50	2.10	.35
1869ds	50¢ Pf.11.2, Overall Tag. Shiny Gum ..	165.00	10.00	1.75	...

1981 Commemoratives

| 1874 | 1875 | 1876-79 |

Scott's No.		Mint Sheet	Plate Block	F-VF NH	F-VF Used
1874-79,1910-45	Set of 42...............................	...	...	24.95	6.50
1874	15¢ Everett Dirksen........................	19.50	1.80	.42	.15
1875	15¢ Whitney Young..........................	19.50	1.80	.42	.15
1876-79	18¢ Flowers, attd ....(48)	26.75	2.60	2.30	1.75
1876-79	Set of 4 Singles.................................	...	...	2.10	.80

1981-82 Regular Issues

| 1890 | 1891 |

1880	1881	1892	1893	1894-96
1882	1883			
1884	1885			
1886	1887			
1888	1889			

Scott's No.		Mint Sheet	Plate Block	F-VF NH	F-VF Used
1880-89	18¢ Wildlife Bklt. Singles.................	...	...	9.00	2.00
1889a	Wildlife Bklt., Pane of 10	...	...	9.75	7.50
1890	18¢ Flag & "Amber Waves" ....(100)	52.50 (20)	11.50	.55	.15
1891	18¢ Flag "Sea", Coil ....(Pl. # Strip)	6.75 (5)	5.00 (3)	.55	.15
1892	6¢ Circle of Stars, Bklt. Sgl................	...	...	.75	.25
1893	18¢ Flag & "For Purple" Bklt. Sgl.....	...	...	.50	.15
1892-93	6¢ & 18¢, Vertical Pair	...	...	1.25	1.20
1893a	Bklt Pn of 8 (2 #1892, 6 #1893)........	...	...	4.00	3.75
1894	20¢ Flag over Supreme Court, Line Pf. 11, Dry Gum ....(100)	95.00 (20)	21.00	1.00	.25
1894e	20¢ Bullseye Pf. 11.2...................(100)	57.50 (20)	12.50	.60	.15
1895	20¢ Flag over S.C., Coil ......Pl. # Strip	4.75 (5)	3.00 (3)	.55	.15
1895e	20¢ Flag, Precancelled ....Pl. # Strip	90.00 (5)	85.00 (3)	1.30	.75
1896	20¢ Flag over S.C., Bk. Sgl	...	...	.70	.15
1896a	20¢ Booklet Pane of 6	...	...	3.95	3.50
1896b	20¢ Booklet Pane of 10 (1982)	...	...	6.50	5.25

1981-91 Transportation Coil Series

11¢ RR Untagged Issue not included in Set.
Pl. #s must appear on center stamp

| 1897 | 1897A | 1898 | 1898A |

| 1899 | 1900 | 1901 | 1902 |

| 1903 | 1904 | 1905 | 1906 |

| 1907 | 1908 |

Scott's No.		Pl# Strip of 5	Pl# Strip of 3	F-VF NH	F-VF Used
1897-1908	Mint (14 values)	130.00	59.75	3.75	1.85
1897	1¢ Omnibus (1983)	.85	.50	.20	.15
1897A	2¢ Locomotive (1982)	.65	.55	.20	.15
1898	3¢ Handcar (1983)	.85	.75	.20	.15
1898A	4¢ Stagecoach (1982)	1.60	1.25	.20	.15
1899	5¢ Motorcycle (1983)	1.50	1.10	.20	.15
1900	5.2¢ Sleigh (1983)	11.75	5.95	.20	.15
1901	5.9¢ Bicycle (1982)	18.50	6.75	.22	.18
1902	7.4¢ Baby Buggy (1984)	12.75	7.00	.30	.20
1903	9.3¢ Mail Wagon	17.50	6.75	.30	.20
1904	10.9¢ Hansom Cab (1982)	57.50	19.75	.50	.20
1905	11¢ RR Caboose (1984)	5.25	3.50	.35	.15
1905b	11¢ Untagged, not precanc. ('91)	3.25	2.75	.35	.25
1906	17¢ Electric Car	3.25	2.25	.50	.15
1907	18¢ Surrey	4.25	3.25	.55	.15
1908	20¢ Fire Pumper	3.50	2.50	.60	.15

#1897-97A: See #2225-26 for designs without "¢" signs.
#1898A: See #2228 for "B" Press

1981-91 Transportation Coil Series
Precancelled Stamps

Scott's No.		Pl# Strip of 5	Pl# Strip of 3	F-VF NH	F-VF Used
1898Ab/1906a	Precancelled (8 values)	125.00	115.00	2.65	1.75
1898Ab	4¢ Stagecoach (1982)	7.50	6.75	.23	.18
1900a	5.2¢ Sleigh (1983)	15.00	13.50	.20	.18
1901a	5.9¢ Bicycle (1982)	49.50	47.50	.30	.25
1902a	7.4¢ Baby Buggy (1984)	6.50	5.95	.35	.25
1903a	9.3¢ Mail Wagon	4.50	3.75	.35	.25
1904a	10.9¢ Hansom Cab (1982)	39.50	37.50	.50	.25
1905a	11¢ RR Caboose (1984)	4.75	4.25	.40	.22
1906a	17¢ Electric Car, Type "A"	6.50	5.75	.50	.35
1906ab	17¢ Type "B"	37.50	35.00	1.50	.75
1906ac	17¢ Type "C"	14.50	12.75	1.00	.50

Type "A" - "Presorted" 11.5mm Length
Type "B" - "Presorted" 12.5mm Length
Type "C" - "Presorted" 13.5mm Length

NOTE: FROM 1935 TO DATE, AVERAGE QUALITY STAMPS, WHEN AVAILABLE, WILL BE PRICED AT APPROXIMATELY 20% BELOW THE APPROPRIATE F-VF QUALITY PRICE.

1983 Express Mail Issue

1909

Scott's No.		Mint Sheet	Plate Block	F-VF NH	F-VF Used
1909	$9.35 Eagle, Booklet Single	...	...	28.50	22.50
1909a	$9.35 Booklet Pane of 3	...	...	82.50	...

1981 Commemoratives (continued)

| 1910 | 1911 | 1920 |

| 1912 | 1913 | 1914 | 1915 |
| 1916 | 1917 | 1918 | 1919 |

| 1921 | 1922 |
| 1923 | 1924 |

1910	18¢ American Red Cross	26.50	2.80	.55	.15
1911	18¢ Savings & Loan	25.00	2.50	.55	.15
1912-19	18¢ Space Achievement, attd (48)	32.50 (8)	6.00	5.50	3.75
1912-19	Set of 8 Singles	...	...	5.25	2.00
1920	18¢ Professional Management	25.00	2.40	.55	.15
1921-24	18¢ Wildlife Habitats, attd	26.50	2.50	2.30	1.50
1921-24	Set of 4 Singles	...	...	2.10	.70

1925   1926   1927

1928   1929
1930   1931

1932   1934   1933

1935   1936   1939

1937   1938   1940

Scott's No.		Mint Sheet	Plate Block	F-VF NH	F-VF Used
1925	18¢ Disabled Persons	25.00	2.40	.55	.15
1926	18¢ Edna St. Vincent Millay.............	25.00	2.40	.55	.15
1927	18¢ Alcoholism...............................	55.00 (20)40.00		.60	.15
1928-31	18¢ Architecture, attd ....(40)	27.50	3.00	2.75	2.25
1928-31	Set of 4 Singles..............................	...	...	2.50	.70
1932	18¢ Babe Didrikson Zaharias............	37.50	4.00	.80	.15
1933	18¢ Bobby Jones	75.00	7.75	1.60	.15
1934	18¢ F. Remington Sculpture..............	25.00	2.40	.55	.15
1935	18¢ James Hoban	25.00	2.40	.55	.15
1936	20¢ James Hoban	26.00	2.50	.55	.15
1937-38	18¢ Yorktown - Capes, attd	28.75	3.00	1.40	.90
1937-38	Set of Singles.................................	...	...	1.30	.40
1939	(20¢)Christmas Madonna.............(100)	50.00	2.50	.55	.15
1940	(20¢)Christmas-Teddy Bear..............	26.00	2.50	.55	.15

1941   1942   1943
1944   1945

Scott's No.		Mint Sheet	Plate Block	F-VF NH	F-VF Used
1941	20¢ John Hanson	26.50	2.50	.55	.15
1942-45	20¢ Desert Plants, attached .... (40)	26.00	3.25	2.75	1.50
1942-45	Set of 4 Singles	...	...	2.50	.70

1981-82 Regular Issues

1946-1948   1949

1946	(20¢) "C" & Eagle, Pf. 11x10½.......(100)	52.50	2.50	.55	.15
1947	(20¢) "C" & Eagle, Coil	Line Pr. 1.95		.75	.15
1948	(20¢) "C" & Eagle,Perf.10,Bklt. Sgl......	...	.60	.15	
1948a	(20¢)Booklet Pane of 10	...	...	5.95	5.00
1949	20¢ Ty. I,Bighorn Sheep,Bklt. Sgl.......	...	...	.70	.15
1949a	20¢ Ty. I, Booklet Pane of 10	...	...	7.25	5.00
1949c	20¢ Type II, Bklt Single	...	...	1.50	.50
1949d	20¢ Ty. II, Booklet Pane of 10............	...	...	14.50	...

* Ty. I is 18¾ mm wide and has overall tagging.
  Ty. II is 18½ mm wide and has block tagging.

1982 Commemoratives

1950   1951   1952

1950-52,2003-4,2006-30 Set of 30		...	...	20.95	4.25
1950	20¢ Franklin D. Roosevelt ....(48)	26.50	2.50	.55	.15
1951	20¢ "LOVE", Perf. 11	29.50	2.75	.60	.15
1951a	20¢ Perf. 11x 10½	45.00	5.50	.95	.35
1952	20¢ George Washington.....................	28.50	2.75	.60	.15

1982 State Birds & Flowers Issue

1953	Alabama	1971	Maine	1989	Oregon
1954	Alaska	1972	Maryland	1990	Pennsylvania
1955	Arizona	1973	Massachusetts	1991	Rhode Island
1956	Arkansas	1974	Michigan	1992	South Carolina
1957	California	1975	Minnesota	1993	South Dakota
1958	Colorado	1976	Mississippi	1994	Tennessee
1959	Connecticut	1977	Missouri	1995	Texas
1960	Delaware	1978	Montana	1996	Utah
1961	Florida	1979	Nebraska	1997	Vermont
1962	Georgia	1980	Nevada	1998	Virginia
1963	Hawaii	1981	New Hampshire	1999	Washington
1964	Idaho	1982	New Jersey	2000	West Virginia
1965	Illinois	1983	New Mexico	2001	Wisconsin
1966	Indiana	1984	New York	2002	Wyoming
1967	Iowa	1985	North Carolina		
1968	Kansas	1986	North Dakota		
1969	Kentucky	1987	Ohio		
1970	Louisiana	1988	Oklahoma		

1982 State Birds & Flowers Issue

| 1957 | 1961 | 1966 | 1972 |

Scott's No.		Mint Sheet	Plate Block	F-VF NH	F-VF Used
1953-2002	20¢ 50 States, attd, Pf. 10½ x 11	37.50	...	...	...
1953a-2002a	20¢ 50 States, attd., Pf. 11 42.50		...	...	...
1953-2002	Set of Singles,......................	...	...	36.50	19.50
1953-2002	20¢ Individual Singles	...	...	1.00	.50

NOTE: Sets of singles may contain mixed perforation sizes.

1982 Commemoratives (continued)

| 2003 | 2004 | 2005 |

2003	20¢ U.S. & Netherlands	32.50 (20)	13.95	.60	.15
2004	20¢ Library of Congress.................	27.50	2.50	.55	.15

1982 Consumer Education Coil

| 2005 | 20¢ Clothing Label............(Pl# Strip) | 125.00(5) | 25.00(3) | 1.00 | .15 |

1982 Commemoratives (continued)

| 2006 2008 | 2007 2009 | 2010 |

| 2012 | 2011 | 2013 |

2006-09	20¢ Knoxville Fair, attd	32.50	3.25	2.80	1.50
2006-09	Set of 4 Singles......................	...	...	2.70	.80
2010	20¢ Horatio Alger........................	26.50	2.50	.55	.15
2011	20¢ "Aging Together"....................	26.50	2.50	.55	.15
2012	20¢ Arts - The Barrymores	26.50	2.50	.55	.15
2013	20¢ Mary Walker, Surgeon............	28.75	2.75	.60	.15

1982 Commemoratives (continued)

| 2015 | 2014 | 2016 |

| 2019 2021 | 2020 2022 | 2017 |
| | | 2018 |

| 2023 | 2024 | 2025 |

| 2026 | 2027 2029 | 2028 2030 |

Scott's No.		Mint Sheet	Plate Block	F-VF NH	F-VF Used
2014	20¢ Peace Garden.........................	26.50	2.50	.55	.15
2015	20¢ Libraries of America	26.50	2.50	.55	.15
2016	20¢ Jackie Robinson.....................	95.00	8.95	2.00	.20
2017	20¢ Touro Synagogue....................	29.50 (20)	13.75	.60	.15
2018	20¢ Wolf Trap Farm Park	26.50	2.50	.55	.15
2019-22	20¢ Architecture, attached ....(40)	32.50	4.25	3.50	2.50
2019-22	Set of 4 Singles............................	...	...	3.25	.80
2023	20¢ St. Francis of Assisi	28.50	2.75	.60	.15
2024	20¢ Ponce de Leon	35.00 (20)	16.00	.75	.15
#2025-30	Christmas Issues				
2025	13¢ Christmas, Kitten & Puppy	18.75	1.80	.40	.15
2026	20¢ Christmas, Tiepolo Madonna ..	29.50 (20)	13.75	.60	.15
2027-30	20¢ Christmas Winter Scenes, attd.	39.50	4.00	3.50	1.60
2027-30	Set of 4 Singles............................	...	...	3.30	.80

NOTE: FROM 1935 TO DATE, WITH FEW LISTED EXCEPTIONS, UNUSED PRICES ARE FOR NEVER HINGED STAMPS. HINGED STAMPS, WHEN AVAILABLE, ARE PRICED AT APPROXIMATELY 20% BELOW THE NEVER HINGED PRICE.

1983 Commemoratives

2032 2033 2035
2034

2036 2031 2037

2039 2038 2040

2041 2042 2043

2044 2045 2046 2047

1983 Commemoratives (cont.)

2048 2049
2050 2051

2052 2053 2054

2055 2056
2057 2058

2059 2060
2061 2062

2063 2064 2065

Scott's No.		Mint Sheet		Plate Block	F-VF NH	F-VF Used
2031-65	Set of 35	...		...	22.50	5.15
2031	20¢ Sciences & Industry	26.50		2.50	.55	.15
2032-35	20¢ Ballooning, attached..............	26.00	(40)	3.00	2.75	1.50
2032-35	Set of 4 Singles	...		...	2.50	.80
2036	20¢ Sweden, B. Franklin..................	26.50		2.50	.55	.15
2037	20¢ Civilian Conservation Corp	26.50		2.50	.55	.15
2038	20¢ Joseph Priestley	29.00		2.75	.60	.15
2039	20¢ Voluntarism	29.00	(20)	13.95	.60	.15
2040	20¢ German Immigration	26.50		2.50	.55	.15
2041	20¢ Brooklyn Bridge......................	26.50		2.50	.55	.15
2042	20¢ Tennessee Valley Authority	29.75	(20)	13.95	.60	.15
2043	20¢ Physical Fitness........................	29.75	(20)	13.95	.60	.15
2044	20¢ Scott Joplin	29.00		2.75	.60	.15
2045	20¢ Medal of Honor.......................	27.50	(40)	3.00	.70	.15
2046	20¢ Babe Ruth	105.00		9.75	2.25	.20
2047	20¢ Nathaniel Hawthorne	26.50		2.50	.55	.15

Scott's No.		Mint Sheet		Plate Block	F-VF NH	F-VF Used
2048-51	13¢ Summer Olympics, attd	29.50		3.75	3.00	1.50
2048-51	Set of 4 Singles	...		...	2.90	.80
2052	20¢ Treaty of Paris........................	23.50	(40)	2.75	.60	.15
2053	20¢ Civil Service............................	29.75	(20)	13.95	.60	.15
2054	20¢ Metropolitan Opera	29.50		2.75	.60	.15
2055-58	20¢ Inventors, attd	35.00		4.25	3.35	1.75
2055-58	Set of 4 Singles	...		...	3.00	.80
2059-62	20¢ Streetcars, attd	29.50		3.75	3.00	1.75
2059-62	Set of 4 Singles	...		...	2.90	.80
2063	20¢ Christmas, Raphael Madonna	26.50		2.50	.55	.15
2064	20¢ Christmas, Santa Claus.............	30.00	(20)	13.95	.60	.15
2065	20¢ Martin Luther	26.50		2.50	.55	.15

		2066	2067 2069	2068 2070	2071
		2072	2073	2074	2075
		2076 2078	2077 2079		
		2080	2081	2086	

| 2082
2084 | 2083
2085 |
| 2087 | 2091 | 2092 |

| 2088 | 2089 | 2090 | 2093 |

| 2094 | 2095 | 2096 | 2097 |

Scott's No.		Mint Sheet	Plate Block	F-VF NH	F-VF Used
2066-2109	Set of 44	...	...	32.75	6.50
2066	20¢ Alaska Statehood	26.50	2.50	.55	.15
2067-70	20¢ Winter Olympics, attd	38.50	4.25	3.50	1.75
2067-70	Set of 4 Singles	...	...	3.25	.80
2071	20¢ Fed. Deposit Insurance	26.50	2.50	.55	.15
2072	20¢ Love, Hearts	29.50 (20)	14.50	.60	.15
2073	20¢ Carter G. Woodson	29.50	2.75	.60	.15
2074	20¢ Soil & Water Conservation......	26.50	2.50	.55	.15
2075	20¢ Credit Union Act	26.50	2.50	.55	.15
2076-79	20¢ Orchids, attached.................(48)	30.00	3.50	2.75	1.75
2076-79	Set of 4 Singles	...	...	2.50	.80
2080	20¢ Hawaii Statehood	29.50	2.75	.65	.15
2081	20¢ National Archives....................	29.50	65	.15	

Scott's No.		Mint Sheet	Plate Block	F-VF NH	F-VF Used
2082-85	20¢ Summer Olympics, attd	47.50	5.50	4.65	2.25
2082-85	Set of 4 Singles	...	...	4.50	.90
2086	20¢ Louisiana World's Fair .... (40)	23.50	2.75	.60	.15
2087	20¢ Health Research	31.50	3.00	.65	.15
2088	20¢ Douglas Fairbanks	35.00 (20)	17.50	.65	.15
2089	20¢ Jim Thorpe	33.50	3.00	.70	.15
2090	20¢ John McCormack	26.50	2.50	.55	.15
2091	20¢ St. Lawrence Seaway	26.50	2.50	.55	.15
2092	20¢ Waterfowl Preservation	42.50	4.15	.90	.15
2093	20¢ Roanoke Voyages...................	31.00	2.80	.65	.15
2094	20¢ Herman Melville......................	26.50	2.50	.55	.15
2095	20¢ Horace Moses	37.50 (20)	17.00	.75	.15
2096	20¢ Smokey Bear	32.50	3.00	.70	.15
2097	20¢ Roberto Clemente...................	130.00	12.75	2.75	.20

NOTE: PRICES THROUGHOUT THIS LIST ARE SUBJECT TO CHANGE WITHOUT NOTICE IF MARKET CONDITIONS REQUIRE. MINIMUM ORDER MUST TOTAL AT LEAST $20.00.

1984 Commemoratives (cont.)

2098 2099 2102
2100 2101

2103 2104 2105

2106 2107 2108 2110

2109

Scott's No.		Mint Sheet	Plate Block	F-VF NH	F-VF Used
2098-2101	20¢ Dogs, attd .... (40)	29.50	4.25	3.50	2.50
2098-2101	Set of 4 Singles			3.00	.80
2102	20¢ Crime Prevention	26.50	2.50	.55	.15
2103	20¢ Hispanic Americans .... (40)	21.50	2.50	.55	.15
2104	20¢ Family Unity	40.00	(20) 17.75	.85	.15
2105	20¢ Eleanor Roosevelt .... (48)	25.00	2.50	.55	.15
2106	20¢ Nation of Readers	32.50	2.95	.70	.15
#2107-8	Christmas Issues				
2107	20¢ Madonna & Child	26.50	2.50	.55	.15
2108	20¢ Santa Claus	26.50	2.50	.55	.15
2109	20¢ Vietnam Memorial .... (40)	35.00	4.25	.90	.15

1985 Commemoratives

2110,2137-47,52-66	Set of 27	...	...	35.75	5.15
2110	22¢ Jerome Kern...............	31.50	3.00	.65	.15

1985-87 Regulars

2111-2113 2114-2115 2115b 2116

		Mint Sheet	Plate Block	F-VF NH	F-VF Used
2111	(22¢) "D" Stamp Perf 11 .... (100)	90.00	(20) 32.50	.75	.15
2113	(22¢) "D" Booklet Single	...	...	1.00	.15
2113a	(22¢) "D" Bklt. Pane of 10	...	...	9.75	5.00
2114	22¢ Flag over Capitol............ (100)	60.00	3.00	.65	.15
2116	22¢ Flag over Cap. Bklt. Sgl	...	...	.85	.15
2116a	22¢ Booklet Pane of 5	...	...	4.25	2.50

Scott's No.		Pl/ # Strip of 5	Pl # Strip of 3	F-VF NH	F-VF Used
2112	(22¢) "D" Coil, Perf 10 Vert.	8.50	6.50	.70	.15
2115	22¢ Flag over Cap. Coil Perf 10 Vert.	4.50	3.50	.65	.15
2115b	Flag "T" Test Coil ('87)...............	5.50	4.25	.65	.15
#2115b has a tiny "T" below capitol building					

1985-89 Regulars

2117 2118 2119 2120 2121

2122

Scott's No.		Mint Sheet	Plate Block	F-VF NH	F-VF Used
2117-21	22¢ Seashells, Strip of 5	...	...	3.25	2.25
2117-21	Set of 5 Singles...............	...	...	3.15	1.00
2121a	22¢ Bklt. Pane of 10	...	...	5.95	5.00
2122	$10.75 Express Mail, Eagle & Moon, Booklet Single, Type I...............	...	...	27.50	10.75
2122a	$10.75 Bklt. Pane of 3 (Pl. #11111)..	...	...	80.00	...
2122b	$10.75 Ty. II, Bklt. Sgl (1989)..........	...	...	37.50	13.95
2122c	$10.75 Ty. II Bklt.Pane of 3(Pl.#22222)	...	...	110.00	...

* Ty. I: washed out appearance; "$10.75" is grainy.
* Ty. II: brighter colors; "$10.75" is smoother and less grainy.

1985-89 TRANSPORTATION COIL SERIES II

2123 2124 2125 2126

2127 2128 2129 2130

2131 2132 2133 2134

2135 2136

1985-89 TRANSPORTATION COIL SERIES II

* Pl. #s must appear on center stamp. Sets do not include "B" press issue.

Scott's No.		Pl.# Strip of 5	Pl.# Strip of 3	F-VF NH	Used
2123-36	Mint (14 values)........................	36.75	30.00	4.50	2.25
2123	3.4¢ School Bus............................	1.20	1.00	.20	.15
2124	4.9¢ Buckboard............................	1.20	1.00	.20	.18
2125	5.5¢ Star Route Truck ('86)	2.00	1.60	.20	.18
2126	6¢ Tricycle..................................	1.85	1.60	.20	.15
2127	7.1¢ Tractor (1987)......................	2.95	2.50	.30	.20
2128	8.3¢ Ambulance............................	1.95	1.65	.30	.20
2129	8.5¢ Tow Truck ('87)	3.50	3.00	.30	.20
2130	10.1¢ Oil Wagon..........................	3.25	2.65	.30	.20
2131	11¢ Stutz Bearcat.........................	2.00	1.65	.32	.15
2132	12¢ Stanley Steamer, Type I	2.95	2.50	.50	.15
2133	12.5¢ Pushcart.............................	3.50	3.00	.35	.25
2134	14¢ Iceboat, Type I	2.75	2.25	.40	.20
2134b	14¢ "B" Press (no line) Ty.II ('86) .	6.75	5.50	.50	.25
2135	17¢ Dog Sled (1986)....................	4.25	3.50	.60	.20
2136	25¢ Bread Wagon (1986)..............	4.75	3.75	.75	.15

NOTE: #2134 17½ MM WIDE, #2134b 17¼ MM WIDE

PRECANCELLED COILS

Scott's No.		Pl.# Strip of 5	Pl.# Strip of 3	F-VF NH	Used
2123a/33a	Precanc. (12 values)	35.75	31.75	3.25	2.40
2123a	3.4¢ School Bus............................	6.75	6.50	.20	.18
2124a	4.9¢ Buckboard............................	2.10	1.85	.22	.18
2125a	5.5¢ Star Route Truck ('86)	2.60	2.35	.20	.18
2126a	6¢ Tricycle..................................	2.15	1.75	.20	.18
2127a	7.1¢ Tractor ('87)	3.95	3.50	.30	.20
2127av	7.1¢ Zip + 4 Precancel ('89).........	2.65	2.25	.30	.25
2128a	8.3¢ Ambulance............................	1.95	1.65	.30	.22
2129a	8.5¢ Tow Truck ('87)	3.65	3.15	.30	.22
2130a	10.1¢ Oil Wagon, Black Prec.........	3.25	2.75	.30	.25
2130av	10.1¢ Oil Wagon,Red Prec.('88) ...	2.90	2.50	.30	.25
2132a	12¢ Stanley Steamer, Type I	3.00	2.50	.50	.25
2132b	12¢ "B" Press,Ty.II(no line) ('87) ..	27.50	25.00	1.50	.75
	#2132, 2132a "Stanley Steamer 1909" 18mm.				
	#2132b "Stanley Steamer 1909" 17½ mm.				
2133a	12.5¢ Pushcart.............................	3.50	3.00	.35	.30

1985 Commemoratives (cont.)

2137	2138		2139
	2140		2141

2142	2143	2144

2145	2146	2147

Scott's No.		Mint Sheet	Plate Block	F-VF NH	F-VF Used
2137	22¢ Mary Mcleod Bethune..............	32.50	3.25	.70	.15
2138-41	22¢ Duck Decoys, attached............	95.00	11.50	8.75	3.25
2138-41	Set of 4 Singles	...	...	8.25	.90
2142	22¢ Winter Spec. Olympics....(40)	25.00	2.95	.65	.15
2143	22¢ Love	33.50	3.25	.70	.15
2144	22¢ Rural Electrification Ad...........	55.00 (20)	32.50	.80	.15
2145	22¢ Ameripex '86, Chicago ......(48)	28.75	2.75	.60	.15
2146	22¢ Abigail Adams........................	28.50	2.75	.60	.15
2147	22¢ Fredic A. Bartholdi.................	28.50	2.75	.60	.15

2149	2150	2152

2153	2159	2154

2155-58

2160-63	2165

2164	2166	2167

1985 Regular Issue Coil Stamps Perf. 10 Vert.

Scott's No.		Pl# Strip of 5	Pl# Strip of 3	F-VF NH	F-VF Used
2149	18¢ Wash. Pre-Sort Coil.................	3.95	2.75	.65	.18
2149a	18¢ Precancelled	4.50	3.50	.55	.35
2149b	18¢ Precan., Dry Gum	6.25	5.50	.70	...
2150	21.1¢ Envelope Coil	4.75	3.50	.60	.25
2150a	21.1¢ Zip + 4 Precancel	5.00	4.00	.60	.50

1985 Commemoratives (continued)

Scott's No.		Mint Sheet	Plate Block	F-VF NH	F-VF Used
2152	22¢ Korean War Vetrans.................	36.50	3.50	.75	.15
2153	22¢ Social Security Act	28.50	2.75	.60	.15
2154	22¢ World War I Vetrans.................	36.50	3.50	.75	.15
2155-58	22¢ Horses, attached ....(40)	115.00	15.00	13.00	7.00
2155-58	Set of 4 Singles	...	...	11.00	1.40
2159	22¢ Public Education	67.50	6.50	1.35	.15
2160-63	22¢ Int'l. Youth Year, attd	59.50	7.95	5.25	3.00
2160-63	Set of 4 Singles	...	...	4.00	1.20
2164	22¢ Help End Hunger	31.50	3.00	.65	.15
#2165-66 Christmas					
2165	22¢ Madonna and Child	28.50	2.75	.60	.15
2166	22¢ Poinsettia Plants	28.50	2.75	.60	.15

1986 Commemoratives

Scott's No.		Mint Sheet	Plate Block	F-VF NH	F-VF Used
2167,2202-04,2210-11, 2220-24,2235-45	Set of 22 (1986)...................	...	...	16.75	3.50
2167	22¢ Arkansas Statehood...................	31.50	3.00	.65	.15

2168	2169	2170	2171

2172	2173	2175	2176

2177	2178	2179	2180	2181

2182,2197	2183	2184	2185	2186

2187	2188	2189	2190	2191

2192	2193	2194	2195	2196

1986-94 Great Americans, Perforated 11
(Sheets of 100)

Scott's No.		Mint Sheet	Plate Block	F-VF NH	F-VF Used
2168/96	Set of 28	...	160.00	35.00	6.50
2168	1¢ Margaret Mitchell	6.00	.40	.20	.15
2169,	2¢ Mary Lyon (1987)	6.75	.45	.20	.15
2169a	2¢ Untagged (1996)	7.75	.90	.20	.18
2170	3¢ Dr.Paul Dudley White,Dull Gum .	10.00	.60	.20	.15
2170g	3¢ Glossy Gum (1995)	10.00	.70	.20	...
2171	4¢ Father Flanagan	11.75	.75	.20	.15
2171a	4¢ Untagged................................	12.95	.85	.22	.18
2172	5¢ Hugo Black	14.50	.85	.20	.15
2173	5¢ Luis Munoz Marin (1990)	16.50	.90	.20	.15
2173v	5¢ Marin, Pl No &Zip Blk of 4 Combo,LL or LR		1.25	...	...
2173a	5¢ Marin, Untagged (1991)	18.00	.95	.20	.18
2175	10¢ Red Cloud, Block Tag Lake('87)	40.00	1.95	.45	.20
2175a	10¢ Overall Tagging (1990)	47.50	2.50	.50	.35
2175c	10¢ Surface Tagged	...	9.95	1.75	.50
2175d	10¢ Carmine, Phosphored Paper.......	32.50	1.65	.35	.20
2176	14¢ Julia Ward Howe (1987)	35.00	1.85	.38	.15
2177	15¢ Buffalo Bill Cody, Block Tag (1988)	60.00	3.95	.65	.25
2177a	15¢ Overall Tagging (1990)	37.50	2.30	.40	.15
2177b	15¢ Surface Tagged	...	6.50	1.00	.40
2178	17¢ Belva Ann Lockwood	47.50	2.25	.50	.15
2179	20¢ Virginia Agpar, Pf 11 x 11.1 (1994)	41.50	3.00	.45	.15

1986-94 Great Americans, Perforated II
(Sheets of 100)

Scott's No.		Mint Sheet	Plate Block	F-VF NH	F-VF Used
2180	21¢ Chester Carlson (1988)..............	57.50	3.25	.60	.20
2181	23¢ Mary Cassatt, Block Tag (1988)	60.00	3.50	.65	.20
2181a	23¢ Overall Tagging	75.00	4.75	.80	.30
2181b	23¢ Phosphored, Dull Gum	65.00	3.85	.70	.20
2181bs	23¢ Phosphored, Shiny Gum	75.00	4.95	.80	...
2182	25¢ Jack London, Perf. 11	60.00	3.00	.65	.15
2182a	25¢ Bklt. Pn/10, Perf. 11 (1988)......	...	...	6.75	5.00
2183	28¢ Sitting Bull (1989)	75.00	4.00	.80	.20
2184	29¢ Earl Warren (1992)	75.00	3.85	.80	.18
2185	29¢ Jefferson Pf 11½ x 11 (1993) ...	75.00	3.85	.80	.18
2185	Jefferson, Plate Block of 8............		7.50	...	...
2186	35¢ Dennis Chavez (1991)	80.00	5.00	.85	.18
2187	40¢ Chennault, Overall ('90)	90.00	5.00	1.00	.18
2187a	40¢ Phosphored, Dull Gum	120.00	6.00	1.25	.35
2187as	40¢ Phosphored, Shiny Gum	125.00	6.50	1.25	...
2188	45¢ Dr. H. Cushing, Block Tag (1988)	125.00	6.00	1.30	.20
2188a	45¢ Overall Tagging (1990)	220.00	11.75	2.35	.75
2189	52¢ Hubert Humphrey, Dull ('91)	150.00	7.75	1.60	.20
2189s	52¢ Shiny Gum (1993)	170.00	8.75	1.80	...
2190	56¢ John Harvard	150.00	7.50	1.60	.22
2191	65¢ Gen. "Hap" Arnold (1988)........	150.00	8.00	1.60	.22
2192	75¢ Wendell Willkie, Dull (1992).....	160.00	8.75	1.75	.18
2192s	75¢ Shiny Gum	160.00	8.75	1.75	...
2193	$1 Dr. Bernard Revel	350.00	16.75	3.75	.30
2194	$1 Johns Hopkins, Block Tag (1989)(20)	48.50	11.75	2.50	.25
2194b	$1 Overall Tagging (1990) ....(20)	48.50	11.75	2.50	.25
2194d	$1 Phosphored, Dull Gum ....(20)	43.50	10.75	2.35	.25
2194ds	$1 Phosphored, Shiny Gum ....(20)	52.50	12.75	2.75	...
2195	$2 William Jennings Bryan............	450.00	20.00	4.75	.55
2196	$5 Bret Harte, Blk.Tag. ('87) ....(20)	215.00	49.50	11.50	2.50
2196b	$5 Surface Tagged (1992) ....(20)	220.00	50.00	11.75	2.25
2197	25¢ J. London Bklt. Sgl., Pf.10 ('88).	...	...	.75	.15
2197a	25¢ Bklt. Pane of 6 (1988)	...	...	4.50	3.00

NOTE: SETS CONTAIN OUR CHOICE OF TAGGED OR UNTAGGED, ETC.

1986 Commemoratives (cont.)

2198	2199	2200	2201

2202	2203	2204	2211

2205	2206	2207

2208	2209	2210

		Mint Sheet	Plate Block	F-VF NH	F-VF Used
2198-2201	22¢ Stamp Coll. Bklt.				
	Set of 4 Singles	...	...	2.60	.90
2201a	22¢ Booklet Pane of 4	...	...	2.75	2.50
2202	22¢ Love, Puppy	32.50	2.95	.70	.15
2203	22¢ Sojourner Truth	32.50	2.95	.70	.15
2204	22¢ Texas, 150th Anniv.	32.50	2.95	.70	.15
2205-09	22¢ Fish Set of 5 Booklet Sgls	...	...	9.50	1.00
2209a	22¢ Booklet Pane of 5	...	...	9.75	3.75
2210	22¢ Public Hospitals	33.50	3.25	.70	.15
2211	22¢ Duke Ellington	31.50	3.00	.65	.15

54

2216

| 2220 | 2221 |
| 2222 | 2223 |

2224

Scott's No.		Mint Sheet	Plate Block	F-VF NH	F-VF Used
1986 Presidents Miniature Sheets of 9					
2216-19	22¢ Ameripex '86, Set of 4	...	...	20.75	20.75
2216a-19i	Presidents, Set of 36 Singles.............	...	...	19.75	13.75
1986 Commemoratives (continued)					
2220-23	22¢ Arctic Explorers, attd	60.00	8.00	5.50	3.75
2220-23	Set of 4 Singles...............................	...	...	4.50	.80
2224	22¢ Statue of Liberty........................	31.50	3.00	.65	.15

| 2225 | 2226 | 2228 | 2231 |

1986-96 Transportation "B" Press Coils

Scott's No.		Pl.# Strip of 5	Pl.# Strip of 3	F-VF NH	F-VF Used
2225-31	Set of 4	11.50	9.50	1.50	.65
2225	1¢ Omnibus,Dull Gum("B" Press)..	.80	.70	.20	.15
2225a	1¢ Untagged, Dull (1991)................	.80	.70	.20	.18
2225s	1¢ Shiny Gum (1996)	8.00	7.50	.25	...
2225sv	1¢ Shiny, Untagged (1996)............	1.30	1.10	.20	...
2225sg	1¢ Semi-Gloss................................	1.40	1.30	.20	...
2226	2¢ Locomotive (1987)....................	.95	.75	.20	.15
2226a	2¢ Untagged Dull Gum (1994)	.95	.75	.20	.18
2226s	2¢ Shiny, Untagged	1.40	1.30	.20	...
2228	4¢ Stagecoach, Block Tagging	1.25	.95	.20	.20
2228a	4¢ Overall Tagging (1990)	15.00	14.50	.50	.25
2231	8.3¢ Ambulance, Precancel	9.00	7.50	1.10	.25

4¢ Stagecoach:
1898A: "Stagecoach 1890s" is 19½ mm. long
2228: "Stagecoach 1890s" is 17 mm. long

8.3¢ Ambulance:
2128: "Ambulance 1860s" is 18½ mm. long
2231: "Ambulance 1860s" is 18 mm. long

| 2235 | 2236 | 2240 | 2241 |
| 2237 | 2238 | 2242 | 2243 |

| 2239 | 2244 | 2245 |

Scott's No.		Mint Sheet	Plate Block	F-VF NH	F-VF Used
2235-38	22¢ Navajo Art, attd	37.50	4.25	3.25	2.75
2235-38	Set of 4 Singles..............................	...	...	3.00	.80
2239	22¢ T.S. Eliot	28.50	2.75	.60	.15
2240-43	22¢ Woodcarved Figurines., attd	37.50	4.50	3.25	2.75
2240-43	Set of 4 Singles..............................	...	...	3.00	.80
2244-45	Christmas Issues				
2244	22¢ Madonna & Child ....(100)	57.50	2.75	.60	.15
2245	22¢ Village Scene.........................(100)	57.50	2.75	.60	.15

1987 Commemoratives

| 2246 | 2247 | 2248 |

| 2249 | 2250 | 2251 |

2246-51,75,2336-38,2349-54,2360-61,2367-68	Set of 20	...		15.95	3.00
2246	22¢ Michigan Statehood	28.50	2.75	.60	.15
2247	22¢ Pan American Games	28.50	2.75	.60	.15
2248	22¢ Love, Heart ....(100)	55.00	2.75	.60	.15
2249	22¢ Jean Baptiste, Pointe du Sable	32.50	3.25	.70	.15
2250	22¢ Enrico Caruso	28.50	2.75	.60	.15
2251	22¢ Girl Scouts	32.50	3.25	.70	.15

1987-94 TRANSPORTATION COILS III

2252   2253   2254   2255

2256   2257   2258   2259

2260   2261   2262   2263

2264   2265   2266

Scott's No.		Pl.# Strip of 5	Pl.# Strip of 3	F-VF NH	Used
2252-66	Set of 15 Different Values............	62.50	50.00	6.50	3.15
2252	3¢ Conestoga Wagon ('88)...........	.90	.80	.20	.15
2252a	3¢ Untagged, Dull Gum (1992)......	1.45	1.30	.20	.18
2252b	3¢ Untagged, Shiny Gum	1.60	1.40	.20	...
2253	5¢ Milk Wagon	1.20	1.00	.20	.15
2254	5.3¢ Elevator, Prec. (1988)............	2.30	1.85	.30	.22
2255	7.6¢ Carretta, Prec. (1988)	3.00	2.65	.30	.22
2256	8.4¢ Wheelchair, Prec. (1986)........	2.50	2.00	.30	.20
2257	10¢ Canal Boat, Block Tagging......	2.25	1.80	.28	.15
2257a	10¢ Overall Tagged (1992)	4.00	3.50	.35	.30
2257ad	10¢ Overall Tagged, dull gum ('91)	6.25	5.75	.35	...
2258	13¢ Police Wagon, Prec. ('88)........	5.00	4.25	.50	.25
2259	13.2¢ R.R. Coat Car, Prec. ('88).....	4.00	3.35	.35	.20
2260	15¢ Tugboat, Block Tagging ('88) ..	3.25	2.50	.45	.18
2260a	15¢ Overall Tagging (1990)	4.35	3.75	.60	.25
2260b	15¢ Untagged	200.00	190.00	4.25	...
2261	16.7¢ Popcorn Wagon, Prec.('88)...	4.00	3.50	.50	.25
2262	17.5¢ Marmon Wasp......................	5.00	4.25	.50	.25
2262a	17.5¢ Precancelled	5.50	4.75	.55	.35
2263	20¢ Cable Car (1988)...................	4.50	3.75	.55	.20
2263b	20¢ Overall Tagged (1990)	9.75	8.00	1.10	.35
2264	20.5¢ Fire Engine, Prec. (1988).....	8.75	6.95	1.00	.35
2265	21¢ R.R. Mail Car, Prec. (1988).....	7.00	5.25	.60	.30
2266	24.1¢ Tandem Bic., Prec. (1988)....	5.75	4.75	.70	.35

1987 Special Occasions Issue

2267

2268   2269

2270

2274   2272

2273

2271   2272

2275   2276   2277/82

2278,2285A   2280   2281   2283

2284   2285

2286-2335 Examples

Scott's No.		Mint Sheet	Plate Block	F-VF NH	F-VF Used
1987 Special Occasions Issue					
2267-74	22¢ Spec. Occ. Bklt. Sgls. (8)	...	...	14.50	2.95
2274a	22¢ Bklt. Pane of 10.......................	...	...	16.50	12.00
	Booklet Pane contains 2 each of # 2267 and # 2272				
1987 Commemoratives (cont)					
2275	22¢ United Way	28.50	2.75	.60	.15
1987-89 Regular Issues					
2276	22¢ Flag & Fireworks...................(100)	57.50	3.00	.60	.15
2276a	22¢ Fireworks B. Pane of 20	...	...	11.50	11.00
2276v	22¢ Flag, Booklet Single	...	...	.65	.20
2277	(25¢) "E" Earth Issue ('88)............(100)	70.00	3.50	.75	.15
2278	25¢ Flag & Clouds ('88) ....(100)	67.50	3.25	.70	.15
2279	(25¢) "E" Earth Coil ('88)........Pl# Strip	4.50 (5)	3.50 (3)	.70	.15
2280	25¢ Flag/Yosem Coil Block Tagging('88)				
	Pl# Strip	4.50 (5)	3.50 (3)	.70	.15
2280v	25¢ Phosphor Paper ('89) ....Pl# Strip	4.95 (5)	3.95 (3)	.70	.15
2281	25¢ Honeybee Coil................Pl# Strip	4.50 (5)	3.50 (3)	.75	.15
2282	(25¢) "E" Bklt. Sgl. ('88)	...	...	.80	.15
2282a	(25¢) Bklt. Pane of 10.................	...	...	7.75	6.00
2283	25¢ Pheas. Bk. Sgl., **red & blue sky** ('88)	...	...	.80	.15
2283a	25¢ Bklt. Pane of 10.................	...	...	7.75	6.00
2283b	25¢ Blue Sky, **(red omitted)**, bklt. sgl. ('89)	...	...	8.75	2.00
2283c	25¢ Bklt. Pn. 10 **(Pl# A3111,A3222)**	...	...	85.00	...
2284	25¢ Grosbeak Bklt. Sgl. ('88)	...	...	.70	.18
2285	25¢ Owl Bklt. Sgl. ('88)	...	...	.70	.18
2284-85	Attached Pair.............................	...	...	1.40	.95
2285b	25¢ Bklt. Pn. (5 ea. #2284,2285)......	...	...	6.75	5.75
2285A	25¢ Flag/Cloud Bk. Sgl. ('88)	...	...	.75	.18
2285Ac	25¢ Bklt. Pn. 6	...	...	4.25	4.00
1987 North American Wildlife Series					
2286-2335	22¢ American Wildlife	69.50	...	...	...
2286-2335	Set of 50 Singles	...	...	65.00	22.50
2286-2335	22¢ Individual Singles	...	...	1.50	.55

2286	Barn Swallow	2303	Blackbird	2320	Bison
2287	Monarch Butterfly	2304	Lobster	2321	Snowy Egret
2288	Bighorn Sheep	2305	Jack Rabbit	2322	Gray Wolf
2289	Hummingbird	2306	Scarlet Tanager	2323	Mountain Goat
2290	Cottontail	2307	Woodchuck	2324	Deer Mouse
2291	Osprey	2308	Spoonbill	2325	Prairie Dog
2292	Mountain Lion	2309	Bald Eagle	2326	Box Turtle
2293	Luna Moth	2310	Brown Bear	2327	Wolverine
2294	Mule Deer	2311	Iiwi	2328	American Elk
2295	Gray Squirrel	2312	Badger	2329	Sea Lion
2296	Armadillo	2313	Pronghorn	2330	Mockingbird
2297	Eastern Chipmunk	2314	River Otter	2331	Raccoon
2298	Moose	2315	Ladybug	2332	Bobcat
2299	Black Bear	2316	Beaver	2333	Ferret
2300	Tiger Swallowtail	2317	Whitetailed Deer	2334	Canada Goose
2301	Bobwhite	2318	Blue Jay	2335	Red Fox
2302	Ringtail	2319	Pika		

2336	2337	2338	2339
2340	2341	2342	2343
2344	2345	2346	2347

2348	2349	2350

1987-90 Ratification of the Constitution Bicentennial

Scott's No.		Mint Sheet	Plate Block	F-VF NH	F-VF Used
2336-48	Set of 13....................	465.00	45.00	9.75	1.95
2336	22¢ Delaware......................	31.50	3.00	.65	.18
2337	22¢ Pennsylvania...........................	37.50	3.95	.75	.18
2338	22¢ New Jersey.......................	35.75	3.50	.75	.18
2339	22¢ Georgia ('88).....................	35.75	3.50	.75	.18
2340	22¢ Connecticut ('88)	35.75	3.50	.75	.18
2341	22¢ Massachusetts ('88)	35.75	3.50	.75	.18
2342	22¢ Maryland ('88)	35.75	3.50	.75	.18
2343	25¢ South Carolina ('88)	40.00	3.95	.85	.18
2344	25¢ New Hampshire ('88)...............	40.00	3.95	.85	.18
2345	25¢ Virginia ('88)	40.00	3.95	.85	.18
2346	25¢ New York ('88).................	40.00	3.95	.85	.18
2347	25¢ North Carolina ('89).............	40.00	3.95	.85	.18
2348	25¢ Rhode Island ('90)	40.00	3.95	.85	.18

1987 Commemoratives (cont.)

2351	2352
2353	2354

2355	
2356	
2357	
2358	
2359	

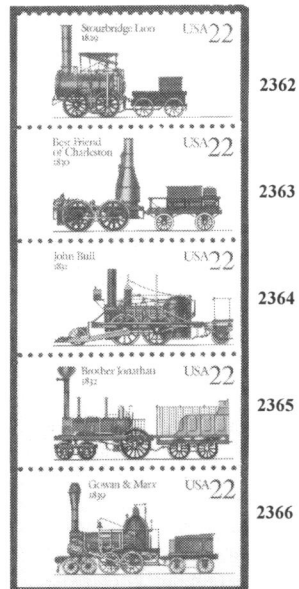

2362
2363
2364
2365
2366

2360	2361

2367	2368

Scott's No.			Mint Sheet	Plate Block	F-VF NH	F-VF Used
2349	22¢ U.S.-Morocco Relations..........		28.50	2.75	.60	.15
2350	22¢ William Faulkner....................		28.50	2.75	.60	.15
2351-54	22¢ Lacemaking, attd..............(40)		35.00	5.00	3.50	2.50
2351-54	Set of 4 Sgls......................		...	...	3.35	1.00
2355-59	22¢ Drafting of Constitution, Bklt. Sgls. (5)........................		...	...	3.95	1.10
2359a	22¢ Bklt. Pane of 5		...	...	4.25	3.50
2360	22¢ Signing the Constitution		31.75	3.25	.70	.15
2361	22¢ Cert. Public Accounting		150.00	15.00	3.50	.15
2362-66	22¢ Locomotives Bklt. Sgls. (5).....		...	...	3.75	1.10
2366a	22¢ Bklt. Pane of 5		...	...	3.95	3.50
#2367-68 Christmas Issues						
2367	22¢ Madonna & Child ....(100)		57.50	2.75	.60	.15
2368	22¢ Ornaments.........................(100)		57.50	2.75	.60	.15

1988 Commemoratives

2369	2370	2371

2339-46,69-80,86-93,99-2400	Set of 30........	...	...	25.75	4.75
2369	22¢ 1988 Winter Olympics	32.50	3.25	.75	.15
2370	22¢ Australia Bicent...................(40)	24.00	2.75	.60	.15
2371	22¢ J.W. Johnson.........................	31.50	3.00	.70	.15

1988 Commemoratives (cont.)

2372
2374   2373
2375   2376

2377

2378   2379   2380

2381   2382

2383   2384

2385

2386   2387
2388   2389   2390   2391
                       2392   2393

Scott's No.		Mint Sheet	Plate Block	F-VF NH	F-VF Used
2372-75	22¢ Cats, attd .... (40)	37.50	5.75	3.75	2.50
2372-75	Set of 4 Sgls	...	3.50	3.50	1.00
2376	22¢ Knute Rockne........................	38.50	3.95	.80	.15
2377	25¢ Francis Ouimet	52.50	5.75	1.10	.20
2378	25¢ Love, Roses.................... (100)	67.50	3.25	.70	.15
2379	45¢ Love, Roses..........................	65.00	5.75	1.35	.20
2380	25¢ Summer Olympics	37.50	3.50	.80	.15
2381-85	25¢ Classic Cars, Bklt. Sgls.	...	...	9.50	1.00
2385a	25¢ Bk. Pn. 5	...	...	10.00	4.75

1988 Commemoratives (cont.)

2386-89	25¢ Antarctic Exp., attd.................	56.75	7.95	5.25	3.00
2386-89	Set of 4 Singles...........................	...	...	4.75	.80
2390-93	25¢ Carousel, attd.......................	55.00	6.00	5.25	3.00
2390-93	Set of 4 Singles...........................	...	...	4.75	.80

2394

2399   2400

2395   2396
2397   2398

1988 Express Mail Issue

Scott's No.		Mint Sheet	Plate Block	F.VF NH	F.VF Used
2394	$8.75 Eagle .... (20)	450.00	100.00	23.75	8.75

1988 Special Occasions Issue

2395-98	25¢ Special Occasions, Bklt. Sgls. ...	...	3.75	.80	
2396a	25¢ Happy Birthday & Best Wishes B. Pn. of 6 (3&3) w/gutter	...	...	5.00	4.00
2398a	25¢ Thinking of You & Love You B. Pn. of 6 (3&3) w/gutter	...	...	5.00	4.00

1988 Commemoratives (cont.)

2399	25¢ Madonna & Child	31.50	3.00	.65	.15
2400	25¢ Horse & Sleigh	31.50	3.00	.65	.15

2401   2402

2403

2404

2405
2406
2407
2408
2409

2410   2411   2412   2413

2417   2416   2418

2419   2420   2421

2422   2433   2426
2424   2425

1989 Commemoratives

Scott's No.		Mint Sheet	Plate Block	F-VF NH	F-VF Used
2347,2401-04,10-18,20-28,34-37	Set of 27 ...	...	...	23.75	3.95
2401	25¢ Montana Sthd. Cent................	40.00	4.00	.90	.15
2402	25¢ A. Philip Randolph	39.50	3.75	.85	.15
2403	25¢ North Dakota Sthd. Cent	31.50	3.00	.65	.15
2404	25¢ Washington Sthd. Cent	35.00	3.50	.75	.15
2405-09	25¢ Steamboats, Bklt. Sgls.............	...	...	4.00	1.10
2409a	25¢ Bklt. Pane of 5 ....(Unfolded 7.00)	...	4.25	3.50
2410	25¢ World Stamp Expo	31.50	3.00	.65	.15
2411	25¢ Arturo Toscanini	35.00	3.50	.75	.15
2412-15	Constitution Bicent., Set of 4..........	150.00	15.00	3.25	.55
2412	25¢ House of Representatives	37.50	3.75	.80	.15
2413	25¢ U.S. Senate	37.50	3.75	.80	.15
2414	25¢ Exec. Branch/G.W. Inaug........	40.00	4.25	.90	.15
2415	25¢ U.S. Supreme Court (1990)	38.50	4.00	.85	.15
2416	25¢ South Dakota Sthd. Cent	31.50	3.00	.65	.15
2417	25¢ Lou Gehrig	52.50	5.25	1.10	.18
2418	25¢ Ernest Hemingway	31.50	3.00	.65	.15
1989 Priority Mail Issue					
2419	$2.40 Moon Landing...................(20)	125.00	28.50	6.75	2.75
1989 Commemoratives (cont.)					
2420	25¢ Letter Carriers ....(40)	25.00	3.00	.65	.15
2421	25¢ Drafting Bill of Rights	45.00	4.75	.95	.15
2422-25	25¢ Prehistoric Animals, attd ......(40)	50.00	5.75	5.25	2.75
2422-25	Set of 4 Singles	...	...	4.85	.90
2426	25¢ Pre-Columbian Customs	31.50	3.00	.65	.15

2427   2428,2429   2431

1989 Christmas Issues

Scott's No.		Mint Sheet	Plate Block	F-VF NH	F-VF Used
2427	25¢ Madonna & Child....................	31.50	3.00	.65	.15
2427v	Madonna, Booklet Single	...	...	.75	.18
2427a	25¢ Bklt. Pane of 10.......................(Unfolded 15.00)		7.50	5.50
2428	25¢ Sleigh & Presents	31.50	3.00	.65	.15
2429	25¢ Sleigh, Bklt. Single	...	...	.90	.18
2429a	25¢ Bklt. Pane of 10...........	(Unfolded 19.50)		8.25	5.50
1989 Regular Issue					
2431	25¢ Eagle & Shield, self adhesive ...	...	.90	.30	
2431a	25¢ Pane of 18.............................	...		15.95	...
2431v	25¢ Eagle & Shield, Coil (No#)......	Strip of 3	2.70	.90	...

1989 World Stamp Expo '89, Washington, DC

2433

2438

		Mint Sheet	Plate Block	F-VF NH	F-VF Used
2433	90¢ World Stamp Expo S/S of 4.......	...	...	19.50	15.00
2434-37	25¢ Traditional Mail Deliv., attd ...(40)	45.00	6.00	5.00	3.25
2434-37	Set of 4 Singles	...	...	4.70	1.00
2438	25¢ Traditional Mail S/S of 4	...	...	6.50	5.00
	Also see #C122-26				

2439   2440,2441   2442   2443

2444

2449   2445   2446
         2447   2448

1990 Commemoratives

Scott's No.		Mint Sheet	Plate Block	F-VF NH	F-VF Used
2348,2439-40,2442,44-49,96-2500,2506-15 Set of 25 ...				26.95	3.75
2439	25¢ Idaho Sthd. Centenary	31.50	3.00	.65	.15
2440	25¢ Love, Doves	31.50	3.00	.65	.15
2441	25¢ Love, Bklt. Single	...	...	.75	.18
2441a	25¢ Booklet Pane of 10 ....(Unfolded 42.50)		...	7.50	6.50
2442	25¢ Ida B. Wells	38.50	3.75	.80	.15

1990 Regular Issue

| 2443 | 15¢ Beach Umbrella, Bklt. Sgl ..... | ... | ... | .45 | .15 |
| 2443a | 15¢ Booklet Pane of 10 ..... (Unfolded 8.95) | | ... | 4.35 | 3.95 |

1990 Commemoratives (continued)

2444	25¢ Wyoming Sthd. Centenary	36.50	3.50	.75	.15
2445-48	25¢ Classic Films, attd .... (40)	85.00	10.00	9.00	5.00
2445-48	Set of 4 Singles	...	...	8.75	1.00
2449	25¢ Marianne Moore....................	31.50	3.00	.65	.15

1990-95 Transportation Coils IV

2451   2452   2452B   2452D   2453,2454

2457   2458   2463

2464   2466   2468

Scott's No.		Pl# Strip of 5	Pl# Strip of 3	F-VF NH	FVF Used
2451/2468 Set of 12 values		42.75	33.50	4.95	2.10
2451	4¢ Steam Carriage (1991).............	1.20	1.00	.20	.15
2451b	4¢ Untagged................................	1.30	1.10	.20	.18
2452	5¢ Circus Wagon, Engraved	1.35	1.10	.20	.15
2452a	5¢ Untagged................................	1.75	1.40	.22	.18
2452B	5¢ Circus Wagon, Gravure ('92)	1.60	1.25	.20	.15
2452D	5¢ Circus Wagon(¢ sign) ('95)	1.95	1.75	.20	.18

1990-95 Transportation Coils (continued)

Scott's No.		Pl#Strip of 5	Pl#Strip of 3	F-VF NH	F-VF Used
2453	5¢ Canoe, Brown (1991)	1.50	1.25	.20	.18
2454	5¢ Canoe, Red (1991)...................	1.85	1.60	.20	.18
2457	10¢ Tractor Trailer, Intaglio ('91)..	3.00	2.50	.25	.18
#2457	"Additional Presort Postage Paid" In Gray.				
2458	10¢ Tractor Trailer, Gravure ('94)	3.50	2.95	.30	.18
#2458	"Additional, etc." in black. Whiter paper.				
2463	20¢ Cog Railway (1995).................	5.50	4.75	.40	.18
2464	23¢ Lunch Wagon, Block Tag (1991)	4.50	3.65	.60	.15
2464p	23¢ Phosphored, Dull Gum............	6.25	5.25	.65	.35
2464ps	23¢ Phosphored, Shiny Gum...........	6.75	5.25	.70	...
2466	32¢ Ferryboat, Shiny (1995)	7.75	6.75	.70	.15
2466b	32¢ Bronx blue	120.00	115.00	7.50	...
2466v	32¢ Low Gloss Gum......................	8.75	7.50	.85	...
2468	$1.00 Seaplane, Dry Gum..............	13.95	9.50	2.25	.60
2468s	$1.00 Shiny Gum..........................	13.95	9.50	2.25	...
2468v	$1.00 Low Gloss Gum....................	13.95	9.50	2.25	...

Circus Wagon: #2452 Short letters and date, #2452B Taller, thinner letters and date

2470   2471   2472   2473   2474

2475

1990 Commemorative Booklet Pane

Scott's No.		Mint Sheet	Plate Block	F-VF NH	F-VF Used
2470-74	25¢ Lighthouse Bklt. Singles	...	...	6.75	1.00
2474a	25¢ Booklet Pane of 5 ......(Unfolded 8.95)			6.95	3.95

1990 Flag Regular Issue

| 2475 | 25¢ ATM Self Adhesive, Plastic Stamp | ... | ... | .85 | .50 |
| 2475a | 25¢ Pane of 12............................ | ... | ... | 9.95 | ... |

1990-95 Flora and Fauna

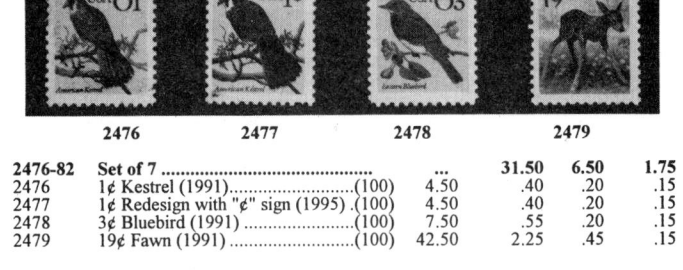

2476   2477   2478   2479

2476-82	Set of 7	...	31.50	6.50	1.75
2476	1¢ Kestrel (1991)............(100)	4.50	.40	.20	.15
2477	1¢ Redesign with "¢" sign (1995) .(100)	4.50	.40	.20	.15
2478	3¢ Bluebird (1991) ....(100)	7.50	.55	.20	.15
2479	19¢ Fawn (1991) ....(100)	42.50	2.25	.45	.15

2480   2481   2482

2480	30¢ Cardinal (1991)....................(100)	55.00	3.50	.65	.20
2481	45¢ Pumpkinseed Sunfish('92) .....(100)	95.00	5.00	1.00	.30
2482	$2.00 Bobcat ....(20)	75.00	18.00	3.95	.90

1991-95 Flora and Fauna Booklet Stamps

	2483	2484,2485	2486	2487,2493, 2495	2488,2494, 2495A

Scott's No.				F-VF NH	F-VF Used
2483	20¢ Blue Jay, Booklet Single ('95)... ...	...	.60		.15
2483a	20¢ Booklet Pane of 10 ....(Unfolded 6.95)	...	5.75	4.95
2484	29¢ Wood Duck, BEP bklt sgl Pf 10...	...	.90		.18
2484a	29¢ BEP Bklt Pane of 10 ('91)..........(Unfolded 9.95)	...	7.95	7.75
2485	29¢ Wood Duck, KCS bklt sgl Pf 11...	...	1.00		.18
2485a	29¢ KCS Bklt Pane of 10 ('91) ....(Unfolded 10.95)	...	8.75	8.95
2486	29¢ African Violet........................	...	...	.85	.18
2486a	29¢ Booklet Pane of 10 (1993).........(Unfolded 9.50)	...	8.50	7.50
2487	32¢ Peach, booklet single	...	...	.95	.20
2488	32¢ Pear, booklet single	...	...	.95	.20
2487-88	32¢ Peach & Pear, Attached Pair.....	...	...	1.90	1.10
2488a	32¢ Booklet Pane of 10 (1995).........(Unfolded 9.95)	...	9.00	7.50

1993-96 Self Adhesive Booklets & Coils

	2489	2490	2491	2492

2489	29¢ Red Squirrel, ...	...	...	.90	.40
2489a	29¢ Pane of 18		...	14.95	...
2489v	Squirrel Coil (No Plate #) ....Strip of 3	2.70	.90	.40
2490	29¢ Rose		...	.90	.40
2490a	29¢ Pane of 18		...	14.95	...
2490v	Rose coil (No Plate #) ....Strip of 3	2.70	.90	.40
2491	29¢ Pine Cone		...	.90	.40
2491a	29¢ Pane of 18 ('93)....................		...	14.95	...
2491v	Pine Cone coil ....Pl. #Strip (5) 8.00	(3) 6.75	.90	...
2492	32¢ Pink Rose		...	.90	.30
2492a	32¢ Pane of 20 (1995)		...	16.50	...
2492v	32¢ Pink Rose, Coil ....Pl.#Strip (5) 6.75	(3) 5.50	.90	...
2492b	32¢ Pink Rose, Folded Pane of 15 ('96)	...	...	12.95	...
2492e	32¢ Pink Rose, Folded Pane of 14 ('96)	...	...	25.95	...
2492f	32¢ Pink Rose, Folded Pane of 16 ('96)	...	...	28.95	...
2492r	32¢ Pane of 20 with Die-cut "Time to Reorder" (1995)................	...	...	17.75	...
2493	32¢ Peach, Self-adhesive single........	...	...	.90	.30
2494	32¢ Pear, Self-adhesive single	...	...	.90	.30
2493-94	32¢ Peach & Pear, Attached Pair.... ...	...	...	1.90	...
2494a	32¢ Pane of 20, Self-adhesive ('95)...	...	...	16.50	...
2495	32¢ Peach, Coil, Self-adhesive	...	...	.95	...
2495A	32¢ Pear, Coil, Self-adhesive...........	...	...	.95	...
2495-95A	32¢ Peach & Pear, Coil Pair ('95) Pl # Strip	(5)6.75	(3) 5.25	1.90	...

1990 Commemoratives (continued)

	2496	2497	2498

	2499	2500

Scott's No.		Mint Sheet	Plate Block	F-VF NH	F-VF Used
2496-2500	25¢ Olympians,Strip of 5..............(35)	38.50	(10)12.50	5.75	4.35
2496-2500	Set of 5 Singles	...	...	5.50	1.00
2496-2500	Tab singles, attd, Top or Bottom ...	...	...	6.75	5.75

1990 Commemoratives (continued)

2501	2502	2503
2504		2505

2506	2607

2508	2509
2510	2511

2512	2513

2514, 2514v	2515,2516

Scott's No.		Mint Sheet	Plate Block	F-VF NH	F-VF Used
2501-05	25¢ Indian Headdresses bklt. sgls. ...	...	...	4.50	1.00
2505a	25¢ Booklet Pane of 10 (2 ea.).........(Unfolded 14.95)	...	8.95	7.50
2506-07	25¢ Micronesia/Marshall Isl., attd....	39.50	3.85	1.75	.90
2506-07	Set of 2 Singles	...	...	1.60	.40
2508-11	25¢ Sea Creatures, attd. ....(40)	33.50	3.95	3.50	2.50
2508-11	Set of 4 Singles	...	...	3.25	.80
2512	25¢ America, Grand Canyon...........	31.50	3.00	.65	.15
2513	25¢ Dwight Eisenhower ....(40)	42.50	5.00	1.10	.15
2514	25¢ Christmas Madonna & Child.....	31.50	3.00	.65	.15
2514v	25¢ Madonna, Booklet Single	...	...	.80	.18
2514a	25¢ Booklet Pane of 10 .....(Unfolded 14.95)...7.95		5.95	
2515	25¢ Christmas Tree, Perf. 11...........	31.50	3.00	.65	.15
2516	25¢ Tree, Bklt. Sgl., Perf. 11½x11	...	...	.90	.18
2516a	25¢ Booklet Pane of 10 ....(Unfolded 18.95)	...	8.95	5.95

1991-94 Regular Issues

| 2517-2520 | 2521 | 2522 |

| 2523 | 2523A | 2524 | 2526 |

| 2528 | 2529 | 2530 | 2531 | 2531A |

1991 Regular Issues

Scott's No.		Mint Sheet	Plate Block	F-VF NH	F-VF Used
2517	(29¢) "F" Flower Stamp .... (100)	70.00	3.50	.75	.15
2519	(29¢) "F" Flower, BEP bklt. sgl.	...	...	.85	.18
2519a	(29¢)Bklt.Pane of 10,BEP,bullseye perfs	...	...	8.50	6.95
2520	(29¢) "F" Flower, KCS bklt. sgl.	...	...	2.75	.35
2520a	(29¢) Bklt. Pane of 10..........	...	...	26.95	19.95

#2519: Bullseye perforations (11.2). Horizontal and vertical perforations meet exactly in stamp corners.
#2520: Normal (line) perforations, Perf. 11

2521	(4¢) Non-Denom. "make-up" .... (100)	12.50	.60	.20	.15
2522	(29¢) "F" Flag Stamp, ATM self adhesive	...	...	.95	.60
2522a	(29¢) Pane of 12	...	...	9.95	...
2524	29¢ Flower, Perf. 11 .... (100)	75.00	4.25	.80	.18
2524a	29¢ Flower, Perf. 12½x13............ (100)	90.00	5.50	.95	.25
2527	29¢ Flower Bklt. Sgl.	...	...	.85	.18
2527a	29¢ Booklet Pane of 10.......... (Unfolded 9.75)	...	8.25	5.95
2528	29¢ Flag with Olympic Rings, bklt. sgl.	...	...	.85	.18
2528a	29¢ Booklet Pane of 10.......... (Unfolded 9.75)	...	8.50	5.95
2530	19¢ Hot-Air Balloons, bklt. sgl	...	...	.55	.20
2530a	19¢ Booklet Pane of 10.......... (Unfolded 6.75)	...	5.25	4.50
2531	29¢ Flags/Mem. Day Anniv .... (100)	70.00	3.50	.75	.18
2531A	29¢ Liberty & Torch, ATM self adh .	...	...	.90	.30
2531Ab	29¢ Pane of 18, Original back	...	...	16.75	...
2531Av	29¢ Pane of 18, Revised back	...	...	14.95	...

1991-94 Coil Stamps, Perforated Vertically

Scott's No.		Pl. Strip of 5	Pl. Strip of 3	F-VF NH	F-VF Used
2518	(29¢) "F" Flower Coil	5.00	3.75	.80	.15
2523	29¢ Flag/Mt. Rushmore Intaglio Coil	5.25	4.50	.80	.25
2523c	29¢ Toledo Brown	200.00	190.00	3.25	...
2523A	29¢ Flag, Gravure	5.75	4.50	.80	.25

* On # 2523A, "USA" & "29" are not outlined in white.

2525	29¢ Flower Coil, rouletted, ...	6.00	4.75	.80	.18
2526	29¢ Flower Coil, perf ('92)	5.50	4.25	.80	.15
2529	19¢ Fishing Boat Coil, Ty. I	4.50	3.75	.55	.15
2529a	19¢ Boat Coil, Ty. II ('93)	4.50	3.75	.55	.18
2529b	19¢ Type II, Untagged	12.50	10.00	.90	.55
2529C	19¢ Boat Coil, Ty. III (94)	7.50	6.75	.70	.22

*Type I: Darker color & large color cells, Perf. 10
Type II: Lighter color & small color cells, Perf. 10
Type III: Numerals & U.S.A. taller and thinner, only 1 loop of rope around piling, Perf. 9.8

1991 Commemoratives

| 2533 | 2532 | 2534 |

Scott's No.		Mint Sheet	Plate Block	F-VF NH	F-VF Used
2532-35,37-38,50-51,53-58,60-61,67,78-79 Set of 19		...	...	16.35	3.25
2532	50¢ Switzerland joint issue .... (40)	52.50	6.50	1.30	.35
2533	29¢ Vermont Bicentennial.................	36.50	3.50	.75	.18
2534	29¢ Savings Bond, 50th Anniv..........	39.50	3.75	.80	.18

1991 Commemoratives (continued)

| 2535,2536 | 2537 | 2538 |

Scott's No.		Mint Sheet	Plate Block	F-VF NH	F-VF Used
2535	29¢ Love Stamp, Pf. 12½x13	37.50	3.75	.80	.15
2535a	Same, Perf. 11	47.50	5.00	1.00	.25
2536	29¢ Booklet Sgl., Pf. 11 on 2-3 sides.	...	...	.85	.20
2536a	Booklet Pane of 10 ....(Unfolded 9.50)	...	8.50	5.75

NOTE: "29" is further from edge of design on #2536 than on #2535.

2537	52¢ Love Stamp, two ounces............	60.00	5.75	1.30	.35
2538	29¢ William Saroyan	36.50	3.50	.75	.18

1991-96 Regular Issues

| 2539 | 2540 | 2541 |

| 2542 | 2543 |

| 2544 | 2544A |

2539	$1.00 USPS Logo&Olym. Rings .....(20)	52.50	12.50	2.75	.75
2540	$2.90 Priority Mail, Eagle.................(20)	150.00	35.00	7.95	3.00
2541	$9.95 Express Mail, Domestic...........(20)	465.00	105.00	24.50	10.75
2542	$14.00 Express Mail, Internat'l. ....(20)	585.00	130.00	30.00	21.50
2543	$2.90 Priority Mail, Space ('93) ....(40)	265.00	29.50	6.95	2.75
2544	$3 Challng.Shuttle,Pr.Mail('95).....(20)	115.00	25.00	5.95	2.75
2544b	$3 with 1996 Date ('96) ....(20)	115.00	25.00	5.95	3.00
2544A	$10.75 Endvr.Shtl.,Exp.Mail('95) .....(20)	395.00	92.50	21.00	8.95

1991 Commemoratives (continued)

| 2545 | 2546 | 2547 |

| 2548 | 2549 |

2545-49	29¢ Fishing Flies, bklt. singles..........	...	...	7.00	1.10
2549a	29¢ Booklet Pane of 5 ....(Unfolded 11.75)	...	7.50	4.25

2550   2551   2552

2553   2554   2555

2556   2557

2558   2561   2560

2559

Scott's No.		Mint Sheet	Plate Block	F-VF NH	F-VF Used
2550	29¢ Cole Porter	38.50	3.75	.85	.18
2551	29¢ Desert Shield/Desert Storm	35.00	3.50	.75	.18
2552	29¢ Desert Storm, Bklt. Sgl., ABNCo	...	...	.85	.20
2552a	29¢ Booklet Pane of 5 .... (Unfolded 6.50)			4.25	4.25
2553-57	29¢ Summer Olympics, attd .... (40) 35.00 (10)		9.75	4.75	3.00
2553-57	Set of 5 Singles	...	...	4.50	1.00
2558	29¢ Numismatics	42.50	3.95	.90	.18
2559	29¢ World War II S/S of 10 .... (20)	17.50	...	8.75	6.75
2559a-j	Set of 10 Singles	...	...	8.50	5.00
2559s	Se-Tenant Center Block of 10	...	...	9.50	8.95

2562   2563   2564

2565   2566

2568	2569	2570	2571	2572
2573	2574	2575	2576	2577

2567   2578   2579   2580   2581

2582   2583   2584   2585

Scott's No.		Mint Sheet	Plate Block	F-VF NH	F-VF Used
2560	29¢ Basketball, 100th Anniversary ...	47.50	4.50	1.00	.20
2561	29¢ District of Columbia Bicent	35.00	3.50	.75	.18
2562-66	29¢ Comedians, bklt. sgls.................	...	...	4.25	1.10
2566a	29¢ Booklet Pane of 10 (2 each)......(Unfolded 10.75)			8.50	6.95
2567	29¢ Jan Matzeliger	40.00	4.25	.85	.18
2568-77	29¢ Space Exploration bklt. sgls.......	...	...	9.75	2.75
2577a	29¢ Booklet Pane of 10 .... (Unfolded 12.75)			9.95	7.95

1991 Christmas Issues

2578	(29¢) Christmas, Madonna & Child..	35.00	3.50	.75	.15
2578v	(29¢) Madonna, Booklet single.........			.85	.18
2578a	(29¢) Booklet Pane of 10 ....(Unfolded 10.75)			8.50	6.50
2579	(29¢) Christmas, Santa & Chimney ..	35.00	3.50	.75	.15
2580-85	(29¢) Santa & Chimney, Set of 6 Booklet Singles	...	...	12.50	1.95
2580-81	(29¢) Bklt. Singles, Ty. I & II, attd...	...	...	10.00	...

* Ty. II, the far left brick from the top row of the chimney is missing from #2581

| 2582-85 | Booklet Singles, Set of 4 .... | | | 3.00 | .70 |
| 2581b-2585a | Bklt. Panes of 4, Set of 5 ....(Unfolded 31.75) | | | 24.95 | 22.50 |

2587   2590   2592

2593,2594   2595-97   2598   2599

1994-95 Definitives Designs of 1869 Essays

2587	32¢ James S. Polk (1995)............(100)	60.00	3.25	.65	.18
2590	$1 Surrender of Burgoyne.............(20)	38.75	9.00	1.95	.95
2592	$5 Washington & Jackson ....(20)	190.00	45.00	9.75	3.95

1992-93 Pledge of Allegiance

Scott's No.		Mint Sheet	Plate Block	F-VF NH	F-VF Used
2593	29¢ **black** denom. bklt.sgl.,Perf.10 ...	...		.85	.15
2593a	29¢ Booklet Pane of 10, Perf. 10 ......(Unfolded 9.75)	...		8.25	5.95
2593b	29¢ Black denom.,bklt.sgl.,Perf.11x10	...	...	1.35	.85
2593c	29¢ Bklt. Pane of 10, Perf. 11x10	...	...	12.95	8.50
2594	29¢,**red** denom,bklt.sgl.('93)...........	...		.80	.18
2594a	29¢ Booklet Pane of 10 ....(Unfolded 9.95)	...		7.75	6.75

1992 Eagle & Shield Self-Adhesive Stamps

2595	29¢ **"Brown"** denomination	...	...	.90	.30
2595a	29¢ "Brown" denomination, Pane of 17	...	...	13.75	...
2596	29¢ **"Green"** denomination	...	...	.90	.30
2596a	29¢ "Green" denomination, Pane of 17	...	...	13.75	...
2597	29¢ **"Red"** denomination	...	...	.90	.30
2597a	29¢ "Red" denomination, Pane of 17...	...	13.75		...

1992 Eagle & Shield Self-Adhesive Coils

2595v	29¢ "Brown" denomination...............Strip of 3	2.70		.90	...
2596v	29¢ "Green" denomination...............Strip of 3	2.70		.90	...
2597v	29¢ "Red" denomination...................Strip of 3	2.70		.90	...

NOTE: #2595v-2597v do not have plate numbers.

1994 Eagle Self-Adhesive Issue

2598	29¢ Eagle, self-adhesive	...	...	.90	.30
2598a	29¢ Pane of 18.............................	...	...	13.75	...
2598v	29¢ Eagle Coil, self-adhesive				
	....Pl#Strip (5)8.00 (3)	6.75		.95	...

1994 Statue of Liberty Self-Adhesive Issue

2599	29¢ Statue of Liberty, self-adhesive ..	...		.90	.30
2599a	29¢ Pane of 18.............................	...	...	13.75	...
2599v	29¢ Liberty Coil, Self-adhesive				
	....Pl#Strip (5)8.00 (3)	6.75		.95	...

1991-93 Coil Issues

2602   2603,2604,2907   2605

2606   2607   2608   2609

1991-93 Coil Issues

Scott's No.		Pl# Strip of 5	Pl# Strip of 3	F-VF NH	F-VF Used
2602	(10¢) Eagle, Bulk rate **ABNCo**............	3.00	2.35	.28	.18
2603	(10¢) Eagle,Bulk rate **BEP** (1993)......	2.90	2.50	.28	.18
2603v	(10¢) Dull Gum................................	4.25	3.50	.35	...
2603b	(10¢) Tagged..................................	16.75	15.75	.50	.50
2603l	(10¢) Low Gloss Gum (1998)...........	4.00	3.50	.25	...
2604	(10¢) Eagle, Blk rate, **Stamp Venturers**	3.65	2.95	.30	.18

#2603 Orange yellow & multicolored, #2604 Gold & multicolored.

2605	23¢ Flag, Pre-sort First Class........	4.75	3.75	.65	.30
2606	23¢ USA, Pre-sort 1st Cl., **ABNCo**('92)	4.75	3.75	.65	.30
2607	23¢ USA, Pre-sort 1st Cl., **BEP** ......('92)	6.00	5.00	.65	.30
2607v	23¢ Dull Gum................................	6.25	5.25	.75	...
2607t	23¢ Tagged	POR	POR	2.65	...
2608	23¢ USA, Pre-sort 1st Cl., **S.V.**........('93)	6.50	5.50	.70	.30

#2606 Light blue at bottom, "23" 6 mm wide, "First Class" 9½ mm wide.
#2607 Dark blue at bottom, "23" 7 mm wide, "First Class" 9½ mm wide.
#2608 Violet blue, "23" 6 mm wide, "First Class" 8½ mm wide.

2609	29¢ Flag/White House ('92).................		5.95	4.75	.80	.15

1992 Commemoratives

2611   2612   2613

2614   2615

2616   2617   2618   2619

Scott's No.		Mint Sheet	Plate Block	F-VF NH	F-VF Used
2611-23,2630-41,2698-2704,2710-14,2720 **Set of 38**			...	**33.75**	**8.75**
2611-15	29¢ Winter Olympics, attd ....(35)	35.00 (10)	9.75	4.75	3.50
2611-15	Set of 5 Singles................................	...	...	4.50	1.10
2616	29¢ World Columbian Expo.............	35.00	3.50	.75	.18
2617	29¢ W.E.B. DuBois, Black Heritage .	37.50	3.75	.80	.18
2618	29¢ Love, Envelope	35.00	3.50	.75	.18
2619	29¢ Olympic Baseball.....................	52.50	4.75	1.10	.20

2596a Sample of Self-Adhesive Pane

2620
2622

2621
2623

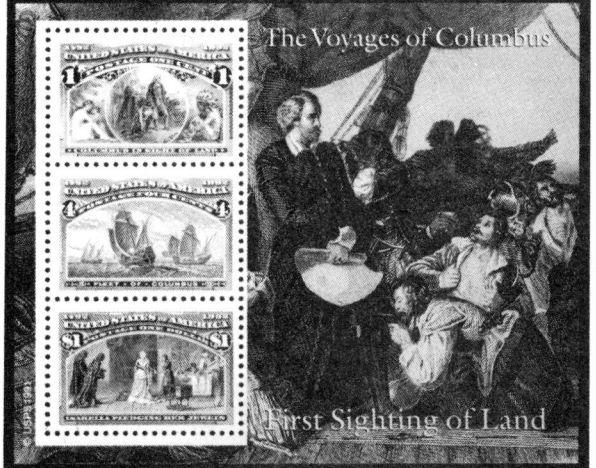

The Voyages of Columbus

First Sighting of Land

2624

The Voyages of Columbus

Claiming a New World

2625

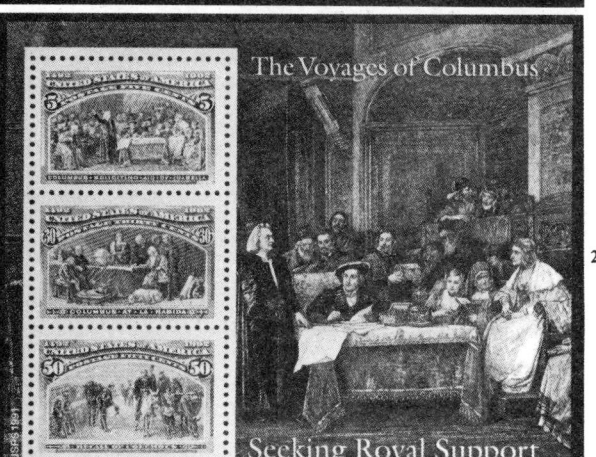

The Voyages of Columbus

Seeking Royal Support

2626

2627

The Voyages of Columbus

Royal Favor Restored

2628

The Voyages of Columbus

Reporting Discoveries

2629

The United States Postal Service celebrates the 500th anniversary of the voyages of Christopher Columbus. This set is based on the first U.S. stamps in commemorative format, engraved a century ago.

Christopher   Columbus

Scott's No.		Mint Sheet	Plate Block	F-VF NH	F-VF Used
2620-23	29¢ Voyage of Columbus, attd...... (40)	35.00	4.35	3.95	3.00
2620-23	Set of 4 Singles.................................	...	...	3.75	.90
2624-29	1¢-$5 Columbian Expo S/S, Set of 6...	...	39.50	37.50	
2624a-29	1¢-$5 Set of 16 Singles	...	...	38.50	35.00

#2624	1¢, 4¢, $1	1893 Designs of #230, 233, 241
#2625	2¢, 3¢, $4	1893 Designs of # 231, 232, 244
#2626	5¢, 30¢, 50¢	1893 Designs of # 234, 239, 240
#2627	6¢, 8¢, $3	1893 Designs of # 235, 236, 243
#2628	10¢, 15¢, $2	1893 Designs of # 237, 238, 242
#2629	$5	1893 Design of # 245

2631   2632
2633   2634

2630   2635   2636

2637   2638   2639

2640   2641

2642   2643   2644   2645   2646

Scott's No.		Mint Sheet	Plate Block	F-VF NH	F-VF Used
2630	29¢ New York Stock Exchange.....(40)	28.00	3.50	.75	.18
2631-34	29¢ Space Accomplishments, attd	41.50	4.25	3.85	2.75
2631-34	Set of 4 Singles	...	...	3.75	.90
2635	29¢ Alaska Highway	35.00	3.50	.75	.18
2636	29¢ Kentucky Statehood..................	35.00	3.50	.75	.18
2637-41	29¢ Summer Olympics, attd...........(35)	31.50 (10)	10.00	4.75	3.95
2637-41	Set of 5 Singles	...	...	4.35	1.10
2642-46	29¢ Hummingbirds, Set of 5 bklt. sgls.	...	...	4.35	1.10
2646a	29¢ Booklet Pane of 5 ....(Unfolded 5.50)			4.50	3.50

2647-96 Examples

2697

2698   2699   2704

2700   2701
2702   2703

Scott's No.		Mint Sheet	Plate Block	F-VF NH	F-VF Used
2647-96	29¢ Wildflowers, Pane of 50 diff......	42.50	...	...	...
2647-96	Set of 50 Singles	...	...	39.50	24.75
2647-96	29¢ Individual Singles	...	...	1.00	.60
2697	29¢ World War II S/S of 10 ....(20)	17.50	...	8.75	6.75
2697a-j	Set of 10 Singles	...	...	8.50	5.00
2697s	Se-Tenant Center Block of 10	...	...	9.50	8.95
2698	29¢ Dorothy Parker, Literary Arts	35.00	3.50	.75	.18
2699	29¢ Dr. Theodore von Karman	35.00	3.50	.75	.18
2700-03	29¢ Minerals, attd ....(40)	37.50	4.50	4.00	3.00
2700-03	29¢ Strip of 4	...	...	4.00	3.00
2700-03	Set of 4 Singles	...	...	3.75	.90
2704	29¢ Juan Rodriguez Cabrillo	35.00	3.50	.75	.18

Giraffe
2705

Giant Panda
2706

Flamingo
2707

King Penguins
2708

White Bengal Tiger
2709

2719

2710

2711, 2715
2713, 2717

2712, 2716
2714, 2718

2720

Scott's No.		Mint Sheet	Plate Block	F-VF NH	F-VF Used
2705-09	29¢ Wild Animals, bklt. sgls	...	...	4.50	1.10
2709a	29¢ Booklet Pane of 5 .... (Unfolded 6.00)			4.75	3.50
#2710-19a Christmas Issues					
2710	29¢ Madonna & Child......................	35.00	3.50	.75	...
2710v	29¢ Madonna, booklet single	...	...	.85	.18
2710a	29¢ Booklet Pane of 10 .... (Unfolded 9.75)			7.95	7.50
2711-14	29¢ Toys, **offset**, attd.	41.50	4.25	3.75	3.00
2711-14	Set of 4 Singles	...	...	3.50	.80
2715-18	29¢ Toys, **gravure**, 4 bklt. sgls	...	...	3.50	.80
2718a	29¢ Booklet Pane of 4 .... (Unfolded 4.75)			3.75	3.50
2719	29¢ Locomotive, ATM, self adhes. sgl.	...	...	.80	.40
2719a	29¢ Locomotive, ATM, pane of 18	...	14.50		
2720	29¢ Happy New Year .... (20)	19.50	4.50	1.00	.18

1993 Commemoratives

ELVIS
2721

OKLAHOMA!
2722

HANK WILLIAMS
2723

2721-30,2746-59,2766,2771-74,2779-89,2791-94, 2804-06	Set of 47..	...	...	40.75	9.25
2721	29¢ Elvis Presley ....(40)	28.00	3.50	.75	.18
2722	29¢ "Oklahoma!" ....(40)	28.00	3.50	.75	.18
2723	29¢ Hank Williams, Perf. 10 ....(40)	28.00	3.50	.75	.18
2723a	Same, Perf. 11.2 x 11.4	...	150.00	23.95	14.95

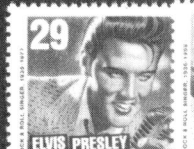
ELVIS PRESLEY
2724, 31

BUDDY HOLLY
2729, 36

RITCHIE VALENS
2727, 34

BILL HALEY
2725, 32

DINAH WASHINGTON
2730, 37

OTIS REDDING
2728, 35

CLYDE McPHATTER
2726, 33

2724-30	29¢ Rock 'n Roll, R & B attd.........(35)	32.50 (8)	7.95	6.95	6.50
2724-30	Top Horiz. Plate Block of 10	...	9.95	...	...
2724-30	Rock 'n Roll, R & B, set of 7 sgls	...	...	...	2.10
2731-37	29¢ Rock 'n Roll, R & B, 7 bklt. sgls.	...	...	6.25	2.10

2741   2742   2743   2744   2745

2747   2746   2748

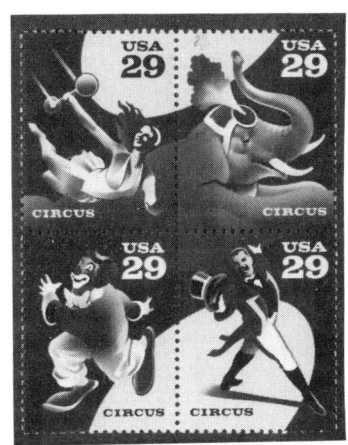
2749   2754   2755

2752   2753
2750   2751

Scott's No.		Mint Sheet	Plate Block	F-VF NH	F-VF Used
2737a	29¢ Booklet Pane of 8 ....(Unfolded 8.95)...			6.75	6.50
2737b	29¢ Booklet Pane of 4 ....(Unfolded 4.95)...			4.00	3.85
2741-45	29¢ Space Fantasy, bklt. sgls............	...	...	4.35	1.10
2745a	29¢ Booklet Pane of 5 ....(Unfolded 5.50)			4.50	3.75
2746	29¢ Percy Lavon Julian	37.50	3.75	.80	.18
2747	29¢ Oregon Trail	35.00	3.50	.75	.18
2748	29¢ World University Games	37.50	3.75	.80	.18
2749	29¢ Grace Kelly	35.00	3.50	.75	.18
2750-53	29¢ Circus, attd ....(40)	35.00 (6)	6.75	3.75	3.00
2750-53	Set of 4 Singles	...	...	3.60	.90
2754	29¢ Cherokee Strip.......................(20)	15.75	3.50	.80	.18
2755	29¢ Dean Acheson	35.00	3.50	.75	.18

2756   2757
2758   2759

2760   2761   2762   2763   2764

2765

2766

2771, 2755   2772, 2777   2767
2768
2769
2770

Scott's No.		Mint Sheet	Plate Block	F-VF NH	F-VF Used
2756-59	29¢ Sporting Horses, blk. of 4 ....(40)	37.50	4.25	4.00	3.00
2756-59	Set of 4 Singles	...	...	3.80	.80
2760-64	29¢ Spring Garden Flowers, 5 bklt. sgls.	...	...	4.35	1.10
2764a	29¢ Booklet Pane of 5 ....(Unfolded 5.50)...			4.50	3.50
2765	29¢ World War II S/S of 10 ....(20)	17.50		8.75	6.75
2765a-j	Set of 10 Singles	...		8.50	5.00
2765s	Se-Tenant Center Block of 10	...		9.50	8.95
2766	29¢ Joe Louis...................................	47.50	4.75	1.00	.20
2767-70	29¢ Broadway Musicals, 4 bklt. sgls......	...		3.35	1.00
2770a	29¢ Booklet Pane of 4 ....(Unfolded 4.95)	...		3.50	3.35
2771-74	29¢ Country Music, Block attd ....(20)	16.50	3.95	3.50	3.00
2771-74	Horizontal Strip of 4	...		3.50	3.00
2771-74	Horiz. Pl. Block of 8 with Label..........	...	7.50	...	...
2771-74	Set of 4 Singles	...	...	3.35	.90
2775-78	29¢ Country Music, 4 bklt. sgls...........	...		3.35	1.00
2778a	29¢ Booklet Pane of 4 ....(Unfolded 4.95)	...		3.50	3.35

2779   2780
2781   2782

2783   2784   2789, 2790   2803

2785   2786   2791,98,2801   2792,97,2802
2787   2788   2793,96,2799   2794,95,2800

2779-82	29¢ Nat'l. Postal Museum, Block .....(20)	18.00	4.25	3.75	3.00
2779-82	Horizontal Strip of 4..........................	...	...	3.75	3.00
2779-82	Set of 4 Singles	...		3.60	1.00
2783-84	29¢ Deaf Communication, pair.........(20)	16.50	3.95	1.80	1.25
2783-84	Set of 2 Singles	...		1.70	.40
2785-88	29¢ Children's Classics, Block ....(40)	37.50	4.50	4.00	3.00
2785-88	Horizontal Strip of 4..........................	...	...	4.00	3.00
2785-88	Set of 4 Singles	...		3.80	1.00
2789	29¢ Christmas Madonna	35.00	3.50	.75	.15
2790	29¢ Madonna, Booklet Single	...		.80	.18
2790a	29¢ Booklet Pane of 4 ....(Unfolded 4.95)	...		3.50	2.75
2791-94	29¢ Christmas Designs, block of 4	45.00	4.50	4.00	3.50
2791-94	Strip of 4	...	...	4.00	3.50
2791-94	Set of 4 Singles	...		3.85	.80
2795-98	29¢ Christmas Designs, set of 4 bklt. sgls.	...		3.50	.90
2798a	29¢ Booklet Pane of 10 (3 Snowmen)(Unfolded 11.75)			9.50	7.50
2798b	29¢ Booklet Pane of 10 (2 Snowmen)(Unfolded 11.75)			9.50	7.50
2799-2802	29¢ Christmas Designs, self adhes.,4 sgls	...		4.50	1.80
2802a	29¢ Pane of 12, self-adhesive	...		12.75	...
2799-2802 var.	Coil, self-adhesive.........Plate Strip of 8 10.95			5.00	...
2803	29¢ Christmas Snowman, self adhes......	...	...	.90	.35
2803a	29¢ Pane of 18, self adhesive	...		14.75	...

2804   2805   2806

2807   2808   2809   2810   2811

2819   2820   2821   2822   2823
2824   2825   2826   2827   2828

2812   2813   2814,2814C   2815

2829   2830   2831   2832   2833

1993 Commemoratives (cont.)

Scott's No.		Mint Sheet	Plate Block	F-VF NH	F-VF Used
2804	29¢ No. Mariana Is. Comm'nwlth.......(20)	15.75	3.75	.80	.18
2805	29¢ Columbus at Puerto Rico................	36.50	3.50	.75	.18
2806	29¢ AIDS Awareness, Perf.11.2............	40.00	3.95	.85	.18
2806a	29¢ AIDS Booklet Single, Perf.11........	...	...	.90	.20
2806b	29¢ Booklet Pane of 5 ....(Unfolded 5.75)			4.50	3.75

1994 Commemoratives

Scott's No.		Mint Sheet	Plate Block	F-VF NH	F-VF Used
2807-12,2814C-28,2834-36,2839, 2848-68,2871-72,2876 Set of 49		...	...	26.95	11.95
2807-11	29¢ Winter Olympics, attd ....(20)	16.75	(10)9.50	4.50	4.00
2807-11	Set of 5 Singles	...	...	4.35	1.20
2812	29¢ Edward R. Murrow	36.50	3.50	.75	.20
2813	29¢ Love & Sunrise, self adhesive	...	...	.85	.30
2813a	29¢ Pane of 18	...	...	14.75	...
2813v	29¢ Love Coil, self adhesive Pl# Strip....................................	(5) 8.00	(3) 6.75	.85	...
2814	29¢ Love & Dove, Booklet Single.........	...	...	.80	.22
2814a	29¢ Booklet Pane of 10 ....(Unfolded 8.95)			7.95	5.95
2814C	29¢ Love & Dove, sheet stamp	36.50	3.50	.75	.18
2815	52¢ Love & Doves................................	63.50	6.75	1.35	.35

2834   2835   2836

2816   2817   2818

2816	29¢ Dr. Allison Davis ....(20)	16.00	4.00	.85	.20
2817	29¢ Chinese New Year, Dog............(20)	18.75	4.35	.95	.20
2818	29¢ Buffalo Soldiers........................(20)	16.00	4.00	.85	.20

2837

Scott's No.		Mint Sheet	Plate Block	F-VF NH	F-VF Used
2819-28	29¢ Silent Screen Stars, attd............(40)	32.50 (10)	8.95	8.50	7.25
2819-28	Half-Pane of 20 with selvedge.............	...	...	16.75	14.75
2819-28	Set of 10 singles	...	...	8.25	3.00
2829-33	29¢ Summer Garden Flowers, set of 5 bklt. sgls....	...	...	4.15	1.20
2833a	29¢ Booklet Pane of 5 ....(Unfolded 5.50)			4.25	3.00
2834	29¢ World Cup Soccer ....(20)	15.00	3.75	.80	.20
2835	40¢ World Cup Soccer ....(20)	21.50	5.25	1.10	.35
2836	50¢ World Cup Soccer ....(20)	25.75	6.25	1.30	.50
2837	29¢,40¢,50¢ World Cup Soccer, Souvenir Sheet of 3	...	...	4.25	3.50

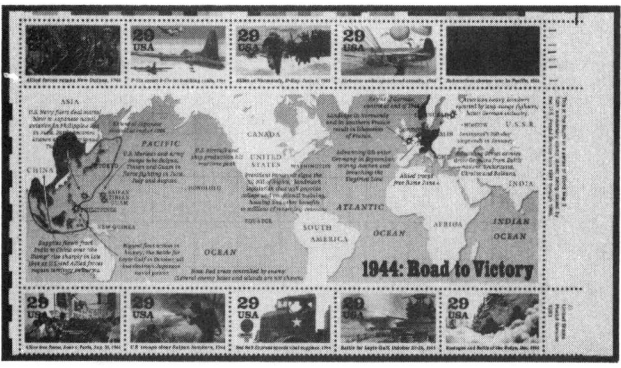

2838

2840

| 2839 | 2841a | 2842 | 2848 |

| 2843 | 2844 | 2845 |

| 2846 | 2847 |

1994 Commemoratives (continued)

Scott's No.		Mint Sheet	Plate Block	F-VF NH	F-VF Used
2838	29¢ World War II S/S of 10 ....(20)	17.50	...	8.75	6.75
2838a-j	Set of 10 Singles....................	...	...	8.50	5.00
2838v	Se-Tenant Center Block of 10	...	...	9.50	8.95
2839	29¢ Norman Rockwell............................	36.50	3.50	.75	.20
2840	50¢ N. Rockwell, Souvenir Sheet of 4	...	...	5.95	4.95
1994 Moon Landing, 25th Anniversary					
2841	29¢ Moon Landing Miniature Sheet of 12. ...	...	...	9.95	7.50
2841a	29¢ Single Stamp from sheet	...	...	.90	.30
2842	$9.95 Moon Landing Express Mail ....(20)	425.00	95.00	22.50	11.50
1994 Commemoratives (continued)					
2843-47	29¢ Locomotives, set of 5 bklt.singls	...	...	4.15	1.20
2847a	29¢ Booklet Pane of 5	(Unfolded 5.50)		4.25	3.50
2848	29¢ George Meany	36.50	3.50	.75	.20

| 2849 | 2850 | 2851 |

| 2852 | 2853 |

| 2854 | 2855 | 2856 | 2857 |

| 2858 | 2859 | 2860 | 2861 |

Scott's No.		Mint Sheet	Plate Block	F-VF NH	F-VF Used
2849-53	29¢ Popular Singers, attd.....................(20)	21.75	(6) 7.50	5.50	3.25
2849-53	Top Plate Block of 12	...	14.95	...	...
2849-53	Set of 5 Singles	...	...	5.25	1.30
2854-61	29¢ Blues & Jazz Artists, attd. ....(35)	32.50	(10)10.95	(10)9.95	6.95
2854-61	Top Plate Block of 10 with Label	...	11.75	...	...
2854-61	Set of 8 Singles	...	...	8.50	3.00

NOTE: BECAUSE OF SHEET LAYOUT THERE ARE NO BLOCKS OF EIGHT POSSIBLE.

| 2862 | 2867 | 2868 |

| 2863 | 2864 |
| 2865 | 2866 |

2862	29¢ James Thurber	36.50	3.50	.75	.20
2863-66	29¢ Wonders of the Sea, attd.................(24)	19.95	3.85	3.50	2.50
2863-66	Set of 4 Singles	...	...	3.35	1.00
2867-68	29¢ Cranes, attd. ....(20)	18.95	4.75	2.00	1.20
2867-68	Set of 2 Singles	...	...	1.90	.45

SE-TENANT NOTE: MANY MODERN SE-TENANTS ARE ISSUED IN "STAGGERED" FORM. STAMP DESIGNS IN BLOCKS AND PLATE BLOCKS WILL NOT ALWAYS FOLLOW "SCOTT ORDER" BUT WILL VARY DEPENDING UPON THEIR LOCATION IN SHEET.

2869

2870

1994 Legends of the West Miniature Sheet

Scott's No.		Mint Sheet	Plate Block	F-VF NH	F-VF Used
2869	29¢ Revised Sheet of 20 .... (6)	100.00	...	16.95	13.95
2869a-t	Set of 20 Singles..................................	...	...	16.00	9.95
2869a/t	Horiz. Gutter Block of 10	...	...	13.95	...
2869a/t	Vert. Gutter Block of 8	...	...	11.95	...
2869a/t	Set of 4 Vert.Gutter Pairs....................	...	...	10.95	...
2869a/t	Set of 5 Horiz. Gutter Pairs.................	...	...	12.95	...
2869a/t	Center Gutter Block of 4	...	...	14.95	...
2869a/t	Cross Gutter Block of 20	...	...	17.75	...
2869a/t	Block of 24 with Vertical Gutter............	...	...	20.95	...
2869a/t	Block of 25 with Horiz. Gutter.............	...	...	21.95	...
2870	29¢ Original (recalled) sheet of 20	...	...	295.00	...

NOTE; #2870 was the original sheet-it contained an incorrect picture of Bill Pickett (second stamp in second row). It was withdrawn and released in quantities via lottery. #2869 contains the correct picture of Bill Pickett.

| 2871 | 2872 | 2873 | 2874 |

Scott's No.		Mint Sheet	Plate Block	F-VF NH	F-VF Used
#2871-74a Christmas Issues					
2871	29¢ Madonna & Child	36.50	3.50	.75	.18
2871a	29¢ Madonna & Child, Bklt. Single	...	...	.80	.20
2871b	29¢ Booklet Pane of 10...........................	(Unfolded 8.95)		7.75	6.35
2872	29¢ Christmas Stocking	36.50	3.50	.75	.18
2872v	29¢ Stocking Booklet Single			.85	.20
2872a	29¢ Booklet Pane of 20...........................	(Unfolded 19.50)		16.50	12.50
2873	29¢ Santa Claus, self-adhesive...................	...	...	.85	.25
2873a	29¢ Pane of 12, self-adhesive....................	...	...	9.95	7.50
2873v	29¢ Santa Claus Coil, self-adhesive				
	Pl# Strip	(5) 8.25	(3) 7.00	.85	...
2874	29¢ Cardinal in Snow, self-adhesive	...	...	.85	.25
2874a	29¢ Pane of 18, self-adhesive.....................	...	...	14.95	11.00

2875

2876

2875	$2 Bureau of Engraving Centennial Souvenir Sheet of 4	...	...	18.75	14.50
2875a	$2 Madison, Single Stamp from S/S...........	...	...	4.75	3.50
2876	29¢ Year of the Boar, New Year............. (20)	18.75	4.35	.95	.20

| 2877,2878 | 2879,2880 | 2881-87,2889-92 | 2888 | 2893 |

1994 Interim Regular Issues

Scott's No.		Mint Sheet	Plate Block	F-VF NH	F-VF Used
2877	(3¢) Dove, ABN, Light Blue .... (100)	8.50	.75	.20	.18
2878	(3¢) Dove, SVS, Darker Blue .... (100)	8.50	.75	.20	.18
	#2877 Thin, taller letters. #2878 Heavy, shorter letters.				
2879	(20¢)"G",Postcard Rate, BEP, Black "G:............................... (100)	52.50	3.75	.55	.18
2880	(20¢) "G",Postcard Rate, SVS,Red "G".......................... (100)	55.00	7.95	.55	.18
2881	(32¢) "G",BEP, Black "G" .... (100)	165.00	49.95	1.25	.18
2881v	(32¢) Black "G" Booklet Single...............	...	...	1.00	.20
2881a	(32¢) Booklet Pane of 10, Perf. 11.2 x 11.1	...	...	9.95	8.95
2882	(32¢) "G", SVS, Red "G"................ (100)	82.50	4.95	.90	.18
2883	(32¢) "G", BEP, Black "G", bklt. sgl..........	...	...	1.00	.20
2883a	(32¢) Booklet Pane of 10, BEP, Perf. 10 x 9.9	...	...	...	9.95
	7.95				
2884	(32¢) "G", ABN, Blue "G", bklt. sgl.........	...	...	1.00	.18
2884a	(32¢) Booklet Pane of 10, ABN...............	...	...	9.95	7.95
2885	(32¢) "G", KCS, Red "G", bklt. sgl.	...	...	1.00	.20
2885a	(32¢) Booklet Pane of 10, KCS...............	...	...	9.95	7.95
2886	(32¢) "G", Surface Tagged, self-adhesive ..	...	...	1.00	.30
2886a	(32¢) Pane of 18, self-adhesive, AD..........	...	...	16.50	...
2886v	(32¢) "G", Coil, self-adhesive Pl.# Strip	(5)7.50	(3) 6.00	.85	...
2887	(32¢) "G", Overall Tagging, self-adhesive, AD	...	...	1.00	.45
2887a	(32¢) Pane of 18, self-adhesive, thin paper..	...	...	16.50	...

#2886 Limited amount of blue shading in the white stripes below field of stars.
#2887 Stronger blue shading in the white stripes.

1994-95 Interim Coil Stamps, Perf. Or Roul. 9.8 Vert.

Scott's No.		Pl.Strip of 5	Pl.Strip of 3	F-VF NH	F-VF Used
2888	(25¢) "G" Presort, Coil, SVS	6.95	5.75	.85	.25
2889	(32¢) "G" Coil, BEP, Black "G"...............	10.50	8.75	1.00	.20
2890	(32¢) "G" Coil, ABN, Blue "G"	6.50	5.25	.90	.20
2891	(32¢) "G" Coil, SVS, Red "G"	6.50	5.25	.90	.20
2892	(32¢) "G" Coil, SVS, Rouletted	7.75	6.50	.90	.20
2893	(5¢) "G" Non-Profit, green ABN (1995)....	2.30	2.00	.22	.18

BEP=Bureau of Engraving and Printing ABN=American Bank-Note Co.
SVS=Stamp Venturers KCS=KCS Industries
AD = Avery–Dennison

1995-97 Regular Issues

| 2897,2913-16 | 2902,2902B | 2903-4B | 2905,7 | 2908-10 |

| 2911-12B | 2919 | 2920-21 |

Scott's No.		Mint Sheet	Plate Block	F-VF NH	F-VF Used
2897	32¢ Flag over Porch, Dull gum.....(100)	67.50	3.95	.70	.15
2897s	32¢ Shiny Gum......................(100)	67.50	3.95	.70	...
2897v	Folded Block of 15 in Booklet (BK243)......			14.95	...

1995-97 Coil Stamps, Perf. Or Die-cut Vertically
Note: S.A. indicates Self-adhesive. Otherwise, stamps are moisture activated.

Scott's No.		Pl.Strip of 5	Pl.Strip of 3	F-VF NH	F-VF Used
2902	(5¢) Butte, Perf. 9.8	1.75	1.50	.20	.18
2902B	(5¢) Butte, SA, Die-cut 11.5 (1996)	2.00	1.75	.20	.18
2903	(5¢) Mountain, BEP, Perf. 9.8 (1996).......	2.25	1.95	.20	.15
2904	(5¢) Mountain, SVS, Perf. 9.8 (1996)	2.25	1.95	.20	.15
2904A	(5¢) Mountain, SA Die-cut 11.5 (1996)	2.25	1.95	.20	.18
2904B	(5¢) Mountain, SA Die-cut 9.8 (1997)........	2.25	1.95	.20	.18
	NOTE: #2903, 2904B Letters outlined in purple. #2904, 2904A No outline on letters.				
2905	(10¢) Automobile, Perf. 9.8	3.25	2.75	.28	.18
2906	(10¢) Automobile, SA, Die-cut 11.5 (1996)2.95	2.65	.35		.25
2907	(10¢) Eagle & Shield, SA, (Design of 1993) Die-cut 11.5 (1996)	2.95	2.65	.35	.25
2908	(15¢) Auto Tail Fin, BEP, Perf. 9.8	3.75	3.00	.40	.25
2909	(15¢) Auto Tail Fin, SVS, Perf. 9.8	3.75	3.00	.40	.25
	Note: #2908 has darker colors and heavier shading than #2909				
2910	(15¢) Auto Tail Fin, SA Die-cut 11.5 (1996)	3.50	3.00	.45	.30
2911	(25¢) Juke Box, BEP, Perf. 9.8	6.25	5.25	.65	.40
2912	(25¢) Juke Box, SVS, Perf. 9.8	5.75	4.75	.65	.40
	Note: #2911 has darker colors and heavier shading than #2912				
2912A	(25¢) Juke Box, SA, Die-cut 11.5 (1996) ...	5.75	4.75	.65	.30
2912B	(25¢) Juke Box, SA, Die-cut 9.8 (1997)	5.75	4.75	.65	.30
2913	32¢ Flag over Porch, BEP, Perf. 9.8	6.25	5.25	.80	.15
2913v	32¢ Dull Gum	6.25	5.25	.80	
2914	32¢ Flag over Porch, SVS, Perf. 9.8	5.75	4.75	.80	.15
	Note: #2913 has Red "1995" Date. #2914 has Blue "1995" Date.				
2915	32¢ Flag over Porch, SA, Die-cut 8.7	6.95	5.75	.90	.30
2915A	32¢ Flag over Porch, SA, Die-cut 9.7 Red "1996", multiple stamps touch (1996).	8.95	7.50	1.10	.30
2915B	32¢ Flag over Porch, SA, Die-cut 11.5 (1996).	8.95	7.50	.90	.30
2915C	32¢ Flag over Porch, SA, Die-cut 10.9(1996)	17.50	15.00	1.75	.50
2915D	32¢ Flag over Porch, SA, Die-cut 9.8, Red "1997" Stamps separate on backing (1997)	6.95	5.75	.90	.30
	Note: See #3133 for Blue "1996" Date Die-cut 9.9				

1995-97 Booklets and Panes

Scott's No.		Mint Sheet	Plate Block	F-VF NH	F-VF Used
2916	32¢ Flag over Porch, booklet single	...	...	.85	.20
2916a	32¢ Booklet Pane of 10 ....(Unfolded 10.75)	8.50	6.95		
2919	32¢ Flag over Field, self-adhesive sgl........	...	...	.90	.30
2919a	32¢ Pane of 18, Self-adhesive	...	...	15.75	...
2920	32¢ Flag over Porch, self-adhesive single large Blue "1995" date Die-cut 8.8	...	...	.90	.30
2920a	32¢ Pane of 20, Self-adhesive, large "1995"	...	...	17.50	...
2920b	32¢ Flag over Porch, self adhesive single, small Blue "1995" date Die-cut 8.8			5.00	.75
2920c	32¢ Pane of 20, self-adhesive,small "1995"	...	...	99.50	...
2920d	32¢ Flag over Porch, self-adhesive, Blue "1996" date (1996) Die-cut 11.3	...	...	.90	.35
2920e	32¢ Booklet Pane of 10, self-adhesive.......	...	...	8.50	...
2920f	32¢ Flag over Porch, folded bklt of 15(1996)	...	...	12.95	...
2920h	32¢ Flag over Porch, folded bklt of 16 with lower right stamp removed (1996)......	...	...	14.95	...
	Note: #2920f and 2920h have large "1995" dates like #2920				

Scott's No.		Mint Sheet	Plate Block	F-VF NH	F-VF Used
	1995-97 Booklet and Panes (cont.)				
2921	32¢ Flag over Porch, self-adhesive booklet single, Red "1996" Date (1996).....	...	...	.90	.30
2921a	32¢ Booklet Pane of 10, self-adhesive Die-cut 9.8 Red "1996" Date (1996)..........(Unfolded 9.75)	8.50	...		
2921b	32¢ Flag over Porch, self-adhesive booklet single, Red "1997" Date (1997).....	...	...	.90	.30
2921c	32¢ Booklet Pane of 10, self-adhesive Die-cut 9.8 Red "1997" Date (1997)	...	...	8.50	...
2921d	32¢ Booklet Pane of 5, self-adhesive Die-cut 9.8 Red "1997" Date (1997) ....(Unfolded 5.75)	4.25	...		

1995-98 Great American Series

| 2933 | 2934 | 2935 | 2936 |

| 2938 | 2940 | 2942 | 2943 |

		Mint Sheet	Plate Block	F-VF NH	F-VF Used
2933-43	**Set of 8....................................**	...	37.50	7.25	1.50
2933	32¢ Milton S. Hershey ....(100)	62.50	3.75	.65	.18
2934	32¢ Cal Farley (1996) ....(100)	62.50	3.75	.65	.18
2935	32¢ Henry R.Luce (1998) ....(20)	12.95	3.35	.65	.18
2936	32¢ Lila & DeWitt Wallace (1998) ..... (20)	12.95	3.35	.65	.18
2938	46¢ Ruth Benedict ....(100)	90.00	4.75	.95	.25
2940	55¢ Alice Hamilton, MD ....(100)	105.00	5.50	1.10	.25
2942	77¢ Mary Breckenridge, SA (1998)...... (20)	29.50	7.00	1.50	.22
2943	78¢ Alice Paul, Dull gum ....(100)	155.00	7.95	1.60	.25
2943g	78¢ Shiny gum (1996) ....(100)	155.00	7.95	1.60	...

1995 Commemoratives

| 2948 | 2949 | 2950 | 2955 |

2951	2952
2953	2954
		2956

		Mint Sheet	Plate Block	F-VF NH	F-VF Used
2948,2950-58,2961-68,2974,2976-80, 2982-92,2998-99,3001-7,3019-23 Set of 49		...	...	39.95	11.75
2948	(32¢) Love & Cherub	37.50	3.75	.80	.20
2949	(32¢) Love & Cherub, Self-adhesive	...	...	1.00	.25
2949a	(32¢) Pane of 20, Self-adhesive	...	...	18.75	...
2950	32¢ Florida Statehood ....(20)	15.00	3.75	.80	.20
2951-54	32¢ Earth Day/Kids Care, attd. ....(16)	14.00	3.95	3.50	2.00
2951-54	Set of 4 Singles			3.25	1.00
2955	32¢ Richard Nixon	37.50	3.75	.80	.20
2956	32¢ Bessie Coleman, Black Heritage Series	37.50	3.75	.80	.20

2957,2958   2958   2960

2961   2962   2963

2964   2965

2966   2967   2968

2969   2970   2971   2972   2973

Scott's No.		Mint Sheet	Plate Block	F-VF NH	F-VF Used
2957	32¢ Love Cherub	37.50	3.75	.80	.20
2957v	Folded Block of 15 in Booklet (BK244)	...	...	14.95	...
2958	55¢ Love Cherub	67.50	6.25	1.40	.60
2959	32¢ Love Cherub, booklet single................	...	...	.90	.20
2959a	32¢ Booklet Pane of 10 .... (Unfolded 9.95)			8.75	5.95
2960	55¢ Love Cherub, Self-Adhesive single......	...	...	1.35	.65
2960a	55¢ Pane of 20, Self-Adhesive	...	...	25.95	...
2960d	55¢ Pane of 20 with Die-cut "Time to Reorder" (1996)	...	...	26.95	...
2961-65	32¢ Recreational Sports Strip .... (20)	17.50	(10)9.50	4.50	2.95
2961-65	Set of 5 Singles.....................................	...	...	4.25	1.30
2966	32¢ POW & MIA .... (20)	15.00	3.50	.80	.20
2967	32¢ Marilyn Monroe	...	...	1.30	.25
2967	M. Monroe Miniature Sheet of 20	...	...	5.95	...
2967	32¢ Monroe Uncut Sheet of 120 (6 Panes)	175.00	...	23.75	16.50
2967	Block of 8 with Vertical Gutter	...	...	15.75	...
2967	Cross Gutter Block of 8	...	...	19.00	...
2967	Vertical Pair with Horizontal Gutter	...	...	4.95	...
2967	Horizontal Pair with Vertical Gutter	...	...	5.95	...
2968	32¢ Texas Statehood........................... (20)	15.00	3.50	.80	.20
2969-73	32¢ Great Lakes Lighthouses 5 booklet singles	...	...	4.35	1.25
2973a	32¢ Booklet Pane of 5 .... (Unfolded 5.75) ...			4.50	3.50

2974   2980

2975   2976   2977
              2978   2979

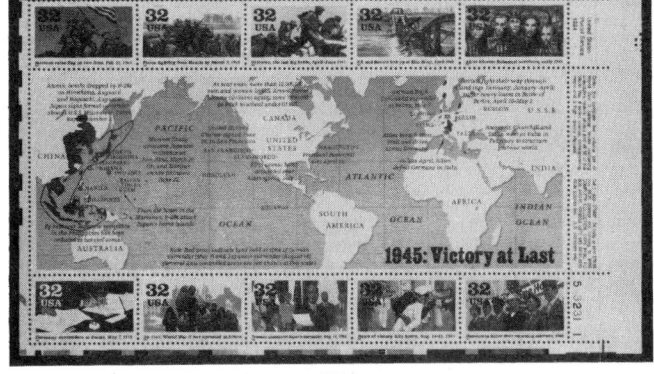

2981

Scott's No.		Mint Sheet	Plate Block	F-VF NH	F-VF Used
2974	32¢ United Nations................................(20)	15.00	3.50	.80	.20
1995 Civil War Miniature Sheet					
2975	32¢ Civil War, Miniature Sheet of 20 ....(6)	100.00	...	16.95	13.95
2975a-t	Set of 20 Singles	...	...	16.75	11.95
2975a/t	Horizontal Gutter, Block of 10	...	...	11.95	...
2975a/t	Vert. Gutter, Block of 8	...	...	9.95	...
2975a/t	Set of 4 Vert. Gutter Pairs	...	...	8.95	...
2975a/t	Set of 5 Horiz. Gutter Pairs......................	...	...	10.95	...
2975a/t	Center Gutter Block of 4	...	...	13.50	...
2975a/t	Cross Gutter Block of 20	...	...	18.50	...
2975a/t	Block of 24 with Vertical Gutter.................	...	...	21.95	...
2975a/t	Block of 25 with Horiz. Gutter...................	...	...	22.95	...
1995 Commemoratives (cont.)					
2976-79	32¢ Carousel Horses, attd ....(20)	16.50	3.95	3.50	2.50
2976-79	Set of 4 Singles	...	...	3.35	1.00
2980	32¢ Woman Suffrage..............................(40)	30.00	3.75	.80	.20
2981	32¢ World War II S/S of 10 ....(20)	17.50	...	8.75	6.75
2981a-j	Set of 10 Singles	...	...	8.50	5.00
2981v	Se-Tenant Center Block of 10.................. ...	...	...	9.50	8.95

2982   2983   2984

2985   2986   2987

2988   2989   2990

2991   2992   2999

2993   2994   2995   2996   2997

2998   3000

Scott's No.		Mint Sheet	Plate Block	F-VF NH	F-VF Used
2982	32¢ Louis Armstrong............................(20)	15.00	3.50	.80	.20
2983-92	32¢ Jazz Musicians, attd ....(20)	16.50(10)9.50		8.50	6.95
2983-92	Set of 10 Singles	...	...	8.25	3.00
2993-97	32¢ Fall Garden Flowers, 5 bklt.Sgls........	...	...	4.35	1.25
2997a	32¢ Booklet Pane of 5.............................(Unfolded 5.75)...			4.50	2.95
2998	60¢ Eddie Rickenbacker	72.50	6.75	1.50	.50
2999	32¢ Republic of Palau	37.50	3.50	.80	.20

1995 Comic Strips Miniature Sheet

3000	32¢ Comic Strips, Min. Sheet of 20........(6)	100.00	...	16.95	13.95
3000a-t	Set of 20 Singles		...	16.75	11.95
3000a/t	Horiz. Gutter Block of 8..........................		...	10.75	...
3000a/t	Vert. Gutter Block of 10		...	12.75	...
3000a/t	Set of 5 Vert. Gutter Pairs		...	11.95	...
3000a/t	Set of 4 Horiz. Gutter Pairs		...	9.50	...
3000a/t	Center Gutter Block of 4		...	13.50	...
3000a/t	Cross Gutter Block of 20..........................		...	17.50	...
3000a/t	Block of 25 with Vertical Gutter		...	21.75	...
3000a/t	Block of 24 with Horiz. Gutter		...	20.75	...

3001   3003   3002

3004,3010,3016   3005,3009,3015   3006,3011,3017   3007,3008,3014

3012,3018   3013

Scott's No.		Mint Sheet	Plate Block	F-VF NH	F-VF Used
3001	32¢ U.S. Naval Academy .... (20)	15.00	3.50	.80	.20
3002	32¢ Tennessee Williams .... (20)	15.00	3.50	.80	.20
#3003-18 Christmas Issues					
3003	32¢ Madonna and Child........................	37.50	3.75	.80	.18
3003a	32¢ Madonna and Child, Bklt.Single	...	...	.80	.18
3003b	32¢ Booklet Pane of 10 ....(Unfolded 9.95)7.95			5.95	
3004-7	32¢ Santa & Children	39.50	3.95	3.50	2.50
3004-7	Strip of 4	...	...	3.50	2.50
3004-7	Set of 4 Singles......................................	...	...	3.35	1.00
3007b	32¢ Booklet Pane of 10, 3 each ....(Unfolded 10.75)			8.50	5.95
	#3004-5, 2 each #3006-7				
3007c	32¢ Booklet Pane of 10, 2 each ....(Unfolded 10.75)			8.50	5.95
	#3004-5, 3 each #3006-7				
Self-Adhesive Stamps					
3008-11	32¢ Santa & Children, Block of 9............	...	...	7.95	...
3008-11	Set of 4 Singles	...	...	3.50	1.80
3011a	32¢ Pane of 20..	...	...	16.75	...
3012	32¢ Midnight Angel	...	...	.90	.45
3012a	32¢ Pane of 20..	...	...	16.00	...
3012c	Folded Block of 15 in Booklet	...	...	12.75	...
3012d	Folded Pane of 16 with one stamp missing(15)	...	...	13.95	...
3013	32¢ Children Sledding	...	...	.90	.45
3013a	32¢ Pane of 18..	...	...	15.00	...
Self-Adhesive Coil Stamps					
3014-17	32¢ Santa & Children ....Pl.Strip 8		8.25	3.75	...
3014-17	Set of 4 Singles	...	...	3.50	1.80
3018	32¢ Midnight Angel....................Pl.# Strip (5) 6.95		(3) 5.75	.90	.45

3019   3021   3023

3020   3022

3019-23	32¢ Antique Automobiles, Strip............ (25)	20.75	(10)9.75	4.25	3.00
3019-23	Set of 5 Singles	...	...	4.15	1.25

1996 Commemoratives

3024	3030

3025	3026	3027	3028	3029

Scott's No.		Mint Sheet	Plate Block	F-VF NH	F-VF Used
3024,3030,3058-67,3069-70,3072-88					
3090-3104,3106-11,3118 Set of 53		...	...	43.95	11.75
3024	32¢ Utah Statehood	37.50	3.75	.80	.20
3024v	Folded Block of 15 in Booklet(BK 245)	...	...	13.95	...
3025-29	32¢ Winter Garden Flowers, 5 Bklt Sgls	...	...	4.35	1.25
3029a	32¢ Booklet Pane of 5	...	(Unfolded 5.50)	4.50	3.25
3030	32¢ Love Cherub, Self-adhesive single	...	...	.85	.30
3030a	32¢ Pane of 20, Self-adhesive	...	...	16.50	...
3030b	32¢ Folded Pane of 15 + Label	...	...	12.95	...

1996-99 Flora and Fauna Series

3032	3033	3036	3044

3048,3053	3049,3054	3050,3055

3032	2¢ Red-headed Woodpecker	(100)	5.25	.50	.20	.15
3033	3¢ Eastern Bluebird	(100)	6.75	.55	.20	.15
3036	1¢ Red Fox, Self-adhesive	(20)	38.50	8.95	1.95	.75
3044	1¢ Kestrel, Coil	(PS5)	.75	(PS3)	.60	.20	.15
3048	20¢ Blue Jay, Self-adhesive Single	...	...	...	.45	.25
3048a	20¢ Pane of 10	...	...	...	4.50	...

1996 Commemoratives (continued)

3059	3058	3060

3061	3062	3065
3063	3064	

1996 Commemoratives (continued)

3066	3067

Scott's No.		Mint Sheet	Plate Block	F-VF NH	F-VF Used
3049	32¢ Yellow Rose, Self-adhesive Single	...	...	.75	.25
3049a	32¢ Pane of 20	...	...	13.95	...
3049b	32¢ Booklet Pane of 4	...	...	3.95	...
3049c	32¢ Booklet Pane of 5 + Label	...	...	4.95	...
3049d	32¢ Booklet Pane of 6	...	...	4.25	...
3050	20¢ Ringnecked Pheasant, SA Single	...	...	.40	.20
3050a	20¢ Pane of 10	...	...	3.95	...
....	2¢ Woodpecker Coil (1999)	(PS5)	.60(PS3)	.50	.20	.15
3053	20¢ Blue Jay Coil	(PS5)	4.65(PS3)	3.95	.40	.22
3054	32¢ Yellow Rose Coil, SA	(PS5)	5.75(PS3)	4.50	.80	.20
3055	20¢ Ringnecked Pheasant Coil, SA	(PS5)	4.65(PS3)	3.95	.40	.20
3058	32¢ Ernest E. Just	(20)	15.00	3.50	.80	.22
3059	32¢ Smithsonian Institution	(20)	15.00	3.50	.80	.22
3060	32¢ Year of the Rat	(20)	18.50	4.25	.95	.25
3061-64	32¢ Pioneers of Communication	(20)	15.00	3.50	3.25	2.25
3061-64	32¢ Strip of 4	...	...	3.25	2.25
3061-64	Set of 4 singles	...	...	3.15	1.00
3065	32¢ Fulbright Scholarships	37.50	3.75	.80	.22
3065v	Folded Block of 15 in Booklet (BK246)	...	...	12.95	...
3066	50¢ Jacqueline Cochran	58.50	5.50	1.20	.45
3067	32¢ Marathon	(20)	15.00	3.50	.80	.22

1996 Atlanta '96 Summer Olympics Miniature Sheet

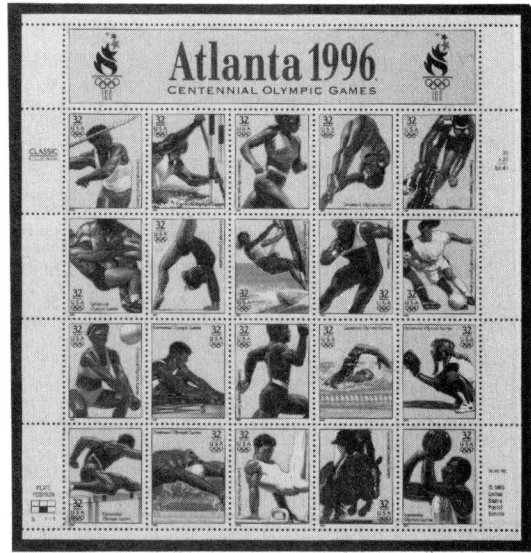

3068

3068	32¢ Centen. Olympic Games, Mini Sht/20	(6)100.00	...	15.95	13.75
3068a-t	Olympics Set of 20 Singles	...	...	15.75	10.95
3068a/t	Vert. Gutter Block of 8	...	...	10.75	...
3068a/t	Horiz. Gutter Block of 10	...	...	12.75	...
3068a/t	Set of 4 Vert. Gutter Pairs	...	...	9.50	...
3068a/t	Set of 5 Horiz. Gutter Pairs	...	...	11.95	...
3068a/t	Center Gutter Block of 4	...	...	13.50	...
3068a/t	Center Gutter Block of 20	...	...	17.50	...
3068a/t	Block of 24 with Vertical Gutter	...	...	20.75	...
3068a/t	Block of 25 with Horiz. Gutter	...	...	21.75	...

1996 Commemoratives (cont.)

3069	3070	3071

3069	32¢ Georgia O'Keeffe	(15)	11.50	3.50	.80	.22
3069v	Folded Block of 15 in Booklet (BK247)	...	...	12.95	...
3070	32¢ Tennessee Statehood	37.50	3.75	.80	.22
3070v	Folded Block of 15 in Booklet (BK248)	...	...	12.95	...
3071	Tennessee Self-adhesive single	...	...	.90	.30
3071a	Tennessee Self-adhesive Pane of 20	...	...	16.85	...

3072   3073   3074   3705   3076

3079   3078
3077   3080   3081

Scott's No.		Mint Sheet	Plate Block	F-VF NH	F-VF Used
3072-76	32¢ American Indian Dances, 5 Designs, Strip. .... (20)	15.00	(10)8.95	4.00	2.95
3072-76	Set of 5 singles	...	...	3.90	1.25
3072-76v	Folded Block of 15 in Booklet (BK249) ...	...	12.95	...	
3077-80	32¢ Prehistoric Animals, 4 Designs, attd., Block. .... (20)	16.50	3.95	3.50	2.25
3077-80	32¢ Strip of 4	...	...	3.50	2.25
3077-80	Set of 4 singles	...	...	3.40	1.00
3081	32¢ Breast Cancer .... (20)	15.00	3.75	.80	.22

3082   3083   3084   3087
         3085   3086

3082	32¢ James Dean.................................... (20)	17.00	3.95	.90	.22
3082	32¢ Dean Uncut Sheet of 120 (6 panes)......	110.00	...	...	...
3082	Block of 8 with Vertical Gutter..................	...	...	13.75	...
3082	Cross Gutter Block of 8	...	...	16.50	...
3082	Vert. Pair with Horiz. Gutter.....................	...	...	3.75	...
3082	Horiz. Pair with Vert. Gutter......................	...	...	4.75	...
3082v	Folded Block of 15 in Booklet (BK250)......	...	...	12.95	...
3083-86	32¢ Folk Heroes, 4 Designs, Block. ...... (20)	15.00	3.95	3.50	2.25
3083-86	32¢ Strip of 4	...	...	3.50	2.25
3083-86	Folk Heroes Set of 4 singles	...	...	3.40	1.00
3083-86v	Folded Block of 15 in Booklet (BK251) ...	...	12.95	...	
3087	32¢ Olympic Games, Discobolus .... (20)	15.00	3.75	.80	.22
3087v	Folded Block of 15 in Booklet (BK252)......	...	...	12.95	...

3090   3088-89   3104

3095
3091
3092
3093
3094

3096   3097
3098   3099

3100   3101
3102   3103

Scott's No.		Mint Sheet	Plate Block	F-VF NH	F-VF Used
3088	32¢ Iowa Statehood	37.50	3.75	.80	.22
3088v	Folded Block of 15 in Booklet (BK253).....	...	...	12.95	...
3089	Iowa Self-Adhesive single..........................	...	...	1.00	.30
3089a	Iowa Self-Adhesive Pane of 20	...	...	18.75	...
3090	32¢ Rural Free Delivery .... (20)	15.00	3.50	.80	.22
3090v	Folded Block of 30 in Booklet (BK254).....	...	...	24.95	...
3091-95	32¢ Riverboats, self-adhesive, attd. .... (20)	15.95	(10)8.95	4.25	2.95
3091-95	Riverboats, Set of 5 singles.......................	...	...	4.15	1.25
3091-95b	32¢ Riverboats, self-adhesive attd, with "missing 3 perforations" special die cutting.............................. (20)	295.00	(10)160.00	79.50	...
3091-95v	Folded Block of 15 in Booklet (BK255)..	...	...	12.95	...
3096-99	32¢ Big Band Leaders, Block .... (20)	16.50	3.95	3.50	2.25
3096-99	32¢ Strip of 4	...	...	3.50	2.25
3096-99	32¢ Horiz. Pl. Block of 8 with selvedge......	7.75	...	...	...
3096-99	Big Band Leaders set of 4 singles	...	...	3.40	1.00
3100-3	32¢ Songwriters Block .... (20)	16.50	3.95	3.50	2.25
3100-3	32¢ Strip of 4	...	...	3.50	2.25
3100-3	32¢ Horiz. Pl. Block of 8 with selvedge......	7.75	...	...	...
3100-3	Songwriters set of 4 singles	...	...	3.40	1.00
3104	23¢ F. Scott Fitzgerald	28.50	2.95	.60	.22

1996 Endangered Species Miniature Sheet

3105

3105	32¢ Endangered Species Miniature Sheet of 15..............................	...	...	12.75	9.75
3105a-o	Set of 15 singles	...	...	12.50	6.95
3105v	Folded Block of 15 in Booklet (BK256).....	...	...	13.95	...

NOTE: S.A.=SELF ADHESIVE STAMPS WHICH DON'T REQUIRE MOISTURE-ACTIVATION.

1996 Commemoratives (cont.)

3106   3108,3113   3109,3114
3110,3115   3111,3116

3107,3112   3118

3119

Scott's No.		Mint Sheet	Plate Block	F-VF NH	F-VF Used
3106	32¢ Computer Technology ....(40)	30.95	3.75	.80	.22
#3107-3117a Christmas Issues					
3107	32¢ Madonna and Child	37.50	3.95	.80	.18
3107v	Folded Block of 15 in Booklet (BK257)	...	...	12.95	..
3108-11	32¢ Family Scenes, Block	39.50	3.95	3.50	2.25
3108-11	32¢ Strip of 4	...	...	3.50	2.25
3108-11	Family Scenes set of 4 singles	...	...	3.40	.90

Self-Adhesive Stamps Booklet

3112	32¢ Madonna and Child Single.................	...	...	.90	.30
3112a	32¢ Pane of 20	...	...	15.95	...
3113-16	32¢ Family Scenes	...	...	3.60	1.40
3116a	32¢ Pane of 20	...	...	15.95	...
3117	32¢ Skaters single	...	...	.90	.30
3117a	32¢ Pane of 18	...	...	14.95	...

1996 Commemoratives (cont.)

3118	32¢ Hanukkah, Self-adhesive ....(20)	15.00	3.50	.80	.25
3118v	Folded Block of 15 in Booklet (BK258)	...	...	12.95	...
3118b	32¢ Hanukkah, revised backing SA 1997	(20) 15.00	3.50	.80	...
3119	50¢ Cycling Souvenir Sheet of 2................	...	...	2.50	2.25
3119a-b	Set of 2 Singles	...	...	2.40	1.20

3120   3121   3122

1997 Commemoratives

Scott's No.		Mint Sheet	Plate Block	F-VF NH	F-VF Used
3120-21, 3125, 3130-31, 3134-35, 3141, 3143-50, 3152-75					
	Set of 40..	...	...	28.75	8.95
3120	32¢ Chinese Year of the Ox	(20) 17.50	3.95	.90	.22
3121	32¢ Benjamin O. Davis, Sr, S.A...........	(20) 15.00	3.50	.80	.22

1997 Statue of Liberty Self-Adhesive Regular Issue

3122	32¢ Liberty, Single, die-cut 11.............	...	...	.90	.25
3122a	32¢ Pane of 20	...	...	16.95	...
3122b	32¢ Booklet Pane of 4	...	...	4.25	...
3122c	32¢ Booklet Pane of 5 + Label	...	...	3.95	...
3122d	32¢ Booklet Pane of 6, die-cut 11	...	...	5.50	...
3122E	32¢ Die-cut 11.5x11.8	...	...	1.50	...
3122Ef	32¢Bklt.Pane of 20, 11.5x11.8	...	...	45.00	...
3122Eg	32¢Bklt.Pane of 6, 11.5x11.8	...	...	5.95	...

3123   3124   3125

1997 Commemoratives (continued)

3123	32¢ Love, Swans, SA Single..................	...	...	.80	.25
3123a	32¢ Pane of 20, SA..............................	...	...	14.95	...
3124	55¢ Love, Swans, SA Single..................	...	...	1.35	.50
3124a	55¢ Pane of 20, SA..............................	...	...	24.75	...
3125	32¢ Helping Children Learn, SA............	(20) 15.00	3.50	.80	.25

3127   3126   3129   3128

1997 Merian Botanical Prints Booklets, SA

#3126-27a Serpentine Die Cut 10.9 x 10.2 on 2,3,4 sides					
3126	32¢ Citron Moth, booklet single	...	...	.80	.25
3127	32¢ Flowering Pineapple, Cockroaches, bklt sgle	...	...	.80	.25
3127a	32¢ Booklet Pane of 20	...	...	14.95	...
#3128-29b Serpentine Die Cut 11.2 x 10.8 on 2 or 3 sides					
3128	32¢ Citron Moth, booklet single	...	...	.80	.25
3128a	32¢ Large perforation on right side	...	...	1.10	.50
3128b	32¢ Booklet Pane of 5, 2-#3128-29, 1-#3128a	...	...	3.95	...
3129	32¢ Flowering Pineapple, Cockroaches, bklt sgle	...	...	.80	.25
3129a	32¢ Large Perforations on right side	...	...	1.50	.60
3129b	32¢ Booklet Pane of 5, 2-#3128-29, 1-#3129a	...	...	4.50	...
3128-29	32¢ Attached Pair..............................	...	...	1.60	...

3130   3131

1997 Pacific '97 Commemoratives

3130	32¢ Clipper Ship	...	...	.80	.25
3131	32¢ Stagecoach	...	...	.80	.25
3130-31	32¢ Pair	(16) 12.75	3.50	1.60	1.00
3131a	32¢ Uncut Sheet of 96	85.00	...	...	...
3131a	32¢ Block of 32	...	...	29.50	...
3131a	32¢ Vert. Pair with Horizontal Gutter	...	...	6.75	...
3131a	32¢ Horiz. Pair with Vertical Gutter	...	...	6.75	...
3131a	32¢ Cross Gutter Block of 16	...	...	19.50	...

NOTE: SA=SELF-ADHESIVE STAMPS WHICH DO NOT REQUIRE MOISTURE-ACTIVATION.

1997 Linerless Coil Stamps

3132   3133

Scott's No.		Pl.Strip of 5	Pl.Strip of 3	F-VF NH	F-VF Used
3132	(25¢) Juke Box, SA, Imperf.	5.75	4.75	.65	...
3133	32¢ Flag over Porch, SA, Die-cut 9.9....	8.75	7.50	.75	...

NOTE: #3133 has Blue "1996" Date at bottom

3134   3135

3136

3137

1997 Commemoratives (continued)

Scott's No.		Mint Sheet	Plate Block	F-VF NH	F-VF Used
3134	32¢ Thornton Wilder..........................	(20) 14.50	3.25	.75	.22
3135	32¢ Raoul Wallenberg........................	(20) 14.50	3.25	.75	.22

1997 World of Dinosaurs Miniature Sheet

Scott's No.		Mint Sheet	Plate Block	F-VF NH	F-VF Used
3136	32¢ World of Dinosaurs, Miniature Pane of 15......................	...	...	10.75	10.00
3136a-o	Dinosaurs Set of 15 singles................	...	...	10.65	7.95

1997 Bugs Bunny Self-Adhesive Special Edition

Scott's No.		Mint Sheet	Plate Block	F-VF NH	F-VF Used
3137	32¢ Souvenir Sheet of 10	...	...	7.50	7.25
3137a	32¢ Single stamp...............................	...	...	.80	.25
3137b	32¢ Booklet Pane of 9 (left side)..........	...	...	6.25	...
3137c	32¢ Booklet Pane of 1 (right side)........	...	...	1.75	...
3137v	32¢ Top Press Sheet of 6 Panes	500.00	...	...	...
3137v	32¢ Bottom Press Sheet of 6 Panes	850.00	...	...	...
3137v	32¢ Souvenir Sheet of 10 from uncut sheet	...	...	90.00	...
3137v	32¢ Souvenir Sheet of 10 with plate number	...	...	450.00	...
3138	32¢ Souvenir Sheet of 10 with special Die-cut that extends thru paper backing	...	...	225.00	...
3138a	32¢ Single stamp...............................	...	...	3.00	...
3138b	32¢ Booklet Pane of 9 (left side)..........	...	...	27.50	...
3138c	32¢ Booklet Pane of 1 imperf (right side)	...	...	210.00	...

NOTE: Souvenir sheets from the uncut sheet do not have vertical roulette lines dividing the two halves of the souvenir sheet. Bottom press sheets contain a plate number.

1997 Pacific '97 Souvenir Sheets

3139

3140

				F-VF NH	F-VF Used
3139	50¢ Benjamin Franklin Sheet of 12	...	...	14.50	13.95
3139a	50¢ single stamp from souvenir sheet....	...	...	1.25	.95
3140	60¢ George Washington Sheet of 12	...	...	17.00	14.95
3140a	60¢ single stamp from souvenir sheet....	...	...	1.50	1.10

3141

1997 Commemoratives (continued)

3141	32¢ Marshall Plan	(20) 14.50	3.25	.75	.22

1997 Classic American Aircraft Miniature Sheet

3142

Scott's No.		Mint Sheet	Plate Block	F-VF NH	F-VF Used
3142	32¢ Classic Am. Aircraft, Mini Sht of 20	(6) 90.00	...	14.95	14.50
3142a-t	Aircraft Set of 20 Singles			14.50	9.95
3142a/t	Vertical Gutter Block of 10	...	...	12.50	...
3142a/t	Horiz. Gutter Block of 10	...	...	10.50	...
3142a/t	Set of 5 Vert. Gutter Pairs	...	...	10.75	...
3142a/t	Set of 4 Horiz. Gutter Pairs	...	...	8.75	...
3142a/t	Center Gutter Block of 4	...	...	12.95	...
3142a/t	Center Gutter Block of 20	...	...	16.50	...
3142a/t	Block of 25 with Vertical Gutter	...	...	21.75	...
3142a/t	Block of 24 with Horiz. Gutter	...	...	20.75	...

3143, 3148   3144, 3149   3145, 3147

3146, 3150   3152   3153

3151

1997 Commemoratives (continued)

Scott's No.		Mint Sheet	Plate Block	F-VF NH	F-VF Used
3143-46	32¢ Legendary Football Coaches, attached	(20) 14.50	3.25	3.00	2.50
3143-46	32¢ Coaches, strip of 4	...	...	3.00	2.50
3143-46	Set of 4 singles	...	...	2.90	1.00
3143-46	Top Plate Block of 8 with Label	...	6.50	...	...
3147	32¢ Vince Lombardi	(20) 14.50	3.25	.75	.22
3148	32¢ Bear Bryant	(20) 14.50	3.25	.75	.22
3149	32¢ Pop Warner	(20) 14.50	3.25	.75	.22
3150	32¢ George Halas	(20) 14.50	3.25	.75	.22

NOTE: #3147-50 HAVE A RED BAR ABOVE THE COACHES NAME. THIS BAR IS MISSING ON THE SE-TENANT ISSUE #3143-46

1997 American Dolls Miniature Sheet

3151	32¢ American Dolls, Miniature Sht of 15	...	...	11.50	11.00
3151a-o	32¢ American Dolls, set of 15 singles	...	...	11.25	7.50
3151v	Folded Block of 15 in Booklet (BK266)	...	...	13.95	...

1997 Commemoratives (continued)

3152	32¢ Humphrey Bogart	(20) 15.95	3.95	.85	.25
3152	Sheet of 120 (6 panes)	95.00	...	...	...
3152	Block of 8 with Vertical Gutter	...	...	13.75	...
3152	Cross Gutter Block of 8	...	...	16.50	...
3152	Vertical Pair with Horiz. Gutter	...	...	3.75	...
3152	Horiz. Pair with Vertical Gutter	...	...	4.75	...
3152v	Folded Block of 15 in Booklet (BK267)	...	...	13.95	...
3153	32¢ Stars and Stripes Forever	35.75	3.50	.75	.22
3153v	Folded Block of 15 in Booklet (BK268)	...	...	13.95	...

3154   3155
3156   3157

3158   3159   3160

3161   3162   3163

3164   3165

3154-57	32¢ Opera Singers, 4 designs	(20) 14.50	3.25	3.00	2.50
3154-57	Top Plate Block of 8 with Label	...	6.50	...	...
3154-57	Set of 4 singles	...	...	2.95	1.00
3158-65	32¢ Conductors and Composers attd	(20) 14.50	(8) 6.50	5.95	4.75
3158-65	Set of 8 singles	...	...	5.85	2.20

Looking For Those Missing Stamps, Covers & Supplies
And at Bargain Prices Too!!!
Do You Enjoy Great Articles from the Leading Philatelic Writers?
You'll Find the Answer in the

BROOKMAN TIMES

"The Brookman Times" is published 6 times a year and has ads from leading stamp dealers and articles from leading Philatelic writers, such as Les Winick, Marjory Sente, Barry Schreiber & George Griffenhagen. In addition we have added a classified advertisement section. There are bargains galore and of particular note is that only dealer's who advertise in the Brookman Price Guide can advertise in "The Brookman Times." We feel these dealers are the "cream of the crop" and heartily endorse them.

SOME OF THE LEADING DEALERS YOU WILL FIND IN "THE BROOKMAN TIMES:"

American Philatelic Society
American Topical Assoc.
Artmaster
Brooklyn Gallery
Brookman Barrett & Worthen
Brookman Stamp Co.
Champion Stamp Co., Inc.
Dale Enterprises
D & N Petro
Eric Jackson
Henry Gitner Philatelists, Inc.
Global Stamp News
Michael Jaffe Stamps, Inc.
Kenmore Stamp Co.

Krause Publications
Linn's Stamp News.
James T. McCusker, Inc.
Mekeel's Weekly Stamp News
Alan Miller Stamps
Miller's Stamp Shop
Plate Block Stamp Co.
Gary Posner, Inc.
Regency Stamp, Ltd.
Scott Publishing
Stamp Collector
Stamp Finder
United Nations
U.S. Stamp News
Vidiforms Co., Inc.

Now You Can Get This $9.95 Value FREE!!!

Everyone who purchases a Brookman Price Guide can *receive the Brookman Times FREE*. All you have to do is fill out the coupon below (or a copy of coupon). (If you purchased your copy directly from Brookman/Barrett & Worthen you will automatically receive the Brookman Times)

| 3166 | 3167 | 3173 |

| 3168 | 3169 | 3170 |

| 3171 | 3172 |

1997 Commemoratives (continued)

Scott's No.		Mint Sheet	Plate Block	F-VF NH	F-VF Used
3166	32¢ Padre Felix Varela	(20) 14.50	3.25	.75	.22
3167	32¢ U.S. Air Force 50th Anniv.	(20) 14.50	3.25	.75	.22

1997 Classic Movie Monsters

3168-72	32¢ Movie Monsters, attd.	(20) 15.75 (10)	8.50	4.00	3.25
3168-72	Set of 5 singles.............................	...	...	3.90	1.30
3168-72	Sheet of 180 (9 Panes)	140.00	...	...	...
3168/72	Vertical Gutter Block of 8	...	...	10.50	...
3168/72	Horiz. Gutter Block of 10	...	...	12.50	...
3168/72	Set of 4 Vert. Gutter Pairs	...	...	8.75	...
3168/72	Set of 5 Horiz. Gutter Pairs	...	...	10.75	...
3168/72	Center Gutter Block of 8	...	...	14.50	...
3168/72v	Folded Block of 15 in Booklet (BK 269)	...	...	12.95	...

1997 Commemoratives (continued)

3173	32¢ First Supersonic Flight 1947 self-adhesive........................	(20) 14.50	3.25	.75	.22

| 3174 | 3175 | 3176 | 3177 |

3178

3174	32¢ Women in the Military............	(20) 14.50	3.25	.75	.22
3175	32¢ Kwanza, self-adhesive..............	36.50	3.50	.75.	.22
3175	Sheet of 250-5 Panes of 50..............	700.00	...	...	...
3176	32¢ Madonna & Child, self-adhesive	...	...	.75	.20
3176a	32¢ Madonna , Pane of 20..............	...	...	13.95	...
3177	32¢ American Holly , self-adhesive ..	...	...	.75	.20
3177a	32¢ Holly, Pane of 20	...	...	13.95	...
3177b	32¢ Holly, Booklet Pane of 4	...	...	4.25	...
3177c	32¢ Holly, Booklet Pane of 5 plus label	...	...	5.25	...
3177d	32¢ Holly, Booklet Pane of 6	...	...	4.75	...

1997 Priority Rate Souvenir Sheet

Scott's No.		Mint Sheet	Plate Block	F-VF NH	F-VF Used
3178	$3 Mars Rover Sojourner.................	...	...	6.25	5.95

NOTE: #3178 IS IMPERFORATE ON ALL 4 SIDES AND MEASURES 146mm WIDE BY 82mm TALL. #3178v IS AN UNCUT SHEET OF 18 WITH VERTICAL PERFORATIONS BETWEEN THE SOUVENIR SHEETS AND WIDE HORIZONTAL GUTTERS. AN INDIVIDUAL SOUVENIR SHEET MEASURES APPROX. 152mm WIDE BY 87mm TALL.

3178v	Uncut sheet of 18 souv. sheets	175.00	...	...	...
3178vc	Perforated on 2 sides......................	...	...	17.50	...
3178vc	Vertical Pair with Horiz. Gutter	...	...	35.00	...
3178vl	Perforated on left side	...	...	17.50	...
3178vl	Vertical Pair with Horiz. Gutter	...	...	35.00	...
3178vr	Perforated on right side	...	...	17.50	...
3178vr	Vertical Pair with Horiz. Gutter	...	...	35.00	...
3178v	Block of 6 (3 wide by 2 tall)	...	...	100.00	...

1998 Commemoratives

| 3179 | 3180 | 3181 |

3179-81, 3192-3203, 3206, 3211-27, 3230-35, 3237-48 Set of 51		...	...	30.75	10.95
3179	32¢ Happy New Year, Year of the Tiger	(20) 15.75	3.75	.80	.22
3180	32¢ Alpine Skiing	(20) 14.50	3.25	.70	.22
3181	32¢ Madam C.J. Walker, SA	(20) 14.50	3.25	.70	.22

1998 Celebrate the Century Souvenir Sheets

3182

3182	32¢ 1900's, Sheet of 15	(Uncut Sheet of 4 49.50)		9.50	...
3182a-o	Set of 15 singles.............................		...	9.50	7.50
3183	32¢ 1910's, Sheet of 15	(Uncut Sheet of 4 49.50)		9.50	...
3183a-o	Set of 15 singles.............................		...	9.50	7.50
3184	32¢ 1920's, Sheet of 15	(Uncut Sheet of 4 49.50)		9.50	...
3184a-o	Set of 15 singles.............................		...	9.50	7.50
3185	32¢ 1930's, Sheet of 15	(Uncut Sheet of 4 49.50)		9.50	...
3185a-o	Set of 15 singles.............................		...	9.50	7.50
3186	33¢ 1940's, Sheet of 15	(Uncut Sheet of 4 49.50)		9.75	...
3186a-o	Set of 15 singles.............................		...	9.75	7.50
3187	33¢ 1950's, Sheet of 15	(Uncut Sheet of 4 49.50)		9.75	...
3187a-o	Set of 15 singles.............................		...	9.75	7.50
3188	33¢ 1960's, Sheet of 15	(Uncut Sheet of 4 49.50)		9.75	...
3188a-o	Set of 15 singles.............................		...	9.75	7.50

NOTE: SA=SELF-ADHESIVE STAMPS WHICH DO NOT REQUIRE MOISTURE-ACTIVATION.

1998 Commemoratives (continued)

3192

3193   3194

3195   3196   3197

3198   3199   3200

3201   3202   3203

Scott's No.		Mint Sheet		Plate Block	F-VF NH	F-VF Used
3192	32¢ Remember the Maine	(20) 14.50		3.25	.70	.22
3193-97	32¢ Flowering Trees, SA, attd.	(20) 14.50	(10)	7.50	3.50	2.75
3193-97	32¢ Trees, Set of 5 Singles	...		...	3.45	1.25
3198-3202	32¢ Alexander Calder, attd.	(20) 14.50	(10)	7.50	3.50	2.75
3198-3202	32¢ Calder, Set of 5 Singles	...		...	3.45	1.25
3198-3202	Sheet of 120 (6 Panes of 20)	140.00		...	...	...
3203	32¢ Cinco de Mayo, SA.	(20) 14.50	(10)	3.25	.70	.22
3203	Sheet of 180 9 Panes of 20)	140.00		...	...	...

1998 Tweety & Sylvester Self-Adhesive Souvenir Sheets

3204

1998 Tweety & Sylvester Self-Adhesive Souvenir Sheets

Scott's No.		Mint Sheet	Plate Block	F-VF NH	F-VF Used
3204	32¢ Souvenir Sheet of 10	...	...	6.75	...
3204a	32¢ Single Stamp	...	...	.70	.22
3204b	32¢ Booklet Pane of 9 (left side)	...	...	5.95	...
3204c	32¢ Booklet Pane of 1(right side)	...	...	1.50	...
3204v	32¢ Top Press Sheet of 6 Panes	115.00	...	...	...
3204v	32¢ Bottom Press Sheet of 6 Panes	195.00	...	...	...
3204v	32¢ Souvenir Sheet of 10 from uncut sheet	...	...	22.50	...
3204v	32¢ Souvenir Sheet of 10 with plate number	...	...	95.00	...
3205	32¢ Souvenir Sheet of 10 with special Die-cut that extends thru paper backing	...	...	22.95	...
3205a	32¢ Single Stamp	...	...	.95	...
3205b	32¢ Booklet Pane of 9 (left side)	...	...	7.95	...
3205c	32¢ Imperf Bklt. Pane of 1(right side)	...	...	17.95	...

NOTE: Souvenir sheets from the uncut sheet do not have vertical roulette lines dividing the two halves of the souvenir sheet. Bottom press sheets contain a plate number.

3206   3207   3208

1998 Commemoratives (continued)

		Mint Sheet	Plate Block	F-VF NH	F-VF Used
3206	32¢ Wisconsin Statehood SA	(20) 14.50	3.25	.70	.22

1999 Nondenominated Coil Stamps

				F-VF NH	F-VF Used
3207	(5¢) Wetlands, Non-Profit	(PS5) 1.95	(PS3)1.70	.20	.18
3207A	(5¢) Wetlands, Self Adhesive	(PS5) 1.95	(P53)1.70	.20	.18
3208	(25¢) Diner, Water-Activated	(PS5) 5.85	(PS3) 4.75	.50	.30
3208A	(25¢) Diner, Self-Adhesive	(PS5) 5.85	(PS3) 4.75	.50	.30

1998 Trans-Mississippi Centennial Souvenir Sheets

3209-10

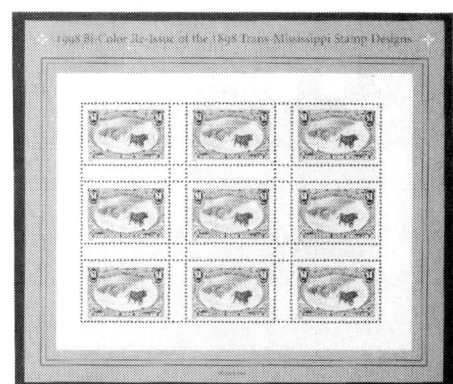

3209-10

Scott's No.		Mint Sheet	Plate Block	F-VF NH	F-VF Used
3209	1c-$2 Souvenir Sheet of 9	...	...	7.95	6.75
3209a-i	Set of 9 singles	...	...	7.75	5.95
3210	$1 Cattle in Storm, Souvenir Sheet of 9	...	...	17.50	15.75
3210a	Single from Souvenir Sheet	...	...	2.25	1.75
3209-10	Uncut Sheet of 54 (3 each #3209 & 3210)	...	...	190.00	...

NOTE: #3209-10 contain bicolored versions of the designs of the 1898 Trans-Mississippi issue. (#285-93)

3211

3214
3212

3215
3213

3219
3216

3218
3217

3220

3211	32¢ Berlin Airlift	(20)	12.95	2.95	.65	.22
3212-15	32¢ Folk Musicians, block attd.	(20)	12.95	2.95	2.60	2.25
3212-15	32¢ Strip of 4		...	...	2.60	2.25
3212-15	32¢ Folk, Set of 4 Singles		...	...	2.55	1.00
3216-19	32¢ Gospel Singers, block attd.	(20)	12.95	2.95	2.60	2.25
3216-19	32¢ Strip of 4		...	...	2.60	2.25
3216-19	32¢ Gospel, Set of 4 Singles		...	...	2.55	1.00
3220	32¢ Spanish Settlement of Southwest in 1598	(20)	12.95	2.95	.65	.22

3221

3224
3222

3225
3223

3221	32¢ Stephen Vincent Benet	(20)	12.95	2.95	.65	.22
3222-25	Tropical Birds, attd.	(20)	12.95	2.95	2.60	2.25
3222-25	32¢ Birds, Set of 4 Singles		...	...	2.55	1.00

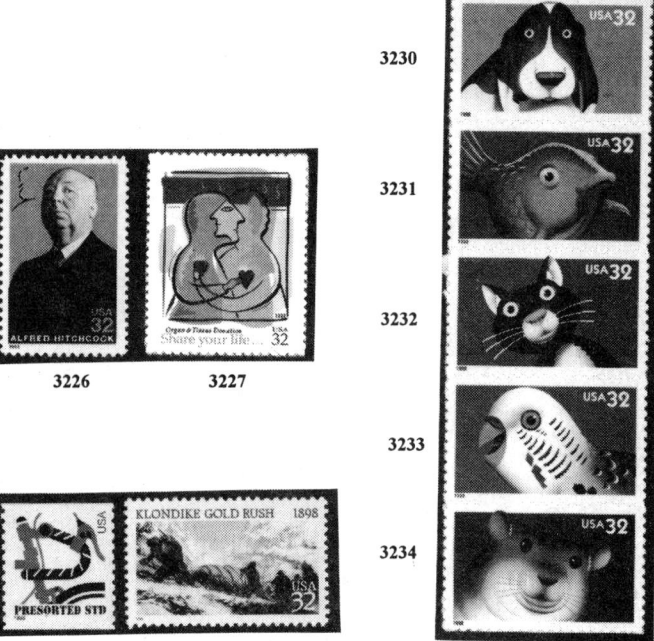

3226   **3227**

3230

3231

3232

3233

3234

3228-29   **3235**

Scott's No.			Mint Sheet	Plate Block	F-VF NH	F-VF Used
3226	32¢ Alfred Hitchcock	(20)	12.95	2.95	.65	.22
3226	Uncut Press Sheet of 120		79.50	...	...	...
3227	32¢ Organ & Tissue Donation, SA	(20)	12.95	2.95	.65	.22

1998 Nondenominated Coil Stamps

3228	(10¢) Green Bicycle, Self-adh	(PS5)3.75	(PS3)3.25	.20	.18
3229	(10¢) Green Bicycle, Water-Act.......	(PS5)3.75	(PS3)3.25	.20	.18

1998 Commemoratives (continued)

3230-34	32¢ Bright Eyes, SA, attd................	(20)	12.95	(10) 6.95	3.25	2.75
3230-34	32¢ Bright Eyes, St of 5 Singles		...	...	3.20	1.25
3235	32¢ Klondike Gold Rush.................	(20)	12.95	2.95	.65	.22

1998 Four Centuries of American Art Miniature Sheets

3236

3236	32¢ American Art, Pane of 20		...	...	12.95	12.50
3236-a-t	32¢ Art, Set of 20 Singles		...	...	12.75	9.95
3236	32¢ Art, Uncut Press Sheet of 120 ...		79.50	...	...	...

1998 Commemoratives (Continued)

3237   3243   3244

3238   3239   3240   3241   3242

3245   3246   3251   3249
3247   3248   3252   3250

Scott's No.		Mint Sheet	Plate Block	F-VF NH	F-VF Used
3237	32¢ Ballet .... (20)	12.95	2.95	.65	.22
3237	Sheet of 120 (6 Panes of 20)	90.00	...	...	...
3238-42	32¢ Space Discovery, attd...............	12.95	(10)6.95	3.25	2.75
3238-42	32¢ Space, Set of 5 singles.............	...	...	3.20	1.25
3238-42	32¢ Space, Press Sheet of 180.........	119.50	...	...	...
3243	32¢ Giving and Sharing .... (20)	12.95	2.95	.65	.22
3244	32¢ Madonna & Child, Self-adhesive ...	...	...	.65	.22
3244a	32¢ Madonna, Pane of 20................	...	...	12.95	...
3245-48	32¢ Christmas Wreaths, SA, attd......	...	...	2.60	...
3245-48	32¢ Wreaths, set of 4 singles...........	...	...	2.55	1.00
3248a	32¢ Wreaths, Booklet Pane of 4	...	...	2.65	...
3248b	32¢ Wreaths, Booklet Pane of 5	...	...	3.35	...
3248c	32¢ Wreaths, Booklet Pane of 6	...	...	3.95	...
3249-52	32¢ Christmas Wreaths, SA, att. (20)	12.95	2.95	2.60	...
3249-52	32¢ Wreaths, Set of 4 Singles...........	...	...	2.55	1.10
3249v-52v	32¢ Wreaths, from #3252b booklet of 20	...	...	2.60	...
3252b	32¢ Wreaths, Booklet of 20...........	...	...	12.95	...

NOTE: #3245-48 are considerably smaller designs than #3249-52.

1998 Regular Issues

3257-58   3259,3263   3260,3264-69   3270-71

3261   3262

1998 Regular Issue Sheet Stamps

Scott's No.		Mint Sheet	Plate Block	F-VF NH	F-VF Used
3257	(1¢) Weather Vane, Make-Up Stamp, White "USA," 1998 Date, BCA......	2.00	.40	.20	.15
3258	(1¢) Weather Vane, Pale blue "USA," Black "1998" Date, AP..................	2.00	.40	.20	.15
3259	22¢ Uncle Sam, self-adhesive .... (20)	8.75	2.25	.45	.15
3260	(33¢) Hat, water-activated	31.75	3.35	.65	.15
3261	$3.20 Space Shuttle Landing, Priority Mail....................... (20)	125.00	27.50	6.35	2.95
3262	$11.75 Piggyback Space Shuttle, Express Mail.............................. (20)	450.00	99.50	23.00	9.75

1998 Regular Issue Coil Stamps

Scott's No.		Pl. Strip of 5	Pl. Strip of 3	F-VF NH	F-VF Used
3263	22¢ Uncle Sam, Self-adhesive.........	4.50	3.50	.45	.15
3264	(33¢) Hat, water-activated	6.50	5.25	.65	.18
3265	(33¢) Hat, SA, Die-cut 9.9 vert.	6.50	5.25	.65	.18
3266	(33¢) Hat, SA, Die-cut 9.7 vert.	6.50	5.25	.65	.18

Note: Unused #3266 is on paper larger than stamp, #3265 is same size as stamp

3270	(10¢) Eagle & Shield, Water-act.	2.40	1.95	.20	.18
3271	(10¢) Eagle & Shield, Self-adhesive.	2.40	1.95	.20	.18

Note: See #2602-4 for varieties with "Bulk Rate"

1998 Regular Issue Booklet Stamps and Panes

Scott's No.				F-VF NH	F-VF Used
3267	(33¢) Hat, Booklet single, SA, BEP, Small "1998" Date, Die-cut 9.9	...	...	.65	.20
3267a	(33¢) Hat, Booklet Pane of 10..........	...	...	6.50	...
3268	(33¢) Hat, single from pane of 10 SA, AV, Large "1998" Date, Die-cut 11.2 x 11.1	...	...	.65	.20
3268a	(33¢) Hat, Pane of 10....................	...	...	12.95	...
3268v	(33¢) Hat, single from pane of 20, SA, AV, Large "1998" Date, Die-cut 11	...	...	.65	.20
3268b	(33¢) Hat, Pane of 20....................	...	...	12.95	...
3269	(33¢) Hat, single from pane of 18,SA, AV	...	...	.65	.20
3269a	(33¢) Hat, Pane of 18	...	...	11.65	...

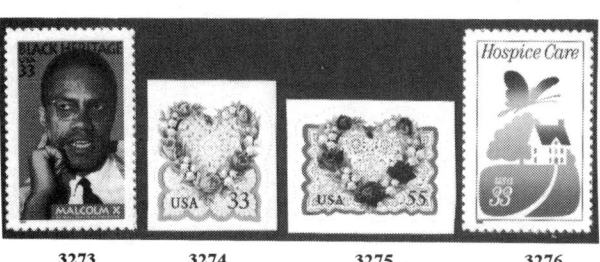

3273   3274   3275   3276

3272   3277-82   3283

1999 Commemoratives

Scott's No.	Sheet	Mint Block	Plate Block	F-VF NH	F-VF Used
3272	33¢ Year of the Hare .... (20)	12.95	2.95	.65	.25
3273	33¢ Malcolm X, Black Heritage, SA .. (20)	12.95	2.95	.65	.25
3274	33¢ Victorian-Love Self-adhesive single	...	...	.65	.25
3274	33¢ Victorian-Love Pane of 20	...	...	12.95	...
3275	55¢ Victorian-Love SA .... (20)	21.50	4.95	1.10	.50
3276	33¢ Hospice-Care, SA .... (20)	12.95	2.95	.65	.25

1999 Flag over City Regular Issues

3277	33¢ Red date, Water-activated ..... (100)	62.50	3.35	.65	.15
3278	33¢ Black date, SA, Die-cut 11.1 ..... (20)	12.95	2.95	.65	.18
3278v	33¢ Black date, SA, Die-cut 11.1	...	...	.65	.18
3278vs	33¢ Bklt Sgl., Die-cut on 4 sides, from booklet of 20	...	...	.95	.35
3278a	33¢ Booklet Pane of 4	...	...	2.60	...
3278b	33¢ Booklet Pane of 5	...	...	3.25	...
3278c	33¢ Booklet Pane of 6	...	...	3.90	...
3278d	33¢ Convertible Booklet of 10...........	...	...	6.45	...
3279	33¢ Red date, Booklet Single, SA, Die-cut 9.8	...	...	.65	.18
3279a	33¢ Red date, Booklet Pane of 10.......	...	...	6.45	...
3280	33¢ Coil, Red date, Water Activated ..	5.50	4.25	.65	.18
3281	33¢ Coil, Red date, SA Square...........	5.50	4.25	.65	.18
3282	33¢ Coil, Red date, SA, Rounded.......	5.50	4.25	.65	.18

Note: #3281 has square corners with backing same size as stamp.
        #3282 has square corners with backing same size as stamp.

1999 Flag Over Chalkboard

Scott's No.		Mint Sheet	Plate Block	F-VF NH	F-VF Used
3283	33¢ Flag. Self-adhesive single...........	...	...	.65	.18
3283a	33¢ Self-adhesive Pane of 18............	...	...	11.65	...

1999 Commemoratives (continued)

3286   3287

3288	3289	3290	3291	3292

3286	33¢ Irish Immigrants........................	(20)	12.95	2.95	.65	.25
3287	33¢ Alfred Lunt & Lynn Fontaine	(20)	12.95	2.95	.65	.25
3288-92	33¢ Arctic Animals, Strip of 5	(15)	9.75 (10)	6.95	3.25	2.75
3288-92	33¢ Arctic, Set of 5 Singles		...	...	3.20	1.50

1999 Sonoran Desert Miniature Sheet

3293

		Mint Sheet	Plate Block	F-VF NH	F-VF Used
3293	33¢ Sonoran Desert, Self-adh. Min. Sheet of 10	...	...	6.50	...
3293a-j	33¢ Desert, Set of 10 Singles.............	...	...	6.40	5.00
3293	33¢ Desert. Uncut Sheet of 60 (6 Panes)	...	...	49.50	...

1999 Fruit Berries Self-Adhesive Regular Issues

3296,99,3305	3294,98,3302	3295,3300,3303	3297,3301,3304

3294-97	33¢ Booklet Singles, Die-cut 11.2 x 11.7	...	...	2.60	.80
3297a	33¢ Booklet Pane of 5	...	...	3.25	...
3298-3301	33¢ Booklet Singles, Die-cut 9.5 x 10	...	...	2.60	...
3301a	33¢ Booklet Pane of 15	...	...	9.70	...
3302-5	33¢ Coils, Die-Cut 8.5 Vert., attd.	(PS8) 7.50	(PS5) 5.50	2.60	...
3302-5	33¢ Set of 4 Coil Singles	...	...	2.55	.80

1999 Daffy Duck Self-adhesive Souvenir Sheets

3306

Scott's No.		Mint Sheet	Plate Block	F-VF NH	F-VF Us
3306	33¢ Souvenir Sheet of 10..................	...	...	6.50	
3306a	33¢ Single Stamp.............................			.65	
3306b	33¢ Booklet Pane of 9 (left side).......	...	...	5.95	
3306c	33¢ Booklet Pane of 1 (right side).....	...	...	1.25	
3306v	33¢ Top Press Sheet of 6 Panes........	115.00	...	...	
3306v	33¢ Bottom Press Sheet of 6 Panes...	185.00	...	...	
3306v	33¢ S/S of 10 from uncut Sheet	...	...	19.95	
3306v	33¢ Souvenir Sheet with Plate Number	...	...	95.00	
3307	33¢ Souvenir Sheet of 10 with Special Die-cut that extends through paper backing	...	...	14.95	
3307a	33¢ Single stamp with special Die-cut	...	...	.85	
3307b	33¢ Booklet Pane of 9, Special Die-cut (left side)	...	...	6.95	
3307c	33¢ Imperforate Bklt. Pane of 1 (right side)	...	...	8.95	

1999 Commemoratives (continued)

3308   3309

3310	3311
3312	3313

3308	33¢ Ayn Rand, Literary	(20)	12.95	2.95	.85
3309	33¢ Cinco de Mayo	(20)	12.95	2.95	.65
3310-13	33¢ Tropical Flowers, SA, block	...	...	2.60	
3313b	33¢ Flowers, Self Adhesive Pane of 20	...	...	12.95	
3310-13	33¢ Flowers, set of 4 singles............	...	...	2.55	
3313v	33¢ Flowers, 2 blocks of 4 back-to-back	...	...	5.20	

Note: SA= Self-adhesive stamps

Stop Collecting Stamps.

Collect plate blocks! Plate blocks are just as much fun to collect as singles, but eminently more profitable as the examples below indicate.

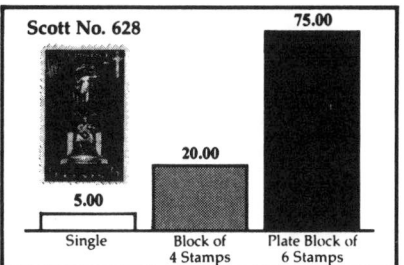

Scott No. 628
Single 5.00
Block of 4 Stamps 20.00
Plate Block of 6 Stamps 75.00

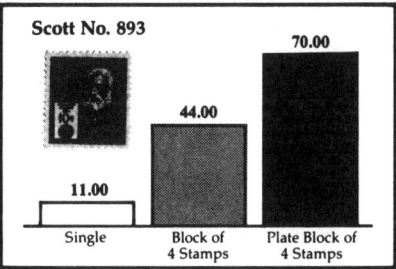

Scott No. 893
Single 11.00
Block of 4 Stamps 44.00
Plate Block of 4 Stamps 70.00

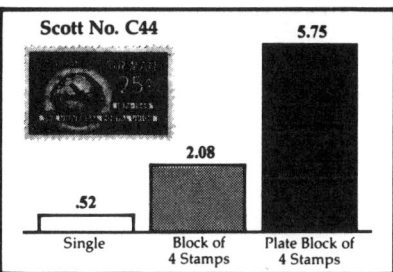

Scott No. C44
Single .52
Block of 4 Stamps 2.08
Plate Block of 4 Stamps 5.75

These are not isolated examples. There is no instance in which a plate block does not have a higher catalog value than the single stamps that comprise it.

Why now is a great time to start collecting plate blocks.

Since the USPS returned to a plate block of only four stamps in January of 1986, an unprecedented resurgence of interest has occurred. And as demand increases so will the value of your plate blocks.

Why buy from us?

The Plate Block Stamp Co. has been in business since 1977 and has grown to be America's premier plate block dealer. Our inventory always exceeds a quarter million plate blocks of consistent Fine-Very Fine Never Hinged condition...always at very competitive prices. Ordering is super-easy with our 11 page catalog and we offer 800 telephone service for Visa and Mastercard holders. Orders are routinely processed within hours. And if for any reason you wish to return a stamp, we will happily refund your money in full.

Inside Information

In addition to great prices, our customers receive the information-packed *Plate Block Market Analyst*. Every quarter we tell you what's hot and what's not. Had you been informed by *The Market Analyst* you would have been able to take advantage of some of the following recommendations we made:

In Volume 26, January 1986, the "D" official stamp, Scott No. 0138 retail was $1.49- Now $25-$30

In Volume 32, October 1987, the 17¢ postage due stamp, Scott No. J104 retail was $6.95- Now $22-$27

The Plate Block Market Analyst...a great opportunity for you to learn more about the hobby you love.

Whatever your goal or interest in collecting stamps might be, plate blocks are the answer. If you collect solely for enjoyment, you can certainly enjoy the beauty of a plate block collection. If you collect for the knowledge to be gained, plate blocks add another dimension. If you are building a legacy for your children or grandchildren, plate blocks add excitement...if you're investing, plate blocks provide a consistent history of appreciation.

So stop collecting stamps! Contact us for a free plate block catalog and newsletter today!

THE PLATE BLOCK STAMP COMPANY

1-800-829-6777 www.plateblockstamps.com
P.O. Box 6417 B/Leawood, KS 66206

1999 Commemoratives (Continued)

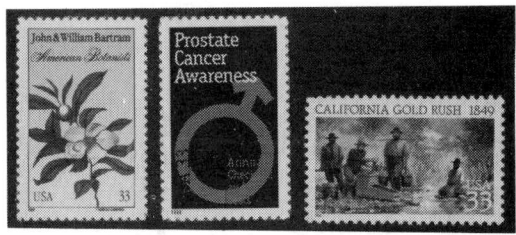

...	33¢ John & William Bartram, SA.... (20) 12.95	2.95	.65	.25
...	33¢ Prostrate Cancer, SA .... (20) 12.95	2.95	.65	.25
...	33¢ California Gold Rush................ (20) 12.95	2.95	.65	.25

...	33¢ Aquarium Fish, attd; SA........... (20) 12.95 (8)	5.85	2.60	...	
...	33¢ Fish, set of 4 singles................. ...	...	2.55	1.20	
...	33¢ Fish, uncut sheet of 120 (6 Panes) 85.00	...	...		
...	33¢ Xtreme Sports, block, SA.......... (20) 12.95	2.95	2.60	...	
...	33¢ Sports, strip of 4	...	2.60	...	
...	33¢ Sports, Set of 4 singles............. ...	...	2.55	1.20	
...	33¢ Sports, uncut sheet of 80 (4 panes) 59.95	...	...	...	
...	33¢ American Glass, block.............. (15) 9.70	2.95	2.60	2.25	
...	33¢ Glass, strip of 4	...	2.60	2.25	
...	33¢ Glass, Set of 4 singles............... ...	...	2.55	1.20	

1999 Great American Series

Scott's No.		Mint Sheet	Plate Block	F-VF NH	F-VF Used
...	55¢ Justin S. Morrill, SA..................... (20) 19.95		4.95	1.10	.30

1999 Commemoratives (continued)

		Mint Sheet	Plate Block	F-VF NH	F-VF Used
...	33¢ James Cagney, Legends of Hollywood Series.....................	(20) 12.95	2.95	.65	.25
...	55¢ Gen. William "Billy" Mitchell, SA	(20) 19.95	4.95	1.10	.50
...	33¢ Honoring Those Who Served......	(20) 12.95	2.95	.65	.25
...	33¢ All Aboard, 5 Trains, attd.........	(20) 12.95	(10) 6.95	3.25	...
...	33¢ Trains, Set of 5 singles.............	...	...	3.20	1.50

Note: Listings for stamps issued after editing is complete are tentative and subject to change.

SEMI POSTAL STAMPS

1998 Breast Cancer Research

B1	(32¢ + 8¢) Breast Cancer, 1st Class Rate	(20) 15.75	3.50	.80	.25

MINT COMMEMORATIVE YEAR SETS

Year	Scott's No.	Qty.	F-VF NH	Year	Scott's No.	Qty.	F-VF NH	Year	Scott's No.	Qty.	F-VF NH	Year	Scott's No.	Qty.	F-VF NH
1935	772-75	4	.65	1958	1100,04-23	21	2.75	1978	1731-33,44-69	29	13.95	1991	2532-35,37-38,50-51, 2553-58,60-61,67, 2578-79	19	16.35
1936	776-84	6	3.35	1959	1124-38	15	1.95	1979	1770-1802	33	14.85				
1937	795-802	8	2.00	1960	1139-73	35	4.95	1980	1803-10,21-43	31	14.65	1992	2611-23,30-41,98-99, 2700-04,10-14,20	38	33.75
1938	835-38	4	.90	1961	1174-90	17	3.95	1981	1874-79,1910-45	42	24.95				
1939	852-58	7	3.95	1962	1191-1207	17	2.35	1982	1950-52,2003-4,955 2006-30	30	20.95	1993	2721-30,46-59,66, 2771-74,79-89,91-94, 2804-06	47	40.75
1940	894-902	9	1.75	1963	1230-41	12	1.80				
1941-3	903-08	6	1.40	1964	1242-60	19	3.95	1983	2031-65	35	22.50				
1944	922-26	5	.85	1965	1261-76	16	2.75	1984	2066-2109	44	32.75	1994	2807-12,14C-28,2834-36, 39,48-68,2871-72, 76	49	26.95
1945	927-38	12	1.60	1966	1306-22	17	2.75	1985	2110,37-47,52-66	27	35.75				
1946	939-44	6	.75	1967	1323-37	15	3.95	1986	2167,2202-4,10-11, 2220-24,2235-2245		16.75	1995	2948,50-58,61-68,74 76-80,82-92,98-99 3001-7,19-23	49	39.95
1947	945-52	8	1.75	1968	1339-40,42-64	25	6.65				
1948	953-80	28	3.25	1969	1365-86	22	7.85	1987	2246-51,75, 2336-38,2349-54, 2360-61,2367-68	20	15.95				
1949	981-86	6	.75	1970	1387-92,1405-22	24	6.75					1996	3024,30,58-67,69-70 3072-88,90-3104, 3106-11,18	53	43.95
1950	987-97	11	1.50	1971	1423-45	23	5.50				
1951	998-1003	6	.70	1972	1446-74	29	6.75	1988	2339-46,69-80, 86-93,2399-2400	30	25.75				
1952	1004-16	13	1.60	1973	1475-1508	34	8.25					1997	3120-21, 3125, 30-31, 34-35, 3141, 43-50, 52-75	40	28.75
1953	1017-28	12	1.50	1974	1525-52	28	8.50	1989	2347,2401-04, 10-18,20-28,34-37	27	23.75				
1954	1029,60-63	5	.65	1975	1553-80	28	7.95				
1955	1064-72	9	1.25	1976	1629-32,83-85 1690-1703	21	8.95	1990	2348,2349-40,2442, 44-49,96-2500, 2506-15	25	26.95	1998	3179-81,3192-3203,3206 3211-27,30-35,37-48	51	30.75
1956	1073-85	13	3.65				
1957	1086-99	14	1.75	1977	1704-30	27	10.00				

UNITED STATES POSTAL SERVICE MINT SETS

Commemoratives and Definitives

Commemoratives

Year	Scott's Nos.	# Stamps	Price
1968 (1)	"Cover #334-890", #1339-40, 1342-64,C74	26	175.00
1968 (2)	"Cover #369-245", Contents same as (1)		150.00
1969	#1365-86,C76	23	120.00
1970	#1387-92,1405-22	24	175.00
1971 (1)	"Mini Album" #1396,1423-45	24	40.00
1971 (2)	Black strips, Contents same as (1)	120.00	
1972	#1446-74,C84-85	31	22.50
1973	#1475-1504,1507-08,C86	33	18.00
1974	#1505-06,1525-51	29	15.00
1975	#1553-80	28	17.50
1976	#1629-32,1633/82 (1 single), 1683-85,1690-1702	21	29.50
1977	#1704-30	27	15.00
1978	#1731-33,44-56,58-69	28	17.50
1979	#1770-94,1799-1802,C97	30	18.50
1980	#1795-98,1803-04,21,23-43	28	23.50
1981	#1874-79,1910-26,28-45	41	30.00
1982	#1950,52,1953/2002 (1 single), 2003-04,06-24,26-30	29	26.50
1983	#2031-65,C101-12	47	45.00
1984	#2066-71,73-2109	43	26.75
1985	#2110,37-47,52-66	27	35.00
1986	#2167,2201a,2202-04,2209a, 2210-11,2216a-9i (1 single), 2220-24,35-45	25	27.50
1987	Soft Cover, #2246-51,2274a,75, 2286/2335 (1 single), 2336-38, 2349-54,59a,60-61,66a,67-68	24	39.50

Year	Scott's Nos.	# Stamps	Price
1987	Hard Cover, Same contents		57.50
1988	Soft Cover, #2339-46,69-80, 85a,86-93,95-99,2400,C117	37	42.50
1988	Hard Cover, Same contents		57.50
1989	#2347,2401-04,09a,10-14, 2416-18,20-28	22	45.00
1990	#2348,2415,39-40,42,44-49,74a, 2496-2515	32	50.00
1991	#2532-35,37-38,49a,50-51,53-67, 2577a,78,80 or 81,82-85, C130-31	33	57.50
1992	Hard Cover, #2611-23,30-41,46a, 2647/96 (1 single), 2697-99, 2700-04,2709a,10-14	41	57.50
1993	Hard Cover, #2721-23,31-37,45a, 2746-59,64a,65-66,70a,78a,79-89, 2791-94,2804-05	47	59.50
1994	Hard Cover, #2807-12,2814-28, 2833a,34-36,38-40,2841a,2847a, 2848-69,71-72	52	69.50
1995	Hard Cover, #2587,2876,2948, 2950-58,61-68,73a,74-92,97a, 2999-3007,3019-23	55	79.50
1996	Hard Cover #3024-29,58-65,67-70 3072-88,90-3111,3118-19	59	69.50
1996	Soft Cover,#3024,3025-29(1),3058-60 ,61-64(1),65,67,68a-t(1),3069-70,72- 76(1),77- 80(1),81-82, 3083-86(1),87-88,90,91-95(1),3096-99(1),3100- 3(1),3104,3105a-o(1)3106-7, 3108-11(1),18,19a-b(1)	29	45.00

Year	Scott's Nos.	# Stamps	Price
1997	Hard Cover #3120-21, 23-27, 3130-31, 34-37, 39a, 40a 3141-46, 51-52, 54-77	47	65.00
1998	Hard Cover #3179-81, 92-3204, 3206 10a, 11-19, 21-27, 30-44, 3249-52	52	59.95

Definitives & Stationery

Year	Scott's Nos.	# Stamps	Price
1980	#1738-42,1805-11,13,22,59,C98-100, U590,U597-99,UC53,UX82-86	27	55.00
1981	#1582b,1818,1819-20 PRS,57-58, 65,89a,90,91 PR,93a,94,95 PR, 96a,1903 PR,1906-08 PRS,1927, 46,47-48 PRS	22	37.50
1982	#1615v PR,1845,55,60,66,97A PR, 1698A PR,1901 PR,1904 PR,49a, 1951,2005 PR,2025,U591,U602-03, UC55,UX94-97,UXC20	22	22.50
1983	#1844,46-48,61,97 PR,98 PR,99 PR, 1900 PR,O127-29,O130,32,35 PR, U604-05,UC56-57,UO73,UX98-100, UXC21,UZ2	25	17.50
1984	#1853,62,64,68,1902 PR, 1905 PR, 2072,U606,UX101-04	12	12.50
1987-88	#2115b,2127,29,30av,69,76-78,80, 2182,83,88,92,2226,52-66,C118-19, O138A-B,40-41	35	50.00
1989-90	#2127av,73,84,86,94A,2280v,2419, 2431 (6),43a,52,75a,76,O143,U611, U614-18,UC62,UO79-80,UX127-38, UX143-48,UX150-52	44	62.50

AIR MAIL STAMPS

| C1 | C4 | C5 | C6 |

1918 First Issue VF Used + 35% (B)

| Scott's No. | | NH | | Unused | | Used |
	VF	F-VF	VF	F-VF		F-VF
C1-3	Set of 3	425.00	315.00	285.00	210.00	99.50
C1	6¢ Curtiss Jenny, Orange	120.00	90.00	80.00	60.00	28.50
C2	16¢ Green	165.00	120.00	110.00	80.00	32.50
C3	24¢ Carmine Rose & Blue	165.00	120.00	110.00	80.00	45.00

1923 Second Issue VF Used + 35% (B)

		NH		Unused		Used
C4-6	Set of 3	370.00	275.00	250.00	185.00	65.00
C4	8¢ Propeller, Dark Green	49.50	37.50	32.50	25.00	13.00
C5	16¢ Emblem, Dark Blue...............	165.00	120.00	110.00	80.00	27.50
C6	24¢ Biplane, Carmine	180.00	135.00	120.00	90.00	28.50

| PLATE BLOCKS | | | | ARROW BLOCKS | | | |
| | | NH | Unused | | | NH | Unused |
Scott #	VF	F-VF	F-VF	Scott #	VF	F-VF	F-VF
C1 (6)	1200.00	900.00	650.00	C1	525.00	395.00	265.00
C2 (6)	2200.00	1650.00	1150.00	C2	700.00	525.00	350.00
C3 (12)	2300.00	1700.00	1200.00	C3	700.00	525.00	350.00
C4 (6)	485.00	365.00	250.00	CENTER LINE BLOCKS			
C5 (6)	3600.00	2700.00	1850.00	C1	600.00	450.00	300.00
C6 (6)	4000.00	3000.00	2100.00	C2	835.00	625.00	425.00
				C3	835.00	625.00	425.00

| C7 | C10 |

| C11 | C12, C16 |

| Scott's No. | | NH | | Unused | | Used |
		VF	F-VF	VF	F-VF	F-VF

1926-27 Map & Mail Planes VF Used + 30% (B)

C7-9	Set of 3........................	26.50	19.50	18.50	13.95	4.25
C7	10¢ Map, Dark Blue 5.15	3.85	3.60	2.75	.40
C8	15¢ Map, Brown 6.00	4.50	4.25	3.25	2.25
C9	20¢ Map, Green (1927) 16.50	12.25	11.50	8.75	1.90

1927 Lindbergh Tribute VF + 30% (B)

C10	10¢ Lindbergh, Dark Blue 13.00	10.00	9.00	7.00	2.25
C10a	Booklet Pane of 3 ....150.00	115.00	110.00	80.00	...

1928 Beacon VF Used + 40% (B)

C11	5¢ Carmine & Blue.........................8.50	5.75	5.65	3.95	.65

1930 Winged Globe, Flat Press, Perf. 11 VF Used + 30% (B)

C12	5¢ Violet 17.00	13.00	11.75	8.75	.40

1930 GRAF ZEPPELIN ISSUE VF Used + 25% (B)

| C13 | C15 | C14 |

C13-15	Set of 3.....................................	2650.00	2150.00	2000.00	1650.00	1175.00
C13	65¢ Zeppelin, Green	435.00	350.00	340.00	270.00	210.00
C14	$1.30 Zeppelin, Brown	900.00	750.00	700.00	575.00	425.00
C15	$2.60 Zeppelin, Blue	1425.00	1150.00	1100.00	875.00	600.00

1931-32 Rotary Press, Perf. 10½x11, Designs of #C12 VF Used + 30% (B)

C16	5¢ Winged Globe, Violet..............	10.50	8.00	7.00	5.25	.50
C17	8¢ Winged Globe (1932) 3.75	2.85	2.70	2.00	.30

| PLATE BLOCKS | | | | PLATE BLOCKS | | | |
| | | NH | Unused | | | NH | Unused |
Scott #	VF	F-VF	F-VF	Scott #	VF	F-VF	F-VF
C7 (6)	75.00	55.00	40.00	C12 (6)	295.00	225.00	160.00
C8 (6)	85.00	65.00	45.00	C13 (6)	3500.00	2800.00	2300.00
C9 (6)	185.00	140.00	100.00	C14 (6)	8750.00	7000.00	5500.00
C10 (6)	250.00	190.00	135.00	C15 (6)	13750.00	11000.00	8500.00
C11 (6)	75.00	52.50	40.00	C16	140.00	110.00	75.00
C11 (6) Double "TOP"				C17	56.50	42.50	30.00
	185.00	125.00	90.00	ARROW BLOCKS			
C11 (8) No "TOP"				C11	36.50	25.00	18.00
	325.00	225.00	175.00				

C18   C19

Scott's No.		VF	NH F-VF	Unused VF	F-VF	Used F-VF

1933 Century of Progress VF Used + 20% (B)

| C18 | 50¢ Graf Zeppelin, Green | 135.00 | 110.00 | 100.00 | 80.00 | 77.50 |

1934 Winged Globe, Design of #C12 VF Used + 30% (B)

| C19 | 6¢ Orange | 3.90 | 3.00 | 3.15 | 2.40 | .20 |

C20   C21-22

C23   C24

1935-37 Trans-Pacific Issue (VF Used + 25%)

C20-22	Clipper Set of 3	27.75	22.00	22.00	17.50	6.50
C20	25¢ China Clipper	2.00	1.60	1.60	1.25	1.10
C21	20¢ China Clipper (1937)	13.50	10.75	10.50	8.50	1.50
C22	50¢ China Clipper ('37)	13.50	10.75	10.50	8.50	4.50

1938 Eagle (VF Used + 30%)

| C23 | 6¢ Dark Blue & Carmine | .65 | .50 | .50 | .40 | .15 |

1939 Trans-Atlantic Issue (VF Used + 30%)

| C24 | 30¢ Winged Globe, Blue | 13.50 | 10.00 | 10.50 | 8.00 | 1.35 |

PLATE BLOCKS				ARROW BLOCKS		
	NH		Unused		NH	Unused
Scott #	VF	F-VF	F-VF	Scott #	VF	F-VF	F-VF
C18 (6)	1075.00	900.00	700.00	C23	3.00	2.50	2.00
C19	37.50	28.50	21.75				
C20 (6)	35.00	27.50	22.50	**CENTER LINE BLOCKS**		
C21 (6)	170.00	135.00	110.00	C23	3.35	2.75	2.25
C22 (6)	170.00	135.00	110.00				
C23	12.50	9.50	7.50				
C24 (6)	235.00	185.00	150.00				

U.S. AIRMAIL AND SPECIAL DELIVERY MINT SHEETS

Scott No. (Size)	F-VF NH	Scott No. (Size)	F-VF NH	Scott No. (Size)	F-VF NH	Scott No. (Size)	F-VF NH
C7 (50)	245.00	C16 (50)	435.00	C23 (50)	30.00	E16 (50)	45.00
C8 (50)	280.00	C17 (50)	175.00	C24 (50)	625.00	E17 (50)	33.50
C9 (50)	700.00	C19 (50)	175.00	CE1 (50)	50.00	E18 (50)	165.00
C10 (50)	650.00	C20 (50)	95.00	CE2 (50)	35.00	E19 (50)	85.00
C11 (50)	315.00	C21 (50)	600.00	E14 (50)	150.00		
C12 (50)	700.00	C22 (50)	600.00	E15 (50)	50.00		

C25   C32   C33,C39

1941-44 Transport Plane

Scott's No.		Mint Sheet	Plate Block	F-VF NH	F-VF Used
C25-31	Set of 7	...	130.00	21.95	4.00
C25	6¢ Carmine	9.75	1.00	.20	.15
C25a	6¢ Booklet Pane of 3	...	...	3.35	3.00
C26	8¢ Olive Green (1944)	11.50	1.85	.24	.15
C27	10¢ Violet	70.00	9.00	1.35	.20
C28	15¢ Brown Carmine	140.00	12.50	2.75	.35

Scott's No.		Mint Sheet	Plate Block	F-VF NH	F-VF Used
C29	20¢ Bright Green	115.00	10.75	2.30	.30
C30	30¢ Blue	125.00	11.75	2.50	.35
C31	50¢ Orange	700.00	80.00	12.00	3.00

1946-1948 Issues

| C32 | 5¢ DC-4 Skymaster | 7.50 | .65 | .20 | .15 |
| C33 | 5¢ Small Plane (1947) .... (100) | 15.00 | .65 | .20 | .15 |

C34   C35   C36

C34	10¢ Pan-Am Building (1947)	13.75	1.35	.30	.15
C34a	10¢ Dry Printing	21.75	2.10	.45	.25
C35	15¢ New York Skyline (1947)	19.50	1.80	.40	.15
C35b	15¢ Dry Printing	29.50	2.75	.60	.25
C36	25¢ Oakland Bay Bridge (1947)	47.50	4.25	.95	.15
C36a	25¢ Dry Printing	65.00	5.75	1.35	.30

C38   C40   C42

C43   C44   C45

1948-49 Issues

		Line Pair		
C37	5¢ Small Plane, Coil	8.50	.85	.80
		Plate Blocks		
C38	5¢ New York City Jubilee .... (100)	18.50	4.25	.20	.15
C39	6¢ Plane (Design of C33) ('49) .... (100)	18.50	.70	.20	.15
C39a	6¢ Booklet Pane of 6	...	...	9.75	7.50
C39b	6¢ Dry Printing .... (100)	115.00	7.50	1.25	.50
C39c	6¢ Bk. Pane of 6, Dry Printing	...	...	25.00	...
C40	6¢ Alexandria Bicentennial ('49)	8.50	.70	.20	.15
		Line Pair		
C41	6¢ Small Plane, Coil (1949)	...	12.75	2.95	.15
		Plate Blocks		
C42-44	Univ. Postal Un., Set of 3 (1949)	8.25	1.30	1.00	
C42	10¢ Post Office Building	14.50	1.30	.27	.25
C43	15¢ Globe & Doves	19.75	1.80	.40	.35
C44	25¢ Stratocruiser & Globe	35.00	5.50	.70	.50
C45	6¢ Wright Brothers Flight (1949)	10.50	1.00	.20	.15

C46

1952 Hawaii Issue

| C46 | 80¢ Diamond Head | 260.00 | 27.50 | 5.25 | 1.25 |

1953-58 Issues

C47   C48, C50   C49   C51,C52,C60,C61

C47	6¢ Anniv. of Powered Flight	8.25	.70	.20	.15
C48	4¢ Eagle in Flight (1954) ....(100)	12.75	1.60	.20	.15
C49	6¢ Air Force 50th (1957)	9.75	.85	.20	.15
C50	5¢ Eagle (as C48) (1958) ....(100)	15.00	1.40	.20	.15
C51	7¢ Jet Silhouette, Blue (1958) ......(100)	17.50	.75	.20	.15
C51a	7¢ Booklet Pane of 6	...	...	11.75	6.75
		Line Pair		
C52	7¢ Jet Blue Coil, LargeHoles (1958).	...	17.00	1.85	.15
C52s	7¢ Small Holes	...	85.00	9.75	...

1959-60 Issues

| C53 | C54 | C55 |

| C57 | C56 | C58 |

Scott's No.		Mint Sheet	Plate Block	F-VF NH	F-VF Used
C53	7¢ Alaska Statehood	11.75	.95	.25	.15
C54	7¢ Balloon Jupiter	11.75	.95	.25	.15
C55	7¢ Hawaii Statehood	11.75	.95	.25	.15
C56	10¢ Pan-Am Games, Chicago	13.75	1.40	.30	.25
C57	10¢ Liberty Bell (1960)	65.00	5.75	1.35	.80
C58	15¢ Statue of Liberty (1959)	21.50	1.95	.45	.15

1960-67 Issues

| C59 | C62 | C63 |

| C64,C65 | C66 | C67 |

C59	25¢ Abraham Lincoln	32.50	2.85	.65	.15
C59a	25¢ Tagged (1966)	40.00	3.75	.80	.35
C60	7¢ Jet Silh., Carmine	(100) 17.50	.80	.20	.15
C60a	7¢ Bk. Pane of 6	...	...	12.50	7.75
C61	7¢ Jet, Carmine Coil	Line Pair 37.50	4.00	.30	
C62	13¢ Liberty Bell (1961)	21.00	1.80	.40	.15
C62a	13¢ Tagged (1967)	65.00	12.00	1.20	.65
C63	15¢ Liberty, Re-engraved (1961)	21.00	1.85	.40	.15
C63a	15¢ Tagged (1967)	23.00	2.10	.45	.25

#C58 has wide border around statue, #C63 is divided in center.

C64	8¢ Jet over Capitol (1962)	(100) 20.75	.90	.22	.15
C64a	8¢ Tagged (1963)	(100) 22.75	1.00	.25	.20
C64b	8¢ B. Pane of 5, Sl. 1, "Your Mailman"	...	...	4.50	2.75
C64b	8¢ B. Pane of 5, Sl. 2, "Use Zone Numbers"	...	...	57.50	...
C64b	8¢ B. Pane of 5, Sl. 3, "Always Use Zip"	...	...	11.50	...
C64c	8¢ Pane/5, Tagged, Slogan 3	...	...	1.50	1.25
C65	8¢ Capitol & Jet Coil (1962)	Line Pair 5.95	.45	.15	
C65a	8¢ Tagged	Line Pair 2.75	.35	.15	
C66	15¢ Montgomery Blair	32.50	2.75	.65	.55
C67	6¢ Bald Eagle	(100) 18.50	1.75	.20	.15
C67a	6¢ Tagged (1967)	...	75.00	3.50	3.00

1963-68 Issues (cont.)

| C68 | C69 | C70 | C71 |

| C72,C73 | C74 | C75 |

Scott's No.		Mint Sheet	Plate Block	F-VF NH	F-VF Used
C68	8¢ Amelia Earhart	15.00	1.30	.30	.18
C69	8¢ Robert H. Goddard (1964)	20.00	1.75	.40	.18
C70	8¢ Alaska Purchase (1967)	13.50	1.50	.28	.18
C71	20¢ Columbian Jays (1967)	45.00	3.85	.90	.15
C72	10¢ 50-Star Runway (1968)	(100) 27.00	1.15	.28	.15
C72b	10¢ Booklet Pane of 8	...	...	2.35	2.25
C72c	10¢ B. Pane of 5 with Sl. 4 or Sl. 5	...	...	3.50	3.25
C72v	10¢ Congressional Precancel	...	110.00	2.00	...
C73	10¢ 50-Star Runway Coil (1968)	Line Pair	1.65	.30	.15
C74	10¢ Air Mail Service 50th Anniv ('68)	16.50	2.25	.30	.18
C75	20¢ "USA" and Jet (1968)	24.50	2.35	.50	.18

1969-73 Issues

| C76 | C77 | C78,C82 |

| C79,C83 | C80 | C81 |

C76	10¢ Moon Landing	(32) 11.75	1.50	.35	.20
C77	9¢ Delta Wing Plane Silh. ('71)	(100) 21.50	1.10	.22	.20
C78	11¢ Jet Airliner Silhouette ('71)	(100) 27.50	1.35	.30	.15
C78a	11¢ Booklet Pane of 4	...	...	1.20	1.15
C78b	11¢ Congressional Precancel	...	25.75	.65	.40
C79	13¢ Winged Envelope (1973)	(100) 33.50	1.50	.35	.15
C79a	13¢ Booklet Pane of 5	...	...	1.60	1.50
C79b	13¢ Congressional Precancel	...	9.50	.50	.35
C80	17¢ Statue of Lib. Head (1971)	22.50	1.95	.45	.22
C81	21¢ "USA" and Jet (1971)	26.75	2.25	.55	.15
C82	11¢ Jet Silhouette Coil (1971)	Line Pair	.75	.30	.15
C83	13¢ Winged Env. Coil (1973)	Line Pair	.95	.35	.15

| C85 | C84 | C86 |

| C87 | C88 |

C89   C90

Scott's No.		Mint Sheet	Plate Block	F-VF NH	F-VF Used
C84	11¢ City of Refuge Park ('72)...........	14.75	1.40	.30	.18
C85	11¢ Olympic Games - Skiing ('72)	14.75 (10)	3.25	.30	.18
C86	11¢ Electronics (1973)......................	13.75	1.20	.28	.18
C87	18¢ Statue of Liberty (1974)...............	24.50	2.10	.45	.45
C88	26¢ Mt. Rushmore Memorial (1974)...	31.50	2.75	.65	.15
C89	25¢ Plane & Globes (1976).......	31.50	2.75	.65	.18
C90	31¢ Plane, Globe and Flag (1976).......	36.50	3.25	.75	.18

1978-80 Issues

C91   C93   C95   C97
C92   C94   C96

C99   C98   C100

C91-92	31¢ Wright Bros., attd ....(100)	80.00	3.75	1.65	1.60
C91-92	Set of 2 Singles.................................	...	...	1.60	.80
C93-94	21¢ Octave Chanute, attd. ('79)......(100)	80.00	4.25	1.75	1.60
C93-94	Set of 2 Singles.................................	...	...	1.65	.90
C95-96	25¢ Wiley Post, attd. ('79)..............(100)	145.00	9.50	2.95	2.00
C95-96	Set of 2 Singles.................................	...	...	2.85	1.20
C97	31¢ Olympics - High Jump ('79).........	45.00	(12)11.50	.90	.35
C98	40¢ Philip Mazzei, Perf. 11 (1980)	50.00	(12)12.50	1.00	.25
C98a	40¢ Perf. 10½x11 (1982).................	...	(12)110.00	5.00	2.00
C99	28¢ Blanche Scott	36.50	(12)9.50	.75	.25
C100	35¢ Glenn Curtiss.............................	42.50	(12)11.00	.85	.25

1983 Los Angeles Olympic Issues

C101   C102
C103   C104

C105   C106
C107   C108

C109   C110
C111   C112

Scott's No.		Mint Sheet	Plate Block	F-VF NH	F-VF Used
C101-4	28¢ Summer Olympics, attd	62.50	6.00	5.50	3.00
C101-4	Set of 4 Singles	...	...	4.75	1.20
C105-8	40¢ Summer Olympics, Bullseye Perfs Pf. 11.2, attd	60.00	5.75	5.25	4.00
C105-8	Set of 4 Singles	...	...	5.00	1.60
C105a-8a	40¢ Line Perfs Pf. 11, attd	110.00	12.75	8.75	7.50
C105a-8a	Set of 4 Singles	...	...	8.00	3.00
C109-12	35¢ Summer Olympics, attd	67.50	8.75	5.25	4.50
C109-12	Set of 4 Singles	...	...	4.75	2.40

1985-1989 Issues

C113   C114   C115

C116   C117   C118

C119   C120   C121

C113	33¢ Alfred Verville	41.50	3.85	.85	.25
C114	39¢ Sperry Brothers	50.00	4.50	1.00	.35
C115	44¢ Transpacific Airmail................	52.50	5.25	1.10	.30
C116	44¢ Father Junipero Serra	67.50	9.00	1.35	.40
C117	44¢ New Sweden (1988)	57.50	7.50	1.15	.40
C118	45¢ Samuel Langley (1988)	60.00	5.25	1.20	.30
C118a	45¢ Overall Tagging	165.00	33.50	3.00	2.00
C119	36¢ Igor Sikorsky (1988)	43.50	4.25	.90	.35
C120	45¢ French Revolution ('89) ....(30)	35.00	5.25	1.15	.45
C121	45¢ Pre-Columbian Customs ('89).	57.50	5.25	1.15	.40

1989 Universal Postal Congress Issues

C122   **C123**
C124   **C125**

C126

Scott's No.		Mint Sheet	Plate Block	F-VF NH	F-VF Used
C122-25	45¢ Futuristic Mail Deliv., Attd....(40)	60.00	7.00	5.75	4.50
C122-25	Set of 4 Singles.............................	...	...	5.50	2.40
C126	$1.80 Future Mail Delivery Souvenir Sheet, Imperforate...........................	...	...	5.75	5.25

1990-93 Airmail Issues

C127   **C128**   **C129**

1990-93 Airmail Issues (cont.)

Scott's No.		Mint Sheet	Plate Block	F-VF NH	F-VF Used
C127	45¢ America, Caribbean Coast........	57.50	6.25	1.20	.40
C128	50¢ Harriet Quimby, Pf. 11 (1991)...	65.00	7.00	1.35	.45
C128b	H.Quimby, Perf. 11.2 ('93).............	67.50	7.50	1.40	.50
C129	40¢ William T. Piper (1991)............	50.00	5.00	1.10	.45

1991-93 Airmail Issues

C130   **C131**   **C132**

Scott's No.		Mint Sheet	Plate Block	F-VF NH	F-VF Used
C130	50¢ Antarctic Treaty (1991).............	60.00	6.00	1.25	.65
C131	50¢ America (1991)........................	60.00	6.00	1.25	.60
C132	40¢ W.T. Piper, new design ('93)....	68.50	7.50	1.40	.60

1999 American Landmarks International Rate Regular Issues

C133

Scott's No.		Mint Sheet	Plate Block	F-VF NH	F-VF Used
...	40¢ Rio Grande, SA........................ (20)	15.50	3.65	.80	.30
C133	48¢ Niagara Falls, SA..................... (20)	18.50	4.40	.75	.35

#C129: Blue sky clear along top of design, Perf. 11
#C132: Piper's hair is touching top of design, Bullseye Perf. 11.2

1934-36 AIR MAIL SPECIAL DELIVERY VF Used + 20%

CE1,CE2

Scott's No.		NH VF	NH F-VF	Unused VF	Unused F-VF	F-VF Used
CE1	16¢ Great Seal, Dark Blue	.90	.70	.70	.55	.70
CE2	16¢ Seal, Red & Blue	.70	.55	.55	.45	.25

PLATE BLOCKS				ARROW BLOCKS			
	NH		Unused		NH		Unused
Scott #	VF	F-VF	F-VF	Scott #	VF	F-VF	F-VF
CE1 (6)	27.00	22.50	18.00	CE2	3.00	2.50	2.00
CE2	10.50	8.50	6.75		CENTER LINE BLOCKS		
				CE2	3.35	2.75	2.25

See after #C24 for CE1-2 mint sheet prices.

SPECIAL DELIVERY STAMPS

E1   E2,E3   E4,E5

1885 "At A Special Delivery Office", Unwmkd., Perf. 12 (VF+60%)(C)

Scott's No.		NH Fine	Unused Fine	Ave.	Used Fine	Ave.
E1	10¢ Messenger, Blue..................	350.00	200.00	115.00	35.00	20.75

1888-93 "At Any Post Office", No Line Under "TEN CENTS"
Unwatermarked, Perf. 12 VF + 60% (C)

E2	10¢ Blue	335.00	195.00	120.00	12.00	7.25
E3	10¢ Orange (1893).....................	210.00	125.00	75.00	15.00	9.50

1894 Line Under "TEN CENTS", Unwmkd., Perf. 12 VF + 60% (C)

E4	10¢ Blue	700.00	425.00	265.00	25.00	16.00

1895 Line Under "TEN CENTS, Double Line Wmk. Perf. 12 VF + 50% (C)

E5	10¢ Blue	175.00	100.00	65.00	2.50	1.60

E6,E8-11   E7

Scott No.		NH VF	F-VF	Unused VF	F-VF	Used F-VF
1902-08 Double Line Watermark VF Used + 50% (B)						
E6	10¢ Ultramarine, Perf. 12............	160.00	110.00	95.00	65.00	2.75
E7	10¢ Mercury, Green (1908)........	110.00	70.00	67.50	45.00	29.50
1911-14 Single Line Watermark VF Used + 50% (B)						
E8	10¢ Ultramarine, Perf. 12............	170.00	115.00	110.00	75.00	4.00
E9	10¢ Ultra., Perf. 10 (1914)..........	315.00	210.00	200.00	135.00	5.00
1916-17 Unwatermarked VF Used + 50% (B)						
E10	10¢ Pale Ultra., Perf. 10..............	525.00	350.00	340.00	225.00	22.50
E11	10¢ Ultra., Perf. 11 (1917)...........	29.00	19.75	18.00	12.75	.45

E12-13,E15-18   E14,E19

1922-1925 Flat Press Printings, Perf. 11 VF Used + 30% (B)

E12	10¢ Motorcycle, Gray Violet........	39.50	28.00	27.50	21.50	.25
E13	15¢ Deep Orange (1925)..............	37.50	27.50	26.00	19.50	1.10
E14	20¢ P.O. Truck, Black (1925)	3.50	2.75	2.65	2.00	1.50

1927-1951 Rotary Press Printings, Perf. 11x10½ VF Used + 20%

E15-19	Set of 5..	8.75	7.00	7.25	5.50	2.95
E15	10¢ Motorcycle, Gray Violet..........	1.35	1.10	1.10	.85	.15
E16	15¢ Orange (1931).........................	1.20	.95	.95	.75	.18
E17	13¢ Blue (1944)	.80	.65	.70	.55	.18
E18	17¢ Orange Yellow (1944).............	4.00	3.25	3.35	2.65	2.50
E19	20¢ P.O. Truck, Black (1951)	2.10	1.70	1.70	1.40	.20

See after #C24 for E14-19 mint sheet prices.

PLATE BLOCKS				PLATE BLOCKS			
	NH		Unused		NH		Unused
Scott#	VF	F-VF	F-VF	Scott #	VF	F-VF	F-VF
E11 (6)	320.00	215.00	150.00	E15	7.50	5.75	4.25
E12 (6)	450.00	350.00	250.00	E16	5.75	4.75	3.75
E13 (6)	400.00	315.00	225.00	E17	4.75	3.75	3.00
E14 (6)	60.00	47.50	32.50	E18	33.50	26.50	19.50
				E19	10.50	8.75	6.50

E20,E21   E22,E23

1954-1971

Scott's No.		Mint Sheet	Pl. Block NH	F-VF NH	F-VF Used
E20-23	Set of 4	...	16.50	3.60	.75
E20	20¢ Letter & Hands.......................	30.00	2.75	.55	.15
E21	30¢ Letter & Hands (1957)	37.50	3.50	.75	.18
E22	45¢ Arrows (1969)........................	62.50	5.50	1.25	.30
E23	60¢ Arrows (1971)........................	67.50	6.00	1.35	.20

F1   FA1

1911 REGISTRATION VF Used + 40% (B)

Scott's No.		NH VF	F-VF	Unused VF	F-VF	Used F-VF
F1	10¢ Eagle, Ultramarine..............	130.00	90.00	77.50	55.00	5.25

1955 CERTIFIED MAIL

Scott's No.		Mint Sheet	Pl.Block NH	F-VF NH	F-VF Used
FA1	15¢ Postman, Red	22.50	5.00	.45	.30

POSTAGE DUE STAMPS

J1/J22   **J29/61**   **J35/65**

1879 Perforated 12 (NH + 100%, VF OG & Used + 60%, VF NH + 175%) (C)

Scott's No.		Unused Fine	Unused Ave.	Used Fine	Used Ave.
J1	1¢ Brown	33.50	20.00	6.50	3.75
J2	2¢ Brown	210.00	125.00	6.00	3.50
J3	3¢ Brown	30.00	18.50	3.50	2.10
J4	5¢ Brown	350.00	215.00	32.50	19.50
J5	10¢ Brown	350.00	215.00	18.75	11.50
J6	30¢ Brown	175.00	110.00	39.50	25.00
J7	50¢ Brown	265.00	160.00	46.50	27.50

1884-1889, Same Design Perf. 12 (NH + 100%, VF OG & Used + 60%, VF NH + 175%)

J15	1¢ Red Brown	32.50	19.50	3.25	1.95
J16	2¢ Red Brown	39.50	23.50	3.75	2.25
J17	3¢ Red Brown	575.00	350.00	120.00	70.00
J18	5¢ Red Brown	260.00	150.00	17.50	10.75
J19	10¢ Red Brown	260.00	150.00	13.50	8.50
J20	30¢ Red Brown	125.00	75.00	37.50	22.50
J21	50¢ Red Brown	1100.00	650.00	135.00	82.50

* Red Brown issues can be distinguished from Bright Claret issues by placing the stamps under long wave UV light. Bright Clarets give off a warm orange glow, Red Browns do not.

1891-93 Same Design Perf. 12 (NH + 75%, VF OG & Used + 60%, VF NH + 150%)

J22	1¢ Bright Claret	15.00	8.75	.75	.45
J23	2¢ Bright Claret	20.00	12.00	.75	.45
J24	3¢ Bright Claret	40.00	24.00	6.00	3.65
J25	5¢ Bright Claret	45.00	28.00	6.00	3.65
J26	10¢ Bright Claret	77.50	45.00	13.75	8.25
J27	30¢ Bright Claret	275.00	165.00	110.00	65.00
J28	50¢ Bright Claret	290.00	175.00	110.00	65.00

1894-95 Unwatermarked, Perf. 12 VF Used + 60% (C)

Scott's No.		NH VF	NH F-VF	Unused VF	Unused F-VF	Used F-VF
J29	1¢ Vermilion	2000.00	1300.00	1375.00	875.00	225.00
J30	2¢ Vermilion	1000.00	600.00	650.00	400.00	85.00
J31	1¢ Claret	67.50	41.50	42.50	27.50	4.95
J32	2¢ Claret	62.50	38.00	40.00	25.00	3.00
J33	3¢ Claret (1895)	265.00	170.00	175.00	110.00	25.00
J34	5¢ Claret (1895)	365.00	225.00	240.00	150.00	27.50
J35	10¢ Claret	365.00	225.00	240.00	150.00	20.00
J36	30¢ Claret (1895)	625.00	385.00	400.00	250.00	70.00
J36b	Pale Rose	535.00	320.00	335.00	210.00	65.00
J37	50¢ Claret (1895)	1700.00	1075.00	1100.00	700.00	195.00
J37a	Pale Rose	1600.00	1000.00	1050.00	650.00	185.00

1895-97, Double Line Watermark, Perf. 12 VF Used + 60% (C)

J38	1¢ Claret	14.50	8.50	8.75	5.50	.55
J39	2¢ Claret	14.50	8.50	8.75	5.50	.55
J40	3¢ Claret	85.00	50.00	55.00	32.50	1.40
J41	5¢ Claret	100.00	60.00	65.00	37.50	1.35
J42	10¢ Claret	100.00	62.50	65.00	40.00	2.75
J43	30¢ Claret (1897)	825.00	500.00	550.00	325.00	37.50
J44	50¢ Claret (1896)	525.00	325.00	325.00	200.00	30.00

1910-12, Single Line Watermark, Perf. 12 VF Used + 60% (C)

J45	1¢ Claret	50.00	30.00	32.50	20.00	2.50
J46	2¢ Claret	50.00	30.00	32.50	20.00	.75
J47	3¢ Claret	875.00	550.00	575.00	350.00	22.50
J48	5¢ Claret	135.00	85.00	90.00	55.00	5.25
J49	10¢ Claret	175.00	110.00	115.00	70.00	9.75
J50	50¢ Claret (1912)	1375.00	900.00	975.00	575.00	90.00

1914-16, Single Line Watermark, Perf. 10 VF Used + 50% (C)

J52	1¢ Carmine	90.00	56.50	57.50	37.50	8.00
J53	2¢ Carmine	70.00	45.00	46.50	30.00	.40
J54	3¢ Carmine	1300.00	850.00	850.00	550.00	29.50
J55	5¢ Carmine	56.50	36.50	36.00	23.50	1.85
J56	10¢ Carmine	90.00	56.50	57.50	37.50	1.50
J57	30¢ Carmine	385.00	250.00	250.00	160.00	13.50
J58	50¢ Carmine	...	...	...	6000.00	500.00
J59	1¢ Rose (No Watermark) (1916)	...	...	2300.00	1500.00	230.00
J60	2¢ Rose (No Watermark) ('16)	250.00	150.00	160.00	100.00	15.00

1917-25 Unwatermarked, Perf. 11 VF Used + 50% (B)

J61	1¢ Carmine Rose	4.50	3.00	2.75	1.85	.20
J62	2¢ Carmine Rose	4.00	2.60	2.50	1.65	.20
J63	3¢ Carmine Rose	19.00	12.00	11.50	7.75	.20
J64	5¢ Carmine Rose	19.00	12.00	11.50	7.75	.20
J65	10¢ Carmine Rose	27.50	17.50	17.00	11.50	.30
J66	30¢ Carmine Rose	140.00	92.50	90.00	60.00	.60
J67	50¢ Carmine Rose	180.00	115.00	120.00	75.00	.25
J68	½¢ Dull Red (1925)	1.60	1.10	1.10	.75	.20

POSTAGE DUE STAMPS (continued)

J69,J79   **J77,J87**   **J88**   **J101**

1930-31 Flat Press, Perf. 11 VF Used + 40% (B)

Scott's No.		NH VF	NH F-VF	Unused VF	Unused F-VF	Used F-VF
J69	½¢ Carmine	6.75	5.00	5.25	3.75	1.10
J70	1¢ Carmine	4.75	3.35	3.50	2.50	.20
J71	2¢ Carmine	5.50	4.00	4.00	3.00	.25
J72	3¢ Carmine	37.50	25.00	25.00	17.50	1.35
J73	5¢ Carmine	32.50	22.50	22.50	16.00	2.00
J74	10¢ Carmine	90.00	52.50	50.00	35.00	.75
J75	30¢ Carmine	185.00	125.00	120.00	85.00	1.50
J76	50¢ Carmine	295.00	165.00	160.00	115.00	.55
J77	$1 Carmine or Scarlet	42.50	30.00	27.50	20.00	.20
J78	$5 Carmine or Scarlet, Dry	60.00	42.50	38.50	27.50	.25
J78b	$5 Scarlet, Wet Printing	65.00	45.00	42.50	30.00	.30

1931-56 Rotary Press, Perf. 11x10½ or 10½x11

Scott's No.		Mint Sheet	Pl.Blk NH	F-VF NH	F-VF Used
J79-87	Set of 9	...	...	62.50	1.40
J79	½¢ Carmine	(100) 110.00	27.50	.85	.18
J80	1¢ Carmine, dry printing	(100) 16.50	2.00	.20	.15
J80b	1¢ Carmine, wet printing	(100) 17.00	2.25	.20	.18
J81	2¢ Carmine, dry printing	(100) 17.50	2.00	.20	.15
J81b	2¢ Carmine, wet printing	(100) 18.00	2.25	.20	.18
J82	3¢ Carmine, dry printing	(100) 27.50	3.00	.30	.15
J82b	3¢ Carmine, wet printing	(100) 29.50	3.25	.35	.18
J83	5¢ Carmine, dry printing	(100) 42.50	4.50	.45	.15
J83b	5¢ Carmine, wet printing	(100) 50.00	5.50	.50	.18
J84	10¢ Carmine, dry printing	(100) 110.00	8.50	1.20	.15
J84b	10¢ Carmine, wet printing	(100) 120.00	9.00	1.25	.18
J85	30¢ Carmine	...	57.50	8.00	.20
J86	50¢ Carmine	...	65.00	11.50	.20
J87	$1 Red ('56)	...	225.00	42.50	.20

1959-85 Rotary Press, Perf. 11x10½

Scott's No.		Mint Sheet	Pl.Blk NH	F-VF NH	F-VF Used
J88-104	Set of 17	...	...	18.50	3.85
J88	½¢ Carmine Rose & Black	(100) 275.00	175.00	1.15	1.10
J89	1¢ Carmine Rose & Black	(100) 5.00	.50	.20	.15
J89v	1¢ Dull Gum	(100) 6.50	.55	.22	...
J90	2¢ Carmine Rose & Black	(100) 6.50	.50	.20	.15
J90v	2¢ Dull Gum	(100) 9.00	.55	.22	...
J91	3¢ Carmine Rose & Black	(100) 8.75	.50	.20	.15
J91v	3¢ Dull Gum	(100) 12.75	.60	.22	...
J92	4¢ Carmine Rose & Black	(100) 11.50	.90	.20	.15
J93	5¢ Carmine Rose & Black	(100) 13.75	.85	.20	.15
J93v	5¢ Dull Gum	(100) 18.75	1.25	.22	...
J94	6¢ Carmine Rose & Black	(100) 15.75	1.10	.20	.15
J94v	6¢ Dull Gum	(100) ...	...	165.00	...
J95	7¢ Carmine Rose & Black	(100) 22.50	2.00	.22	.15
J95v	7¢ Dull Gum	(100) ...	...	350.00	...
J96	8¢ Carmine Rose & Black	(100) 19.75	1.25	.22	.15
J97	10¢ Carmine Rose & Black	(100) 25.00	1.50	.25	.15
J97v	10¢ Dull Gum	(100) 29.50	1.85	.30	...
J98	30¢ Carmine Rose & Black	(100) 72.50	3.95	.75	.18
J98v	30¢ Dull Gum	(100) 87.50	4.95	.90	...
J99	50¢ Carmine Rose & Black	(100) 120.00	5.25	1.15	.15
J99v	50¢ Dull Gum	(100) 130.00	6.25	1.25	...
J100	$1 Carmine Rose & Black	(100) 225.00	10.75	2.25	.15
J100v	$1 Dull Gum	(100) 250.00	12.75	2.50	...
J101	$5 Carmine Rose & Black	...	47.50	10.75	.20
J101v	$5 Dull Gum	...	52.50	11.75	...
J102	11¢ Carmine Rose & Blk. ('78)	(100) 28.50	3.50	.30	.30
J103	13¢ Carmine Rose & Blk. ('78)	(100) 33.50	2.00	.35	.30
J104	17¢ Carmine Rose & Blk. ('85)	(100) 79.50	39.50	.45	.35

OFFICIAL DEPARTMENTAL STAMPS

O3,O95   O12   O16,O97   O27,O106   O40

1873 Continental Bank Note Co. - Thin Hard Paper
(NH + 100%, VF OG & Used + 60%, VF NH + 175%) (C)

NOTE: Unused stamps without gum sell for about 30% less
DESIGNS: With the exception of the Post Office Dept., busts are the same as the 1873 Regular Issue.

AGRICULTURE

Scott's No.		Unused Fine	Ave.	Used Fine	Ave.
O1	1¢ Franklin, Yellow	95.00	57.50	75.00	45.00
O2	2¢ Jackson	85.00	50.00	32.50	18.75
O3	3¢ Washington	70.00	45.00	6.00	3.65
O4	6¢ Lincoln	80.00	47.50	25.00	15.00
O5	10¢ Jefferson	170.00	100.00	95.00	60.00
O6	12¢ Clay	225.00	135.00	130.00	80.00
O7	15¢ Webster	190.00	45.00	110.00	65.00
O8	24¢ Scott	190.00	115.00	95.00	57.50
O9	30¢ Hamilton	240.00	145.00	140.00	85.00

EXECUTIVE

O10	1¢ Franklin, Carmine	365.00	210.00	200.00	120.00
O11	2¢ Jackson	235.00	140.00	100.00	60.00
O12	3¢ Washington	285.00	170.00	100.00	60.00
O13	6¢ Lincoln	435.00	260.00	275.00	165.00
O14	10¢ Jefferson	400.00	240.00	300.00	180.00

INTERIOR

O15	1¢ Franklin, Vermilion	22.50	13.50	5.25	3.15
O16	2¢ Jackson	18.50	11.50	3.50	2.15
O17	3¢ Washington	31.00	18.50	3.00	1.75
O18	6¢ Lincoln	23.00	13.50	3.15	1.85
O19	10¢ Jefferson	22.50	13.00	6.25	3.75
O20	12¢ Clay	31.75	18.50	4.75	2.65
O21	15¢ Webster	52.50	30.00	10.75	6.50
O22	24¢ Scott	39.50	22.00	9.00	5.50
O23	30¢ Hamilton	52.50	30.00	8.75	5.50
O24	90¢ Perry	125.00	72.50	33.50	14.00

JUSTICE

O25	1¢ Franklin, Purple	67.50	40.00	50.00	30.00
O26	2¢ Jackson	115.00	70.00	50.00	30.00
O27	3¢ Washington	115.00	70.00	10.75	6.25
O28	6¢ Lincoln	105.00	65.00	15.75	9.50
O29	10¢ Jefferson	120.00	70.00	35.00	18.00
O30	12¢ Clay	95.00	60.00	21.50	12.75
O31	15¢ Webster	175.00	100.00	80.00	47.50
O32	24¢ Scott	425.00	250.00	165.00	100.00
O33	30¢ Hamilton	375.00	225.00	110.00	65.00
O34	90¢ Perry	550.00	325.00	260.00	150.00

NAVY

O35	1¢ Franklin, Ultramarine	47.50	27.50	23.00	14.50
O36	2¢ Jackson	37.50	22.50	10.00	6.00
O37	3¢ Washington	37.50	22.50	5.00	3.00
O38	6¢ Lincoln	37.50	22.50	8.75	5.25
O39	7¢ Stanton	250.00	150.00	95.00	55.00
O40	10¢ Jefferson	52.50	31.50	17.50	10.75
O41	12¢ Clay	60.00	35.00	14.75	8.75
O42	15¢ Webster	115.00	70.00	30.00	18.50
O43	24¢ Scott	115.00	70.00	33.50	20.00
O44	30¢ Hamilton	95.00	55.00	16.50	10.00
O45	90¢ Perry	425.00	250.00	110.00	70.00

O49,O108   O60   O74,O109   O83,O114

POST OFFICE

O47	1¢ Black	8.25	5.00	3.50	2.10
O48	2¢	10.00	6.00	2.75	1.55
O49	3¢	3.50	2.10	.90	.50
O50	6¢	10.00	6.00	2.10	1.25
O51	10¢	45.00	27.00	20.00	12.00
O52	12¢	22.50	13.50	5.50	3.00
O53	15¢	30.00	18.50	8.50	5.00
O54	24¢	37.50	22.50	10.50	6.00
O55	30¢	37.50	22.50	10.00	5.50
O56	90¢	60.00	35.00	10.00	6.00

OFFICIAL DEPARTMENTAL STAMPS (continued)

STATE

Scott's No.		Unused Fine	Ave.	Used Fine	Ave.
O57	1¢ Franklin, Green	67.50	40.00	25.00	15.00
O58	2¢ Jackson	130.00	75.00	40.00	24.50
O59	3¢ Washington	52.50	30.00	10.50	5.85
O60	6¢ Lincoln	52.50	30.00	13.00	7.50
O61	7¢ Stanton	100.00	60.00	23.50	13.00
O62	10¢ Jefferson	85.00	50.00	17.50	10.00
O63	12¢ Clay	125.00	75.00	50.00	29.50
O64	15¢ Webster	135.00	85.00	34.50	21.00
O65	24¢ Scott	275.00	165.00	90.00	55.00
O66	30¢ Hamilton	250.00	150.00	70.00	42.50
O67	90¢ Perry	500.00	300.00	150.00	95.00
O68	$2 Seward Green & Black	575.00	335.00	400.00	240.00
O69	$5 Green & Black	4250.00	2600.00	2000.00	1350.00
O70	$10 Green & Black	2800.00	1575.00	1400.00	950.00
O71	$20 Green & Black	2250.00	1300.00	1050.00	595.00

TREASURY

O72	1¢ Franklin, Brown	24.00	14.50	2.85	1.70
O73	2¢ Jackson	30.00	18.00	2.85	1.70
O74	3¢ Washington	20.00	12.00	1.25	.75
O75	6¢ Lincoln	27.50	16.50	2.50	1.50
O76	7¢ Stanton	60.00	36.50	13.50	7.95
O77	10¢ Jefferson	60.00	36.50	5.25	3.00
O78	12¢ Clay	60.00	36.50	3.75	2.25
O79	15¢ Webster	55.00	32.50	5.00	2.75
O80	24¢ Scott	275.00	165.00	42.50	23.50
O81	30¢ Hamilton	95.00	55.00	6.00	3.50
O82	90¢ Perry	100.00	60.00	6.50	3.75

WAR

O83	1¢ Franklin, Rose	90.00	55.00	4.50	2.65
O84	2¢ Jackson	80.00	50.00	6.25	3.50
O85	3¢ Washington	85.00	52.50	1.75	1.00
O86	6¢ Lincoln	275.00	165.00	4.00	2.25
O87	7¢ Stanton	80.00	47.50	42.50	25.00
O88	10¢ Jefferson	27.50	16.50	6.75	4.00
O89	12¢ Clay	95.00	55.00	5.50	3.00
O90	15¢ Webster	23.75	14.00	6.75	4.00
O91	24¢ Scott	23.75	14.00	4.00	2.35
O92	30¢ Hamilton	25.00	15.00	4.00	2.35
O93	90¢ Perry	60.00	36.50	25.00	14.50

1879 American Bank Note Co. - Soft Porous Paper
(NH + 75%, VF OG & Used + 60%, VF NH + 150%) (C)

O94	1¢ Agric. Dept. (Issued w/o gum)	1400.00	800.00	...	...
O95	3¢ Washington	200.00	120.00	40.00	24.00
O96	1¢ Interior Department, Franklin	140.00	80.00	125.00	75.00
O97	2¢ Jackson	2.50	1.40	1.00	.60
O98	3¢ Washington	2.25	1.35	.75	.40
O99	6¢ Lincoln	3.50	2.10	3.50	2.10
O100	10¢ Jefferson	40.00	24.00	35.00	21.00
O101	12¢ Clay	80.00	45.00	62.50	38.50
O102	15¢ Webster	185.00	110.00	160.00	100.00
O103	24¢ Scott	1795.00	1100.00	...	...
O106	3¢ Justice Department	57.50	33.50	35.00	21.00
O107	6¢ Lincoln	120.00	70.00	95.00	57.50
O108	3¢ Post Office Department	9.50	5.50	3.00	1.80
O109	3¢ Treasury Department	29.50	17.00	4.00	2.25
O110	6¢ Lincoln	55.00	31.50	21.00	12.50
O111	10¢ Jefferson	85.00	50.00	25.00	15.00
O112	30¢ Hamilton	850.00	500.00	175.00	105.00
O113	90¢ Perry	1150.00	675.00	175.00	105.00
O114	1¢ Franklin, War Department	2.25	1.35	1.80	1.10
O115	2¢ Jackson	3.35	2.00	2.00	1.20
O116	3¢ Washington	3.35	2.00	.95	.55
O117	6¢ Lincoln	3.00	1.65	.90	.50
O118	10¢ Jefferson	25.00	15.00	22.50	14.00
O119	12¢ Clay	18.50	11.00	6.00	3.75
O120	30¢ Hamilton	50.00	29.50	42.50	25.75

1910-11 Official Postal Savings VF Used + 50% (B)

O122   O123   O124

Scott's No.		NH VF	F-VF	Unused VF	F-VF	Used F-
VF						
O121	2¢ Black, D.L. Wmk	23.00	14.50	13.75	8.75	1.25
O122	50¢ Dark Green, D.L. Wmk	235.00	140.00	145.00	95.00	30.00
O123	$1 Ultramarine, D.L. Wmk	225.00	135.00	135.00	90.00	9.00
O124	1¢ Dark Violet, S.L. Wmk	12.50	7.75	7.50	5.00	1.15
O125	2¢ Black, S.L. Wmk	65.00	40.00	42.50	27.50	3.75
O126	10¢ Carmine, S.L. Wmk	22.50	15.00	14.00	9.50	1.10

MODERN OFFICIAL ISSUES

| | O127 | O133 | O135 | O138 | O139 |

1983-85 Official Stamps

Scott's No.		Mint Sheet	Pl# Blk. F-VF NH	F-VF NH	F-VF Used
O127	1¢ Eagle ....(100)	7.50	.50	.20	.15
O128	4¢ Eagle ....(100)	12.50	.70	.20	.25
O129	13¢ Eagle ....(100)	37.50	1.80	.40	.70
O129A	14¢ Eagle (No Pl.#) ('85) ..(100)	38.50	...	.40	.50
O130	17¢ Eagle ....(100)	45.00	2.35	.50	.40
O132	$1 Eagle($1.00).............(100)	270.00	12.50	2.75	1.50
O133	$5 Eagle	...	50.00	11.75	5.50
O135	20¢ Eagle, Coil ....**(Pl.# Strip)**	70.00(5)	12.50(3)	.95	1.50
O136	22¢ Eagle, Coil (No Pl.#) ('85)	...	...	1.10	1.50
O138	(14¢) "D" Postcard rate ('85)......(100)	365.00	35.00	4.00	4.25
O139	(22¢) "D" Coil ('85)........**(Pl.# Strip)**	90.00(5)	47.50(3)	3.25	2.50

| | O138A | O138B | O140 | O143 | O144 |

| | O146 | O152 | O154 | O155 | O156 |

1988-95 Official Stamps
(Sheets and Coils do not have Plate #s)

O138A	15¢ Coil (1988)................	...	...	.45	.50
O138B	20¢ Coil (No ¢ sign) ('88)................	...	...	.60	.65
O140	(25¢) "E" Coil ('88)...............	...	...	1.10	1.70
O141	25¢ Coil ('88)...............	...	...	.80	.45
O143	1¢ Offset (No ¢ sign) ('89).........(100)	9.50	...	.20	.20
O144	(29¢) "F" Coil ('91)...............	...	...	1.60	.75
O145	29¢ Coil ('91)...............	...	...	.85	.40
O146	4¢ Make-up rate ('91)...........(100)	12.75	...	.20	.30
O146A	10¢ Eagle (1993)...........(100)	27.50	...	.30	.50
O147	19¢ Postcard rate ('91)..........(100)	52.50	...	.55	.55
O148	23¢ 2nd Ounce rate ('91).........(100)	65.00	...	.70	.50
O151	$1 Eagle ($1)(1993)...........(100)	230.00	...	2.50	1.50
O152	(32¢) "G" Coil (94)...............	...	...	.90	1.00
O153	32¢ Eagle, Coil (1995)...............	...	...	.90	.95
O154	1¢ "¢" Sign added,No "USA"('95)(100)	8.75	...	.20	.20
O155	20¢ Sheet Stamp (1995)..........(100)	47.50	...	.50	.50
O156	23¢ Reprint, Line above "23"('95)(100)	57.50	...	.60	.60

| Q1 | QE1 | JQ1 |

1913 PARCEL POST STAMPS VF Used + 40% (B)

Scott's No.		NH VF	NH F-VF	Unused VF	Unused F-VF	Used F-VF
Q1	1¢ Post Office Clerk 7.25		5.00	4.65	3.25	1.20
Q2	2¢ City Carrier 8.75		6.25	5.50	4.00	.90
Q3	3¢ Railway Clerk.............16.00		11.00	9.50	6.75	4.75
Q4	4¢ Rural Carrier.............46.50		31.50	28.50	20.00	2.25
Q5	5¢ Mail Train.............42.50		26.50	25.00	16.50	1.80
Q6	10¢ Steamship & Tender 70.00		50.00	43.00	30.00	2.25
Q7	15¢ Automobile Service 100.00		67.50	60.00	42.50	8.75
Q8	20¢ Airplane Carrying Mail........210.00		130.00	115.00	82.50	17.50
Q9	25¢ Manufactured 100.00		65.00	57.50	40.00	5.50
Q10	50¢ Dairying 400.00		280.00	250.00	180.00	32.50
Q11	75¢ Harvesting 125.00		85.00	77.50	55.00	26.50
Q12	$1 Fruit Growing.............500.00		365.00	315.00	225.00	22.50

1925-1955 SPECIAL HANDLING STAMPS VF + 30% (B)

QE1	10¢ Yellow Green, Dry (1955).......2.25		1.65	1.60	1.25	1.00
QE1a	10¢ Wet Printing (1928).............4.00		2.90	2.75	2.25	1.10
QE2	15¢ Yellow Green, Dry (1955).......2.25		1.75	1.65	1.25	1.00
QE2a	15¢ Wet Printing (1928).............4.75		3.50	3.25	2.60	1.10
QE3	20¢ Yellow Green, Dry (1955).......3.65		2.65	2.50	1.90	1.50
QE3a	20¢ Wet Printing (1928).............5.50		3.75	3.75	3.00	1.65
QE4	25¢ Yellow Green (1929).......28.50		22.50	21.00	16.50	7.50
QE4a	25¢ Deep Green (1925).......42.50		31.50	29.50	22.50	5.25

1912 PARCEL POST DUE VF + 40% (B)

JQ1	1¢ Dark Green.............14.50		10.00	9.00	6.50	3.75
JQ2	2¢ Dark Green.............120.00		80.00	70.00	50.00	13.00
JQ3	5¢ Dark Green.............20.00		13.50	12.50	8.50	4.25
JQ4	10¢ Dark Green.............260.00		170.00	160.00	110.00	40.00
JQ5	25¢ Dark Green.............170.00		95.00	90.00	62.50	3.75

PLATE BLOCKS

	NH VF	NH F-VF	Unused F-VF		NH VF	NH F-VF	Unused F-VF
Q1 (6)	170.00	120.00	75.00	QE1 (6)	23.75	17.50	13.50
Q2 (6)	180.00	125.00	85.00	QE2 (6)	37.50	18.50	22.50
Q3 (6)	315.00	210.00	150.00	QE3 (6)	42.50	32.50	25.00

U.S. OFFICES IN CHINA

| K1 | K2 | K13 | K17 |

1919 U.S. Postal Agency in China
VF Used + 50% (B)

K1	2¢ on 1¢ Green (on #498) 42.50		29.50	26.00	18.00	22.50
K2	4¢ on 2¢ Rose (on #499).............42.50		29.50	26.00	18.00	22.50
K3	6¢ on 3¢ Violet (#502).............80.00		50.00	45.00	32.50	50.00
K4	8¢ on 4¢ Brown (#503).............95.00		60.00	52.50	37.50	50.00
K5	10¢ on 5¢ Blue (#504).............105.00		65.00	60.00	42.50	50.00
K6	12¢ on 6¢ Red Orange(#506)........130.00		82.50	75.00	52.50	75.00
K7	14¢ on 7¢ Black (#507).............135.00		85.00	77.50	55.00	85.00
K8	16¢ on 8¢ Olive Bister (#508).............105.00		65.00	60.00	42.50	55.00
K8a	16¢ on 8¢ Olive Green.............100.00		62.50	57.50	40.00	45.00
K9	18¢ on 9¢ Salmon Red (#509).............105.00		65.00	60.00	42.50	55.00
K10	20¢ on 10¢ Or. Yellow (#510).............105.00		65.00	57.50	40.00	50.00
K11	24¢ on 12¢ Brn. Carm. (#512).............115.00		72.50	62.50	45.00	57.50
K11a	24¢ on 12¢ Claret Brown.............160.00		100.00	92.50	65.00	90.00
K12	30¢ on 15¢ Gray (#514).............140.00		87.50	77.50	55.00	95.00
K13	40¢ on 20¢ Deep Ultra (#515) 210.00		130.00	115.00	80.00	140.00
K14	60¢ on 30¢ Or. Red (#516).............185.00		120.00	105.00	75.00	125.00
K15	$1 on 50¢ Lt. Violet (#517).............800.00		500.00	450.00	325.00	425.00
K16	$2 on $1 Vlt. Brown (#518).............650.00		425.00	375.00	275.00	335.00

1922 Surcharged in Shanghai, China

K17	2¢ on 1¢ Green (#498).............200.00		125.00	115.00	80.00	80.00
K18	4¢ on 2¢ Carmine (#528B).............185.00		110.00	105.00	70.00	70.00

SAVINGS STAMPS (B) PS & WS (NH + 20%) VF + 30%, S (NH + 10%) VF + 20%

| PS8 | PS14 | S2 | S7 | WS8 |

Scott's No.	F-VF Unused
1911-41 Postal Savings	
PS1	10¢ Orange.........................6.75
PS2	10¢ Orange, Card...........140.00
PS4	10¢ D. Blue, Pf. 12 ....4.00
PS5	10¢ Dp. Blue, Card 125.00
PS6	10¢ Blue, Perf. 11 ('36).....4.75
PS7	10¢ Ultramarine (1940) 14.75
PS8	25¢ Carmine Rose ('40) ...16.50
PS9	50¢ Blue Green ('40) 45.00
PS10	$1 Gray Black (1940).....125.00
PS11	10¢ Rose Red (1941)............60
PS11	Plate Block of 4................7.50
PS11b	Bklt. Pane of 10 ....45.00
PS12	25¢ Blue Green ("41) 1.75
PS12	Plate Block of 4..............18.75
PS12b	Bklt. Pane of 10 ....55.00
PS13	50¢ Ultramarine ('41)........6.50
PS13	Plate Block of 4..............50.00
PS14	$1 Gray Black ('41) 11.00
PS15	$5 Sepia (1941)...............35.00
1954-61 Savings	
S1	10¢ Rose Red......................45
S1	Plate Block of 4................3.00
S1a	Bklt. Pane of 10 ....140.00
S2	25¢ Blue Green 6.00
S2	Plate Block of 4..............30.00
S2a	Bklt. Pane of 10 ....775.00
S3	50¢ Ultramarine ('56).........7.50

Scott's No.	F-VF Unused
S3	50¢ Plate Block of 4 ....47.50
S4	$1 Gray Black (1957) 21.50
S5	$5 Sepia (1956)...............75.00
S6	25¢ 48 Star Flag (1958) 1.60
S6	Plate Block of 4 ....8.00
S6a	Bklt. Pane of 10 ....67.50
S7	25¢ 50 Star Flag (1961) 1.20
S7	Plate Block of 4 ....9.00
S7a	Bklt. Pane of 10 ....275.00
1917-45 War Savings	
WS1	25¢ Thrift Stamp...............14.50
WS2	$5 Washington..................75.00
WS4	$5 Franklin ('19)............270.00
WS7	10¢ Rose Red (1942)...........45
WS7	Plate Block of 4 ....4.75
WS7b	Bklt. Pane of 10 ....45.00
WS8	25¢ Blue Green (1942) 1.00
WS8	Plate Block of 4 ....8.00
WS8b	Bklt. Pane of 10 ....45.00
WS9	50¢ Ultramarine (1942).....3.75
WS9	Plate Block of 4 ....21.50
WS10	$1 Gray Black (1942) 10.00
WS10	Plate Block of 4 ....65.00
WS11	$5 Violet Brown (1945)....45.00
WS12	10¢ Rose Red, Coil ('43) ..2.50
WS12	Line Pair 9.50
WS13	25¢ Blue Green,Coil '43)...4.50
WS13	Line Pair.........................18.50

U.S. TEST COILS

| 11 etc. | 31etc. | 41 etc. | SV1 |

Scott's No.		Line Pair	Pair	F-VF NH
Blank Coils				
11	Imperforate	...	57.50	27.50
15	Perforated 10, Shiny Gum...................	...	1.40	.70
16	Perforated, 10½	...	4.00	2.00
17	Perforated 11	...	9.00	4.50
18	Perf. 10, Tagged, Dull Gum	65.00	11.50	5.75
21	Perf. 10, Two Horiz. Red Lines	...	2.80	1.40
1938-60 Solid Design Coil				
31	Purple	30.00	11.00	5.50
32	Carmine (1954)..................................	...	...	...
33	Red Violet, Large Holes (1960)	25.00	6.00	3.00
33s	Red Violet, Small Holes......................	...	10.00	5.00
1962-98 "FOR TESTING PURPOSES ONLY"				
41	Black, untagged, shiny gum	8.25	2.60	1.30
41a	Black, tagged, shiny gum	5.50	1.60	.80
41b	Black, tagged, pebble-surfaced gum....	17.50	3.00	1.50
41d	Black, tagged, dull gum	19.50	9.00	4.50
41e	Black, untagged, dull gum	8.75	2.20	1.10
42	Carmine, tagged (1970)	...	...	...
43	Green, tagged.....................................	...	170.00	85.00
43c	Green, untagged..................................	...	170.00	85.00
44	Brown, untagged..................................	32.50	5.50	2.75
45	Black, "B" Press, 19mm wide (1988).....	1.70	.85	
47	Black, on white paper,Self-adhesive(1998)..	1.40	.70	
47	Same, Plate #V1, Strip of 5.................	...	12.95	...
48	Black,on blue paper, self-adhesive......	...	1.40	.70
48	Same, Plate #1111, Strip of 5..............	...	12.95	

STAMP VENTURERS TEST COILS

| SV1 | Eagle, Perforated .... | ... | 2.20 | 1.10 |
| SV2 | Eagle, Rouletted .... | ... | 6.50 | 3.25 |

U.S. AUTOPOST ISSUES
Computer Vended Postage

Type I

Type II

Washington, D.C., Machine 82
CV1a 25¢ First Class, Ty. 1.............
CV2a $1.00 3rd Class, Ty. 1...........
CV3a $1.69 Parcel Post, Ty. 1...........
CV4a $2.40 Priority Mail, Ty. 1......
CV5a $8.75 Express Mail, Ty. 1......
   Set of 5 ....$95.00

Washington, D.C., Machine 83
CV6a 25¢ First Class, Ty. 1...........
CV7a $1.00 3rd Class, Ty. 1...........
CV8a $1.69 Parcel Post, Ty. 2.........
CV9a $2.40 Priority Mail, Ty. 1......
CV10a $8.75 Express Mail, Ty. 1......
   Set of 5 ....$77.50

Kensington, MD, Machine 82
CV11a 25¢ First Class, Ty. 1.........

Washington, D.C., Machine 83
CV12a $1.00 3rd Class, Ty. 1..........
CV13a $1.69 Parcel Post, Ty. 2..........
CV14a $2.40 Priority Mail, Ty. 1......
CV15a $8.75 Express Mail, Ty. 1......
   Set of 5 ....$77.50

Kensington, MD, Machine 83
CV16a 25¢ First Class, Ty. 1..........
CV17a $1.00 3rd Class, Ty. 1..........
CV18a $1.69 Parcel Post, Ty. 2......
CV19a $2.40 Priority Mail, Ty. 1......
CV20a $8.75 Express Mail, Ty. 1......
   Set of 5 ....$77.50

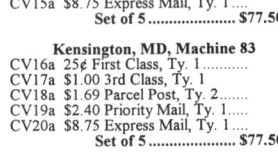

| CV31,31a,31b,31c | CV32,CV33 |

1992-96 Variable Rate Coils (Computer Vending)

Scott's No.		Pl# Strip of 5	Pl# Strip of 3	F-VF NH	F-VF Used
CV31	29¢ Shield, horiz.design, Dull Gum	12.00	10.75	1.25	.50
CV31a	29¢ Shield, Shiny Gum	12.00	10.75	1.40	...
CV31b	32¢ Shield, Dull Gum (1995)	14.75	12.75	1.50	.65
CV31c	32¢ Shield, Shiny Gum (1995)..	14.75	12.75	1.50	...
CV32	29¢ Shield, vertical design (1994)	9.75	8.75	1.00	.50
CV33	32¢ Shield, Vertical Design ('96)	9.75	8.75	1.10	.50

NOTE: #CV31- CV32 COME IN A NUMBER DIFFERENT DENOMINATIONS BUT THE FIRST CLASS RATE OF 29¢ AND 32¢ ARE THE ONLY RATES REGULARLY AVAILABLE.

PLATE NUMBER COIL STRIPS

1897

2127

Scott No.	F-VF,NH	Pl.Strip of 5	Pl.Strip of 3
	1981		
1891	**18¢ Flag**		
	Pl# 1	350.00	100.00
	Pl# 2	40.00	19.50
	Pl# 3	875.00	250.00
	Pl# 4	9.00	6.00
	Pl# 5	6.75	5.00
	Pl# 6	P.O.R.	P.O.R.
	Pl# 7	35.00	32.50
1895	**20¢ Flag**		
	Pl# 1	75.00	6.50
	Pl# 2,11,12	9.75	7.00
	Pl# 3,5,9-10,13-14	4.75	3.00
	Pl# 4	675.00	45.00
	Pl# 6	165.00	90.00
	Pl# 8	13.00	6.50
1895e	Pl# 14	90.00	85.00
	1981-91 Transportation Coils		
1897	**1¢ Omnibus**		
	Pl# 1,2,5,6	.60	.50
	Pl# 3,4	1.00	.80
1897A	**2¢ Locomotive**		
	Pl# 2,6	.75	.60
	Pl# 3,4,8,10	.65	.55
1898	**3¢ Handcar**		
	Pl# 1-4	.85	.75
1898A	**4¢ Stagecoach**		
	Pl# 1,2,3,4	1.60	1.25
	Pl# 5,6	3.25	2.50
1898Ab	Pl# 3,4,5,6	7.50	6.75
1899	**5¢ Motorcycle**		
	Pl# 1-4	1.50	1.10
1900	**5.2¢ Sleigh**		
	Pl# 1,2	11.75	5.95
	Pl# 3	375.00	225.00
	P1#5	215.00	185.00
1900a	Pl# 1-3, 5	15.00	13.50
	P1#4,6	18.50	17.00
1901	**5.9¢ Bicycle**		
	Pl# 3,4	18.50	6.75
1901a	Pl# 3,4	49.50	47.50
	Pl# 5,6	90.00	85.00
1902	**7.4¢ Baby Buggy**		
	Pl# 2	12.75	7.00
1902a	Pl# 2	6.50	5.95
1903	**9.3¢ Mail Wagon**		
	Pl# 1,2	17.50	6.75
	Pl# 3,4	45.00	25.00
	Pl# 5,6	375.00	350.00
1903a	Pl# 1,2	16.50	14.50
	Pl# 3	57.50	39.50
	Pl# 4	25.00	19.50
	Pl# 5,6	4.50	3.75
	Pl# 8	285.00	275.00
1904	**10.9¢ Hansom Cab**		
	Pl# 1,2	57.50	19.75
1904a	Pl# 1,2	45.00	39.50
	Pl# 3,4	415.00	375.00
1905	**11¢ Caboose**		
	Pl# 1	5.25	3.50
1905b	Pl# 2, untagged	3.25	2.75
1905a	Pl# 1	4.75	4.25
1906	**17¢ Electric Car**		
	Pl# 1-5	3.25	2.25
	Pl# 6	18.75	17.50
	Pl# 7	7.75	7.00
1906a	Pl# 3A-5A	6.50	5.75
	Pl# 6A,7A	19.50	17.00
1906ab	Pl# 3B,4B	37.50	35.00
	Pl# 5B,6B	42.50	39.50
1906ac	Pl# 1C,2C,3C,4C	14.50	12.75
	Pl# 5C,7C	37.50	35.00

Scott No.	F-VF,NH	Pl.Strip of 5	Pl.Strip of 3
1907	**18¢ Surrey**		
	Pl# 1	110.00	85.00
	Pl# 2,5,6,8	4.25	3.25
	Pl# 3,4	70.00	65.00
	Pl# 7	40.00	35.00
	Pl# 9,10	15.00	13.50
	Pl# 11,12	18.00	16.00
	Pl# 13-14,17-18	8.75	6.50
	Pl# 15-16	55.00	37.50
1908	**20¢ Fire Pumper**		
	Pl# 1	175.00	25.00
	Pl# 2	950.00	160.00
	Pl# 3,4,13,15,16	5.25	4.00
	Pl# 5,9,10	3.50	2.50
	Pl# 6	45.00	30.00
	Pl# 7,8	210.00	70.00
	Pl# 11	90.00	25.00
	Pl# 12,14	7.95	6.50
	1982-1987		
2005	**20¢ Consumer**		
	Pl# 1,2	190.00	35.00
	Pl# 3,4	125.00	25.00
2112	**(22¢) "D" Eagle Coil**		
	Pl# 1,2	8.50	6.50
2115	**22¢ Flag/Capitol**		
	Pl# 1	13.75	8.75
	Pl# 2,8,10,12	4.50	3.50
	Pl# 3	65.00	13.00
	Pl# 4,5,6,11	7.50	6.50
	Pl# 7,13	15.00	10.00
	Pl# 14	33.50	30.00
	Pl# 15,19,22	4.50	3.50
	Pl# 16,17,18,20,21	8.75	7.50
2115b	**22¢ Flag Test Coil**		
	Pl# T1	5.50	4.25
	1985-89 Transportation Coils		
2123	**3.4¢ School Bus**		
	Pl# 1,2	1.20	1.00
2123a	Pl# 1,2	6.75	6.50
2124	**4.9¢ Buckboard**		
	Pl# 3,4	1.20	1.00
2124a	Pl# 1-6	2.10	1.85
2125	**5.5¢ Star Route Truck**		
	Pl# 1,2	2.00	1.60
2125a	Pl# 1,2	2.60	2.35
2126	**6¢ Tricycle**		
	Pl# 1	1.85	1.60
2126a	Pl# 1	2.15	1.75
	Pl# 2	8.75	8.00
2127	**7.1¢ Tractor**		
	Pl# 1	2.95	2.50
2127a	Pl# 1	3.95	3.50
2127av	Zip + 4		
	Pl# 1	2.65	2.25
2128	**8.3¢ Ambulance**		
	Pl# 1,2	1.95	1.65
2128a	Pl# 1,2	1.95	1.65
	Pl# 3,4	6.50	5.50
2129	**8.5¢ Tow Truck**		
	Pl# 1	3.50	2.65
2129a	Pl# 1	3.65	3.15
	Pl# 2	13.50	12.50
2130	**10.1¢ Oil Wagon**		
	Pl# 1	3.25	2.65
2130a	Pl# 1	3.25	2.75
2130av	Pl# 2,3 Red Prec.	2.90	2.50
2131	**11¢ Stutz Bearcat**		
	Pl# 1-4	2.00	1.65
2132	**12¢ Stanley Steamer**		
	Pl# 1,2	2.95	2.50
2132a	Pl# 1,2	3.00	2.50
2132b	12¢ "B" Press, Prec.		
	Pl# 1	27.50	25.00

Scott No.	F-VF,NH	Pl.Strip of 5	Pl.Strip of 3
2133	**12.5¢ Pushcart**		
	Pl# 1	3.50	3.00
	P1#2	6.00	5.25
2133a	Pl# 1	3.50	3.00
	P1#2	6.00	5.25
2134	**14¢ Iceboat**		
	Pl# 1-4	2.75	2.25
2134b	**"B" Press**		
	Pl# 2	6.75	5.50
2135	**17¢ Dog Sled**		
	Pl# 2	4.25	3.50
2136	**25¢ Bread Wagon**		
	Pl# 1-5	4.75	3.75
	1985		
2149	**18¢ GW Monument**		
	Pl# 1112,3333	3.95	2.75
2149a	Pl# 11121,33333	4.50	3.50
2149b	Pl# 33333 Dry Gum	6.25	5.50
	Pl# 43444 Dry Gum	11.50	10.00
2150	**21.1¢ Pre-Sort**		
	Pl# 111111	4.75	3.50
	Pl# 111121	6.00	4.75
2150a	Pl# 111111	5.00	4.00
	Pl# 111121	6.25	5.00
	1986-96 Transportation Coils		
2225	**1¢ Omnibus "B" Press**		
	Pl# 1,2	.80	.70
2225a	Pl# 2,3 untagged	.80	.70
2225s	Pl# 3 Shiny, Tag	8.00	7.50
2225sv	Pl# 3 Shiny, Untag	1.30	1.10
2225sg	P1# 3,Semi-gloss	1.40	1.30
2226	**2¢ Locomotive "B" Press**		
	Pl# 1	.95	.75
2226a	Pl# 2 untagged	.95	.75
2226s	P1# 2, Shiny Gum	1.40	1.30
2228	**4¢ Stagecoach "B"**		
	Pl# 1, block tag	1.25	.95
2228a	Pl# 1, overall tag	15.00	14.50
2231	**8.3¢ Ambul."B" Press,Precancel**		
	Pl# 1	9.00	7.50
	Pl# 2	12.00	10.75
	1987-94 Transportation Coils		
2252	**3¢ Conestoga Wagon**		
	Pl# 1	.90	.80
2252a	Pl# 2,3 untagged	1.45	1.30
2252b	Pl# 3 Shiny Gum	1.60	1.40
	Pl# 5,6 Shiny Gum	2.95	2.50
2253	**5¢ Milk Wagon**		
	Pl# 1	1.20	1.00
2254	**5.3¢ Elevator, Precancel**		
	Pl# 1	2.30	1.85
2255	**7.6¢ Carreta, Precancel**		
	Pl# 1,2	3.00	2.65
	Pl# 3	6.50	6.00
2256	**8.4¢ Wheel Chair, Precancel**		
	Pl# 1,2	2.50	2.00
	Pl# 3	15.00	14.00
2257	**10¢ Canal Boat**		
	Pl# 1	2.25	1.80
2257a	Pl# 1 overall tag	4.00	3.50
	P1# 3-4	6.00	5.50
2257ad	Pl# 1, o.t., dull gum	6.25	5.75
2258	**13¢ Patrol Wagon, Prec.**		
	Pl# 1	5.00	4.25
2259	**13.2¢ Coal Car, Prec.**		
	Pl# 1,2	4.00	3.35
2260	**15¢ Tugboat**		
	Pl# 1,2	3.25	2.50
2260a	Pl# 2, overall tag	4.35	3.75
2261	**16.7¢ Popcorn Wagon, Prec.**		
	Pl# 1	4.00	3.50
	P1# 2	5.25	4.50
2262	**17.5¢ Marmon Wasp**		
	Pl# 1	5.00	4.25
2262a	Pl# 1	5.50	4.75

PLATE NUMBER COIL STRIPS

2281

2904B

Scott No.	F-VF,NH	Pl.Strip of 5	Pl.Strip of 3
2263	20¢ Cable Car		
	Pl# 1,2 block tag........	4.50	3.75
2263b	Pl# 2, overall tag........	9.75	8.00
2264	20.5¢ Fire Engine, Prec.		
	Pl# 1	8.75	6.95
2265	20.5¢ RR Mail Car, Prec.		
	Pl# 1,2	7.00	5.25
2266	24.1¢ Tandem Bike, Prec.		
	Pl# 1	5.75	4.75
	1988		
2279	(25¢) "E" Series		
	Pl# 1111,1222............	4.50	3.50
	Pl# 1211, 2222............	6.00	5.00
2280	25¢ Yosemite Block tagged		
	Pl# 1,7	8.50	7.50
	Pl# 2-5,8	4.50	3.50
	Pl# 9	15.00	13.75
2280v	25¢ Yosemite Phos. tag.		
	Pl# 1	55.00	52.50
	Pl# 2-3,7-11,13-14.....	4.95	3.95
	Pl# 5,15	8.50	7.50
	Pl# 6	15.75	14.00
2281	25¢ Honeybee		
	Pl# 1,2	4.50	3.50
	1990-95 Transportation Coils		
2451	4¢ Steam Carriage		
	Pl# 1	1.20	1.00
2451b	Pl# 1, untagged	1.30	1.10
2452	5¢ Circus Wagon, Engr.		
	Pl# 1	1.35	1.10
2452a	Pl# 1, untagged	1.75	1.40
2452B	5¢ Circus Wagon, Gravure		
	Pl# A1,A2...............	1.60	1.25
	Pl# A3 Hi-Brite........	3.95	3.50
2452D	5¢ Circus Wagon (¢ sign)		
	Pl# S1,S2	1.95	1.75
2453	5¢ Canoe, Brown, Engr.		
	Pl# 1,2,3	1.50	1.25
2454	5¢ Canoe, Red, Gravure		
	Pl# S11	1.85	1.60
2457	10¢ Tractor Trailer,intaglio		
	Pl# 1	3.00	2.50
2458	10¢ Tractor Trailer, Gravure		
	Pl#11	6.75	6.00
	Pl# 22	3.50	2.95
2463	20¢ Cog Railway		
	Pl# 1,2	5.50	4.75
2464	23¢ Lunch Wagon		
	Pl# 2,3	4.50	3.65
2464p	23¢ Phosphored, Dull Gum		
	Pl# 3, 4	6.25	5.25
2464ps	23¢ Phosphored, Shiny Gum		
	Pl# 3, 4, 5	6.75	5.75
2466	32¢ Ferry Boat,Shiny		
	Pl# 2,3,4	7.75	6.75
	P1# 5	14.50	13.50
2466v	32¢ Low Gloss Gum		
	Pl# 3,5	8.75	7.50
	Pl# 4	21.75	19.75
2466b	32¢ Bronx Blue		
	Pl# 5	120.00	115.00
2468	$1 Seaplane, Dry Gum		
	Pl# 1	13.95	9.50
2468s	$1 Shiny Gum		
	Pl# 3	13.95	9.50
2468v	$1 Low Gloss Gum		
	P1# 3	13.95	9.50
	1993-95 Flora & Fauna		
2491v	29¢ Pine Cone, SA		
	Pl# B1	8.00	6.75
2492v	32¢ Pink Rose, SA		
	Pl# S111	6.75	5.50
2495-95Av	32¢ Peach & Pear, SA		
	Pl# V11111...............	6.75	5.25

NOTE: SA= SELF-ADHESIVE

Scott No.	F-VF,NH	Pl.Strip of 5	Pl.Strip of 3
	1991-1994		
2518	(29¢) "F" Flower		
	Pl# 1111,22221,2222	5.00	3.75
	Pl# 1211	16.50	15.00
	Pl# 2211	6.50	5.50
2523	29¢ Flag/Mt. Rushmore		
	Pl# 1-8	5.25	4.25
	Pl# 9	17.00	15.75
2523c	29¢ Toledo Brown		
	P1#7	200.00	190.00
2523A	29¢ Rushmore/Gravure		
	Pl# A11111,A22211.......	5.75	4.50
2525	29¢ Flower, rouletted		
	Pl# S1111,S2222	6.00	4.75
2526	29¢ Flower, perforated		
	Pl# S2222	5.50	4.25
2529	19¢ Fishing Boat, Ty. I		
	Pl# A1111,A1212,A2424	4.50	3.75
	Pl# A1112	14.75	13.50
2529a	Ty. II, Andreotti Gravure		
	Pl# A5555,A5556,		
	A6667	4.50	3.75
	P1# A7667, A7679		
	A7766, A7779.............	5.95	4.95
2529b	Type II,untagged		
	A5555	12.50	10.00
2529C	Type III, S111	7.50	6.75
2598v	29¢ Eagle, SA		
	Pl# 111	8.00	6.75
2599v	Statue of Liberty, SA		
	Pl# D1111	8.00	6.75
2602	(10¢) Eagle &Shield		
	A11111,A11112,A21112,		
	A22112,A22113,A33333,		
	A43334,A43335,A53335.........	3.00	2.35
	A12213	16.50	15.00
	A21113,A33335,		
	A43324,A43325,A43326,		
	A34424,A34426, ...	3.50	2.65
	A32333	6.50	5.75
	A33334	365.00	350.00
	A77777,A88888,A88889,	97.50	90.00
	A89999,A99998,A99999.....	3.50	2.65
	A1010101010,A1110101010,		
	A1011101011,etc..........	4.00	3.00
	A111010101011	14.00	13.00
2603	(10¢) Eagle & Shield (BEP)		
	Pl# 11111,22221,		
	22222, 33333	3.75	2.95
2603v	(10¢) Dull Gum,		
	22222, 33333	4.25	3.50
2603b	(10¢) Tagged		
	Pl# 11111, 22221	16.75	15.75
2603l	(10¢) Low Gloss Gum		
	P1# 44444	4.00	3.50
2604	(10¢) Eagle & Shield (SV)		
	Pl# S11111,S22222	3.65	2.95
2605	23¢ Flag, Bulk Rate		
	Pl# A111,A212,		
	A222 (FAT)	4.75	3.75
	Pl# A112,A122,A333,		
	A222(THIN)	4.75	3.75
2606	23¢ USA Pre-sort, ABNCo.		
	Pl# A1111,A2222,A2232,	4.75	3.75
	P1# A2233,A3333,A4443,		
	A4444,A4453,A4364	5.75	4.75
2607	23¢ USA Pre-sort, BEP		
	Pl# 1111	6.00	5.00
2607v	23¢ Dull Gum #1111............	6.25	5.25
2608	23¢ USA Pre-sort, S.V.		
	Pl# S1111	6.50	5.50
2609	29¢ Flag/White House		
	Pl# 1-11	5.95	4.75
	Pl# 13-16,18...................	6.75	5.50

Scott No.	F-VF,NH	Pl.Strip of 5	Pl.Strip of 3
	1993 Self-Adhesive		
2799-2802v	29¢ Christmas		
	Pl#V1111111..............(8)	10.95	...
2813v	29¢ Love		
	Pl# B1	8.00	6.75
2873v	29¢ Santa Claus		
	Pl# V1111	8.25	7.00
2886v	(32¢) "G"		
	Pl# V11111	7.50	6.00
	1994-95 "G" Coils		
2888	(25¢) "G"		
	Pl# S11111	6.75	5.75
2889	(32¢) Black "G"		
	Pl# 1111, 2222	10.50	8.75
2890	(32¢) Blue "G"		
	Pl# A1111,A1112,A1113,		
	A1211,A1212,A1311,A1313		
	A1314,A1324,A1417,A1433		
	A2211,A2212,A2213,A2214,		
	A2223,A2313,A3113,A3314,		
	A3315,A3323,A3324,A3423,		
	A3433,A3435,A3436,A4426,		
	A4427,A5327,A5417,A5427,		
	A5437,...................	6.50	5.25
	P1#A1113, A1222, A1313,		
	A1314...................	15.75	12.75
	Pl# A3114, ...A3426	9.00	7.75
	Pl# A4435	170.00	165.00
2891	(32¢) Red "G"		
	Pl# S1111	6.50	5.25
2892	(32¢) "G" Rouletted		
	Pl# S1111,S2222	7.75	6.50
2893	(5¢) "G" Non-Profit		
	Pl# A11111,A21111	2.30	2.00
	1995-97 Non Denominated Coils		
2902	(5¢) Butte,		
	Pl# S111,S222, S 333	1.75	1.50
2902B	(5¢) Butte, SA		
	Pl# S111	2.00	1.75
2903	(5¢) Mountain, BEP		
	Pl# 11111	2.25	1.95
2904	(5¢) Mountain, SVS		
	Pl# S111	2.25	1.95
2904A	(5¢) Mountain, 11.5		
	Pl# V222222, V333323,		
	V333333, V333342,		
	V333343.................	2.25	1.95
2904B	(5¢) Mountain, 9.8		
	Pl# 1111	2.25	1.95
2905	(10¢) Automobile		
	Pl# S111,S222,S 333 ..	3.25	2.75
2906	(10¢) Automobile		
	Pl# S111	2.95	2.65
2907	(10¢) Eagle & Shield		
	Pl# S11111	2.95	2.65
2908	(15¢) Auto Tail Fin, BEP		
	Pl# 11111	3.75	3.00
2909	(15¢) Auto Tail Fin, SVS		
	Pl# S11111	3.75	3.00
2910	(15¢) Auto Tail Fin, SA		
	Pl# S11111	3.50	3.00
2911	(25¢) Juke Box, BEP		
	Pl# 111111,212222,		
	222222,332222...........	6.25	5.25
2912	(25¢) Juke Box, SVS		
	Pl# S11111,S22222	5.75	4.75
2912A	(25¢) Juke Box, 11.5, SA		
	Pl# S11111, S22222	5.75	4.75
2912B	(25¢) Juke box, 9.8, SA		
	Pl# 111111	5.75	4.75

PLATE NUMBER COIL STRIPS

3132   0135

Scott No.	F-VF, NH	Pl. Strip of 5	Pl. Strip of 3
	1995-97 Flag over Porch		
2913	32¢ Flag over Porch, BEP		
	Pl# 11111,22221,22222,33333, 34333,44444, 45444,66646, 77767,78767,91161, 99969	6.25	5.25
	Pl# 22322	37.50	35.00
	P1#66666	17.50	12.50
2913a	32¢ Dull Gum		
	Pl# 11111,22221,22222	6.25	5.25
2914	32¢ Flag over Porch, SVS		
	Pl# S11111	5.75	4.75
2915	32¢ Flag over Porch, 8.7, SA		
	Pl# V11111	6.95	5.75
2915A	32¢ Flag over Porch, 9.7, SA		
	Pl#11111,22222,23222, 33333,44444,45444, 55555,66666,78777, 88888,89878,89888,97898 99999	8.95	7.50
	P1#87898,89898,	19.75	18.50
	P1#87888,	45.00	42.50
	P1#88898, 89899	POR	POR
	P1#99899	31.50	29.50
2915B	32¢ Flag over Porch, 11.5, SA		
	Pl# S11111	8.95	7.50
2915C	32¢ Flag over Porch, 10.9, SA		
	PL# 55555,66666	17.50	15.00
2915D	32¢ Flag over Porch, 9.8,SA		
	Stamps Separate		
	Pl# 11111	6.95	5.75
	1995-97		
3014-17	32¢ Santa & Children, SA		
	Pl# V1111	(8)8.25	...
3018	32¢ Midnight Angel, SA		
	Pl# B1111	6.95	5.75
3044	1¢ Kestrel		
	Pl# 1111	.75	.60
3053	20¢ Blue Jay, SA		
	Pl# S1111	4.65	3.95
3054	32¢ Yellow Rose, SA		
	Pl # 1111, 1112, 1122 2222, 2223,2233,2333, 3344, 4455, 5455, 5555, 5556, 5566, 5666, 6666,6677, 6777, 7777, 8888	5.75	4.75
3055	20¢ Ringnecked Pheasant, SA		
	P1#1111	4.65	3.95
3132	(25¢) Juke Box, SA		
	Linerless Pl #M11111	5.75	4.75
3133	32¢ Flags over Porch, SA		
	Linerless Pl #M11111	8.75	7.50
3207	(5¢) Wetlands		
	Pl#S111	1.95	1.70
3207A	(5¢) Wetlands, SA		
	Pl#1111	1.95	1.70
3208	(25¢) Diner, SA		
	Pl#S11111	5.85	4.75
3208A	(25¢) Diner, SA		
	Pl#11111	5.85	4.75
3228	(10¢) Green Bicycle		
	Pl# 221	3.75	3.25
3229	(10¢) Green Bicycle, SA		
	Pl#5111	3.75	3.25
3263	22¢ Uncle Sam, SA		
	Pl#1111	4.50	3.50
3264	(33¢) Hat		
	Pl#1111,3333,3343,3344	6.50	5.25
3265	(33¢) Hat, SA, Die-cut 9.9		
	Pl#1111,1131,2222,3333	6.50	5.25
3266	(33¢) Hat, SA Die-cut 9.7		
	Pl# 1111	6.50	5.25
3270	(10¢) Eagle, Pre-sorted		
	P1#1111	2.40	1.95
3271	(10¢) Eagle, Pre-sorted, SA		
	P1#11111	2.40	1.95
	1983-85 Official Stamps		
O135	20¢ Official		
	Pl# 1	70.00	12.50
O139	(22¢) "D" Official		
	Pl# 1	90.00	47.50
	VARIABLE RATE COILS		
CV31	29¢ Shield, Dull Gum		
	Pl# 1	12.00	10.75
CV31a	29¢ Shiny Gum		
	Pl# 1	12.00	10.75
CV31b	32¢ Dull Gum		
	Pl# 1	14.75	12.75
CV31c	32¢ Shiny Gum		
	Pl# 1	14.75	12.75
CV32	29¢ Vertical Design		
	Pl# A11	9.75	8.75
CV33	32¢ Vertical Design		
	Pl# 11	9.75	8.75

UNFOLDED BOOKLET PANES WITH PLATE NUMBERS

2833a

Scott N.	Description	FVF,NH
2409a	25¢ Steamboats, Pl#1	7.00
	Pl# 2	22.50
2427a	25¢ Madonna (10) Pl# 1	15.00
2429a	25¢ Sleigh (10) Pl# 1111	19.50
	Pl#2111	25.75
2441a	25¢ Love (10), Pl# 1211	42.50
2474a	25¢ Lighthouse (5) Pl# 3,5	8.95
	Pl# 1,2	10.95
2483a	20¢ Blue Jay (10) Pl#S1111	6.95
2484a	29¢ Wood Duck, BEP(10) Pl#1111	9.95
2485a	29¢ Wood Duck, KCS (10)	
	Pl#K11111	10.95
2486a	29¢ African Violet (10) Pl# K1111	9.50
2488a	32¢ Peach & Pear (10) Pl#11111	9.00
	Pl# 1111 Without Perf. Hole	11.95
2505a	25¢ Indian Headresses (10)	
	Pl# 1,2	14.95
2514a	25¢ Madonna (10) Pl# 1	14.95
2516a	25¢ Christmas Tree (10) Pl#1211	18.95
2527a	29¢ Flower (10) Pl# K1111	9.75
2528a	29¢ Olympic Rings (10) Pl#K11111	9.75
2530a	19¢ Hot-Air Balloons (10) Pl# 1111	6.75
2536a	29¢ Love (10) Pl# 1111,1112	9.50
2549a	29¢ Fishing Flies (5) Pl# A23213	11.75
	Pl# A23133	15.00
	Pl# A23124	57.50
	pl# A33225,A33233	27.50
2552a	29¢ Desert Storm (5)	
	Pl# A11121111	6.50
2566a	29¢ Comedians (10) Pl#1	10.75
2577a	29¢ Space (10) Pl# 111111	12.75
2578a	(29¢) Madonna (10) Pl# 1	10.75
2581b-85a	(29¢) Santa, set of 5	
	Panes of 4, Pl# A11111	31.75
2593a	29¢ Pledge, black (10) Pl# 1111	9.75
2594a	29¢ Pledge, red (10) Pl# K1111	9.95
2646a	29¢ Hummingbirds (5)	
	Pl# A2212112,A2212122,A2222222	5.50
	Pl# A1111111, A2212222	9.95
2709a	29¢ Wild Animals (5) Pl# K1111	6.00
2710a	29¢ Madonna (10)Pl#1	9.75
2718a	29¢ Toys (4) Pl# A111111, A222222	4.75

Scott N.	Description	F-VF,NH
2737a	29¢ Rock'n Roll (8) Pl#A22222	8.95
2737b	29¢ Rock'n Roll (4) Pl#A22222	4.95
2745a	29¢ Space Fantasy (5)	
	Pl# 1111,1211	5.50
2764a	29¢ Garden Flowers (5) Pl# 1	5.50
2770a	29¢ Broadway Musicals (4)	
	Pl# A11121,A22222	5.50
	Pl# A11111	5.50
2778a	29¢ Country Music (4)	
	Pl# A222222	4.95
2790a	29¢ Madonna (4)	
	Pl# K1-11111, K1-44444	4.95
	Pl# K1-33333	7.50
2798a	29¢ 3 Snowmen (10) Pl#111111	11.75
2798b	29¢ 2 Snowmen (10) Pl#111111	11.75
2806b	29¢ AIDS (5) Pl# K111	5.75
2814a	29¢ Love & Dove (10) Pl# A11111	8.95
2833a	29¢ Garden Flowers (5) Pl# 2	5.50
2847a	29¢ Locomotives (5) Pl# S11111	5.50
2871b	29¢ Madonna (10) Pl# 1,2	8.95
2872a	29¢ Stocking (20)	
	Pl# P11111, P44444	19.50
	Pl# P22222	27.50
2916a	32¢ Flag over Porch (10)	
	Pl# 1111	10.75
2921a	32¢ Flag over Porch SA, (10)	
	Pl# 21221, 22221, 22222	9.75
2921d	32¢ Flag over porch SA, (5)	
	P1# 11111	5.75

Scott N.	Description	F-VF,NH
2959a	32¢ Love Cherub (10) Pl# 1	9.95
2973a	32¢ Great Lakes Lighthouses (5)	
	Pl# S11111	5.75
2997a	32¢ Garden Flowers (5) Pl# 2	5.75
3003b	32¢ Madonna (10) Pl# 1	9.95
3007b	32¢ Santa (10) Pl# P11111	10.75
3007c	32¢ Santa (10) Pl# P11111	10.75
3029a	32¢ Garden Flowers (5) Pl# 1	5.50
3049b	32¢ Yellow Rose (4) No#, SA	3.95
3049c	32¢ Yellow Rose (5), SA	
	Pl#S11111	4.95
3049d	32¢ Yellow Rose (6) No#, SA	4.25
3122b	32¢ Liberty (4) No#, SA	4.25
3122c	32¢ Liberty (5), SA	
	Pl# V1111	3.95
3122d	32¢ Liberty (6), No #, SA	5.50
3128b	32¢ Merian Botanical (5)	
	(2 ea. 3128-29,1-3128a)	
	Pl# S11111	3.95
3129b	32¢ Merian Botanical (5)	
	(2 ea. 3128-29,1-3129a)	
	Pl# S11111	4.50
3177b	32¢ Holly (4) No #, SA	4.25
3177c	32¢ Holly (5) No #, SA	5.25
3177d	32¢ Holly (6) #B111 11	4.75

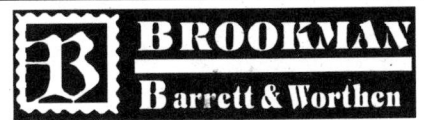

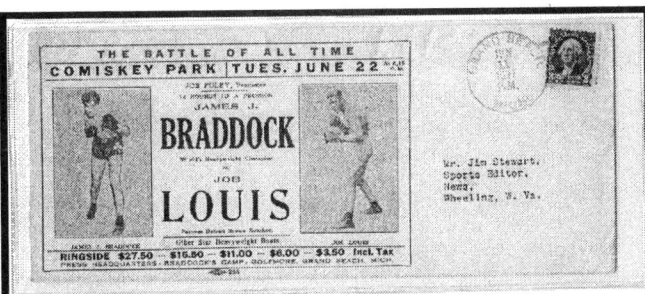

2490a

2960a

3116a

Scott No.	Description	F-VF,NH
2431a	25¢ Eagle & Shield (18)	
	Pl# A1111	15.95
2475a	25¢ Flag, Plastic (12) No #	9.95
2489a	29¢ Red Squirrel (18)	
	Pl# D11111,D22211,D23133	14.95
	Pl#D22221,D22222	18.95
2490a	29¢ Rose (18)	
	Pl# S111	14.95
2491a	29¢ Pine Cone (18)	
	Pl# B2-3,B5-11,B13-16	14.95
	Pl# B4,B12	16.75
	Pl# B1	18.75
2492a	32¢ Pink Rose (20)	
	Pl# S111,S112,S333	16.50
2492r	32¢ Die-Cut "Time to Reorder"	
	S444, S555	17.75
2494a	32¢ Peach & Pear (20)	
	Pl# V11111, V11122, V11132,	
	V12132, V12211, V22212,	
	V22221, V22222, V33333, V33353,	
	V33363, V44424, V44454	16.50
	Pl# V11131, V12131, V12221,	
	V33142, V33143, V33243,	
	V33343, V33453, V44434, V45434,	
	V45464, V54565, V55365	19.75
	Pl# V33323	25.00
2522a	(29¢) "F" Flag (12) No Pl#	9.95
2531Ab	29¢ Liberty & Torch (18) No Pl#	14.75
2531Av	29¢ Revised back No Pl#	14.95
2595a	29¢ Eagle, Brown (17)	
	Pl# B111-1,B1111-2,B2222-1, B3434-1,	
	B2222-2, B3333-1, B4344-1,	13.75
	Pl# B3333-3,B3434-3, B4444-1,	
	B4444-3	17.50
2596a	29¢ Eagle, Green (17)	
	Pl# D21221,D22322, D32322,	13.75
	Pl# D11111,D23322, D33352,D43452,	
	D43453,D54563,D54571,	
	D54573,D54673,D65784	15.95
	Pl# D61384	19.50
	Pl# D54561	23.50
	Pl# D32342,D42342	35.00
2597a	29¢ Eagle, Red (17)	
	Pl# S1111	13.75
2598a	29¢ Eagle (18)	
	Pl# M1111,M1112	13.75
2599a	29¢ Statue of Liberty (18)	
	Pl# D1111,D1212	13.75
2719a	29¢ Locomotive (18)	
	Pl# V11111	14.50
2802a	29¢ Christmas (12)	
	Pl# V111-1111,V222-1222,	
	V222-2112,V222-2122,V222-2221,	
	V222-2222,	12.75
	Pl# V333-3333	14.75
2803a	29¢ Snowman (18)	
	Pl# V11111	14.75
	Pl# V22222	17.50

Scott No.	Description	F-VF,NH
2813a	29¢ Love & Sunrise (18)	
	Pl# B111-1,B111-2,B111-3,B111-4,	
	B121-5,B222-4,B222-5,B222-6, B333-9,	
	B333-10,B333-11,B333-12, B333-17,	
	B344-12,B344-13,B444-9,B444-10,	
	B444-13,B444-14, B444-15,B444-17,	
	B444-18,B444-19,B555-20,B555-21.	14.75
	Pl# B221-5,B444-7,B444-8,B444-16.	17.50
	Pl# B333-5,B333-7,B333-8	22.50
	Pl# B344-11	50.00
	Pl# 333-14	85.00
2873a	29¢ Santa Claus (12)	
	Pl# V1111	9.95
2874a	29¢ Cardinal in Snow (18)	
	Pl# V1111,V2222	14.95
2886a	(32¢) "G" Surface (18)	
	Pl# V11111,V22222	16.50
2887a	(32¢) "G" Overall (18)	
	No Plate Number	16.50
2919a	32¢ Flag over Field (18)	
	Pl# V1111	15.75
2920a	32¢ Flag over Porch, Large "1995"(20)	
	Pl# V12211,V12212,V12312,V12321,	
	V12322,V12331,V13322,V13831,V13834	
	V13836,V22211,V23322,V23422,	
	V34743,V34745,V36743,V42556,	
	V45554,V56663,V56665,V56763,	
	V57663,V65976,V78989	17.50
	Pl# V23522	45.00
2920c	32¢ Flag over Porch, Small "1995"(20)	
	Pl# V11111	79.50
2920e	32¢ Flag over Porch, 11.3 (10)	
	Pl# V11111,V12111,V23222,	
	V31121,V32111,V32121,V44322,	
	V44333,V44444,V55555,V66666,	
	V66886,V67886,V68886,V68896,V76989,	
	V77666,V77668,V77766,V78698,V78886,	
	V78896,V78898,V78986,V78989	8.50
2949a	(32¢) Love & Cherub (20)	
	Pl# B1111-1,B2222-1	
	B2222-2,B3333-2	18.75
2960a	55¢ Love Cherub (20)	
	Pl# B1111-1,B2222-1	25.95
3011a	32¢ Santa & Children (20)	
	Pl# V1111,V1211,	
	V3233,V3333,V4444	16.75
	Pl# V1212	25.00
3012a	32¢ Midnight Angel (20)	
	Pl# B1111,B2222,B3333	16.00
3013a	32¢ Children Sledding (20)	
	Pl# V1111	15.00
3030a	32¢ Love Cherub (20)	
	Pl#B1111-1,B1111-2	
	B2222-1,B2222-2	16.50
3048a	20¢ Blue Jay (10) SA	
	Pl# S1111, S2222	4.50

Scott No.	Description	F-VF,NH
3049a	32¢ Yellow Rose)20)	
	Pl# S1111, S2222, S3333	13.95
3050a	20¢ Ringnecked Pheasant (10) SA	
	Pl# V1111	3.95
3071a	32¢ Tennessee (20)	
	Pl# S11111	16.85
3089a	32¢ Iowa (20), Pl# B11111	18.75
3112a	32¢ Madonna (20)	
	Pl# 11111,12111,22121,22221,	
	23111,33231,33331,33341,	
	44441,55441,55562,56562,66661,	
	66662,67661,78871,78872,	
	78882,79882	15.95
	Pl# 6656-2	25.00
	Pl# 5556-1	30.00
	Pl# 5555-1	70.00
3116a	32¢ Family Scenes (20)	
	Pl# B1111,B2222,B3333,	15.95
3117a	32¢ Skaters (18)	
	Pl# V1111,V2111	14.95
3122a	32¢ Liberty & Torch (20)	
	Pl# V1111,V1211,V1311,V2122,	
	V2222,V2311,V2331,V3233,V3333,	
	V3532,V4532	16.95
3123a	32¢ Love & Swans (20)	
	Pl# B1111,B2222,B3333,B4444,	
	B5555,B6666,B7777	14.95
3124a	55¢ Love & Swans (20)	
	Pl#B1111,B2222,B3333,B4444	24.75
3127a	32¢ Merian Botanical,SA	
	Prints (20) Pl#S11111,S22222,	
	S33333	14.95
3176a	32¢ Madonna (20)	
	Pl# 1111, 2222, 3333	13.95
3177a	32¢ American Holly (20)	
	Pl# B1111, B2222, B3333	12.95
3244a	32¢ Madonna (20)	
	Pl# 1111, 2222, 3333	12.95
3268a	(33¢) Hat (10)	
	Pl# V1111, V1211, V2211, V2222	6.50
3268b	(33¢) Hat (20)	
	Pl# V1111, V1112, V1213, V2122,	
	V2213, V2223	12.95
3269a	(33¢) Hat (18)	
	Pl# V1111	11.65

UNEXPLODED BOOKLETS

BK58

BK113

Scott No.	Cover Value, Pane No. and Description(Number of Panes)	F-VF NH
1914 Flat Press, Perf. 10, Single-Line Wtmk.		
BK41	25¢ #424d,1¢ Washington (4)	275.00
BK42	97¢ #424d,1¢ Washington (16)	125.00
BK43	73¢ #424d,1¢(4) + #425e,2¢ (4)	300.00
BK44	25¢ #425e,2¢ Washington (2)	400.00
1916 Flat Press, Perf. 10, Unwatermarked		
BK47	25¢ #462a,1¢ Washington(4)	575.00
BK48	97¢ #462a 1¢ Washington(16)	425.00
BK50	25¢ #463a,2¢ Washington(2)	550.00
1917-23 Flat Press, Perforated 11		
BK53	25¢ #498e,1¢ Wash.,"POD"(4)	275.00
BK54	97¢ #498e,1¢ Washington(16)	65.00
BK55	25¢ #498e,1¢ "City Carrier"(4)	85.00
BK56	73¢ #498e,1¢(4) + #499e,2¢(4)	77.50
BK57	73¢ #498e,1¢(4) + #554c,2¢(4)	115.00
BK58	25¢ #499e,2¢ Washington (2)	195.00
BK59	49¢ #499e,2¢ Washington(4)	425.00
BK60	97¢ #499e,2¢ Washington(8)	575.00
BK62	37¢ #501b,3¢ Wash.,Type I(2)	575.00
BK63	37¢ #502b,3¢ Wash., Type II(2)	195.00
1923 Flat Press, Perforated 11		
BK66	25¢ #552a,1¢ Franklin(4)	70.00
BK67	97¢ #552a,1¢ Franklin(16)	550.00
BK68	73¢ #552a,1¢(4) + #554c,2¢(4)	115.00
BK69	25¢ #554a,2¢ Washington (2)	400.00
BK70	49¢ #554a,2¢ Washington(4)	125.00
1926 Rotary Press, Perforated 10		
BK72	25¢ #583a,2¢ Washington(2)	400.00
BK73	49¢ #583a,2¢ Washington(4)	550.00
1927-32 Rotary Press, Perf. 11 x 10½		
BK75	25¢ #632a,1¢ Franklin(4)	82.50
BK76	97¢ #632a,1¢ "P.O.D."cvr.(16)	565.00
BK77	97¢ #632a,1¢ "Postrider"cvr.(16)	550.00
BK79	73¢ #632a,1¢(4) + #634a,2¢(4) "Postrider" Cover	85.00
BK80	25¢ #634d,2¢ Washington(2)	9.00
BK81	49¢ #634d,2¢ Washington(4)	16.50
BK82	97¢ #634d,2¢ "Postrider"cvr.(8)	57.50
BK84	37¢ #720b,3¢ Washington(2)	125.00
BK85	73¢ #720b,3¢ Washington(4)	295.00
1939 Presidential Series - 3mm Gutters		
BK86	25¢ #804bv,1¢ Washington(4)	65.00
BK87	97¢ #804bv,1¢ Washington(16)	550.00
BK89	73¢ #804bv,1¢(4) + #806bv,2¢(4)	165.00
BK94	97¢ #806bv,2¢ John Adams(8)	
BK100	37¢ #807av,3¢ Jefferson(2)	95.00
1942 Presidential Series - 2½mm Gutters		
BK90	25¢ #804b,1¢ Washington(4)	9.00
BK91	97¢ #804b,1¢ "P.O.D."cover(16)	550.00
BK92	73¢ #804b,1¢(4) + #806b,2¢(4) "Postrider" cover	32.50
BK93	73¢ #804b,1¢(4) + #806b,2¢(4)] "P.O. Seal" cover	42.50
BK96	25¢ #806b,2¢ Adams "Postrider"(2)	18.50
BK97	25¢ #806b,2¢ Adams "P.O.Seal"(2)	110.00
BK98	49¢ #806b,2¢ Adams "Postrider"(4)	70.00
BK99	49¢ #806b,2¢ Adams "P.O. Seal"(4)	65.00
BK102	37¢ #807a,3¢ Jefferson(2)	25.00
BK103	73¢ #807a,3¢ Jefferson(4)	45.00
1954-58 Liberty Series		
BK104	37¢ #1035a,3¢ Liberty, Wet(2)	20.00
BK104a	37¢ #1035f,3¢ Dry Printing(2)	25.00
BK105	73¢ #1035a,3¢ Liberty, Wet(4)	27.50
BK105a	73¢ #1035f,3¢ Dry Printing(4)	35.00
BK106	97¢ on 37¢ #1036a,4¢ Lincoln(4)	75.00
BK107	97¢ on 73¢ #1036a,4¢ Lincoln(4)	42.50
BK108	97¢ "Yellow" paper #1036a(4)	125.00
BK109	97¢ "Pink" paper #1036a(4)	12.50

Scott No.	Cover Value, Pane No. and Description(Number of Panes)	F-VF NH
1962-64 George Washington Issue		
BK110	$1 #1213a,5¢ Slog.1 "Mailman"(4)	35.00
BK111	$1 #1213a,5¢ Slogan 2 "Zone"(4) "Postrider" Cover	150.00
BK112	$1 #1213a,5¢ Slogan 2 "Zone"(4) "Mr. Zip" Cover	125.00
BK113	$1 #1213a,5¢ Slogan 3 "Zip"(4)	19.50
BK114	$1 #1213c,5¢ Tagged, Slogan 2(4)	395.00
BK115	$1 #1213c,5¢ Tagged, Slogan 3(4)	5.50
1967-78 Regular Issues		
BK116	$2 #1278a,1¢(1) + 1284b,6¢(4)	6.50
BK117	$1 #1280c,2¢(1) + #1284c,6¢(3)	6.00
BK117A	$3.60 #1288Bc,15¢ Holmes(3)	9.75
BK117B	$2 #1278a,1¢(1) + #1393a,6¢(4) "P.O. Seal" Cover	13.75
BK118	$2 #1278a,1¢(1) + #1393a,6¢(4) "Eisenhower" Cover	7.50
BK119	$2 #1278ae,1¢(1) + #1393ae,6¢(4) Dull Gum,"Eisenhower"Cover	6.75
BK120	$1 #1280a,2¢(1) + #1393b,6¢(3)	5.95
BK121	$1.92 #1395a,8¢ Eisenhower-8(3)	7.00
BK122	$1 #1278b,1¢(1) + #1395b,8¢(2)	5.25
BK123	$2 #1395c,8¢(1) + #1395d,8¢(3)	8.50
BK124	$1 #1510b,10¢ Jeff. Meml. - 5(2)	3.50
BK125	$4 #1510c,10¢ Jeff. Meml. - 8(5)	12.00
BK126	$1.25 #1510d,10¢(1)+#C79a,13¢(1)	7.75
1975-80 Regular Issues		
BK127	90¢ #1280c,2¢(1) + 1595a,13¢(1)	3.75
BK128	$2.99 #1595b,13¢(1)+#1595c,13¢(2)	7.95
BK129	$1.30 #1595d,13¢ Liberty Bell-5(2)	6.50
BK130	$1.20 #1598a,15¢ Fort McHenry Flag-8(1)	5.25
BK131	$1 #1623a,9¢ + 13¢, Pf. 11x10½(1)	2.95
BK132	$1 #1623c,9¢ + 13¢, Perf. 10(1)	29.75
BK133	$3.60 #1736a,(15¢) "A"(3)	8.75
BK134	$2.40#1737a,15¢ Roses(2)	6.50
BK135	$3 #1742a,15¢ Windmills(2)	9.50
BK136	$4.32 #1819a,(18¢) "B"(3)	12.50
1981-83 Regular Issues		
BK137	$3.60 #1889a,18¢Wildlife(2)Pl#1-10	20.00
BK137	Pl# 11-13	50.00
BK137	Pl# 14-16	45.00
BK138	$1.20 #1893a,6¢ + 18¢ Flag(1)Pl# 1	4.00
BK139	$1.20 #1896a,20¢ Flag - S.C. -6(1)	
BK139	Pl# 1	4.25
BK140	$2 #1896b,20¢ Flag-S. Court-10(1)	
BK140	Pl#1	6.75
BK140	Pl#4	52.50
BK140A	$4 #1896b,20¢ Flag-S. Court-10(2)	
BK140A	Pl# 2	13.50
BK140A	Pl#3	17.50
BK140B	$28.05#1909a,$9.35 Exp.Mail(1) #1111	83.50
BK141	$4#1948a,(20¢) "C"(2)No Pl#	11.95
BK142	$4 #1949a,20¢ Bighorn Sheep(2) Pl#1-6, 9-10	14.50
BK142	Pl# 11,12,15	37.50
BK142	Pl# 14	30.00
BK142	Pl# 16	85.00
BK142	Pl# 17-19	70.00
BK142	Pl# 20	110.00
BK142a	$4 #1949d,20¢ Sheep, Type II(2) Pl# 34	29.50

Scott No.	Cover Value, Pane No. and Description(Number of Panes)	F-VF NH
1985-89 Regular Issues		
BK143	$4.40 #2113a,(22¢) "D"(2)Pl#1,3,4	21.50
BK144	$1.10 #2116a,22¢ Flag - Capitol(1) Pl# 1,3	5.00
BK145	$2.20 #2116a,22¢ Flag - Capitol(2) Pl# 1,3	10.00
BK146	$4.40 #2121a,22¢ Seashells(2) Multi-Seashells Cover (7 covers needed for all 25 shells)Pl#1,3	12.75
BK146	Pl# 2	14.75
BK147	$4.40 #2121a,22¢(2)"Beach"Cover Pl#1,3,5,7,10	11.95
BK147	Pl# 8	13.75
BK148	$32.25 #2122a,$10.75 Express Mail Type I(1) Pl#11111	82.50
BK149	$32.25 #2122c, Type II(1) Pl# 22222	115.00
BK150	$5 #2182a, 25¢ Jack London-10(2) Pl# 1,2	13.50
BK151	$1.50 #2197a,25¢ Jack London-6(1) Pl# 1	4.75
BK152	$3 #2197a,25¢ Jack London-6(2) Pl#1	9.25
1986 Commemoratives		
BK153	$1.76 #2201a,22¢ Stamp Coll(2) Pl# 1	5.50
BK153a	$1.76 #2201b Black Missing(2) Pl# 1	160.00
BK154	$2.20 #2209a,22¢ Fish(2) Pl# 11111,22222	19.75
1987-88 Regular Issues		
BK155	$2.20 #2274a,22¢ Sp. Occasions(1) Pl# 111111,222222	16.50
BK156	$4.40 #2276a,22¢ Flag-Fireworks(1) No Pl#	12.00
BK156	Pl# 1111,2222	14.75
BK156	Pl# 2122	22.50
BK157	$5 #2282a,(25¢) "E"(2) Pl#1111,2222	16.00
BK157	Pl# 2122	18.75
BK158	$5 #2283a,25¢ Pheasant(2) Pl# A1111	16.00
BK159	$5 #2283c Bluer sky(2) Pl# A3111,A3222	170.00
BK160	$5 #2285b,25¢ Owl-Grosbeak(2) Pl#1111,1112,1211,1433,1434 1734,2121,2321,3333,5955	13.50
BK160	Pl# 1133,2111,2122,2221,2222, 3133,3233,3412,3413,3422,3521 4642,4644,4911,4941	22.75
BK160	Pl# 1414	100.00
BK160	Pl# 1634,3512,3822	47.50
BK160	Pl# 5453	150.00
BK161	$3 #2285Ac,25¢ Flag-Clouds(2) Pl# 1111	8.50
1987-90 Commemoratives		
BK162	$4.40 #2359a,22¢ Constitution (4) Pl# 1111,1112	16.95
BK163	$4.40 #2366a,22¢ Locomotives (4) Pl# 1,2	15.95
BK164	$5 #2385a,25¢ Classic Cars(4) Pl#1	39.95

BK215

BK191

BK176

BK202

Scott No.	Cover Value, Pane No. and Description(Number of Panes)	F-VF NH
BK165	$3 #2396a(1),2398a(1), 25¢ Special OccasionsPl# A1111	10.00
BK166	$5 #2409a,25¢ Steamboats(4) Pl#1,2	14.95
BK167	$5 #2427a,25¢ 1989 Madonna(2) Pl#1	15.00
BK168	$5 #2429a,25¢ Sleigh(2) Pl# 1111,2111	16.50
BK169	$5 #2441a,25¢ Love,Doves(2) Pl# 1211	14.95
BK169	Pl# 2111,2222	22.50
BK169	Pl# 2211	32.50
	1990 Regular Issue	
BK170	$3 #2443a,15¢ Beach Umbrella(2) Pl#111111	8.75
BK170	Pl# 221111	11.75
	1990 Commemorative	
BK171	$5 #2474a,25¢ Lighthouses(4) Pl#1-5	28.75
	1991-96 Flora and Fauna Regular Issues	
BK172	$2 #2483a,20¢ Blue Jay(1)Pl# S1111	5.75
BK173	$2.90 #2484a,29¢ Duck,BEP(1) Pl# 4444	8.50
BK174	$5.80 #2484a,29¢ Duck,BEP(2) Pl# 1111,2222,4444	15.95
BK174	Pl# 1211,3221	100.00
BK174	Pl# 2122,3222,3333	22.50
BK175	$5.80 #2485a,29¢ Duck,KCS(2) Pl# K11111	17.50
BK176	$2.90 #2486a,29¢ African Violet(1) Pl# K11111	8.50
BK177	$5.80 #2486a,29¢ African Violet(2 Pl# K11111)	16.95
BK178	$6.40 #2488a,32¢ Peach-Pear(2) Pl# 11111	17.95
BK178A	$4.80 #2492b,32¢ Pink Rose(1)	12.95
BK178B	$9.60 #2492e (1), 2492f(1), 32¢ Pink Rose No Pl#	54.95
BK178C	$9.60 #2492b,32¢ Pink Rose (2) No Pl#	29.75
BK178D	$9.60 #2492f,32¢ Pink Rose (2) 2 Panes with missing stamp No Pl#	33.75
	1990 Commemoratives	
BK179	$5 #2505a,25¢ Indian Headdress(2) Pl# 1,2	17.95
BK180	$5 #2514a,25¢ Madonna(2) Pl# 1	15.95
BK181	$5 #2516a,25¢ Christmas Tree(2) Pl# 1211	17.95
	1991 Regular Issues	
BK182	$2.90 #2519a,(29¢) "F",BEP(1) Pl # 2222	8.50
BK183	$5.80 #2519a,(29¢) "F",BEP(2) Pl# 1111,2121,2222	17.00
BK183	Pl# 1222,2111,2212	27.50
BK184	$2.90 #2520a,(29¢) "F",KCS(1) Pl# K1111	27.50
BK185	$5.80 #2527a,29¢ Flower(2) Pl# K1111,K2222,K3333	16.50

Scott No.	Cover Value, Pane No. and Description(Number of Panes)	F-VF NH
BK186	$2.90 #2528a,29¢ Olympic(1) Pl# K11111	8.50
BK186A	$2.90 #2528a, WCSE Ticket Cover	11.95
BK187	$3.80 #2530a,19¢ Balloons(2) Pl# 1111,2222	10.50
BK187	Pl# 1222	27.50
	1991 Commemoratives	
BK188	$5.80 #2536a,29¢ Love(2) Pl# 1111,1112	16.95
BK188	Pl# 1113,1123,2223	18.95
BK188	Pl# 1212	45.00
BK189	$5.80 #2549a,29¢ Fishing Flies(4) Pl# A22122,A23123,A23124,A33235 A44446,A45546,A45547	29.95
BK189	Pl# A11111,A22113,A23133, A23313	42.50
BK189	Pl#A22132,A32224,A33233	25.00
BK190	$5.80 #2552a,29¢ Desert Storm(2) Pl# A11111111,A11121111	16.95
BK191	$5.80 #2566a,29¢ Comedians(2) Pl# 1,2	16.95
BK192	$5.80 #2577a,29¢ Space(2) Pl#111111,111112	17.50
BK193	$5.80 #2578a,(29¢) Madonna(2) Pl# 1	16.95
BK194	$5.80 #2581b-85a,(29¢) Santa & Chimney(5 Panes, 1 each) Pl# A11111,A12111	25.00
	1992-93 Regular Issues	
BK195	$2.90 #2593a,29¢ Pledge,Pf.10(1) Pl# 1111,2222	9.95
BK196	$5.80 #2593a,29¢ Pledge,Pf.10(2) Pl# 1111,2222	16.50
BK197	$5.80 #2593c,29¢ Perf. 11x10(2) Pl# 1111,2222,3333,	25.95
BK197	Pl# 1211,2122,2232	27.95
BK197	Pl#4444	42.50
BK198	$2.90 #2594a,29¢ Pledge, Red(1) Pl# K1111	10.95
BK199	$5.80 #2594a,29¢ Pledge, Red(2) Pl# K1111	15.75
	1992 Commemoratives	
BK201	$5.80 #2646a 29¢ Hummingbirds(4) Pl# A1111111,A2212112,A2212222 A2222222	17.95
BK201	Pl# A2212122	21.95
BK202	$5.80 #2709a,29¢ Wild Animals(4) Pl# K1111	18.95
BK202A	$5.80 #2710a,29¢ Madonna(2)Pl# 1	15.95
BK203	$5.80 #2718a,29¢ Toys(5) Pl# A111111,A112211,A222222	18.75
	1993 Commemoratives	
BK204	$5.80 #2737a(2),2737b(1), 29¢ Rock'n Roll, Rythym & Blues Pl# A11111,A22222	17.50
BK204	Pl# A13113,A44444	19.75
BK207	$5.80 #2745a,29¢ Space Fantasy(4) Pl# 1111,1211,2222	17.95
BK208	$5.80 #2764a,29¢ Garden Flowers(4) Pl# 1,2	17.95

Scott No.	Cover Value, Pane No. and Description(Number of Panes)	F-VF NH
BK209	$5.80 #2770a,29¢ Broadway(5) Pl# A11111,A11121,A22222, A23232,A23233	17.50
BK210	$5.80 #2778a,29¢ Country Music(5) Pl# A111111,A222222,A333333 A422222	17.50
BK211	$5.80 #2790a,29¢ Madonna(5) Pl# K111111,K133333,K144444 K255555,K266666	17.50
BK211	Pl# 222222	35.00
BK212	$5.80 #2798a(1),2798b(1) 29¢ Christmas Designs Pl# 111111,222222	18.95
BK213	$2.90 #2806b,29¢ AIDS(2) Pl# K111	8.95
	1994 Commemoratives	
BK214	$5.80 #2814a,29¢ Love & Dove(2) Pl# A11111,A11311,A12112 A21222,A22112.A22222,A22332	15.95
BK214	Pl# A12111,A12211,A12212, A21311	22.75
BK215	$5.80 #2833a,29¢ Garden Flowers(4) Pl# 1,2	16.95
BK216	$5.80 #2847a,29¢ Locomotives(4) Pl# S11111	16.95
BK217	$5.80 #2871b,29¢ Madonna(2)Pl#1,2	15.50
BK218	$5.80 #2872a,29¢ Stocking(1) Pl# P11111,P22222,P33333, P44444	16.50
	1994 "G" Regular Issues	
BK219	$3.20 #2881a,(32¢) BEP,Pf.11(1) Pl# 1111	9.95
BK220	$3.20 #2883a,(32¢) BEP.Pf.10(1) Pl# 1111,2222	9.95
BK221	$6.40 #2883a,(32¢)BEP,Pf.10(2) Pl# 1111,2222	19.95
BK222	$6.40 #2884a,(32¢)ABN,Blue(2) Pl# A1111,A1211,A2222 A3333,A4444	19.95
BK223	$6.40 #2885a,(32¢)KCS,Red(2) Pl# K1111	19.95
	1995-97 Regular Issues	
BK225	$3.20 #2916a,32¢ Flag-Porch(1) Pl# 11111,22222,33332	8.95
BK226	$6.40 #2916a,32¢ Flag-Porch(2) Pl# 11111,22222,23222,33332, 44444	16.95
BK226A	$4.80#2920f 32¢ Flag-Porch (1)No Pl#	12.95
BK226B	$4.80#2920h 32¢ Flag-Porch(1)No Pl#	14.95
BK227	$9.60#2920f 32¢ Flag-Porch(2)No Pl#	25.95
BK227A	$4.80#2921c(1), 2921d(1) 32¢ Flag-Porch Pl# 11111	12.50
BK228	$6.40 2921a 32¢ Flag-Porch (2) Pl# 11111,13111,21221,22221,22222, 44434,44444,55555,66666,77777	17.00
BK228A	$9.60 2921c 32¢ Flag-Porch (3) Pl# 11111	25.75

BK246

BKC19

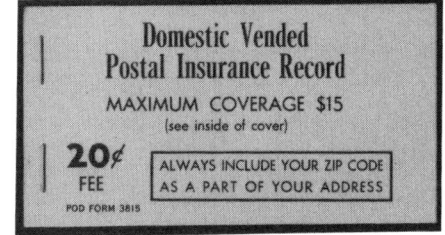

QI2

BK264

Scott No.	Cover Value, Pane No. and Description(Number of Panes)	F-VF NH
1995 Commemoratives		
BK229	$6.40 #2959a,32¢ Love (2) Pl#1	17.50
BK230	$6.40 #2973a,32¢ Great Lakes Lighthouses(4) Pl# S11111	16.95
BK231	$6.40 #2997a,32¢ Garden Flowers(4) Pl #2	17.95
BK232	$6.40 #3003b,32¢ Madonna(2) Pl# 1	15.95
BK233	$6.40 #3007a(1),3007b(1), 32¢ Santa & Children Pl# P1111,P2222	16.95
BK233A	$4.80 #3012c,32¢ Midnight Angel(1) Pl# B1111,B2222,B3333	12.75
BK233B	$9.60 #3012b,32¢ Midnight Angel(2) Pl# B1111,B2222,B3333	25.75
BK233C	$9.60 #3012d,32¢ Midnight Angel(2) No Pl#	27.95
BK233D	$9.60 #3012c,3012d	39.50
1996 Commemoratives		
BK234	$6.40 #3029a,32¢ Winter Garden Flowers(4) Pl# 1	17.95
BK235	$4.80 3030b 32¢ Love (1)	12.95
BK236	$9.60 3030b 32¢ Love (2)	25.95
1996-97 Issues		
BK241	$4.80 3049b (1), 3049c (1), 3049d (1) 32¢ Yellow Rose Pl# S1111	12.75
BK242	$9.60 3049d 32¢ Yellow Rose (5) Pl# S1111	19.95
1996 Makeshift Vending Machine Booklets		
BK243	$4.80 2897 32¢ Flag Over Porch(15)	14.95
BK244	$4.80 2957 32¢ Love Cherub (15)	14.95
BK245	$4.80 3024 32¢ Utah Statehood (15)	13.95
BK246	$4.80 3065 32¢ Fulbright (15)	12.95
BK247	$4.80 3069 32¢ Geo. O'Keefe (15)	12.95
BK248	$4.80 3070 32¢ Tennessee (15)	12.95
BK249	$4.80 3072-76 32¢Indian Dances(15)	12.95
BK250	$4.80 3082 32¢ James Dean (15)	12.95
BK251	$4.80 3083-86 32¢ Folk Heroes (15)	12.95
BK252	$4.80 3087 32¢ Discobolus (15)	12.95
BK253	$4.80 3088 32¢ Iowa (15)	12.95
BK254	$4.80 3090 32¢ Rural Free (30)	24.95
BK255	$4.80 3091-95 32¢ Riverboats (15)	12.95
BK256	$4.80 3105a/o 32¢ End Species (15)	13.95
BK257	$4.80 3107 32¢ Madonna (15)	12.95
BK258	$4.80 3118 32¢ Hanukkah (15)	12.95
1997 Issues		
BK259	$4.80 3122b (1), 3122c (1), 3122d (1) 32¢ Statue of Liberty Pl# V1111	13.50
BK260	$9.60 3122c 32¢ Statue of Liberty(5) Pl# V1111	19.75
BK260A	$9.60 3122Eg32¢ Stat. of Liberty(5)	27.00
BK261	$4.80 3128b (2), 3129b (1), 32¢ Merian Botanical Prints Pl#S11111	12.95
BK262	$3.20 3137b (1) 3137c (1) 32¢ Bugs Bunny, No Pl#	7.50
BK263	$3.20 3138b (1) 3138c (1) 32¢ Bugs,die-Cut Variety	195.00
BK264	$4.80 3177b (1) 3177c (1) 3177d (1) 32¢ Holly, Pl# B1111	12.75
BK265	$9.60 3177d (1) 32¢ Holly,Pl# B1111	22.75

Scott No.	Cover Value, Pane No. and Description(Number of Panes)	F-VF NH
1997 Makeshift Vending Machine Booklets		
BK266	$4.80 3151a-o 32¢ Dolls	13.95
BK267	$4.80 3152 32¢ Bogart	13.95
BK268	$4.80 3153 32¢ Stars & Stripes	13.95
BK269	$4.80 3168-72 32¢ Monsters	12.95
1998 Issues		
BK270	$4.80 3248a(1), 3248b(1) 3248c(1) 32¢ Wreaths Pl# B111111	9.75
BK271	$6.60 3267a (33¢) Hat (2)	12.95
1927-60 Airmail Issues		
BKC1	61¢ #C10a.10¢ Lindbergh(2)	265.00
BKC2	37¢ #C25a,6¢ Transport(2)	9.50
BKC3	73¢ #C25a,6¢ Transport(4)	18.75
BKC4	73¢ #C39a,6¢ Small Plane, Wet(2)	22.50
BKC4a	73¢ #C39c,6¢ Small Plane, Dry(2)	50.00
BKC5	85¢ on 73¢ #C51a,7¢ Blue Jet(2)	45.00
BKC6	85¢ #C51a,7¢ Blue Jet(2)	29.50
BKC7	85¢ #C60a,7¢ Red Jet(2),Blue Cvr.	30.00
BKC8	85¢ #C60a,7¢ Red Jet (2),Red Cvr.	40.00
1962-64 Jet over Capitol		
BKC9	20¢ #C64b,8¢ Slog.1,"Mailman"(2)	15.00
BKC10	$2 #C64b,8¢ Slog.1,"Mailman"(5)	25.00
BKC11	80¢ #C64b,8¢ Slogan 3, "Zip"(2)	25.00
BKC12	$2 #C64b,8¢ Slogan 2, "Zone"(5) "Wings" Cover	385.00
BKC13	$2 #C64b,8¢ Slog.2(5) Mr. Zip Cvr.	375.00
BKC15	$2 #C64b,8¢ Slogan 3, "Zip"(5)	100.00
BKC16	80¢ #C64c,8¢ Tagged Slogan 3(2)	38.75
BKC18	$2 #C64c,8¢ Tagged, Sl.3,Pink(5)	395.00
BKC19	$2 #C64c,8¢ Tagged, Sl.3,Red(5)	7.75
1968-73 Airmail Issues		
BKC20	$4 #C72b,10¢ 50-Star Runway-8(5)	12.00
BKC21	$1 #C72c,10¢ 50-Star Runway-5(2)	8.95
BKC22	$1 #1280c,2¢(1) + #C78a,11¢(2)	4.75
BKC23	$1.25 #1510d,10¢(1)+#C79a,13¢(1)	7.50
1965-81 Postal Insurance Booklets		
QI1	(10¢) "Insured P.O.D. V"	125.00
QI2w	(20¢) "Insured U.S.Mail" White Cvr.	6.00
QI2b	(20¢) "Insured U.S.Mail" Black Cvr.	4.50
QI3	(40¢) "Insured U.S.Mail" Black	4.00
QI4	(50¢) "Insured U.S.Mail" Green	3.50
QI5	(45¢) "Insured U.S.Mail" Red	4.50

Due to the increasing popularity of modern errors, listings of this nature, formerly scattered throughout the catalogue, have been consolidated in an effort to provide a more useful format. Several new listings have been included as well.

While the listing is not intended to be complete, additions will be considered for subsequent editions of this catalogue.

1519a   **1895a**

IMPERFORATE MAJOR ERRORS

Scott's No.		F-VF NH
525c	1¢ Washington, horiz. pair, Imperf. Between	95.00
554a	2¢ Washington, horiz. pair, Imperf. Vert.	225.00
744a	5¢ Yellowstone, horiz. pair, imperf. vert	550.00
805b	1.5¢ M. Washington, horiz. pair, imperf. between	170.00
805b	1.5¢ M. Washington, horiz. pair, imperf. between, precancelled	25.00
899b	1¢ Defense, Horizontal Pair, Imperf. Between	45.00
900a	2¢ Defense, Horizontal Pair, Imperf. Between	47.50
901a	3¢ Defense, Horizontal Pair, Imperf. Between	32.50
966a	3¢ Palomar, vert. pair, imperf. between	625.00
1055b	2¢ Jefferson, coil pair, imperf., precancelled	575.00
1055c	2¢ Jefferson, coil pair, imperf.	600.00
1058a	4¢ Lincoln, Coil Pair, Imperf	115.00
1058a	4¢ Same, Line Pair	225.00
1059Ac	25¢ Revere, Coil Pair, Imperf.	50.00
1059Ac	Same, Line Pair	90.00
1125a	4¢ San Martin, Horizontal Pair, Imperf. between	1350.00
1138a	4¢ McDowell, Vert. Pair, Imperf. between	450.00
1138b	4¢ McDowell, vert. pair, imperf. horizontal	325.00
1151a	4¢ SEATO, vertical pair, imperf. between	175.00
1229a	5¢ Washington, Coil Pair, Imperf.	350.00
1297a	3¢ Parkman, Coil Pair, Imperf	27.50
1297a	Same, Line Pair	65.00
1297c	Same, Precancelled	10.00
1297c	Same, Precancelled, Line Pair	25.00
1299b	1¢ Jefferson, Coil Pair, Imperf	30.00
1299b	Same, Line Pair	65.00
1303b	4¢ Lincoln, Coil Pair, Imperf	895.00
1304b	5¢ Washington, Coil Pair Imperf	200.00
1304e	Same, Precancelled	425.00
1305a	6¢ FDR, Coil Pair, Imperf.	95.00
1305a	Same, Line Pair	150.00
1305Eg	15¢ Holmes, Coil Pair, Imperf	40.00
1305Eg	Same, Line Pair	100.00
1305Ej	Holmes, Type II, Dry Gum, Coil Pair, Imperf	85.00
1305Ej	Same, Line Pair	175.00
1338k	6¢ Flag, vert. pair, imperf. between	550.00
1338Ab	6¢ Flag, Coil Pair, Imperf	500.00
1338De	6¢ Flag, horiz. pair, imperf. between	165.00
1338Fi	8¢ Flag, Vert. Pair, Imperf	50.00
1338Fj	8¢ Flag, horiz. pair, imperf. between	60.00
1338Gh	8¢ Flag, Coil Pair	60.00
1355b	6¢ Disney, Vert. pair, imperf. horiz	875.00
1355c	6¢ Disney, Imperf. Pair	900.00
1362a	6¢ Waterfowl, vertical pair, imperf. between	600.00
1363b	6¢ Christmas, imperf. tagged	250.00
1363d	6¢ Christmas, Imperf. Pair, untagged	350.00
1370a	6¢ Grandma Moses, horiz. pair, imperf. between	265.00
1402a	8¢ Eisenhower, Coil Pair, Imperf.	60.00
1402a	Same, Line Pair	95.00
1484a	8¢ Gershwin, vert. pair, imperf. horiz	265.00
1485a	8¢ Jefferson, vert. pair, imperf. horiz	275.00
1487a	8¢ Cathers, vert. pair, imperf. horiz	300.00
1503a	8¢ Johnson, horiz. pair, imperf. vert.	325.00
1508a	8¢ Christmas, vert. pair, imperf. between	400.00
1509a	10¢ Flags, Horiz. Pair, Imperf. Between	55.00
1510e	10¢ Jefferson Memorial, Vert. Pair, imperf. horiz	475.00
1518b	6.3¢ Bell Coil Pair, Imperf	225.00
1518c	Same, Precancelled Pair	125.00
1518c	Same, Line Pair	325.00
1519a	10¢ Flag Coil Pair, Imperf	42.50
1520b	10¢ Jefferson Memorial, Coil Pair, Imperf	45.00
1520b	Same, Line Pair	80.00
1563a	10¢ Lexington-Concord, vert. pair, imperf. horiz	500.00
1579a	10¢ Madonna, Imperf. Pair	125.00
1580a	10¢ Prang, Imperf. Pair.	125.00
1596a	13¢ Eagle & Shield, Imperf. Pair	50.00
1597a	15¢ Flag (from Sheet), Imperf. Pair	20.00
1615b	7.9¢ Drum, Coil Pair, Imperf.	650.00
1615Ce	8.4¢ Piano, Coil, Precancelled Pr., Imperf. Between	55.00
1615Cf	8.4¢ Piano, Coil, Precancelled Pair, Imperf.	17.50
1615Cf	Same, Line Pair	35.00
1616a	9¢ Capitol, Coil Pair, Imperf. (VG)	75.00
1616a	Same, Line Pair (VG)	175.00
1616a	Same, Pair F-VF	180.00

IMPERFORATE MAJOR ERRORS (cont.)

Scott's No.		F-VF NH
1616a	Same, Line Pair F-VF	475.00
1617b	10¢ Petition, Coil Pair, Imperf	75.00
1617b	Same, Line Pair.	150.00
1617bv	Same, Pair, dull finish gum.	65.00
1618b	13¢ Liberty Bell, Coil Pair, Imperf.	30.00
1618b	Same, Line Pair.	75.00
1618Cd	15¢ Flag, Coil Pair, Imperf.	25.00
1618Ce	Same, Strip of 4, middle pair imperf. between	175.00
1622a	13¢ Flag, Horiz. Pair, Imperf. Between	50.00
1622d	Same, Imperf. Pair	175.00
1625a	13¢ Flag, Coil Pair, Imperf	25.00
1695-98b	13¢ Winter Olympics, Imperf. Block of 4	850.00
1699a	13¢ Maass, horiz. pair, imperf. vert.	525.00
1701a	13¢ Nativity, Imperf. Pair	125.00
1702a	13¢ Currier & Ives, Imperf. Pair	135.00
1703a	13¢ Currier & Ives, Imperf. Pair	135.00
1704a	13¢ Princeton, Horiz. Pair, Imperf. Vert.	550.00
1711a	13¢ Colorado, Horiz. Pair, Imperf. between	675.00
1711a	13¢ Colorado, Horizontal Pair, Imperf. Vertically	950.00
1729a	13¢ G.W. at Valley Forge, Imperf. Pair.	90.00
1730a	13¢ Christmas Mailbox, Imperf. Pair	295.00
1734a	13¢ Indian Head Penny, Horiz. Pair, Imperf. Vert	350.00
1735a	(15¢) "A" Eagle, Vert. Pair, Imperf	95.00
1735b	(15¢) "A" Eagle, Vert. Pair, Imperf. horiz.	675.00
1743a	(15¢) "A" Eagle, Coil Pair, Imperf	100.00
1743a	Same, Line Pair.	225.00
1768a	15¢ Christmas Madonna, Imperf. Pair.	100.00
1769a	15¢ Hobby Horse, Imperf. Pair	125.00
1783-86b	15¢ Flora, Block of 4, Imperf	675.00
1787a	15¢ Seeing Eye Dog, Imperf. Pair	475.00
1789	15¢ J. Paul Jones, Imperf. Pair.	75.00
1789c	Same, Perf. 12, vert. pair, imperf. horiz.	210.00
1789d	Same, Perf. 11, vert. pair, imperf. horiz.	165.00
1799a	15¢ 1979 Madonna & Child, Imperf. Pair	110.00
1801a	15¢ Will Rogers, Imperf. Pair	275.00
1804a	15¢ B. Banneker, Horiz. Pair, Imperf. Vert.	850.00
1811a	1¢ Quill Pen, Coil Pair, Imperf.	175.00
1811a	Same, Line Pair.	325.00
1813b	3.5¢ Violin, Coil Pair, Imperf. (VG)	120.00
1813b	Same, F-VF	265.00
1813b	Same, F-VF Line Pair	450.00
1816b	12¢ Torch, Coil Pair, Imperf	200.00
1816b	Same, Line Pair.	400.00
1820a	(18¢) "B" Eagle, Coil Pair, Imperf	120.00
1820a	Same, Line Pair.	210.00
1823a	15¢ Bissell, vert. pair, imperf. horiz	400.00
1825a	15¢ Veterans, horiz. pair, imperf. vert	525.00
1831a	15¢ Organized Labor, Imperf. Pair.	390.00
1833a	15¢ Learning, horiz. pair, imperf. vert	265.00
1842a	15¢ 1980 Madonna, Imperf. Pair.	100.00
1843a	15¢ Toy Drum, Imperf. Pair.	100.00
1844a	1¢ Dorothea Dix, Imperf. Pair.	500.00
1856a	14¢ S. Lewis, Vert. Pair, Imperf. Horiz.	175.00
1856b	14¢ S. Lewis, Horizontal Pair, Imperf. Between	12.50
1867a	39¢ Clark, vert. pair, imperf. horiz	675.00
1890a	18¢ "Amber" Flag, Imperf. Pair.	120.00
1891a	18¢ "Shining Sea", Coil Pair, Imperf.	22.50
1893b	6¢/18¢ Booklet, Imperf. Vertical Between, Perfs at Left	95.00
1894a	20¢ Flag, Vert. Pair, Imperf	50.00
1895a	20¢ Flag, Coil Pair, Imperf.	12.50
1897b	1¢ Omnibus, Imperf. Pair.	750.00
1897Ae	2¢ Locomotive, Coil Pair, Imperf.	50.00
1898Ac	4¢ Stagecoach, Imperf. Pair, Precancelled	750.00
1898Ad	4¢ Stagecoach, Imperf. Pair	850.00
1901b	5.9¢ Bicycle, Precancelled Coil Pair, Imperf	225.00
1903b	9.3¢ Mail Wagon, Precancelled Coil Pair, Imperf	150.00
1904b	10.9¢ Hansom Cab, Prec. Coil Pair, Imperf.	175.00
1906b	17¢ Electric Car, Coil Pair, Imperf.	190.00
1906c	Same, Precancelled Pair, Imperf.	775.00
1907a	18¢ Surrey, Coil Pair, Imperf.	135.00
1908a	20¢ Fire Pumper, Coil Pair, Imperf	125.00
1927a	18¢ Alcoholism, Imperf. Pair.	400.00
1934a	18¢ Remington, vert. pair, imperf. between	265.00
1939a	20¢ 1981 Madonna, Imperf. Pair.	115.00
1940a	20¢ Teddy Bear, Imperf. Pair.	275.00
1949b	20¢ Ram Bklt. Booklet Pane Vert. Imperf. Btwn., Perfs. at Left	110.00
1951b	20¢ Love, Imperf. Pair.	325.00
2003a	20¢ Netherlands, Imperf. Pair	375.00
2005a	20¢ Consumer, Coil Pair, Imperf.	120.00
2015a	20¢ Libraries, vert. pair, imperf. horiz	350.00
2024a	20¢ Ponce de Leon, Imperf. Pair.	650.00
2025a	13¢ Christmas, Imperf. Pair	675.00
2026a	20¢ Madonna & Child, Imperf. Pair.	160.00
2039a	20¢ Voluntarism, Imperf. Pair.	850.00
2044a	20¢ Joplin, Imperf. Pair.	500.00
2064a	20¢ 1983 Santa Claus, Imperf. Pair.	185.00
2072a	20¢ Love, horiz. pair, imperf. vert.	200.00
2092a	20¢ Waterfowl, horiz. pair, imperf. vert	475.00
2096a	20¢ Smokey Bear, horiz. pair, imperf. between	350.00
2096b	Same, vert. pair, imperf. between	250.00
2104a	20¢ Family Unity, horiz. pair, imperf. vert	600.00
2108a	20¢ Santa Claus, Horiz. Pair, Imperf. Vert.	975.00
2111a	(22¢) "D" Eagle, Vert. Pair, Imperf.	65.00
2112a	(22¢) "D" Eage, Coil Pair, Imperf.	57.50
2115a	22¢ Flag, Coil Pair, Imperf.	14.00
2121a	22¢ Seashells Booklet Pane, Imperf. Vert.	700.00
2126b	6¢ Tricycle, Precancelled Coil Pair, Imperf.	225.00
2130b	10.1¢ Oil Wagon, Black Precancel, Coil Pair, Imperf.	100.00

Scott's No.		F-VF NH
2130b var	10.1¢ Oil Wagon, Red Precancel, Coil Pair, Imperf	20.00
2133b	12.5¢ Pushcart, Precancelled Coil Pair, Imperf	50.00
2134a	14¢ Iceboat, Coil Pair, Imperf	125.00
2135a	17¢ Dogsled, Coil Pair, Imperf. Miscut	575.00
2136a	25¢ Bread Wagon, Coil Pair, Imperf	15.00
2142a	22¢ Winter Special Olympics, vert. pair, imperf. horiz	700.00
2146a	22¢ A. Adams, Imperf. Pair	325.00
2165a	22¢ 1985 Madonna, Imperf. Pair	120.00
2166a	22¢ Poinsettia, Imperf. Pair	150.00
2210a	22¢ Public Hospitals, vert. pair, imperf. horiz	325.00
2228b	4¢ Stagecoach "B" Press, Coil Pair, Imperf	350.00
2256a	8.4¢ Wheel Chair, Coil Pair, Imperf.	700.00
2259a	13.2¢ Coal Car, Coil Pair, Imperf	110.00
2260c	15¢ Tugboat, Coil Pair, Imperf	800.00
2261a	16.7¢ Popcorn Wagon Pair, Imperf	210.00
2263a	20¢ Cable Car, Coil Pair, Imperf	95.00
2265a	21¢ Railway Car, Coil Pair, Imperf	80.00
2279a	(25¢) "E" Earth, Coil Pair, Imperf	100.00
2280a	25¢ Flag Over Yosemite, Coil Pair, Block Tagged, Imperf	30.00
2280a var	25¢ Flag Over Yosemite, Coil Pair, Prephosphor paper, Impf	15.00
2281a	25¢ Honeybee Coil, Imperf. Pair	70.00
2440a	25¢ Love, Imperf. Pair	900.00
2451a	4¢ Steam Carriage, Imperf. Pair	750.00
2453a	5¢ Canoe, Coil Pair, Imperf	425.00
2457a	10¢ Tractor Trailer, Coil Pair, Imperf	500.00
2463a	20¢ Cog Railway, Coil Pair, Imperf.	150.00
2464a	23¢ Lunch Wagon, Coil Pair, Imperf.	185.00
2517a	(29¢) Flower, Imperf. Pair	800.00
2518a	(29¢) "F" Coil, Imperf. Pair	37.50
2521a	4¢ Non-denominated, vert. pair, imperf. horiz.	150.00
2523b	29¢ Mt. Rushmore, Coil Pair, Imperf.	25.00
2550a	29¢ Cole Porter, vert. pair, imperf. horiz	675.00
2579a	(29¢) Santa in Chimney, horiz. pair, imperf. vertically	400.00
2579b	(29¢) Santa in Chimney, Vert. Pair, Imperf. Horiz	600.00
2594b	29¢ Pledge Allegiance, Imperf. Pair.	950.00
2603a	(10¢) Eagle & Shield, Coil Pair, Imperf	35.00
2607c	23¢ USA Pre-sort, Coil Pair, Imperf	110.00
2609a	29¢ Flag over White House, Coil Pair, Imperf	20.00
2609b	Same, Imperf. Between	110.00
2897a	32¢ Flag over Porch, Imperf. Pair	325.00
2902a	(5¢) Butte Coil Imperf. Pair	950.00
2904c	(5¢) Mountain Imperf. Pair	800.00
2913a	32¢ Flag over Porch Coil, Imperf. Pair	85.00
3069a	32¢ Georgia O'Keeffe, Imperf. Pair	275.00
3082a	32¢ James Dean, Imperf. Pair	425.00

AIRMAILS & SPECIAL DELIVERY

C23a	6¢ Eagle Vertical Pair, Imperf. Horizontal	350.00
C73a	10¢ Stars, Coil Pair, Imperf	850.00
C82a	11¢ Jet, Coil Pair, Imperf.	350.00
C82a	Same, Line Pair	450.00
C83a	13¢ Winged Env., Coil Pair, Imperf.	90.00
C83a	Same, Line Pair	185.00
C113	33¢ Verville, Imperf. Pair	850.00
C115	44¢ Transpacific, Imperf. Pair	850.00
E15c	10¢ Motorcycle, horiz. pair, imperf. between	325.00

COLOR ERRORS & VARIETIES

499 var.	2¢ Washington, "Boston Lake", with PFC	175.00
1895 var.	20¢ Flag, Blue "Supreme Court" color var	175.00
2115 var.	22¢ Flag, Blue "Capitol Bldg." color var	12.00
C23c	6¢ Ultramarine & Carmine	200.00

COLOR OMITTED - MAJOR ERRORS

1271a	5¢ Florida, ochre omitted	500.00
1331-32 var.	5¢ Space Twins, red stripes of capsule flag omitted, single in block of 9	195.00
1338Fp	8¢ Flag and White House, Slate green omitted	475.00
1355a	6¢ Disney, ochre omitted	750.00
1362b	6¢ Waterfowl, red & dark blue omitted	1250.00
1363c	6¢ Christmas, 1968, light yellow omitted	95.00
1370b	6¢ Grandma Moses, black and prussian blue omitted	950.00
1381a	6¢ Baseball, black omitted	1100.00
1384c	6¢ Christmas, 1969, light green omitted	25.00
1414b	6¢ Christmas, 1970, black omitted	700.00
1420a	6¢ Pilgrims, orange & yellow omitted	975.00
1432a	8¢ Revolution, gray & black omitted	795.00
1436a	8¢ Emily Dickinson, black & olive omitted	1000.00
1444a	8¢ Christmas, gold omitted	575.00
1471a	8¢ Christmas, 1972, pink omitted	225.00
1501a	8¢ Electronics, black omitted	750.00

Scott's No.		F-VF NH
1506a	10¢ Wheat Fields, black & blue omitted	950.00
1509b	10¢ Crossed Flags, blue omitted	175.00
1511a	10¢ Zip, yellow omitted	60.00
1542a	10¢ Kentucky, dull black omitted	950.00
1547a	10¢ Energy Conservation, blue & orange omitted	975.00
1547b	10¢ Energy Conservation, orange & green omitted	800.00
1547c	10¢ Energy Conservation, green omitted	950.00
1551a	10¢ Christmas, buff omitted	40.00
1555a	10¢ D.W. Griffith, brown omitted	800.00
1557a	10¢ Mariner, red omitted	650.00
1559a	8¢ Ludington, green inscription on gum omitted	300.00
1560a	10¢ Salem Poor, green inscription on gum omitted	275.00
1561a	10¢ Salomon, green inscription on gum omitted	300.00
1561b	10¢ Salomon, red color omitted	275.00
1596b	13¢ Eagle & Shield, yellow omitted	225.00
1597b	15¢ McHenry Flag, gray omitted	675.00
1608a	50¢ Lamp, black color omitted	400.00
1610a	$1.00 Lamp, dark brown color omitted	325.00
1610b	$1.00 Lamp, tan, yellow & orange omitted	375.00
1618Cf	15¢ Flag Coil, grey omitted	45.00
1690a	13¢ Franklin, light blue omitted	325.00
1800a	15¢ Christmas, green & yellow omitted	700.00
1800b	15¢ Christmas, yellow, green & tan omitted	775.00
1826a	15¢ de Galvez, red, brown & blue omitted	850.00
1843b	15¢ Wreath, buff omitted	25.00
1894c	20¢ Flag, dark blue omitted	100.00
1894d	20¢ Flag, black omitted	350.00
1895b	20¢ Flag Coil, black omitted	525.00
1926a	18¢ Millay, black omitted	525.00
1934b	18¢ Remington, brown omitted	600.00
1937-38b	18¢ Yorktown, se-tenant pair, black omitted	500.00
1951c	20¢ Love, blue omitted	225.00
2014a	20¢ Peace Garden, black, green & brown omitted	290.00
2045a	20¢ Medal of Honor, red omitted	325.00
2055-58b	20¢ Inventors, Block of 4, black omitted	490.00
2059-62b	20¢ Streetcars, Block of 4, black omitted	550.00
2145a	22¢ Ameripex, black, blue & red omitted	250.00
2201b	22¢ Stamp Collecting, cplt. bklt. of 2 panes, black omitted	140.00
2235-38b	22¢ Navajo Art, black omitted	425.00
2281b	25¢ Honeybee, black (engraved) omitted	75.00
2281c	25¢ Honeybee, Black (litho) omitted	550.00
2349a	22¢ U.S./Morocco, black omitted	350.00
2361a	22¢ CPA, black omitted	950.00
2399a	25¢ Christmas, 1988, gold omitted	40.00
2421a	25¢ Bill of Rights, black (engraved) omitted	365.00
2474b	25¢ Lighthouse bklt., white omitted, cplt. bklt. of 4 panes	350.00
	Same, Individual Pane	90.00
2481a	45¢ Sunfish, black omitted	600.00
2482a	$2 Bobcat, black omitted	350.00
2561a	29¢ Washington, DC Bicentennial, black "USA 29¢" omitted	200.00
2595c	29¢ Eagle & Shield, brown omitted	475.00
2635a	29¢ Alaska Highway, black omitted	900.00
2764b	29¢ Garden Flowers, booklet pane, black omitted	450.00
2833b	29¢ Garden Flowers, booklet pane, black omitted	450.00
3066a	50¢ Jacqueline Cochran, black omitted	90.00
C76a	10¢ Man on the Moon, red omitted	550.00
C76 var.	10¢ Man on the Moon, patch only omitted	250.00
C91-92b	31¢ Wright Bros., ultramarine & black omitted	850.00
J89a	1¢ Postage Due, Black Numeral omitted	350.00

POSTAL STATIONERY ENTIRES

U571a	10¢ Compass, brown omitted	150.00
U572a	13¢ Homemaker, brown omitted	150.00
U573a	13¢ Farmer, brown omitted	150.00
U575a	13¢ Craftsman, brown omitted	150.00
U583a	13¢ Golf, black & blue omitted	750.00
U584d	13¢ Conservation, black & red omitted	450.00
U586a	15¢ Star, brown surcharge omitted	350.00
U587a	15¢ Auto Racing, black omitted	150.00
U595 var.	15¢ Veterinarians, brown & grey omitted	125.00
U596a	15¢ Olympics, red & green omitted	250.00
U596b	15¢ Olympics, black omitted	250.00
U596c	15¢ Olympics, black & green omitted	250.00
U597a	15¢ Bicycle, blue omitted	95.00
U599a	15¢ Honeybee, brown omitted	165.00
U611a	25¢ Stars, dark red omitted	100.00
U612a	8.4¢ Constellation, black omitted	625.00
UX50a	4¢ Customs, blue omitted	450.00

U 362

U546

Scott's No.		Mint Entire	Scott's No.		Mint Entire	Scott's No.		Mint Entire	Scott's No.		Mint Entire
	1886 Grant Letter Sheet		U360	2¢ Carmine, or. buff	29.75	U421	1¢ Green, amber	.55	U515	1½¢ on 1¢ (U420)	.60
U293	2¢ Green, folded	21.50	U361	2¢ Carmine, blue	75.00	U422	1¢ Green, or. buff	2.40	U516	1½¢ on 1¢ (U421)	57.50
	1887-94 Issues		U362	2¢ Carmine	.60	U423	1¢ Green, blue	.70	U517	1½¢ on 1¢ (U422)	6.50
U294	1¢ Blue	.75	U363	2¢ Carmine, amber	.3.25	U424	1¢ Green, manila	8.50	U518	1½¢ on 1¢ (U423)	6.50
U295	1¢ Dark blue	9.00	U364	2¢ Carmine, or. buff	.2.75	W425	1¢ Wrapper	.35	U519	1½¢ on 1¢ (U424)	32.50
U296	1¢ Blue, amber	4.50	U365	2¢ Carmine, blue	.3.50	U428	1¢ Green, brown	12.50	U521	1½¢ on 1¢ (U420)	5.00
U297	1¢ Dk. blue, amber	52.50	W366	2¢ Wrapper	12.50	U429	2¢ Carmine	.30		**1926-58 Issues**	
U300	1¢ Blue, manila	1.00	U367	2¢ Carmine	.8.50	U430	2¢ Carmine, amber	.50	U522	2¢ Sesquicent	1.75
W301	1¢ Blue, wrapper	1.50	U368	2¢ Carmine, amber	15.00	U431	2¢ Carmine, or. buff	4.50	U522a	Same, Die 2	10.75
U302	1¢ Dk. blue, manila	35.00	U369	2¢ Carmine, or. buff	30.00	U432	2¢ Carmine, blue	.60	U523	1¢ Wash. Bicent. ('32)	1.95
W303	1¢ Dk. blue, wrapper	25.00	U370	2¢ Carmine, blue	22.50	W433	2¢ Wrapper	.35	U524	1½¢ Wash. Bicent	3.25
U304	1¢ Blue, amber manila	7.50	U371	4¢ Brown	26.75	U436	3¢ Dark violet	.70	U525	2¢ Wash. Bicent	.60
U305	2¢ Green, die 1	20.00	U372	4¢ Brown, amber	32.50	U436f	3¢ Purple (1932)	.60	U526	3¢ Wash. Bicent	3.50
U306	2¢ Green, amber	29.50	U374	4¢ Brown	22.50	U437	3¢ Dark violet, amber	7.75	U527	4¢ Wash. Bicent	30.00
U307	2¢ Green, oriental buff	100.00	U375	4¢ Brown, amber	50.00	U437a	3¢ Purple, amber (1932)	1.10	U528	5¢ Wash. Bicent	5.50
U311	2¢ Green, die 2	.55	W376	4¢ Wrapper	26.75	U438	3¢ Dark violet, buff	32.50	U529	6¢ Orange	7.50
U312	2¢ Green, amber	.60	U377	5¢ Blue	15.75	U439	3¢ Dark violet, blue	12.50	U530	6¢ Orange, amber	15.00
U313	2¢ Green, oriental buff	.95	U378	5¢ Blue, amber	20.75	U439a	3¢ Purple, blue (1932)	.80	U531	6¢ Orange, blue	15.00
U314	2¢ Green, blue	1.00		**1903-04 Issues**		U440	4¢ Black	2.50	U532	1¢ Franklin (1950)	7.00
U315	2¢ Green, manila	3.00	U379	1¢ Green	.85	U441	4¢ Black, amber	4.00	U533	2¢ Washington	1.35
W316	2¢ Green, wrapper	7.00	U380	1¢ Green, amber	18.75	U442	4¢ Black, blue	5.00	U534	3¢ Washington	.55
U317	2¢ Green, amber manila	4.50	U381	1¢ Green, or. buff	18.50	U443	5¢ Blue	5.50	U535	1½¢ Washington (1952)	5.50
U324	4¢ Carmine	3.25	U382	1¢ Green, blue	19.50	U444	5¢ Blue, amber	5.00	U536	2¢ Franklin (1958)	.95
U325	4¢ Carmine, amber	4.75	U383	1¢ Green, manila	.4.35	U445	5¢ Blue, blue	7.75	U537	2¢ + 2¢ Sur., Circle	3.95
U326	4¢ Carmine, oriental buff	11.00	W384	1¢ Wrapper	.1.60		**1920-21 Surcharge Issues**		U538	2¢ + 2¢ Sur., Oval	1.00
U327	4¢ Carmine, blue	8.75	U385	2¢ Carmine	.60	U446	2¢ on 3¢ (U436)	14.50	U539	3¢ + 1¢ Sur., Circle	16.00
U328	4¢ Carmine, manila	9.00	U386	2¢ Carmine, amber	.3.25	U447	2¢ on 3¢ (U436)	9.50	U540	3¢ + 1¢ Sur., Oval	.65
U329	4¢ Carmine, amber manila	8.00	U387	2¢ Carmine, or. buff	.2.25	U448	2¢ on 3¢ (U436)	2.75		**1960-74 Issues**	
U330	5¢ Blue, die 1	6.00	U388	2¢ Carmine, blue	.3.25	U449	2¢ on 3¢ (U437)	7.00	U541	1¼¢ Franklin	.90
U331	5¢ Blue, amber	9.00	W389	2¢ Wrapper	21.50	U450	2¢ on 3¢ (U438)	21.50	U542	2½¢ Washington	.95
U332	5¢ Blue, oriental buff	13.00	U390	4¢ Chocolate	23.50	U451	2¢ on 3¢ (U439)	13.75	U543	4¢ Pony Express	.70
U333	5¢ Blue, blue	13.00	U391	4¢ Chocolate, amber	23.50	U458	2¢ on 3¢ (U436)	.70	U544	5¢ Lincoln (1962)	.95
U334	5¢ Blue, die 2	15.00	W392	4¢ Wrapper	25.00	U459	2¢ on 3¢ (U437)	4.25	U545	4¢ + 1¢ Sur., Frank	1.65
U335	5¢ Blue, amber	15.00	U393	5¢ Blue	22.50	U460	2¢ on 3¢ (U438)	3.75	U546	5¢ NY World's Fair ('64)	.70
U336	30¢ Red brown	50.00	U394	5¢ Blue, amber	22.50	U461	2¢ on 3¢ (U439)	6.75	U547	1¼¢ Liberty Bell (1965)	.95
U337	30¢ Red brown, amber	57.50	U395	2¢ Carmine (1904)	.1.00	U468	2¢ on 3¢ (U436)	.90	U548	1-4/10¢ Liberty Bell ('68)	1.00
U338	30¢ Red brown,		U396	2¢ Carmine, amber	11.75	U469	2¢ on 3¢ (U437)	4.50	U548A	1-6/10¢ Liberty Bell ('69)	.90
	oriental buff	52.50	U397	2¢ Carmine, or. buff	7.50	U470	2¢ on 3¢ (U438)	7.75	U549	4¢ Old Ironsides ('65)	.95
U339	30¢ Red brown, blue	52.50	U398	2¢ Carmine, blue	5.75	U471	2¢ on 3¢ (U439)	9.50	U550	5¢ Eagle	.90
U340	30¢ Red brown, manila	50.00	W399	2¢ Wrapper	22.50	U472	2¢ on 4¢ (U390)	25.00	U551	6¢ Liberty Head (1968)	.90
U341	30¢ Red brown,			**1907-16 Issues**		U473	2¢ on 4¢ (U391)	20.00	U552	4¢ + 2¢ Surcharge	4.50
	amber manila	57.50	U400	1¢ Green	.40		**1925 Issues**		U553	5¢ + 1¢ Surcharge	3.75
U342	90¢ Purple	80.00	U401	1¢ Green, amber	1.10	U481	1½¢ Brown	.55	U554	6¢ Moby Dick (1970)	.65
U343	90¢ Purple, amber	110.00	U402	1¢ Green, or. buff	5.95	U482	1½¢ Brown, amber	1.60	U555	6¢ Brotherhood (1971)	.80
U344	90¢ Purple, oriental buff		U403	1¢ Green, blue	5.95	U483	1½¢ Brown, blue	1.95	U556	1-7/10¢ Liberty Bell	.40
		110.00	U404	1¢ Green, manila	4.50	U484	1½¢ Brown, manila	11.00	U557	8¢ Eagle	.65
U345	90¢ Purple, blue	115.00	W405	1¢ Wrapper	.55	W485	1½¢ Wrapper	1.35	U561	6¢ + 2¢ Liberty	1.15
U346	90¢ Purple, manila	120.00	U406	2¢ Brown red	1.50	U490	1½¢ on 1¢ (U400)	6.50	U562	6¢ + 2¢ Brotherhood	2.75
U347	90¢ Purple,		U407	2¢ Brown red, amber	7.50	U491	1½¢ on 1¢ (U401)	14.50	U563	8¢ Bowling	.65
	amber manila	125.00	U408	2¢ Brown red, or. buff	10.75	U495	1½¢ on 1¢ (U420)	.60	U564	8¢ Aging	.65
	1893 Columbian Issue		U409	2¢ Brown red, blue	5.75	U496	1½¢ on 1¢ (U421)	25.00	U565	8¢ Transpo. '72 (1972)	.75
U348	1¢ Deep Blue	2.75	W410	2¢ Wrapper	57.50	U497	1½¢ on 1¢ (U422)	5.25	U566	8¢ + 2¢ Sur., Eagle ('73)	.50
U349	2¢ Violet	2.65	U411	2¢ Carmine	.60	U498	1½¢ on 1¢ (U423)	2.25	U567	10¢ Liberty Bell	.45
U350	5¢ Chocolate	13.50	U412	2¢ Carmine, amber	.85	U499	1½¢ on 1¢ (U424)	18.50	U568	1-8/10¢ Volunteer ('74)	.35
U351	10¢ Slate Brown	60.00	U413	2¢ Carmine, or. buff	.55	U500	1½¢ on 1¢ (U428)	70.00	U569	10¢ Tennis	.55
	1899 Issues		U414	2¢ Carmine, blue	1.00	U501	1½¢ on 1¢ (U426)	75.00		**1975-82 Issues**	
U352	1¢ Green	1.25	W415	2¢ Wrapper	8.50	U508	1½¢ on 1¢ (U353)	70.00	U571	10¢ Seafaring	.50
U353	1¢ Green, amber	7.75	U416	4¢ Black	8.75	U509	1½¢ on 1¢ (U380)	25.00	U572	13¢ Homemaker (1976)	.50
U354	1¢ Green, or. buff	13.50	U417	4¢ Black, amber	10.50	U509B	1½¢ on 1¢ (U381)	60.00	U573	13¢ Farmer (1976)	.50
U355	1¢ Green, blue	12.75	U418	5¢ Blue	11.50	U510	1½¢ on 1¢ (U400)	3.75	U574	13¢ Doctor (1976)	.50
U356	1¢ Green, manila	5.50	U419	5¢ Blue, amber	18.00	U512	1½¢ on 1¢ (U402)	10.50	U575	13¢ Craftsman (1976)	.50
W357	1¢ Wrapper	11.00		**1916-32 Issues**		U513	1½¢ on 1¢ (U403)	8.50	U576	13¢ Liberty Tree (1975)	.45
U358	2¢ Carmine	7.00	U420	1¢ Green	.30	U514	1½¢ on 1¢ (U404)	35.00	U577	2¢ Star & Pinwheel ('76)	.35
U359	2¢ Carmine, amber	26.75									

MINT POSTAL STATIONERY ENTIRES

U597

UC17

Scott's No.	Mint Entire
U578	2.1¢ Hexagon (1977) .... .35
U579	2.7¢ U.S.A (1978) .... .40
U580	(15¢) "A" & Eagle .... .50
U581	15¢ Uncle Sam.................. .50
U582	13¢ Bicentennial (1976).... .50
U583	13¢ Golf (1977) .... .60
U584	13¢ Conservation.............. .50
U585	13¢ Development.............. .50
U586	15¢ on 16¢ Surch ('78) ..... .55
U587	15¢ Auto Racing............... .65
U588	15¢ on 13¢ Tree................ .55
U589	3.1¢ Non Profit .... .35
U590	3.5¢ Violins .... .35
U591	5.9¢ Circle (1982)............ .35
U592	(18¢) "B" & Eagle (1981 ..) .55
U593	18¢ Star .... .55
U594	(20¢) "C" & Eagle .... .55
U595	15¢ Veterinary (1979)....... .55
U596	15¢ Soccer .... .80
U597	15¢ Bicycle (1980)........... .55
U598	15¢ America's Cup .... .55
U599	15¢ Honeybee .... .55
U600	18¢ Blinded Veteran .... .60
U601	20¢ Capitol Dome .... .55
U602	20¢ Great Seal (1982)...... .55
U603	20¢ Purple Heart .... .60
1983-89 Issues	
U604	5.2¢ Non Profit .... .45
U605	20¢ Paralyzed Vets .... .55
U606	20¢ Small Business ('84) .. .70
U607	(22¢) "D" & Eagle (1985). .65
U608	22¢ Bison .... .60
U609	6¢ Old Ironsides............... .35
U610	8.5¢ Mayflower (1986) ..... .35
U611	25¢ Stars (1988)............... .70
U612	8.4¢ USS Const .... .35
U613	25¢ Snowflake.................. .80
U614	25¢ Philatelic Env. ('89) ... .65
U615	25¢ Stars Security Env...... .65
U616	25¢ Love........................... .65
U617	25¢ WSE Space Sta .... .75
1990-94 Issues	
U618	25¢ Football..................... .65
U619	29¢ Star (1991)................. .85
U620	11.1¢ Non Profit .... .40
U621	29¢ Love........................... .75
U622	29¢ Magazine Industry...... .75
U623	29¢ Stars & Bars............... .75
U624	29¢ Country Geese .... .75

Scott's No.	Mint Entire
U625	29¢ Space Station ('92).... .75
U626	29¢ Western Americana.... .75
U627	29¢ Environmen................ .75
U628	19.8¢ Bulk Rate .... .55
U629	29¢ Disabled Americans ... .75
U630	29¢ Kitten (1993)............. .75
U631	29¢ Football (1994) .... .75
1995-96 Issues	
U632	32¢ Liberty Bell .... .80
U633	(32¢) "G" #6 ¾ .... .80
U634	(32¢) "G", Security Envelope #10 .... .80
U635	(5¢) Sheep .... .35
U636	(10¢) Eagle .... .45
U637	(32¢) Spiral Heart .... .80
U638	32¢ Liberty Bell, Security Envelope.................. .80
U639	32¢ Space Shuttle .... .80
U640	32¢ Environment ('96)..... .75
U641	32¢ Paralympics ('96)...... .75
1999 Issues	
U642	33¢ Flag........................... .75
U643	33¢ Flag, Security Env.... .75
U644	33¢ Love........................... .75
U645	33¢ Lincoln...................... .75

AIR MAIL ENTIRES
1929-44 Issues

Scott's No.	Mint Entire
UC1	5¢ Blue, Die 1 .... 4.25
UC2	5¢ Blue, Die 2 .... 16.50
UC3	6¢ Orange, Die 2a (1934) 2.00
UC3v	6¢ No Border 1.75
UC4	6¢ Orange, Die 2b (1942) 57.50
UC4v	6¢ No Border 4.50
UC5	6¢ No Border, Die 2c (1944)............ 1.25
UC6	6¢ Orange, Die 3 ('42) 1.75
UC6v	6¢ No Border 2.00
UC7	8¢ Olive Green ('32)........ 15.00
1945-47 Issues	
UC8	6¢ on 2¢ Sur., Wash........ 1.65
UC9	6¢ on 2¢ Wash. Bic...... 100.00
UC10	5¢ on 6¢ Orange Die 2a (1946)............ 4.50
UC11	5¢ on 6¢ Or. Die 2b 11.00
UC12	5¢ on 6¢ Or. Die 2c 1.50
UC13	5¢ on 6¢ Or. Die 3 .... 1.25
UC14	5¢ Plane, Die 1 .... 1.00
UC15	5¢ Plane, Die 2 .... 1.00

Scott's No.	Mint Entire
UC17	5¢ CIPEX (1947)............. .55
1950-58 Issues	
UC18	6¢ Skymaster .... .55
UC19	6¢ on 5¢, Die 1 ('51).... 1.30
UC20	6¢ on 5¢, Die 2 .... 1.30
UC21	6¢ on 5¢, Die 1 ('52).... 35.00
UC22	6¢ on 5¢, Die 2 .... 5.50
UC25	6¢ FIPEX (1956) 1.00
UC26	7¢ Skymaster (1958) 1.00
UC27	6¢ + 1¢ Or., Die 2a.... 250.00
UC28	6¢ + 1¢ Or., Die 2b ... 90.00
UC29	6¢ + 1¢ Or., Die 2c.... 45.00
UC30	6¢ + 1¢ Skymaster.......... 1.25
UC31	6¢ + 1¢ FIPEX 1.50
UC33	7¢ Jet, Blue .... .80
1960-73 Issues	
UC34	7¢ Jet, Carmine .... .70
UC36	8¢ Jet Airliner (1962) ...... .80
UC37	8¢ Jet, Triangle (1965) ... .55
UC37a	Same, Tagged (1967)...... 2.00
UC40	10¢ Jet, Triangle ('68) ..... .80
UC41	8¢ + 2¢ Surcharge .... .90
UC43	1¢ Three Circles ('71) ...... .65
UC45	10¢ + 1¢ Triangle 2.00
UC47	13¢ Bird in Flight ('73)... .65

AIRLETTER SHEETS
1947-71 Issues

Scott's No.	Mint Entire
UC16	10¢ DC3, 2 Lines 7.50
UC16a	10¢ 4 Lines Letter (1951) 12.50
UC16c	10¢ Aero., 4 Lines (1953) 52.50
UC16d	10¢ Aero., 3 Lines (1955) 6.50
UC32	10¢ Jet, 2 Lines ('59)...... 5.50
UC32a	10¢ Jet, 3 Lines ('58)..... 9.00
UC35	11¢ Jet & Globe ('61)..... 2.25
UC38	11¢ J.F. Kennedy (1965) 3.00
UC39	13¢ J.F. Kennedy (1967) 3.00
UC42	13¢ Human Rights (1968) 6.00
UC44	15¢ Birds,Letter ('71)..... 1.30
UC44a	15¢ w/"Aerogramme".... 1.30
1973-81 Issues	
UC46	15¢ Ballooning................ .85
UC48	18¢ "USA" (1974) .... .80
UC49	18¢ NATO .... .80
UC50	22¢ "USA" (1976) .... .85

Scott's No.	Mint Entire
UC51	22¢ "USA" (1978) .... .85
UC52	22¢ Moscow Olym. ('79) 1.65
UC53	30¢ "USA", Blue, Red & Brown (1980). .85
UC54	30¢ "USA", Yel., Bl.&Blk (1981) .... .85
1982-95 Issues	
UC55	30¢ World Trade .... .85
UC56	30¢ Comm. Year (1983). .85
UC57	30¢ Olympics .... .85
UC58	36¢ Landsat Satellite (85) .85
UC59	36¢ Travel .... .85
UC60	36¢ Mark Twain/ Halley's Comet......... .85
UC61	39¢ Styl. Aero (1988) ..... .90
UC62	39¢ Mont. Blair (1989)... .90
UC63	45¢ Eagle,blue paper (1991) 1.10
UC63a	Eagle, white paper 1.10
UC64	50¢T.Lowe (1995)......... 1.20
UC65	60¢ Voyaguers Park (1999) 1.15

POSTAL SAVINGS OFFICIAL ENVELOPES

UO70	1¢ Green (1911) 85.00
UO71	1¢ Green, Oriental buff (1911) 225.00
UO72	2¢ Carmine (1911).......... 15.00

OFFICIAL MAIL ENTIRES

UO73	20¢ Eagle ('83).............. 1.00
UO74	22¢ Eagle ('85).............. .90
UO75	22¢ Bond Env. ('87)....... .90
UO76	(25¢) "E" Bond Env ('88) .90
UO77	25¢ Eagle .... .80
UO78	25¢ Bond Env.................. .80
UO79	45¢ Passport 2 oz (90)..... 1.50
UO80	65¢ Passport env.3 oz..... 1.80
UO81	45¢ Self-sealing 2 oz 1.30
UO82	65¢ Self-sealing 3 oz 1.80
UO83	(29¢) "F" Sav. Bond (91) 1.25
UO84	29¢ Official Mail .... .75
UO85	29¢ Sav. Bond Env.......... .75
UO86	52¢ Consular Service (92) 2.25
UO87	75¢ Consular Service....... 4.50
UO88	32¢ Official Mail ('95)..... .95
UO89	33¢ Great Seal (99) .... .75

MINT POSTAL CARDS

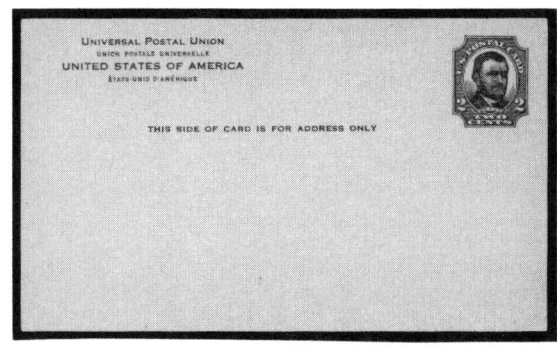

UX 25

UX 174

Scott's No.		Mint Card
1873-98 Issues		
UX1	1¢ Liberty, brown, large watermark	335.00
UX1	Preprinted	60.00
UX3	Same, small watermark	75.00
UX3	Preprinted	20.00
UX5	1¢ Liberty, black, "Write" (1875)	65.00
UX5	Preprinted	8.00
UX6	2¢ Liberty, blue on buff (1879)	28.50
UX6	Preprinted	11.00
UX7	1¢ Liberty, black, "Nothing" (1881)	57.50
UX7	Preprinted	7.50
UX8	1¢ Jefferson, brown (85)	50.00
UX8	Preprinted	9.50
UX9	1¢ Jeff., black (1886)	16.50
UX9	Preprinted	1.95
UX10	1¢ Grant, black (1891)	32.50
UX10	Preprinted	8.00
UX11	Same, blue	15.00
UX11	Preprinted	5.00
UX12	1¢ Jeff., black, small wreath (1894)	40.00
UX12	Preprinted	5.00
UX13	2¢ Liberty, blue on cream (1897)	155.00
UX13	Preprinted	80.00
UX14	1¢ Jeff., black, large wreath	27.50
UX14	Preprinted	3.00
UX15	1¢ Adams, black (1898)	42.50
UX15	Preprinted	12.75
UX16	2¢ Liberty, black, "No Frame" (1898)	11.50
UX16	Preprinted	6.50
1902-18 Issues		
UX18	1¢ McKinley, oval	12.00
UX18	Preprinted	2.25
UX19	1¢ McKinley ('07)	40.00
UX19	Preprinted	2.75
UX20	1¢ Correspond Space at L (1908)	50.00
UX20	Preprinted	9.50
UX21	1¢ McKnly, shaded ('10)	100.00
UX21	Preprinted	19.50
UX22	Same, White backgrd	15.00
UX22	Preprinted	2.00
UX23	1¢ Lincoln, red ('11)	9.50
UX23	Preprinted	3.75
UX24	1¢ McKinley, red	12.00
UX24	Preprinted	2.00
UX25	2¢ Grant, red	1.65
UX25	Preprinted	.85
UX26	1¢ Lincoln, green ('13)	11.50
UX26	Preprinted	3.50
UX27	1¢ Jeff, Die 1 (1914)	.35
UX27	Preprinted	.20
UX28	1¢ Lincoln, green ('17)	.75
UX28	Preprinted	.35
UX29	2¢ Jeff, Die 1	45.00
UX29	Preprinted	8.00
UX30	2¢ Jeff, Die 2 (1918)	28.50
UX30	Preprinted	7.00
1920-64 Issues		
UX32	1¢ on 2¢ red, die 1	52.50
UX32	Preprinted	18.00
UX33	1¢ on 2¢ red, die 2	13.50
UX33	Preprinted	4.00
UX37	3¢ McKinley (1926)	5.00
UX37	Preprinted	2.50
UX38	2¢ Franklin (1951)	.40
UX38	Preprinted	.30
UX39	2¢ on 1¢ Jeff, green ('52)	.65

Scott's No.		Mint Card
UX39	Preprinted	.40
UX40	2¢ on 1¢ Linc., grn	.75
UX40	Preprinted	.50
UX41	2¢ on 1¢ Jeff, dk grn	5.50
UX41	Preprinted	3.00
UX42	2¢ on 1¢ Linc, dk grn	5.75
UX42	Preprinted	3.00
UX43	2¢ Lincoln, carmine	.30
UX43	Preprinted	.25
UX44	2¢ FIPEX (1956)	.30
UX45	4¢ Liberty	1.60
UX46	3¢ Liberty (1958)	.50
UX46c	Precancelled ('61)	5.00
UX48	4¢ Linc., precan ('62)	.30
UX48a	Same, Tagged ('66)	.65
UX49	7¢ "USA" (1963)	4.50
UX50	4¢ Customs (1964)	.55
UX51	4¢ Social Security	.50
1965-73 Issues		
UX52	4¢ Coast Guard	.40
UX53	4¢ Census	.40
UX54	8¢ "USA" (1967)	4.75
UX55	5¢ Lincoln (1968)	.32
UX56	5¢ Women Marines	.40
UX57	5¢ Weather (1970)	.35
UX58	6¢ Paul Revere (1971)	.35
UX59	10¢ "USA"	4.75
UX60	6¢ Hospitals	.35
UX61	6¢ Constellation ('72)	1.00
UX62	6¢ Monument Valley	.50
UX63	6¢ Gloucester	.50
UX64	6¢ John Hanson	.30
UX64a	Coarse Paper	1.25
UX65	6¢ Liberty (1973)	.30
UX66	8¢ Samuel Adams	.40
1974-79 Issues		
UX67	12¢ Visit USA	.40
UX68	7¢ Thomson (1975)	.35
UX69	9¢ Witherspoon	.35
UX70	9¢ Rodney (1976)	.35
UX71	9¢ Galveston (1977)	.35
UX72	9¢ Nathan Hale	.35
UX73	10¢ Music Hall (1978)	.40
UX74	(10¢) John Hancock	.40
UX75	10¢ John Hancock	.35
UX76	14¢ Cutter "Eagle"	.45
UX77	10¢ Molly Pitcher	.35
UX78	10¢ G.R. Clark (1979)	.35
UX79	10¢ Pulaski	.35
UX80	10¢ Olympics	.65
UX81	10¢ Iolani Palace	.35
1980-83 Issues		
UX82	14¢ Winter Olympics	.70
UX83	10¢ Salt Lake Temple	.35
UX84	10¢ Rochambeau	.35
UX85	10¢ King's Mt	.35
UX86	19¢ Golden Hinde	.90
UX87	10¢ Cowpens (1981)	.35
UX88	(12¢) Eagle	.40
UX89	12¢ Isaiah Thomas	.40
UX90	12¢ N. Greene	.35
UX91	12¢ Lewis & Clark	.35
UX92	(13¢) Morris	.35
UX93	13¢ Morris	.35
UX94	13¢ F. Marion (1982)	.35
UX95	13¢ LaSalle	.35
UX96	13¢ Music Academy	.35
UX97	13¢ St. Louis P.O.	.35
UX98	13¢ Georgia (1983)	.35
UX99	13¢ Old P. Office	.35
UX100	13¢ Yachting	.35
1984-88 Issues		
UX101	13¢ Maryland	.35
UX102	13¢ Olympics	.35
UX103	13¢ Baraga	.35

Scott's No.		Mint Card
UX104	13¢ Rancho S.Pedro	.35
UX105	(14¢) Charles Carroll(85)	.35
UX106	14¢ Charles Carroll	.55
UX107	25¢ Flying Cloud	.75
UX108	14¢ George Wythe	.35
UX109	14¢ Conn. Anniv	.35
UX110	14¢ Stamp Coll (1986)	.35
UX111	14¢ Francis Vigo	.35
UX112	14¢ Rhode Island	.35
UX113	14¢ Wisconsin Ty	.35
UX114	14¢ Nat'l. Guard	.35
UX115	14¢ Steel Plow (1987)	.35
UX116	14¢ Const. Conv	.35
UX117	14¢ U.S. Flag	.35
UX118	14¢ Pride in America	.35
UX119	14¢ Timberline Ldg	.35
UX120	15¢ Am. the Beaut ('88)	.35
UX121	15¢ Blair House	.35
UX122	28¢ Yorkshire	.70
UX123	15¢ Iowa Terr	.35
UX124	15¢ NW/Ohio Terr	.35
UX125	15¢ Hearst Castle	.35
UX126	15¢ Fed. Papers	.35
1989-92 Issues		
UX127	15¢ The Desert	.35
UX128	15¢ Healy Hall	.35
UX129	15¢ Wetlands	.35
UX130	15¢ Oklahoma	.35
UX131	21¢ Can. Geese/Mtns.	.60
UX132	15¢ Seashore	.35
UX133	15¢ Woodlands	.35
UX134	15¢ Hull House	.35
UX135	15¢ Independence Hall	.35
UX136	15¢ Balt. Inner Harbor	.35
UX137	15¢ 59th St.Bridge,NY	.35
UX138	15¢ Capitol Bldg	.35
UX139-42	15¢ Cityscape sheet of 4 postcards	19.50
UX143	15¢ The White House	1.40
UX144	15¢ Jefferson Memorial	1.40
UX145	15¢ Papermaking ('90)	.35
UX146	15¢ World Literacy Yr.	.35
UX147	15¢ Geo. Bingham Art	1.25
UX148	15¢ Isaac Royall House	.45
UX150	15¢ Stanford Univ	.45
UX151	15¢ DAR/Const. Hall	1.25
UX152	15¢ Chicago Orch.Hall	.45
UX153	19¢ Flag (1991)	.50
UX154	19¢ Carnegie Hall	.50
UX155	19¢ "Old Red", U of TX	.50
UX156	19¢ Bill of Rights Bicent	.50
UX157	19¢ Notre Dame	.50
UX158	30¢ Niagara Falls	.80
UX159	19¢ Old Mill, U of VT	.50
UX160	19¢ Wadsw'th Athen (92)	.50
UX161	19¢ Cobb Hall, U of Chi	.50
UX162	19¢ Waller Hall	.50
UX163	19¢ America's Cup	1.40
UX164	19¢ Columbia River	.50
UX165	19¢ Grt. Hall, Ellis Island	.50
1993-94 Issues		
UX166	19¢ National Cathedral	.50
UX167	19¢ Wren Building	.50
UX168	19¢ Holocaust Mem'l	1.40
UX169	19¢ Ft. Recovery	.50
UX170	19¢ Playmaker's Theater	.50
UX171	19¢ O'Kane Hall	.50
UX172	19¢ Beecher Hall	.50
UX173	19¢ Massachusetts Hall	.50
UX175	19¢ Myers Hall	.50
UX176	19¢ Canyon de Chelly	.50
UX177	19¢ St. Louis Station	.50
UX178-97	19¢ Legends of the West (20)	16.95

Scott's No.		Mint Card
1995-96 Issues		
UX198	20¢ Red Barn	.50
UX199	(20¢) "G"	.50
UX200-19	20¢ Civil War (20)	20.95
UX220	20¢ Clipper Ship	.45
UX221-40	20¢ Comic Strip (20)	15.95
UX241	20¢ Winter Farm Scene (1996)	.45
UX242-61	20¢ Atlanta Olympics (20)(1996)	20.95
UX262	20¢ McDowell Hall (96)	.45
UX263	20¢ Alexander Hall (96)	.45
UX264-78	20¢ Endangered Species (15) (1996)	23.95
1997-98 Issues		
UX279	20¢ Love-Swans	1.50
UX279a	Same, Package of 12	14.95
Note: UX279 is sold in packages of 12 with 8 different stamp designs without values.		
UX280	20¢ City College of New York	.45
UX281	20¢ Bugs Bunny	1.25
UX281a	20¢ Bugs Bunny Booklet of 10	11.95
UX282	20¢ Golden Gate Bridge	.45
UX283	50¢ Golden Gate Bridge	1.10
UX284	20¢ Fort McHenry	.45
UX285-89	20¢ Movie Monsters(5)	3.50
UX289a	Same, booklet of 20	12.95
UX290	20¢ University of Mississippi (1998)	.45
UX291	20¢ Tweety & Sylvester (1998)	1.25
UX291a	20¢ Tweety Booklet of 10	11.95
UX292	20¢ Girard College	1.15
UX293-96	20¢ Tropical Birds (4)	2.80
UX296a	same, booklet of 10	11.50
UX297	20¢ Ballet	1.15
UX297a	same, booklet of 10	11.50
UX298	20¢ Northeastern Univ	.45
UX299	20¢ Brandeis Univ	.45
1999 Issues		
UX300	20¢ Love	.70
UX300a	Love Booklet of 20	12.95
UX301	20¢ Univ. of Wisconsin	.45
UX302	20¢ Wash. & Lee Univ	.45
UX303	20¢ Redwood Library	.45
UX304	20¢ Daffy Duck	1.35
UX304a	Daffy Duck Pack-10	12.95
...	20¢ Mount Vernon	.45
...	55¢ Mount Rainier	1.10
...	20¢ Block Island Light House	.45

MINT POSTAL CARDS

UXC 24

UZ 2

UY 29

Scott's No.		MintCard
AIRMAIL POSTAL CARDS		
UXC1	4¢ Eagle	.50
UXC2	5¢ Eagle (1958)	1.75
UXC3	5¢ Eagle, redrawn (60) .	6.50
UXC4	6¢ Bald Eagle ('63)	.55
UXC5	11¢ SIPEX, Travel (66)	.60
UXC6	6¢ Virgin Islands ('67)..	.50
UXC7	6¢ Boy Scouts	.50
UXC8	13¢ Travel USA	1.60
UXC9	8¢ Eagle, Precan ('68) ..	70
UXC9a	Same, Tagged ('69)	2.65
UXC10	9¢ Eagle, Precan ('71)	.60
UXC11	15¢ Travel USA	1.75
UXC12	9¢ Grand Canyon ('72).	.55
UXC13	15¢ Niagara Falls.........	.70
UXC14	11¢ Mail Early (1974) ..	.75
UXC15	18¢ Visit USA	.90
UXC16	21¢ Visit USA (1975)...	.85
UXC17	21¢ Curtiss Jenny ('78).	.80
UXC18	21¢ Olympics (1979)....	1.10
UXC19	28¢ Trans-Pacific ('81).	1.00
UXC20	28¢ Soaring (1982).......	1.00
UXC21	28¢ Speedskating ('83).	.90
UXC22	33¢ China Clipper ('85).	.90
UXC23	33¢ Ameripex (1986)....	.85
UXC24	36¢ DC-3 (1988)	.85
UXC25	40¢ Yankee Clipper (91)	.90
UXC26	50¢ Eagle (1995)	1.15

Scott's No.		Mint Card
OFFICIAL POSTAL CARDS		
UZ2	13¢ Emblem (1983)	.60
UZ3	14¢ Emblem ('85)	.60
UZ4	15¢ Emblem ('88)	.60
UZ5	19¢ Emblem ('91)	.60
UZ6	20¢ Emblem ('95).............	.60
"POSTAL BUDDY" CARDS		
PB1	15¢ (1990) Eagle	8.00
	Sheet of 4	32.50
PB2	19¢ (1991) Eagle	3.75
PB3	19¢ (1992) Plain, star........	10.00
PB3	Sheet of 4	42.50
PB3a	With Logo	11.00
PB3b	New Back	75.00
PB3b	Sheet of 4	300.00
PB3c	New Back w\ Logo .	135.00

Scott's No.		Mint Card
POSTAL REPLY CARDS		
1892-1920 Issues		
Unsevered Cards-Folded		
UY1	1¢ Grant, black............	37.50
UY1	Preprinted....................	17.50
UY2	2¢ Liberty, blue ('93) ...	18.50
UY2	Preprinted....................	14.50
UY3	1¢ Grant, no frame(98).	70.00
UY3	Preprinted....................	16.50
UY4	1¢ + 1¢ Sherman and Sheridan (1904)	55.00
UY4	Preprinted....................	12.50
UY5	1¢ + 1¢ M&G Wash., Blue (1910)	150.00
UY5	Preprinted....................	50.00
UY6	Same, Green (1911)	150.00
UY6	Preprinted....................	65.00
UY7	Same,sgl.frm. line ('15)	1.50
UY7	Preprinted....................	.60
UY8	2¢ + 2¢ M&G Wash., red (1918)	80.00
UY8	Preprinted....................	35.00
UY9	1¢ on 2¢ + 1¢ on 2¢, red (1920)	20.00
UY9	Preprinted....................	11.50
Note: Add 50% for unfolded on UY1-9		
1924-68		
Unsevered cards-Unfolded		
UY11	2¢ + 2¢ Liberty, red	3.00
UY11	Preprinted....................	1.50
UY12	3¢ + 3¢ McKinley ('26)	15.00
UY12	Preprinted....................	6.50
UY13	2¢ + 2¢ M&G Wash.(51)	1.75
UY13	Preprinted....................	.80
UY14	2¢ on 1¢ + 2¢ on 1¢ M&G Wash (1952)	1.75
UY14	Preprinted....................	1.00
UY15	2¢ on 1¢ + 2¢ on 1¢, green	150.00
UY15	Preprinted....................	60.00
UY16	4¢ + 4¢ Liberty ('56)....	1.50
UY17	3¢ + 3¢ Liberty ('58)....	5.25
UY18	4¢ + 4¢ Lincoln ('62) ...	6.00
UY19	7¢ + 7¢ "USA" (1963)..	3.75
UY20	8¢ + 8¢ "USA" (1967)	3.50
UY21	5¢+5¢ Lincoln (1968)	2.00

Scott's No.		Mint Card
1971-99		
Unsevered Cards-Unfolded		
UY22	6¢ + 6¢ Revere................	1.25
UY23	6¢ + 6¢ Hanson (1972)....	1.35
UY24	8¢ + S. Adams (1973)....	1.10
UY25	7¢ + 7¢ Thomson ('75) ...	1.10
UY26	9¢ + 9¢ Witherson...........	1.10
UY27	9¢ + 9¢ Rodney (1976) ...	1.10
UY28	9¢ + 9¢ Hale (1977)........	1.30
UY29	(10¢+10¢) Hancock ('78).	10.75
UY30	10¢ + 10¢ Hancock	1.25
UY31	(12¢ + 12¢) Eagle ('81)...	1.25
UY32	12¢ + 12¢ Thomas	1.75
UY33	(13¢ + 13¢) Morris...........	2.25
UY34	13¢ + 13¢ Morris	1.25
UY35	(14¢ + 14¢) Carroll ('85)..	3.25
UY36	14¢ + 14¢ Carroll	1.25
UY37	14¢ + 14¢ Wythe	1.25
UY38	14¢ + 14¢ U.S. Flag ('87)	1.25
UY39	15¢ + 15¢ Am./Beaut ('88)	1.25
UY40	19¢ + 19¢ Flag (1991).....	1.25
UY41	20¢ + 20¢ Red Barn ('95)	1.25
...	20¢ + 20¢ Block Island Light House..................	1.25

UNITED STATES REVENUES

| R15 | R24c | R36c | R44c | R60c |

| R71c | R82c | R85c |

1862-71 (All Used) (C) (VF + 50%)

Scott's No.		Imperforate(a) Fine	Ave.	Part Perforate(b) Fine	Ave.	Perforated(c) Fine	Ave.
R1	1¢ Express	47.50	25.00	37.50	21.00	1.00	.60
R2	1¢ Play Cards	895.00	525.00	600.00	375.00	150.00	90.00
R3	1¢ Proprietary	575.00	325.00	95.00	52.50	.45	.25
R4	1¢ Telegraph	375.00	200.00	...	...	9.75	6.00
R5	2¢ Bank Ck.,Blue	1.10	.70	1.50	.90	.25	.18
R6	2¢ Bank Ck.,Orange	...	...	65.00	37.50	.25	.18
R7	2¢ Certif.,Blue	11.00	6.00	...	...	22.50	12.00
R8	2¢ Certif.,Orange	...	...	...	...	22.50	13.00
R9	2¢ Express,Blue	11.00	6.00	15.00	8.50	.35	.25
R10	2¢ Express,Orange	...	...	...	...	6.50	3.85
R11	2¢ Ply.Cds.,Blue	...	...	140.00	85.00	3.50	2.00
R12	2¢ Ply.Cds.,Orange	...	...	...	...	30.00	18.00
R13	2¢ Propriet.,Blue	275.00	200.00	100.00	57.50	.40	.25
R14	2¢ Propriet.,Orange	...	...	...	...	30.00	16.00
R15	2¢ U.S.I.R.	...	...	...	...	.20	.15
R16	3¢ Foreign Exchange	...	...	230.00	130.00	3.15	1.75
R17	3¢ Playing Cards	...	...	...	...	100.00	60.00
R18	3¢ Proprietary	...	...	250.00	160.00	2.75	1.60
R19	3¢ Telegraph	47.50	25.00	16.50	9.50	2.35	1.25
R20	4¢ Inland Exchange	...	...	...	...	1.50	1.00
R21	4¢ Playing Cards	...	...	...	...	425.00	225.00
R22	4¢ Proprietary	...	...	185.00	110.00	5.75	3.50
R23	5¢ Agreement	...	...	...	...	.25	.18
R24	5¢ Certificate	2.25	1.25	9.00	5.00	.25	.18
R25	5¢ Express	3.75	2.25	4.25	2.60	.30	.20
R26	5¢ Foreign Exch	...	...	...	...	.30	.20
R27	5¢ Inland Exch	4.50	2.65	3.25	1.95	.25	.18
R28	5¢ Playing Cards	...	...	...	...	15.00	9.00
R29	5¢ Proprietary	...	...	...	...	19.50	11.00
R30	6¢ Inland Exch	...	...	...	...	1.60	.95
R32	10¢ Bill of Lading	42.50	25.00	170.00	95.00	.85	.50
R33	10¢ Certificate	110.00	60.00	170.00	95.00	.25	.18
R34	10¢ Contract,Blue	...	...	130.00	75.00	.35	.22
R35	10¢ For.Exch.,Blue	...	...	...	...	6.00	4.00
R36	10¢ Inland Exch.	150.00	85.00	3.25	1.95	.22	.15
R37	10¢ Power of Atty	400.00	225.00	18.50	11.00	.45	.30
R38	10¢ Proprietary	...	...	...	...	12.50	7.50
R39	15¢ Foreign Exch	...	...	...	...	12.00	7.00
R40	15¢ Inland Exch	25.00	14.00	11.00	6.00	1.10	.65
R41	20¢ Foreign Exch	38.50	21.50	...	...	30.00	15.00
R42	20¢ Inland Exch	13.00	7.50	15.00	8.50	.35	.20
R43	25¢ Bond	130.00	75.00	5.25	3.15	2.25	1.30
R44	25¢ Certificate	8.50	4.75	5.00	2.75	.25	.18
R45	25¢ Entry Goods	15.00	8.50	57.50	32.50	.70	.40
R46	25¢ Insurance	9.00	5.50	9.00	5.00	.25	.15
R47	25¢ Life Insurance	28.50	16.00	180.00	110.00	6.00	4.00
R48	25¢ Power of Atty	5.50	3.25	22.50	13.75	.30	.20
R49	25¢ Protest	25.00	15.00	230.00	130.00	6.50	4.00
R50	25¢ Wareh'se. Rct	36.00	20.00	200.00	115.00	19.50	10.50
R51	30¢ Foreign Exch	60.00	36.50	800.00	450.00	42.50	23.50
R52	30¢ Inland Exch.	42.50	23.00	51.50	28.75	3.00	1.80
R53	40¢ Inland Exch.	500.00	285.00	6.00	3.50	3.00	1.80
R54	50¢ Convey.,Blue	12.00	6.75	1.30	.80	.20	.15
R55	50¢ Entry of Goods	...	...	10.00	5.50	.35	.22
R56	50¢ Foreign Exch	37.50	21.00	35.00	20.00	4.75	3.00
R57	50¢ Lease	19.50	11.00	50.00	27.50	7.25	4.50
R58	50¢ Life Insurance	25.00	14.00	47.50	26.00	.85	.50
R59	50¢ Mortgage	12.00	7.00	2.10	1.20	.45	.30
R60	50¢ Orig.Process	2.65	1.50	450.00	325.00	.50	.30
R61	50¢ Passage Ticket	60.00	32.50	130.00	75.00	1.15	.70
R62	50¢ Probate of Will	28.50	16.00	55.00	30.00	17.00	10.00
R63	50¢ Sty. Bond,Blue	125.00	70.00	2.35	1.30	.30	.20
R64	60¢ Inland Exch.	70.00	38.50	40.00	22.00	5.25	3.00
R65	70¢ Foreign Exch	265.00	150.00	85.00	50.00	7.25	4.25
R66	$1 Conveyance	11.00	6.00	365.00	200.00	12.50	7.50
R67	$1 Entry of Goods	26.50	15.00	...	...	1.75	1.00
R68	$1 Foreign Exch	55.00	30.00	...	...	.65	.37
R69	$1 Inland Exch	10.50	6.00	250.00	140.00	.45	.25
R70	$1 Lease	29.50	16.00	...	...	2.00	1.25
R71	$1 Life Insurance	125.00	72.50	...	...	5.75	3.50
R72	$1 Manifest	40.00	22.50	...	...	25.00	14.50
R73	$1 Mortgage	16.50	9.75	...	...	160.00	95.00
R74	$1 Passage Ticket	210.00	120.00	...	...	160.00	95.00
R75	$1 Power of Atty	62.50	35.00	...	...	1.80	1.10
R76	$1 Probate of Will	60.00	32.50	...	...	30.00	16.50

1862-71 Issue (continued) (All Used) (C)

Scott's No.		Imperforate(a) Fine	Ave.	Part Perforate(b) Fine	Ave.	Perforated(c) Fine	Ave.
R77	$1.30 Foreign Exch	...	...	...	...	45.00	25.00
R78	$1.50 Inland Exch	19.00	10.50	...	...	2.85	1.75
R79	$1.60 Foreign Exch	775.00	425.00	...	...	90.00	50.00
R80	$1.90 Foreign Exch	...	1650.00	...	...	80.00	47.50
R81	$2 Conveyance	90.00	50.00	1100.00	650.00	2.50	1.40
R82	$2 Mortgage	90.00	50.00	...	...	2.65	1.50
R83	$2 Probate of Will	...	1500.00	...	...	42.50	22.50
R84	$2.50 Inland Exch	2000.00	1100.00	...	...	5.25	3.25
R85	$3 Charter Party	95.00	55.00	...	...	4.25	2.50
R86	$3 Manifest	90.00	50.00	...	...	22.50	12.50
R87	$3.50 Inland Exch	...	1500.00	...	...	40.00	22.50
R88	$5 Charter Party	200.00	115.00	...	...	5.75	3.50
R89	$5 Conveyance	30.00	16.50	...	...	5.75	3.50
R90	$5 Manifest	90.00	50.00	...	...	75.00	41.50
R91	$5 Mortgage	100.00	55.00	...	...	15.00	8.25
R92	$5 Probate of Will	425.00	250.00	...	...	15.00	8.25
R93	$10 Charter Party	450.00	250.00	...	...	22.50	12.50
R94	$10 Conveyance	75.00	42.50	...	...	50.00	27.50
R95	$10 Mortgage	300.00	165.00	...	...	22.50	12.50
R96	$10 Probate of Will	950.00	525.00	...	...	22.50	12.00
R97	$15 Mortgage,Blue	950.00	525.00	...	...	100.00	65.00
R98	$20 Conveyance	110.00	65.00	...	...	52.50	37.50
R99	$20 Probate of Will	975.00	550.00	...	...	875.00	575.00
R100	$25 Mortgage	775.00	435.00	...	...	100.00	60.50
R101	$50 U.S.I.R	160.00	95.00	...	...	80.00	45.00
R102	$200 U.S.I.R.	1150.00	650.00	...	...	575.00	325.00

1ST ISSUE HANDSTAMPED CANCELLATIONS ARE GENERALLY AVAILABLE FOR A 20% PREMIUM.

1871 SECOND ISSUE (C) (VF + 50%)

| R104,R135 | R107,R137 | R113,R140 | R118,R144 |

Scott's No.		Used Fine	Ave.	Scott's No.		Used Fine	Ave.
R103	1¢	32.50	16.50	R118	$1	2.75	1.50
R104	2¢	1.10	.55	R119	$1.30	230.00	125.00
R105	3¢	13.00	8.00	R120	$1.50	10.00	5.50
R106	4¢	55.00	30.00	R121	$1.60	290.00	160.00
R107	5¢	1.30	.70	R122	$1.90	140.00	80.00
R108	6¢	80.00	42.50	R123	$2	12.75	7.00
R109	10¢	.80	.45	R124	$2.50	22.50	12.75
R110	15¢	22.50	13.00	R125	$3	25.00	14.00
R111	20¢	5.00	2.75	R126	$3.50	125.00	70.00
R112	25¢	.60	.33	R127	$5	15.00	8.50
R113	30¢	52.50	30.00	R128	$10	85.00	50.00
R114	40¢	32.50	18.75	R129	$20	265.00	165.00
R115	50¢	.50	.33	R130	$25	265.00	165.00
R116	60¢	77.50	45.00	R131	$50	325.00	200.00
R117	70¢	28.50	17.50				

R103 through R131 have blue frames and a black center.
1871-72 Third Issue - Same Designs as Second Issue (C) (VF + 50%)

		Fine	Ave.			Fine	Ave.
R134	1¢ Claret	25.00	14.00	R143	70¢ Green	32.50	17.50
R135	2¢ Orange	.20	.15	R144	$1 Green	1.35	.75
R136	4¢ Brown	30.00	16.50	R145	$2 Vermillion	18.00	9.50
R137	5¢ Orange	.25	.15	R146	$2.50 Claret	28.50	16.00
R138	6¢ Orange	28.50	16.00	R147	$3 Green	28.50	16.00
R139	15¢ Brown	10.50	6.50	R148	$5 Vermillion	16.00	9.50
R140	30¢ Orange	13.00	8.50	R149	$10 Green	60.00	35.00
R141	40¢ Brown	26.50	15.00	R150	$20 Orange	425.00	235.00
R142	60¢ Orange	50.00	28.75				

Note : Cut cancels are priced at 40% to 60% of the above prices.

R134 through R150 have black centers.

1874 Fourth Issue (C)

Scott's No.		Uncancelled Fine	Ave.	Used Fine	Ave.
R151	2¢ Orange and Black, Green Paper...	...	.20	.15	

1875-78 Fifth Issue (C)(VF + 50%)

R152a	2¢ Liberty, Blue, Silk Paper	1.50	.90	.20	.15
R152b	2¢ Blue, Watermarked	1.50	.90	.20	.15
R152c	2¢ Blue, Rouletted, Watermarked	...	28.50	14.50	

* 1898 Postage Stamps Overprinted "I.R." (C) (VF + 50%)

R153	1¢ Green, Small I.R. (#279)	2.50	1.50	2.75	1.65
R154	1¢ Green, Large I.R. (#279)	.25	.20	.20	.15
R154a	1¢ Green, Inverted Surcharge	17.50	10.00	15.00	8.50
R155	2¢ Carmine, Large I.R. (#267)	.25	.20	.20	.15

* 1898 Newspaper Stamps Surcharged "INT. REV./$5/DOCUMENTARY" (C)

R159	$5 Blue, Surcharge down (#PR121)	210.00	130.00	140.00	85.00
R160	$5 Blue, Surcharge up (#PR121)90.00	50.00	60.00	35.00	

*** Used prices are for stamps with contemporary cancels.**

R163 R174 R197,R208 R219

1898 Documentary "Battleship" Designs (C) (VF +30%) (Rouletted 5½)

R161	½¢ Orange	2.00	1.25	6.50	4.00
R162	½¢ Dark Gray	.30	.20	.20	.15
R163	1¢ Pale Blue	.25	.20	.20	.15
R163p	1¢ Hyphen Hole Perf. 7	.35	.22	.30	.20
R164	2¢ Carmine	.25	.20	.20	.15
R164p	2¢ Hyphen Hole Perf. 7	.35	.22	.30	.20
R165	3¢ Dark Blue	1.10	.60	.20	.15
R165p	3¢ Hyphen Hole Perf. 7	10.00	6.25	.50	.35
R166	4¢ Pale Rose	.75	.45	.20	.15
R166p	4¢ Hyphen Hole Perf. 7	3.75	2.25	1.00	.60
R167	5¢ Lilac	.25	.20	.20	.15
R167p	5¢ Hyphen Hole Perf. 7	3.75	2.25	.30	.20
R168	10¢ Dark Brown	1.00	.60	.20	.15
R168p	10¢ Hyphen Hole Perf. 7	3.25	1.95	.30	.20
R169	25¢ Purple Brown	1.10	.60	.20	.15
R169p	25¢ Hyphen Hole Perf. 7	5.00	3.00	.35	.25
R170	40¢ Blue Lilac (cut .25)	90.00	50.00	1.80	1.00
R170p	40¢ Hyphen Hole Perf. 7	140.00	85.00	24.00	15.00
R171	50¢ Slate Violet	11.00	7.50	.20	.15
R171p	50¢ Hyphen Hole Perf. 7	16.50	10.75	.30	.20
R172	80¢ Bistre (cut .15)	52.50	32.50	.35	.20
R172p	80¢ Hyphen Hole Perf. 7	140.00	85.00	27.50	16.50

Commerce Design (C) (Rouletted 5½) (VF + 30%)

R173	$1 Commerce, Dark Green	6.50	3.75	.20	.15
R173p	1¢ Hyphen Hole Perf. 7	14.50	9.00	.70	.45
R174	$3 Dark Brown (cut .18)	15.00	9.00	.75	.45
R174p	3¢ Hyphen Hole Perf. 7(cut .30)	19.50	12.00	2.50	1.50
R175	$5 Orange Red Perf. 7 (cut .20) 19.50	12.50	1.35	.80	
R176	$10 Black Perf. 7 (cut .60)	60.00	38.50	2.50	1.50
R177	$30 Red Perf. 7 (cut 35.00)	180.00	100.00	95.00	57.50
R178	$50 Gray Brown Perf.7(cut 1.80)85.00	50.00	5.50	3.50	

1899 Documentary Stamps Imperforated (C) (VF + 30%)

R179	$100 Marshall, Brn. & Blk.(cut 17.50)	100.00	62.50	25.00	16.00
R180	$500 Hamilton,Car.Lk/Blk(cut 210.00)	650.00	400.00	400.00	250.00
R181	$1000 Madison,Grn&Blk (cut 95.00)	650.00	400.00	300.00	240.00

1900 Documentary Stamps (C) (Hyphen Hole Perf 7) (VF + 30%)

R182	$1 Commerce, Carmine (cut .15) ...	14.00	8.50	.50	.30
R183	$3 Lake (cut 7.50)	110.00	65.00	40.00	24.50

1900 Surcharged Large Black Numerals (C) (VF + 30%)

R184	$1 Gray (cut .15)	10.00	5.75	.20	.15
R185	$2 Gray (cut .15)	7.50	4.25	.20	.15
R186	$3 Gray (cut $2.00)	47.50	25.00	10.00	5.50
R187	$5 Gray (cut $1.00)	33.50	20.00	6.50	3.95
R188	$10 Gray (cut 3.35)	57.50	35.00	15.00	9.00
R189	$50 Gray (cut 70.00)	550.00	300.00	325.00	185.00

1902 Surcharged Ornamental Numerals (C) (VF + 30%)

R190	$1 Green (cut .25)	15.00	8.50	3.25	1.95
R191	$2 Green (cut .25)	13.50	7.50	1.30	.80
R192	$5 Green (cut $4.00)	110.00	65.00	26.50	16.50
R193	$10 Green (cut 45.00)	265.00	150.00	130.00	70.00
R194	$50 Green (cut 210.00)	875.00	495.00	725.00	400.00

1914 Documentary Single Line Watermark "USPS" (VF + 40%) (B)

Scott's No.		Unused Fine	Ave.	Used Fine	Ave.
R195	½¢ Rose	6.25	3.85	3.00	1.85
R196	1¢ Rose	1.25	.70	.20	.15
R197	2¢ Rose	1.65	.95	.20	.15
R198	3¢ Rose	40.00	21.50	25.00	14.50
R199	4¢ Rose	12.50	7.50	1.75	1.00
R200	5¢ Rose	3.50	1.95	.20	.15
R201	10¢ Rose	3.00	1.65	.20	.15
R202	25¢ Rose	24.75	15.75	.60	.35
R203	40¢ Rose	15.00	9.00	.85	.50
R204	50¢ Rose	5.00	3.00	.20	.15
R205	80¢ Rose	75.00	45.00	9.00	5.50

1914 Documentary Double Line Watermark "USIR" (VF + 40%) (B)

R206	½¢ Rose	1.20	.65	.50	.30
R207	1¢ Rose	.25	.20	.20	.15
R208	2¢ Rose	.25	.20	.20	.15
R209	3¢ Rose	1.35	.70	.20	.15
R210	4¢ Rose	3.25	1.85	.40	.25
R211	5¢ Rose	1.60	.90	.25	.18
R212	10¢ Rose	1.00	.65	.20	.15
R213	25¢ Rose	4.50	2.70	1.10	.65
R214	40¢ Rose (cut .50)	55.00	31.75	11.00	6.50
R215	50¢ Rose	12.50	8.00	.25	.18
R216	80¢ Rose (cut .90)	80.00	43.50	16.00	8.75
R217	$1 Liberty, Green (cut .15)	26.50	16.00	.30	.20
R218	$2 Carmine (cut .15)	40.00	24.00	.45	.30
R219	$3 Purple (cut .20)	45.00	25.00	2.00	1.10
R220	$5 Blue (cut .60)	42.50	23.00	2.50	1.50
R221	$10 Orange (cut .90)	95.00	55.00	4.50	2.65
R222	$30 Vermillion (cut 2.00)	200.00	120.00	9.75	6.00
R223	$50 Violet (cut 275.00)	1000.00	575.00	700.00	385.00

1914-15 Documentary stamps - Perforated 12, without gum (B)

R224	$60 Lincoln, Brown (cut 42.50)	...	...	100.00	60.00
R225	$100 Wash., Green (cut 16.50)	50.00	32.50	37.50	20.00
R226	$500 Hamilton, Blue (cut 185.00)	...	450.00	250.00	
R227	$1000 Madison, Orange (cut 165.00)	...	...	400.00	225.00

R228,R251 R240 R733

1917-33 Documentary Stamps - Perf. 11 (VF + 30%) (B)

R228	1¢ Rose	.25	.20	.20	.15
R229	2¢ Rose	.25	.20	.20	.15
R230	3¢ Rose	1.20	.70	.30	.20
R231	4¢ Rose	.40	.25	.20	.15
R232	5¢ Rose	.25	.20	.20	.15
R233	8¢ Rose	1.65	1.00	.30	.20
R234	10¢ Rose	.35	.25	.20	.15
R235	20¢ Rose	.80	.50	.20	.15
R236	25¢ Rose	1.00	.60	.20	.15
R237	40¢ Rose	1.35	.80	.35	.25
R238	50¢ Rose	1.75	1.10	.20	.15
R239	80¢ Rose	4.25	2.25	.20	.15
R240	$1 Green, Without Date	5.75	3.50	.20	.15
R241	$2 Rose	9.50	5.75	.20	.15
R242	$3 Violet (cut .15)	31.50	19.00	.65	.35
R243	$4 Brown (cut .15)	23.00	14.00	1.50	.90
R244	$5 Blue (cut .15)	12.50	7.00	.25	.18
R245	$10 Orange (cut .15)	25.00	15.00	.85	.50

1917 Documentary Stamps - Perforated 12, Without Gum (B)

R246	$30 Grant, Orange (cut 1.25)	40.00	25.00	8.50	5.25
R247	$60 Lincoln, Brown (cut .85)	47.50	30.00	6.50	4.00
R248	$100 Wash., Green (cut .40)	28.00	17.00	1.10	.65
R249	$500 Hamilton, Blue (cut 9.00)	175.00	120.00	30.00	17.50
R250	$1000 Madison, Orange (cut 4.25).	110.00	62.50	13.00	7.50

1928-29 Documentary Stamps - Perf. 10 (20%) (B)

R251	1¢ Carmine Rose	1.90	1.15	1.30	.80
R252	2¢ Carmine Rose	.50	.30	.20	.15
R253	4¢ Carmine Rose	5.50	3.00	3.75	2.25
R254	5¢ Carmine Rose	1.15	.65	.55	.35
R255	10¢ Carmine Rose	1.50	.90	1.10	.70
R256	20¢ Carmine Rose	5.75	3.25	5.00	3.00
R257	$1 Green (cut 4.50)	75.00	45.00	25.00	15.00
R258	$2 Rose	28.50	16.50	2.25	1.30
R259	$10 Orange (cut 20.00)	95.00	60.00	37.50	22.50

1929-30 Documentary Stamps - Perf. 11x10 (VF + 30%) (B)

R260	2¢ Carmine Rose	2.75	1.50	2.50	1.40
R261	5¢ Carmine Rose	1.75	1.10	1.75	1.10
R262	10¢ Carmine Rose	7.50	4.00	6.50	4.00
R263	20¢ Carmine Rose	16.50	10.00	8.50	5.00

#R264-R732 1940-1958 Documentary Stamps (Dated)
We will be glad to quote prices on any of these items we have in stock.

1962-1963 Documentary Stamps

Scott's No.		Plate Block	F.VF NH	F.VF Used
R733	10¢ Internal Revenue Bldg	12.75	2.50	.40
R734	10¢ Bldg., Without Date (1963)	27.50	4.25	.40

RB1   RB12   RB33,RB45   RB66

1871-74 Proprietary (All Used) (C)

Scott's No.		Violet Paper(a) Fine	Ave.	Green Paper(b) Fine	Ave.
RB1	1¢ Green and Black	4.25	2.65	6.50	4.00
RB2	2¢ Green and Black	5.25	3.00	13.00	7.75
RB3	3¢ Green and Black	12.50	7.50	40.00	22.50
RB4	4¢ Green and Black	8.25	4.75	12.50	7.50
RB5	5¢ Green and Black	120.00	70.00	125.00	75.00
RB6	6¢ Green and Black	30.00	18.00	75.00	41.50
RB7	10¢ Green and Black	215.00	130.00	40.00	22.50
RB8	50¢ Green and Black	525.00	300.00	825.00	450.00

1875-81 Proprietary (All Used) (C)

Scott's No.		Silk Paper(s) Fine	Ave.	Watermarked(b) Fine	Ave.	Rouletted(c) Fine	Ave.
RB11	1¢ Green	1.65	1.00	.40	.25	60.00	33.50
RB12	2¢ Brown	2.25	1.30	1.35	.75	70.00	42.50
RB13	3¢ Orange	10.75	5.75	4.00	2.50	70.00	42.50
RB14	4¢ Red Brown	5.25	3.00	5.25	2.95	...	...
RB15	4¢ Red	...	...	4.00	2.25	115.00	70.00
RB16	5¢ Black	87.50	50.00	75.00	37.50	...	...
RB17	6¢ Violet Blue	21.50	13.00	16.00	9.50	200.00	120.00
RB18	6¢ Violet	...	...	25.00	16.00	...	...
RB19	10¢ Blue	...	...	265.00	160.00	...	...

1898 Proprietary Stamps (Battleship) (C) (Roulette 5½)

Scott's No.		Uncancelled Fine	Ave.	Used Fine	Ave.
RB20	1/8¢ Yellow Green	.25	.20	.20	.15
RB20p	1/8¢ Hyphen Hole Perf 7	.25	.20	.20	.15
RB21	1/4¢ Pale Brown	.25	.20	.20	.15
RB21p	1/4¢ Hyphen Hole Perf 7	.25	.20	.20	.15
RB22	3/8¢ Deep Orange	.25	.20	.20	.15
RB22p	3/8¢ Hyphen Hole Perf 7	.30	.20	.20	.15
RB23	5/8¢ Deep Ultramarine	.25	.20	.20	.15
RB23p	5/8¢ Hyphen Hole Perf 7	.30	.20	.20	.15
RB24	1¢ Dark Green	.95	.60	.30	.20
RB24p	1¢ Hyphen Hole Perf 7	23.50	14.75	14.50	9.00
RB25	1¼¢ Violet	.25	.20	.20	.15
RB25p	1¼¢ Hyphen Hole Perf 7	.30	.20	.20	.15
RB26	1 1/8¢ Dull Blue	6.25	4.00	1.10	.70
RB26p	1 1/8¢ Hyphen Hoe Perf 7	18.75	11.00	6.50	4.25
RB27	2¢ Violet Brown	.70	.45	.20	.15
RB27p	2¢ Hyphen Hole Perf 7	3.85	2.25	.30	.20
RB28	2½¢ Lake	2.10	1.25	.20	.15
RB28p	2½¢ Hyphen Hole Perf 7	2.40	1.50	.25	.18
RB29	3¾¢ Olive Gray	25.00	16.50	6.50	4.50
RB29p	3¾¢ Hyphen Hole Perf 7	47.50	27.50	14.50	8.50
RB30	4¢ Purple	6.25	4.00	.85	.50
RB30p	4¢ Hyphen Hole Perf 7	47.50	27.50	14.50	8.50
RB31	5¢ Brown Orange	7.00	4.25	.75	.45
RB31p	5¢ Hyphen Hole Perf 7	47.50	27.50	7.50	4.50

1914 Black Proprietary Stamps - S.L. Wmk. "USPS" (VF + 40%) (B)

Scott's No.		Unused Fine	Ave.	Used Fine	Ave.
RB32	1/8¢ Black	.25	.20	.20	.15
RB33	1/4¢ Black	1.50	.90	1.10	.65
RB34	3/8¢ Black	.25	.20	.20	.15
RB35	5/8¢ Black	3.00	1.80	2.25	1.35
RB36	1¼¢ Black	2.10	1.40	1.10	.70
RB37	1 7/8¢ Black	30.00	17.50	15.00	9.50
RB38	2½¢ Black	6.00	3.75	2.35	1.50
RB39	3 1/8¢ Black	70.00	40.00	42.50	25.00
RB40	3¼¢ Black	30.00	18.50	20.00	12.50
RB41	4¢ Black	42.50	25.00	23.50	14.00
RB42	4⅜¢ Black	...	695.00	...	...
RB43	5¢ Black	95.00	57.50	60.00	35.00

1914 Black Proprietary Stamps - D.L. Wmk. "USIR" (40%) (B)

RB44	1/8¢ Black	.25	.20	.20	.15
RB45	1/4¢ Black	.25	.20	.20	.15
RB46	3/8¢ Black	.55	.33	.30	.18
RB47	½¢ Black	3.25	1.95	2.25	1.40
RB48	5/8¢ Black	.25	.20	.20	.15
RB49	1¢ Black	4.50	2.50	3.25	1.90
RB50	1¼¢ Black	.40	.25	.35	.22
RB51	1½¢ Black	3.25	1.90	2.00	1.10

1914 Black Proprietary Stamps - D.L. Wmk. "USIR" (VF + 40%) (cont)

Scott's No.		Unused Fine	Ave.	Used Fine	Ave.
RB52	1 7/8¢ Black	1.10	.65	.65	.40
RB53	2¢ Black	5.50	3.50	3.25	1.95
RB54	2½¢ Black	1.10	.65	1.10	.65
RB55	3¢ Black	3.75	2.10	2.25	1.35
RB56	3 1/8¢ Black	5.00	3.00	2.50	1.50
RB57	3¾¢ Black	9.00	5.50	8.00	4.75
RB58	4¢ Black	.50	.30	.20	.15
RB59	4 3/8¢ Black	12.00	7.00	7.00	4.25
RB60	5¢ Black	2.65	1.50	2.50	1.40
RB61	6¢ Black	47.50	29.50	36.50	21.75
RB62	8¢ Black	15.00	9.00	11.00	6.75
RB63	10¢ Black	9.00	5.50	7.50	4.50
RB64	20¢ Black	18.75	11.50	16.00	9.75

1919 Proprietary Stamps (VF + 30%) (B)

RB65	1¢ Dark Blue	.25	.20	.20	.15
RB66	2¢ Dark Blue	.25	.20	.20	.15
RB67	3¢ Dark Blue	1.10	.65	.65	.40
RB68	4¢ Dark Blue	1.10	.65	.55	.30
RB69	5¢ Dark Blue	1.35	.80	.65	.40
RB70	8¢ Dark Blue	11.50	7.00	9.00	5.50
RB71	10¢ Dark Blue	4.25	2.75	2.10	1.30
RB72	20¢ Dark Blue	6.25	4.00	3.25	1.95
RB73	40¢ Dark Blue	40.00	25.00	10.50	6.50

1918-34 Future Delivery Stamps (VF + 30%) (B)
1917 Documentary Stamps overprinted "FUTURE DELIVERY" in black or red

Horizontal Overprints

RC1	2¢ Carmine Rose	3.15	2.00	.20	.15
RC2	3¢ Carmine Rose (cut 10.75)	25.00	15.00	20.00	12.50
RC3	4¢ Carmine Rose	5.00	3.00	.20	.15
RC3A	5¢ Carmine Rose	67.50	40.00	6.50	3.75
RC4	10¢ Carmine Rose	9.50	6.00	.20	.15
RC5	20¢ Carmine Rose	12.50	7.50	.20	.15
RC6	25¢ Carmine Rose (cut .15)	30.00	18.00	.75	.45
RC7	40¢ Carmine Rose (cut .15)	35.00	21.50	.85	.50
RC8	50¢ Carmine Rose	7.50	4.50	.35	.20
RC9	80¢ Carmine Rose (cut .85)	62.50	38.50	8.00	5.00

Vertical Overprints

RC10	$1 Green (cut .15)	25.00	15.00	.25	.18
RC11	$2 Rose (cut .15)	30.00	18.00	.25	.18
RC12	$3 Violet (cut .20)	70.00	40.00	2.25	1.30
RC13	$5 Dark Blue (cut .15)	50.00	30.00	.50	.25
RC14	$10 Orange (cut .20)	70.00	40.00	1.00	.60
RC15	$20 Olive Bistre (cut .50)	125.00	75.00	5.00	3.00

Horizontal Overprints, Without Gum

RC16	$30 Vermillion (cut 1.50)	65.00	40.00	3.25	1.95
RC17	$50 Olive Green (cut .55)	50.00	28.50	1.10	.65
RC18	$60 Brown (cut .80)	65.00	35.00	2.10	1.30
RC19	$100 Yellow Green (cut 5.75)	70.00	38.50	22.50	13.50
RC20	$500 Blue (cut 4.50)	65.00	37.50	10.50	6.25
RC21	$1000 Orange (cut 1.65)	75.00	45.00	5.25	3.25
RC22	1¢ Carm. Rose, Narrow Overprt	1.10	.70	.20	.15
RC23	80¢ Narrow Overprint (cut .30)	57.50	37.50	2.50	1.50

Horizontal Serif Overprints

RC25	$1 Green (cut .15)	25.00	16.50	.75	.45
RC26	$10 Orange (cut 8.75)	80.00	50.00	15.00	10.00

1918-22 Stock Transfer Stamps, Perf. 11 or 12 (VF + 30%) (B)
1917 Documentary Stamps overprinted "STOCK TRANSFER" in black or red

Horizontal Overprints

RD1	1¢ Carmine Rose	.80	.45	.20	.15
RD2	2¢ Carmine Rose	.25	.20	.20	.15
RD3	4¢ Carmine Rose	.25	.20	.20	.15
RD4	5¢ Carmine Rose	.25	.20	.20	.15
RD5	10¢ Carmine Rose	.25	.20	.20	.15
RD6	20¢ Carmine Rose	.50	.30	.20	.15
RD7	25¢ Carmine Rose (cut .15)	1.25	.70	.25	.20
RD8	40¢ Carmine Rose (cut .15)	1.25	.70	.20	.15
RD9	50¢ Carmine Rose	.55	.35	.20	.15
RD10	80¢ Carmine Rose (cut .15)	2.50	1.50	.30	.20

Vertical Overprints

RD11	$1 Green, Red Overprint (cut 4.00)	57.50	33.50	16.50	10.00
RD12	$1 Green, Black Overprint	2.10	1.25	.25	.20
RD13	$2 Rose	2.10	1.25	.20	.15
RD14	$3 Violet (cut .22)	15.00	8.50	3.75	2.30
RD15	$4 Brown (cut .15)	7.50	4.25	.25	.18
RD16	$5 Blue (cut .15)	5.00	3.00	.25	.18
RD17	$10 Orange (cut .15)	13.00	8.00	.30	.20
RD18	$20 Bistre (cut 3.00)	65.00	40.00	18.00	11.00

Horizontal Serif Overprints, Without Gum

RD19	$30 Vermillion (cut 2.00)	16.00	9.75	4.25	2.50
RD20	$50 Olive Green (cut 17.50)	95.00	52.50	52.50	28.75
RD21	$60 Brown (cut 7.75)	95.00	52.50	20.00	13.00
RD22	$100 Green (cut 2.00)	21.50	13.00	5.25	3.00
RD23	$500 Blue (cut 60.00)	285.00	190.00	100.00	65.00
RD24	$1000 Orange (cut 26.75)	150.00	95.00	65.00	40.00

1928 Transfer Stamps, Pf. 10 (VF + 30%)

Scott's No.		Fine Unused	Used
RD25	1¢ Carm rose	2.10	.25
RD26	4¢ Carm rose	2.10	.25
RD27	10¢ Carm rose	1.80	.25
RD28	20¢ Carm rose	2.50	.25
RD29	50¢ Carm rose	3.00	.25
RD30	$1 Green	25.00	.20
RD31	$2 Carm rose	25.00	.20
RD32	$10 Orng (cut .15)	27.50	.30

1920 Transfers, Serif Ovpts. (VF + 30%) RD33-38, Pf. 11; RD39-41, Pf. 10

RD33	2¢ Carm rose	6.25	.60
RD34	10¢ Carm rose	1.00	.25
RD35	20¢ Carm rose	1.00	.25
RD36	50¢ Carm rose	2.50	.25
RD37	$1 Green (cut .25)	35.00	8.50
RD38	$2 Rose (cut .25)	30.00	8.50
RD39	2¢ Carm rose	5.00	.45
RD40	10¢ Carm rose	1.10	.45
RD41	20¢ Carm rose	2.00	.25

We will be glad to quote on any of the following Revenue categories: 1940-58 Dated Documentaries

CORDIAL AND WINE STAMPS (VF + 30%)

RE27 RE37

1914 Single-line Wtmk. "USPS", Perf. 10

RE1	¼¢ Green	.70	.50
RE2	½¢ Green	.45	.25
RE3	1¢ Green	.40	.30
RE4	1½¢ Green	2.00	1.35
RE5	2¢ Green	2.75	2.75
RE6	3¢ Green	3.00	1.15
RE7	4¢ Green	2.50	1.50
RE8	5¢ Green	1.00	.55
RE9	6¢ Green	5.00	3.25
RE10	8¢ Green	3.50	1.40
RE11	10¢ Green	3.00	2.65
RE12	20¢ Green	4.00	1.65
RE13	24¢ Green	13.00	7.50
RE14	40¢ Green	3.00	1.00
RE15	$2 Imperf	6.50	.20

1914 Double-Line Wtmk. "USIR", Perf. 10

RE16	¼¢ Green	5.50	4.50
RE17	½¢ Green	3.50	2.75
RE18	1¢ Green	.25	.15
RE19	1½¢ Green	40.00	30.00
RE20	2¢ Green	.15	.15
RE21	3¢ Green	2.50	2.25
RE22	4¢ Green	.95	.95
RE23	5¢ Green	11.75	10.00
RE24	6¢ Green	.50	.30
RE25	8¢ Green	1.80	.45
RE26	10¢ Green	.50	.25
RE27	20¢ Green	.70	.45
RE28	24¢ Green	12.50	.75
RE29	40¢ Green	27.50	9.50
RE30	$2 Imperf	28.00	2.95
RE31	$2 Perf.11	72.50	80.00

1916 Rouletted 3½
Inscribed "Series of 1916"

RE32	1¢ Green	.35	.30
RE33	3¢ Green	3.75	3.50
RE34	4¢ Green	.30	.30
RE35	6¢ Green	1.40	.75
RE36	7½¢ Green	6.75	3.75
RE37	10¢ Green	1.10	.40
RE38	12¢ Green	2.75	3.75
RE39	15¢ Green	1.60	1.75
RE40	18¢ Green	23.00	21.00
RE41	20¢ Green	.30	.30
RE42	24¢ Green	3.75	2.75
RE43	30¢ Green	3.00	2.35
RE44	36¢ Green	18.50	14.00
RE45	50¢ Green	.55	.40

1916 Rouletted 3½ (continued)

Scott No.		Fine Unused	Used
RE46	60¢ Green	3.50	2.00
RE47	72¢ Green	32.50	25.00
RE48	80¢ Green	.75	.55
RE49	$1.20 Green	6.50	5.50
RE50	$1.44 Green	8.00	2.75
RE51	$1.60 Green	23.50	16.50
RE52	$2 Green	1.65	1.35
RE53	$4 Green	.90	.20
RE54	$4.80 Green	3.50	2.75
RE55	$9.60 Green	1.15	.25
RE56	$20 Pf. 11½	80.00	37.50
RE57	$40 Pf. 11½	160.00	45.00
RE58	$50 Pf. 11½	55.00	42.50
RE59	$100 Pf. 11½	225.00	130.00

1933 Rouletted 7

RE60	1¢ Lt. green	2.50	.30
RE61	3¢ Lt. green	6.50	2.25
RE62	4¢ Lt. green	1.40	.25
RE63	6¢ Lt. green	10.00	4.50
RE64	7½¢ Lt. green	2.75	.50
RE65	10¢ Lt. green	1.75	.15
RE66	12¢ Lt. green	8.50	4.25
RE67	15¢ Lt. green	3.50	.25
RE69	20¢ Lt. green	4.00	.15
RE70	24¢ Lt. green	4.00	.15
RE71	30¢ Lt. green	4.00	.25
RE72	36¢ Lt. green	10.00	.55
RE73	50¢ Lt. green	3.75	.25
RE74	60¢ Lt. green	6.75	.15
RE75	72¢ Lt. green	11.50	.30
RE76	80¢ Lt. green	11.50	.15
RE77	$1.20 Lt. green	9.00	1.50
RE78	$1.44 Lt. green	11.50	4.00
RE79	$1.60 Lt. green	...	150.00
RE80	$2 Lt. green	31.75	3.75
RE81	$4 Lt. green	27.50	6.25
RE82	$4.80 Lt. green	27.50	13.75
RE83	$9.60 Lt. green	120.00	75.00

RE83A RE133

1934-40 "Series of 1934" Rouletted 7

RE83A	1/5¢ Green	.65	.18
RE84	½¢ Green	.50	.35
RE85	1¢ Green	.60	.15
RE86	1¼¢ Green	1.00	.70
RE87	1½¢ Green	6.00	4.75
RE88	2¢ Green	1.75	.60
RE89	2½¢ Green	1.75	.50
RE90	3¢ Green	4.50	3.75
RE91	4¢ Green	2.25	.15
RE92	5¢ Green	.55	.15
RE93	6¢ Green	1.65	.50
RE94	7½¢ Green	2.00	.15
RE95	10¢ Green	.45	.15
RE96	12¢ Green	1.50	.15
RE96A	14 2/5¢ Green	135.00	3.00
RE97	15¢ Green	.75	.15
RE98	18¢ Green	1.40	.15
RE99	20¢ Green	1.10	.15
RE100	24¢ Green	1.80	.20
RE101	30¢ Green	1.30	.20
RE102	40¢ Green	3.00	.25
RE102A	43 1/5¢ Green	12.50	2.00
RE103	48¢ Green	12.75	1.50
RE104	$1 Green	16.00	10.00
RE105	$1.50 Green	26.50	13.50
RE106	$2.50 Green	32.50	15.00
RE107	$5 Green	23.75	6.75

1942 "Series of 1941" Rouletted 7

RE108	1/5¢ Grn. & Bk.	.60	.40
RE109	¼¢ Green & Bk.	2.00	1.60
RE110	½¢ Green & Bk.	2.50	1.80
RE111	1¢ Green & Bk.	1.00	.75
RE112	2¢ Green & Bk.	5.00	5.00
RE113	3¢ Green & Bk.	4.25	3.75
RE115	3¾¢ Green & Bk.	8.00	6.00
RE116	4¢ Green & Bk.	3.25	2.75
RE117	5¢ Green & Bk.	2.25	2.00
RE118	6¢ Green & Bk.	2.75	2.50
RE119	7¢ Green & Bk.	5.00	4.00
RE120	7½¢ Green & Bk.	8.00	5.00
RE121	8¢ Green & Bk.	4.00	3.50
RE122	9¢ Green & Bk.	9.00	8.00
RE123	10¢ Green & Bk.	4.00	1.00

RE153

1942 "Series of 1941" (continued)

Scott No.		Fine Unused	Used
RE124	11¼¢ Green & Bk.	4.50	4.50
RE125	12¢ Green & Bk.	6.50	5.50
RE126	14¢ Green & Bk.	22.50	22.50
RE127	15¢ Green & Bk.	4.25	2.75
RE128	16¢ Green & Bk.	10.00	7.50
RE129	19 1/5¢ Grn & Bk.	135.00	7.50
RE130	20¢ Green & Bk.	5.50	1.75
RE131	24¢ Green & Bk.	4.00	.15
RE133	30¢ Green & Bk.	1.15	.20
RE134	32¢ Green & Bk.	140.00	7.00
RE135	36¢ Green & Bk.	2.75	.20
RE136	40¢ Green & Bk.	2.25	.15
RE137	45¢ Green & Bk.	5.50	.25
RE138	48¢ Green & Bk.	16.00	6.50
RE139	50¢ Green & Bk.	8.75	6.75
RE140	60¢ Green & Bk.	3.00	.15
RE141	72¢ Green & Bk.	9.00	1.00
RE142	80¢ Green & Bk.	...	9.00
RE143	84¢ Green & Bk.	...	55.00
RE144	90¢ Green & Bk.	15.00	.20
RE145	96¢ Green & Bk.	11.50	.20
RE146-RE172 Denomination in 2 lines			
RE146	$1.20 Yellow Green and Black	5.50	.15
RE147	$1.44 Y.G. & Bk.	1.50	.15
RE148	$1.50 Y.G. & Bk.	100.00	60.00
RE149	$1.60 Y.G. & Bk.	9.00	1.00
RE150	$1.68 Y.G. & Bk.	95.00	45.00
RE151	$1.80 Y.G. & Bk.	2.75	.15
RE152	$1.92 Y.G. & Bk.	50.00	35.00
RE153	$2.40 Y.G. & Bk.	8.25	1.00
RE154	$3 Y. green & Bk.	65.00	35.00
RE155	$3.36 Y.G. & Bk.	70.00	25.00
RE156	$3.60 Y.G. & Bk.	115.00	5.50
RE157	$4 Y. green & Bk.	22.50	5.00
RE158	$4.80 Y.G. & Bk.	115.00	3.00
RE159	$5 Y.green & Bk.	13.50	9.00
RE160	$7.20 Y.G. & Bk.	17.50	.45
RE161	$10 Y.G. & Bk.	185.00	135.00
RE162	$20 Y.G. & Bk.	100.00	70.00
RE163	$50 Y.G. & Bk.	100.00	70.00
RE164	$100 Y.G. & Bk.	275.00	27.50
RE165	$200 Y.G. & Bk.	140.00	18.50
RE166	$500 Y.G. & Bk.	...	140.00
RE167	$600 Y.G. & Bk.	...	120.00
RE169	$1000 Y.G. & Bk.	...	185.00
RE171	$3000 Y.G. & Bk.	...	180.00

1949 "Series of 1941" Rouletted 7
#RE173-RE182 Denominations in one line.

RE173	$1 Y.green & Bk.	4.00	1.40
RE174	$2 Y.green & Bk.	6.50	1.85
RE175	$4 Y.green & Bk.	...	350.00
RE176	$5 Y.green & Bk.	...	75.00
RE177	$6 Y.green & Bk.	...	350.00
RE178	$7 Y.green & Bk.	...	50.00
RE179	$8 Y.green & Bk.	...	325.00
RE180	$10 Y.green & Bk.	8.75	5.00
RE181	$20 Y.green & Bk.	18.00	3.50

1951-54 "Series of 1941" Rouletted 7

RE183	3 2/5¢ Grn. & Bk.	50.00	45.00
RE184	8½¢ Green & Bk.	27.50	18.50
RE185	13 2/5¢ Grn. & Bk.	90.00	70.00
RE186	17¢ Green & Bk.	14.00	13.50
RE187	20 2/5¢ Gr. & Bk.	100.00	55.00
RE188	33½¢ Green & Bk.	80.00	65.00
RE189	38¼¢ Green & Bk.	110.00	80.00
RE190	40 4/5¢ Grn. & Bk.	3.50	.60
RE191	51¢ Green & Bk.	3.50	1.00
RE192	67¢ Green & Bk.	10.75	3.50
RE193	68¢ Green & Bk.	3.50	.60
RE194	80 2/5¢ Grn. & Bk.	110.00	90.00
RE195-RE197 Denominations in two lines in smaller letters			
RE195	$1.50¾ Y.G. & Bk.	45.00	35.00
RE196	$1.60 4/5 Y.G. & Bk.	4.00	.55
RE197	$1.88 3/10 YG & Bk.	200.00	70.00
RE198	$1.60 4/5 YG & Bk.	27.50	5.50
RE199	$2.01 Y.green & bk.	3.50	.75

1951-54 "Series of 1941" Rouletted 7

Scott No.		Fine Unused	Used
#RE198-RE204 Denominations in two lines in large letters as #RE146-72			
RE200	$2.68 Y.green & Bk.	3.50	1.20
RE201	$4.08 Y.green & Bk.	60.00	30.00
RE202	$5.76 Y.& Bk.	200.00	100.00
RE203	$8.16 Y.green & Bk.	16.00	6.00

PLAYING CARD STAMPS (VF+ 30%)

1894-1902 Rouletted

RF2 RF19

RF1	2¢ Lake "On Hand".	.60	.40
RF2	2¢ Ultramarine, "Act of.", Unwmk.	12.50	2.50
RF3	2¢ Blue, Wmtk.	4.50	.50
RF4	2¢ Blue, Perf. 12	...	41.50

1917 Various Surcharges

RF6	7¢ on 2¢ Blue "17" ...		40.00
RF9	7¢ on 2¢ "7 CENTS"	...	8.75
RF10	7¢ on 2¢ Blue "7¢"..	...	55.00
RF11	Blue, Imperf.	37.50	27.50
RF12	Blue, Roul. 14	...	200.00
RF13	7¢ Blue, Roul. 9½	...	32.50
RF14	8¢ on 2¢ Roul. 7	...	70.00
RF16	8¢ on 2¢ Blue	100.00	1.00
RF17	(8¢) Blue, Roul. 7	16.50	1.25
RF18	8¢ Blue, Roul. 7	...	32.50
RF19	10¢ Blue, Roul. 7	10.00	.40
RF20	10¢ Perf. 10 Coil	...	.25
RF21	10¢ Flat, Perf. 11	21.00	5.00
RF22	10¢ Blue, Perf. 10	11.00	4.00

1929-1940

RF23

RF23	10¢ Perf. 10 Coil	...	.15
RF24	10¢ Flat, Perf. 10	11.50	1.25
RF25	10¢ Flat, Perf. 11	11.50	1.25
RF26	Blue, Perf. 10 Coil	...	.40
RF27	Blue, Perf. 10 Coil	2.75	.15
RF28	Blue, Flat. Pf. 11	5.00	.75
RF29	Blue, Perf. 10x11	160.00	...

SILVER TAX STAMPS (VF + 30%)

RG 1

RG 111

1934 Documentary Stamps of 1917 Overprinted, D.L. Wmk., Perf. 11

Scott's No.		Fine Unused	Used
RG1	1¢ Carm rose	1.00	.75
RG2	2¢ Carm rose	1.50	.50
RG3	3¢ Carm rose	1.50	.75
RG4	4¢ Carm rose	2.00	1.50
RG5	5¢ Carm rose	3.25	1.50
RG6	8¢ Carm rose	4.25	2.75
RG7	10¢ Carm rose	4.50	2.25
RG8	20¢ Carm rose	6.50	3.00
RG9	25¢ Carm rose	6.75	4.00
RG10	40¢ Carm rose	7.25	5.00
RG11	50¢ Carm rose	6.50	6.00
RG12	80¢ Carm rose	12.50	8.50
RG13	$1 Green	20.00	10.00
RG14	$2 Rose	25.00	13.50
RG15	$3 Violet	52.50	23.50
RG16	$4 Yellow brn	40.00	16.00
RG17	$5 Dark blue	47.50	16.00
RG18	$10 Orange	67.50	16.00

SILVER TAX (continued)

Scott No.		Fine Unused	Used
	Without Gum, Perf. 12		
RG19	$30 Vermillion	110.00	40.00
	Cut cancel	...	17.50
RG20	$60 Brown	130.00	62.50
	Cut cancel	...	25.00
RG21	$100 Green	130.00	27.50
RG22	$500 Blue	375.00	195.00
	Cut cancel	...	85.00
RG23	$1000 Orange	...	90.00
	Cut cancel	...	52.50

1936 Same Ovpt., 11 mm between words "SILVER TAX"

RG26	$100 Green	150.00	60.00
RG27	$1000 Orange	...	450.00

1940 Documentary Stamps of 1917
D.L. Wmk., Perf. 11, Overprinted
SERIES 1940

SILVER TAX

RG37	1¢ Rose pink	16.00	...
RG38	2¢ Rose pink	16.00	...
RG39	3¢ Rose pink	16.00	...
RG40	4¢ Rose pink	17.00	...
RG41	5¢ Rose pink	9.50	...
RG42	8¢ Rose pink	17.00	...
RG43	10¢ Rose pink	16.00	...
RG44	20¢ Rose pink	17.00	...
RG45	25¢ Rose pink	16.00	...
RG46	40¢ Rose pink	22.50	...
RG47	50¢ Rose pink	22.50	...
RG48	80¢ Rose pink	22.50	...
RG49	$1 Green	100.00	...
RG50	$2 Rose	160.00	...
RG51	$3 Violet	210.00	...
RG52	$4 Yellow brn	425.00	...
RG53	$5 Dark blue	525.00	...
RG54	$10 Orange	575.00	...

Ovpt in Blk. SERIES OF 1941 pf.11 (Gray)

RG58	1¢ Hamilton	3.50	...
RG59	2¢ Wolcott, Jr	3.50	...
RG60	3¢ Dexter	3.50	...
RG61	4¢ Gallatin	4.50	...
RG62	5¢ Campbell	6.00	...
RG63	8¢ Dallas	6.50	...
RG64	10¢ Crawford	7.50	...
RG65	20¢ Rush	12.00	...
RG66	25¢ Ingham	15.00	...
RG67	40¢ McLane	23.00	...
RG68	50¢ Duane	30.00	...
RG69	80¢ Taney	52.50	...
RG70	$1 Woodbury	65.00	25.00
RG71	$2 Ewing	170.00	45.00
RG72	$3 Forward	140.00	55.00
RG73	$4 Spencer	210.00	65.00
RG74	$5 Bibb	160.00	65.00
RG75	$10 Walker	275.00	85.00
RG76	$20 Meredith	425.00	265.00

Without Gum, Perf. 12

RG77	$30 Corwin	225.00	125.00
	Cut cancel	...	65.00
RG79	$60 Cobb	...	175.00
	Cut cancel	...	85.00
RG80	$100 Thomas	...	275.00
	Cut cancel	...	90.00

#RG58-82 Overprinted SERIES OF 1942

RG83	1¢ Hamilton	2.00	...
RG84	2¢ Wolcott, Jr	2.00	...
RG85	3¢ Dexter	2.00	...
RG86	4¢ Gallatin	2.00	...
RG87	5¢ Campbell	2.00	...
RG88	8¢ Dallas	4.50	...
RG89	10¢ Crawford	5.00	...
RG90	20¢ Rush	7.50	...
RG91	25¢ Ingham	15.00	...
RG92	40¢ McLane	17.50	...
RG93	50¢ Duane	17.50	...
RG94	80¢ Taney	50.00	...
RG95	$1 Woodbury	60.00	...
RG96	$2 Ewing	60.00	...
RG97	$3 Forward	110.00	...
RG98	$4 Spencer	110.00	...
RG99	$5 Bibb	120.00	...
RG100	$10 Walker	375.00	...
RG101	$20 Meredith	475.00	...

1944 Silver Stamps of 1941 w/o ovpt.

RG108	1¢ Hamilton	1.00	...
RG109	2¢ Wolcutt, Jr	1.00	...
RG110	3¢ Dexter	1.00	...
RG111	4¢ Gallatin	1.00	...
RG112	5¢ Campbell	2.10	...
RG113	8¢ Dallas	3.15	...
RG114	10¢ Crawford	3.15	...
RG115	20¢ Rush	6.50	...
RG116	25¢ Ingham	8.25	...

SILVER TAX (continued)

Scott No.		Fine Unused	Used
RG117	40¢ McLane	12.75	...
RG118	50¢ Duane	12.75	...
RG119	80¢ Taney	18.50	...
RG120	$1 Woodbury	40.00	15.00
RG121	$2 Ewing	57.50	35.00
RG122	$3 Forward	65.00	26.50
RG123	$4 Spencer	85.00	60.00
RG124	$5 Bibb	90.00	28.50
RG125	$10 Walker	125.00	50.00
	Cut cancel	...	13.50
RG126	$20 Meredith	425.00	375.00

Without Gum, Perf. 12

RG127	$30 Corwin	250.00	110.00
	Cut cancel	...	50.00
RG128	$50 Gutherie	525.00	500.00
	Cut cancel	...	285.00
RG129	$60 Cobb	...	350.00
	Cut cancel	...	150.00
RG130	$100 Thomas	...	32.50
	Cut cancel	...	12.50
RG131	$500 Dix	...	400.00
	Cut cancel	...	225.00
RG132	$1000 Chase	...	135.00
	Cut cancel	...	65.00

CIGARETTE TUBE STAMPS
(Very Fine + 30%)

RH 1
Doc. Stamp of 1917 ovpt., D.L. Wmk.

RH1	1¢ Carm rose ('19)	.50	.25
	Perf. 11		
RH2	1¢ Carm rose ('29)	27.50	9.50
	RH4		
RH3	1¢ Rose (1933)	2.25	.90

RH4	2¢ Rose (1933)	6.75	1.75

POTATO TAX STAMPS (VF + 20%)

RI 1

Issue of 1935

Scott's No.		F-VF Unused
RI1	¾¢ Carm rose	.25
RI2	1¼¢ Black brn	.50
RI3	2¼¢ Yellow grn	.50
RI4	3¢ Light Violet	.50
RI5	3¾¢ Olive Bistre	.50
RI6	7½¢ Orange brn	1.35
RI7	11¼¢ Deep orange	1.65
RI8	18¾¢ Violet brn	4.00
RI9	37½¢ Red orange	4.00
RI10	75¢ Blue	4.00
RI11	93¾¢ Rose lake	6.50
RI12	$1.12½¢ Green	11.50
RI13	$1.50 Yellow brn	10.50

TOBACCO SALE TAX STAMPS
1934 Doc. Issue of 1917, Ovpt.
D.L. Wmk., pf. 11 (VF + 30%)

RJ 1   **RJ 7**

Scott's No.		Fine Unused	Used
RJ1	1¢ Carm rose	.35	.15
RJ2	2¢ Carm rose	.35	.20
RJ3	5¢ Carm rose	1.25	.35
RJ4	10¢ Carm rose	1.50	.35
RJ5	25¢ Carm rose	4.00	1.50
RJ6	50¢ Carm rose	4.00	1.50
RJ7	$1 Green	8.50	1.75
RJ8	$2 Rose	16.00	1.75
RJ9	$5 Dark blue	22.50	3.75
RJ10	$10 Orange	32.50	10.00
RJ11	$20 Olive bistre	80.00	12.50

NARCOTIC TAX STAMPS (VF + 30%)

1919 Doc. Issue of 1914, D.L. Wmk., pf. 10, Handstamped "NARCOTIC" in Magenta, Blue or Black

RJA1	1¢ Rose	75.00	50.00

1919 Doc. Issue of 1917, D.L. Wmk., perf. 11, Handstamped "NARCOTIC," "Narcotic," "NARCOTICS," or "ACT/NARCOTIC/1918" in Magenta, Blue, Black, Violet or Red

RJA9	1¢ Carm rose	1.75	1.70
RJA10	2¢ Carm rose	4.50	3.75
RJA11	3¢ Carm rose	25.00	25.00
RJA12	4¢ Carm rose	9.00	8.00
RJA13	5¢ Carm rose	12.75	12.50
RJA14	8¢ Carm rose	10.50	10.00
RJA15	10¢ Carm rose	45.00	16.50
RJA16	20¢ Carm rose	50.00	50.00
RJA17	25¢ Carm rose	37.50	30.00
RJA18	40¢ Carm rose	80.00	80.00
RJA19	50¢ Carm rose	17.50	15.00
RJA20	80¢ Carm rose	95.00	85.00
RJA21	$1 Green	85.00	45.00

RJA 33

1919 Doc. Issue of 1917, D.L. Wmk., perf. 11, Overprinted
NARCOTIC
17½ mm wide

RJA33	1¢ Carm rose	1.00	.60
RJA34	2¢ Carm rose	1.50	1.00
RJA35	3¢ Carm rose	32.50	22.50
RJA36	4¢ Carm rose	5.00	3.00
RJA37	5¢ Carm rose	12.00	9.00
RJA38	8¢ Carm rose	21.50	16.50
RJA39	10¢ Carm rose	3.00	3.00
RJA40	25¢ Carm rose	24.00	16.50

Overprint Reading Up

RJA41	$1 Green	40.00	17.50

Narcotic Issues of 1919-1970, D.L. Wmk.

RJA44b

NARCOTICS TAX (cont.)

Scott's No.		Fine Used a.Impf.	b.roult.
RJA42	1¢ Violet	4.25	.25
RJA43	1¢ Violet	.50	.25
RJA44	2¢ Violet	1.00	.50
RJA45	3¢ Violet	...	100.00
RJA46	1¢ Violet	2.25	.75
RJA47	2¢ Violet	1.75	.75
RJA49	4¢ Violet	...	7.00
RJA50	6¢ Violet	38.50	5.00
RJA51	6¢ Violet	...	1.00
RJA52	8¢ Violet	45.00	3.00
RJA53	9¢ Violet	75.00	16.50
RJA54	10¢ Violet	25.00	.50
RJA55	16¢ Violet	52.50	4.00
RJA56	18¢ Violet	100.00	8.50
RJA57	18¢ Violet	135.00	20.00
RJA58	20¢ Violet	350.00	175.00
	"Cents" below value		
RJA59	1¢ Violet	50.00	10.00
RJA60	2¢ Violet	...	18.50
RJA61	4¢ Violet	42.50	37.50
RJA62	5¢ Violet	...	25.00
RJA63	6¢ Violet	65.00	22.50
RJA64	8¢ Violet	...	40.00
RJA65	9¢ Violet	21.50	17.00
RJA66	10¢ Violet	12.50	14.00
RJA67	16¢ Violet	15.00	12.50
RJA68	18¢ Violet	350.00	400.00
RJA69	19¢ Violet	10.00	...
RJA70	20¢ Violet	350.00	195.00
RJA71	25¢ Violet	...	23.50
RJA72	40¢ Violet	425.00	...
RJA73	$1 Green	...	1.25
RJA74	$1.28 Green	25.00	10.50

Imperf.

1963 Denom. added in blk. by rubber plate (similar to 1959 Postage Dues)

		Fine Unused	Used
RJA105	1¢ Violet	85.00	75.00

1964 Denomination on Stamp Plate

RJA106	1¢ Violet	80.00	5.50

CONSULAR SERVICE FEE STAMPS
(Very Fine + 30%)

RK 5   **RK 36**

1906 "Consular Service" Pf. 12

Scott No.		Fine Used
RK1	25¢ Dark green	40.00
RK2	50¢ Carmine	52.50
RK3	$1 Dark violet	5.75
RK4	$2 Brown	4.25
RK5	$2.50 Dark blue	1.50
RK6	$5 Brown red	15.00
RK7	$10 Orange	47.50

Perf. 10

RK8	25¢ Dark green	40.00
RK9	50¢ Carmine	45.00
RK10	$1 Dark violet	250.00
RK11	$2 Brown	52.50
RK12	$2.50 Dark blue	13.50
RK13	$5 Brown red	70.00

Consular Service, Pf. 11

RK14	25¢ Dark green	47.50
RK15	50¢ Carmine	70.00
RK16	$1 Dark violet	1.70
RK17	$2 Brown	2.25
RK18	$2.50 Dark blue	.75
RK19	$5 Brown red	3.25
RK20	$9 Gray	11.00
RK21	$10 Orange	22.50

1924 "Foreign Service" Pf. 11

RK22	$1 Dark violet	52.50
RK23	$2 Brown	60.00
RK24	$2.50 Dark blue	8.75
RK25	$5 Brown red	40.00
RK26	$9 Gray	165.00

CONSULAR SERVICE (cont.)

Scott No.		Fine Used

Issue of 1925-52 Perf. 10

RK27	$1 Violet	17.00
RK28	$2 Brown	43.50
RK29	$2.50 Ultramarine	1.35
RK30	$5 Carmine	8.00
RK31	$9 Gray	30.00

Perf. 11

RK32	25¢ Green	47.50
RK33	50¢ Orange	47.50
RK34	$1 Violet	2.50
RK35	$2 Brown	2.50
RK36	$2.50 Blue	.50
RK37	$5 Carmine	3.25
RK38	$9 Gray	12.00
RK39	$10 Blue gray	57.50
RK40	$20 Violet	65.00

1887 CUSTOMS FEES (VF + 30%)

RL 5

RL1	20¢ Dull Rose	1.00
RL2	30¢ Orange	1.75
RL3	40¢ Green	2.00
RL4	50¢ Dark blue	3.75
RL5	60¢ Red violet	1.75
RL6	70¢ Brown violet	27.50
RL7	80¢ Brown	67.50
RL8	90¢ Black	80.00

MOTOR VEHICLE USE STAMPS
(Very Fine + 30%)

RV 6   RV 42

1942 Gum on Back

Scott No.		F-VF Unused
RV1	$2.09 Lt.green (used .50)	1.00

Gum on Face, Inscription on Back

RV2	$1.67 Light green	13.50
RV3	$1.25 Light green	10.00
RV4	84¢ Light green	12.00
RV5	42¢ Light green	11.00

1942 Gum and Control # on Face

RV6	$5.00 Rose red (used .90)	2.50
RV7	$4.59 Rose red	20.00
RV8	$4.17 Rose red	25.00
RV9	$3.75 Rose red	25.00
RV10	$3.34 Rose red	25.00
RV11	$2.92 Rose red	25.00

1943

RV12	$2.50 Rose red	25.00
RV13	$2.09 Rose red	20.00
RV14	$1.67 Rose red	15.00
RV15	$1.25 Rose red	15.00
RV16	84¢ Rose red	15.00
RV17	42¢ Rose red	15.00
RV18	$5.00 Yellow (used .75)	2.50
RV19	$4.59 Yellow	25.00
RV20	$4.17 Yellow	35.00
RV21	$3.75 Yellow	35.00
RV22	$3.34 Yellow	42.50
RV23	$2.92 Yellow	50.00

MOTOR VEHICLE (cont.)

Scott No.		F-VF Unused

1944

RV24	$2.50 Yellow	52.50
RV25	$2.09 Yellow	36.50
RV26	$1.67 Yellow	25.00
RV27	$1.25 Yellow	25.00
RV28	84¢ Yellow	21.00
RV29	42¢ Yellow	21.00

**Gum on Face
Control # and Inscription on Back**

RV30	$5.00 Violet (used .75)	2.50
RV31	$4.59 Violet	41.50
RV32	$4.17 Violet	30.00
RV33	$3.75 Violet	30.00
RV34	$3.34 Violet	25.00
RV35	$2.92 Violet	25.00

1945

RV36	$2.50 Violet	25.00
RV37	$2.09 Violet	20.00
RV38	$1.67 Violet	20.00
RV39	$1.25 Violet	20.00
RV40	84¢ Violet	15.00
RV41	42¢ Violet	12.50

1945
Bright blue green
& Yellow green

RV42	$5.00 (used .75)	2.50
RV43	$4.59	30.00
RV44	$4.17	30.00
RV45	$3.75	26.50
RV46	$3.34	25.00
RV47	$2.92	20.00

1946
Bright blue green
& Yellow green

RV48	$2.50	20.00
RV49	$2.09	20.00
RV50	$1.67	14.50
RV51	$1.25	12.50
RV52	84¢	12.50
RV53	42¢	9.50

BOATING STAMPS (VF+20%)

RVB 2

		NH F-VF
	1960 Rouletted	
RVB1	$1.00 Rose red,blk.#	35.00
	Plate Blk. of 4	160.00
RVB2	$3.00 Blue, red #	40.00
	Plate Blk. of 4	180.00

DISTILLED SPIRITS (VF + 20%)

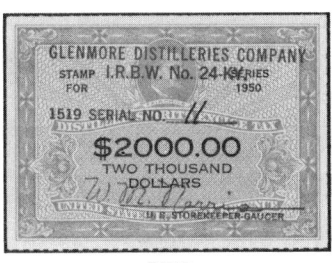

RX18

1950
Inscribed
"STAMP FOR SERIES 1950"
Yellow, Green & Black

DISTILLED SPIRITS (cont.)

Scott's No.		Fine Unused	Used
RX1	1¢	27.50	22.50
RX2	3¢	90.00	85.00
RX3	5¢	18.50	15.00
RX4	10¢	16.50	13.50
RX5	25¢	9.50	7.50
RX6	50¢	9.50	7.50
RX7	$1	2.50	2.00
RX8	$3	20.00	16.50
RX9	$5	6.50	5.00
RX10	$10	3.00	2.50
RX11	$25	13.50	11.50
RX12	$50	7.50	6.50
RX13	$100	5.50	4.00
RX14	$300	25.00	22.50
RX15	$500	16.50	12.50
RX16	$1000	9.50	7.50
RX17	$1500	52.50	42.50
RX18	$2000	5.50	4.50
RX19	$3000	23.50	17.50
RX20	$5000	23.50	17.50
RX21	$10,000	27.50	22.50
RX22	$20,000	35.00	28.50
RX23	$30,000	75.00	55.00
RX24	$40,000	800.00	600.00
RX25	$50,000	85.00	75.00

1952
DISTILLED SPIRITS
Inscription
"STAMP FOR SERIES 1950"
omitted

Yellow, Green & Black

		Fine Punch Cancel
RX28	5¢	35.00
RX29	10¢	4.00
RX30	25¢	15.00
RX31	50¢	11.50
RX32	$1	1.75
RX33	$3	21.50
RX34	$5	23.50
RX35	$10	1.75
RX36	$25	9.50
RX37	$50	23.50
RX38	$100	2.25
RX39	$300	7.50
RX40	$500	32.50
RX41	$1000	6.50
RX43	$2000	57.50
RX44	$3000	800.00
RX45	$5000	45.00
RX46	$10,000	65.00

FIREARMS TRANSFER TAX STAMPS
(VF + 30%)
Documentary Stamp of 1917
Overprinted Vertically in Black

NATIONAL FIREARMS ACT

		Without Gum	Fine Unused
RY1	$1 Green (1934)		300.00

RY 2,4,6
Without Gum
$200 Face Value

RY2	Dark blue & red Serial #1-1500 (1934)	1250.00
RY4	Dull blue & red Serial #1501-3000 (1950)	500.00
RY6	Dull blue & red Serial #3001 & up (1974)	225.00

Firearm Transfer Tax (cont.)
With Gum

		Fine Unused
RY3	$1 Green (1938)	75.00
RY5	$5 Red (1960)	20.00

1946 RECTIFICATION TAX STAMPS
(VF+20%)

Rectification Tax Stamps were for the use of rectifiers in paying tax on liquor in bottling tanks. Used stamps have staple holes.

RZ12

		Fine Unused	Used
RZ1	1¢	7.50	3.00
RZ2	3¢	25.00	8.50
RZ3	5¢	16.50	2.50
RZ4	10¢	16.50	2.50
RZ5	25¢	16.50	3.00
RZ6	50¢	20.00	5.00
RZ7	$1	20.00	5.00
RZ8	$3	90.00	17.50
RZ9	$5	37.50	10.00
RZ10	$10	30.00	3.25
RZ11	$25	90.00	10.50
RZ12	$50	90.00	8.00
RZ13	$100	...	9.50
RZ14	$300	...	9.50
RZ15	$500	...	9.50
RZ16	$1000	...	15.00
RZ17	$1500	...	40.00
RZ18	$2000	...	75.00

RW 1

RW 12

On each stamp the words "Void After ..." show a date 1 year later than the actual date of issue.
Even though RW1 has on it "Void After June 30, 1935," the stamp was issued in 1934.
RW1-RW25, RW31 Plate Blocks of 6 Must Have Margins on Two Sides

RW1-RW10 VF Used + 50% (B)

Scott's No.		VF	NH F-VF	Unused VF	F-VF	Used F-VF
RW1	1934, $1 Mallards....................	875.00	600.00	495.00	350.00	125.00
RW2	1935, $1 Canvasbacks	775.00	525.00	450.00	350.00	145.00
RW3	1936, $1 Canada Geese	400.00	290.00	240.00	170.00	65.00
RW4	1937, $1 Scaup Duck	340.00	250.00	185.00	140.00	45.00
RW5	1938, $1 Pintails.................	450.00	285.00	225.00	160.00	45.00
RW6	1939, $1 Teal	230.00	150.00	120.00	90.00	40.00
RW7	1940, $1 Mallards.................	230.00	150.00	120.00	90.00	40.00
RW8	1941, $1 Ruddy Ducks............	230.00	150.00	120.00	90.00	40.00
RW9	1942, $1 Baldplates.........	235.00	150.00	125.00	90.00	40.00
RW10	1943, $1 Ducks	90.00	60.00	60.00	45.00	40.00

RW1-RW12 VF Used + 50%   RW13-RW15 VF Used + 40%

RW11	1944, $1 Geese.................	105.00	65.00	65.00	50.00	25.00
RW12	1945, $1 Shovellers.............	75.00	50.00	45.00	30.00	25.00
RW13	1946, $1 Redheads.............	55.00	37.50	45.00	30.00	14.00
RW14	1947, $1 Snow Geese.........	55.00	37.50	45.00	30.00	14.00
RW15	1948, $1 Buffleheads.........	60.00	45.00	45.00	30.00	14.00

Plate Blocks	VF	NH F-VF	Unused F-VF	Plate Blocks	VF	NH F-VF	Unused F-VF
RW10 (6)	695.00	475.00	395.00	RW13 (6).....	360.00	300.00	225.00
RW11 (6)	750.00	475.00	395.00	RW14 (6).....	360.00	300.00	225.00
RW12 (6)	475.00	350.00	250.00	RW15 (6).....	395.00	300.00	225.00

RW 16

RW 21

1949-58 Issues VF Used + 40%

RW16	1949, $2 Goldeneyes	72.50	55.00	45.00	35.00	15.00
RW17	1950, $2 Swans	85.00	55.00	50.00	40.00	12.00
RW18	1951, $2 Gadwalls...................	85.00	60.00	50.00	40.00	12.00
RW19	1952, $2 Harlequins	85.00	60.00	50.00	40.00	8.00
RW20	1953, $2 Teal	90.00	60.00	50.00	40.00	8.00
RW21	1954, $2 Ring-necked.................	85.00	60.00	50.00	40.00	8.00
RW22	1955, $2 Blue-necked.........	85.00	60.00	50.00	40.00	8.00
RW23	1956, $2 Merganser...........	90.00	60.00	50.00	40.00	8.00
RW24	1957, $2 Eider	85.00	60.00	50.00	40.00	8.00
RW25	1958, $2 Canada Geese	85.00	60.00	50.00	40.00	8.00

Plate Blocks	VF	NH F-VF	Unused F-VF	Plate Blocks	VF	NH F-VF	Unused F-VF
RW16 (6)....	425.00	350.00	275.00	RW21 (6)....	550.00	400.00	325.00
RW17 (6)....	550.00	400.00	295.00	RW22 (6)....	550.00	400.00	325.00
RW18 (6)....	550.00	400.00	295.00	RW23 (6)....	575.00	400.00	325.00
RW19 (6)....	550.00	400.00	295.00	RW24 (6)....	550.00	400.00	325.00
RW20 (6)....	565.00	400.00	325.00	RW25 (6)....	550.00	400.00	325.00

RW 26

RW 32

1959-71 Issues VF Used + 30%

Scott's No.		Pl# Blocks F-VF NH	VF NH	F-VF NH	F-VF Unus.	Used
RW26	1959, $3 Retriever........................	425.00	120.00	90.00	65.00	8.00
RW27	1960, $3 Redhead Ducks..............	375.00	105.00	75.00	50.00	8.00
RW28	1961, $3 Mallard.......................	395.00	115.00	80.00	52.50	8.00
RW29	1962, $3 Pintail Ducks..................	435.00	125.00	90.00	60.00	9.00
RW30	1963, $3 Brant Landing.............	410.00	125.00	90.00	60.00	9.00
RW31	1964, $3 Hawaiian Nene...........(6)	2200.00	125.00	90.00	60.00	9.00
RW32	1965, $3 Canvasback Ducks..........	410.00	125.00	90.00	60.00	9.00
RW33	1966, $3 Whistling Swans........	435.00	125.00	90.00	60.00	9.00
RW34	1967, $3 Old Squaw Ducks	435.00	125.00	90.00	60.00	9.00
RW35	1968, $3 Hooded Mergansers........	280.00	70.00	55.00	37.50	9.00
RW36	1969, $3 White-winged Scooters....	280.00	70.00	55.00	37.50	7.00
RW37	1970, $3 Ross's Geese..............	280.00	70.00	55.00	35.00	7.00
RW38	1971, $3 Cinnamon Teals..............	160.00	47.50	35.00	25.00	7.00

RW 39

RW 46

1972-79 Issues VF Used + 25%

Scott's No.		VF Pl# Blk	NH VF	F-VF	Used F-VF
RW39	1972, $5 Emperor Geese	135.00	30.00	22.50	7.00
RW40	1973, $5 Steller's Eiders	115.00	27.50	20.00	7.00
RW41	1974, $5 Wood Ducks	95.00	24.00	18.00	7.00
RW42	1975, $5 Decoy & Canvasbacks	70.00	18.75	14.00	7.00
RW43	1976, $5 Canada Geese	60.00	18.75	14.00	7.00
RW44	1977, $5 Pair of Ross's Geese	62.50	18.75	14.00	7.00
RW45	1978, $5 Hooded Merganser Drake	60.00	18.75	14.00	7.00
RW46	1979, $7.50 Green-winged Teal	70.00	20.00	17.00	7.00

RW 51

RW 54

1980-89 Issues VF Used + 25%

RW47	1980, $7.50 Mallards	70.00	21.00	17.00	7.00
RW48	1981, $7.50 Ruddy Ducks	70.00	21.00	17.00	7.00
RW49	1982, $7.50 Canvasbacks	70.00	21.00	17.00	7.00
RW50	1983, $7.50 Pintails	70.00	21.00	17.00	7.00
RW51	1984, $7.50 Wigeon	70.00	21.00	17.00	7.00
RW52	1985, $7.50 Cinnamon Teal	70.00	21.00	17.00	7.00
RW53	1986, $7.50 Fulvous Whistling Duck	70.00	21.00	17.00	7.00
RW54	1987, $10 Red Head Ducks	90.00	25.00	20.00	10.00
RW55	1988, $10 Snow Goose	90.00	25.00	20.00	10.00
RW56	1989, $12.50 Lesser Scaups	100.00	28.00	22.50	10.00

RW 57

RW 64

1990-98 Issues VF Used + 25%

RW57	1990, $12.50 Blk-Bellied Whistl. Duck.........	100.00	28.00	22.50	10.00
RW58	1991, $15.00 King Eiders	135.00	32.50	27.50	12.50
RW59	1992, $15.00 Spectacled Eider	135.00	32.50	27.50	12.50
RW60	1993, $15.00 Canvasbacks	135.00	32.50	27.50	12.50
RW61	1994, $15.00 Redbreasted Merganser...........	135.00	32.50	27.50	12.50
RW62	1995, $15.00 Mallards	135.00	32.50	27.50	12.50
RW63	1996, $15.00 Surf Scoter.............................	135.00	32.50	27.50	12.50
RW64	1997, $15.00 Canada Goose........................	135.00	32.50	27.50	12.50
RW65	1998, $15.00 Barrow's Goldeneye	135.00	32.50	27.50	12.50
RW65	1998, Same, Self-Adhesive............................	...	32.50	27.50	12.50
RW66	1999, $15.00 Greater Scaup.........................	135.00	32.50	27.50	12.50
RW66A	1999, Same, Self-Adhesive............... ...	...	32.50	27.50	

Michael Jaffe Stamps is Your Full Service Duck Dealer

MICHAEL JAFFE STAMPS IS YOUR FULL-SERVICE HEADQUARTERS FOR:
* Federal Hunting Permit Stamps
* State & Foreign Duck Stamps
* Duck Stamp Prints
* Indian Reservation Stamps
ALL AT BUDGET-FRIENDLY PRICES!!

Why shop around when you can find 99% of all pictorial Duck stamps ever issued (including foreign) in stock at Michael Jaffe for very competitive prices? Michael Jaffe is also your best source for Duck prints...albums...first day covers... and just about everything else related to Ducks. *And Michael Jaffe guarantees 100% satisfaction on every purchase.*

The Beginning of State Duck Stamps

One of the main purposes of the state waterfowl stamp programs have been to generate revenue for waterfowl conservation and restoration projects. In addition, waterfowl stamps validate hunting licenses and often serve as a control to limit the harvest within a specific geographical area.

The federal government recognized the need to protect waterfowl in the U.S. with the Migratory Bird Treaty Act of 1918. On March 16, 1934, President Franklin Roosevelt signed the Migratory Bird Hunting Stamp Act into law. Sale of Federal waterfowl stamps provided funding for the purchase and development of federal waterfowl areas.

Soon, state and local governments began requiring hunters to purchase waterfowl hunting stamps. Since these agencies did not have collectors in mind, most of the early stamps are printed text only. These include Pymatuning, Marion County, Honey Lake and the states of California, Illinois, North and South Dakota as well as several Indian Reservations.

Pictorial state waterfowl stamps saw their beginning in 1971, when California commissioned Paul Johnson to design the state's first duck stamp, a relatively simple rendition of a pair of pintails in flight. California's decision to issue pictorial stamps were prompted by the growing number of collectors interested in fish and game stamps. State officials estimated that any added production costs could be more than made up through the increased sale of stamps to collectors. In 1971, Iowa became the second state to initiate a pictorial waterfowl stamp program..

The appearance of new pictorial issues, combined with the publication of E.L. Vanderford's *Handbook of Fish and Game Stamps* in 1973, led to a surge in waterfowl stamp collecting.

Maryland and Massachusetts began to issue their stamps in 1974. All Massachusetts stamps depict waterfowl decoys by famous carvers. Illinois started a pictorial stamp program in 1975. The face value of this stamp was $5, and half of the revenue obtained through its sale went to Ducks Unlimited, a private conservation organization which has done much to aid in waterfowl restoration throughout North America.

These pictorial stamp programs were so successful in raising funds for waterfowl conservation projects that many additional states adopted similar stamp programs. Between 1976 and 1980, 13 additional states began issuing pictorial waterfowl stamps. Tennessee became the first state to issue separate pictorial waterfowl stamps for non-residents. These non-resident stamps were discontinued after only two years.

In response to an increasing demand for waterfowl stamps on the part of stamp collectors, many states started to print their stamps in two different formats in the 1980's. There was one type, usually printed in booklet panes, for license agents to issue to hunters, and a second type, usually printed in sheets, that was sold to collectors.

The 1981 Arkansas stamp was printed in booklet panes of thirty and issued with protective booklet covers to license agents. Sheets of thirty, without protective covers, were kept in Little Rock for sale to collectors. South Carolina issued their first stamp in 1981. They were printed in sheets of thirty. Starting with their second issues in 1982, a portion of the stamps were serially numbered on the reverse and distributed to license agents. Collectors who bought stamps directly from the state were sold stamps from sheets lacking the serial numbers. The agent, or "hunter type" stamps as they are often called, were only sold to those collectors who especially requested them.

When North Dakota introduced their first pictorial stamps in 1982, the first 20,000 stamps were set aside to be sold with prints or to be signed by the artist. These were printed in sheets of ten. Stamps numbered 20,001-150,000 were printed in booklet panes of five and distributed to license agents. Stamps with serial numbers higher than 150,000 were printed in sheets of thirty and reserved for sale to collectors. The stamps that were distributed to license agents were available to collectors for a brief period of time following the end of the hunting season and then destroyed. The collector type stamps, on the other hand, were kept on sale for three years. This accounts for the relative difficulty in obtaining unused examples of early North Dakota booklet-type (hunter stamps.

New Hampshire's first stamp was printed in two different formats. When collectors placed their orders, they were asked whether they wanted stamps with straight edges on three sides (booklet type) or fully perforated (from sheets printed for collectors). Not understanding the difference between the two types, the majority of collectors requested fully perforated stamps.

Collector interest in state duck stamps exploded in the mid 1980's. This can be attributed to the large number of states issuing stamps by this time and the fact that an album containing spaces for federal and state waterfowl stamps was published in 1987. In the years since, every state has initiated a waterfowl stamp program.

Nearly half of the states print their stamps in two formats today. Hunter stamps from Montana are printed in booklet panes of ten (2x5) with selvage on both sides. These are most often collected in horizontal pairs. (Connecticut 1993-1996 and Virginia 1988-1995 issued stamps in the same format). The selvage on each side of the pair makes it easy to differentiate them from the collector-type stamps, which are printed in sheets of thirty. When the 1986 Montana stamps were issued, some representatives at the state agency did not recognize a difference between the booklet and sheet type stamps. Therefore, only a small number of booklet-type stamps were obtained by collectors.

There have been some occasions when the waterfowl season was ready to begin and the state license sections had not yet received their stamps from the printer. This occurred in 1989 for Oregon and in 1991 for Idaho. In these instances "temporary" non-pictorial stamps were printed and distributed to license agents for issue to hunters until the regular pictorial stamps were received.

In the late 1980's the U.S. Fish and Wildlife Service encouraged many tribal governments to formally organize their fish and wildlife programs. Many of these programs were made to include stamp and license requirements in their general provisions. In 1989 the Crow Creek Sioux of South Dakota became the first tribal government to issue pictorial waterfowl stamps. These stamps were not printed with collectors in mind. Rather, tribal Department of Natural Resources officials were simply attempting to conform to standards set by the South Dakota Game, Fish and Parks Commission for their pictorial stamps. Separate stamps were printed for reservation residents, South Dakota residents who did not live on the reservation and non-residents of the state. For each classification only 200 stamps were printed.

In the last few years, several tribal governments have issued waterfowl stamps that are more readily available to collectors.

Michael Jaffe

STATE DUCK STAMPS

State Duck Stamps provide a natural area for the person who wishes to expand his or her field of interest beyond the collecting of Federal Ducks. In 1971, California became the first state to issue a pictorial duck stamp. Other states followed with the sales providing a much needed source of revenue for wetlands. By 1994, all 50 states will have issued duck stamps.

Similar to Federal policy, many states hold an art competition to determine the winning design. Other states commission an artist. Beginning in 1987, some states started to issue a "Governor's" stamp. These stamps with high face values were designed to garner additional wetland funds. In 1989, the Crow Creek Sioux Tribe of South Dakota became the first Indian Reservation to issue a pictorial duck stamp.

Hunter or Agent stamps generally come in booklets with a tab attached to the stamp, or specific serial numbers on the stamp issued in sheet format that allows collectors' orders to be filled more easily. Many of these stamps exist with plate numbers in the margin. The items illustrated below represent just a sampling of the interesting varieties which have been produced by the various states.

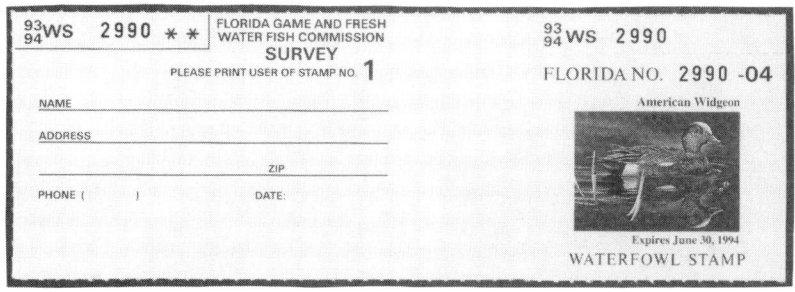

FL 15T SURVEY TAB

OR 3A HUNTER TYPE WITH TAB

WA 6AN MINI SHEET

MT 4A HZ. PAIR WITH SIDE MARGINS

AR 12 PROOF PAIR, IMPERF.

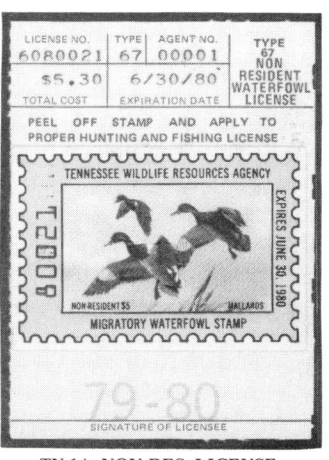

TN 1A NON-RES. LICENSE

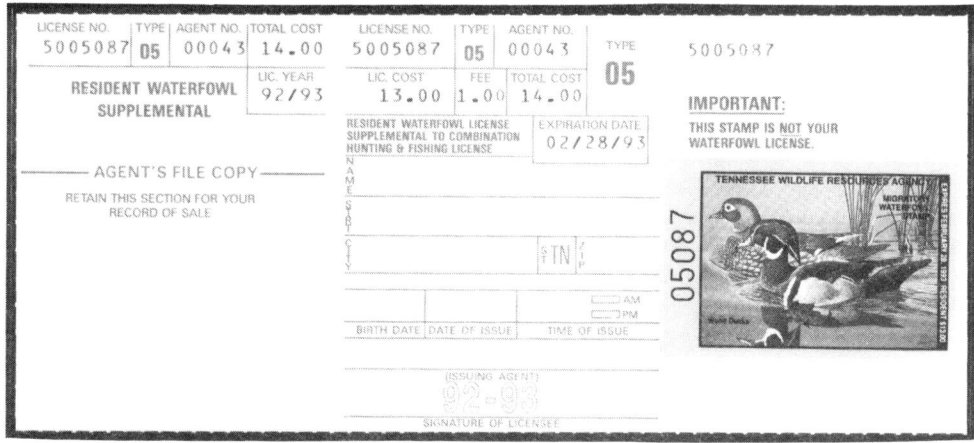

TN 14B 3 PART CARD

STATE HUNTING PERMIT STAMPS

ALABAMA

AL 1

No.	Description	F-VF NH
AL 1	'79 $5 Wood Ducks	10.00
AL 2	'80 $5 Mallards	10.00
AL 3	'81 $5 Canada Geese	10.00
AL 4	'82 $5 Grn Winged Teal	10.00
AL 5	'83 $5 Widgeon	10.00
AL 6	'84 $5 Buffleheads	10.00
AL 7	'85 $5 Wood Ducks	14.00
AL 8	'86 $5 Canada Geese	14.00
AL 9	'87 $5 Pintails	14.00
AL 10	'88 $5 Canvasbacks	10.00
AL 11	'89 $5 Hooded Mergan	10.00
AL 12	'90 $5 Wood Ducks	10.00
AL 13	'91 $5 Redheads	10.00
AL 14	'92 $5 Cinnamon Teal	10.00
AL 15	'93 $5 Grn Winged Teal	10.00
AL 16	'94 $5 Canvasbacks	10.00
AL 17	'95 $5 Canda Geese	10.00
AL 18	'96 $5 Wood Ducks	10.00
AL 19	'97 $5 Snow Goose	10.00
AL 20	'98 $5 Barrow's goldeneye	10.00
Alabama Set 1979-98 (20)		**205.00**

ALASKA

AK 1

No.	Description	F-VF NH
AK 1	'85 $5 Emperor Geese	10.00
AK 2	'86 $5 Steller's Elders	10.00
AK 3	'87 $5 Spectacled Elders	10.00
AK 3A	'87 $5 Hunted Full Tab	10.00
AK 4	'88 $5 Trumpeter Swan	10.00
AK 4A	'88 $5 Hunter/Full Tab	10.00
AK 5	'89 $5 Goldeneyes	9.00
AK 5A	'89 $5 Hunter/Full Tab	10.00
AK 6	'90 $5 Oldsquaw	9.00
AK 6A	'90 $5 Hunter/Full Tab	9.50
AK 7	'91 $5 Snowgeese	9.00
AK 7A	'91 $5 Hunter/Full Tab	9.50
AK 8	'92 $5 Canvasbacks	9.00
AK 8A	'92 $5 Hunter/Full Tab	9.50
AK 9	'93 $5 Wh. Fronted Geese	9.00
AK 9A	'93 $5 Hunter/Full Tab	9.50
AK 10	'94 $5 Harlequin	9.00
AK 10A	'94 $5 Hunter/Full Tab	9.50
AK 11	'95 $5 Pacific Brant	9.00
AK 11A	'95 $5 Hunter w/ Full Tab	9.50
AK 12	'96 $5 Aleutian Canada Geese	9.00
AK 12A	'96 $5 Hunter w/ Full Tab	9.50
AK 13	'97 $5 King Eiders	9.00
AK 13A	'97 $5 Hunter w/ Full Tab	9.50
AK 14	'98 Barrow's Goldeneye	9.00
AK 14 A	'98 Hunter w/ full tab	9.50

NOTE: Governor's stamps available upon request.

Alaska Set 1985-98 (14)		**130.00**
Alaska Hunter type, cplt. set (11)		**85.00**

ARIZONA

AZ 1

No.	Description	F-VF NH
AZ 1	'87 $5.50 Pintails	11.00
AZ 1A	'87 $5.50 Hunter w/tab	11.00

ARIZONA (cont.)

No.	Description	F-VF NH
AZ 2	'88 $5.50 Grn. Winged Teal	11.00
AZ 2A	'88 $5.50 Hunter w/tab	11.00
AZ 3	'89 $5.50 Cinnamon Teal	11.00
AZ 3A	'89 $5.50 Hunter w/tab	11.00
AZ 4	'90 $5.50 Canada Geese	11.00
AZ 4A	'90 $5.50 Hunter w/tab	11.00
AZ 5	'91 $5.50 Bl. Winged Teal	9.50
AZ 5A	'91 $5.50 Hunter w/tab	11.00
AZ 6	'92 $5.50 Buffleheads	9.50
AZ 6A	'92 $5.50 Hunter w/tab	11.00
AZ 7	'93 $5.50 Mexican Duck	9.50
AZ 7A	'93 $5.50 Hunter w/tab	9.50
AZ 8	'94 $5.50 Mallards	9.50
AZ 8A	'94 $5.50 Hunter w/tab	9.50
AZ 9	'95 $5.50 Wigeon	9.50
AZ 9A	'95 $5.50 Hunter w/tab	9.50
AZ 10	'96 $5.50 Canvasback	9.50
AZ 10A	'96 $5.50 Hunter w/ Tab	9.50
AZ 11	'97 $5.50 Gadwall	9.50
AZ 11A	'97 $5.50 Hunter w/ Tab	9.50
AZ 12	'98 $5.50 Wood Duck	9.50
AZ 12 A	'98 $5.50 Hunter w/ tab	9.50

NOTE: Governor's stamps available upon request.

Arizona Set 1987-98 (12)		**110.00**
Arizona Hunter type, cplt. set		**110.00**

ARKANSAS

AR 1

No.	Description	F-VF NH
AR 1	'81 $5.50 Mallards	40.00
AR 1B	'81 Hunter (S# 110,001-200,000)	55.00
AR 1P	'81 Imperf Proof Pair	20.00
AR 2	'82 $5.50 Wood Ducks	40.00
AR 2B	'82 Hunter (S# 110,001-200,000)	55.00
AR 2P	'82 Imperf Proof Pair	25.00
AR 3	'83 $5.50 Grn.Wngd Teal	55.00
AR 3B	'83 Hunter (S# 70,001-160,000)	900.00
AR 3P	'83 Imperf Proof Sgl	70.00
AR 4	'84 $5.50 Pintails	25.00
AR 4B	'84 Hunter (S# 25,001-100,000)	35.00
AR 4P	'84 Imperf Proof Pair	20.00
AR 5	'85 $5.50 Mallards	14.00
AR 5B	'85 Hunter (S# 25,001-100,000)	28.00
AR 5P	'85 Imperf Proof Pair	20.00
AR 6	'86 $5.50 Blk. Swamp Mallards	12.00
AR 6B	'86 Hunter (S# 25,001-100,000)	17.00
AR 6P	'86 Imperf Proof Pair	20.00
AR 7	'87 $7 Wood Ducks	12.00
AR 7A	'87 $5.50 Wood Ducks	13.00
AR 7B	'87 Hunter (S# 25,001-100,000)	14.00
AR 7P	'87 Imperf Proof Pair	20.00
AR 8	'88 $7 Pintails	11.00
AR 8A	'88 $5.50 Pintails	13.00
AR 8B	'88 Hunter (S# 25,001-100,000)	14.00
AR 8P	'88 Imperf Proof Pair	23.00
AR 9	'89 $7 Mallards	11.00
AR 9B	'89 Hunter (S# 30,001-100,000)	12.00
AR 9P	'89 Imperf Proof Pair	23.00
AR 10	'90 $7 Blk Duck/Mallards	11.00
AR 10B	'90 Hunter (S# 30,001-100,000)	12.00
AR 10P	'90 Imperf Proof Pair	23.00
AR 11	'91 $7 Widgeons	11.00
AR 11B	'91 Hunter (S# 30,001-100,000)	11.00
AR 11P	'91 Imperf Proof Pair	17.00
AR 12	'92 $7 Shovelers	11.00
AR 12B	'92 Hunter (S# 30,001-100,000)	11.00
AR 12P	'92 Imperf Proof Pair	17.00
AR 13	'93 $7 Mallards	11.00
AR 13B	'93 Hunter (S# 30,001-100,000)	11.00
AR 13P	'93 Imperf Proof Pair	17.00

ARKANSAS (cont.)

No.	Description	F-VF NH
AR 14	'94 $7 Canada Geese	11.00
AR 14B	'94 Hunter (S# 25,001-100,000)	11.00
AR 14P	'94 Imperf Proof Pair	16.00
AR 15	'95 $7 Mallard	11.00
AR 15B	'95 Hunter (S# 25,001-100,000)	11.00
AR 15P	'95 Imperf Proof Pair	16.00
AR 16	'96 $7.00 Black Lab	11.00
AR 16B	Hunter (SN# 13,001-100,000)	11.00
AR 16P	'96 Imperf Proof Pair	16.00
AR 17	'97 $7.00 Chocolate Lab	11.00
AR 17B	Hunter (SN# 13,001-100,000)	11.00
AR 17P	'97 Imperf Proof Pair	16.00
AR 18	'98 Mallards / Yellow Lab	11.00
AR 18B	Hunter (SN 13,001-100,000)	11.00
AR 18P	'98 Imperf Proof Pair	16.00

Arkansas Set 1981-98 (20)		**330.00**
Arkansas Hunter, cplt (18)		**1200.00**
Arkansas Imperfs, cplt (18)		**345.00**

CALIFORNIA

CA 8

No.	Description	F-VF NH
CA 1	'71 $1 Pintails Original Backing	825.00
CA 1	'71 $1 Unsigned w/o Orig. Backing	165.00
CA 2	'72 $1 Canvasback Original Backing	3200.00
CA 2	'72 $1 Unsigned w/o Orig. Backing	300.00
CA 3	'73 $1 Mallards	12.00
CA 4	'74 $1 Wh. Fronted Geese	3.00
CA 5	'75 $1 Grn. Winged Teal Clear Wax Back	165.00
CA 5R	'75 $1 Same, Ribbed Back	40.00
CA 6	'76 $1 Widgeon	18.00
CA 7	'77 $1 Cinnamon Teal	45.00
CA 7A	'78 $5 Cinnamon Teal	10.00
CA 8	'78 $5 Hooded Mergans	150.00
CA 9	'79 $5 Wood Ducks	9.00
CA 9P	'79 Imperf Proof Pair	55.00
CA 10	'80 $5 Pintails	9.00
CA 10P	'80 Imperf Proof Pair	55.00
CA 11	'81 $5 Canvasbacks	9.50
CA 12	'82 $5 Widgeon	9.50
CA 13	'83 $5 Grn.Winged Teal	9.50
CA 14	'84 $7.50 Mallard Decoy	12.00
CA 15	'85 $7.50 Ring Neck Duck	12.00
CA 16	'86 $7.50 Canada Goose	12.00
CA 17	'87 $7.50 Redheads	12.00
CA 18	'88 $7.50 Mallards	12.00
CA 19	'89 $7.50 Cinnamon Teal	12.00
CA 20	'90 $7.50 Canada Goose	12.00
CA 21	'91 $7.90 Gadwalls	12.00
CA 22	'92 $7.90 Wh.Frntd Goose	12.00
CA 23	'93 $10.50 Pintails	14.50
CA 24	'94 $10.50 Wood Ducks	14.50
CA 25	'95 $10.50 Snow Geese	14.50
CA 25a	Strip of 4 designs	58.00
CA 25m	Mini sheet of 4	90.00
CA 26	'96 $10.50 Mallard	14.50
CA 27	'97 $10.50 Pintails	14.50
CA 28	'98 $10.50 Green Wingedteal (PR)	32.00
California Set 1973-98 (29)		**635.00**

COLORADO

CO 1

No.	Description	F-VF NH
CO 1	'90 $5 Canada Geese	12.00
CO 1A	'90 $5 Hunter w/tab	12.00
CO 2	'91 $5 Mallards	18.00

COLORADO (cont.)

No.	Description	F-VF NH
CO 2A	'91 $5 Hunter w/tab	12.00
CO 3	'92 $5 Pintails	9.00
CO 3A	'92 $5 Hunter w/tab	11.00
CO 4	'93 $5 Grn. Winged Teal	9.00
CO 4A	'93 $5 Hunter w/tab	9.50
CO 5	'94 $5 Wood Ducks	9.00
CO 5A	'94 $5 Hunter w/tab	9.50
CO 6	'95 $5 Buffleheads	9.00
CO 6A	'95 $5 Hunter w/tab	9.50
CO 7	'96 $5.00 Cinnamon Teal	9.00
CO 7A	'96 $5.00 Hunter w/Tab	9.50
CO 8	'97 $5.00 Widgeon	9.00
CO 8A	'97 $5.00 Hunter w/tab	9.50
CO 9	'98 $5.00 Cinnamon Teal	9.00
CO 9 A	'98 $ 5.00 Hunter w/ tab	9.50

NOTE: Governor's stamps available upon request.

Colorado Set 1990-98 (9)		**85.00**
Colorado Hunter Set 1990-98 (9)		**85.00**

CONNECTICUT

CT 2

No.	Description	F-VF NH
CT 1	'93 $5 Black Ducks	9.00
CT 1A	'93 $5 Hunter Hz. Pair	18.00
CT 1M	'93 Commem. Sht. of 4	80.00
CT 2	'94 $5 Canvasbacks	8.50
CT 2A	'94 $5 Hunter Horiz. Pair	17.00
CT 2M	'94 Commem Sheet of 4	40.00
CT 3	'95 $5 Mallards	8.50
CT 3A	'95 $5 Hunter Horiz. Pair	17.00
CT 4	'96 $5 Old Squaw	8.50
CT 4A	'96 $5 Hunter Horiz. Pair	17.00
CT 5	'97 $5 Green Winged Teal	8.50
CT 5A	'97 $5 Hunter "H" Prefix	8.50
CT 6	'98 $ 5 Mallards	8.50
CT 6A	'98 $ 5 Hunter "H" prefix	8.50

NOTE: Governor's stamps available upon request.

Connecticut Set 1993-98 (6)		**50.00**
Ct. Hunter Set (6)		**80.00**

DELAWARE

DE 2

No.	Description	F-VF NH
DE 1	'80 $5 Black Ducks	95.00
DE 2	'81 $5 Snow Geese	70.00
DE 3	'82 $5 Canada Geese	70.00
DE 4	'83 $5 Canvasbacks	40.00
DE 5	'84 $5 Mallards	15.00
DE 6	'85 $5 Pintail	12.00
DE 7	'86 $5 Widgeon	12.00
DE 8	'87 $5 Redheads	12.00
DE 9	'88 $5 Wood Ducks	10.00
DE 10	'89 $5 Buffleheads	9.50
DE 11	'90 $5 Green Winged Teal	9.50
DE 12	'91 $5 Hooded Mergans	9.50
DE 12A	'91 Hunter-SN# on Back	11.00
DE 13	'92 $5 Bl. Wngd. Teal	9.50
DE 13A	'92 Hunter-SN# on Back	9.50
DE 14	'93 $5 Goldeneyes	9.50
DE 14A	'93 Hunter-SN# on Back	9.50
DE 15	'94 $5 Blue Geese	9.50
DE 15A	'94 Hunter-SN# on back	9.50
DE 16	'95 $5 Scaup	9.00
DE 16A	'95 Hunter-SN# on back	9.50
DE 17	'96 $6 Gadwall	9.00
DE 17A	'96 Hunter-SN# on back	9.50
DE 18	'97 $6 Wh. Winged Scoter	9.00
DE 18A	'97 Hunter-SN# on back	9.50
DE 19	'98 Blue Winged Teal	9.00
DE 19A	'98 Hunter SN# on back	9.50

NOTE: Governor's stamps available upon request.

Delaware Set 1980-98 (19)		**405.00**
Delaware Hunters (8)		**75.00**

STATE HUNTING PERMIT STAMPS

FLORIDA

FL 5

No.	Description	F-VF NH
FL 1	'79 $3.25 Grn Wngd Teal	170.00
FL 1T	'79 $3.25 Full Tab Attd.	185.00
FL 2	'80 $3.25 Pintails	20.00
FL 2T	'80 $3.25 Full Tab Attd	24.00
FL 3	'81 $3.25 Widgeon	17.00
FL 3T	'81 $3.25 Full Tab Attd	24.00
FL 4	'82 $3.25 Ring-Neck Duck	24.00
FL 4T	'82 $3.25Full Tab Attd	35.00
FL 5	'83 $3.25 Buffleheads	50.00
FL 5T	'83 $3.25Full Tab Attd	60.00
FL 6	'84 $3.25 Hooded Merg	12.00
FL 6T	'84 $3.25 Full Tab Attd	18.00
FL 7	'85 $3.25 Wood Ducks	12.00
FL 7T	'85 $3.25 Full Tab Attd	10.00
FL 8	'86 $3.00 Canvasbacks	11.00
FL 8T	'86 $3.00 Survey Tab Attd	18.00
FL 9	'87 $3.50 Mallards	9.50
FL 9T	'87 $3.50 Survey Tab Attd	25.00
FL 10	'88 $3.50 Redheads	9.50
FL 10T	'88 $3.50 Survey Tab Attd	23.00
FL 11	'89 $3.50 Bl. Winged Teal	7.50
FL 11T	'89 $3.50 Survey Tab Attd	23.00
FL 12	'90 $3.50 Wood Ducks	7.50
FL 12T	'90 $3.50 Survey Tab Attd	23.00
FL 13	'91 $3.50 Northern Pintail	7.50
FL 13T	'91 $3.50 Survey Tab Attd	17.00
FL 14	'92 $3.50 Ruddy Duck	7.50
FL 14T	'92 $3.50 Survey Tab Attd	14.00
FL 15	'93 $3.50 Amer. Widgeon	7.00
FL 15T	'93 $3.50 Survey Tab Attd	14.00
FL 16	'94 $3.50 Mottled Duck	6.50
FL 16T	'94 $3.50 Survey Tab Attd.	14.00
FL 17	'95 $3.50 Fulvous Whistling Duck	6.50
FL 17T	'95 $3.50 Survey Tab Attd.	14.00
FL 18	'96 $3.50 Goldeneyes	6.50
FL 18T	'96 $3.50 Survey Tab Attchd.	15.00
FL 19	'97 $3.50 Hooded Mergansers	6.50
FL 19T	'97 $3.50 Survey Tab Attchd.	15.00
FL 20	'98 $3.50 Shoveler	6.50
FL 20T	'98 $3.50 Survey Tab Attchd.	15.00

Florida Set 1979-98 (20) 390.00
Florida Tabs Set 1979-98 (20) 580.00

GEORGIA

GA 5

No.	Description	F-VF NH
GA 1	'85 $5.50 Wood Ducks	11.00
GA 2	'86 $5.50 Mallards	8.50
GA 3	'87 $5.50 Canada Geese	8.50
GA 4	'88 $5.50 Ring Neck Ducks	8.50
GA 5	'89 $5.50 Duckling/Puppy	11.00
GA 6	'90 $5.50 Wood Ducks	8.50
GA 7	'91 $5.50 Grn. Winged Teal	8.50
GA 8	'92 $5.50 Buffleheads	8.50
GA 9	'93 $5.50 Mallards	8.50
GA 10	'94 $5.50 Ringnecks	8.50
GA 11	'95 $5.50 Widgeons/Blk Lab	8.50
GA 12	'96 $5.50 Black Ducks	8.50
GA 13	'97 $5.50 Lesser Scaup	8.50
GA 14	'98 $5.50 Blk Lab w/Ringneks	8.50

Georgia Set 1985-97 (13) 120.00

HAWAII

HI 1

No.	Description	F-VF NH
HI 1	'96 $5 Nene Geese	10.00
HI 1A	'96 $5 Hunter Type	10.00
HI 1B	'96 $5 Booklet	10.00
H11M	'96 $5 Mini Sheet of 4	40.00
HI 2	'97 $5 Hawaiian Duck	8.50
HI 2A	'97 $5 Hunter Type	9.00
HI 3	'98 $5 Wild Turkey	8.50
HI 3A	'98 $5 Hunter Type	9.00

IDAHO

ID 1

No.	Description	F-VF NH
ID 1	'87 $5.50 Cinnamon Teals	15.00
ID 1A	'87 $5.50 Bklt. sgl. w/Tab	11.00
ID 2	'88 $5.50 Grn. Winged Teal	13.00
ID 2A	'88 $5.50 Bklt. sgl. w/Tab	13.00
ID 3	'89 $6 Bl. Winged Teal	11.00
ID 3A	'89 $6 Bklt. sgl. w/Tab	11.00
ID 4	'90 $6 Trumpeter Swan	18.00
ID 4A	'90 $6 Bklt. sgl. w/Tab	11.00
ID 5	'91 $6 Amer. Widgeons	9.50
ID 5A	'91 $6 Bklt. sgl. w/Tab	11.00
ID 5X	'91 $6 Provisional	130.00
ID 6	'92 $6 Canada Geese	9.50
ID 6A	'92 $6 Bklt. sgl. w/Tab	9.50
ID 7	'93 $6 Com'n Goldeneye	10.00
ID 7A	'93 $6 Bklt. sgl. w/Tab	9.50
ID 8	'94 $6 Harlequin	9.50
ID 8A	'94 $6 Bklt. sgl. w/Tab	9.50
ID 9	'95 $6 Wood Ducks	9.50
ID 9A	'95 $6 Bklt. Sgl. w/tab	9.50
ID 10	'96 $6 Mallard	9.50
ID 11	'97 $6.50 Shovelers	9.50
ID 12	'98 $6.50 Canada Geese	9.50

Idaho Set 1987-98 (12) 120.00
Idaho Bklt. Set 1987-95 (9) 90.00

ILLINOIS

IL 1

No.	Description	F-VF NH
IL 1	'75 $5 Mallard	695.00
IL 2	'76 $5 Wood Ducks	290.00
IL 3	'77 $5 Canada Goose	195.00
IL 4	'78 $5 Canvasbacks	110.00
IL 5	'79 $5 Pintail	110.00
IL 6	'80 $5 Grn. Winged Teal	110.00
IL 7	'81 $5 Widgeon	110.00
IL 7A	'81 $5 G.W. Teal Error	585.00
IL 8	'82 $5 Black Ducks	70.50
IL 9	'83 $5 Lesser Scaup	70.50
IL 10	'84 $5 Bl. Winged Teal	70.50
IL 11	'85 $5 Red Head	15.00
IL 11T	'85 $5 Full Tab Attd	20.00
IL 12	'86 $5 Gadwalls	15.00
IL 12T	'86 $5 Full Tab Attd	17.00
IL 13	'87 $5 Buffleheads	12.00
IL 13T	'87 $5 Full Tab Attd	14.00
IL 14	'88 $5 Com'n Goldeneye	12.00
IL 14T	'88 $5 Full Tab Attd	14.00
IL 15	'89 $5 Ring Neck Duck	10.00
IL 15T	'89 $5 Full Tab Attd	11.00
IL 16	'90 $10 Lesser Snow Gs.	16.00
IL 16T	'90 $10 Full Tab Attd	17.00
IL 17	'91 $10 Blk. Lab/Can. Gs.	15.00

ILLINOIS (cont.)

No.	Description	F-VF NH
IL 17T	'91 $10 Full Tab Attd	17.00
IL 18	'92 $10 Retvr./Mallards	15.00
IL 18T	"92 $10 Full Tab Attd.	17.00
IL 19	'93 $10 Puppy/Decoy	15.00
IL 19T	'93 $10 Full Tab Attd	17.00
IL 20	'94 $10 Chessies & Canvasbacks	15.00
IL 20T	'94 $10 Full Tab Attd.	16.00
IL 21	'95 $10 Green Winged Teal/C. Lab	14.50
IL 21T	'95 $10 Full Tab Attd.	16.00
IL 22	'96 $10 Wood Ducks	14.50
IL 23	'97 $10 Canvasbacks	14.50
IL 24	'98 $10 Canada Geese	14.50

NOTE: Governor's stamps available upon request.

Illinois Set 1975-98 Without Error (24) 1950.00

INDIANA

IN 1

No.	Description	F-VF NH
IN 1	'76 $5 Grn. Winged Teal	9.00
IN 2	'77 $5 Pintail	9.00
IN 3	'78 $5 Canada Geese	9.00
IN 4	'79 $5 Canvasbacks	9.00
IN 5	'80 $5 Mallard Ducklings	9.00
IN 6	'81 $5 Hooded Mergans	9.00
IN 7	'82 $5 Bl. Winged Teal	9.00
IN 8	'83 $5 Snow Geese	9.00
IN 9	'84 $5 Redheads	9.00
IN 10	'85 $5 Pintail	9.00
IN 10T	'85 $5 Full Tab Attd	12.00
IN 11	'86 $5 Wood Duck	9.00
IN 11T	'86 $5 Full Tab Attd	12.00
IN 12	'87 $5 Canvasbacks	9.00
IN 12T	'87 $5 Full Tab Attd	12.00
IN 13	'88 $6.75 Redheads	11.00
IN 13T	'88 $6.75 Full Tab Attd	12.00
IN 14	'89 $6.75 Canada Goose	11.00
IN 14T	'89 $6.75 Full Tab Attd	12.00
IN 15	'90 $6.75 Bl. Winged Teal	11.00
IN 15T	'90 $6.75 Full Tab Attd	12.00
IN 16	'91 $6.75 Mallards	11.00
IN 16T	'91 $6.75 Full Tab Attd	12.00
IN 17	'92 $6.75 Grn. Winged Tl.	11.00
IN 17T	'92 $6.75 Full Tab Attd	12.00
IN 18	'93 $6.75 Wood Ducks	11.00
IN 18T	'93 $6.75 Full Tab Attd	12.00
IN 19	'94 $6.75 Pintail	11.00
IN 19T	'94 $6.75 Full Tab Attd.	12.00
IN 20	'95 $6.75 Goldeneyes	11.00
IN 20T	'95 $6.75 Full Tab Attd.	12.00
IN 21	'96 $6.75 Black Ducks	11.00
IN 21T	'96 $6.75 Full Tab Attchd.	12.00
IN 22	'97 $6.75 Canada Geese	11.00
IN 22T	'97 $6.75 Full Tab Attchd.	12.00
IN 23	'98 $6.75 Widgeon	11.00
IN 23T	'98 $6.75 Full Tab Attchd.	12.00

Indiana Set 1976-98 (23) 220.00

IOWA

IA 9

No.	Description	F-VF NH
IA 1	'72 $1 Mallards	195.00
IA 2	'73 $1 Pintails	45.00
IA 3	'74 $1 Gadwalls	100.00
IA 4	'75 $1 Canada Geese	125.00

IOWA (cont.)

No.	Description	F-VF NH
IA 5	'76 $1 Canvasbacks	25.00
IA 6	'77 $1 Lesser Scaup	25.00
IA 7	'78 $1 Wood Ducks	50.00
IA 8	'79 $5 Buffleheads	420.00
IA 9	'80 $5 Redheads	30.00
IA 10	'81 $5 Grn. Winged Teal	30.00
IA 11	'82 $5 Snow Geese	18.00
IA 12	'83 $5 Widgeon	20.00
IA 13	'84 $5 Wood Ducks	40.00
IA 14	'85 $5 Mallard & Decoy	24.00
IA 15	'86 $5 Bl. Wngd. Teal	16.00
IA 16	'87 $5 Canada Goose	14.00
IA 17	'88 $5 Pintails	12.00
IA 18	'89 $5 Bl. Winged Teal	12.00
IA 19	'90 $5 Canvasback	8.00
IA 19A	'90 Serial #26001-80000	12.00
IA 20	'91 $5 Mallards	8.00
IA 21	'92 $5 Blk. Lab/Ducks	9.50
IA 22	'93 $5 Mallards	9.50
IA 23	'94 $5 Grn. Winged Teal	9.00
IA 24	'95 $5 Canada Geese	9.00
IA 25	'96 $5 Canvasbacks	9.00
IA 26	'97 $5 Canada Geese	9.00
IA 27	'98 $5 Pintails	9.00

Iowa Set 1972-98 (27) 1200.00

KANSAS

KS 1AS

No.	Description	F-VF NH
KS 1	'87 $3 Grn. Winged Teal	8.50
KS 1	'87 $3 Horiz. Pair	18.00
KS 1AD	'87 Hunter sgl. with DD in Serial Number	8.50
KS 1AD	'87 Horiz. Pair with DD in Serial Number	18.00
KS 1AS	'87 Hunter sgl. with SS in Serial Number	8.50
KS 1AS	'87 Horiz. Pair with SS in Serial Number	18.00
KS 2	'88 $3 Canada Geese	6.50
KS 2A	'88 Hunter sgl.	8.50
KS 2A	'88 $3 Horiz. Pair	18.00
KS 3	'89 $3 Mallards	6.50
KS 3A	'89 Hunter sgl.	7.00
KS 3A	'89 $3 Horiz. Pair	14.00
KS 4	'90 $3 Wood Ducks	6.50
KS 4A	'90 Hunter sgl.	7.00
KS 4A	'90 $3 Horiz. Pair	12.50
KS 5	'91 $3 Pintail	6.00
KS 5A	'91 Hunter sgl.	7.00
KS 5A	'91 $3 Horiz. Pair	12.50
KS 6	'92 $3 Canvasbacks	6.00
KS 7	'93 $3 Mallards	6.00
KS 8	'94 $3 Blue Winged Teal	6.00
KS 9	'95 $3 Barrow's Goldeneyes	6.00
KS 10	'96 $3 Wigeon	6.00
KS 11	'97 $3 Mallard	6.00
KS 12	'98 $3 Mallard	6.00

Kansas Set 1987-97 (11) 75.00
Kansas Hunters Pairs Set 1987-91 (5) 85.00

KENTUCKY

KY 7

No.	Description	F-VF NH
KY 1	'85 $5.25 Mallards	14.00
KY 1T	'85 $5.25 Full Tab Attd	15.00

STATE HUNTING PERMIT STAMPS

KENTUCKY (cont.)

No.	Description	F-VF NH
KY 2	'86 $5.25 Wood Ducks	9.50
KY 2T	'86 $5.25 Full Tab Attd	12.00
KY 3	'87 $5.25 Black Ducks	9.50
KY 3T	'87 $5.25 Full Tab Attd	12.00
KY 4	'88 $5.25 Canada Goose	9.50
KY 4T	'88 $5.25 Full Tab Attd	12.00
KY 5	'89 $5.25 Cnvsbk/Retrvr	9.50
KY 5T	'89 $5.25 Full Tab Attd	12.00
KY 6	'90 $5.25 Widgeons	9.50
KY 6T	'90 $5.25 Full Tab Attd	12.00
KY 7	'91 $5.25 Pintails	9.50
KY 7T	'91 $5.25 Full Tab Attd	12.00
KY 8	'92 $5.25 Grn.Winged Teal	12.00
KY 8T	'92 $5.25 Full Tab Attd	12.00
KY 9	'93 $5.25 Canvasbk/Decoy	15.00
KY 9T	'93 $5.25 Full Tab Attd	16.00
KY 10	'94 $5.25 Canada Goose	9.50
KY 10T	'94 $5.25 Full Tab Attd	10.00
KY 11	'95 $7.50 Ringnecks/ Black Lab	11.50
KY 11T	'95 $7.50 Full tab attd.	12.00
KY 12	'96 $7.50 Bl. Winged Teal	11.50
KY 13	'97 $7.50 Shovelers	11.50
KY 14	'98 $7.50 Gadwalls	11.50

Kentucky Set 1985-97 (13)............ 149.00

LOUISIANA

LA 2

No.	Description	F-VF NH
LA 1	'89 $5 Bl. Winged Teal	12.00
LA 1A	'89 $7.50 Non-Resident	16.00
LA 2	'90 $5 Grn. Winged Teal	9.00
LA 2A	'90 $7.50 Non-Resident	13.00
LA 3	'91 $5 Wood Ducks	9.50
LA 3A	'91 $7.50 Non-Resident	13.00
LA 4	'92 $5 Pintails	8.50
LA 4A	'92 $7.50 Non-Resident	11.75
LA 5	'93 $5 Amer. Widgeons	8.50
LA 5A	'93 $7.50 Non-Resident	11.75
LA 6	'94 $5 Mottled Duck	8.50
LA 6A	'94 $7.50 Non-Resident	11.50
LA 7	'95 $5 Speckled Belly Goose	8.50
LA 7A	'95 $7.50 Non-Resident	11.50
LA 8	'96 $5 Gadwall	8.50
LA 8A	'96 $7.50 Non-Resident Gadwall	11.50
LA 9	'97 $5 Ring Necked Duck	8.50
LA 9A	'97 $13.50 Ring Necked Duck	17.50
LA 10	'98 $5 Mallard	8.50
LA 10A	'98 $13.50 Non-Resident Mallard	17.50

NOTE: Governor's stamps available upon request.

Louisiana Set Resident & Non-Res. 1989-98 (20) 195.00

MAINE

ME 1

No.	Description	F-VF NH
ME 1	'84 $2.50 Black Ducks	25.00
ME 2	'85 $2.50 Common Eiders	55.00
ME 3	'86 $2.50 Wood Ducks	10.00
ME 4	'87 $2.50 Buffleheads	8.50
ME 5	'88 $2.50 Grn Winged Teal	8.50
ME 6	'89 $2.50 Goldeneyes	6.00
ME 7	'90 $2.50 Canada Geese	6.00
ME 8	'91 $2.50 Ring Neck Duck	6.00
ME 9	'92 $2.50 Old Squaw	6.00

MAINE (cont.)

No.	Description	F-VF NH
ME 10	'93 $2.50 Hooded Mergans	6.00
ME 11	'94 $2.50 Mallards	6.00
ME 12	'95 $2.50 White Winged Scoter	6.00
ME 13	'96 $2.50 Blue Winged Teal	6.00
ME 14	'97 $2.50 Greater Sceup	6.00
ME 15	'98 $2.50 Surf Scoter	6.50

Maine Set 1984-98 (15)................... 140.00

MARYLAND

MD 7

No.	Description	F-VF NH
MD 1	'74 $1.10 Mallards	12.00
MD 2	'75 $1.10 Canada Geese	12.00
MD 3	'76 $1.10 Canvasbacks	12.00
MD 4	'77 $1.10 Greater Scaup	12.00
MD 5	'78 $1.10 Redheads	12.00
MD 6	'79 $1.10 Wood Ducks	12.00
MD 7	'80 $1.10 Pintail Decoy	12.00
MD 8	'81 $3 Widgeon	7.00
MD 9	'82 $3 Canvasbacks	10.00
MD 10	'83 $3 Wood Duck	14.00
MD 11	'84 $6 Black Duck	12.00
MD 12	'85 $6 Canada Geese	11.00
MD 13	'86 $6 Hooded Mergan	11.00
MD 14	'87 $6 Redheads	11.00
MD 15	'88 $6 Ruddy Duck	11.00
MD 16	'89 $6 Bl. Wngd. Teal	12.00
MD 17	'90 $6 Lesser Scaup	10.00
MD 18	'91 $6 Shovelers	10.00
MD 19	'92 $6 Bufflehead	10.00
MD 20	'93 $6 Canvasbacks	10.00
MD 21	'94 $6 Redheads	10.00
MD 22	'95 $6 Mallards	10.00
MD 23	'96 $6 Canada Geese	10.00
MD 24	'97 $6 Canvasbacks	10.00
MD 25	'98 $6 Pintail	10.00

Maryland Set 1974-98 (25)............ 260.00

MASSACHUSETTS

MA 18

No.	Description	F-VF NH
MA 1	'74 $1.25 Wood Duck	16.00
MA 2	'75 $1.25 Pintail	16.00
MA 3	'76 $1.25 Canada Goose	16.00
MA 4	'77 $1.25 Goldeneye	16.00
MA 5	'78 $1.25 Black Duck	16.00
MA 6	'79 $1.25 Ruddy Turnstone	16.00
MA 7	'80 $1.25 Old Squaw	16.00
MA 8	'81 $1.25 Rd Brstd Mrgnsr	15.00
MA 9	'82 $1.25 Grtr. Yellowlegs	15.00
MA 10	'83 $1.25 Redhead	15.00
MA 11	'84 $1.25 Wh. Ringed Scooter	15.00
MA 12	'85 $1.25 Ruddy Duck	15.00
MA 13	'86 $1.25 Preening Bluebill	12.00
MA 14	'87 $1.25 Amer. Widgeon	12.00
MA 15	'88 $1.25 Mallard Drake	12.00
MA 16	'89 $1.25 Brant	9.00
MA 17	'90 $1.25 Whistler Hen	9.00
MA 18	'91 $5 Canvasback	11.00
MA 19	'92 $5 Blk-Bellied Plover	11.00
MA 20	'93 $5 Rd Breasted Merg	11.00
MA 21	'94 $5 Wh. Winged Scoter	11.00
MA 22	'95 $5 Hooded Merganser	10.00
MA 23	'96 $5 Eider Decoy	10.00
MA 24	'97 $5 Curlew Shorebird	10.00
MA 25	'98 $5 Canada Goose	10.00

Massachusetts Set 1974-98 (25) 310.00

MICHIGAN

MI 6

No.	Description	F-VF NH
MI 1	'76 $2.10 Wood Duck	5.00
MI 2	'77 $2.10 Canvasbacks	330.00
MI 3	'78 $2.10 Mallards	28.00
MI 3T	'78 $2.10 Full Tab	50.00
MI 4	'79 $2.10 Canada Geese	50.00
MI 4T	'79 $2.10 Full Tab	67.50
MI 5	'80 $3.75 Lesser Scaup	23.00
MI 5T	'80 $3.75 Full Tab	34.00
MI 6	'81 $3.75 Buffleheads	28.00
MI 7	'82 $3.75 Redheads	28.00
MI 8	'83 $3.75 Wood Ducks	28.00
MI 9	'84 $3.75 Pintails	28.00
MI 10	'85 $3.75 Ring Neck Duck	28.00
MI 11	'86 $3.75 Com'n Gldneyes	21.00
MI 12	'87 $3.85 Grn. Winged Teal	12.00
MI 13	'88 $3.85 Canada Goose	10.00
MI 14	'89 $3.85 Widgeon	8.00
MI 15	'90 $3.85 Wood Ducks	8.00
MI 16	'91 $3.85 Bl. Wngd. Teal	7.00
MI 17	'92 $3.85 Rd Breasted Merg	7.00
MI 18	'93 $3.85 Hooded Mergan	7.00
MI 19	'94 $3.85 Black Duck	7.00
MI 20	'95 $4.35 Blue Winged Teal	8.00
MI 21	'96 $4.35 Canada Geese	8.00
MI 22	'97 $5 Canvasbacks	8.00
MI 23	'98 $5 Pintail	8.00

Michigan Set 1976-98 (23)............ 660.00

MINNESOTA

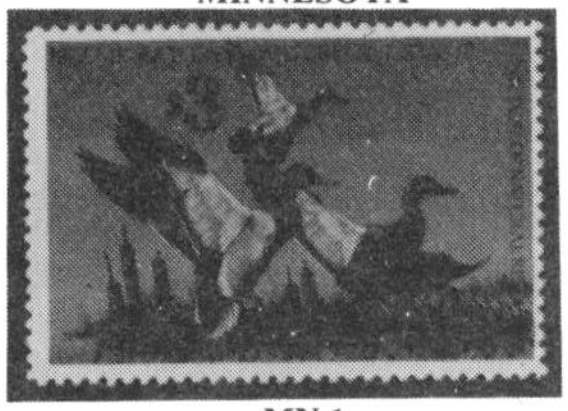

MN 1

No.	Description	F-VF NH
MN 1	'77 $3 Mallards	17.00
MN 2	'78 $3 Lesser Scaup	11.00
MN 3	'79 $3 Pintails	11.00
MN 4	'80 $3 Canvasbacks	11.00
MN 5	'81 $3 Canada Geese	10.00
MN 6	'82 $3 Redheads	11.00
MN 7	'83 $3 Bl & Snow Geese	11.00
MN 8	'84 $3 Wood Ducks	11.00
MN 9	'85 $3 Wh. Front Geese	9.00
MN 10	'86 $5 Lesser Scaup	10.00
MN 11	'87 $5 Goldeneyes	12.00
MN 11T	'87 $5 Full Tab	14.50
MN 12	'88 $5 Buffleheads	11.00
MN 12T	'88 $5 Full Tab	14.50
MN 13	'89 $5 Amer. Widgeons	11.00
MN 13T	'89 $5 Full Tab	14.50
MN 14	'90 $5 Hooded Mergan	18.00
MN 14T	'90 $5 Full Tab	22.00
MN 15	'91 $5 Ross' Goose	9.00
MN 15T	'91 $5 Full Tab	9.50
MN 16	'92 $5 Barrow's Gold'eye	9.00
MN 16T	'92 $5 Full Tab	9.50
MN 17	'93 $5 Bl. Winged Teal	9.00
MN 17T	'93 $5 Full Tab	9.50
MN 18	'94 $5 Ring Necked Duck	9.00
MN 18T	'94 $5 Full Tab	9.50
MN 19	'95 $5 Gadwalls	9.00
MN 19T	'95 $5 Full Tab	9.50
MN 20	'96 $5 Scaup	9.00
MN 20T	'96 $5 Full Tab	9.50
MN 21	'97 $5 Shoveler w/Decoy	9.00
MN 21T	'97 $5 Full Tab	9.50
MN 22	'98 $5 Harlequin Ducks	9.00
MN 22T	'98 $5 Full Tab	9.50

Minnesota Set 1977-98 (22).......... 230.00

MISSISSIPPI

MS 2

No.	Description	F-VF NH
MS 1	'76 $2 Wood Duck	23.00
MS 1B	'76 $2 Full Comput. Card	28.00
MS 2	'77 $2 Mallards	9.00
MS 3	'78 $2 Grn. Winged Teal	9.00
MS 4	'79 $2 Canvasbacks	9.00
MS 5	'80 $2 Pintails	9.00
MS 5	'81 $2 Redheads	9.00
MS 6	'82 $2 Canada Geese	8.00
MS 7	'82 $2 Canada Geese	9.00
MS 8	'83 $2 Lesser Scaup	9.00
MS 9	'84 $2 Black Ducks	9.00
MS 10	'85 $2 Mallards	9.00
MS 10A	'85 Serial # Error-No Hz#	165.00
MS 10B	'85 Serial # Var.- No Silver Bar	575.00
MS 11	'86 $2 Widgeon	9.00
MS 12	'87 $2 Ring Neck Ducks	9.00
MS 13	'88 $2 Snow Geese	9.00
MS 14	'89 $2 Wood Ducks	6.50
MS 15	'90 $2 Snow Geese	14.00
MS 16	'91 $2 Blk. Lab/ Canvasbk Decoy	5.50
MS 17	'92 $2 Grn. Winged Teal	5.00
MS 18	'93 $5 Mallards	8.00
MS 19	'94 $5 Canvasbacks	8.00
MS 20	'95 $5 Blue Winged Teal	8.00
MS 21	'96 $5 Hooded Merganser	8.00
MS 22	'97 $5 Wood Duck	9.00
MS 23	'98 $5 Pin Tails	9.00

NOTE: Governor's stamps available upon request.

Mississippi Set 1976-98 (23)............. 205.00

MISSOURI

MO 2

No.	Description	F-VF NH
MO 1	'79 $3.40 Canada Geese	695.00
MO 1T	'79 $3.40 Full Tab Attd.	895.00
MO 2	'80 $3.40 Wood Ducks	120.00
MO 2T	'80 $3.40 Full Tab Attd	145.00
MO 3	'81 $3 Lesser Scaup	55.00
MO 3T	'81 $3 Full Tab Attd	70.00
MO 4	'82 $3 Buffleheads	60.00
MO 4T	'82 $3 Full Tab Attd	75.00
MO 5	'83 $3 Bl. Wngd. Teal	50.00
MO 5T	'83 $3 Full Tab Attd	60.00
MO 6	'84 $3 Mallards	40.00
MO 6T	'84 $3 Full Tab Attd	60.00
MO 7	'85 $3 Widgeon	20.00
MO 7T	'85 $3 Full Tab Attd	25.00
MO 8	'86 $3 Hooded Mergans	15.00
MO 8T	'86 $3 Full Tab Attd	18.00
MO 9	'87 $3 Pintails	12.00
MO 9T	'87 $3 Full Tab Attd	15.00
MO 10	'88 $3 Canvasbacks	11.00
MO 10T	'88 $3 Full Tab Attd	12.00
MO 11	'89 $3 Ring Neck Ducks	8.50
MO 11T	'89 $3 Full Tab Attd	9.50
MO 12	'90 $3 Redheads	8.00
MO 12T	'90 $3 Full Tab Attd	10.00
MO 13	'91 $5 Snow Geese	8.00
MO 13T	'91 $5 Full Tab Attd	11.00
MO 14	'92 $5 Gadwalls	8.00
MO 14T	'92 $5 Full Tab Attd	11.00
MO 15	'93 $5 Grn. Winged Teal	8.00
MO 15T	'93 $5 Full Tab Attd	10.00
MO 16	'94 $5 Wh Fronted Geese	8.00
MO 16T	'94 $5 Full Tab Attd	9.00
MO 17	'95 $5 Goldeneyes	8.00
MO 17T	'95 $5 Full Tab Attached	9.00
MO 18	'96 $5 Black Duck	8.00

STATE HUNTING PERMIT STAMPS

MISSOURI (cont.)

NOTE: Governor's stamps available upon request.

No.	Description	F-VF NH
Missouri	**Set 1979-96 (18)**	**1100.00**
Missouri	**Tab Set 1979-95 (17)**	**1450.00**

MONTANA

MT 1

No.	Description	F-VF NH
MT 1	'86 $5 Canada Geese	13.00
MT 1A	'86 $5 Horiz. Pair w/ Side Margins	2800.00
MT 2	'87 $5 Redheads	17.00
MT 2A	'87 $5 Hz.Pr./side mgns	35.00
MT 3	'88 $5 Mallards	14.00
MT 3A	'88 $5 Hz.Pr./side mgns	25.00
MT 4	'89 $5 Blk. Lab & Pintail	9.00
MT 4A	'89 $5 Hz.Pr./side mgns	34.00
MT 5	'90 $5 Cinn & Bl.Wng.Teal	8.50
MT 5A	'90 $5 Hz.Pr./side mgns	22.00
MT 6	'91 $5 Snow Geese	8.50
MT 6A	'91 $5 Hz.Pr./side mgns	23.00
MT 7	'92 $5 Wood Ducks	8.50
MT 7A	'92 $5 Hz.Pr./side mgns	23.00
MT 8	'93 $5 Harlequin	8.50
MT 8A	'93 $5 Hz.Pr./side mgns	23.00
MT 9	'94 $5 Widgeon	8.50
MT 9A	'94 $5 Hz.Pr./side mgns.	23.00
MT 10	'95 $5 Tundra Swans	8.50
MT 10A	'95 $5 Horz. Pr/side mgns.	23.00
MT 11	'96 $5 Canvasbacks	8.50
MT 11A	'96 $5 Horz.Pr./side Mgns	23.00
MT 12	'97 $5 Golden Retriever	10.00
MT 12A	'97 $5 Horz.Pr./side Mgns	23.00
MT 13	'98 $5 Gadwalls	8.50
MT 13A	'98 $5 Horz. Pr. / side Mgns	23.00

NOTE: Governor's stamps available upon request.

Montana Set 1986-98 (13) 120.00

NEBRASKA

NE 2

No.	Description	F-VF NH
NE 1	'91 $6 Canada Goose	11.00
NE 2	'92 $6 Pintails	9.00
NE 3	'93 $6 Canvasbacks	9.00
NE 4	'94 $6 Mallard	9.00
NE 5	'95 $6 Wood Ducks	9.00

NOTE: Governor's stamps available upon request.

Nebraska Set 1991-95 (5) 45.00

NEVADA

NV1

No.	Description	F-VF NH
NV1	'79 $2 Canvasbks/Decoy	45.00
NV 1T	'79 $2 Serial # Tab Attd	55.00
NV 2	'80 $2 Cinnamon Teal	6.00
NV 2T	'80 $2 Serial # Tab Attd	7.00
NV 3	'81 $2 Whistling Swans	7.00
NV 3T	'81 $2 Serial # Tab Attd	9.00

NEVADA (cont.)

No.	Description	F-VF NH
NV 4	'82 $2 Shovelers	7.00
NV 4T	'82 $2 Serial # Tab Attd.	9.00
NV 5	'83 $2 Gadwalls	12.00
NV 5T	'83 $2 Serial # Tab Attd.	14.00
NV 6	'84 $2 Pintails	12.00
NV 6T	'84 $2 Serial # Tab Attd.	14.00
NV 7	'85 $2 Canada Geese	17.00
NV 7T	'85 $2 Serial # Tab Attd.	19.00
NV 8	'86 $2 Redheads	15.00
NV 8T	'86 $2 Serial # Tab Attd.	16.00
NV 9	'87 $2 Buffleheads	12.00
NV 9T	'87 $2 Serial # Tab Attd.	14.00
NV 10	'88 $2 Canvasback	12.00
NV 10T	'88 $2 Serial # Tab Attd.	14.00
NV 11	'89 $2 Ross' Geese	8.00
NV 11T	'89 $2 Serial # Tab Attd.	11.00
NV 11A	'89 Hunter Tab #50,001-75,000	21.00
NV 12	'90 $5 Grn. Winged Teal	9.00
NV 12T	'90 $5 Serial # Tab Attd.	12.00
NV 12A	'90 Hunter Tab #50,001-75,000	16.00
NV 13	'91 $5 Wh. Faced Ibis	19.00
NV 13T	'91 $5 Serial # Tab Attd.	12.00
NV 13A	'91 Hunter Tab #50,001-75,000	13.00
NV 14	'92 $5 Amer. Widgeon	8.50
NV 14T	'92 $5 Serial # Tab Attd.	9.00
NV 14A	'92 Hunter Tab #50,001-75,000	12.00
NV 15	'93 $5 Com'n Goldeneye	8.50
NV 15T	'93 $5 Serial # Tab Attd.	9.00
NV 15A	'93 Hunter Tab #50,001-75,000	9.00
NV 16	'94 $5 Mallard	8.50
NV 16T	'94 $5 Serial # Tab Attd.	9.00
NV 16A	'94 Hunter Tab #50,001-75,000	9.00
NV 17	'95 $5 Wood Ducks	8.50
NV 17T	'95 $5 Serial # Tab Attd.	9.00
NV17A	'95 Hunter Tab #50,001-75,000	9.00
NV 18	'96 $5 Ring Necked Duck.	8.50
NV 18T	'96 $5 Serial # Tab Attd.	9.00
NV 18A	'96 Hunter Tab #50,001-75,000	9.00
NV 19	'97 $5 Ruddy Duck	8.50
NV 19T	'97 $5 Serial # Tab Attd.	9.00
NV 19A	'97 Hunter Tab #50,001-75,000	9.00
NV 20	'98 $5 Hooded Merganser.	8.50
NV 20T	'98 Serial # Tab Attd.	9.00
NV 20A	'98 Hunter Tab	9.00

Nevada Set 1979-98 (20) 220.00
Nevada Tab Set 1979-98 (20) 250.00

NEW HAMPSHIRE

NH 9

No.	Description	F-VF NH
NH 1	'83 $4 Wood Ducks	150.00
NH 1A	'83 3 Part Bklt. Type	150.00
NH 2	'84 $4 Mallards	105.00
NH 2A	'84 3 Part Bklt. Type	200.00
NH 3	'85 $4 Bl. Wngd. Teal	110.00
NH 3A	'85 3 Part Bklt. Type	110.00
NH 4	'86 $4 Mergansers	25.00
NH 4A	'86 3 Part Bklt. Type	30.00
NH 5	'87 $4 Canada Geese	12.00
NH 5A	'87 3 Part Bklt. Type	14.00
NH 6	'88 $4 Buffleheads	8.50
NH 6A	'88 3 Part Bklt. Type	12.00
NH 7	'89 $4 Black Ducks	8.50
NH 7A	'89 3 Part Bklt. Type	12.00
NH 8	'90 $4 Grn. Winged Teal	8.00
NH 8A	'90 3 Part Bklt. Type	9.00
NH 9	'91 $4 Gldn Retr/Mallard	10.00
NH 9A	'91 3 Part Bklt. Type	10.00
NH 10	'92 $4 Ring Neck Ducks	8.00
NH 10A	'92 3 Part Bklt. Type	9.00
NH 11	'93 $4 Hooded Mergans	8.00
NH 11A	'93 3 Part Bklt. Type	8.00
NH 12	'94 $4 Common Gldneyes	8.00
NH 12A	'94 3 Part Bklt. Type	8.00
NH 13	'95 $4 Pintails	8.00
NH 13A	'95 3 Part Bklt. Type	8.00
NH 14	'96 $4 Surf Scoters	8.00
NH 14A	'96 3 Part Booklet Type	8.00
NH 15	'97 $4 Old Squaws	8.00

NEW HAMPSHIRE (cont.)

No.	Description	F-VF NH
NH 15A	'97 $4 - 3 Part Booklet Type	8.00
NH 16	'98 $4 Canada Goose	8.00

NOTE: Governor's stamps available upon request.

New Hampshire Set '83-'98 (16) 470.00
NH Bklt. Type Set '83-'98 (16) 585.00

NEW JERSEY

NJ 6

No.	Description	F-VF NH
NJ 1	'84 $2.50 Canvasbacks	45.00
NJ 1A	'84 $5.00 Non-Resident	60.00
NJ 1B	'84 $2.50 Hunter Bklt. Sgl	65.00
NJ 2	'85 $2.50 Mallards	15.00
NJ 2A	'85 $5.00 Non-Resident	20.00
NJ 2B	'85 $2.50 Hunter Bklt. Sgl	30.00
NJ 3	'86 $2.50 Pintails	12.00
NJ 3A	'86 $5.00 Non-Resident	15.00
NJ 3B	'86 $2.50 Hunter Bklt. Sgl	12.00
NJ 4	'87 $2.50 Canada Geese	12.00
NJ 4A	'87 $5.00 Non-Resident	12.00
NJ 4B	'87 $2.50 Hunter Bklt. Sgl	12.00
NJ 4AB	'87 $5.00 Hunter Bklt. Sgl	12.00
NJ 5	'88 $2.50 Grn.Winged Teal	8.50
NJ 5A	'88 $5.00 Non-Resident	10.00
NJ 5B	'88 $2.50 Hunter Bklt. Sgl	10.00
NJ 5AB	'88 $5.00 Hunter Bklt. Sgl	12.00
NJ 6	'89 $2.50 Snow Geese	6.00
NJ 6A	'89 $5.00 Non-Resident	10.00
NJ 6B	'89 $2.50 Hunter Bklt. Sgl	7.00
NJ 6AB	'89 $5.00 Hunter Bklt. Sgl	10.00
NJ 7	'90 $2.50 Wood Ducks	6.00
NJ 7A	'90 $5.00 Non-Resident	9.50
NJ 7B	'90 $2.50 Hunter Bklt. Sgl	6.00
NJ 7AB	'90 $5.00 Hunter Bklt. Sgl	10.00
NJ 8	'91 $2.50 Atlantic "Brandt"	6.00
NJ 8A	'91 $5.00 Non-Resident	9.50
NJ 8B	'91 $2.50 Hunter Bklt. Sgl	6.00
NJ 8AB	'91 $5.00 Hunter Bklt. Sgl	10.00
NJ 8AV	'91 $5.00 Atlantic"Brandt"	32.00
NJ 8V	'91 $2.50 Atlantic"Brandt"	18.00
NJ 9	'92 $2.50 Bluebills	6.00
NJ 9A	'92 $5.00 Non-Resident	8.50
NJ 9B	'92 $2.50 Hunter Bklt. Sgl	6.00
NJ 9AB	'92 $5.00 Hunter Bklt. Sgl	10.00
NJ 10	'93 $2.50 Buffleheads	6.00
NJ 10A	'93 $5.00 Non-Resident	8.50
NJ 10B	'93 $2.50 Hunter Bklt. Sgl	6.00
NJ 10AB	'93 $5.00 Hunter Bklt. Sgl	10.00
NJ 10M-NJ 10AM	Comm.Shts.of 4	69.00
NJ 11	'94 $2.50 Black Ducks	6.00
NJ 11A	'94 $5.00 Black Ducks	8.00
NJ 11B	'94 $2.50 Hunter Bklt. Sgl	6.00
NJ 11AB	'94 $5.00 Hunter Bklt. Sgl	10.00
NJ 12	'95 $2.50 Widgeon	6.00
NJ 12A	'95 $5 Widgeon	8.00
NJ 12B	'95 $2.50 Hunter Bklt. Sgl	6.00
NJ 12AB	'95 $5 Hunter Bklt. Sgl	10.00
NJ 13	'96 $2.50 Goldeneyes	8.00
NJ 13A	'96 $5 Goldeneyes	15.00
NJ 13B	'96 $2.50 Hunter Bklt.Sgl.	10.00
NJ 13AB	'96 $5 Hunter Bklt.Single	15.00
NJ 13C	'96 $2.50 Goldeneyes	7.00
NJ 14	'97 $5 Old Squaws	8.50
NJ 14A	'97 $10 Old Squaws	15.00
NJ 14B	'97 $5 Hunter Bklt Single	8.50
NJ 14AB	'97 $10 HunterBklt Single	15.00
NJ 15	'98 $5 Mallards	8.50
NJ 15A	'98 $10 Mallards	15.00
NJ 15B	'98 $5 Hunter Bklt Single	8.50
NJ 15AB	'98 $10 Hunter Bklt Single	15.00

NOTE: Governor's stamps available upon request.

New Jersey Set 1984-98 (31) 350.00
NJ Bklt. Type Set '84-'98 (27) 340.00

NEW MEXICO

NM 1

No.	Description	F-VF NH
NM 1	'91 $7.50 Pintails	11.00
NM 1A	'91 $7.50 Booklet sgl	12.00
NM 2	'92 $7.50 Amer. Widgeon	11.00
NNM 2A	'92 $7.50 Booklet sgl	12.00
NM 3	'93 $7.50 Mallards	11.00
NM 3A	'93 $7.50 Booklet sgl	12.00
NM 3M	'93 Commem. Sheet of 4	60.00
NM 3MI	'93 Imperf. Commem. Sheet of 4	85.00
NM 4	'94 $7.50 Grn.Wngd.Teal	11.00
NM 4A	'94 $7.50 Booklet sgl	12.50
NM 4A	'94 Strip of 4 different attd.	52.00
NM 4M	'94 Commem. Sheet of 4	60.00
NM 4MI	'94 Imperf. Commem. Sheet of 4	120.00

NOTE: Governor's stamps available upon request.

New Mexico Set 1991-94 (7) 75.00
N.M. Hunter Set 1991-94 (7) 75.00

NEW YORK

NY 1

No.	Description	F-VF NH
NY 1	'85 $5.50 Canada Geese	15.00
NY 2	'86 $5.50 Mallards	10.00
NY 3	'87 $5.50 Wood Ducks	9.00
NY 4	'88 $5.50 Pintails	9.00
NY 5	'89 $5.50 Greater Scaup	9.00
NY 6	'90 $5.50 Canvasbacks	9.00
NY 7	'91 $5.50 Redheads	8.50
NY 8	'92 $5.50 Wood Duck	8.50
NY 9	'93 $5.50 Bl. Wngd. Teal	8.50
NY 10	'94 $5.50 Canada Geese	8.50
NY 11	'95 $5.50 Canada Geese	8.50
NY 12	'96 $5.50 Common Loon	8.50
NY 13	'97 $5.50 Hooded Merganser	8.50
NY 14	'98 $5.50 Osprey	8.50

New York Set 1985-98 (14) 115.00

NORTH CAROLINA

NC 1

No.	Description	F-VF NH
NC 1	'83 $5.50 Mallards	80.00
NC 2	'84 $5.50 Wood Ducks	55.00
NC 3	'85 $5.50 Canvasbacks	25.00
NC 4	'86 $5.50 Canada Geese	18.00
NC 5	'87 $5.50 Pintails	15.00
NC 6	'88 $5 Grn. Winged Teal	10.00
NC 7	'89 $5 Snow Geese	10.00
NC 8	'90 $5 Redheads	10.00
NC 9	'91 $5 Bl. Wngd. Teal	8.50
NC 10	'92 $5 Amer. Widgeon	8.50
NC 11	'93 $5 Tundra Swan	8.50
NC 12	'94 $5 Buffleheads	8.50
NC 13	'95 $5 Brant	8.50
NC 14	'96 $5 Pintails	8.50
NC 15	'97 $5 Wood Ducks	8.50
NC 15B	'97 $5 Self Adhesive	11.00
NC 16	'98 $5 Canada Geese	8.50
NC 16B	'98 $5 Self Adhesive	10.00

North Carolina Set '83-'98 (16) 270.00

NORTH DAKOTA

ND 1

STATE HUNTING PERMIT STAMPS

NORTH DAKOTA

North Dakota Hunter Stamps have the following serial #'s:
1982-86 #20,001-150,000
1987-95 #20,001-140,000

No.	Description	F-VF NH
ND 1	'82 $9 Canada Geese	140.00
ND 1A	'82 $9 Hunter Type with Selvedge	1750.00
ND 2	'83 $9 Mallards	35.00
ND 2A	'83 $9 Hunter Type with Selvedge	3500.00
ND 3	'84 $9 Canvasbacks	35.00
ND 3A	'84 $9 Hunter Type	3000.00
ND 4	'85 $9 Blue Bills	24.00
ND 4A	'85 $9 Hunter Type	4000.00
ND 5	'86 $9 Pintails	20.00
ND 5A	'86 $9 Hunter Type	900.00
ND 6	'87 $9 Snow Geese	20.00
ND 6A	'87 $9 Hunter Type	50.00
ND 7	'88 $9 Wh.Wngd.Scooter	15.00
ND 7A	'88 $9 Hunter Type	34.00
ND 8	'89 $6 Redheads	12.00
ND 8A	'89 $6 Hunter Type	17.00
ND 9	'90 $6 Blk Labs/Mallards	12.00
ND 9A	'90 $6 Hunter Type	17.00
ND 10	'91 $6 Grn. Winged Teal	11.00
ND 10A	'91 $6 Hunter Type	14.50
ND 11	'92 $6 Bl. Winged Teal	9.00
ND 11A	'92 $6 Hunter Type	14.00
ND 12	'93 $6 Wood Ducks	9.00
ND 12A	'93 $6 Hunter Type	11.00
ND 13	'94 $6 Canada Geese	9.00
ND 13A	'94 $6 Hunter Type	12.00
ND 14	'95 $6 Widgeon	9.00
ND 14A	'95 $6 Hunter Type	12.00
ND 15	'96 $6 Mallards	9.00
ND 15A	'96 $6 Hunter Type	12.00
ND 16	'97 $6 White Fronted Geese	9.00
ND 16A	'97 $6 Hunter Type	12.00
ND 17	'98 $6 Blue Winged Teal	9.00
ND 17A	'98 $6 Hunter Type	12.00

North Dakota Set 1982-98 (17)...... 405.00

OHIO

OH 4

No.	Description	F-VF NH
OH 1	'82 $5.75 Wood Ducks	75.00
OH 2	'83 $5.75 Mallards	75.00
OH 3	'84 $5.75 Grn.Winged Teal	75.00
OH 4	'85 $5.75 Redheads	35.00
OH 5	'86 $5.75 Canvasbacks	30.00
OH 6	'87 $5.75 Bl.Winged Teal	12.00
OH 7	'88 $5.75 Goldeneyes	12.00
OH 8	'89 $5.75 Canada Geese	12.00
OH 9	'90 $9 Black Ducks	14.00
OH 10	'91 $9 Lesser Scaup	14.00
OH 11	'92 $9 Wood Ducks	13.00
OH 12	'93 $9 Buffleheads	13.00
OH 13	'94 $11 Mallard	16.00
OH 14	'95 $11 Pintails	16.00
OH 15	'96 $11 Hooded Mergansers	16.00
OH 16	'97 $11 Widgeons	16.00
OH 17	'98 $11 Gadwall	16.00

Ohio Set 1982-98 (17)..................... 440.00

OKLAHOMA

OK 4

No.	Description	F-VF NH
OK 1	'80 $4 Pintails	70.00
OK 2	'81 $4 Canada Goose	25.00
OK 3	'82 $4 Grn.Wngd.Teal	10.00
OK 4	'83 $4 Wood Ducks	10.00
OK 5	'84 $4 Ring Neck Ducks	9.00
OK 5T	'84 $4 Same, with Tab	10.00
OK 6	'85 $4 Mallards	7.50
OK 6T	'85 $4 Full Tab Attd	9.00
OK 7	'86 $4 Snow Geese	7.50
OK 7T	'86 $4 Full Tab Attd	9.00

OKLAHOMA (cont.)

No.	Description	F-VF NH
OK 8	'87 $4 Canvasbacks	7.50
OK 8T	'87 $4 Full Tab Attd	9.00
OK 9	'88 $4 Widgeons	7.50
OK 9T	'88 $4 Full Tab Attd	9.00
OK 9TV	'88 $4 Full Tab Attd. Serial #>30,000	18.00
OK 10	'89 $4 Redheads	7.50
OK 10A	'89 $4 Hunter Ty., w/Tab	9.00
OK 11	'90 $4 Hood'd Mergans'r	7.50
OK 11A	'90 $4 Hunter Ty., w/Tab	9.00
OK 12	'91 $4 Gadwalls	7.50
OK 12A	'91 $4 Hunter Ty., w/Tab	9.00
OK 13	'92 $4 Lesser Scaup	7.00
OK 13A	'92 $4 Hunter Ty.,w/ Tab	9.00
OK 14	'93 $4 Wh. Frnt'd Geese	7.00
OK 14A	'93 $4 Hunter Ty.,w/ Tab	8.00
OK 15	'94 $4 Widgeon	7.00
OK 15A	'94 $4 Hunter Ty.,w/ Tab	7.00
OK 16	'95 $4 Ruddy Ducks	7.00
OK 16A	'95 $4 Hunter Ty.,w/ Tab	7.00
OK 17	'96 $4 Buffleheads	7.00
OK 17A	'96 $4 Hunter Type w/Tab	7.00
OK 18	'97 $4 Goldeneyes	7.00
OK 18A	'97 $4 Hunter Type w/Tab	7.00
OK 19	'98 $4 Shoveler	7.00

Oklahoma Set 1980-98 (19)............ 205.00
NOTE: Governor's stamps available upon request.

OREGON

OR 2

No.	Description	F-VF NH
OR 1	'84 $5 Canada Geese	30.00
OR 2	'85 $5 Snow Geese	42.00
OR 2A	'85 $5 Hunter Ty. w/Tab	675.00
OR 2A	'85 $5 Same, w/o Tab	105.00
OR 3	'86 $5 Pacific Brant	15.00
OR 3A	'86 $5 Hunter Ty. w/Tab	20.00
OR 3A	'86 $5 Same, w/o Tab	11.00
OR 4	'87 $5 Wh. Frnt'd Geese	10.00
OR 4A	'87 $5 Hunter Ty. w/Tab	14.00
OR 4A	'87 $5 Same, w/o Tab	10.00
OR 5	'88 $5 Grt. Basin Geese	10.00
OR 5A	'88 $5 Hunter Ty (89X197mm)	17.00
OR 6	'89 $5 Blk. Lab/Pintail	10.00
OR 6A	'89 $5 Hunter Ty (89X197mm)	14.00
OR 6YB	'89 $5 Provisional Issue, Black Serial #	30.00
OR 6VR	'89 $5 Provisional Issue, Red Serial #	12.50
OR 7	'90 $5 Gldn. Retr/Mallard	12.00
OR 7A	'90 $5 Hunter Ty (89X197mm)	12.00
OR 8	'91 $5 Ch'pk Bay Retrvr	10.00
OR 8A	'91 $5 Hunter Ty. w/Tab	12.00
OR 9	'92 $5 Grn. Winged Teal	8.50
OR 9A	'92 $5 Hunter Ty(216X152mm)	11.00
OR 10	'93 $5 Mallards	8.50
OR 10A	'93 $5 Hunter Type	12.00
OR 10M	'93 Mini. Sheet of 2	25.00
OR 10MI	'93 Same, Imperf.	180.00
OR 11	'94 $5 Pintails	10.00
OR 11A	'94 $5 Hunter Ty(216X152mm)	12.00
OR 11AN	'94 $25 Hunter Type	40.00
OR 12	'95 $5 Wood Ducks	10.00
OR 12A	'95 $5 Hunter Type	12.00
OR 12AN	'95 $25 Hunter Booklet	60.00
OR 13	'96 $5 Mallard/Widgeon/ Pintail	10.00
OR 13B	'96 $5 Mallards..in Folder	10.00
OR 13AN	'96 $25 Hunter Booklet	60.00
OR 14	'97 $5 Canvasbacks	10.00
OR 14AN	'97 $25 Hunter Booklet	40.00
OR 14B	'97 $5 Canvasbacks inFldr	10.00
OR 15	'98 $5 Pintail	10.00
OR 15AN	'98 $25 Hunter Booklet	35.00
OR 15B	'98 Pin Tail in Folder	10.00

NOTE: Governor's stamps available upon request.

Oregon Set 1984-98 (15)................ 195.00

PENNSYLVANIA

PA 1

No.	Description	F-VF NH
PA 1	'83 $5.50 Wood Ducks	18.00
PA 2	'84 $5.50 Canada Geese	15.00
PA 3	'85 $5.50 Mallards	10.00
PA 4	'86 $5.50 Bl. Winged Teal	10.00
PA 5	'87 $5.50 Pintails	10.00
PA 6	'88 $5.50 Wood Ducks	10.00
PA 7	'89 $5.50 Hood'd Mergans'r	10.00
PA 8	'90 $5.50 Canvasbacks	9.00
PA 9	'91 $5.50 Widgeon	9.00
PA 10	'92 $5.50 Canada Geese	9.00
PA 11	'93 $5.50 North'n Shovelers	9.00
PA 12	'94 $5.50 Pintails	8.50
PA 13	'95 $5.50 Buffleheads	8.50
PA 14	'96 $5.50 Black Ducks	8.50
PA 15	'97 $5.50 Hooded Mergans'r	8.50
PA 16	'98 $5.50 Wood Ducks	8.50

Pennsylvania Set '83-'98 (16)........ 155.00

RHODE ISLAND

RI 1

No.	Description	F-VF NH
RI 1	'89 $7.50 Canvasbacks	12.00
RI 1A	'89 $7.50 Hunter Type	17.00
RI 2	'90 $7.50 Canada Geese	12.00
RI 2A	'90 $7.50 Hunter Type	15.00
RI 3	'91 $7.50 Blk. Lab/Wd Dks.	13.00
RI 3A	'91 $7.50 Hunter Type	14.50
RI 4	'92 $7.50 Bl. Winged Teal	12.00
RI 4A	'92 $7.50 Hunter Type	12.00
RI 5	'93 $7.50 Pintails	11.00
RI 5A	'93 $7.50 Hunter Type	12.00
RI 5M	'93 Commem. Sheet of 4	55.00
RI 5MI	'93 Same, Imperf.	85.00
RI 6	'94 $7.50 Wood Duck	11.00
RI 6A	'94 $7.50 Hunter Type	12.00
RI 7	'95 $7.50 Hooded Mergan.	11.00
RI 7A	'95 $7.50 Hunter Type	12.00
Ri 8	'96 $7.50 Harlequin	11.00
RI 8A	'96 $7.50 Hunter Type	12.00
RI 9	'97 $7.50 Greater Scaup	11.00
RI 9A	'97 $7.50 Hunter Type	12.00
RI 10	'98 $7.50 Black Ducks	11.00
RI 10A	'98 $7.50 Hunter Type	12.00

NOTE: Governor's stamps available upon request.
Rhode Island Set 1989-98 (10)....... 110.00
RI Hunter Type Set 1989-98 (10).. 110.00

SOUTH CAROLINA

SC 1

No.	Description	F-VF NH
SC 1	'81 $5.50 Wood Ducks	65.00
SC 2	'82 $5.50 Mallards	115.00
SC 2A	'82 Hunter-Ser'l # on Rev	550.00
SC 3	'83 $5.50 Pintails	100.00
SC 3A	'83 Hunter-Ser'l # on Rev	525.00
SC 4	'84 $5.50 Canada Geese	65.00
SC 4A	'84 Hunter-Ser'l # on Rev	230.00
SC 5	'85 $5.50 Grn. Winged Teal	65.00
SC 5A	'85 Hunter Ser'l # on Rev	130.00
SC 6	'86 $5.50 Canvasbacks	25.00
SC 6A	'86 Hunter-Ser'l # on Rev	45.00
SC 7	'87 $5.50 Black Ducks	20.00
SC 7A	'87 Hunter-Ser'l # on Rev	25.00

SOUTH CAROLINA (cont.)

No.	Description	F-VF NH
SC 8	'88 $5.50 Spaniel/Widg'n	20.00
SC 8A	'88 Hunter-Ser'l # on Rev	40.00
SC 9	'89 $5.50 Bl. Wingd. Teal	10.00
SC 9A	'89 Hunter-Ser'l # on Rev	15.00
SC 10	'90 $5.50 Wood Ducks	10.00
SC 10A	'90 Hunter-Ser'l # on Rev	10.00
SC 11	'91 $5.50 Blk. Lab/Pintails	9.00
SC 11A	'91 Hunter-Ser'l # on Rev	9.00
SC 12	'92 $5.50 Buffleheads	9.00
SC 12A	'92 Hunter-Ser'l # on Front	9.00
SC 13	'93 $5.50 Lesser Scaup	8.50
SC 13A	'93 Hunter-Ser'l # on Front	9.00
SC 14	'94 $5.50 Canvasbacks	8.50
SC 14A	'94 Hunter-Ser'l # on Front	9.00
SC 15	'95 $5.50 Shovelers	8.50
SC 15A	'95 Hunter, Serial # on Front	9.00
SC 16	'96 $5.50 Redhds/Lighthouse	8.50
SC 16A	'96 Hunter-Serial# on Front	9.00
SC 17	'97 $5.50 Old Squaws	8.50
SC 17A	'97 Hunter-Serial# on Front	9.00
SC 18	'98 $5.50 Ruddy Ducks	8.50
SC 18A	'98 Hunter-Serial # on Front	9.00

NOTE: Governor's stmps avail upon request.

South Carolina Set 1981-98 (18) 540.00
SC Hunter Type Set '81-'98 (17) 1560.00

SOUTH DAKOTA

SD 1

No.	Description	F-VF NH
SD 1	'76 $1 Mallards	35.00
SD 1V	'76 Small Serial # Variety	75.00
SD 2	'77 $1 Pintails	23.00
SD 3	'78 $1 Canvasbacks	14.00
SD 4	'86 $2 Canada Geese	10.00
SD 5	'87 $2 Blue Geese	8.00
SD 6	'88 $2 Wh. Fronted Geese	6.00
SD 7	'89 $2 Mallards	6.00
SD 8	'90 $2 Bl. Winged Teal	5.00
SD 9	'91 $2 Pintails	5.00
SD 10	'92 $2 Canvasbacks	5.00
SD 11	'93 $2 Lesser Scaup	5.00
SD 12	'94 $2 Redhead	5.00
SD 13	'95 $2 Wood Ducks	5.00
SD 14	'96 $2 Canada Goose	5.00
SD 15	'97 $2 Widgeons	5.00
SD 16	'98 $2 Green Winged Teal	5.00

South Dakota Set 1976-98 (16)...... 140.00

TENNESSEE

TN 1

No.	Description	F-VF NH
TN 1	'79 $2.30 Mallards	50.00
TN 1A	'79 $5.30 Non-Resident	1050.00
TN 2	'80 $2.30 Canvasbacks	60.00
TN 2A	'80 $5.30 Non-Resident	400.00
TN 2B	'80 $2.30 3 Part Card	925.00
TN 3	'81 $2.30 Wood Ducks	40.00
TN 3B	'81 $2.30 3 Part Card	...
TN 4	'82 $6.50 Canada Geese	60.00
TN 5	'83 $6.50 Pintails	60.00
TN 5B	'83 $6.50 3 Part Card	75.00
TN 6	'84 $6.50 Black Ducks	60.00

STATE HUNTING PERMIT STAMPS

TENNESSEE (cont.)

No.	Description	F-VF NH
TN 6B	'84 $6.50 3 Part Card	75.00
TN 7	'85 $6.50 Bl. Winged Teal	25.00
TN 7B	'85 $6.50 3 Part Card	50.00
TN 8	'86 $6.50 Mallards	15.00
TN 8B	'86 $6.50 3 Part Card	50.00
TN 9	'87 $6.50 Canada Geese	12.00
TN 9B	'87 $6.50 3 Part Card	18.00
TN 10	'88 $6.50 Canvasbacks	14.00
TN 10B	'88 $6.50 3 Part Card	23.00
TN 11	'89 $6.50 Grn Wngd Teal	12.00
TN 11B	'89 $6.50 3 Part Card	14.00
TN 12	'90 $13 Redheads	18.00
TN 12B	'90 $13 3 Part Card	22.00
TN 13	'91 $13 Mergansers	18.00
TN 13B	'91 $13 3 Part Card	22.00
TN 14	'92 $14 Wood Ducks	18.50
TN 14B	'92 $14 3 Part Card	22.00
TN 15	'93 $14 Pintail/Decoy	18.50
TN 15B	'93 $14 3 Part Card	22.00
TN 16	'94 $16 Mallard	21.00
TN 16B	'94 $16 3 Part Card	22.50
TN 17	'95 $16 Ring Nckd Ducks	22.00
TN 17B	'95 $16 3 Part Card	22.50
TN 18	'96 $18 Black Ducks	24.00
TN 18B	'96 $18 3 Part Card	25.00

Tennessee Set 1979-96 (20) 1950.00
Tennessee Set 1979-96 (18) w/o Non-Res 600.00

TEXAS

TX 1

No.	Description	F-VF NH
TX 1	'81 $5 Mallards	50.00
TX 2	'82 $5 Pintails	30.00
TX 3	'83 $5 Widgeon	175.00
TX 4	'84 $5 Wood Ducks	30.00
TX 5	'85 $5 Snow Geese	10.00
TX 6	'86 $5 Grn. Winged Teal	10.00
TX 7	'87 $5 Wh. Frnt'd Geese	10.00
TX 8	'88 $5 Pintails	10.00
TX 9	'89 $5 Mallards	10.00
TX 10	'90 $5 Widgeons	10.00
TX 11	'91 $7 Wood Duck	10.00
TX 12	'92 $7 Canada Geese	10.00
TX 13	'93 $7 Bl. Wngd. Teal	10.00
TX 14	'94 $7 Shovelers	10.00
TX 15	'95 $7 Buffleheads	10.00
TX 16	'96 $20 Book of 8 Different	20.00
TX 17	'97 $20 Book of 8 Different	20.00
TX 18	'98 $20 Book of 8 Different	20.00

Texas Set 1981-98 (18) 420.00

UTAH

UT 6

No.	Description	F-VF NH
UT 1	'86 $3.30 Whistling Swans	10.00
UT 2	'87 $3.30 Pintails	8.00
UT 3	'88 $3.30 Mallards	8.00
UT 4	'89 $3.30 Canada Geese	7.00
UT 5	'90 $3.30 Canvasbacks	7.00
UT 5A	'90 $3.30 Bklt, sgl. w/Tab	8.00
UT 6	'91 $3.30 Tundra Swans	6.50
UT 6A	'91 $3.30 Bklt. sgl w/Tab	7.00
UT 7	'92 $3.30 Pintails	6.50
UT 7A	'92 $3.30 Bklt. sgl w/Tab	7.00
UT 8	'93 $3.30 Canvasbacks	6.50
UT 8A	'93 $3.30 Bklt. sgl w/Tab	7.00
UT 9	'94 $3.30 Chesepeake	20.00
UT 9A	'94 $3.30 Bklt. sgl. w/Tab	18.00
UT10	'95 $3.30 Grn Winged Teal	6.50
UT 10A	'95 $3.30 Bklt. Sgl. w/Tab	7.00
UT 11	'96 $7.50 Wh.FrontedGoose	13.00
UT 12	'97 $7.50 Redheads PR(2)	26.00

NOTE: Governor's stamps available upon request.

UTAH (cont.)

Utah Set 1986-97 (13) 115.00
Utah Set Bklt. Sgl. 1990-95 (6) 50.00

VERMONT

VT 2

No.	Description	F-VF NH
VT 1	'86 $5 Aut'mn Wd Ducks	12.00
VT 2	'87 $5 Wintr Goldeneyes	10.00
VT 3	'88 $5 Spring Blk. Ducks	9.00
VT 4	'89 $5 Summer Canada Geese	9.00
VT 5	'90 $5 Grn Wngd Teal	9.00
VT 6	'91 $5 H'ded Mergans'r	9.00
VT 7	'92 $5 Snow Geese	9.00
VT 8	'93 $5 Mallards	9.00
VT 9	'94 $5 Ring Necked Duck	8.00
VT 10	'95 $5 Bufflehead	8.00
VT 11	'96 $5 Bluebills	8.00
VT 12	'97 $5 Pintail	8.00
VT 13	'98 $5Blue Winged Teal	8.00

Vermont Set 1986-98 (13) 99.00

VIRGINIA

VA 2

No.	Description	F-VF NH
VA 1	'88 $5 Mallards	12.00
VA 1A	'88 $5 Bklt. Single	15.00
VA 1A	'88 $5 Hz. pr./side mgns	25.00
VA 2	'89 $5 Canada Geese	15.00
VA 2A	'89 $5 Bklt. Single	14.50
VA 2A	'89 $5 Hz. pr./side mgns	28.00
VA 3	'90 $5 Wood Ducks	9.00
VA 3A	'90 $5 Bklt. Single	12.00
VA 3A	'90 $5 Hz. pr./side mgns	23.00
VA 4	'91 $5 Canvasbacks	9.00
VA 4A	'91 $5 Bklt. Single	12.00
VA 4A	'91 $5 Hz. pr./side mgns	23.00
VA 5	'92 $5 Buffleheads	9.00
VA 5A	'92 $5 Bklt. Single	12.00
VA 5A	'92 $5 Hz. pr./side mgns	23.00
VA 6	'93 $5 Black Ducks	8.50
VA 6A	'93 $5 Bklt. Single	8.50
VA 6A	'93 $5 Hz. pr./side mgns	17.00
VA 7	'94 $5 Lesser Scaup	8.00
VA 7A	'94 $5 Hz. pr./side mgns.	17.00
VA 8	'95 $5 Snow Geese	8.00
VA 8A	'95 $5 hz. pr./side Mgns.	17.00
VA 9	'96 $5 Hooded Merganser	8.00
VA 10	'97 $5 Lab	8.00
VA 11	'98 $5 Mallards	8.00

Virginia Set 1988-98 (11) 100.00
VA Hunter Pairs Set 1988-95 (8) 165.00

WASHINGTON

WA 2

No.	Description	F-VF NH
WA 1	'86 $5 Mallards	9.00
WA 1A	'86 $5 Hunter Type (77X82MM)	15.00
WA 2	'87 $5 Canvasbacks	15.00
WA 2A	'87 $5 Hunter Type (77X82MM)	10.00
WA 3	'88 $5 Harlequin	9.00
WA 3A	'88 $5 Hunter Type (77X82MM)	10.00

WASHINGTON (cont.)

No.	Description	F-VF NH
WA 4	'89 $5 Amer. Widgeon	9.00
WA 4A	'89 $5 Hunter Type (77X82MM)	10.00
WA 5	'90 $5 Pintails/Sour Duck	9.00
WA 5A	'90 $5 Hunter Type (77X82MM)	10.00
WA 6	'91 $5 Wood Duck	9.00
WA 6A	'91 $5 Hunter Type (77X82MM)	10.00
WA 6V	'91 $6 Wood Duck	12.00
WA 6AN	'91 $6 Mini Sheet/ No Staple Holes	40.00
WA 6AV	'91 $6 Hunter Type (77X82MM)	10.00
WA 7	'92 $6 Puppy/Can. Geese	10.00
WA 7N	'92 $6 Mini Sheet/ No Staple Holes	40.00
WA 7A	'92 $6 Hunter Type (77X82MM)	10.00
WA 8	'93 $6 Snow Geese	10.00
WA 8N	'93 $6 Mini Sheet/ No Staple Holes	17.00
WA 8A	'93 $6 Hunter Type (77X82MM)	10.00
WA 9	'94 $6 Black Brant	10.00
WA 9A	'94 $6 Hunter Type (77X82MM)	10.00
WA 9N	'94 $6 Mini Sheet, No staple holes	17.00
WA 10	'95 $6 Mallards	10.00
WA 10A	'95 $6 Hunter Type (77 x 82 MM)	10.00
WA 10N	'95 $6 Mini Sheet No staple holes	17.00
WA 11	'96 $6 Redheads	9.00
WA 11A	'96 $6 Hunter Type (77x82MM)	10.00
WA 11N	'96 $6 Mini Sheet No staple holes	17.00
WA 12	'97 $6 Canada Geese	9.00
WA 12A	'97 $6 Hunter Type (77x82MM)	9.00
WA 12AN	'97 $6 Mini Sheet No staple holes	18.00
WA 13	'98 $6 Goldeneye	9.00
WA 13A	'98 $6 Hunter Type (61x137mm)	9.00
WA 13N	'98 $6 Mini Sheet No staple holes	15.00

Washington Set 1986-98 (14) 120.00
WA Hunter Set 1986-98 (14) 125.00

WEST VIRGINIA

WV 4A

No.	Description	F-VF NH
WV 1	'87 $5 Can. Geese/Res	15.00
WV 1A	'87 $5 Non-Resident	15.00
WV 1B	'87 $5 Bklt. sgl-Resident	45.00
WV 1AB	'87 Same, Non-Res	45.00
WV 2	'88 $5 Wood Ducks/Res	12.00
WV 2A	'88 $5 Non-Resident	12.50
WV 2B	'88 $5 Bklt. sgl-Resident	28.00
WV 2AB	'88 Same, Non-Res	28.00
WV 3	'89 $5 Decoys/Res	12.50
WV 3A	'89 $5 Non-Resident	12.50
WV 3B	'89 $5 Bklt. sgl-Resident	13.00
WV 3AB	'89 Same, Non-Res	13.00
WV 4	'90 Lab/Decoys/Res	12.00
WV 4A	'90 $5 Non-Resident	12.00
WV 4B	'90 $5 Bklt. sgl-Resident	12.00
WV 4AB	'90 Same, Non-Res	12.00
WV 5	'91 $5 Mallards/Res	8.50
WV 5A	'91 $5 Non-Resident	8.50
WV 5B	'91 $5 Bklt. sgl-Resident	12.00
WV 5AB	'91 Same, Non-Res	12.00
WV 5S	'91 WV Ohio Riv. Sht of 6	55.00
WV 6	'92 $5 Can. Geese/Res	9.50
WV 6A	'92 $5 Non-Resident	9.50
WV 6B	'92 $5 Bklt. sgl-Resident	9.50
WV 6AB	'92 Same, Non-Res	9.50
WV 7	'93 $5 Pintails/Res	9.00
WV 7A	'93 $5 Non-Resident	9.00
WV 7B	'93 $5 Bklt. sgl-Resident	9.00
WV 7AB	'93 Same, Non-Res	9.00
WV 8	'94 $5 Grn. Winged Teal	8.50
WV 8A	'94 Same, Non-Res	8.50
WV 8B	'94 $5 Pintails-Hunter	9.00
WV 8AB	'94 Same, Non-Res	9.00
WV 9	'95 $5 Wood Duck	8.50
WV 9A	'95 Same, Non-Resident	8.50
WV 9B	'95 $5 Hunter Type	9.00

WEST VIRGINIA (cont.)

No.	Description	F-VF NH
WV 9AB	'95 Same, Non-Resident	9.00
WV 10	'96 $5 American Widgeons	8.50
WV 10A	'96 $5 Widgeon Non-Res.	8.50
WV 10B	'96 $5 Widgeon Hunter Typ	9.00
WV 10AB	'96 $5 Widgeon NR Hunter	9.00

NOTE: Governor's stamps available upon request.

West Virginia Set 1987-96 (20) 210.00
WV Hunter Ty.Set 1987-96 (20) 275.00

WISCONSIN

WI 1

No.	Description	F-VF NH
WI 1	'78 $3.25 Wood Ducks	115.00
WI 2	'79 $3.25 Buffleheads	30.00
WI 3	'80 $3.25 Widgeon	12.00
WI 4	'81 $3.25 Lesser Scaup	10.00
WI 5	'82 $3.25 Pintails	8.00
WI 5T	'82 $3.25 Full Tab Attd	10.00
WI 6	'83 $3.25 Bl. Winged Teal	8.50
WI 6T	'83 $3.25 Full Tab Attd	12.00
WI 7	'84 $3.25 Hd'd Mergans'r	8.50
WI 7T	'84 $3.25 Full Tab Attd	12.00
WI 8	'85 $3.25 Lesser Scaup	10.00
WI 8T	'85 $3.25 Full Tab Attd	12.00
WI 9	'86 $3.25 Canvasbacks	10.00
WI 9T	'86 $3.25 Full Tab Attd	12.00
WI 10	'87 $3.25 Canada Geese	6.50
WI 10T	'87 $3.25 Full Tab Attd	8.00
WI 11	'88 $3.25 Hd'd Mergans'r	6.50
WI 11T	'88 $3.25 Full Tab Attd	8.00
WI 12	'89 $3.25 Cm'n Gldneye	6.50
WI 12T	'89 $3.25 Full Tab Attd	8.00
WI 13	'90 $3.25 Redheads	6.50
WI 13T	'90 $3.25 Full Tab Attd	8.00
WI 14	'91 $5.25 Grn. Wngd. Teal	8.50
WI 14T	'91 $5.25 Full Tab Attd	9.50
WI 15	'92 $5.25 Tundra Swans	8.50
WI 15T	'92 $5.25 Full Tab Attd	9.50
WI 16	'93 $5.25 Wood Ducks	8.50
WI 16T	'93 $5.25 Full Tab Attd	9.50
WI 17	'94 $5.25 Pintails	8.50
WI 17A	'94 $5.25 Full Tab Attd	9.50
WI 18	'95 $5.25 Mallards	8.50
WI 18A	'95 $5.25 Full Tab Attd	9.50
WI 19	'96 $5.25 Gr. Winged Teal	8.50
WI 19T	'96 $5.25 Full Tab Attchd.	9.50
WI 20	'97 $7 Canada Goose	8.50
WI 20T	'97 $7 Full Tab Attchd.	9.50
WI 21	'98 $7 Snow Goose	10.00
WI 21T	'98 Full Tab Arrow Head	11.00

Wisconsin Set 1978-98 (21) 290.00

WYOMING

WY 2

No.	Description	F-VF NH
WY 1	'84 $5 Meadowlark	40.00
WY 2	'85 $5 Canada Geese	45.00
WY 3	'86 $5 Prnghrn Antelope	45.00
WY 4	'87 $5 Sage Grouse	45.00
WY 5	'88 $5 Cut-Throat Trout	45.00
WY 6	'89 $5 Mule Deer	50.00
WY 7	'90 $5 Grizzly Bear	40.00
WY 8	'91 $5 Big Horn Sheep	40.00
WY 9	'92 $5 Bald Eagle	25.00
WY 10	'93 $5 Elk	20.00
WY 11	'94 $5 Bobcat	15.00
WY 12	'95 $5 Moose	10.00
WY 13	'96 $5 Turkey	10.00
WY 14	'97 $5 Rocky Mntn Goats	10.00
WY 15	'98 $5 Thunder Swans	10.00

Wyoming Set 1984-98 (12) 420.00

NOTE: SEE PAGE 253 FOR CANADA FEDERAL AND PROVINCIAL DUCK STAMPS.

INDIAN RESERVATION STAMPS

NEW MEXICO - JICARILLA

**NORTH DAKOTA
STANDING ROCK SIOUX**

CHEYENNE RIVER SIOUX

CROW CREEK SIOUX

FORT PECK TRIBES

PINE RIDGE - OGLALA SIOUX

LAKE TRAVERSE

MONTANA - CROW

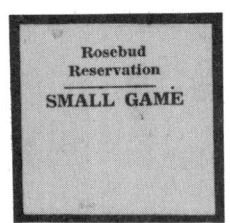

ROSEBUD

MONTANA - FLATHEAD

No.		Description	F-VF NH
		MONTANA CROW	
W #3	1992	Waterfowl	110.00
W #2	1992	Upland Game	60.00
W #3V	1993	Waterfowl, undated	12.00
W #2V	1993	Upland, undated	12.00
		FLATHEAD	
H #1	1987	Bird	1450.00
H #3	1988	Bird/Fish	1100.00
H #4	1989	Bird/Fish Pr w/Dupe	18.00
H #5	1989	Shiny Paper	55.00
H #7	1990	Shiny Paper	575.00
H #9	1990	Bird/Fish Pr w/Dupe	18.00
H #10	1991	Joint Bird	11.00
H #12	1992	Bird Annual	10.00
H #13	1992	Bird 3-Day	9.00
H #16	1993	Bird Annual	9.00
H #17	1993	Bird 3-Day	9.00
H #20	1994	Bird Annual	9.00
H #21	1994	Bird 3-Day	8.00
H #24	1995	Bird Resident	10.00
H #25	1995	Bird Non-Resident	15.00
H #28	1996	Bird Resident	12.00
H #29	1996	Bird Non-Resident	16.00
H #33	1997	Bird Resident	12.00
H #34	1997	Bird Non-Resident	16.00
H #8		Bird/Fish "Fasson" Backing	40.00
H #38		Bird Resident	12.00
H #39		Bird Non-Resident	15.00
		FORT PECK	
P #3	1975	Bird	1550.00
P #5	1976	Bird	110.00
P #9	1978	Bird	350.00
P #16	1988	$10 Upland Game(yellow)	25.00
P #16a	1988	$10 Plate Flaw	125.00
P #14	1988	$25 Upland Game(yellow)	40.00
P #17	1994	$40 Upland Game(yellow)	75.00
P #15	1988	$50 Upland Game(yellow)	75.00
P #18	1994	$15 Upland Game (drawing)	22.00
P #19	1994	$45 Upland Game (drawing)	60.00
P #20	1995	$45 Upland Game(wht,brn)	60.00
P #25	1996	$25 Upland Game(blue)	25.00
P #26	1996	$25 Upland Game(brn)	55.00
P #27	1997	$10 Waterfowl (orange)	20.00
P #28	1997	$40 Waterfowl (green)	35.00
P #31	1997	$25 Upland (blue)	25.00
P #32	1997	$40 Upland (plum)	45.00

No.		Description	F-VF NH
		NEW MEXICO JICARILLA	
JI #2	1988	Wildlife Stamp	15.00
		NORTH DAKOTA STANDING ROCK SIOUX TRIBE:	
SR #10	1992	Waterfowl	17.00
SR #20	1993	Waterfowl	12.00
SR $30	1994	Waterfowl	11.00
SR #39	1995	Waterfowl	15.00
SR #48	1996	Waterfowl	15.00
SR #57	1997	Waterfowl	15.00
SR #70	1998	Waterfowl	15.00
		SOUTH DAKOTA CHEYENNE RIVER SIOUX TRIBE	
CR#2	1984-91	Birds&Small Game,Member	
CR #7	1984-91	Same,Non-Member	
CR #29	1989-94	Birds & Small Game Member	15.00
CR #34		Same, Non-Member	30.00
CR #12	1989-94	Birds & Small Game Member, Shiny Paper	30.00
Cr #18		Non-Member, Shiny Paper	55.00
Cr #32	1994	Waterfowl, Member	20.00
Cr #42	1994	Same, Non-Member	30.00
		CROW CREEK SIOUX TRIBE	
CC #27	1989	$10 Canada Geese Reservation	600.00
CC #28	1989	$30 SD Resident	
CC #29	1989	$65 Non-Resident	1500.00
CC #30	1990	$10 Canada Geese Reservation	425.00
CC #31	1990	$30 SD Resident	350.00
CC #32	1990	$65 Non-Resident	1400.00
		1989-1990 Sportsman Set (8 stamps)	
CC #33-40		**($770 Face Val.)**	**4200.00**
		1989-1990 Upland Game Set	
CC #15-20		**(6 stamps)**	**1050.00**
CC #61	1994	$5 Tribal Member	55.00
CC #62	1994	$15 Resident	80.00
CC #63	1994	$30 Non-Res. Daily	115.00
CC #64	1994	$75 Non-Resident	195.00

No.		Description	F-VF NH
CC #91-94	1995		
		$5 Tribal Member	
		$15 Resident Member,	
		$30 Non-Resident Daily	
		$75 Non-Resident	
		Set of 4	295.00
CC #121-124	1996		
		Set of 4	295.00
CC #152-155	1997		
		Set of 4	295.00
		LOWER BRULE	
LB #26-30	1995	Set of 5 Waterfowl	50.00
LB #31-33	1996	Set of 3 Waterfowl	35.00
LB #34-36	1997	Set of 3 Waterfowl	35.00
LB #37-39	1998	Set of 3 Waterfowl	35.00
		LAKE TRAVERSE INDIAN RESERVATION (SISSETON-WAHPETON)	
LT #5	1986	Game Bird	180.00
LT #9	1986	Upland Game	500.00
LT #27	1991	Waterfowl - Bright Green	125.00
LT #24	1991	Small Game	50.00
LT #26	1991	Upland Bird	70.00
LT #32	1992	Small Game - Green	25.00
LT #31	1992	Small Game - Orange	12.50
LT #34	1992	Upland Game	4.00
LT #35	1992	Wood Duck	17.00
LT #42	1993	Upland Bird	12.00
LT #40	1993	Small Game	12.00
LT #43	1993	Waterfowl-Bright Red	25.00
LT #56	1994	Waterfowl-Yellow Orange	10.00
LT #52	1994	Small Game	6.00
LT #55	1994	Upland Bird	6.00
LT #62	1995	Waterfowl	12.00
LT #59	1995	Small Game	8.00
LT #65	1996	Small Game	8.00
LT #67	1996	Upland Bird	7.00
LT #68	1996	Waterfowl	225.00
LT #71	1997	Small Game	8.00
LT #72	1997	Sportsman	35.00
LT #73	1997	Upland Bird	7.00
LT #74	1997	Waterfowl	10.00
LT #77	1998	Small Game	7.00
LT #78	1998	Sportsman	35.00
LT #79	1998	Upland Bird	6.00
LT #80	1998	Waterfowl	40.00

No.		Description	F-VF NH
		ROSEBUD	
RB #10	1970's	Small Game Ser.#	1600.00
RB #11	1980's	Small Game Ser.#	275.00
RB #52	1988	$10 Small Game	45.00
RB #53	1989	$45 Small Game	190.00
		PINE RIDGE (OGLALA SIOUX)	
PR #11	1988-92	$4 Waterfowl, Rouletted	375.00
PR #30	1988-92	$4 Waterfowl, Perforated	30.00
PR #47	1992	$4 Canada Geese	12.50
PR #48	1993	$6 Canada Geese	12.50
PR #49	1994	$6 '94 ovrprntd on '93	15.00
		FORT BERTHOLD	
TT #12	1990	Small Game	85.00
TT #14	1990	Upland Game	140.00
TT #15	1990	Waterfowl	2500.00
TT #19	1991	Small Game	80.00
TT #21	1991	Upland Game	105.00
TT #22	1991	Waterfowl	900.00
TT #26	1992	Small Game	80.00
TT #28	1992	Upland Game	85.00
TT #33	1993	Small Game	175.00
TT #35	1993	Upland Game	85.00
TT #36	1993	Waterfowl	600.00
TT #39	1994	Small Game	70.00
TT #41	1994	Upland Game	295.00
TT #42	1994	Waterfowl	615.00
TT #45	1995	Small Game	100.00
TT #47	1995	Upland Bird	85.00
TT #48	1995	Waterfowl	275.00
TT #51	1996	Small Game	55.00
TT #53	1996	Upland Game	85.00
TT #54	1996	Waterfowl	225.00
TT #57	1997	Small Game	50.00
TT #60	1997	Waterfowl	260.00
TT #63	1998	Small Game	40.00
TT #66	1998	Waterfowl	300.00
		NAVAJO	
NA #1	1991	Habitat	65.00
NA #2	1992	Habitat	12.00
NA #3	1993	Habitat	12.00
NA #4	1994	Habitat	10.00
NA #5	1995	Habitat	10.00
NA #6	1996	Habitat	10.00
NA #7	1997	Habitat	10.00

Welcome to First Day Cover Collecting!

by Barry Newton, Editor *FIRST DAYS*, the official journal of the American First Day Cover Society

A First Day Cover (FDC) is an envelope or card with a stamp postmarked on the day the stamp was sold. The postmark may be pictorial, like the one shown above, or it can simply have the slogan "FIRST DAY OF ISSUE" (FDOI) between the killer bars of the cancel. Most new stamps are first sold in a city related to the subject of the stamp. Sometimes a stamp subject will be considered so popular or important that it is issued in every PO all across the county on the First Day (FD).

A cachet (pronounced ka-shay) is the design on the envelope. It usually shows something more about the new stamp and is usually on the left side of the envelope. Some cachets cover the entire face of the envelope with the design.

Combination FDCs or Combo FDCs can be made for any subject. Some research into a new stamp you like is all you need to do. Find some inexpensive stamps that help to tell the full story of the stamp. Many stamps going all the way back into the 1940s will be inexpensive enough to put on your Combo. The Combo shown here contains eight stamps from the Black Heritage series issued by the U.S. Postal Service.

A Joint Issue First Day Cover has two or more stamps issued by different countries to commemorate the same event, topic, place or person. The cover shown above has the US and Canadian Year of the Tiger stamps, both cancelled with the First Day of Issue cancel of their own country. In 1998, more than 20 countries issued Year of the Tiger stamps, including countries with significant Chinese ethnic groups, like the US, Canada and Australia.

Autographs on First Day Covers are very popular. This FDC was made by AFDCS Member Florence Villasenor. Florence met Captain Lillian Kinkela Keil through a friend and was able to honor her on this cachet. Captain Keil then autographed the covers. For more information on autograph collecting, send a 55¢ self-addressed stamped envelope to the Autograph Chapter of the AFDCS, Box 42, Audubon, NJ 08106.

FIRST CACHETS

by Marjory J. Sente

Stamp collectors are always interested in the oldest, first, best, rarest, most expensive items. So it is not unusual for First Day Cover enthusiasts to search for the earliest known cachet by a particular manufacturer or designer. First cachets are a fascinating and challenging speciality. They have been researched and documented for thousands of artists and cachetmakers. Yet, the search for other first cachets continues.

A first cachet is the initial design commercially produced by a cachetmaker. To qualify as commercially produced, the cacheted First Day Cover is made and sold in a quantity greater than the maker's personal needs. An example is the design prepared by Colorano "Silk"

cachets for the 1971 American Wool Industry commemorative, issued on January 19 at Las Vegas, NV. Ray Novak had seen silk cachets produced by the French firm, Ceres, and decided to market the same type of cachet for United States postal issues. For the first Colorano "Silk" cachet, Ray produced 1200 covers. The press run increased to 2400 in 1972 and by the cachet line's tenth anniversary, production had increased to 10,000 per issue.

Sometimes it is difficult to identify a cachetmaker's initial production, because it is not signed. So researchers need to rely on philatelic publications released about the time the cachet was produced and advertised for

distribution. Stuffers in the FDCs also provide good clues as to the cachet's producer. The first Fleetwood cachet, prepared for the Vermont Statehood commemorative, released on March 4, 1941, was not signed, but a stuffer identifies Staehle as the designer and Fleetwood as the producer. The line has undergone many changes over the years, and today, the colorful Fleetwood designs produced by Unicover are likely the most mass-marketed First Day Covers.

Other cachets are relatively easy to identify, because most of designs including the first one are signed. Fluegel cachets, produced from the mid-1940's until the late 1960's, are nearly always signed "Fluegel." Herman "Cap" Fluegel

prepared his first commercial venture for the 3-cent Roosevelt commemorative issued on June 27, 1945. Known for their brilliant colors, his early cachets were printed in letterpress in five or six colors.

Addresses on FDCs are sometimes a tip to their origin. Cachetmakers frequently send covers to themselves or relatives. Ernest J. Weschcke produced his first and only cachet for the Norse-American Centennial commemorative pair, released on May 18, 1925. The distinctive red cachet printed on Norwegian Blue envelopes is unsigned but most of the FDCs are addressed to him. It is estimated that Weschcke made about 200 of these FDCs, but few were sold. The others were treasured by the family and kept in pristine condition.

Sometimes a first cachet gives birth to a line with a formal trademark. Of the four major cachet lines that are marketed today-- Artcraft, Artmaster, House of Farnum and Fleetwood--only the first Artmaster cachet appeared with its well known script trademark. The other three cachet lines adopted trademarks later.

Robert Schmidt of Louisville, Kentucky, prepared the first Artmaster cachet for the Honor Discharge issue released on May 9, 1946. For this initial cachet 15,000 covers were sold and 10,000 distributed free for advertising and publicity purposes.

Dabbling or creating of multiple cachet lines are other confusing issues for the positive identification of first cachets. Cachetmakers frequently will dabble at making cachets before launching into commercial production. They will design a cachet as an experiment, for their own amusement, or as a favor for an organization. Do these forerunners qualify as first cachets? Part of the answer is whether you collect first cachets by artist or designer or by cachetmaker or the cachet line.

Sometimes an artist will prepare cachets for earlier FDCs than the one that is considered to be a first because it is defined by cachetmaker or the name of the cachet line. For example, Ludwig Staehle prepared his first cachet for the Swedish-Finnish Tercentenary commemorative issued in 1938, several years earlier than the first Fleetwood cachet that he designed for the 1941 Vermont Statehood issue.

Doris Gold's cachetmaking career provides another example. She began making one-of-a-kind handdrawn/handpainted covers. Her first endeavor for a U.S. issue was for the 1975 Benjamin West issue. Her first commercial special events cover was prepared for the 1976 Writer's day INTERPHIL show cancellation. Her first commercial handdrawn/handpainted FDC was made for the 1976 Olympics block-of-four commemoratives. The release of the 1977 Lindbergh Transatlantic commemorative was the birth of the DG Series. And in 1987 she started the DGHC Series beginning with Enrico Caruso commemorative. With this series an outline is printed in black outline, and then the cover is painted by hand. The first cachet for the DGX Series, which employs laser color printing, was prepared for the 1990 Movie Classics issue.

Sometimes a cachetmaker is involved in commercially producing event covers before making FDCs. This is true for John Adlen, producer of Pilgrim cachets. He started making event covers in the early 1930s, his first cachet on an FDC was for the 1937 Constitution commemorative. Most of his covers are signed and include a return address at the bottom of the cachet.

Along with first cachets come one-time cachets. These designs are the works of cachetmakers who produce only one cachet in their lifetime. Some collectors call the one-timers, first cachets. Others say to have a first cachet, you must have a second. An excellent discussion on "Collecting First Cachets" appeared in the September/October 1980 *First Days*.

The systematic compilation of data on first cachets resulted in the publication of *Mellone's First Cachets A FDC Reference Catalog* by Hal Ansink, Lois Hamilton and Dr. Richard A. Monty in 1980. Three years later an updated version was published, followed by a third in 1989. A fourth edition, *First Cachets Revisited*, is the latest comprehensive update of the list. In the interim, *First Days,* the official journal of the American First Day Cover Society, publishes an ongoing column updating the research.

Marjory Sente has written about First Day Covers for more than two decades. Her monthly column appears in MeKeel's Weekly and Stamps. *She also teach an independent learning course on FDCs offered through Penn State.*

Brookman's Subscription Bonanza

Here's your chance to see photos of the best covers in the comfort of your home.

Cover Line is designed for the collector who is looking for 1000's of covers.
Cover Line features: U.S. First Days, Akron/Macons, Zeppelins, Flights, WWII Patriotics, Catapults, Hawaii/Pacific Rim, Fluegels, Collins, Our Bargain Bonanza Section with covers as low as 99¢ and many, many more.......
Cover Line is published in the Spring, Summer, Fall, and Winter.

Subscribe today for $9.95 per year

Coverline Express is our newest publication used to highlight only very recent cover purchases. It goes out to about 10% of our customers before it is seen by 1000's of buyers.
This is your chance to get first shot at buying that special cover you've been hunting for. The Cover Line Express features all of the same types of covers featured in the Cover Line. All subscribers will receive their issues via *First Class Mail*.
The Cover Line Express is published monthly.

Subscribe today for $19.95 per year.

Subscribe today for both CoverLine and Coverline Express and receive a $25 gift certificate

❑ **Cover Line $9.95** ____

❑ **Cover Line Express $19.95** ____
<u>**Save & Subscribe to Both**</u>

❑ **Cover Line & Coverline Express $24.95** ____
  + receive a $25 Gift Certificate
  good on any Cover Order

Total Due ____

Name: _____

Address: _____

City: _____ State: ____ Zip: _____

Daytime Phone: _____

Visa / MC: _____

Expiration Date: _____

BROOKMAN
Barrett & Worthen

Brookman, Barrett & Worthen
10 Chestnut Drive, Bedford, NH 03110

1-800-332-3382
E-mail: sales@brookmancovers.com

FAX 1-603-472-8795
Web Site: www.brookmancovers.com

138

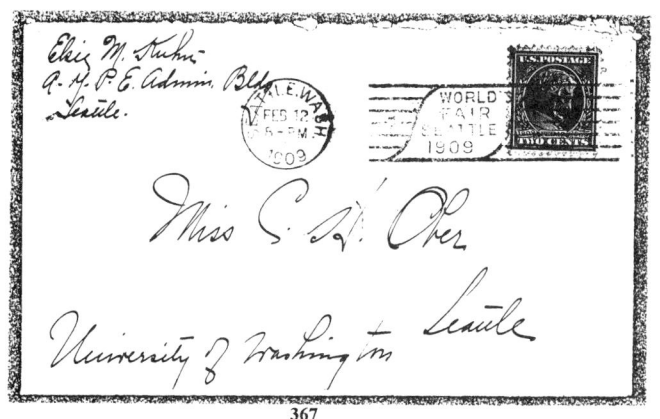

367

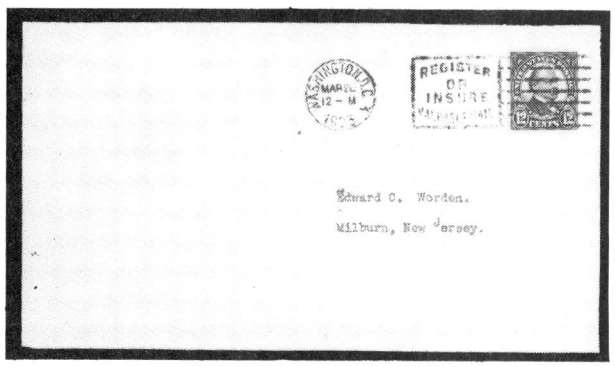

564

FDC's will be addressed from #5A-952 and unaddressed from 953 to date
Cacheted prices are for FDC's with common printed cachets. From #704 all FDC's will be cacheted. Multiples are generally priced @ 1.25x for blocks & 2x for plate blks. or line pairs

Scott #	Description	Uncacheted
1851-1890		
5A	1¢ Franklin, Blue, Type 1b, 7/1/1851 Any City	135,000.00
7	1¢ Franklin, Blue, Type II 7/1/1851 Any City	4500.00
10	3¢ Washington, Orange Brown 7/1/1851 Any City	17,500.00
64B	3¢ Washington, Rose Pink 8/17/1861 Any City	26,000.00
79	3¢ Washington "A" Grill 8/13/1867 Any City	15,000.00
210	2¢ Washington, Red Brown 10/1/1883 Any City	2700.00
210-211	2¢ Wash., 4¢ Jackson on one cvr, 10/1/1883	40,000.00
219D	2¢ Washington, Lake 2/22/1890 Any City	17,500.00
1893 COLUMBIAN ISSUE		
230	1¢ Columbian 1/2/1893 Any City	5000.00
	Salem, MA 12/31/1892	15,000.00
231	2¢ Columbian 1/2/1893 Any City	4000.00
	New York, NY or Boston, MA 1/1/1893	7500.00
	Salem, MA 12/31/1892	15,000.00
232	3¢ Columbian 1/2/1893 Any City	10,000.00
233	4¢ Columbian 1/2/1893 Any City	10,500.00
234	5¢ Columbian 1/2/1893 Any City	17,500.00
235	6¢ Columbian 1/2/1893 Any City	22,500.00
237	10¢ Columbian 1/2/1893 Any City	25,000.00
	East Lexington, MA 12/31/92 bkstp	25,000.00
242	$2.00 Columbian 1/2/1893 New York, NY	65,000.00
265	2¢ Washington 5/2/1895 Any City	9500.00

* Since Jan. 1, 1893 was a Sunday and few post offices were open, both Jan. 1 and Jan. 2 covers are considered FDC's by collectors.

	1898 TRANS-MISSISSIPPI ISSUE	
285	1¢ Trans-Mississippi 6/17/1898 Any City	13,500.00
286	2¢ Trans-Mississippi 6/17/1898 DC	11,500.00
	6/17/1898 Pittsburgh, PA	12,500.00
287	4¢ Trans-Mississippi 6/17/1898 Any City	20,000.00
288	5¢ Trans-Mississippi 6/17/1898 DC	20,000.00
289	8¢ Trans-Mississippi 6/17/1898 DC	25,000.00
290	10¢ Trans-Mississippi 6/17/1898 Any City	30,000.00
291	50¢ Trans-Mississippi 6/17/1898 DC	35,000.00
292	$1 Trans-Mississippi 6/17/1898 DC	60,000.00
	1901 PAN AMERICAN ISSUE	
294	1¢ Pan-American 5/1/01 Any City	5000.00
	294,296, 297 on one cover, Boston, MA	30,000.00
295	2¢ Pan-American 5/1/01 Any City	2750.00
296	4¢ Pan-American 5/1/01 Any City	10,000.00
297	5¢ Pan-American 5/1/01 Any City	17,500.00
298	8¢ Pan-American 5/1/01 Any City	17,500.00
298,296	4¢ & 8¢ on one FDC Boston, MA	22,500.00
294-299	1¢-10¢ Pan-American, cplt. set on one FDC, Any City	37,500.00
	1904 LOUISIANA PURCHASE 1907 JAMESTOWN ISSUES	
323	1¢ Louisiana Purchase 4/30/04 Any City	7500.00
324	2¢ Louisiana Purchase 4/30/04 Any City	6000.00
325	3¢ Louisiana Purchase 4/30/04 Any City	18,000.00
326	5¢ Louisiana Purchase 4/30/04 Any City	26,000.00
327	10¢ Louisiana Purchase 4/30/04 Any City	27,500.00
323-327	1¢-10¢ Louisiana Purchase, complete set on 1 FDC	100,000.00
328	1¢ Jamestown Expedition 4/26/07 Any City	10,000.00
328-30	On one cover, 5/10/07 Norwalk, VA (eku)	22,000.00
329	2¢ Jamestown Expedition 4/26/07 Any City	12,000.00
330	5¢ Jamestown Expedition 5/10/07 Norfolk, VA (eku)	17,500.00
331a	1¢ Franklin, bklt. sgl. 12/2/08 DC	20,000.00
332a	2¢ Washington, bklt. sgl. 11/16/08 DC	35,000.00
	1909 COMMEMORATIVES	
367	2¢ Lincoln 2/12/09 Any City	400.00
367	2¢ Lincoln 2/12/09 Any City on Lincoln-related post-card	600.00
368	2¢ Lincoln Imperf. 2/12/09 Canton, OH	17,000.00
370	2¢ Alaska-Yukon 6/1/09 Any City	5000.00
370	On related card	5500.00
370	On card, Any City	6000.00
372	2¢ Hudson-Fulton, 9/25/09, Any City, (100-200 Known)	800.00
372	2¢ Hudson-Fulton, 9/25/09, Any City on related post-card	1500.00
373	2¢ Hudson-Fulton Imperf. 9/25/09 Any City	8500.00

Scott #	Description	Uncacheted
1913 PAN-PACIFIC ISSUE		
397	1¢ Pan-Pacific Expo 1/1/13 Any City	5000.00
398	2¢ Pan-Pacific Expo 1/18/13 Washington, D.C.	2000.00
399	5¢ Pan-Pacific Expo 1/1/13 Any City	22,000.00
400	10¢ Pan-Pacific Expo 1/1/13 Any City	17,500.00
403	5¢ Pan-Pacific Expo, Perf. 10, 2/6/15 Chicago, Ill	7500.00
397,399,400	1¢,5¢ & 10¢ Pan-Pacific on one FDC, SF, CA	30,000.00
497	10¢ Franklin Coil 1/31/22 DC (all are Hammelman cvrs)	5300.00
526	2¢ Offset Ty. IV 3/15/20 Any City (eku)	1100.00
537	3¢ Victory 3/3/19 Any City	800.00
542	1¢ Rotary Perf. 10 x 11 5/26/20 Any City	2400.00
1920 PILGRIM TERCENTENARY		
548	1¢ "Mayflower" Pair 12/21/20 DC	1250.00
549	2¢ "Landing of the Pilgrims" 12/21/20 DC	1000.00
	12/21/20 Philadelphia, PA	2000.00
	12/21/20 Plymouth, MA	2500.00
548-50	1¢-5¢ Complete set on one cover, Phila., PA	3200.00
	Complete set on one cover, DC	3200.00
1922-25 FLAT PLATE PERF. 11		
551	½¢ Hale (Block of 4) 4/4/25 DC	18.00
	New Haven, CT	23.00
	Unofficial City	150.00
	551 & 576 on one FDC 4/4/25 DC	125.00
552	1¢ Franklin 1/17/23 DC	22.50
	Philadelphia, PA	45.00
	Unofficial City	175.00
553	1½¢ Harding 3/19/25 DC	25.00
554	2¢ Washington 1/15/23 DC	35.00
555	3¢ Lincoln 2/12/23 DC	35.00
	Hodgenville, KY	200.00
	Unofficial City	300.00
556	4¢ Martha Washington 1/15/23 DC	70.00
557	5¢ Teddy Roosevelt 10/27/22 DC	115.00
	New York, NY	175.00
	Oyster Bay, NY	2500.00
558	6¢ Garfield 11/20/22 DC	250.00
559	7¢ McKinley 5/1/23 DC	150.00
	Niles, OH	210.00
560	8¢ Grant 5/1/23 DC	160.00
	559-560 on one FDC, DC	750.00
	565 & 560 on one FDC, DC	2500.00
561	9¢ Jefferson 1/15/23 DC	160.00
	556-561 on one FDC, DC	900.00
562	10¢ Monroe 1/15/23 DC	160.00
	562,554,556 & 561 on one FDC	2000.00
562 & 554	On one FDC	800.00
563	11¢ Hayes 10/4/22 DC	650.00
	Fremont, OH	3750.00
564	12¢ Cleveland 3/20/23 DC	175.00
	Boston, MA	250.00
	Caldwell, NJ	175.00
	Lynn, MA	4500.00
565	14¢ Indian 5/1/23 DC	325.00
	Muskogee, OK	2000.00
566	15¢ Statue of Liberty 11/11/22 DC	550.00
567	20¢ Golden Gate 5/1/23 DC	550.00
	Oakland, CA	8000.00
	San Francisco, CA	3750.00
568	25¢ Niagara Falls 11/11/22 DC	650.00
569	30¢ Bison 3/20/23 DC	800.00
	569 & 564 on one FDC, DC	6000.00
570	50¢ Arlington 11/11/22 DC	1500.00
	570,566 & 568 on one FDC	7500.00
571	$1 Lincoln Memorial 2/12/23 DC	6500.00
	Springfield, IL	6500.00
	571 & 555 on one FDC, DC	9500.00
572	$2 U.S. Capitol 3/20/23 DC	17,500.00
573	$5 Freedom Statue 3/20/23 DC	32,500.00
1925-26 ROTARY PRESS PERF. 10		
576	1½¢ Harding Imperf. 4/4/25 DC	50.00
581	1¢ Franklin, unprecancelled 10/17/23 DC	7500.00
582	1½¢ Harding 3/19/25 DC	45.00
583a	2¢ Washington bklt pane of 6, 8/27/26 DC	1400.00

* eku: earliest known use

598

Scott #	Description	Uncacheted
584	3¢ Lincoln 8/1/25 DC	60.00
585	4¢ Martha Washington 4/4/25 DC	60.00
585-587	On one FDC	750.00
586	5¢ T. Roosevelt 4/4/25 DC	65.00
587	6¢ Garfield 4/4/25 DC	65.00
588	7¢ McKinley 5/29/26 DC	70.00
589	8¢ Grant 5/29/26 DC	80.00
590	9¢ Jefferson 5/29/26 DC	80.00
	590, 588 & 589 on one FDC	350.00
591	10¢ Monroe 6/8/25 DC	100.00

Scott #	Description	Uncacheted	Line Pairs
	1923-25 COIL ISSUES		
597	1¢ Franklin 7/18/23 DC	750.00	1750.00
598	1½¢ Harding 3/19/25 DC	55.00	175.00
*599	2¢ Washington 1/15/23 DC (37 known)	2250.00	3500.00
	1/10/23 Lancaster, PA (1 known)	4000.00	...

* These are the eku from DC and prepared by Phil Ward.
Other covers are known date 1/10, 1/11 & 1/13.

600	3¢ Lincoln 5/10/24 DC	125.00	275.00
602	5¢ T. Roosevelt 3/5/24 DC	100.00	275.00
603	10¢ Monroe 12/1/24 DC	110.00	350.00
604	1¢ Franklin 7/19/24 DC	85.00	225.00
605	1½¢ Harding 5/9/25 DC	75.00	175.00
606	2¢ Washington 12/31/23 DC	150.00	450.00
	1923 Issues		
610	2¢ Harding 9/1/23 DC	30.00	...
	Marlon, OH	20.00	...
	George W. Linn cachet (1st modern cachet)	875.00	
611	2¢ Harding Imperf. 11/15/23 DC	90.00	...
612	2¢ Harding Perf. 10 9/12/23 DC	110.00	...

Scott #	Description	Uncacheted	Cacheted
	1924 HUGENOT-WALLOON ISSUE		
614	1¢ Hugenot-Walloon 5/1/24 DC	40.00	...
	Albany, NY	40.00	...
	Allentown, PA	40.00	...
	Charleston, SC	40.00	...
	Jacksonville, FL	40.00	...
	Lancaster, PA	40.00	...
	Mayport, FL	40.00	...
	New Rochelle, NY	40.00	...
	New York, NY	40.00	...
	Philadelphia, PA	40.00	...
	Reading, PA	40.00	...
	Unofficial CIty	100.00	...
615	2¢ Hugenot-Walloon 5/1/24 DC	60.00	...
	Albany, NY	60.00	...
	Allentown, PA	60.00	...
	Charleston, SC	60.00	...
	Jacksonville, FL	60.00	...
	Lancaster, PA	60.00	...
	Mayport, FL	60.00	...
	New Rochelle, NY	60.00	...
	New York, NY	60.00	...
	Philadelphia, PA	60.00	...
	Reading, PA	60.00	...
	Unofficial City	125.00	...
616	5¢ Hugenot-Walloon 5/1/24 DC	85.00	...
	Albany, NY	85.00	...
	Allentown, PA	85.00	...
	Charleston, SC	85.00	...
	Jacksonville, FL	85.00	...
	Lancaster, PA	85.00	...
	Mayport, FL	85.00	...
	New Rochelle, NY	85.00	...
	New York, NY	85.00	...
	Philadelphia, PA	85.00	...
	Reading, PA	85.00	...
	Unofficial CIty	150.00	...
614-16	1¢-5¢ Comp. set on 1 cover, any official city	175.00	...
614-16	Same, Any Unofficial City	400.00	...
	1925 LEXINGTON-CONCORD ISSUE		
617	1¢ Lexington-Concord 4/4/25 DC	30.00	125.00
	Boston, MA	30.00	125.00
	Cambridge, MA	30.00	125.00
	Concord, MA	30.00	125.00
	Concord Junction, MA	35.00	...
	Lexington, MA	35.00	125.00
	Unofficial City	75.00	...

U.S. FIRST DAY COVERS

Scott #	Description	Uncacheted	Cacheted
618	2¢ Lexington-Concord 4/4/25 DC	35.00	125.00
	Boston, MA	35.00	125.00
	Cambridge, MA	35.00	125.00
	Concord, MA	35.00	125.00
	Concord Junction, MA	40.00	...
	Lexington, MA	40.00	125.00
	Unofficial City	100.00	...
619	5¢ Lexington-Concord 4/4/25 DC	80.00	175.00
	Boston, MA	80.00	175.00
	Cambridge, MA	80.00	175.00
	Concord, MA	80.00	175.00
	Concord Junction, MA	90.00	...
	Lexington, MA	90.00	175.00
	Unofficial City	125.00	...
617-19	1¢-5¢ **1st Jackson cachet** (see above listings for prices)		
617-19	1¢-5¢ Lexington-Concord, cplt. set on one cover	150.00	...
	Same, Concord-Junction or Lexington	175.00	...
	Same, Any Unofficial City	250.00	...
	1925 NORSE-AMERICAN ISSUE		
620	2¢ Norse-American 5/18/25 DC	20.00	...
	Algona, IA	20.00	...
	Benson, MN	20.00	...
	Decorah, IA	20.00	...
	Minneapolis, MN	20.00	...
	Northfield, MN	20.00	...
	St. Paul, MN	20.00	...
	Unofficial City	60.00	...
621	5¢ Norse-American 5/18/25 DC	30.00	...
	Algona, IA	30.00	...
	Benson, MN	30.00	...
	Decorah, IA	30.00	...
	Minneapolis, MN	30.00	...
	Northfield, MN	30.00	...
	St. Paul, MN	30.00	...
	Unofficial City	90.00	...
620-21	2¢-5¢ Norse-Amer., one cover 5/18/25 DC	50.00	275.00
	2¢-5¢ Algona, IA	50.00	275.00
	2¢-5¢ Benson, MN	50.00	275.00
	2¢-5¢ Decorah, IA	50.00	275.00
	2¢-5¢ Minneapolis, MN	50.00	275.00
	2¢-5¢ Northfield, MN	50.00	275.00
	2¢-5¢ St. Paul, MN	50.00	275.00
	Unofficial City	150.00	...
	1st Ernest J. Weschcke cachet	...	275.00
	1st A.C. Roessler cachet	...	300.00
622	13¢ Harrison 1/11/26 DC	15.00	...
	Indianapolis, IN	25.00	...
	North Bend, OH	150.00	...
	Unofficial CIty	200.00	...
623	17¢ Wilson 12/28/25	20.00	275.00
	New York, NY	20.00	275.00
	Princeton, NJ	30.00	275.00
	Staunton, VA	25.00	275.00
	Unofficial City	125.00	...
	1st Nickles cachet	...	275.00
627	2¢ Sesquicentennial 5/10/26 DC	10.00	65.00
	Boston, MA	10.00	65.00
	Philadelphia, PA	10.00	65.00
	1st Griffin cachet	...	150.00
	1st Baxter cachet	...	75.00
628	5¢ Ericsson Memorial 5/29/26 DC	25.00	450.00
	Chicago, IL	25.00	450.00
	Minneapolis, MN	25.00	450.00
	New York, NY	25.00	450.00
629	2¢ White Plains 10/18/26 New York, NY	8.00	70.00
	New York, NY Int. Phil. Ex. Agency	8.00	70.00
	White Plains, NY	8.00	70.00
630a	2¢ White Plains S/S, sgl. 10/18/26 NY, NY	12.00	75.00
	New York, NY Int. Phil. Ex. Agency	12.00	75.00
	White Plains, NY	12.00	75.00
	Block of 10 with selvage	250.00	...
630	Complete Sheet 10/18/26	1700.00	...
630	10/28/26	1300.00	...
631	1½¢ Harding Rotary Imperf. 8/27/26 DC	50.00	...
	1926-27 ROTARY PRESS PERF. 11 X 10½		
632	1¢ Franklin 6/10/27 DC	42.50	...
632a	Bklt. Pane of 6 11/27	4000.00	...
633	1½¢ Harding 5/17/27 DC	42.50	...
634	2¢ Washington 12/10/26 DC	45.00	...
634EE	Experimental Electric Eye 3/28/35	1200.00	...
635	3¢ Lincoln 2/3/27 DC	45.00	...
635a	3¢ Lincoln Re-issue 2/7/34 DC	25.00	45.00
636	4¢ Martha Washington 5/17/27 DC	55.00	...
637	5¢ T. Roosevelt 3/24/27 DC	55.00	...
638	6¢ Garfield 7/27/27 DC	65.00	...
639	7¢ McKinley 3/24/27 DC	60.00	...
639, 637	on one FDC	300.00	...
640	8¢ Grant 6/10/27 DC	65.00	...
	640, 632 on one FDC	300.00	...
641	9¢ Jefferson 5/17/27 DC	70.00	...
	641, 633, & 636 on one FDC	450.00	...
642	10¢ Monroe 2/3/27 DC	85.00	...
	632-42, set of 12	700.00	...

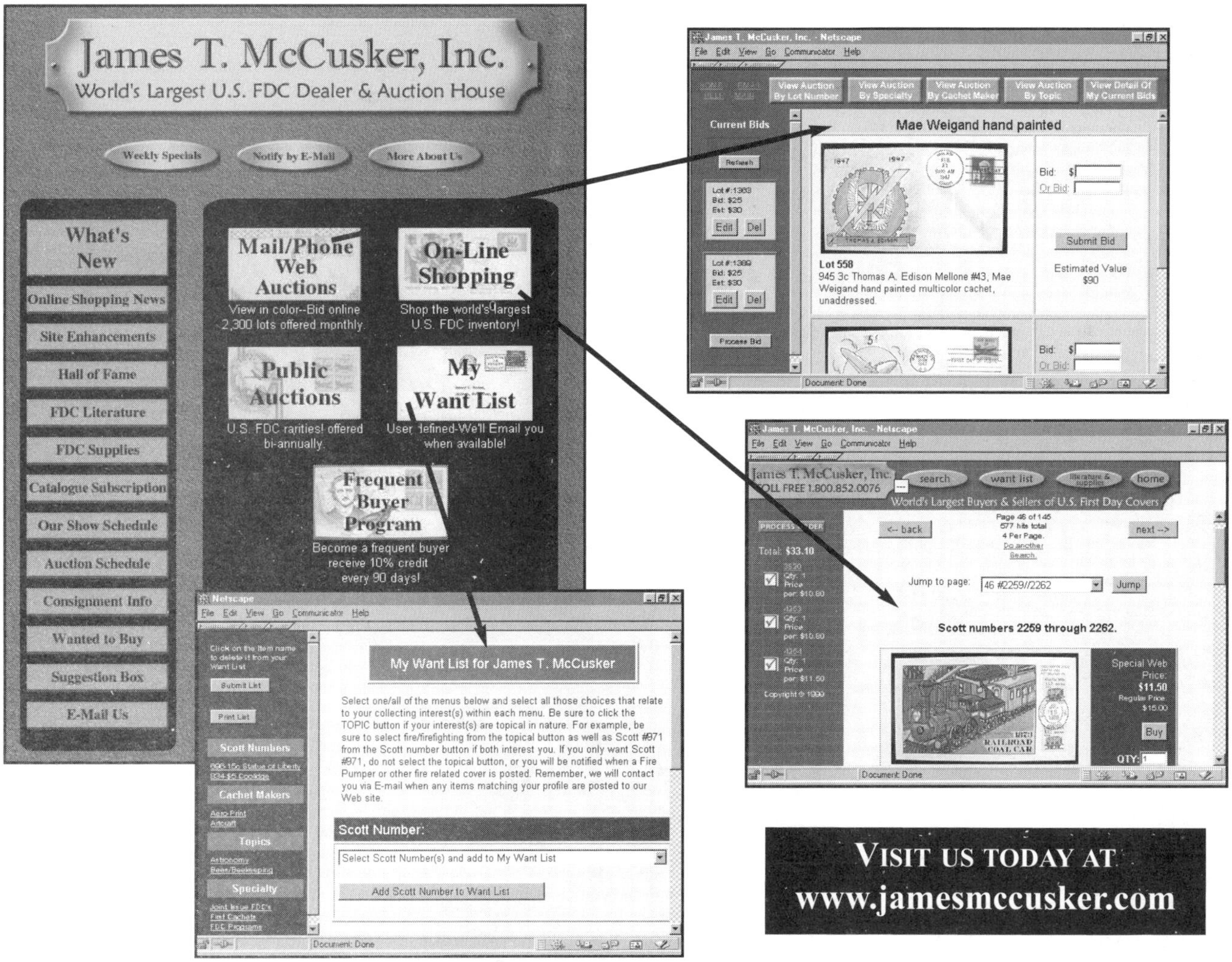

650

Scott #	Description	Uncacheted	Cacheted
	1927		
643	2¢ Vermont 8/3/27 DC.................................	8.00	60.00
	Bennington, VT..	8.00	60.00
	1st Joshua Gerow cachet............................	...	**200.00**
	1st Harris Hunt cachet..............................	...	**150.00**
	1st Kirkjian cachet...................................		**250.00**
644	2¢ Burgoyne 8/3/27 DC..............................	12.00	75.00
	Albany, NY...	12.00	75.00
	Rome, NY...	12.00	75.00
	Syracuse, NY..	12.00	75.00
	Utica, NY...	12.00	75.00
	1st Ralph Dyer cachet..............................	...	**300.00**
	Any Official City......................................	40.00	125.00
	1928		
645	2¢ Valley Forge 5/26/28 DC........................	5.00	60.00
	Cleveland, OH..	60.00	140.00
	Lancaster, PA...	5.00	60.00
	Norristown, PA...	5.00	60.00
	Philadelphia, PA.......................................	5.00	60.00
	Valley Forge, PA.......................................	5.00	60.00
	West Chester, PA......................................	5.00	60.00
	Cleveland Midwestern Phil. Sta..................	5.00	60.00
	1st J.W. Stoutzenberg cachet....................	...	**275.00**
	1st Adam K. Bert cachet...........................	...	**75.00**
	1st Egolf cachet.......................................		**90.00**
646	2¢ Molly Pitcher 10/20/28 DC.....................	12.50	85.00
	Freehold, NJ...	12.50	85.00
	Red Bank, NJ..	12.50	85.00
647	2¢ Hawaii 8/13/28 DC.................................	25.00	125.00
	Honolulu, HI...	25.00	125.00
648	5¢ Hawaii 8/13/28 DC.................................	25.00	150.00
	Honolulu, HI...	30.00	150.00
647-48	Hawaii on one cover..................................	50.00	250.00
	1st F.W. Reid Cachet...............................	...	**325.00**
	1st Best Cachet..	...	**325.00**
649	2¢ Aeronautics Conf., green pmk. 12/12/28 DC ...	6.00	40.00
	Black pmk...	10.00	40.00
650	5¢ Aeronautics Conf., green pmk. 12/12/28 DC ...	10.00	50.00
	Black pmk...	12.50	50.00
649-50	Aero. Conf., one cover, green pmk...............	15.00	70.00
	One cover, black pmk.................................	17.50	75.00
	1929		
651	2¢ Clark 2/25/29 Vincennes, in....................	5.00	30.00
	1st Harry Loor cachet..............................	...	**175.00**
653	½¢ Hale (block of 4) 5/25/29 DC..................	40.00	...
	Unofficial City..	150.00	...
654	2¢ Electric Lt., flat press 6/5/29 Menlo Park, NJ ..	10.00	45.00
	1st Klotzbach cachet................................	...	**225.00**
655	2¢ Electric Light, rotary press 6/11/29 DC.....	100.00	250.00
656	2¢ Electric Light, coil 6/11/29 DC.................	100.00	250.00
656	Coil Line Pair...	150.00	275.00
655-56	Rotary & Coil sgls. on one FDC...................	175.00	375.00
657	2¢ Sullivan 6/17/29 Auburn, NY..................	4.00	30.00
	Binghamton, NY..	4.00	30.00
	Canajoharie, NY..	4.00	30.00
	Canandaigua, NY.......................................	4.00	30.00
	Elmira, NY...	4.00	30.00
	Geneva, NY..	4.00	30.00
	Geneseo, NY...	4.00	30.00
	Horseheads, NY..	4.00	30.00
	Owego, NY...	4.00	30.00
	Penn Yan, NY...	4.00	30.00
	Perry, NY...	4.00	30.00
	Seneca Falls, NY.......................................	4.00	30.00
	Waterloo, NY..	4.00	30.00
	Watkins Glen, NY......................................	4.00	30.00
	Waverly, NY...	4.00	30.00
	1st Robert Beazell cachet.........................	...	**400.00**
	1st A.C. Elliot cachet...............................	...	**75.00**

Scott #	Description	Uncacheted	Cacheted
	KANSAS OVERPRINTS		
658	1¢ Franklin 5/1/29 DC................................	50.00	...
	4/15/29 Newton, KS...................................	500.00	...
659	1½¢ Harding 5/1/29 DC..............................	60.00	...
660	2¢ Washington 5/1/29 DC...........................	60.00	75.00
661	3¢ Lincoln 5/1/29 DC.................................	75.00	...
662	4¢ Martha Washington 5/1/29 DC.................	100.00	...
663	5¢ T. Roosevelt 5/1/29 DC..........................	100.00	200.00
664	6¢ Garfield 5/1/29 DC................................	125.00	...
	4/15/29 Newton, KS...................................	900.00	...
665	7¢ McKinley 5/1/29 DC..............................	150.00	...
666	8¢ Grant 5/1/29 DC...................................	150.00	...
	4/15/29 Newton, KS...................................	900.00	...
667	9¢ Jefferson 5/1/29 DC...............................	150.00	...
668	10¢ Monroe 5/1/29 DC...............................	200.00	...
658-68	1¢-10¢ Kansas cplt. set on one FDC 5/1/29 DC...	1300.00	2000.00
658-68	Kansas Set of 11 covers..............................	1250.00	2000.00
658,664,666	4/15 Newton...	1900.00	
	NEBRASKA OVERPRINTS		
669-79	Nebraska Set of 11 Covers..........................	1250.00	2000.00
669	1¢ Franklin 5/1/29 DC................................	50.00	...
	4/15/29 Beatrice, NE..................................	400.00	...
670	1½¢ Harding 5/1/29 DC..............................	60.00	...
	4/15/29 Hartington, NE..............................	350.00	...
671	2¢ Washington 5/1/29 DC...........................	60.00	...
	4/15/29 Auburn, NE...................................	350.00	...
	4/15/29 Beatrice, NE..................................	350.00	...
	4/15/29 Hartington, NE..............................	350.00	...
672	3¢ Lincoln 5/1/29 DC.................................	75.00	...
	4/15/29 Beatrice, NE..................................	450.00	...
	4/15/29 Hartington, NE..............................	450.00	...
673	4¢ Martha Washington 5/1/29 DC.................	100.00	...
	4/15/29 Beatrice, NE..................................	500.00	...
	4/15/29 Hartington, NE..............................	500.00	...
674	5¢ T. Roosevelt 5/1/29 DC..........................	100.00	200.00
	4/15/29 Beatrice, NE..................................	500.00	...
	4/15/29 Hartington, NE..............................	500.00	...
675	6¢ Garfield 5/1/29 DC................................	125.00	...
676	7¢ McKinley 5/1/29 DC..............................	150.00	...
677	8¢ Grant 5/1/29 DC...................................	150.00	...
678	9¢ Jefferson 5/1/29 DC...............................	150.00	...
679	10¢ Monroe 5/1/29 DC...............................	200.00	...
669-79	1¢-10¢ Nebraska cplt. set on one FDC 5/1/29 DC...	1300.00	1700.00
658-79	all 22 values on 1 cover (2 known)................	4500.00	...
680	2¢ Fallen Timbers 9/14/29 Erie, PA..............	3.00	35.00
	Maumee, OH...	3.00	35.00
	Perrysburgh, OH..	3.00	35.00
	Toledo, OH...	3.00	35.00
	Waterville, OH..	3.00	35.00
681	2¢ Ohio River 10/19/29 Cairo, IL.................	3.00	35.00
	Cincinnati, OH..	3.00	35.00
	Evansville, IN...	3.00	35.00
	Homestead, PA..	3.00	35.00
	Louisville, KY...	3.00	35.00
	Pittsburgh, PA...	3.00	35.00
	Wheeling, WV...	3.00	35.00
	1930-31		
682	2¢ Mass. Bay Colony 4/8/30 Boston, MA...........	3.00	35.00
	Salem, MA...	3.00	35.00
683	2¢ Carolina-Charleston 4/10/30 Charleston, SC	3.00	35.00
684	1½¢ Harding 12/1/30 Marion, OH..................	4.00	45.00
685	4¢ Taft 6/4/30 Cincinnati, OH......................	6.00	60.00
686	1½¢ Harding, coil 12/1/30 Marion, OH...........	5.00	60.00
686	Coil Line Pair...	15.00	90.00
687	4¢ Taft, coil 9/18/30 DC.............................	40.00	150.00
687	Coil Line Pair...	75.00	250.00
688	2¢ Braddock 7/9/30 Braddock, PA.................	4.00	35.00
689	2¢ Von Steuben 9/17/30 New York, NY..........	4.00	35.00
690	2¢ Pulaski 1/16/31 Brooklyn, NY..................	4.00	35.00
	Buffalo, NY..	4.00	35.00
	Chicago, IL...	4.00	35.00
	Cleveland, OH..	4.00	35.00
	Detroit, MI...	4.00	35.00
	Gary, IN..	4.00	35.00
	Milwaukee, WI..	4.00	35.00

680

707

Scott #	Description	Uncacheted	Cacheted
690	New York, NY	4.00	35.00
	Pittsburgh, PA	4.00	35.00
	Savannah, GA	4.00	35.00
	South Bend, IN	4.00	35.00
	Toledo, OH	4.00	35.00
	1st Truby cachet	...	**125.00**

1931 ROTARY PRESS HI-VALUES

Scott #	Description	Uncacheted	Cacheted
692	11¢ Hayes 9/4/31 DC	125.00	...
693	12¢ Cleveland 8/25/31 DC	125.00	...
694	13¢ Harrison 9/4/31 DC	125.00	...
695	14¢ Indian 9/8/31 DC	125.00	...
696	15¢ Statue of Liberty 8/27/31 DC	140.00	...
697	17¢ Wilson 7/27/31 DC	400.00	...
	7/25/31 Brooklyn, NY	3000.00	...
698	20¢ Golden Gate 9/8/31 DC	300.00	...
699	25¢ Niagara Falls 7/27/31 DC	400.00	...
	7/25/31 Brooklyn, NY	1500.00	...
	697, 699 on one FDC, Brooklyn, NY	4000.00	...
700	30¢ Bison 9/8/31 DC	300.00	...
701	50¢ Arlington 9/4/31 DC	450.00	...

1931

Scott #	Description	Uncacheted	Cacheted
702	2¢ Red Cross 5/21/31 DC	3.00	35.00
	Dansville, NY	3.00	35.00
	1st Edward Hacker cachet	...	**150.00**
703	2¢ Yorktown 10/19/31 Wethersfield, CT	3.00	45.00
	Yorktown, VA	3.00	45.00
	Any Predate	200.00	...
	Unofficial City	45.00	...
	1st Crosby cachet	...	**400.00**
	1st Aeroprint cachet	...	**150.00**

1932 WASHINGTON BICENTENNIAL ISSUE

Scott #	Description	Uncacheted	Cacheted
704-15	Bicentennial Set of 12 Covers	220.00	
704	½¢ olive brown 1/1/32 DC		20.00
705	1¢ green 1/1/32 DC		20.00
706	1½¢ brown 1/1/32 DC		20.00
707	2¢ carmine rose 1/1/32 DC		20.00
708	3¢ deep violet 1/1/32 DC		20.00
709	4¢ light brown 1/1/32 DC		20.00
710	5¢ blue 1/1/32 DC		20.00
711	6¢ red orange 1/1/32 DC		20.00
712	7¢ black 1/1/32 DC		20.00
713	8¢ olive bistre 1/1/32 DC		20.00
714	9¢ pale red 1/1/32 DC		20.00
715	10¢ orange yellow 1/1/32 DC		20.00
	1st Rice cachet (on any single)		**25.00**
	1st Raley cachet (on any single)		**40.00**
704-15	Wash. Bicent. on one cover		250.00

1932

Scott #	Description	Uncacheted	Cacheted
716	2¢ Winter Olympic Games 1/25/32 Lake Placid, NY		35.00
	1st Beverly Hills cachet		**250.00**
717	2¢ Arbor Day 4/22/32 Nebraska City, NE		25.00
	1st Linnprint cachet		**40.00**
718	3¢ Summer Olympics 6/15/32 Los Angeles, CA		40.00
719	5¢ Summer Olympics 6/15/32 Los Angeles, CA		40.00
718-19	Summer Olympics cplt. set on one FDC		60.00
720	3¢ Washington 6/16/32 DC		40.00
720b	3¢ Booklet Pane 7/25/32 DC		200.00
721	3¢ Washington, coil, vert. 6/24/32 DC		50.00
721	Coil Line Pair		90.00
722	3¢ Washington, coil, horiz. 10/12/32 DC		50.00
722	Coil LIne Pair		90.00
723	6¢ Garfield, coil 8/18/32 Los Angeles, CA		60.00
723	Coil Line Pair		95.00
724	3¢ William Penn 10/24/32 New Castle, DE		25.00
	Chester, PA		25.00
	Philadelphia, PA		25.00
725	3¢ Daniel Webster 10/24/32 Franklin, NH		25.00
	Exeter, NH		25.00
	Hanover, NH		25.00

1933-34

Scott #	Description	Uncacheted	Cacheted
726	3¢ Gen'l Oglethorpe 2/12/33 Savannah, GA		25.00
	1st Anderson cachet		**150.00**
727	3¢ Peace Proclamation 4/19/33 Newburgh, NY		25.00
	1st Grimsland cachet		**350.00**
728	1¢ Century of Progress 5/25/33 Chicago, IL		20.00
729	3¢ Century of Progress 5/25/33 Chicago, IL		20.00

Scott #	Description	Cacheted
728-29	Progress on one cover	25.00
730	1¢ Amer. Phil. Soc., sht. of 25 8/25/33 Chicago, IL	200.00
730a	1¢ Amer. Phil. Soc., single 8/25/33 Chicago, IL	20.00
731	3¢ Amer. Phil. Soc., sht. of 25 8/25/33 Chicago, IL	200.00
731a	3¢ Amer. Phil. Soc., single 8/25/33 Chicago, IL	20.00
730-731	On one Uncacheted Cover	850.00
730a-31a	Amer. Phil. Soc. on one cover	25.00
732	3¢ National Recovery Act 8/15/33 DC	20.00
	Nira, IA 8/17/33, unofficial	25.00
733	3¢ Byrd Antarctic 10/9/33 DC	30.00
734	5¢ Kosciuszko 10/13/33 Boston, MA	20.00
	Buffalo, NY	20.00
	Chicago, NY	20.00
	Detroit, MI	20.00
	Pittsburgh, PA	50.00
	Kosciuszko, MS	20.00
	St. Louis, MO	20.00
735	3¢ Nat'l Exhibition, sht. of 6 2/10/34 New York, NY	75.00
735a	3¢ National Exhibition, single 2/10/34 New York NY	20.00
736	3¢ Maryland 3/23/34 St. Mary's City, MD	20.00
	1st Torkel Gundel cachet	**300.00**
	1st Don Kapner cachet	**25.00**
	1st Louis Nix cachet	**250.00**
	1st Top Notch cachet	**25.00**
737	3¢ Mothers of Am., rotary 5/2/34 any city	15.00
738	3¢ Mothers of Am., flat 5/2/34 any city	15.00
737-38	Mothers of Am. on one cover	35.00
739	3¢ Wisconsin 7/7/34 Green Bay, WI	20.00

1934 NATIONAL PARKS ISSUE

Scott #	Description	Cacheted
740-49	National Parks set of 10 covers	125.00
740-49	On 1 Cover 10/8/34	150.00
740	1¢ Yosemite 7/16/34 Yosemite, CA	12.50
	DC	12.50
741	2¢ Grand Canyon 7/24 34 Grand Canyon, AZ	12.50
	DC	12.50
742	3¢ Mt. Rainier 8/3/34 Longmire, WA	12.50
	DC	12.50
743	4¢ Mesa Verde 9/25/34 Mesa Verde, CO	12.50
	DC	12.50
744	5¢ Yellowstone 7/30/34 Yellowstone, WY	12.50
	DC	12.50
745	6¢ Crater Lake 9/5/34 Crater Lake, OR	12.50
	DC	12.50
746	7¢ Acadia 10/2/34 Bar Harbor, ME	12.50
	DC	12.50
747	8¢ Zion 9/18/34 Zion, UT	12.50
	DC	12.50
748	9¢ Glacier Park 8/27/34 Glacier Park, MT	12.50
	DC	12.50
749	10¢ Smoky Mts. 10/8/34 Sevierville, TN	12.50
	DC	12.50
750	3¢ Amer. Phil. Soc., sheet of 6 8/28/34 Atlantic City, NJ	75.00
750a	3¢ Amer. Phil. Soc., single 8/28/34 Atlantic City, NJ	20.00
751	1¢ Trans-Miss. Phil. Expo., sht. of 6 10/10/34 Omaha, NE	75.00
751a	1¢ Trans-Miss. Phil. Expo., single 10/10/34 Omaha, NE	20.00

Scott #	Description	Center Gutter or Line Blk	Cacheted Gutter or Line Pair	Singles
	1935 FARLEY SPECIAL PRINTING			
752-71	Set of 20 covers	...	...	500.00
752-71	Set on 1 cover 3/15/35	...	...	450.00
752-55,766a-71	10 varieties on 1 cover 3/15/35	...	...	250.00
752	3¢ Peace Proclamation 3/15/35 DC	150.00	50.00	35.00
753	3¢ Byrd 3/15/35 DC	175.00	50.00	35.00
754	3¢ Mothers of America 3/15/35 DC	150.00	45.00	35.00
755	3¢ Wisconsin 3/15/35 DC	150.00	45.00	35.00
756-65	Parks set of 10 covers	1750.00	400.00	300.00
756-65	Set on 1 cover 3/15/35	...	...	175.00
756	1¢ Yosemite 3/15/35 DC	150.00	40.00	30.00
757	2¢ Grand Canyon 3/15/35 DC	150.00	40.00	30.00
758	3¢ Mount Rainier 3/15/35	150.00	40.00	30.00
759	4¢ Mesa Verde 3/15/35 DC	150.00	40.00	30.00
760	5¢ Yellowstone 3/15/35 DC	150.00	40.00	30.00
761	6¢ Crater Lake 3/15/35 DC	150.00	40.00	30.00
762	7¢ Acadia 3/15/35 DC	150.00	40.00	30.00
763	8¢ Zion 3/15/35 DC	150.00	40.00	30.00
764	9¢ Glacier Park 3/15/35 DC	150.00	40.00	30.00
765	10¢ Smoky Mountains 3/15/35 DC	150.00	40.00	30.00
766	1¢ Century of Progress 3/15/35, DC Imperf, pane of 25,	...	500.00	...
766a	Strip of 3,	150.00	50.00	40.00
767	3¢ Century of Progress 3/15/35, DC Imperf, pane of 25	...	500.00	...
767a	Single	150.00	50.00	40.00
768	3¢ Byrd 3/15/35 DC Imperf, pane of 25	...	500.00	...
768a	Single	175.00	70.00	40.00
769	1¢ Yosemite 3/15/35 DC Imperf, pane of 6	...	500.00	...
769a	Strip of 3	150.00	55.00	40.00
770	3¢ Mount Rainier 3/15/35 Imperf, pane of 6	...	500.00	...
770a	Single	150.00	55.00	40.00
771	16¢ Air Mail-Spec. Del. 3/15/35 DC	175.00	60.00	40.00

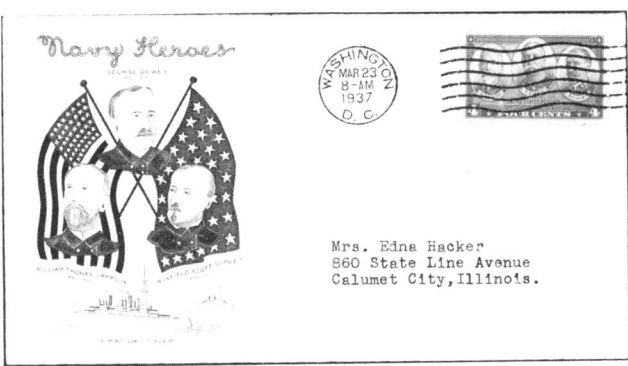

793

Scott #	Description	Cacheted
	1935-36	
772	3¢ Connecticut 4/26/35 Hartford, CT	17.50
	1st Winfred Grandy cachet	**30.00**
773	3¢ Calif. Exposition 5/29/35 San Diego, CA	17.50
	1st W. Espenshade cachet	**30.00**
774	3¢ Boulder Dam 9/30/35 Boulder City, NV	17.50
775	3¢ Michigan 11/1/35 Lansing, MI	17.50
	1st Risko Art Studio cachet	**200.00**
776	3¢ Texas 3/2/36 Gonzales, TX	20.00
	1st John Sidenius cachet	**60.00**
	1st Walter Czubay cachet	**75.00**
777	3¢ Rhode Island 5/4/36 Providence, RI	17.50
	1st J.W. Clifford cachet	**30.00**
778	3¢ TIPEX sheet 5/9/36 New York, NY	17.50
	1st House of Farnam cachet	**500.00**
778a-78d	Single from sheet	10.00
782	3¢ Arkansas 6/15/36 Little Rock, AK	15.00
783	3¢ Oregon 7/14/36 Astoria, OR	12.50
	Daniel, WY	12.50
	Lewiston, ID	12.50
	Missoula, MT	12.50
	Walla Walla, WA	12.50
784	3¢ Susan B. Anthony 8/26/36 DC	17.50
	1st Historic Arts cachet	**25.00**

Scott #	Description	Price
	1936-37 ARMY - NAVY	
785-94	Army-Navy set of 10 covers	70.00
785	1¢ Army 12/15/36 DC	7.00
786	2¢ Army 1/15/37 DC	7.00
787	3¢ Army 2/18/37 DC	7.00
	1st William Von Ohlen cachet	75.00
788	4¢ Army 3/23/37 DC	7.00
789	5¢ Army 5/26/37 West Point, NY	7.00
	#785-89, Army set on one cover, 5/26/37	35.00
790	1¢ Navy 12/15/36 DC	7.00
791	2¢ Navy 1/15/37 DC	7.00
792	3¢ Navy 2/18/37 DC	7.00
793	4¢ Navy 3/23/37 DC	7.00
794	5¢ Navy 5/26/37 Annapolis, MD	7.00
	#790-94, Navy set on one cover, 5/26/37	35.00
	#785-94, Army-Navy set on one cover, 5/26/37	75.00

	1937	
795	3¢ Ordinance of 1787 7/13/37 Marietta, OH	12.00
	New York, NY	12.00
	1st Cachet Craft cachet	**60.00**
	1st Linto cachet	**150.00**
796	5¢ Virginia Dare 8/18/37 Manteo, NC	15.00
797	10¢ S.P.A. sheet 8/26/37 Asheville, NC	12.00
798	3¢ Constitution 9/17/37 Philadelphia, PA	12.00
	1st Pilgrim cachet	**90.00**
	1st Fidelity Stamp Co. cachet	**15.00**
799-802	Territory set of 4 covers	60.00
799-802	On 1 Cover 12/15/37	40.00
799	3¢ Hawaii 10/18/37 Honolulu, HI	20.00
800	3¢ Alaska 11/12/37 Juneau, AK	15.00
801	3¢ Puerto Rico 11/25/37 San Juan, PR	15.00
802	3¢ Virgin Islands 12/15/37 Charlotte Amalie, VI	15.00

	1938-1954 PRESIDENTIAL SERIES	
803-34	Presidents set of 32 covers	450.00
803-31	Presidents set of 29 covers	110.00
803	½¢ Franklin 5/19/38 Philadelphia, PA	3.00
804	1¢ Washington 4/25/38 DC	3.00
804b	booklet pane 1/27/39 DC	15.00
805	1½¢ Martha Washington 5/5/38 DC	3.00
806	2¢ J. Adams 6/3/38 DC	3.00
806b	booklet pane 1/27/39 DC	15.00
807	3¢ Jefferson 6/16/38 DC	3.00
807a	booklet pane 1/27/39 DC	15.00
	#804b, 806b, 807a Bklt. set on one cover, 1/27/38 DC	60.00
808	4¢ Madison 7/1/38 DC	3.00
809	4½¢ White House 7/11/38 DC	3.00
810	5¢ Monroe 7/21/38 DC	3.00
811	6¢ J.Q. Adams 7/28/38 DC	3.00

Scott #	Description	Price
812	7¢ Jackson 8/4/38 DC	3.00
813	8¢ Van Buren 8/11/38 DC	3.00
814	9¢ Harrison 8/18/38 DC	3.00
815	10¢ Tyler 9/2/38 DC	3.00
816	11¢ Polk 9/8/38 DC	5.00
817	12¢ Taylor 9/14/38 DC	5.00
818	13¢ Fillmore 9/22/38 DC	5.00
819	14¢ Pierce 10/6/38 DC	5.00
820	15¢ Buchanan 10/13/38 DC	5.00
821	16¢ Lincoln 10/20/38 DC	6.00
822	17¢ Johnson 10/27/38 DC	6.00
823	18¢ Grant 11/3/38 DC	6.00
824	19¢ Hayes 11/10/38 DC	6.00
825	20¢ Garfield 11/10/38 DC	6.00
	#824-825 on one FDC	40.00
826	21¢ Arthur 11/22/38 DC	7.00
827	22¢ Cleveland 11/22/38 DC	7.00
	#826-827 on one FDC	40.00
828	24¢ Harrison 12/2/38 DC	8.00
829	25¢ McKinley 12/2/38 DC	8.00
	#828-829 on one FDC	40.00
830	30¢ Roosevelt 12/8/38 DC	10.00
831	50¢ Taft 12/8/38 DC	15.00
	#830-831 on one FDC	40.00
832	$1 Wilson 8/29/38 DC	65.00
832c	$1 Wilson, dry print 8/31/54 DC	30.00
833	$2 Harding 9/29/38 DC	125.00
834	$5 Coolidge 11/17/38 DC	210.00

	PRESIDENTIAL ELECTRIC EYE FDC's	
803-31EE	Presidents set of 29 Covers	550.00
803EE	½¢ Electric Eye 9/8/41 DC	10.00
804EE	1¢ Electric Eye 9/8/41 DC	10.00
	#803, 804, E15 on one FDC	30.00
805EE	1½¢ Electric Eye 1/16/41 DC	10.00
806EE	2¢ Electric Eye (Type I) 6/3/38 DC	15.00
806EE	2¢ Electric Eye (Type II) 4/5/39 DC	8.00
807EE	3¢ Electric Eye 4/5/39 DC	8.00
	#806-807 on one FDC 4/5/39	15.00
807EE	3¢ Electric Eye convertible 1/18/40	12.50
808EE	4¢ Electric Eye 10/28/41 DC	17.50
809EE	4½¢ Electric Eye 10/28/41 DC	17.50
810EE	5¢ Electric Eye 10/28/41 DC	17.50
811EE	6¢ Electric Eye 9/25/41 DC	15.00
812EE	7¢ Electric Eye 10/28/41 DC	17.50
813EE	8¢ Electric Eye 10/28/41 DC	17.50
814EE	9¢ Electric Eye 10/28/41 DC	17.50
815EE	10¢ Electric Eye 9/25/41 DC	15.00
	#811, 815 on one FDC	25.00
816EE	11¢ Electric Eye 10/8/41 DC	20.00
817EE	12¢ Electric Eye 10/8/41 DC	20.00
818EE	13¢ Electric Eye 10/8/41 DC	20.00
819EE	14¢ Electric Eye 10/8/41 DC	20.00
820EE	15¢ Electric Eye 10/8/41 DC	20.00
	#816-820 on one FDC	30.00
821EE	16¢ Electric Eye 1/7/42 DC	25.00
822EE	17¢ Electric Eye 10/28/41 DC	25.00
	#808-10, 812-14, 822 on one FDC	60.00
823EE	18¢ Electric Eye 1/7/42 DC	25.00
824EE	19¢ Electric Eye 1/7/42 DC	25.00
825EE	20¢ Electric Eye 1/7/42 DC	25.00
	#824-825 on one FDC	30.00
826EE	21¢ Electric Eye 1/7/42 DC	25.00
	#821, 823-26 on one FDC	60.00
827EE	22¢ Electric Eye 1/28/42 DC	35.00
828EE	24¢ Electric Eye 1/28/42 DC	35.00
829EE	25¢ Electric Eye 1/28/42 DC	40.00
830EE	30¢ Electric Eye 1/28/42 DC	40.00
831EE	50¢ Electric Eye 1/28/42 DC	50.00
	#827-831 on one FDC	75.00
	1938	
835	3¢ Ratification 6/21/38 Philadelphia, PA	15.00
836	3¢ Swedes and Finns 6/27/38 Wilmington, DE	15.00
	1st Staehle cachet	**50.00**
837	3¢ NW Territory 7/15/38 Marietta, OH	15.00
838	3¢ Iowa Territory 8/24/38 Des Moines, IA	15.00

832

855

1939 PRESIDENTIAL COILS

Scott #	Description	Line Pr	Price
839-51	Presidents set of 13 covers	...	65.00
839	1¢ Washington, pair 1/20/39 DC	12.00	5.00
840	1½¢ M. Wash., pair 1/20/39 DC	12.00	5.00
841	2¢ J. Adams, pair 1/20/39 DC	12.00	5.00
842	3¢ Jefferson 1/20/39 DC	12.00	5.00
842	Same, pair	...	7.00
843	4¢ Madison 1/20/39 DC	12.00	6.00
844	4½¢ White House 1/20/39 DC	12.00	6.00
845	5¢ Monroe 1/20/39 DC	15.00	6.00
846	6¢ J.Q. Adams, vert. 1/20/39 DC	17.50	7.00
847	10¢ Tyler 1/20/39 DC	20.00	10.00
839-847	On 1 Cover	125.00	60.00
848	1¢ Washington, pair, vert. coil 1/27/39 DC	12.00	6.00
849	1½¢ M. Wash., pair, vert. coil 1/27/39 DC	12.00ea	6.00
850	2¢ J. Adams, pair, vert. coil 1/27/39 DC	12.00	6.00
851	3¢ Jefferson 1/27/39 DC	12.00	6.00
848-51	On 1 Cover	75.00	40.00
839-51	On 1 cover	200.00	110.00

1939

		Price
852	3¢ Golden Gate 2/18/39 San Francisco, CA	15.00
853	3¢ World's Fair 4/1/39 New York, NY	15.00
	1st Artcraft cachet	**300.00**
854	3¢ Wash. Inauguration 4/30/39 NY, NY	15.00
855	3¢ Baseball 6/12/39 Cooperstown, NY	40.00
856	3¢ Panama Canal 8/15/39 USS Charleston	20.00
857	3¢ Printing Tercent. 9/25/39 NY, NY	15.00
858	3¢ 50th Anniv. 4 States 11/2/39 Bismarck, ND	10.00
	11/2/39 Pierre, SD	10.00
	11/8/39 Helena, MT	10.00
	11/11/39 Olympia, WA	10.00

1940 FAMOUS AMERICANS

859-93	**Famous Americans set of 35 covers**	**135.00**
859	1¢ Washington Irving 1/29/40 Terrytown, NY	4.00
860	2¢ James Fenimore Cooper 1/29/40 Cooperstown, NY	4.00
861	3¢ Ralph Waldo Emerson 2/5/40 Boston, MA	4.00
862	5¢ Louisa May Alcott 2/5/40 Concord, MA	5.00
863	10¢ Samuel Clemens 2/13/40 Hannibal, MO	9.00
859-63	Authors on one cover 2/13/40	40.00
864	1¢ Henry W. Longfellow 2/16/40 Portland, ME	4.00
865	2¢ John Greenleaf Whittier 2/16/40 Haverhill, MA	4.00
866	3¢ James Russell Lowell 2/20/40 Cambridge, MA	4.00
867	5¢ Walt Whitman 2/20/40 Camden, NJ	5.00
868	10¢ James Whitcomb Riley 2/24/40 Greenfield, IN	6.00
864-68	Poets on one cover 2/24/40	40.00
869	1¢ Horace Mann 3/14/40 Boston, MA	4.00
870	2¢ Mark Hopkins 3/14/40 Williamstown, MA	4.00
871	3¢ Charles W. Eliot 3/28/40 Cambridge, MA	4.00
872	5¢ Frances E. Willard 3/28/40 Evanston, IL	5.00
873	10¢ Booker T. Washington 4/7/40 Tuskegee Inst., AL	12.00
869-73	Educators on one cover 4/7/40	45.00
874	1¢ John James Audubon 4/8/40 St. Francesville, LA	5.00
875	2¢ Dr. Crawford W. Long 4/8/40 Jefferson, GA	5.00
876	3¢ Luther Burbank 4/17/40 Santa Rosa, CA	4.00
877	5¢ Dr. Walter Reed 4/17/40 DC	5.00
878	10¢ Jane Addams 4/26/40 Chicago, IL	6.00
874-78	Scientists on one cover 4/26/40	40.00
879	1¢ Stephen Collins Foster 5/3/40 Bardstown, KY	4.00
880	2¢ John Philip Sousa 5/3/40 DC	4.00
881	3¢ Victor Herbert 5/13/40 New York, NY	4.00
882	5¢ Edward A. MacDowell 5/13/40 Peterborough, NH	5.00
883	10¢ Ethelbert Nevin 6/10/40 Pittsburg, PA	6.00
879-83	Composers on one cover 6/10/40	40.00
884	1¢ Gilbert Charles Stuart 9/5/40 Narragansett, RI	4.00
885	2¢ James A. McNeill Whistler 9/5/40 Lowell, MA	4.00
886	3¢ Augustus Saint-Gaudens 9/16/40 New York, NY	4.00
887	5¢ Daniel Chester French 9/16/40 Stockbridge, MA	5.00
888	10¢ Frederic Remington 9/30/40 Canton, NY	6.00
884-88	Artists on one cover 9/30/40	40.00
889	1¢ Eli Whitney 10/7/40 Savannah, GA	4.00
890	2¢ Samuel F.B. Morse 10/7/40 NY, NY	4.00
891	3¢ Cyrus Hall McCormick 10/14/40 Lexington, VA	4.00
892	5¢ Elias Howe 10/14/40 Spencer, MA	5.00
893	10¢ Alexander Graham Bell 10/28/40 Boston, MA	7.00

Scott #	Description	Price
889-93	Inventors on one cover 10/28/40	40.00
859-93	Famous American set on one cover 10/28/40	200.00

1940-43

894	3¢ Pony Exxpress 4/3/40 St. Joseph, MO	7.00
	Sacramento, CA	7.00
	1st Aristocrats cachet	**15.00**
895	3¢ Pan American Union 4/14/40 DC	6.00
896	3¢ Idaho Statehood 7/3/40 Boise, ID	6.00
897	3¢ Wyoming Statehood 7/10/40 Cheyenne, WY	6.00
	1st Spartan cachet	**40.00**
898	3¢ Coronado Expedition 9/7/40 Albuquerque, NM	6.00
899	1¢ National Defense 10/16/40 DC	5.00
900	2¢ National Defense 10/16/40 DC	5.00
901	3¢ National Defense 10/16/40 DC	5.00
899-901	National Defense on one cover	10.00
902	3¢ 13th Amend. 10/20/40 World's Fair, NY	9.00
903	3¢ Vermont Statehood 3/4/41 Montpelier, VT	8.00
	1st Fleetwood cachet	**90.00**
	1st Dorothy Knapp hand painted cachet	**1600.00**
904	3¢ Kentucky Statehood 6/1/42 Frankfort, KY	6.00
	1st Signed Fleetwood cachet	**75.00**
905	3¢ Win the War 7/4/42 DC	5.00
906	5¢ China Resistance 7/7/42 Denver, CO	10.00
907	2¢ United Nations 1/14/43 DC	5.00
908	1¢ Four Freedoms 2/12/43 DC	5.00

1943-44 OVERRUN NATIONS (FLAGS)

		Name Blks.	Singles
909-21	**Flags set of 13 covers**	**130.00**	**40.00**
909	5¢ Poland 3/22/43 Chicago, IL	10.00	6.00
	DC	10.00	6.00
	1st Penn Arts cachet	...	**20.00**
	1st Smartcraft cachet	...	**15.00**
910	5¢ Czechoslovakia 7/12/43 DC	10.00	5.00
911	5¢ Norway 7/27/43 DC	10.00	5.00
912	5¢ Luxembourg 8/10/43 DC	10.00	5.00
913	5¢ Netherlands 8/24/43 DC	10.00	5.00
914	5¢ Belgium 9/14/43 DC	10.00	5.00
915	5¢ France 9/28/43 DC	10.00	5.00
916	5¢ Greece 10/12/43 DC	10.00	5.00
917	5¢ Yugoslavia 10/26/43 DC	10.00	5.00
918	5¢ Albania 11/9/43 DC	10.00	5.00
919	5¢ Austria 11/23/43 DC	10.00	5.00
920	5¢ Denmark 12/7/43 DC	10.00	5.00
	#909-920 on one cover, 12/7/43	...	70.00
921	5¢ Korea 11/2/44 DC	10.00	6.00
	#909-921 on one cover, 11/2/44	...	85.00

1944

922	3¢ Railroad 5/10/44 Ogden, UT	7.00
	Omaha, NE	7.00
	San Francisco, CA	7.00
923	3¢ Steamship 5/22/44 Kings Point, NY	7.00
	Savannah, GA	7.00
924	3¢ Telegraph 5/24/44 DC	7.00
	Baltimore, MD	7.00
925	3¢ Corregidor 9/27/44 DC	7.00
926	3¢ Motion Picture 10/31/44 Hollywood, CA	7.00

1945

927	3¢ Florida 3/3/45 Tallahassee, FL	7.00
928	5¢ UN Conference 4/25/45 San Francisco, CA	9.00
929	3¢ Iwo Jima 7/11/45 DC	15.00
930	1¢ Roosevelt 7/26/45 Hyde Park, NY	4.00
931	2¢ Roosevelt 8/24/45 Warm Springs, GA	4.00
932	3¢ Roosevelt 6/27/45 DC	4.00
	1st Fluegel cachet	**75.00**
933	5¢ Roosevelt 1/30/46 DC	4.00
	#930-933 on one cover 1/30/46 DC	12.00
934	3¢ Army 9/28/45 DC	8.00
935	3¢ Navy 10/27/45 Annapolis, MD	8.00
936	3¢ Coast Guard 11/10/45 New York, NY	7.00
937	3¢ Alfred E. Smith 11/26/45 New York, NY	5.00
938	3¢ Texas Centennial 12/29/45 Austin, TX	6.00

921

976

Scott #	Description	Price
	1946	
939	3¢ Merchant Marine 2/26/46 DC	7.00
	#929, 934-36, 939 on one cover 2/26/46	30.00
940	3¢ Honorable Discharge 5/9/46 DC............................	7.00
	1st Artmaster cachet	**20.00**
	#929, 934-36, 939-940 on one cover 5/9/46	35.00
941	3¢ Tennessee Sthd. 6/1/46 Nashville, TN................	3.00
942	3¢ Iowa Statehood 8/3/46 Iowa City, IA..................	3.00
943	3¢ Smithsonian 8/10/46 DC	3.00
944	3¢ New Mexico 10/16/46 Santa Fe, NM	3.00
	1947	
945	3¢ Thomas A. Edison 2/11/47 Milan, OH................	4.00
946	3¢ Joseph Pulitzer 4/10/47 New York, NY	3.00
947	3¢ Stamp Centenary Sheet 5/17/47 New York, NY....	3.00
	1st Fulton cachet (10 different)..................	**30.00**
948	5¢-10¢ Stamp Centenary Sheet 5/19/47 New York, NY......	4.00
949	3¢ Doctors 6/9/47 Atlantic City, NJ	7.00
950	3¢ Utah Cent. 7/24/47 Salt Lake City, UT	3.00
951	3¢ Constitution 10/21/47 Boston, MA	4.00
	1st C.W. George cachet	**75.00**
	1st Suncraft cachet	**25.00**
952	3¢ Everglades 12/5/47 Florida City, FL	3.00
	1948	
953	3¢ G. Washington Carver 1/5/48 Tuskegee Inst., AL	4.50
	1st Jackson cachet	**35.00**
954	3¢ Discovery of Gold 1/24/48 Coloma, CA................	2.00
955	3¢ Mississippi 4/7/48 Natchez, MS	2.00
956	3¢ Four Chaplains 5/28/48 DC	2.50
957	3¢ Wisconsin Cent. 5/29/48 Madison, WI	2.00
958	5¢ Swedish Pioneers 6/4/48 Chicago, IL	2.00
959	3¢ Women's Prog. 7/19/48 Seneca Falls, NY	2.00
960	3¢ William A. White 7/31/48 Emporia, KS	2.00
961	3¢ US-Canada 8/2/48 Niagara Falls, NY	2.00
962	3¢ Francis Scott Key 8/9/48 Frederick, MD............	2.25
963	3¢ Youth of America 8/11/48 DC	2.00
964	3¢ Oregon Terr. 8/14/48 Oregon City, OR	2.00
965	3¢ Harlan Fisk Stone 8/25/48 Chesterfield, NH........	2.00
966	3¢ Palomar Observatory 8/30/48 Palomar Mt., CA......	2.25
967	3¢ Clara Barton 9/7/48 Oxford, MA........................	3.50
968	3¢ Poultry Industry 9/9/48 New Haven, CT..............	2.00
969	3¢ Gold Star Mothers 9/21/48 DC	2.00
970	3¢ Fort Kearny 9/22/48 Minden, NE	2.00
971	3¢ Fireman 10/4/48 Dover, DE	4.00
972	3¢ Indian Centennial 10/15/48 Muskogee, OK..........	2.00
973	3¢ Rough Riders 10/27/48 Prescott, AZ	2.00
974	3¢ Juliette Low 10/29/48 Savannah, GA	4.00
975	3¢ Will Rogers 11/4/48 Claremore, OK	2.00
	1st Kolor Kover cachet	**100.00**
976	3¢ Fort Bliss 11/5/48 El Paso, TX	3.00
977	3¢ Moina Michael 11/9/48 Athens, GA....................	2.00
978	3¢ Gettysburgh Address 11/19/48 Gettysburg, PA	3.00
979	3¢ Amer. Turners 11/20/48 Cincinnati, OH	2.00
980	3¢ Joel Chandler Harris 12/9/48 Eatonton, GA	2.00
	1949	
981	3¢ Minnesota Terr. 3/3/49 St. Paul, MN..................	2.00
982	3¢ Washington & Lee Univ. 4/12/49 Lexington, VA	2.00
983	3¢ Puerto Rico 4/27/49 San Juan, PR	2.00
984	3¢ Annapolis 5/23/49 Annapolis, MD	2.00
985	3¢ G.A.R. 8/29/49 Indianapolis, IN	2.50
986	3¢ Edgar Allan Poe 10/7/49 Richmond, VA	2.50
	1950	
987	3¢ Bankers 1/3/50 Saratoga Springs, NY	3.00
988	3¢ Samuel Gompers 1/27/50 DC	2.00
989	3¢ Statue of Freedom 4/20/50 DC	2.00
990	3¢ White House 6/12/50 DC	2.00
991	3¢ Supreme Court 8/2/50 DC	2.00
992	3¢ Capitol 11/22/50 DC	2.00
	#989-992 on one cover 11/22/50	7.50
993	3¢ Railroad Engineers 4/29/50 Jackson, TN	5.00
994	3¢ Kansas City 6/3/50 Kansas City, MO	2.00

Scott #	Description	Price
995	3¢ Boy Scouts 6/30/50 Valley Forge, PA	4.50
996	3¢ Indiana Terr. 7/4/50 Vincennes, IN....................	2.00
997	3¢ California Sthd. 9/9/50 Sacramento, CA	2.00
	1951	
998	3¢ Confederate Vets. 5/30/51 Norfolk, VA	3.00
999	3¢ Nevada Territory 7/14/51 Genoa, NY	2.00
1000	3¢ Landing of Cadillac 7/24/51 Detroit, MI..............	2.00
1001	3¢ Colorado Statehood 8/1/51 Minturn, CO	2.50
1002	3¢ Amer. Chem. Soc. 9/4/51 New York, NY	2.00
1003	3¢ Battle of Brooklyn 12/10/51 Brooklyn, NY	2.00
	1st Velvatone cachet..................................	**75.00**
	1952	
1004	3¢ Betsy Ross 1/2/52 Philadelphia, PA....................	2.50
	1st Steelcraft cachet	**30.00**
1005	3¢ 4-H Clubs 1/15/52 Springfield, OH	2.00
1006	3¢ B. & O. Railroad 2/28/52 Baltimore, MD	5.00
1007	3¢ Am. Automobile Assoc. 3/4/52 Chicago, IL	2.00
1008	3¢ NATO 4/4/52 DC	2.00
1009	3¢ Grand Coulee Dam 5/15/52 Grand Coulee, WA	2.00
1010	3¢ Lafayette 6/13/52 Georgetown, SC	2.00
1011	3¢ Mount Rushmore 8/11/52 Keystone, SD	2.00
1012	3¢ Civil Engineers 9/6/52 Chicago, IL	2.00
1013	3¢ Service Women 9/11/52 DC	2.50
1014	3¢ Gutenberg Bible 9/30/52 DC	2.00
1015	3¢ Newspaper Boys 10/4/52 Phila., PA	2.00
1016	3¢ Red Cross 11/21/52 New York, NY	3.00
	1953	
1017	3¢ National Guard 2/23/53 DC	2.00
1018	3¢ Ohio Statehood 3/2/53 Chillicothe, OH	2.00
	1st Boerger cachet	**25.00**
1019	3¢ Washington Terr. 3/2/53 Olympia, WA	2.00
1020	3¢ Louisiana Pur. 4/30/53 St. Louis, MO	2.00
1021	3¢ Opening of Japan 7/14/53 DC	2.00
	1st Overseas Mailers cachet	**75.00**
1022	3¢ Amer. Bar Assoc. 8/24/53 Boston, MA	4.50
1023	3¢ Sagamore Hill 9/14/53 Oyster Bay. NY	2.00
1024	3¢ Future Farmers 10/13/53 KS City, MO	2.00
1025	3¢ Trucking Ind. 10/27/53 Los Angeles, CA	2.00
1026	3¢ General Patton 11/11/53 Fort Knox, KY	2.00
1027	3¢ Founding of NYC 11/20/53 New York, NY	2.00
1028	3¢ Gadsden Purchase 12/30/53 Tucson, AZ	2.00
	1954	
1029	3¢ Columbia Univ. 1/4/54 New York, NY	2.00
	1954-61 LIBERTY SERIES	
1030-53	Liberty set of 27	100.00
1030	½¢ Franklin 10/20/55 DC	1.75
1031	1¢ Washington 8/26/54 Chicago, IL	1.75
1031A	1¼¢ Palace 6/17/60 Santa Fe, NM	1.75
1032	1½¢ Mt. Vernon 2/22/56 Mt. Vernon, VA	1.75
1033	2¢ Jefferson 9/15/54 San Francisco, CA	1.75
1034	2½¢ Bunker Hill 6/17/59 Boston, MA	1.75
1035	3¢ Statue of Liberty 6/24/54 Albany, NY	1.75
1035a	booklet pane 6/30/54	4.00
1035b	Luminescent 7/6/66 DC	50.00
1035b & 1225a	Luminescent, combo	60.00
1036	4¢ Lincoln 11/19/54 New York, NY	1.75
1036a	booklet pane 7/31/58 Wheeling, WV	3.00
1036b	Luminescent 11/2/63 DC	100.00
1037	4½¢ Hermitage 3/16/59 Hermitage, TN	1.75
1038	5¢ Monroe 12/2/54 Fredericksburg, VA	1.75
1039	6¢ Roosevelt 11/18/55 New York, NY	1.75
1040	7¢ Wilson 1/110/56 Staunton, VA	1.75
1041	8¢ Statue of Liberty 4/9/54 DC	1.75
1042	8¢ Stat. of Lib. (Giori Press) 3/22/58 Cleveland, OH......	1.75
1042A	8¢ Pershing 11/17/61 New York, NY	2.25
1043	9¢ The Alamo 6/14/56 San Antonio, TX	2.00
1044	10¢ Independence Hall 7/4/56 Phila., PA	2.00
1044b	Luminescent 7/6/66	50.00
1044A	11¢ Statue of Liberty 6/15/61 DC	2.50
1044Ac	Luminescent 1/11/67	50.00
1045	12¢ Harrison 6/6/59 Oxford, OH	2.00
1045a	Luminescent 5/6/68	40.00
1045a & 1055a	Luminescent, combo	40.00
1046	15¢ John Jay 12/12/58 DC	2.50
1046a	Luminescent 5/6/68	50.00

1045

1053

Scott #	Description	Price
	1954-61 LIBERTY SERIES (con't.)	
1047	20¢ Monticello 4/13/56 Charlottesville, VA	2.50
1048	25¢ Paul Revere 4/118/58 Boston, MA	2.50
1049	30¢ Robert E. Lee 9/21/55 Norfolk, VA	4.00
1050	40¢ John Marshall 9/24/55 Richmond, VA	4.00
1051	50¢ Susan Anthony 8/25/55 Louisville, KY	6.00
1052	$1 Patrick Henry 10/7/55 Joplin, MO	10.00
1053	$5 Alex Hamilton 3/19/56 Patterson, NJ	50.00
	1954-65 LIBERTY SERIES COILS	
1054	1¢ Washington 10/8/54 Baltimore, MD	1.75
1054A	1¼¢ Palace 6/17/60 Santa Fe, NM	1.75
1055	2¢ Jefferson 10/22/54 St. Louis, MO	1.75
1055a	Luminescent 5/6/68 DC	40.00
1055a & 1045a	Luminescent, combo	50.00
1056	2½¢ Bunker Hill 9/9/59 Los Angeles, CA	1.75
1057	3¢ Statue of Liberty 7/20/54 DC	1.75
1057b	Luminescent 5/12/67 DC	60.00
1058	4¢ Lincoln 7/31/58 Mandan, ND	1.75
1059	4½¢ Hermitage 5/1/59 Denver, CO	1.75
1059A	25¢ Paul Revere 2/25/65 Wheaton, MD	2.50
1059b	Luminescent 4/3/73 NY, NY	40.00
1060	3¢ Nebraska Ter. 5/7/54 Nebraska City, NE	1.75
1061	3¢ Kansas Terr. 5/31/54 Fort Leavenworth, KS	1.75
1062	3¢ George Eastman 7/12/54 Rochester, NY	1.75
1063	3¢ Lewis & Clark 7/28/54 Sioux City, IA	1.75
	1955	
1064	3¢ Fine Arts 1/15/55 Philadelphia, PA	1.75
1065	3¢ Land Grant Colleges 2/12/55 East Lansing, MI	2.50
1066	3¢ Rotary Int. 2/23/55 Chicago, IL	2.50
1067	3¢ Armed Forces Reserve 5/21/55 DC	2.00
1068	3¢ New Hampshire 6/21/55 Franconia, NH	1.75
1069	3¢ Soo Locks 6/28/55 Sault St. Marie, MI	1.75
1070	3¢ Atoms for Peace 7/28/55 DC	1.75
1071	3¢ Fort Ticonderoga 9/18/55 Ticonderoga, NY	1.75
1072	3¢ Andrew W. Mellon 12/20/55 DC	1.75
	1956	
1073	3¢ Benjamin Franklin 1/17/56 Phila., PA	1.75
	Poor Richard Station	1.75
1074	3¢ Booker T. Washington 4/5/56	
	Booker T. Washington Birthplace, VA	2.50
1075	11¢ FIPEX Sheet 4/28/56 New York, NY	4.50
1076	3¢ FIPEX 4/30/56 New York, NY	1.75
1077	3¢ Wild Turkey 5/5/56 Fond du Lac, WI	2.50
1078	3¢ Antelope 6/22/56 Gunnison, CO	2.00
1079	3¢ King Salmon 11/9/56 Seattle, WA	2.00
1080	3¢ Pure Food and Drug Laws 6/27/56 DC	1.75
1081	3¢ Wheatland 8/5/56 Lancaster, PA	1.75
1082	3¢ Labor Day 9/3/56 Camden, NJ	1.75
1083	3¢ Nassau Hall 9/22/56 Princeton, NJ	1.75
1084	3¢ Devils Tower 9/24/56 Devils Tower, NY	1.75
1085	3¢ Children 12/15/56 DC	1.75
	1957	
1086	3¢ Alex Hamilton 1/11/57 New York, NY	1.75
1087	3¢ Polio 1/15/57 DC	2.50
1088	3¢ Coast & Geodetic Survey 2/11/57 Seattle, WA	1.75
1089	3¢ Architects 2/23/57 New York, NY	2.25
1090	3¢ Steel Industry 5/22/57 New York, NY	1.75
1091	3¢ Naval Review 6/10/57 USS Saratoga, Norfolk, VA	1.75
1092	3¢ Oklahoma Statehood 6/14/57 Oklahoma City, OK	1.75
1093	3¢ School Teachers 7/1/57 Phila., PA	2.50
	"Philadelpia" error cancel	7.50
1094	4¢ American Flag 7/4/57 DC	1.75
1095	3¢ Shipbuilding 8/15/57 Bath, ME	1.75
1096	8¢ Ramon Magsaysay 8/31/57 DC	1.75
1097	3¢ Lafayette 9/6/57 Easton, PA	1.75
	Fayetteville, NC	1.75
	Louisville, KY	1.75
1098	3¢ Whooping Crane 11/22/57 New York, NY	1.75
	New Orleans, LA	1.75
	Corpus Christi, TX	1.75
1099	3¢ Religious Freedom 12/27/57 Flushing, NY	1.75

Scott #		Price
	1958-59	
1100	3¢ Horticulture 3/15/58 Ithaca, NY	1.75
1104	3¢ Brussels Exhibit. 4/17/58 Detroit, MI	1.75
1105	3¢ James Monroe 4/28/58 Montross, VA	1.75
1106	3¢ Minnesota Sthd. 5/11/58 St. Paul, MN	1.75
1107	3¢ Int'l. Geo. Year 5/31/58 Chicago, IL	1.75
1108	3¢ Gunston Hall 6/12/58 Lorton, VA	1.75
1109	3¢ Mackinaw Bridge 6/25/58 Mackinaw Bridge, MI	1.75
1110	4¢ Simon Bolivar 7/24/58 DC	1.75
1111	8¢ Simon Bolivar 7/24/58 DC	1.75
1110-11	Bolivar on one cover	2.50
1112	4¢ Atlantic Cable 8/15/58 New York, NY	1.75
1113	1¢ Lincoln 2/12/59 Hodgenville, NY	1.75
1114	3¢ Lincoln 2/27/59 New York, NY	1.75
1115	4¢ Lincoln & Douglas 8/27/58 Freeport, IL	1.75
1116	4¢ Lincoln Statue 5/30/59 DC	1.75
1113-16	On 1 Cover	8.00
1117	4¢ Lajos Kossuth 9/19/58 DC	1.75
1118	8¢ Lajos Kossuth 9/19/58 DC	1.75
1117-18	Kossuth on one cover	2.50
1119	4¢ Freedom of Press 9/22/58 Columbia, MO	1.75
1120	4¢ Overland Mail 10/10/58 San Fran., CA	1.75
	1958 (cont.)	
1121	4¢ Noah Webster 10/16/58 W. Hartford, CT	1.75
1122	4¢ Forest Conserv. 10/27/58 Tucson, AZ	1.75
1123	4¢ Fort Duquesne 11/25/58 Pittsburgh, PA	1.75
	1959	
1124	4¢ Oregon Sthd. 2/14/59 Astoria, OR	1.75
1125	4¢ Jose de San Martin 2/25/59 DC	1.75
1126	8¢ Jose de San Martin 2/25/59 DC	1.75
1125-26	San Martin on one cover	2.50
1127	4¢ NATO 4/1/59 DC	1.75
1128	4¢ Arctic Explorers 4/6/59 Cresson, PA	1.75
1129	8¢ World Trade 4/20/59 DC	1.75
1130	4¢ Silver Cent. 6/8/59 Virginia City, NV	1.75
1131	4¢ St. Lawrence Seaway 6/26/59 Massena, NY	2.00
1131	Combo w/Canada	10.00
1131	Combo w/Canada, dual cancel	250.00
1132	4¢ 49-Star Flag 7/4/59 Auburn, NY	1.75
1133	4¢ Soil Conserv. 8/26/59 Rapid City, SD	1.75
1134	4¢ Petroleum Ind. 8/27/59 Titusville, PA	2.00
1135	4¢ Dental Health 9/14/59 New York, NY	5.00
1136	4¢ Ernst Reuter 9/29/59 DC	1.75
1137	8¢ Ernst Reuter 9/29/59 DC	1.75
1136-37	Reuter on one cover	2.50
1138	4¢ Dr. McDowell 12/3/59 Danville, KY	1.75
	1960	
1139	4¢ Washington Credo 1/20/60 Mt. Vernon, VA	1.75
1140	4¢ Franklin Credo 3/31/60 Phila., PA	1.75
1141	4¢ Jefferson Credo 5/18/60 Charlottesville, VA	1.75
1142	4¢ Francis Scott Key Credo 9/14/60 Baltimore, MD	1.75
1143	4¢ Lincoln Credo 11/19/60 New York, NY	1.75
1144	4¢ Patrick Henry Credo 1/11/61 Richmond, VA	1.75
	#1139-1144 on one cover, 1/11/61	6.00
1145	4¢ Boy Scouts 2/8/60 DC	3.50
1146	4¢ Winter Olympics 2/18/60 Olympic Valley, CA	1.75
1147	4¢ Thomas G. Masaryk 3/7/60 DC	1.75
1148	8¢ Thomas G. Masaryk 3/7/60 DC	1.75
1147-48	Masaryk on one cover	2.50
1149	4¢ World Refugee Year 4/7/60 DC	1.75
1150	4¢ Water Conservation 4/18/60 DC	1.75
1151	4¢ SEATO 5/31/60 DC	1.75
1152	4¢ American Women 6/2/60 DC	2.00
1153	4¢ 50-Star Flag 7/4/60 Honolulu, HI	1.75
1154	4¢ Pony Express Centennial 7/19/60 Sacramento, CA	2.25
1155	4¢ Employ the Handicapped 8/28/60 New York, NY	1.75
1156	4¢ World Forestry Co. 8/29/60 Seattle, WA	1.75
1157	4¢ Mexican Indep. 9/16/60 Los Angeles, CA	1.75
1157	Combo w/Mexico	20.00
1157	Combo w/Mexico, dual cancel	375.00
1158	4¢ US-Japan Treaty 9/28/60 DC	1.75
1159	4¢ Paderewski 10/8/60 DC	1.75
1160	8¢ Paderewski 10/8/60 DC	1.75
1159-60	Paderewski on one cover	2.50
1161	4¢ Robert A. Taft 10/10/60 Cincinnati, OH	1.75

1152

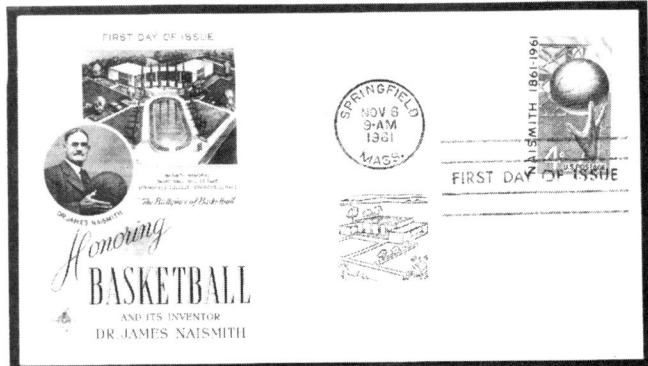

1189

Scott #	Description	Price
	1960 (cont.)	
1162	4¢ Wheels of Freedom 10/15/60 Detroit, MI	1.75
1163	4¢ Boys Clubs 10/18/60 New York, NY	1.75
1164	4¢ Automated P.O. 10/20/60 Providence, RI	1.75
1165	4¢ Gustav Mannerheim 10/26/60 DC	1.75
1166	8¢ Gustav Mannerheim 10/26/60 DC	1.75
1165-66	Mannerheim on one cover	2.50
1167	4¢ Camp Fire Girls 11/1/60 New York, NY	2.50
1168	4¢ Giuseppe Garibaldi 11/2/60 DC	1.75
1169	8¢ Guiseppe Garibaldi 11/2/60 DC	1.75
1168-69	Garibaldi on one cover	2.50
1170	4¢ Walter F. George 11/5/60 Vienna, GA	1.75
1171	4¢ Andrew Carnegie 11/25/60 New York, NY	1.75
1172	4¢ John Foster Dulles 12/6/60 DC	1.75
1173	4¢ Echo 1 12/15/60 DC	3.00
	1961-65	
1174	4¢ Mahatma Gandhi 1/26/61 DC	1.75
1175	8¢ Mahatma Gandhi 1/26/61 DC	1.75
1174-75	Gandhi on one cover	2.50
1176	4¢ Range Cons. 2/2/61 Salt Lake City, UT	1.75
1177	4¢ Horace Greeley 2/3/61 Chappaqua, NY	1.75
1178	4¢ Fort Sumter 4/12/61 Charleston, SC	5.00
1179	4¢ Battle of Shiloh 4/7/62 Shiloh, TN	5.00
1180	5¢ Battle of Gettysburg 7/1/63 Gettysburg, PA	5.00
1181	5¢ Battle of Wilderness 5/5/64 Fredericksburg, VA	5.00
1182	5¢ Appomattox 4/9/65 Appomattox, VA	5.00
1178-82	Civil War on 1 cover 4/9/65	12.00
1183	4¢ Kansas Statehood 5/10/61 Council Grove, KS	1.75
1184	4¢ George Norris 7/11/611 DC	1.75
1185	4¢ Naval Aviation 8/20/61 San Diego, CA	2.00
1186	4¢ Workmen's Comp. 9/4/61 Milwaukee, WI	1.75
1187	4¢ Frederic Remington 10/4/61 DC	2.00
1188	4¢ Sun Yat-Sen 10/10/61 DC	5.00
1189	4¢ Basketball 11/6/61 Springfield, MA	8.00
1190	4¢ Nursing 12/28/61 DC	12.00
	1962	
1191	4¢ New Mexico Sthd. 1/6/62 Santa Fe, NM	2.25
1192	4¢ Arizona Sthd. 2/14/62 Phoenix, AZ	2.25
	1st Glory cachet	**35.00**
1193	4¢ Project Mercury 2/20/62 Cape Canaveral, FL	4.00
	1st Marg cachet	**25.00**
1194	4¢ Malaria Eradication 3/30/62 DC	2.00
1195	4¢ Charles Evans Hughes 4/11/62 DC	1.75
1196	4¢ Seattle Fair 4/25/62 Seattle, WA	1.75
1197	4¢ Louisiana 4/30/62 New Orleans, LA	1.75
1198	4¢ Homestead Act 5/20/62 Beatrice, NE	1.75
1199	4¢ Girl Scouts 7/24/62 Burlington, VT	3.50
1200	4¢ Brien McMahon 7/28/62 Norwalk, CT	1.75
1201	4¢ Apprenticeship 8/31/62 DC	1.75
1202	4¢ Sam Rayburn 9/16/62 Bonham, TX	1.75
1203	4¢ Dag Hammarskjold 10/23/62 NY, NY	1.75
1204	4¢ Hammarskjold Invert. 11/16/62 DC	5.00
1205	4¢ Christmas 11/1/62 Pittsburgh, PA	2.00
1206	4¢ Higher Education 11/14/62 DC	2.25
1207	4¢ Winslow Homer 12/15/62 Gloucester, MA	2.25
	1962-63 REGULAR ISSUES	
1208	5¢ 50-Star Flag 1/9/63 DC	1.75
1208a	5¢ Luminescent 8/25/66 DC	35.00
1209	1¢ Andrew Jackson 3/22/63 New York, NY	1.75
1209a	Luminescent 7/6/66 DC	35.00
1213	5¢ Washington 11/23/62 New York, NY	1.75
1213a	Booklet Pane 11/23/62 New York, NY	3.00
1213b	Luminescent 10/28/63 Dayton, OH	35.00
1213c	Luminescent bklt. pair 10/28/63 Dayton, OH	40.00
1213c	Luminescent bklt. pane 10/28/63 Dayton, OH	100.00
	DC	125.00
1225	1¢ Jackson, coil 5/31/63 Chicago, IL	1.75
1225a	Luminescent 7/6/66 DC	35.00
1225a & 1035b	Luminescent combo	40.00
1229	5¢ Washington, coil 11/23/62 New York, NY	1.75
1229a	Luminescent 10/28/63 Dayton, OH	35.00
	DC	35.00
1229a,1213b, & 1213c	On one FDC 10/28/63 Dayton, OH	60.00

Scott #	Description	Price
	1963	
1230	5¢ Carolina Charter 4/6/63 Edenton, NC	1.75
1231	5¢ Food for Peace 6/4/63 DC	1.75
1232	5¢ W. Virginia Sthd. 6/20/63 Wheeling, WV	1.75
1233	5¢ Emancipation Proc. 8/16/63 Chicago, IL	2.50
1234	5¢ Alliance for Progress 8/17/63 DC	1.75
1235	5¢ Cordell Hull 10/5/63 Carthage, TN	1.75
1236	5¢ Eleanor Roosevelt 10/11/63 DC	1.75
1237	5¢ Science 10/14/63 DC	2.00
1238	5¢ City Mail Delivery 10/26/63 DC	2.00
1239	5¢ Red Cross 10/29/63 DC	2.50
1240	5¢ Christmas 11/1/63 Santa Claus, IN	2.00
1240a	5¢ Luminescent 11/2/63 DC	60.00
1241	5¢ Audobon 12/7/63 Henderson, KY	2.00
	1964	
1242	5¢ Sam Houston 1/10/64 Houston, TX	2.00
1243	5¢ Charle Russell 3/19/64 Great Falls, MT	2.50
1244	5¢ NY World's Fair 4/22/64 World's Fair, NY	2.00
	1st Sarzin Metallic cachet	**20.00**
1245	5¢ John Muir 4/29/64 Martinez, CA	1.75
1246	5¢ John F. Kennedy 5/29/64 Boston, MA	2.50
	1st Cover Craft cachet	**40.00**
1247	5¢ New Jersey Terc. 6/15/64 Elizabeth, NJ	1.75
1248	5¢ Nevada Sthd. 7/22/64 Carson City, NV	1.75
1249	5¢ Register & Vote 8/1/64 DC	2.00
1250	5¢ Shakespeare 8/14/64 Stratford, CT	2.00
1251	5¢ Doctors Mayo 9/11/64 Rochester, MN	5.00
1252	5¢ American Music 10/15/64 New York, NY	2.50
1253	5¢ Homemakers 10/26/64 Honolulu, HI	1.75
1254-57	5¢ Christmas attd. 11/9/64 Bethlehem, PA	4.00
1254-57	Christmas set of 4 singles	10.00
1254-57a	Luminescent Christmas attd 11/10/64 Dayton, OH	60.00
1254-57a	Luminescent Christmas set of 4 singles	80.00
1258	5¢ Verrazano-Narrows Bridge 11/21/64 Stat. Is., NY	1.75
1259	5¢ Fine Arts 12/2/64 DC	1.75
1260	5¢ Amateur Radio 12/15/64 Anchorage, AK	2.50
	1965	
1261	5¢ Battle of New Orleans 1/8/65 New Orleans, LA	1.75
1262	5¢ Physical Fitness 2/15/65 DC	2.00
1263	5¢ Cancer Crusade 4/1/65 DC	3.50
1264	5¢ Winston Churchill 5/13/65 Fulton, MO	2.00
1265	5¢ Magna Carta 6/15/65 Jamestown, VA	1.75
1266	5¢ Int'l. Cooperation Year 6/26/65 San Francisco, CA	1.75
1267	5¢ Salvation Army 7/2/65 New York, NY	1.75
1268	5¢ Dante 7/17/65 San Francisco, CA	1.75
1269	5¢ Herbert Hoover 8/10/65 West Branch, IA	1.75
1270	5¢ Robert Fulton 8/19/65 Clermont, NY	1.75
1271	5¢ 400th Anniv. of FL 8/28/65 St. Augustine, FL	1.75
1271	Combo w/Spain	90.00
1271	Combo w/Spain, dual cancel	450.00
1272	5¢ Traffic Safety 9/3/65 Baltimore, MD	1.75
1273	5¢ John Copley 9/17/65 DC	1.75
1274	11¢ Int'l. Telecomm. Union 10/6/65 DC	1.75
1275	5¢ A. Stevenson 10/23/65 Bloominton, IL	1.75
1276	5¢ Christmas 11/2/65 Silver Bell, AZ	1.75
1276a	Luminescent 11/16/65 DC	50.00
	1965-68 PROMINENT AMERICANS SERIES	
1278	1¢ Jefferson 1/12/68 Jeffersonville, IN	1.75
1278a	bklt. pane of 8 1/12/68 Jeffersonville, IN	2.00
1278a	bklt. pane of 8, dull gum 3/1/71 DC	90.00
1278a & 1393a	Combo, 3/1/71	150.00
1278b	booklet pane of 4 5/10/71 DC	15.00
1279	1¼¢ Gallatin 1/30/67 Gallatin, MO	1.75
1280	2¢ Wright 6/8/66 Spring Green, WI	1.75
1280a	booklet pane of 5 1/8/68 Buffalo, NY	3.00
1280c	booklet pane of 6 5/7/71 Spokane, WA	15.00
1280c var.	bklt. pane of 6, dull gum 10/31/75 Cleveland, OH	100.00
1281	3¢ Parkman 9/16/67 Boston, MA	1.75
1282	4¢ Lincoln 11/19/65 New York, NY	1.75
1282a	Luminescent 12/1/65 Dayton, OH	40.00
	DC	45.00
1283	5¢ Washington 2/22/66 DC	1.75
1283a	Luminescent 2/23/66 Dayton, OH	100.00
	DC	27.50
1283B	5¢ Washington, redrawn 11/17/67 New York, NY	1.75

1261

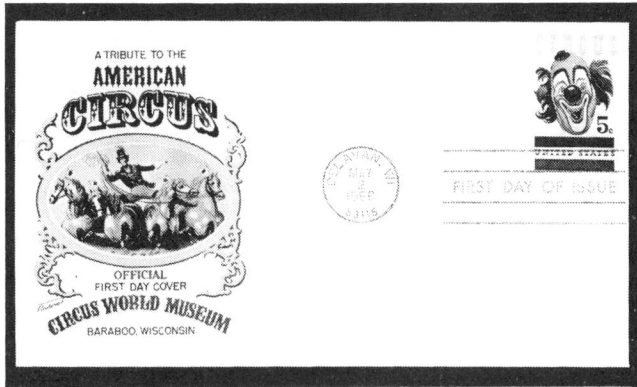

1309

Scott #	Description	Price
	1965-68 PROMINENT AMERICANS SERIES (con't.)	
1284	6¢ Roosevelt 1/29/66 Hyde Park, NY	1.75
1284a	Luminescent 12/29/66	40.00
1284b	booklet pane of 8 12/28/67 DC	2.50
1284bs	booklet single	1.75
1284c	booklet pane of 5 1/9/68 DC	125.00
1285	8¢ Einstein 3/14/66 Princeton, NJ	2.00
1285a	Luminescent 7/6/66 DC	40.00
1286	10¢ Jackson 3/15/67 Hermitage, TN	1.75
1286A	12¢ Ford 7/30/68 Greenfield Village, MI	2.50
1287	13¢ Kennedy 5/29/67 Brookline, MA	2.50
1288	15¢ Holmes 3/8/68 DC	1.75
1288B	booklet single 6/14/78 Boston, MA	1.75
1288Bc	15¢ bklt. pane of 8 6/14/78 Boston, MA	3.50
1289	20¢ Marshall 10/24/67 Lexington, VA	2.00
1289a	Luminescent 4/3/73 New York, NY	40.00
1290	25¢ Douglass 2/14/67 DC	3.50
1290a	Luminescent 4/3/73 DC	45.00
1291	30¢ Dewey 10/21/68 Burlington, VT	2.50
1291a	Luminescent 4/3/73 New York, NY	45.00
1292	40¢ Paine 1/29/68 Philadelphia, PA	3.00
1292a	Luminescent 4/3/73 New York, NY	45.00
1293	50¢ Stone 8/13/68 Dorchester, MA	4.00
1293a	Luminescent 4/3/73 New York, NY	50.00
1294	$1 O'Neill 10/16/67 New London, CT	7.00
1294a	Luminescent 4/3/73 New York, NY	65.00
1295	$5 Moore 12/3/66 Smyrna, DE	40.00
1295a	Luminescent 4/3/73 New York NY	125.00
	#1295 & 1295a on one cover 4/3/73	250.00
	1966-81 PROMINENT AMERICAN COILS	
1297	3¢ Parkman 11/4/75 Pendleton, OR....................	1.75
1298	6¢ Roosevelt, vert. coil 12/28/67 DC.................	1.75
1299	1¢ Jefferson 1/12/68 Jeffersonville, IN	1.75
1303	4¢ Lincoln 5/28/66 Springfield, IL.....................	1.75
1304	5¢ Washington 9/8/66 Cincinnati, OH	1.75
1304C	5¢ Washington re-engraved 3/31/81 DC	25.00
1305	6¢ Roosevelt, horiz. coil 2/28/68 DC	1.75
1305E	15¢ Holmes 6/14/78 Boston, MA	1.75
1305C	$1 O'Neill 1/12/73 Hampstead, NY	4.00
	1966	
1306	5¢ Migratory Bird 3/16/66 Pittsburgh, PA	2.50
1307	5¢ Humane Treatment 4/9/66 New York, NY	2.00
1308	5¢ Indiana Sthd. 4/16/66 Corydon, IN	1.75
1309	5¢ Circus 5/2/66 Delevan, WI	2.50
1310	5¢ SIPEX 5/21/66 DC	1.75
1311	5¢ SIPEX sheet 5/23/66 DC	2.00
1312	5¢ Bill of Rights 7/1/66 Miami Beach, FL	1.75
1313	5¢ Polish Millenium 7/30/66 DC	1.75
1314	5¢ Nat'l. Park Service 8/25/66 Yellowstone Nat'l. Park	2.00
1314a	Luminescent 8/26/66	50.00
1315	5¢ Marine Corps Reserve 8/29/66 DC	2.50
1315a	Luminescent 8/29/66 DC	50.00
1316	5¢ Women's Clubs 9/12/66 New York, NY	2.00
1316a	Luminescent 9/13/66 DC	50.00
1317	5¢ Johnny Appleseed 9/24/66 Leominster, MA	1.75
1317a	Luminescent 9/26/66 DC	50.00
1318	5¢ Beautification 10/5/66 DC	1.75
1318a	Luminescent 10/5/66 DC	50.00
1319	5¢ Great River Road 10/21/66 Baton Rouge, LA...	1.75
1319a	Luminescent 10/22/66 DC	50.00
1320	5¢ Savings Bonds 10/26/66 Sioux City, IA	1.75
1320a	Luminescent 10/27/66 DC	50.00
1321	5¢ Christmas 11/1/66 Christmas, MI	1.75
1321a	Luminescent 11/2/66	50.00
1322	5¢ Mary Cassatt 11/17/66 DC	2.00
1322a	Luminescent 11/17/66 DC	50.00
	1967	
1323	5¢ National Grange 4/17/67 DC	1.75
1324	5¢ Canada Centenary 5/25/67 Montreal, CAN	1.75
1325	5¢ Erie Canal 7/4/67 Rome, NY........................	1.75
1326	5¢ Search for Peace 7/5/67 Chicago, IL..............	1.75
1327	5¢ Henry Thoreau 7/12/67 Concord, MA	1.75

Scott #	Description	Price
1328	5¢ Nebraska Statehood. 7/29/67 Lincoln, NE	1.75
1329	5¢ Voice of America 8/1/67	1.75
1330	5¢ Davy Crockett 8/17/67 San Antonio, TX	1.75
1331-32	5¢ Space Twins attd. 9/29/67 Kennedy Space Ctr., FL	8.00
1331-32	Space Twins set of 2 singles	8.00
1333	5¢ Urban Planning 10/2/67 DC..........................	1.75
1334	5¢ Finland Indep. 10/6/67 Finland, MI	1.75
1335	5¢ Thomas Eakins 11/2/67 DC	2.00
1336	5¢ Christmas 11/6/67 Bethlehem, GA	2.00
1337	5¢ Mississippi Statehood 12/11/67 Natchez, MS ...	1.75
	1968-71 REGULAR ISSUES	
1338	6¢ Flag & White House 1/24/68 DC	1.75
1338A	6¢ Flag & W.H., coil 5/30/69 Chicago, IL	1.75
1338D	6¢ Flag & W.H. (Huck Press) 8/7/70 DC..............	1.75
1338F	8¢ Flag & White House 5/10/71 DC	1.75
1338G	8¢ Flag & White House, coil 5/10/71 DC	1.75
	1968	
1339	6¢ Illinois Statehood 2/12/68 Shawneetown, IL	1.75
1340	6¢ Hemis Fair '68 3/30/68 San Antonio, TX	1.75
1341	$1 Airlift 4/4/68 Seattle, WA	7.50
1342	6¢ Support Our Youth 5/1/68 Chicago, IL	1.75
1343	6¢ Law and Order 5/17/68 DC	3.50
1344	6¢ Register and Vote 6/27/68 DC	2.50
1345-54	6¢ Historic Flags attd. 7/4/68 Pittsburgh, PA	8.50
1345-54	Historic Flags set of 10 singles	30.00
1355	6¢ Walt Disney 9/11/68 Marceline, MO	35.00
1356	6¢ Marquette 9/20/68 Sault Ste. Marie, MI..........	1.75
1357	6¢ Daniel Boone 9/26/68 Frankfort, KY	1.75
1358	6¢ Arkansas River 10/1/68 Little Rock, AR	1.75
1359	6¢ Leif Ericson 10/9/68 Seattle, WA	1.75
1360	6¢ Cherokee Strip 10/15/68 Ponca, OK	1.75
1361	6¢ John Trumbull 10/18/66 New Haven, CT	2.50
1362	6¢ Waterfowl Cons. 10/24/68 Cleveland, OH	2.00
1363	6¢ Christmas, tagged 11/1/68 DC	2.00
1363a	6¢ Not tagged 11/2/68 DC	15.00
1364	6¢ American Indian 11/4/68 DC	2.00
	1969	
1365-68	6¢ Beautification attd. 1/16/69 DC	5.00
1365-68	Beautification set of 4 singles	10.00
1369	6¢ American Legion 3/15/69 DC	1.75
1370	6¢ Grandma Moses 5/1/69 DC	2.00
1371	6¢ Apollo 8 5/5/69 Houston, TX	3.00
1372	6¢ W.C. Handy 5/17/69 Memphis, TN	2.50
1373	6¢ California 7/16/69 San Diego, CA	1.75
1374	6¢ John W. Powell 8/1/69 Page, AZ	1.75
1375	6¢ Alabama Sthd. 8/2/69 Huntsville, AL	1.75
1376-79	6¢ Botanical Congress attd. 8/23/69 Seattle, WA ..	6.00
1376-79	Botanical Congress set of 4 singles	10.00
1380	6¢ Dartmouth Case 9/22/69 Hanover, NH	1.75
1381	6¢ Baseball 9/24/69 Cincinnati, OH....................	12.00
1382	6¢ Football 9/26/69 New Brunswick, NJ	6.00
1383	6¢ Eisenhower 10/14/69 Abilene, KS	1.75
1384	6¢ Christmas 11/3/69 Christmas, FL	2.00
1384a	6¢ Christmas - Precancel 11/4/69 Atlanta, GA	175.00
	Baltimore, MD	175.00
	Memphis, TN	200.00
	New Haven, CT	175.00
1385	6¢ Hope for Crippled 11/20/69 Columbus, OH	2.00
1386	6¢ William Harnett 12/3/69 Boston, MA	1.75
	1970	
1387-90	6¢ Natural History attd. 5/6/70 NY, NY	4.00
1387-90	Natural History set of 4 singles	8.00
1391	6¢ Maine Statehood 7/9/70 Portland, ME	1.75
1392	6¢ Wildlife - Buffalo 7/20/70 Custer, SD	1.75
	1970-74 REGULAR ISSUES	
1393	6¢ Eisenhower 8/6/70 DC	1.75
1393a	booklet pane of 8 8/6/70 DC	2.50
1393a	booklet pane of 8, dull gum 3/1/71 DC	75.00
1393a & 1278a	Combo, 3/1/71	150.00
1393b	booklet pane of 6 8/6/70 DC	3.00
1393bs	booklet single, 8/6/70	1.75
1393D	7¢ Franklin 10/20/72 Philadelphia, PA	1.75
1394	8¢ Eisenhower 5/10/71 DC	1.75
1395	8¢ Eisenhower, claret 5/10/71 DC	2.00

1387-90

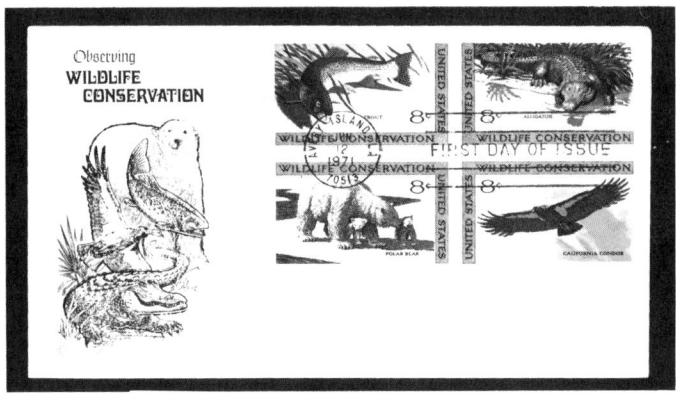

1427-30

Scott #	Description	Price
	1970-74 REGULAR ISSUE (con't.)	
1395a	booklet pane of 8 5/10/71 DC	2.50
1395b	booklet pane of 6 5/10/71 DC	2.50
1395c	bklt. pane of 4 1/28/72 Casa Grande, AZ	2.00
1395cs	Booklet Single 1/28/72 Casa Grande, AZ	1.75
1395d	bklt. pane of 7 1/28/72 Casa Grande, AZ	2.00
1395ds	Booklet Single 1/28/72 Casa Grande, AZ	1.75
1396	8¢ Postal Service Emblem 7/1/71 any city	1.75
1397	14¢ LaGuardia 4/24/72 New York, NY	1.75
1398	16¢ Ernie Pyle 5/7/71 DC	2.50
1399	18¢ Eliz. Blackwell 1/23/74 Geneva, NY	2.00
1400	21¢ Giannini 6/27/73 San Mateo, CA	2.25
1401	6¢ Eisenhower, coil 8/6/70 DC	1.75
1402	8¢ Eisenhower, coil 5/10/71 DC	1.75
	1970	
1405	6¢ Edgar Lee Masters 8/22/70 Petersburg, IL	1.75
1406	6¢ Woman Suffrage 8/26/70 Adams, MA	1.75
1407	6¢ South Carolina 9/12/70 Charleston, SC	1.75
1408	6¢ Stone Mountain 9/19/70 Stone Mt., GA	1.75
1409	6¢ Ft. Snelling 10/17/70 Ft. Snelling, MT	1.75
1410-13	6¢ Anti-Pollution attd. 10/28/70 San Clemente, CA	5.00
1410-13	Anti-Pollution set of 4 singles	8.00
1414	6¢ Christmas - Religious 11/5/70 DC	1.75
1414a	6¢ Christmas Precancel 11/5/70 DC	3.00
1415-18	6¢ Christmas Toys attd. 11/5/70 DC	6.00
1415-18	Christmas Toys set of 4 singles	10.00
1415a-18a	Christmas Toys-Precancel attd. 11/5/70 DC	15.00
1415a-18a	Christmas Toys-Precancel set of 4 singles	50.00
1414a-18a	Religious & Toys (5) on one FDC 11/5/70 DC	30.00
1419	6¢ UN 25th Anniv. 11/20/70 New York, NY	1.75
1420	6¢ Pilgrims' Landing 11/21/70 Plymouth, MA	1.75
1421-22	6¢ Disabled Vets - US Servicemen attd. 11/24/70 Cincinnati or Montgomery	2.00
1421-22	D.A.V. - Serv. set of 2 singles	3.50
	1971	
1423	6¢ Wool Industry 1/19/71 Las Vegas, NV	1.75
	1st Bazaar cachet	**30.00**
	1st Colorano Silk cachet	**300.00**
1424	6¢ MacArthur 1/26/71 Norfolk, VA	2.00
1425	6¢ Blood Donor 3/12/71 New York, NY	1.75
1426	6¢ Missouri 5/8/71 Independence, MO	1.75
1427-30	8¢ Wildlife Conservation attd. 6/12/71 Avery Island, LA	4.00
1427-30	Wildlife set of 4 singles	8.00
1431	8¢ Antarctic Treaty 6/23/71 DC	1.75
1432	8¢ American Revolution Bic. 7/4/71 DC	1.75
	1st Medallion cachet	**30.00**
1433	8¢ John Sloan 8/2/71 Lock Haven, PA	1.75
1434-35	8¢ Space Achievement Decade attd. 8/2/71	
	Kennedy Space Center, FL	2.50
	Houston, TX	2.50
	Huntsville, AL	2.50
1434-35	Space Achievement set of 2 singles	
	Kennedy Space Center, FL	3.50
	Houston, TX	3.50
	Huntsville, AL	3.50
1436	8¢ Emily Dickinson 8/28/71 Amherst, MA	1.75
1437	8¢ San Juan 9/12/71 San Juan, PR	1.75
1438	8¢ Drug Abuse 10/4/71 Dallas, TX	1.75
1439	8¢ CARE 10/27/71 New York, NY	1.75
1440-43	8¢ Historic Preservation attd. 10/29/71 San Diego, CA	4.00
1440-43	Historic Preservation set of 4 singles	8.00
1444	8¢ Christmas - Religious 11/10/71 DC	2.00
1445	8¢ Christmas - Partridge 11/10/71 DC	2.00
1444-45	Christmas on one cover	2.50
	1972	
1446	8¢ Sidney Lanier 2/3/72 Macon, GA	1.75
1447	8¢ Peace Corps 2/11/72 DC	1.75
1448-51	2¢ Cape Hatteras 4/5/72 Hatteras, NC	1.75
1452	6¢ Wolf Trap Farm 6/26/72 Vienna, VA	1.75
1453	8¢ Yellowstone 3/1/72 DC	1.75
	Yellowstone Nat'l. Park, WY	1.75
1454	15¢ Mt. McKinley 7/28/72 Mt. McKinley Nat'l. Park, AK	1.75
1448-54,C84	Parks on one cover 7/28/72	6.00

Scott #	Description	Price
	1972 (cont.)	
1455	8¢ Family Planning 3/18/72 New York, NY	1.75
1456-59	8¢ Colonial Craftsmen attd. 7/4/72 Williamsburg, VA	4.00
1456-59	Colonial Craftsmen set of 4 singles	8.00
1460	6¢ Olympic - Bicycling 8/17/72 DC	1.75
1461	8¢ Olympic - Bobsledding 8/17/72 DC	1.75
1462	15¢ Olympic - Runners 8/17/72 DC	1.75
1460-62,C85	Olympics on one cover	4.00
1463	8¢ P.T.A. 9/15/72 San Francisco, CA	1.75
1464-67	8¢ Wildlife attd. 9/20/72 Warm Springs, OR	4.00
1464-67	Wildlife set of 4 singles	8.00
1468	8¢ Mail Order 9/27/72 Chicago, IL	1.75
1469	8¢ Osteopathic Medicine 10/9/72 Miami, FL	2.50
1470	8¢ Tom Sawyer 10/13/72 Hannibal, MO	2.50
1471	8¢ Christmas - Religious 11/9/72 DC	1.75
1472	8¢ Christmas - Santa Claus 11/9/72 DC	1.75
1471-72	Christmas on one cover	2.50
1473	8¢ Pharmacy 11/10/72 Cincinnati, OH	10.00
1474	8¢ Stamp Collecting 11/17/72 NY, NY	2.00
	1973	
1475	8¢ Love 1/26/73 Philadelphia, PA	2.25
1476	8¢ Pamphleteer 2/16/73 Portland, OR	1.75
1477	8¢ Broadside 4/13/73 Atlantic City, NJ	1.75
1478	8¢ Post Rider 6/22/73 Rochester, NY	1.75
1479	8¢ Drummer 9/28/73 New Orleans, LA	1.75
1480-83	8¢ Boston Tea Party attd. 7/4/73 Boston, MA	4.00
1480-83	Boston Tea Party set of 4 singles	8.00
1484	8¢ Geo. Gershwin 2/28/73 Beverly Hills, CA	1.75
1485	8¢ Robinson Jeffers 8/13/73 Carmel, CA	1.75
1486	8¢ Henry O. Tanner 9/10/73 Pittsburgh, PA	2.50
1487	8¢ Willa Cather 9/20/73 Red Cloud, NE	1.75
1488	8¢ Nicolaus Copernicus 4/23/73 DC	2.00
1489-98	8¢ Postal People attd. 4/30/73 any city	7.00
1489-98	Postal People set of 10 singles	20.00
1499	8¢ Harry Truman 5/8/73 Independence, MO	2.00
1500	6¢ Electronics 7/10/73 New York, NY	1.75
1501	8¢ Electronics 7/10/73 New York, NY	1.75
1502	15¢ Electronics 7/10/73 New York, NY	1.75
1500-02,C86	Electronics on one cover	7.00
1503	8¢ Lyndon B. Johnson 8/27/73 Austin, TX	1.75
1504	8¢ Angus Cattle 10/5/73 St. Joseph, MO	1.75
1505	10¢ Chautauqua 8/6/74 Chautauqua, NY	1.75
1506	10¢ Wheat 8/16/74 Hillsboro, KS	1.75
1507	8¢ Christmas - Madonna 11/7/73 DC	1.75
1508	8¢ Christmas - Tree 11/7/73 DC	1.75
1507-08	Christmas on one cover	2.75
	1973-74 REGULAR ISSUES	
1509	10¢ Crossed Flags 12/8/73 San Fran., CA	1.75
1510	10¢ Jefferson Memorial 12/14/73 DC	1.75
1510b	booklet pane of 5 12/14/73 DC	2.00
1510bs	booklet pane single, 12/14/73	1.75
1510c	booklet pane of 8 12/14/73 DC	2.25
1510d	booklet pane of 6 8/5/74 Oakland, CA	5.25
1510ds	booklet pane single, 8/5/74	1.75
1511	10¢ Zip Code 1/4/74 DC	1.75
1518	6.3¢ Liberty Bell, coil 10/1/74 DC	1.75
1518	Untagged, 10/2/74 DC	5.00
1519	10¢ Crossed Flags, coil 12/8/73 San Francisco, CA	1.75
1520	10¢ Jefferson Memorial, coil 12/14/73 DC	1.75
	1974	
1525	10¢ Veterans of Foreign Wars 3/11/74 DC	1.75
1526	10¢ Robert Frost 3/26/74 Derry, NH	1.75
1527	10¢ EXPO '74 4/18/74 Spokane, WA	1.75
1528	10¢ Horse Racing 5/4/74 Louisville, KY	3.00
1529	10¢ Skylab 5/14/74 Houston, TX	2.00
1530-37	10¢ UPU Centenary attd. 6/6/74 DC	5.00
1530-37	UPU Centenary set of 8 singles	20.00
1538-41	10¢ Mineral Heritage attd. 6/13/74 Lincoln, NE	4.00
1538-41	Mineral Heritage set of 4 singles	8.00
1542	10¢ Fort Harrod 6/15/74 Harrodsburg, KY	1.75
1543-46	10¢ Continental Congr. attd. 7/4/74 Philadelphia, PA	4.00
1543-46	Continental Congress set of 4 singles	8.00
1547	10¢ Energy Conserv. 9/23/74 Detroit, MI	1.75
1548	10¢ Sleepy Hollow 10/10/74 North Tarrytown, NY	2.00

1525

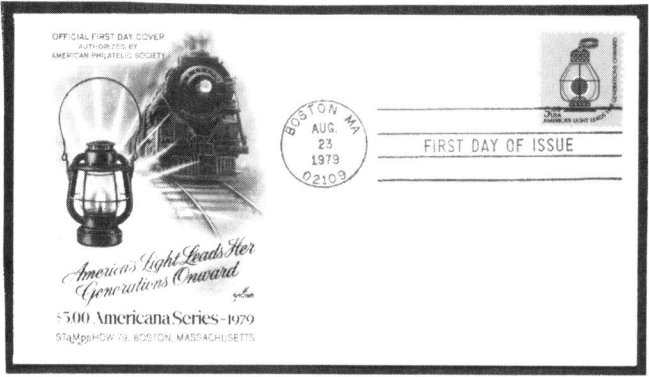

1612

Scott #	Description	Price
	1974 (cont.)	
1549	10¢ Retarded Children 10/12/74 Arlington, TX	1.75
1550	10¢ Christmas - Angel 10/23/74 NY, NY	1.75
1551	10¢ Christmas - Currier & Ives 10/23/74 NY, NY	1.75
1550-51	Christmas on one cover	2.25
1552	10¢ Christmas - Weathervane 11/15/74 New York, NY	3.00
1550-52	Christmas, dual cancel	5.00
	1975	
1553	10¢ Benjamin West 2/10/75 Swarthmore, PA	1.75
1554	10¢ Paul Dunbar 5/1/75 Dayton, OH	2.50
1555	10¢ D.W. Griffith 5/27/75 Beverly, Hills, CA	1.75
1556	10¢ Pioneer - Jupiter 2/28/75 Mountain View, CA	1.75
1557	10¢ Mariner 10 4/4/75 Pasadena, CA	1.75
1558	10¢ Collective Bargaining 3/13/75 DC	1.75
1559	8¢ Sybil Ludington 3/25/75 Carmel, NY	1.75
1560	10¢ Salem Poor 3/25/75 Cambridge, MA	2.50
1561	10¢ Haym Salomon 3/25/75 Chicago, IL	1.75
1562	18¢ Peter Francisco 3/25/75 Greensboro, NC	1.75
1559-62	Contributions on one cover, any city	8.00
1563	10¢ Lexington-Concord 4/19/75 Lexington, MA	1.75
	Concord, MA	1.75
1564	10¢ Bunker Hill 6/17/75 Charlestown, MA	1.75
1565-68	10¢ Military Uniforms attd. 7/4/75 DC	4.00
1565-68	Military Uniforms set of 4 singles	8.00
1569-70	10¢ Apollo-Soyuz attd. 7/15/75 Kennedy Sp. Ctr., FL	3.00
1569-70	Apollo-Soyuz set of 2 singles	4.00
1569-70	Apollo-Soyuz, combo, dual cancel	450.00
1571	10¢ Women's Year 8/26/75 Seneca Falls, NY	1.75
1572-75	10¢ Postal Serv. Bicent. attd. 9/3/75 Philadelphia, PA	4.00
1572-75	Postal Service set of 4 singles	8.00
1576	10¢ World Peace through Law 9/29/75 DC	2.00
1577-78	10¢ Banking - Commerce attd. 10/6/75 New York, NY	2.00
1577-78	Banking-Commerce set of 2 singles	3.00
1579	(10¢) Christmas - Madonna 10/14/75 DC	1.75
1580	(10¢) Christmas - Card 10/14/75 DC	1.75
1579-80	Christmas on one cover	2.50
	1975-81 AMERICANA SERIES REGULAR ISSUES	
1581	1¢ Inkwell & Quill 12/8/77 St. Louis, MO	1.75
1582	2¢ Speaker's Stand 12/8/77 St. Louis, MO	1.75
1584	3¢ Ballot Box 12/8/77 St. Louis, MO	1.75
1585	4¢ Books & Eyeglasses 12/8/77 St. Louis, MO	1.75
1581-85	4 values on one cover	3.00
1590	9¢ Capitol Dome, bklt. single	
	perf. 11 x 10½ 3/11/77 New York, NY	10.00
1590a	9¢ Capitol Dome, bklt. single	
	perf. 10 3/11/77 New York, NY	15.00
1591	9¢ Capitol Dome 11/24/75 DC	1.75
1592	10¢ Justice 11/17/77 New York, NY	1.75
1593	11¢ Printing Press 11/13/75 Phila., PA	1.75
1594	12¢ Liberty's Torch 4/8/81 Dallas, TX	1.75
1595	13¢ Liberty Bell, bklt. sgl. 10/31/75 Cleveland, OH	1.75
1595b	bklt. pane of 6 10/31/75 Cleveland, OH	2.25
1595c	bklt. pane of 7 10/31/75 Cleveland, OH	2.50
1595c	bklt. pane of 8 10/31/75 Cleveland, OH	2.75
1595d	bklt. pane of 5 4/2/76 Liberty, MO	2.00
1595ds	bklt. pane single, 4/2/76	1.75
1596	13¢ Eagle & Shield 12/1/75 Juneau, AK	1.75
1597	15¢ Ft. McHenry Flag 6/30/78 Baltimore, MD	1.75
1598	15¢ Ft. McHenry Flag,bklt. sgl. 6/30/78 Baltimore, MD..........	1.75
1598a	booklet pane of 8 6/30/78 Baltimore, MD	2.75
1599	16¢ Statue of Liberty 3/31/78 NY, NY	1.75
1603	24¢ Old North Church 11/14/75 Boston, MA	1.75
1604	28¢ Ft. Nisqually 8/11/78 Tacoma, WA	1.75
1605	29¢ Lighthouse 4/14/78 Atlantic City, NJ	1.75
1606	30¢ School House 8/27/79 Devils Lake, ND	1.75
1608	50¢ Betty Lamp 9/11/79 San Jaun, PR	2.00
1610	$1 Rush Lamp 7/2/79 San Francisco, CA	3.50
1611	$2 Kerosene Lamp 11/16/78 New York, NY	7.00
1612	$5 Railroad Lantern 8/23/79 Boston, MA	15.00

Scott #	Description	Price
	1975-79 AMERICANA SERIES COILS	
1613	3.1¢ Guitar 10/25/79 Shreveport, LA	1.75
1614	7.7¢ Saxhorns 11/20/76 New York, NY	1.75
1615	7.9¢ Drum 4/23/76 Miami, FL	1.75
1615C	8.4¢ Grand Piano 7/13/78 Interlochen, MI	1.75
1616	9¢ Capitol Dome 3/5/76 Milwaukee, WI	1.75
1617	10¢ Justice 11/4/77 Tampa, FL	1.75
1618	13¢ Liberty Bell 11/25/75 Allentown, PA	1.75
1618C	15¢ Ft. McHenry Flag 6/30/78 Baltimore, MD	1.75
1619	16¢ Statue of Liberty 3/31/78 NY, NY	1.75
	1975-77 REGULAR SERIES	
1622	13¢ Flag over Ind. Hall 11/15/75 Philadelphia, PA	1.75
1623	13¢ Flag over Capitol, bklt. single	
	perf. 11 x 10½ 3/11/77 NY, NY	2.50
1623a	13¢ & 9¢ booklet pane of 8 (7 #1623 & 1 #1590)	
	perf. 11 x 10½ 3/11/77 NY, NY	25.00
1623b	13¢ Flag over Capitol, bklt. single	
	perf. 10 3/11/77 New York, NY	2.00
1623c	13¢ & 9¢ booklet pane of 8 (7 #1623b & 1 #1590a)	
	perf. 10 3/11/77 New York, NY	15.00
1625	13¢ Flag over Ind. Hall, coil 11/15/75 Phila., PA	1.75
	1976	
1629-31	10¢ Spirit of '76 attd. 1/1/76 Pasadena, CA	3.00
1629-31	Spirit of '76 set of 3 singles	5.75
1632	13¢ Interphil '76 1/17/76 Phila., PA	1.75
	1976 STATE FLAGS	
1633-82	13¢ State Flags 2/23/76 set of 50 DC	75.00
	State Capitals	80.00
	State Capital & DC cancels, set of 50 combo FDC's	150.00
1682a	Full sheet on one FDC (Uncacheted)	40.00
1683	13¢ Telephone 3/10/76 Boston, MA	1.75
1684	13¢ Aviation 3/19/76 Chicago, IL	2.00
1685	13¢ Chemistry 4/6/76 New York, NY	1.75
1686-89	13¢-31¢ Bicent. Souv. Shts. 5/29/76 Philadelphia, PA	30.00
1686a-89e	Set of 20 singles from sheets	90.00
1686a-89e	Set of 20 singles on 4 covers	40.00
1690	13¢ Franklin 6/1/76 Philadelphia, PA	1.75
1690	U.S. & Canada joint issue	5.00
1690	U.S. & Canada joint issue, dual cancel	15.00
1691-94	13¢ Decl. of Indep. attd. 7/4/76 Philadelphia, PA	4.00
1691-94	Decl. of Indep. set of 4 singles	8.00
1695-98	13¢ Olympics attd. 7/16/76 Lake Placid, NY	4.00
1695-98	Olympics set of 4 singles	8.00
1699	13¢ Clara Maass 8/18/76 Belleville, NJ	2.00
1700	13¢ Adolph S. Ochs 9/18/76 New York, NY	1.75
1701	13¢ Nativity 10/27/76 Boston, MA	1.75
1702	13¢ "Winter Pastime" 10/27/76 Boston, MA	1.75
1701-02	Christmas on one cover	2.00
1703	13¢ "Winter Pastime", Grav.-Int. 10/27/76 Boston, MA	2.00
1701,03	Christmas on one cover	2.25
1702-03	Christmas on one cover	2.50
1701-03	Christmas on one cover	3.00
	1977	
1704	13¢ Washington 1/3/77 Princeton, NJ	1.75
	1st Carrollton cachet	**20.00**
1705	13¢ Sound Recording 3/23/77 DC	2.00
1706-09	13¢ Pueblo Pottery attd. 4/13/77 Santa Fe, NM	4.00
1706-09	Pueblo Pottery set of 4 singles	8.00
1710	13¢ Lindbergh 5/20/77 Roosevelt Field Sta., NY	2.50
	1st Doris Gold cachet	**65.00**
	1st GAMM cachet	**50.00**
	1st Spectrum cachet	**25.00**
	1st Tudor House cachet	**20.00**
	1st Z-Silk cachet	**20.00**
1711	13¢ Colorado Sthd. 5/21/77 Denver, CO	1.75
1712-15	13¢ Butterflies attd. 6/6/77 Indianapolis, IN	4.00
1712-15	Butterflies set of 4 singles	8.00
	1st Ham cachet	**450.00**
1716	13¢ Lafayette 6/13/77 Charleston, SC	1.75
1717-20	13¢ Skilled Hands attd. 7/4/77 Cincinnati, OH	4.00
1717-20	Skilled Hands set of 4 singles	8.00
1721	13¢ Peace Bridge 8/4/77 Buffalo, NY	1.75
	US and Canadian stamps on one cover	2.50
	Dual US & Canadian FD cancels	7.50
1722	13¢ Herkimer 8/6/77 Herkimer, NY	1.75
1723-24	13¢ Energy Conservation attd. 10/20/77 DC	2.50
1723-24	Energy Conservation set of 2 singles	3.00
1725	13¢ Alta California 9/9/77 San Jose, CA	1.75
1726	13¢ Articles of Confed. 9/30/77 York, PA	1.75
1727	13¢ Talking Pictures 10/6/77 Hollywood, CA	2.25
1728	13¢ Surrender at Saratoga 10/7/77 Schuylerville, NY	1.75
1729	13¢ Christmas - Valley Forge 10/21/77 Valley Forge, PA	1.75
1730	13¢ Christmas - Mailbox 10/21/77 Omaha, NE	1.75
1729-30	Christmas on one cover, either city	2.50
1729-30	Christmas on one cover, dual FD cancels	4.00
	1978	
1731	13¢ Carl Sandburg 1/6/78 Galesburg, IL	1.75
	1st Western Silk cachet	**35.00**
1732-33	13¢ Captain Cook attd. 1/20/78 Honolulu, HI	2.00
	Anchorage, AK	2.00
1732-33	Captain Cook set of 2 singles Honolulu, HI	3.50
	Anchorage, AK	3.50

1749-52

Scott #	Description	Price
	1978 (con't.)	
1732-33	Set of 2 on one cover with dual FD cancels	15.00
	1st K.M.C. Venture cachet (set of 3)	**70.00**
1734	13¢ Indian Head Penny 1/11/78 Kansas City, MO	1.75
	1978-80 REGULAR ISSUES	
1735	(15¢) "A" & Eagle 5/22/78 Memphis, TN	1.75
1736	(15¢) "A", booklet single 5/22/78 Memphis, TN	1.75
1736a	(15¢) Booklet Pane of 8 5/22/78 Memphis, TN	3.00
1737	15¢ Roses, booklet single 7/11/78 Shreveport, LA	1.75
1737a	Booklet Pane of 8 7/11/78 Shreveport, LA	3.50
1738-42	15¢ Windmills set of 5 singles 2/7/80 Lubbock, TX	10.00
1742av	15¢ Windmills, strip of 5	5.00
1742a	Windmills booklet pane of 10	5.00
1743	(15¢) "A" & Eagle, coil 5/22/78 Memphis, TN	1.75
	1st Kribbs Kover cachet	**40.00**
1744	13¢ Harriet Tubman 2/1/78 DC	2.50
1745-48	13¢ American Quilts attd. 3/8/78 Charleston, WV	4.00
1745-48	American Quilts set of 4 singles	8.00
	1st Collins cachet	**450.00**
1749-52	13¢ American Dance attd. 4/26/78 New York, NY	4.00
1749-52	American Dance set of 4 singles	8.00
	1st Andrews cachet	**40.00**
1753	13¢ French Alliance 5/4/78 York, PA	1.75
1754	13¢ Dr. Papanicolaou 5/18/78 DC	1.75
1755	13¢ Jimmie Rodgers 5/24/78 Meridian, MS	1.75
1756	15¢ George M. Cohan 7/3/78 Providence, RI	1.75
1757	13¢ CAPEX Sheet 6/10/78 Toronto, Canada	3.50
1757a-h	CAPEX set of 8 singles	16.00
1758	15¢ Photography 6/26/78 Las Vegas, NV	1.75
1759	15¢ Viking Mission 7/20/78 Hampton, VA	1.75
1760-63	15¢ American Owls attd. 8/26/78 Fairbanks, AK	4.00
1760-63	American Owls set of 4 singles	8.00
1764-67	15¢ Amer. Trees attd. 10/9/78 Hot Springs Nat'l. Park, AR	4.00
1764-67	American Trees set of 4 singles	8.00
1768	15¢ Christmas - Madonna 10/18/78 DC	1.75
1769	15¢ Christmas - Hobby Horse 10/18/78 Holly, MI	1.75
1768-69	Christmas on one cover	2.50
	1979	
1770	15¢ Robert F. Kennedy 1/12/79 DC	2.00
	1st DRC cachet	**75.00**
1771	15¢ Martin Luther King 1/13/79 Atlanta, GA	2.50
1772	15¢ Int'l. Yr. of the Child 2/15/79 Philadelphia, PA	1.75
1773	15¢ John Steinbeck 2/27/79 Salinas, CA	1.75
1774	15¢ Albert Einstein 3/4/79 Princeton, NJ	1.75
1775-78	15¢ Toleware attd. 4/19/79 Lancaster, PA	4.00
1775-78	Toleware set of 4 singles	8.00
1779-82	15¢ Architecture attd. 6/4/79 Kansas City, MO	4.00
1779-82	Architecture set of 4 singles	8.00
1783-86	15¢ Endangered Flora attd. 6/7/79 Milwaukee, WI	4.00
1783-86	Endangered Flora set of 4 singles	8.00
1787	15¢ Seeing Eye Dogs 6/15/79 Morristown, NJ	1.75
1788	15¢ Special Olympics 8/9/79 Brockport, NY	1.75
1789	15¢ John Paul Jones, perf. 11x12 9/23/79 Annapolis, MD	2.00
1789a	15¢ John Paul Jones, perf. 11 9/23/79 Annapolis, MD	2.00
1789,89a	Both Perfs. on 1 Cover	12.00
1790	10¢ Olympic Javelin 9/5/79 Olympia, WA	1.75
1791-94	15¢ Summer Olympics attd. 9/28/79 Los Angeles, CA	4.00
1791-94	Summer Olympics set of 4 singles	8.00
1795-98	15¢ Winter Olympics attd. 2/1/80 Lake Placid, NY	4.00
1795-98	Winter Olympics set of 4 singles	8.00
1799	15¢ Christmas - Painting 10/18/79 DC	1.75
1800	15¢ Christmas - Santa Claus 10/18/79 North Pole, AK	1.75
1799-1800	Christmas on one cover, either city	2.50
1799-1800	Christmas, dual cancel	2.50
1801	15¢ Will Rogers 11/4/79 Claremore, OK	1.75
1802	15¢ Vietnam Vets 11/11/79 Arlington, VA	2.50
	1980	
1803	15¢ W.C. Fields 1/29/80 Beverly Hills, CA	2.50
	1st Gill Craft cachet	**30.00**
	1st Kover Kids cachet	**20.00**
1804	15¢ Benj. Banneker 2/15/80 Annapolis, MD	2.50
1805-06	15¢ Letters - Memories attd. 2/25/80 DC	2.00
1805-06	Letters - Memories set of 2 singles	3.00
1807-08	15¢ Letters - Lift Spirit attd. 2/25/80 DC	2.00
1807-08	Letters - Lift Spirit set of 2 singles	3.00

Scott #	Description	Price
1809-10	15¢ Letters - Opinions attd. 2/25/80 DC	2.00
1809-10	Letters - Opinions set of 2 singles	3.00
1805-10	15¢ Letter Writing attd. 2/25/80 DC	4.00
1805-10	Letter Writing set of 6 singles	7.50
1805-10	Letters, Memories, 6 on 3	5.00
	1980-81 REGULAR ISSUES	
1811	1¢ Inkwell, coil 3/6/80 New York, NY	1.75
1813	3½¢ Williamsburg, coil 6/23/80 Williamsburg, PA	1.75
1816	12¢ Liberty's Torch, coil 4/8/81 Dallas, TX	1.75
1818	(18¢) "B" & Eagle 3/15/81 San Fran., CA	2.00
1819	(18¢) "B" & Eagle, bklt. sngl. 3/15/81 San Francisco, CA	1.75
1819a	(18¢) Bklt. Pane of 8 3/15/81 San Francisco, CA	4.00
1820	(18¢) "B" & Eagle, coil 3/15/81 San Francisco, CA	1.75
	1980	
1821	15¢ Frances Perkins 4/10/80 DC	1.75
1822	15¢ Dolly Madison 5/20/80 DC	1.75
	1st American Postal Arts Society cachet (Post/Art)	**35.00**
1823	15¢ Emily Bissell 5/31/80 Wilmington, DE	1.75
1824	15¢ Helen Keller 6/27/80 Tuscumbia, AL	2.00
1825	15¢ Veterans Administration 7/21/80 DC	2.00
1826	15¢ Bernardo de Galvez 7/23/80 New Orleans, LA	1.75
1827-30	15¢ Coral Reefs attd. 8/26/80 Charlotte Amalie, VI	4.00
1827-30	Coral Reefs set of 4 singles	8.00
1831	15¢ Organized Labor 9/1/80 DC	1.75
1832	15¢ Edith Wharton 9/5/80 New Haven, CT	1.75
1833	15¢ Education 9/12/80 Franklin, MA	2.00
1834-37	15¢ Indian Masks attd. 9/25/80 Spokane, WA	4.00
1834-37	Indian Masks set of 4 singles	8.00
1838-41	15¢ Architecture attd. 10/9/80 New York, NY	4.00
1838-41	Architecture set of 4 singles	8.00
1842	15¢ Christmas - Madonna 10/31/80 DC	1.75
1843	15¢ Christmas - Wreath & Toys 10/31/80 Christmas, MI	1.75
1842-43	Christmas on one cover	2.50
1842-43	Christmas, dual cancel	3.00
	1980-85 GREAT AMERICANS SERIES	
1844	1¢ Dorothea Dix 9/23/83 Hampden, ME	1.75
1845	2¢ Igor Stravinsky 11/18/82 New York, NY	1.75
1846	3¢ Henry Clay 7/13/83 DC	1.75
1847	4¢ Carl Shurz 6/3/83 Watertown, WI	1.75
1848	5¢ Pearl Buck 6/25/83 Hillsboro, WV	1.75
1849	6¢ Walter Lippman 9/19/85 Minneapolis, MN	1.75
1850	7¢ Abraham Baldwin 1/25/85 Athens, GA	1.75
1851	8¢ Henry Knox 7/25/85 Thomaston, ME	1.75
1852	9¢ Sylvanus Thayer 6/7/85 Braintree, MA	2.00
1853	10¢ Richard Russell 5/31/84 Winder, GA	1.75
1854	11¢ Alden Partridge 2/12/85 Norwich Un., VT	2.00
1855	13¢ Crazy Horse 1/15/82 Crazy Horse, SD	1.75
1856	14¢ Sinclair Lewis 3/21/85 Sauk Centre, MN	1.75
1857	17¢ Rachel Carson 5/28/81 Springdale, PA	1.75
1858	18¢ George Mason 5/7/81 Gunston Hall, VA	1.75
1859	19¢ Sequoyah 12/27/80 Tahlequah, OK	1.75
1860	20¢ Ralph Bunche 1/12/82 New York, NY	2.50
1861	20¢ Thomas Gallaudet 6/10/83 West Hartford, CT	2.00
1862	20¢ Harry S. Truman 1/26/84 DC	2.00
1863	22¢ John J. Audubon 4/23/85 New York, NY	2.00
1864	30¢ Frank Laubach 9/2/84 Benton, PA	1.75
1865	35¢ Charles Drew 6/3/81 DC	2.50
1866	37¢ Robert Millikan 1/26/82 Pasadena, CA	1.75
1867	39¢ Grenville Clark 3/20/85 Hanover, NH	2.00
1868	40¢ Lillian Gilbreth 2/24/84 Montclair, NJ	2.00
1869	50¢ Chester W. Nimitz 2/22/85 Fredericksburg, TX	3.00
	1981	
1874	15¢ Everett Dirksen 1/4/81 Pekin, IL	1.75
1875	15¢ Whitney Moore Young 1/30/81 NY, NY	2.50
1876-79	15¢ Flowers attd. 4/23/81 Ft. Valley, GA	4.00
1876-79	Flowers set of 4 singles	8.00
1880-89	18¢ Wildlife set of 10 sgls. 5/14/81 Boise, ID	17.50
1889a	Wildlife booklet pane of 10	6.00
	1981-82 REGULAR ISSUES	
1890	18¢ Flag & "Waves of Grain" 4/24/81 Portland, ME	1.75
1891	18¢ Flag & "Sea" coil 4/24/81 Portland, ME	1.75
1892	6¢ Circle of Stars, bklt. sngl. 4/24/81 Portland, ME	2.00
1893	18¢ Flag & "Mountain", bklt. sgl. 4/24/81 Portland, ME	1.75

1822

First Day Cover Collecting Made Easy!

For over fifty years, Artmaster Incorporated has provided the philatelic community with the most courteous and complete First Day Cover services available. Our convenient First Day Cover and Envelope Clubs are automatic shipment plans that insure you never miss another issue, and we offer three different cachet lines from which to choose. **Artmaster** First Day Covers have been produced since 1946 and feature two-color offset printed cachets including an historical synopsis of the stamp subject printed on the reverse. **House of Farnam** is the oldest continuously produced First Day Cover in existence and features multicolor engraved cachets. And **Cover Craft Cachets** are limited edition versions of the House of Farnam engravings printed on tinted envelopes, and include an informative insert card detailing the stamp subject and exact quantities of covers produced for each issue. Our services our guaranteed - you will be completely satisfied with your covers, or they will be replaced. Send for a free stamp schedule and samples of our cachets, and see for yourself!

Name _____

Address _____

City _____ State _____ Zip _____

Artmaster
INCORPORATED

P.O. Box 7156 ◆ Louisville, Ky 40257-0156
Toll Free 1-888-200-6466
www.firstdaycover.com

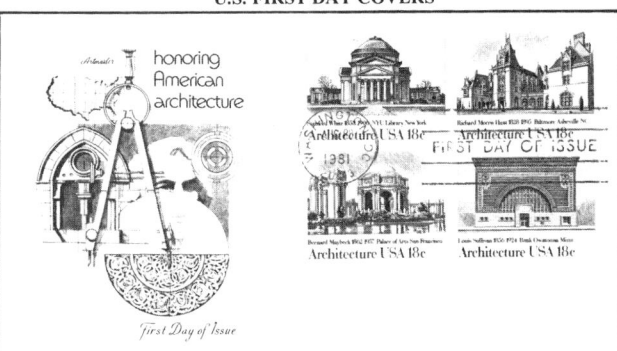

1928-31

Scott #	Description	Price
	1981-82 REGULAR ISSUES (con't.)	
1892-93	6¢ & 18¢ Booklet Pair 4/24/81 Portland, ME	3.75
1893a	18¢ & 6¢ B. Pane of 8 (2 #1892 & 6 #1893) 4/24/81 Portland, ME	5.00
1894	20¢ Flag over Supreme Court 12/17/81 DC	1.75
1895	20¢ Flag, coil 12/17/81 DC	1.75
1896	20¢ Flag, bklt. single 12/17/81 DC	1.75
1896a	Flag, bklt. pane of 6 12/17/81 DC	4.00
	#1894, 1895 & 1896a on one FDC	7.00
1896b	Flag, bklt. pane of 10 6/1/82 DC	6.00
1896bv	Flag, booklet single from pane of 20 11/17/83 DC	1.75
1896bv	Reissue-Flag bklt single, 11/17/83, NY	2.50
1896bv	Reissue-Flag, pane of 10 from 20, 11/17/83, NY	20.00
	1981-84 TRANSPORTATION COIL SERIES	
1897	1¢ Omnibus 8/19/83 Arlington, VA	2.00
1897A	2¢ Locomotive 5/20/82 Chicago, IL	2.50
1898	3¢ Handcar 3/25/83 Rochester, NY	2.00
1898A	4¢ Stagecoach 8/19/82 Milwaukee, WI	2.00
1899	5¢ Motorcycle 10/10/83 San Francisco, CA	2.00
1900	5.2¢ Sleigh 3/21/83 Memphis, TN	2.00
1900a	Precancelled	150.00
1901	5.9¢ Bicycle 2/17/82 Wheeling, WV	2.00
1901a	Precancelled	200.00
1902	7.4¢ Baby Buggy 4/7/84 San Diego, CA	2.00
1902a	Precancelled	300.00
1903	9.3¢ Mail Wagon 12/15/81 Shreveport, LA	2.00
1903a	Precancelled	300.00
1904	10.9¢ Hansom Cab 3/26/82 Chattanooga, TN	2.00
1904a	Precancelled	300.00
1905	11¢ Caboose 2/3/84 Rosemont, IL	2.50
1906	17¢ Electric Car 6/25/81 Greenfield Village, MI	2.00
1907	18¢ Surrey 5/18/81 Notch, MO	2.00
1908	20¢ Fire Pumper 12/10/81 Alexandria, VA	2.00
1909	$9.35 Express Mail, single 8/12/83 Kennedy Sp. Ctr., FL	60.00
1909a	Express Mail, booklet pane of 3	175.00
	1981 Commemoratives (continued)	
1910	18¢ American Red Cross 5/1/81 DC	2.00
1911	18¢ Savings and Loans 5/8/81 Chicago, IL	1.75
1912-19	18¢ Space Ach. attd. 5/21/81 Kennedy Sp. Ctr., FL	6.00
1912-19	Space Achievement set of 8 singles	16.00
1920	18¢ Professional Management 6/18/81 Philadelphia, PA	1.75
1921-24	18¢ Wildlife Habitats attd. 6/26/81 Reno, NV	4.00
1921-24	Wildlife Habitats set of 4 singles	8.00
1925	18¢ Disabled Persons 6/29/81 Milford, MI	1.75
1926	18¢ Edna St. Vincent Millay 7/10/81 Austeritz, NY	1.75
1927	18¢ Alcoholism 8/19/81 DC	3.00
1928-31	18¢ Architecture attd. 8/28/81 DC	4.00
1928-31	Architecture set of 4 singles	8.00
1932	18¢ Babe Zaharias 9/22/81 Pinehurst, NC	8.00
1933	18¢ Bobby Jones 9/22/81 Pinehurst, NC	12.00
1932-33	Zaharias & Jones on one cover	15.00
1934	18¢ Frederic Remington 10/9/81 Oklahoma City, OK	1.75
1935	18¢ James Hoban 10/13/81 DC	1.75
1936	20¢ James Hoban 10/13/81 DC	1.75
1935-36	Hoban on one cover	3.50
1935-36	Combo w/Irish Stamp-(US cancel)	3.00
1935-36	Combo w/Irish Stamp-(Ireland cancel)	9.00
1937-38	18¢ Battle of Yorktown attd. 10/16/81 Yorktown, VA	2.00
1937-38	Battle of Yorktown set of 2 singles	3.00
1939	(20¢) Christmas - Madonna 10/28/81 Chicago, IL	1.75
1940	(20¢) Christmas - Teddy Bear 10/28/81 Christmas Valley, OR	1.75
1939-40	Christmas on one cover	2.50
1939-40	Christmas, dual cancel	3.00
1941	20¢ John Hanson 11/5/81 Frederick, MD	1.75
1942-45	20¢ Desert Plants attd. 12/11/81 Tucson, AZ	4.00
1942-45	Desert Plants set of 4 singles	8.00
	1st Pugh cachet	**75.00**
	1981-82 REGULAR ISSUES	
1946	(20¢) "C" & Eagle 10/11/81 Memphis, TN	1.75
1947	(20¢) "C" Eagle, coil 10/11/81 Memphis, TN	1.75
1948	(20¢) "C" Eagle, bklt. single 10/11/81 Memphis, TN	1.75
1948a	(20¢) "C" Booklet Pane of 10	5.50
1949	20¢ Bighorn Sheep, bklt. single 1/8/82 Bighorn, MT	1.75
	1st New Direxions cachet	**25.00**
1949a	20¢ Booklet Pane of 10	6.00

Scott #	Description	Price
	1982 Commemoratives	
1950	20¢ Franklin D. Roosevelt 1/30/82 Hyde Park, NY	1.75
1951	20¢ Love 2/1/82 Boston, MA	1.75
1952	20¢ George Washington 2/22/82 Mt. Vernon, VA	2.00
	1982 STATE BIRDS AND FLOWERS	
1953-2002	20¢ Birds & Flowers 4/14/82 Set of 50 DC	70.00
	Set of 50 State Capitals	75.00
2002a	Complete pane of 50 (Uncacheted)	45.00
	1982 Commemoratives (continued)	
2003	20¢ US & Netherlands 4/20/82 DC	1.75
...	Combo FDC with Netherland issue	7.50
...	20¢ US & Netherlands-combo, dual cancel	15.00
2004	20¢ Library of Congress 4/21/82 DC	1.75
2005	20¢ Consumer Education, coil 4/27/82 DC	1.75
2006-09	20¢ Knoxville World's Fair, attd. 4/29/82 Knoxville, TN	4.00
2006-09	20¢ Knoxville World's Fair, Knoxville, TN, set of 4 sngls	8.00
2010	20¢ Horatio Alger 4/30/82 Willow Grove, PA	1.75
2011	20¢ "Aging Together" 5/21/82 Sun City, AZ	1.75
2012	20¢ The Barrymores 6/8/82 New York, NY	1.75
2013	20¢ Dr. Mary Walker 6/10/82 Oswego, NY	1.75
2014	20¢ Peace Garden 6/30/82 Dunseith, ND	1.75
2015	20¢ Libraries 7/13/82 Philadelphia, PA	1.75
2016	20¢ Jackie Robinson 8/2/82 Cooperstown, NY	7.00
2017	20¢ Touro Synagogue 8/22/82 Newport, RI	2.00
2018	20¢ Wolf Trap 9/1/82 Vienna, VA	1.75
2019-22	20¢ Architecture attd. 9/30/82 DC	4.00
2019-22	Architecture set of 4 singles	8.00
2023	20¢ St. Francis of Assisi 10/7/82 San Francisco, CA	1.75
2024	20¢ Ponce de Leon 10/12/82 San Juan, PR	1.75
2025	13¢ Christmas - Kitten & Puppy 11/3/82 Danvers, MA	2.00
2026	20¢ Christmas - Madonna & Child 10/28/82 DC	1.75
2027-30	20¢ Christmas - Winter Scene, attd. 10/28/82 Snow, OK	4.00
2027-30	Christmas set of 4 singles	8.00
2026-30	Christmas on one cover either city	3.00
2026-30	Christmas, dual cancel	3.50
	1983 Commemoratives	
2031	20¢ Science & Industry 1/19/83 Chi., IL	1.75
2032-35	20¢ Ballooning 3/31/83 DC	4.00
	Albuquerque, NM	4.00
2032-35	Ballooning set of 4 singles DC	8.00
	Albuquerque, NM	8.00
2036	20¢ Sweden, 3/24/83 Philadelphia, PA	1.75
	20¢ US & Sweden, joint Issue, dual cancel	15.00
	20¢ US & Sweden, joint issue	5.00
	1st Panda Cachet	**25.00**
2036	w/Swedish issue on one cover	5.00
2037	20¢ Civilian Conservation Corps 4/5/83 Luray, VA	1.75
2038	20¢ Joseph Priestley 4/13/83 Northumberland, PA	1.75
2039	20¢ Voluntarism 4/20/83 DC	1.75
2040	20¢ German Immigration 4/29/83 Germantown, PA	1.75
2040	w/German Issue, dual cancel	8.00
2041	20¢ Brooklyn Bridge 5/17/83 Brooklyn, NY	2.00
2042	20¢ Tennessee Valley Authority 5/18/83 Knoxville, TN	1.75
2043	20¢ Physical Fitness 5/14/83 Houston, TX	2.00
2044	20¢ Scott Joplin 6/9/83 Sedalia, MO	2.50
2045	20¢ Medal of Honor 6/7/83 DC	6.00
2046	20¢ Babe Ruth 7/6/83 Chicago, IL	6.00
2047	20¢ Nathaniel Hawthorne 7/8/83 Salem, MA	1.75
2048-51	13¢ Summer Olympics attd. 7/28/83 South Bend, IN	4.00
2048-51	Summer Olympics set of 4 singles	8.00
2052	20¢ Treaty of Paris 9/2/83 DC	1.75
2053	20¢ Civil Service 9/9/83 DC	1.75
2054	20¢ Metropolitan Opera 9/14/83 NY, NY	1.75
2055-58	20¢ Inventors attd. 9/21/83 DC	4.00
2055-58	Inventors set of 4 singles	8.00
2059-62	20¢ Streetcars attd. 10/8/83 Kennebunkport, ME	4.00
2059-62	Streetcars set of 4 singles	8.00
2063	20¢ Christmas - Madonna & Child 10/28/83 DC	1.75
2064	20¢ Christmas - Santa Claus 10/28/83 Santa Claus, IN	1.75
2063-64	Christmas on one cover either city	2.50
2063-64	Christmas, dual cancel	3.00
2065	20¢ Martin Luther 11/11/83 DC	1.75
2065	w/German Issue, dual cancel	7.50

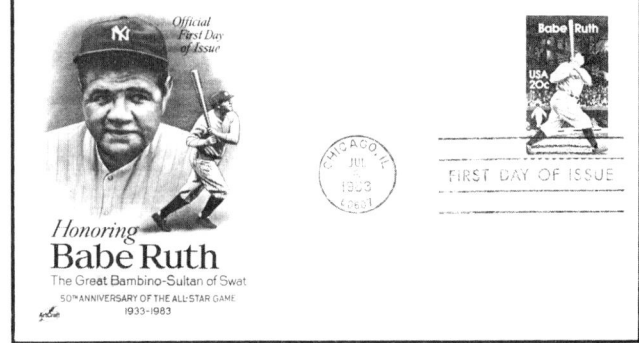

2046

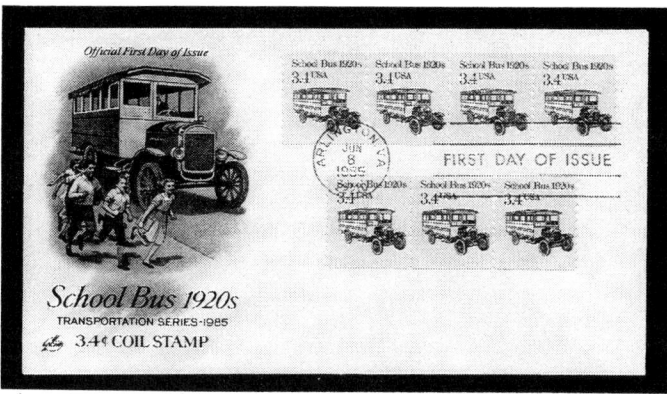

2123

Scott #	Description	Price
	1984 Commemoratives	
2066	20¢ Alaska Sthd. 1/3/84 Fairbanks, AK	1.75
2067-70	20¢ Winter Olympics attd. 1/6/84 Lake Placid, NY	4.00
2067-70	Winter Olympics set of 4 singles	8.00
2071	20¢ Fed. Deposit Ins. Corp. 1/12/84 DC	1.75
2072	20¢ Love 1/31/84 DC	1.75
2073	20¢ Carter Woodson 2/1/84 DC	2.50
2074	20¢ Soil & Water Cons. 2/6/84 Denver, CO	1.75
2075	20¢ Credit Union Act 2/10/84 Salem, MA	1.75
2076-79	20¢ Orchids attd. 3/5/84 Miami, FL	4.00
2076-79	Orchids set of 4 singles	8.00
2080	20¢ Hawaii Sthd. 3/12/84 Honolulu, HI	2.00
2081	20¢ National Archives 4/16/84 DC	1.75
2082-85	20¢ Summer Olympics attd. 5/4/84 Los Angeles, CA	4.00
2082-85	Summer Olympics set of 4 singles	8.00
2086	20¢ Louisiana World's Fair 5/11/84 New Orleans, LA	1.75
2087	20¢ Health Research 5/17/84 New York, NY	1.75
2088	20¢ Douglas Fairbanks 5/23/84 Denver, CO	1.75
2089	20¢ Jim Thorpe 5/24/84 Shawnee, OK	5.00
2090	20¢ John McCormack 6/6/84 Boston, MA	1.75
	20¢ John McCormack, combo, dual cancel	15.00
	20¢ John McCormack, combo	5.00
2091	20¢ St. Lawrence Swy. 6/26/84 Massena, NY	1.75
	20¢ St. Lawrence Swy. w/Canada combo	5.00
	20¢ St. Lawrence Swy. w/Canada, combo, dual cancel	15.00
2092	20¢ Waterfowl Preservation 7/2/84 Des Moines, IA	1.75
	1st George Van Natta cachet	**40.00**
2093	20¢ Roanoke Voyages 7/13/84 Manteo, NC	1.75
2094	20¢ Herman Melville 8/1/84 New Bedford, MA	1.75
2095	20¢ Horace Moses 8/6/84 Bloomington, IN	1.75
2096	20¢ Smokey the Bear 8/13/84 Capitan, NM	2.00
2097	20¢ Roberto Clemente 8/17/84 Carolina, PR	10.00
2098-2101	20¢ Dogs attd. 9/7/84 New York, NY	4.00
2098-2101	Dogs set of 4 singles	8.00
2102	20¢ Crime Prevention 9/26/84 DC	2.00
2103	20¢ Hispanic Americans 10/31/84 DC	1.75
2104	20¢ Family Unity 10/1/84 Shaker Heights, OH	1.75
2105	20¢ Eleanor Roosevelt 10/11/84 Hyde Park, NY	1.75
2106	20¢ Nation of Readers 10/16/84 DC	1.75
2107	20¢ Christmas - Madonna & Child 10/30/84 DC	1.75
2108	20¢ Christmas - Santa 10/30/84 Jamaica, NY	1.75
2107-08	Christmas on one cover, either city	2.50
2107-08	Christmas, dual cancel	3.00
2109	20¢ Vietnam Memorial 11/10/84 DC	3.00
	1985 REGULARS & COMMEMS.	
2110	22¢ Jerome Kern 1/23/85 New York, NY	1.75
2111	(22¢) "D" & Eagle 2/1/85 Los Angeles, CA	1.75
2112	(22¢) "D" coil 2/1/85 Los Angeles, CA	1.75
2113	(22¢) "D" bklt. single 2/1/85 L.A., CA	1.75
2111-13	(22¢) "D" Stamps on 1	5.00
2113a	(22¢) Booklet Pane of 10	7.00
2114	22¢ Flag over Capitol 3/29/85 DC	1.75
2115	22¢ Flag over Capitol, coil 3/29/85 DC	1.75
2115b	Same, Phosphor Test Coil 5/23/87 Secaucus, NJ	2.50
2116	22¢ Flag over Capitol, bklt. single 3/29/85 Waubeka, WI	1.75
2116a	Booklet Pane of 5	3.00
2117-21	22¢ Seashells set of 5 singles 4/4/85 Boston, MA	10.00
2121a	Seashells, booklet pane of 10	7.00
2122	$10.75 Express Mail, bklt. sgl. 4/29/85 San Francisco, CA	50.00
2122a	Express Mail, booklet pane of 3	135.00
2122b	$10.75 Re-issue, bklt. sgl. 6/19/89 DC	250.00
2122c	Re-issue, booklet pane of 3	700.00
	1985-89 TRANSPORTATION COILS	
2123	3.4¢ School Bus 6/8/85 Arlington, VA	1.75
2123a	Precancelled 6/8/85 (earliest known use)	250.00
2124	4.9¢ Buckboard 6/21/85 Reno, NV	1.75
2124a	Precancelled 6/21/85 DC (earliest known use)	250.00
2125	5.5¢ Star Route Truck 11/1/86 Fort Worth, TX	1.75
2125a	Precancelled 11/1/86 DC	5.00
2126	6¢ Tricycle 5/6/85 Childs, MD	1.75

U.S. FIRST DAY COVERS

Scott #	Description	Price
2127	7.1¢ Tractor 2/6/87 Sarasota, FL	1.75
2127a	Precancelled 2/6/87 Sarasota, FL	5.00
2127av	Zip + 4 Prec., 5/26/89 Rosemont, IL	1.75
2128	8.3¢ Ambulance 6/21/85 Reno, NV	1.75
2128a	Precancelled 6/21/85 DC (earliest known use)	250.00
2129	8.5¢ Tow Truck 1/24/87 Tucson, AZ	1.75
2129a	Precancelled 1/24/87 DC	5.00
2130	10.1¢ Oil Wagon 4/18/85 Oil Center, NM	1.75
2130a	Black Precancel 4/18/85 DC (earliest known use)	250.00
2130a	Red. Prec. 6/27/88 DC	1.75
2131	11¢ Stutz Bearcat 6/11/85 Baton Rouge, LA	1.75
2132	12¢ Stanley Steamer 4/2/85 Kingfield, ME	1.75
2132b	"B" Press cancel 9/3/87 DC	60.00
	1985-89 TRANSPORTATION COILS (cont.)	
2133	12.5¢ Pushcart 4/18/85 Oil Center, NM	1.75
2134	14¢ Iceboat 3/23/85 Rochester, NY	1.75
2135	17¢ Dog Sled 8/20/86 Anchorage, AK	1.75
2136	25¢ Bread Wagon 11/22/86 Virginia Bch., VA	1.75
	1985 (cont.)	
2137	22¢ Mary McLeod Bethune 3/5/85 DC	2.50
2138-41	22¢ Duck Decoys attd. 3/22/85 Shelburne, VT	4.00
2138-41	Duck Decoys set of 4 singles	8.00
2142	22¢ Winter Special Olympics 3/25/85 Park City, UT	1.75
2143	22¢ Love 4/17/85 Hollywood, CA	1.75
2144	22¢ Rural Electrification Admin. 5/11/85 Madison, SD	1.75
2145	22¢ Ameripex '86 5/25/85 Rosemont, IL	1.75
2146	22¢ Abigail Adams 6/14/85 Quincy, MA	1.75
2147	22¢ Frederic A. Bartholdi 7/18/85 NY, NY	1.75
2149	18¢ Washington Pre-Sort, coil 11/6/85 DC	1.75
2149a	18¢ Washington, Precanceled, pair w/2149	5.00
2150	21.1¢ Zip + 4, coil 10/22/85 DC	1.75
2150a	21.1¢ Zip + 4, Precanceled, pair w/2150	5.00
2152	22¢ Korean War Veterans 7/26/85	2.00
2153	22¢ Social Security Act 8/14/85 Baltimore, MD	1.75
2154	22¢ World War I Vets 8/26/85 Milwaukee, WI	2.00
2155-58	22¢ Horses attd. 9/25/85 Lexington, KY	4.00
2155-58	Horses set of 4 singles	8.00
2159	22¢ Public Education 10/1/85 Boston, MA	2.00
2160-63	22¢ Int'l. Youth Year attd. 10/7/85 Chicago, IL	4.00
2160-63	Set of 4 singles	8.00
2164	22¢ Help End Hunger 10/15/85 DC	1.75
2165	22¢ Christmas - Madonna 10/30/85 Detroit, MI	1.75
2166	22¢ Christmas - Poinsettia 10/30/85 Nazareth, MI	1.75
2165-66	Christmas on one cover, either city	2.50
	1986	
2167	22¢ Arkansas Sthd. 1/3/86 Little Rock, AR	1.75
	1986-94 GREAT AMERICANS SERIES	
2168	1¢ Margaret Mitchell 6/30/86 Atlanta, GA	2.50
2169	2¢ Mary Lyon 2/28/87 South Hadley, MA	1.75
2170	3¢ Dr. Paul Dudley White 9/15/86 DC	1.75
2171	4¢ Father Flanagan 7/14/86 Boys Town, NE	1.75
2172	5¢ Hugo L. Black 2/27/86 DC	1.75
2173	5¢ Luis Munoz Marin 2/18/90 San Juan, PR	1.75
2175	10¢ Red Cloud 8/15/87 Red Cloud, NE	2.00
2176	14¢ Julia Ward Howe 2/12/87 Boston, MA	1.75
2177	15¢ Buffalo Bill Cody 6/6/88 Cody, WY	1.75
2178	17¢ Belva Ann Lockwood 6/18/86 Middleport, NY	1.75
2179	20¢ Virginia Apgar 10/24/94 Dallas, TX	1.75
2180	21¢ Chester Carlson 10/21/88 Rochester, NY	1.75
2181	23¢ Mary Cassatt 11/4/88 Phila., PA	1.75
2182	25¢ Jack London 1/11/86 Glen Ellen, CA	2.00
2182a	Bklt. Pane of 10 Perf, 11 5/3/88 San Francisco, CA	8.00
2182as	Perf. 11 bklt. single 5/3/88 San Francisco, CA	2.00
2183	28¢ Sitting Bull 9/14/89 Rapid City, SD	2.25
2184	29¢ Earl Warren 3/9/92 DC	2.00
2185	29¢ Thomas Jefferson 4/13/93 Charlottesville, VA	2.00
2186	35¢ Dennis Chavez 4/3/91 Albuquerque, NM	2.00
2187	40¢ General Claire Chennault 9/6/90 Monroe, LA	2.00
2188	45¢ Dr. Harvey Cushing 6/17/88 Cleveland, OH	2.00
2189	52¢ Hubert H. Humphrey 6/3/91 Minneapolis, MN	2.00
2190	56¢ John Harvard 9/3/86 Cambridge, MA	2.00
2191	65¢ General "Hap" Arnold 11/5/88 Gladwyne, PA	2.50
2192	75¢ Wendell Wilkie 2/16/92 Bloomington, IN	3.00
2193	$1 Dr. Bernard Revel 9/23/86 NY, NY	4.00
2194	$1 Johns Hopkins 6/7/89 Baltimore, MD	5.00
2195	$2 William Jennings Bryan 3/19/86 Salem, IL	8.00
2196	$5 Bret Harte 8/25/87 Twain Harte, CA	17.50
2197	25¢ Jack London, perf. 10 bklt. sgl. 5/3/88 San Fran., CA	1.75
2197a	Bklt. Pane of 6	4.00

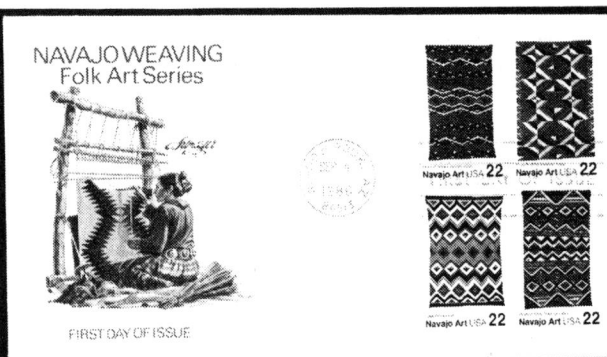

NAVAJO WEAVING
Folk Art Series

FIRST DAY OF ISSUE

2235-38

Scott #	Description	Price
	1986 (cont.)	
2198-2201	22¢ Stamp Coll. set of 4 1/23/86 State College, PA	8.00
2201a	Stamp Collecting, bklt. pane of 4	5.00
2201b	Color error, Black omitted on #2198 & 2201	300.00
2201b	Same, set of 4 singles	300.00
2202	22¢ Love 1/30/86 New York, NY	1.75
2203	22¢ Sojourner Truth 1/4/86 New Paltz, NY	2.50
2204	22¢ Texas 3/2/86 San Antonio, TX	2.00
	Washington-on-the-Brazos, TX	2.00
2205-09	22¢ Fish set of 5 singles 3/21/86 Seattle, WA	10.00
2209a	Fish, booklet pane of 5	6.00
2210	22¢ Public Hospitals 4/11/86 NY, NY	1.75
2211	22¢ Duke Ellington 4/29/86 New York, NY	2.75
2216-19	22¢ U.S. Presidents 4 sheets of 9 5/22/86 Chicago, IL	24.00
2216a-19a	US President set of 36 singles	60.00
2220-23	22¢ Explorers attd. 5/28/86 North Pole, AK	5.00
2220-23	22¢ Explorers set of 4 singles	10.00
2224	22¢ Statue of Liberty 7/4/86 NY, NY	2.00
2224	w/French Issue, combo	5.00
2224	22¢ Statue of Liberty w/French combo, dual cancel	15.00
2225	1¢ Omnibus Coil Re-engraved 11/26/86 DC	1.75
2226	2¢ Locomotive Coil Re-engraved 3/6/87 Milwaukee, WI	1.75
2228	4¢ Stagecoach Coil "B" Press 8/15/86 DC (eku)	150.00
2231	8.3¢ Ambulance Coil "B" Press 8/29/86 DC (eku)	150.00
2235-38	22¢ Navajo Art attd. 9/4/86 Window Rock, AZ	4.00
2235-38	Set of 4 singles	8.00
2239	22¢ T.S. Eliot 9/26/86 St. Louis, MO	1.75
2240-43	22¢ Woodcarved Figurines attd. 10/1/86 DC	4.00
2240-43	Set of 4 singles	8.00
2244	22¢ Christmas - Madonna & Child 10/24/86 DC	2.00
2245	22¢ Christmas Village Scene 10/24/86 Snow Hill, MD	2.00
	1987	
2246	22¢ Michigan Statehood 1/26/87 Lansing, MI	1.75
2247	22¢ Pan American Games 1/29/87 Indianapolis, IN	1.75
2248	22¢ Love 1/30/87 San Francisco, CA	1.75
2249	22¢ Jean Baptiste Point du Sable 2/20/87 Chicago, IL	2.50
2250	22¢ Enrico Caruso 2/27/87 NY, NY	1.75
2251	22¢ Girl Scouts 3/12/87 DC	3.00
	1987-88 TRANSPORTATION COILS	
2252	3¢ Conestoga Wagon 2/29/88 Conestoga, PA	1.75
2253	5¢ Milk Wagon 9/25/87 Indianapolis, IN	1.75
2254	5.3¢ Elevator, Prec. 9/16/88 New York, NY	1.75
2255	7.6¢ Carretta, Prec. 8/30/88 San Jose, CA	1.75
2256	8.4¢ Wheelchair, Prec. 8/12/88 Tucson, AZ	1.75
2257	10¢ Canal Boat 4/11/87 Buffalo, NY	1.75
2258	13¢ Police Patrol Wagon, Prec. 10/29/88 Anaheim, CA	1.75
2259	13.2¢ RR Car, Prec. 7/19/88 Pittsburgh, PA	1.75
2260	15¢ Tugboat 7/12/88 Long Beach, CA	1.75
2261	16.7¢ Popcorn Wagon, Prec. 7/7/88 Chicago, IL	1.75
2262	17.5¢ Marmon Wasp 9/25/87 Indianapolis, IN	1.75
2262a	Precancelled	5.00
2263	20¢ Cable Car 10/28/88 San Francisco, CA	1.75
2264	20.5¢ Fire Engine, Prec. 9/28/88 San Angelo, TX	2.00
2265	21¢ R.R. Mail Car, Prec. 8/16/88 Santa Fe, NM	1.75
2266	24.1¢ Tandem Bicycle, Prec. 10/26/88 Redmond, WA	1.75
	1987-88 REGULAR & SPECIAL ISSUES	
2267-74	22¢ Special Occasions, bklt. sgls. 4/20/87 Atlanta, GA	16.00
2274a	Booklet Pane of 10	7.00
2275	22¢ United Way 4/28/87 DC	1.75
2276	22¢ Flag and Fireworks 5/9/87 Denver, CO	1.75
2276a	Booklet Pane of 20 11/30/87 DC	12.00
2277	(25¢) "E" Earth Issue 3/22/88 DC	1.75
2278	25¢ Flag & Clouds 5/6/88 Boxborough, MA	1.75
2279	(25¢) "E" Earth Coil 3/22/88 DC	1.75
2280	25¢ Flag over Yosemite Coil 5/20/88 Yosemite, CA	1.75
2280 var.	Phosphor paper 2/14/89 Yosemite, CA	1.75
2281	25¢ Honeybee Coil 9/2/88 Omaha, NE	1.75
2282	(25¢) "E" Earth Bklt. Sgl. 3/22/88 DC	1.75
2282a	Bklt. Pane of 10	7.50
2283	25¢ Pheasant Bklt. Sgl. 4/29/88 Rapid City, SD	1.75
2283a	Bklt. Pane of 10	8.00

Scott #	Description	Price
	1987-88 REGULAR & SPECIAL ISSUES	
2284	25¢ Grosbeak Bklt. Sgl. 5/28/88 Arlington, VA	1.75
2285	25¢ Owl Bklt. Sgl. 5/28/88 Arlington, VA	1.75
2284-85	attached pair	3.50
2285b	Bklt. Pane of 10 (5 of ea.)	8.00
2285A	25¢ Flag & Clouds bklt. sgl. 7/5/88 DC	1.75
2285Ac	Bklt. Pane of 6	4.50
2286-2335	22¢ American Wildlife 6/13/87 Toronto, Canada	
	Set of 50 singles	75.00
2335a	Complete Pane of 50	40.00
	RATIFICATION OF CONSTITUTION	
	STATE BICENTENNIAL ISSUES 1987-90	
2336	22¢ Delaware Statehood Bicent. 7/4/87 Dover, DE	2.00
2337	22¢ Pennsylvania Bicent. 8/26/87 Harrisburg, PA	2.00
2338	22¢ New Jersey Bicent. 9/11/87 Trenton, NJ	2.00
2339	22¢ Georgia Bicent. 1/6/88 Atlanta, GA	2.00
2340	22¢ Connecticut Bicent. 1/9/88 Hartford, CT	2.00
2341	22¢ Massachusetts Bicent. 2/6/88 Boston, MA	2.00
2342	22¢ Maryland Bicent. 2/15/88 Annapolis, MD	2.00
2343	25¢ South Carolina Bicent. 5/23/88 Columbia, SC	2.00
2344	25¢ New Hampshire Bicent. 6/21/88 Concord, NH	2.00
2345	25¢ Virginia Bicent. 6/25/88 Williamsburg, VA	2.00
2346	25¢ New York Bicent. 7/26/88 Albany, NY	2.00
2347	25¢ North Carolina Bicent. 8/22/89 Fayetteville, NC	2.00
2348	25¢ Rhode Island Bicent. 5/29/90 Pawtucket, RI	2.00
2349	22¢ US & Morocco, combo w/Morocco, Dual cancel	15.00
2349	22¢ US & Morocco, combo w/Morocco	5.00
2336-48	Set of 13 on one cover, each with a different FD cancel	100.00
2349	22¢ U.S.-Morocco Relations 7/17/87 DC	1.75
2349	22¢ U.S.-Morocco, Combo w/Morocco, Dual Cancel	15.00
2349	22¢ U.S.-Morocco, Combo w/Morocco	5.00
2349	**1st Anagram cachet**	**25.00**
2350	22¢ William Faulkner 8/3/87 Oxford, MS	1.75
2351-54	22¢ Lacemaking attd. 8/14/87 Ypsilanti, MI	4.00
2351-54	Set of 4 singles	8.00
2355-59	22¢ Drafting of Constitution bklt. sgls. (5) 8/28/87 DC	10.00
2359a	Booklet Pane of 5	5.00
2360	22¢ Signing the Constitution 9/17/87 Philadelphia, PA	2.00
2361	22¢ Certified Public Accounting 9/21/87 NY, NY	12.00
2362-66	22¢ Locomotives, bklt. sgls. (5) 10/1/87 Baltimore, MD	10.00
2366a	Booklet Pane of 5	4.00
2367	22¢ Christmas - Madonna & Child 10/23/87 DC	2.00
2368	22¢ Christmas Ornaments 10/23/87 Holiday, CA	2.00
	1988	
2369	22¢ 1988 Winter Olympics 1/10/88 Anchorage, AK	1.75
2370	22¢ Australia Bicentennial 1/26/88 DC	1.75
2370	22¢ Australia Bicentennial combo, dual cancel	15.00
2370	22¢ Australia Bicentennial combo	5.00
2371	22¢ James Weldon Johnson 2/2/88 Nashville, TN	2.50
2372-75	22¢ Cats attd. 2/5/88 New York, NY	8.00
2372-75	Set of 4 singles	12.00
2376	22¢ Knute Rockne 3/9/88 Notre Dame, IN	4.00
2377	25¢ Francis Ouimet 6/13/88 Brookline, MA	7.50
2378	25¢ Love, 7/4/88 Pasadena, CA	1.75
2379	45¢ Love, 8/8/88 Shreveport, LA	2.00
2380	25¢ Summer Olympics 8/19/88 Colo. Springs, CO	1.75
2381-85	25¢ Classic Cars, Bklt. Sgls. 8/25/88 Detroit, MI	10.00
2385a	Bklt. Pane of 5	4.00
2386-89	25¢ Antarctic Explorers attd. 9/14/88 DC	4.00
2386-89	Set of 4 singles	8.00
2390-93	25¢ Carousel Animals attd. 10/1/88 Sandusky, OH	4.00
2390-93	Set of 4 singles	8.00
2394	$8.75 Eagle 10/4/88 Terra Haute, IN	30.00
2395-98	25¢ Sp. Occasions Bklt. Sgls. 10/22/88 King of Prussia, PA..	7.00
2396a	Happy Birthday & Best Wishes, Bklt. Pane of 6	5.00
2398a	Thinking of You & Love You, Bklt. Pane of 6	5.00
2399	25¢ Christmas Madonna & Child 10/20/88 DC	2.00
2400	25¢ Christmas Sleigh & Village 10/20/88 Berlin, NH	2.00
	1989	
2401	25¢ Montana Statehood 1/15/89 Helena, MT	2.00
2402	25¢ A. Philip Randolph 2/3/89 New York, NY	2.50
2403	25¢ North Dakota Statehood 2/21/89 Bismarck, ND	1.75
2404	25¢ Washington Statehood 2/22/89 Olympia, WA	1.75
2405-09	25¢ Steamboats, Bklt. Sgls. 3/3/89 New Orleans, LA	10.00
2409a	Bklt. Pane of 5	4.00
2410	25¢ World Stamp Expo 3/16/89 New York, NY	1.75
2411	25¢ Arturo Toscanini 3/25/89 New York, NY	1.75
2412	25¢ U.S. House of Representatives 4/4/89 DC	2.00
2413	25¢ U.S. Senate 4/6/89 DC	2.00

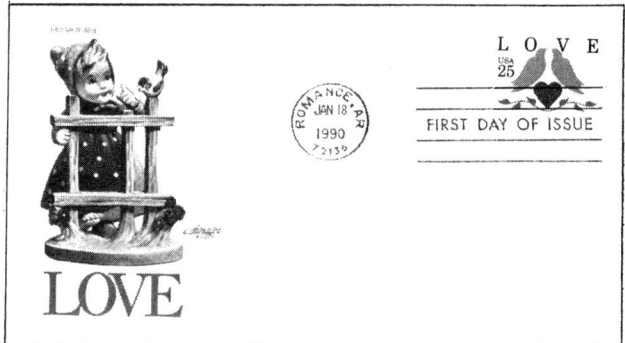

2440

Scott #	Description	Price
	1989 (cont.)	
2414	25¢ Exec. Branch & George Washington Inaugural 4/16/89 Mt. Vernon, VA......	2.00
2415	25¢ U.S. Supreme Court 2/2/90 DC......	2.00
2416	25¢ South Dakota Statehood 5/3/89 Pierre, SD......	1.75
2417	25¢ Lou Gehrig 6/10/89 Cooperstown, NY......	5.50
2418	25¢ Ernest Hemingway 7/17/89 Key West, FL......	1.75
2419	$2.40 Moon Landing, Priority Mail, 7/20/89 DC......	7.00
2420	25¢ Letter Carriers 8/30/89 Milwaukee, WI......	2.00
2421	25¢ Drafting the Bill of Rights 9/25/89 Philadelphia, PA.........	1.75
2422-25	25¢ Prehistoric Animals attd. 10/1/89 Orlando, FL......	5.00
2422-25	Set of 4 singles......	10.00
2426, C21(1)	25¢ Pre-Columbian w/45¢ Air Combo......	7.50
2426	25¢ Pre-Columbian Customs 10/12/89 San Juan, PR......	1.75
2427	25¢ Christmas Madonna & Child 10/19/89 DC......	1.75
2427a	Booklet Pane of 10......	8.00
2428	25¢ Christmas Sleigh & Presents 10/19/89 Westport, CT........	1.75
2429	25¢ Christmas Sleigh, bklt. sgl. Westport, CT......	1.75
2429a	Booklet Pane of 10......	8.00
2431	25¢ Eagle & Shield, self-adhes. 11/10/89 Virginia Bch., VA	1.75
2431a	Booklet Pane of 18......	15.00
2433	90¢ World Stamp Expo S/S of 4 11/17/89 DC......	14.50
2434-37	25¢ Traditional Mail Transportation attd. 11/19/89 DC......	4.00
2434-37	Set of 4 singles......	8.00
2438	25¢ Traditional Mail Transportation, S/S of 4 11/28/89 DC......	4.50
	1990	
2439	25¢ Idaho Statehood 1/6/90 Boise, ID......	2.00
2440	25¢ Love 1/18/90 Romance, AR......	2.00
2441	25¢ Love, bklt. sgl. 1/18/90 Romance, AR......	1.75
2441a	Booklet Pane of 10......	8.00
2442	25¢ Ida B. Wells 2/1/90 Chicago, IL......	2.50
2443	15¢ Beach Umbrella, bklt. sgl. 2/3/90 Sarasota, FL......	1.75
2443a	Booklet Pane of 10......	6.00
2444	25¢ Wyoming Statehood 2/23/90 Cheyenne, WY......	1.75
2445-48	25¢ Classic Films attd. 3/23/90 Hollywood, CA......	7.50
2445-48	Set of 4 singles......	12.00
2449	25¢ Marianne Moore 4/18/90 Brooklyn, NY......	2.00
	1990-95 TRANSPORTATION COILS	
2451	4¢ Steam Carriage 1/25/91 Tucson, AZ......	1.75
2452	5¢ Circus Wagon 8/31/90 Syracuse, NY......	1.75
2452B	5¢ Circus Wagon, Gravure 12/8/92 Cincinnati, OH......	1.75
2452D	5¢ Circus Wagon, Reissue (5¢) 3/20/95, Kansas City,MO.......	1.90
2453	5¢ Canoe, brown 5/25/91 Secaucus, NJ......	1.75
2454	5¢ Canoe, red, Gravure print 10/22/91 Secaucus, NJ......	1.75
2457	10¢ Tractor Trailer,Intaglio 5/25/91 Secaucus, NJ......	1.75
2458	10¢ Tractor Trailer, Gravure 5/25/91 Secaucus, NJ......	1.75
2463	20¢ Cog Railway Car 6/9/95 Dallas, TX......	1.90
2464	23¢ Lunch Wagon 4/12/91 Columbus, OH......	1.75
2466	32¢ Ferry Boat 6/2/95 McLean, VA......	1.90
2468	$1.00 Seaplane 4/20/90 Phoenix, AZ......	3.00
	1990-93	
2470-74	25¢ Lighthouse bklt. sgls. 4/26/90 DC......	10.00
2474a	Booklet Pane of 5......	4.00
2475	25¢ Flag Stamp, ATM self-adhes. 5/18/90 Seattle, WA......	1.75
2475a	Pane of 12......	10.00
2476	1¢ Kestrel 6/22/91 Aurora, CO......	1.75
2477	1¢ Reprint 5/10/95 Aurora,CO w "¢" sign......	1.75
2478	3¢ Bluebird 6/22/91 Aurora, CO......	1.75
2479	19¢ Fawn 3/11/91 DC......	1.75
2480	30¢ Cardinal 6/22/91 Aurora, CO......	1.75
2481	45¢ Pumpkinseed Sunfish 12/2/92 DC......	2.00
2482	$2 Bobcat 6/1/90 Arlington, VA......	7.00
2483	20¢ Blue Jay, Bklt.sgl. 6/15/95 Kansas City, MO......	1.90
2483a	Booklet Pane of 10......	8.50
2484	29¢ Wood Duck, BEP bklt. single 4/12/91 Columbus, OH.......	1.75
2484a	BEP Booklet Pane of 10......	9.00
2485	29¢ Wood Duck, KCS bklt. single 4/12/91 Columbus, OH.......	1.75
2485a	KCS Booklet Pane of 10......	9.00
2486	29¢ African Violet, Bklt. Sgl. 10/8/93 Beaumont, TX......	1.75
2486a	Booklet Pane of 10......	8.00
2487	32¢ Peach, Bklt. sgl. 7/8/95 Reno, NV......	1.90
2488	32¢ Pear, Bklt. sgl. 7/8/95 Reno, NV......	1.90

Scott #	Description	Price
	1990-93 (cont.)	
2487-88	32¢ Peach & Pear, Attached Pair......	2.50
2488A	Booklet Pane of 10......	8.50
	1993-95 SELF ADHESIVE BOOKLETS & COILS	
2489	29¢ Red Squirrel, Self adhesive,sgl. 6/25/93 Milwaukee, WI....	1.75
2489a	Pane of 18......	14.00
2490	29¢ Rose, Self adhesive sgl. 8/19/93 Houston, TX......	1.75
2490a	Pane of 18......	14.00
2491	29¢ Pine Cone, Self adhesive sgl. 11/5/93 Kansas City, MO.....	1.75
2491a	Pane of 18......	14.00
2492	32¢ Pink Rose, Self-adhesive 6/2/95 McLean, VA......	1.90
2492a	Pane of 20, Self-adhesive......	15.50
2493	32¢ Peach, self-adhesive 7/8/95 Reno, NV......	1.90
2494	32¢ Pear, self-adhesive 7/8/95 Reno, NV......	1.90
2493-94	32¢ Peach & Pear, attd......	2.50
2494a	Pane of 20, self-adhesive......	15.50
2495	32¢ Peach, Coil Self adhesive 7/8/95 Reno, NV......	1.90
2495A	32¢ Pear, Coil, Self-adhesive 7/8/95 Reno, NV......	1.90
2495-95A	Peach & Pear, Coil Pair......	2.50
	1990 COMMEMORATIVES (cont.)	
2496-2500	25¢ Olympians attd. 7/6/90 Minneapolis, MN......	5.00
2496-2500	Set of 5 singles......	12.50
2496-2500	Olympians with Tab singles attd......	8.00
2496-2500	Set of 5 singles with Tabs......	12.00
2501-05	25¢ Indian Headdresses bklt. singles 8/17/90 Cody, WY......	10.00
2505a	Booklet Pane of 5......	8.00
2506-07	25¢ Micronesia & Marshall Isles joint issue 9/28/90 DC......	3.00
2506-07	Set of 2 singles......	4.00
2506-07	25¢ Micronesia & Marshall Isles, dual cancel......	15.00
2506-07	25¢ Micronesia & Marshall Isles, combo......	5.00
2508-11	25¢ Sea Creatures attd. 10/3/90 Baltimore, MD......	5.00
2508-11	Set of 4 singles......	10.00
2508-11	25¢ Sea Creatures attd, combo, dual cancel......	15.00
2508-11	25¢ Sea Creatures attd, combo......	5.00
2512	25¢ Pre-Columbian Customs 10/12/90 Grand Canyon, AZ ...	2.00
2513	25¢ Dwight D. Eisenhower 10/13/90 Abilene, KS......	2.00
2514	25¢ Christmas Madonna & Child 10/18/90 DC......	2.00
2514a	Booklet Pane of 10 10/18/90 DC......	6.50
2515	25¢ Christmas Tree 10/18/90 Evergreen, CO......	2.00
2516	25¢ Christmas Tree bklt. sgl. 10/18/90 Evergreen, CO......	2.00
2516a	Booklet Pane of 10 10/18/90......	6.50
	1991-94	
2517	(29¢) "F" Flower stamp 1/22/91 DC......	1.75
2518	(29¢) "F" Flower coil 1/22/91 DC......	1.75
2519	(29¢) "F" Flower, BEP bklt. single 1/22/91 DC......	1.75
2519a	Bklt. Pane of 10, BEP......	7.50
2520	(29¢) "F" Flower, KCS bklt. single 1/22/91 DC......	1.75
2520a	Bklt. Pane of 10, KCS......	9.50
2521	(4¢) Make-up rate stamp 1/22/91 DC, non-denom......	1.75
2522	(29¢) "F" Flag stamp, ATM self-adhes. 1/22/91 DC......	1.75
2522a	Pane of 12......	10.00
2523	29¢ Flag over Mt. Rushmore Coil 3/29/91 Mt. Rushmore, SD ..	1.75
2523A	29¢ Same, Gravure print 7/4/91 Mt. Rushmore, SD......	1.75
	* On #2523A "USA" and "29" are **not** outlined in white	
2524	29¢ Flower 4/5/91 Rochester, NY......	1.75
2525	29¢ Flower coil, rouletted 8/16/91 Rochester, NY......	1.75
2526	29¢ Flower coil, perforated 3/3/92 Rochester, NY......	1.75
2527	29¢ Flower, bklt. single 4/5/91 Rochester, NY......	1.75
2527a	Booklet Pane of 10......	7.50
2528	29¢ Flag with Olympic Rings, bklt. sgl. 4/21/91 Atlanta, GA....	1.75
2528a	Booklet Pane of 10......	7.50
2529	19¢ Fishing Boat, coil 8/8/91 DC......	1.75
2529C	19¢ Fishing Boat, coil, Type III 6/25/94 Arlington, VA......	1.75
2530	19¢ Ballooning, bklt. sgl. 5/17/91 Denver, CO......	1.75
2530a	Booklet Pane of 10......	7.00
2531	29¢ Flags/Memorial Day, 125th Anniv. 5/30/91 Waterloo,NY..	1.75
2531A	29¢ Liberty Torch, ATM self-adhes. 6/25/91 New York, NY...	1.75
2531Ab	Pane of 18......	14.00
	1991 COMMEMORATIVES	
2532	50¢ Switzerland, joint issue 2/22/91 DC......	2.00
2532	50¢ Switzerland, combo, dual cancel......	15.00
2532	50¢ Switzerland, combo......	5.00
2533	29¢ Vermont Statehood 3/1/91 Bennington, VT......	2.25
2534	29¢ Savings Bonds 4/30/91 DC......	1.75
2535	29¢ Love 5/9/91 Honolulu, HI......	1.75
2536	29¢ Love, Booklet Sgl. 5/9/91 Honolulu, HI......	1.75
2536a	Booklet Pane of 10......	7.50
2537	52¢ Love, 2 ounce rate 5/9/91 Honolulu, HI......	2.00
2538	29¢ William Saroyan 5/22/91 Fresno, CA......	2.25
2538	29¢ WIlliam Saroyan, combo, dual cancel......	15.00
2538	29¢ William Saroyan, combo......	5.00

U.S. FIRST DAY COVERS

2540

Scott #	Description	Price
	1991-95 REGULAR ISSUES	
2539	$1.00 USPS & Olympic Rings 9/29/91 Orlando, FL	3.00
2540	$2.90 Priority Mail 7/7/91 San Diego, CA	9.00
2541	$9.95 Express Mail,Domestic rate 6/16/91 Sacramento,CA	25.00
2542	$14.00 Express Mail,Internat'l rate 8/31/91 Indianapolis,IN	32.50
2543	$2.90 Priority Mail, Space 6/3/93 Titusville, FL	7.50
2544	$3 Challenger Shuttle, Priority Mail 6/22/95 Anaheim, CA	7.75
2544A	$10.75 Endeavor Shuttle Express Mail 8/4/95 Irvine, CA	25.00
	1991 COMMEMORATIVES (continued)	
2545-49	29¢ Fishing Flies, bklt. sgls. 5/31/91 Cudlebackville, NY	10.00
2549a	Booklet Pane of 5	5.00
2550	29¢ Cole Porter 6/8/91 Peru, IN	1.75
2551	29¢ Desert Shield / Desert Storm 7/2/91 DC	2.00
2552	29¢ Desert Shield / Desert Storm bklt. sgl. 7/2/91 DC	2.00
2552a	29¢ Booklet Pane of 5	4.50
2553-57	29¢ Summer Olympics,strip of 5 7/12/91 Los Angeles, CA	4.50
2553-57	Set of 5 singles	10.00
2558	29¢ Numismatics 8/13/91 Chicago, IL	2.00
2559	29¢ World War II S/S of 10 9/3/91 Phoenix, AZ	12.00
2559a-j	Set of 10 singles	30.00
2560	29¢ Basketball 8/28/91 Springfield, MA	3.00
2561	29¢ District of Columbia Bicent. 9/7/91 DC	1.75
2562-66	29¢ Comedians .,set of 5 8/29/91 Hollywood, CA	10.00
2562-66	Set of 5 on 1	4.50
2566a	Booklet Pane of 10	7.50
2567	29¢ Jan Matzeliger 9/15/91 Lynn, MA	2.50
2568-77	29¢ Space Exploration bklt. sgls. 10/1/91 Pasadena, CA	20.00
2577a	Booklet Pane of 10	8.00
2578	(29¢) Christmas, Madonna & Child 10/17/91 Houston,TX	1.75
2578a	Booklet Pane of 10	8.00
2579	(29¢) Christmas, Santa & Chimney 10/19/91 Santa, ID	1.75
2580-85	(29¢) Christmas, bklt. pane sgls. 10/17/91 Santa, ID	12.00
2581b-85a	Booklet Panes of 4, set of 5	20.00
	1994-95 DEFINITIVES DESIGNS OF 1869 ESSAYS	
2587	32¢ James S. Polk 11/2/95 Columbia, TN	1.90
2590	$1 Surrender of Burgoyne 5/5/94 New York, NY	4.00
2592	$5 Washington & Jackson 8/19/94 Pittsburgh, PA	20.00
	1992-93 REGULAR ISSUES	
2593	29¢ "Pledge" Black denom., bklt. sgl. 9/8/92 Rome, NY	1.75
2593a	Booklet Pane of 10	7.00
	1992 Eagle & Shield Self-Adhesives Stamps (9/25/92 Dayton, OH)	
2595	29¢ "Brown" denomination, sgl	2.00
2595a	Pane of 17 + label	12.00
2596	29¢ "Green" denomination, sgl	2.00
2596a	Pane of 17 + label	12.00
2597	29¢ "Red" denomination, sgl	2.00
2597a	Pane of 17 + label	12.00
	1992 Eagle & Shield Self-Adhesive Coils	
2595v	29¢ "Brown" denomination, pair with paper backing	2.25
2596v	29¢ "Green" denomination, pair with paper backing	2.25
2597v	29¢ "Red" denomination, pair with paper backing	2.25
	1994 Eagle Self-Adhesive Issues	
2598	29¢ Eagle, single 2/4/94 Sarasota, FL	1.75
2598a	Pane of 18	12.50
2598v	29¢ Coil Pair with paper backing	2.25
	1994 Statue of Liberty Self-Adhesive Issue	
2599	29¢ Statue of Liberty, single 6/24/94 Haines, FL	1.75
2599a	Pane of 18	12.50
2599v	29¢ Coil pair with paper backing	2.25
	1991-93 Coil Issues	
2602	(10¢) Eagle & Shield, bulk-rate 12/13/91 Kansas City, MO	1.75
2603	(10¢) Eagle & Shield, **BEP** 5/29/93 Secaucus, NJ	1.75
2604	(10¢) Eagle & Shld., **Stamp Venturers** 5/29/93 Secaucus, NJ	1.75
2605	23¢ Flag, First Class pre-sort 9/27/91 DC	1.75
2606	23¢ USA, 1st Cl, pre-sort, **ABNCo.** 7/21/92 Kansas City, MO	1.75
2607	23¢ USA, 1st Cl, pre-sort, **BEP** 10/9/92 Kansas City, MO	1.75
2608	23¢ USA, 1st Cl, p.s., **Stamp Venturers** 5/14/93 Denver, CO	1.75
2609	29¢ Flag over White House 4/23/92 DC	1.75

U.S. FIRST DAY COVERS

Scott #	Description	Price
	1992 Commemoratives	
2611-15	29¢ Winter Olympics, strip of 5 1/11/92 Orlando, FL	5.00
2611-15	Set of 5 singles	10.00
2616	29¢ World Columbian Expo 1/24/92 Rosemont, IL	1.75
2617	29¢ W.E.B. DuBois 1/31/92 Atlanta, GA	2.50
2618	29¢ Love 2/6/92 Loveland. CO	1.75
2619	29¢ Olympic Baseball 4/3/92 Atlanta, GA	3.50
	1992 Columbus Commemoratives	
2620-23	29¢ First Voyage of Columbus 4/24/92 Christiansted, VI	4.00
2620-23	Set of 4 singles	8.00
2620-23	Joint Issue	15.00
2620-23	Joint Issue w/Italy, Dual with blue cancel	450.00
2620-23	Joint Issue w/Italy, set of 4	30.00
2624-29	1¢-$5.00 Voyages of Columbus S/S 5/22/92 Chicago, IL	50.00
2624a-29	Set of 16 singles	90.00
	1992 Commemoratives (cont.)	
2630	29¢ New York Stock Exchange 5/17/92 New York, NY	3.00
2631-34	29¢ Space: Accomplishments 5/29/92 Chicago, IL	4.00
2631-34	Set of 4 singles	10.00
2635	29¢ Alaska Highway 5/30/92 Fairbanks, AK	1.75
2636	29¢ Kentucky Statehood Bicent. 6/1/92 Danville, KY	1.75
2637-41	29¢ Summer Olympics, strip of 5 6/11/92 Baltimore, MD	5.00
2637-41	Set of 5 singles	10.00
2642-46	29¢ Hummingbirds, bklt. sgls. 6/15/92 DC	10.00
2646a	Booklet Pane of 5	5.00
2647-96	29¢ Wildflowers, set of 50 singles 7/24/92 Columbus, OH	87.50
2697	29¢ World War II S/S of 10 8/17/92 Indianapolis, IN	10.00
2697a-j	Set of 10 singles	25.00
2698	29¢ Dorothy Parker 8/22/92 West End, NJ	1.75
2699	29¢ Dr. Theodore von Karman 8/31/92 DC	1.75
2700-03	29¢ Minerals 9/17/92 DC	4.00
2700-03	Set of 4 singles	8.00
2704	29¢ Juan Rodriguez Cabrillo 9/28/92 San Diego, CA	1.75
2705-09	29¢ Wild Animals, bklt. sgls. 10/1/92 New Orleans, LA	10.00
2709a	Booklet Pane of 5	5.00
2710	29¢ Christmas, Madonna & Child 10/22/92 DC	2.00
2710a	Booklet Pane of 10 10/22/92 DC	8.00
2711-14	29¢ Christmas Toys,offset, 10/22/92 Kansas City, MO	4.00
2711-14	Set of 4 singles	10.00
2715-18	29¢ Christmas Toys,gravure,bklt.sgls.10/22/92 Kansas City,MO	10.00
2718a	Booklet Pane of 4.	4.00
2719	29¢ Christmas Train self-adhes. ATM 10/28/92 NY, NY	1.75
2719a	Pane of 18	14.00
2720	29¢ Happy New Year 12/30/92 San Francisco, CA	3.00
	1993 Commemoratives	
2721	29¢ Elvis Presley 1/8/93 Memphis, TN	2.00
2722	29¢ Oklahoma! 3/30/93 Oklahoma City, OK	1.75
2723	29¢ Hank Williams 6/9/93 Nashville, TN	1.75
2724-30	29¢ R 'n' R/R & B 6/16/93 on one cover Cleveland, OH & Santa Monica, CA (same cancel ea. city)	8.00
2724-30	Set of 7 singles on 2 covers	11.00
2724-30	Set of 7 singles	17.50
2731-37	29¢ R 'n' R/R & B, Set/7 bklt. sgls. 6/16/93 Cleveland, OH & Santa Monica, CA (same cancel ea. city)	17.50
2731-37	Set of 7 singles on 2 covers	10.00
2737a	Booklet Pane of 8.	8.00
2737b	Booklet Pane of 4.	4.50
2737a,2737b	Booklet Panes on 1 cover.	12.00
2741-45	29¢ Space Fantasy, bklt. sgls. 1/25/93 Huntsville, AL	10.00
2745a	Booklet Pane of 5.	5.00
2746	29¢ Percy Lavon Julian 1/29/93 Chicago, IL	2.50
2747	29¢ Oregon Trail 2/12/93 Salem, OR	1.75
2748	29¢ World University Games 2/25/93 Buffalo, NY	2.00
2749	29¢ Grace Kelly 3/24/93 Hollywood, CA	2.50
2750-53	29¢ Circus 4/6/93 DC	4.00
2750-53	Set of 4 singles	10.00
2754	29¢ Cherokee Strip 4/17/93 Enid, OK	1.75
2755	29¢ Dean Acheson 4/21/93 DC	1.75
2756-59	29¢ Sport Horses 5/1/93 Louisville, KY	4.00
2756-59	Set of 4 singles	10.00
2760-64	29¢ Garden Flowers, bklt. sgls. 5/15/93 Spokane, WA	10.00
2764a	Booklet Pane of 5.	5.00
2765	29¢ World War II S/S of 10 5/31/93 DC	10.00
2765a-j	Set of 10 singles	25.00
2766	29¢ Joe Louis 6/22/93 Detroit, MI	3.00
2767-70	29¢ Broadway Musicals, bkt. sgls. 7/14/93 New York, NY	10.00
2770a	Booklet Pane of 4.	5.00
2771-74	29¢ Country Music attd. 9/25/93 Nashville, TN	5.00
2771-74	Set of 4 singles	10.00
2775-78	29¢ Country Music, bklt. sgls. 9/25/93 Nashville, TN	10.00
2778a	Booklet Pane of 5.	5.00
2779-82	29¢ National Postal Museum 7/30/93 DC	4.00
2779-82	Set of 4 singles	10.00
2783-84	29¢ Deaf Communication, pair 9/20/93 Burbank, CA	2.25
2783-84	Set of 2 singles	4.00
2785-88	29¢ Children's Classics, block of 4 10/23/93 Louisville, KY	4.00
2785-88	Set of 4 singles	10.00
2789	29¢ Madonna & Child 10/21/93 Raleigh, NC	1.75
2790	Booklet Single	1.75
2790a	Booklet Pane of 4.	4.00
2791-94	29¢ Christmas Designs attd. 10/21/93 New York, NY	4.00
2791-94	Set of 4 singles	10.00
2795-98	29¢ Contemp. Christmas, 4 bklt.singles 10/21/93 NY, NY	10.00
2798a	Booklet Pane of 10 (3 snowmen).	8.00
2798b	Booklet Pane of 10 (2 snowmen).	8.00
2799-2802	29¢ Contemp. Christmas, self-adhes. Set of 4 10/28/93 NY, NY	9.00
2802a	Pane of 12.	10.00
2803	29¢ Snowman, self-adhesive 10/28/93 New York, NY	1.75

2817

Scott #	Description	Price
	1993 Commemoratives (cont.)	
2803a	Pane of 18	14.00
2804	29¢ Northern Mariana Isles 11/4/93 DC	1.75
2805	29¢ Columbus-Puerto Rico 11/19/93 San Juan, PR	1.75
2806	29¢ AIDS Awareness 12/1/93 New York, NY	1.75
2806a	29¢ AIDS, booklet single 12/1/93 New York, NY	1.75
2806b	Booklet Pane of 5	5.00
	1994 Commemoratives	
2807-11	29¢ Winter Olympics, Strip of 5, 1/6/94 Salt Lake City, UT	5.00
2807-11	Set of 5 Singles	10.00
2812	29¢ Edward R. Murrow 1/21/94 Pullman, WA	1.75
2813	29¢ Love & Sunrise, self-adhesive sgl. 1/27/94 Loveland, OH	1.75
2813a	Pane of 18	14.00
2813v	Coil Pair with paper backing	2.25
2814	29¢ Love & Dove, booklet single 2/14/94 Niagara Falls, NY	1.75
2814a	Booklet Pane of 10	7.00
2814C	29¢ Love & Dove, Sheet Stamp 6/11/94 Niagara Falls, NY	1.75
2815	52¢ Love & Doves 2/14/94 Niagara Falls, NY	2.00
2816	29¢ Dr. Allison Davis 2/1/94 Williamstown, MA	2.75
2817	29¢ Chinese New Year, Dog 2/5/94 Pomona, CA	2.50
2818	29¢ Buffalo Soldiers 4/22/94 Dallas, TX	2.50
2819-28	29¢ Silent Screen Stars, attd. 4/27/94 San Francisco, CA	8.00
2819-28	Set of 10 Singles	20.00
2819-28	Set of 10 on 2 covers	9.50
2829-33	29¢ Summer Garden Flowers 4/28/94 Cincinnati, OH	5.00
2833a	Set of 5 Singles	10.00
2834	29¢ World Cup Soccer 5/26/94 New York, NY	1.75
2834-36	29¢, 40¢, 50¢ Soccer on 1 cover	3.00
2834-36	29¢, 40¢, 50¢ Soccer on 3 covers	5.75
2835	40¢ World Cup Soccer 5/26/94 New York, NY	2.00
2836	50¢ World Cup Soccer 5/26/94 New York, NY	2.00
2837	29¢,40¢,50¢ Soccer Souvenir Sheet of 3 5/26/94 NY,NY	3.50
2838	29¢ World War II Souvenir Sht of 10 6/6/94 U.S.S. Normandy	10.00
2838a-j	Set of 10 Singles	25.00
2839	29¢ Norman Rockwell 7/1/94 Stockbridge, MA	1.75
2840	50¢ Norman Rockwell, S/S of 4 7/1/94 Stockbridge, MA	5.75
2840A-D	Singles from Souvenir Sheet	8.00
	1994 Moon Landing, 25th Anniversary	
2841	29¢ Moon Landing Souvenir Sheet of 12 7/20/94 DC	10.75
2841a	Single from Souvenir Sheet	1.75
2842	$9.95 Moon Landing, Express Mail 7/20/94 DC	25.00
	1994 Commemoratives (continued)	
2843-47	29¢ Locomotives, booklet singles 7/28/94 Chama, NM	10.00
2847a	Booklet Pane of 5	5.00
2848	29¢ George Meany 8/16/94 DC	1.75
2849-53	29¢ Popular Singers 9/1/94 New York, NY	6.00
2849-53	Set of 5 Singles	12.50
2854-61	29¢ Blues & Jazz Artists 9/17/94 Greenville, MI	10.00
2854-61	Set of 8 on 2 covers	10.00
2854-61	Set of 8 Singles	20.00
2862	29¢ James Thurber 9/10/94 Columbus, OH	1.75
2863-66	29¢ Wonders of the Sea 10/1/94 Honolulu, HI	4.00
2863-66	Set of 4 Singles	8.00
2867-68	29¢ Cranes, attd. 10/9/94 DC	2.25
2867-68	Set of 2 Singles	4.00
2867-68	Joint Issue	5.00
2867-68	Joint Issue - Dual Cancel	15.00
	1994 Legends of the West Miniature Sheet	
2869	29¢ Legends of the West, Pane of 20 10/18/94 Tucson, AZ, Laramie, WY and Lawton, OK	25.00
2869a-t	Set of 20 Singles	50.00
2869a-t	Set of four covers, 2 blocks of 4 and 2 blocks of 6	22.50
	1994 Commemoratives (continued)	
2871	29¢ Madonna & Child 10/20/94 DC	1.75
2871a	Booklet single	1.75
2871b	Booklet Pane of 10	8.50
2872	29¢ Christmas Stocking 10/20/94 Harmony, MN	1.75
2872a	Booklet Pane of 20	15.50
2872v	Booklet single	1.75
2873	29¢ Santa Claus, self-adhesive 10/20/94 Harmony, MN	1.75
2873a	Pane of 12	10.00
2873v	Coil pair on paper backing	2.25
2874	29¢ Cardinal in Snow, self-adhesive 10/20/94 Harmony, MN	1.75
2874a	Pane of 18	14.00
2875	$2 Bureau of Engraving Centennial Souvenir sheet of 4 11/3/94 New York, NY	24.00

U.S. FIRST DAY COVERS

Scott #	Description	Price
	1994 Commemoratives (continued)	
2875a	$2 Madison single from souvenir sheet	7.00
2876	29¢ Year of the Boar 12/30/94 Sacramento, CA	2.50
	1994-95 Interim Regular Issues	
2877	(3¢) Dove, ABN, Light blue 12/13/94 DC	1.90
2878	(3¢) Dove, SVS, Darker blue 12/13/94 DC	1.90
2879	(20¢) "G" Postcard Rate, BEP, Black "G" 12/13/94 DC	1.95
2880	(20¢) "G" Postcard Rate, SVS, Red "G" 12/13/94 DC	1.95
2881	(32¢) "G" BEP, Black "G" 12/13/94 DC	1.90
2881a	Booklet Pane of 10	8.50
2882	(32¢) "G" SVS, Red "G" 12/13/94 DC	1.90
2881-82	(32¢) "G" Combo 12/13/94 DC	2.75
2883	(32¢) "G" BEP, Black "G", Booklet Single 12/13/94 DC	1.90
2883a	Booklet Pane of 10, BEP	8.50
2884	(32¢) "G" ABN, Blue "G", Booklet Single 12/13/94 DC	1.90
2884a	Booklet Pane of 10, ABN	8.50
2885	(32¢) "G" KCS, Red "G", Booklet Single 12/13/94 DC	1.90
2885a	Booklet Pane of 10, KCS	8.50
2886	(32¢) "G"Surface Tagged,self-adh.,strip format 12/13/94 DC	1.90
2886a	Pane of 18, Self-Adhesive	15.00
2887	(32¢) "G" Overall Tagging, self-adhesive 12/13/94 DC	1.90
2887a	Pane of 18, self-adhesive	15.00
2888	(25¢) "G" Presort, Coil 12/13/94 DC	1.90
2888,2393	(25¢) "G" Presort and (5¢) "G" Non-profit Combo 12/13/94 DC	2.40
2889	(32¢) "G" Coil, BEP, Black "G" 12/13/94 DC	1.90
2890	(32¢) "G" Coil, ABN, Blue "G" 12/13/94 DC	1.90
2891	(32¢) "G" Coil, SVS, Red "G" 12/13/94 DC	1.90
2892	(32¢) "G" Coil, Rouletted, Red "G" 12/13/94 DC	1.90
2893	(5¢) "G" Non-Profit, Green, 12/13/94 date, available for mail order sale 1/12/95 DC	1.90
2897	32¢ Flag over Porch, sheet stamp 5/19/95 Denver, CO	1.90
2902	(5¢) Butte 3/10/95 State College, PA	1.90
2902B	(5¢) Butte - S/A Coil 6/15/96 State College, PA	1.90
2903	(5¢) Mountain, Coil, BE (Letters outlined in purple) 3/16/96, San Jose, Ca	1.90
2904	(5¢) Mountain, Coil, SV, (outlined letters) 3/16/96 San Jose, Ca.	1.90
2904A	(5¢) Mountain, S/A, Coil, 6/15/96	1.90
2904B	(5¢) Mountain, S/A, BEP, 1/24/97	1.90
2905	(10¢) Automobile 3/10/95 State College, PA	1.90
2906	(10¢) Auto, S/A. Coil, 6/15/96	1.90
2907	(10¢) Eagle & Shield, S/A, Coil, 5/21/96	1.90
2908	(15¢) Auto Tail Fin, BEP 3/17/95 New York, NY	1.90
2909	(15¢) Auto Tail Fin, SVS 3/17/95 New York, NY	1.90
2908-9	(15¢) Auto Tail Fin, Combo with BEP and SVS Singles	2.25
2910	(15¢) Auto Tail Fin, S/A, Coil, 6/15/96, New York, NY	1.90
2911	(25¢) Juke Box, BEP 3/17/95 New York, NY	1.90
2912	(25¢) Juke Box, SVS 3/17/95 New York, NY	1.90
2912A	(25¢) Juke Box, S/A, Coil, 6/15/96, New York, NY	1.90
2912B	(25¢) Juke Box, S/A, BEP, 1/24/97	1.90
2911-12	(25¢) Juke Box, Combo with BEP and SVS singles	2.35
2913	32¢ Flag over Porch, BEP, coil 5/19/95 Denver, CO	1.90
2914	32¢ Flag over Porch, SVS, coil 5/19/95 Denver, CO	1.90
2913-14	32¢ Flag over Porch, Combo with BEP and SVS singles	2.50
2915	32¢ Flag over Porch, self-adhesive strip format 4/18/95 DC	2.00
2915A	32¢ Flag over Porch, S/A, Coil, 5/21/96	1.90
2915B	32¢ Flag over Porch, S/A, Coil, (serpentine diecut 11.5 vert.) SV, 6/15/96, San Antonio, TX	1.90
2915D	32¢ Flag over Porch, S/A, Coil, BEP, 1/24/97	1.90
2916	32¢ Flag over Porch, booklet single 5/19/95 Denver, CO	1.90
2916a	Booklet Pane of 10	8.50
2919	32¢ Flag over Field, self-adhesive 3/17/95 New York, NY	1.90
2919a	Pane of 18, Self-adhesive	14.50
2920	32¢ Flag over Porch, self-adhesive 4/19/95 DC	1.90
2920a	Pane of 20, self-adhesive w/large "1995"	15.50
2920b	Small Date	1.90
2920c	32¢ Pane of 20 S/A w/small "1995" 4/18/95 (fairly scarce)	45.00
2920d	Serpentine die cut 11.3, S/A, Single, 1/20/96	1.90
2920e	Booklet Pane of 10, S/A, 1/20/96	8.50
2921	32¢ Flag over Porch, S/A, Booklet Single, (Serpentine die cut 9.8), 5/21/96	1.90
2921a	Booklet Pane of 10, 5/21/96	8.50
2921v	32¢ Flag over Porch, bklt. single S/A, (1997 date)	1.90
	1995 Great American Series	
2933	32¢ Milton S. Hershey 9/13/95 Hershey, PA	1.90
2934	32¢ Cal Farley 4/26/96 Amarillo, TX	1.90
2935	32¢ Henry R. Luce (1998)	1.90
2936	32¢ Lila & DeWitt Wallace (1998)	1.90
2938	46¢ Ruth Benedict 10/20/95 Virginia Beach, VA	2.25
2940	55¢ Alice Hamilton, M.D. 7/11/95 Boston, MA	2.25
2942	77¢ Mary Breckinridge, 11/9/98, Troy, NY	2.75
2943	78¢ Alice Paul 8/18/95 Mount Laurel, NJ	2.75
	1995 Commemoratives	
2948	(32¢) Love & Cherub 2/1/95 Valentines, VA	1.90
2949	(32¢) Love & Cherub, self-adhesive 2/1/95 Valentines, VA	1.90
2949a	Pane of 20, self-adhesive	15.50
2950	32¢ Florida Statehood 3/3/95 Tallahassee, FL	1.90
2951-54	32¢ Earth Day/Kids Care attd. 4/20/95 DC	4.35
2951-54	Set of 4 singles	8.00
2955	32¢ Richard Nixon 4/26/95 Yorba Linda, CA	1.90
2956	32¢ Bessie Coleman 4/27/95 Chicago, IL	3.00
2957	32¢ Love-Cherub 5/12/95 Lakeville, PA	1.90
2958	55¢ Love-Cherub 5/12/95 Lakeville, PA	2.25
2959	32¢ Love-Cherub, booklet single	1.90
2959a	Booklet Pane of 10	8.50
2960	55¢ Love-Cherub, self-adhesive single 5/12/95 Lakevilla, PA	2.25
2960a	55¢ Pane of 20, self-adhesive	21.50
2961-65	32¢ Recreational Sports, Strip of 5 5/20/95 Jupiter, FL	5.50
2961-65	Set of 5 singles	10.00
2966	32¢ POW/MIA 5/29/95 DC	1.90

3024

Scott #	Description	Price
2967	32¢ Marilyn Monroe 6/1/95 Hollywood, CA	4.00
2967a	Pane of 20 on one cover	16.50
2968	32¢ Texas Statehood 6/16/95 Austin, TX	1.90
2969-73	32¢ Great Lakes Lighthouses,bklt.sgls. 6/17/95 Cheboygan,MI	10.00
2973a	Booklet Pane of 5	5.50
2974	32¢ United Nations 6/26/95 San Francisco, CA	1.90
2975	32¢ Civil War, Miniature Sht. of 20, 6/29/95 Gettysburg, PA	20.00
2975a-t	Set of 20 singles	40.00
2976-79	32¢ Carousel Horses attd. 7/21/95 Lahaska, PA	4.35
2976-79	Set of 4 singles	8.00
2980	32¢ Women's Suffrage 8/26/95 DC	1.90
2981	32¢ World War II S/S of 10 9/2/95 Honolulu, HI	10.00
2981a-j	Set of 10 singles	25.00
2982	32¢ Louis Armstrong 9/1/95 New Orleans, LA	2.75
2983-92	32¢ Jazz Musicians 9/16/95 Monterey, CA	10.00
2983-92	Set of 10 singles	25.00
2993-97	32¢ Fall Garden Flowers, bklt. sgles. 9/19/95 Encinitas, CA	10.00
2997a	Booklet Pane of 5	5.50
2998	60¢ Eddie Rickenbacker 9/25/95 Columbus, OH	2.25
2999	32¢ Republic of Palau 9/29/95 Agana, Guam	1.90
3000	32¢ Comic Strips, Min. Sheet of 20 10/2/95 Boca Raton, FL	25.00
3000a-t	Set of 20 Singles	50.00
3000a-t	Set of 5 combos (incl. Plate Block)	15.00
3001	32¢ U.S. Naval Academy, 150 Anniv. 10/10/95 Annapolis, MD	1.90
3002	32¢ Tennessee Williams 10/13/95 Clarksdale, MS	1.90
3003	32¢ Madonna and Child 10/19/95 Washington, DC	1.90
3003a	Booklet Single	1.90
3003b	Booklet Pane of 10	8.50
3004-7	32¢ Santa + Children 9/30/95 North Pole, NY, set of 4	8.00
3007a	32¢ Christmas (secular) sheet, 9/30/95, North Pole, NY	3.50

1995 Self-Adhesive Stamps

Scott #	Description	Price
3008-11	32¢ Santa + Children 9/30/95 North Pole, NY	3.50
3008-11	Set of 4 Singles	7.00
3011a	Pane of 20	15.50
3012	32¢ Midnight Angel 10/19/95 Christmas, FL	1.90
3012a	Pane of 20	15.50
3013	32¢ Children Sledding 10/19/95 Christmas, FL	1.90
3013a	Pane of 18	14.00

1995 Self-Adhesive Coil Stamps

Scott #	Description	Price
3014-17	32¢ Santa + Children 9/30/95 North Pole, NY	3.50
3014-17	Set of 4 Singles	7.00
3018	32¢ Midnight Angel 10/19/95 Christmas, FL	1.90

1995 Commemoratives (continued)

Scott #	Description	Price
3019-23	32¢ Antique Automobiles 11/3/95 New York, NY	3.75
3019-23	Set of 5 Singles	8.50

1996 Commemoratives

Scott #	Description	Price
3024	32¢ Utah Statehood 1/4/96 Salt Lake City, UT	1.90
3025-29	32¢ Winter Garden Flowers Bklt.Singles 1/19/96 Kennett Square, PA	10.00
3029a	Booklet Pane of 5	5.50
3030	32¢ Love Cherub, Self-adhesive 1/20/96 New York, NY	1.90
3030a	Booklet Pane of 20	15.50

1996 Flora and Fauna Series

Scott #	Description	Price
3032	2¢ Red-headed Woodpecker 2/2/96 Sarasota, FL	1.90
3033	3¢ Eastern Bluebird 4/3/96 DC	1.90
3036	$1.00 Red Fox, 8/14/98	3.50
3044	1¢ Kestrel, Coil 1/20/96 New York, NY	1.90
3048	20¢ Blue Jay, S/A, 8/2/96 St. Louis, MO	1.90
3048a	Booklet Pane of 10	8.50
3048 + 53	Combo - Blue Jays, 8/2/96, St. Louis, MO	5.00
3049	32¢ Yellow Rose, single, 10/24/96, Pasadena, Ca.	1.90
3049a	Booklet Pane of 20, S/A	15.50
3050	20¢ Ring-Neck Pheasant S/A, 7/31/98, Somerset, NJ	1.90
3050a	20¢ Ring-Neck Pheasant, S/A BP10, 7/31/98	8.50
3053	20¢ Blue Jay, Coil, S/A, 8/2/96, St. Louis, MO	1.90
3054	32¢ Yellow Rose, S/A Coil 8/1/97	1.90
3055	20¢ Ring-Neck Pheasant, S/A Coil, 7/31/98, Somerset, NJ	1.90

1996 Commemoratives (continued)

Scott #	Description	Price
3058	32¢ Ernest E. Just 2/1/96 DC	2.75
3059	32¢ Smithsonian Institution 2/5/96 DC	1.90
3060	32¢ Year of the Rat 2/8/96 San Francisco, CA	2.00
3061-64	32¢ Pioneers of Communication Set of 4 2/22/96 NY, NY	7.00
3061-64a	Block of 4 on one cover	3.50
3065	32¢ Fulbright Scholarship 2/28/96 Fayetteville, AR	1.90
3066	50¢ Jacqueline Cochran 3/9/96 Indio, CA	2.25
3067	32¢ Marathon 4/11/96 Boston, MA	1.90

Scott #	Description	Price

1996 Commemoratives (continued)

Scott #	Description	Price
3068	32¢ Centennial Olympic Games, Min. Sheet of 20 5/2/96 DC	20.00
3068a-t	Set of 20 Singles	40.00
3068a-t	Set of 20 on 4 covers	13.00
3069	32¢ Georgia O'Keeffe 5/23/96 Santa Fe, NM	1.90
3069	Souvenir Sheet of 15	11.50
3070	32¢ Tennessee Statehood 5/31/96 Nashville, Knoxville or Memphis, TN	1.90
3071	32¢ Tennessee Statehood, Self-adhesive single	1.90
3071a	Booklet Pane of 20	13.00
3076a	32¢ American Indian Dances, 5 designs attached 6/7/96 Oklahoma City, OK	4.00
3072-76	Set of 5 Singles	8.50
3077-80	32¢ Prehistoric Animals, 4 designs attached 6/8/96 Toronto, Canada	4.00
3077-80	Set of 4 Singles	8.00
3081	32¢ Breast Cancer Awareness 6/15/96 DC	2.00
3082	32¢ James Dean 6/24/96 Hollywood, CA	2.00
3083-86	32¢ Folk Heroes, 4 designs attached 7/11/96 Anaheim, CA	4.00
3083-86	Set of 4 Singles	8.00
3087	32¢ Olympic Games, Discobolus 7/19 /96	1.90
3088	32¢ Iowa Statehood 8/1/96 Dubuque, IA	1.90
3089	Self-adhesive Single	1.90
3089a	Self-adhesive Pane of 20	15.50
3090	32¢ Rural Free Delivery 8/6/96 Charleston, WV	1.90
3091-95	32¢ River Boats, S/A, 8/22/96, set of 5, Orlando, Fl.	10.00
3095a	Strip of 5	5.50
3096-99	32¢ Big Band Leaders, set of 4, 9/11/96, New York, NY	10.00
3099a	32¢ Big Band Leaders, attd., 9/11/96, New York, NY	5.00
3100-03	32¢ Songwriters, set of 4, 9/11/96, New York, NY	10.00
3103a	32¢ Songwriters, att'd., 9/11/96, New York	5.00
3104	23¢ F. Scott Fitzgerald, 9/27/96, St. Paul, MN	2.00
3105	32¢ Endangered Species, pane of 15,10/2/96, San Diego, Ca.	14.50
3105a-o	Set of 15 covers	30.00
3106	32¢ Computer Tech., 10/8/96, Aberdeen Proving Ground, MD	2.00
3107	32¢ Madonna & Child, 11/1/96, Richmond, Va.	2.00
3108-11	32¢ Christmas Family Scenes,set of 4,10/8/96,North Pole,AK	8.00
3111a	Block or strip of 4	4.25
3112	32¢ Madonna & Child, single, 11/1/96, Richmond, Va.	2.00
3112a	Pane of 20, S/A	15.50
3116a	Booklet Pane of 20, S/A	15.50
3113-16	32¢ Christmas Family Scene, set of 4, Bklt Pane Singles	8.00
3117	32¢ Skaters - for ATM, 10/8/96, North Pole, AK	2.00
3117a	Booklet Pane of 18, S/A	14.75
3118	32¢ Hanukkah, S/A, 10/22/96, Washington, DC	2.00
3118	32¢ Hanukkah, Combo	5.00
3118	32¢ Hanukkah, Combo w/Dual Cancel	15.00
3119	50¢ Cycling, sheet of 2, 11/1/96, New York, NY	3.75
3119	50¢ Cycling, sheet of 2, 11/1/96, Hong Kong	3.75
3119	50¢ Cycling, set of 2, 11/1/96, New York, NY	4.50
3119	50¢ Cycling, set of 2, 11/1/96, Hong Kong	4.50

1997 Commemoratives

Scott #	Description	Price
3120	32¢ Lunar New Year (Year of the Ox), 1/5/97	2.10
3121	32¢ Benjamin O' Davis Sr., S/A, 1/28/97, Wash. DC	2.75
3122	32¢ Statue of Liberty, S/A, Bklt Single, 2/1/97	2.00
3122a	Pane of 20 w/Label	15.50
3122c	Pane of 5 w/Label	5.50
3122d	Pane of 6	6.00
3123	32¢ Love Swan, S/A, Single, 2/4/97	2.00
3123a	Booklet Pane of 20 w/Label	15.50
3124	55¢ Love Swan, S/A, Single, 2/4/97	2.00
3124a	Booklet Pane of 20 w/Label	15.50
3125	32¢ Helping Children Learn, S/A, 2/18/97	2.00
3126-27	Citron Moth & Flowering Pineapple, attd, 3/3/97, Wash. DC	2.50
3126-27	Pane of 20	15.50
3126-27	Set of 2	5.00
3128-29	Slightly smaller than 3126-27, set of 2	5.00
3128-29b	Booklet pane of 5, Vendor Bklt, From booklet of 15	5.50
3128a-29a	(2) Mixed die-cut	5.00
3130-31	32¢ Pacific '97 Stagecoach & Ship, 3/13/97, New York, NY	2.50
3130-31	Set of Singles	4.00
3132	25¢ Jukebox (Linerless Coil) 3/14/97 NY,NY	1.90
3133	32¢ Flag over Porch (LInerless Coil) 3/14/97 NY,NY	1.90
3134	32¢ Thornton Wilder, 4/17/97, Hamden, Ct.	2.00
3135	32¢ Raoul Wallenberg, 4/24/97, Wash. DC	2.00
3136	32¢ The World of Dinosaurs, set of 15, 5/1/97	30.00
3136a-o	15 on 1 miniature pane	12.00
3137	32¢ Bugs Bunny, S/A, pane of 10, 5/22/97	11.00
3137a	32¢ Bugs Bunny, S/A Single, 5/22/97, Burbank CA	2.50
3137c	32¢ Bugs, single pane (right side) 5/22/97, Burbank,CA	5.00
3138	32¢ Bugs, Pane of 10 (9/1) imperf, 5/22/97, Burbank,CA	275.00
3138c	32¢ Bugs, Pane of 1, imperf, 5/22/97, Burbank,CA	250.00
3139	50¢ Pacific '97 - 1847 Franklin, S/S, 5/29/97, S.F., Ca.	24.00
3139a	50¢ single from S/S	2.00
3140	60¢ Pacific '97 - 1847 Washington, 5/30/97, S.F., Ca.	24.00
3140a	60¢ single from S/S	2.00
3141	32¢ Marshall Plan 6/4/97 Cambridge, MA	2.00
3142a-t	32¢ Classic American Aircraft,set of 20,7/19/97,Dayton, OH.	40.00
3142	Sheet of 20	15.50
3143-46	32¢ Legendary Football Coaches, att'd., 7/25/97	4.00
3146a	Set of 4 singles	8.00
3147-50	32¢ Legendary Football Coaches,set of 4 w/red bar	8.00
3147	32¢ Vince Lombardi,single, Green Bay WI,8/5/97	2.00
3148	32¢ Paul (Bear) Bryant, single, 8/7/97, Tuscaloosa, AL	2.00
3149	32¢ Glenn (Pop) Warner,single, 8/8/97, Phil. PA	2.00
3150	32¢ George Halas, single, 8/16/97, Chicago, IL	2.00
3151a-o	32¢ Classic American Dolls, set of 15, 7/28/97, Anaheim, Ca.	30.00

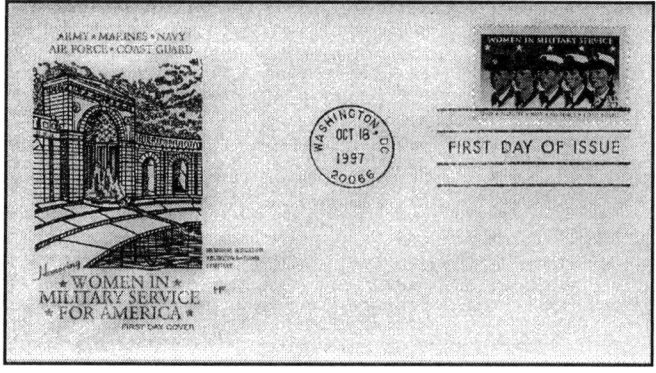

3174

1997 Commemoratives (continued)

Scott #	Description	Price
3151	Sheet of 15	12.00
3152	32¢ Humphrey Bogart, Legends of Hollywood series, 7/31/97	2.00
3153	32¢ Stars & Stripes Forever, 8/21/97, Milwaukee, WI	2.00
3154-57	Set of 4	8.00
3157a	32¢ Opera Singers, att'd., 9/10/97	4.25
3158-65	Set of 8	16.00
3165a	32¢ Conductors & Composers, Set of 2, 9/12 /97	11.00
3166	32¢ Padre Felix Varela 9/15/97 Miami, FL	2.00
3167	32¢ U.S. Air Force, 9/18/97	2.00
3172a	32¢ Classic Movie Monsters, att'd., 9/30/97	5.50
3168-72	Set of 5	10.00
3173	32¢ 1st Supersonic Flight, S/A, 10/14/97,Edwards AF Base,CA...2.00	
3174	32¢ Women in the Military, 10/18/97 Wash. DC	2.00
3175	32¢ Kwanzaa 10/22/97, LA,CA	2.25
3176	32¢ Madonna & Child, 10/27/97, Wash. DC	2.00
3176a	32¢ Madonna & Child, pane of 20, Wash. DC	15.00
3177	32¢ American Holly, S/A, 10/30/97,NY,NY	2.00
3177a	32¢ American Holly, S/A, Pane of 20, 10/30/97,NY,NY	15.50
3177b	32¢ American Holly, S/A, Pane of 6, 10/30/97,NY,NY	6.00
3177c	32¢ American Holly, S/A, Pane of 5&Label,10/30/97,NY,NY	5.50
3178	$3 Mars Rover Sojourner, S/S, 12/10/97,Pasadena,CA	10.00

1998 Commemoratives

Scott #	Description	Price
3179	32¢ Year of the Tiger, 1/5/98, Seattle WA	2.25
3180	32¢ Alpine Skiing, 1/22/98, Salt Lake City UT	2.00
3181	32¢ Madam C.J. Walker, 1/28/98, Ind., IN	2.25
3182	1900's 32¢ Celebrate the Century, Pane of 15,2/3/98, Wash.DC	12.50
3182a-o	1900's 32¢ Celebrate the Century, Set of 15,2/3/98, Wash.DC	27.50
3183	1910's 32¢ Celebrate the Century, Pane of 15,2/3/98, Wash.DC	12.50
3183a-o	1910's 32¢ Celebrate the Century, Set of 15,2/3/98, Wash.DC	27.50
3184	1920's 32¢ Celebrate the Century, Pane of 15, 5/28/98, Chicago, IL	12.50
3184a-o	1920's 32¢ Celebrate the Century, Set of 15, 5/28/98, Chicago, IL	27.50
3185	1930's 32¢ Celebrate the Century, Pane of 15, 9/10/98	12.50
3185a-o	1930's 32¢ Celebrate the Century, Set of 15, 9/10/98	27.50
3186	1940's 33¢ Celebrate the Century, Pane of 15, 2/18/99, Dobins AFB, GA	12.50
3186	0-1940's 33¢ Celebrate the Century Set of 15, 2/18/99	30.00
3187	1950's 33¢ Celebrate the Century, pane of 15, 5/26/99	12.50
3087a-o	Set of 15	30.00
3192	32¢ Remember the Maine, 2/15/98, Key West FL	2.00
3193-97	32¢ Flowering Trees, S/A, Set of 5, 3/19/98	10.00
3197a	32¢ Flowering Trees, S/A, Pane of 5, 3/19/98, NY,NY	5.50
3198-3202	32¢ Alexander Calder, S/A, Set of 5, 3/25/98, Wash, DC	10.00
3202a	32¢ Alexander Calder, S/A, Pane of 5, 3/25/98, Wash, DC	5.50
3203	32¢ Cinco de Mayo, S/A, 4/16/98, San Antonio, TX	2.00
3203	32¢ Cinco de Mayo, Joint Issue , with Mexican single only	3.00
3203	32¢ Cinco de Mayo, U.S./Mexican Cancel	5.00
3204	32¢ Tweety&Sylvester, S/S of 10, perf. 4/27/98, NY,NY	10.00
3204a	32¢ Tweety&Sylvester, single, perf. 4/27/98, NY, NY	2.00
3204c	32¢ Tweety&Sylvester, pane of 1, perf. 4/27/98, NY, NY	5.00
3205	32¢ Tweety&Sylvester, S/S of 10, imperf. 4/27/98, NY, NY	15.00
3205c	Tweety&Sylvester, imperf single	10.00
3205c	32¢ Tweety&Sylvester, pane of 1, imperf. 4/27/98, NY, NY	12.00
3205c	Tweety&Sylvester, perf and imperf pane on 1 Cover	20.00
3206	32¢ Wisconsin Statehood, 5/29/98, Madison WI	2.25
3207	5¢ Wetlands, Coil, 6/5/98, McLean, VA	1.90
3207a	5¢ Wetlands, S/A Coil Strips, 12/14/98 Wash. DC	2.00
3208	25¢ Diner, coil, 6/5/98, McLean, VA	2.20
3208a	25¢ Diner, coil, S/A Coil Pair, 9/30/98, Wash DC	3.50
3209	1¢-$2 Trans Mississippi Centennial 9 diff., 6/18/98, Anaheim,CA	25.00
3209a	1¢-$2 Trans Mississippi Centennial 9 diff., plus pair of $1.00 issue .	30.00
3209	1¢-$2 Trans Mississippi Centennial Full sheet, 6/18/98, Anaheim,CA	10.75
3209	1¢-$2 Trans Mississippi Centennial Full sheet, plus Pair of $1.00 issue	15.00
3210	$1 Cattle in Storm, pane of 9, 6/18/98, Anaheim,CA	16.50
3211	32¢ Berlin Airlift, 6/26/98, Berlin Station, APOAE	2.00
3215a	32¢ Folk Musicians, 7 designs attd., 6/26/98, (1) Wash. DC	4.25
3212-3215	32¢ Set of 4 Wash. DC	8.00

1998 Commemoratives (continued)

Scott #	Description	Price
3219a	32¢ Gospel Singers, att'd., 7/15/98, New Orleans, LA	5.00
3216-19	32¢ Gospel Singers, Set of 4 7/15/98,	10.00
3221	32¢ Stephen Vincent Benet, 7/22/98, Harper's Ferry, WV	2.00
3225a	32¢ Tropical Birds, 7/29/98, Puerto Rico. Bof 4	5.50
3222-25	32¢ Tropical Birds, 7/29/98, Set of 4	10.00
3226	32¢ Alfred Hitchcock, 8/3/98, LA, CA	2.00
3234a	32¢ Bright Eyes, strip of 5, 8/20/98, Boston, MA	5.50
3230-34	32¢ Bright Eyes, Set of 5, 8/20/98,	10.00
3220	32¢ Spanish Settlement of SW 1598, 7/11/98,Espana, NM	2.00
3227	32¢ Organ & Tissue Donation, 8/5/98, Columbus, OH	2.00
3228	(10¢) Bicycle, S/A Coil, 8/14/98, Wash. DC (Amer. Transportation)	1.90
3229	(10¢) Bicycle, W/A Coil, 8/14/98, Wash. DC (Amer. Transportation)	1.90
3228-29	(10¢) Bicycle W/A & S/A coil pairs on one cover	2.20
3236	32¢ Four Centuries of American Art, pane of 20 8/27/98, Santa Clara, CA	15.50
3236a-t	32¢ Four Centuries of American Art, (20), 8/27/98, Santa Clara, CA	40.00
3235	32¢ Klondike Gold Rush, 8/21/98, Nome, Alaska	2.00
3237	32¢ Ballet, 9/16/98, NY, NY	2.00
3242a	32¢ Space Discovery, Strip of 5, 10/1/98	2.00
3238-42	32¢ Space Discovery, Set of 5, 10/1/98	10.00
3243	32¢ Giving & Sharing, 10/7/98, Atlanta GA	2.00
3244	32¢ Madonna and Child, 10/15/98, Wash. DC Kennedy Space Center, FL	5.50
3245-48	32¢ Wreath Set of 4 Vending Bklt sgls, S/A, 10/15/98, Christmas, MI	8.00
3248a	Pane of 4	4.00
3248b	Pane of 5	4.50
3248c	Pane of 6	5.25
3249-52	32¢ Wreathes, set of 4 sheet singles, S/A, (larger than vending) S/A, 10/15/98, Christmas, MI	8.00
3249-52	32¢ Wreathes, attd.	4.00
3252b	32¢ Wreathes, Bklt of 20	15.50
3257	(1¢) Make up Rate – Weathervane, A.P., 11/9/98, Troy, NY	1.90
3258	(1¢) Make up Rate – Weathervane, BCA, 11/9/98, Troy, NY	1.90
3257,3258	On 1	2.00
3259	22¢ Uncle Sam, S/A from sheet, 11/9/98, Troy, NY	2.00
3260	(33¢) "H" Hat, W/A from sheet, 11/9/98, Troy, NY	2.00
3261	$3.20 Space Shuttle, Priority Mail, 11/9/98, Troy, NY	8.00
3262	$11.75 Piggyback Space Shuttle, Express Mail, 11/19/98, NY, NY .	30.00
3263	22¢ Uncle Sam, coil, pair, S/A, 11/9/98, Troy, NY	2.00
3264	(33¢) "H" Hat, Coil, 11/9/98, Troy, NY	2.00
3265	(33¢) "H" Hat, S/A, single, 11/9/98, Troy, NY	2.00
3266	(33¢) "H" Hat, S/A (w/gaps between stamps) 11-9-98, Troy, NY	2.00
3267	(33¢) "H" Hat, Folded Bklt, Pane of 10, 10/9/98, Troy, NY	8.50
3268	(33¢) "H" Hat, Convertible Bklt, Pane of 10, 10/9/98, Troy, NY	8.50
3268a	Single from Convertible Pane of 10	3.00
3268b	Convertible Pane of 20	15.50
3269	(33¢) "H" Hat, ATM, Pane 18, 11/9/98, Troy, NY	14.00
3269a	Single from ATM Pane 18	3.00
3270	(10¢) Eagle & Shield, W/A, 12/14/98, Wash. DC	1.90
3271	(10¢) Eagle & Shield, S/A Coil, Presort; 12/14/98, Wash. DC	1.90
3270-71	(10¢) Eagle & Shield, Both W/A & S/A on 1	2.20

1999 Commemoratives

Scott #	Description	Price
3272	33¢ Year of the Rabbit, 1/5/99, LA, CA	2.25
3273	33¢ Malcolm X, BH Series, 1/20/99NY, NY	2.50
2374	33¢ Love, S/A, 1/28/99, Loveland, CO	1.90
3274a	33¢ Love, Bklt of 20, 1/28/99	15.50
3275	55¢ Love, S/A, 1/28/99, Loveland, CO	2.25
3276	33¢ Hospice Care, 2/9/99, Largo, FL	2.25
3277	33¢ Flag & City, Single W/A sheet, 2/25/99, Orlando, FL	1.90
3278	33¢ Flag & City, S/A Sheet, 2/25/99, Orlando, FL	1.90
3278 a-c	33¢ Flag & City, (3) Convertible Bklts, 2/25/99, Orlando, FL	10.50
3278d	33¢ Flag & City, Convertible Bklt of 10	8.50
3278e	33¢ Flag & City, Convertible Bklt of 20	15.50
3279	33¢ Flag & City, S/A Bklt Stamp, 2/25/99, Orlando, FL	1.90
3279a	33¢ Flag & City, S/A Bklt Pane of 10, 2/25/99, Orlando, FL	1.90
3280	33¢ Flag & City, W/A coil, 2/25/99, Orlando, FL	1.90
3281	33¢ Flag & City, S/A Coil Square die-cut corners, 2/25/99, Orlando, FL	1.90
3282	33¢ Flag & City, S/A Coil Rounded die-cut corners, 2/25/99, Orlando, FL	1.90
3283s	33¢ Flag & Chalkboard, S/A, Cleveland, OH, 3/13/99	2.00
3283	33¢ Flag & Chalkboard, S/A, Pane of 18 OH, 3/13/99	14.50
3286	33¢ Irish Immigration, 2/26/99, Boston, MA	1.90
3286	33¢ Irish Immigration, 2/26/99, Combo with Ireland	2.75
3287	33¢ Alfred Hunt & Lynn Fontanne, 3/2/99	1.90

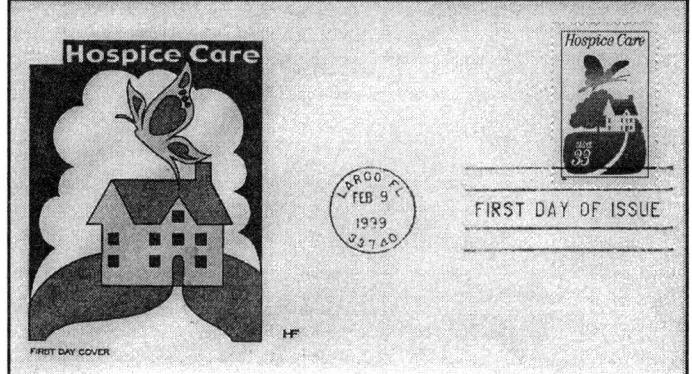

3286

3306a

Scott #	Description	Price
3292	33¢ Arctic Animals, strip of 5, 3/12/99, Barrow, AK	5.50
3288-92	33¢ Arctic Animals, set of 5, 3/12/99, Barrow, AK	10.00
3293	33¢ Sonora Dessert, pane of 10, 4/6/99	10.00
3293a-j	33¢ Sonora Dessert, set of 10, 4/6/99	25.00
3297a	33¢ Fruits & Berries, S/A Pane of 20, 4/10/99	15.50
3294-97	33¢ Fruits & Berries, S/A set of 4, 4/10/99	8.00
3294-97	33¢ Fruits & Berries on one cover	5.50
3301a	33¢ Fruits & Berries, S/A vend. Bklt of 15, 4/10/99	12.50
3302-5	33¢ Fruits & Berries, set of 4 singles from coil, 4/10/99	8.00
3306	33¢ Daffy Duck, S/A Imperf Pane of 10, 4/16/99, LA, CA	15.00
3306a	33¢ Daffy Duck, S/A Imperf single, 4/16/99, LA, CA	6.00
3306c	33¢ Daffy Duck, S/A Imperf Pane (right side), 4/16/99, LA, CA	10.00
3307	33¢ Daffy Duck, S/A Perf Pane of 10, 4/16/99, LA, CA	15.00
3307a	33¢ Daffy Duck, S/A Perf Single, 4/16/99, LA, CA	2.50
3307c	33¢ Daffy Duck, S/A Perf Pane (right side), 4/16/99	6.00
3306c & 3307c	33¢ Daffy Duck combo	15.00
3308	33¢ Ayn Rand, 4/22/99	1.90
3309	33¢ Cinco de Mayo, 4/27/99	1.90
3313a	33¢ Tropical Flowers (1), 5/1/99	5.50
3313b	33¢ Tropical Flowers Bklt Pane of 8 plus label	7.50
3310-13	Set of 4	10.00
3314	33¢ John & William Bartram, 5/18/99,	1.90
3315	33¢ Prostrate Cancer Awarenedss, 5/28/99, Austin, TX	1.90
....	33¢ Cal. Gold Rush, 6/18/99, Sacremento, CA	1.90
....	2¢ Woodpecker, coil, 6/22/99	1.90
....	33¢ Aquarium Fish, 6/24/99, Anaheim, CA	5.50
....	Set of 4	10.00
....	33¢ Extreme Sports, 6/25/99, SF., CA	5.50
....	Set of 4	10.00
....	33¢ American Glass, 6/29/99, Corning, NY	5.50
....	Set of 4	10.00
....	33¢ James Cagney, 7/17/99, LA, CA	1.90
....	55¢ Justin S. Morill, S/A, 7/17/99, Strafford, VT	2.00
....	40¢ Rio Garde, 7/30/99, Strafford, VT	1.90
....	55¢ Bill Mitchell, 7/30/99, Strafford, VT	2.00
....	33¢ Coral Rose, S/A, 8/13/99, Ind., IN	1.90
....	33¢ Honoring Those Who Served, 8/16/99, Kansas City, MO	1.90
....	33¢ Trains (1), 8/26/99, Cleveland, OH	5.50
....	33¢ Trains, set of 5	10.50
....	33¢ 1960's 33¢ Celebrate the Century	
	Pane of 15, 8/ /99	12.50
....	33¢ Set of 15	30.00

Semi-Postal Stamps

B1	1st Class Rate+8¢ Breast Cancer Research,8/13/98, Wash,DC	2.25

1901

The listing below omits prices on FDC's which are extremely rare or where sufficient pricing information is not available. *Due to market volatility, prices are subject to change without notice.* **Prices are for unaddressed FDC's with common cachets and cancels which do not obscure the Pl. #. Strips of 3 must have a plate # on the center stamp.**

Scott #	Description	Pl# Pr.	Pl# Str of 3
1891	18¢ Flag 4/24/81		
	Pl# 1	75.00	120.00
	Pl# 2	180.00	340.00
	Pl# 3	260.00	420.00
	Pl# 4	160.00	280.00
	Pl# 5	125.00	...
1895	20¢ Flag 12/17/81		
	Pl# 1	17.50	36.00
	Pl# 2	100.00	160.00
	Pl# 3	160.00	320.00
1897	1¢ Omnibus 8/19/83		
	Pl # 1,2	7.00	10.50
1897A	2¢ Locomotive 5/20/82		
	Pl# 3,4	10.50	17.00
1898	3¢ Handcar 3/25/83		
	Pl# 1,2,3,4	8.00	17.00
1898A	4¢ Stagecoach 8/19/82		
	Pl# 1,2,3,4	8.00	16.00
1899	5¢ Motorcycle 10/10/83		
	Pl# 1,2	9.00	13.50
	Pl# 3,4	...	...
1900	5.2¢ Sleigh 3/21/83		
	Pl# 1,2	13.50	27.00
1900a	Pl# 1,2	...	...
1901	5.9¢ Bicycle 2/17/82		
	Pl# 3,4	13.50	22.50
1901a	Pl# 3,4	...	...
1902	7.4¢ Baby Buggy 4/7/84		
	Pl# 2	8.50	18.00
1903	9.3¢ Mail Wagon 12/15/81		
	Pl# 1,2	18.00	34.00
	Pl# 3,4	...	...
1904	10.9¢ Hansom Cab 3/26/82		
	Pl# 1,2	14.50	32.50
1904a	Pl# 1,2	...	...
1905	11¢ Caboose 2/3/84, Pl# 1	13.50	32.50
1905a	11¢ Caboose, "B" Press 9/25/91		
	Pl#2	...	...
1906	17¢ Electric Car 6/25/82		
	Pl# 1,2	14.50	27.00
1907	18¢ Surrey 5/18/81		
	Pl# 1	27.00	...
	Pl# 2	17.50	40.00
	Pl# 3,4,7,9,10	...	...
	Pl# 5	100.00	...
	Pl# 6,8	100.00	...
1908	20¢ Fire Pumper 12/10/81		
	Pl# 1,7,8	...	...
	Pl# 2	150.00	240.00
	Pl# 3,4	13.50	36.00
	Pl# 5,6	100.00	175.00
2005	20¢ Consumer 4/27/82		
	Pl# 1,2,3,4	22.50	...
2112	(22¢) "D" Coil 2/1/85		
	Pl# 1,2	8.50	16.00
2115	22¢ Flag over Capitol 3/29/85		
	Pl# 1	32.50	57.50
	Pl# 2	13.50	20.00
2115b	22¢ Test Coil 5/23/87		
	Pl# T1	...	11.00
2123	3.4¢ School Bus 6/8/85		
	Pl# 1,2	5.50	8.50
2124	4.9¢ Buckboard 6/21/85		
	Pl# 3,4	6.00	11.50
2125	5.5¢ Star Route Truck 11/1/86		
	Pl# 1	6.00	11.50
2125a	Pl# 1	...	36.00
2126	6¢ Tricycle 5/6/85		
	Pl# 1	5.50	8.50

Scott #	Description	Pl# Pr.	Pl# Str of 3
2126a	Pl# 1	...	...
2127	7.1¢ Tractor Coil 2/6/87, Pl# 1	6.50	11.50
2127a	Pl# 1	...	32.50
2127a	7.1¢ Zip + 4 Pl# 1 5/26/89	...	6.50
2128	8.3¢ Ambulance 6/21/86		
	Pl# 1,2	6.50	11.00
2128a	Pl# 1,2	...	...
2129	8.5¢ Tow Truck 1/24/87		
	Pl# 1	5.50	8.50
2129a	Pl# 1	...	15.50
2130	10.1¢ Oil Wagon 4/18/85		
	Pl# 1	6.50	10.50
2130a	10.1¢ Red Prec. Pl# 2 6/27/88	...	7.50
2131	11¢ Stutz Bearcat 6/11/85		
	Pl# 3,4	...	11.00
2132	12¢ Stanley Steamer 4/2/85		
	Pl# 1,2	6.50	11.00
2132a	Pl# 1	...	...
2133	12.5¢ Pushcart 4/18/85		
	Pl# 1	6.50	11.00
2134	14¢ Iceboat 3/23/85		
	Pl# 1,2	8.50	13.50
2135	17¢ Dog Sled 8/20/86		
	Pl# 2	6.50	10.50
2136	25¢ Bread Wagon 11/22/86		
	Pl# 1	6.50	11.00
2149	18¢ GW Monument 11/6/85		
	Pl# 1112,3333	17.50	32.50
2149a	Pl# 11121	40.00	...
	Pl# 33333	40.00	...
2150	21.1¢ Pre-Sort 10/22/85		
	Pl# 111111	13.50	22.50
2150a	Pl# 111111	35.00	...
2225	1¢ Omnibus Re-engraved 11/26/86		
	Pl# 1	5.50	11.00
2226	2¢ Locomotive Re-engraved 3/6/87		
	Pl# 1	...	7.00
2228	4¢ Stagecoach, "B" Press 8/15/86 (eku)		
	Pl# 1	...	260.00
2231	8.3¢ Ambulance, "B" Press 8/29/86 (eku)		
	Pl# 1	...	...
2252	3¢ Conestoga Wagon 2/29/88		
	Pl# 1	...	6.00
2253	5¢ Milk Wagon 9/25/87		
	Pl# 1	...	6.00
2254	5.3¢ Elevator 9/16/88		
	Pl# 1	...	6.00
2255	7.6¢ Carreta 8/30/88		
	Pl# 1	...	6.50
2256	8.4¢ Wheelchair 8/12/88		
	Pl# 1	...	6.50
2257	10¢ Canal Boat 4/11/87		
	Pl# 1	...	7.50
2258	13¢ Patrol Wagon 10/29/88		
	Pl# 1	...	6.50
2259	13.2¢ Coal Car 7/19/88		
	Pl# 1	...	6.50
2260	15¢ Tugboat 7/12/88		
	Pl# 1	...	6.50
2261	16.7¢ Popcorn Wagon 7/7/88		
	Pl# 1	...	6.50
2262	17.5¢ Racing Car 9/25/87		
	Pl# 1	...	7.50
2263	20¢ Cable Car 10/28/88		
	Pl# 1	...	6.50
	Pl# 2	...	60.00
2264	20.5¢ Fire Engine 9/28/88		
	Pl# 1	...	6.50
2265	21¢ Railroad Mail Car 8/16/88		
	Pl# 1	...	6.50
	Pl# 2	...	...
2266	24.1¢ Tandem Bicycle 10/26/88		
	Pl# 1	...	6.50
2279	(25¢) "E" & Earth 3/22/88		
	Pl# 1111,1222	...	6.50
	Pl# 1211	...	8.50
	Pl# 2222	...	22.50

2259/1

Scott #	2005 Description	Pl# Pr.	Pl# Str of 3
2280	25¢ Flag over Yosemite 5/20/88		
	Pl# 1,2	...	8.50
	Pl# 3,4	...	125.00
2280v	Pre-Phosphor Paper 2/14/89		
	Pl# 5	...	16.00
	Pl# 6,9	...	32.50
	Pl# 7,8	...	7.50
	Pl# 10	...	...
2281	25¢ Honeybee 9/2/88		
	Pl# 1	...	8.50
	Pl# 2	...	27.00
2451	4¢ Steam Carriage 1/25/91, Pl# 1	...	5.50
2452	5¢ Circus Wagon 8/31/90, Pl# 1	...	5.50
2452B	5¢ Circus Wagon, Gravure 12/8/92, Pl# A1,A2 ...	...	5.50
2452D	5¢ Circus Wagon, SV 3/20/95, Pl# S1	...	5.50
2453	5¢ Canoe 5/25/91, Pl# 1	...	5.50
2454	5¢ Canoe, Gravure Print 10/22/91, Pl# S11	...	5.50
2457	10¢ Tractor Trailer 5/25/91, Pl# 1	...	5.50
2463	20¢ Cog Railroad 6/9/95, Pl#1	...	6.50
2464	23¢ Lunch Wagon 4/12/91		
	Pl# 2	...	7.50
	Pl# 3	...	6.50
2466	32¢ Ferryboat 6/2/95		
	Pl# 2-3	...	6.50
	Pl# 4	...	13.50
	Pl# 5	...	32.50
2468	$1.00 Seaplane 4/20/90, Pl# 1	...	8.50
2480	29¢ Pine Cone (self-adhesive)11/5/93, Pl# B1	...	8.50
2492	32¢ Rose (self-adhesive) 7/8/95, Pl# V11111	...	8.50
2495A	32¢ Peaches and Pears (self-adhesive) 7/8/95		
	Pl# V11111	...	8.50
2518	(29¢) "F" & Flower 1/22/91		
	Pl# 1111,1222,2222,1211	...	8.50
	Pl# 2211	...	22.50
2523	29¢ Flag over Mt. Rushmore 3/29/91, Pl# 1-7	6.50	...
2523A	29¢ Mt. Rushmore, Gravure Print 7/4/91		
	Pl# 11111	...	6.50
2525	29¢ Flower, rouletted 8/16/91, Pl# S1111	...	6.50
2526	29¢ Flower, perforated 3/3/92, Pl# 2222	6.50	...
2529	(19¢) Fishing Boat 8/8/91		
	Pl# 1111,1212	...	6.50
2529c	(19¢) Fishing Boat 6/25/94, Pl# 11	...	6.50
2598	29¢ Statue of Liberty (self-adhesive) 6/24/94		
	Pl# D1111	...	8.50
2604	10¢ Eagle & Shield, **ABNCo** 12/13/91	...	5.50
	Any Pl# (except A12213 & A32333).....................	...	5.50
	Pl# A12213	...	24.00
	Pl# A32333	...	125.00
2605	10¢ Eagle & Shield, **BEP** 5/29/93, Pl# 11111	...	5.50
2606	10¢ Eagle & Shield, **SV**, Pl# S11111	...	5.50
2607	23¢ Flag, First Class pre-sort 9/27/91	...	6.50
2608	23¢ "USA" First Class pre-sort **ABNCo**, 7/21/92		
	Pl# A1111, A2222	...	6.50
2608A	23¢ "USA" First Class pre-sort **BEP**, 10/9/92		
	Pl# 1111	...	6.50
2608B	23¢ "USA" First Class pre-sort **SV**, 5/14/93		
	Pl# S111	...	6.50
2609	29¢ Flag over White House 4/23/92		
	Pl# 1-7	...	5.25
	Pl# 8	...	...
2799-2809	29¢ Christmas (self-adhesive) 10/28/93		
	Pl# V1111111	...	8.50
2813	29¢ Love (self-adhesive) 1/27/94		
	Pl# B1	...	8.50
2873	29¢ Santa (self-adhesive) 10/20/94		
	Pl# V1111	...	8.50
2886	(32¢) "G" Flag (self-adhesive) 12/13/94		
	Pl# V11111	...	6.50
2888	(32¢) "G" Flag 12/13/94, Pl# S11111	...	6.50

Scott #	2266 Description	Pl# Pr.	Pl# Str of 3
2889	(32¢) "G" Flag 12/13/94		
	Pl# 1111, 2222	...	6.50
2890	(32¢) "G" Flag 12/13/94		
	Pl# A1111, A1112, A1113, A1211, A1212,		
	A1222, A1311, A1313, A1314, A1324, A1417,		
	A1433, A2211, A2212, A2213, A2214, A2223,		
	A2313, A3113, A3114, A3315, A3323, A3423,		
	A3324, A3426, A3433, A3435, A3536, A4426,		
	A4427, A5327, A5417, A5427, A5437	...	8.50
2890	(32¢) "G" Flag 12/13/94 ,Pl# A4435	...	200.00
2891	(32¢) "G" Flag 12/13/94, Pl# S1111	...	6.50
2892	(32¢) "G" Flag 12/13/94, Pl# S1111,S2222	...	6.50
2893	(32¢) "G" Flag 12/13/94, Pl# A11111, A21111	...	6.50
2902	5¢ Butte 3/10/95, Pl# S111	...	5.50
2902b	5¢ ButteSV, self-adhesive 6/15/96		
	Pl# S111	...	5.50
2903	5¢ Mountains, BEP, 3/16/96, Pl# 11111	...	5.50
2904	5¢ Mountains,SV, 3/16/96, Pl# S11	...	5.50
2904a	5¢ Mountains,SA 6/15/96		
	Pl# V222222,V333333,V333323		
	V333342,V333343	...	5.50
	Pl# S11111	...	6.50
2911	25¢ Juke Box, BEP 3/17/95		
	Pl# S111111	...	6.50
2905	10¢ Auto, 3/10/95, Pl # S111	...	6.50
2906	10¢ Auto,SA 6/15/96, Pl # S111	...	5.50
2907	10¢ Eagle & Shield, SA 5/21/96, Pl # S1111	...	5.50
2908	15¢ Auto Tail Fin, BEP, 3/17/95, Pl# 11111	...	6.50
2909	15¢ Auto Tail Fin, SV, 3/17/95, Pl# S11111	...	6.50
2912	25¢ Juke Box, 3/17/95, Pl# 111	...	6.50
2912a	25¢ Juke Box,SV,SA 6/15/96, Pl# S11111	...	6.50
2912b	25¢ Juke Box, BEP,SA 6/15/96, Pl# 11111	...	6.50
2913	32¢ Flag over Porch 4/18/95		
	Pl# 11111,22222,33333,44444,S11111	...	6.50
	Pl# 22221	...	13.50
	Pl# 45444,66646	...	30.00
2914	32¢ Flag over Porch SV 5/19/95, Pl# S11111	...	8.50
2915a	32¢ Flag over Porch BEP (self-adhesive) 5/21/96		
	Pl# 55555,66666,78777	...	8.50
	Pl# 87888	...	50.00
	Pl# 87898,88888	...	8.50
	Pl# 88898	...	500.00
	Pl# 89878	...	8.50
	Pl# 89888	...	50.00
	Pl# 89898	...	17.50
	Pl# 97898,99999	...	8.50
2915b	32¢ Flag over Porch SV (self-adhesive) 6/15/96		
	Pl# S11111	...	8.50
2915c	32¢ Flag over Porch BEP (self-adhesive) 5/21/96		
	serpentine die-cut Pl# 66666	...	22.50
3017	32¢ Christmas (self-adhesive) 9/30/95		
	Pl# V1111	...	8.50
3018	32¢ Christmas Angel (self-adhesive) 10/31/95		
	Pl# B1111	...	8.50
3044	1¢ Kestrel 1/20/96, Pl# 1111	...	5.50
3053	20¢ Blue Jay (self-adhesive)8/2/96, Pl# S111	...	6.50

OFFICIAL STAMPS

		Pl# Pr.	Pl# Str of 3
O135	20¢ Official, Pl# 1	25.00	75.00
O139	(22¢) "D" Official, Pl# 1....................................	30.00	75.00

COMPUTER VENDED POSTAGE

		Pl# Pr.	Pl# Str of 3
CV31	29¢ Variable Rate Coil 8/20/92		
	Pl# 1	...	7.00
CV31	29¢ Variable Rate 8/20/92, 1st Print		
	Pl# 1	...	7.00
CV31b	29¢ Variable Rate 8/20/92, 2nd Print		
	Pl# 1	...	22.50
CV32	29¢ Variable Rate 8/20/92		
	Pl# A11	...	7.00

C23

Cacheted prices are for FDC's with common printed cachets.
From #C4 - C31, FDC's will usually be addressed.
Prices and Dates for #C1-3 are for First Flight Covers, AND FDC's.

Scott #	Description	Uncacheted	Cacheted
C1	6¢ Jenny 12/10/18 Washington, DC FDC	25000.00	...
C1	6¢ Jenny 12/16/18 NYC; Phila.,PA; DC FFC	2500.00	...
C2	16¢ Jenny 7/11/18 Washington, DC FDC	25000.00	...
C2	16¢ Jenny 7/15/18 NYC; Phila.,PA; DC FFC	800.00	...
C3	24¢ Jenny 5/15/18 NYC; Phila.,PA; DC FFC	800.00	...
C4	8¢ Propeller 8/15/23 DC	350.00	...
C5	16¢ Air Service Emblem 8/17/23 DC	525.00	...
C6	24¢ DeHavilland Biplane 8/21/23 DC	650.00	...
C7	10¢ Map 2/13/26 DC	80.00	...
	Chicago, IL	90.00	...
	Detroit, MI	90.00	...
	Cleveland, OH	120.00	...
	Dearborn, MI	120.00	...
	Unofficial city	175.00	...
C8	15¢ Map 9/18/26 DC	90.00	...
C9	20¢ Map 1/25/27 DC	100.00	...
	New York, NY	110.00	...
	1st Albert E. Gorham cachet	...	250.00
C10	10¢ Lindbergh 6/18/27 DC	30.00	175.00
	St. Louis, MO	30.00	175.00
	Detroit, MI	40.00	175.00
	Little Falls, MN	40.00	175.00
	Air Mail Field, Chicago, unofficial	150.00	...
	Unofficial city (other than AMF Chicago)	175.00	...
	1st Milton Mauck cachet	...	250.00
C10a	10¢ **Booklet Single** 5/26/28 DC	100.00	175.00
	Booklet Sgl., Cleveland Midwest Phil. Sta.	100.00	175.00
	#C10a sgl. & 645 Cleveland Midwest Sta	150.00	200.00
C10a	10¢ **Booklet Pane of 3** 5/26/28 DC	875.00	1000.00
	B. Pane of 3, Cleveland Midwest Sta.	825.00	1000.00
	#C10a & 645 on one FDC, Clev. Midwst.	900.00	1100.00
	Booklet Pane w/o tab, DC or Cleveland	425.00	750.00
C11	5¢ Beacon, pair 7/25/28 DC	60.00	250.00
	Single on FDC	200.00	...
	Single on FDC with postage due	250.00	...
	Unofficial city (pair)	250.00	...
	Predate 7/24/28	1500.00	...
C12	5¢ Winged Globe 2/10/30 DC	15.00	90.00
C13	65¢ Graf Zeppelin 4/19/30 DC	1100.00	2500.00
	On flight cover, any date	250.00	...
C14	$1.30 Graf Zeppelin 4/19/30 DC	800.00	2500.00
	On flight cover, any date	400.00	...
C15	$2.60 Graf Zeppelin 4/19/30 DC	950.00	2500.00
	On flight cover, any date	600.00	...
C13-15	Graf Zeppelin, cplt. set on one cover	16000.00	...
	Complete set on one Flight Cover, any date	2400.00	...
C16	5¢ Winged Globe, Rotary 8/19/31 DC	175.00	...
C17	8¢ Winged Globe 9/26/32 DC	16.50	50.00
	Combo with UC7	60.00	...
C18	50¢ Zeppelin 10/2/33 New York, NY	175.00	250.00
	Akron, OH 10/4/33	250.00	400.00
	DC 10/5/33	225.00	425.00
	Miami, FL 10/6/33	200.00	325.00
	Chicago, IL 10/7/33	250.00	400.00
	On flight cover, any date	110.00	150.00
C19	6¢ Winged Globe 6/30/34 Baltimore, MD	200.00	600.00
	New York, NY	1250.00	1750.00
	First Day of Rate 7/1/34 DC	20.00	40.00
	Combo with UC3	60.00	...

1935-39

C20	25¢ China Clipper 11/22/35 DC		45.00
	San Francisco, CA		45.00
C21	20¢ China Clipper 2/15/37 DC		55.00
C22	50¢ China Clipper 2/15/37 DC		60.00
C21-22	China Clipper on one cover		125.00
C23	6¢ Eagle Holding Shield 5/14/38 Dayton, OH		17.50
	St. Petersburg, FL		17.50
C24	30¢ Winged Globe 5/16/39 New York, NY		60.00

Scott #	Description	Price
C25	6¢ Plane 6/25/41 DC	7.50
C25a	Booklet Pane of 3 (3/18/43) DC	30.00
	Booklet single	10.00
C26	8¢ Plane 3/21/44 DC	6.00
C27	10¢ Plane 8/15/41 Atlantic City, NJ	9.00
C28	15¢ Plane 8/19/41 Baltimore, MD	9.00
C29	20¢ Plane 8/27/41 Philadelphia, PA	12.00
C30	30¢ Plane 9/25/41 Kansas City, MO	20.00
C31	50¢ Plane 10/29/41 St. Louis, MO	30.00
C25-31,C25a	Transport Plane set of 8 covers	95.00

From #C32 - Date, prices are for unaddressed FDC's & common cachets.

1946-59

Scott #	Description	Price
C32	5¢ DC-4 Skymaster 9/25/46 DC	1.75
C33	5¢ Small Plane (DC-4) 3/26/47 DC	1.75
C34	10¢ Pan Am. Building 8/30/47 DC	1.75
C35	15¢ New York Skyline 8/20/47 NY, NY	2.00
C36	25¢ Bay Bridge 7/30/47 San Francisco, CA	2.50
C37	5¢ Small Plane, coil 1/15/48 DC	1.75
C38	5¢ NY City Jubilee 7/31/48 New York, NY	2.00
C39	6¢ DC-4 Skymaster 1/18/49 DC	1.75
C39a	Booklet Pane of 6 11/18/49 NY, NY	12.00
C39as	Booklet Pane, single,	4.00
C40	6¢ Alexandria 5/11/49 Alexandria, VA	2.00
C41	6¢ DC-4 Skymaster, coil 8/25/49 DC	1.75
C42	10¢ Post Office Bldg. 11/18/49 New Orleans, LA	1.75
C43	15¢ Globe & Doves 10/7/49 Chicago, IL	3.00
C44	25¢ Boeing 11/30/49 Seattle, WA	4.00
C45	6¢ Wright Brothers 12/17/49 Kitty Hawk, NC	3.00
C46	80¢ Diamond Head 3/26/52 Honolulu, HI	15.00
C47	6¢ Powered Flight 5/29/53 Dayton, OH	2.50
C48	4¢ Eagle in Flight 9/3/54 Phila., PA	1.75
C49	6¢ Air Force 8/1/57 DC	2.00
C50	5¢ Eagle 7/31/58 Colorado Springs, CO	1.75
C51	7¢ Blue Jet 7/31/58 Philadelphia, PA	1.75
C51a	Booklet Pane of 6 7/31/58 San Antonio, TX	7.00
C51as	Booklet Pane, single,	4.00
C52	7¢ Blue Jet, coil 7/31/58 Miami, FL	1.75
C53	7¢ Alaska 1/3/59 Juneau, AK	2.00
C54	7¢ Balloon 8/17/59 Lafayette, IN	2.00
C55	7¢ Hawaii Sthd. 8/21/59 Honolulu, HI	2.00
C56	10¢ Pan Am Games 8/27/59 Chicago, IL	2.00

1959-68

Scott #	Description	Price
C57	10¢ Liberty Bell 6/10/60 Miami, FL	1.75
C58	15¢ Statue of Liberty 11/20/59 NY, NY	1.75
C59	25¢ Lincoln 4/22/60 San Francisco, CA	1.75
C59a	Luminescent 12/29/66 DC	60.00
C60	7¢ Red Jet 8/12/60 Arlington, VA	1.75
C60a	Booklet Pane of 6 8/19/60 St. Louis, MO	8.00
C60as	Booklet Pane, single,	4.00
C61	7¢ Red Jet, coil 10/22/60 Atlantic City, NJ	1.75
C62	13¢ Liberty Bell 6/28/61 New York, NY	1.75
C62a	Luminescent 2/15/67 DC	60.00
C63	15¢ Statue of Liberty 1/31/61 Buffalo, NY	1.75
C63a	Luminescent 1/11/67 DC	60.00
C64	8¢ Jet over Capitol, single 12/5/62 DC	1.75
C64a	Luminescent 8/1/63 Dayton, OH	1.75
C64b	Booklet Pane of 5 12/5/62 DC	1.75
C64bs	Booklet Pane, single,	4.00
C65	8¢ Jet over Capitol, 12/5/62 DC, single	1.75
C65a	Luminescent 1/14/65 New Orleans, LA	60.00
C66	15¢ Montgomery Blair 5/3/63 Silver Springs, MD	2.50
C67	6¢ Bald Eagle 7/12/63 Boston, MA	1.75
C67a	Luminescent 2/15/67 DC	60.00
C68	8¢ Amelia Earhart 7/24/63 Atchinson, KS	4.00
C69	8¢ Robert Goddard 10/5/64 Roswell, NM	2.50
C70	8¢ Alaska Purchase 3/30/67 Sitka, AK	2.00
C71	20¢ Columbia Jays 4/26/67 New York, NY	2.50
C72	10¢ 50-Star Runway 1/5/68 San Fran., CA	1.75
C72	Precancelled, 5/19/71, Wash, DC	75.00
C72b	Bklt. Pane of 8 1/5/68 San Fran., CA	3.00
C72bs	Booklet Pane, single,	4.00
C72c	Bklt. Pane of 5 1/6/68 DC	125.00
C73	10¢ 50-Star Runway, coil 1/5/68 San Francisco, CA	1.75

C46

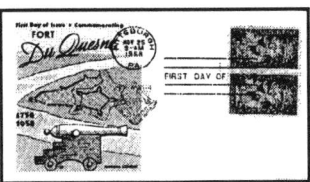

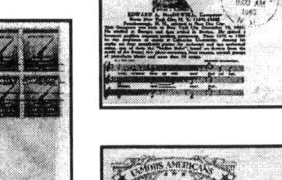

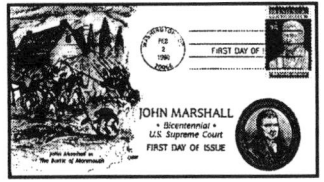

AIR MAIL FIRST DAY COVERS

C91-92

Scott #	Description	Price
	1969-91	
C74	10¢ Jenny 5/15/68 DC	2.00
C75	20¢ "USA" & Jet 11/22/68 New York, NY	1.75
C76	10¢ First Man on Moon 9/9/69 DC	5.00
C77	9¢ Delta Plane 5/15/71 Kitty Hawk, NC	1.75
C78	11¢ Jet Silhouette 5/7/71 Spokane, WA	1.75
C78	Precancel, 5/19/71, Wash, DC	75.00
C78a	Booklet Pane of 4 5/7/71 Spokane, WA	3.00
C78as	Booklet Pane Single	4.00
C79	13¢ Winged Envelope 11/16/73 NY, NY	1.75
C79	Precancel, 3/4/74, Wash, DC	75.00
C79a	Bklt. Pane of 5 12/27/73 Chicago, IL	3.00
C79as	Blklt.Pane, single	4.00
C80	17¢ Statue of Liberty 7/13/71 Lakehurst, NJ	1.75
C81	21¢ "USA" & Jet 5/21/71 DC	1.75
C82	11¢ Jet Silhouette, coil 5/7/71 Spokane, WA	1.75
C83	13¢ Winged Envelope, coil 12/27/73 Chicago, IL	1.75
C84	11¢ City of Refuge 5/3/72 Honaunau, HI	1.75
C85	11¢ Olympics 8/17/72 DC	1.75
C86	11¢ Electronics 7/10/73 New York, NY	1.75
C87	18¢ Statue of Liberty 1/11/74 Hampstead, NY	1.75
C88	26¢ Mt. Rushmore 1/2/74 Rapid City, SD	1.75
C89	25¢ Plane and Globe 1/2/76 Honolulu, HI	1.75
C90	31¢ Plane, Globe & Flag 1/2/76 Honolulu, HI	1.75
C89-90	On one FDC	3.00
C91-92	31¢ Wright Bros. attd. 9/23/78 Dayton, OH	2.50
C91-92	Wright Bros. set of 2 singles	3.50
C93-94	21¢ Octave Chanute attd. 3/29/79 Chanute, KS	2.50
C93-94	Octave Chanute set of 2 singles	3.50
C95-96	25¢ Wiley Post attd. 11/20/79 Oklahoma City, OK	2.50
C95-96	Wiley Post set of 2 singles	3.50
C97	31¢ Olympic - High Jump 11/1/79 Col. Springs, CO	1.75
C98	40¢ Philip Mazzei 10/13/80 DC	1.75
C99	28¢ Blanche Scott 12/30/80 Hammondsport, NY	1.75
C100	35¢ Glenn Curtiss 12/30/80 Hammondsport, NY	1.75
C99-100	Scott & Curtiss on one cover	3.50
C101-04	28¢ Olympics attd. 6/17/83 San Antonio, TX	4.00
C101-04	Olympics set of 4 singles	8.00
C105-08	40¢ Olympics attd. 4/8/83 Los Angeles, CA	4.50
C105-08	Olympics set of 4 singles	8.00
C109-12	35¢ Olympics attd. 11/4/83 Colorado Springs, CO	4.50
C109-12	Olympics set of 4 singles	8.00
C113	33¢ Alfred Verville 2/13/85 Garden City, NY	1.75
C114	39¢ Sperry Bros. 2/13/85 Garden City, NY	1.75
C115	44¢ Transpacific Airmail 2/15/85 San Francisco, CA	2.50
C116	44¢ Junipero Serra 8/22/85 San Diego, CA	2.00
C117	44¢ New Sweden, 350th Anniv. 3/29/88 Wilmington, DE	2.00
C118	45¢ Samuel P. Langley 5/14/88 San Diego, CA	2.00
C119	36¢ Igor Sikorsky 6/23/88 Stratford, CT	2.00
C120	45¢ French Revolution 7/14/89 DC	2.00
C121	45¢ Pre-Columbian Customs 10/12/89 San Juan, PR	2.00
C122-25	45¢ Future Mail Transportation attd. 11/27/89 DC	8.00
C122-25	Set of 4 singles	10.00
C126	$1.80 Future Mail Trans. S/S of 4, imperf. 11/24/89 DC	7.00
C127	45¢ America, Caribbean Coast 10/12/90 Grand Canyon, AZ	2.00
C128	50¢ Harriet Quimby 4/27/91 Plymouth, MI	2.00
C129	40¢ William T. Piper 5/17/91 Denver, CO	2.00
C130	50¢ Antarctic Treaty 6/21/91 DC	2.00
C131	50¢ America 10/12/91 Anchorage, AK	2.00

1934-36 AIRMAIL SPECIAL DELIVERY ISSUES

CE1	16¢ Great Seal, blue 8/30/34 Chic., IL (AAMS Conv. Sta.)	30.00
CE2	16¢ Great Seal, red & blue 2/10/36 DC	25.00

Scott #	Description	Uncacheted	Cacheted
	1885-1931 SPECIAL DELIVERY		
E1	10¢ Messenger 10/1/85 Any City	8500.00	...
E12	10¢ Motorcycle,Flat plate,perf.11 7/12/22 DC	375.00	...
E13	15¢ Motorcycle,Flat plate,perf.11 4/11/25 DC	225.00	...
E14	20¢ Truck, Flat plate, perf.11 4/25/25 DC	110.00	...
E15	10¢ Motorcycle, Rotary 11/29/27 DC	95.00	...
E15EE	Electric Eye 9/8/41 DC	...	25.00
E16	15¢ Motorcycle, Rotary 8/6/31 Easton, PA	2300.00	...
	Motorcycle, Rotary 8/13/31 DC	125.00	...

SPECIAL SERVICE FIRST DAY COVERS

Scott #	Description	Uncacheted	Cacheted
	1944-1971 SPECIAL DELIVERY		
E17	13¢ Motorcycle 10/30/44	...	10.00
E18	17¢ Motorcycle 10/30/44	...	10.00
E17-18	Motorcycles on one cover	...	15.00
E19	20¢ Post Office Truck, Rotary 11/30/51 DC	...	4.50
E20	20¢ Letter & Hands 10/13/54 Boston, MA	...	2.00
E21	30¢ Letter & Hands 9/3/57 Indpls., IN	...	2.00
E22	45¢ Arrows 11/21/69 New York, NY	...	2.25
E23	60¢ Arrows 5/10/71 Phoenix, AZ	...	2.50
	1911 REGISTERED MAIL		
F1	10¢ Eagle, blue 12/1/11 Any city	12500.00	...
	10¢ Eagle, blue 11/28/11 Pre Date	13,000.00	...
	1955 CERTIFIED MAIL		
FA1	15¢ Postman, red 6/6/55 DC	...	2.00
	POSTAGE DUE		
	1925		
J68	½¢ P. Due (4/15/25 EKU) Phil., PA	900.00	
	Rahway, NJ	2200.00	
	1959		
J88	½¢ Red & Black 6/19/59 Any city	75.00	...
J89	1¢ Red & Black 6/19/59 Any city	75.00	...
J90	2¢ Red & Black 6/19/59 Any city	75.00	...
J91	3¢ Red & Black 6/19/59 Any city	75.00	...
J92	4¢ Red & Black 6/19/59 Any city	75.00	...
J93	5¢ Red & Black 6/19/59 Any city	115.00	...
J94	6¢ Red & Black 6/19/59 Any city	115.00	...
J95	7¢ Red & Black 6/19/59 Any city	115.00	...
J96	8¢ Red & Black 6/19/59 Any city	115.00	...
J97	10¢ Red & Black 6/19/59 Any city	115.00	...
J98	30¢ Red & Black 6/19/59 Any city	115.00	...
J99	50¢ Red & Black 6/19/59 Any city	115.00	...
J100	$1 Red & Black 6/19/59 Any city	125.00	...
J101	$5 Red & Black 6/19/59 Any city	125.00	...
	1978-85		
J102	11¢ Red & Black 1/2/78 Any city	...	5.00
J103	13¢ Red & Black 1/2/78 Any city	...	5.00
	#J102-103 on one FDC	...	7.50
J104	17¢ Red & Black 6/10/85 Any city	...	5.00
	1983-95 OFFICIAL STAMPS		
O74	3¢ Treasury 7/1/1873 Washington, DC	5000.00	...
O127	1¢ Eagle 1/12/83 DC	...	1.75
O128	4¢ Eagle 1/12/83 DC	...	1.75
O129	13¢ Eagle 1/12/83 DC	...	1.75
O129A	14¢ Eagle 5/15/85 DC	...	2.00
O130	17¢ Eagle 1/12/83 DC	...	1.75
O132	$1 Eagle 1/12/83 DC	...	5.00
O133	$5 Eagle 1/12/83 DC	...	15.00
O136	22¢ Eagle 5/15/85 DC	...	1.75
O138	(14¢) "D" Eagle 2/4/85 DC	...	1.75
O143	1¢ Eagle, Offset Printing, No ¢ sign 7/5/89 DC	...	1.75
O146	4¢ Official Mail 4/6/91 Oklahoma City, OK	...	1.75
O146A	10¢ Official Mail 10/19/93	...	1.75
O147	19¢ Official Postcard rate 5/24/91 Seattle, WA	...	1.75
O148	23¢ Official 2nd oz. rate 5/24/91 Seattle, WA	...	1.75
O151	$1 Eagle Sept 1993	...	7.00
O154	1¢ Eagle, with ¢ sign 5/9/95 DC	...	1.90
O155	20¢ Eagle, postcard rate 5/9/95 DC	...	1.90
O156	23¢ Eagle, 2nd oz. rate 5/9/95 DC	...	1.90
O154-56	1¢, 20¢, 23¢, 32¢ Coil Combo cover, 5/9/95 DC (1)	...	2.50
	1983-95 OFFICIAL COILS		
O135	20¢ Eagle, with ¢ sign 1/12/83 DC	...	1.75
	#O127-129,O130-135 on one FDC	...	15.00
O138A	15¢ Official Mail 6/11/88 Corpus Christi, TX	...	1.75
O138B	20¢ Official Mail, No ¢ sign 5/19/88 DC	...	1.75

0138B

SPECIAL SERVICE FIRST DAY COVERS

RW49

Scott #	Description	Uncacheted	Cacheted
O139	(22¢) "D" Eagle 2/4/85 DC	...	1.75
O140	(25¢) "E" Official 3/22/88 DC	...	1.75
O141	25¢ Official Mail 6/11/88 Corpus Christi, TX	...	1.75
O144	(29¢) "F" Official 1/22/91 DC	...	1.75
O145	29¢ Official Mail 5/24/91 Seattle, WA	...	1.75
O152	(32¢) "G" Official 12/13/94	...	1.90
O153	32¢ Official Mail 5/9/95 DC	...	1.90

POSTAL NOTES

Scott #	Description	Uncacheted	Cacheted
PN1-18	1¢-90¢ Black, cplt. set on 18 forms	750.00	...
PN1	1¢ Black 2/1/45 on cplt 3 part M.O. form, any city	45.00	...
PN2	2¢ 2/1/45 on cplt 3 part M.O. form, any city	45.00	...
PN3	3¢ 2/1/45 on cplt 3 part M.O. form, any city	45.00	...
PN4	4¢ 2/1/45 on cplt 3 part M.O. form, any city	45.00	...
PN5	5¢ 2/1/45 on cplt 3 part M.O. form, any city	45.00	...
PN6	6¢ 2/1/45 on cplt 3 part M.O. form, any city	45.00	...
PN7	7¢ 2/1/45 on cplt 3 part M.O. form, any city	45.00	...
PN8	8¢ 2/1/45 on cplt 3 part M.O. form, any city	45.00	...
PN9	9¢ 2/1/45 on cplt 3 part M.O. form, any city	45.00	...
PN10	10¢ 2/1/45 on cplt 3 part M.O. form, any city	45.00	...
PN11	20¢ 2/1/45 on cplt 3 part M.O. form, any city	45.00	...
PN12	30¢ 2/1/45 on cplt 3 part M.O. form, any city	45.00	...
PN13	40¢ 2/1/45 on cplt 3 part M.O. form, any city	45.00	...
PN14	50¢ 2/1/45 on cplt 3 part M.O. form, any city	45.00	...
PN15	60¢ 2/1/45 on cplt 3 part M.O. form, any city	45.00	...
PN16	70¢ 2/1/45 on cplt 3 part M.O. form, any city	45.00	...
PN17	80¢ 2/1/45 on cplt 3 part M.O. form, any city	45.00	...
PN18	90¢ 2/1/45 on cplt 3 part M.O. form, any city	45.00	...

POSTAL SAVINGS

Scott #	Description	Uncacheted	Cacheted
PS11	10¢ Minuteman, red 5/1/41 Any city	175.00	...

PARCEL POST

Scott #	Description	4th Class (1/1/13)	1st Class (7/1/13)
Q1	1¢ Post Office Clerk, any city	3500.00	2500.00
Q2	2¢ City Carrier, any city	4500.00	2500.00
Q3	3¢ Railway Postal Clerk, any city	...	4500.00
Q4	4¢ Rural Carrier, any city	...	5500.00
Q5	5¢ Mail Train, any city	4000.00	7000.00

1925-28 SPECIAL HANDLING

Scott #	Description	Uncacheted	Cacheted
QE1	10¢ Yellow Green 6/25/28 DC	50.00	...
QE2	15¢ Yellow Green 6/25/28 DC	50.00	...
QE3	20¢ Yellow Green 6/25/28 DC	50.00	...

1925-28 SPECIAL HANDLING

Scott #	Description	Uncacheted	Cacheted
QE1-3	Set of 3 on one FDC	250.00	...
QE4a	25¢ Deep Green 4/11/25 DC	225.00	...

REVENUE STAMPS

Scott #	Description	Uncacheted	Cacheted
R155	2¢ Carmine, 7/1/98	1000.00	...
R733	10¢ Documentary	200.00	...

FEDERAL DUCK STAMP FIRST DAY COVERS

Scott #	Description	Uncacheted	Cacheted
RW47	$7.50 Mallards 7/1/80 DC		150.00
RW48	$7.50 Ruddy Ducks 7/1/81 DC		75.00
RW49	$7.50 Canvasbacks 7/1/82 DC		55.00
RW50	$7.50 Pintails 7/1/83 DC		55.00
RW51	$7.50 Widgeons 7/2/84 DC		60.00
RW52	$7.50 Cinnamon Teal 7/1/85		45.00
RW53	$7.50 Fulvous Whistling Duck 7/1/86		45.00
RW54	$10.00 Red Head Ducks 7/1/87		45.00
RW55	$10.00 Snow Goose 7/1/88 Any city		45.00
RW56	$12.50 Lesser Scaups 6/30/89 DC		45.00
RW57	$12.50 Black-Bellied Whistling Duck 6/30/90 DC		45.00
RW58	$15.00 King Eiders 6/30/91 DC		45.00
RW59	$15.00 Spectacled Eiders 6/30/92 DC		45.00
RW60	$15.00 Canvasbacks 6/30/93 DC		37.50
RW60	Same, Mound, MN		37.50
RW61	$15.00 Redbreasted Merganser 6/30/94 DC		37.50
RW62	$15.00 Mallard 6/30/95 DC		37.50
RW63	$15.00 Surf Scoter 6/27/96 DC		37.50
RW64	$15.00 Canada Goose 6/21/97 DC		37.50
RW65	$15.00 Barrow's Goldeneye, W/A 7/1/98, Wash., DC		37.50
RW66	$15.00 Barrow's Goldeneye, S/A		37.50
RW67	$15.00 Greater Scaup, W/A, 7/1/99, Washington DC		37.50
RW67	$15.00 Greater Scaup, S/A, 7/1/99, Washington DC		37.50

POSTAL STATIONERY FIRST DAY COVERS

Prices are for standard 6¾ size envelopes, unless noted otherwise.

Scott #	Description	Uncacheted	Cacheted
	1925-32		
U436a	3¢ G. Washington, white paper, extra quality		
	6/16/32 DC, size 5, die 1, wmk. 29	75.00	...
	Size 8, die 1, wmk. 29	18.00	
U436e	3¢ G. Washington, white paper, extra quality		
	6/16/32 DC, size 5, die 1, wmk. 29	12.00	30.00
U436f	3¢ G. Washington, white paper, extra quality		
	6/16/32 DC, size 5, die 9, wmk. 29	12.00	50.00
	Size 12, die 9, wmk. 29	18.00	...
U437a	3¢ G. Washington, amber paper, standard qual.		
	7/13/32 DC, size 5, wmk. 28	50.00	...
	7/19/32 DC, size 5, wmk. 29, extra qual.	35.00	...
U439	3¢ G. Washington, blue paper, standard qual.		
	7/13/32, size 5, wmk. 28	40.00	...
	Size 13, die 9, wmk. 28	65.00	...
	9/9/32 DC, size 5, wmk. 28	85.00	...
U439a	3¢ G. Washington, blue paper, extra quality		
	7/19/32 DC, size 5, die 29	40.00	...
U481	1½¢ G. Wash. 3/19/25 DC, size 5, wmk. 27	35.00	...
	Size 8, wmk. 27	70.00	...
	Size 13, wmk. 26	50.00	...
	Size 5, wmk. 27 with Sc#553, 582 & 598	150.00	...
	Size 8, wmk. 27 with Sc#553, 582 & 598	125.00	...
	Size 13, wmk. 26 with Sc#553	60.00	...
U495	1½¢ on 1¢ B. Franklin 6/1/25 DC, size 5	50.00	...
	6/3/25 DC, size 8	65.00	...
	6/2/25 DC, size 13	60.00	...
U515	1½¢ on 1¢ B. Franklin 8/1/25 Des Moines, IA		
	size 5, die 1	50.00	...
U521	1½¢ on 1¢ B. Franklin 10/22/25 DC		
	size 5, die 1, watermark 25	100.00	...
U522a	2¢ Liberty Bell 7/27/26 Philadelphia, PA		
	Size 5, wmk. 27	20.00	30.00
	Size 5, wmk. 27 DC	22.50	32.50
	Unofficial city, Size 5, wmk. 27	35.00	45.00
	WASHINGTON BICENTENNIAL ISSUE		
U523	1¢ Mount Vernon 1/1/32 DC, size 5, wmk. 29	10.00	32.50
	Size 8, wmk. 29	12.50	37.50
	Size 13, wmk. 29	10.00	32.50
U524	1½¢ Mount Vernon 1/1/32 DC, size 5, wmk.29	10.00	32.50
	Size 8, wmk. 29	12.50	37.50
	Size 13, wmk. 29	10.00	32.50
U525	2¢ Mount Vernon 1/1/32 DC, size 5, wmk. 29	8.00	30.00
	Size 8, wmk. 29	10.00	30.00
	Size 13, wmk. 29	8.00	30.00
U526	3¢ Mount Vernon 6/16/32 DC, size 5, wmk.29	18.00	40.00
	Size 8, wmk. 29	25.00	80.00
	Size 13, wmk. 29	20.00	60.00
U527	4¢ Mount Vernon 1/1/32 DC, size 5, wmk. 29	30.00	80.00
U528	5¢ Mount Vernon 1/1/32 DC, size 5, wmk. 29	18.00	40.00
	Size 8, wmk. 29	20.00	45.00
	Size 13, wmk. 29	10.00	32.50
	1932-71		
U529	6¢ G. Washington, white paper, 8/18/32		
	Los Angeles, CA, size 8, wmk 29	15.00	...
	8/19/32 DC, size 7, wmk. 29	20.00	...
	8/19/32 DC, size 9, wmk. 29	20.00	...
U530	6¢ G. Washington, amber paper, 8/18/32		
	Los Angeles, CA, size 8, wmk 29	15.00	...
	8/19/32 DC, size 7, wmk. 29	20.00	...
	8/19/32 DC, size 9, wmk. 29	20.00	...
	size 8, wmk 29 with Sc#723 pair	40.00	...
U531	6¢ G. Washington, blue paper, 8/18/32		
	Los Angeles, CA, size 8, wmk 29	15.00	...
	8/19/32 DC, size 7, wmk. 29	20.00	...
	8/19/32 DC, size 9, wmk. 29	20.00	...
U532	1¢ Franklin 11/16/50 NY, NY, size 13, wmk 42	...	1.75
U533a	2¢ Wash. 11/17/50 NY, NY, size 13, wmk 42	...	1.75
U534a	3¢ Wash.,die 1 11/18/50 NY,NY,size 13,wmk 42	1.75	...
U534b	3¢ Wash.,die 2 11/19/50 NY,NY,size 8,wmk 42	4.00	...

U532

POSTAL STATIONERY FIRST DAY COVERS

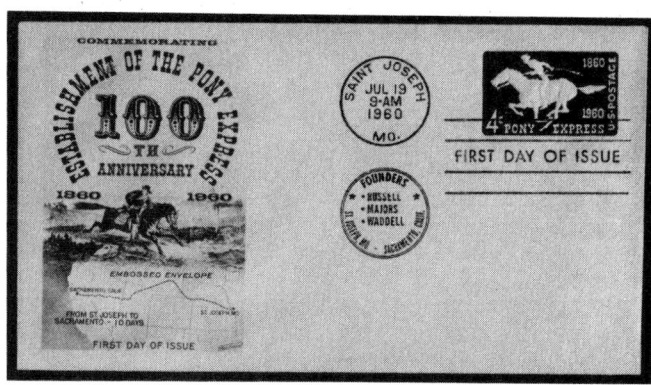

U543

Scott #	Description	Uncacheted	Cacheted
U536	4¢ Franklin 7/31/58 Montpelier, VT......................	...	1.75
	Size 8, wmk 46	60.00	...
	Size 12, wmk 46	60.00	...
	Size 13, window	25.00	...
	Wheeling, WV, size 6¾, wmk 46, w/#1036a	35.00	...
U540	3¢+1¢ G.Washington (U534c) 7/22/58 Kenvil, NJ		
	Size 8, wmk 46, die 3 (earliest known use)	50.00	...
U541	1¼¢ Franklin 6/25/60 Birmingham, AL		1.75
U542	2½¢ Washington 5/28/60 Chicago, IL		1.75
U543	4¢ Pony Express 7/19/60 St. Joseph, MO		1.75
	Sacramento, CA		3.50
U544	5¢ Lincoln 11/19/62 Springfield, IL		1.75
U546	5¢ World's Fair 4/22/64 World's Fair, NY		1.75
U547	1¼¢ Liberty Bell 1/6/65 DC		1.75
	1/8/65 DC, size 10, wmk 48		15.00
U548	1.4¢ Liberty Bell 3/26/68 Springfield, MA		1.75
	3/27/68 DC, size 10, wmk 48		8.00
U548A	1.6¢ Liberty Bell 6/16/69 DC		1.75
	Size 10, wmk 49		1.75
U549	4¢ Old Ironsides 1/6/65 DC		1.75
	1/8/65, window		15.00
	Size 10		15.00
	Size10, window		15.00
U550	5¢ Eagle 1/5/65 Williamsburg, PA		1.75
	1/8/65, window		15.00
	Size 10		15.00
	Size 10, window		15.00
U550a	5¢ Eagle, tagged 8/15/67 DC, wmk 50		3.50
	Dayton, OH		15.00
	Wmk 48		5.00
	Size 10, wmk 48		5.00
	Size 10, wmk 49, Dayton, OH only		7.50
	Size 10, wmk 49, window		5.00
U551	6¢ Liberty 1/4/68 New York, NY		1.75
	1/5/68 DC, window		3.00
	Size 10, wmk 47		3.00
	Size 10, window, wmk 49		3.00
	11/15/68 DC, shiny plastic window, wmk 48		5.00
U552	4 + 2¢ Old Ironsides, revalued 2/5/68 DC, wmk 50		7.50
	Window, wmk 48		7.50
	Size 10, wmk 47		7.50
	Size 10, window, wmk 49		7.50
U553	5 + 1¢ Eagle, revalued 2/5/68 DC		7.50
	Size 10		7.50
U553a	5 + 1¢ Eagle, revalued, tagged 2/5/68 DC, wmk 48		15.00
	Size 10, wmk 47 or 49		7.50
	Size 10, window, wmk 49		7.50
U554	6¢ Moby Dick 6/7/70 New Bedford, MA		1.75
U554	**1st Colonial Cachet**		**30.00**
U555	6¢ Youth Conf. 2/24/71 DC		1.75
U556	1.7¢ Liberty Bell 5/10/71 Balt., MD, wmk 48A		1.75
	5/10/71 DC, wmk 49 with #1394		15.00
	5/10/71 Phoenix, AZ, wmk 48A with #E23		30.00
	5/10/71 DC, with #1283		3.00
	5/11/71 DC, size 10, wmk 47 or 49		12.00
	5/11/71 DC, size 10, wmk 48A		6.00

Scott #	Description	Price
	1971-78	
U557	8¢ Eagle 5/6/71 Williamsburg, PA, wmk 48A	1.75
	Wmk 49	2.50
	5/7/71 DC, window, wmk 48A	3.50
	Size 10, wmk 49	3.50
	Size 10, window, wmk 47	3.50
U561	6 + 2¢ Liberty Bell, revalued 5/16/71 DC, wmk 47	3.00
	Wmk 48A	25.00
	Wmk 49	4.00
	Window, wmk 47	3.00
	Size 10, wmk 48A	3.00
	Size 10, wmk 49	6.00
	Size 10, window, wmk 47	3.00
	Size 10, window, wmk 49	5.00
U562	6 + 2¢ Youth Conf., revalued 5/16/71 DC, wmk 49	3.00
	Wmk 47	30.00

POSTAL STATIONERY FIRST DAY COVERS

Scott #	Description	Price
U563	8¢ Bowling 8/21/71 Milwaukee, WI	2.50
	Size 10	2.00
U564	8¢ Aging Conference 11/15/71 DC	1.75
U565	8¢ Transpo '72 5/2/72 DC, wmk 49	1.75
	Wmk 47	3.00
U566	8 + 2¢ Eagle, revalued 12/1/73 DC	2.50
	Window, wmk 48A ....(uncacheted)	7.50
	Window, wmk 49	4.50
	Size 10, wmk 47	4.50
	Size 10, window, wmk 47	4.50
U567	10¢ Liberty Bell 12/5/73 Phila., PA knife depth 58 mm	1.75
	Knife depth 51 mm	1.75
U568	1.8¢ Volunteer 8/23/74 Cincinnati, OH	1.75
	Size 10	1.75
U569	10¢ Tennis 8/31/74 Forest Hills, NY	3.00
	Size 10	3.00
	9/3/74 DC, window	4.00
	Size 10, window	4.00
U571	10¢ Seafaring 10/13/75 Minneapolis, MN	1.75
	Size 10	1.75
U572	13¢ Homemaker 2/2/76 Biloxi, MS	1.75
	Size 10	1.75
U573	13¢ Farmer 3/15/76 New Orleans, LA	1.75
	Size 10	1.75
U574	13¢ Doctor 3/30/76 Dallas, TX	2.50
	Size 10	3.00
U575	13¢ Craftsman 8/6/76 Hancock, MA	1.75
	Size 10	1.75
U576	13¢ Liberty Tree 11/8/75 Memphis, TN	1.75
	Size 10	1.75
U577	2¢ Star & Pinwheel 9/10/76 Hempstead, NY	1.75
	Size 10	1.75
U578	2.1¢ Non-Profit 6/3/77 Houston, TX	1.75
	Size 10	1.75
U579	2.7¢ Non-Profit 7/5/78 Raleigh, NC	1.75
	Size 10	1.75
U580	(15¢) "A" Eagle 5/22/78 Memphis, TN, wmk 47	2.00
	Wmk 48A	1.75
	Window, wmk 47 or 48A	2.50
	Size 10	1.75
	Size 10, window	2.50
	Size 6¾, wmk 48A with sheet, coil & bklt. pane.	10.00
U581	15¢ Uncle Sam 6/3/78 Williamsburg, PA	1.75
	Window	2.50
	Size 10	1.75
	Size 10, window	2.50
U582	13¢ Bicentennial 10/15/76 Los Angeles, CA, wmk 49	1.75
	Wmk 49, dark green	7.50
	Wmk 48A	3.00
	Size 10	1.75
U583	13¢ Golf 4/7/77 Augusta, GA	7.00
	Size 10	7.50
	4/8/77 DC, Size 6¾, window	9.50
	Size 10, window	9.50
	1977-85	
U584	13¢ Conservation 10/20/77 Ridley Park, PA.............	1.75
	Window	2.50
	Size 10	1.75
	Size 10, window	2.50
U585	13¢ Development 10/20/77 Ridley Park, PA.............	1.75
	Window	2.50
	Size 10	1.75
	Size 10, window	2.50
U586	15¢ on 16¢ Surcharged USA 7/28/78 Williamsburg, PA	1.75
	Size 10	1.75
U587	15¢ Auto Racing 9/2/78 Ontario, CA	1.75
	Size 10	1.75
U588	13 + 2¢ Lib. Tree, revalued 11/28/78 Williamsburg, PA	1.75
	Size 10	1.75
	11/29/78 DC, size 6¾, window	2.00
	Size 10, window	2.00
U589	3.1¢ Non-Profit 5/18/79 Denver, CO	1.75
	Size 6¾, window	2.00
	Size 10	1.75
	Size 10, window	2.00

U583

POSTAL STATIONERY FIRST DAY COVERS

U619

Scott #	Description	Price
U590	3.5¢ Non-Profit 6/23/80 Williamsburg, PA	1.75
	Size 10	1.75
U591	5.9¢ Non-Profit 2/17/82 Wheeling, WV	1.75
	Size 6¾, window	2.00
	Size 10	1.75
	Size 10, window	2.00
U592	(18¢) "B" Eagle 3/15/81 Memphis, TN	1.75
	Size 6¾, window	2.00
	Size 10	1.75
	Size 10, window	2.00
U593	18¢ Star 4/2/81 Star City, IN	1.75
	Size 10	1.75
U594	(20¢) "C" Eagle 10/11/81 Memphis, TN	1.75
	Size 10	1.75
U595	15¢ Veterinary Med. 7/24/79 Seattle, WA	1.75
	Size 10	1.75
	7/25/79 Seattle, WA, size 6¾, window, ...(uncacheted)	4.00
	Size 10, window ....(uncacheted)	4.00
U596	15¢ Olympics 12/10/79 E. Rutherford, NJ	1.75
	Size 10	1.75
U597	15¢ Bicycle 5/16/80 Baltimore, MD	1.75
	Size 10	1.75
U598	15¢ America's Cup 9/15/80 Newport, RI	1.75
	Size 10	1.75
U599	15¢ Honey Bee 10/10/80 Paris, IL	1.75
	Size 10	1.75
U600	18¢ Blinded Veteran 8/13/81 Arlington, VA	1.75
	Size 10	1.75
U601	20¢ Capitol Dome 11/13/81 Los Angeles, CA	1.75
	Size 10	1.75
U602	20¢ Great Seal 6/15/82 DC	1.75
	Size 10	1.75
U603	20¢ Purple Heart 8/6/82 DC	2.00
	Size 10	2.00
U604	5.2¢ Non-Profit 3/21/83 Memphis, TN	1.75
	Size 6¾, window	1.75
	Size 10	1.75
	Size 10, window	1.75
U605	20¢ Paralyzed Vets 8/3/83 Portland, OR	1.75
	Size 10	1.75
U606	20¢ Small Business 5/7/84 DC	1.75
	Size 10	1.75
U607	(22¢) "D" Eagle 2/1/85 Los Angeles, CA	1.75
	Size 6¾, window	1.75
	Size 10	1.75
	Size 10, window	1.75
U608	22¢ Bison 2/25/85 Bison, SD	1.75
	Size 6¾, window	1.75
	Size 10	1.75
	Size 10, window	1.75

Scott #	Description 1985-96	Cacheted
U609	6¢ Old Ironsides, Non-Profit 5/3/85 Boston, MA	1.75
	Size 10	2.00
U610	8.5¢ Mayflower 12/4/86 Plymouth, MA	1.75
	Size 10	2.00
U611	25¢ Stars 3/26/88 Star, MS	1.75
	Size 10	2.00
U612	9.4¢ USS Constellation 4/12/88 Baltimore, MD	1.75
	Size 10	2.00
U613	25¢ Snowflake 9/8/88 Snowflake, AZ	1.75
U614	25¢ Philatelic Mail Return Env. 3/10/89 Cleveland, OH ..	1.75
U615	25¢ Security Envelope 7/10/89 DC	1.75
U616	25¢ Love 9/22/89 McLean, VA	1.75
U617	25¢ Space Hologram, World Stamp Expo 12/3/89 DC	1.75
U618	25¢ Football 9/9/90 Green Bay, WI	4.00
U619	29¢ Star 1/24/91 DC	1.75
U620	11.1¢ Non-Profit 5/3/91 Boxborough, MA	1.75
U621	29¢ Love 5/9/91 Honolulu, HI	1.75
U622	29¢ Magazine Industry 10/7/91 Naples, FL	1.75
U623	29¢ USA & Star, Security Envelope 7/20/91 DC	1.75
U624	29¢ Country Geese 11/8/91 Virginia Beach, VA	1.75
U625	29¢ Space Station Hologram 1/21/92 Virginia Beach, VA ..	1.75

POSTAL STATIONERY FIRST DAY COVERS

Scott #	Description	Cacheted
U626	29¢ Western Americana 4/10/92 Dodge City, KS	1.75
U627	29¢ Protect the Environment 4/22/92 Chicago, IL	1.75
U628	19.8¢ Bulk-rate, third class 5/18/92 Las Vegas, NV	1.75
U629	29¢ Disabled Americans 7/22/92 DC	1.75
U630	29¢ Kitten 10/2/93 King of Prussia, PA	1.75
	Size 10	2.00
U631	29¢ Football size 10 9/17/94 Canton, OH	3.00
U632	32¢ Liberty Bell 1/3/95 Williamsburg, VA	2.00
U633	(32¢) Old Glory 12/13/94 Cancel, released 1/12/95	2.00
U634	(32¢) Old Glory, Security Envelope	2.00
U635	(5¢) Sheep 3/10/95 State College, PA	2.00
U636	(10¢) Eagle 3/10/95 State College,PA	2.00
U637	32¢ Spiral Heart 5/12/95 Lakeville, PA	2.00
U638	32¢ Liberty Bell Security Size 9 5/15/95 DC	2.00
U639	32¢ Space Hologram (Legal size only) 9/22/95	
	Milwaukee, WI	2.00
U640	32¢ Environment 4/20/96 Chicago, IL	2.00
U641	32¢ Paralympics 5/2/96 DC	2.00
U642	33¢ Flag, 3 colors, 1/11/99, Washington DC	2.00
U643	33¢ Flag, 2 colors, 1/11/99, Washington DC	2.00
U644	33¢ Love, 1/28/99, Loveland, CO	2.00
U645	33¢ Lincoln, 6/5/99	2.00

Scott #	Description **AIRMAIL POSTAL STATIONERY** 1929-46	Uncacheted
UC1	5¢ Blue 1/12/29 DC, size 13	40.00
	2/1/29, DC, size 5	75.00
	2/1/29, DC, size 8	75.00
UC3	6¢ Orange 7/1/34, size 8	25.00
	Size 13	14.00
UC3	Combo with C19 .... ,	60.00
UC7	8¢ Olive green 9/26/32, size 8	30.00
	Size 13	11.00
UC7	Combo with C17	60.00
UC10	5¢ on 6¢ Orange 10/1/46 Aiea Hts, HI, die 2a	150.00
UC11	5¢ on 6¢ Orange 10/1/46 Aiea Hts, HI die 2b	200.00
UC12	5¢ on 6¢ Orng. 10/1/46 Aiea Hts, HI, APO & NY, NY die 2c	100.00
UC13	5¢ on 6¢ Orng. 10/1/46 Aiea Hts, HI, die 3	100.00

Scott #	Description 1946-67	Cacheted
UC14	5¢ Skymaster 9/25/46 DC	2.25
UC16	10¢ Air Letter 4/29/47 DC	5.00
UC17	5¢ CIPEX, Type 1 5/21/47 New York, NY	2.50
UC17a	5¢ CIPEX, Type 2 5/21/47 New York, NY	2.50
UC18	6¢ Skymaster 9/22/50 Philadelphia, PA	1.75
UC20	6¢ on 5¢ 9/17/51 U.S. Navy Cancel ....(uncacheted)	400.00
UC22	6¢ on 5¢ die 2 (UC15) 8/29/52 Norfolk, VA ....(uncacheted)	35.00
	Cacheted	30.00
UC25	6¢ FIPEX 5/2/56 New York, NY, "short clouds"	1.75
	"Long clouds"	1.75
UC26	7¢ Skymaster 7/31/58 Dayton, OH, "straight left wing" ..	1.75
	"Crooked left wing"	3.00
	Size 8 ....(uncacheted)	35.00
UC32a	10¢ Jet Air Letter 9/12/58 St. Louis, MO	2.00
UC33	7¢ Jet, blue 11/21/58 New York, NY	1.75

Scott #	Description	Cacheted
UC34	...7¢ Jet, red 8/18/60 Portland, OR	1.75
UC35	...11¢ Jet Air Letter 6/16/61 Johnstown, PA	1.75
UC36	...8¢ Jet 11/17/62 Chantilly, VA	1.75
UC37	...8¢ Jet Triangle 1/7/65 Chicago, IL	1.75
	Size 10	15.00
UC37a	..8¢ Jet Triangle, tagged 8/15/67 DC	15.00
	Dayton, OH	15.00
	Size 10	7.50

	1965-95	
UC38	...11¢ Kennedy Air Letter 5/29/65 Boston, MA	1.75
UC39	...13¢ Kennedy Air Letter 5/29/67 Chic., IL	1.75
UC40	...10¢ Jet Triangle 1/8/68 Chicago, IL	7.50
	1/9/68 DC, size 10	10.00
UC41	8 + 2¢ revalued UC37 2/5/68 DC	10.00
	Size 10	10.00
UC42	13¢ Human Rights Air Letter 12/3/68 DC	1.75
UC43	11¢ Jet & Circles 5/6/71 Williamsburg, PA	1.75
	Size 10	6.00

UC43

POSTAL CARD FIRST DAY COVERS

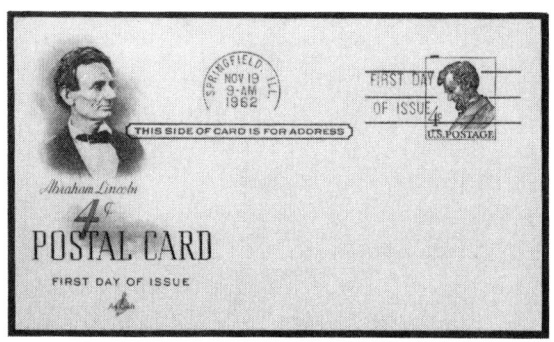

UX48

Scott #	Description	Cacheted
UC44	15¢ Birds Air Letter 5/28/71 Chicago, IL	1.75
UC44a	15¢ Birds AEROGRAMME 12/13/71 Phila., PA	1.75
UC45	10¢+1¢ revalued UC40 6/28/71 DC	5.00
	Size 10	10.00
UC46	15¢ Balloon Air Letter 2/10/73 Albuquerque, NM	1.75
UC47	13¢ Dove 12/1/73 Memphis, TN	1.75
	1/5/74, size 10, earliest known use	5.00
UC48	18¢ USA Air Letter 1/4/74 Atlanta, GA	1.75
UC49	17¢ NATO Air Letter 4/4/74 DC	1.75
UC50	22¢ USA Air Letter 1/16/76 Tempe, AZ	1.75
UC51	22¢ USA Air Letter 11/3/78 St. Petersburg, FL	1.75
UC52	22¢ Olympics 12/5/79 Bay Shore, NY	1.75
UC53	30¢ USA 12/29/80 San Francisco, CA	1.75
UC54	30¢ USA 9/21/81 Honolulu, HI	1.75
UC55	30¢ USA & Globe 9/16/82 Seattle, WA	1.75
UC56	30¢ Communications 1/7/83 Anaheim, CA	1.75
UC57	30¢ Olympics 10/14/83 Los Angeles, CA	1.75
UC58	30¢ Landsat Sat. 2/14/85 Goddard Flight Ctr., MD ..	1.75
UC59	36¢ Travel 5/21/85 DC	1.75
UC60	36¢ Twain / Halley's Comet 12/4/85 DC	1.75
UC61	39¢ Stylized Aerogramme 5/9/88 Miami, FL	1.75
UC62	39¢ Montgomery Blair 11/20/89 DC	1.75
UC63	45¢ Eagle 5/17/91 Denver, CO	2.00
UC64	50¢ Thaddeus Lowe – Aerogramme 9/23/95 Tampa, FL	2.25
UC65	60¢ Scenic America – Aerogramme 5/15/99	2.50

OFFICIAL POSTAL STATIONERY
1983-95

UO73	20¢ Eagle 1/12/83 DC, size 10	2.00
	Window	3.00
UO74	22¢ Eagle 2/26/85 CD, size 10	1.75
	Window	2.00
UO75	22¢ Savings Bond Env. Window 3/2/87 DC	4.00
UO76	(25¢) Official "E" Savings Bond Env. Window 3/22/52 DC ...	2.00
UO77	25¢ Official Mail 4/11/88 DC	1.75
	Window	2.00
UO78	25¢ Savings Bond Env. 4/14/88 DC	1.75
	Window	2.00
UO79	45¢ Passport Envelope (2 oz.) 3/17/90 Springfield, VA ...	2.00
UO80	65¢ Passport Envelope (3 oz.) 3/17/90 Springfield, VA ...	2.50
UO81	45¢ "Stars" clear, "Official" 14.5 mm long, 8/10/90 DC ..	2.00
UO82	65¢ "Stars" clear, "Official" 14.5 mm long, 8/10/90 DC ..	2.50
UO83	(29¢) "F" Savings Bond Env. 1/22/91 DC	1.75
UO84	29¢ Official 4/6/91 Oklahoma City, OK	1.75
UO85	29¢ Savings Bond Env. 4/17/91 DC	1.75
UO86	52¢ U.S. Consular Service, Passport Env. 7/10/92 DC ...	2.25
UO87	75¢ U.S. Consular Service, Passport Env. 7/10/92 DC ...	2.75
UO88	32¢ Eagle (Legal size only) 5/9/95 DC	2.00
UO89	33¢ 2/22/99	2.00

Scott #	Description	Uncacheted	Cacheted
	1873-1966		
UX1	1¢ Liberty 5/13/1873 Boston, NY, or DC	3000.00	...
UX37	3¢ McKinley 2/1/26 DC	250.00	...
UX38	2¢ Franklin 11/16/51 New York, NY	...	1.75
UX39	2¢ on 1¢ Jefferson (UX27) 1/1/52 DC	12.50	25.00
UX40	2¢ on 1¢ Lincoln (UX28) 3/22/52 DC	100.00	250.00
UX43	2¢ Lincoln 7/31/52 DC	...	1.75
UX44	2¢ FIPEX 5/4/56 New York, NY	...	1.75
UX45	4¢ Liberty 11/16/56 New York, NY	...	1.75
UX46	3¢ Liberty 8/1/58 Philadelphia, PA	...	1.75
UX46a	Missing "I"/"N God We Trust"	175.00	250.00
UX46c	Precancelled 9/15/61	50.00	
UX48	4¢ Lincoln 11/19/62 Springfield, IL	...	1.75
UX48a	4¢ Lincoln, tagged 6/25/66 Bellevue, OH	35.00	50.00
	7/6/66 DC	4.50	10.00
	Bellevue, OH	20.00	35.00
	Cincinnati, OH	15.00	20.00
	Cleveland, OH	18.00	30.00
	Columbus, OH	20.00	35.00
	Dayton, OH	10.00	18.00
	Indianapolis, IN	20.00	35.00
	Louisville, KY	20.00	35.00
	Overlook, OH	15.00	20.00
	Toledo, OH	20.00	35.00

POSTAL CARD FIRST DAY COVERS

Scott #	Description	Cacheted
	1963-80	
UX49	7¢ USA 8/30/63 New York, NY	1.75
UX50	4¢ Customs 2/22/64 DC	1.75
UX51	4¢ Social Security 9/26/64 DC	1.75
	Official Gov't. Printed Cachet.................	12.00
	Blue hand cancel and gov't. cachet	20.00
UX52	4¢ Coast Guard 8/4/65 Newburyport, MA	1.75
UX53	4¢ Census Bureau 10/21/65 Phila, PA	1.75
UX54	8¢ USA 12/4/67 DC	1.75
UX55	5¢ Lincoln 1/4/68 Hodgenville, KY	1.75
UX56	5¢ Women Marines 7/26/68 San Fran., CA	1.75
UX57	5¢ Weathervane 9/1/70 Fort Myer, VA	1.75
UX58	6¢ Paul Revere 5/15/71 Boston, MA	1.75
UX59	10¢ USA 6/10/71 New York, NY	1.75
UX60	6¢ America's Hospitals 9/16/71 NY, NY.........	1.75
UX61	6¢ US Frigate Constellation 6/29/72 Any City	1.75
UX62	6¢ Monument Valley 6/29/72 Any City	1.75
UX63	6¢ Gloucester, MA 6/29/72 Any City...........	1.75
UX64	6¢ John Hanson 9/1/72 Baltimore, MD	1.75
UX65	6¢ Liberty Centenary 9/14/73 DC	1.75
UX66	8¢ Samuel Adams 12/16/73 Boston, MA	1.75
UX67	12¢ Ship's Figurehead 1/4/74 Miami, FL	1.75
UX68	7¢ Charles Thomson 9/14/75 Bryn Mawr, PA	1.75
UX69	9¢ J. Witherspoon 11/10/75 Princeton, NJ	1.75
UX70	9¢ Caeser Rodney 7/1/76 Dover, DE	1.75
UX71	9¢ Galveston Court House 7/20/77 Galveston, TX ..	1.75
UX72	9¢ Nathan Hale 10/14/77 Coventry, CT	1.75
UX73	10¢ Music Hall 5/12/78 Cincinnati, OH	1.75
UX74	(10¢) John Hancock 5/19/78 Quincy, MA	1.75
UX75	10¢ John Hancock 6/20/78 Quincy, MA	1.75
UX76	14¢ Coast Guard Eagle 8/4/78 Seattle, WA......	1.75
UX77	10¢ Molly Pitcher 9/8/78 Freehold, NJ.........	1.75
UX78	10¢ George R. Clark 2/23/79 Vincennes, IN	1.75
UX79	10¢ Casimir Pulaski 10/11/79 Savannah, GA	1.75
UX80	10¢ Olympics 9/17/79 Eugene, OR	1.75
UX81	10¢ Iolani Palace 10/1/79 Honolulu, HI	2.00
UX82	14¢ Olympic Skater 1/15/80 Atlanta, GA	1.75
UX83	10¢ Mormon Temple 4/5/80 Salt Lake City, UT ..	1.75
UX84	10¢ Count Rochambeau 7/11/80 Newport, RI	1.75
UX85	10¢ King's Mountain 10/7/80 King's Mountain, NC ..	1.75
UX86	19¢ Golden Hinde 11/21/80 San Rafael, CA	1.75
	1981-87	
UX87	10¢ Battle of Cowpens 1/17/81 Cowpens, SC	1.75
UX88	(12¢) "B" Eagle 3/15/81 Memphis, TN	1.75
UX89	12¢ Isaiah Thomas 5/5/81 Worcester, MA	1.75
UX90	12¢ Nathaniel Greene 9/8/81 Eutaw Springs, SC .	1.75
UX91	12¢ Lewis & Clark 9/23/81 St. Louis, MO.......	1.75
UX92	(13¢) Robert Morris 10/11/81 Memphis, TN	1.75
UX93	13¢ Robert Morris 11/10/81 Phila., PA	1.75
UX94	13¢ Frances Marion 4/3/82 Marion, SC	1.75
UX95	13¢ LaSalle 4/7/82 New Orleans...............	1.75
UX96	13¢ Philadelphia Academy 6/18/82 Philadelphia, PA .	1.75
UX97	13¢ St. Louis P.O. 10/14/82 St. Louis, MO	1.75
UX98	13¢ Oglethorpe 2/12/83 Savannah, GA	1.75
UX99	13¢ Old Washington P.O. 4/19/83 DC	1.75
UX100	13¢ Olympics - Yachting 8/5/83 Long Beach, CA..	1.75
UX101	13¢ Maryland 3/25/84 St. Clemente Island, MD ..	1.75
UX102	13¢ Olympic Torch 4/30/84 Los Angeles, CA....	1.75
UX103	13¢ Frederic Baraga 6/29/84 Marquette, MI	1.75
UX104	13¢ Rancho San Pedro 9/16/84 Compton, CA....	1.75
UX105	(14¢) Charles Carroll 2/1/85 New Carrollton, MD .	1.75
UX106	14¢ Charles Carroll 3/6/85 Annapolis, MD	1.75
UX107	25¢ Flying Cloud 2/27/85 Salem, MA	1.75
UX108	14¢ George Wythe 6/20/85 Williamsburg, VA ...	1.75
UX109	14¢ Settling of CT 4/18/86 Hartford, CT........	1.75
UX110	14¢ Stamp Collecting 5/23/86 Chicago, IL	1.75
UX111	14¢ Frances Vigo 5/24/86 Vincennes, IN	1.75
UX112	14¢ Rhode Island 6/26/86 Providence, RI	1.75
UX113	14¢ Wisconsin Terr. 7/3/86 Mineral Point, WI ..	1.75
UX114	14¢ National Guard 12/12/86 Boston, MA	1.75
UX115	14¢ Steel Plow 5/22/87 Moines, IL............	1.75
UX116	14¢ Constitution Convention 5/25/87 Philadelphia, PA .	1.75
UX117	14¢ Flag 6/14/87 Baltimore, MD...............	1.75
UX118	14¢ Pride in America 9/22/87 Jackson, WY	1.75
UX119	14¢ Historic Preservation 9/28/87 Timberline, OR .	1.75
	1988-91	
UX120	15¢ America the Beautiful 3/28/88 Buffalo, NY ..	1.75
UX121	15¢ Blair House 5/4/88 DC	1.75
UX122	28¢ Yorkshire 6/29/88 Mystic, CT.............	1.75
UX123	15¢ Iowa Territory 7/2/88 Burlington, IA	1.75
UX124	15¢ Northwest/Ohio Territory 7/15/88 Marietta, OH .	1.75
UX125	15¢ Hearst Castle 9/20/88 San Simeon, CA	1.75
UX126	15¢ Federalist Papers 10/27/88 New York, NY ..	1.75
UX127	15¢ The Desert 1/13/89 Tucson, AZ	1.75
UX128	15¢ Healy Hall 1/23/89 DC	1.75
UX129	15¢ The Wetlands 3/17/89 Waycross, GA	1.75
UX130	15¢ Oklahoma Land Run 4/22/89 Guthrie, OK ...	1.75
UX131	21¢ The Mountains 5/5/89 Denver, CO	1.75
UX132	15¢ The Seashore 6/19/89 Cape Hatteras, NC ...	1.75
UX133	15¢ The Woodlands 8/26/89 Cherokee, NC	1.75
UX134	15¢ Hull House 9/16/89 Chicago, IL	1.75
UX135	15¢ Independence Hall 9/25/89 Philadelphia, PA .	1.75
UX136	15¢ Baltimore Inner Harbor 10/7/89 Baltimore, MD .	1.75
UX137	15¢ Manhattan Skyline 11/8/89 New York, NY ..	1.75

POSTAL CARD FIRST DAY COVERS

UX166

Scott #	Description	Cacheted
UX138	15¢ Capitol Dome 11/26/89 DC	1.75
UX139-42	15¢ Cityscapes sheet of 4 diff.views,rouletted 12/1/89 DC	7.00
UX139-42	Cityscapes, set of 4 different, rouletted	8.00
UX143	(15¢) White House, Picture PC (cost 50¢) 11/30/89 DC	1.75
UX144	(15¢) Jefferson Mem. Pict. PC (cost 50¢) 12/2/89 DC	1.75
UX145	15¢ American Papermaking 3/13/90 New York, NY	1.75
UX146	15¢ Literacy 3/22/90 DC	1.75
UX147	(15¢)Geo. Bingham Pict.PC (cost 50¢) 5/4/90 St. Louis, MO	1.75
UX148	15¢ Isaac Royall House 6/16/90 Medford, MA	1.75
UX150	15¢ Stanford University 9/30/90 Stanford, CA	1.75
UX151	15¢ DAR Mem., Continental/Constitution Hall 10/11/91 DC	1.75
UX152	15¢ Chicago Orchestra Hall 10/19/91 Chicago, IL	1.75
UX153	19¢ Flag 1/24/91 DC	1.75
UX154	19¢ Carnegie Hall 4/1/91 New York, NY	1.75
UX155	19¢ "Old Red" Bldg., U.of Texas 6/14/91 Galveston, TX	1.75
UX156	19¢ Bill of Rights Bicent. 9/25/91 Notre Dame, IN	1.75
UX157	19¢ Notre Dame Admin. Bldg. 10/15/91 Notre Dame, IN	1.75
UX158	30¢ Niagara Falls 8/21/91 Niagara Falls, NY	1.75
UX159	19¢ Old Mill, Univ. of Vermont 10/29/91 Burlington, VT	1.75
	1992-96	
UX160	19¢ Wadsworth Atheneum 1/16/92 Hartford, CT	1.75
UX161	19¢ Cobb Hall, Univ. of Chicago 1/23/92 Chicago, IL	1.75
UX162	19¢ Waller Hall 2/1/92 Salem, OR	1.75
UX163	19¢ America's Cup 5/6/92 San Diego, CA	1.75
UX164	19¢ Columbia River Gorge 5/9/92 Stevenson, WA	1.75
UX165	19¢ Great Hall, Ellis Island 5/11/92 Ellis Island, NY	1.75
UX166	19¢ National Cathedral 1/6/93 DC	1.75
UX167	19¢ Wren Building 2/8/93 Williamsville, VA	1.75
UX168	19¢ Holocaust Memorial 3/23/93 DC	2.25
UX169	19¢ Ft. Recovery 6/13/93 Fort Recovery, OH	1.75
UX170	19¢ Playmaker's Theater 9/14/93 Chapel Hill, NC	1.75
UX171	19¢ O'Kane Hall 9/17/93 Worcester, MA	1.75
UX172	19¢ Beecher Hall 10/9/93 Jacksonville, IL	1.75
UX173	19¢ Massachusetts Hall 10/14/93 Brunswick, ME	1.75
UX174	19¢ Lincoln Home 2/12/94 Springfield, IL	1.75
UX175	19¢ Myers Hall 3/11/94 Springfield, OH	1.75
UX176	19¢ Canyon de Chelly 8/11/94 Canyon de Chelly, AZ	1.75
UX177	19¢ St. Louis Union Station 9/1/94 St. Louis, MO	1.75
UX178-97	19¢ Legends of the West, set of 20 10/18/94	
	Tucson, AZ Lawton, OK or Laramie, WY	35.00
	19¢ Legends of the West, Combo w/2689a-t	50.00
UX198	20¢ Red Barn 1/3/95 Williamsburg, PA	1.75
UX199	(20¢) "G" Old Glory, 12/13/94 cancel, released 1/12/95	1.75
UX200-19	20¢ Civil War Set of 20 6/29/95 Gettysburg, PA	35.00
	20¢ Civil War, combo w/2975a-t	50.00
UX220	20¢ Clipper Ship 9/23/95 Hunt Valley, MD	1.75
UX221-40	20¢ Comic Strips Set of 20 10/1/95 Boca Raton, FL	35.00
UX241	20¢ Winter Farm Scene 2/23/96 Watertown, NY	1.75
UX242-61	20¢ Olympics, Set of 20 5/2/96 DC	35.00
UX262	20¢ McDowell Hall, Hist.Pres.Series 6/1/96, Anapolis, Md	1.75
UX263	20¢ Alexander Hall, Hist.Pres.Series 9/20/96,Princeton, NJ	1.75
UX264-78	20¢ Endangered Species, Set of 15, 10/2/96, San Diego, Ca.	35.00
UX279	20¢ Love Swan Stamp 2/4/97, L.A., CA	1.75
UX280	20¢ City College of NY, Hist.Pres.Series, NY,NY 5/7/97	1.75
UX281	32¢ Bugs Bunny, 5/22/97, Burbank, CA	2.00
UX282	20¢ Pacific '97, Golden Gate in Daylight 6/2/97 S.F.,Ca.	1.75
UX283	40¢ Pacific '97, Golden Gate at Sunset 6/2/97 S. F., Ca.	1.75
UX284	20¢ Fort McHenry, Hist. Pres. Series 9/97	1.75
UX285-89	20¢ Classic Movie Monsters, 9/30/97,	
	Set of 5, Universal City, CA	9.00
UX290	20¢ University of Mississippi, 4/20/98, Univ. of Ms	1.75
UX291	20¢ Tweety & Sylvester, 4/27/98 NY, NY	2.00
UX292	20¢ Girard College, 5/1/98. Phil. PA	1.75
UX293-96	20¢ Tropical Birds, Set of 4, 7/29/98, Ponce, PR	8.50
UX297	20¢ Ballet, 9/16/98, NY, NY	2.00
UX298	20¢ Northeastern Univ., 10/3/98, Boston, MA	1.90
UX299	20¢ Brandies Univ. 10/17/98, Waltham, MA	1.90
UX300	20¢ Love, 1/28/99, Loveland, CO	2.25
UX301	20¢ Univ. of Wisconsin, 2/5/99, Madison, IW	1.90
UX302	20¢ Washington & Lee Univ., 2/11/99, Lexington, VA	1.90
UX303	20¢ Redwood Library & Anthenaeum, 3/11/99	1.90
UX304	20¢ Daffy Duck, 4/16/99	2.25
UX305	20¢ Mount Vernon, 5/14/99, Mount Vernon, VA	1.75
UX...	20¢ Block Island Lighthouse, 7/24/99	1.75

AIRMAIL POST CARDS 1949-95

Scott #	Description	Cacheted
UXC1	4¢ Eagle 1/10/49 DC, round "O" in January 10	2.00
	Oval "O" in January 10	5.00
UXC2	5¢ Eagle 7/31/58 Wichita, KS	2.00
UXC3	5¢ Eagle w/border 6/18/60 Minneapolis, MN	2.00
	"Thin dividing line" at top	5.00
UXC4	6¢ Bald Eagle 2/15/63 Maitland, FL	2.00
UXC5	11¢ Visit the USA 5/27/66 DC	1.75

AIRMAIL POST CARDS (continued)

Scott #	Description	Cacheted
UXC6	6¢ Virgin Islands 3/31/67 Charlotte Amalie, VI	1.75
UXC7	6¢ Boy Scouts 8/4/67 Farragut State Park, ID	1.75
UXC8	13¢ Visit the USA 9/8/67 Detroit, MI	1.75
UXC9	8¢ Eagle 3/1/68 New York, NY	1.75
UXC9a	8¢ Eagle, tagged 3/19/69 DC	15.00
UXC10	9¢ Eagle 5/15/71 Kitty Hawk, NC	1.75
UXC11	15¢ Visit the USA 6/10/71 New York, NY	1.75
UXC12	9¢ Grand Canyon 6/29/72 any city	1.75
UXC13	15¢ Niagara Falls 6/29/72 any city	1.75
UXC13a	Address side blank **(uncacheted)**	600.00
UXC14	11¢ Modern Eagle 1/4/74 State College, PA	1.75
UXC15	18¢ Eagle Weathervane 1/4/74 Miami, FL	1.75
UXC16	21¢ Angel Weathervane 12/17/75 Kitty Hawk, NC	1.75
UXC17	21¢ Jenny 9/16/78 San Diego, CA	1.75
UXC18	21¢ Olympic-Gymnast 12/1/79 Fort Worth, TX	1.75
UXC19	28¢ First Transpacific Flight 1/2/81 Wenatchee, WA	1.75
UXC20	28¢ Soaring 3/5/82 Houston, TX	1.75
UXC21	28¢ Olympic-Speedskating 12/29/83 Milwaukee, WI	1.75
UXC22	33¢ China Clipper 2/15/85 San Fran., CA	1.75
UXC23	33¢ AMERIPEX '86 2/1/86 Chicago, IL	1.75
UXC24	36¢ DC-3 5/14/88 San Diego, CA	2.00
UXC25	40¢ Yankee Clipper 6/28/91	2.00
UXC26	50¢ Eagle 8/24/95 St. Louis, MO	2.25
UXC27	55¢ Mt. Ranier, 5/15/99	2.25

1892-1956 POSTAL REPLY CARDS

Scott #	Description	Uncacheted	Cacheted
UY1	1¢ + 1¢ U.S. Grant 10/25/1892 any city	350.00	...
UY12	3¢ + 3¢ McKinley 2/1/26 any city	250.00	...
UY13	2¢ + 2¢ Washington 12/29/51 DC	...	1.75
UY14	2¢ on 1¢ + 2¢ on 1¢ G. Wash. 1/1/52 any city	50.00	75.00
UY16	4¢ + 4¢ Liberty 11/16/56 New York, NY	...	1.75
UY16a	Message card printed on both halves	75.00	100.00
UY16b	Reply card printed on both halves	50.00	75.00
UY...	20¢ + 20¢ Block Island Lighthouse, 7/14/99	21.25	...
	1958-75		
UY17	3¢ + 3¢ Liberty 7/31/58 Boise, ID		1.75
UY18	4¢ + 4¢ Lincoln 11/19/62 Springfield, IL		1.75
UY18a	4¢ + 4¢ Lincoln, Tagged 3/7/67 Dayton, OH		500.00
UY19	7¢ + 7¢ USA 8/30/63 New York, NY		1.75
UY20	8¢ + 8¢ USA 12/4/67 DC		1.75
UY21	5¢ + 5¢ Lincoln 1/4/68 Hodgenville, KY		1.75
UY22	6¢ + 6¢ Paul Revere 5/15/71 Boston, MA		1.75
UY23	6¢ + 6¢ John Hanson 9/1/72 Baltimore, MD		1.75
UY24	8¢ + 8¢ Samuel Adams 12/16/73 Boston, MA		1.75
UY25	7¢ + 7¢ Charles Thomson 9/14/75 Bryn Mawr, PA		1.75
UY26	9¢ + 9¢ John Witherspoon 11/10/75 Princeton, NJ		1.75

POSTAL CARD FIRST DAY COVERS

Scott #	Description	Cacheted
	1976-95	
UY27	9¢ + 9¢ Caeser Rodney 7/1/76 Dover, DE	1.75
UY28	9¢ + 9¢ Nathan Hale 10/14/77 Coventry, CT	1.75
UY29	(10¢ + 10¢) John Hancock 5/19/78 Quincy, MA	2.50
UY30	10¢ + 10¢ John Hancock 6/20/78 Quincy, MA	1.75
UY31	(12¢ + 12¢) "B" Eagle 3/15/81 Memphis, TN	1.75
UY32	12¢ + 12¢ Isaiah Thomas 5/5/81 Worcester, MA	1.75
UY32a	"Small die"	5.00
UY33	(13¢ + 13¢) Robert Morris 10/11/81 Memphis, TN	1.75
UY34	13¢ + 13¢ Robert Morris 11/10/81 Philadelphia, PA	1.75
UY35	(14¢ + 14¢) Charles Carroll 2/1/85 New Carrollton, MD	1.75
UY36	14¢ + 14¢ Charles Carroll 3/6/85 Annapolis, MD	1.75
UY37	14¢ + 14¢ George Wythe 6/20/85 Williamsburg, PA	1.75
UY38	14¢ + 14¢ American Flag 9/1/87 Baltimore, MD	1.75
UY39	15¢ + 15¢ America the Beautiful 7/11/88 Buffalo, NY	1.75
UY40	19¢ + 19¢ American Flag 3/27/91 DC	2.00
UY41	20¢+20¢ Red Baron 1/3/95 Williamsburg, PA	2.25
	OFFICIAL POSTAL CARDS	
	1983-95	
UZ2	13¢ Eagle 1/12/83 DC	1.75
UZ3	14¢ Eagle 2/26/85 DC	1.75
UZ4	15¢ Eagle (4 colors) 6/10/88 New York, NY	1.75
UZ5	19¢ Eagle 5/24/91 Seattle, WA	1.75
UZ6	20¢ Eagle 5/9/95 DC	1.75
	"POSTAL BUDDY" CARDS	
PB1	15¢ 7/5/90 Merriifield, VA	2.50
PB2	19¢ 2/3/91 Any city	...
PB3	19¢ Stylized Flag 11/13/92 Any city	27.50

CHRISTMAS SEAL FIRST DAY COVERS

Beginning in 1936, Santa Claus, Indiana has been used as the First Day City of U.S. National Christmas Seals. In 1936 the Postmaster would not allow the seal to be tied to the front of the cover and seals for that year are usually found on the back. Since 1937, all seals were allowed to be tied on the front of the FDC's. **All prices are for cacheted FDC's.**

YEAR	PRICE	YEAR	PRICE	YEAR	PRICE	
1936 (500 processed)	55.00	1958	10.00	1980	5.00	
1937	35.00	1959	10.00	1981	5.00	
1938	35.00	1960	20.00	1982	5.00	
1939	35.00	1961	10.00	1983	10.00	
1940	35.00	1962	10.00	1984	5.00	
1941	30.00	1963	10.00	1985	5.00	
1942	40.00	1964	40.00	1986	5.00	
1943	25.00	1965	10.00	1987	5.00	
1944	30.00	1966	10.00			
1945	12.00	1967	20.00	**YEAR**	**PERF**	**IMPERF**
1946	12.00	1968	10.00	1988	7.50	30.00
1947	12.00	1969	10.00	1989	7.50	30.00
1948	20.00	1970	6.00	1990	5.00	20.00
1949	12.00	1971	6.00	1991	5.00	20.00
1950	12.00	1972	6.00	1991-Foil	10.00	...
1951	15.00	1973	6.00	1992	7.50	35.00
1952	12.00	1974	6.00	1993	5.00	20.00
1953	10.00	1975	7.00	1994	5.00	20.00
1954	10.00	1976	6.00	1995	5.00	20.00
1955	10.00	1977	6.00	1996	20.00	5.00
1956	10.00	1978	10.00	1997	20.00	5.00
1957	10.00	1979	6.00			

WORLD WAR II PATRIOTIC EVENT COVERS

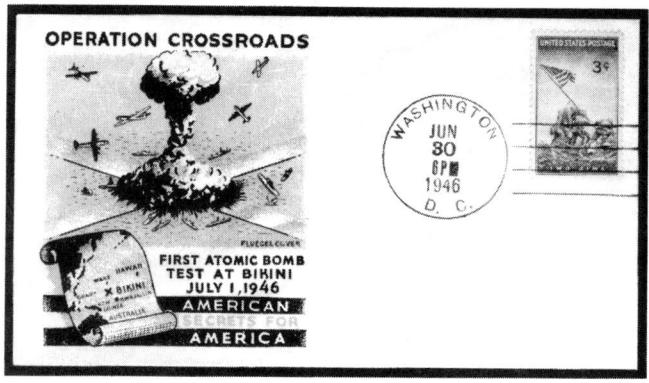

6/30/46

The listing below features the dates of significant patriotic events of World War II. The values listed are for standard size covers bearing related, printed cachets, and cancelled on the appropriate date.
Cachets produced by Minkus and others, which feature general patriotic themes such as "Win the War" are valued at 75¢ unused and $2.00 used.
Covers with Naval cancels, when available, usually sell for twice the listed prices.
From 1943 to date, prices are for unaddressed covers.

WORLD WAR II EVENT	CACHETED COVER
Pearl Harbor 12/7/41	100.00
U.S. Declares War on Japan 12/8/41	75.00
Germany and Italy Declare War on U.S. 12/11/41	75.00
U.S. Declares War on Germany and Italy 12/11/41	75.00
Churchill Arrives at the White House 12/22/41	60.00
Manila and Cavite Fall 1/2/42	60.00
Roosevelt's Diamond Jubilee Birthday 1/30/42	60.00
Singapore Surrenders 2/15/42	60.00
Japan Takes Java 3/10/42	60.00
Marshall Arrives in London 4/8/42	60.00
Dedication of MacArthur Post Office 4/15/42	60.00
Doolittle Air Raid on Tokyo 4/18/42	60.00
Fort Mills Corregidor Island Surrenders 5/6/42	60.00
Madagascar Occupied by U.S. 5/9/42	60.00
Mexico at War with Axis 5/23/42	60.00
Bombing of Cologne 6/6/42	60.00
Japan Bombs Dutch Harbor, AK 6/3/42	60.00
Six German Spies Sentenced to Death 8/7/42	60.00
Brazil at War 8/22/42	60.00
Battle of El Alamein 10/23/42	70.00
Operation Torch (Invasion of North Africa) 11/8/42	50.00
Gas Rationing in U.S. 12/1/42	50.00
The Casablanca Conference 1/14/43	50.00
The Casablanca Conference (You must remember this!) 1/22/43	40.00
Point Rationing 3/1/43	50.00
Battle of the Bismarck Sea 3/13/43	40.00
U.S. Planes Bomb Naples 4/5/43	50.00
Bizerte & Tunis Occupied 5/8/43	40.00
Invasion of Attu 5/11/43	40.00
Siciliy Invaded 7/14/43	35.00
Mussolini Kicked Out 7/25/43	35.00
The Quebec Conference 8/14/43	40.00
Sicily Encircled 8/17/43	35.00
Japenese Flee From Kiska 8/21/43	35.00
Italy Invaded 9/3/43	40.00
Italy Surrenders 9/8/43	40.00
Mussolini Escapes 9/18/43	35.00
U.S. Drives Germans out of Naples 10/2/43	35.00
Italy Declares War on Germany 10/13/43	35.00
Hull, Eden, Stalin Conference 10/25/43	35.00
U.S. Government takes over Coal Mines 11/3/43	35.00
The Cairo Meeting 11/25/43	40.00
The Teheran Meeting 11/28/43	40.00
Roosevelt, Churchill, Kai-Shek at Cairo 12/2/43	40.00
FDR, Stalin, Churchill Agree on 3 fronts 12/4/43	40.00
Soviets Reach Polish Border 1/4/44	35.00
Marshalls Invaded 2/4/44	35.00
Truk Attacked 2/18/44	35.00
U.S. Captures Cassino 3/16/44	35.00
Invasion of Dutch New Guinea 4/24/44	35.00
Sevastopol Seige 5/11/44	35.00
Rome Falls 6/4/44	35.00
D-Day Single Face Eisenhower 6/6/44	100.00
D-Day: Invasion of Normandy 6/6/44	35.00
B29's Bomb Japan 6/15/44	35.00
Cherbourg Surrenders 6/27/44	40.00
Paris Revolts 6/23/44	35.00
Caen Falls to Allies 10/14/44	35.00
Marines Invade Guam 7/21/44	35.00
Yanks Enter Brest, etc. 8/7/44	35.00
U.S. Bombs Phillipines 8/10/44	35.00
Invasion of Southern France 8/16/44	25.00
Liberation of Paris 8/23/44	30.00
Romania Joins Allies 8/23/44	35.00
Florence Falls to Allies 8/23/44	30.00
Liberation of Brussels 9/4/44	25.00
We Invade Holland, Finland Quits 9/5/44	30.00
Soviets Invade Yugoslavia 9/6/44	30.00
Russians Enter Bulgaria 9/9/44	30.00

WORLD WAR II EVENT	CACHETED COVER
We Invade Luxembourg 9/9/44	30.00
Liberation of Luxembourg 9/10/44	25.00
Albania Invaded 9/27/44	35.00
Phillippines, We Will Be Back 9/27/44	25.00
Greece Invaded 10/5/44	35.00
Liberation of Athens 10/14/44	25.00
Liberation of Belgrade 10/16/44	25.00
Russia Invades Czechoslovakia 10/19/44	30.00
Invasion of the Philippines 10/20/44	25.00
The Pied Piper of Leyte-Philippine Invasion 10/21/44	35.00
Invasion of Norway 10/25/44	25.00
Liberation of Tirana 11/18/44	25.00
100,000 Yanks Land on Luzon 1/10/45	25.00
Liberation of Warsaw 1/17/45	30.00
Warsaw Recaptured 1/17/45	30.00
Russians Drive to Oder River 2/2/45	25.00
Liberation of Manila 2/4/45	25.00
Yalta Conference 2/12/45	25.00
Liberation of Budapest 2/13/45	25.00
Corregidor is Ours 2/17/45	25.00
Turkey Wars Germany and Japan 2/23/45	25.00
Egypt at War 2/25/45	25.00
Yanks Enter Cologne 3/5/45	25.00
Cologne is Taken 3/6/45	20.00
Historical Rhine Crossing 3/8/45	20.00
Bombing of Tokyo 3/10/45	25.00
Russia Crosses Oder River 3/13/45	25.00
Capture of Iwo Jima 3/14/45	20.00
Battle of the Inland Sea 3/20/45	20.00
Crossing of the Rhine 3/24/45	20.00
Danzig Invaded 3/27/45	25.00
Okinawa Invaded 4/1/45	20.00
Vienna Invaded 4/5/45	25.00
Japanese Cabinet Resigns 4/7/45	20.00
6 Japanese Warships Sunk 4/7/45	25.00
Liberation of Vienna 4/10/45	20.00
We Invade Bremen, etc. 4/10/45	25.00
FDR Dies - Truman becomes President 4/12/45	50.00
Liberation of Vienna 4/13/45	25.00
Patton Invades Czechoslovakia 4/18/45	25.00
Berlin Invaded 4/21/45	25.00
Berlin Encircled 4/25/45	20.00
"GI Joe" and "Ivan" Meet at Torgau-Germany 4/26/45	20.00
Yanks Meet Reds 4/27/45	25.00
Mussolini Executed 4/28/45	35.00
Hitler Dead 5/1/45	35.00
Liberation of Italy 5/2/45	20.00
Berlin Falls 5/2/45	25.00
Liberation of Rangoon 5/3/45	20.00
5th and 7th Armies Meet at Brenner Pass 5/4/45	20.00
Liberation of Copenhagen 5/5/45	20.00
Liberation of Amsterdam 5/5/45	25.00
Over a Million Nazis Surrender 5/5/45	25.00
Liberation of Oslo 5/8/45	25.00
Liberation of Prague 5/8/45	25.00
V-E Day 5/8/45	35.00
Atomic Bomb Test 5/16/45	25.00
Invasion of Borneo 6/11/45	25.00
Eisenhower Welcomed Home 6/19/45	20.00
Okinawa Captured 6/21/45	25.00
United Nations Conference 6/25/45	25.00
American Flag Raised over Berlin 7/4/45	25.00
Churchill Defeated 7/26/45	25.00
Big Three Meet at Potsdam 8/1/45	25.00
Atomic Bomb Dropped on Hiroshima 8/6/45	65.00
Russia Declares War on Japan 8/8/45	25.00
Japan Capitulates 8/14/45	25.00
Japan Signs Peace Treaty 9/1/45	50.00
Liberation of China 9/2/45	35.00
V-J Day 9/2/45	35.00
Liberation of Korea 9/2/45	35.00
Flag Raising over Tokyo - Gen. MacArthur Takes Over 9/8/45	25.00
Gen. Wainwright Rescued from the Japanese 9/10/45	25.00
Nimitz Post Office 9/10/45	25.00
Wainright Day 9/10/45	25.00
Marines Land in Japan 9/23/45	40.00
Nimitz Day-Washington 10/5/45	25.00
War Crimes Commission 10/18/45	25.00
Premier Laval Executed as Traitor 10/15/45	25.00
Fleet Reviewed by President Truman 10/27/45	35.00
Trygue Lie Elected 1/21/46	25.00
2nd Anniversary of D-Day 6/6/46	25.00
Operation Crossroads 6/30/46	100.00
Bikini Atomic Bomb Test 7/1/46	125.00
Philippine Republic Independence 7/3/46	25.00
Atomic Age 7/10/46	25.00
Victory Day 8/14/46	25.00
Opening of UN Post Office at Lake Success 9/23/46	25.00
Goering Commits Suicide 10/16/46	40.00
Opening Day of UN in Flushing, NY 10/23/46	25.00
Marshall is Secretary of State 1/21/47	25.00
Moscow Peace Conference 3/10/47	25.00

Values listed below from 1901 thru 1925 are for Picture Postcards with Washington DC Cancels
with or without content relating to the Inauguration or Washington DC related items.

 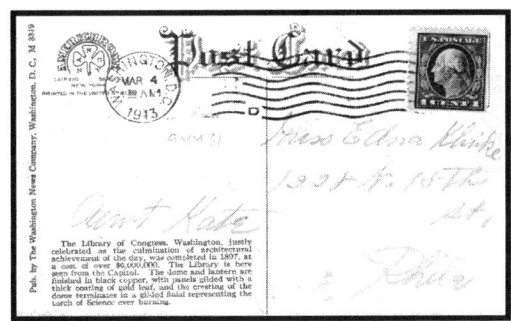

1913 WILSON WITHOUT CONTENT

		Without Content	With Content
1901	McKinley, 3/4/01	1000.00	1500.00
1901	McKinley, 9/7/01, Assignment Day on cover with add-on cachet		650.00
1901	McKinley, 9/14/01, Day of Death with add-on cachet		1500.00
1905	Teddy Roosevelt, 3/4/05	350.00	500.00
1909	Taft, 3/4/09	200.00	250.00
1913	Wilson, 3/4/13	300.00	400.00
1917	Wilson, 3/4/17	400.00	500.00
1921	Harding, 3/4/21	350.00	⌐450.00

1933 FRANKLIN D. ROOSEVELT

1985 RONALD REAGAN

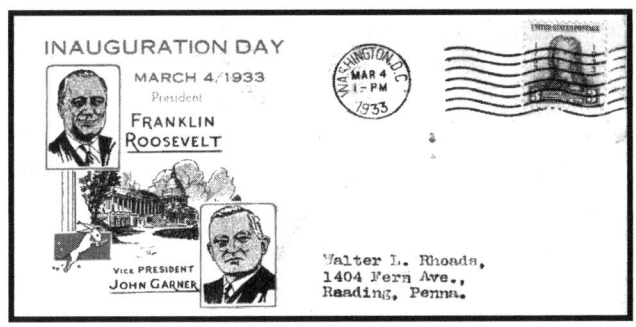 

Prices are for covers with **PRINTED CACHETS** and Wash, D.C. cancels.
Covers with cancels from other cities, except as noted, sell for somewhat less.

1929	Hoover 3/4/29	250.00
1929	Hoover 3/4/29 (**Rubber Stamp Cachet**)	150.00
1933	Roosevelt 3/4/33	60.00
1937	Roosevelt 1/20/37	225.00
1941	Roosevelt 1/20/41	225.00
1945	Roosevelt 1/20/45	225.00
1945	Truman 4/12/45	250.00
1949	Truman 1/20/49	70.00
1953	Eisenhower 1/20/53	16.00
1957	Eisenhower 1/21/57	12.00

1961	Kennedy 1/20/61	20.00
1963	Johnson 11/22/63 Any City	100.00
1965	Johnson 1/20/65	8.00
1969	Nixon 1/20/69	10.00
1973	Nixon 1/20/73	8.00
1974	Ford 8/9/74	6.00
1977	Carter 1/20/77	4.00
1981	Reagan 1/20/81	4.00
1985	Reagan 1/20/85	3.50
1989	Bush 1/20/89	3.50
1993	Clinton 1/20/93	3.00
1997	Clinton 1/20/97	3.00

UNITED STATES SOUVENIR CARDS

UNITED STATES POSTAL SERVICE

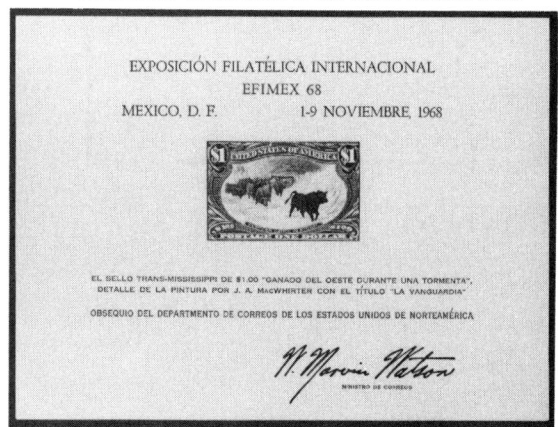

PS2

PS45

SCCS Number	Event and Description	First Day Show/Issue	Mint Card	Cancelled Card
FPS1939Aa	Philatelic Truck with Gum	1939	50.00	..
FPS1939Ab	Philatelic Truck without Gum	1939	10.00	..
PS1	Barcelona'60-Columbus Landing ($) (2)	3/26/60	450.00	425.00
PS2	Efimex'68-#292 (4)	11/1/68	2.50	7.50
	1970-1975			
PS3	Philympia - #548-550 (9)	9/18/70	1.25	sc/12.00
PS4	Exfilima'71 - #1110, 1125, Peru (15)	11/6/71	1.25	50.00
PS5	Belgica'72 - #914, 1026, 1104 (20)	6/24/72	1.25	sc/22.50
PS6	Olympia Philatelie Munchen'72 - #1460, 1461, 1462, C85 (21)	8/18/72	1.25	25.00
PS7	Exfilbra'72 - #C14, Brazil (22)	8/26/72	1.25	45.00
PS8	Postal Forum VI - #1396 Block (23)	8/27/72	1.25	20.00
PS9	Postal People (#1489-98 (11''x14'')	1973	110.00	200.00
PS10	Ibra'73 - #C13, Germany (28)	5/11/73	1.50	10.00
PS11	Apex'73 - #C3a, Newfld., Honduras (30)	7/4/73	1.50	20.00
PS12	Polska'73 - #1488 (31)	8/19/73	1.50	150.00
PS13	Hobby Show Chicago - #1456-59 (35)	2/3/74	1.75	15.00
PS14	Internaba'74 - #1530-37 (37)	6/6/74	2.75	12.00
PS15	Stockholmia'74 - #836, Sweden (38)	9/21/74	2.75	15.00
PS15	Swedish First Day Cancel			22.50
PS16	Exfilmex'74 - #1157, Mexico (39)	10/26/74	2.75	sc/37.50
PS17	Espana'75 - #233, 1271, Spain (40)	4/4/75	1.50	35.00
PS17	Spanish First Day Cancel			75.00
PS18	Arphila'75 - #1187, 1207, France (42)	6/6/75	2.35	35.00
	1976-1980			
PS19	Weraba'76 - #1434-35 (45)	4/1/76	2.50	4.00
PS20	Science & Technology - #C76 (48)	5/30/76	2.75	4.00
PS21	Colorado Centennial - #288, 743, 1670 (50)	8/1/76	2.50	4.00
PS22	Hafnia'76 - #5, Denmark (51)	8/20/76	2.50	4.00
PS23	Italia'76 - #1168, Italy (52)	10/14/76	2.50	4.00
PS23	Italian First Day Cancel			40.00
PS24	Nordposta'76 - #689, Germany, Hamburg(53)	10/30/76	2.25	4.00
PS25	Amphilex'77 - #1027, Netherlands (56)	5/26/77	2.50	4.00
PS26	San Marino'77 - #1, 2, San Marino (57)	8/28/77	2.50	4.00
PS27	Rocpex'78 - #1706-9, Taiwan (60)	3/20/78	2.75	100.00
PS28	Naposta'78 - $555, 563, Germany (61)	5/20/78	2.50	4.00
PS28	German First Day Cancel			22.50
PS29	Brasiliana'79 - #C91-92, Brazil (63)	9/15/79	3.25	6.00
PS30	Japex'79 - #1158, Japan (64)	11/2/79	3.50	6.00
PS31	London'80 - #329 (65)	5/6/80	3.50	75.00
PS32	Norwex'80 - #620-21, Norway (66)	6/13/80	3.25	5.00
PS33	Essen'80 - #1014, German (69)	11/15/80	3.25	5.00
	1981-1985			
PS34	Wipa'81 - #1252, Austria (71)	5/22/81	3.25	5.00
PS35	Stamp Collecting Month - #245, 1913 (72)	10/1/81	3.00	5.00
PS36	Philatokyo'81 - #1531, Japan (73)	10/9/81	3.00	5.00
PS37	Nordposta'81 - #923, Germany (74)	11/7/81	3.00	5.00
PS38	Canada'82 - #116, Canada #15 (76)	5/20/82	3.25	5.00
PS39	Philexfrance'82 - #1753, France (77)	6/11/82	3.25	5.00
PS40	Stamp Collecting Month - #C3a (78)	10/1/82	3.25	5.00
PS41	Espamer'82 - #801, 1437, 2024 (80)	10/12/82	3.25	5.00
PS42	U.S.-Sweden - #958, 2036, Sweden (81)	3/24/83	3.00	5.00
PS43	Concord, German Settlers - #2040, Germany (82)	4/29/83	3.00	5.00

SCCS Number	Event and Description	First Day Show/Issue	Mint Card	Cancelled Card
PS44	Tembal'83 - #C71, Switzerland (83)	5/21/83	3.00	5.00
PS45	Brasiliana'83 - #2, Brazil (85)	7/29/83	3.00	5.00
PS46	Bangkok'83 - #210, Siam (86)	8/4/83	3.00	5.00
PS47	Philatelic Memento'83 - #1387 (87)	8/19/83	3.00	4.50
PS48	Stamp Collecting Month - #293 (88)	10/4/83	4.25	6.00
PS49	Espana'84 - #233, Spain (92)	4/27/84	3.00	5.00
PS50	Hamburg'84 - #C66, Germany (95)	6/19/84	3.00	5.00
PS51	St. Lawrence Seaway - #1131, Canada #387 (96)	6/26/84	3.25	5.00
PS52	Ausipex'84 - #290, Australia (97)	9/21/84	3.00	5.00
PS53	Stamp Collecting Month - #2104 (98)	10/1/84	3.00	5.00
PS54	Philakorea'84 - #741, Korea (99)	10/22/84	3.00	5.00
PS55	Philatelic Memento'85 - #2 (101)	2/26/85	3.00	5.00
PS56	Olymphilex'85 - #C106, Switzerland (102)	3/18/85	3.00	5.00
PS57	Israphil'85 - #566, Israel (103)	5/14/85	3.00	5.00
PS58	Argentina'85 - #1737, Argentina (107)	7/5/85	3.00	5.00
PS59	Mophila'85 - #296, Germany (108)	9/11/85	3.00	5.00
PS60	Italia'85 - #1107, Italy (109)	10/25/85	3.00	5.00
PS61	Statue of Liberty - #2147	7/18/85	32.50	25.00
	1986-1992			
PS62	Statue of Liberty - #C87 (110)	2/21/86	5.00	7.00
PS62v	Stampex Overprint - #2204, Australia	8/4/86	15.00	25.00
PS63	Stockholmia'86 - #113, Sweden (113)	8/28/86	5.00	7.00
PS64	Capex'87 - #569, Canada #883 (117)	6/13/87	5.00	7.00
PS65	Hafnia'87 - #299, Denmark (118)	10/16/87	5.00	7.00
PS66	Monte Carlo - #2286, 2300, Monaco (121)	11/13/87	5.00	7.00
PS67	Finlandia'88 - #836, Finland (122)	6/1/88	5.00	7.00
PS68	Philexfrance'89 - #C120, France (125)	7/7/89	9.00	12.00
PS69	World Stamp Expo'89 - #2433 (127)	11/17/89	8.00	9.00
PS70	Stamp World London - #1, G.B. #1 (130)	5/3/90	8.00	9.00
PS71	Olymphilex'92 - #2619, 2637-41		60.00	125.00

BUREAU OF ENGRAVING AND PRINTING

		1954-1970		
F1954A	National Philatelic Museum, DC (1)	3/13/54	1875.00	..
F1966A	Sipex Scenes'66 - Washington D.C. Scenes (3)	5/21/66	125.00	160.00
B1	Sandipex - 3 Washington D.C. Scenes(5)	7/16/69	50.00	150.00
B2	ANA'69 - Eagle "Jackass" Notes ($) (N1)	8/12/69	75.00	..
B3	Fresno Fair - 3 Wash. D.C. Scenes (N2)	10/2/69	400.00	..
B4	ASDA'69 - #E4 Block (6)	11/21/69	22.50	85.00
B5	Interpex'70 - #1027, 1035, C35, C38 (7)	3/13/70	50.00	150.00
B6	Compex'70 - #C18 Block (8)	5/29/70	12.50	175.00
B7	ANA'70 - Currency Collage ($) (N3)	8/18/70	95.00	..
B8	Hapex APS'70 - #799, C46, C55 (10)	11/5/70	12.00	..
		1971-1973		
B9	Interpex'71 - #1193 Block,1331-32, 1371,C76 (11)	3/12/71	2.25	50.00
B10	Westpex San Francisco - #740,852,966,997 (12)	4/23/71	2.25	130.00
B11	Napex'71 - #990-92 (13)	5/12/71	2.25	125.00
B12	ANA'71- 80th Anniv. Convention ($) (N4)	8/10/71	5.50	..
B13	Texanex'71 - #938, 1043, 1242 (14)	8/26/71	2.00	250.00
B14	ASDA'71 - #C13-15 (16)	11/19/71	3.25	37.50
B15	Anphilex, Collectors Club - #1-2 (17)	11/26/71	1.00	..
B16	Interpex'72 - #1173 Block, 976, 1434-35 (18)	3/17/72	1.00	10.00
B17	Nopex, New Orleans - #1020 (19)	4/6/72	1.00	150.00
B18	ANA'72 - $2 Science Allegory ($) (N5)	8/15/72	5.50	135.00
B19	Sepad'72, SPA - #1044 Block (24)	10/20/72	1.00	30.00
B20	ASDA'72 - #863, 868, 883, 888 (25)	11/17/72	1.00	10.00
B21	Stamp Expo'72 - #C36 Block (26)	11/24/72	2.00	25.00
B22	Interpex'73 - #976 Block (27)	3/9/73	1.25	10.00
B23	Compex'73 - #245 Block (29)	5/25/73	3.00	40.00
B24	ANA'73 - $5 "America" ($) (N6)	8/23/73	9.00	25.00

BUREAU OF ENGRAVING AND PRINTING

B26

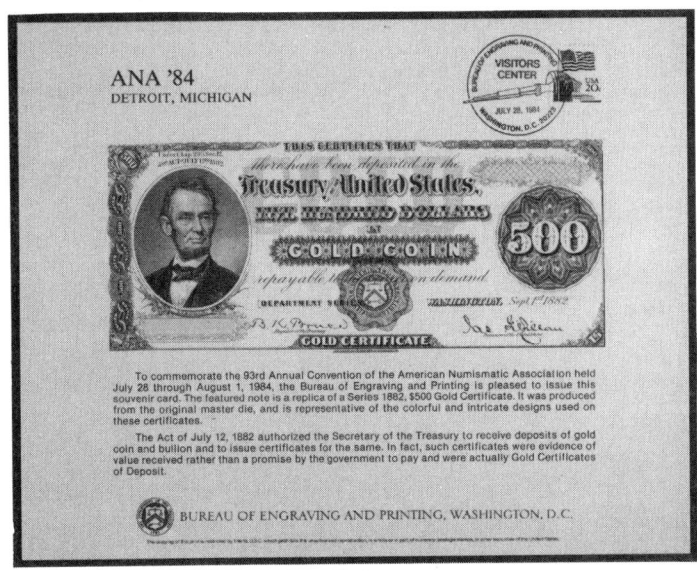

B71

SCCS Number	Event and Description	First Day Show/Issue	Mint Card	Cancelled Card
B25	Napex'73 - #C3 Block, C4-6 (32)	9/14/73	2.00	35.00
B26	ASDA'73 - #908 Block, 1139-44 (33)	11/16/73	1.00	8.00
B27	Stamp Expo'73 - #C20 Block (34)	12/7/73	2.00	20.00
	1974-1976			
B28	Micopex'74 - #C43 Block (36)	3/8/74	1.50	8.50
B29	ANA'74 - $10 Education ($) (N7)	8/13/74	11.00	40.00
B30	Napex'75 - #708 Block (41)	5/9/75	5.75	18.50
B31	Women's Year (with folder) - #872, 878, #959, $1 Martha Washington ($) (43)	5/2/75	22.50	250.00
B32	ANA'75 - $1 George & Martha Wash. ($)(N8)	8/19/75	9.00	40.00
B33	ASDA'75 - #1003 Block, Washington (44)	11/21/75	27.50	50.00
B34	Interphil'76 - #120 Block, Jefferson (46)	5/29/76	5.00	15.00
B35	Card from Interphil program - #1044	5/29/76	5.50	100.00
B36	Bicentennial Expo on Science and Technology, Kitty Hawk/Space	5/30/76	5.50	150.00
B37	Stamp Expo'76, Citizen Soldier - #1348, #1348, 51, 52 (49)	6/11/76	5.50	40.00
B38	ANA'76 - $2 Fulton & Morse (N9)	8/24/76	7.50	32.50
	1977-1980			
B39	Milcopex'77, Polar Theme - #733, 1128 (54)	3/4/77	2.00	15.00
B40	Rompex'77, Mountains - #1001 Block (55)	5/20/77	2.00	9.50
B41	ANA'77 - $5 Indian Chief ($) (N10)	8/23/77	5.75	10.00
B42	Puripex'77 - #801 Block, San Juan Gate (58)	9/2/77	1.50	6.00
B43	ASDA'77 - #C45 Block, Wright Bros (59).	11/16/77	2.00	6.00
B44	Paper Money Show'78 - De Soto Vignette(N11)	6/2/78	4.50	8.00
B45	Cenjex'78 - #785 Block, 646, 680, 689, #1086, 1716 (62)	6/23/78	2.00	6.00
B46	ANA'80 - $5 Grant & Sheridan ($) (N12)	2/15/80	17.50	40.00
B47	Paper Money Show'80 - 2 $10 Lewis-Clark ($) (N13)	6/6/80	13.50	20.00
B48	Napex'80 - #573 Block, Capitol (67)	7/4/80	9.00	30.00
B49	Visitor Center - Eagle & Freedom	9/8/80	7.00	15.00
B50	ASDA Stamp Festival - #962 Block, Francis S.Key (68)	9/25/80	11.00	35.00
	1981-1983			
B51	Stamp Expo'81 South - #1287 Block, 1331-32 (70)	3/20/81	13.00	37.50
B52	Visitor Center - G.Wash. & D.C.Views	4/22/81	7.50	12.00
B53	Paper Money Show'81 - $20 G.Wash.($)(N14)	6/19/81	16.75	25.00
B54	ANA'81 - $5 Silver Certificate ($) (N15)	7/27/81	12.50	22.50
B55	Milcopex'82 - #1136 Block, Reuter (75)	3/5/82	12.50	17.50
B56	Paper Money Show'82 -"Brown Backs"($)(N16)	6/18/82	12.00	20.00
B57	ANA'82 - $1 Great Seal ($) (N17)	8/17/82	12.50	20.00
B58	Espamer'82 - #244 Block, Isabella (79)	10/12/82	25.00	65.00
B59	FUN'83 - $100 "Watermelon" ($) (N18)	1/5/83	22.50	30.00
B60	Texanex-Topex'83 - #776 Block, 1660 (84)	6/17/83	18.00	30.00
B61	ANA'83 - $20 1915 Note ($) (N19)	8/16/83	17.50	25.00
B62	Philatelic Show'83, Boston - #718-19 (89)	10/21/83	10.00	25.00
B63	ASDA'83 - #881, Metropolitan Opera (90)	11/17/83	10.00	20.00
	1984-1985			
B64	FUN'84 - $1 1880 Note ($) (N20)	1/4/84	22.50	25.00
B65	Spider Press, Intaglio, Brown Eagle	1/4/84	350.00	425.00
B66	Espana'84 - #241 Block (91)	4/27/84	13.50	30.00
B67	Stamp Expo'84 - #1791-94, Torch (93)	4/27/84	20.00	27.50
B68	Compex'84 - #728 (94)	5/25/84	20.00	27.50
B69	Money Show'84, Memphis - $10,000 1878 Note ($) (N21)	6/15/84	22.50	25.00

SCCS Number	Event and Description	First Day Show/Issue	Mint Card	Cancelled Card
B70	Spider Press, Intaglio, Blue Eagle	6/15/84	350.00	450.00
B71	ANA'84 - $500 1882 Gold Certificate($) (N22)	7/28/84	15.00	20.00
B72	Spider Press, Intaglio, Green Eagle	7/28/84	350.00	425.00
B73	ASDA'84 - #1470 Block, Youth (100)	11/15/84	13.00	25.00
B74	Spider Press, Intaglio, Green Eagle	11/15/84	140.00	200.00
B75	Long Beach'85 #954, $20 1865 Note $(104)	1/31/85	10.00	14.00
B76	Milcopex'85 - #880 Block, Sousa (105)	3/1/85	11.00	25.00
B77	Coin Club of El Paso-$50 1902 Note ($)(N23)	4/19/85	12.50	25.00
B78	Spider Press, Maroon Statue of Liberty	4/19/85	150.00	180.00
B79	Pacific NW Numismatics -$50 1914 ($) (N24)	5/17/85	13.50	25.00
B80	Napex'85 - #2014 Block, Peace Garden(106)	6/7/85	10.00	22.50
B81	Paper Money Show, Memphis - $10,000 1878 Note ($) (N25)	6/14/85	15.00	20.00
B82	ANA'85 - $500 1882 Gold Cert. ($) (N26)	8/20/85	15.00	18.00
B83	Spider Press, Green Statue of Liberty	8/20/85	175.00	200.00
B84	Paper Money Show, Cherry Hill - $10 1882 ($) (N27)	11/14/85	17.50	23.50
B85-86	Spider Press, Blue Liberty Bell with card (100)	11/14/85	175.00	200.00
	1986-1987			
B87	FUN'86 - $100 1890 Treasury ($) (N28)	1/2/86	15.00	18.00
B88	ANA Midwinter, Salt Lake C. - $10 1901($)(N29)	2/19/86	12.50	20.00
B89	Garfield-Perry - #306 Block, Martha Wash (111)	3/21/86	10.00	25.00
B90	Ameripex'86 - #134, 2052, 1474, Franklin (112)	5/22/86	10.00	20.00
B91-92	Spider Press, Green Liberty Bell with card	5/22/86	65.00	100.00
B93	Paper Money Show'86 - $5 1902 ($)(N30)	6/20/86	11.00	17.50
B94	ANA'86, Milwaukee - 5¢ Fractional ($) (N31)	8/5/86	11.00	17.50
B95-96	Spider Press, Brown Liberty Bell with card	8/5/86	65.00	100.00
B97	Houpex'86 - #1035, 1041, 1044A (114)	9/5/86	12.00	25.00
B98	Lobex'86 - $10 1907 Gold Cert. ($) (115)	10/2/86	13.00	22.50
B99	NW Paper Money - Fractional Currency ($)(N32)	11/13/86	13.00	22.50
B100	Dallas Expo - #550 Block, $10,000 1918 ($) (116)	12/11/86	14.00	22.50
B101	BEP 125th Anniv. - Cherry Blossoms (100)	1/7/87	45.00	70.00
B101A	same, "FUN" Embossed (100)	1/7/87	75.00	100.00
B101B	same, ANA Midwinter Seals (100)	2/27/87	75.00	90.00
B101C	same, BEP & WMPG Seals (100)	4/9/87	85.00	135.00
B101D	same, BEP & IPMS Seals (100)	6/19/87	85.00	100.00
B101E	same, BEP & ANA'87 Seals (100)	8/26/87	80.00	95.00
B101F	same, BEP & GENA Seals (100)	9/18/87	50.00	75.00
B102	FUN'87 - $1 1874 Columbus, Wash. ($)(N33)	1/7/87	14.00	18.50
B103	ANA Midwinter'87 - $500,000,000 Treasury Note ($) (N34)	2/27/87	15.00	18.50
B104	BEP 125th Anniv., Fort Worth - $5 1902 Harrison (N35)	4/25/87	18.00	115.00
B105	Paper Money Show'87 - $20 1922 Seal ($)(N36)	6/19/87	11.00	15.00
B106	ANA'87, Atlanta - $2 1886 ($) (N37)	8/26/87	11.00	15.00
B108	GENA'87 Numismatics - $10 1907 ($)(N38)	9/18/87	15.00	18.00
B109	Spider Press, Brown State Shields, Intaglio	9/18/87	85.00	150.00
B110	Sescal'87 - #798 Constitution (119)	10/16/87	12.50	22.50
B111	Hawaii Numismatist - $5 1923 ($), #C55(120)	11/12/87	22.50	26.50
	1988-1989			
B112	FUN'88 - 50¢ Fractional Currency ($) (N39)	1/7/88	12.00	17.50
B113	Spider Press, Green State Shields, Intaglio	1/7/88	85.00	125.00
B114	ANA Midwinter, Little Rock, $10,000 1882 Jackson, Gold Certificate ($) (N40)	3/11/88	13.50	16.50
B115	Paper Money Show - $5 1899 ($) (N41)	6/24/88	13.00	16.00
B116	ANA'88, Cincinnati - $2 1918 Battleship ($) (N42)	7/20/88	14.50	18.00
B117	Spider Press, Blue State Shields, Intaglio	7/20/88	85.00	140.00
B118	APS Stampshow, Detroit - #835 Constitution (123)	8/25/88	11.00	20.00

BUREAU OF ENGRAVING AND PRINTING

B119

SCCS Number	Event and Description	First Day Show/Issue	Mint Card	Cancelled Card
B119	Illinois Numismatist - $10 1915 ($) (N43)	10/6/88	10.00	15.00
B120	Midaphil'88 - #627, Steamboat (124)	11/18/88	10.00	22.50
B121	FUN '89 - $50 1891 Seward ($) (N44)	1/5/89	10.00	15.00
B122	FUN, Indian Mourning Civilization, Intaglio	1/5/89	45.00	75.00
B124	ANA Midwinter, Colorado Springs - $5,000 1878 ($) (N45)	3/3/89	11.50	17.50
B125	Texas Numismatics, El Paso - $5,000 1918 ($) (N46)	4/28/89	11.50	15.00
B126	Paper Money Show - $5 1907 U.S. Note ($) (N47)	6/23/89	10.00	15.00
B127	Paper Money S., Agriculture Scene, Intag.	6/23/89	45.00	70.00
B129	ANA'89, Pittsburgh - $1,000 1891 ($) (N48)	8/9/89	15.00	17.50
B130	ANA, Declaration of Independence, Intag.	8/9/89	45.00	75.00
B132	APS Stampshow, Anaheim - #565, Indians (126)	8/24/89	10.00	18.00
1990-1991				
B133	FUN'90 - $5 1897 Silver ($) (N49)	1/4/90	10.00	16.00
B134	FUN, Brown Eagle & Ships, Intaglio	1/4/90	35.00	70.00
B135	ANA Midwinter, San Diego - $2 1897 ($)(N50)	3/2/90	10.00	16.00
B136	Central States Numismatics, Milwaukee - $1 1897 Silver ($) (N51)	4/6/90	10.00	16.00
B137	CSNS, Blue Eagle & Ships, Intaglio	4/6/90	35.00	70.00
B138	Aripex'90 - #285 Trans-Mississippi (128)	4/20/90	10.00	17.50
B139	DCSE'90, Dallas - $10 1890 Note ($) (N52)	6/14/90	12.50	18.00
B140	ANA Seattle - $1,000 1891 Silver ($) (N53)	8/22/90	12.50	18.00
B141	ANA, Green Eagle & Ships, Intaglio	8/22/90	35.00	70.00
B142	APS Stampshow - #286 Trans-Mississippi (129)	8/23/90	10.00	18.00
B143	Westex Numismatic, Denver - $2 1890 ($) (N54)	9/21/90	12.50	16.00
B144	Hawaii Numis. - $50 1874 Legal Tender($) (N55)	11/1/90	15.00	25.00
B145	FUN - $20 1875 Legal Tender ($)(N49)	1/3/91	11.50	16.00
B146	FUN, Green "Freedom & Capitol, Intaglio	1/3/91	39.50	70.00
B147	ANA Midwinter - $2 1917 Legal Tender ($) (N50)	3/1/91	11.50	16.00
B148	Paper Money Show, Memphis - $20 1890 ($) (N58)	6/14/91	11.50	16.00
B149	ANA, Chicago - $5,000 1878 Legal T. ($) (N59)	8/13/91	16.50	19.50
B150	ANA, Gray "Freedom" & Capitol, Intaglio	8/13/91	42.50	70.00
B151	APS Stampshow, Philadelphia - #537 (131)	8/22/91	10.00	20.00
B152	Fort Worth, Five BEP Buildings	4/26/91	40.00	160.00
1992-1993				
B153	FUN - $1 1862 Legal Tender ($) (N60)	1/9/92	10.00	16.00
B154	FUN, Blue Columbus Voyage, Intaglio	1/9/92	40.00	70.00
B155	Central States Numis. - $1,000 1875 Legal Tender ($) (N61)	4/30/92	13.00	18.50
B156	World Columbian Stamp Expo - #118 (132)	5/22/92	11.00	18.00
B157	WCSE, Red Columbus Voyage, Intaglio	5/22/92	40.00	80.00
B158	Paper Money Show - $5 1914 ($) (N62)	6/19/92	10.00	16.00
B159	ANA, Orlando - $5 1865 Note ($) (N63)	8/12/92	12.50	16.00
B160	ANA, Green Columbus Voyage, Intaglio	8/12/92	40.00	85.00
B161	APS, Oakland - #118 Block (134)	8/27/92	10.00	17.00
B162	Savings Bonds - #WS7, $25 Sav. Bond (133)	6/15/92	12.50	30.00
B163	Green Fleet of Columbus 1492, Intaglio	10/13/92	40.00	75.00

SCCS Number	Event and Description	First Day Show/Issue	Mint Card	Cancelled Card
B164	CFC, Red Cross - #1016 + 1155, 1263, 1385, 1425, 1438, 1549 (135)	1/13/93	11.50	30.00
B165	FUN - $1,000 1890 Treasury Note Back ($) (N64)	1/7/93	12.50	16.00
B166	FUN, 3 National Parks Scenes, Intaglio	1/7/93	45.00	65.00
B167	ANA, Colorado Springs - $2 1880 Legal Tender Back($) (N65)	3/11/93	12.00	16.00
B168	ASDA'93 - #859, 864, 869, 874, 879, 884, 889, 893 1¢ Famous Americans (136)	5/5/93	10.00	16.00
B169	Texas Numismatics - $500 1902 Back ($)(N66)	5/6/93	12.50	16.00
B170	Georgia Numism. - $1,000 1878 Back ($) (N67)	5/13/93	12.50	16.00
B171	Paper Money Show - $500 1918 Back ($) (N69)	6/18/93	12.50	16.00
B172	IPMS, 3 National Parks Scenes,Purple, Int.	6/18/93	45.00	55.00
B173	ANA, Baltimore - $100 1914 Back ($)	7/28/93	12.50	16.00
B174	ANA, 3 National Parks Scenes, Green, Int.	7/28/93	45.00	60.00
B175	Savings Bond - #WS8, $200 Bond (137)	8/2/93	11.50	25.00
B176	Omaha Philatelic - #QE4, JQ5, E7, Newspaper (138)	9/3/93	12.00	20.00
B178	ASDA - Unfinished Masterpieces, Wash (139)	10/28/93	10.00	16.00
1994-1995				
B179	FUN'94 - $20 1923 Proposed ($) (N70)	1/6/94	10.00	16.00
B180	FUN, Justice Orlando, Intaglio	1/6/94	35.00	50.00
B181	SANDICAL - #E1 Block (140)	2/11/94	10.00	17.50
B182	ANA, New Orleans -$10 1899 Proposed($) (N71)	3/3/94	12.50	17.50
B183	European Paper Money Show, Netherlands - $100 1908 Proposed Note (N72)	4/16/94	13.50	37.50
B184	Paper Money Show - $10 Proposed Note ($) (N73)	6/17/94	12.50	16.00
B185	IPMS, Justice Memphis, Intaglio	6/17/94	33.50	50.00
B186	BEP Stamp Centennial - #246/263 Black (13)	7/1/94	150.00	175.00
B187	ANA, Detroit - $10 1915 Prop. Back ($)(N74)	7/27/94	12.50	16.00
B188	ANA, 1915 3 Female Figures Allegory, Int	7/27/94	70.00	90.00
B189	Savings Bonds - #S1-5, Minuteman (141)	8/1/94	15.00	25.00
B190	APS, Pittsburg - #J31, J32, J35 (142)	8/18/94	10.00	16.00
B191	ASDA, N.Y. - 1894 Newspaper Stamps(143)	11/3/94	10.00	16.00
B192	FUN'95 - $1 1899 Silver Certificate ($)(N75)	1/5/95	12.50	16.50
B193	FUN, Red-Brown Seated Eagle, Intaglio	1/5/95	32.50	45.00
B194	COLOPEX, Columbus, OH - #261 Block (144)	4/7/95	10.00	16.50
B195	New York Numismatics - $1 1917 ($) (N76)	5/5/95	11.50	22.50
B196	Paper Money Show, Memphis - $1 1880 ($) (N77)	6/16/95	11.50	18.00
B197	BEP Stamp Centennial - #246/263, Blue (13) (145)	6/30/95	90.00	115.00
B198	Savings Bond - #905, 908, 940 WWII (146)	8/16/95	10.00	25.00
B199	ANA, Anaheim - $1 1918 Back ($) (N78)	8/16/95	12.50	20.00
B200	ANA, Blue Eagle & Flag, Intaglio	8/16/95	35.00	45.00
B201	Long Beach Numism. - $1 1923 Back ($) (N79)	10/4/95	10.00	18.00
B202	ASDA, N.Y. - #292 Block and background (147)	11/2/95	10.00	18.00
1996-1997				
B203	FUN'96 - $500 1878 Silver Cert. ($) (N80)	1/4/96	10.00	18.00
B204	FUN, Miners Panning for Gold, Brown Int	1/4/96	35.00	45.00
B205	Suburban Washington / Baltimore Coin Show - $500 1878 Back Silver Cert. ($) (N81)	3/22/96	10.00	18.00
B206	Central States Numism. - $1,000 1907 ($) (N82)	4/25/96	10.00	18.00
B207	CAPEX'96, Toronto - #291 Block (148)	6/8/96	10.00	20.00
B208	Olymphilex, Atlanta - #718 Block (149)	7/19/96	10.00	18.00
B209	Olymphiles, Miners Panning Gold, Green Intaglio	7/19/96	35.00	45.00
B210	Savings Bond - Brown Eagle in Flight	8/12/96	11.50	25.00
B211	ANA, Denver - $1,000 1907 Back ($) (N83)	8/14/96	10.00	18.00
B212	ANA, Miners Panning for Gold, Blue Int	8/14/96	35.00	45.00
B213	Billings Stamp Club (150)	10/19/96	10.00	24.00
B214	FUN'96 201886 Silver Cert. ($) (N84)	1/9/97	12.00	20.00
B215	Long Beach C&C, Lock Seal (151)	2/19/97	12.00	20.00
B216	Bay State Coin Show, $20 1882 BN (N85)	4/17/97	12.00	20.00
B217	Pacific '97, Butter Revenue	5/29/97	12.00	20.00
B218	Pacific '97 Handprint	5/29/97	...	...
B219	1PMS, Memphis, TN, $10 1902 ($) (N86)	6/20/97	12.00	20.00
B220	1PMS, intaglio	6/20/97	40.00	50.00
B221	ANA 106th, $100 1874 LT ($) (N87)	7/30/97	12.00	20.00
B222	Milcopex, Newspaper Stamps (153)	9/17/97	12.00	20.00
1998-1999				
B224	FUN'98 (N88)	1/8/98	12.00	20.00
B225	Okpex'98 #922 Block (154)	5/1/98	12.00	20.00
B226	IPMS, Memphis ($) (N89)	6/19/98	12.00	20.00
B227	ANA, Portland, OR ($)	8/5/98	12.00	20.00
B228	Long Beach C&C ($)	9/23/98	12.00	20.00
B229	Long Beach C&C, Trans-Mississippi (155)	9/23/98	40.00	50.00
B230	Savings Bond, Washington, DC	12/21/98	12.00	20.00
B231	FUN'99 ($)	1/7/99	12.00	20.00
B232	Bay State Coin ($)	2/26/99	12.00	20.00
B233	1PMS, Memphis ($)	6/18/99	12.00	20.00
B234	ANA, Rosemont, IL ($)	8/11/99	12.00	20.00

AMERICAN BANK NOTE COMPANY

OFFICIAL SOUVENIR CARD OF
FLORIDA UNITED NUMISMATISTS, INC.
27th ANNUAL CONVENTION, ORLANDO, FLORIDA, JANUARY 6-9, 1982

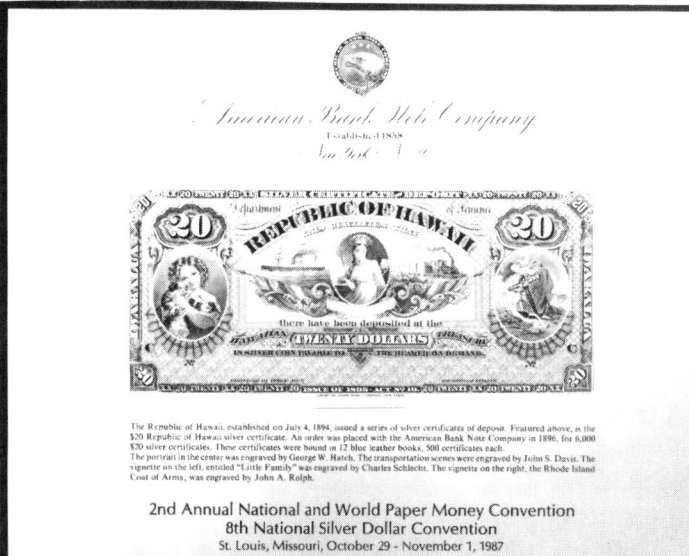

2nd Annual National and World Paper Money Convention
8th National Silver Dollar Convention
St. Louis, Missouri, October 29 - November 1, 1987

SO58

SCCS Number	Event and Description	First Day Show/Issue	Mint Card	Cancelled Card
	SO22			
	1966-1980			
SO1	SIPEX Miner - United States Bank Note Company	5/21/66	10.00	(sc)95.00
SO2	Interphil "America 1776-1976"	5/29/76	60.00	100.00
SO3	Interphil "Lincoln's Gettysburg Address"	5/29/76	75.00	100.00
SO4	Interphil "Awards Banquet, Scenes"	6/5/76	135.00	300.00
SO5	Interphil "Awards Banquet Menu"	6/5/76	225.00	400.00
SO9	Paper Money Show - $2 Liberty Bank of Providence, RI ($)	6/15/79	35.00	50.00
SO10	ANA'79 - $10 Exchange Bank, St.Louis ($)	7/28/79	8.00	35.00
SO11	Paper Money Show - $100 Bank of Lebanon, NH ($)	6/6/80	20.00	35.00
SO12	ANA'80 - $3 Bank of the Ohio Valley ($)	8/13/80	8.00	50.00
SO13	Bank Note Reporter - $3 Bank of the State of Kansas ($)	9/9/80	7.00	500.00
	1981-1984			
SO14	ANA Midyear, Honolulu - $5 Republic of Hawaii Silver Certificate ($)	2/5/81	15.00	85.00
SO15	Paper Money Show - $50 Bank of Selma,AL($)	6/19/81	13.50	20.00
SO16	INTERPAM - $1 Grenville County Bank of Prescott, ON & $2 Cataract City Bank of Paterson, NJ ($)	6/15/81	9.00	100.00
SO17	ANA'81 - $5,000 Canal Bank of New Orl.($)	7/28/81	12.50	22.50
SO18	ANA Building Fund - $10 Artisan Bank of Trenton, NJ ($)	7/28/81	18.50	150.00
SO20	Chester County, PA - 4 Vignettes, Green	12/10/81	9.00	95.00
SO21	Chester County, PA - 4 Vignettes, Brown	21/10/81	9.00	95.00
SO22	FUN'82 - $10 Bank of St. Johns, FL ($)	1/6/82	10.00	300.00
SO23	ANA Midyear, Colorado Springs - Certificate of Deposit, Bank of Ruby, CO	2/18/82	9.50	20.00
SO24	Paper Money Show - $1 Baton Rouge ($)	6/18/82	17.50	20.00
SO25	ANA'82 - $3 Tremont Bank of Boston ($)	8/17/82	11.00	20.00
SO32	ANA Midwinter, Tucson - $1 Lord & Williams Arizona Territory ($)	1/5/83	11.50	17.00
SO33	Paper Money Show - $2 White Mountains Bank of Lancaster, NH ($)	1/5/83	14.00	18.00
SO34	ANA'83 - $1,000 Felix Argenti & Co. ($)	8/16/83	14.00	18.00
SO35	ANA Midwinter, Colorado Springs - Colorado National Bank Advertising Card	2/23/84	17.50	35.00
SO37	Paper Money Show - $100 Bank of the State of Indiana ($)	6/15/84	16.50	25.00
SO38	Statue of Liberty, Black	7/4/84	7.75	18.00
SO39	ANA'84 - $10 Michigan State Bank ($)	7/28/84	25.00	32.50
	1985-1988			
SO40	FUN'85 - $10 Bank of Commerce at Fernandina, FL ($)	1/3/85	9.00	45.00
SO41	ANA Midwinter, San Antonio - $3 Commercial and Agricultural Bank of Galveston ($)	2/21/85	27.50	40.00
SO42	Natl. Assoc. of Tobacco Distributors	3/27/85	9.00	..
SO43	SPMC & IBNS - Hologram with Statue of Liberty		50.00	..
SO53	INS'87 - Statue of Liberty	2/6/87	30.00	95.00
SO54	200th Anniv.-Constitution - Independence Hall	6/19/87	10.00	20.00
SO56	AFL-CIO Trade Show - Eagle	6/19/87	125.00	175.00
SO57	ANA'87 - $10 Republic of Hawaii ($)	8/26/87	16.00	20.00
SO58	NWPMC, St.Louis - $20 Rep. of Hawaii ($)	10/29/87	17.00	20.00
SO59	200th Anniv.-Constitution - 8 States & Eagle	1988	9.00	..
SO60	Paper Money Show - $50 Rep.of Hawaii($)	6/24/88	17.50	20.00
SO61	ANA'88 - $100 Republic of Hawaii ($)	7/20/88	15.00	20.00
	1989-1991			
SO62	FUN'89 - $5 Republic of Hawaii ($)	1/5/89	15.00	20.00
SO63	Miami Stamp Expo - 3 Railroad Vignettes	1/27/89	24.00	35.00
SO64	ANA'89 - #SO34 with Museum Overprint on Back($)	3/3/89	20.00	25.00
SO65	Washington Inauguration - $20 Bank of Pittsylvania ($)	3/15/89	12.00	..
SO66	200th Anniv.-Constitution - 3 States		12.00	..
SO67	Paper Money Show - $10 Rep. Hawaii ($)	6/23/89	18.00	20.00
SO68	ANA'89 - $20 Republic of Hawaii ($)	8/9/89	18.00	22.50
SO69	200th Anniv.-N.Carolina - $5 Bank of North Carolina ($)	11/2/89	13.50	....
SO71	Miami Stamp Expo - Native Americans	1/12/90	20.00	35.00
SO72	200th Anniv.-Rhode I. - $100 Bank-America($)	6/15/90	14.00	20.00
SO73	ANA'90 - #SO12 overprinted on back ($)	..	15.00	18.00
SO74	Paper Money Show -$5 City of Memphis($)	6/14/91	15.00	20.00
SO75	IPMS - America, American Flag Hologram	6/14/91	15.00	20.00
SO76	ANA'91 - $3 Marine Bank of Chicago ($)	8/13/91	15.00	20.00
SO77	Souvenir Card Collectors Soc.10th Anniv.	8/13/91	15.00	20.00
SO78	APS'91 - #114 and Railroad Scene	8/22/91	15.00	25.00
SO79	APS - William Penn Treaty with Indians	8/22/91	115.00	175.00
SO80	Baltimore Phil.Soc.- #120 Decl.of Indep.	8/31/91	15.00	25.00
SO81	ASDA - #117 and S.S.Adriatic	11/7/91	15.00	25.00
SO82	ASDA - Brooklyn Bridge Harbor Scene	11/7/91	110.00	175.00
SO83	PSNE - #118 and Landing of Columbus	11/15/91	15.00	25.00
	1992-1994			
SO84	FUN'92 - Cuban 50 Centavo Note ($)	1/9/92	15.00	25.00
SO85	FUN - Columbus with Globe Hologram	1/9/92	17.00	30.00
SO86	ANA - Costa Rica 100 Colones Gold Ct.($)	2/27/92	18.00	25.00
SO87	Interpex - Venezuela 25¢ Land.-Columbus	3/12/92	15.00	25.00
SO88	World Columbian Stamp Expo - Costa Rica 12¢ Christopher Columbus	5/22/92	15.00	25.00
SO89	WCSE - #230 1¢ Columbian	5/22/92	15.00	25.00
SO90	WCSE - 1921 El Salvador & Statue (Red)	5/22/92	110.00	165.00
SO90A	WCSE - 1921 El Salvador & Statue (Blue)	5/22/92	250.00	375.00
SO91-96	WCSE - set of 6 1893 Columbian Exposition Tickets	5/22/92	165.00	275.00
SO97	WCSE - Folder for #2624-29 with insert bearing "Landing of Columbus"	5/22/92	35.00	45.00
SO102	Paper Money Show -$10 City -Memphis($)	6/19/92	15.00	25.00
SO103	ANA, Orlando - $4 Bank of Florida ($)	8/12/92	15.00	27.50
SO104	APS, Oakland - #234, Costa Rica #122	8/27/92	15.00	25.00
SO105	APS, 3 El Salvador stamps in brown	8/27/92	70.00	100.00
SO105A	same as SO105 in Green, Purple, Orge.	8/27/92	250.00	375.00
SO106	ASDA - 2 El Salvador stamps plus vignette of Columbus	10/28/92	15.00	25.00
SO107	ASDA, Historic Event, Dominican Rep. 50 Pesos Columbus Note ($)	10/28/92	18.00	25.00
SO108	ASDA, Grey Columbus Vignette	10/28/92	100.00	175.00
SO108A	same, Maroon Hand Pulled Proof	10/28/92	250.00	375.00
SO109	Orcoexpo, Anaheim - Hawaii #79 Block	1/8/93	15.00	25.00
SO110	Orcoexpo, Iron-Horse Hologram	1/8/93	18.00	25.00
SO111	Milcopex - Hawaii #76 Block	3/5/93	15.00	25.00

AMERICAN BANK NOTE COMPANY

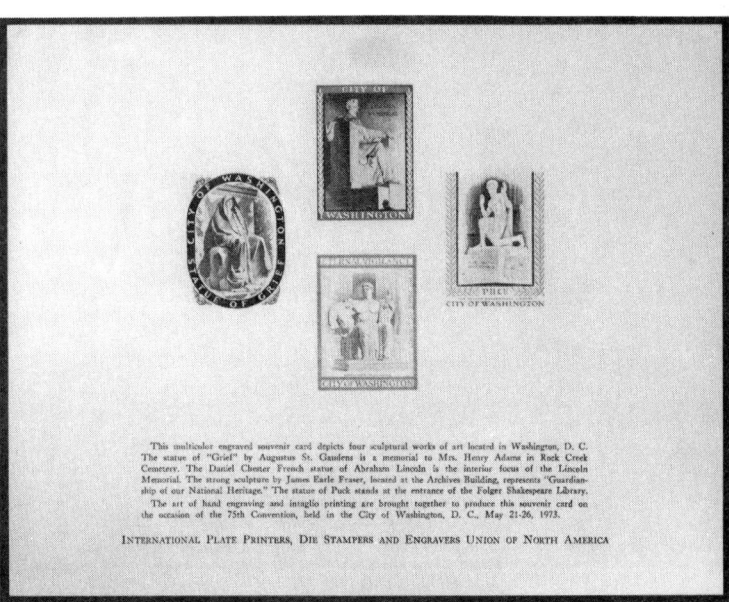

SO112

SCCS Number	Event and Description	First Day Show/Issue	Mint Card	Cancelled Card
SO112	ANA - 50 Peso Banco de Minero,Mexico($)	3/11/93	15.00	25.00
SO113	Plymouth, MI - Hawaii #75 Block	4/24/93	15.00	60.00
SO114	ASDA Mega Event - Hawaii #77 Block	5/5/93	15.00	25.00
SO115	Paper Money Show - $20 City-Memphis($)	6/18/93	15.00	25.00
SO116	ANA, Baltimore - $20 Peoples' Bank of Baltimore ($)	7/28/93	14.00	25.00
SO117	ANA, $100 Chesepeake Bank Proof ($)	7/28/93	80.00	120.00
SO118	APS, Houston - Hawaii #74 Block	8/19/93	14.00	22.50
SO119	APS, $1 Hawaii Revenue Blue Proof	8/19/93	70.00	110.00
SO119A	same, Black Hand pulled Proof	8/19/93	250.00	375.00
SO120	ASDA Mega Event - Hawaii #78 Block	10/28/93	13.50	22.50
SO121	ASDA - Holiday, Bank Draft for the Shetucket Bank of Norwich, CT	10/28/93	13.50	22.50
SO122	ASDA, 3 Hawaii Foreign Affairs, Green	10/28/93	80.00	120.00
SO122A	same, Green, Blue, Red Proof	10/28/93	250.00	375.00
SO123	Aripex, Mesa,AZ - U.S. #1 Franklin	1/7/94	16.00	25.00
SO124	ANA, New Orleans - 1 Peso Medellin, Colombia ($)	3/3/94	16.00	25.00
SO125	Milcopex - #73, 2¢ Andrew Jackson	3/4/94	16.00	25.00
SO126	Garfield-Perry - #13, 10¢ Washington	3/18/94	16.00	25.00
SO127	Central States Numism. - $2 Indiana's Pioneer Association ($)	4/8/94	16.00	25.00
SO128	Paper Money Show - $100 Union Bank ($)	6/17/94	16.00	25.00
SO129	ANA, Detroit - $5 Bank of the Capitol, Lansing, Michigan ($)	7/27/94	16.00	25.00
SO130	ANA - Winged Majesty / Eagle Hologram	7/27/94	20.00	30.00
SO131	ANA - $1 White Mountain Bank 0f NH ($)	7/27/94	80.00	120.00
SO132	APS, Pittsburgh - #39, 90¢ Washington	8/18/94	16.00	25.00
SO133	APS - #1 Proof of 5¢ Franklin	8/18/94	80.00	120.00
SO134	Balpex'94 - #226, 10¢ D. Webster	9/3/94	16.00	25.00
SO135	ASDA Mega Event - #122, 90¢ Lincoln	11/3/94	16.00	25.00
SO136	ASDA - #2 Proof of 10¢ Washington	11/3/94	80.00	120.00
SO137	Paper Money Show - 100 Peso El Banco of Uruguay ($)	11/11/94	16.00	25.00

Note: From 1995 on, ABNC Souvenir Cards were limited editions.

PLATE PRINTERS UNION

F1973B

SCCS Number	Event and Description	First Day Show/Issue	Mint Card	Cancelled Card
F1973B	Four Statues with IPP Text line	5/21/73	9.50	70.00
F1981B	$2 Embarkation of the Pilgrims ($)	5/17/81	35.00	95.00
F1982A	Napex'82 - Flag with Pledge of Allegiance	7/2/82	10.00	20.00
F1982B	Balpex'82 - Great Seal	9/4/82	15.00	40.00
F1983A	IPPDS & EU - $1 North Berwick Bank($)	1983	10.00	40.00
F1983C	Napex'83 - "Medal of Honor"	6/10/83	10.00	25.00
F1983F	Balpex'83 - George Washington	9/3/83	10.00	15.00
F1984A	Napex'84 - G.Washington & U.S. Capitol	6/24/84	10.00	20.00
F1984C	"Men in Currency" 11 faces	1984	250.00	275.00
F1985D	IPPDS & EU - Eagle resting on Rock	5/12/85	30.00	..
F1987A-B	IPPDS & EU - 6 Train Vignettes on 2 cards	5/3/87	35.00	90.00
F1987G	IPPDS & EU - 6 Train Vignettes on 1 card	5/3/87	70.00	150.00
F1988C	IPPDS & EU - Canadian Parliament, Statue of Liberty, Indep.Hall, U.S. Capitol	1988	30.00	..
F1990D	Napex'90 - #F1983C with 60th Ann. Ovpt	6/1/90	80.00	100.00
F1991F	GENA'91 - "1000" Breakfast Card	9/27/91	125.00	..
F1992A	SCCS Annual Meeting - Trolley Scene	1992	25.00	..
F1993A	GENA'93 - Woman with Sword & Shield	3/5/93	9.50	..
F1993F	ANA'93 - SCCS "$" Card	7/28/93	10.00	12.00
F1993G	SCCS'93 - Farming Scene	1993	25.00	28.50
F1993J	MANA'93 - SCCS, Eagle & Shield	1993	11.50	..

STAMP VENTURES SOUVENIR CARDS

SO98	World Columbian Stamp Expo - Vignette of Columbus by Canadian Bank Note Co.	5/22/92	42.50	90.00
SO99	WCSE - Czeslae Slania, Engraver	5/22/92	75.00	80.00
SO100	WCSE - Bonnie Blair Olympic Champion	5/22/92	70.00	80.00
SO101	WCSE - Eagle in Flight Hologram	5/22/92	50.00	90.00

1266

1453

Each Souvenir Page has one or more stamps affixed and cancelled with a "FD of Issue" postmark. Each page also has a picture of the issued stamp(s) and important technical data. Prior to March 1, 1972 these pages were privately distributed. The most prominent servicer was W.C. Bates, who began with Scott #1232 (West Virginia). **These pages were folded twice in order to fit into a #10 envelope.** These are known as "Unofficial" Souvenir Pages.

UNOFFICIAL

1329

Scott No.	Subject	Price	Scott No.	Subject	Price
1962-64 Issues			**1965-81 Prominent Americans(cont.)**		
1232	West Virginia	10.00	1280a	Zip pane of 5	12.50
1233	Emancipation Proc	16.50	1280a	Mail early pn. of 5	12.50
1234	Alliance/Progress	10.00	1281	3¢ Parkman	10.00
1235	Cordell Hull	10.00	1282	4¢ Lincoln	13.00
1236	Eleanor Roosevelt	12.00	1283	5¢ Washington	10.00
1237	Science	10.00	1283B	5¢ Wash. re-engr	11.00
1238	City Mail	16.00	1284	6¢ F.D. Roosevelt	13.00
1239	Red Cross	11.00	1285	8¢ Einstein	13.00
1240	Christmas 1963	14.00	1286	10¢ Jackson	10.00
1241	Audubon	10.00	1286A	12¢ Henry Ford	15.00
1242	Sam Houston	15.00	1287	13¢ J.F. Kennedy	22.50
1243	C.M. Russell	13.00	1288	15¢ Holmes	10.00
1244	N.Y. World's Fair	10.00	1289	20¢ Marshall	11.00
1245	Muir	15.00	1290	25¢ Douglass	20.00
1246	John F. Kennedy	15.00	1291	30¢ Dewey	30.00
1247	NJ Tercentenary	10.00	1292	40¢ Paine	65.00
1248	Nevada Statehood	10.00	1293	50¢ Lucy Stone	80.00
1249	Register & Vote	10.00	1294	$1 O'Neill	80.00
1250	Shakespeare	10.00	1295	$5 Moore	225.00
1251	Mayo Brothers	10.00	1298	6¢ FDR end coil	13.00
1252	Music	10.00	1299	1¢ Jefferson coil	10.00
1253	Homemakers	10.00	1303	4¢ Lincoln coil	10.00
1254-57	Christmas 1964	65.00	1304	5¢ Wash. coil	10.00
1258	Verrazano Bridge	11.00	1305	6¢ FDR side coil	10.00
1259	Modern Art	10.00			
1260	Radio	10.00	**1966 Commemoratives**		
			1306	Migrat. Bird Treaty	13.00
1965 Commemoratives			1307	Hum. Treat./Animal	10.00
1261	Battle/New Orleans	10.00	1308	Indiana Statehood	10.00
1262	Sokol Society	10.00	1309	Circus	13.00
1263	Cancer	10.00	1310	SIPEX	11.00
1264	Churchill	10.00	1311	SIPEX Souv. Sht	10.00
1265	Magna Carta	10.00	1312	Bill of Rights	10.00
1266	Int'l Cooperation Year	10.00	1313	Polish Millenium	10.00
1267	Salvation Army	10.00	1314	Nat'l. Parks Service	10.00
1268	Dante	10.00	1315	Marine Reserves	10.00
1269	Herbert Hoover	10.00	1316	Women's Clubs	10.00
1270	Robert Fulton	10.00	1317	Johnny Appleseed	12.00
1271	St. Augustine, FL	10.00	1318	Beautif./America	10.00
1272	Traffic Safety	10.00	1319	Great River Road	10.00
1273	Copley	10.00	1320	Sav. Bond/Srvcmen	11.00
1274	ITU	11.00	1321	Christmas 1966	11.00
1275	Adlai Stevenson	10.00	1322	Mary Cassatt	11.00
1276	Christmas 1965	10.00			
			1967 Commemoratives		
1965-81 Prominent Americans			1323	Nat'l. Grange	10.00
1278	1¢ Jefferson	10.00	1324	Canada Centenary	10.00
1278a	Pane of 8	11.00	1325	Erie Canal	10.00
1279	1¼¢ Gallatin	11.00	1326	Peace/Lions	10.00
1280	2¢ Wright	13.00			

OFFICIAL SOUVENIR PAGES

Scott No.	Subject	Price	Scott No.	Subject	Price
1967 Commemoratives (cont.)			**1970 Commemoratives (cont.)**		
1327	Thoreau	10.00	1407	SC Founding	10.00
1328	NE Statehood	10.00	1408	Stone Mountain	13.00
1329	Voice of America	10.00	1409	Fort Snelling	10.00
1330	Davy Crockett	11.00	1410-13	Anti-Pollution	25.00
1331-32	Space Twins	35.00	1414	Christmas 1970	13.00
1333	Urban Planning	10.00	1415-18	Christmas Toys	25.00
1334	Finnish Independ	10.00	1415a-18a	Toys Precancelled	100.00
1335	Thomas Eakins	11.00	1419	U.N. 25th Anniv	10.00
1336	Christmas 1967	11.00	1420	Mayflower	13.00
1337	MS Statehood	10.00	1421-22	D.A.V./Servicemen	60.00
1968-71 Regular Issues					
1338	6¢ Flag	10.00	**1970-74 Regular Issues**		
1338A	6¢ Flag coil	10.00	1393	6¢ Eisenhower	13.00
1338D	6¢ Flag huck press	10.00	1393a	Pane of 8	30.00
1338F	8¢ Flag	10.00	1393b	Zip pane of 5	35.00
1341	$1 Airlift	100.00	1939b	Mail early p./5	35.00
			1394	8¢ Eisen., multi	13.00
1968 Commemoratives			1395a	8¢ Eisen., claret,	
1339	IL Statehood	10.00		pane of 8	40.00
1340	Hemisfair	10.00	1395b	Pane of 6	40.00
1342	Youth/Elks	9.00	1396	8¢ USPS	35.00
1343	Law & Order	9.00	1398	16¢ Ernie Pyle	15.00
1344	Register and Vote	9.00	1401	6¢ Eisen., coil	13.00
1345-54	Historic Flags	165.00	1402	8¢ Eisen., coil	15.00
1355	Walt Disney	30.00			
1356	Marquette	10.00			
1357	Daniel Boone	11.00	**1971 Commemoratives**		
1358	AK River Navigation	10.00	1423	American Wool Ind.	13.00
1359	Leif Erikson	16.00	1424	Douglas MacArthur	16.00
1360	Cherokee Strip	13.00	1425	Blood Donors	10.00
1361	Trumbull Painting	10.00	1426	MO Sesquicent	13.00
1362	Waterfowl Conserv.	13.00			
1363	Christmas 1968	9.00			
1364	Chief Joseph	13.00	**Airmails & Special Delivery**		
			C67	6¢ Eagle	18.00
1969 Commemoratives			C68	Amel. Earhart	20.00
1365-68	Beautification	30.00	C69	Goddard	25.00
1369	American Legion	10.00	C70	Alaska	30.00
1370	Grandma Moses	13.00	C71	Audubon Jays	13.00
1371	Apollo 8	15.00	C72	10¢ Stars	13.00
1372	W.C. Handy	10.00	C72b	Pane of 8	35.00
1373	CA Settlement	10.00	C72c	Pane of 5	60.00
1374	John Wesley Powell	13.00	C73	10¢ Stars coil	15.00
1375	AL Statehood	10.00	C74	Air Service	10.00
1376-79	Botanical Congress	27.50	C75	20¢ USA	20.00
1380	Daniel Webster	10.00	C76	Moon Landing	16.00
1381	Baseball	150.00	C77	9¢ Delta Wing	25.00
1382	Football	20.00	C78	11¢ Jet	12.50
1383	Eisenhower Memor.	10.00	C78a	Pane of 4	30.00
1384	Christmas 1969	10.00	C80	17¢ Liberty	35.00
1385	Hope/Crip. Child	10.00	C81	21¢ USA	35.00
1386	Harnett Painting	10.00	C82	11¢ Jet coil	12.50
			E22	45¢ Arrows	50.00
1970 Commemoratives			E23	60¢ Arrows	40.00
1387-90	Natural History	55.00			
1391	Maine Statehood	13.00			
1392	Wildlife Conserv.	20.00			
1405	Edgar Lee Masters	10.00			
1406	Women's Suffrage	10.00			

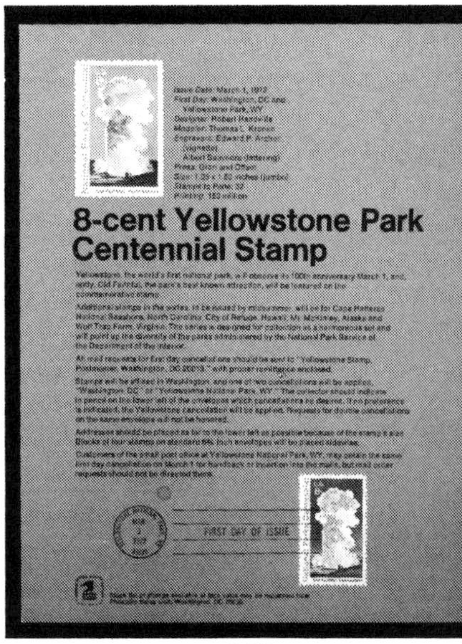

1453

OFFICIAL SOUVENIR PAGES

Since March 1, 1972 the U.S. Postal Service has offered, by subscription, Souvenir Pages with first day cancels. They are known as "Official" Souvenir Pages. **These were issued flat and unfolded.**

Scott No.	Subject	Price
	1972-78 Regular Issues	
1297	3¢ Fran. Parkman	4.00
1305C	$1 O'Neill coil	17.50
1305E	15¢ O.W. Holmes	3.00
1393D	7¢ B. Franklin	6.00
1397	14¢ LaGuardia	110.00
1399	18¢ Eliz. Blackwell	3.00
1400	21¢ A. Giannini	4.50
	1972 Commemoratives	
1448-51	2¢ Cape Hatteras	85.00
1452	6¢ Wolf Trap Farm	30.00
1453	8¢ Yellowstone Park	100.00
1454	15¢ Mt. McKinley	22.50
1455	8¢ Family Planning	750.00
1456-59	8¢ Colonial Craftsmen	16.00
1460-62	C85 Olympics	12.00
1463	8¢ PTA	6.50
1464-67	8¢ Wildlife	7.50
1468	8¢ Mail Order	6.00
1469	8¢ Osteopathic Med	6.00
1470	8¢ Tom Sawyer	8.50
1471-72	8¢ Christmas 1972	7.50
1473	8¢ Pharmacy	6.50
1474	8¢ Stamp Collecting	6.00
	1973 Commemoratives	
1475	8¢ Love	7.50
1476	8¢ Pamphleteers	5.00
1477	8¢ Broadside	6.00
1478	8¢ Post Rider	4.50
1479	8¢ Drummer	4.00
1480-83	8¢ Boston Tea Party	6.00
1484	8¢ George Gershwin	5.50
1485	8¢ Robinson Jeffers	4.50
1486	8¢ Henry O. Tanner	6.50
1487	8¢ Willa Cather	4.00
1488	8¢ Copernicus	5.50
1489-98	8¢ Postal People	7.00
1499	8¢ Harry S. Truman	5.00
1500-02,C86	Electronics	8.00
1503	8¢ Lyndon B. Johnson	4.50
1504	8¢ Angus Cattle	4.00
1505	10¢ Chautauqua	3.50
1506	10¢ Kansas Wheat	3.00
1507-08	8¢ Christmas 1973	6.50
	1973-74 Regular Issues	
1509	10¢ Crossed Flags	3.50
1510	10¢ Jeff. Memorial	3.50
1511	10¢ Zip Code	4.50
1518	6.3¢ Bulk Rate coil	4.00
	1974 Commemoratives	
1525	10¢ VFW	3.50
1526	10¢ Robert Frost	4.00
1527	10¢ Expo '74	5.00
1528	10¢ Horse Racing	6.50
1529	10¢ Skylab	7.00
1530-37	10¢ Univ. Postal Un	7.50
1538-41	10¢ Mineral Heritage	7.50
1542	10¢ Fort Harrod	3.50
1543-46	10¢ Cont. Congress	5.00

Scott No.	Subject	Price
1547	10¢ Energy Conserv	3.00
1548	10¢ Sleepy Hollow	4.00
1549	10¢ Retarded Children	3.50
1550-52	10¢ Christmas 1974	5.50
	1975 Commemoratives	
1553	10¢ Benjamin West	3.75
1554	10¢ Paul L. Dunbar	4.00
1555	10¢ D.W. Griffith	4.00
1556	10¢ Pioneer – Jupiter	7.50
1557	10¢ Mariner 10	6.00
1558	10¢ Coll. Bargaining	3.00
1559	8¢ Sybil Ludington	3.00
1560	10¢ Salem Poor	3.50
1561	10¢ Haym Salomon	3.00
1562	18¢ Peter Francisco	3.50
1563	10¢ Lexington-Con.	3.50
1564	10¢ Bunker Hill	3.50
1565-68	10¢ Military Uniforms	7.50
1569-70	10¢Apollo Soyuz	7.50
1571	10¢ Women's Year	3.00
1572-75	10¢ Postal Bicent	4.25
1576	10¢ Peace thru Law	3.00
1577-78	10¢ Bank /Commerce.	4.00
1579-80	10¢Christmas 1975	4.50
	1975-81 Americana Issues	
1581-82,84-85	1¢-4¢ Issues	3.50
1591	9¢ Rt. to Assemble	3.00
1592	10¢ Petit./Redress	3.50
1593	11¢ Free./Press	2.50
1594,1816	12¢ Conscience	3.25
1596	13¢ Eagle/Shield	3.50
1597,1618C	15¢ Ft. McHenry	3.00
1599,1619	16¢ Liberty	3.00
1603	24¢ Old No. Church	3.00
1604	28¢ Rem. Outpost	3.00
1605	29¢ Lighthouse	3.25
1606	30¢ Am. Schools	3.50
1608	50¢ "Betty" Lamp	3.75
1610	$1 Rush Lamp	4.75
1611	$2 Kero. Lamp	6.50
1612	$5 R.R. Lantern	11.00
1613	3.1¢ Non Prof coil	6.00
1614	7.7¢ Bulk Rate coil	3.00
1615	7.9¢ Bulk Rate coil	3.00
1615C	8.4¢ Bulk Rate coil	4.00
1616	9¢ Assembly coil	3.00
1617	10¢ Redress coil	3.50
1618	13¢ Libty. Bell coil	3.00
1622,25	13¢ Flag/Ind. Hall	3.00
1623c	$1 Vend bk. p. 10	21.50
	1976 Commemoratives	
1629-31	13¢Spirit of '76	5.00
1632	13¢ INTERPHIL '76	4.50
1633-82	13¢ State Flags (5 pgs.)	37.50
1683	13¢ Telephone Cent.	2.50
1684	13¢ Comm. Aviation	3.25
1685	13¢ Chemistry	3.25
1686-89	Bicentennial S/S (4)	37.50

Scott No.	Subject	Price
1690	13¢ Ben Franklin	3.00
1691-94	13¢ Dec. of Indepen	5.00
1695-98	13¢ Olympics	5.00
1699	13¢ Clara Maass	2.50
1700	13¢ Adolph S. Ochs	3.50
1701-03	13¢ Christmas 1976	4.00
	1977 Commemoratives	
1704	13¢Wash./Princeton	3.00
1705	13¢ Sound Record	3.50
1706-09	13¢ Pueblo Art	5.00
1710	13¢ Lindbergh Flight	4.00
1711	13¢ Colorado	3.50
1712-15	13¢ Butterflies	4.50
1716	13¢ Lafayette	2.50
1717-20	13¢ Skilled Hands	4.00
1721	13¢ Peace Bridge	3.25
1722	13¢ Herkimer/Oriskany	3.00
1723-24	13¢ Energy	3.00
1725	13¢ Alta California	2.75
1726	13¢ Art. of Confed.	2.75
1727	13¢ Talking Pictures	3.00
1728	13¢ Saratoga	3.50
1729-30	Christmas, Omaha	3.00
1729-30	Valley Forge	3.00
	1978 Issues	
1731	13¢ Carl Sandburg	3.00
1732-3	13¢ Cook, Anchorage	3.50
1732-3	13¢ Cook/Honolulu	3.50
1734	13¢ Ind. Hd. Penny	3.00
1735,43	(15¢)"A" Stamp (2)	5.00
1737	15¢ Rose bklt. sgl	3.00
1742a	15¢ Windmills bklt. pane/10 (1980)	7.50
1744	13¢ Harriet Tubman	4.25
1745-48	13¢ Quilts	4.00
1749-52	13¢ Dance	4.00
1753	13¢ French Alliance	2.75
1754	13¢ Dr. Papanicolaou.	3.00
1755	13¢ Jimmie Rodgers	4.50
1756	15¢ George M. Cohan	3.00
1757	13¢ CAPEX '78	7.50
1758	15¢ Photography	3.50
1759	15¢ Viking Missions	6.25
1760-63	15¢ American Owls	3.75
1764-67	15¢ American Trees	4.00
1768	15¢ Madonna & Child	3.00
1769	15¢ Hobby Horse	3.00
	1979 Commemoratives	
1770	15¢ Robert F. Kennedy	3.50
1771	15¢ Martin L. King, Jr.	5.00
1772	15¢ Year of the Child.	2.75
1773	15¢ John Steinbeck	3.50
1774	15¢ Albert Einstein	4.50
1775-78	15¢ PA Toleware	4.50
1779-82	15¢ Architecture	3.50
1783-86	15¢ Endang Flora	4.00
1787	15¢ Seeing Eye Dogs.	3.00
1788	15¢ Special Olympics	3.00
1789	15¢ John Paul Jones	3.85
1790	10¢ Olympics	3.75
1791-94	15¢ Summer Olym	5.50
1795-98	15¢ Winter Olym(80).	5.00
1799	15¢Virgin & Child	3.50
1800	15¢ Santa Claus	3.50
1801	15¢ Will Rogers	3.50
1802	15¢ Vietnam Vets	3.50
	1980-81 Issues	
1803	15¢ W.C. Fields	4.00
1804	15¢ Ben Banneker	4.00
1805-10	15¢ Letter Writing	3.50
1811	1¢ Quill Pen coil	3.00
1813	3.5¢ Non Profit coil	3.50
1818,20	"B"18¢ sht./coil stamps	3.00
1819a	"B" bklt. pane of 8	3.25
1821	15¢ Frances Perkins	3.00
1822	15¢ Dolly Madison	4.00
1823	15¢ Emily Bissell	3.25
1824	15¢ Keller/Sullivan	3.00
1825	15¢ Veterans. Admin.	3.00
1826	15¢ B. de Galvez	3.25
1827-30	15¢ Coral Reefs	3.50
1831	15¢ Organized Labor.	3.50
1832	15¢ Edith Wharton	3.50
1833	15¢ Education	3.50
1834-37	15¢ Indian Masks	5.00
1838-41	15¢ Architecture	3.50
1842	15¢ St. Glass Window.	3.00
1843	15¢ Antique Toys	3.50
	1980-85 Great Americans	
1844	1¢ Dorothea Dix	3.00
1845	2¢ I. Stravinsky	3.50
1846	3¢ Henry Clay	3.00
1847	4¢ Carl Shurz	3.00
1848	5¢ Pearl S. Buck	3.00
1849	6¢ W. Lippmann	3.00
1850	7¢ A. Baldwin	3.00
1851	8¢ Henry Knox	3.00
1852	9¢ S. Thayer	3.00

Scott No.	Subject	Price
	1980-85 Gr. Americans (cont)	
1853	10¢ R. Russell	3.00
1854	11¢ A. Partridge	3.00
1855	13¢ Crazy Horse	3.00
1856	14¢ S. Lewis	3.00
1857	17¢ R. Carson	3.00
1858	18¢ G. Mason	2.50
1859	19¢ Sequoyah	3.00
1860	20¢ Ralph Bunche	5.00
1861	20¢ T. Gallaudet	3.50
1862	20¢ Truman	3.00
1863	22¢ Audubon	3.50
1864	30¢ Dr. Laubach	3.00
1865	35¢ Dr. C. Drew	3.00
1866	37¢ R. Millikan	3.00
1867	39¢ G. Clark	3.00
1868	40¢ L. Gilbreth	3.00
1869	50¢ C. Nimitz	3.00
	1981-82 Issues	
1874	15¢ Everett Dirksen	3.00
1875	15¢ Whitney Young	4.50
1876-79	18¢ Flowers	3.50
1889a	18¢ Wildlife bk/10	6.50
1890-91	18¢ Flag	3.50
1893a	6¢ & 18¢ Flag & Stars bklt. pn	3.50
1894-95	20¢ Flag	4.00
1896a	20¢ Flag bklt. pn./6	3.50
1896b	20¢ Flag bklt. pn./10	4.50
	1981-84 Transportation Coils	
1897	1¢ Omnibus	3.00
1897A	2¢ Locomotive	3.75
1898	3¢ Handcar	3.75
1898A	4¢ Stagecoach	4.25
1899	5¢ Motorcycle	5.75
1900	5.2¢ Sleigh	4.50
1901	5.9¢ Bicycle	6.50
1902	7.4¢ Baby Buggy	5.00
1903	9.3¢ Mail Wagon	4.00
1904	10.9¢ Hansom Cab	4.50
1905	11¢ Caboose	4.00
1906	17¢ Electric Car	3.25
1907	18¢ Surrey	3.50
1908	20¢ Pumper	6.00
	1981-83 Regulars & Commem.	
1909	$9.35 Eagle bklt. sgl.	125.00
1909a	$9.35 Bklt.pane of 3	175.00
1910	18¢ Red Cross	3.00
1911	18¢ Savings & Loan	3.00
1912-19	18¢ Space Achieve	8.50
1920	18¢ Prof. Manage	3.00
1921-24	18¢ Wildlife Habitats.	3.50
1925	18¢ Disable Person	3.00
1926	18¢ St. Vincent Millay	3.00
1927	18¢ Alcoholism	3.00
1928-31	18¢ Architecture	3.50
1932	18¢ Babe Zaharias	7.50
1933	18¢ Bobby Jones	9.00
1934	18¢ Frederic Remington	4.00
1935-36	18¢ & 20¢ J. Hoban	3.00
1937-38	18¢ Yrktwn/V Capes.	3.50
1939	20¢ Madonna/Child	3.50
1940	20¢ "Teddy Bear"	3.50
1941	20¢ John Hanson	3.00
1942-45	20¢ Desert Plants	3.75
1946-47	"C" sht./coil stamps	3.50
1948a	"C" bklt. pane/10	3.75
1949a	20¢ Sheep bk pn/10	5.00
	1982 Commemoratives	
1950	20¢ F.D. Roosevelt	3.00
1951	20¢ Love	3.00
1952	20¢ G. Washington	3.25
1953/2002	20¢ State Birds & Flowers Mixed Perfs (5)	50.00
2003	20¢ Netherlands	3.00
2004	20¢ Library of Congress	3.00
2005	20¢ Consumer Coil	3.75
2006-09	20¢ World's Fair	3.00
2010	20¢ Horatio Alger	2.50
2011	20¢ Aging	2.50
2012	20¢ Barrymores	4.00
2013	20¢ Dr. Mary Walker	2.50
2014	20¢ Int'l Peace Garden	2.50
2015	20¢ Libraries	2.50
2016	20¢ Jackie Robinson	15.00
2017	20¢ Touro Synagogue	3.00
2018	20¢ Wolf Trap	2.50
2019-22	20¢ Architecture	3.00
2023	20¢ Francis of Assisi.	2.75
2024	20¢ Ponce de Leon	2.75
2025	13¢ Kitten & Puppy	3.50
2026	20¢ Madonna	3.50
2027-30	20¢ Snow Scene	3.50
	1983 Commemoratives	
2031	20¢ Science & Industry	3.00
2032-35	20¢ Balloons	3.00

OFFICIAL SOUVENIR PAGES

Scott No.	Subject	Price
2036	20¢ Sweden/US	3.00
2037	20¢ Civ.Conserv.	2.50
2038	20¢ Joseph Priestley	3.00
2039	20¢ Volunteerism	2.50
2040	20¢ German Immigr	3.00
2041	20¢ Brooklyn Bridge	3.25
2042	20¢ Tenn. Valley Auth	3.00
2043	20¢ Physical Fitness	3.00
2044	20¢ Scott Joplin	4.00
2045	20¢ Medal of Honor	5.00
2046	20¢ Babe Ruth	12.50
2047	20¢ Hawthorne	3.00
2048-51	13¢ Olympics	4.50
2052	20¢ Treaty of Paris	2.50
2053	20¢ Civil Service	2.50
2054	20¢ Metropolitan Opera	3.00
2055-58	20¢ Inventors	3.50
2059-62	20¢ Streetcars	4.50
2063	20¢ Madonna	3.00
2064	20¢ Santa Claus	3.00
2065	20¢ Martin Luther	3.25

1984 Commemoratives

Scott No.	Subject	Price
2066	20¢ Alaska Statehood.	3.00
2067-70	20¢ Winter Olympics	4.00
2071	20¢ FDIC	3.00
2072	20¢ Love	2.50
2073	20¢ Carter G. Woodson	4.00
2074	20¢ Soil/Water Con	2.50
2075	20¢ Credit Un.Act	3.00
2076-79	20¢ Orchids	4.00
2080	20¢ Hawaii Statehood	3.00
2081	20¢ Nat'l. Archives	2.50
2082-85	20¢ Summer Olympics	4.25
2086	20¢ LA World Expo	2.50
2087	20¢ Health Research	2.50
2088	20¢ Douglas Fairbanks	4.00
2089	20¢ Jim Thorpe	10.00
2090	20¢ John McCormack	4.25
2091	20¢ St. Lawren. Seaway	2.50
2092	20¢ Mig. Bird Stamp Act	4.50
2093	20¢ Roanoke Voyages	2.50
2094	20¢ Herman Melville	2.50
2095	20¢ Horace Moses	2.50
2096	20¢ Smokey Bear	8.50
2097	20¢ Roberto Clemente	14.00
2098-2101	20¢ Dogs	4.00
2102	20¢ Crime Prevention.	3.00
2103	20¢ Hispanic Americans	2.50
2104	20¢ Family Unity	3.50
2105	20¢ Eleanor Roosevelt	4.50
2106	20¢ Nation of Readers	3.00
2107	20¢ Xmas Traditional.	3.00
2108	20¢ Xmas Santa Claus	3.00
2109	20¢ Vietnam Vets Mem	5.00

1985-87 Issues

Scott No.	Subject	Price
2110	22¢ Jerome Kern	3.00
2111-12	"D" sht./coil stamps	3.00
2113a	22¢ "D" bklt. pane/10.	4.50
2114-15	22¢ Flag	3.00
2115b	22¢ Flag "T" coil	3.00
2116a	22¢ Flag bklt. bk./5	4.00
2121a	22¢ Seashells bk/10	5.50
2122	$10.75 Eagle bklt.sgl.	47.50
2122a	$10.75 Bklt. pane/3	90.00

1985-89 Transportation Coils

Scott No.	Subject	Price
2123	3.4¢ School Bus	4.25
2124	4.9¢ Buckboard	4.50
2125	5.5¢ Star Rt. Truck	4.00
2126	6¢ Tricycle	4.00
2127	7.1¢ Tractor	2.75
2127a	7.1¢ Tractor Zip+4	3.00
2128	8.3¢ Ambulance	4.50
2129	8.5¢ Tow Truck	3.00
2130	10.1¢ Oil Wagon	3.25
2130a	10.1¢ Red Prec	3.50
2131	11¢ Stutz Bearcat	4.00
2132	12¢ Stanley Stmr	4.25
2133	12.5¢ Pushcart	4.00
2134	14¢ Iceboat	5.00
2135	17¢ Dog Sled	3.50
2136	25¢ Bread Wagon	4.00

1985 Issues (cont.)

Scott No.	Subject	Price
2137	22¢ Mary Bethune	4.50
2138-41	22¢ Duck Decoys	3.50
2142	22¢ Winter Spec. Olymp.	2.50
2143	22¢ Love	3.50
2144	22¢ Rural Electr	2.50
2145	22¢ AMERIPEX '86	2.75
2146	22¢ Abigail Adams	2.50
2147	22¢ Fred Bartholdi	3.50
2149	18¢ G. Wash. coil	4.00
2150	21.1¢ Zip+4 coil	4.25
2152	22¢ Korean War Vets.	3.75
2153	22¢ Social Security	2.50
2154	22¢ W War I Vets	2.50
2155-58	22¢ Horses	5.00
2159	22¢ Public Education	3.00

Scott No.	Subject	Price
2160-63	22¢ Youth Year	4.25
2164	22¢ End Hunger	2.75
2165	22¢ Madonna	3.00
2166	22¢ Poinsettia	4.00

1986 Issues

Scott No.	Subject	Price
2167	22¢ Arkansas Statehd	2.75

1986-94 Great Americans

Scott No.	Subject	Price
2168	1¢ M. Mitchell	3.00
2169	2¢ Mary Lyon	3.00
2170	3¢ Dr. P.D. White	2.75
2171	4¢ Fr. Flanagan	3.00
2172	5¢ Hugo Black	3.50
2173	5¢ Munoz Marin	3.00
2175	10¢ Red Cloud	3.00
2176	14¢ Julia W. Howe	2.50
2177	15¢ Buffalo Bill	3.00
2178	17¢ B. Lockwood	2.50
2179	20¢ Virginia Agpar	5.00
2180	21¢ C. Carlson	2.50
2181	23¢ M. Cassatt	3.00
2182	25¢ Jack London	2.50
2182a	Bklt. pn./10	5.75
2183	28¢ Sitting Bull	2.50
2184	29¢ Earl Warren	4.00
2185	29¢ T. Jefferson	3.50
2186	35¢ Dennis Chavez	3.75
2187	40¢ C.L. Chennault	3.75
2188	45¢ Cushing	2.50
2189	52¢ H. Humphrey	3.00
2190	56¢ John Harvard	3.00
2191	65¢ H. Arnold	3.00
2192	75¢ Wendell Wilkie	3.00
2193	$1 Dr. B. Revel	3.00
2194	$1 Johns Hopkins	4.00
2195	$2 W.J. Bryan	5.00
2196	$5 B. Harte	11.00
2197a	25¢ London, bk/6	3.50

1986 Issues

Scott No.	Subject	Price
2201a	22¢ Stamp Collect	4.50
2202	22¢ Love	3.00
2203	22¢ Sojourner Truth	3.25
2204	22¢ Republic Texas	2.75
2209a	22¢ Fish bklt. pane/5	5.00
2210	22¢ Public Hospitals	2.75
2211	22¢ Duke Ellington	5.00
2216-19	US Pres. shts.,4 pgs.	22.50
2220-23	22¢ Polar Explorers	4.50
2224	22¢ Statue of Liberty	3.50
2226	2¢ Locom. re-engr	3.00
2235-38	22¢ Navajo Art	4.25
2239	22¢ T.S. Elliot	2.75
2240-43	22¢ Woodcarv Figs	4.25
2244	22¢ Madonna	3.00
2245	22¢ Christmas Trees	3.00

1987 Issues

Scott No.	Subject	Price
2246	22¢ Michigan	3.50
2247	22¢ Pan-Am. Games	3.50
2248	22¢ Love	3.00
2249	22¢ J. Bap. Pnt. du Sable	5.50
2250	22¢ Enrico Caruso	3.00
2251	22¢ Girl Scouts	5.50

1987-88 Transportation Coils

Scott No.	Subject	Price
2252	3¢ Con. Wag	3.50
2253,62	5¢,17.5¢	3.75
2254	5.3¢ Elevator, Prec.	3.00
2255	7.6¢ Carretta, Prec	3.00
2256	8.4¢ Wheelchair, Prec.	3.75
2257	10¢ Canal Boat	3.00
2258	13¢ Police Wag,Prec.	3.50
2259	13.2¢ RR Car, Prec	4.00
2260	15¢ Tugboat	3.50
2261	16.7¢ Pop.Wag,Prec.	3.50
2263	20¢ Cable Car	3.50
2264	20.5¢ Fire Eng, Prec.	4.50
2265	21¢ RR Mail Car,Prec	4.00
2266	24.1¢ Tand. Bike,Pre.	3.00

1987-89 Issues

Scott No.	Subject	Price
2274a	22¢ Sp. Occ. Bk	5.50
2275	22¢ United Way	2.50
2276	222¢ Flag/Fireworks	2.50
2276a	Bklt. pair	3.00
2277,79	(25¢) "E" sheet/coil	3.50
2278	25¢ Flag/Clouds	2.50
2280	25¢ Flag/Yosem. coil.	3.00
2280var	Pre-phos. paper	3.00
2281	25¢ Honeybee coil	4.00
2282a	(25¢) "E" Bklt. Pane/10	5.00
2283a	25¢ Pheasant Bk/10	5.00
2284-85b	25¢ Owl/Grosbeak. Bk	4.25
2285Ac	25¢ Flag/Clouds Bk	4.50
2286-2335	22¢ Wildlife (5)	30.00

1987-90 Bicentennial Issues

Scott No.	Subject	Price
2336	22¢ Delaware	3.00
2337	22¢ Penn	3.00
2338	22¢ New Jersey	3.00
2339	22¢ Georgia	3.00
2340	22¢ Conn	3.00
2341	22¢ Mass	3.50
2342	22¢ Maryland	3.50
2343	25¢ S. Carolina	3.00
2344	25¢ New Hampshire	3.00
2345	25¢ Virginia	3.00
2346	25¢ New York	3.50
2347	25¢ North Carolina	3.50
2348	25¢ Rhode Island	3.50

1987-88 Issues

Scott No.	Subject	Price
2349	22¢ U.S.-Moroc. Rel.	2.50
2350	22¢ Faulkner	2.50
2351-54	22¢ Lacemaking	6.50
2359a	22¢ Const. Bklt	4.00
2360	22¢ Sign. Const	2.75
2361	22¢ CPA	4.75
2366a	22¢ Loco. Bklt	9.00
2367	22¢ Madonna	2.50
2368	22¢ Ornament	2.50
2369	22¢ '88 Wnt. Olym	2.75
2370	22¢ Australia Bicent.	3.00
2371	22¢ J.W. Johnson	4.00
2372-75	22¢ Cats	6.00
2376	22¢ Knute Rockne	10.00
2377	25¢ F. Ouimet	11.00
2378	25¢ Love	3.00
2379	45¢ Love	3.00
2380	25¢ Sum. Olym	3.00
2385a	25¢ Classic Cars bk	6.50
2386-89	25¢ Ant. Expl	4.00
2390-93	25¢ Carousel Anim	5.00
2394	$8.75 Express Mail	25.00
2396a-98a	25¢ Occas.bk.(2)	45.00
2399	25¢ Madonna	2.75
2400	25¢ Village Scene	2.75

1989-90 Issues

Scott No.	Subject	Price
2401	25¢ Montana Sthd	3.00
2402	25¢ A.P. Randolph	4.25
2403	25¢ N.Dakota Sthd	3.00
2404	25¢ Washington sthd	3.00
2409a	25¢ Steamboats bklt	6.00
2410	25¢ Wld. Stamp Expo	2.50
2411	25¢ A. Toscanini	3.00
2412	25¢ House of Reps	2.50
2413	25¢ U.S. Senate	2.50
2414	25¢ Exec.Branch/GW	2.50
2415	25¢U.S.Sup.Ct.('90)	2.50
2416	25¢ S.Dakota sthd	2.50
2417	25¢ Lou Gehrig	12.50
2418	25¢ E. Hemingway	4.00
2419	$2.40 Moon Landing	18.00
2420	25¢ Letter Carriers	3.00
2421	25¢ Bill of Rights	2.50
2422-25	25¢ Prehis. Animals	10.00
2426/C121	25¢/45¢ Pre-Columbian Customs	3.50
2427,27a	25¢ Christmas Art, Sht. & Bklt. Pn	6.75
2428,29a	25¢ Christmas Sleigh, Sht. & Bklt. Pn	6.75
2431	25¢ Eagle, self-adhes	3.00
2433	90¢ WSE S/S of 4	10.00
2434-37	25¢ Classic Mail	5.00
2438	25¢ Cl.Mail S/S of 4	7.00

1990-91 Issues

Scott No.	Subject	Price
2439	25¢ Idaho Sthd	2.50
2440,41a	25¢ Love, sht. & bklt.	5.00
2442	25¢ Ida B. Wells	4.00
2443a	15¢ Bch. Umbr., bklt.	4.25
2444	25¢ Wyoming Sthd	3.50
2445-48	25¢ Classic Films	7.50
2449	25¢ Marianne Moore	2.50

1990-95 Transportation Coils

Scott No.	Subject	Price
2451	4¢ Steam Carriage	3.75
2452	5¢ Circus Wagon	4.00
2452B	5¢ Wagon, gravure	5.00
2452D	5¢ Circus Wagon, (¢)Sign	4.50
2453,57	5¢/10¢ Canoe/Trailer	3.75
2454	5¢ Canoe, gravure	4.50
2458	10¢ Tractor Trailer	4.00
2463	20¢ Cog Railway	4.00
2464	23¢ Lunch Wagon	3.00
2466	32¢ Ferryboat	4.00
2468	$1.00 Seaplane coil	6.50

1990-95

Scott No.	Subject	Price
2474a	25¢ Lighthouse bklt	7.50
2475	25¢ ATM Plastic Flag	4.00

1990-95 (cont)

Scott No.	Subject	Price
2476,78,80	1¢/30¢ Birds	3.00
2477	1¢ Kestrel	4.00
2479	19¢ Fawn	3.00
2481	45¢ Pumpkinseed	4.50
2482	$2 Bobcat	5.50
2483	20¢ Blue Jay	4.00
2484a,85a	29¢ Wood Duck bklts. BEP & KCS	15.00
2486a	29¢ African Violet, booklet pane of 10	6.00
2487-88,93-94	Peach & Pear	6.00
2489	29¢ Red Squirrel	4.50
2490	29¢ Rose	4.00
2491	29¢ Pine Cone	4.00
2492	32¢ Pink Rose	5.50
2493-94	32¢ Peach/Pear	10.00
2496-2500	25¢ Olympics	6.00
2505a	25¢ Indian Headress	7.00
2506-07	25¢ Marsh Is. & Micro. Joint Issue	3.00
2508-11	25¢ Sea Creatures	6.00
2512/C127	25¢,45¢ America	3.00
2513	25¢ D.D. Eisenhower	3.50
2514,14a	25¢ Christmas sht. & Bklt. Pn./10	6.50
2515,16a	25¢ Christmas Tree sht. & Bklt. Pn./10	6.50

1991-94 Issues

Scott No.	Subject	Price
2517,18	(29¢) "F" Flower, sht. & Coil pr	3.75
2519a,20a	(29¢) "F" Flower, Bklt. Pns. of 10	11.00
2521	(4¢) Make-up rate	3.00
2522	(29¢) "F" Self Adh	3.00
2523	29¢ Flag/Rushmore	4.00
2523A	29¢ Mt. Rush, grav	3.50
2524,27a	29¢ Flower,sht./bklt	7.00
2525	29¢ Flwr. coil,roulette	3.00
2526	29¢ Flower coil,perf.	3.50
2528a	29¢ Flag/Olympic Rings Bklt. pane	7.00
2529	19¢ Fishing Boat coil	3.00
2529C	19¢ Fishing Boat III	5.00
2530a	19¢ Balloons, bklt	5.50
2531	29¢ Flags on Parade	3.00
2531A	29¢ Liberty, ATM	3.00

1991-95 Issues

Scott No.	Subject	Price
2532	50¢ Switzerland	3.50
2533	29¢ Vermont	3.75
2534	29¢ Savings Bonds	3.00
2535,36a,37	29¢,52¢ Love, shts. & Bklt.	2.00
2538	29¢ William Saroyan	3.50
2539	$1.00 USPS & Olym	4.00
2540	$2.90 Priority Mail	10.00
2541	$9.95 Express Mail	30.00
2542	$14.00 Express Mail	37.50
2543	$2.90 Space P.M.	11.00
2544	$3 Challenger	13.50
2544A	$10.75 Endeavor	30.00
2549a	29¢ Fishing Flies bklt.	7.50
2550	29¢ Cole Porter	3.00
2551	29¢ Desert Storm/ Shield	7.00
2553-57	29¢ Summer Olymp	7.00
2558	29¢ Numismatics	3.75
2559	29¢ WW II S/S	8.75
2560	29¢ Basketball	10.00
2561	29¢ Washington, D.C.	3.50
2566a	29¢ Comedians bklt	7.00
2567	29¢ Jan Matzeliger	6.00
2577a	29¢ Space bklt	9.00
2578,78a	29¢ Madonna,...sht/bklt	11.00
2579,80, or 81,82-85	29¢ Santa Claus sht./bklt	17.50
2587	32¢ James Polk	6.50
2590	$1.00 Burgoyne	6.00
2592	$5.00 Washington	13.50
2593a	29¢ Pledge bklt.	6.00
2595-97	29¢ Eagle & Shield/ Die Cut (3 Pgs.)	5.50
2598	29¢ Eagle S/A	4.00
2599	29¢ Liberty	4.00
2602	(10¢)Eagle&Shld. coil	5.00
2603-4	(10¢) BEP & SV	4.50
2605	23¢ Flag/Pre-sort	3.50
2606	23¢ USA/Pre-sort	4.00
2607	23¢ Same, BEP	4.00
2608	23¢ Same, SV	3.75
2609	29¢ Flag/W.H. Coil	3.25

1992 Issues

Scott No.	Subject	Price
2611-15	29¢ Winter Olympics	5.50
2616	29¢ World Columbian	3.50
2617	29¢ W.E.B. DuBois	6.00
2618	29¢ Love	3.50
2619	29¢ Olympic BB	17.50

OFFICIAL SOUVENIR PAGES

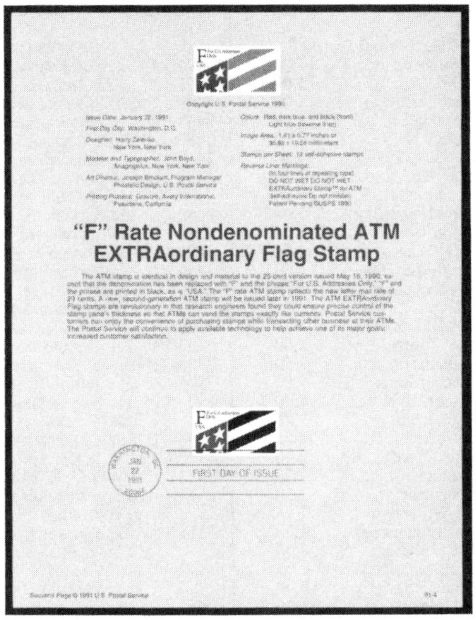

2522

Scott No.	Subject	Price
	1992 Issues (continued)	
2620-23	29¢ Columb. Voyages..	5.50
2624-29	1¢-$5 Columbus S/S	55.00
2630	29¢ NY Stock Exchg....	3.00
2631-34	29¢ Space Accomp	7.00
2635	29¢ Alaska Hwy..........	3.00
2636	29¢ Kentucky Sthd.......	3.00
2637-41	29¢ Summer Olymp	5.50
2646a	29¢ Hummingbird Pn ...	7.00
2647-96	29¢ Wildflowers (5).....	40.00
2697	29¢ WW II S/S	7.50
2698	29¢ Dorothy Parker.	4.00
2699	29¢ Dr. von Karman	6.00
2700-03	29¢ Minerals..........	6.00
2704	29¢ Juan Cabrillo	3.00
2709a	29¢ Wild Animals Bklt.	7.00
2710,10a	29¢ Christmas Trad. Sheet & Bklt.	10.00
2711-14,18a,19	29¢ Toys, sheet bklt.& Die Cut	7.50
2720	29¢ Chinese New Yr....	11.00
	1993 Issues	
2721	29¢ Elvis Presley.....	13.00
2722	29¢ Oklahoma.........	3.50
2723	29¢ Hank Williams..	6.00
2724/30,2737a	29¢ Rock 'n Roll Bklt. & Single	20.00
2745a	29¢ Space Fantasy, Bklt. Pane of 5	8.00
2746	29¢ Perry L. Julian	5.00
2747	29¢ Oregon Trail.....	3.50
2748	29¢ World Games	3.50
2749	29¢ Grace Kelly	6.00
2750-3	29¢ Circus..............	5.50
2754	29¢ Cherokee Strip	4.25
2755	29¢ Dean Acheson	3.00
2756-9	29¢ Sports Horses	7.50
2764a	29¢ Garden Flowers, Bklt. Pane of 5	5.50
2765	29¢ WW II S/S	7.50
2766	29¢ Joe Louis..............	11.50
2770a	29¢ Broadway, Booklet of 4	7.00
2771/4,2778a	Country Music, Booklet & Single..........	15.00
2779-82	29¢ Postal Museum......	4.50
2783-4	29¢ Deaf Commun	4.00
2785-8	29¢ Youth Classics	4.50
2789,2790a	29¢ Madonna	7.50
2791/4,2798b,2799/2802,2803	29¢ Christmas	18.00
2804	29¢ N. Marianas	4.00
2805	29¢ Columbus Landing in Puerto Rico	5.00
2806,2806b	29¢ AIDS..................	8.00
	1994 Issues	
2807-11	29¢ Winter Olympics ...	7.00
2812	29¢ Edward R.Murrow	4.00
2813	29¢ Sunrise Love	4.50
2814a,15	29¢-52¢ Love................	9.50
2814C	29¢ Love......................	4.50
2816	29¢ Dr. Allison Davis...	6.50
2817	29¢ Chinese New Year	6.00
2818	29¢ Buffalo Soldiers.....	7.50
2819-28	29¢ Silent Scrn. ... Stars	8.50

Scott No.	Subject	Price
	1994 Issues (continued)	
2833a	29¢ Garden Flowers, Bklt. Pane of 5	8.50
2834-36	29¢-50¢ Soccer	8.50
2837	Soccer Sv. Sheet	9.00
2838	29¢ WWII S/S	7.50
2839-40	29¢ Rockwell Stamp & S/S	13.00
2841-42	29¢/$9.95 Moon...........	30.00
2847a	29¢ Locomotive Pn.	9.50
2848	29¢ George Meany.......	4.50
2849-53	29¢ Pop Singers	8.50
2854-61	29¢ Blues/Jazz	11.50
2862	29¢ J. Thurber	6.00
2863-66	29¢ Wonders-Sea.........	7.00
2867-68	29¢ Cranes..................	4.00
2869	29¢ Legends-West	22.50
2871,71b	29¢ Madonna	10.00
2872,72a	29¢ Stocking	7.50
2873-74	29¢ Santa/Cardinal.......	9.00
2875	$2 BEP S/S	19.50
2876	29¢ Happy New Year...	7.50
2877,84,90,93	"G" ABNC	6.00
2878,80,82,85	"G" SVS................	6.00
2879,81,83,89	"G" BEP.................	6.00
2886-87	"G" Self. Adh.	12.50
	1995-98 Issues	
2897/2916	32¢ Flag-Porch...........	6.50
2902	(5¢)Butte Coil	7.00
2902B,4A,	6,10,12A,15B Coils.....	8.00
2903-4	(5¢) Mountain Coil.......	6.50
2905	(10¢) Automobile Coil .	5.50
2907,20d,21	Regulars....................	6.50
2908-9	(15¢) Tail Fin Coil........	5.50
2911-12	(25¢) Juke Box Coil	4.50
2912B/15	Self Adhesives	8.00
2919	32¢ Flag - Field, S.A. ...	4.00
2933	32¢ M. Hershey	4.00
2934	32¢ Cal Farley.............	5.00
2935	32¢ Henry R. Luce	9.00
2936	32¢ Wallaces	9.00
2938	46¢ Ruth Benedict........	5.00
2940	55¢ A. Hamilton..........	4.00
2942	77¢ M. Breckenridge....	5.00
2943	78¢ Alice Paul.............	4.00
	1995 Issues	
2948-49	(32¢) Love	5.00
2950	32¢ Florida..................	4.00
2951-54	32¢ Kids Care	5.00
2955	32¢ Richard Nixon	4.50
2956	32¢ Bessie Coleman......	5.50
2957-60	32¢ - 55¢ Angel	5.00
2961-65	32¢ Rec. Sports...........	8.50
2966	32¢ POW/MIA	4.50
2967	32¢ Marilyn Monroe	8.00
2968	32¢ Texas	6.00
2973a	32¢ Lighthouses Pn.	8.00
2974	32¢ U.N. Nations.........	4.00
2975	32¢ Civil War	20.00
2976-79	32¢ Carousel	7.50
2980	32¢ Suffrage................	4.00
2981	32¢ World War II.........	10.00
2982	32¢ L. Armstrong.........	6.00
2983-92	32¢ Jazz......................	11.00
2997a	32¢ Garden Flowers, ... Pane of 5	10.00
2998	60¢ E. Rickenbacker....	6.00
2999	32¢ Republic-Palau	5.00

Scott No.	Subject	Price
	1995 Issues (continued)	
3000	32¢ Comic Strips	20.00
3001	32¢ Naval Academy......	6.00
3002	32¢ Tenn. Williams......	6.00
3003,3b	32¢ Madonna..............	8.50
3004-7,8-11	32¢ Christmas	7.50
3012	32¢ Midnight Angel.....	6.50
3013	32¢ Children Sledding..	6.50
3019-23	32¢ Antique Autos.......	8.50
	1996 Issues	
3024	32¢ Utah Statehood	5.00
3029a	32¢ Garden Flowers, Pane of 5..................	8.50
3030	32¢ Love	6.50
3032	2¢ Woodpeckers..........	5.00
3033	3¢ Bluebird..................	5.00
3036	$1 Red Fox	10.75
3048,53	20¢ Bluejay	7.00
3050,55	20¢ Pheasant...............	9.00
3054	32¢ Yellow Rose Coil (97)	9.00
3058	32¢ Ernest Just	7.50
3059	32¢ Smithsonian	5.00
3060	32¢ Chinese New Year	8.50
3061-64	32¢ Communications ...	6.50
3065	32¢ Fulbright	5.00
3066	50¢ J Cochran.............	5.00
3067	32¢ Marathon	5.00
3068	32¢ Atlanta Games	21.50
3069	32¢ Georgia O'Keefe...	6.50
3070	32¢ Tennessee	5.00
3072-76	32¢ American Indian Dances..........	6.50
3077-80	32¢ Prehist. Animals....	6.50
3081	32¢ Breast Cancer	6.50
3082	32¢ James Dean...........	6.50
3083-86	32¢ Folk Heroes	7.00
3087	32¢ Olympic Games	7.00
3088-89	32¢ Iowa......................	7.00
3090	32¢ Rural Free Delivery	5.50
3091-95	32¢ Riverboats............	9.00
3096-99	32¢ Big Band Leaders..	9.00
3100-3	32¢ Songwriters..........	9.00
3104	32¢ F.Scott Fitzgerald..	5.50
3105	32¢ Endangered Species	22.50
3106	32¢ Computer Technology.......	5.50
3107/12	32¢ Madonna..............	9.00
3108/16	32¢ Family Scenes.......	9.00
3117	32¢ Skaters..................	9.00
3118	32¢ Hanukkah.............	7.00
3119	50¢ Cycling S.S.	9.00
3120	32¢ Chinese New Year	9.00
	1997 Issues	
3121	32¢ B.O. Davis, Jr.	9.00
3122	32¢ Liberty	8.00
3123-24	32¢-55¢ Love	8.00
3125	32¢ Children Learn	7.00
3126-29	32¢ Merian Prints	8.00
3130-31	32¢ PAC-97 Triangles .	7.00
3132-33	Linerless Coils	8.00
3134	32¢ Thorton Wilder	7.00
3135	32¢ R. Wallenberg.......	7.00
3136	32¢ Dinosaurs.............	22.50
3137a	32¢ Bugs Bunny	9.00
3139	50¢ B. Franklin Sh.	18.00
3140	60¢ G.Washington Sh ..	18.00
3141	32¢ Marshall Plan........	7.00
3142	32¢ Aircraft	22.50
3143-46	32¢ Football Coaches ..	13.50
3147	32¢ Vince Lombardi	9.00
3148	32¢ Bear Bryant...........	9.00
3149	32¢ Pop Warner...........	9.00
3150	32¢ George Halas	9.00
3151	32¢ Dolls.....................	18.50
3152	32¢ Humphry Bogart ...	9.00
3153	32¢ Stars & Stripes......	9.00
3154-57	32¢ Opera Singers	13.00
3158-65	32¢ Composers & Conductors	15.00
3166	32¢ Felix Varela	9.00
3167	32¢ Air Force..............	12.50
3168-72	32¢ Movie Monsters....	15.00
3173	32¢ Supersonic Flight ..	13.00
3174	32¢ Women in Military	9.00
3175	32¢ Kwanza................	11.00
3176	32¢ Madonna..............	11.00
3177	32¢ Holly....................	11.00
3178	$3 Mars Pathfinder	17.50
	1998 Issues	
3179	32¢ Chinese New Yr....	9.00
3180	32¢ Alpine Skiing	9.00
3181	32¢ Mdm. CJ Walker...	9.00
3182	32¢ 1900's..................	15.00
3183	32¢ 1910's..................	15.00
3184	32¢ 1920's..................	15.00
3185	32¢ 1930's	15.00
3186	33¢ 1940's (1999)	15.00
3192	32¢ Remember-Maine .	9.00
3193-97	32¢ Flowering Trees	12.00
3198-3202	32¢ A. Calder	12.00
3203	32¢ Cinco de Mayo	9.00
3204a	32¢ Sylvester & Tweety	9.00

Scott No.	Subject	Price
3206	32¢ Wisconsin	9.00
3207-8	Wetlands, Diner Coils..	9.00
3207A,70-71	Wetlands, Eagle & Shield Coils.	10.00
3208A	Diner Coil	9.00
3211	32¢ Berlin Airlift..........	9.00
3212-15	32¢ Folk Musicians.....	11.00
3216-19	32¢ Gospel Singers	11.00
3220	32¢ Spanish Sett.	9.00
3221	32¢ Stephen Benet	9.00
3222-25	32¢ Tropical Birds	11.00
3226	32¢ Alfred Hitchcock...	9.00
3227	32¢ Organ & Tissue....	9.00
3229	(10¢) Green Bicycle.....	9.00
3230-34	32¢ Bright Eyes	12.00
3235	32¢ Klondlike Gold......	9.00
3236	32¢ American Art	15.00
3237	32¢ Ballet	9.00
3238-42	32¢ Space Discovery ...	12.00
3243	32¢ Giving & Sharing ..	9.00
3244	32¢ Madonna & Child .	9.00
3245-52	32¢ Wreaths	12.00
3257-58,60	1¢ W.Vane, 33¢ Hat.......................	10.00
3259,63	22¢ Uncle Sam	9.00
3261	$3.20 Shuttle...............	12.00
3262	$11.75 Shuttle.............	22.50
3264,66	33¢ Hat, Coils..............	10.50
3267-69	33¢ Hat, Booklet Singles..........	11.00
	1998 Semi-Postal	
B1	32¢+8¢ Breast Cancer	
	Airmails (1973-85)	
C79	13¢ Winged Env	3.00
C83	13¢ Winged Coil..........	3.50
C84	11¢ City of Refuge.......	85.00
C87	18¢ Stat. of Liberty	7.00
C88	26¢ Mt. Rushmore	5.50
C89-90	25¢ & 31¢ Airmails	3.50
C91-92	31¢ Wright Brothers	4.00
C93-94	21¢ Octave Chanute.....	3.50
C95-96	25¢ Wiley Post	4.00
C97	31¢ Olym. Games	4.50
C98	40¢ P. Mazzei..............	3.00
C99	28¢ Blanche Scott	3.00
C100	35¢ Glenn Curtiss	3.00
C101-04	28¢ Olympics..............	4.00
C105-08	40¢ Olympics..............	4.00
C109-12	35¢ Olympics..............	4.50
C113	33¢ A. Verville	2.50
C114	39¢ L.& E. Sperry........	3.00
C115	44¢ Transpacific Flt	3.00
C116	44¢ Fr.J. Serra	3.00
	Airmails (1988-91)	
C117	44¢ New Sweden.........	3.00
C118	45¢ S.P. Langley..........	3.00
C119	36¢ Sikorsky.............. .	3.50
C120	45¢ French Rev.......... .	3.50
C122-25	45¢ Future Mail	6.50
C126	$1.80 Future Mail S/S .	6.50
C128	50¢ Harriet Quimby	3.50
C129	40¢ William Piper	3.50
C130	50¢ Antarctic Treaty .. .	4.00
C131	50¢ America	3.50
	1983-95 Official Issues	
O127-29,30-35	1¢/$5 (5 pgs)	22.50
O129A,136	14¢&22¢ Issues	3.00
O138-39	(14¢&22¢)"D" Sht.&Coil	3.00
O138A,141	15¢,25¢ Coils.......... .	3.50
O138B	20¢ Coil..................... .	3.00
O140	(25¢) "E" Coil	3.00
O143	1¢ Offset.................... .	3.50
O144	(29¢) "F" Coil	3.50
O145,47-48	19¢,23¢,29¢ Sgls. & Coil	3.00
O146	4¢ Make-up rate......... .	3.00
O146A	10¢ Official................ .	3.50
O153/56	1¢/32¢ Officials	4.50
	1992-94 Variable Rate Coils	
CV31	29¢ Variable Rate...... .	4.00
CV32	29¢ Vert. Design....... .	5.25
CV33	32¢ Variable Rate...... .	6.00

1474

The U.S. Postal Service has provided panels for commemorative and Christmas issues since Scott #1464-67 (Sept. 20, 1972). Each panel features mint stamps along with appropriate steel engravings and interesting stories about the subject. Prices are for with or without the original sleeves. Please add 20% if you require sleeves.

Scott No.	Subject	Price
1972 Commemoratives		
1464-67	8¢ Wildlife	6.00
1468	8¢ Mail Order	6.00
1469	8¢ Osteopathic Med.	6.00
1470	8¢ Tom Sawyer	9.00
1471	8¢ Christmas 1972	8.00
1472	8¢ 'Twas Night	8.00
1473	8¢ Pharmacy	7.50
1474	8¢ Stamp Collecting	7.50
1973 Commemoratives		
1475	8¢ Love	8.00
1476	8¢ Pamphleteers	6.00
1477	8¢ Posting Broadside	6.00
1478	8¢ Post Rider	8.00
1479	8¢ Drummer	10.00
1480-83	8¢ Boston Tea Party	20.00
1484	8¢ George Gershwin	8.00
1485	8¢ Robinson Jeffers	6.50
1486	8¢ Henry O. Tanner	6.50
1487	8¢ Willa Cather	6.50
1488	8¢ Copernicus	6.50
1489-98	8¢ Postal People	7.00
1499	8¢ Harry S Truman	10.00
1500-02,C86	Electronics	10.00
1503	8¢ Lyndon B. Johnson	8.00
1504	8¢ Angus Cattle	8.00
1505	10¢ Chautauqua (74)	8.00
1506	10¢ Kansas Wheat(74)	8.00
1507	8¢ Christmas (73)	10.00
1508	8¢ Needlepoint	9.00
1974 Commemoratives		
1525	10¢ Vet. Foreign Wars	6.00
1526	10¢ Robert Frost	6.00
1527	10¢ Expo '74	8.00
1528	10¢ Horse Racing	9.50
1529	10¢ Skylab	10.00
1530-37	10¢ Univ. Postal Un.	8.00
1538-41	10¢ Mineral Heritage	10.00
1542	10¢ Fort Harrod	6.00
1543-46	10¢ Cont. Congress	7.50
1547	10¢ Energy Conserv.	6.50
1548	10¢ Sleepy Hollow	8.00
1549	10¢ Retarded Children	6.00
1550	10¢ Angel	7.50
1551	10¢ Currier R Ives	8.00
1975 Commemoratives		
1553	10¢ Benjamin West	7.50
1554	10¢ Paul L. Dunbar	8.00
1555	10¢ D.W. Griffith	9.00
1556	10¢ Pioneer	9.50
1557	10¢ Mariner	10.75
1558	10¢ Coll Bargaining	6.00

Scott No.	Subject	Price
1559-62	10¢ Contrib. to Cause	7.50
1563	10¢ Lexing. & Concord	7.00
1564	10¢ Bunker Hill	8.00
1565-68	10¢ Military	7.50
1569-70	10¢ Apollo Soyuz	11.00
1571	10¢ Women's Year	7.00
1572-75	10¢ Postal Bicent	7.00
1576	10¢ Peace thru Law	7.00
1577-78	10¢ Bank/Commerce	6.50
1579	10¢ Madonna	7.50
1580	10¢ Christmas Card	8.00
1976 Commemoratives		
1629-31	13¢ Spirit of '76	8.50
1632	13¢ INTERPHIL '76	9.00
1633/82	State Flags,Blk.4	16.50
1683	13¢ Telephone Cent.	8.00
1684	13¢ Commer. Aviation	9.00
1685	13¢ Chemistry	8.00
1690	13¢ Benj Franklin	8.00
1691-94	13¢ Dec. of Indepen.	8.00
1695-98	13¢ Olympics	9.00
1699	13¢ Clara Maass	10.75
1700	13¢ Adolph S. Ochs	9.00
1701	13¢ Copley Nativity	10.00
1702	13¢ Currier Winter Past	9.00
1977 Commemoratives		
1704	13¢ Wash. Princeton	10.00
1705	13¢ Sound Recording	22.50
1706-09	13¢ Pueblo Art	80.00
1710	13¢ Lindbergh Flight	80.00
1711	13¢ Colorado	13.50
1712-15	13¢ Butterflies	15.00
1716	13¢ Lafayette	13.00
1717-20	13¢ Skilled Hands	13.00
1721	13¢ Peace Bridge	13.00
1722	13¢ Herkimer	13.00
1723-24	13¢ Energy	14.00
1725	13¢ Alta California	13.50
1726	13¢ Art. of Confed	16.00
1727	13¢ Talking Pictures	15.00
1728	13¢ Saratoga	16.50
1729	13¢ Valley Forge	22.50
1730	13¢ Rural Mailbox	25.00
1978 Issues		
1731	13¢ Carl Sandburg	8.50
1732-33	13¢ Captain Cook	15.00
1744	13¢ Harriet Tubman	15.00
1745-48	13¢ Quilts	15.00
1749-52	13¢ Dance	12.00
1753	13¢ French Alliance	13.00
1754	13¢ Dr. Papanicolaou	11.00
1755	13¢ Jimmie Rodgers	12.00
1756	15¢ George M. Cohan	15.00

Scott No.	Subject	Price
1758	15¢ Photography	12.00
1759	15¢ Viking Missions	32.50
1760-63	15¢ Owls	32.50
1764-67	15¢ Trees	25.00
1768	15¢ Madonna	14.00
1769	15¢ Hobby Horse	14.00
1979 Commemoratives		
1770	15¢ Robert Kennedy	11.00
1771	15¢ Martin L. King, Jr.	10.00
1772	15¢ Year of the Child	8.00
1773	15¢ John Steinbeck	7.50
1774	15¢ Albert Einstein	9.50
1775-78	15¢ Toleware	11.00
1779-82	15¢ Architecture	9.50
1783-86	15¢ Endang. Flora	9.50
1787	15¢ Seeing Eye Dogs	8.00
1788	15¢ Special Olympics	7.50
1789	15¢ John Paul Jones	9.50
1790/C97	Olympic Games	9.50
1791-94	15¢ Summer Olym	10.00
1795-98	15¢ Winter Olym (80)	8.00
1799	15¢ Virgin & Child	11.00
1800	15¢ Santa Claus	11.00
1801	15¢ Will Rogers	10.00
1802	15¢ Vietnam Vets	10.00
1980 Commemoratives		
1803	15¢ W.C. Fields	12.50
1804	15¢ Benj. Banneker	8.00
1821	15¢ Frances Perkins	7.00
1823	15¢ Emily Bissell	8.00
1824	15¢ Keller/Sullivan	7.00
1825	15¢ Vet. Admin	6.50
1826	15¢ Gen. B. de Galvez	6.50
1827-30	15¢ Coral Reefs	8.00
1831	15¢ Organized Labor	7.00
1832	15¢ Edith Wharton	6.50
1833	15¢ Amer. Education	7.00
1834-37	15¢ Indian Masks	11.00
1838-41	15¢ Architecture	7.50
1842	15¢ St. Glass Window	8.00
1843	15¢ Antique Toys	8.50
1981 Commemoratives		
1874	15¢ Everett Dirksen	7.00
1875	15¢ Whitney Young	8.00
1876-79	18¢ Flowers	8.50
1910	18¢ Red Cross	7.50
1911	18¢ Savings & Loan	7.50
1912-19	18¢ Space Achieve	11.00
1920	18¢ Prof. Manage	7.00
1921-24	18¢ Wildlife Habitats	10.00
1925	18¢ Yr. Disable Per.	7.00
1926	18¢ Vincent Millay	7.50
1928-31	18¢ Architecture	7.50
1932-33	18¢ Jones/Zaharias	32.50
1934	18¢ Fred Remington	8.50
1935-36	18¢ & 20¢ J. Hoban	7.00
1937-38	18¢ Yorktown Capes	7.00
1939	20¢ Madonna	8.00
1940	20¢ "Teddy Bear"	9.00
1941	20¢ John Hanson	7.00
1942-45	20¢ Desert Plants	10.00
1982 Commemoratives		
1950	20¢ Roosevelt	8.50
1951	20¢ Love	10.75
1952	20¢ G. Washington	10.00
1953/2002	20¢ State Birds/Fl Blk	30.00
2003	20¢ Netherlands	11.00
2004	20¢ Library Congress	10.00
2006-09	20¢ World's Fair	8.50
2010	20¢ Horatio Alger	9.00
2011	20¢ Aging	9.00
2012	20¢ Barrymores	11.00
2013	20¢ Mary Walker	9.00
2014	20¢ Peace Garden	9.00
2015	20¢ Libraries	9.00
2016	20¢ Robinson	30.00
2017	20¢ Touro Synag	9.00
2018	20¢ Wolf Trap	9.50
2019-22	20¢ Architecture	10.00
2023	20¢ Francis Assisi	10.00
2024	20¢ Ponce de Leon	9.00
2025	20¢ Kitten & Puppy	14.00
2026	20¢ Madonna	13.50
2027-30	20¢ Snow Scene	13.50
1983 Commemoratives		
2031	20¢ Science/Industry	6.00
2032-35	20¢ Balloons	6.50
2036	20¢ Sweden/US	6.00
2037	20¢ Conserv.Corps	6.00
2038	20¢ Priestley	6.00
2039	20¢ Voluntarism	6.00
2040	20¢ German Immigr	6.00
2041	20¢ Brooklyn Bridge	6.00
2042	20¢ Tenn. Valley Auth	6.00
2043	20¢ Physical Fitness	6.00

Scott No.	Subject	Price
2044	20¢ Scott Joplin	6.50
2045	20¢ Medal of Honor	7.00
2046	20¢ Babe Ruth	22.50
2047	20¢ Nath. Hawthorne	6.00
2048-51	13¢ Olympics	6.50
2052	20¢ Treaty of Paris	6.50
2053	20¢ Civil Service	6.50
2054	20¢ Met. Opera	7.00
2055-58	20¢ Inventors	7.50
2059-62	20¢ Streetcars	8.00
2063	20¢ Madonna	8.00
2064	20¢ Santa Claus	8.00
2065	20¢ Martin Luther	7.50
1984 Commemoratives		
2066	20¢ Alaska Statehood	6.00
2067-70	20¢ Winter Olympics	7.50
2071	20¢ FDIC	6.00
2072	20¢ Love	6.00
2073	20¢ Carter Woodson	6.00
2074	20¢ Soil/Water Cons.	6.00
2075	20¢ Credit Un.Act	6.00
2076-79	20¢ Orchids	7.00
2080	20¢ Hawaii Statehood	6.50
2081	20¢ Nat'l. Archives	6.00
2082-85	20¢ Summer Olympics	6.50
2086	20¢ Louisiana Expo	6.00
2087	20¢ Health Research	6.00
2088	20¢ Doug Fairbanks	6.50
2089	20¢ Jim Thorpe	7.50
2090	20¢ J McCormack	7.00
2091	20¢ St. Lawr. Seaway	6.50
2092	20¢ Migratory Bird	8.00
2093	20¢ Roanoke	6.00
2094	20¢ Herman Melville	6.50
2095	20¢ Horace Moses	6.00
2096	20¢ Smokey Bear	17.50
2097	20¢ Clemente	30.00
2098-2101	20¢ Dogs	8.00
2102	20¢ Crime Prevent	6.00
2103	20¢ Hispanic Amer	6.00
2104	20¢ Family Unity	6.00
2105	20¢ E. Roosevelt	10.00
2106	20¢ Nation Readers	6.00
2107	20¢ Madonna	7.00
2108	20¢ Santa Claus	6.50
2109	20¢ Vietnam Vets	9.00
1985 Issues Commemoratives		
2110	22¢ Jerome Kern	6.50
2137	22¢ Mary M. Bethune	7.00
2138-41	22¢ Duck Decoys	12.50
2142	22¢ Winter Special Olympics	6.00
2143	22¢ Love	6.00
2144	22¢ Rural Electric	6.00
2145	22¢ AMERIPEX '86	6.50
2146	22¢ Abigail Adams	6.00
2147	22¢ Bartholdi	8.50
2152	22¢ Korean War Vets	8.00
2153	22¢ Social Security	6.00
2154	22¢ World War I Vets	6.50
2155-58	22¢ Horses	11.00
2159	22¢ Public Education	7.00
2160-63	22¢ Youth Year	11.00
2164	22¢ Help End Hunger	6.50
2165	22¢ Madonna	7.50
2166	22¢ Poinsettias	8.00
1986 Commemoratives		
2167	22¢ Arkansas Statehood	6.00
2201a	22¢ Stamp Col.	7.50
2202	22¢ Love	8.50
2203	22¢ Sojourner Truth	8.00
2204	22¢ Republic Texas	7.00
2209a	22¢ Fish booklet	9.50
2210	22¢ Public Hospitals	6.00
2211	22¢ Duke Ellington	9.00
2216-19	22¢ US Presidents 4 panels	30.00
2220-23	22¢ Polar Explorers	9.00
2224	22¢ Statue of Liberty	7.50
2235-38	22¢ Navajo Art	9.00
2239	22¢ T.S. Elliot	6.50
2240-43	22¢ Woodcarved	8.00
2244	22¢ Madonna	7.00
2245	22¢ Village	7.00
1987 Commemoratives		
2246	22¢ Michigan	6.50
2247	22¢ P-Am. Games	6.00
2248	22¢ Love	6.50
2249	22¢ J.Bap. Sable	6.50
2250	22¢ Enrico Caruso	7.00
2251	22¢ Girls Scouts	9.00
2274a	22¢ Sp. Occ. Bk	7.00
2275	22¢ United Way	6.00
2286-2335	22¢ Am.Wildlife(5)	37.50

2381-85

Scott No.	Subject	Price
1993 Commemoratives		
2721	29¢ Elvis Presley	20.00
2722	29¢ Oklahoma	10.00
2723	29¢ Hank Williams	20.00
2737b	29¢ Rock 'n Roll	25.00
2745a	29¢ Space Fantasy	13.00
2746	29¢ Percy L. Julian	11.00
2747	29¢ Oregon Trail	11.00
2748	29¢ World Games	11.00
2749	29¢ Grace Kelly	18.00
2750-3	29¢ Circus	12.00
2754	29¢ Cherokee Strip	11.00
2755	29¢ Dean Acheson	12.00
2756-9	29¢ Sports Horses	13.00
2764a	29¢ Garden Flowers	11.00
2765	29¢ WW II S/S	15.00
2766	29¢ Joe Louis	30.00
2770a	29¢ Broadway Musicals, Booklet Pane	15.00
2775-8	29¢ Country-Western	22.50
2779-82	29¢ Postal Museum	11.00
2783-4	29¢ Deaf Commun	11.00
2785-8	29¢ Youth Classics	13.50
2789,91-4	29¢ Christmas	14.00
2804	29¢ Nthn.Marianas	11.00
2805	29¢ Columbus Lands in Puerto Rico	14.00
2806	29¢ AIDS	11.00
1994 Commemoratives		
2807-11	29¢ Winter Olympics	20.00
2812	29¢ Edward R.Murrow	12.00
2814a	29¢ Love, Bklt Pane	13.00
2816	29¢ Allison Davis	14.00
2817	29¢ Chinese New Year	18.00
2818	29¢ Buffalo Soldiers	16.00
2819-28	29¢ Silent Screen Stars	18.00
2833a	29¢ Garden Flowers, Pane of 5	14.00
2837	29¢,40¢,50¢ World Cup Soccer, S/S of 3	15.00
2838	29¢ WWII S/S	18.00
2839	29¢ Norman Rockwell	25.00
2841	29¢ Moon Landing	22.50
2847a	29¢ Locomotives, Pane of 5	16.00
2848	29¢ George Meany	11.00
2849-53	29¢ Pop. Singers	16.00
2854-61	29¢ Jazz/Blues	20.00
2862	29¢ J. Thurber	10.00
2863-66	29¢ Wonders - Sea	15.00
2867-68	29¢ Cranes	15.00
2871	29¢ Madonna	11.00
2872	29¢ Stocking	11.00
2876	29¢ Year of Bear	16.00
1995 Commemoratives		
2950	32¢ Florida	12.00
2951-54	32¢ Kids Care	12.00
2955	32¢ R. Nixon	18.00
2956	32¢ B. Coleman	17.00
2957-58	32¢-55¢ Love	17.00
2961-65	32¢ Rec. Sports	17.00
2966	32¢ POW/MIA	14.00
2967	32¢ M. Monroe	30.00
2968	32¢ Texas	15.00
2973a	32¢ Lighthouses	17.00
2974	32¢ Un. Nations	13.00
2976-79	32¢ Carousel	15.00
2980	32¢ Women's Suffrage	13.00
2981	32¢ WWII S/S	19.50
2982	32¢ L. Armstrong	20.00
2983-92	32¢ Jazz Musicians	21.50
2997a	32¢ Garden Flowers Pane of 5	13.00
2999	32¢ Palau	13.00
3001	32¢ Naval Academy	17.00
3002	32¢ Tennessee Williams	15.00
3003	32¢ Madonna	17.00
3004-7	32¢ Christmas	17.00
3019-23	32¢ Antique Autos	22.50
1996 Commemoratives		
3024	32¢ Utah	13.00
3029a	32¢ Garden Flowers	13.00
3058	32¢ Ernest E. Just	18.00
3059	32¢ Smithsonian	13.00
3060	32¢ Chinese New Year	22.00
3061-4	32¢ Communications	17.00
3065	32¢ Fulbright	13.00
3067	32¢ Marathon	17.00
3068	32¢ Olympics Sheet	39.50
3069	32¢ Georgia O'Keeffe	13.00
3070	32¢ Tennessee	13.00
3071-6	32¢ Indian Dances	21.50
3077-80	32¢ Prehistoric Animals	21.50

Scott No.	Subject	Price
1996 Comm. (continued)		
3081	32¢ Breast Cancer	13.00
3082	32¢ James Dean	21.50
3083-86	32¢ Folk Heroes	21.50
3087	32¢ Olympic Games	15.00
3088	32¢ Iowa	13.00
3090	32¢ Rural Free Delivery	13.00
3091-95	32¢ Riverboats	21.50
3096-99	32¢ Big Band Leaders	21.50
3100-3	32¢ Songwriters	21.50
3104	32¢ Scott Fitzgerald	17.00
3105	32¢ Endangered Species	35.00
3106	32¢ Computer Tech	17.00
3107	32¢ Madonna	17.00
3108-11	32¢ Family	18.00
3118	32¢ Hanukkah	18.00
3119	50¢ Cycling Sv. Sheet	18.00
1997 Commemoratives		
3120	32¢ Chinese New Year	20.00
3121	32¢ Benjamin Davis	17.00
3124	55¢ Love	15.00
3125	32¢ Children Learn	13.00
3130-31	32¢ Triangles	17.00
3134	32¢ Thorton Wilder	13.00
3135	32¢ R. Wallenberg	15.00
3136	32¢ Dinosaurs	27.50
3137c	32¢ Bugs Bunny	22.50
3139	50¢ B. Franklin Sh	37.50
3140	60¢ G.Washington Sh	37.50
3141	32¢ Marshall Plan	13.00
3142	32¢ Aircraft Sheet	36.50
3143-46	32¢ Football Coaches	20.00
3151	32¢ Dolls Sheet	22.50
3152	32¢ Humphrey Bogart	18.00
3153	32¢ Stars and Stripes	16.00
3154-57	32¢ Opera Singers	18.00
3158-65	32¢ Composers & Conductors	18.50
3166	32¢ Felix Varela	16.00
3167	32¢ Air Force	16.00
3168-72	32¢ Movie Monsters	20.00
3173	32¢ Supersonic Flight	18.50
3174	32¢ Women in Military	16.00
3175	32¢ Kwanza	18.50
3176a	32¢ Madonna	23.50
3177a	32¢ Holly	23.50
1998 Commemoratives		
3179	32¢ Chinese New Yr	16.00
3180	32¢ Alpine Skiing	16.00
3181	32¢ Mdm. CJ Walker	16.00
3182	32¢ 1900's	25.00
3183	32¢ 1910's	25.00
3184	32¢ 1920's	25.00
3185	32¢ 1930's	25.00
3186	33¢ 1940's (1999)	25.00
3192	32¢ Remember-Maine	16.00
3193-97	32¢ Flowering Trees	19.50
3198-3202	32¢ A. Calder	19.50
3203	32¢ Cinco de Mayo	16.00
3204c	32¢ Sylvester/Tweety	16.00
3206	32¢ Wisconsin	16.00
3209-10	Trans-Mississippi (2)	27.50
3211	32¢ Berlin Airlift	16.00
3212-15	32¢ Folk Musicians	16.00
3216-19	32¢ Gospel Singers	16.00
3220	32¢ Spanish Settlem	16.00
3221	32¢ Stephen V. Benet	16.00
3222-25	32¢ Tropical Birds	16.00
3226	32¢ Alfred Hitchcock	16.00
3227	32¢ Organ & Tissue	16.00
3230-34	32¢ Bright Eyes	17.00
3235	32¢ Klondike Gold	16.00
3236	32¢ Art	22.50
3237	32¢ Ballet	16.00
3238-42	32¢ Space Discovery	17.00
3243	32¢ Giving/Sharing	16.00
3244a	32¢ Madonna	21.00
3249-52	32¢ Wreaths	16.00
1999 Commemoratives		
3272	33¢ Year of the Rabbit	16.00
3273	33¢ Malcolm X	16.00
3274a	33¢ Love, Pane	25.00
3275	55¢ Love	18.00
3276	33¢ Hospice Care	16.00
3286	33¢ Irish Immigration	16.00
1998 Semi-Postal		
B1	32¢+8¢ Breast Cancer	16.00
Airmails		
C101-04	28¢ Olympics	7.50
C105-06	40¢ Olympics	7.00
C109-12	35¢ Olympics	8.00
C117	44¢ New Sweden	7.50
C120	45¢ French Revolution	8.00
C122-25	45¢ Future Mail	9.00
C130	50¢ Antarctic Treaty	8.00
C131	50¢ America	8.00

Scott No.	Subject	Price
1987-90 Bicentennial Issues		
2336	22¢ Delaware	8.00
2337	22¢ Pennsylvania	6.50
2338	22¢ New Jersey	6.50
2239	22¢ Georgia	7.00
2340	22¢ Connecticut	7.00
2341	22¢ Massachusetts	7.00
2342	22¢ Maryland	7.00
2343	25¢ South Carolina	7.00
2344	25¢ New Hampshire	7.00
2345	25¢ Virginia	7.00
2346	25¢ New York	7.00
2347	25¢ North Carolina	7.00
2348	25¢ Rhode Island	7.00
1987 Commemoratives (cont)		
2349	22¢ U.S.-Morocco	6.00
2350	22¢ Faulkner	6.00
2351-54	22¢ Lacemaking	8.00
2359a	22¢ Const. Bklt.	7.50
2360	22¢ Const. Signing	6.50
2361	22¢ CPA	20.00
2366a	22¢ Locom. Bklt.	8.00
2367	22¢ Madonna	7.00
2368	22¢ Ornaments	7.00
1988 Commemoratives		
2369	22¢ '88 Wint. Olympics	7.00
2370	22¢ Australia Bicent.	8.00
2371	22¢ J.W. Johnson	7.50
2372-75	22¢ Cats	8.50
2376	22¢ K. Rockne	12.00
2377	25¢ F. Ouimet	16.50
2378-79	25¢-45¢ Love	7.50
2380	25¢ Sum. Olympics	7.50
2385a	25¢ Classic Cars bk	8.50
2386-89	25¢ Ant. Explorers	7.50
2390-93	25¢ Carousel	8.50
2395-98	25¢ Occasions bk	7.50
2399-2400	25¢ Christmas	7.50
1989 Commemoratives		
2401	25¢ Montana	7.00
2402	25¢ Randolph	8.50
2403	25¢ North Dakota	7.00
2404	25¢ Washington	7.00
2409a	25¢ Steamboats bklt.	8.50
2410	25¢ Wld. Stamp Expo	7.00
2411	25¢ Arturo Toscanini	8.00
2412	25¢ House of Reps	8.00
2413	25¢ U.S. Senate	8.00
2414	25¢ Exec./GW Inaug.	8.50
2415	25¢ Supr Court(1990)	7.50
2416	25¢ South Dakota	7.00
2417	25¢ Lou Gehrig	30.00
2418	25¢ E. Hemingway	7.50
2420	25¢ Letter Carriers	7.50
2421	25¢ Bill of Rights	7.50
2422-25	25¢ Prehis. Animals	16.00
2426/C121	25¢/45¢ Pre-Columbian Customs	9.00
2427-28	25¢ Christmas	9.50
2434-37	25¢ Classic Mail	8.00

Scott No.	Subject	Price
1990 Commemoratives		
2439	25¢ Idaho Sthd	7.00
2440,41a	25¢ Love	7.50
2442	25¢ Ida B. Wells	10.00
2444	25¢ Wyoming Sthd	7.00
2445-48	25¢ Classic Films	14.00
2449	25¢ Marianne Moore	6.50
2474a	25¢ Lighthouse bklt	14.00
2496-2500	25¢ Olympians	11.00
2505a	25¢ Headress Bklt.	11.00
2506-07	25¢ Marshalls & Micronesia Joint Issue	7.00
2508-11	25¢ Sea Creatures	12.00
2512/C127	25¢,45¢ America	9.00
2513	25¢ D.D. Eisenhower	8.50
2514,15	25¢ Christmas	10.00
1991 Commemoratives		
2532	50¢ Switzerland	9.00
2533	29¢ Vermont	7.00
2534	29¢ Savings Bonds	7.50
2535,37	29¢ Love	9.50
2538	29¢ William Saroyan	7.50
2549a	29¢ Fishing Flies bk	11.00
2550	29¢ Cole Porter	9.00
2551	29¢ Desert Shield	25.00
2553-57	29¢ Summer Olymp	9.50
2558	29¢ Numismatics	8.00
2559	29¢ WW II	15.00
2560	29¢ Basketball	16.50
2561	29¢ Dist.of Columbia	9.00
2566a	29¢ Comedians bklt.	11.00
2567	29¢ Jan Matzeliger	9.50
2577a	29¢ Space bklt	14.00
2578-79	29¢ Christmas	12.00
2587	32¢ J. S.Polk(1995)	11.50
1992 Commemoratives		
2611-15	29¢ Winter Olympics	10.00
2616	29¢ World Columbian	10.00
2617	29¢ W.E.B. DuBois	13.50
2618	29¢ Love	12.00
2619	29¢ Olympic Baseball	35.00
2620-23	29¢ Columb.Voyages	12.00
2624-29	1¢/$5 Columbus S/S Set of 3 Panels	180.00
2630	29¢ Stock Exchg	15.00
2631-34	29¢ Space Accomp	12.00
2635	29¢ Alaska Highway	9.50
2636	29¢ Kentucky Sthd	7.50
2637-41	29¢ Summer Olymp	9.50
2646a	29¢ Humming. B. Pn	13.00
2647-96	29¢ Wildflowers (5)	175.00
2697	29¢ WW II S/S	13.00
2698	29¢ Dorothy Parker	7.50
2699	29¢ Dr. von Karman	12.00
2700-03	29¢ Minerals	12.00
2704	29¢ Juan Cabrillo	10.00
2709a	29¢ Wild Animals Pn	12.50
2710,14a	29¢ Christmas	13.50
2720	29¢ Chinese New Yr	20.00

CONFEDERATE STATES OF AMERICA

1,4 2,5 6,7 8

11 12 13 14

1861-62 (OG + 40%) (C)

Scott's No.		Unused Fine	Unused Ave.	Used Fine	Used Ave.
1	5¢ Jefferson Davis, Green	165.00	95.00	140.00	85.00
2	10¢ T. Jefferson, Blue	210.00	130.00	175.00	110.00
3	2¢ Andrew Jackson, Green	465.00	275.00	600.00	350.00
4	5¢ Jefferson, Rose	125.00	75.00	95.00	55.00
5	10¢ T. Jefferson, Rose	825.00	500.00	450.00	275.00
6	5¢ J. Davis, London Print, Clear	7.50	4.50	25.00	16.00
7	5¢ J. Davis, Local Print, Coarse	10.75	6.50	17.50	11.00

1862-63 (OG + 30%) (C)

8	2¢ A. Jackson, Brown Red	49.50	29.50	300.00	180.00
9	10¢ J. Davis, Blue "TEN CENTS"	650.00	395.00	475.00	280.00
10	10¢ Blue "TEN CENTS", Frame Line	2750.00	1600.00	1150.00	675.00
11	10¢ Blue, No Frame Line, Die A	8.50	5.50	13.00	7.75
12	10¢ Same, Filled in Corners, Die B	10.00	6.00	15.00	9.00
13	20¢ Washington, Green	27.50	17.00	350.00	210.00
14	1¢ J.C. Calhoun, Orange (unissued)	65.00	42.50	...	...

CANAL ZONE

5 73 84/101 96

1904 U.S. 1902-03 Issue Ovptd. "CANAL ZONE" "PANAMA" VF Used + 50% (C)

Scott's No.		NH VF	NH F-VF	Unused VF	Unused F-VF	Used F-VF
4	1¢ Frank., Bl. Grn. (#300)	79.50	52.50	48.50	32.50	22.50
5	2¢ Wash., Carmine (#319)	72.50	47.50	42.50	27.50	23.50
6	5¢ Lincoln, Blue (#304)	275.00	180.00	160.00	110.00	70.00
7	8¢ M. Wash., V.Blk. (#306)	400.00	265.00	240.00	160.00	95.00
8	10¢ Webster, Red Brn.(#307)	425.00	280.00	265.00	175.00	100.00

1924-25 U.S. Stamps of 1923-25 Overprinted "CANAL ZONE" (Flat Top "A") Flat Press, Perf. 11 VF Used + 30% (B)

70	½¢ N. Hale (#551)	2.10	1.50	1.30	.95	.65
71	1¢ Franklin (#552)	2.40	1.80	1.60	1.20	.80
71e	1¢ Bklt. Pane of 6 (#552a)	275.00	175.00	160.00	120.00	...
72	1½¢ Harding (#553)	4.25	3.15	2.75	2.10	1.50
73	2¢ Washington (#554)	14.50	10.50	9.50	7.00	1.65
73a	2¢ Bklt. Pane of 6 (#554c)	400.00	300.00	275.00	200.00	...
74	5¢ T. Roosevelt (#557)	36.50	27.50	24.00	18.00	8.00
75	10¢ Monroe (#562)	82.50	61.50	53.50	40.00	21.50
76	12¢ Cleveland (#564)	77.50	55.00	47.50	35.00	30.00
77	14¢ Indian (#565)	57.50	41.50	37.50	27.50	21.00
78	15¢ Liberty (#566)	100.00	77.50	65.00	50.00	32.50
79	30¢ Buffalo (#569)	60.00	45.00	40.00	30.00	21.50
80	50¢ Amphitheater (#570)	135.00	100.00	87.50	65.00	42.50
81	$1 Lincoln Mem. (#571)	500.00	380.00	330.00	250.00	100.00

1925-28 Same as Preceding but with Pointed "A", VF Used + 30% (B)

84	2¢ Washington (#554)	70.00	50.00	45.00	32.50	8.50
84d	2¢ Bklt. Pane of 6 (#554c)	395.00	275.00	285.00	195.00	...
85	3¢ Lincoln (#555)	8.25	6.25	5.35	3.95	3.25
86	5¢ T. Roosevelt (#557)	8.75	6.50	5.50	4.15	2.25
87	10¢ Monroe (#562)	75.00	56.50	48.50	36.50	12.50
88	12¢ Cleveland (#564)	52.50	38.50	33.50	25.00	13.00
89	14¢ Indian (#565)	41.50	30.00	26.50	19.50	16.50
90	15¢ Liberty (#566)	13.50	10.00	8.50	6.50	4.25
91	17¢ Wilson (#623)	7.50	5.50	4.85	3.65	3.25

CANAL ZONE

1925-28 Pointed "A" (cont.)

Scott's No.		NH VF	NH F-VF	Unused VF	Unused F-VF	Used F-VF
92	20¢ Golden Gate (#567)	13.00	10.00	8.50	6.50	3.75
93	30¢ Buffalo (#569)	11.50	8.50	7.25	5.50	4.25
94	50¢ Amphitheater (#570)	500.00	385.00	325.00	250.00	210.00
95	$1 Lincoln Mem (#571)	265.00	200.00	170.00	130.00	75.00

1926 Sesquicentennial Issue Overprinted "CANAL ZONE" VF Used + 30%

96	2¢ Liberty Bell (#627)	7.50	5.50	5.25	4.00	3.75

1926-27 Rotary Press, Perf. 10, Overprinted "CANAL ZONE" VF Used + 60% (B)

97	2¢ Washington (#583)	100.00	60.00	65.00	42.50	11.50
98	3¢ Lincoln (#584)	19.50	11.50	12.50	7.50	4.35
99	10¢ Monroe (#591)	32.50	19.50	21.50	13.00	7.25

1927-31 Rotary Press, Perf. 11x10½, Overprinted "CANAL ZONE" VF Used + 30% (B)

100	1¢ Franklin (#632)	3.35	2.50	2.50	1.85	1.20
101	2¢ Washington (#634)	3.85	2.85	2.80	2.10	1.10
101a	2¢ Bklt. Pane of 6 (#634d)	450.00	300.00	300.00	200.00	...
102	3¢ Lincoln (#635) (1931)	8.50	6.25	5.75	4.25	3.00
103	5¢ T. Roosevelt (#637)	50.00	37.50	33.50	25.00	10.75
104	10¢ Monroe (#642) (1930)	35.00	26.75	23.75	18.00	11.50

105 107 110 112

1928-40 Flat Plate Printing VF Used + 20% (B)

105-14	Set of 10	13.50	10.50	9.75	7.75	4.95
105	1¢ General Gorgas	.30	.25	.25	.20	.18
106	2¢ General Goethels	.30	.25	.25	.20	.18
106a	2¢ Booklet Pane of 6	36.50	28.00	26.50	20.00	...
107	5¢ Gaillard Cut (1929)	1.85	1.40	1.40	1.10	.70
108	10¢ General Hodges (1932)	.70	.55	.50	.40	.20
109	12¢ Colonel Gaillard (1929)	2.20	1.70	1.50	1.25	.75
110	14¢ Gen. W.L. Sibert (1937)	1.70	1.30	1.25	1.00	1.00
111	15¢ Jackson Smith (1932)	1.10	.85	.75	.60	.55
112	20¢ Adm. Rousseau (1932)	1.35	1.10	1.00	.80	.25
113	30¢ Col. Williamson (1940)	1.75	1.40	1.25	1.00	.85
114	50¢ J. Blackburn (1929)	3.50	2.75	2.50	2.00	.75

PLATE BLOCKS

	NH VF	NH F-VF	Unused F-VF		NH VF	NH F-VF	Unused F-VF
105 (6)	1.25	1.00	.70	110 (6)	20.00	16.00	11.50
106 (6)	3.50	2.75	2.00	111 (6)	16.50	12.50	8.50
107 (6)	19.50	15.00	11.00	112 (6)	18.00	13.00	9.00
108 (6)	11.50	9.50	6.75	113 (6)	19.00	13.75	9.50
109 (6)	21.00	16.50	12.00	114 (6)	33.50	27.50	20.00

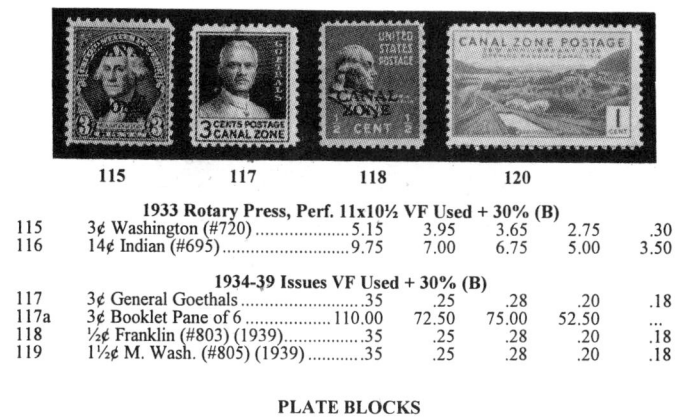

115 117 118 120

1933 Rotary Press, Perf. 11x10½ VF Used + 30% (B)

115	3¢ Washington (#720)	5.15	3.95	3.65	2.75	.30
116	14¢ Indian (#695)	9.75	7.00	6.75	5.00	3.50

1934-39 Issues VF Used + 30% (B)

117	3¢ General Goethals	.35	.25	.28	.20	.18
117a	3¢ Booklet Pane of 6	110.00	72.50	75.00	52.50	...
118	½¢ Franklin (#803) (1939)	.35	.25	.28	.20	.18
119	1½¢ M. Wash. (#805) (1939)	.35	.25	.28	.20	.18

PLATE BLOCKS

	NH VF	NH F-VF	Unused F-VF		NH VF	NH F-VF	Unused F-VF
115	65.00	50.00	35.00	118	5.25	4.00	3.00
116	100.00	75.00	50.00	119	5.25	4.00	3.00
117 (6)	2.35	1.80	1.40				

CANAL ZONE

1939 25th Anniversary Series VF + 30%

Scott's No.		Plate Blocks F-VF NH	Plate Blocks F-VF Unus.	F-VF NH	F-VF Unus.	F-VF Used
120-35	Set of 16	...	...	120.00	85.00	65.00
120	1¢ Balboa, before...................(6)	13.50	10.00	.75	.55	.35
121	2¢ Balboa, after ....(6)	13.50	10.00	.75	.55	.40
122	3¢ Gaillard Cut, before ....(6)	13.50	10.00	.75	.55	.22
123	5¢ Gaillard Cut, after..............(6)	22.00	16.00	1.75	1.25	1.00
124	6¢ Bas Obispo, before ....(6)	47.50	35.00	3.25	2.35	2.35
125	7¢ Bas Obispo, after ....(6)	47.50	35.00	3.50	2.50	2.35
126	8¢ Gatun Locks, before..........(6)	60.00	45.00	5.25	3.75	2.75
127	10¢ Gatun Locks, after............(6)	60.00	45.00	3.75	2.85	2.65
128	11¢ Canal Channel, before......(6)	130.00	100.00	9.00	6.50	7.00
129	12¢ Canal Channel, after.........(6)	110.00	80.00	8.50	6.00	6.50
130	14¢ Gamboa, before ....(6)	130.00	100.00	8.50	6.00	6.75
131	15¢ Gamboa, after ....(6)	165.00	125.00	11.50	8.00	4.75
132	18¢ P. Miguel Locks, before....(6)	160.00	120.00	11.50	8.00	7.50
133	20¢ P. Miguel Locks, after.......(6)	200.00	150.00	14.00	10.00	6.75
134	25¢ Gatun Spillway, before......(6)	335.00	250.00	20.00	14.00	13.50
135	50¢ Gatun Spillway, after.......(6)	365.00	275.00	25.75	18.00	4.75

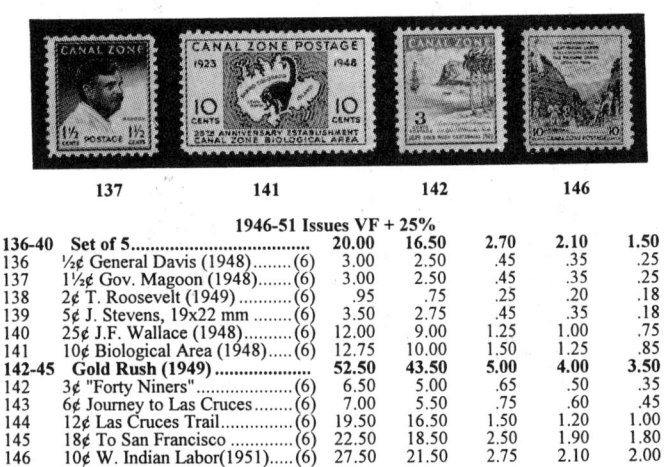

137   141   142   146

1946-51 Issues VF + 25%

Scott's No.		Plate Blocks F-VF NH	Plate Blocks F-VF Unus.	F-VF NH	F-VF Unus.	F-VF Used
136-40	Set of 5..................................	20.00	16.50	2.70	2.10	1.50
136	½¢ General Davis (1948)........(6)	3.00	2.50	.45	.35	.25
137	1½¢ Gov. Magoon (1948).......(6)	3.00	2.50	.45	.35	.25
138	2¢ T. Roosevelt (1949) ....(6)	.95	.75	.25	.20	.18
139	5¢ J. Stevens, 19x22 mm ....(6)	3.50	2.75	.45	.35	.18
140	25¢ J.F. Wallace (1948)..........(6)	12.00	9.00	1.25	1.00	.75
141	10¢ Biological Area (1948).....(6)	12.75	10.00	1.50	1.25	.85
142-45	Gold Rush (1949)	52.50	43.50	5.00	4.00	3.50
142	3¢ "Forty Niners"...................(6)	6.50	5.00	.65	.50	.35
143	6¢ Journey to Las Cruces ......(6)	7.00	5.50	.75	.60	.45
144	12¢ Las Cruces Trail...............(6)	19.50	16.50	1.50	1.20	1.00
145	18¢ To San Francisco ....(6)	22.50	18.50	2.50	1.90	1.80
146	10¢ W. Indian Labor(1951).....(6)	27.50	21.50	2.75	2.10	2.00

1955-58 Commemoratives

148   149   150

Scott's No.		Plate Blocks NH	F-VF NH	F-VF Used
147	3¢ Panama Railroad ....(6)	7.50	.75	.55
148	3¢ Gorgas Hospital (1957)	4.35	.45	.40
149	4¢ S.S. Ancon (1958)	3.25	.45	.35
150	4¢ T. Roosevelt (1958).............................	3.50	.50	.40

1960-62 Issues

151   152   153   157

151	4¢ Boy Scouts	4.50	.50	.40
152	4¢ Administration Bldg..............................	1.10	.20	.17
		Line Pairs		
153	3¢ Goethals, Coil.......................................	1.10	.20	.18
154	4¢ Admin. Bldg., Coil................................	1.15	.20	.18
155	5¢ Stevens, Coil (1962)	1.50	.30	.25

CANAL ZONE
1960-62 Issues (cont.)

Scott's No.		Plate Blocks NH	F-VF NH	F-VF Used
156	4¢ Girl Scouts (1962)..	2.75	.40	.30
157	4¢ Thatcher Ferry Bridge ('62)	3.35	.35	.30

1968-78 Issues

158   159   163   165

158	6¢ Goethals Monument Balboa	2.25	.35	.30
159	8¢ Fort San Lorenzo (1971)	2.95	.45	.25
160	1¢ Gorgas,Coil,Pf.10 Vert.(1975)......Line Pair	1.10	.20	.18
161	10¢ Hodges,Coil,Pf.10 Vert.(1975)....Line Pair	5.50	.85	.50
162	25¢ Wallace,Coil,Pf.10 Vert.(1975)....Line Pair	21.50	3.00	2.85
163	13¢ Dredge Cascadas (1976)	2.35	.40	.30
163a	13¢ Booklet Pane of 4	...	3.00	...
164	5¢ Stevens, Rotary, 19x22½mm (1977)	5.75	1.00	.95
164a	5¢ Stevens, Tagged	...	11.00	...
165	15¢ Towing Locomotive (1978)	3.00	.60	.40

AIR MAIL STAMPS

C3   C5   C6   C17

Scott's No.		NH VF	NH F-VF	Unused VF	Unused F-VF	Used F-VF
	1929-31 Surcharges on Issues of 1928-29 VF Used + 30% (B)					
C1	15¢ on 1¢ Gorgas T.I (#105)	16.00	12.00	9.75	7.50	5.75
C2	15¢ on 1¢ Gorgas T.II (1931)	210.00	155.00	130.00	87.50	90.00
	Type I: Flag "5" points up. Type II: Flag of "5" is curved up.					
C3	25¢ on 2¢ Goethals (#106) 7.50		5.25	4.75	3.50	2.10
C4	10¢ on 50¢ Blackburn (#114) 15.00		11.00	9.75	7.50	7.00
C5	20¢ on 2¢ Goethals (#106) 11.00		7.50	6.75	5.00	1.85
	1931-49 Series Showing "Gaillard Cut" VF Used + 25% (B)					
C6-14	Set of 9...32.75		24.50	22.50	18.00	6.75
C6	4¢ Red Yellow (1949) 1.10		.90	.85	.70	.75
C7	5¢ Yellow Green 90		.65	.65	.50	.45
C8	6¢ Yellow Brown (1946) 1.20		.95	.90	.70	.35
C9	10¢ Orange 1.50		1.20	1.15	.90	.35
C10	15¢ Blue.....................................1.85		1.50	1.40	1.10	.30
C11	20¢ Red Violet 3.25		2.50	2.40	1.90	.30
C12	30¢ Rose Lake (1941) 5.25		4.00	3.75	2.95	1.10
C13	40¢ Yellow 5.25		4.00	3.75	2.95	1.25
C14	$1 Black 13.50		10.00	9.50	7.50	2.25

PLATE BLOCKS

	NH VF	NH F-VF	Unused F-VF		NH VF	NH F-VF	Unused F-VF
C6 (6)	8.50	6.75	5.50	C11 (6)	28.00	21.50	16.50
C7 (6)	6.50	5.00	4.00	C12 (6)	45.00	36.50	27.50
C8 (6)	8.50	6.75	5.50	C13 (6)	45.00	36.50	27.50
C9 (6)	15.75	12.00	9.50	C14 (6)	125.00	97.50	75.00
C10 (6)	16.75	12.75	10.00				

1939 25th Anniversary of Canal Opening VF + 30%

Scott's No.		Plate Blocks NH	Plate Blocks Unused	F-VF NH	F-VF Unused	F-VF Used
C15-20	Set of 6................................			79.50	58.75	42.50
C15	5¢ Plane over Sosa Hill ....(6)	45.00	33.50	4.75	3.50	2.65
C16	10¢ Map of Central America...(6)	55.00	40.00	4.00	3.00	2.60
C17	15¢ Fort Amador......................(6)	59.50	45.00	4.75	3.50	1.20
C18	25¢ Cristobal Harbor...............(6)	235.00	175.00	15.00	11.00	8.50
C19	30¢ Gaillaird Cut ....(6)	170.00	125.00	13.75	10.00	7.00
C20	$1 Clipper Landing ....(6)	535.00	400.00	40.00	30.00	23.50

NOTE: FROM 1955 TO DATE, UNLESS OTHERWISE NOTED, CANAL ZONE UNUSED PRICES ARE FOR NEVER HINGED STAMPS. HINGED STAMPS, WHEN AVAILABLE, ARE PRICED AT APPROXIMATELY 20% BELOW THE NEVER HINGED PRICE. VERY FINE QUALITY IS PRICED AT 20% OVER THE APPROPRIATE F-VF PRICE. MINIMUM 10¢ PER STAMP.

NOTE: PRICES THROUGHOUT THIS LIST ARE SUBJECT TO CHANGE WITHOUT NOTICE IF MARKET CONDITIONS REQUIRE. MINIMUM ORDER MUST TOTAL AT LEAST $20.00

| C21 | C32 | C33 |

1951 "Globe and Wing" Issue VF + 25%

Scott's No.		Plate Blocks NH	Plate Blocks Unus.	F-VF NH Unus.	F-VF Used
C21-26	Set of 6	210.00	160.00	24.50 17.95	11.00
C21	4¢ Red Violet ....(6)	7.50	5.75	.80 .60	.40
C22	6¢ Brown ....(6)	5.75	4.25	.75 .55	.35
C23	10¢ Red Orange ....(6)	9.50	7.50	1.15 .90	.50
C24	21¢ Blue ....(6)	75.00	57.50	8.50 6.50	4.25
C25	31¢ Cerise ....(6)	75.00	57.50	8.50 6.50	4.25
C26	80¢ Gray Black.......................(6)	42.50	33.75	5.25 4.00	1.75

1958 "Globe and Wing" Issue

Scott's No.		Plate Blocks F-VF NH	F-VF NH	F-VF Used
C27-31	Set of 5	170.00	24.75	9.00
C27	5¢ Yellow Green	7.00	1.25	.75
C28	7¢ Olive	6.00	1.15	.60
C29	15¢ Brown	30.00	4.50	2.25
C30	25¢ Orange Yellow	90.00	10.75	3.00
C31	35¢ Dark Blue	47.50	8.00	3.25

1961-63 Issues

C32	15¢ U.S. Army Carib. School	15.00	1.50	.95
C33	7¢ Anti-Malaria (1962)........................	3.25	.55	.50
C34	8¢ Globe & Wing (1963)	5.00	.65	.35
C35	15¢ Alliance for Progress (1963)	12.50	1.20	.90

1964 50th Anniversary of Canal Opening

C36-41	Set of 6	60.00	10.95	8.75
C36	6¢ Jet over Cristobal	2.00	.40	.40
C37	8¢ Gatun Locks	2.75	.50	.45
C38	15¢ Madden Dam	8.00	1.20	.80
C39	20¢ Gaillard Cut	10.50	2.00	1.10
C40	30¢ Miraflores Lock	16.50	2.70	2.50
C41	80¢ Balboa	25.00	4.50	3.75

1965 Seal & Jet Plane

C42-47	Set of 6	28.50	5.50	2.65
C42	6¢ Green & Black	2.25	.40	.30
C43	8¢ Rose Red & Black	2.50	.45	.18
C44	15¢ Blue & Black	2.75	.45	.35
C45	20¢ Lilac & Black	3.00	.70	.45
C46	30¢ Reddish Brown & Black	5.00	1.00	.50
C47	80¢ Bistre & Black	15.00	2.75	1.00

1968-76 Seal & Jet Plane

C48-53	Set of 6	24.95	4.65	3.00
C48	10¢ Dull Orange & Black	2.00	.40	.20
C48a	10¢ Booklet Pane of 4 (1970)	...	5.25	...
C49	11¢ Olive & Black (1971)	2.25	.45	.25
C49a	11¢ Booklet Pane of 4	...	4.25	...
C50	13¢ Emerald & Black (1974)	5.50	1.10	.35
C50a	13¢ Booklet Pane of 4	...	7.00	...
C51	22¢ Violet & Black (1976)	5.50	1.10	1.00
C52	25¢ Pale Yellow Green & Black	4.25	.85	.65
C53	35¢ Salmon & Black (1976)	7.00	1.15	.95

1941-47 OFFICIAL AIRMAIL STAMPS VF Used + 30%
Issue of 1931-46 Overprinted OFFICIAL PANAMA CANAL
"PANAMA CANAL" 19-20 mm long

Scott's No.		VF	NH F-VF	Unused VF	F-VF	Used F-VF
CO1-7,14	Set of 8	165.00	140.00	125.00	100.00	45.00
CO 1	5¢ Yellow Green (#C7)	7.50	6.00	5.50	4.50	2.00
CO 2	10¢ Orange (#C9)	14.50	11.50	10.50	8.75	2.50
CO 3	15¢ Blue (#C10)	18.00	13.50	12.50	10.00	3.50
CO 4	20¢ Rose Violet (#C11)	21.00	17.00	15.50	13.00	6.00
CO 5	30¢ Rose Lake (#C12) (1942)	25.50	21.50	20.00	16.50	6.50
CO 6	40¢ Yellow (#C13)...................	27.50	22.50	21.00	17.00	9.00
CO 7	$1 Black (#C14)....................	40.00	30.00	27.50	22.50	13.50
CO 14	6¢ Yel. Brown (#C8) (1947)	21.00	16.50	14.75	11.75	5.00

1941 OFFICIAL AIRMAIL STAMPS
Issue of 1931-46 Overprinted OFFICIAL PANAMA CANAL
"PANAMA CANAL" 17 mm long

		Used VF	Used F-VF
CO 8	5¢ Yellow Green (#C7)	175.00	135.00
CO 9	10¢ Orange (#C9)	290.00	225.00
CO 10	20¢ Red Violet (#C11)	215.00	165.00
CO 11	30¢ Rose Lake (#C12)	70.00	55.00
CO 12	40¢ Yellow (#C13)	225.00	175.00

NOTE: ON #CO1-CO14 AND O1-9, USED PRICES ARE FOR CANCELLED-TO-ORDER. POSTALLY USED COPIES SELL FOR MORE.

POSTAGE DUE STAMPS
1914 U.S. Dues Ovptd. "CANAL ZONE", Perf. 12 VF Used + 50% (C)

Scott' No.		VF	NH F-VF	Unused VF	F-VF	Used F-VF
J1	1¢ Rose Carmine (#J45a)	140.00	95.00	95.00	65.00	16.00
J2	2¢ Rose Carmine (#J46a)	475.00	320.00	315.00	210.00	55.00
J3	10¢ Rose Carmine (#J49a)	...	975.00	...	750.00	50.00

1924 U.S. Dues Ovptd. "CANAL ZONE", Flat "A" VF Used + 40% (B)

J12	1¢ Carmine Rose (#J61)	240.00	170.00	150.00	110.00	30.00
J13	2¢ Claret (#J62b)..................	140.00	100.00	85.00	60.00	12.00
J14	10¢ Claret (#J65b).................	575.00	390.00	350.00	250.00	55.00

1925 U.S. Ovptd. "CANAL ZONE POSTAGE DUE" VF Used + 40% (B)

J15	1¢ Franklin (#552)............	215.00	150.00	140.00	100.00	18.50
J16	2¢ Washington (#554)	47.50	35.00	31.50	22.50	7.75
J17	10¢ Monroe (#562)..............	120.00	80.00	75.00	52.50	13.00

1925 U.S. Dues Ovptd. "CANAL ZONE", Sharp "A" VF Used + 40% (B)

J18	1¢ Carmine Rose (#J61)	21.00	15.00	13.50	9.50	4.25
J19	2¢ Carmine Rose (#J62)	38.00	26.50	25.00	17.50	5.00
J20	10¢ Carmine Rose (#J65)	295.00	215.00	195.00	140.00	23.50

1929-30 Issue of 1928 Surcharged "POSTAGE DUE" VF Used + 30% (B)

J21	1¢ on 5¢ Gaillard Cut (#107)..	7.25	5.50	5.00	3.75	2.00
J22	2¢ on 5¢ Blue	12.75	9.50	8.50	6.50	3.00
J23	5¢ on 5¢ Blue	12.75	9.50	8.50	6.50	3.50
J24	10¢ on 5¢ Blue	12.75	9.50	8.50	6.50	3.50

1932-41 Canal Zone Seal VF Used + 30% (B)

J25-29	Set of 5	5.25	3.95	4.15	3.00	3.15
J25	1¢ Claret	.35	.25	.27	.20	.20
J26	2¢ Claret	.35	.25	.27	.20	.20
J27	5¢ Claret	.70	.50	.50	.40	.30
J28	10¢ Claret	2.50	1.85	1.80	1.35	1.50
J29	15¢ Claret (1941)	1.90	1.50	1.50	1.15	1.10

1941-47 OFFICIAL STAMPS VF Used + 30% (B)
Issues of 1928-46 Overprinted "OFFICIAL PANAMA CANAL"

O1	1¢ Gorgas, Type 1 (#105).......	3.35	2.50	2.50	1.85	.50
O2	3¢ Goethals, T. 1 (#117).......	5.85	4.50	4.35	3.25	.95
O3	5¢ Gaillard Cut, T. 2 (#107)...	...	...	...	...	35.00
O4	10¢ Hodges, Type 1 (#108).....	11.75	8.75	8.85	6.50	2.25
O5	15¢ Smith, Type 1 (#111)......	20.00	15.00	15.00	11.00	2.50
O6	20¢ Rousseau, T. 1 (#112)......	24.75	18.75	18.50	13.75	3.25
O7	50¢ Blackburn, T. 1 (#114).....	70.00	50.00	50.00	37.50	6.75
O8	50¢ Blackburn, T. 1A (#114)...	...	...	...	625.00	
O9	5¢ Stevens, T. 1 (#139) ('47)14.50	10.75	10.75	7.75	3.85	

Type 1: Ovptd. "10mm", Type 1A: Ovptd. "9mm", Type 2: Ovptd. "19½mm".

CUBA VF + 50% (C)

| 223 | 228 | E2 | J4 |

1899 U.S. Stamps of 1895-98 Surcharged for Use in Cuba

Scott's No.		NH Fine	Unused Fine	Ave.	Used Fine	Ave.
221	1¢ on 1¢ Franklin (#279) 8.00	5.00	3.25	.60	.35	
222	2¢ on 2¢ Wash. T. III (#267) 13.00	8.00	4.75	.75	.45	
222A	2¢ on 2¢ Wash. T. IV (#279B) 10.75	6.50	4.00	.50	.30	
223	2½¢ on 2¢ Wash. (#267) 7.00	4.50	2.75	.85	.55	
223A	2½¢ on 2¢ Wash. (#279B) 5.75	3.75	2.25	.60	.35	
224	3¢ on 3¢ Jackson (#268)............17.00	11.00	7.00	1.65	1.00	
225	5¢ on 5¢ Grant (#281a) 17.00	11.00	7.00	1.75	1.10	
226	10¢ on 10¢ Webster (#282C) 38.50	25.00	15.00	9.75	6.00	

1899 Issues of Republic under U.S. Military Rule, Wtmk. "US-C"

227	1¢ Statue of Columbus.............8.00	5.25	3.00	.30	.18	
228	2¢ Royal Palms 8.00	5.25	3.00	.30	.18	
229	3¢ Allegory "Cuba" 7.50	5.00	2.85	.35	.25	
230	5¢ Ocean Liner 11.50	7.50	4.35	.35	.25	
231	10¢ Cane Field 26.00	16.50	9.75	.95	.60	

NOTE: A RE-ENGRAVED SET WAS ISSUED BY THE REPUBLIC OF CUBA IN 1905-07. THEY ARE UN-WATERMARKED.

1899 SPECIAL DELIVERY

E1	10¢ on 10¢ Blue (#E5) 185.00	120.00	80.00	95.00	60.00	
E2	10¢ Messenger, Orange 75.00	50.00	32.50	15.00	9.00	

#E2 IS INSCRIBED "IMMEDIATE". THE REPUBLIC OF CUBA ISSUED A CORRECTED VERSION IN 1902 INSCRIBED "INMEDIATA".

1899 POSTAGE DUE

J1	1¢ on 1¢ Claret (#J38) 65.00	42.50	25.00	5.75	3.50	
J2	2¢ on 2¢ Claret (#J39) 65.00	42.50	25.00	5.75	3.50	
J3	5¢ on 5¢ Claret (#J41) 65.00	42.50	25.00	5.75	3.50	
J4	10¢ on 10¢ Claret (#J42) 55.00	35.00	21.50	3.25	1.95	

GUAM VF + 60% (C)

| | 1 | 4 | 12 | E1 |

1899 U.S. Stamps of 1895-98 Overprinted "GUAM"

Scott's No.		NH Fine	Unused Fine	Unused Ave.	Used Fine	Used Ave.
1	1¢ Franklin (#279)................	29.50	18.50	12.00	27.50	16.00
2	2¢ Wash., Red (#279B)	26.50	17.50	10.50	26.50	16.00
2a	2¢ Rose Carmine (#279Bc)	32.50	20.00	13.50	35.00	22.50
3	3¢ Jackson (#268)	170.00	110.00	65.00	150.00	90.00
4	4¢ Lincoln (#280a)	170.00	110.00	65.00	150.00	90.00
5	5¢ Grant (#281a)	45.00	28.50	18.00	45.00	27.50
6	6¢ Garfield (#282)	160.00	100.00	60.00	175.00	110.00
7	8¢ Sherman (#272)	160.00	100.00	60.00	175.00	110.00
8	10¢ Webster (#282C)	62.50	40.00	25.00	55.00	35.00
10	15¢ Clay (#284)	210.00	135.00	85.00	150.00	90.00
11	50¢ Jefferson (#275)	425.00	275.00	165.00	350.00	215.00
12	$1 Perry (#276)	575.00	375.00	225.00	425.00	240.00

1899 SPECIAL DELIVERY

E1	10¢ Blue (on U.S. #E5)	220.00	140.00	85.00	175.00	110.00

HAWAII

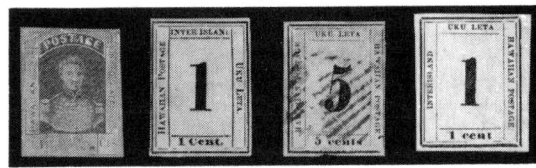

| | 11 | 15,23 | 21 | 25 |

1857-68 Issues (OG + 30%) (C)

Scott's No.		Unused Fine	Unused Ave.	Used Fine	Used Ave.
8	5¢ Kamehameha III, Blue	500.00	300.00	475.00	285.00
9	5¢ Blue, Bluish Paper	325.00	195.00	225.00	135.00
10	5¢ Blue, Reissue	22.50	13.75	...	...
11	13¢ Dull Rose, Reissue	225.00	140.00	...	...
15	1¢ Numeral, Black, Grayish	425.00	275.00	...	...
16	2¢ Black, Grayish Paper	700.00	450.00	550.00	350.00
19	1¢ Black	400.00	250.00	...	...
20	2¢ Black	575.00	350.00	...	...
21	5¢ Blue, Bluish Paper	600.00	365.00	425.00	265.00
22	5¢ Blue, Interisland	450.00	275.00	700.00	425.00
23	1¢ Black, Laid Paper	230.00	140.00	...	...
24	2¢ Black, Laid Paper	230.00	140.00	...	...
25	1¢ Dark Blue	230.00	140.00	...	...
26	2¢ Dark Blue	230.00	140.00	...	...

1861-86 Issues (OG + 20%, NH + 100) (VF + 50%) (C)

| | 27-29 | 30 | 32,39,52C | 35,38,43 | 36,46 |

		Unused Fine	Unused Ave.	Used Fine	Used Ave.
27	2¢ Kamehameha IV, Pale Rose	250.00	150.00	225.00	135.00
28	2¢ Pale Rose, Vert. Laid Paper.........	250.00	150.00	135.00	85.00
29	2¢ Red, Thin Wove Paper Reprint	40.00	25.00	...	...
30	1¢ Victoria Kamamalu, Purple	8.50	5.00	6.25	3.75
31	2¢ Kamehameha IV, Vermilion	14.50	9.00	8.25	4.75
32	5¢ Kamehameha V, Blue	130.00	85.00	27.50	16.50
33	6¢ Kamehameha V, Green...............	21.00	12.00	7.75	4.75
34	18¢ Kekuanaoa, Dull Rose, Gum......	75.00	42.50	32.50	18.75
34v	18¢ Without Gum	19.50	13.50	...	...
35	2¢ Kalakaua, Brown	6.50	4.00	2.75	1.60
36	12¢ Leleiohoku, Black....................	47.50	28.50	25.00	15.00

HAWAII

1882-91 Issues (OG + 20%) (VF + 50%) (C)

| | 37,42 | 40,44-45 | 41 | 47 | 52 |

Scott's No.		NH Fine	Unused Fine	Unused Ave.	Used Fine	Used Ave.
37	1¢ Likelike, Blue	8.25	5.25	3.25	9.00	5.75
38	2¢ Kalakaua, Lilac Rose	170.00	110.00	67.50	40.00	25.00
39	5¢ Kamehameha V, Ultra	22.50	14.50	9.00	3.00	1.85
40	10¢ Kalakaua, Black...............	50.00	32.50	20.00	18.50	11.00
41	15¢ Kapiolani, Red Brown	77.50	50.00	30.00	25.00	15.00
42	1¢ Likelike, Green	3.85	2.50	1.50	1.75	1.00
43	2¢ Kalakaua, Rose	6.50	4.25	2.50	.90	.55
44	10¢ Kalakaua, Red Brown	42.50	27.50	16.50	9.00	5.50
45	10¢ Kalakaua, Vermilion	45.00	29.75	18.00	12.00	7.50
46	12¢ Leleiohoku, Red Lilac	125.00	80.00	50.00	31.50	19.50
47	25¢ Kamehameha I, Dk. Viol. ..	190.00	120.00	75.00	50.00	30.00
48	50¢ Lunalilo, Red	230.00	150.00	90.00	75.00	46.50
49	$1 Kaleleonalani, Rose Red....	350.00	225.00	140.00	130.00	80.00
50	2¢ Orange Verm., Imperf........	...	150.00	95.00	...	...
51	2¢ Carmine, Imperf.................	...	30.00	17.50	...	...
52	2¢ Liliuokalani, Dull Violet	12.00	7.50	4.50	2.25	1.35
52C	5¢ Kamehameha, V.D. Ind.	170.00	110.00	65.00	125.00	75.00

1893 Issues of 1864-91 Overprinted "Provisional Government 1893" VF + 40% (C)

Red Overprints

53	1¢ Purple (#30)	11.00	7.00	4.25	11.00	6.50
54	1¢ Blue (#37)	8.50	5.50	3.35	11.00	6.50
55	1¢ Green (#42)	2.50	1.65	1.00	2.50	1.50
56	2¢ Brown (#35)	14.00	9.00	5.50	17.50	10.75
57	2¢ Dull Violet (#52)	5.75	3.75	2.25	3.25	1.95
58	5¢ Deep Indigo (#52C) ...	15.75	10.00	6.25	22.50	14.50
59	5¢ Ultramarine (#39)	8.75	5.75	3.50	4.00	2.50
60	6¢ Green (#33)	21.00	13.50	8.25	22.75	14.50
61	10¢ Black (#40)	13.50	8.75	5.25	13.75	8.75
62	12¢ Black (#36)	13.50	8.75	5.25	16.00	10.00
63	12¢ Red Lilac (#46).........	215.00	140.00	85.00	225.00	135.00
64	25¢ Dark Violet (#47)	35.00	22.50	13.50	35.00	22.00

Black Overprint

65	2¢ Rose Vermilion (#31)	95.00	60.00	37.50	65.00	40.00
66	2¢ Rose (#43)	2.15	1.40	.85	2.25	1.35
67	10¢ Vermilion (#45)	21.50	13.50	8.25	26.50	17.50
68	10¢ Red Brown (#44)	11.50	7.50	4.50	12.00	7.50
69	12¢ Red Lilac (#46)	385.00	250.00	155.00	450.00	275.00
70	15¢ Red Brown (#41)	28.50	18.50	11.50	27.50	16.50
71	18¢ Dull Rose (#34)	35.00	22.50	14.00	31.00	18.75
72	50¢ Red (#48)	80.00	52.50	32.50	85.00	50.00
73	$1 Rose Red	160.00	100.00	60.00	160.00	95.00

| | 74,80 | 76 | 79 | O1 |

1894-99 Issues VF + 40% (B)

74	1¢ Coat of Arms, Yellow........	2.70	1.80	1.10	1.25	.75
75	2¢ Honolulu, Brown	3.25	2.10	1.25	.70	.40
76	5¢ Kameha I, Rose Lake.........	6.50	4.25	2.60	2.00	1.35
77	10¢ Star & Palms, Yel. Grn.	8.50	5.50	3.75	4.50	2.75
78	12¢ S.S. "Arawa", Blue	18.50	12.00	7.25	20.00	13.50
79	25¢ Dole, Deep Blue	18.50	12.00	7.25	20.00	13.50
80	1¢ Arms, Green (1899)..........	2.25	1.50	.90	1.20	.75
81	2¢ Honolulu, Rose (1899).......	2.25	1.50	.90	1.20	.75
82	5¢ Kameha I, Blue (1899).......	8.00	5.25	3.25	3.00	1.80

1896 OFFICIALS VF + 40% (B)

O1	2¢ Thurston, Green................	57.50	37.50	23.00	20.00	12.50
O2	5¢ Black Brown	57.50	37.50	23.00	20.00	12.50
O3	6¢ Deep Ultramarine	57.50	37.50	23.00	20.00	12.50
O4	10¢ Bright Rose...................	57.50	37.50	23.00	20.00	12.50
O5	12¢ Orange.........................	80.00	50.00	30.00	20.00	12.50
O6	25¢ Gray Violet...................	100.00	60.00	40.00	20.00	12.50

PHILIPPINE ISLANDS VF + 50% (C)

213 226 E1 J1

1899 U.S. Stamps of 1894-98 Overprinted "PHILIPPINES"

Scott's No.		NH Fine	Unused Fine	Unused Ave.	Used Fine	Used Ave.
212	50¢ Jefferson (#260)	650.00	400.00	250.00	250.00	160.00
213	1¢ Franklin (#279)	5.75	3.75	2.25	1.00	.60
214	2¢ Wash., Red (#279)	2.75	1.75	1.20	.75	.45
215	3¢ Jackson (#268)	10.00	6.50	4.00	1.95	1.15
216	5¢ Grant (#281)	10.00	6.50	4.00	1.50	.90
217	10¢ Webster Ty. I (#282C)	33.50	21.50	13.00	4.25	2.75
217A	10¢ Webster, Ty. II (#283).....	325.00	210.00	130.00	40.00	25.00
218	15¢ Clay (#284)	60.00	38.00	25.00	8.25	4.95
219	50¢ Jefferson (#275)	230.00	145.00	90.00	40.00	25.00

1901 U.S. Stamps of 1895-98 Overprinted "PHILIPPINES"

220	4¢ Lincoln (#280b)	36.50	23.50	15.00	5.25	3.00
221	6¢ Garfield (#282)	45.00	28.50	17.50	7.50	4.50
222	8¢ Sherman (#272)	52.50	32.50	21.00	7.50	4.50
223	$1 Perry, Ty. I (#276)...........	700.00	450.00	280.00	250.00	160.00
223A	$1 Perry, Ty. II (#276A)........	3,200.00	2,000.00	1,375.00	1,050.00	650.00
224	$2 Madison (#277a)	825.00	525.00	350.00	300.00	185.00
225	$5 Marshall (#278)	1500.00	950.00	625.00	650.00	425.00

1903-04 U.S. Stamps of 1902-03 Overprinted "PHILIPPINES"

226	1¢ Franklin (#300)................	7.00	4.50	2.75	.45	.27
227	2¢ Wash. (#301)..................	12.50	8.00	5.00	1.85	1.10
228	3¢ Jackson (#302)................	115.00	75.00	47.50	16.00	9.00
229	4¢ Grant (#303)...................	130.00	80.00	52.50	24.00	14.50
230	5¢ Lincoln (#304)................	19.00	12.50	7.50	1.40	.85
231	6¢ Garfield (#305)................	140.00	90.00	55.00	23.50	13.75
232	8¢ M. Wash. (#306)..............	77.50	50.00	30.00	15.00	9.00
233	10¢ Webster (#307)..............	38.75	25.00	15.00	3.25	1.95
234	13¢ Harrison (#308)..............	57.50	37.50	23.00	18.00	11.00
235	15¢ Clay (#309)	100.00	65.00	40.00	17.00	10.50
236	50¢ Jefferson (#310).............	275.00	175.00	110.00	40.00	27.50
237	$1 Farragut (#311)...............	725.00	450.00	290.00	275.00	175.00
238	$2 Madison (#312)...............	...	1,050.00	700.00	825.00	500.00
239	$5 Marshall (#313)...............	...	1,250.00	850.00	950.00	550.00
240	2¢ Wash. (#319)...................	10.00	6.50	4.00	3.00	1.85

1901 SPECIAL DELIVERY U.S. #E5 Ovptd. "PHILIPPINES"

E1	10¢ Messenger, Dark Blue	180.00	115.00	75.00	110.00	65.00

1899-1901 POSTAGE DUES U.S. Dues Ovptd. "PHILIPPINES"

J1	1¢ Deep Claret (#J38)	9.50	6.00	3.75	2.25	1.40
J2	2¢ Deep Claret (#J39)	9.75	6.25	3.90	2.25	1.40
J3	5¢ Deep Claret (#J41)	26.00	16.50	10.00	3.75	2.30
J4	10¢ Deep Claret (#J42)	31.50	20.00	13.00	7.50	4.50
J5	50¢ Deep Claret (#J44)	300.00	190.00	120.00	110.00	70.00
J6	3¢ Deep Claret (#J40)	27.50	17.50	11.00	9.50	5.65
J7	30¢ Deep Claret (#J43)	335.00	215.00	135.00	100.00	65.00

PUERTO RICO VF + 50% (C)

210a 211 212 215 J2

1899 U.S. Stamps of 1895-98 Overprinted "PORTO RICO"

210	1¢ Franklin (36° Angle).........	11.00	7.00	4.25	2.25	1.40
210a	1¢ (#279) (25° Angle)	15.00	9.50	5.75	2.75	1.70
211	2¢ Wash. (36° Angle)............	11.00	7.00	4.25	2.50	1.60
211a	2¢ (#279Bf) (25° Angle)........	15.00	9.50	5.75	2.75	1.70
212	5¢ Grant, Blue (#281a)..........	15.00	9.50	5.75	2.35	1.45
213	8¢ Sherman (36° Angle).........	55.00	35.00	21.50	16.00	12.50
213a	8¢ (#272) (25° Angle)............	65.00	40.00	25.00	18.50	13.50
214	10¢ Webster (#282C).............	35.00	22.50	14.00	5.75	3.50

1900 U.S. Stamps of 1895-98 Overprinted "PUERTO RICO"

215	1¢ Franklin (#279)................	11.00	7.00	4.25	1.95	1.20
216	2¢ Wash. (#279B).................	12.50	8.00	5.00	2.25	1.40

1899 Postage Dues; U.S. Dues Overprinted "PORTO RICO"

J1	1¢ (#J38) (36° Angle)...........	36.50	23.50	14.00	7.50	4.50
J1a	1¢ Claret (25° Angle)	40.00	26.50	16.00	9.00	5.50
J2	2¢ (#J39) (36° Angle)...........	27.50	17.50	11.00	7.50	4.50
J2a	2¢ Claret (25° Angle)	35.00	22.50	14.00	9.00	5.50
J3	10¢ (#J42) (36° Angle)..........	260.00	165.00	100.00	55.00	32.50
J3a	10¢ Claret (25° Angle)	315.00	200.00	120.00	70.00	42.50

U.S. TRUST TERRITORY OF THE PACIFIC

THE MARSHALL ISLANDS, MICRONESIA, AND PALAU WERE PART OF THE U.S. TRUST TERRITORY OF THE PACIFIC. THE MARSHALL'S BECAME INDEPENDENT IN 1986.

MARSHALL ISLANDS

31 35 50

1984 Commemoratives

Scott's No.		Mint Sheetlet	Plate Block	F-VF NH
31-34	20¢ Postal Service Inaugural, attd..............	...	3.50	2.50
50-53	40¢ U.P.U., attd	...	3.75	3.00
54-57	20¢ Ausipex '84, Dolphins, attd	...	3.00	2.25
58	20¢ Christmas, 3 Kings, Strip of 4, attd	(16) 11.75	(8) 6.75	3.00
58	Christmas with tabs, attd..................	...	(8) 7.00	4.50
59-62	20¢ Marshalls Constitution, attd.................	...	3.50 ·	2.35

1984-85 Maps and Navigational Instruments

35-49A	1¢-$1 Definitives (16)	...	49.50	11.95
39a	13¢ Booklet Pane of 10	...	...	11.75
40a	14¢ Booklet Pane of 10	...	...	12.50
41a	20¢ Booklet Pane of 10	...	...	11.75
41b	13¢/20¢ Bklt. Pane of 10 (5 #39, 5 #41).....	...	...	12.50
42a	22¢ Booklet Pane of 10	...	...	12.50
42b	14¢/22¢ Bklt. Pane of 10 (5 #40, 5 #42).....	...	...	13.50

63-64

1985 Commemoratives

63-64	22¢ Audubon, attd................................	...	3.35	1.60
65-69	22¢ Sea Shells, strip of 5 attd	(10)	5.50	2.40
70-73	22¢ Decade for Women, attd.....................	...	2.50	1.85
74-77	22¢ Reef and Lagoon Fish, attd	...	2.50	1.95
78-81	22¢ International Youth Year, attd	...	2.65	2.10
82-85	14¢,22¢,33¢,44¢ Christmas, Missions (4)...	...	15.00	2.75
86-90	22¢ Halley's Comet, strip of 5 attd..............	(15) 45.00	(10) 14.00	5.75
86-90	Halley's Comet with tabs, attd	...	...	35.00
91-94	22¢ Medicinal Plants, attd	...	2.65	2.10

1986-87 Maps and Navigational Instruments

107	$2 Wotje & Erikub, 1871 Terrestrial Globe...	...	27.50	5.95
108	$5 Bikini, Stick Chart	...	65.00	14.75
109	$10 Stick Chart (1987)	...	95.00	21.50

110 163

1986-87 Commemoratives

110-13	14¢ Marine Invertebrates, attd	...	2.35	1.90
114	$1 Ameripex S/S (C-54 Globemaster)........	...	...	4.00
115-18	22¢ Operation Crossroads, attd.................	...	2.85	2.35
119-23	22¢ Seashells, strip of 5, attd	...	(10) 6.50	2.95
124-27	22¢ Game Fish, attd..............................	...	3.00	2.35
128-31	22¢ Christmas / Year of Peace, attd	...	3.75	2.95
132-35	22¢ Whaling Ships, attd (1987)	...	3.00	2.50
136-41	22¢ Pilots (3 pairs)	...	(12)13.50	6.00
142	$1.00 Amelia Earhart / CAPEX S/S............	...	...	3.25
143-51	14¢,22¢,44¢ U.S. Const. Bicent (9)...........	(15) 32.50	...	6.50
152-56	22¢ Seashells, strip of 5, attd	...	(10) 6.95	3.00
157-59	44¢ Copra Industry, strip of 3, attd	...	(6) 6.00	2.75
160-63	14¢,22¢,33¢,44¢ Christmas, Bible Verses (4)...	...	12.00	2.50

164   184

Scott's No.		Mint Sheetlet	Plate Block	F-VF NH
1988 Commemoratives				
164-67	44¢ Marine Birds, attd	...	5.25	4.50
188	15¢ Olympics, Javelin, Strip of 5	(10) 5.00		2.25
189	25¢ Olympics, Runner, Strip of 5	(10) 6.75		3.15
190	25¢ Robt. Louis Stevenson S/S of 9	...	...	9.50
191-94	25¢ Colonial Ships and Flags, attd	...	3.50	3.00
195-99	25¢ Christmas, strip of 5	(10) 7.25		3.25
200-04	25¢ John F. Kennedy, Strip of 5	(15) 17.50	...	3.95
205-08	25¢ Space Shuttle, Strip of 4	(12) 8.95	(8) 6.75	3.00
205-08	Space ShuttleTab Strip	...	...	3.75
1988-89 Fish Definitives				
168-83	1¢-$5.00 Fish (16)	...	125.00	26.50
170a	14¢ Booklet Pane of 10	...	...	5.75
171a	15¢ Booklet Pane of 10	...	...	7.50
173a	22¢ Booklet Pane of 10	...	...	7.75
173b	14¢ & 22¢ Bklt. Pane of 10 (5 ea.)	...	...	6.00
174a	25¢ Booklet Pane of 10	...	...	7.75
174b	15¢ & 25¢ Booklet Pane of 10	...	...	8.00
184	$10 Fish Definitive ('89)	...	105.00	23.75

1989 Commemoratives

209   222

209-12	45¢ Links to Japan, attd	...	5.00	4.50
213-15	45¢ Alaska State 30th Anniv., Strip of 3	(9) 12.75		3.50
216-20	25¢ Seashells, Strip of 5	(10) 7.95		3.85
221	$1.00 Hirohito Memorial S/S	...	...	2.95
222-25	45¢ Migrant Birds, attd	...	5.50	4.50
226-29	45¢ Postal History, attd	...	5.75	4.75
230	25¢ Postal History, S/S of 6	...	...	12.75
231	$1.00 PHILEXFRANCE, S/S	...	...	12.50
232-38	25¢ (6)$1 Moon Landing, 20th Ann., Bklt. sgls..	...	...	21.75
238a	$2.50 Booklet Pane of 7 (6x25¢,$1)	...	...	21.95
	Also See #341-45			

239   298

* WW II Anniversaries 1939-1989

239	25¢ Invasion of Poland	(12) 13.50	4.50	.90
240	45¢ Sinking of HMS Royal Oak	(12) 24.50	8.00	1.65
241	45¢ Invasion of Finland	(12) 24.50	8.00	1.65
242-45	45¢ Battle of River Platte, attd	(16) 32.50	8.00	6.75

* WW II Anniversaries 1940-1990

246-47	25¢ Invas. of Norway & Denmark, attd.	(12) 20.75	4.00	1.85
248	25¢ Katyn Forest Massacre	(12) 11.00	3.75	.75
249-50	25¢ Invasion of Belgium, attd	(12) 13.50	4.50	1.80
251	45¢ Churchill Becomes Prime Minister	(12) 24.50	8.00	1.65
252-53	45¢ Evacuation at Dunkirk	(12) 23.50	7.95	3.50
254	45¢ Occupation of Paris	(12) 25.00	8.00	1.65
255	25¢ Mers-el-Kebir & Burma Rd	(12) 13.00	4.35	.90
256	25¢ Burma Road	(12) 13.00	4.35	.90
257-60	25¢ U.S. Destroyers for G.B., atd	(16) 32.50	8.00	6.50
261-64	45¢ Battle of Britain, attd	(16) 32.50	8.00	6.50
265	45¢ Tripartite Pact, 1940	(12) 24.50	8.00	1.65
266	25¢ FDR Elected to Third Term	(12) 13.50	4.50	.90
267-70	25¢ Battle of Taranto, attd	(16) 17.75	4.50	3.75

Scott's No.		Mint Sheetlet	Plate Block	F-VF NH
* WW II Anniversaries 1941-1991				
271-74	30¢ Four Freedoms, attd	(16) 23.50	5.50	4.50
275	30¢ Battle of Beda Fomm	(12) 13.50	4.50	.90
276-77	29¢ German Invasion of Greece & Yugoslavia, attd.	(12) 16.50	5.50	2.25
278-81	50¢ Sinking of the Bismarck, attd	(16) 29.50	10.00	7.50
282	30¢ Germany Invades Russia	(12) 16.50	5.50	1.10
283-84	29¢ Atlantic Charter, attd. pair	(12) 14.50	4.75	2.25
285	29¢ Siege of Moscow	(12) 16.50	5.50	1.10
286-87	30¢ Sinking of the USS Reuben James, attd.(16)	19.50	4.752.25	
288-91	50¢ Japanese Attack Pearl Harbor, attd.	(16) 35.00	8.95	7.50
288a-91a	50¢ Pearl Harbor Reprint,attd.	(16) 60.00	16.50	12.75
292	29¢ Japanese Capture Guam	(12) 16.50	5.50	1.10
293	29¢ Fall of Singapore	(12) 16.50	5.50	1.10
294-95	50¢ Flying Tigers, attd	(16) 26.50	8.95	3.75
296	29¢ Fall of Wake Island	(12) 16.50	5.50	1.10
* WW II Anniversaries 1942-1992				
297	29¢ FDR & Churchill at Arcadia Conference	(12) 16.50	5.50	1.10
298	50¢ Japanese enter Manila	(12) 27.75	9.25	1.85
299	29¢ Japanese take Rabaul	(12) 16.50	5.50	1.10
300	29¢ Battle of Java Sea	(12) 16.50	5.50	1.10
301	50¢ Fall of Rangoon	(12) 27.75	9.25	1.85
302	29¢ Battle for New Guinea	(12) 16.50	5.50	1.10
303	29¢ MacArthur Leaves Corregidor	(12) 16.50	5.50	1.10
304	29¢ Raid on Saint-Nazaire	(12) 16.50	5.50	1.10
305	29¢ Surrender of Bataan	(12) 16.50	5.50	1.10
306	50¢ Doolittle Raid on Tokyo	(12) 27.75	9.25	1.85
307	29¢ Fall of Corregidor	(12) 16.50	5.50	1.10
308-11	50¢ Battle of the Coral Sea, attd	(12) 35.00	8.95	7.50
308a-11a	50¢ Coral Sea Reprint, attd.	(16) 60.00	16.50	12.75
312-15	50¢ Battle of Midway, attd	(16) 35.00	8.95	7.50
316	29¢ Village of Lidice Destroyed	(12) 16.50	5.50	1.10
317	29¢ Fall of Sevastopol	(12) 16.50	5.50	1.10
318-19	29¢ Convoy, attd	(12) 16.50	5.00	2.25
320	29¢ Marines Land on Guadalcanal	(12)16.50	5.50	1.10
321	29¢ Battle of Savo Island	(12) 16.50	5.50	1.10
322	29¢ Dieppe Raid	(12) 16.50	5.50	1.10
323	50¢ Battle of Stalingrad	(12) 27.50	9.25	1.85
324	29¢ Battle of Eastern Solomons	(12) 16.50	5.50	1.10
325	50¢ Battle of Cape Esperance	(12) 27.50	9.25	1.85
326	29¢ Battle of El Alamein	(12) 16.50	5.50	1.10
327-28	29¢ Battle of Barents Sea, attd. pair	(12) 16.50	5.50	2.25
* WW II Anniversaries 1943-1993				
329	29¢ Casablanca Conference	(12) 16.50	5.50	1.10
330	29¢ Liberation of Kharkov	(12) 16.50	5.50	1.10
331-34	50¢ Battle of Bismarck Sea, attd	(16) 35.00	8.95	7.50
335	50¢ Interception of Yamamoto	(12) 27.50	9.25	1.85
336-37	29¢ Battle of Kursk	(16) 24.00	6.00	2.50

364   381   383

1989 Commemoratives (cont.)

341-44	25¢ Christmas 1989, attd	...	4.75	4.00
345	45¢ Milestones in Space, Sheet of 25 diff. designs	...	...	43.50

1990-92 Birds Definitives

346-65A	1¢-$2 Birds (21)	...	175.00	29.50
361a	95¢ Essen '90 Min. Sht. of 4 (#347,350,353,361) ...	...		5.75

1990 Commemoratives

366-69	25¢ Children's Games, attd	...	5.25	4.50
370-76	25¢, (6)$1 Penny Black, 150th Anniv., Booklet Singles	...	...	17.75
376a	Booklet Pane of 7 (6x25¢,$1)	...	...	18.50
377-80	25¢ Endangered Sea Turtles, attd	...	4.95	4.50
381	25¢ Joint Issue with Micronesia & U.S.	...	11.75	1.30
382	45¢ German Reunification	...	6.75	1.50
383-86	25¢ Christmas, attd	...	4.75	4.00
387-90	25¢ Breadfruit, attd	...	4.50	3.75

399   411

Scott's No.		Mint Sheetlet	Plate Block	F-VF NH
391-94	50¢ US Space Shuttle Flights, 10th Anniv., attd	...	5.50	4.50
395-98	52¢ Flowers, attd	...	8.50	6.75
398a	52¢ Phila Nippon, min. sht. of 4	...	...	6.95
399	29¢ Operation Desert Storm	...	8.75	1.45
400-06	29¢, (6)$1 Birds, set of 7 booklet singles .	...	...	28.75
406a	Booklet Pane of 7 (6x29¢,$1)	...	...	29.50
407-10	12¢,29¢,50¢ (2) Air Marshall Island Aircraft (4)	18.75		4.25
411	29¢ Admission to United Nations	...	12.75	.95
412	30¢ Christmas, Peace Dove	...	5.75	1.20
413	29¢ Peace Corps in Marshall Islands	...	6.50	1.20

425-28

1992 Commemoratives

414-17	29¢ Ships, Strip of 4	...	(8) 12.50	5.50
418-24	50¢, (6) $1 Voyages of Discovery, set of 7 booklet sgls	...	...	22.50
424a	Booklet Pane of 7 (6x50¢ + $1)	...	...	23.00
425-28	29¢ Traditional Handcrafts, attd	...	(8) 8.00	3.50
429	29¢ Christmas	...	5.50	1.00

1992 Birds Definitives

430-33	9¢,22¢,28¢,45¢ Birds	...	45.00	7.95

1993 Commemoratives

434-40	50¢, (6) $1 Reef Life, 7 booklet sgls	...	...	19.75
440a	Booklet Pane of 7 (6x50¢,$1)	...	...	20.00

441   464

1993-95 Ship Definitives

441/65	10¢-$3.00 Ships (24)	...	170.00	35.00
463	$1.00 Canoe	...	17.50	3.25
464	$2.00 Canoe	...	25.00	5.25
466A	$5.00 Canoe (1994)	...	75.00	12.50
466B	$10.00 Canoe (1994)	...	150.00	32.50
466C	15¢-75¢ Sailing Vessels, S/S of 4 (1994)	...	...	4.75

474

* WW II Anniversaries 1943-1993 (continued)

467-70	52¢ Invasion of Sicily, attd. blk. of 4	(16)36.50	9.25	7.95
471	50¢ Bombing Raids on Schweinfurt	(12)27.50	9.25	1.85
472	29¢ Liberation of Smolensk	(12)16.50	5.50	1.10
473	29¢ Landing at Bougainville	(12)16.50	5.50	1.10
474	50¢ US Invasion of Tarawa	(12)27.50	9.25	1.85
475	52¢ Tehran Conference	(12)27.50	9.25	1.85
476-77	29¢ Battle of North Cape, attd. pair	(12)18.75	6.25	2.60

Scott's No.		Mint Sheetlet	Plate Block	F-VF NH
478	29¢ Eisenhower Commands SHAEF	(12)16.50	5.50	1.10
479	50¢ Invasion of Anzio	(12)27.50	9.25	1.85
480	52¢ Siege of Leningrad Ends	(12)27.50	9.25	1.85
481	29¢ U.S. Frees Marshall Islands	(12)16.50	5.50	1.10
482	29¢ Japanese Defeat at Truk	(12)16.50	5.50	1.10
483	52¢ Bombing of Germany	(12)27.50	9.25	1.85
484	50¢ Rome Falls to Allies	(12)27.50	9.25	1.85
485-88	75¢ D-Day Landings, attd	(16)52.50	13.00	11.50
485a-88a	75¢ D-Day, Reprint, attd	(16)75.00	20.00	17.50
489	50¢ V-1 Bombs Strike England	(12)27.50	9.25	1.85
490	29¢ Landing on Saipan	(12)16.50	5.50	1.10
491	50¢ Battle of Philippine Sea	(12)27.50	9.25	1.85
492	29¢ U.S. Liberates Guam	(12)16.50	5.50	1.10
493	50¢ Warsaw Uprising	(12)27.50	9.25	1.85
494	50¢ Liberation of Paris	(12)27.50	9.25	1.85
495	29¢ Marines Land on Peliliu	(12)16.50	5.50	1.10
496	52¢ MacArthur Returns to Philippines	(12)16.50	9.25	1.85
497	52¢ Battle of Leyte Gulf	(12)16.50	9.25	1.85
498-99	50¢ Battleship "Tirpitz" Sunk, attd	(16)38.50	10.75	4.50
500-3	50¢ Battle of the Bulge	(16)45.00	12.50	10.75

WWII Anniversaries 1945-1995

504	32¢ Yalta Conference	(12)22.50	7.00	1.40
505	55¢ Bombing of Dresden	(12)31.50	11.75	2.50
506	$1 Iwo Jima Invaded	(12)57.50	19.75	4.50
507	32¢ Remagen Bridge Taken	(12)22.50	7.00	1.40
508	55¢ Marines Invade Okinawa	(12)36.50	11.75	2.60
509	50¢ Death of F.D. Roosevelt	(12)45.00	11.00	2.50
510	32¢ US/USSR Troops Link	(12)23.50	7.00	1.50
511	60¢ Soviet Troops Conquer Berlin	(12)45.00	11.50	2.50
512	55¢ Allies liberate concentration camps	(12)45.00	11.50	2.50
513-16	75¢ V.E. Day, Block of 4	(16)75.00	19.50	17.75
517	32¢ United Nations Charter	(12)22.50	7.00	1.50
518	55¢ Postdam Conference	(12)45.00	11.00	2.50
519	60¢ Churchill's Resignati	(12)45.00	11.50	2.50
520	$1 Atomic Bomb dropped on Hiroshima	(12)75.00	21.75	4.85
521-24	75¢ V.J. Day, Block of 4	(16)87.50	19.50	17.75

* WW II Anniversary Issues are are available in Tab singles, Tab pairs and Tab blocks for an additional 25%.

1994-95 WWII Anniversary Souvenir Sheets

562	50¢ MacArthur Returns to Philippines, Souvenir Sheet of 2	...	...	3.75
563	$1 U.N. Charter Souvenir Sheet (1995)	...	...	3.95

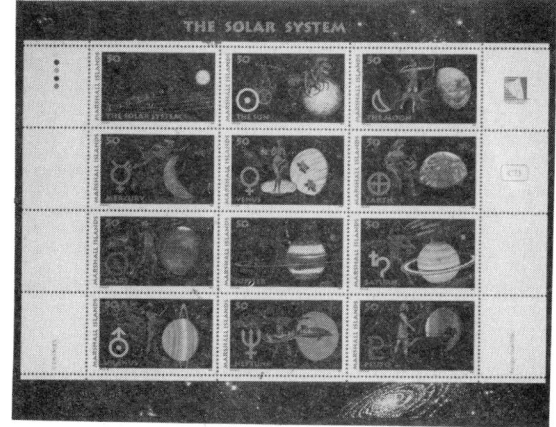

567   572   576

1993 Commemoratives (continued)

567-70	29¢ Capitol Complex	...	18.50	2.50
571	50¢ Mobil Oil Tanker, Eagle Souv. Sheet	...	...	1.20
572-75	29¢ Life in 1800's, attd	...	3.85	3.00
576	29¢ Christmas	...	5.25	1.00

582

1994 Commemoratives

577	$2.90 15th Anniv. Constitution Souv. Sht. (1994)	...	...	6.50
578	29¢ 10th Anniv. Postal Service Souv. Sht. (1994)	...	...	.95
579-80	50¢ Soccer Cup, attd	...	14.00	6.25
582	50¢ Solar System, sheet of 12	...	...	18.95
583-86	75¢ Moon Landing, 25th Anniv. attd	...	8.50	7.00
586b	75¢ Moon Landing, Souv. Sheet of 4	...	...	6.75
587	29¢, 52¢, $1 Butterflies, Souv. Sheet of 3	...	...	5.25
588	29¢ Christmas	...	5.75	1.00

1995 Commemoratives

Scott's No.		Mint Sheetlet	Plate Block	F-VF NH

592 Part   **596 Part**   **599**

Scott's No.		Mint Sheetlet	Plate Block	F-VF NH
589	50¢ Year of the Boar, Souv. Sheet		...	2.20
590	55¢ Underseas Glory, Block of 4		15.00	12.50
591	55¢ John F. Kennedy, Strip of 6		(12) 19.50	7.95
592	75¢ Marilyn Monroe, Block of 4	(12) 23.75	9.75	7.95
593	32¢ Cats, Block of 4		... 5.25	3.65
594	75¢ Mir-Shuttle Docking, Block of 4		7.75	6.75
595	60¢ Game Fish, Block of 8		(8) 21.50	16.75
596	32¢ Island Legends, Block of 4		4.00	3.50
597	32¢ Singapore '95 Orchids Souv. Sheet of 4		...	3.35
598	50¢ Beijing '95, Suzhou Gardens, Souv. Sheet .		1.25	
599	32¢ Christmas		4.75	1.00
600	32¢ Jet Fighter Planes, Min.Sheet of 25		...	18.75
601	32¢ Yitzhak Rabin	(8) 10.50	7.50	1.20

604 Part   **608**   **616**

1996 Commemoratives

Scott's No.		Mint Sheetlet	Plate Block	F-VF NH
602	50¢ Year of the Rat Souvenir Sheet		... ...	1.25
603	32¢ Local Birds, Block of 4		12.00	10.50
604	55¢ Wild Cats, Block of 4		6.75	5.50
605	32¢ Millenium of Navigation, Mini Sht of 25			18.50
606	60¢ Modern Olympics, Block of 4		7.25	6.00
607	55¢ Marshall Island Chronology, Shtlt of 12			16.50
608	32¢ Elvis Presley	(20) 67.50(6)26.50		2.25
609	50¢ China '96 Palace Museum Souv. Sheet			1.95
610	32¢ James Dean	(20) 52.50(6) 19.50		1.75
611	60¢ Ford Motor 100th Anniv., S/S of 8			9.75
612	32¢ Island Legends, Block of 4		4.25	3.25
613	55¢ Steam Locomotives, sheetlet of 12			16.50
614	32¢ Taipei 1996 Souvenir Sheet of 4		...	2.80
615	$3 Compact with U.S.		40.00	7.95
616	32¢ Christmas Angels	(16) 14.95	...	.85
617	32¢ Biplanes Sheetlet of 25			18.50

621   **638**

1997 Commemoratives

Scott's No.		Mint Sheetlet	Plate Block	F-VF NH
618	32¢ Handicrafts, Block of 4		3.50	2.80
619	60¢ Year of the Ox, Souvenir Sheet		...	1.15
620-21	32¢-60¢ Amata Kabua (2)	(8) 16.50	4.25	2.10
622	32¢ Elvis Presley, Strip of 3	(15) 13.50	(6) 5.95	2.75
623-24	32¢ Hong Kong '97, Souvenir Sheets of 2 (2)			2.80
625	60¢ Twelve Apostles, Sheetlet of 12		...	15.75
626	$3 Last Supper, Souvenir Sheet		...	6.50
627	60¢ 20th Century, 1900-1909, Sheetlet of 15		...	19.50
628	60¢ Deng Xiaoping		6.50	1.30

1997 Commemoratives (continued)

Scott's No.		Mint Sheetlet	Plate Block	F-VF NH
629	32¢ Traditional Crafts, Self-adhesive block of 4 (2x10 design)	(20) 15.95	4.00	3.25
630	32¢ Traditional Crafts, Self-adhesive strip of 4 (4x5 design)	(20) 15.95	(8) 7.95	3.25
631-37	50¢, (6) $1 Pacific '97, 1st Marshall Is. and U.S. stamps, set of 7 singles	...	...	9.85
636a,37a	50¢-$1 Pacific '97 Booklet (6-50¢, 1-$1 Souvenir Sheet)	...	...	9.95
638	16¢ World Wildlife Fund, Birds (4)	(16) 6.35	...	1.60
639	50¢ Bank of China, Hong Kong S/S	...	...	1.25

640

Scott's No.		Mint Sheetlet	Plate Block	F-VF NH
640	32¢ Canoes, 4 designs	...	3.75	3.25
641	32¢ Air Force, Sheetlet of 25	...	...	19.95

642   **647-48**

Scott's No.		Mint Sheetlet	Plate Block	F-VF NH
642	32¢ Old Ironsides	(15) 12.00	3.75	.80
643	32¢ Folklore, 4 designs	(8) 6.50	3.75	3.25
644	60¢ Underseas Glory, 4 designs	(24) 21.75	4.50	3.75
645	60¢ Princess Diana, 3 designs	(15) 22.50	...	4.50
646	60¢ 20th Century, 1910-1919, Sheetlet of 15	...	...	22.50
647-648	32¢ Christmas, Raphael's Angel, Pair	(16) 12.75	(8) 7.50	1.60
649	20¢ U.S. Warships of 50 States	(50)	...	24.75
650	50¢ Shanghai '97 Souvenir Sheet	...	...	1.25

1998 Commemoratives

Scott's No.		Mint Sheetlet	Plate Block	F-VF NH
651	60¢ Year of the Tiger Souvenir Sheet	...	...	1.50
652	32¢ Elvis Presley TV Special, Strip of 3	(15) 11.95	...	2.40
653	32¢ Seashells, 4 Designs	(20) 13.75	3.35	2.80

654

Scott's No.		Mint Sheetlet	Plate Block	F-VF NH
654	60¢ 20th Century, 1920-29, Sheetlet of 15	...	...	19.50
655	32¢ Canoes of the Pacific, Sheetlet of 8	...		5.35
656	60¢ Berlin Airlift	(16) 20.75	6.25	5.25
657	60¢ 20th Century, 1930-39, Sheetlet of 15	...	...	19.50

1998 Commemoratives (continued)

Scott's No.		Mint Sheetlet	Plate Block	F-VF NH
664a	60¢-$3 Czar Nicholas II Booklet (6-60¢ , 1-$3)....	...		14.50
658-64	60¢-$3 Czar Nicholas, set of 7 singles (6-60¢, 1-$3 Souvenir Sheet)	...		14.35
665	32¢ Babe Ruth	(15) 10.50	3.50	.70
666	32¢ Legendary Aircraft of the U.S. Navy Sheetlet of 25	...	...	17.50
667	60¢ Chevrolet Automobiles, Sheetlet of 8	...	...	10.50
668	33¢ Alphabet & Language, Sheetlet of 24	...	...	17.50
669	33¢ New Buildings, Strip of 3	(12) 8.50	(6) 4.75	2.15
670	32¢ Christmas Angel	...	3.50	.70
677a	60¢-3$ John Glenn, Hero in Spaces Booklet (6-60¢, $3 Souvenir Sheet)	...		13.95
671-77	60¢-$3 John Glenn, set of 7 singles..........	...		13.85

678

678	$3 Drought Relief Priority Mail Souvenir Sheet	...	...	6.25
679	60¢ 20th Century, 1940-49, Sheetlet of 15............	...	...	19.95
680	33¢ History's Greatest Fighting Ships, Sheetlet of 25	...	...	18.00
681	60¢ Year of the Rabbit Souvenir Sheet	...	...	1.30
682-89	1¢, 3¢, 20¢, 22¢, 33¢, 55¢, $1, $10, (8)	...	115.00	26.75
690	33¢ Canoes of the Pacific, Sheetlet of 8	...	...	5.50
691-98	33¢ Canoes of the Pacific, Self-adhesive.............. 8 designs.........................	(20) 13.75	...	5.50
699	60¢ Great American Indian Chiefs, Sheetlet of 12.	...	...	15.75
700	33¢ Marshallese Flag	(16) 11.00	3.40	.70
701	33¢ Flowers of the Pacific, 6 designs	(12) 8.65	...	4.35
702	60¢ 20th Century, 1950-59, Sheetlet of 15............	...	...	19.50
703	$1.20 Australia '99 Souvenir Sheet......................	...	...	2.60
704	33¢ Elvis Presley, Artist of the Century	(20) 13.75	3.40	.7

705

705	60¢ IBRA '99 Stamp Exhibition Souvenir Sheet of 4	...	...	5.25
...	33¢ RMI Constitution 20th Anniversary ..	(6) 4.15	...	.70
...	33¢ 15th Anniversary RMI Postal Service (4)	(24) 16.50	3.35	2.80
...	33¢ Legendary Aircraft, Sheetlet of 25......	...	...	17.50
...	$1 Philexfrance '99, Transportation .... on the Moon, Souvenir Sheet..................	...	...	2.15

B1

Scott's No.		Mint Sheetlet	Plate Block	F-VF NH
	1996 Semi-Postals			
B1	32¢ + 8¢ Operations Crossroads, Sheetlet of 6	...	...	6.75

C8   C9-12

1985-89 Airmails

C1-2	44¢ Audubon, attd	...	6.95	3.35
C3-6	44¢ Ameripex - Planes, attd (1986)	...	6.50	5.50
C7	44¢ Operation Crossroads, S/S (1986)	...	...	5.75
C8	44¢ Statue of Liberty/Peace Year (1986)	...	6.25	1.40
C9-12	44¢ Girl Scouts, attd (1986)...................	...	4.50	4.00
C13-16	44¢ Marine Birds, attd (1987)................	...	4.85	4.25

C17   C22

C17-20	44¢ Amelia Earhart/CAPEX attd (1987)	...	5.50	4.50
C21	45¢ Astronaut and Space Shuttle (1988)	...	5.75	1.30
C22-25	12¢,36¢,39¢,45¢ Aircraft (1989) (4)	...	19.75	4.25
C22a	12¢ Bklt. Pane of 10	...	...	4.85
C23a	36¢ Bklt. Pane of 10	...	...	13.00
C24a	39¢ Bklt. Pane of 10	...	...	13.75
C25a	45¢ Bklt. Pane of 10	...	...	15.75
C25b	36¢-45¢ Bklt. Pane of 10 (5 each)	...	...	14.75

UX1
Postal Cards

UX1	20¢ Elvis Presley (1996)................................	...	...	2.50
UX2-5	20¢ Canoes, Set of 4	...	...	4.75
UX6	20¢ Heavenly Angels, Christmas (1996)	...	...	1.35
UX7	32¢ Turtle (1997)	...	...	1.25

MICRONESIA
MICRONESIA BECAME INDEPENDENT IN 1986

| | **1** | **21** | **22** |

1984 Commemoratives

Scott's No.		Mint Sheetlet	Plate Block	F-VF NH
1-4	20¢ Postal Service Inaugural, attd	...	3.00	2.50
21,C4-6	20¢,28¢,35¢,40¢ AUSIPEX (4)	...	17.50	3.75
22,C7-9	20¢,28¢,35¢,40¢ Christmas (4)	...	45.00	9.00

1984 Explorers and Views Definitives

5-20	1¢-$5 Definitives (16)	...	110.00	25.75

| | **23** | **C36** | **45** |

1985 Commemoratives

23,C10-12	22¢,33¢,39¢,44¢ Ships (4)	...	21.50	3.75
24,C13-14	22¢,33¢,44¢ Christmas (3)	...	23.50	3.75
25-28,C15	22¢,44¢ Audubon (5)	...	10.00	4.50
45,C16-18	22¢,33¢,39¢,44¢ Ruins (4)	...	22.50	4.50

1985-88 Definitives

31-39,C34-36	3¢-$10 Definitives & Airs (12)	...	140.00	29.50
33a	15¢ Booklet Pane of 10	...	...	9.95
36a	25¢ Booklet Pane of 10	...	...	9.95
36b	15¢ & 25¢ Booklet Pane of 10 (5 ea.)	...	...	11.75

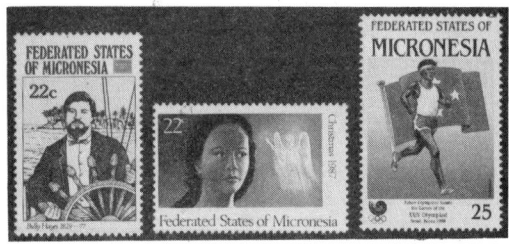

| | **52** | **58** | **63** |

1986 Commemoratives

46,C19-20	22¢, 44¢ Int'l Peace Year (3)	...	25.00	5.25
48-51	22¢ on 20¢ Postal Service (#1-4), attd...	...	2.85	2.50
52,C21-24	22¢,33¢,39¢,44¢ AMERIPEX (4)	...	24.50	5.00
53	22¢ Passport	...	4.50	1.00
54-5,C26-7	5¢,22¢,33¢,44¢ Christmas Paintings (4)	...	22.95	4.75

1987 Commemoratives

56,C28-30	22¢,33¢,39¢,44¢ Homeless, Events (4)	...	23.50	4.25
57	$1.00 CAPEX Souvenir Sheet..............	...	...	3.75
58,C31-33	22¢,33¢,39¢,44¢ Christmas (4)	(25)130.00	21.75	4.25

1988 Commemoratives

59-62,C37-8	22¢,44¢ Colonial Flags, attd (6)	...	10.75	5.75
59-62,C37-8	Center Blocks of 8	...	...	22.50
63-66	25¢ Olympics, attd., two pair	...	7.75	3.25
67-70	25¢ Christmas Tree, attd	...	2.95	2.65
71	25¢ Truk Lagoon S/S of 18	...	...	12.50

| | **72** | **102** | **107** |

FEDERATED STATES OF MICRONESIA (continued)

1989 Commemoratives

Scott's No.		Mint Sheetlet	Plate Block	F-VF NH
72-75	45¢ Flowers, attd	...	4.50	3.95
76	$1.00 Hirohito Memorial S/S	...	...	2.25
77-80	25¢-45¢ Sharks, attd. two pair	...	8.50	3.50
81	25¢ Moon Landing, 20th Anniv., S/S of 9...	...	...	6.95
82	$2.40 Moon Landing, 20th Anniv.	...	26.50	5.75
103	25¢ WSE, Fruits & Flowers, Sht. of 18	...	...	11.75
104-05	25¢,45¢ Christmas (2)..........................	...	11.75	2.50

1989 Seashells Definitives

83-102	1¢/$5 Seashell definitives (12)	...	105.00	24.75
85a	15¢ Booklet Pane of 10 (1990)	...	...	10.00
88a	25¢ Booklet Pane of 10 (1990)	...	...	15.00
88b	15¢ & 25¢ Booklet Pane of 10 (5 ea.)(1990)	...	...	15.00

1990 Commemoratives

106-09	10¢,15¢,20¢,25¢ World Wildlife Fund (4)	...	26.50	4.95
110-113	45¢ Stamp World London '90 Whalers, attd	...	5.00	4.00
114	$1.00 S.W. London '90, Whalers, S/S	...	...	2.75
115	$1.00 Penny Black, 150th Anniv., S/S	...	...	2.75
116-20	25¢ Pohnpei Agric. & School, Strip of 5 (15)	9.75	...	3.25
121	$1.00 Int'l. Garden Expo, Osaka, Japan S/S	...	...	2.25
122-23	25¢,45¢ Loading Mail, Airport & Truk Lagoon (2)	...	8.75	2.60
124-26	25¢ Joint issue w/Marsh. Isl. & U.S........ (12)	10.00	(6) 5.75	2.50
127-30	45¢ Moths, attd	...	4.50	3.95
131	25¢ Christmas, S/S of 9	...	...	5.75

| | **134-35** | | **142** |

1991 Commemoratives

132	25¢,45¢ New Capital of Micronesia, S/S...	...	...	2.25
133	$1 New Capital, S/S.............................	...	...	2.85
134-37	29¢-50¢ Turtles, attd. two pairs	...	20.75	8.75
138-41	29¢ Operation Desert Storm, strip of 4.....	...	4.00	3.25
142	$2.90 Frigatebird, Flag	...	...	5.50
142a	$2.90 Frigatebird, S/S	...	...	5.75
143	29¢ Phila Nippon '91, min. sht. of 3	...	...	2.95
144	50¢ Phila Nippon '91, min. sht. of 3	...	...	4.75
145	$1 Phila Nippon S/S	...	...	3.25
146-48	29¢,40¢,50¢ Christmas (3)	...	...	2.95
149	29¢ Pohnpei Rain Forest, min. sht. of 18...	...	...	16.75

1992 Commemoratives

150	29¢ Peace Corps, strip of 5	(15)12.75	...	3.50
151	29¢ Discovery of America, strip of 3........	...	(6) 12.75	5.95
152-53	29¢,50¢ U.N. Membership Anniv (2).......	...	...	6.75
153a	Same, S/S of 2	...	...	7.95
154	29¢ Christmas..	...	18.50	3.50

| | **160** | **172** | **179** |

1993 Commemoratives

155	29¢ Pioneers of Flight, se-ten. Blk. Of 8	...	7.50	6.25
168	29¢ Golden Age of Sail, min. sht. Of 12	...	...	19.95
172	29¢ Thomas Jefferson	...	5.75	1.10
173-76	29¢ Pacific Canoes, attd	...	4.50	3.95
177	29¢ Local Leaders, strip of 4	(8)	2.25	3.50
178	50¢ Pioneers of Flight, block of 8........	(8)	10.00	8.50
179-80	29¢-50¢ Pohnpei	...	11.95	2.85
181	$1 Pohnpei Souvenir Sheet...................	...	...	2.60
182-83	29¢-50¢ Butterflies, two pairs	...	10.00	4.25
184-185	29¢-50¢ Christmas	...	11.95	2.60
186	29¢ Yap Culture, sheet of 18..............	...	...	16.50

1993-94 Fish Definitives

156-57	10¢-$2.90 Fish, set of 16	...	115.00	23.95

Note: From #151 to date, Plate Blocks have Logos instead of Plate Numbers

| 187 | 192 Part | 202 |

1994 Commemoratives

Scott's No.		Mint Sheetlet	Plate Block	F-VF NH
187-89	29¢,40¢,50¢ Kosrae	...	13.00	2.95
190	29¢-50¢ Butterflies, Hong Kong, sheet of 4	...		5.50
191	29¢ Pioneers of Flight, block of 8	...	8.95	7.75
192	29¢ Micronesian Games, block of 4	...	4.25	3.50
193	29¢ Native Costumes, block of 4	...	4.25	3.50
194	29¢ Anniversary of Constitution	...	9.50	2.15
195	29¢ Flowers, Strip of 4	(8)	7.75	3.50
196-97	50¢ World Cup Soccer, attd	...	12.95	5.95
198	29¢ Postal Service, 10th Anniv., Block of 4	...	8.75	6.95
199	29¢, 52¢, $1 Philakorea Dinosaurs, Souvenir Sheet of 3	...	...	6.95
200	50¢ Pioneers of Flight, Block of 8	...	9.95	8.95
201	29¢ Migratory Birds, Block of 4	...	8.75	6.75
202-3	29¢-50¢ Christmas (2)	...	26.50	5.50
204-7	32¢ Local Leaders (4)	...	30.00	7.25

| 211 | 236 |

1995 Commemoratives

208	50¢ Year of the Boar Souvenir Sheet	...	...	1.85
209	32¢ Chuuk Lagoon, underwater scenes, Blk/4		13.75	11.95
210	32¢ Pioneers of Flight, block of 8	...	6.25	5.75
211	32¢ Dogs of the World, block of 4	...	4.25	3.65
228	32¢ Hibiscus, Strip of 4	(8)	7.50	3.15
229	$1 United Nations 50th Anniv. Souv. Sheet	...	...	2.40
230	32¢ Singapore '95, Orchids S/S of 4	...	...	2.85
231	60¢ End of World War II, Block of 4	...	6.95	5.75
232	50¢ Beijing '95 Souvenir Sheet	...	...	1.20
233	60¢ Pioneers of Flight, Block of 8	...	11.50	10.50
234-35	32¢-60¢ Christmas (2)	...	11.95	2.20
236	32¢ Yitzhak Rabin	(8) 13.95	...	1.10

1995-96 Fish Definitives

213-26	23¢-$5.00 Fish Set of 9	...	115.00	23.95
227	32¢ Native Fish Shtlt of 25 (96)	...	...	27.50

239

1996 Commemoratives

Scott's No.		Mint Sheetlets	Plate Block	F-VF NH
237	50¢ Year of the Rat Souvenir Sheet	...	...	1.60
238	32¢ Pioneers of Flight, Block of 8	...	11.50	9.95
239	32¢ Tourism in Yap, Block of 4	...	4.35	3.65
240	55¢ Starfish, Block of 4	...	7.50	6.25
241	60¢ Modern Olympics, Block of 4	...	7.25	6.25
242	50¢ China '96 Souvenir Sheet	...	...	2.25
243-44	32¢ Patrol Boats, Pair	...	8.25	3.75
245	55¢ Ford Motor 100th Anniversary, S/S of 8	...	...	11.75
247	32¢ Officer Reza, Police Dog	...	11.50	2.00
248	50¢ Citrus Fruits, strip of 4	(8) 16.50	7.75
249	60¢ Pioneers of Flight, Block of 8	...	19.75	18.50
250	32¢ Taipei '96, Souvenir sheet of 4	...	...	4.50
251-52	32¢-60¢ Christmas (2)	...	18.75	2.95
253	$3 Compact with US	...	39.50	8.25

1997 Commemoratives

254	60¢ Deng Xiaoping, Sheetlet of 4	...	...	5.95
255	$3 Deng Xiaoping, Souvenir Sheet	...	...	7.50
256	$2 Hong Kong, Souvenir Sheet	...	...	7.50

| 257 | 260 |

257	32¢ Year of the Ox	...	7.50	1.50
258	$2 Year of the Ox, Souvenir Sheet	...	...	4.95
259	60¢ Hong Kong return to China, Sheet of 6	...	...	8.95
260	$3 Hong Kong return to China, S/S	...	...	7.50
261	32¢ Pacific '97, Goddesses of the Sea, sheetlet of 6	...	...	4.75
262-64	20¢,50¢,60¢ Hiroshige Sheetlets of 3	...	...	9.75
265-66	$2 Hiroshige Souvenir Sheets (2)	...	...	9.95

| 267 | 273 |

267	32¢ Pre-Olympics, 4 designs	(16) 12.95	3.95	3.25
268	50¢ Elvis Presley, Sheetlet of 6	...	...	7.50
269	32¢ Underwater Exploration, Sheetlet of 9	...	...	7.25
270-72	$2 Underwater Exploration, Souvenir Sheets (3)..	...		14.95
273	60¢ Diana, Princess of Wales, ...	(6) 6.95	...	1.25
274	50¢ WWF, Butterfly Fish, 4 designs	(16) 19.75	5.95	4.95
275-76	32¢ Christmas, Fra Angelico, 2 designs	(16) 12.75	3.95	1.60
277-78	60¢ Christmas, Simon Marmion, 2 des.	(16) 23.50	7.50	2.95

279 **287**

Scott's No.		Mint Sheetlet	Plate Block	F-VF NH
	1998 Commemoratives			
279-80	50¢ Year of the Tiger Souvenir Sheets (2)	...	...	2.50
281	$1 Micronesia's admission to the United Nations Souvenir Sheet..............	...	...	2.50
282	32¢ Disney "Winnie the Pooh" Sheetlet of 8	...	...	8.50
283-84	$2 Disney "Winnie the Pooh" Souvenir Sheets (2)	...	...	11.50
285	32¢ Soccer, Sheetlet of 8......................	...	...	6.50
286-87	$2 Soccer, Souvenir Sheets (2)................	...	...	9.75
288	$3 Olympics, Souvenir Sheet..................	...	...	7.50
289-91	32¢, 40¢, 60¢ Israel '98 Sheetlets of 3 (3)	...	...	8.50
292-94	$2 Israel '98, Souvenir Sheets (3)..........	...	...	12.75

295

295	32¢ Year of the Ocean, Deep-Sea Research, Sheetlet of 9		...	6.25
296-98	$2 Year of the Ocean, Souvenir Sheets (3)........	...	...	12.95
299	50¢ Native Birds, Block of 4	(16) 16.75	...	4.25
300	$3 Native Birds, Souvenir Sheet..............	...	...	6.50
	1998-99 Definitives			
301-19	1¢-$5 Fish (19)......................	...	110.00	24.95
319A	$10.75 Fish Definitive..................	...	90.00	20.95
328-32	33¢-$3.20 Fish, Part II (5).....................	...	47.50	11.50
333	$11.75 Fish Definitive..................	...	100.00	22.95
	1998 Commemoratives (continued)			
320	32¢ F.D. Roosevelt Memorial, Fala, Sheetlet of 6	...	...	4.25
321-22	32¢-60¢ Christmas, Madonna in 20th Century Art, Sheetlet-3	...	...	5.85
323	$2 Christmas Souvenir Sheet..................	...	...	4.25
324-25	60¢ John Glenn's Return to Space Sheetlets of 8 (2)	...	...	19.95
326-27	$2 John Glenn's Return to Space Souvenir Sheets (2)	...	...	8.75
	1999 Commemoratives			
334	33¢ Russian Space Accomplishments, Sheetlet of 20	...	...	13.95
335-36	$2 Russian Space Souvenir Sheets (2).....	...	...	8.75

340-41

337-38	33¢ Romance of the Three Kingdoms, Sheetlets of 5 (2)	...	...	7.25
339	$2 Romance of Three Kingdoms, Souvenir Sheet	...	...	4.35
340-41	55¢ IBRA'99, Caroline Is. Stamps (2).....	...	4.95	2.35
342	$2 IBRA'99, Caroline Is. Stamps, Souvenir Sheet	...	...	4.35

Scott's No.		Mint Sheetlet	Plate Block	F-VF NH
	1999 Commemoratives (continued)			
343	33¢ Australia '99 WSE, Voyages of the Pacific, Sheetlet of 20	...	...	13.95
...	33¢ United States Space Achievements Sheetlet of 20...	...	...	13.95
...	$2 U.S. Space Achievements Souvenir Sheets (2)	...	...	8.75
...	33¢ Earth Day: Endangered, Extinct and Prehistoric Species, Sheetlet of 20..	...	...	13.95
...	$2 Earth Day, Souvenir Sheets (2)..........	...	...	8.75
...	33¢ Hokusai, Sheetlets of 6 (2).............	...	...	8.75
...	$2 Hokusai, Souvenir Sheets (2).............	...	...	8.75

Airmails

C39-42

1984-94

		Mint Sheetlet	Plate Block	F-VF NH
C1-3	28¢,35¢,40¢ Aircraft (1984)..............................	...	12.75	2.50
C25	$1.00 Ameripex S/S (1986).........................		...	4.25
C39-42	45¢ Federated State Flags, attd (1989)	...	4.85	4.50
C43-46	22¢,36¢,39¢,45¢ Aircraft Serving Micronesia ('90).................	...	31.50	6.75
C47-48	40¢,50¢ Aircraft (1992).........................	...	21.95	4.85
C49	$2.90 Moon Landing Souvenir Sheet (1994)......	...	...	6.35
	Postal Stationary Entires			
U1	20¢ National Flag (1984).........................	...	...	18.50
U2	22¢ Tall Ship Senyavin (1986).........................	...	...	10.75
U3	29¢ on 30¢ New Capital (1991)	...	...	6.95
	Postal Cards			
UX1-4	20¢ Scenes, Set of 4 (1997).........................	...	...	5.95

REPUBLIC OF PALAU
PALAU BECAME INDEPENDENT IN 1994.
1983 Commemoratives

	1	5	9	21

Scott's No.		Mint Sheetlet	Plate Block	F-VF NH
1-4	20¢ Postal Service Inaugural, attd	...	3.95	2.85
5-8	20¢ Birds, attd	...	2.75	2.25
24-27	20¢ Whales, attd	...	3.25	2.50
28-32	20¢ Christmas, Strip of 5.....................	... (10)	7.50	3.25
33-40	20¢ Henry Wilson, Block of 8.................	...	5.75	4.50

1983-84 Marine Definitives

9-21	1¢-$5 Definitives, Set of 13.....................	...	125.00	25.75
13a	13¢ Booklet Pane of 10........................	...	...	12.75
13b	13¢/20¢ Bklt. Pane of 10 (5 #13, 5 #14)...	...	...	14.75
14b	20¢ Booklet Pane of 10.......................	...	...	13.75

	59	95	99

1984 Commemoratives

41-50	20¢ Seashells, Block of 10, attd)	...	6.50	5.50
51-54	40¢ 19th UPU Congress.........................	...	5.25	4.35
55-58	20¢ Ausipex, attd	...	2.95	2.15
59-62	20¢ Christmas, attd	...	3.00	2.25

1985 Commemoratives

63-66	22¢ Audubon, attd..............................	...	4.95	4.25
67-70	22¢ Shipbuilding, attd	...	3.00	2.50
86-89	44¢ International Youth Yr., attd.............	...	4.75	4.00
90-93	14¢,22¢,33¢,44¢ Christmas....................	...	23.50	3.75
94	$1.00 Trans-Pacific Air Anniv. S/S	...	...	3.65
95-98	44¢ Halley's Comet, attd......................	...	5.00	4.25

1985 Marine Definitives

75-85	14¢/$10 Marine Life (7)........................	...	140.00	30.75
75a	14¢ Booklet Pane of 10........................	...	...	10.75
76a	22¢ Booklet Pane of 10........................	...	...	13.50
76b	14¢/22¢ Bklt. Pane of 10 (5 #75, 5 #76)...	...	...	14.75

1986 Commemoratives

99-102	44¢ Songbirds, attd	...	5.25	4.65
103	14¢ AMERIPEX Sea & Reef, Sht of 40 ...	...	...	50.00
104-08	22¢ Seashells, attd	... (10)	8.35	3.85
109-12,C17	22¢ Int'l. Peace Year, attd................	...	10.00	4.85
113-16	22¢ Reptiles, attd	...	3.95	3.15
117-21	22¢ Christmas,Strip of 5, attd..............	(15) 10.50 (10)	5.95	2.75
117-21	Christmas with Tabs............................	... (10)	7.50	3.50

	122	123	141

Scott's No.		Mint Sheetlet	Plate Block	F-VF NH

1987 Commemoratives

121B-E	44¢ Butterflies, attd	...	5.95	4.85
122-25	44¢ Fruit Bats, attd	...	5.50	4.75
146-49	22¢ CAPEX, attd...............................	...	3.25	2.65
150-54	22¢ Seashells, Strip of 5 attd	... (10)	7.95	3.50
155-63	14¢,22¢,44¢ U.S. Constitution Bicentennial, attd. (3 strips of 3)	(15) 28.50	...	6.25
164-67	14¢,22¢,33¢,44¢ Japanese Links (4)........	...	14.50	2.95
168	$1 S/S Japanese Links to Palau.............	...	...	2.95
173-77	22¢ Christmas, Strip of 5 attd	... (10)	8.50	3.35
178-82	22¢ "Silent Spring" Symb. Species,attd(15)	12.50(10) 8.95	3.65	

1987-88 Indigenous Flowers Definitives

126-42	1¢ - $10 Flowers (17)	...	250.00	52.50
130a	14¢ Bklt. Pane of 10	...	...	5.25
131a	15¢ Bklt. Pane of 10 (1988)	...	...	4.25
132a	22¢ Bklt. Pane of 10	...	...	8.25
132b	14¢/22¢ Bklt. Pane of 10 (5 ea.).............	...	...	8.25
133a	25¢ Bklt. Pane of 10 (1988)	...	...	7.00
133b	15¢/25¢ Bklt. Pane of 10 (5 ea.) (1988) ...	...	...	6.75

	191-95

1988 Commemoratives

183-86	44¢ Butterflies & Flowers, attd...............	...	5.00	4.35
187-90	44¢ Ground Dwelling Birds, attd	...	5.25	4.50
191-95	25¢ Seashells, Strip of 5, attd...............	... (10)	9.00	3.75
196	25¢ Postal Indep. S/S of 6 (FINLANDIA)...	...	...	3.75
197	45¢ USPPS S/S of 6 (PRAGA '88)	...	...	5.95
198-202	25¢ Christmas, strip of 5.....................	(15) 9.50	(8) 7.00	3.35
198-202	Christmas with Tabs	...	(8) 8.75	4.35
203	25¢ Palauan Nautilus, S/S of 5................	...	...	4.15

1989 Commemoratives

204-07	45¢ Endangered Birds, attd....................	...	5.25	4.50
208-11	45¢ Exotic Mushrooms, attd..................	...	5.50	4.75
212-16	25¢ Seashells, strip of 5 ....(10)		7.75	3.65
217	$1 Hirohito Memorial S/S......................	...	...	2.95
218	25¢ Moon Landing, 20 Anniv., S/S of 25...	...	...	14.95
219	$2.40 Moon Landing, 20th Anniv	...	26.75	5.85
220	25¢ Literacy, block of 10......................	...	6.95	5.95
221	25¢ World Stamp Expo, Fauna, Min. sheet of 25	...	...	13.50
222-26	25¢ Christmas, Strip of 5, attd	(15)11.00	(10) 7.50	3.65
222-26	25¢ Christmas with Tabs	...	(10) 9.50	3.95

	258

1990 Commemoratives

227-30	25¢ Soft Coral, attd	...	3.25	2.85
231-34	45¢ Forest Birds, attd	...	4.85	4.50
235	25¢ Stamp World London '90, S/S of 9....	...	5.25	
236	$1.00 Penny Black, 150th Anniv. S/S	...	...	2.65
237-41	45¢ Orchids, strip of 5	(15) 16.50 (10)	10.75	4.95
237-41	45¢ Orchids with Tabs.........................	...	...	5.50
242-45	45¢ Butterflies & Flowers, attd...............	...	4.75	4.25
246	25¢ Lagoon Life, Sheetlet of 25...............	...	...	16.50
247-48	45¢ Pacifica/Mail Delivery, attd	(10) 23.95	9.75	4.25
249-53	25¢ Christmas, Strip of 5, attd	(15) 8.25	(10)6.50	2.75
249-53	Christmas with Tabs	...	...	3.25
254-57	45¢ U.S. Forces in Palau, 1944, attd........	...	5.95	5.25
258	$1 U.S. Forces in Palau, 1944, S/S	...	...	3.50

259   266   291

1991 Commemoratives

Scott's No.		Mint Sheetlets	Plate Block	F-VF NH
259-62	30¢ Coral, attd..............................	...	4.25	3.50
263	30¢ Angaur, The Phospate Island, Sheet/16. ...	...	...	11.50
288	29¢ Cent. of Christianity in Palau, Sheet of 6...	...	...	3.75
289	29¢ Marine Life, Sheet of 20..........................	...	...	16.95
290	20¢ Desert Shield/Desert Storm, min. Sheet/9 ...	...	4.75	
291	$2.90 Fairy tern, Yellow/Ribbon......................	...	...	6.25
292	$2.90 Same, S/S	...	...	6.25
293	29¢ Women's Conf. & Palau,10th Anniv,min sht of 8	...	...	5.25
294	50¢ Giant Clam Cultivation, S/S of 4	...	...	5.50
295	29¢ Japanese Heritage, Phila Nippon,Shtlt of 6	...	...	3.95
296	$1.00 Phila Nippon S/S	...	...	2.35
297	29¢ Peace Corps in Palau, min. sht. of 6	...	...	3.95
298	29¢ Christmas, strip of 5, attd..........................	(15) 10.50	(10) 7.50	3.50
298	Christmas with Tabs	...	...	4.25
299	29¢ WWII in the Pacific, min. sht. of 10.........	...	...	10.50

1991-92 Birds Definitives

266-83	1¢-$10 Birds (18)	...	230.00	49.75
269b	19¢ Palau Fantail, Bklt. Pane of 10..................	...	...	4.50
272a	29¢ Fruit Dove, Bklt. Pane of 10....................	...	...	6.75
272b	19¢ Fantail & 29¢ Fruit Dove, Bklt. Pane/10(5 ea)	...	...	5.75

300   312

1992 Commemoratives

300	50¢ Butterflies, Block of 4............................	...	5.00	4.50
301	29¢ Shells, strip of 5..................................	...	(10) 9.50	3.75
302	29¢ Columbus & Age of Discovery, min. sht/20...	...	14.75	
303	29¢ Biblical Creation/Earth Summit, min sht/24	...	...	16.95
304-09	50¢ Summer Olympics, Souvenir Sheets (6) ..	...	...	7.50
310	29¢ Elvis Presley, min. sht. of 9	...	...	8.50
311	50¢ WWII, Aircraft - Pacific Theater, min sht/10	...	...	14.95
312	29¢ Christmas, strip of 5..............................	(15) 11.50	(10) 8.25	3.95
312	Christmas with Tabs	...	...	4.35

313 Part   315 Part

Scott's No.		Mint Sheetlets	Plate Block	F-VF NH

1993 Commemoratives

313	50¢ Animal Families, block of 4	...	5.00	4.50
314	29¢ Seafood, block of 4	...	...	3.00
315	50¢ Sharks, block of 4	...	...	4.50
316	29¢ WWII, Pacific Theater, min. sheet of 10...	...	...	10.75
317	29¢ Christmas, strip of 5..............................	(15) 10.00	(10) 7.75	3.65
317	29¢ Christmas with Tabs	...	...	4.25
318	29¢ Prehistoric & Legendary Sea Creatures, Sheet of 25	...	...	16.50
319	29¢ Indigenous People, sheet of 4.................	...	...	2.95
320	$2.90 Indigenous People, Souvenir Sheet........	...	...	7.50
321	29¢ Jonah and the Whale, sheet of 25	...	...	17.95

323

1994 Commemoratives

322	40¢ Palau Rays, block of 4............................	...	...	3.95
323	20¢ Crocodiles, block of 4	...	3.25	2.95
324	50¢ Seabirds, block of 4	...	...	4.50
325	29¢ WWII, Pacific Theater, min. sheet of 10...	...	...	10.50
326	50¢ WWII, D-Day, min. sheet of 10	...	...	13.50
327	29¢ Baron Pierre de Coubertin	...	...	.90
328-33	50¢, $1, $2 Coubertin and Winter Olympics Stars, Set of 6 Souv. Sheets	...	...	14.95
334-36	29¢, 40¢, 50¢ Philakorea '94 Philatelic Fantasies, Wildlife, 3 Souv. Sheets of 8..........	...	...	31.95
337	29¢ Apollo XI Moon Landing 25th Anniv., Miniature Sheet of 20	...	...	14.75
338	29¢ Independence Day Strip of 5	(15) 10.75	...	3.65
339	$1 Invasion of Peleliu Souvenir Sheet	...	...	3.25
340	29¢ Disney Tourism Sheetlet of 9...................	...	...	7.50
341-43	$1, $2.90 Disney Tourism, 3 Souv. Sheets......	...	...	13.50
344	20¢ Year of the Family, Min. Sheet of 12........	...	...	5.25
345	29¢ Christmas '94 Strip of 5	(15) 10.00	...	3.75
345	Christmas with Tabs	...	...	4.25
346-48	29¢, 50¢ World Cup of Soccer, Set of 3 Sheetlets of 12...............................	...	...	29.95

365   378

1995 Commemoratives

350	32¢ Elvis Presley, Sheetlet of 9......................	...	...	7.50
368	32¢ Tourism, Lost Fleet, Sheetlet of 18..........	...	...	14.50
369	32¢ Earth Day '95, Dinosaurs, Shtlt of 18........	...	...	13.95
370	50¢ Jet Aircraft, Sheetlet of 12......................	...	...	14.50
371	$2 Jet Aircraft, Souvenir Sheet.......................	...	...	4.85
372	32¢ Underwater Ships, Sheetlet of 18.............	...	...	14.50
373	32¢ Singapore '95 Hidden Treasures, Blk of 4. ...	3.75	3.25	
374	60¢ U.N., FAO 50th Anniv., Block of 4.............	...	6.25	5.50
375-76	$2 U.N. FAO 50th Anniv., Souv. Sheets	...	...	8.75
377	20¢ Independence, Block of 4	...	2.60	2.10
378	32¢ Independence, Marine Life	...	3.95	.85
379	32¢ End of World War II, Sheetlet of 12...........	...	...	10.75
380	60¢ End of World War II, Sheetlet of 5............	...	...	9.75
381	$3 End of World War II Souvenir Sheet........	...	...	7.75
382	32¢ Christmas Strip of 5	(15) 11.50	(10) 8.50	3.75
382	32¢ Christmas with Tabs	...	...	4.25
383	32¢ Life Cycle of the Sea Turtle, Shtlt/12	...	...	12.75
384	32¢ John Lennon	(16) 29.95	...	1.50

1995 Fish Definitives

351-64	1¢-$5 Fish Definitives (14)	...	125.00	25.95
365	$10 Fish Definitive......................................	...	100.00	22.50
366	20¢ Fish, Booklet Single	...	...	.55
366a	20¢ Fish, Booklet Pane of 10	...	...	4.75
367	32¢ Fish, Booklet Single	...	...	.85
367a	32¢ Fish, Booklet Pane of 10	...	...	7.75
367b	20¢, 32¢ Fish, Bklt. Pane of 10 (5 each)..........	...	...	6.50

| | 387 | | 392A | |

Scott's No.			Mint Sheetlets	Plate Block	F-VF NH
385	10¢ Year of the Rat Strip of 4	(8)	4.50	...	2.25
386	60¢ Year of the Rat Souvenir Sheet			...	2.85
387	32¢ 50th Anniversary of UNICEF Blk/4	(16)	11.50	3.50	2.85
388	32¢ China '96 Underwater Strip of 5	(15)	11.00	...	3.60
389	32¢ Capex '96 Circumnavigators Shtlt/9		...	...	6.50
390	60¢ Capex '96 Air & Space Sheetlet of 9		...	...	12.95
391	$3 Capex '96 Air & Space Souvenir Sheet		...	...	7.50
392	$3 Capex '96 Circumnavigators S/S		...	...	7.50
393	60¢ Disney Sweethearts Sheetlet of 9		...	...	14.95
394-95	$2 Disney Sweethearts Souv. Sheets (2)		...	...	11.00
392A-F	1¢ - 6¢ Disney Sweethearts (6)		...	...	1.00
396	20¢ 3000th Anniversary of Jerusalem Shtlt/30		...	...	14.95

| | | 399-400 | | | |

397-400	40¢-60¢ Atlanta '96, 2 Pairs	(20)	65.00	11.50	5.50
401	32¢ Atlanta '96, Sheetlet of 20		...	...	15.95
402	50¢ Lagoon Birds, Sheetlet of 20..................		...	...	25.00
403	40¢ "Spies in the Sky", Sheetlet of 12		...	...	12.50
404	60¢ Oddities of the Air, Sheetlet of 12..........		...	...	16.50
405	$3 Stealth Bomber, Souvenir Sheet..............		...	...	7.50
406	$3 Martin Marietta X-24B, Souv. Sheet........		...	...	7.50
407-8	20¢ Independence..	(16)	7.95	...	1.00
409	32¢ Christmas, Strip of 5	(15)	12.00	...	3.95
409	32¢ Christmas with Tabs		...	...	4.25
410	32¢ Voyages to Mars, Sheetlet of 12		...	...	9.95
411-12	$3 Voyages to Mars, Souvenir Sheet ....(2)		...	...	13.50

1997 Commemoratives

412	$2 Year of the Ox, Souvenir Sheet................		...	...	5.00
413	$1 South Pacific Commission, 50th Anniv., Souvenir Sheet		...	...	2.50

| | 414 | | 425 | |
| | | 1997 Pacific '97, Flowers | | |

414-19	1¢-$3 Flowers (6)		...	37.50	7.95
420-21	32¢-50¢ Shoreline Plants, 2 Blocks of 4	(16)	32.50	9.75	8.25

Scott's No.			Mint Sheetlets	Plate Block	F-VF NH
422-23	32¢-60¢ Parachutes, Sheetlets of 8 (2)..............................		...	...	17.95
424-25	$2 Parachutes, Souvenir Sheets (2)		...	...	9.75
426	20¢ Avian Environment, Sheetlet of 12		...	...	5.95
427-28	32¢-60¢ UNESCO, 50th Anniversary, Sheetlets of 8 and 5 (2)		...	...	13.50
429-30	$2 UNESCO, Souvenir Sheets (2).................		...	...	9.75
431	32¢ Hiroshige Poetic Prints, Sheetlet of 5......		...	...	3.95
432-33	$2 Hiroshige Souvenir Sheets (2)		...	...	9.75
434	32¢ Volcano Goddesses of the Pacific, Pacific '97, Sheetlet of 6		...	...	4.75

| | 435 | 440 | | |

435	32¢ 3rd Anniv. of Independence	(12)	9.50	3.95	.80
436	32¢ Underwater Exploration, Sheetlet of 9....		...	...	6.95
437-39	$2 Underwater Exploration, Souvenir Sheets (3)		...	...	14.75
440	60¢ Diana, Princess of Wales, ...	(6)	8.95	...	1.50
441-46	1¢-10¢ Disney "Let's Read (6)		...	...	.75
447	32¢ Disney "Let's Read" Sheetlet of 9..........		...	...	6.50
448-49	$2-$3 Disney "Let's Read" Souvenir Sheets (2)		...	...	12.00
450	32¢ Christmas song, 5 designs	(15)	11.75	...	3.95

1998 Commemoratives

451-52	Year of the Tiger Souvenir Sheets (2)		...	...	2.50
453	32¢ Hubble Space Telescope Sheetlet of 6....		...	...	4.75
454-56	$2 Hubble, Souvenir Sheets (3).....................		...	...	4.95

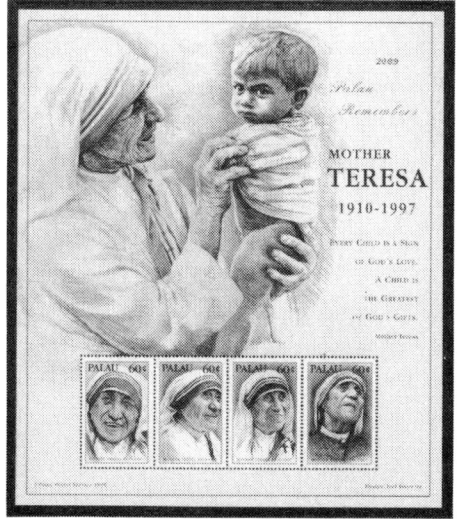

| | | 457 | | |

457	60¢ Mother Teresa, Souvenir Sheet of 4		...	...	5.95
458	32¢ Deep Sea Robots Sheetlet of 18		...	...	13.95
459-60	$2 Deep Sea Robots, Souvenir Sheets (2)		...	...	9.75
461	20¢ "Israel 98" Overprint on Jerusalem Sheetlet of 30 (#396)		...	...	13.00
462	40¢ Legend of Orachel, Sheetlet of 12		...	...	10.50
463	50¢ World Cup Soccer, Sheetlet of 8		...	...	8.65
464	$3 World Cup Soccer, Souvenir Sheet		...	...	6.50
465	32¢ 4th Micronesian Games, Sheetlet of 9		...	...	6.35
466	32¢ Christmas, Rudolph, Strip of 5	(15)	10.50	...	3.50
467-70	20¢, 32¢, 50¢, 60¢ Disney's "A Bug's Life" Sheetlets of 4 (4)		...	...	16.00
471-74	$2 Disney's "A Bug's Life" Souvenir Sheets (4)		...	...	20.00

Scott's No.		Mint Sheetlets	Plate Block	F-VF NH
475-76	60¢ John Glenn's Return to Space Sheetlets of 8 (2)	...		19.95
477-78	$2 John Glenn's Return to Space Souvenir Sheets (2)	...		8.75
479	33¢ Environmental Heroes of 20th Century Sheetlet of 16	...		11.50
480	33¢ Mir and the Space Shuttles Sheetlet of 6	...		4.35
481-84	$2 Mir and the Space Shuttles Souvenir Sheets (4)	...		17.50

485-94 (Ex)

1999 Famous Persons Regular Issues

485-94	1¢-$3.20 set of 10	...		59.50	13.50

1999 Commemoratives (continued)

496-97 (Ex)

495	33¢ Vanishing Turtles, Frogs and Amphibians, Sheetlet of 12	...		8.50
496-97	$2 Vanishing Turtles, etc. Souvenir Sheets (2)	...		8.75
498-99	55¢ IBRA '99, Caroline Is. Stamps (2)		4.95	2.35
500	$2 IBRA '99, Caroline Is. Stamps, Souvenir Sheet	...		4.35
...	33¢ Exploring Mars, Sheetlet of 6	...		4.25
...	$2 Exploring Mars, Souvenir Sheets (4)	...		17.50
...	33¢ Space Station, Sheetlet of 6	...		4.25
...	$2 Space Station, Souvenir Sheets (4)	...		17.50
...	33¢ Earth Day, Pacific Insects, Sheetlet of 20.	...		13.95
...	33¢ Information Age, Visionaries of the 20th Century, Sheetlet of 25	...		17.50

1988 Semi-Postals

B1-2

Scott's No.		Mint Sheetlets	Plate Block	F-VF NH
B1-4	25¢ + 5¢,45¢ + 5¢ Olympic Sports, 2 pairs	...	10.00	4.85

Airmails

C5   **C10**

1984-95

C1-4	40¢ Birds, attd (1984)		...	4.75	3.95
C5	44¢ Audubon (1985)		...	7.50	1.50
C6-9	44¢ Palau-Germany Exchange Cent., attd......		...	6.00	4.95
C10-13	44¢ Trans-Pacific Anniv., attd		...	5.50	4.50
C14-16	44¢ Remelik Memorial, Strip of 3 (1986)......	(9) 16.50	(6) 9.50	4.50
C14-16	Remelik Mem., with tabs, attd.....................	...	(6) 12.00	5.95
C14-16	Remelik Sheetlet of 9	...	...	15.95

C17   **C18-20**

C17	44¢ Peace Year, St. of Liberty......................		...	7.00	1.35
C18-20	36¢,39¢,45¢ Aircraft (1989).......................		...	15.75	3.25
C18a	36¢ Bklt. Pane of 10..................................		...	...	8.75
C19a	39¢ Bklt. Pane of 10..................................		...	...	9.50
C20a	45¢ Bklt. Pane of 10..................................		...	...	10.50
C20b	36¢/45¢ Bklt. Pane of 10 (5 each)		...	...	9.50
C21	50¢ Palauan Bai (#293a), self adh (1991)......		...	9.75	1.95
C22	50¢ Birds, Block of 4 (1995).......................		...	...	4.95

Postal Stationery

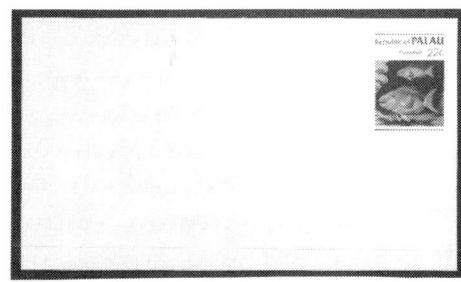

U1

U1	22¢ Parrotfish (1989)	...	...	4.50
U2	22¢ Spearfishing	...	...	7.95
U3	25¢ Chambered Nautilus (1991)....................	...	...	4.25
UC1	36¢ Birds (1985).....................................	...	...	11.95
UX1	14¢ Giant Clam (1985)...............................	...	...	3.50

UNITED NATIONS

| | 1 | 2 | 8 | 11 |

1951 Regular Issue

Scott's No.		MI Block of 4	F-VF NH	F-VF Used
1-11	1¢-$1 Regular Issue	32.50	7.00	6.75
1	1¢ Peoples, Magenta	.60	.20	.15
2	1½¢ U.N. Hdqtrs. Blue Green	.60	.20	.15
2p	1½¢ Precancelled	...	...	50.00
3	2¢ Peace, Justice, Sec. Purple	.60	.20	.15
4	3¢ Flag, Magenta & Blue	.60	.20	.15
5	5¢ UNICEF, Blue	.60	.20	.15
6	10¢ Peoples, Chocolate	1.25	.25	.20
7	15¢ Flag, Violet & Blue	1.35	.30	.20
8	20¢ World Unity, Dark Brown	3.50	.75	.50
9	25¢ Flag, Olive Gray & Blue	2.75	.60	.50
10	50¢ U.N. Hdqtrs., Indigo	19.50	4.25	4.00
11	$1 Peace, Justice Sec., Red	8.00	1.80	1.50

| | 13 | 17 | 21 |

1952

12	5¢ War Memorial Building, U.N. Charter	.85	.20	.20
13-14	3¢-5¢ Human Rights, Flame	1.65	.35	.30

1953

15-16	3¢-5¢ Refugee Family	2.25	.50	.45
17-18	3¢-5¢ Universal Postal Union	4.25	.95	.90
19-20	3¢-5¢ Technical Assistance	2.25	.50	.50
21-22	3¢-5¢ Human Rights, Hands	6.75	1.50	.60

| | 23 | 25 | 27 | 30 |

1954

23-24	3¢-8¢ Food & Agriculture Org	7.00	1.50	.75
25-26	3¢-8¢ Int'l. Labor Organization	8.00	1.75	.95
27-28	3¢-8¢ U.N. European Office, Geneva	11.50	2.50	1.50
29-30	3¢-8¢ Human Rights, Mother and Child	40.00	9.00	2.75

| | 31 | 35 | 47 |

1955

31-32	3¢-8¢ Int'l Civil Aviation Organization	14.50	3.00	1.65
33-34	3¢-8¢ UNESCO Emblem	2.25	.50	.50
35-37	3¢, 4¢, 8¢ 10th Anniversary United Nations	8.25	1.75	1.15
38	3¢, 4¢, 8¢ 10th Anniv. Souv. Sheet of 3	...	130.00	50.00
38v	3¢, 4¢, 8¢ Second Print, Retouched	...	140.00	60.00
39-40	3¢-8¢ Human Rights, Torch	2.25	.50	.50

NOTE : "MI" REFERS TO MARGINAL INSCRIPTION BLOCKS FROM THE CORNERS OF U.N. MINT SHEETS.

Scott's No.		MI Block of 4	F-VF NH	F-VF Used
41-42	3¢-8¢ Telecommunications	2.25	.50	.55
43-44	3¢-8¢ World Health Organ	2.00	.45	.55
45-46	3¢-8¢ General Assembly, U.N. Day	1.25	.30	.25
47-48	3¢-8¢ Human Rights, Flame and Globe	1.00	.30	.20

| | 53 | 55 | 63 | 67 |

1957

49-50	3¢-8¢ Meteorological, Weather Balloon	1.00	.30	.20
51-52	3¢-8¢ U.N. Emergency Force	1.00	.30	.20
53-54	3¢-8¢ Same, re-engraved	2.25	.50	.30

#53-54 The area around the circles is shaded, giving a halo effect.

55-56	3¢-8¢ Security Council, Emblem and Globe	1.00	.30	.20
57-58	3¢-8¢ Human Rights, Flaming Torch	1.00	.30	.20

1958

59-60	3¢-8¢ Atomic Energy Agency	1.10	.30	.20
61-62	3¢-8¢ Central Hall, London	.90	.30	.20
63-64	4¢-8¢ Regulars, U.N. Seal	.90	.30	.20
65-66	4¢-8¢ Economic & Social Council	1.10	.30	.20
67-68	4¢-8¢ Human Rights, Hands and Globe	.90	.30	.20

| | 69 | 73 | 77 | 86 |

1959

69-70	4¢-8¢ Flushing Meadows, Gen. Assembly	1.10	.30	.22
71-72	4¢-8¢ Economic Comm. - Europe	1.50	.35	.35
73-74	4¢-8¢ Trusteeship Council	1.70	.35	.25
75-76	4¢-8¢ World Refugee Year	1.15	.30	.20

1960

77-78	4¢-8¢ Chaillot Palace Paris	1.15	.30	.20
79-80	4¢-8¢ Economic Council - Asia & Far East	1.15	.30	.20
81-82	4¢-8¢ World Forestry Congress	1.15	.30	.20
83-84	4¢-8¢ 15th Anniversary, United Nations	1.15	.30	.20
85	4¢-8¢ 15th Anniv. Souvenir Sheet	...	.70	.65
85v	Same broken "v" Variety	...	55.00	50.00
86-87	4¢-8¢ Bank for Reconstruction & Develop	1.15	.30	.20

| | 88 | 97 | 108 | 112 |

1961

88-89	4¢-8¢ Int'l Court of Justice	1.15	.30	.20
90-91	4¢-7¢ Monetary Fund	1.15	.30	.20
92	30¢ Regular, Flags	2.25	.50	.45
93-94	4¢-11¢ Economic Council - Latin America	2.00	.45	.40
95-96	4¢-11¢ Economic Comm. - Africa	1.60	.35	.25
97-99	3¢, 4¢, 13¢ Children's Fund, UNICEF	1.90	.40	.35

1962

100-01	4¢-7¢ Housing & Urban Development	1.15	.30	.25
102-03	4¢-11¢ World Health Org., Anti-Malaria	1.50	.35	.30
104-07	1¢, 3¢, 5¢, 11¢ Regulars	2.75	.60	.40
108-09	5¢-15¢ Dag Hammarskjold	1.70	.40	.45
110-11	4¢-11¢ Operations in Congo	1.70	.40	.45
112-13	4¢-11¢ Peaceful Uses of Outer Space	1.85	.40	.30

NOTE: PRICES THROUGHOUT THIS LIST ARE SUBJECT TO CHANGE WITHOUT NOTICE IF MARKET CONDITIONS REQUIRE. MINIMUM MAIL ORDER MUST TOTAL AT LEAST $20.00.

| | | 114 | 119 | 133 | | 134 | |

| | | 192 | 197 | 203 | 209 |

Scott's No.		MI Block of 4	F-VF NH	F-VF Used
114-15	5¢-11¢ Science & Technology	1.50	.35	.30
116-17	5¢-11¢ Freedom from Hunger	1.50	.35	.30
118	25¢ UN in West New Guinea (UNTEA)	2.25	.50	.45
119-20	5¢-11¢ General Assembly Bldg.,N.York	1.50	.35	.30
121-22	5¢-11¢ Human Rights, Flame	1.50	.35	.30
	1964			
123-24	5¢-11¢ Maritime Consultative Org	1.50	.35	.30
125-28	2¢,7¢,10¢,50¢ Regulars	6.25	1.40	1.10
129-30	5¢-11¢ Trade & Development	1.50	.35	.30
131-32	5¢-11¢ Control Narcotics	1.95	.40	.35
133	5¢ Ending Nuclear Tests	.60	.20	.15
134-36	4¢,5¢,11¢ Education Progress	1.70	.35	.35

| | | 137 | 139 | 154 | 161 |

	1965			
137-38	5¢-11¢ Development Fund	1.50	.35	.30
139-40	5¢-11¢ Peace Keeping Force - Cyprus	1.50	.35	.30
141-42	5¢-11¢ Telecommunications Union	1.50	.35	.30
143-44	5¢-15¢ 20th Anniv. Cooperation Year	1.60	.35	.35
145	5¢-12¢ 20th Anniv. Souvenir Sheet of 2	...	.50	.50
146-50	1¢,15¢,20¢,25¢,$1 Regulars	14.50	3.00	2.75
151-53	4¢,5¢,11¢ Population Trends	2.10	.45	.40
	1966			
154-55	5¢-15¢ Fed. of U.N. Associations	1.50	.35	.30
156-57	5¢-11¢ W.H.O. Headqtrs. Geneva	1.50	.35	.27
158-59	5¢-11¢ Coffee Agreement	1.50	.35	.27
160	15¢ Peacekeeping - Observers	1.50	.30	.30
161-63	4¢,5¢,11¢ UNICEF 20th Anniv.	1.85	.45	.35

| | | 164 | 170 | 185 | 190 |

	1967			
164-65	5¢-11¢ Development Program	1.60	.35	.30
166-67	1½¢-5¢ Regulars	.90	.30	.20
168-69	5¢-11¢ Independent Nations, Fireworks	1.60	.35	.30
170-74	4¢,5¢,8¢,10¢,15¢ Expo '67, Montreal	3.00	.70	.65
175-76	5¢-15¢ Tourist Year	1.80	.40	.30
177-78	6¢-13¢ Disarmament	1.85	.40	.30
179	6¢ Chagall Souvenir Sheet of 6	...	.60	.60
180	6¢ Chagall Window Stamp	.70	.20	.15
	1968			
181-82	6¢-13¢ Secretariat	1.60	.35	.35
183-84	6¢-75¢ Art, Starcke Statue	6.75	1.40	1.30
185-86	6¢-13¢ Industrial Development	1.40	.30	.30
187	6¢ Regular, U.N. Headquarters	.70	.20	.15
188-89	6¢-20¢ World Weather Watch	1.95	.40	.35
190-91	6¢-13¢ Human Rights, Flame	1.60	.35	.35

Scott's No.		MI Block of 4	F-VF NH	F-VF Used
192-93	6¢-13¢ Training & Research Inst.	1.50	.35	.35
194-95	6¢-15¢ U.N. Building, Santiago	1.65	.35	.35
196	13¢ Regular "U.N." & Emblem	1.20	.30	.25
197-98	6¢-13¢ Peace Through Law	1.60	.35	.30
199-200	6¢-20¢ Labor & Development	2.10	.45	.40
201-02	6¢-13¢ Art, Tunisian Mosaic	1.50	.35	.30
	1970			
203-04	6¢-25¢ Art, Japanese Peace Bell	2.50	.55	.45
205-06	6¢-13¢ Mekong Basin Development	1.50	.35	.30
207-08	6¢-13¢ Fight Against Cancer	1.60	.35	.30
209-11	6¢,13¢,25¢ 25th Anniversary of U.N.	3.50	.75	.70
212	6¢,13¢,25¢ 25th Anniv. Souv. Sheet of 3	...	.75	.70
213-14	6¢-13¢ Peace, Justice & Progress	1.85	.40	.35

| | | 215 | 216 | 220 | 224 |

	1971			
215	6¢ Peaceful Uses of the Sea Bed	.70	.20	.15
216-17	6¢-13¢ Support for Refugees	1.50	.35	.30
218	13¢ World Food Program	1.15	.25	.25
219	20¢ U.P.U. Headquarters, Bern	1.65	.35	.35
220-21	8¢-13¢ Racial Discrimination	1.85	.40	.35
222-23	8¢-60¢ Regulars	5.25	1.15	1.00
224-25	8¢-21¢ U.N. Int'l. School	2.25	.45	.45

| | | 228 | 232 | 236 | 242 |

	1972			
226	95¢ Regular, Letter	7.00	1.60	1.50
227	8¢ No More Nuclear Weapons	.75	.20	.15
228	15¢ World Health Day, Man	1.15	.25	.25
229-30	8¢-15¢ Human Environment, Stockholm	2.35	.50	.40
231	21¢ Economic Comm. - Europe	1.90	.40	.35
232-33	8¢-15¢ Art, Jose Maria Sert Mural	2.25	.50	.45
	1973			
234-35	8¢-15¢ Disarmament Decade	2.25	.50	.45
236-37	8¢-15¢ Against Drug Abuse	2.25	.50	.45
238-39	8¢-21¢ Volunteer Program	2.50	.55	.50
240-41	8¢-15¢ Namibia, Map of Africa	2.25	.50	.50
242-43	8¢-21¢ Human Rights, 25th Anniv	2.25	.50	.50

NOTE: PRICES ARE FOR SETS OR SINGLES AS LISTED.

| 244 | 252 | 256 | 260 |

Scott's No.		MI Block of 4	F-VF NH	F-VF Used
244-45	10¢-21¢ Labor Organization Headquarters	2.50	.55	.50
246	10¢ U.P.U. Centenary	1.10	.25	.20
247-48	10¢-18¢ Art, Brazil Peace Mural	2.75	.60	.60
249-51	2¢,10¢,18¢ Regulars	2.75	.60	.60
252-53	10¢-18¢ Population Year	3.25	.70	.70
254-55	10¢-25¢ Law of the Sea	3.25	.70	.65

1975

256-57	10¢-26¢ Peaceful Use of Outer Space............	3.25	.70	.70
258-59	10¢-18¢ Women's Year	3.25	.70	.65
260-61	10¢-26¢ 30th Anniversary of U.N, ...	3.65	.80	.75
262	10¢-26¢ 30th Anniv. Souv. Sheet of 2	...	.75	.75
263-64	10¢-18¢ Namibia, Hand..................................	2.95	.65	.55
265-66	13¢-26¢ Peacekeeping Operations	3.50	.75	.70

| 272 | 278 | 283 | 289 |

1976

267-71	3¢,4¢,9¢,30¢,50¢ Regulars	7.25	1.65	1.50
272-73	13¢-26¢ U.N. Associations(WFUNA)	3.00	.65	.60
274-75	13¢-31¢ Trade & Development	3.35	.75	.70
276-77	13¢-25¢ Human Settlement, Habitat	3.00	.65	.65
278-79	13¢-31¢ 25th Postal Anniversary	9.50	2.15	2.10
278-79	Sheetlets of 20	...	39.50	...
280	13¢ World Food Council	1.40	.30	.25

1977

281-82	13¢-31¢ Intellectual Property(WIPO)	3.35	.75	.70
283-84	13¢-25¢ Water Conference	3.50	.75	.65
285-86	13¢-31¢ Security Council	3.75	.75	.70
287-88	13¢-25¢ Racial Discrimination	3.00	.65	.65
289-90	13¢-18¢ Peaceful - Atomic Energy	3.00	.65	.65

| 296 | 298 | 310 | 312 |

| 299 | 301 | 302 |

1978

291-93	1¢,25¢,$1 Regulars...............................	9.00	2.10	1.95
294-95	13¢-31¢ Smallpox-Eradication	3.50	.75	.75
296-97	13¢-18¢ Namibia, Open Handcuff	3.00	.65	.60
298-99	13¢-25¢ Civil Aviation Organ (ICAO)...........	3.25	.70	.70
300-01	13¢-18¢ General Assembly..............................	3.25	.70	.70
302-03	13¢-31¢ Technical Cooperation	3.95	.85	.85

Scott's No.		MI Block of 4	F-VF NH	F-VF Used

1979

304-07	5¢,14¢,15¢,20¢ Regulars	5.00	1.10	1.00
308-09	15¢-20¢ Disaster Relief (UNDRO)	2.75	.60	.60
310-11	15¢-31¢ Year of the Child	3.50	.75	.75
310-11	Sheetlets of 20	...	14.50	...
312-13	15¢-31¢ Namibia, Olive Branch......................	3.75	.80	.70
314-15	15¢-20¢ Court of Justice, The Hague	3.25	.70	.70

| 316 | 325 | 344 | 346 |

1980

316-17	15¢-31¢ New Economic Order	3.95	.85	.85
318-19	15¢-20¢ Decade for Women	3.00	.65	.65
320-21	15¢-31¢ Peacekeeping Operations.	3.95	.85	.80
322-23	15¢-31¢ 35th Anniversary of U.N.	3.75	.80	.70
324	15¢-31¢ 35th Anniv. - Souv. Sheet of 2	...	.85	.85
*325-40	15¢ World Flag Series of 16	10.50	2.65	2.50
325-40	Se-Tenant Block of 4(4)	...	6.50	...

325	Turkey	329	Guinea	333	Jugoslavia	337	Madagascar
326	Luxembourg	330	Surinam	334	France	338	Cameroun
327	Fiji	331	Bangladesh	335	Venezuela	339	Rwanda
328	Vietnam	332	Mali	336	El Salvador	340	Hungary

341-42	15¢-20¢ Economic & Social Council	3.75	.80	.70

1981

343	15¢ Palestinian People	1.50	.30	.25
344-45	20¢-35¢ Disabled Persons	4.50	.95	.90
346-47	20¢-31¢ Art, Bulgarian Mural	4.25	.90	.80
348-49	20¢-40¢ Energy Conference	5.00	1.10	1.10
*350-65	20¢ World Flag Series of 16	17.50	4.25	4.25
350-65	Se-Tenant Blocks of 4(4)	...	9.50	...

350	Djibouti	354	Malta	358	Ukraine	362	U.S.
351	Sri Lanka	355	Czech.	359	Kuwait	363	Singapore
352	Bolivia	356	Thailand	360	Sudan	364	Panama
353	Eq. Guinea	357	Trinidad & T.	361	Egypt	365	Costa Rica

366-67	18¢-28¢ Volunteers Program	4.95	1.10	.95

| 371 | 390 | 394 | 397 |

1982

368-70	17¢,28¢,40¢ Regulars	8.75	1.90	1.75
371-72	20¢-40¢ Human Environment	5.75	1.25	1.15
373	20¢ Peaceful Use of Outer Space	3.25	.70	.60
*374-89	20¢ World Flag Series of 16	17.50	4.25	4.25
374-89	Se-Tenant Blocks of 4(4)	...	10.75	...

374	Austria	378	Mozambique	382	Philippines	386	Cape Verde
375	Malaysia	379	Albania	383	Swaziland	387	Guyana
376	Seychelles	380	Dominica	384	Nicaragua	388	Belgium
377	Ireland	381	Solomon Isl.	385	Burma	389	Nigeria

390-91	20¢-28¢ Nature Conservation	5.25	1.15	1.00

1983

392-93	20¢-40¢ Communications Year........................	5.25	1.15	1.00
394-95	20¢-37¢ Safety at Sea	5.50	1.20	1.15
396	20¢ World Food Program	2.50	.50	.50
397-98	20¢-28¢ Trade & Development	5.50	1.20	1.20
*399-414	20¢ World Flag Series of 16	22.50	5.50	5.25
399-414	Se-Tenant Blocks of 4(4)	...	12.50	...

399	U. Kingdom	403	Malawi	407	China	411	Somalia
400	Barbados	404	Byelorussia	408	Peru	412	Senegal
401	Nepal	405	Jamaica	409	Bulgaria	413	Brazil
402	Israel	406	Kenya	410	Canada	414	Sweden

415-16	20¢-40¢ Human Rights, 35th Anniv.	5.50	1.20	1.15
415-16	Same, Sheetlets of 16	...	19.75	...

NOTE: WORLD FLAGS ARE ISSUED IN SHEETS OF 16, EACH WITH 4 DIFFERENT BLOCKS. SHEETS OF 16 WILL BE SUPPLIED AT MI BLOCK PRICE.

417   419   421

Scott's No.		MI Block of 4	F-VF NH	F-VF Used
417-18	20¢-40¢ Population Conference.	5.00	1.10	1.10
419-20	20¢-40¢ FAO Food Day	5.25	1.15	1.10
421-22	20¢-50¢ UNESCO World Heritage	5.75	1.25	1.20
423-24	20¢-50¢ Refugee Futures	7.50	1.65	1.50
*425-40	20¢ World Flag Series of 16	42.50	10.50	10.00
425-40	Se-Tenant Blocks of 4(4)	...	19.50	...

425	Burundi	429	Tanzania	433	Poland	437	Paraguay
426	Pakistan	430	United Arab	434	Papua New	438	Bhutan
427	Benin		Emirates		Guinea	439	Central Afric.
428	Italy	431	Ecuador	435	Uruguay		Republic
		432	Bahamas	436	Chile	440	Australia

441-42	20¢-35¢ Youth Year	7.50	1.65	1.50

466   468   473

	1985			
443	23¢ ILO-Turin Centre	3.00	.65	.60
444	50¢ U.N. University in Japan	6.50	1.40	1.40
445-46	22¢-$3 Regulars	25.00	5.35	4.50
447-48	22¢-45¢ 40th Anniversary of U.N.	8.50	1.80	1.75
449	22¢-45¢ 40th Anniv. Souvenir Sheet of 2	...	1.95	1.90
*450-65	22¢ World Flag Series of 16	43.50	10.75	10.00
450-65	Se-Tenant Blocks of 4(4)	...	21.50	...

450	Grenada	454	Uganda	455 458	Liberia	462	Sultanate of
451	Federal Rep.	455	St. Thomas	459	Mauritius		Oman
	of Germ.		& Prince	460	Chad	463	Ghana
452	Saudi Arabia	456	USSR	461	Dominican	464	Sierra Leone
453	Mexico	457	India		Republic	465	Finland

466-67	22¢-33¢ UNICEF Child Survival	5.50	1.20	1.15

	1986			
468	22¢ Africa in Crisis, Against Hunger	2.75	.60	.55
469-72	22¢ UN Development Program, attd.	8.75	7.95	7.50
469-72	Sheet of 40	...	95.00	...
473-74	22¢-44¢ Philately, Stamp Collecting	6.25	1.35	1.25
475-76	22¢-33¢ International Peace Year	11.50	2.50	2.25
*477-92	22¢ World Flag Series of 16	45.00	11.00	10.75
477-92	Se-Tenant Blocks of 4(4)	...	20.75	...

477	New Zealand	481	Maldives	485	Iceland	489	Romania
478	Lao PDR	482	Ethiopia	486	Antigua &	490	Togo
479	Burkina Faso	483	Jordan		Barbuda	491	Mauritania
480	Gambia	484	Zambia	487	Angola	492	Colombia
				488	Botswana		

493	22¢,33¢,39¢,44¢ WFUNA S/S of 4	...	4.75	4.50

516   517   518

	1987			
494	22¢ Trygve Lie, Secretary-General	4.50	.95	.85
495-96	22¢-44¢ Shelter for the Homeless	9.50	2.10	1.85
497-98	22¢-33¢ Life Yes/Drugs No	9.50	2.10	1.85
*499-514	22¢ 1987 World Flag Series of 16	47.50	11.50	10.50
499-514	Se-Tenant Blocks of 4 (4)	...	20.75	...

499	Comoros	503	Japan	507	Argentina	511	Bahrain
500	DPRYemen	504	Gabon	508	Congo	512	Haiti
501	Mongolia	505	Zimbabwe	509	Niger	513	Afghanistan
502	Vanuatu	506	Iraq	510	St. Lucia	514	Greece

Scott's No.		MI Block of 4	F-VF NH	F-VF Used
515-16	22¢-39¢ U.N. Day, Multinational	6.75	1.50	1.50
515-16	Miniature Sheets of 12	...	20.75	
517-18	22¢-44¢ Child Immunization	16.00	3.50	2.00

519   524   544

	1988			
519-20	22¢-33¢ World Without Hunger(IFAO)	9.00	2.00	1.85
521	3¢ Regular, UN For a Better World	.70	.20	.15
522-23	25¢-44¢ Forestry, pair	15.00	6.50	6.25
522-23	Miniature Sheet of 12	...	35.00	
524-25	25¢-50¢ Int'l. Volunteers Day	11.00	2.25	2.00
526-27	25¢-38¢ Health in Sports	11.50	2.35	2.10
*528-43	25¢ World Flag Series of 16	47.50	11.50	10.75
528-43	Se-Tenant Blocks of 4 (4)	...	20.75	...

528	Spain	532	Yemen Arab	536	Qatar	540	Iran
529	St. Vincent		Rep.	537	Zaire	541	Tunisia
	& Gren.	533	Cuba	538	Norway	542	Samoa
530	Ivory Coast	534	Denmark	539	German	543	Belize
531	Lebanon	535	Libya		Dem. Rep.		

544	25¢ Human Rights 40th Anniv.	3.35	.75	.65
545	$1 Human Rights Anniv. S/S	...	1.95	1.85

	1989			
546-47	25¢-45¢ World Bank	12.75	2.75	2.35
548	25¢ UN Peace Keeping, Nobel Prize	3.75	.65	.60
549	45¢ Regular UN Headquarters	4.50	.90	.90
550-51	25¢-36¢ World Weather Watch	13.50	3.00	2.75
552-53	25¢-90¢ UN Offices Vienna, 10th Anniv.	27.50	6.00	5.25
552-53	Sheets of 25	...	195.00	...
*554-69	25¢ World Flags Series of 16	51.50	12.50	11.00
554-69	Se-Tenant Blocks of 4 (4)	...	21.75	...

554	Indonesia	558	South Africa	562	Honduras	566	Algeria
555	Lesotho	559	Portugal	563	Kampucea	567	Brunei
556	Guatemala	560	Morocco	564	Guinea-Bissau	568	St.Kitts-Nevis
557	Netherlands	561	Syrian Arab	565	Cyprus	569	United Nations
			Republic				

570-71	25¢-45¢ Declaration of Human Rights	...	2.00	1.75
570-71	Strips of 3 with Tabs at Bottom	...	6.00	...
570-71	Miniature Sheets of 12	...	28.50	...

572   580   592   597

	1990			
572	25¢ International Trade Center	8.25	1.75	1.60
573-74	25¢-40¢ Fight Against AIDS	11.50	2.50	2.25
575-76	25¢-90¢ Medicinal Plants	13.50	3.00	2.75
577-78	25¢-45¢ UN 45th Anniversary	19.50	4.25	3.75
579	25¢-45¢ UN 45th Anniversary S/S of 2	...	9.00	8.50
580-81	25¢-36¢ Crime Prevention	17.50	3.75	3.25
582-83	25¢-45¢ Declaration of Human Rights	...	2.25	2.25
582-83	Strips of 3 with Tabs at Bottom	...	6.75	...
582-83	Miniature Sheets of 12	...	30.00	...
	1991			
584-87	30¢ Europe Econ. Commission attd.	6.50	5.50	5.00
588-89	30¢-50¢ Namibia Independence	16.50	3.50	2.75
590-91	30¢-50¢ Regulars	13.75	2.75	2.40
592	$2 Regular U.N. Headquarters	16.50	3.50	3.25
593-94	30¢-70¢ Children's Rights	19.75	4.25	3.75
595-96	30¢-90¢ Chemical Weapons Ban	22.50	5.00	4.50
597-98	30¢-40¢ UNPA 40th Anniv.	13.50	3.00	2.75
599-600	30¢-50¢ Declaration of Human Rights	...	2.40	2.25
599-600	Strips of 3 with Tabs at Bottom	...	7.20	...
599-600	Miniature Sheets of 12	...	30.00	...

	601	611		624

Scott's No.		MI Block of 4	F-VF NH	F-VF Used
601-02	30¢-50¢ World Heritage, UNESCO	11.00	2.40	2.25
603-04	29¢ Clean Oceans attd	6.00	1.35	1.25
603-04	Miniature Sheet of 12	...	12.00	
605-08	29¢ UNICED: Earth Summit attd	3.50	3.00	3.00
605-08	29¢ UNICED Sheet of 40	...	32.50	...
609-10	29¢ Mission to Planet Earth attd.	18.50	8.00	7.95
609-10	Miniature Sheet of 10	...	50.00	...
611-12	29¢-50¢ Science & Technology	7.75	1.70	1.50
613-15	4¢,29¢,40¢ Regulars	7.75	1.80	1.60
616-17	29¢-50¢ Declaration of Human Rights		2.50	2.50
616-17	Strips of 3 with Tabs at Bottom		7.50	
616-17	Miniature Sheet of 12	...	37.50	...

1993

618-19	29¢-52¢ Aging with Dignity	16.00	3.50	3.50
620-23	29¢ Endangered Species attd	3.65	3.25	3.00
620-23	Miniature sheet of 16	...	14.50	...
624-25	29¢-50¢ Healthy Environments	11.00	2.40	2.25
626	5¢ Regular	.85	.20	.18
627-28	29¢-35¢ Human Rights		2.75	2.75
627-28	Strips of 3 with Tabs at Bottom		8.25	
627-28	Miniature Sheets of 12		40.00	
629-32	29¢ Peace Day, attd	12.00	11.00	9.50
629-32	Sheet of 40		115.00	...
633-36	29¢ Environment - Climate ......(8)	8.25	3.75	3.25
633-36	Miniature Sheet of 24		25.00	...

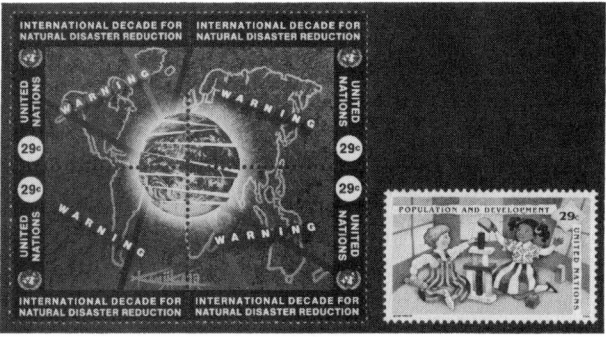

	647-50		651

1994

637-38	29¢-45¢ Year of the Family	18.75	3.95	3.50
639-42	29¢ Endangered Species, attd	3.95	3.25	3.00
639-42	Miniature Sheets of 16	...	13.50	...
643	50¢ Refugees	7.50	1.60	1.25
644-46	10¢,19¢,$1 Regulars	14.50	2.95	2.75
647-50	29¢ Natural Disaster, block of 4	11.00	9.75	8.75
647-50	Sheet of 40	...	95.00	...
651-52	29¢-52¢ Population Development	11.50	2.50	2.40
653-54	29¢-50¢ Development Partnership	8.75	1.90	1.75

	655	661		663

1995

655	32¢ U.N. 50th Anniversary	9.00	1.90	1.50
656	50¢ Social Summit, Copenhagen	6.00	1.35	1.15
657-60	32¢ Endangered Species, attd	3.75	3.25	3.00
657-60	Miniature Sheet of 16	...	15.00	...
661-62	32¢-55¢ Youth: Our Future	17.50	3.75	3.00
663-64	32¢-50¢ 50th Anniv. of U.N.	19.50	4.25	3.50
665	82¢ 50th Anniversary Souv. Sheet of 2		4.50	3.75
666-67	32¢-40¢ Conference on Women	11.50	2.50	2.00
668	20¢ Regular Issue, U.N. Headquarters	2.30	.50	.45
669	32¢ U.N. 50th Anniv. Sheetlet - 12	...	14.75	...
670	32¢ U.N. 50th Anniv. Souvenir, Booklet of 12	...	16.50	...

	671	672-73	

Scott's No.		MI Block of 4	F-VF NH	F-VF Used
671	32¢ WFUNA 50th Anniv	3.65	.75	.65
672-73	32¢-60¢ Regular Issues	10.50	2.15	1.75
674-77	32¢ Endangered Species	3.35	2.85	2.50
674-77	Miniature Sheet of 16	...	13.50	...
678-82	32¢ City Summit, Strip of 5 ......(10)	11.50	5.25	4.50
678-82	Miniature Sheet of 25		28.50	...
683-84	32¢-50¢ Sport & Environment	11.75	2.75	2.35
685	32¢-50¢ Sport & Environment Souv. Sheet	2.75	2.25	
686-87	32¢-60¢ Plea For Peace	10.50	2.25	1.75
688-89	32¢-60¢ UNICEF 50th Anniv.	11.50	2.50	2.00
688-89	Miniature Sheet of 8	...	24.50	...

1997

	690	698	699

690-97	32¢ Flags of New Countries (8)	...	5.95	4.75
690-97	Sheetlets of 16 (2)	...	23.75	...
	690 Tadjikistan 692 Armenia 694 Liechtenstein 696 Kazakhstan			
	691 Georgia 693 Namibia 695 Rep. Of Korea 697 Latvia			
698-99	8¢-55¢ Regulars, Flowers	7.00	1.50	1.30
700-3	32¢ Endangered Species	3.50	2.95	2.50
700-3	Miniature Sheets of 16	...	13.75	...
704-7	32¢ Earth Summit	3.50	2.95	2.50
704-7	Miniature Sheet of 16	...	19.50	...

708

718

708	$1 Earth Summit, Souvenir Sheet	...	2.25	2.15
708a	$1 Pacific "97 Overprint on #708		11.95	10.95
709-13	32¢ Transportation, 5 designs ......(10)	7.95	3.75	3.75
709-13	Sheetlet of 20		14.75	...
714-15	32¢ Tribute to Philately, set of 2	8.25	1.75	1.75
716-17	32¢-60¢ Heritage, Terracotta Warriors	9.00	1.95	1.95
718	$1.92 Terracotta Warriors Prestige Booklet with 6 8¢ Blocks of 4	...	4.75	...
718a-f	Set of Singles From #718(6)	...	1.75	1.65

Scott's No.		MI Block of 4	F-VF NH	F-VF Used
719-26	32¢ Flags of New Countries (8)	...	5.25	4.25
719-26	Sheetlet of 16 (2)	...	20.95	...

719 Micronesia	721 Dem. Rep. Korea	723 Uzbekistan	725 Czech Rep.
720 Slovakia	722 Azerbaijan	724 Monaco	726 Estonia

727-29

		MI Block of 4	F-VF NH	F-VF Used
727-29	1¢, 2¢, 21¢ Regulars	2.50	.50	.50
730-33	32¢ Endangered Species	3.50	2.95	2.10
730-33	Miniature Sheet of 16	...	13.75	...

734

735   **737-38**

734	32¢ Year of the Ocean, Min. Sheet of 12	...	8.25	...
735	32¢ Rainforests	3.50	.75	.65
735	Rainforests, Sheet of 20	...	14.50	...
736	$2 Rainforests, Souvenir Sheet	...	4.35	4.25
737-38	33¢-40¢ Peacekeeping (2)	7.50	1.60	1.50
737-38	Peacekeeping, Sheets of 20	...	31.50	...
739-40	32¢-55¢ Human Rights (2)	8.40	1.80	1.65
739-40	Human Rights, Sheets of 20	...	35.00	...
741-42	33¢-60¢ Schonbrun Palace (2)	8.75	1.90	1.80
741-42	Schonbrun Palace, Sheets of 20	...	37.50	...
743	Schonbrun Palace, Prestige Booklet with Six Booklet Panes of 3 or 4	...	5.95	...
743a-f	11¢-15¢ Set of 6 Singles from booklet	...	1.75	...

Scott's No.		MI Block of 4	F-VF NH	F-VF Used
744-51	33¢ Flags of New Countries (8)	...	5.75	4.75
744-51	Flags, Sheetlets of 16 (2)	...	22.75	...
752	33¢ Banner of Flags Regular Issue	3.35	.70	.65
753	$5 Roses Regular Issue	43.50	9.95	7.95
754-55	33¢-60¢ World Heritage-Australia (2)	8.75	1.90	1.75
754-55	Australia, Sheetlets of 20 (2)	...	37.50	...
756	Australia, Prestige Booklet with Six Bk. Panes of 4		5.75	...
756a-f	5¢-15¢ Set of 6 singles from booklet	...	1.50	...
757-60	33¢ Endangered Species (4)	3.35	2.80	2.50
757-60	Endangered Species, Sheetlet of 16	...	11.75	...
...	33¢ UNISPACE III, Pair	...	1.40	...
...	UNISPACE III, Miniature Sheet of 10	...	6.95	...
...	$2 UNISPACE III, Souvenir Sheet	...	4.25	...
...	33¢ Universal Postal Union (4)	3.35	2.80	2.50
...	U.P.U, Sheetlet of 20	...	13.75	...

UNITED NATIONS AIRMAILS

C1   C5   C7

Scott's No.		MI Block of 4	F-VF NH	F-VF Used
1951 First Airmail Issue				
C1-4	6¢,10¢,15¢,25¢ Airmail Issue..........................	5.75	1.25	1.25
1957-59				
C5-7	4¢,5¢,7¢ Airmails..	1.85	.45	.40

C8   C11   C14

	1963-69			
C8-10	6¢,8¢,13¢ Airmails................................	2.25	.50	.50
C11-12	15¢ & 25¢ Airmails (1964)	4.50	.95	.85
C13	20¢ Jet Plane (1968)	1.85	.40	.40
C14	10¢ Wings & Envelopes (1969)	1.10	.25	.25

C15   C19   C22

	1972-77			
C15-18	9¢,11¢, 17¢, 21¢ Airmails	4.50	1.00	.90
C19-21	13¢, 18¢, 26¢ Airmails (1974)......................	4.25	.95	.95
C22-23	25¢ & 31¢ Airmails (1977)	4.25	.95	.95

U.N. IN NEW YORK 1951-98

1-743,C1-23	Complete..	...	635.00	...
1/743,C1-23	Without Souvenir Sheet #38	...	515.00	...

**FOR VERY FINE, ADD 20% TO PRICE LISTED.
MINIMUM-10¢ PER STAMP**

UNITED NATIONS POSTAL STATIONERY

U1

UXC 3

Scott's No.		Mint Entire	Scott's No.		Mint Entire
ENVELOPE ENTIRES			**POSTAL CARDS**		
U1	3¢ Emblem (1953)	.60	UX1	2¢ Hdqtrs (1952)..........	.25
U2	4¢ Emblem (1958)	.50	UX2	3¢ Hdqtrs (1958)	.25
U3	5¢ Wthr. Vane (1963).....	.25	UX3	4¢ Map (1963)	.25
U4	6¢ Wthr. Vane (1969).....	.25	UX4	5¢ Post Horn (1969)	.25
U5	8¢ Hdqtrs (1973)............	.60	UX5	6¢ "UN" (1973)	.28
U6	10¢ Hdqtrs (1975)..........	.50	UX6	8¢ "UN" (1975)	.65
U7	22¢ Bouquet (1985)........	10.75	UX7	9¢ Emblem (1977)........	.75
U8	25¢ NY Headqtrs ('89)....	3.50	UX8	13¢ Letters (1982).........	.45
U9	25¢+4¢ Schg on U8 ('91).	2.95	UX9-13	15¢ NY HQ Views(89)	7.50
U10	32¢ Cripticondina ('97)...	2.50	UX14-18	36¢ NY HQ Views	
U11	32¢ Cripticondina,			(1989............................	10.00
	larger design (1997)	1.75	UX19	40¢ UN HQ (1992)	3.50
U12	32¢+1¢ Cripticondina		UX20	21¢ Rose Garden(1998)	.50
	(1999).	.90	UX21	50¢ NY Skyline (1998)	1.20
AIRMAIL ENVELOPE ENTIRES					
UC3	7¢ Flag (1959)	1.95	**AIRMAIL POSTAL CARDS**		
UC6	8¢ Emblem (1963)	.40	UXC1	4¢ Wing (1957)	.30
UC8	10¢ Emblem (1969)	.45	UXC2	4¢ + 1¢ Surch (1959)....	.40
UC10	11¢ Birds (1973).............	.75	UXC3	5¢ Wing (1959)	.80
UC11	13¢ Globe (1975)............	.45	UXC4	6¢ Space (1963)	.85
AIRLETTER SHEETS			UXC5	11¢ Earth (1966)	.40
UC1	10¢ Air Letter (1952)	27.95	UXC6	13¢ Earth (1968)	.45
UC2	10¢ "Air Letter/Aero..."		UXC7	8¢ Planes (1969)..........	.60
	White Border (1954).......	8.50	UXC8	9¢ Wings (1972)..........	.45
UC2a	10¢ Same, No White		UXC9	15¢ Planes (1972).........	.50
	Border (1958)	7.75	UXC10	11¢ Clouds (1975)	.45
UC4	10¢ Flag (1960)	.80	UXC11	18¢ Pathways ('75).......	.45
UC5	11¢ Gull, blue (1961)......	.75	UXC12	28¢ Flying Mailman(82)	.60
UC5a	11¢ Greenish (1965)	1.50			
UC7	13¢ Plane (1968)............	.40			
UC9	15¢ Globe (1972)............	.70			
UC12	18¢ Hdqtrs (1975)..........	.75			
UC13	22¢ Birds (1977).............	.75			
UC14	30¢ Paper Airplane (82)..	1.95			
UC15	30¢+6¢ Surcharge (87) ...	55.00			
UC16	39¢ NY Headqrtrs (89) ...	4.25			
UC17	39¢+6¢ Surcharge				
	on UC16 (1991)..............	17.50			
UC18	45¢ Winged Hand ('92) ...	2.95			
UC19	45¢+5¢ Surcharge				
	on UC18 (95).................	6.50			
UC20	50¢ Cherry Blossom ('97)	2.25			

1   **4**   **8**   **14**

1969-70

Scott's No.		MI Block of 4	F-VF NH	F-VF Used
1-14	5¢,10¢,20¢,30¢,50¢,60¢,70¢,75¢, 80¢,90¢,1fr.,2fr.,3fr.,10 fr. Regular Issue......	35.00	7.75	7.75

16   **18**   **22**

1971

15	30¢ Peaceful Use of Sea Bed........................	.95	.20	.20
16	50¢ Support for Refugees	1.50	.30	.30
17	50¢ World Food Program	1.50	.30	.30
18	75¢ U.P.U. Headquarters.............................	2.15	.45	.45
19-20	30¢-50¢ Racial Discrimination	2.35	.50	.50
21	1.10 fr. U.N. Int'l. School............................	4.75	.95	.90

1972

22	40¢ Palace of Nations,Geneva	.95	.20	.20
23	40¢ No Nuclear Weapons.............................	1.65	.35	.35
24	80¢ World Health Day, Man.........................	2.25	.50	.50
25-26	40¢-80¢ Human Environment	4.25	.90	.90
27	1.10 fr. Economic Comm. - Europe..............	5.50	1.20	1.15
28-29	40¢-60¢ Art, Jose Maria Set Mural..............	5.00	1.10	1.10

36   **37**   **43**   **45**

1973

30-31	60¢-1.10 fr. Disarmament Decade	7.00	1.50	1.50
32	60¢ Against Drug Abuse..............................	2.35	.50	.50
33	80¢ Volunteer Program................................	2.10	.45	.45
34	60¢ Namibia, Map of Africa	2.10	.45	.45
35-36	40¢-80¢ Human Rights, Flame.....................	4.75	1.00	.95

1974

37-38	60¢-80¢ ILO Headquarters,Geneva	5.50	1.20	1.10
39-40	30¢-60¢ U.P.U. Centenary...........................	5.25	1.10	1.00
41-42	60¢-1 fr. Art, Brazil Peace Mural.................	5.50	1.20	1.10
43-44	60¢-80¢ Population Year..............................	7.00	1.50	1.45
45	1.30 fr. Law of the Sea	5.00	1.10	1.00

50   **55**   **59**   **61**

1975

Scott's No.		MI Block of 4	F-VF NH	F-VF Used
46-47	60¢-90¢ Peaceful Use of Outer Space	7.00	1.50	1.40
48-49	60¢-90¢ Women's Year...............................	5.75	1.25	1.25
50-51	60¢-90¢ 30th Anniversary of U.N.	5.75	1.25	1.25
52	60¢-90¢ 30th Anniv. - Souv. Sheet of 2........	...	.90	.90
53-54	50¢-1.30 fr. Namibia, Hand........................	5.75	1.25	1.25
55-56	60¢-70¢ Peacekeeping Operations................	5.75	1.25	1.25

1976

57	90¢ U.N. Association (WFUNA)..................	5.00	1.10	1.10
58	1.10 fr. Trade & Development (UNCTAD) ...	5.00	1.10	1.10
59-60	40¢-1.50 fr. Human Settlements,Habitat	5.75	1.25	1.25
61-62	80¢-1.10 fr. 25th Postal Anniversary	14.00	3.00	2.95
61-62	Sheetlets of 20............................	...	49.50	...
63	70¢ World Food Council	2.75	.60	.55

65   **71**   **73**   **77**

1977

64	80¢ Intellectual Property (WIPO).................	3.25	.70	.70
65-66	80¢-1.10 fr. Water Conference.....................	7.00	1.50	1.40
67-68	80¢-1.10 fr. Security Council......................	7.00	1.50	1.40
69-70	40¢-1.10 fr. Racial Discrimination...............	5.25	1.15	1.10
71-72	80¢-1.10 fr. Peaceful - Atomic Energy	6.75	1.40	1.35

1978

73	35¢ Regular, Tree of Doves.........................	1.30	.25	.25
74-75	80¢-1.10 fr. Smallpox Eradication................	7.00	1.50	1.45
76	80¢ Namibia, Handcuffs..............................	4.25	.95	.85
77-78	70¢-80¢ Civil Aviation Organ (ICAO)	5.75	1.25	1.20
79-80	70¢-1.10 fr. General Assembly.....................	7.50	1.60	1.50
81	80¢ Technical Cooperation...........................	4.25	.90	.80

82   **93**   **96**

1979

82-83	80¢-1.50 fr. Disaster Relief(UNDRO)...........	7.50	1.60	1.50
84-85	80¢-1.10 fr. Year of the Child	5.50	1.20	1.15
84-85	Sheetlets of 20........................	...	19.75	...
86	1.10 fr. Namibia, Map	2.75	.60	.60
87-88	80¢-1.10 fr. Court of Justice, The Hague.......	5.75	1.25	1.20

1980

89	80¢ New Economic Order	4.50	.95	.90
90-91	40¢-70¢ Decade for Women	5.25	1.10	1.00
92	1.10 fr. Peacekeeping Operations	4.50	.95	.90
93-94	40¢-70¢ 35th Anniversary of U.N.	5.25	1.10	1.00
95	40¢-70¢ 35th Anniv. - Souv. Sheet of 2........	...	.90	.90
96-97	40¢-70¢ Economic & Social Council.............	5.25	1.10	1.10

99   **103**   **105**   **107**

1981

98	80¢ Palestinian People................................	3.50	.75	.70
99-100	40¢-1.50 fr. Disabled Persons	6.75	1.50	1.50
101	80¢ Art, Bulgarian Mural	4.50	.95	.95
102	1.10 fr. Energy Conference	4.50	.95	.95
103-04	40¢-70¢ Volunteers Program.......................	6.75	1.50	1.50

1982

Scott's No.		MI Block of 4	F-VF NH	F-VF Used
105-06	30¢-1 fr. Regulars......................................	5.75	1.25	1.20
107-08	40¢-1.20 fr. Human Environment.................	7.50	1.60	1.50
109-10	80¢-1 fr. Peaceful Use of Outer Space.........	7.75	1.65	1.65
111-12	40¢-1.50 fr. Nature Conservation.................	8.50	1.80	1.75

113   114   116

1983

113	1.20 fr. Communications Year	6.75	1.45	1.40
114-15	40¢-80¢ Safety at Sea................................	5.50	1.20	1.15
116	1.50 fr. World Food Program.......................	6.95	1.50	1.40
117-18	80¢-1.10 fr. Trade & Development	6.95	1.50	1.40
119-20	40¢-1.20 fr. Human Rights, 35th Anniv.	8.00	1.75	1.70
119-20	Sheetlets of 16	...	27.50	...

121   131   140

1984

121	1.20 fr. Population Conference	5.75	1.25	1.20
122-23	50¢-80¢ FAO Food Day	5.75	1.25	1.20
124-25	50¢-70¢ UNESCO, World Heritage..............	8.50	1.85	1.80
126-27	35¢-1.50 fr. Refugee Futures......................	8.25	1.80	1.75
128	1.20 fr. Youth Year....................................	7.00	1.50	1.40

1985

129-30	80¢-1.20 fr. ILO - Turin Centre	8.50	1.85	1.80
131-32	50¢-80¢ U.N. Univ. in Japan	7.75	1.70	1.65
133-34	20¢-1.20 fr. Regulars................................	9.00	1.95	1.90
135-36	50¢-70¢ 40th Anniversary of U.N.	7.50	1.60	1.50
137	50¢-70¢ 40th Anniv. Souvenir Sheet of 2.....	...	2.50	2.25
138-39	50¢-1.20 fr. UNICEF Child Survival	9.00	1.95	1.90

140   145   154   160

1986

140	1.40 fr. Africa in Crisis, Anti-Hunger...........	7.00	1.50	1.50
141-44	35¢ UN Development Program, attd	11.00	10.00	9.50
141-44	Sheet of 40	...	100.00	...
145	5¢ Regular, Dove & Sun..............................	.70	.20	.15
146-47	50¢-80¢ Philately, Stamp Collecting	7.75	1.70	1.65
148-49	45¢-1.40 fr. Int'l. Peace Year	16.75	2.50	2.25
150	35¢,45¢,50¢,70¢ WFUNA S/S	...	5.00	4.75

1987

151	1.40 fr. Trygve Lie, Secretary-General.........	7.00	1.50	1.40
152-53	90¢-1.40 fr. Bands/Sphere Regulars.............	10.00	2.25	2.20
154-55	50¢-90¢ Shelter for the Homeless	8.50	1.85	1.80
156-57	80¢-1.20 fr. Life Yes/Drugs No	8.50	1.85	1.80
158-59	35¢-50¢ U.N. Day	7.00	1.50	1.50
158-59	Miniature Sheets of 12...............................	...	19.50	...
160-61	90¢-1.70 fr. Child Immunization	21.75	4.50	4.50

164   171   173   178

Scott's No.		MI Block of 4	F-VF NH	F-VF Used
1988				
162-63	35¢-1.40 fr. World Without Hunger	11.00	2.40	2.25
164	50¢ Regular, UN for a Better World	4.50	.95	.85
165-66	50¢-1.10 fr. Forest Conservation, pair..........	18.00	8.25	8.25
165-66	Miniature Sheet of 12	...	42.50	...
167-68	80¢-90¢ Int'l. Volunteers Day	10.50	2.25	2.20
169-70	50¢-1.40 fr. Health in Sports......................	11.75	2.50	2.25
171	90¢ Human Rights 40th Anniv	5.75	1.20	1.15
172	2 fr. Human Rights 40th Anniv. S/S	...	3.25	3.15
1989				
173-74	80¢-1.40 fr. World Bank............................	17.50	3.75	3.75
175	90¢ Peace Keeping, Nobel Prize..................	5.85	1.25	1.25
176-77	90¢-1.10 fr. World Weather Watch...............	18.50	4.00	3.75
178-79	50¢-2 fr. UN Offices in Vienna,10th Anniv...	23.50	5.00	4.50
178-79	Miniature Sheets of 25	...	130.00	...
180-81	35¢-80¢ Declaration of Human Rights	...	2.90	2.75
180-81	Strips of 3 with Tabs at Bottom...................	...	8.70	...
180-81	Miniature Sheets of 12	...	35.00	...

182   184   199

1990				
182	1.50 fr. International Trade Center	15.00	3.15	2.75
183	5 fr. Regular..	25.00	5.50	5.50
184-85	50¢-80¢ Fight Against AIDS......................	16.00	3.50	3.25
186-87	90¢-1.40 fr. Medicinal Plants.....................	16.50	3.70	3.50
188-89	90¢-1.10 fr. UN 45th Anniversary...............	18.75	4.00	3.75
190	90¢-1.10 fr. UN 45th Anniv. S/S of 2...........	...	7.75	6.50
191-92	50¢-2 fr. Crime Prevention.........................	18.75	4.00	3.85
193-94	35¢-90¢ Declaration of Human Rights	...	3.00	2.50
193-94	Strips of 3 with Tabs at Bottom...................	...	9.00	...
193-94	Miniature Sheets of 12	...	36.50	...
1991				
195-98	90¢ Eur. Econ. Commission, attd	6.50	5.75	5.50
195-98	Sheet of 40	...	55.00	...
199-200	70¢-90¢ Namibia, Independence..................	19.50	4.25	4.00
201-02	80¢-1.50 fr. Regulars................................	19.50	4.25	4.00
203-04	80¢-1.10 fr. Children's Rights.....................	18.50	4.00	3.95
205-06	80¢-1.40 fr. Chemical Weapons Ban.............	22.00	4.75	4.50
207-08	50¢-1.60 fr. UNPA 40th Anniv	18.50	4.00	3.75
207-08	Miniature Sheets of 25	...	80.00	...
209-10	50¢-90¢ Human Rights	...	3.00	2.75
209-10	Strips of 3 with Tabs at Bottom...................	...	9.00	...
209-10	Miniature Sheets of 12	...	36.50	...

211   222   232

1992				
211-12	50¢-1.10 fr. World Heritage........................	20.75	4.50	4.00
213	3 fr. Regular..	16.50	3.75	3.75
214-15	80¢ Clean Oceans, attd	6.25	2.75	2.50
214-15	Miniature Sheet of 12	...	19.50	...
216-19	75¢ UNICED: Earth Summit, attd	6.25	5.25	4.95
216-19	Sheet of 40	...	55.00	...
220-21	1.10 fr. Mission to Planet Earth, attd............	14.50	6.00	5.00
220-21	Miniature Sheet of 10	...	30.00	...
222-23	90¢-1.60 fr. Science & Technology	20.75	4.50	4.25
224-25	50¢-90¢ Human Rights	...	2.75	2.50
224-25	Strips of 3 with Tabs at Bottom...................	...	8.25	...
224-25	Miniature Sheets of 12	...	35.00	...

Scott's No.		MI Block of 4	F-VF NH	F-VF Used
	1993			
226-27	50¢-1.60 fr. Aging with Dignity	20.75	4.25	3.75
228-31	80¢ Endangered Species, attd	23.50	5.00	5.00
228-31	Miniature Sheet of 16	...	22.50	...
232-33	60¢-1 fr. Healthy Environments	21.00	4.50	4.00
234-35	50¢-90¢ Declaration of Human Rights	...	2.90	2.75
234-35	Strips of 3 with Tabs at Bottom	...	9.70	...
234-35	Miniature Sheets of 12	...	40.00	...
236-39	60¢ Peace Day, attd	11.00	10.00	9.00
236-39	Sheet of 40	...	100.00	...
240-43	1.10 fr. Environment - Climate, attd..........(8)	33.50	7.25	6.75
240-43	Miniature Sheet of 24	...	40.75	...

244   255   258

	1994			
244-45	80¢-1 fr. Year of the Family	17.50	3.75	3.25
246-49	80¢ Endangered Species, attd	6.50	5.50	5.00
246-49	Miniature Sheet of 16	...	22.75	...
250	1.20 fr. Refugees	16.00	3.50	3.25
251-54	60¢ Natural Disaster, Block of 4	9.50	8.25	7.95
251-54	Sheet of 40	...	80.00	...
255-57	60¢,80¢,1.80 fr. Regulars	24.50	5.25	4.75
258-59	60¢-80¢ Population Development	17.50	3.75	3.50
260-61	80¢-1 fr. Development Partnership	16.50	3.50	3.50

262   263   268

	1995			
262	80¢ U.N. 50th Anniversary	8.50	1.80	1.65
263	1 fr Social Summit	8.75	1.85	1.85
264-67	80¢ Endangered Species, attd	6.75	5.95	5.95
264-67	Miniature Sheet of 16	...	23.50	...
268-69	80¢ 1 fr Youth: Our Future	22.50	4.95	4.75
270-71	60¢-180 fr 50th Anniv. of U.N.	22.50	4.95	4.75
272	2.40 fr 50th Anniv. Souv. Sheet of 2	...	5.95	5.95
273-74	60¢-1 fr Conference on Women	21.50	4.75	4.50
275	30¢ U.N. 50th Anniv. Sheetlet - 12	...	19.50	19.50
276	30¢ U.N. 50th Anniv. Souvenir, Booklet of 12	...	24.50	...

280-83

Scott's No.		MI Block of 4	F-VF NH	F-VF Used
	1996			
277	80¢ WFUNA 50th Anniversary.	8.25	1.80	1.65
278-79	40¢-70¢ Regular Issues	8.75	1.90	1.70
280-83	80¢ Endangered Species, attd	6.00	5.25	4.50
280-83	Miniature Sheet of 16	...	20.75	...
284-88	70¢ City Summit, Strip of 5 ....(10)	16.50	7.00	6.95
284-88	Miniature Sheet of 25	...	35.00	...
289-90	70¢-1.10 fr Sport & Environment	17.50	3.75	3.75
291	70¢-1.10 fr Sport & Environment, Souv. Sheet...	...	3.75	3.75
292-93	90¢-1.10 fr Plea for Peace	17.50	3.75	3.75
294-95	70¢-1.80 fr UNICEF 50th Anniversary	18.75	4.00	3.95
294-95	Miniature Sheets of 8	...	30.00	...

	1997			

297   298-301

296-97	10¢-1.10 fr Regulars	9.75	2.00	1.95
298-301	80¢ Endangered Species, attd	6.95	5.95	4.95
298-301	Miniature Sheet of 16	...	23.75	...

302-5   312-13

307-11

302-5	45¢ Earth Summit	3.50	3.00	2.25
302-5	Miniature Sheet of 24	...	17.75	...
306	1.10fr Earth Summit, Souvenir Sheet	...	1.90	1.75
307-11	70¢ Transportation, 5 designs ....(10)	10.75	5.00	5.00
307-11	70¢ Transportation, Sheetlet of 20	...	19.95	...
312-13	70¢-1.10fr Tribute to Philately, set of 2	13.95	2.95	2.95
314-15	45¢-70¢ Terracotta Warriors	12.50	2.85	2.75
316	fr. 240 Terracotta Warriors Prestige Booklet with 6 10¢ Blocks of 4	...	4.75	...
316a-f	Set of singles from #316 (6)	...	1.95	1.95

318-21   324

Scott's No.		MI Block of 4	F-VF NH	F-VF Used
317	2 fr. Palais des Nations, Geneva, Regular Issue	14.50	2.95	2.75
318-21	80¢ Endangered Species	5.75	4.95	4.50
318-21	Miniature Sheet of 16	...	19.75	...
322	45¢ Year of the Ocean, Miniature Sheet of 12	...	8.95	...
323	70¢ Rainforest	5.95	1.25	1.15
323	Rainforest, Sheet of 20	...	24.50	...
324	2 fr.Rainforest, Souvenir Sheet	...	3.50	3.25
325-26	70¢ 90¢ Peacekeeping (2)	10.00	2.25	2.10
325-26	Peacekeeping, Sheets of 20	...	43.50	...
327-28	90¢ - 1.80fr Human Rights (2)	16.75	3.75	3.50
327-28	Human Rights, Sheets of 20	...	73.50	...
329-30	70¢-1.10fr Schonnbrun Palace (2)	12.75	2.75	2.65
329-30	Schonnbrun Palace, Sheets of 20	...	54.00	...
331	Schonnbrun Palace, Prestige Booklet with Six Booklet Panes of 3 or 4	...	5.95	...
331a-f	10¢-30¢ Set of Singles from booklet	...	2.10	...

1999

332	1.70fr Palais de Wilson Regular Issue	12.75	2.75	2.35
333-34	90¢-1.10fr World Heritage-Australia	14.75	3.35	2.75
333-34	Australia, Sheetlets of 20 (2)	...	65.00	...
335	Australia, Prestige Booklet with Six Bk. Panes of 4		5.75	...
335a-f	10¢-20¢ Set of singles from booklet	...	2.10	...
336-39	90¢ Endangered Species, (4)	6.35	5.50	4.75
336-39	Endangered Species, Sheetlet of 16	...	21.50	...
...	45¢ UNISPACE III, Pair	...	.75	...
...	UNISPACE III, Miniature Sheet of 10	...	3.75	...
...	2 fr UNISPACE III, Souvenir Sheet	...	3.35	...
...	70¢ Universal Postal Union (4)	4.95	4.25	2.75
...	UPU, Sheetlet of 20	...	20.95	...

U.N. OFFICES IN GENEVA   1969-98

1-331	Complete	...	460.00	...

UX1

Scott's No.		Mint Entire	Scott's No.		Mint Entire
GENEVA AIRLETTER SHEET			**GENEVA POSTAL CARDS**		
UC1	65¢ Plane (1969)	1.00	UX9	50¢+10¢ Surch (93)	2.25
			UX10	80¢ Palais des Nations (1993)	3.00
GENEVA POSTAL CARDS			UX11	50¢ + 20¢ Surcharge on #UX5 (1996)	2.50
UX1	20¢ Post Horn (1969)	.35			
UX2	30¢ Earth (1969)	.35	UX12	80¢ + 30¢ Surcharge on #UX10.(1996)	2.50
UX3	40¢ Emblem (1977)	.40			
UX4	70¢ Ribbons (1977)	.50	UX13	70¢ Assembly Hall	1.20
UX5	50¢ "UN" Emblm (85)	4.50	UX14	1.10 fr.Palais des Nations	1.75
UX6	70¢ Peace Dove(85)	4.00			
UX7	70¢ + 10¢ Surch (86)	3.50			
UX8	90¢ Gen Offices (92)	2.50			

	5	8	9	12

1979 Regular Issue

1-6	50g,1s,4s,5s,6s,10s Regulars	9.50	1.95	1.95

1980

7	4s New Economic Order ....19.50 (TP)	9.50 (B)	.75	.75
8	2.50s Regular, Dove	1.50	.35	.35
9-10	4s-6s Decade for Women	4.75	1.00	1.00
11	6s Peacekeeping Operations	2.75	.60	.60
12-13	4s-6s 35th Anniversary of U.N.	5.25	1.15	1.15
14	4s-6s 35th Anniv. - Souv. Sheet of 2	...	.70	.70
15-16	4s-6s Economic & Social Council	5.25	1.15	1.10

(TP)= Top Position, (B)=Bottom

	21	22	27

1981

17	4s Palestinian People	2.35	.50	.50
18-19	4s-6s Disabled Persons	5.75	1.25	1.25
20	6s Art, Bulgarian Mural	4.50	.95	.90
21	7.50s Energy Conference	4.25	.90	.90
22-23	5s-7s Volunteers Program	7.00	1.50	1.50

1982

24	3s Regular, Better World	2.25	.50	.45
25-26	5s-7s Human Environment	7.00	1.50	1.50
27	5s Peaceful Use of Outer Space	3.50	.75	.70
28-29	5s-7s Nature Conservation	7.00	1.50	1.50

	30	31	33

1983

30	4s Communications Year	2.35	.50	.50
31-32	4s-6s Safety at Sea	5.75	1.25	1.25
33-34	5s-7s World Food Program	6.75	1.40	1.40
35-36	4s-8.50s Trade & Development	7.25	1.50	1.40
37-38	5s-7s Human Rights, 35th Anniversary	7.50	1.60	1.50
37-38	Sheetlets of 16	...	24.50	...

1984

39	7s Population Conference	3.95	.85	.80
40-41	4.50-6s FAO Food Day	5.75	1.25	1.20
42-43	3.50-15s UNESCO, World Heritage	9.25	2.00	2.00
44-45	4.50-8.50s Refugee Futures	9.75	2.10	2.10
46-47	3.50-6.50s Youth Year	8.00	1.75	1.65

	48	49	57

Scott's No.		MI Block of 4	F-VF NH	F-VF Used
	1985			
48	7.50s ILO - Turin Centre	5.25	1.15	1.10
49	8.50s U.N. Univ. in Japan	5.75	1.25	1.20
50-51	4.50-15s Regulars	15.00	3.25	3.25
52-53	6.50-8.50s 40th Anniversary of U.N.	15.00	3.25	3.00
54	6.50-8.50 40th Anniv. Souvenir Sht of 2	...	3.50	3.50
55-56	4s-6s UNICEF, Child Survival	13.50	2.85	2.75
	1986			
57	8s Africa in Crisis, Anti-Hunger	4.25	1.10	1.10
58-61	4.50s UN Dev. Program, attd	10.00	8.75	8.25
58-61	Sheet of 40	...	90.00	...
62-63	3.5s-6.5s Philately, Stamp Collecting	7.50	1.60	1.50
64-65	5s-6s Int'l. Peace Year	11.00	2.25	2.25
66	4s,5s,6s,7s WFUNA S/S of 4	...	5.00	4.95

	67	70	84

	1987			
67	8s Trygve Lie	6.00	1.25	1.20
68-69	4s-9.50s Shelter for Homeless	10.75	2.25	2.25
70-71	5s-8s Life Yes/Drugs No	8.95	1.90	1.85
72-73	2s-17s Regulars	12.00	2.65	2.50
74-75	5s-6s U.N. Day	10.75	2.25	2.25
74-75	Miniature Sheet of 12	...	27.50	...
76-77	4s-9.50s Child Immunization	17.50	3.75	3.50
	1988			
78-79	4s-6s World Without Hunger	9.00	1.95	1.90
80-81	4s-5s Forest Conservation, pair	19.75	8.50	8.00
80-81	Miniature Sheet of 12	...	45.00	...
82-83	6s-7s Int'l. Volunteers Day	13.50	2.75	2.50
84-85	6s-8s Health in Sports	14.00	3.00	2.75
86	5s Human Rights 40th Anniv	4.25	.90	.85
87	11s Human Rights 40th Anniv. S/S	...	2.25	2.15

	90	93	101	121

	1989			
88-89	5.50s-8s World Bank	17.50	3.75	3.50
90	6s Peace Keeping, Nobel Prize	5.35	1.15	1.10
91-92	4s-9.50s World Weather Watch	20.75	4.50	4.00
93-94	5s-7.50s UN Offices in Vienna, 10th Anniv.	29.50	6.75	5.75
94-94	Miniature Sheets of 25	...	195.00	...
95-96	4s-6s Human Rights 40th Anniv	...	2.50	2.50
95-96	Strips of 3 with Tabs at Bottom	...	7.50	...
95-96	Miniature Sheets of 12	...	32.50	...
	1990			
97	12s International Trade Center	9.50	2.00	2.00
98	1.50s Regular	1.95	.40	.35
99-100	5s-11s Fight Against AIDS	18.75	4.00	3.75
101-02	4.5s-9.5s Medicinal Plants	18.75	4.00	4.00
103-04	7s-9s UN 45th Anniversary	20.75	4.35	5.50
105	7s-9s UN 45th Anniversary S/S of 2	...	6.00	3.75
106-07	6s-8s Crime Prevention	18.75	4.00	2.50
108-09	4.5s-7s Human Rights	...	2.50	3.00
108-09	Strips of 3 with Tabs at Bottom	...	7.50	...
108-09	Miniature Sheets of 12	...	32.50	...
	1991			
110-13	5s Europe Econ. Commission, attd	6.50	5.50	5.00
114-15	6s-9.50s Namibia Independence	23.75	5.00	4.75
116	20s Regular	17.50	3.75	3.50
117-18	7s-9s Children's Rights	19.50	4.25	3.75
119-20	5s-10s Chemical Weapons Ban	20.75	4.50	4.25
121-22	5s-8s UNPA 40th Anniv	16.50	3.50	3.25
121-22	Miniature Sheets of 25	...	65.00	...
123-24	4.50s-7s Human Rights	...	3.00	3.00
123-24	Strips of 3 with Tabs at Bottom	...	9.00	...
123-24	Miniature Sheets of 12	...	39.50	...

137   149   150

Scott's No.		MI Block of 4	F-VF NH	F-VF Used
1992				
125-26	5s-9s World Heritage	20.75	4.50	4.00
127-28	7s Clean Oceans, attd	7.25	3.25	3.00
127-28	Miniature Sheet of 12	...	25.00	...
129-32	5.5s UNICED: Earth Summit, attd	7.25	6.50	6.00
129-32	Sheet of 4	...	65.00	...
133-34	10s Mission to Planet Earth, attd	14.00	6.25	6.00
133-34	Miniature Sheet of 10	...	39.50	...
135-36	5.5s-7s Science & Technology	13.50	2.85	2.75
137-38	5.5s-7s Regulars	15.00	3.25	3.00
139-40	6s-10s Human Rights	...	4.00	3.75
139-40	Strips of 3 with Tabs at Bottom	...	12.00	...
139-40	Miniature Sheets of 12	...	50.00	...
1993				
141-42	5.5s-7s Aging with Dignity	15.00	3.25	3.00
143-46	7s Endangered Species, attd	6.50	5.75	5.50
143-46	Miniature Sheet of 16	...	24.50	...
147-48	6s-10s Healthy Environments	20.75	4.50	3.95
149	13s Reglaur, Globe	13.00	2.75	2.50
150-51	5s-6s Human Rights	...	3.50	3.25
150-51	Strips of 3 with Tabs at Bottom	...	10.50	...
150-51	Miniature Sheets of 12	...	42.50	...
152-55	5.5s Peace Day, attd	11.00	9.75	8.75
152-55	Sheet of 40	...	100.00	...
156-59	7s Environment - Climate, attd ......(8)	16.50	7.50	7.00
156-59	Miniature Sheet of 24	...	42.50	...

162-65   166

	1994			
160-61	5.5s-8s Year of the Family	16.50	3.50	3.25
162-65	7s Endangered Species, attd	8.00	6.75	6.25
162-65	Miniature Sheet of 16	...	27.50	...
166	12s Refugees	14.50	2.75	2.50
167-69	50g,4s,30s Regulars	29.75	6.25	5.50
170-73	6s Natural Disaster, Block of 4	10.00	9.00	8.50
170-73	Sheet of 40	...	90.00	...
174-75	5.50s-7s Population Development	18.50	3.95	3.75
176-77	6s-7s Development Partnership	18.00	3.65	3.50

180-83

Scott's No.		**1995** MI Block of 4	F-VF NH	F-VF Used
178	7s U.N. 50th Anniversary	9.50	1.95	1.75
179	14s Social Summit	15.75	3.25	3.00
180-83	7s Endangered Species, attd	6.75	5.75	5.75
180-83	Miniature Sheet of 16	...	25.00	...
184-85	6s-7s Youth: Our Future	18.50	4.00	3.75
186-87	7s-10s 50th Anniv. of U.N.	24.50	4.75	4.50
188	17s 50th Anniv. Souv. Sheet of 2	...	8.00	7.50
189-90	5-50s-6s Conference on Women	17.50	3.75	3.50
191	3s U.N. 50th Anniv. Sheetlet - 12	...	23.50	23.50
192	3s U.N. 50th Anniv. Souvenir Booklet of 12	...	25.00	...

193   194-95

	1996			
193	7s WFUNA 50th Anniv.	8.50	1.75	1.50
194-95	1s-10s Regular Issues	12.00	2.50	2.25
196-99	7s Endangered Species	7.95	6.50	5.75
196-99	Miniature Sheet of 16	...	26.00	...
200-4	6s City Summit, Strip of 5 ......(10)	26.50	9.75	8.75
200-4	Miniature Sheet of 25	...	48.50	...
205-6	6s-7s Sport & Environment	14.50	2.95	2.75
207	6s-7s Sport & Environment Souv Sheet	...	2.95	2.75
208-9	7s-10s Plea for Peace	19.75	4.25	4.25
210-11	5.50s-8s UNICEF 50th Anniversary	15.75	3.25	3.00
210-11	Miniature Sheets of 8	...	30.00	...

212-13   218-21

	1997			
212-13	5s-6s Regulars	10.50	2.30	2.15
214-17	7s Endangered Species	7.75	6.50	5.75
214-17	Miniature Sheet of 16	...	25.75	...
218-21	3.50s Earth Summit	3.85	3.25	3.00
218-21	Miniature Sheet of 24	...	19.50	...
222	11s Earth Summit, Souvenir Sheet	...	2.50	2.25
223-27.	7s Transportation, 5 designs ......(10)	16.50	7.95	7.95

228-29   230-31

223-27	7s Transportation, Sheetlet of 20	...	31.50	..
228-29	6.50s-7s Tribute to Philately, set of 2	13.75	2.95	2.90
230-31	3s-6s Terracotta Warriors	13.50	3.00	2.85
232	24s Terracotta Warriors, Prestige Booklet with 6 1s Blocks of 4	...	5.75	...
232a-f	Set of singles from #232 (6)	...	1.95	1.95

235-38   240

U3

Scott's No.		MI Block of 4	F-VF NH	F-VF Used
1998				
233-34	6.50s-9s Regulars..........................	12.95	2.75	2.65
235-38	7s Endangered Species................	5.75	4.95	4.75
235-38	Miniature Sheet of 16..................	...	19.75	...
239	3.50s Year of the Ocean Miniature Sheet of 12	...	8.25	...
240	6.50s Rainforests	6.25	1.35	1.25
240	Rainforests, Sheet of 20..............	...	24.95	...
241	22s Rainforests, Souvenir Sheet ...	...	4.50	...
242-43	4s-7.50s Peacekeeping (2)...........	9.00	1.95	1.80
242-45	Peacekeeping, Sheets of 20..........	...	37.50	...
244-45	4.50s-7s Human Rights (2)...........	9.00	1.95	1.80
244-45	Human Rights, Sheets of 20..........	...	37.50	...
246-47	3.50's-7's Schonbrunn Palace (2)..	8.95	1.95	1.85
246-47	Schonbrunn Palace, Sheets of 20..	...	38.50	...
248	Schonbrunn Palace, Prestige Booklet with Six Booklet Panes of 3 or 4	...	5.95	...
248a-f	1s-2s Set of 6 singles from booklet.......	...	2.10	...

1999

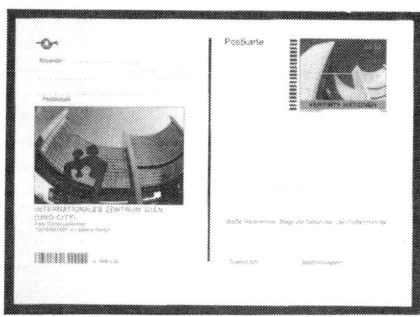

UX1

249	8s Volcanic Landscape, Regular Issue	7.50	1.60	1.50
250-51	4.50s-6.50s World Heritage-Australia	10.50	2.25	1.95
250-51	Australia, Sheetlets of 20 (2)	...	44.50	...
252	Australia, Prestige Booklet with Six B. Panes of 4	...	5.75	...
252a-f	1s-2s Set of 6 singles from booklet...............	...	1.50	...
253-56	7s Endangered Species (4)	5.65	4.75	4.25
253-56	Endangered Species, Sheetlet of 16...............	...	18.75	...
...	3.50s UNISPACE III, Pair	...	1.30	...
...	UNISPACE III, Miniature Sheet of 10	...	6.50	...
...	13s UNISPACE III, Souvenir Sheet	...	2.20	...
...	6.50's Universal Postal Union(4)	5.15	4.30	3.75
...	UPU, Sheetlet of 20	...	20.95	...

U.N. OFFICES IN VIENNA 1979-98

1-248	Complete	...	430.00	...

Scott's No.	Mint Entire	Scott's No.	Mint Entire
VIENNA ENVELOPE ENTIRES		**VIENNA POSTAL CARDS**	
U1 6s Vienna Centre (95)........	3.95	UX1 3s Branch (1982)	1.25
U2 7s Landscape (1995).........	1.95	UX2 5s Glove (1982)...................	1.00
U3 13s Lake Scene (1998).......	2.95	UX3 4s Emblem (1985)................	3.75
VIENNA AIRLETTER SHEET		UX4 5s + 1s Surch (1992)............	21.75
UC1 9s Bird (1982)	2.75	UX5 6s Regschek Paint(92)	3.75
UC2 9s + 2s Surchrg (86)	47.50	UX6 5s Peoples (1993)	11.00
UC3 11s Birds in Flight (87)	3.25	UX7 6s Donaupark (1993)	3.75
UC4 11s + 1s Surchrg (92)	52.50	UX8 5s + 50g (1994)	4.75
UC5 12s Vienna Offices (92).....	4.75	UX9 6.50s (Revalued 1992 6s Postal Card (1997)...	2.50
		UX10 7s (Revalued 1993 6s Postal Card) (1997)...	2.50
		UX11 6.50s Vienna International Center (1998)...	1.30
		UX12 7s Gloriette (1999)..........	1.40

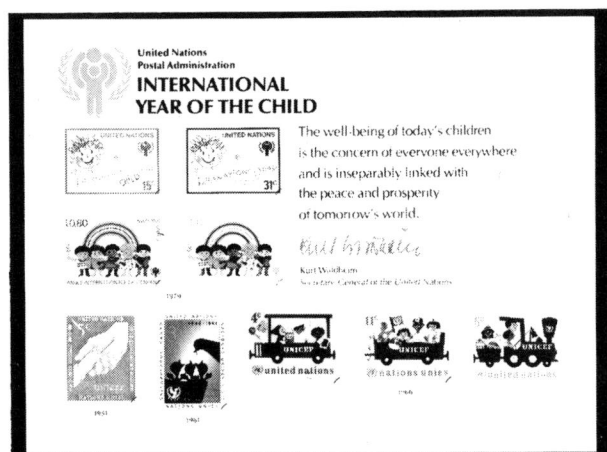

15

33 New York Cancel

			Mint	First Day of Issue		
			Card	N.Y.	Geneva	Vienna
1	World Health Day 1st Print	4/7/72	.95	18.50	175.00	...
1A	World Health Day 2nd Print	4/7/72	8.75	27.50	210.00	...
2	UN Art	11/17/72	.65	.55	.55	...
3	Disarmament	3/9/73	.75	.60	.60	...
4	Human Rights	11/16/73	.90	.55	.60	...
5	Univ. Postal Union	3/22/74	.95	.65	.65	...
6	Population Year	10/18/74	11.75	1.50	1.50	...
7	Outer Space	3/14/75	2.75	1.20	1.20	...
8	Peacekeeping	11/21/75	2.65	1.50	1.40	...
9	WFUNA	3/12/76	4.95	2.25	2.25	...
10	Food Council	11/19/76	3.00	1.50	1.50	...
11	WIPO	3/11/77	1.95	1.15	1.15	...
12	Combat Racism	9/19/77	2.10	1.15	1.15	...
13	NAMIBIA	5/5/78	1.20	1.20	1.20	...
14	Civil Aviation	6/12/78	1.75	1.10	1.10	...
15	Year of the Child	5/4/79	.60	.60	.60	...
16	Court of Justice	11/9/79	.95	1.00	1.00	...
17	Decade of Women	3/7/80	15.00	5.75	5.00	5.75
18	Econ. & Social Council	11/7/80	1.25	1.00	1.00	1.20
19	Disabled Persons	3/6/81	1.00	.90	.90	.90
20	Energy Sources	5/29/81	1.50	1.25	1.15	1.15
21	Environment	3/19/82	2.25	1.25	1.25	1.25
22	Outer Space	6/11/82	1.80	1.50	1.50	1.50
23	Safety at Sea	3/18/83	1.60	1.50	1.50	1.50
24	Trade & Development	6/6/83	2.75	1.95	1.95	1.95
25	Population	2/3/84	2.50	2.50	2.00	2.25
26	Youth Year	11/15/84	3.75	3.00	3.00	3.25
27	ILO - Turin Centre	2/1/85	4.75	3.50	3.50	3.50
28	UNICEF	11/22/85	5.00	2.75	3.25	3.25
29	Stamp Collecting	5/22/86	9.50	4.25	4.25	4.25
30	Int'l. Peace Year	6/20/86	5.00	3.25	3.00	3.00
31	Shelter for Homeless	3/13/87	4.50	3.50	3.50	3.50
32	Child Immunization	11/20/87	5.95	4.25	4.25	4.25
33	Int'l. Volunteers Day	5/6/88	8.25	4.50	4.25	4.25
34	WHO/Sports Health	6/17/88	8.25	4.50	4.25	4.25
35	World Bank	1/27/89	8.25	4.50	4.25	4.25
36	World Weather Watch	4/21/89	8.50	5.00	5.25	5.50
37	Fight Against AIDS	3/16/90	10.75	6.00	6.00	6.25
38	Crime Prevention	9/13/90	11.00	7.50	7.50	7.75
39	European Econ. Commission	3/15/91	11.00	7.50	7.50	7.75
40	Children's Rights	6/14/91	12.50	6.50	6.25	6.25
41	Mission to Planet Earth	9/4/92	23.50	12.50	12.50	12.50
42	Science And Technology	10/2/92	17.50	9.75	9.75	9.75
43	Healthy Environments	5/7/93	17.50	9.50	9.50	9.50
44	Peace	9/21/93	17.50	9.50	9.50	9.50
44A	Peace - Gold Hong Kong overprint		20.00	...	...	...
45	Year of the Family	2/4/94	15.00	9.50	9.50	9.50
46	Population - Development	9/1/94	13.50	9.50	9.75	9.75
47	Social Summit	2/3/95	12.50	9.50	9.75	9.75
48	Youth: Our Future	5/26/95	12.50	9.00	9.50	9.50
49	WFUNA 50th Anniversary	2/2/96	11.75	8.25	8.50	8.50
50	UNICEF 50th Anniversary	9/27/96	8.95	7.50	7.50	7.50

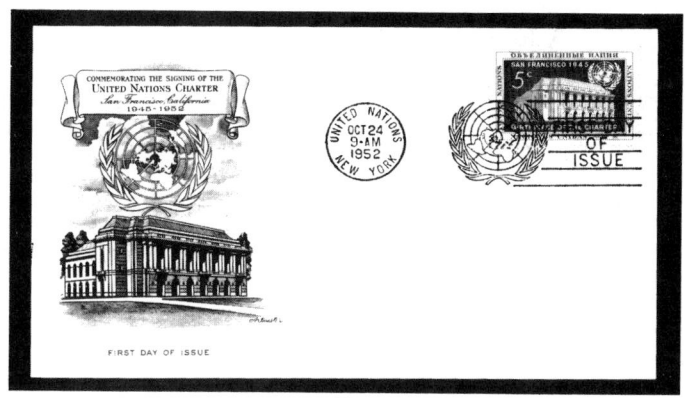

12

Scott #	Description	Separate Covers	One Cover
	NEW YORK		
	1951		
1-11	1¢-$1 Regular Issue 10/24+11/16	75.00	60.00
	1952		
12	5¢ Charter 10/24/52.........................	...	1.25
13-14	3¢-5¢ Human Rights 12/10/52	3.00	2.50
	1953		
15-16	3¢-5¢ Refugee Family 4/24/53	3.50	3.00
17-18	3¢-5¢ Univ. Postal Union 6/12/53	3.75	3.25
19-20	3¢-5¢ Tech. Assistance 10/24/53	4.00	3.50
21-22	3¢-5¢ Human Rights 12/10/54	7.00	6.00
	1954		
23-24	3¢-8¢ F.A.O. 2/11/54	3.00	2.75
25-26	3¢-8¢ Int'l. Labor Organ. 5/10/54	3.00	2.75
27-28	3¢-8¢ U.N. Euro. Office 10/25/54	3.00	2.75
29-30	3¢-8¢ Human Rights 12/10/54	8.00	6.50
	1955		
31-32	3¢-8¢ Int'l. Civil Aviat. 2/9/55	3.50	3.00
33-34	3¢-8¢ UNESCO Emblem 5/11/55	3.50	3.00
35-37	3¢-8¢ 10th Anniv. 10/24/55	4.00	3.50
38	3¢-8¢ 10th Anniversary S/S 10/24/55 ...	...	55.00
39-40	3¢-8¢ Human Rights 12/9/55	2.50	2.00
	1956		
41-42	3¢-8¢ I.T.U 2/17/56........................	2.50	2.00
43-44	3¢-8¢ W.H.O. 4/6/56......................	2.50	2.00
45-46	3¢-8¢ General Assembly 10/24/56	2.50	2.00
47-48	3¢-8¢ Human Rights 12/10/56	2.50	2.00
	1957		
49-50	3¢-8¢ Meteor Org. 1/28/57	2.50	1.50
51-52	3¢-8¢ U.N. Emerg. Force 4/8/57	2.50	1.50
55-56	3¢-8¢ Security Council 10/24/57	2.50	1.50
57-58	3¢-8¢ Human Rights 12/10/57	2.50	1.50
	1958		
59-60	3¢-8¢ Atomic Ener. Agency 2/10/58	2.50	1.50
61-62	3¢-8¢ Central Hall London 4/14/58	2.50	1.50
63-64	4¢-8¢ Reg. U.N. Seal 6/2 & 10/24	2.50	1.50
65-66	4¢-8¢ Economic & Social C. 10/24	2.50	1.50
67-68	4¢-8¢ Human Rights 12/10/58	2.50	1.50
	1959		
69-70	4¢-8¢ Flushing Meadows 3/30/59	2.50	1.50
71-72	4¢-8¢ Econ. Comm. Europe 5/18/59	2.50	1.50
73-74	4¢-8¢ Trusteeship Coun. 10/23/59	2.50	1.50
75-76	4¢-8¢ World Refugee Year 12/10/59	2.50	1.50
	1960		
77-78	4¢-8¢ Chalot Palace Paris 2/29/60	2.50	1.50
79-80	4¢-8¢ ECAFE 4/11/90	2.50	1.50
81-82	4¢-8¢ World Forestry Cong. 8/29/60	2.50	1.50
83-84	4¢-8¢ 15th Anniversary 10/24/60.........	2.50	1.50
85	4¢-8¢ 15th Anniv. S/S 10/24/60..........	...	2.75
85v	Same broken "v" 10/24	...	120.00
86-87	4¢-8¢ International Bank 12/9/60	2.50	1.50
	1961		
88-89	4¢-8¢ Court of Justice 2/13/61	2.50	1.50
90-91	4¢-7¢ Monetary Fund 4/17/61	2.50	1.50
92	30¢ Regular Flags 6/5/61	...	1.50
93-94	4¢-11¢ Econ. C. Lat. Am. 9/18/61	2.50	1.50
95-96	4¢-11¢ Econ. Comm. Africa 10/24/61 ...	2.50	1.50
97-99	3¢-13¢ Children's Fund 12/14/61	2.75	1.75

Scott #	Description	Separate Covers	One Cover
	NEW YORK		
	1962		
100-01	4¢-7¢ House & Urban Dev. 2/28/62	2.50	1.50
102-03	4¢-11¢ Wld. Health Organ. 3/30/62	2.50	1.50
104-07	1¢-4¢ Regulars 5/25/62	5.00	2.00
108-09	5¢-15¢ Hammarskjold 9/17/62	2.50	1.50
110-11	4¢-11¢ Oper. in Congo 10/24/62	2.50	1.50
112-13	4¢-11¢ Outer Space 12/3/62	2.50	1.50
	1963		
114-15	5¢-11¢ Science & Tech. 2/4/63	2.50	1.50
116-17	5¢-11¢ Freedom from Hung. 3/22/63	2.50	1.50
118	25¢ UNTEA 10/1/63	...	1.50
119-20	5¢-11¢ General Assembly 11/4/63	2.50	1.50
121-22	5¢-11¢ Human Rights 12/10/63	2.50	1.50
	1964		
123-24	5¢-11¢ Maritime Organ. 1/13/64	2.50	1.50
125-27	2¢-10¢ Regulars 5/29/64	3.75	1.75
128	50¢ Reg. Weather Vane 3/6/64	...	2.00
129-30	5¢-11¢ Trade & Develop. 6/15/64	2.50	1.50
131-32	5¢-11¢ Control Narcotics 9/21/64	2.50	1.50
133	5¢ End Nuclear Tests 10/23/64	...	1.25
134-36	4¢-11¢ Education Prog. 12/7/64	3.75	1.75
	1965		
137-38	5¢-11¢ Development Fund 1/25/65	2.50	1.50
139-40	5¢-11¢ Peace Force Cyprus 3/4/65	2.50	1.50
141-42	5¢-11¢ Telecomm. Union 5/17/65	2.50	1.50
143-44	5¢-15¢ 20th Anniv. ICY 6/26/65	2.50	1.50
145	5¢-12¢ 20th Anniv. S/S 6/26/65	...	1.75
146-49	1¢-25¢ Regulars 9/20 & 10/25/65	3.75	2.25
150	$1 Regular Emblem 3/25/65	...	3.00
151-53	4¢-11¢ Population 11/29/65	3.75	1.75
	1966		
154-55	5¢-15¢ Fed. U.N. Assoc. 1/31/66	2.50	1.50
156-57	5¢-11¢ W.H.O. Headqtrs. 5/26/66	2.50	1.50
158-59	5¢-11¢ Coffee Agreement 9/19/66	2.50	1.50
160	15¢ Peacekpg. Obsrv. 10/24/66	...	1.75
161-63	4¢-11¢ UNICEF 11/28/66	3.75	1.50
	1967		
164-65	5¢-11¢ Develop. Program 1/23/67	2.50	1.50
166-67	1½¢-5¢ Regulars 3/17 & 1/23/67	2.50	1.50
168-69	5¢-11¢ Independ. Nations 3/17/67	2.50	1.50
170-74	4¢-15¢ Expo '67 Montreal 4/28/67	5.00	4.00
175-76	5¢-15¢ Tourist Year 6/19/67	2.50	1.50
177-78	6¢-13¢ Disarmament 10/24/67	2.50	1.50
179	6¢ Chagall S/S 11/17/67..................	...	1.75
180	6¢ Chagall Window 11/17/67	...	1.50
	1968		
181-82	6¢-13¢ Secretariat 1/16/68...............	2.50	1.00
183-84	6¢-75¢ Art, Starcke Stat. 3/1/68.........	5.75	5.00
185-86	6¢-13¢ Industrial Dev. 4/18/68	2.50	1.00
187	6¢ Regular, U.N. Hdqtrs. 5/31/68	...	.75
188-89	6¢-20¢ Wld. Weather Watch 9/19/68 ...	2.50	1.00
190-91	6¢-13¢ Human Rights 11/22/68	2.50	1.00
	1969		
192-93	6¢-13¢ Train. & Res. Inst. 2/10/69......	2.50	1.50
194-95	6¢-15¢ U.N. Bldg., Chile 3/14/69.......	2.50	1.50
196	13¢ Regular U.N. & Emblem 3/14/69 ...	...	1.25
197-98	6¢-13¢ Peace Through Law 4/21/69	2.50	1.50
199-200	6¢-20¢ Labor & Dev. 6/5/69	2.50	1.50
201-02	6¢-13¢ Tunisian Mosaic 11/21/69	2.50	1.50

175-76

254-55

Scott #	Description NEW YORK 1970	Separate Covers	One Cover
203-04	6¢-25¢ Art, Peace Bell 3/13/70	2.50	1.50
205-06	6¢-13¢ Mekong Basin Dev. 3/13/70	2.50	1.50
207-08	6¢-13¢ Fight Cancer 5/22/70	2.50	1.50
209-11	6¢-25¢ 25th Anniversary 6/26/70	3.75	1.75
212	6¢-25¢ 25th Anniv. S/S 6/26/70	...	1.50
213-14	6¢-13¢ Peace, Just. & Pro. 5/20/70	2.50	1.50
	1971		
215	6¢ Peaceful Uses of the Sea 1/25/71	...	1.25
216-17	6¢-13¢ Support Refugees 3/2/71	2.50	1.50
218	13¢ World Food Program 4/13/71	...	1.25
219	20¢ U.P.U. Headquarters 5/28/71	...	1.25
220-21	8¢-13¢ Racial Discrim. 9/21/71	2.50	1.50
222-23	8¢-60¢ Regulars 10/22/71	3.00	2.00
224-25	8¢-21¢ U.N. Int'l. School 11/19/71	2.50	1.50
	1972		
226	95¢ Regular, Letter 1/5/72	...	2.50
227	8¢ No Nuclear Weapons 2/14/72	...	1.25
228	15¢ World Health Day, Man. 4/7/72	...	1.25
229-30	8¢-15¢ Human Environment 6/5/72	2.50	1.50
231	21¢ Economic Comm. Europe 9/11/72	...	1.75
232-33	8¢-15¢ Maria Sert. Mural 11/17/72	2.50	1.50
	1973		
234-35	8¢-15¢ Disarmament Decade 3/9/73	2.50	1.50
236-37	8¢-15¢ Against Drug Abuse 4/13/73	2.50	1.50
238-39	8¢-21¢ Volunteer Program 5/25/73	2.50	1.50
240-41	8¢-15¢ Namibia 10/1/73	2.50	1.50
242-43	8¢-21¢ Human Rights 11/16/73	2.50	1.50
	1974		
244-45	10¢-21¢ ILO Headquarters 1/11/74	2.50	1.50
246	10¢ U.P.U. Centenary 3/22/74	...	1.25
247-48	10¢-18¢ Art, Brazil Mural 5/6/74	2.50	1.25
249-51	2¢-18¢ Regualrs 6/10/74	3.75	1.75
252-53	10¢-18¢ Population Year 10/18/74	2.50	1.50
254-55	10¢-25¢ Law of the Sea 11/22/74	2.50	1.50
	1975		
256-57	10¢-26¢ Peaceful-O. Space 3/14/75	2.50	1.50
258-59	10¢-18¢ Women's Year 5/9/75	2.50	1.50
260-61	10¢-26¢ 30th Anniversary 6/26/75	2.50	1.50
262	10¢-26¢ 30th Anniv. S/S 6/26/75	...	1.75
263-64	10¢-18¢ Namibia 9/22/75	2.50	1.50
265-66	13¢-26¢ Peacekpg. Force 11/21/75	2.50	1.50
	1976		
267-71	3¢-50¢ Regulars 1/6 & 11/19/76	4.00	2.50
272-73	13¢-26¢ U.N. Assoc. 3/12/76	2.50	1.50
274-75	13¢-31¢ Trade & Dev. 4/23/76	2.50	1.50
276-77	13¢-25¢ Human Settlement 5/28/76	2.50	1.50
278-79	13¢-31¢ 25th Postal Ann. 10/8/76	7.75	6.75
280	13¢ World Food Council 11/18/76	...	1.25
	1977		
281-82	13¢-31¢ Intellect Prop. 3/11/77	2.50	1.50
283-84	13¢-25¢ Water Conference 4/22/77	2.50	1.50
285-86	13¢-31¢ Security Council 5/27/77	2.50	1.50
287-88	13¢-25¢ Racial Discrim. 9/19/77	2.50	1.50
289-90	13¢-18¢ Atomic Energy 11/18/77	2.50	1.50
	1978		
291-93	1¢-$1 Regulars 1/27/78	3.75	3.00
294-95	13¢-31¢ Smallpox-Erad. 3/31/78	2.50	1.50
296-97	13¢-31¢ Namibia 5/5/78	2.50	1.50
298-99	25¢ ICAO 6/12/78	2.50	1.50
300-01	13¢-18¢ General Assembly 9/15/78	2.50	1.50
302-03	13¢-31¢ Technical Coop. 11/17/78	2.50	1.50

Scott #	Description NEW YORK 1979	Separate Covers	One Cover
304-07	5¢-20¢ Regulars 1/19/79	3.75	1.75
308-09	15¢-20¢ Disaster Relief 3/9/79	2.50	1.50
310-11	15¢-31¢ Yr. of the Child 5/4/79	3.50	2.85
312-13	15¢-31¢ Namibia 10/5/79	2.50	1.50
314-15	15¢-20¢ Court of Justice 11/9/79	2.50	1.50
	1980		
316-17	15¢-31¢ New Econ. Order 1/11/80	2.50	1.75
318-19	15¢-20¢ Decade for Women 3/7/80	2.50	1.75
320-21	15¢-31¢ Peacekpg. Oper. 5/16/80	2.50	1.75
322-23	15¢-31¢ 35th Anniversary 6/26/80	2.75	1.75
324	15¢-31¢ 35th Anniv. S/S 6/26/80	...	1.30
325-40	15¢ 1980 Flag Series 9/26/80	12.00	...
341-42	15¢-20¢ Econ. & Soc. 11/21/80	1.50	1.50
	1981		
343	15¢ Palestinian People 1/30/81	...	1.50
344-45	20¢-35¢ Disabled Persons 3/6/81	2.50	1.50
346-47	20¢-31¢ Bulgarian Mural 4/15/81	2.50	1.50
348-49	20¢-40¢ Energy Conf. 5/29/81	2.50	1.50
350-65	20¢ 1981 Flag Series 9/25/81	12.00	...
366-67	18¢-28¢ Volunteers 11/13/81	2.50	1.50
	1982		
368-70	17¢-40¢ Definitives 1/22/82	3.75	2.25
371-72	20¢-40¢ Human Environ. 3/19/82	2.50	2.25
373	20¢ Peaceful, Use of Space 6/11/82	...	1.50
374-89	20¢ 1982 Wld. Flag Series 9/24/82	12.00	...
390-91	20¢-28¢ Nature Conserv. 11/19/82	2.50	2.25
	1983		
392-93	20¢-40¢ Commun. Year 1/28/83	3.00	2.00
394-95	20¢-37¢ Safety at Sea 3/18/83	3.00	2.00
396	20¢ World Food Program 4/22/83	...	1.75
397-98	20¢-28¢ Trade & Develop. 6/6/83	3.00	2.00
399-414	20¢ 1983 Flag Series 9/23/83	13.50	...
415-16	20¢-40¢ Human Rights 12/9/83	3.00	2.25
	1984		
417-18	20¢-40¢ Population Conf. 2/3/84	2.50	1.75
419-20	20¢-40¢ FAO Food Day 3/15/84	2.50	1.75
421-22	20¢-50¢ UNESCO 4/18/84	2.50	2.00
423-24	20¢-50¢ Refugee Futures 5/29/84	2.50	1.85
425-40	20¢ 1984 Flag Series 9/20/84	17.00	...
441-42	20¢-35¢ Youth Year 11/15/84	2.50	1.75
	1985		
443	23¢ ILO-Turin Centre 2/1/85	...	1.75
444	50¢ U.N. Univ. in Japan 3/15/85	...	2.25
445-46	22¢-$3 Definitives 5/10/85	7.00	6.00
447-48	22¢-45¢ 40th Anniv. 6/26/85	3.50	3.00
449	22¢-45¢ 40th Anniv. S/S 6/26/85	...	3.00
450-65	22¢ 1985 Flag Series 9/20/85	18.00	...
466-67	22¢-33¢ UNICEF 11/22/85	2.50	1.75
	1986		
468	22¢ Africa in Crisis 1/31/86	...	1.75
469-72	22¢ UN Dev. & Prog. attd. 3/14/86	...	6.00
469-72	UN Dev. & Prog., set of 4 singles	7.00	...
473-74	22¢-44¢ Philately 5/22/86	3.00	2.00
475-76	22¢-33¢ Int'l. Year of Peace 6/20/86	2.75	1.75
477-92	22¢ 1986 World Flag Series 9-19-86	17.00	...
493	22¢,33¢,39¢,44¢ WFUNA S/S 11/14/86	...	5.50
	1987		
494	22¢ Trygve Lie 1/30/87	...	2.00
495-96	22¢-44¢ Shelter for the Homeless 3/13/87	2.75	2.00
497-98	22¢-33¢ Life Yes/Drugs No 6/12/87	2.50	1.75
499-514	22¢ 1987 World Flag Series 9/18/87	18.00	...
515-16	22¢-39¢ U.N. Day 10/23/87	2.75	2.00
517-18	22¢-44¢ Child Immunization 11/20/87	2.75	2.00

493

C19-21

Scott #	Description NEW YORK	Separate Covers	One Cover
	1988		
519-20	22¢-33¢ World Without Hunger 1/29/88	2.50	1.75
521	3¢ UN For a Better World 1/29/88	...	2.00
522-23	25¢-50¢ Forest Conservation 3/18/88	10.00	8.00
524-25	25¢-50¢ Int'l. Volunteers Day 5/6/88	2.50	2.00
526-27	25¢-38¢ Health in Sports 6/17/88	2.50	2.15
528-43	25¢ World Flag Series of 16 9/19/88	16.00	...
544-45	25¢,$1 S/S Human Rights Anniv. 12/9/88	5.00	3.75
	1989		
546-47	25¢-45¢ World Bank 1/27/89	4.00	3.00
548	25¢ UN Peace Force, Nobel Prize 3/17/89	...	2.50
549	45¢ UN Headquarters 3/17/89	...	2.50
550-51	25¢-36¢ World Weather Watch 4/21/89	2.50	2.00
552-53	25¢-90¢ UN Of. in Vienna Anniv. 8/23/89	3.50	2.50
554-69	25¢ World Flags Series of 16 9/22/89	17.00	...
570-71	25¢-45¢ Human Rights 11/17/89	2.50	2.00
570-71	Strips of 3 with tabs on bottom	8.50	...
	1990		
572	25¢ International Trade Center 2/2/90	...	2.00
573-74	25¢-40¢ Fight Against AIDS 3/16/90	2.50	2.00
575-76	25¢-90¢ Medicinal Plants 5/4/90	3.50	2.50
577-78	25¢-45¢ UN 45th Anniversary 6/26/90	3.50	2.50
579	25¢-45¢ UN 45th Anniversary S/S	...	4.25
580-81	25¢-36¢ Crime Prevention 9/13/90	2.50	2.00
582-83	25¢-45¢ Human Rights 11/16/90	2.50	2.00
582-83	Strips of 3 with tabs on bottom	8.50	...
	1991		
584-87	30¢ Eur. Econ. Commission attd. 3/15/91	8.00	6.00
588-89	30¢-50¢ Namibia 5/10/91	3.00	2.50
590-91	30¢-50¢ Definitives 9/11/91	3.00	2.50
592	$2 UN Headquarters Definitive 5/10/91	...	5.00
593-94	30¢-70¢ Children's Rights 6/14/91	3.50	2.75
595-96	30¢-90¢ Chemical Weapons Ban 9/11/91	4.00	3.25
597-98	30¢-40¢ UNPA 40th Anniv. 10/24/91	3.00	2.25
599-600	30¢-50¢ Human Rights 11/20/91	3.00	2.50
599-600	Strips of 3 with tabs on bottom	8.00	...
	1992		
601-02	30¢-50¢ World Heritage 1/24/92	3.50	3.00
603-04	29¢ Clean Oceans attd. 3/13/92	3.00	2.50
605-08	29¢ UNICED: Earth Summit attd. 5/22/92	6.00	3.50
609-10	29¢ Mission to Planet Earth attd. 9/4/92	4.50	3.75
611-12	29¢-50¢ Science & Technology 10/2/92	3.00	2.50
613-15	4¢,29¢,40¢ Definitives 10/2/92	4.50	2.50
616-17	29¢-50¢ Human Rights S/S 12/10/92	3.50	2.75
616-17	Strips of 3 with tabs on bottom	7.00	...
	1993		
618-19	29¢-52¢ Aging 2/5/93	3.00	2.35
620-23	29¢ Endangered Species attd. 3/3/93	5.00	3.00
624-25	29¢-50¢ Healthy Environments 5/7/93	3.00	2.50
626	5¢ Definitive 5/7/93	...	2.00
627-28	29¢-35¢ Human Rights 6/11/93	3.00	2.50
627-28	Strips of 3 with tabs on bottom	7.50.	...
629-32	29¢ Peace attd. 9/21/93	5.00	4.00
633-36	29¢ Environment - Climate 10/29/93	5.00	4.00
	1994		
637-38	29¢-45¢ Year of the Family 2/4/94	3.00	2.50
639-42	29¢ Endangered Species 3/18/94	5.00	4.00
643	50¢ Refugees 4/29/94	...	1.75
644-46	10¢,19¢,$1 Definitives 4/29/94	3.75	2.75
647-50	29¢ Natural Disaster 5/27/94	5.00	4.00
651-52	29¢-52¢ Population-Development 9/1/94	3.00	2.50
653-54	29¢-50¢ Development Partnership 10/28/94	3.00	2.50
	1995		
655	32¢ U.N. 50th Anniversary 1/1/95	...	2.50
656	50¢ Social Summit 2/3/95	...	2.25
657-60	32¢ Endangered Species 3/24/95	5.00	4.00
661-62	32¢-55¢ Youth: Our Future 5/26/95	4.00	3.00
663-64	32¢-50¢ 50th Anniv. of U.N. 6/26/95	4.00	3.00
665	82¢ 50th Anniv. Souv. Sheet 6/26/95	...	4.50
666-67	32¢-40¢ Conference on Women 9/5/95	3.00	2.50
668	20¢ Definitive 9/5/95	...	1.50
669	32¢ U.N. 50th Anniv. Souv. Sheet 10/24/95	21.00	25.00
670	32¢ U.N. 50th Anniv. Souv. Bklt. of 12 10/24/95	28.00	29.00
671	32¢ WFUNA 50th Anniv. 2/2/96	...	1.50
672-73	32¢-60¢ Regular Issues 2/2/96	3.00	2.50
674-77	32¢ Endangered Species 3/14/96	5.00	4.00

NOTE:"HUMAN RIGHTS" ALL CAN COME AS 6 ON 1, 2 W/STRIP OF 3 EACH, 3 W/2 STAMPS EACH

Scott #	Description NEW YORK	Separate Covers	One Cover
	1996		
678-82	32¢ City Summit, Strip of 5 6/3/96	...	3.25
683-84	32¢-50¢ s/s Sports&Envir.,7/19/96 Atlanta, GA.	3.45	2.75
683-84	32¢-50¢ s/s Sport & Environment, NY, 7/19/96	3.10	2.40
686-87	32¢-60¢ Plea For Peace, 9/17/96	3.20	2.50
688-89	32¢ - 60¢ UNICEF 50th Anniv., 11/20/96	3.20	2.50
	1997		
690-97	32¢ Flags of New Countries (8) 2/12/97	12.50	...
698-99	8¢ - 55¢ Regulars, Flowers 2/12/97	3.00	2.80
700-3	32¢ Endangered Species 3/13/97	5.00	2.75
704-7	32¢ Earth Summit 5/30/97	6.75	3.00
708	$1 Earth Summit, S/S 5/30/97	...	4.00
708a	$1 Pacific '97 Overprint on #708 5/30/97	...	4.50
709-713	32¢ Transportation (strips of 5) 8/29/97	...	4.00
714-715	32¢,50¢ Tribute to Philately,10/14/97	4.00	3.00
716-717	32¢,60¢ Terracotta Warriors,11/19/97	4.00	3.00
	1998		
719-726	32¢ Flags of New Countries (8),2/13/98	14.00	5.50
727-729	1¢,2¢,21¢ Regulars, 2/13/98	4.75	3.00
730-733	32¢ Endaegred Species, 3/13/98	3.20	3.00
734	32¢ Year of the Ocean, Sheet of 12, 5/20/98	...	7.00
735	32¢ Rain Forest, 4 designs, 6/19/98	5.50	3.00
736	$2 Rain Forest, S/S, 6/19/98	...	3.50
737-38	33¢-40¢ Peacekeeping	3.00	2.50
739-40	32¢-55¢ Human Rights	3.25	2.75

Airmail Issues

Scott #	Description	Separate Covers	One Cover
	1951-59		
C1-4	6¢-25¢ 1st Airmail Issue 12/14/51	25.00	17.50
C5-7	4¢-7¢ Airmail 5/27/57 & 2/9/59	2.25	...
	1963-69		
C8-10	6¢-13¢ Airmail 6/17/63	3.75	2.00
C11-12	15¢ & 25¢ Airmail 5/1/64	2.50	1.50
C13	20¢ Jet Plane 4/18/68	...	1.50
C14	10¢ Wings & Envelopes 4/21/69	...	1.50
	1972-77		
C15-18	9¢-21¢ Airmail 5/1/72	3.00	2.00
C19-21	13¢-26¢ Airmail 9/16/74	3.00	2.00
C22-23	25¢ & 31¢ Airmail 6/27/77	3.00	2.00

U.N. Postal Stationery
Stamped Envelopes

Scott #	Description	Separate Covers	One Cover
U1	3¢ Emblem 9/15/53	...	4.25
U2	4¢ Emblem 9/22/58	...	1.50
U3	5¢ Weather Vane 4/26/63	...	1.50
U4	6¢ Weather Vane 4/26/63	...	1.50
U5	8¢ Headquarters 1/12/73	...	1.50
U6	10¢ Headquarters 1/10/75	...	1.50
U7	22¢ Bouquet 5/10/85	...	2.00
U8	25¢ UN Headquarters 3/17/89	...	2.25
U9	25¢ + 4¢ Surcharge on U8 4/15/91	...	2.00
U10	32¢ Cripticondia (97), 2/12/97 (#63/4 env.)	...	2.00
U10	32¢ Cripticondia (97), 2/12/97 (#10 env.)	...	2.50
UC3	7¢ Flag and Plane 9/21/59	...	1.50
UC6	8¢ Emblem 4/26/63	...	1.50
UC8	10¢ Emblem 1/8/69	...	1.50
UC10	11¢ Birds 1/12/73	...	1.50
UC11	13¢ Globe 1/10/75	...	1.50

Airletter Sheets

Scott #	Description	Separate Covers	One Cover
UC1	10¢ Air Letter 8/29/52	...	6.75
UC2	10¢ Air Letter/Aerogramme 9/14/54(white border)	...	75.00
UC2a	10¢ same, no white border, 1958	...	...
UC4	10¢ Flag 1/18/60	...	...
UC5	11¢ Gull, Blue 6/26/61	...	1.50
UC5a	11¢ Gull (greenish) (1965)	...	...
UC7	13¢ Plane 5/31/68	...	1.50
UC9	15¢ Globe 10/16/72	...	1.50
UC12	18¢ Headquarters 1/10/75	...	1.50
UC13	22¢ Birds 6/27/77	...	1.50
UC14	30¢ Airplane 4/28/82	...	3.25
UC15	30¢ + 6¢ Surcharge on UC14 7/7/87	...	12.50
UC16	39¢ UN Headquarters 3/17/89	...	9.00
UC17	39¢ + 6¢ Surcharge on UC16 2/12/91	...	2.50
UC18	45¢ Winged Hand 9/4/92	...	2.00
UC19	45¢,5¢ Surcharge on UC18 (95)	...	...
UC20	50¢ Cherry Blossom Airletter 3/13/97	...	5.00

Postal Cards

Scott #	Description	Separate Covers	One Cover
UX1	2¢ Headquarters 7/18/52	...	1.50
UX2	3¢ Headquarters 9/22/58	...	1.50
UX3	4¢ Map 4/26/63	...	1.50
UX4	5¢ Post Horn 1/8/69	...	1.50
UX5	6¢ "UN" 1/12/73	...	1.50
UX6	8¢ "UN" 1/10/75	...	1.50
UX7	9¢ Emblem 6/27/77	...	1.50
UX8	13¢ Letters 4/28/82	...	1.50
UX9-13	15¢ UN Headquarters, 5 Diff. Views 3/17/89	...	20.00
UX14-18	36¢ UN Headquarters, 5 Diff. Views 3/17/89	...	22.00
UX19	40¢ U.N. Headquarters 9/4/92	...	1.50

Airmail Postal Cards

Scott #	Description	Separate Covers	One Cover
UXC1	4¢ Wing 5/27/57	...	1.50
UXC2	4¢ + 1¢ 6/8/59 (first day of public use)	...	40.00
UXC3	5¢ Wing 9/21/59	...	1.50
UXC4	6¢ Space 4/26/63	...	1.50
UXC5	11¢ Earth 6/9/66	...	1.50
UXC6	13¢ Earth 5/31/68	...	1.50
UXC7	8¢ Plane 1/8/69	...	1.50
UXC8	9¢ Wing 10/16/72	...	1.50
UXC9	15¢ Planes 10/16/72	...	1.50
UXC10	11¢ Clouds 1/10/75	...	1.50
UXC11	18¢ Pathways 1/10/75	...	1.50
UXC12	28¢ Flying Mailmen 4/28/82	...	1.50

1

Scott #	Description GENEVA	Separate Covers	One Cover
	1969-70		
1-14	5¢-10¢ fr. Regular 10/4 + 9/22	40.00	...
	1971		
15	30¢ Peaceful Use of Sea 1/25/71	...	1.50
16	50¢ Support for Refugees 3/12/71	...	1.50
17	50¢ World Food Program 4/13/71	...	1.50
18	75¢ U.P.O. Headquarters 5/28/71	...	1.75
19-20	30¢-50¢ Racial Discrim. 9/21/71	2.50	2.00
21	1.10 fr. Int'l. School 11/19/71	...	3.35
	1972		
22	40¢ Palace of Nations 1/15/72	...	1.50
23	40¢ No Nuclear Weapons 2/14/72	...	2.50
24	80¢ World Health Day 4/7/72	...	1.50
25-26	40¢-80¢ Human Environment 6/5/72	3.50	2.50
27	1.10 fr. Econ. Comm. Europe 9/11/72	...	3.00
28-29	40¢-80¢ Sert Mural 11/17/72	3.35	3.00
	1973		
30-31	60¢-1.10 Disarm. Decade 3/9/73	3.35	3.00
32	60¢ Against Drug Abuse 4/13/73	...	1.50
33	80¢ Volunteer Program 5/25/73	...	2.00
34	60¢ Namibia 10/1/73	...	1.75
35-36	40¢-80¢ Human Rights 11/16/73	2.50	2.00
	1974		
37-38	60¢-80¢ ILO Headqtrs. 1/11/74	2.65	2.15
39-40	30¢-60¢ UPU Centenary 3/22/74	2.50	1.85
41-42	60¢-1 fr. Brazil Mural 5/6/74	2.75	2.40
43-44	60¢-80¢ Population Year 10/18/74	2.40	2.15
45	1.30 fr. Law of the Sea 11/22/74	...	2.15
	1975		
46-47	60¢-90¢ Peace - Out. Space 3/14/75	2.50	2.00
48-49	60¢-90¢ Women's Year 5/9/75	2.65	2.40
50-51	60¢-90¢ 30th Anniv. 6/26/75	2.50	2.00
52	30¢ Anniv. S/S 6/26/75	...	2.50
53-54	50¢-1.30 fr. Namibia 9/22/75	2.75	2.25
55-56	60¢-70¢ Peacekpg. Force 11/21/75	2.50	2.00
	1976		
57	90¢ U.N. Association 3/12/76	...	1.75
58	1.10 fr. Trade & Develop. 4/23/76	...	1.90
59-60	40¢-1.50 fr. Human Settle. 5/28/76	2.75	2.40
61-62	80¢-1.10 fr. 25th Post Ann. 10/8/76	9.00	8.00
63	70¢ World Food Council 11/19/76	...	1.75
	1977		
64	80¢ Intellect Prop. 3/11/77	...	1.75
65-66	80¢-1.10 fr. Water Conf. 4/22/77	2.75	2.40
67-68	80¢-1.10 fr. Sec. Count. 5/29/77	2.75	2.40
69-70	40¢-1.10 fr. Racial Disc. 9/19/77	2.50	2.10
71-72	80¢-1.10 fr. Atom. Energy 11/18/77	2.80	2.45
	1978		
73	35¢ Regular 1/27/78	...	1.50
74-75	80¢-1.10 fr. Smallpox 3/31/78	2.75	2.40
76	80¢ Namibia 5/5/78	...	1.50
77-78	70¢-80¢ Civil Aviat. Org. 6/12/78	2.50	1.90
79-80	70¢-1.10 fr. Gen. Assem 9/15/78	2.85	2.50
81	80¢ Technical Coop. 11/19/78	...	1.50
	1979		
82-83	80¢-1.50 fr. Disaster Relief 3/9/79	2.95	2.60
84-85	80¢--1.10 fr. Year of Child 5/4/79	4.50	3.75
86	1.10 fr. Namibia 10/5/79	...	1.75
87-88	80¢-1.10 fr. Court of Just. 11/9/79	2.85	2.50

Scott #	Description GENEVA	Separate Covers	One Cover
	1980		
89	80¢ New Econ. Organ. 1/11/80	...	1.50
90-91	40¢-70¢ Dec. for Women 3/7/80	2.50	1.60
92	1.10 fr. Peacekpg. Force 5/16/80	...	1.70
93-94	40¢-70¢ 35th Anniv. 6/26/80	2.50	1.60
95	40¢-70¢ 35th Anniv. S/S 6/26/80	...	2.50
96-97	40¢-70¢ Econ. & Social Co. 11/21/80	2.50	1.50
	1981		
98	80¢ Palestinian People 1/30/81	...	1.50
99-100	40¢-1.50 fr. Disabled Persons 3/6/81	2.50	2.25
101	80¢ Bulgarian Mural 4/15/81	...	1.50
102	1.10 fr. Energy Conf. 5/29/81	...	1.50
103-04	40¢-70¢ Volunteers 11/13/81	1.85	1.60
	1982		
105-06	30¢-1 fr. Definitives 1/22/82	1.95	1.70
107-08	40¢-1.20 fr. Human Environ. 3/19	2.25	2.00
109-10	80¢-1 fr. Peac. Use of Space 6/11	2.50	2.25
111-12	40¢-1.50 fr. Nat. Cons. 11/19/82	2.85	2.50
	1983		
113	1.20 fr. Commun. Year 1/28/83	...	2.00
114-15	40¢-80¢ Safety at Sea 3/28/83	1.60	1.50
116	1.50 fr. World Food Prog. 4/22/83	...	2.50
117-18	80¢-1.10 fr. Trade & Dev. 6/6/83	3.00	2.75
119-20	40¢-1.20 fr. Human Rights 12/9	3.25	2.90
	1984		
121	1.20 fr. Population Conf. 2/3/84	...	2.00
122-23	50¢-80¢ FAO Food Day 3/15/84	2.00	1.75
124-25	50¢-70¢ UNESCO 4/18/84	2.35	2.10
126-27	35¢-1.50 fr. Refugee 5/29/84	2.75	2.40
128	1.20 fr. Youth Year 11/15/84	...	2.00
	1985		
129-30	80¢-1.20 fr. ILO-Turin Centre 2/1	3.25	2.50
131-32	50¢-80¢ UN Univ. of Japan 3/15/85	3.00	2.00
133-34	20¢-1.20 fr. Definitives 5/10/85	3.00	2.50
135-36	50¢-70¢ 40th Anniversary 6/26/85	3.00	2.50
137	50¢-70¢ 40th Anniv. S/S 6/26/85	...	3.00
138-39	50¢-4 fr. UNICEF 11/22/85	4.00	3.00
	1986		
140	1.40 fr. Africa in Crisis 1/31	...	2.75
141-44	35¢ UN Dev. attd. 3/14/86	...	7.50
141-44	UN Dev. set of 4 singles	8.50	...
145	5¢ Definitive 3/14/86	...	1.50
146-47	50¢-80¢ Philately 5/22/86	3.00	2.00
148-49	45¢-1.40 fr. Int. Peace 6/20/86	3.25	2.50
150	35¢,45¢,50¢,70¢ WFUNA S/S 11/14/86	...	5.00
	1987		
151	1.40 fr. Trygve Lie 1/30/87	...	3.00
152-53	90¢-1.40 fr. Bands/Sphere Definitives 1/30/87	3.00	2.75
154-55	50¢-90¢ Shelter for the Homeless 3/13/87	3.00	2.50
156-57	80¢-1.20 fr. Life Yes/Drugs No 6/12/87	3.00	2.50
158-59	50¢-1.70 fr. U.N. Day 10/23/87	3.25	2.75
160-61	35¢-90¢ Child Immunization 11/20/87	3.00	2.75
	1988		
162-63	35¢-1.40 fr. World Without Hunger 1/29/88	3.00	2.50
164	50¢ UN For a Better World 1/29/88	...	2.00
165-66	50¢-1.40 fr. Forest Conservation 3/18/88	10.50	9.50
167-68	80¢-90¢ Int'l. Volunteers Day 5/6/88	3.00	2.50
169-70	50¢-1.40 fr. Health in Sports 6/17/88	3.00	2.50
171-72	90¢,2 fr. S/S Human Rts. Decl. Anniv. 12/9/88	4.25	3.75
	1989		
173-74	80¢-1.40 fr. World Bank 1/27/89	3.00	2.50
175	90¢ UN Peace Force, Nobel Prize 3/17/89	...	2.00
176-77	90¢-1.10 fr. World Weather Watch 4/21/89	3.00	2.50
178-79	90¢-2 fr. UN Offices in Vienna Anniv. 8/23/89	3.50	3.00
180-181	35¢-80¢ Human Rights 11/17/89	3.00	2.50
180-181	Strips of 3 with tabs on bottom	8.00	...

119-20

182

UC 1

Scott #	Description	Separate Covers	One Cover
GENEVA			
1990			
182	1.50 fr. International Trade Center 2/2/90	...	2.50
183	5 fr. Definitive 2/2/90	...	7.00
184-85	50¢-80¢ Fight Against AIDS 3/16/90	3.00	2.50
186-87	90¢-1.40 fr. Medicinal Plants 5/4/90	3.25	3.00
188-89	90¢-1.10 fr. UN 45th Anniversary 6/26/90	3.00	2.50
190	90¢-1.10 fr. UN 45th Anniversary S/S 6/26/90	...	8.50
191-92	50¢-2 fr. Crime Prevention 9/13/90	4.00	3.25
193-94	35¢-90¢ Human Rights 11/16/90	3.00	2.50
....	Strips of 3 with tabs on bottom	7.75	...
1991			
195-98	90¢ Eur. Econ. Commission attd. 3/15/91	6.00	5.00
199-200	70¢-90¢ Namibia 5/10/91	4.00	3.00
201-02	80¢-1.50 fr. Definitives 5/10/91	4.50	3.75
203-04	80¢-1.10 fr. Children's Rights 6/14/91	4.00	3.25
205-06	80¢-1.40 fr. Chemical Weapons Ban 9/11/91	4.50	3.75
207-08	50¢-1.60 fr. UNPA 40th Anniv. 10/24/91	4.25	3.50
209-10	50¢-90¢ Human Rights 11/20/91	7.00	5.75
209-10	Strips of 3 with tabs on bottom	8.00	...
1992			
211-12	50¢-1.10 fr. World Heritage 1/24/92	3.50	3.00
213	3 fr. Definitive 1/24/92	...	7.00
214-15	80¢ Clean Oceans attd. 3/13/92	3.50	3.00
216-19	75¢ UNICED: Earth Summit attd. 5/22/92	8.00	5.00
220-21	1.10 fr. Mission to Planet Earth attd. 9/4/92	4.75	3.75
222-23	90¢-1.60 fr. Science & Technology 10/2/92	6.00	4.25
224-25	50¢-90¢ Human Rights 12/10/92	6.00	3.25
224-225	Strips of 3 with tabs on bottom	7.00	...
1993			
226-27	50¢-1.60 fr. Aging 2/5/93	4.25	3.50
228-31	80¢ Endangered Species, block of 4 3/3/93	7.00	4.75
232-33	60¢-1 fr. Healthy Environments 5/7/93	3.75	3.00
234-35	50¢-90¢ Human Rights 6/11/93	6.00	3.50
234-235	Strips of 3 with tabs on bottom	7.00	...
236-39	60¢ Peace, block of 4, attd. 9/21/93	8.00	5.00
240-43	1.10 fr. Environment - Climate 10/29/93	8.00	5.00
1994			
244-45	80¢-1 fr. Year of the Family 2/4/94	4.00	3.00
246-49	80¢ Endangered Species 3/18/94	7.25	5.50
250	1.20 fr. Refugees 4/29/94	...	2.50
251-54	60¢ Natural Disaster 5/24/94 (4)	6.00	4.50
255-57	60¢,80¢,1.80 fr. Definitives 9/1/94	8.00	6.25
258-59	60¢-80¢ Population Development 9/1/94	3.50	2.75
260-61	80¢-1 fr. Development Partnership 10/28/94	4.00	3.25
262	80¢ U.N. 50th Anniversary 1/1/95	...	2.00
263	1 fr Social Summit 2/3/95	...	2.25

Scott #	Description	Separate Covers	One Cover
GENEVA			
1995			
264-67	80¢ Endangered Species 3/24/95	6.95	4.50
268-69	80¢-1 fr Youth: Our Future 5/26/95	4.00	3.25
270-71	60¢-1.80 fr 50th Anniv. of U.N. 6/26/95	5.25	4.25
272	2.40 fr 50th Anniv. Souv. Sheet 6/26/95	...	5.00
273-74	60¢-1 fr Conference on Women 9/5/95	4.00	3.50
275	30¢ U.N. 50th Anniv. Souv. Sheet 10/24/95	40.00	30.00
276	30¢ U.N. 50th Anniv. Souv. Bklt. of 12 10/24/95	42.50	30.00
1996			
277	80¢ WFUNA 50th Anniversary 2/2/96	...	2.00
278-79	40¢-70¢ Definitives 2/2/96	3.75	3.00
280-83	80¢ Endangered Species 3/14/96	7.25	5.50
284-88	70¢ City Summit Strip of 5 6/3/96	...	6.75
289-90	70¢ - 1.10fr Sport & Environment 7/19/96	4.25	3.50
291	70¢ - 1.10fr Sport & Environment s/s 7/19/96	...	4.25
292-93	90¢ - 1.10fr Plea For Peace 9/17/96	4.00	3.50
294-95	70¢ - 1.80fr UNICEF 50th Anniversary 11/20/96	4.25	3.75
1997			
296-97	10¢ - 1.10fr Regulars 2/12/97	3.25	2.75
298-301	80¢ Endangered Species 3/13/97	6.95	5.00
302-5	45¢ Earth Summit 5/30/97	8.75	3.50
306	1.10fr Earth Summit, S/S 5/30/97	...	2.50
307-11	70¢ Transportation , 5 designs 8/29/97	8.90	5.00
312-13	70¢ 1.10fr Tribute to Philately 10/14/97	4.75	4.50
314-15	45¢,70¢ Terracotta Warriors 11/19/97	3.75	3.25
1998			
317	2fr Definitive, 2/13/98	...	3.00
318-21	80¢ Endangered Species, 4/22/99	5.75	4.25
322	45¢ Year of the Ocean	...	7.75
323	70¢ Rain Forest	...	...
327-28	90¢ 1.80 Fr Peacekeeping (2), 9/15/98	4.00	2.25
329-30	70¢ 1.10 Fr Schonburn Palace, 12/4/98	3.00	2.75
GENEVA AIRLETTER SHEETS			
UC1	65¢ Plane 10/4/69	...	4.75
GENEVA POSTAL CARDS			
UX1	20¢ Post Horn 10/4/69	...	1.85
UX2	30¢ Earth 10/4/69	...	2.00
UX3	40¢ Emblem 6/27/77	...	1.90
UX4	70¢ Ribbons 6/27/77	...	2.00
UX5	50¢ "UN" Emblem 5/10/85	...	1.95
UX6	70¢ Peace Dove 5/10/85	...	2.25
UX7	70¢ + 10¢ Surcharge on UX6 1/2/86	...	8.75
UX8	90¢ Letters 9/4/92	...	2.25
UX9	50¢ + 10¢ Surcharge on UX5 5/7/93	...	2.25
UX10	80¢ Palais des Nations 5/7/93	...	2.00
UX11	50¢ + 20¢ Surcharge on UX5	...	8.25
UX12	80¢ + 30¢ Surcharge on UX10	...	8.25
UX13	70¢ Assembly Hall	...	2.00
UX14	$1.10 Fr Palaisdes Nations	...	2.25

UNITED NATIONS
Peace-Keeping
Operations
1980

11

Scott #	Description	Separate Covers	One Cover
	VIENNA		
1-6	50g-10s Regular Issue 8/24/79	6.00	5.00
	1980		
7	4s Economic Order 1/11/80	...	3.35
8	2.50s Regular, Dove 1/11/80	...	1.50
9-10	4s-6s Decade for Women 3/7/80	2.75	2.50
11	6s Peacekeeping Forces 5/16/80	...	1.75
12-13	4s-6s 35th Anniversary 6/26/80	2.85	2.60
14	4s-6s 35th Anniv. S/S 6/26/80	...	3.50
15-16	4s-6s Econ. & Soc. Coun. 11/21/80	2.10	1.85
	1981		
17	4s Palestinian People 1/30/81	...	1.40
18-19	4s-6s Disabled Persons 3/6/81	2.50	2.25
20	6s Art, Bulgarian Mural 4/15/81	...	1.50
21	7.50s Energy Conference 5/29/81	...	1.75
22-23	5s-7s Volunteers 11/13/81	2.75	2.50
	1982		
24	3s Definitive 1/22/81	...	1.50
25-26	5s-7s Human Environment 3/19/82	2.25	2.00
27	5s Peaceful Use of Space 6/11/82	...	1.50
28-29	5s-7s Nature Conserv. 11/16/82	2.25	2.00
	1983		
30	4s Communications Yr. 1/28/83	...	1.50
31-32	4s-6s Safety at Sea 3/18/83	2.50	2.25
33-34	5s-7s World Food Prog. 4/22/83	2.50	2.25
35-36	4s-8.50s Trade & Dev. 6/6/83	2.50	2.25
37-38	5s-7s Human Rights 12/9/83	2.85	2.50
	1984		
39	7s Population Conf. 2/3/84	...	1.75
40-41	4.50s-6s FAO Food Day 3/15/84	2.50	2.00
42-43	4.50s-8.50s UNESCO 3/15/84	3.00	2.75
44-45	4.50s-8.50s Refugee 3/29/84	2.50	2.00
46-47	3.50s-6.50s Youth Year 11/15/84	2.50	2.00
	1985		
48	7.50s ILO-Turin Centre 2/1/85	...	2.00
49	8.50s UN Univ. of Japan 3/15/85	...	2.00
50-51	4.50s-15s Definitives 5/10/85	2.85	2.50
52-53	6.50s-8.50s 40th Anniv. 6/26/85	2.50	2.25
54	6.50s-8.50s 40th Anniv. S/S 6/26/85	...	3.50
55-56	4s-6s UNICEF 11/22/85	2.25	2.00
	1986		
57	8s African Crisis 1/31/86	...	1.50
58-61	4.50s UN Dev. attd. 3/14/86	...	2.75
58-61	UN Dev. set of 4 singles	5.00	...
62-63	3.50s-6.50s Philately 5/22	2.50	2.00
64-65	6s-7s Int. Year 6/20/86	3.00	2.50
66	3.50s,4s,5s,6s WFUNA S/S 11/14/86	...	7.00
	1987		
67	8s Trygve Lie 1/30/87	...	1.50
68-69	4s-9.50s Shelter for Homeless 3/13/87	3.50	3.00
70-71	5s-8s Life Yes/Drugs No 6/12/87	3.50	3.00
72-73	2s-17s Definitives 6/12/87	3.75	3.25
74-75	5s-6s U.N. Day 10/23/87	3.50	3.00
76-77	4s-9.50s Child Immunization 11/20/87	3.50	3.00
	1988		
78-79	4s-6s World Without Hunger 1/29/88	3.00	3.00
80-81	4s-5s Forest Conservation 3/18/88	9.50	8.00
82-83	6s-7.50s Int'l Volunteers Day 5/6/88	3.00	2.50
84-85	6s-8s Health in Sports 6/17/88	2.25	3.00
86-87	5s-11s Human Rights Decl. Anniv. 12/9/88	4.00	3.50
	1989		
88-89	5.5s-8s World Bank 1/27/89	3.75	3.00
90	6s UN Peace Force, Nobel Prize 3/17/89	...	2.00
91-92	4s-9.5s World Weather Watch 4/21/89	3.50	3.00
93-94	5s-7.5s UN Offices in Vienna Anniv. 8/23/89	4.50	4.00
95-96	4s-6s Human Rights 11/17/89	5.00	4.50
95-96	Strips of 3 with tabs on bottom	7.00	...
	1990		
97	12s International Trade Center 2/2/90	...	3.00
98	1.5s Definitive 2/2/90	...	2.00
99-100	5s-11s Fight Against AIDS 3/16/90	3.50	3.00
101-02	4.5s-9.5s Medicinal Plants 5/4/90	3.50	3.00
103-04	7s-9s UN 45th Anniversary 6/26/90	3.50	3.00
105	7s-9s UN 45th Anniversary S/S	...	7.00

Scott #	Description	Separate Covers	One Cover
	VIENNA		
106-07	6s-8s Crime Prevention 9/13/90	3.75	3.25
108-09	4.5s-7s Human Rights 11/16/90	6.75	6.00
108-09	Strips of 3 with tabs on bottom	7.50	...
	1991		
110-13	5s Eur. Econ. Commission attd. 3/15/91	7.00	6.00
114-15	6s-9.50s Namibia 5/10/91	4.75	3.75
116	20s Definitive 5/10/91	...	4.25
117-18	7s-9s Children's Rights 6/14/91	4.00	3.25
119-20	5s-10s Chemical Weapons Ban 9/11/91	4.25	3.50
121-22	5s-8s UNPA 40th Anniv. 10/24/91	3.75	3.00
123-24	4.50s-7s Human Rights 11/20/91	7.00	6.00
123-24	Strips of 3 with tabs on bottom	8.00	...
	1992		
125-26	5s-9s World Heritage 1/24/92	3.75	3.25
127-28	7s Clean Oceans attd. 3/13/92	3.75	3.25
129-32	5.5s UNICED: Earth Summit. 5/22/92	6.00	4.95
133-34	10s Mission to Planet Earth attd. 9/4/92	4.95	4.50
135-36	5.5s-7s Science & Technology 10/2/92	3.40	3.00
137-38	5.5s-7s Definitives 10/2/92	3.40	3.00
139-40	6s-10s Human Rights 12/10/92	4.50	3.75
139-40	Strips of 3 with tabs on bottom	7.75	...
	1993		
141-42	5.5s-7s Aging 2/5/93	3.40	3.00
143-46	7s Endangered Species, block of 4 3/3/93	7.00	5.75
147-48	6s-10s Healthy Environments 5/7/93	4.00	3.75
149	13s Definitive 5/7/93	...	2.75
150-51	5s-6s Human Rights 6/11/93	6.50	5.00
150-511	Strips of 3 with tabs on bottom	7.25	...
152-55	5.5s Peace, block of 4, attd. 9/21/93	12.00	6.00
156-59	7s Environment - Climate 10/29/93	14.00	7.00
	1994		
160-61	5.5s-8s Year of the Family 2/4/94	4.25	3.50
162-65	7s Endangered Species 3/18/94	6.50	5.50
166	12s Refugees 4/29/94	...	2.75
167-69	50g,4s,30s Definitives 4/29/94	8.25	6.75
170-73	6s Natural Disaster 5/24/94 (4)	18.00	8.00
174-75	5.50s-7s Population Development 9/1/94	3.65	2.85
176-77	6s-7s Development Partnership 10/28/94	3.75	2.95
	1995		
178	7s U.N. 50th Anniversary 1/195	...	2.75
179	14s Social Summit 2/3/95	...	3.75
180-83	7s Endangered Species 3/24/95	6.50	5.50
184-85	6s-7s Youth: Our Future 5/26/95	3.75	2.95
186-87	7s-10s 50th Anniv. of U.N. 6/26/95	3.75	3.50
188	17s 50th Anniv. Souv. Sheet 6/2/65	...	4.75
189-90	5.50s-6s Conference on Women 9/5/95	3.75	3.25
191	3s U.N. 50th Anniv. Sheetlet of 12 10/24/95	40.00	27.50
192	3s U.N. 50th Anniv. Souv. Booklet of 12 10/24/95 47.00	42.00	
	1996		
193	7s WFUNA 50th Anniversary 2/2/96	...	2.00
194-95	1s – 10¢ Regular Issues 2/2/96	3.50	3.00
196-99	7s Endangered Species 3/14/96	6.50	5.50
200-4	6s City Summit, Strip of 5 6/3/96	...	5.25
205-6	6s - 7s Sport & Environment 7/19/96	3.75	3.50
207	6s - 7s Sport & Environment S/S 7/19/96	...	3.50
208-9	7s - 10s Plea For Peace 9/17/96	4.25	3.75
210-11	5.50s - 8s UNICEF 50th Anniversary 11/20/96	3.00	2.60
	1997		
212-13	5s - 6s Regulars 2/12/97	3.00	2.75
0214-17s	Endangered Species 3/13/97	6.95	5.25
218-21	3.50s Earth Summit 5/30/97	8.50	5.25
222	11s Earth Summit, S/S, 5/30/97	...	3.00
223-27	7s Transportation, 5 designs, 8/29/97	8.95	5.25
228-29	6.50s – 7s Tribute to Philately, 10/14/97	4.75	4.50
230-31	3s-6s Terracotta Warriors, 11/19/97	3.75	3.25
	1998		
233-34	6.50s – 9s Definitives, 2/13/98	3.50	3.00
239	3.50s Year of Ocean, Mini-sheet	...	6.00
240	6.50s Rain Forests	...	1.50
242-43	4s – 7.50s Peacekeeping, 9/15/98	3.00	2.50
244-45	4.50s – 7 Human Rights	3.00	2.50
246-47	3.50s – 7s Schonbrun Palace, 12/4/98	3.00	2.50
	1999		
235-38	7s Endangered Species, 4/22/99	6.00	5.00
	VIENNA ENVELOPE ENTIRES		
U1	6s Vienna Centre	...	5.95
U2	7s Landscape	...	6.50
	VIENNA AIRLETTER SHEETS		
UC1	9s Bird 4/28/82	...	7.95
UC2	9s + 2s Surcharge on UC1 2/3/86	...	35.00
UC3	11s Birds in Flight 1/30/87	...	11.00
UC4	11s+1s Surcharge (1992)	...	...
UC5	12s Donaupark 9/4/92	...	...
	VIENNA POSTAL CARDS		
UX1	3s Branch 4/28/82	...	3.50
UX2	5s Glove 4/28/82	...	11.00
UX3	4s Emblem 5/10/85	...	6.75
UX4	5s + 1s Surcharge on UX2 1/1/92	...	13.00
UX5	6s Regschek Painting 9/4/92	...	10.50
UX6	5s Peoples 5/7/93	...	12.00
UX7	6s Donaupark 5/7/93	...	11.00
UX8	5s+50g (1994)	...	...

CANADA

| 1,4 | 2,5,10 | 7 | 8 | 9 |

PROVINCE OF CANADA
1851 Laid Paper, Imperforate (OG + 50%) (C)

Scott's No.		Unused		Used	
		Fine	Ave.	Fine	Ave.
1	3p Beaver, Red	...	...	500.00	300.00
2	6p Albert, Grayish Purple	...	...	795.00	435.00

1852-1857 Wove Paper, Imperforate (OG + 50%) (C)

4	3p Beaver, Red, Thick Paper	750.00	450.00	110.00	65.00
4d	3p Thin Paper	825.00...	500.00	130.00	90.00
5	6p Albert, Slate Gray	...	...	700.00	375.00
7	10p Cartier, Blue	...	...	700.00	400.00
8	½p Victoria, Rose	400.00	240.00	300.00	190.00
9	7½p Victoria, Green	...	...	1250.00	675.00
10	6p Albert, Reddish Purple, Thick	...	...	...	1300.00

1858-59 Wove Paper, Perforated 12 (OG + 50%) (C)

11	½p Victoria, Rose	...	850.00	600.00	325.00
12	3p Beaver, Red	...	1300.00	300.00	200.00
13	6p Albert, Brown Violet	...	...	...	1650.00

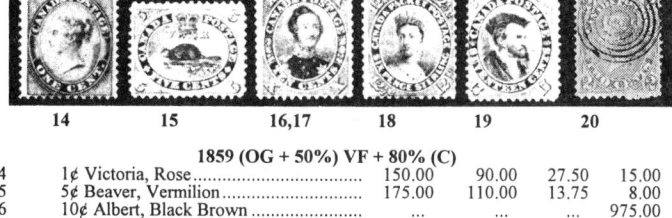

| 14 | 15 | 16,17 | 18 | 19 | 20 |

1859 (OG + 50%) VF + 80% (C)

14	1¢ Victoria, Rose	150.00	90.00	27.50	15.00
15	5¢ Beaver, Vermilion	175.00	110.00	13.75	8.00
16	10¢ Albert, Black Brown	...	...	...	975.00
17	10¢ Red Lilac	375.00	235.00	45.00	27.50

CANADA
1859-64 (OG + 50%) (VF + 60%) (C)

Scott's No.		Unused		Used	
		Fine	Ave.	Fine	Ave.
18	12½¢ Victoria, Yellow Green	350.00	225.00	45.00	25.00
19	17¢ Cartier, Blue	450.00	240.00	70.00	37.50
20	2¢ Victoria, Rose (1864)	225.00	150.00	120.00	80.00

DOMINION OF CANADA
1868-1876 Large "Cents" Issue, Perf. 12 (OG +30%) VF + 80% (C)

| 21 | 22-23,31 | 25,33 | 26 | 29-30 |

21	½¢ Victoria, Black	40.00	23.50	27.50	15.00
21a	½¢ Perf. 11½ x 12	45.00	26.50	30.00	16.50
21c	½¢ Thin Paper	45.00	27.00	37.50	21.50
22	1¢ Brown Red	275.00	165.00	37.50	25.00
22a	1¢ Watermarked	...	...	180.00	105.00
22b	1¢ Thin Paper	290.00	175.00	37.50	25.00
23	1¢ Yellow Orange	475.00	275.00	70.00	40.00
24	2¢ Green	250.00	150.00	30.00	16.50
24a	2¢ Watermarked	...	850.00	150.00	100.00
24b	2¢ Thin Paper	350.00	225.00	35.00	19.50
25	3¢ Red	500.00	280.00	13.50	7.25
25a	3¢ Watermarked	1650.00	850.00	135.00	85.00
25b	3¢ Thin Paper	550.00	325.00	17.50	11.00
26	5¢ Olive Green, Perf. 11½ x 12	575.00	325.00	100.00	55.00
27	6¢ Dark Brown	650.00	395.00	40.00	25.00
27b	6¢ Watermarked	...	1500.00	650.00	375.00
27c	6¢ Thin Paper	850.00	500.00	85.00	50.00
28	12½¢ Blue	350.00	195.00	50.00	27.50
28a	12½¢ Watermarked	1125.00	600.00	140.00	90.00
28b	12½¢ Thin Paper	475.00	275.00	60.00	38.50
29	15¢ Gray Violet	35.00	22.50	18.50	11.50
29a	15¢ Perf. 11½ x 12	475.00	250.00	90.00	52.50
29b	15¢ Red Lilac	450.00	300.00	50.00	25.00
29c	15¢ Gray Violet Wmkd	...	1400.00	375.00	210.00
29e	15¢ Gray Violet, Thin Paper	375.00	235.00	65.00	40.00
30	15¢ Gray	35.00	21.00	17.50	10.00
30a	15¢ Perf. 11½ x 12	500.00	300.00	90.00	50.00

1868 Laid Paper, Perf. 12 (OG + 30%) VF + 80% (C)

Scott's No.		NH Fine	Unused Fine	Unused Ave.	Used Fine	Used Ave.
31	1¢ Brown Red	...	...		2100.00	1100.00
33	3¢ Bright Red	...	...		400.00	225.00

34   35   37,41   44   46

1870-1889 Small "Cents" Issue, Perf. 12 (OG + 20%) VF + 80% (C)

		NH Fine	Fine	Ave.	Fine	Ave.
34	½¢ Victoria Black	10.50	4.75	2.75	4.25	2.40
35	1¢ Yellow	30.75	15.00	8.00	.50	.30
35a	1¢ Orange	110.00	50.00	32.50	5.25	3.15
35d	1¢ Orange, Pf. 11½ x 12	210.00	100.00	60.00	12.50	7.00
36	2¢ Green	42.50	20.00	13.50	.80	.50
36d	2¢ Blue Green	85.00	40.00	22.50	2.50	1.50
36e	2¢ Green, Pf. 11½ x 12	325.00	150.00	85.00	15.00	9.25
37	3¢ Dull Red	90.00	40.00	22.50	1.50	.80
37a	3¢ Rose	550.00	250.00	150.00	6.50	3.75
37b	3¢ Copper Red	...	675.00	375.00	27.50	15.00
37c	3¢ Orange Red	85.00	40.00	22.50	1.15	.65
37d	3¢ Cop. Red 12½ x 12	...	...	...	525.00	350.00
37e	3¢ Red, Perf. 11½ x 12	285.00	135.00	75.00	7.50	4.50
38	5¢ Slate Green	425.00	200.00	110.00	10.75	7.25
38a	5¢ Ol. Gr., Pf. 11½ x 12	650.00	295.00	180.00	30.00	18.75
39	6¢ Yellow Brown	400.00	175.00	90.00	9.50	6.50
39b	6¢ Brown, 11½ x 12	700.00	300.00	185.00	20.00	13.50
40	10¢ Dull Rose Lilac	550.00	240.00	140.00	30.00	20.00
40c	10¢ Rose Ll., 11½ x 12	1200.00	500.00	265.00	165.00	95.00

1888-1893 Small "Cents" Issue, Perf. 12 (OG + 20%) VF + 80% (C)

41	3¢ Bright Vermilion	28.00	13.50	7.00	.25	.15
41a	3¢ Rose Carmine	475.00	225.00	120.00	6.50	4.15
42	5¢ Gray	85.00	40.00	21.50	2.50	1.50
43	6¢ Red Brown	75.00	35.00	18.75	7.50	4.15
43a	6¢ Chocolate	235.00	110.00	60.00	17.50	10.75
44	8¢ Gray (1893)	90.00	42.50	22.50	2.50	1.40
45	10¢ Brown Red	235.00	110.00	60.00	22.50	12.50
46	20¢ Vermilion (1893)	350.00	165.00	95.00	45.00	25.00
47	50¢ Deep Blue (1893)	350.00	165.00	110.00	42.50	23.50

1897 Jubilee Issue VF Used + 60% (B)

50   55   60

Scott's No.		NH VF	NH F-VF	Unused VF	Unused F-VF	Used F-VF
50	½¢ Victoria, Black	185.00	110.00	85.00	50.00	52.50
51	1¢ Orange	20.00	12.00	9.50	5.50	4.00
52	2¢ Green	32.50	18.50	15.00	8.75	7.00
53	3¢ Bright Rose	18.00	10.00	8.50	5.00	1.35
54	5¢ Deep Blue	75.00	42.50	35.00	20.00	13.50
55	6¢ Yellow Brown	375.00	210.00	175.00	100.00	95.00
56	8¢ Dark Violet	75.00	40.00	35.00	20.00	17.50
57	10¢ Brown Violet	160.00	95.00	75.00	45.00	45.00
58	15¢ Steel Blue	335.00	180.00	160.00	87.50	80.00
59	20¢ Vermillion	360.00	210.00	175.00	100.00	85.00
60	50¢ Ultramarine	380.00	225.00	165.00	110.00	95.00
61	$1 Lake	1300.00	800.00	650.00	400.00	325.00
62	$2 Dark Purple	2000.00	1250.00	1000.00	625.00	325.00
63	$3 Yellow Bistre	2500.00	1450.00	1200.00	700.00	575.00
64	$4 Purple	2500.00	1450.00	1200.00	700.00	575.00
65	$5 Olive Green	2500.00	1450.00	1200.00	700.00	550.00

66   74   85-86   87

1897-1898 Issue, Maple Leaves in Four Corners, VF Used + 60% (B)

		NH VF	NH F-VF	Unused VF	Unused F-VF	Used F-VF
66	½¢ Victoria, Black	11.00	7.00	5.75	3.75	3.50
67	1¢ Blue Green	26.50	15.75	13.50	8.00	.65
68	2¢ Purple	29.50	16.50	15.00	8.50	.90
69	3¢ Carmine (1898)	35.00	21.00	18.00	11.00	.25
70	5¢ Dark Blue	130.00	80.00	65.00	40.00	3.50
71	6¢ Brown	125.00	75.00	62.50	37.50	15.75
72	8¢ Orange	195.00	62.50	100.00	60.00	5.50
73	10¢ Brown Violet (1898)	325.00	200.00	165.00	100.00	40.00

1898-1902 Issue, Numerals in Lower Corners VF Used + 60% (B)

74	½¢ Victoria, Black	4.25	2.50	2.25	1.35	1.00
75	1¢ Gray Green	24.75	14.50	13.00	7.75	.15
76	2¢ Purple	24.00	14.00	12.50	7.50	.15
77	2¢ Carmine, Die I (1898)	30.00	18.00	15.75	9.50	.15
77a	2¢ Carmine, Die II	31.50	19.00	16.50	10.00	.25
78	3¢ Carmine	43.50	26.00	22.50	13.50	.40
79	5¢ Blue	170.00	105.00	90.00	55.00	.80
80	6¢ Brown	180.00	110.00	95.00	57.50	23.50
81	7¢ Olive Yellow (1902)	135.00	80.00	72.50	42.50	10.00
82	8¢ Orange	265.00	160.00	140.00	85.00	10.75
83	10¢ Brown Violet	350.00	210.00	185.00	110.00	10.00
84	20¢ Olive Green (1900)	625.00	385.00	325.00	200.00	50.00

1898 Imperial Penny Post VF Used + 50% (B)

85	2¢ Map, Blk. Lav. Carm	37.50	25.00	21.00	13.50	4.00
86	2¢ Black, Blue, Carmine	37.50	25.00	21.00	13.50	4.00

1899 Surcharges VF Used + 60% (B)

87	2¢ on 3¢ Carmine (on #69)	16.00	9.50	8.00	5.00	3.00
88	2¢ on 3¢ Carmine (on #78)	26.50	16.00	14.00	8.50	2.50

89   96   100

1903-1908 King Edward VII VF Used + 60% (B)

89	1¢ Edward VII, Green	25.00	15.00	13.50	8.00	.15
90	2¢ Carmine	25.00	15.00	13.50	8.00	.15
90a	2¢ Imperforate Pair	57.50	37.50	37.50	25.00	...
91	5¢ Blue	125.00	75.00	70.00	42.50	2.00
92	7¢ Olive Bistre	87.50	55.00	47.50	30.00	2.00
93	10¢ Brown Lilac	210.00	120.00	110.00	65.00	4.00
94	20¢ Olive Green	575.00	375.00	315.00	195.00	16.50
95	50¢ Purple (1908)	850.00	525.00	450.00	275.00	50.00

1908 Quebec Tercentenary VF + 65% (B)

96-103	Set of 8	835.00	525.00	450.00	265.00	215.00
96	½¢ Prince & Princess	7.25	4.25	3.75	2.25	2.25
97	1¢ Cartier & Champlain	16.00	9.75	8.75	5.25	2.40
98	2¢ Alexandria & Edward	24.00	14.50	13.00	8.00	.70
99	5¢ Champlain's Home	67.50	40.00	35.00	21.00	20.00
100	7¢ Montcalm & Wolfe	135.00	85.00	72.50	45.00	30.00
101	10¢ 1700 View of Quebec	145.00	90.00	77.50	47.50	40.00
102	15¢ Champlain Heads West	210.00	125.00	110.00	65.00	52.50
103	20¢ Cartier Arrival	290.00	180.00	155.00	95.00	85.00

104-105   116-118   135   140

1912-1925 "Admiral Issue" Perf. 12 VF Used + 50% (B)

104-22	Set of 18	850.00	570.00	500.00	330.00	24.50
104	1¢ George V. Green	12.00	8.00	6.75	4.50	.15
104a	1¢ Booklet Pane of 6	35.00	23.50	23.75	15.00	...
105	1¢ Yellow (1922)	11.50	7.50	6.50	4.25	.15
105a	1¢ Booklet Pane of 4	70.00	47.50	45.00	30.00	...
105b	1¢ Booklet Pane of 6	70.00	47.50	45.00	30.00	...
106	2¢ Carmine	9.50	6.25	5.25	3.50	.15
106a	2¢ Booklet Pane of 6	38.50	25.50	26.50	17.50	...
107	2¢ Yellow Green (1922)	8.75	6.00	4.85	3.25	.15
107a	2¢ Thin Paper	9.50	6.50	5.25	3.50	1.50
107b	2¢ Booklet Pane of 4	87.50	57.50	57.50	37.50	...
107c	2¢ Booklet Pane of 6	425.00	290.00	300.00	200.00	...
108	3¢ Brown (1918)	15.75	9.75	8.50	5.50	.15
108a	3¢ Booklet Pane of 4	115.00	75.00	77.50	52.50	...
109	3¢ Carmine (1923)	9.50	6.25	5.25	3.50	.15
109a	3¢ Booklet Pane of 4	80.00	53.50	52.50	35.00	...
110	4¢ Olive Bistre (1922)	37.50	25.00	20.00	13.50	1.60
111	5¢ Dark Blue	110.00	72.50	65.00	42.50	.35

1912-1925 "Admiral Issue" Perf. 12, VF Used + 50% (B)

Scott's No.	NH VF	NH F-VF	Unused VF	Unused F-VF	Used F-VF
112	5¢ Violet (1922)	21.50	14.50	12.50	8.25	.35
112a	5¢ Thin Paper	22.50	15.00	12.50	8.50	4.25
113	7¢ Yellow Ochre	42.50	28.50	24.00	16.00	1.25
113a	7¢ Olive Bistre	42.50	28.50	24.00	16.00	1.50
114	7¢ Red Brown (1924)	24.00	15.00	13.00	8.50	4.75
115	8¢ Blue (1925)	35.00	22.50	19.00	12.50	4.75
116	10¢ Plum	180.00	120.00	105.00	70.00	.75
117	10¢ Blue (1922)	48.50	32.50	26.50	17.50	.95
118	10¢ Bister Brown (1925)	41.50	27.50	22.50	15.00	.90
119	20¢ Olive Green	80.00	55.00	45.00	30.00	.75
120	50¢ Black Brown (1925)	90.00	60.00	50.00	33.50	1.50
120a	50¢ Black	135.00	90.00	90.00	60.00	3.50
122	$1 Orange (1923)	127.50	85.00	85.00	55.00	5.35

1912 Coil Stamps, Perf. 8 Horizontally VF Used + 50% (B)

| 123 | 1¢ Dark Green | 105.00 | 70.00 | 62.50 | 42.50 | 27.50 |
| 124 | 2¢ Carmine | 105.00 | 70.00 | 62.50 | 42.50 | 27.50 |

1912-1924 Coil Stamps, Perf. 8 Vertically VF Used + 50% (B)

125-30	Set of 6	150.00	105.00	99.50	65.00	9.75
125	1¢ Green	18.00	12.00	11.00	7.50	.55
126	1¢ Yellow (1923)	12.50	8.25	7.50	5.00	3.75
126a	1¢ Block of four	70.00	47.50	45.00	30.00	...
127	2¢ Carmine	26.50	17.50	16.50	11.00	.50
128	2¢ Green (1922)	16.00	11.00	10.00	6.75	.50
128a	2¢ Block of four	70.00	47.50	45.00	30.00	...
129	3¢ Brown (1918)	12.50	8.25	7.50	5.00	.50
130	3¢ Carmine (1924)	77.50	52.50	52.50	35.00	4.50
130a	3¢ Block of four	935.00	625.00	635.00	425.00	...

#126a,128a,130a are from Part.-Perf. Sheets - Pairs are at half block prices.

1915-1924 Coil Stamps, Perf. 12 Horizontally VF Used + 50% (B)

131-34	Set of 4	150.00	99.50	89.50	59.50	51.50
131	1¢ Dark Green	9.00	6.00	5.25	3.50	3.75
132	2¢ Carmine	24.50	16.50	16.50	11.00	6.50
133	2¢ Yellow Green (1924)	115.00	75.00	67.50	45.00	40.00
134	3¢ Brown (1921)	10.00	6.75	6.00	4.00	3.25

1917 Confederation VF Used + 100% (B)

| 135 | 3¢ "Fathers of Confed." | 50.00 | 25.00 | 30.00 | 15.00 | .50 |

1924 Imperforate VF Used + 30% (B)

136	1¢ Yellow	65.00	47.50	37.50	28.50	28.50
137	2¢ Green	65.00	47.50	37.50	28.50	28.50
138	3¢ Carmine	30.00	22.50	18.00	13.75	13.75

1926 Surcharges on #109 VF Used + 50% (B)

| 139 | 2¢ on 3¢ - One Line | 75.00 | 45.00 | 49.50 | 30.00 | 30.00 |
| 140 | 2¢ on 3¢ - Two Lines | 30.00 | 20.00 | 20.00 | 13.50 | 13.50 |

| 141 | 145 | 146 | 148 |

1927 Confederation Issue VF Used + 30% (B)

141-45	Set of 5	38.75	28.50	25.75	19.50	7.85
141	1¢ John A. MacDonald	3.35	2.50	2.25	1.65	.60
142	2¢ "Fathers of Confed."	1.90	1.45	1.25	.95	.15
143	3¢ Parliament Building	9.00	7.00	6.25	4.75	2.95
144	5¢ Sir Wilfrid Laurier	5.75	4.25	3.75	2.75	1.75
145	12¢ Map of Canada	21.50	15.75	13.75	10.50	3.00

1927 Historical Issue VF Used + 30% (B)

146-48	Set of 3	35.75	26.50	23.50	18.50	7.85
146	5¢ Thomas McGee	4.00	3.00	2.60	2.00	1.50
147	12¢ Laurier & MacDonald	11.00	8.25	7.25	5.50	3.00
148	20¢ Baldwin & Lafontaine	22.50	16.50	15.00	11.50	3.75

1928-29 Scroll Series VF Used + 40% (B)

| 149 | 154 | 155 | 156 |

149-59	Set of 11	760.00	550.00	465.00	340.00	100.00
149	1¢ George V, Orange	3.00	2.15	1.90	1.35	.25
149a	1¢ Booklet Pane of 6	25.00	18.00	16.50	12.00	...
150	2¢ Green	1.40	1.00	.95	.70	.15
150a	2¢ Booklet Pane of 6	28.50	20.00	18.00	13.00	...
151	3¢ Dark Carmine	21.00	15.00	13.75	10.00	7.00

1928-29 Scroll Series (cont.)

Scott's No.	NH VF	NH F-VF	Unused VF	Unused F-VF	Used F-VF
152	4¢ Bistre (1929)	16.50	11.75	11.00	7.75	3.25
153	5¢ Deep Violet	7.75	6.00	5.25	4.00	1.50
153a	5¢ Booklet Pane of 6	140.00	100.00	90.00	65.00	...
154	8¢ Blue	13.00	9.75	8.75	6.50	3.50
155	10¢ Mt. Hurd	13.00	9.75	8.75	6.50	.70
156	12¢ Quebec Bridge (1929)	22.50	16.00	15.00	10.75	4.00
157	20¢ Harvest Wheat (1929)	37.50	27.50	23.50	17.00	6.00
158	50¢ "Bluenose" (1929)	315.00	225.00	185.00	135.00	35.00
159	$1 Parliament (1929)	350.00	260.00	215.00	160.00	40.00

1929 Coil Stamps, Perf. 8 Vertically VF Used + 40% (B)

| 160 | 1¢ George V, Orange | 30.00 | 21.50 | 18.75 | 13.50 | 11.50 |
| 161 | 2¢ Green | 23.00 | 17.00 | 15.00 | 11.00 | 1.60 |

1930-31 King George V & Pictorials VF Used + 40% (B)

| 162-63 | 173 | 174 | 175 |

162-77	Set of 16	570.00	395.00	350.00	250.00	39.50
162	1¢ George V. Orange	1.30	.90	.85	.60	.35
163	1¢ Deep Green	1.75	1.35	1.20	.85	.15
163a	1¢ Booklet Pane of 4	125.00	90.00	85.00	60.00	...
163c	1¢ Booklet Pane of 6	27.50	20.00	19.00	13.50	...
164	2¢ Dull Green	1.40	1.00	.90	.65	.15
164a	2¢ Booklet Pane of 6	39.50	27.00	26.00	18.00	...
165	2¢ Deep Red, Die II	2.30	1.65	1.60	1.15	.15
165a	2¢ Deep Red, Die I	1.75	1.25	1.20	.85	.20
165b	2¢ B. Pane of 6, Die I	31.50	21.75	20.75	14.50	...
166	2¢ Dark Br., Die II (1931)	1.50	1.15	1.00	.75	.15
166a	2¢ B. Pane of 4, Die II	140.00	100.00	105.00	75.00	...
166b	2¢ Dark Brown, Die I	6.25	4.25	4.25	3.00	3.25
166c	2¢ B. Pane of 6, Die I	40.00	29.50	28.00	20.00	...
167	3¢ Deep Red (1931)	2.75	1.95	1.75	1.30	.15
167a	3¢ Booklet Pane of 4	45.00	32.50	31.00	22.50	...
168	4¢ Yellow Bistre	12.50	9.00	7.75	5.50	3.00
169	5¢ Dull Violet, Flat Plate	7.00	5.00	4.25	3.00	2.25
169a	5¢ Dull Violet, Rotary	5.00	5.00	4.25	3.00	2.25
170	5¢ Dull Blue	4.00	3.00	2.75	2.00	.15
171	8¢ Dark Blue	20.00	13.50	13.00	9.00	5.00
172	8¢ Red Orange	7.75	5.50	5.00	3.50	2.50
173	10¢ Library of Parliament	10.75	7.75	7.50	5.50	.60
174	12¢ Citadel at Quebec	17.50	12.50	12.00	8.50	3.35
175	20¢ Harvesting Wheat	31.50	22.50	21.00	15.00	.35
176	50¢ Museum-Grand Pre	235.00	160.00	140.00	100.00	7.75
177	$1 Mt. Edith Cavell	260.00	175.00	130.00	110.00	16.50

Die I: Dot of Color in "P" of Postage. Die II: Large Dot in "P".

1930-31 Coil Stamps, Perf. 8½ Vertically VF Used + 40% (B)

178-83	Set of 6	87.50	58.50	53.75	38.50	12.95
178	1¢ George V, Orange	15.75	11.50	10.50	7.50	6.25
179	1¢ Green	9.00	6.50	6.00	4.25	3.25
180	2¢ Dull Green	7.00	5.00	4.35	3.35	1.85
181	2¢ Carmine	21.50	14.50	14.00	9.50	1.50
182	2¢ Dark Brown (1931)	13.00	9.00	8.50	6.00	.40
183	3¢ Deep Red (1931)	21.00	15.00	14.00	10.00	.40

1931 Design of 1912, Perf. 12 x 8 VF Used + 30% (B)

| 184 | 3¢ George V Carmine | 4.75 | 3.50 | 2.95 | 2.25 | 2.10 |

| 190 | 192 | 194 | 195 |

1931 Cartier Issue VF + 30% (B)

| 190 | 10¢ Sir Georges Cartier | 10.75 | 8.25 | 7.25 | 5.50 | .18 |

1932 Surcharges VF + 30% (B)

| 191 | 3¢ on 2¢ Deep Red, Die II | 1.30 | 1.00 | .85 | .65 | .18 |
| 191a | 3¢ on 2¢ Deep Red, Die I | 2.60 | 2.00 | 1.95 | 1.50 | 1.20 |

1932 Imperial Conference VF + 30% (B)

192-94	Set of 3	17.00	12.50	11.95	8.50	5.15
192	3¢ George V	1.00	.75	.65	.50	.15
193	5¢ Prince of Wales	8.00	5.75	5.25	4.00	1.50
194	13¢ Allegory	9.00	6.75	6.00	4.50	3.75

1932 George V, Medallion, VF Used + 30% (B)

Scott's No.		VF	NH F-VF	Unused VF	F-VF	Used F-VF
195-201	Set of 7	115.00	85.00	79.50	62.50	7.50
195	1¢ George V. Dark Green	1.00	.75	.70	.55	.15
195a	1¢ Booklet Pane of 4	120.00	90.00	85.00	65.00	...
195b	1¢ Booklet Pane of 6	30.75	23.75	21.50	16.50	...
196	2¢ Black Brown	1.10	.85	.80	.60	.15
196a	2¢ Booklet Pane of 4	120.00	90.00	85.00	65.00	...
196b	2¢ Booklet Pane of 6	31.50	24.50	22.50	17.00	...
197	3¢ Deep Red	1.75	1.30	1.20	.90	.15
197a	3¢ Booklet Pane of 4	37.00	27.50	26.00	19.50	...
198	4¢ Ocher	45.00	35.00	32.50	25.00	3.50
199	5¢ Dark Blue............................	8.75	6.50	5.95	4.50	.15
200	8¢ Red Orange	26.50	20.00	18.50	14.00	2.35
201	13¢ Citadel at Quebec	45.00	33.00	30.00	22.50	1.75

202   208   209

1933 Pictorials VF + 30%

202	5¢ U.P.U. Meeting 8.75	7.00	6.25	4.75	2.00
203	20¢ Grain Exhib. (on #175) 36.50	27.50	24.00	18.00	8.00
204	5¢ "Royal William" 10.00	7.50	6.50	5.00	2.00

1933 Coil Stamps, Perf. Vertically VF + 30% (B)

205	1¢ George V. Dark Green 17.00	12.50	11.50	8.50	1.50
206	2¢ Black Brown 19.50	15.00	13.00	10.00	.55
207	3¢ Deep Red 17.00	12.50	11.50	8.50	.25

1934 Commemoratives VF + 30%

208	3¢ Cartier at Quebec 3.95	3.00	2.60	2.00	.75
209	10¢ Loyalists Monument 23.50	17.50	16.00	12.00	4.75
210	2¢ Seal of New Brunswick 2.75	2.10	1.85	1.40	1.10

1935 Silver Jubilee VF + 25%

211   213   214   216

Scott's No.		Plate Blocks NH	Unused	F-VF NH	F-VF Unused	Used
211-16	Set of 6	...	...	18.75	14.00	6.50
211	1¢ Princess Elizabeth..............(6)	7.00	5.75	.35	.28	.20
212	2¢ Duke of York ....(6)	7.50	6.25	.50	.40	.15
213	3¢ George V and Mary.............(6)	17.50	13.50	1.70	1.30	.15
214	5¢ Prince of Wales ....(6)	47.50	35.00	4.50	3.50	1.65
215	10¢ Windsor Castle ....(6)	57.50	45.00	5.75	4.25	1.50
216	13¢ Royal Yacht "Brittania" ......(6)	75.00	55.00	7.50	5.25	3.50

1935 George V & Pictorials VF + 25%

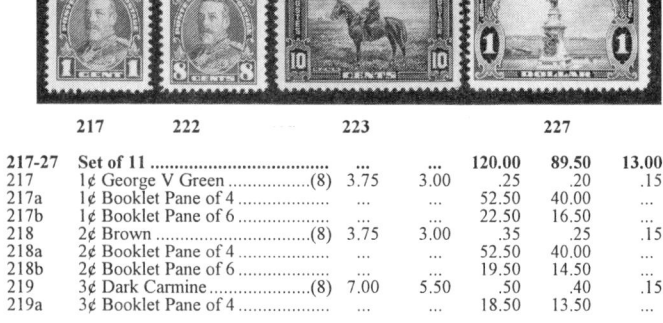

217   222   223   227

217-27	Set of 11	...	...	120.00	89.50	13.00
217	1¢ George V Green ....(8)	3.75	3.00	.25	.20	.15
217a	1¢ Booklet Pane of 4	...	...	52.50	40.00	...
217b	1¢ Booklet Pane of 6	...	...	22.50	16.50	...
218	2¢ Brown ....(8)	3.75	3.00	.35	.25	.15
218a	2¢ Booklet Pane of 4	...	...	52.50	40.00	...
218b	2¢ Booklet Pane of 6	...	...	19.50	14.50	...
219	3¢ Dark Carmine ....(8)	7.00	5.50	.50	.40	.15
219a	3¢ Booklet Pane of 4	...	...	18.50	13.50	...

1935 George V & Pictorials (cont.)

Scott's No.		Plate Blocks NH	Unused	F-VF NH	F-VF Unused	Used
220	4¢ Yellow ....(6)	35.00	27.50	2.35	1.75	.35
221	5¢ Blue ....(6)	35.00	27.50	2.25	1.70	.15
222	8¢ Deep Orange ....(6)	35.00	27.50	2.65	2.00	1.30
223	10¢ Mounted Police ....(6)	55.00	42.50	6.50	4.75	.18
224	13¢ Confederation Conf..........(6)	55.00	42.50	7.00	5.25	.50
225	20¢ Niagara Falls ....(6)	160.00	120.00	18.50	14.00	.35
226	50¢ Parliament, Victoria.........(6)	235.00	175.00	27.50	20.00	3.25
227	$1 Champlain Monument ....(6)	500.00	375.00	60.00	45.00	7.00

1935 Coil Stamps, Perf. 8 Vertically VF + 25% (B)

228	1¢ George V, Green	...	...	12.75	8.75	1.75
229	2¢ Brown	...	...	11.00	7.50	.55
230	3¢ Dark Carmine	...	...	11.00	7.50	.30

231   237   241   242

1937 George VI VF + 25% (B)

231-36	Set of 6	...	...	8.50	6.25	.75
231	1¢ George VI, Green	2.25	1.85	.35	.25	.15
231a	1¢ Booklet Pane of 4	...	...	11.75	8.50	...
231b	1¢ Booklet Pane of 6	...	...	1.80	1.35	...
232	2¢ Brown	2.75	2.25	.45	.35	.15
232a	2¢ Booklet Pane of 4	...	...	13.50	9.75	...
232b	2¢ Booklet Pane of 6	...	...	6.75	4.75	...
233	3¢ Carmine	3.50	2.75	.60	.50	.15
233a	3¢ Booklet Pane of 6	...	...	2.30	1.75	...
234	4¢ Yellow	16.50	12.50	2.50	1.85	.15
235	5¢ Blue	16.50	12.50	2.70	2.00	.15
236	8¢ Orange	16.50	12.50	2.70	2.00	.35

1937 Coronation Issue VF + 25% (B)

237	3¢ George VI and Elizabeth.......	2.25	1.75	.25	.20	.15

1937 Coil Stamps, Perf. 8 Vertically VF + 25% (B)

238	1¢ George VI, Green	...	...	1.60	1.10	.70
239	2¢ Brown	...	...	2.25	1.60	.25
240	3¢ Carmine	...	...	4.25	2.90	.18

1938 Pictorials VF + 25%

241-45	Set of 5.................................	...	...	115.00	79.50	7.50
241	10¢ Memorial Hall....................	35.00	27.50	5.50	4.25	.15
242	13¢ Halifax Harbor	35.00	25.00	7.50	5.25	.35
243	20¢ Ft. Garry Gate, Winnipeg....	90.00	65.00	12.00	8.50	.25
244	50¢ Vancouver Harbor	175.00	120.00	24.50	16.50	3.25
245	$1 Chateau de Ramezay	400.00	275.00	72.50	50.00	4.25

1939 Royal Visit VF + 25%

246   247   248

246-48	Set of 3.................................	3.65	2.90	.65	.50	.30
246	1¢ Elizabeth & Margaret Rose....	1.65	1.35	.24	.20	.15
247	2¢ War Memorial, Ottawa..........	1.65	1.35	.24	.20	.15
248	3¢ George VI and Elizabeth........	1.65	1.35	.24	.20	.15

1942-43 War Set

249   250   253   262

1942-43 War Set VF + 25%

Scott's No.		Plate Blocks NH	Plate Blocks Unused	F-VF NH	F-VF Unused	F-VF Used
249-62	Set of 14	...	...	115.00	80.00	10.75
249	1¢ George VI, Green	1.60	1.25	.25	.20	.15
249a	1¢ Booklet Pane of 4	...	...	5.00	3.75	...
249b	1¢ Booklet Pane of 6	...	...	1.50	1.10	...
249c	1¢ Booklet Pane of 3	...	...	1.35	1.00	...
250	2¢ Brown.............................	2.35	1.75	.45	.35	.15
250a	2¢ Booklet Pane of 4	...	...	5.00	3.75	...
250b	2¢ Booklet Pane of 6	...	...	4.65	3.50	...
251	3¢ Dark Carmine	2.35	1.75	.40	.30	.15
251a	3¢ Booklet Pane of 4	...	...	1.75	1.25	...
252	3¢ Rose Violet (1943)............	2.35	1.75	.40	.30	.15
252a	3¢ Booklet Pane of 4	...	...	1.65	1.20	...
252b	3¢ Booklet Pane of 3	...	...	2.65	2.00	...
252c	3¢ Booklet Pane of 6	...	...	3.50	2.50	...
253	4¢ Grain Elevators	8.50	6.25	1.25	.90	.55
254	4¢ George VI. Carm.(1943)....	2.35	1.75	.40	.30	.15
254a	4¢ Booklet Pane of 6	...	...	2.25	1.35	...
254b	4¢ Booklet Pane of 3	...	...	1.10	1.60	...
255	5¢ George VI, Deep Blue	6.75	5.00	1.00	.80	.15
256	8¢ Farm Scene	12.50	9.00	1.60	1.10	.35
257	10¢ Parliament Buildings	25.00	17.50	4.00	2.75	.15
258	13¢ "Ram" Tank	27.50	20.00	4.75	3.50	2.75
259	14¢ "Ram" Tank (1943)	40.00	30.00	7.00	5.00	.25
260	20¢ Corvette	42.00	30.00	8.50	5.75	.20
261	50¢ Munitions Factory	160.00	110.00	32.50	22.50	1.50
262	$1 Destroyer	395.00	265.00	67.50	45.00	6.00

1942-43 Coil Stamps, Perf. 8 Vertically VF + 25%

				F-VF NH	F-VF Unused	F-VF Used
263-67	Set of 5................................	...	...	10.00	6.85	2.10
263	1¢ George VI, Green	...	...	1.00	.70	.35
264	2¢ Brown.............................	...	...	1.50	1.10	.70
265	3¢ Dark Carmine	...	...	1.50	1.10	.70
266	3¢ Rose Violet (1943)............	...	...	2.60	1.75	.25
267	4¢ Dark Carmine (1943)	...	...	4.00	2.75	.20

1946 Reconversion "Peace" Issue VF + 25%

268   271   273

		Plate Blocks NH	Plate Blocks Unused	F-VF NH	F-VF Unused	F-VF Used
268-73	Set of 6..............................	...	...	63.50	43.50	4.25
268	8¢ Farm Scene	7.75	6.00	1.35	1.00	.45
269	10¢ Great Bear Lake..............	8.25	6.50	1.75	1.30	.15
270	14¢ Hydroelectric Station	17.50	13.75	3.00	2.25	.18
271	20¢ Combine	22.00	16.50	3.75	2.75	.15
272	50¢ Logging	100.00	70.00	17.50	13.00	1.35
273	$1 Train Ferry.....................	225.00	165.00	40.00	28.50	2.25

274   275   276   283

1947-48 Commemoratives

Scott's No.		Plate Blocks NH	F-VF NH	F-VF Used
274-77,282-83	Set of 6	...	.90	.70
274	4¢ Alexander Graham Bell	.85	.20	.15
275	4¢ Citizenship	.85	.20	.15
276	4¢ Royal Wedding (1948)	.85	.20	.15
277	4¢ Parliament (1948)	.75	.20	.15

1948 Coils, Perf. 9½ Vertically

			F-VF NH	F-VF Used
278-81	Set of 4	...	26.00	10.50
278	1¢ George VI, Green	...	3.25	1.35
279	2¢ George VI, Brown	...	10.75	5.50
280	3¢ George VI, Rose Violet	...	6.00	1.85
281	4¢ George VI, Dark Carmine	...	7.50	2.25

1949 Commemoratives

282	4¢ Founding of Newfoundland	.95	.20	.15
283	4¢ Halifax Anniversary..........................	.95	.20	.15

1949 George VI with "Postes-Postage" In Design

284   289   294   302

Scott's No.		Plate Blocks NH	F-VF NH	F-VF Used
284-88	Set of 5	...	2.25	.55
284	1¢ George VI, Green	.85	.20	.15
284a	1¢ Book. Pane of 3 (1950)	...	.60	...
285	2¢ Sepia	1.25	.25	.15
286	3¢ Rose Violet	1.25	.30	.15
286a	3¢ Book. Pane of 3 (1950)	...	1.25	...
286b	3¢ Booklet Pane of 4	...	1.50	...
287	4¢ Dark Carmine	2.25	.50	.15
287a	4¢ Book. Pane of 3 (1950)	...	10.00	...
287b	4¢ Book. Pane of 6 (1951)	...	12.50	...
288	5¢ Deep Blue	5.50	1.10	.15

1950 George VI without "Postes-Postage" In Design

289-93	Set of 5	...	2.00	1.15
289	1¢ George VI, Green	.65	.20	.15
290	2¢ Sepia	1.75	.30	.15
291	3¢ Rose Violet	.95	.20	.15
292	4¢ Dark Carmine	1.35	.25	.15
293	5¢ Deep Blue	5.75	1.25	.75

1950 Regular Issue

294	50¢ Oil Wells, Alberta.............................	50.00	10.50	1.20

1949-50 Coil Stamps, Perf. 9½ Vertically

295-300	Set of 6		15.00	2.90
	(without "Postes-Postage")			
295	1¢ George VI, Green	...	.50	.25
296	3¢ Rose Violet	...	.75	.50
	(with "Postes-Postage")			
297	1¢ George VI, Green (1950)	...	.35	.22
298	2¢ Sepia (1950)	...	2.00	1.35
299	3¢ Rose Violet (1950)	...	1.40	.20
300	4¢ Dark Carmine (1950)	...	11.50	.65

1950-1951 Regular Issue

301	10¢ Fur Resources	4.00	.75	.15
302	$1 Fishing (1951)	275.00	60.00	9.75

303   311   314   315

1951-52 Commemoratives

303-4,11-15,17-19	Set of 10...................................	...	4.65	2.65

1951 Commemoratives

303	3¢ Robert L. Borden................................	1.40	.22	.15
304	4¢ William L. Mackenzie King....................	1.50	.25	.15

1951 Color Changes (with "Postes-Postage")

305	2¢ George VI, Olive Green........................	.70	.20	.15
306	4¢ Orange Vermillion	1.10	.25	.15
306a	4¢ Booklet Pane of 3	...	2.25	...
306b	4¢ Booklet Pane of 6	...	2.75	...
309	2¢ Ol. Gr., Coil Pf. 9½ Vert	...	1.00	.60
310	4¢ Or. Verm., Coil Pf. 9½ Vert	...	2.40	.70

1951 Int'l. Philatelic Exhibition "CAPEX"

311-14	Set of 4	...	3.65	1.90
311	4¢ Trains of 1851 & 1951	2.10	.45	.15
312	5¢ Steamships	7.50	1.50	1.35
313	7¢ Plane & Stagecoach	4.50	.90	.30
314	15¢ 1st Canada Stamp	5.75	1.00	.27

1951 Commemoratives

315	4¢ Royal Visit to Canada and U.S.	.95	.20	.15

FROM 1947 TO PRESENT, ADD 20% FOR VERY FINE QUALITY
Minimum of 10¢ per stamp

| 316 | 317 | 320 |

1952 Regular Issue

Scott's No.		Plate Blocks NH	F-VF NH	F-VF Used
316	20¢ Paper Industry	7.00	1.35	.15

1952 Commemoratives

317	4¢ Red Cross Conference	1.15	.20	.15
318	3¢ John J.C. Abbott	1.00	.20	.15
319	4¢ Alexander Mackenzie	1.10	.22	.15

1952-53 Regular Issues

| 320 | 7¢ Canada Goose .... | 1.50 | .30 | .15 |
| 321 | $1 Totem Pole (1953) .... | 50.00 | 10.00 | .80 |

| 322 | 325 | 330 | 334 |

1953-54 Commemoratives

| 322-24,35-36,49-50 Set of 7 .... | | ... | 1.35 | .95 |

1953 Wildlife Commemoratives

322	2¢ Polar Bear	1.00	.20	.15
323	3¢ Moose	1.10	.20	.15
324	4¢ Bighorn Sheep	1.25	.20	.15

1953 Queen Elizabeth II Issue

325-29	Set of 5	...	.95	.60
325	1¢ Elizabeth II, Brown	.50	.20	.15
325a	1¢ Booklet Pane of 3	...	1.00	...
326	2¢ Green	.60	.20	.15
327	3¢ Carmine Rose	.75	.20	.15
327a	3¢ Booklet Pane of 3	...	1.30	...
327b	3¢ Booklet Pane of 4	...	1.25	...
328	4¢ Violet	1.15	.24	.15
328a	4¢ Booklet Pane of 3	...	1.60	...
328b	4¢ Booklet Pane of 6	...	1.75	...
329	5¢ Ultramarine	1.40	.30	.15

1953 Coronation Issue

| 330 | 4¢ Elizabeth II .... | .85 | .20 | .15 |

1953 Queen Elizabeth II Coils, Perf. 9½ Vertically

331	2¢ Elizabeth II, Green	...	1.35	.80
332	3¢ Carmine Rose	...	1.30	.80
333	4¢ Violet	...	2.95	1.20

1953 Regular Issue

| 334 | 50¢ Textile Industry .... | 19.00 | 3.25 | .15 |

| 336 | 337 | 349 | 351 |

1954 Wildlife Commemoratives

335	4¢ Walrus	1.25	.20	.15
336	5¢ Beaver	1.40	.25	.15
336a	5¢ Booklet Pane of 5	...	1.75	...

1954 Queen Elizabeth II Issue

337-43	Set of 7	...	2.10	.75
337	1¢ Elizabeth II, V. Brown	.50	.20	.15
337a	1¢ Booklet Pane of 5 (1956)	...	.90	...
338	2¢ Green	.60	.20	.15
338a	2¢ Min. Pane of 25 (1961)	...	4.50	...
338a	Pack of 2	...	9.00	...
339	3¢ Carmine Rose	.75	.20	.15
340	4¢ Violet	.90	.20	.15
340a	4¢ Booklet Pane of 5 (1956)	...	1.50	...
340b	4¢ Booklet Pane of 6 (1955)	...	7.75	...
341	5¢ Bright Blue	1.10	.20	.15
341a	5¢ Booklet Pane of 5	...	1.65	...
341b	5¢ Min. Pane of 20 (1961)	...	8.75	...

Scott's No.		Plate Blocks NH	F-VF NH	F-VF Used
342	6¢ Orange...	1.50	.30	.15
343	15¢ Gannet, Gray	4.50	.95	.15

1954 Elizabeth II Coil Stamps, Perf. 9½ Vertically

345	2¢ Elizabeth II, Green...............................	...	.50	.18
347	4¢ Violet	...	1.40	.20
348	5¢ Bright Blue	...	2.00	.18

1954 Commemoratives

| 349 | 4¢ J.S.D. Thompson .... | 1.20 | .20 | .15 |
| 350 | 5¢ M. Bowell .... | 1.20 | .20 | .15 |

1955 Regular Issue

| 351 | 10¢ Eskimo in Kayak.................................. | 1.50 | .30 | .15 |

| 352 | 356 | 359 | 360 |

1955 Commemoratives

352-58	Set of 7	...	1.60	.85
352	4¢ Wildlife - Musk Ox...............................	1.25	.25	.15
353	5¢ Whooping Cranes..................................	1.40	.30	.15
354	5¢ Civil Aviation Org	1.40	.25	.15
355	5¢ Alberta - Saskatchewan	1.40	.25	.15
356	5¢ Boy Scout Jamboreen	1.40	.25	.15
357	4¢ Richard B. Bennett	1.25	.25	.15
358	5¢ Charles Tupper	1.25	.25	.15

1956 Commemoratives

359-61,364	Set of 4..	...	.95	.50
359	5¢ Ice Hockey	1.25	.25	.15
360	4¢ Wildlife - Caribou	1.25	.25	.15
361	5¢ Mountain Goat	1.25	.25	.15

| 362 | 364 | 365 | 369 |

1956 Regular Issues

| 362 | 20¢ Paper Industry..................................... | 6.00 | 1.25 | .15 |
| 363 | 25¢ Chemistry Industry.............................. | 7.50 | 1.50 | .15 |

1956 Commemoratives

| 364 | 5¢ Fire Prevention .... | 1.25 | .25 | .15 |

1957 Commemoratives

365-74	Set of 10..	...	3.95	2.75
365-68	5¢ Outdoor Recreation, attd.......................	1.85	1.50	1.45
365-68	Set of 4 Singles...	...	1.30	.80
369	5¢ Wildlife - Loon	1.25	.25	.15
370	5¢ David Thompson	1.10	.20	.15
371	5¢ U.P.U. - Parliament...............................	1.10	.20	.15
372	15¢ U.P.U. - Post Horn..............................	9.00	1.80	1.50
373	5¢ Mining Industry	1.10	.20	.15
374	5¢ Royal Visit	1.10	.20	.15

1958 Commemoratives

| 376 | 378 | 380 | 381 |

375-82	Set of 8...	...	1.60	1.00
375	5¢ Newspaper Industry...................(Blank)	2.50	.25	.15
376	5¢ Int'l. Geophysical Year ....(Blank)	2.50	.25	.15
377	5¢ British Columbia Cent	2.25	.20	.15
378	5¢ Explorer La Verendrye	1.75	.20	.15
379	5¢ Quebec Anniversary	4.00	.20	.15
380	5¢ National Health	1.35	.20	.15
381	5¢ Petroleum Industry................................	1.35	.20	.15
382	5¢ 1st Elected Assembly.............................	1.40	.20	.15

CANADA

1959 Commemoratives

383   385   387

Scott's No.		Plate Block	F-VF NH	F-VF Used
383-88	**Set of 6**	...	**1.10**	**.75**
383	5¢ Golden Anniv. of Flight	1.35	.20	.15
384	5¢ 10th Anniv. of N.A.T.O.	1.25	.20	.15
385	5¢ Country Women of the World	1.10	.20	.15
386	5¢ Royal Tour	1.10	.20	.15
387	5¢ St. Lawrence Seaway	3.75	.20	.15
388	5¢ Plains of Abraham	1.10	.20	.15

1960-1961 Commemoratives

390   391   393   395

Scott's No.		Plate Block	F-VF NH	F-VF Used
389-95	**Set of 7**	...	**1.30**	**.85**
389	5¢ Girl Guides Association	1.25	.20	.15
390	5¢ Battle of Long Sault	1.25	.20	.15
391	5¢ Northland Development (1961)	1.25	.20	.15
392	5¢ E. Pauline Johnson (1961)	1.25	.20	.15
393	5¢ P. Minister A. Meighen (1961)	1.25	.20	.15
394	5¢ Colombo Plan (1961)	1.25	.20	.15
395	5¢ Resources for Tomorrow (1961)	1.25	.20	.15

396   398   400   401

1962 Commemoratives

		Plate Block	F-VF NH	F-VF Used
396-400	**Set of 5**	...	**.90**	**.65**
396	5¢ Education	1.25	.20	.15
397	5¢ Red River Settlement, Lord Selkirk	1.25	.20	.15
398	5¢ Jean Talon	1.25	.20	.15
399	5¢ Victoria B.C. Centenary	1.25	.20	.15
400	5¢ Trans-Canadian Highway	1.25	.20	.15

1962-63 Queen Elizabeth "Cameo" Issue

		Plate Block	F-VF NH	F-VF Used
401-05	**Set of 5**	...	**.85**	**.60**
401	1¢ Deep Brown (1963)	.50	.20	.15
401a	1¢ Booklet Pane of 5	...	3.75	...
402	2¢ Green (1963)	2.95	.20	.15
402a	2¢ Miniature Pane of 25 .... (pack of 2)	15.00	7.50	...
403	3¢ Purple (1963)	.70	.20	.15
404	4¢ Carmine (1963)	.90	.20	.15
404a	4¢ Booklet Pane of 5	...	3.50	...
404b	4¢ Miniature Pane of 25	...	8.75	...
405	5¢ Violet Blue	1.10	.20	.15
405a	5¢ Booklet Pane of 5 (1963)	...	5.25	...
405b	5¢ Miniature Pane of 20 (1963)	...	11.75	...

1962-63 Coil Stamps, Perf. 9½ Horizontally

		Plate Block	F-VF NH	F-VF Used
406-9	**Set of 4**	...	**13.00**	**4.75**
406	2¢ Elizabeth, Green (1963)	...	3.75	1.75
407	3¢ Purple (1963)	...	2.50	1.25
408	4¢ Carmine (1963)	...	3.75	1.50
409	5¢ Violet Blue	...	3.75	.60

411   413   417

CANADA
1963 Commemoratives

Scott's No.		Plate Block	F-VF NH	F-VF Used
410,412-13	**Set of 3**	...	**.65**	**.35**
410	5¢ Sir Casimir S. Gzowski	1.00	.20	.15

1963 Regular Issues

411	$1 Export Trade, Crate & Map	60.00	12.00	1.75

1963 Commemoratives

412	5¢ Explorer M. Frobisher	1.15	.24	.15
413	5¢ First Post Route	1.15	.24	.15

1963-1964 Regular Issues

414	7¢ Jet at Ottawa Airport (1964)	1.65	.35	.35
415	15¢ Canada Geese (1963)	9.75	1.95	.15

1964 Commemoratives

416,431-35	**Set of 6**	...	**1.15**	**.75**
416	5¢ "Peace on Earth"	1.00	.20	.15

418   431   434

1964-1966 Coat of Arms & Flowers

		Plate Block	F-VF NH	F-VF Used
417-29A	**Set of 14** **14.75**	2.75	1.75	
417	5¢ Canadian Unity, Maple Leaf	1.00	.20	.15
418	5¢ Ontario, White Trillium	1.00	.20	.18
419	5¢ Quebec, White Garden Lily	1.00	.20	.15
420	5¢ Nova Scotia, Mayflower/1965	1.00	.20	.15
421	5¢ New Brunswick, Purple Violet ('65)	1.00	.20	.15
422	5¢ Manitoba, Prairie Crocus ('65)	1.75	.20	.15
423	5¢ British Columbia, Dogwood ('65)	1.00	.20	.15
424	5¢ Pr. Edward I., Lady's Slipper ('65)	1.00	.20	.15
425	5¢ Saskatchewan, Prairie Lily ('66)	1.00	.20	.18
426	5¢ Alberta, Wild Rose ('66)	1.00	.20	.15
427	5¢ Newfoundland, Pitcher Plant ('66)	1.75	.20	.15
428	5¢ Yukon, Firewood ('66)	1.00	.20	.18
429	5¢ Northwest Terr., Mountain Avens ('66)	1.00	.20	.15
429A	5¢ Canada, Maple Leaf ('66)	1.00	.20	.15

1964 Regular Issue

430	8¢ on 7¢ Jet Aircraft (on #414) .... (Blank)	1.50	.30	.30

1964 Commemoratives

431	5¢ Charlottestown Conference	1.00	.20	.15
432	5¢ Quebec Conference	1.00	.20	.15
433	5¢ Queen Elizabeth Visit	1.00	.20	.15
434	3¢ Christmas, Family & Star	.75	.20	.15
434a	3¢ Miniature Pane of 25 .... (pack of 2)	14.00	7.00	...
435	5¢ Christmas, Family & Star	1.15	.20	.15

1964 Regular Issue

436	8¢ Jet at Ottawa Airport	1.75	.35	.20

1965 Commemoratives

437   440   441   443

		Plate Block	F-VF NH	F-VF Used
437-44	**Set of 8**	...	**1.50**	**1.00**
437	5¢ International Cooperation Year	.90	.20	.15
438	5¢ Sir Wilfred Grenfell	.90	.20	.15
439	5¢ National Flag	.90	.20	.15
440	5¢ Sir Winston Churchill	.90	.20	.15
441	5¢ Interparliamentary Union	.90	.20	.15
442	5¢ Ottawa Centennial	.90	.20	.15
443	3¢ Christmas, Gifts of Wise Men	.70	.20	.15
443a	3¢ Miniature Pane of 25 .... (pack of 2)	12.50	6.25	...
444	5¢ Christmas, Gifts of Wise Men	1.25	.20	.15

1966 Commemoratives

| | | 445 | | 448 | | 450 | | 451 | |

Scott's No.			Plate Block	F-VF NH	F-VF Used
445-52	**Set of 8**		...	1.50	1.00
445	5¢ Satellite Alouette II		1.00	.20	.15
446	5¢ LaSalle Arrival Tercentary		1.00	.20	.15
447	5¢ Highway Safety		1.00	.20	.15
448	5¢ London Conf. Centenary		1.00	.20.	.15
449	5¢ Atomic Energy		1.00	.20	.15
450	5¢ Parliamentary Association		1.00	.20	.15
451	3¢ Christmas, Praying Hands		.70	.20	.15
451a	3¢ Miniature Pane of 25 .... (pack of 2)		7.50	3.75	...
452	5¢ Christmas, Praying Hands		1.00	.20	.15

1967 Commemoratives

453,469-77	**Set of 10**		...	1.90	1.30
453	5¢ Canadian Centenary		1.00	.20	.15

1967-72 Centennial Regular Issue, Perf. 12

| | 454 | 459,460 | 461 | 465B |

		Plate Block	F-VF NH	F-VF Used
454-65B	**Set of 14**	...	14.95	2.15
454	1¢ Elizabeth & Dog Team, Brown	.70	.20	.15
454a	1¢ Booklet Pane of 5	...	.95	...
454b	B. Pane of 5 (1 #454 & 4 #459), Perf. 10(1968)	...	3.00	...
454c	B. Pane of 10 (5 #454 & 5 #457) Perf.10(1968)	...	2.50	...
454d	1¢ Booklet Single, Perf. 10 (1968)	...	.35	.20
454e	1¢ Booklet Single, Perf. 12½ x 12 (1969)......	...	.65	.20
455	2¢ Elizabeth & Totem Pole, Green	.75	.20	.15
455a	B. Pane of 8 (4 #455, 4 #456)	...	1.90	...
456	3¢ Elizabeth & Combine, Purple	1.50	.20	.15
456a	3¢ Booklet Single, Perf. 12½ x 12 (1971)......	...	4.75	1.75
457	4¢ Elizabeth & Seaway Lock, Carmine	1.50	.20	.15
457a	4¢ Booklet Pane of 5	...	1.50	...
457b	4¢ Miniature Pane of 25	...	25.00	...
457c	4¢ B. Pane of 25, Perf. 10 (1968)	...	9.50	...
457d	4¢ Booklet Single, Perf. 10(1968)	...	.60	.25
458	5¢ Elizabeth & Fishing Port, Blue	1.25	.20	.15
458a	5¢ Booklet Pane of 5	...	6.95	...
458b	5¢ Miniature Pane of 20	...	32.50	...
458c	5¢ B. Pane of 20, Perf. 10 (1968)	...	8.25	...
458d	5¢ Booklet Single, Perf. 10 (1968)	...	.65	.25
459	6¢ Elizabeth & Trans, Orange, Perf. 10 (1968)	3.00	.35	.15
459a	6¢ Booklet Pane of 25, Perf. 10 (1968)	...	9.00	...
459b	6¢ Orange, Perf. 12½ x 12 (1968)	2.75	.30	.15
460	6¢ Black, Die I, Perf. 12½ x 12 (1970)	1.75	.20	.15
460a	6¢ Die I, B. Pane of 25, Perf. 10 (1970)	...	13.50	...
460g	6¢ Die I, Booklet Single, Perf. 10 (1970)	...	1.60	.35
460b	6¢ Die I, B.Pane of 25, Perf. 12½x12 (1970)...	...	19.50	...
460c	6¢ Black, Die II, Perf. 12½ x 12 (1970)	2.00	.25	.15
460d	6¢ Die II, B. Pane of 4, Perf. 12½ x 12 (1970)	...	4.50	...
460e	6¢ Die II, B. Pane of 4, Perf. 10 (1970)	...	8.25	...
460h	6¢ Die II, Booklet Single, Perf. 10	...	4.00	2.25
460f	6¢ Die II, Perf. 12 (1973)	2.85	.55	.50
461	8¢ "Alaska Highway"..........................	3.00	.30	.15
462	10¢ "The Jack Pine"..........................	1.65	.30	.15
463	15¢ "Bylot Island"..........................	2.75	.40	.15
464	20¢ "The Ferry, Quebec"....................	3.25	.55	.15
465	25¢ "The Solemn Land"....................	5.75	1.00	.15
465A	50¢ "Summer's Stores"......................	16.50	3.50	.15
465B	$1 "Oilfield, Edmonton"..................	40.75	8.25	.50

#460 has weak shading lines around "6"; #460c has lines strengthened.

1967-70 Coil Stamps, Perf. 9½ or 10 Horiz.

			Plate Block	F-VF NH	F-VF Used
466-68B	**Set of 5**		...	4.15	2.75
466	3¢ Elizabeth & Oil Rig.......................		...	1.50	1.25
467	4¢ Elizabeth & Canal Lock		...	.70	.60
468	5¢ Elizabeth & Fishing Port		...	1.50	.80
468A	6¢ Elizabeth, Orange (1969)................		...	.30	.15
468B	6¢ Elizabeth, Black (1970).................		...	.30	.15

1967 Commemoratives (See also #453)

| | 469 | 473 | 476 |

Scott's No.		Plate Block	F-VF NH	F-VF Used
469	5¢ Expo '67, Montreal	1.00	.20	.15
470	5¢ Women's Franchise	1.00	.20	.15
471	5¢ Royal Visit, Elizabeth II	1.00	.20	.15
472	5¢ Pan American Games	1.00	.20	.15
473	5¢ Canadian Press	1.00	.20	.15
474	5¢ Georges P. Vanier	1.00	.20	.15
475	5¢ Toronto Centennial	1.00	.20	.15
476	3¢ Christmas, Singing Children	.80	.20	.15
476a	3¢ Miniature Pane of 25 .... (pack of 2)	6.50	3.25	...
477	5¢ Christmas, Singing Children	.85	.20	.15

1968 Commemoratives

| | | 479 | | 485 | | 486 | | 488 | |

		Plate Block	F-VF NH	F-VF Used
478-89	**Set of 12**	...	3.95	2.50
478	5¢ Wildlife - Gray Jays.........................	3.75	.35	.15
479	5¢ Meteorological Readings	1.00	.20	.15
480	5¢ Wildlife - Narwhal	1.00	.20	.15
481	5¢ Int'l. Hydrological Decade	1.00	.20	.15
482	5¢ Voyage of "Nonsuch"	1.25	.25	.18
483	5¢ Lacrosse Players	1.25	.25	.18
484	5¢ George Brown and "Globe"	1.25	.25	.18
485	5¢ Henry Bourassa - Journalist	1.15	.20	.15
486	15¢ World War I Armistice	8.00	1.65	1.20
487	5¢ John McCrae - Poet	1.15	.20	.15
488	5¢ Christmas - Eskimo Carving	.75	.20	.15
488a	5¢ Booklet Pane of 10	...	3.25	...
489	6¢ Christmas - Mother & Infant.................	1.10	.22	.15

1969 Commemoratives

| | 491 | 496 | 500 | 502 |

		Plate Block	F-VF NH	F-VF Used
490-504	**Set of 15**	...	9.25	7.00
490	6¢ Sports - Curling................................	1.25	.25	.15
491	6¢ Vincent Massey	1.00	.20	.15
492	50¢ Aurele de Fey Suzor-Cote...................	15.00	3.00	2.50
493	6¢ Int'l. Labor Organization	1.25	.25	.15
494	15¢ Non-Stop Atlantic Flight	7.50	1.50	1.40
495	6¢ Sir William Osler	1.25	.25	.15
#496-98 Canadian Birds				
496	6¢ White-Throated Sparrow	1.65	.35	.15
497	10¢ Ipswich Sparrow	3.25	.70	.45
498	25¢ Hermit Thrush	8.50	1.75	1.50
499	6¢ Charlottetown Bicentennial	1.25	.25	.15
500	6¢ Canada Summer Games	1.00	.20	.15
501	6¢ Sir Isaac Brock	1.00	.20	.15
502	5¢ Christmas, Children Praying	.85	.20	.15
502a	5¢ Booklet Pane of 10	...	3.50	...
503	6¢ Christmas, Children Praying	.85	.20	.15
504	6¢ Stephen Leacock	1.25	.25	.15

NOTE: STARTING IN 1967, MANY PLATE BLOCKS HAVE IMPRINTS WITHOUT PLATE NUMBERS.

1970 Commemoratives

505	508	513

Scott's No.		Plate Block	F-VF NH	F-VF Used
505-18,531 Set of 15........................		...	**11.50**	**9.75**
505	6¢ Manitoba Centenary	.95	.20	.15
506	6¢ Northwest Territory	.90	.20	.15
507	6¢ Biological Program...................................	1.15	.25	.15
508-11	25¢ Expo '70, Osaka, Japan, attd.................	9.50	8.50	8.50
508-11	Set of 4 Singles..	...	7.75	7.75
512	6¢ Henry Kelsey - Explorer	1.15	.25	.15
513	10¢ 25th Anniv. of United Nations	2.50	.50	.45
514	15¢ 25th Anniv. of United Nations	4.00	.80	.70
515	6¢ Louis Riel, Metis Leader	1.15	.25	.15
516	6¢ Sir A. Mackenzie - Explorer	.90	.20	.15
517	6¢ Sir Oliver Mowat	1.15	.25	.15
518	6¢ Group of Seven	.95	.20	.15

Note: Prices are for stamps without straight edges.

1970 Christmas - Children's Designs

519	524	530

		Plate Block	F-VF NH	F-VF Used
519-30	**Set of 12 Singles**	...	**4.35**	**2.40**
519-23	5¢ Christmas, attached................................	(10) 6.75	2.75	2.50
519-23	Set of 5 Singles..	...	1.50	.75
524-28	6¢ Christmas, attached................................	(10) 7.25	3.00	2.75
524-28	Set of 5 Singles..	...	1.95	.75
529	10¢ Christ Child in Manger..........................	1.95	.40	.30
530	15¢ Snowmobile & Trees	3.85	.75	.75

1970 Commemoratives (continued)

531	6¢ Donald Alexander Smith	.90	.20	.15

532	533	535	543

1971 Commemoratives

		Plate Block	F-VF NH	F-VF Used
532-42,552-58 Set of 18.............................		...	**5.25**	**3.95**
532	6¢ Emily Carr - Painter	.85	.20	.15
533	6¢ Discovery of Insulin...............................	.85	.20	.15
534	6¢ Sir Ernest Rutherford	.85	.20	.15
535	6¢ Maple Leaf - Spring	1.15	.24	.15
536	6¢ Maple Leaf - Summer	1.15	.24	.15
537	7¢ Maple Leaf - Autumn	1.15	.24	.15
538	7¢ Maple Leaf - Winter	1.15	.24	.15
539	6¢ Louis Papineau..	.85	.20	.15
540	6¢ Samuel Hearne..	.85	.20	.15
541	15¢ Radio Canada Int'l................................	7.00	1.40	1.10
542	6¢ Census Centennial...................................	.85	.20	.15

1971-72 Regular Issue

543	7¢ Elizabeth & Transportation, Green.........	3.00	.25	.15
543a	B. Pane of 5 (1 #454,1 #456,3 #543)	...	4.25	...
543b	B. Pane of 20 (4 #454,4 #456,12 #543).......	...	9.00	...
544	8¢ Elizabeth & Parliament, Slate................	2.50	.20	.15
544a	B. Pane of 6 (3 #454,1 #460c,2 #544).........	...	1.50	...
544b	B. Pane of 18 (6 #454,1 #460c,11 #544).....	...	6.50	...
544c	B. Pane of 10 (4 #454,1 #460c,5 #544) (1972)	...	2.25	...
549	7¢ Green, Coil, Perf. 10 Horiz	...	.35	.15
550	8¢ Slate, Coil, Perf. 10 Horiz	...	.40	.15

1971 Commemoratives (continued)

554	556	561

Scott's No.		Plate Block	F-VF NH	F-VF Used
552	7¢ British Columbia Centenary	.85	.20	.15
553	7¢ Paul Kane - Painter	2.25	.30	.18
554	6¢ Christmas, Snowflake.............................	.85	.20	.15
555	7¢ Christmas, Snowflake.............................	1.00	.20	.15
556	10¢ Christmas, Snowflake...........................	1.60	.35	.30
557	15¢ Christmas, Snowflake...........................	3.00	.65	.60
558	7¢ Pierre Laporte	2.00	.20	.15

1972 Commemoratives

559-61,582-85,606-10 Set of 12		...	**8.95**	**7.50**
559	8¢ Figure Skating	1.00	.20	.15
560	8¢ World Health Day	1.20	.25	.18
561	8¢ Frontenac Anniversary	1.00	.20	.15

1972-76 Canadian Indians

562	564	568	570

1972 Indians of the Plains

562-63	8¢ Plains Indians, attached........................	1.50	.60	.60
562-63	Set of 2 Singles, Horizontal Design	...	.55	.25
564-65	8¢ Plains Indians, attached........................	1.50	.60	.60
564-65	Set of 2 Singles, Vertical Design................	...	.55	.25

1973 Algonkian Indians

566-67	8¢ Algonkians, attached.............................	1.50	.60	.55
566-67	Set of 2 Singles, Horizontal Design	...	.55	.25
568-69	8¢ Algonkians, attached.............................	1.50	.60	.55
568-69	Set of 2 Singles, Vertical Design................	...	.55	.25

1974 Pacific Coast Indians

570-71	8¢ Pacific Indians, attached.......................	1.50	.60	.55
570-71	Set of 2 Singles, Horizontal Design	...	.55	.25
572-73	8¢ Pacific Indians, attached.......................	1.50	.60	.55
572-73	Set of 2 Singles, Vertical Design................	...	.55	.25

576	578	580	582

1975 Subarctic Indians

574-75	8¢ Subarctic, attached	1.20	.50	.45
574-75	Set of 2 Singles, Horizontal Design	...	.45	.25
576-77	8¢ Subarctic, attached	1.20	.50	.45
576-77	Set of 2 Singles, Vertical Design................	...	.45	.25

1976 Iroquois Indians

578-79	10¢ Iroquois, attached................................	1.20	.50	.45
578-79	Set of 2 Singles, Horizontal Design	...	.45	.25
580-81	10¢ Iroquois, attached................................	1.20	.50	.45
580-81	Set of 2 Singles, Vertical Design................	...	.45	.25
562-81	**Canadian Indians, set of 20**	...	**4.95**	**2.25**

1972 Earth Sciences

582-85	15¢ Sciences, attached	(16) 29.50	7.00	7.00
582-85	Set of 4 Singles	...	6.60	6.00

1972-1977 Regular Issue, Perf. 12 x 12½ or 12½ x 12

586 593 594 599

Scott's No.		Plate Block	F-VF NH	F-VF Used
586-601	Set of 17	...	14.50	5.25
#586-92 Famous People				
586	1¢ Sir John A. MacDonald	.40	.20	.15
586a	B. Pane of 6 (3 #586,1 #591,2 #593) ('74) ...	...	1.10	...
586b	B. Pane of 18 (6 #586,1 #591,11 #593)('75)..	...	2.50	...
586c	B. Pane of 10 (2 #586,4 #587,4 #593c)('76)...	...	1.20	...
587	2¢ Sir Wilfred Laurier ('73)	.50	.20	.15
588	3¢ Sir Robert L. Borden ('73)	.50	.20	.15
589	4¢ W.L. Mackenzie King ('73)	.60	.20	.15
590	5¢ Richard B. Bennett ('73)	.80	.20	.15
591	6¢ Lester B. Pearson ('73)	.80	.20	.15
592	7¢ Louis St. Laurent ('74)	.90	.20	.15
593	8¢ Queen Elizabeth II, Perf. 12 x 12½ ('73)..	1.00	.20	.15
593b	8¢ Queen Elizabeth II, Perf. 13 x 13½ ('76)..	4.95	.95	.90
593A	10¢ Queen Elizabeth II, Perf. 13 x 13½ ('76)	1.10	.22	.15
593Ac	10¢ Booklet Single, Perf. 12 x 12½ ('76)	...	.40	.25
#594-601 Scenic Pictorials				
594	10¢ Forests, Tagged, Narrow Side Bars........	1.20	.25	.15
594a	10¢ Redrawn, Perf. 13½ ('76)	1.35	.28	.15
595	15¢ Mountain Sheep, Tagged Narrow Bars ..	1.60	.35	.15
595a	15¢ Redrawn, Perf. 13½ ('76)	1.95	.45	.15
596	20¢ Prairie Mosaic, Tagged Narrow Bars.....	1.90	.40	.15
596a	20¢ Redrawn, Perf. 13½ ('76)	2.40	.50	.15
597	25¢ Polar Bears, Tagged Narrow Bars........	2.50	.50	.15
597a	25¢ Redrawn, Perf. 13½ ('76)	3.00	.65	.15
598	50¢ Seashore	4.75	1.00	.15
598a	50¢ Redrawn, Perf. 13½ ('76)	7.00	1.50	.18
599	$1 Vancouver, Revised ('73)	12.50	2.25	.35
599a	$1 Redrawn, Perf. 13½ ('77)	11.00	2.25	.25
600	$1 Vancouver, Original, Perf. 11	22.50	4.75	1.75
601	$2 Quebec Buildings, Perf. 11	19.00	4.00	1.75
604	8¢ Elizabeth II, Coil, Perf. 10 Vert (1974)....	...	.24	.15
605	10¢ Elizabeth II, Coil, Perf. 10 Vert(1976) ...	...	.30	.15

1972 Commemoratives (continued)

606 608 610

606	6¢ Christmas, Candles...............................	.90	.20	.15
607	8¢ Christmas, Candles...............................	1.00	.20	.15
608	10¢ Christmas, Candles & Fruit....................	1.95	.40	.35
609	15¢ Christmas, Candles & Prayer Book........	2.85	.60	.60
610	8¢ C. Krieghoff, Painter.............................	1.80	.25	.15

1973 Commemoratives

620 623 625

611-28	Set of 18.................................	...	5.15	4.25
611	8¢ Monsignor de Laval	.90	.20	.15
612	8¢ Mounties - G.A. French	.95	.20	.15
613	10¢ Mounties - Spectograph	1.40	.30	.30
614	15¢ Mounties - Municipal Rider	3.15	.65	.60
615	8¢ Jeanne Mance - Nurse	.90	.20	.15
616	8¢ Joseph Howe - Journalist	.90	.20	.15
617	15¢ J.E.H. MacDonald - Painter	2.50	.50	.45

NOTE: STARTING IN 1973, ALL CANADIAN STAMPS ARE TAGGED.

1973 Commemoratives (cont.)

Scott's No.		Plate Block	F-VF NH	F-VF Used
618	8¢ Prince Edward I Centenary	.90	.20	.15
619	8¢ Scottish Settlers Bicentenary...................	.90	.20	.15
620	8¢ Royal Visit, Elizabeth II	.90	.20	.15
621	15¢ Royal Visit, Elizabeth II	2.75	.60	.50
622	8¢ Nellie McClung, Suffragette	.90	.20	.15
623	8¢ 21st Olympics Publicity	.90	.20	.15
624	15¢ 21st Olympics Publicity	2.25	.50	.45
625	6¢ Christmas - Ice Skate	.70	.20	.15
626	8¢ Christmas - Dove	.90	.20	.15
627	10¢ Christmas - Santa Claus	1.25	.25	.25
628	15¢ Christmas - Shepherd and Star	2.25	.50	.50

1974 Commemoratives

629 634 644

648 650 655

629-55	Set of 27	...	8.25	5.50
629-32	8¢ Summer Olympics, attd	1.50	1.25	.95
629-32	Set of 4 Singles	...	1.20	.70
633	8¢ Winnipeg Centenary	.90	.20	.15
634-39	8¢ Letter Carriers, attached (6)...................	3.25	2.50	2.50
634-39	Set of 6 Singles	...	1.90	1.80
640	8¢ Agriculture Education............................	1.00	.22	.15
641	8¢ Telephone Centenary	1.00	.22	.15
642	8¢ World Cycling Champs	1.00	.22	.15
643	8¢ Mennonite Settlement	1.00	.22	.15
644-47	8¢ Winter Olympics, attached	1.50	1.25	.95
644-47	Set of 4 Singles	...	1.20	.70
648	8¢ Universal Postal Union	.90	.20	.15
649	15¢ Universal Postal Union	3.50	.75	.65
650	6¢ Christmas "Nativity".............................	.70	.20	.15
651	8¢ Christmas "Skaters in Hull"....................	.85	.20	.15
652	10¢ Christmas "The Ice Cone"	1.45	.30	.25
653	15¢ Christmas "Village".............................	2.75	.55	.50
654	8¢ Marconi Centenary	.90	.20	.15
655	8¢ William H. Merritt, Welland Canal........	.90	.20	.15

1975 Commemoratives

657 662 664 669

658 670 674

1975 Commemoratives

Scott's No.		Plate Block	F-VF NH	F-VF Used
656-80	Set of 25	...	14.75	10.65
656	$1 Olympics "The Sprinter"	12.00	2.25	1.95
657	$2 Olympics "The Plunger"	23.00	4.50	4.25
658-59	8¢ Writers,Montgomery,Hemon attached	.95	.40	.35
658-59	Set of 2 Singles	...	.38	.30
660	8¢ Marguerite Bourgeoys	.90	.20	.15
661	8¢ Alphonse Desjardins	.90	.20	.15
662-63	8¢ Religious Leaders,Chown,Cook att.......	1.10	.45	.40
662-63	Set of 2 Singles	...	.40	.35
664	20¢ Olympics - Pole Vaulting	2.75	.55	.50
665	25¢ Olympics - Marathon Running...............	3.15	.65	.55
666	50¢ Olympics - Hurdling	5.50	1.25	1.00
667	8¢ Calgary Centennial "Untamed"...............	1.00	.20	.15
668	8¢ Women's Year	1.00	.20	.15
669	8¢ Supreme Court Centenary	1.00	.20	.15
670-73	8¢ Canadian Coastal Ships, attached	1.75	1.30	1.30
670-73	Set of 4 Singles	...	1.25	1.00
674-75	6¢ Christmas, attached	.85	.45	.35
674-75	Set of 2 Singles	...	.40	.30
676-77	8¢ Christmas, attached	1.00	.45	.35
676-77	Set of 2 Singles	...	.40	.30
678	10¢ Christmas, Gift Box	1.10	.22	.20
679	15¢ Christmas, Tree	1.85	.40	.40
680	8¢ Royal Canadian Legion	1.00	.20	.15

1976 Commemoratives

684 692 697 704

687 700

681-703	Set of 23...	...	16.75	13.75
681	8¢ Olympic Torch......................................	.95	.20	.15
682	20¢ Olympic Opening Ceremonies...............	2.75	.60	.50
683	25¢ Olympic Medal Ceremonies..................	3.50	.75	.70
684	20¢ Olympics - Communication Arts	3.75	.80	.65
685	25¢ Olympics - Handcraft Tools	4.75	1.00	.70
686	50¢ Olympics - Performing Arts	8.00	1.75	1.20
687	$1 Olympic Site - Tower and Church	12.00	2.50	2.35
688	$2 Olympic Site - Olympic Stadium	24.75	5.00	4.75
689	20¢ Winter Olympic Games........................	2.85	.65	.65
690	20¢ HABITAT - U.N. Conference	2.00	.45	.45
691	10¢ U.S. Bicentennial - B. Franklin	1.20	.25	.20
692-93	8¢ Royal Military College, attd.	1.00	.45	.40
692-93	Set of 2 Singles	...	.40	.30
694	20¢ Olympiad for Physically Disabled	2.85	.60	.55
695-96	8¢ Authors,R. Service, G. Guevremont att	1.00	.45	.35
695-96	Set of 2 Singles	...	.40	.30
697	8¢ Xmas - Stained Glass Window..............	.75	.45	.15
698	10¢ Xmas - Stained Glass Window.............	1.10	.25	.15
699	20¢ Xmas - Stained Glass Window.............	2.15	.45	.40
700-03	10¢ Canadian Inland Ships, attached...........	1.60	1.25	1.25
700-03	Set of 4 Singles	...	1.20	1.10

1977 Commemoratives

704,732-51	Set of 21...	...	5.95	3.95
704	25¢ Queen Elizabeth II Silver Jubilee	2.75	.60	.50

1977-1979 Definitive Issues, Perf. 12 x 12½

707 723 726

1977-1979 Definitive Issues, Perf. 12 x 12½

Scott's No.		Plate Block	F-VF NH	F-VF Used
705-27	Set of 22...	...	14.75	4.85
705	1¢ Wildflower - Bottle Gentian....................	.40	.20	.15
707	2¢ Wildflower - W. Columbine....................	.45	.20	.15
708	3¢ Wildflower - Canada Lily	.50	.20	.15
709	4¢ Wildflower - Hepatica	.50	.20	.15
710	5¢ Wildflower - Shooting Star	.60	.20	.15
711	10¢ Wildflower - Lady's Slipper	.90	.22	.15
711a	10¢ Same (1978, Perf. 13)	.90	.22	.15
712	12¢ Wildflower - Jewelweed, Pf. 13 x 13½ (1978)..................................	1.50	.30	.20
713	12¢ Elizabeth II, Perf. 13 x 13½	1.20	.25	.15
713a	12¢ Booklet Single., Perf. 12 x 12½...........	...	.35	.25
714	12¢ Houses of Parliament, Perf. 13 ('78)......	1.20	.25	.15
715	14¢ Houses of Parliament, Perf. 13 ('78)......	1.30	.28	.15
716	14¢ Eliz. II, 13 x 13½ ('78)	1.30	.28	.15
716a	14¢ Bklt. Sgl., Perf. 12 x 12½ ('78)............	...	.40	.15
716b	14¢ B. Pane of 25, Perf. 12 x 12½ ('78)......	...	6.50	...
717	15¢ Tree - Trembling Aspen, Perf. 13½.......	1.85	.40	.15
718	20¢ Tree - Doug. Fir, Perf. 13½..................	1.85	.40	.15
719	25¢ Trees - Sugar Maple, Perf. 13½	2.25	.50	.15
720	30¢ Trees - Red Oak, Perf. 13½ ('78)..........	2.75	.60	.18
721	35¢ Trees - Winter Pine, Perf. 13½ ('79)......	3.25	.70	.20
723	50¢ Streets-Prairie Town, Perf.13½ ('78)......	5.25	1.15	.50
723A	50¢ Same, "1978" on License Plate	4.75	1.00	.20
724	75¢ Streets-Row Houses, Perf.13½ ('78)	7.00	1.50	.30
725	80¢ Streets-Maritime, Perf. 13½ ('79)..........	7.00	1.50	.35
726	$1 Bay of Fundy, Perf. 13½ ('79)................	8.75	1.95	.40
726a	$1 Untagged(1981).....................................	9.00	2.00	.65
727	$2 Kluane National Park, Perf.13½ ('79)......	18.00	3.95	.90
729	12¢ Parliament, Coil, Perf. 10 Vert.............	...	.24	.15
730	14¢ Parliament, Coil, Perf. 10 Vert. ('78)......	...	.28	.15

NOTE: Also see #781-806

1977 Commemoratives (continued)

733 736 738

741 744 748

732	12¢ Wildlife - Eastern Cougar.....................	1.20	.25	.15
733-34	12¢ Thomson Paintings, attd......................	1.20	.50	.40
733-34	Set of 2 Singles	...	.48	.30
735	12¢ Canadian-born Gov. Generals	1.20	.25	.15
736	12¢ Order of Canada 10th Anniv.	1.20	.25	.15
737	12¢ Peace Bridge - 50th Anniv.	1.20	.25	.15
738-39	12¢ Pioneers,Bernier,Fleming att...............	1.20	.50	.40
738-39	Set of 2 Singles	...	.48	.30
740	25¢ Parliamentary Conference	3.00	.65	.65
741	10¢ Christmas - Christmas Star	.95	.20	.15
742	12¢ Christmas - Angelic Choir	1.20	.25	.15
743	25¢ Christmas - Christ Child	2.40	.50	.40
744-47	12¢ Sailing Ships, attached	1.20	1.00	.90
744-47	Set of 4 Singles	...	.95	.75
748-49	12¢ Inuit Hunting, attached	1.20	.50	.40
748-49	Set of 2 Singles, Seal, Spear Fishing	...	.48	.30
750	12¢ Inuit Hunting, attached	1.20	.50	.40
750-51	Set of 2 Singles, Caribou, Walrus...............	...	.48	.30

1978 Commemoratives

752-56,757-79	Set of 28	...	10.25	6.35
752	12¢ Peregrine Falcon	1.20	.25	.15
753-56	12¢ -$1.25 Capex, Set of 4........................	16.50	3.50	1.60
753	12¢ CAPEX, 12p Queen Victoria	1.20	.25	.15
754	14¢ CAPEX, 10p Cartier	1.40	.30	.15
755	30¢ CAPEX, ½p Queen Victoria	2.75	.60	.40
756	$1.25 CAPEX, 6p Prince Albert.................	11.50	2.50	.95
756a	$1.69 CAPEX Souvenir Sheet.....................	...	2.85	2.75
757	14¢ Commonwealth Games, Symbol..........	1.30	.28	.15
758	30¢ Commonwealth Games, Badminton.....	2.75	.60	.40

759   765   776

753   763   768

Scott's No.		Plate Block	F-VF NH	F-VF Used
759-60	14¢ Commonwealth Games, attd	1.20	.50	.40
759-60	Set of 2 Singles, Stadium, Running	...	.48	.30
761-62	30¢ Commonwealth Games, attd	2.50	1.10	1.10
761-62	Set of 2 Singles, Edmonton, Bowls	...	1.00	.90
763-64	14¢ Captain Cook, attached	1.20	.50	.40
763-64	Set of 2 Singles	...	.48	.30
765-66	14¢ Resource Development, attd	1.20	.50	.40
765-66	Set of 2 Singles	...	.48	.30
767	14¢ Canadian National Exhibition	1.20	.24	.15
768	14¢ Mere d'Youville, Beatified	1.20	.24	.15
769-70	14¢ Travels of Inuit, attached	1.20	.50	.40
769-70	Set of 2 Singles, Woman Walking, Migration	.48	.30	
771-72	14¢ Travels of Inuit, attached	1.20	.50	.40
771-72	Set of 2 Singles, Plane, Dogteam & Sled	...	.48	.30
773	12¢ Christmas, Madonna	.95	.20	.15
774	14¢ Christmas, Virgin & Child	1.15	.24	.15
775	30¢ Christmas, Virgin & Child	2.25	.50	.45
776-79	14¢ Sailing Ice Vessels, attd	1.40	1.20	1.10
776-79	Set of 4 Singles	...	1.10	.80

1979 Commemoratives

780,813-20,833-46	Set of 23	...	7.85	4.75
780	14¢ Quebec Winter Carnival	1.25	.25	.15

1977-1983 Definitives, Perf. 13 x 13½
Designs of #705-730 plus new designs

781-792	Set of 11	...	2.90	1.45
781	1¢ Wildflower, Bottle Gentian ('79)	.40	.20	.15
781a	1¢ Bklt. Sgl., Perf. 12 x 12½	...	.35	.20
781b	B. Pane of 6 (2 #781a & 4 #713a)	...	1.10	...
782	2¢ Wildflower, W. Columbine (1979)	.40	.28	.18
782a	B. Pane of 7 (4 #782b, 3 #716a) ('78)	...	1.10	...
782b	2¢ B. Sgl. Perf. 12 x 12½ ('78)	...	.28	.18
783	3¢ Wildflower-Canada Lily ('79)	.45	.20	.15
784	4¢ Wildflower-Hepatica ('79)	.50	.20	.15
785	5¢ Wildflower-Shooting Star ('79)	.60	.20	.15
786	10¢ Wildflower-Lady's Slipper (1979)	.80	.20	.15
787	15¢ Wildflower-Canada Violet ('79)	1.40	.30	.15
789	17¢ Elizabeth II ('79)	1.35	.28	.15
789a	B. Sgl. Perf. 12 x 12½ ('79)	...	.35	.30
789b	B. Pane of 25, Perf. 12 x 12½ ('79)	...	7.50	...
790	17¢ Houses of Parliament / 1979	1.35	.28	.15
791	30¢ Elizabeth II (1982)	2.25	.50	.15
792	32¢ Elizabeth II (1983)	2.50	.55	.15
797	1¢ Parl. B. Sgl. Perf. 12 x 12½ ('79)	...	.35	.20
797a	B. Pane/6 (1 #797,3 #800,2 #789a)	...	1.15	...
800	5¢ Parl. B. Sgl. Perf. 12 x 12½ ('79)	...	.20	.15
806	17¢ Parl. Coil, Perf. 10 Vert	...	.32	.15

1979 Commemoratives (continued)

813   815   817

821   839   843

Scott's No.		Plate Block	F-VF NH	F-VF Used
813	17¢ Wildlife, Turtle	1.35	.30	.15
814	35¢ Wildlife, Whale	3.25	.70	.60
815-16	17¢ Postal Code, attached	1.50	.60	.55
815-16	Set of 2 Singles	...	.55	.30
817-18	17¢ Writer F. Grove & Poet E. Nelligan att	1.50	.60	.55
817-18	Set of 2 Singles	...	.55	.30
819-20	17¢ Colonels, De Salaberry & By att	1.50	.60	.55
819-20	Set of 2 Singles	...	.55	.40
821-32	17¢ Provincial Flags, Set of 12 Singles	...	3.80	2.40
832a	Sheetlet of Twelve Flags	...	3.95	3.75
833	17¢ Canoe-Kayak Meet	1.35	.30	.15
834	17¢ Women's Field Hockey	1.35	.30	.15
835-36	17¢ Inuit, attached	1.45	.60	.55
835-36	Set of 2 Singles, Summer Tent, Igloo	...	.55	.30
837-38	17¢ Inuit, attached	1.45	.60	.55
837-38	Set of 2 Singles, Dance, Two Figures	...	.55	.30
839	15¢ Christmas - Antique Toy Train	1.40	.30	.15
840	17¢ Christmas - Antique Toy Horse	1.40	.30	.15
841	35¢ Christmas - Antique Knitted Doll	2.90	.65	.45
842	17¢ Int'l. Year of the Child	1.35	.30	.15
843-44	17¢ Flying Boats, attached	1.45	.60	.55
843-44	Set of 2 Singles	...	.55	.30
845-46	35¢ Flying Boats, attached	3.20	1.35	1.25
845-46	Set of 2 Singles	...	1.30	1.20

1980 Commemoratives

849   856   860   870

847-77	Set of 31	...	11.50	7.50
847	17¢ Arctic Islands	1.35	.28	.15
848	35¢ Winter Olympics, Skier	2.85	.60	.55
849-50	17¢ Artists, Harris, Hebert attached	1.45	.60	.55
849-50	Set of 2 Singles	...	.55	.36
851-52	35¢ Artists, Fuller, O'Brien attached	2.95	1.30	1.25
851-52	Set of 2 Singles	...	1.20	1.20
853	17¢ Wildlife Atlantic Whitefish	1.60	.35	.15
854	17¢ Wildlife Greater Prairie Chicken	1.60	.35	.15
855	17¢ Montreal Flower Show	1.35	.28	.15
856	17¢ Rehabilitation Congress	1.35	.28	.15

857   865   873

Scott's No.		Plate Block	F-VF NH	F-VF Used
857-58	17¢ "O Canada" Centenary, attd	1.45	.60	.55
857-58	Set of 2 Singles	...	.55	.30
859	17¢ John George Diefenbaker	1.35	.28	.15
860-61	17¢ Musicians, Albani, Willan attached	1.45	.60	.55
860-61	Set of 2 Singles	...	.55	.35
862	17¢ Ned Hanlan, Oarsman	1.35	.28	.15
863	17¢ Saskatchewan, Wheat Field	1.35	.28	.15
864	17¢ Alberta, Strip Mining	1.35	.28	.15
865	35¢ Uranium Resources	3.00	.65	.50
866-67	17¢ Inuit Spirits, attached	1.45	.60	.55
866-67	Set of 2 Singles, Sedna, Return-Sun	...	.55	.30
868-69	35¢ Inuit Spirits, attached	2.95	1.30	1.25
868-69	Set of 2 Singles, Bird Spirit, Shaman	...	1.20	1.20
870	15¢ Christmas, "Christmas Morning"	1.30	.28	.15
871	17¢ Christmas, "Sleigh Ride"	1.35	.28	.15
872	35¢ Christmas, "McGill Cab Stand"	2.90	.60	.45
873-74	17¢ Military Aircraft, attached	1.50	.65	.55
873-74	Set of 2 Singles	...	.60	.30
875-76	35¢ Military Aircraft, attached	2.95	1.30	1.25
875-76	Set of 2 Singles	...	1.20	1.20
877	17¢ E.P. Lachapelle, Physician	1.35	.28	.15

1981 Commemoratives

879-82   **889**

Scott's No.		Plate Block	F-VF NH	F-VF Used
878-906	**Set of 29**	...	**9.50**	**5.60**
878	17¢ 18th Century Mandora	1.35	.28	.15
879-82	17¢ Feminists, attached	1.65	1.40	1.35
879-82	Set of 4 Singles	...	1.35	.90
883	17¢ Endangered Wildlife, Marmot	1.35	.30	.15
884	35¢ Endangered Wildlife, Wood Bison	3.25	.75	.70
885-86	17¢ Beatified Women, attached	1.45	.60	.55
885-86	Set of 2 Singles	...	.55	.30
887	17¢ Marc-Aurele Fortin, Painter	1.35	.28	.15
888	17¢ Frederic H. Varley, Painter	1.35	.28	.15
889	35¢ Paul-Emile Borduas, Painter	2.95	.60	.60
890-93	17¢ Historic Maps, attached strip	(8) 3.00	1.25	1.20
890-93	Set of 4 Singles	...	1.20	.90
894-95	17¢ Botanists Marie-Victorin, Macoun, att	1.45	.60	.55
894-95	Set of 2 Singles	...	.55	.30
896	17¢ Montreal Rose	1.35	.28	.15
897	17¢ Niagara-on-the-Lake	1.35	.28	.15
898	17¢ Acadian Congress Centenary	1.35	.28	.15
899	17¢ Aaron Mosher Labor	1.35	.28	.15
900	15¢ 1781 Christmas Tree	1.15	.25	.15
901	15¢ 1881 Christmas Tree	1.15	.25	.15
902	15¢ 1981 Christmas Tree	1.15	.25	.15
903-04	17¢ Aircraft, attached	1.50	.65	.55
903-04	Set of 2 Singles	...	.60	.30
905-06	35¢ Aircraft, attached	2.95	1.25	1.20
905-06	Set of 2 Singles	...	1.20	1.10

907   **909**   **914**

1981 "A" Interim Definitives

907	(30¢) "A" and Maple Leaf, Perf. 13 x 13½	2.50	.55	.15
908	(30¢) "A" and Maple Leaf, Coil	...	.80	.18

1982 Commemoratives

909-13,914-16,954,967-75 Set of 18		...	**11.85**	**6.65**
909-13	30¢-60¢ Youth Exhibition, Set of 5	...	3.35	2.25
909	30¢ 1851 3d Beaver	2.60	.55	.18
910	30¢ 1908 15¢ Champlain	2.60	.55	.18
911	35¢ 1935 10¢ Mountie	3.00	.65	.55
912	35¢ 1928 10¢ Mt. Hurd	3.00	.65	.60
913	60¢ 1929 50¢ Bluenose	5.75	1.15	.90
913a	$1.90 Exhibition Souvenir Sheet	...	4.50	4.50
914	30¢ Jules Leger, Governor-Gen'l	2.60	.55	.15
915	30¢ Marathon of Hope - Terry Fox	2.60	.55	.15
916	30¢ New Consitution	2.60	.55	.15

1982-89 Regular Issue

917   **923**   **927**   **931**

Scott's No.		Plate Block	F-VF NH	F-VF Used
917-37	**Set of 23**	...	**29.95**	**8.95**
#917-22,927-30,932-33 Artifacts				
917	1¢ Decoy, Perf. 14 x 13½	.40	.20	.15
917a	1¢ Perf. 13 x 13½ (1985)	.40	.20	.15
918	2¢ Fishing Spear, Perf. 14 x 13½	.40	.20	.15
918a	2¢ Perf. 13 x 13½ (1984)	.40	.20	.15
919	3¢ Stable Lantern, Perf. 14 x 13½	.40	.20	.15
919a	3¢ Perf. 13 x 13½ (1985)	.40	.20	.15
920	5¢ Bucket, Perf. 14 x 13½	.60	.20	.15
920a	5¢ Perf. 13 x 13½ (1985)	.60	.20	.15
921	10¢ Weathercock, Perf. 14 x 13½	.90	.20	.15
921a	10¢ Perf. 13 x 13½ (1985)	1.10	.28	.15
922	20¢ Ice Skates	1.75	.38	.15
923	30¢ Maple Leaf, Red & Blue Pf.13x13½	2.50	.55	.15
923a	Bklt. Pane of 20, Pf. 12 x 12½	...	11.75	...
923b	Bklt. Sgl., Pf. 12 x 12½	...	.75	.20
924	32¢ Maple Leaf, Red & Brown on Beige, Pf. 13 x 13½ ('83)	2.30	.55	.15
924a	Bklt. Pane of 25, Pf. 12 x 12½ ('83)	...	14.50	...
924b	Bklt. Sgl., Pf. 12 x 12½ ('83)	...	.75	.35
925	34¢ Parliament Library ('85)	2.50	.60	.15
925a	Parl. Bklt. Pane of 25 ('85)	...	14.75	...
925b	Bluer sky, Pf. 13½ x 14, bklt. sgl ('86)	...	.95	.20
925c	Same, Bklt. Pane of 25 (1986)	...	14.95	...
926	34¢ Queen Elizabeth II ('85)	2.50	.60	.15
926A	36¢ Queen Elizabeth II ('87)	19.50	3.75	1.75
926B	36¢ Parliamentary ('87)	2.75	.60	.15
926Bc	Booklet Pane of 10 ('87)	...	6.50	...
926Bd	Booklet Pane of 25 ('87)	...	16.50	...
926Be	Bklt. Sgl., Perf. 13½ x 14 ('87)	...	.75	.25
927	37¢ Wooden Plow ('83)	3.00	.65	.20
928	39¢ Settle Bed ('85)	3.25	.70	.20
929	48¢ Hand Hewn Cradle ('83)	4.25	.90	.25
930	50¢ Sleigh (1985)	4.00	.85	.20
931	60¢ Ontario Street Scene	5.50	1.20	.25
932	64¢ Wood Burning Stove ('83)	5.25	1.10	.35
933	68¢ Spinning Wheel (1985)	5.25	1.15	.35
934	$1.00 Glacier National Park ('84)	8.00	1.75	.40
935	$1.50 Waterton Lakes Nat'l. Park	13.50	3.00	.55
936	$2.00 Banff National Park ('85)	16.00	3.50	.75
937	$5.00 Point Pelee Nat'l. Park ('83)	39.50	9.00	1.75

NOTE: Also see #1080-84

Booklet Stamps

938-48	**Set of 11**	...	**4.75**	**3.00**
938	1¢ Parl. East, Bklt. Sgl. ('87)	...	.20	.15
939	2¢ West Parl. Bldg., Booklet Sgl. ('85)	...	.20	.15
939a	Slate Green, bklt. sgl. ('89)	...	.20	.15
940	5¢ Maple Leaf, Booklet Single	...	.20	.15
941	5¢ East Parl. Bldg., Booklet Sgl. ('85)	...	.30	.20
942	6¢ Parl., West B. Sgl. ('87)	...	.25	.15
943	8¢ Maple Leaf, Bklt. Single ('83)	...	.45	.30
944	10¢ Maple Leaf, Booklet Single	...	.40	.30
945	30¢ Maple Leaf, Red, Bklt. Sgl	...	.70	.50
945a	Bklt. Pane of 4 (2 #940,#944,#945) Pf. 12 x 12½	...	1.20	...
946	32¢ Maple Leaf, Brown, Bklt. Sgl. ('83)	...	.60	.50
946b	Bklt. Pane of 4 (2 #941, #943, #946, Pf. 12 x 12½)	...	1.15	...
947	34¢ Center Parl. Bldg., Bklt. Sgl. ('85)	...	1.10	.50
947a	B. Pane of 6 (3 #939,2 #941 #947)	...	1.50	...
948	36¢ Parl. Library, Bklt. Sgl. ('87)	...	.95	.50
948a	Vend Bklt. of 5 (2 #938,2 #942, #948)	...	1.50	...

Coil Stamps

950-53	**Set of 4**	...	**2.65**	**.55**
950	30¢ Maple Leaf, Red	...	.80	.15
951	32¢ Maple Leaf, Brown ('83)	...	.65	.15
952	34¢ Parliament Red Brown ('85)	...	.65	.15
953	36¢ Parliament Dark Red ('87)	...	.65	.15

1982 Commemoratives (continued)

955   **969**   **973**

954	30¢ Salvation Army	2.60	.55	.15

1982 Canada Day Paintings

955-66	30¢ Canada Day Paintings, Set of 12 Sgls	...	8.75	4.00
966a	Sheetlet of 12 Paintings	...	9.00	9.00

1982 Commemoratives (continued)

Scott's No.		Plate Block	F-VF NH	F-VF Used
967	30¢ Regina Centennial	2.60	.55	.15
968	30¢ Henley Rowing Regatta	2.60	.55	.15
969-70	30¢ Bush Aircraft, attached	2.60	1.20	.90
969-70	Set of 2 Singles	...	1.10	.40
971-72	60¢ Bush Aircraft, attached	5.50	2.20	2.10
971-72	Set of 2 Singles	...	2.10	1.90
973	30¢ Christmas, Nativity	2.60	.55	.15
974	35¢ Christmas, Shepherds	2.95	.65	.55
975	60¢ Christmas, Wise Men	5.25	1.10	.80

1983 Commemoratives

976-82,993-1008 Set of 23		...	**19.95**	**9.95**
976	32¢ Communications Year	2.60	.55	.18
977	$2 Commonwealth Day	32.50	7.00	3.25
978-79	32¢ Poet L. Conan, Author E. Pratt attached	2.60	1.15	1.00
978-79	Set of 2 Singles	...	1.10	.40

980   981   983

980	32¢ St. John Ambulance	2.80	.55	.18
981	32¢ World University Games	2.80	.55	.18
982	64¢ World University Games	5.50	1.10	.75

1983 Historic Forts Commemorative Booklet

983-92	32¢ Historic Forts, Set of 10 Bklt. Sgls	...	6.75	5.25
992a	Booklet Pane of 10	...	7.00	7.00

993   995   996

1983 Commemoratives (continued)

993	32¢ Boy Scout Jamboree	2.50	.55	.18
994	32¢ World Council of Churches	2.50	.55	.18
995	32¢ Sir Humphrey Gilbert	2.50	.55	.18
996	32¢ Discovery of Nickel	2.75	.60	.18
997	32¢ Josiah Henson	2.50	.55	.18
998	32¢ Antoine Labelle	2.50	.55	.18

999   1003   1004

999-1000	32¢ Steam Locomotives, attd	2.50	1.15	1.10
999-1000	Set of 2 Singles	...	1.10	.50
1001	37¢ Locomotive Samson 0-6-0,	3.00	.65	.65
1002	64¢ Locomotive Adam Brown 4-4-0,	5.50	1.10	.95
1003	32¢ Dalhousie Law School	2.50	.55	.18
1004	32¢ Christmas, Urban Church	2.50	.55	.18
1005	37¢ Christmas, Family	2.95	.65	.50
1006	64¢ Christmas, Rural Church	5.50	1.10	.95
1007-08	32¢ Army Regiment Uniforms, attd	2.50	1.15	1.00
1007-08	Set of 2 Singles	...	1.10	.40

FROM 1947 TO PRESENT, ADD 20% FOR VERY FINE QUALITY
Minimum of 10¢ Per Stamp

1984 Commemoratives

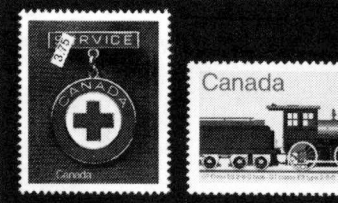

1013   1038

Scott's No.		Plate Block	F-VF NH	F-VF Used
1009-15,1028-39,1040-44 Set of 24		...	**14.95**	**7.95**
1009	32¢ Yellowknife	2.50	.55	.18
1010	32¢ Montreal Symphony	2.50	.55	.18
1011	32¢ Cartier Landing in Quebec	2.50	.55	.18
1012	32¢ Voyage of Tall Ships	2.50	.55	.18
1013	32¢ Red Cross Society	2.50	.55	.18
1014	32¢ New Brunswick	2.50	.55	.18
1015	32¢ St. Lawrence Seaway	2.50	.55	.18

1984 Provincial Landscapes

1016-27	32¢ Canada Day Paintings, Set of 12 Sgls	...	9.75	4.25
1027a	Sheetlet of Twelve Paintings	...	9.95	9.95

1984 Commemoratives (continued)

1028	32¢ United Empire Loyalists	2.50	.55	.18
1029	32¢ Catholic Church in Newfoundland	2.50	.55	.22
1030	32¢ Papal Visit	2.50	.55	.22
1031	64¢ Papal Visit	5.25	1.10	.80
1032-35	32¢ Lighthouses, attd	3.15	2.75	1.20
1032-35	Set of 4 Singles	...	2.60	.90
1036-37	32¢ Steam Locomotives, attd	2.50	1.20	1.00
1036-37	Set of 2 Singles	...	1.10	.40
1038	37¢ Locomotive Grand Trunk 2-6-0	3.15	.65	.65
1039	64¢ Locomotive Canadian Pacific 4-6-0	5.75	1.20	1.00
1039a	$1.65 Locomotive Souvenir Sheet	...	3.95	3.95
1040	32¢ Christmas, Annunciation	2.50	.55	.20
1041	37¢ Christmas, Three Kings	3.10	.65	.60
1042	64¢ Christmas, Snow in Bethlehem	5.25	1.10	.90
1043	32¢ Royal Canadian Air Force	2.50	.55	.20
1044	32¢ Newspaper, La Presse	2.50	.55	.20

1985 Commemoratives

1046   1062   1075   1076

1045-49,1060-66,1067-70,1071-76 Set of 22		...	**14.50**	**6.75**
1045	32¢ Int'l. Youth Year	2.50	.55	.20
1046	32¢ Canadian Astronaut	2.75	.60	.20
1047-48	32¢ Decade of Women T. Casgrain, E. Murphy, attd	2.50	1.20	1.00
1047-48	Set of 2 Singles	...	1.10	.40
1049	32¢ Gabriel Dumont, Metis	2.50	.55	.20

1985 Historic Forts Commemorative Booklet

1050-59	34¢ Historic Forts, Set/10 Bklt Sgls	...	7.75	6.00
1059a	Booklet Pane/10	...	8.00	8.00

1985 Commemoratives (continued)

1060	34¢ Louis Hebert	2.75	.60	.20
1061	34¢ Interparliamentary Union	2.75	.60	.20
1062	34¢ Girl Guides 7th Anniv	2.75	.60	.20
1063-66	34¢ Lighthouses, attd	3.65	3.25	3.00
1063-66	Set of 4 Singles	...	3.15	1.10
1066b	$1.36 Lighthouse Souvenir Sheet of 4	...	3.25	3.15
1067	34¢ Christmas, Santa Claus	2.75	.60	.20
1068	39¢ Christmas, Coach	3.40	.70	.60
1069	68¢ Christmas, Tree	5.95	1.25	.85
1070	32¢ Christmas, Polar Float Bklt. Sgl	...	.90	.30
1070a	Christmas Bklt. Pane/10	...	8.50	8.50
1071-72	34¢ Locomotives, attd	2.75	1.20	.50
1071-72	Set of 2 Singles	...	1.15	.40
1073	39¢ Locomotives #010a	3.25	.70	.70
1074	68¢ Locomotives #H4D	5.95	1.25	1.00
1075	34¢ Royal Canadian Navy	2.75	.60	.20
1076	34¢ Montreal Fine Arts Museum	2.75	.60	.20

1986 Commemoratives

1078 1084 1117

Scott's No.		Plate Block	F-VF NH	F-VF Used
1077-79,1090-1107,1108-21				
	Set of 32	**...**	**25.00**	**10.50**
1077	34¢ 1988 Calgary Winter Olympics, Map	2.75	.60	.20
1078	34¢ EXPO '86 Pavilion	2.75	.60	.20
1079	39¢ EXPO '86 Communications	3.25	.70	.55

1986-87 Regular Issues

1080-84	**Set of 5**	**...**	**13.50**	**2.65**
1080	25¢ Artifact Butter Stamp (1987)	2.30	.50	.18
1081	42¢ Artifact Linen Chest (1987)	4.15	.85	.20
1082	55¢ Artifact Iron Kettle (1987)	6.25	1.35	.30
1083	72¢ Artifact Cart (1987)	8.00	1.70	.40
1084	$5 La Maurice Nat'l. Park	42.50	9.50	1.70

1986 Commemoratives (continued)

1090	34¢ Philippe Aubert de Gaspe	2.75	.60	.20
1091	34¢ Molly Brant, Iroquois	2.75	.60	.20
1092	34¢ EXPO '86, Expo Center	2.75	.60	.20
1093	68¢ EXPO '86, Transportation	6.00	1.25	.55
1094	34¢ Canadian Forces Postal Serv	2.75	.60	.20
1095-98	34¢ Indigenous Birds, attd	5.00	4.25	3.75
1095-98	Set of 4 Singles	...	4.00	1.20
1099-1102	34¢ Canada Day,Inventions attd	3.50	3.00	2.75
1099-1102	Set of 4 Singles	...	2.90	1.10
1103	34¢ Canadian Broadcasting Corp	2.75	.60	.20
1104-07	34¢ Canada Exploration, attd	3.50	3.00	2.75
1104-07	Set of 4 Singles	...	2.90	1.20
1107b	$1.36 CAPEX '87, Exploration Souv. Sheet...	...	3.25	3.15
1108-09	34¢ Frontier Peacemakers, attd	2.75	1.20	1.00
1108-09	Set of 2 Singles	...	1.15	.50
1110	34¢ International Peace Year	2.75	.60	.20
1111-12	34¢ Calgary Winter Olympics, attd	2.75	1.20	.90
1111-12	Set of 2 Singles, Ice Hockey, Biathlon	...	1.15	.40
1113	34¢ Christmas, Angels	2.75	.60	.25
1114	39¢ Christmas, Angels	3.00	.65	.50
1115	68¢ Christmas, Angels	5.50	1.15	.75
1116	29¢ Christmas, Bklt. Sgl. Perf. 13½	...	1.00	.40
1116a	Bklt. Pane of 10, Perf. 13½	...	10.00	...
1116b	Bklt. Sgl., Perf. 12½	...	7.00	2.50
1116c	Bklt. Pane of 10, Perf. 12½	...	70.00	...
1117	34¢ John Molson	2.75	.60	.20
1118-19	34¢ Locomotives, attd	4.25	1.20	.90
1118-19	Set of 2 Singles	...	1.15	.40
1120	39¢ Locomotive CN U2a	4.75	1.10	.80
1121	68¢ Locomotive CP H1c	7.50	1.65	1.40

1122 1130 1134

1987 Commemoratives

1122-25,1126-54	**Set of 33**	**...**	**23.85**	**10.95**
1122-25	34¢-72¢ CAPEX '87 Set of 4	...	3.25	2.15
1122	34¢ 1st Toronto P.O.	2.75	.60	.20
1123	36¢ Nelson-Miramichi P.O.	3.10	.65	.22
1124	42¢ Saint Ours P.O.	4.25	.90	.80
1125	72¢ Battleford P.O.	6.75	1.60	1.25
1125A	$1.84 CAPEX S/S	...	3.95	3.95
1126-29	34¢ Exploration,New France, attd	4.25	3.75	3.50
1126-29	Set of 4 Singles	...	3.60	1.20
#1130-31	1988 Calgary Winter Olympics			
1130	36¢ Speed Skating	2.75	.60	.20
1131	42¢ Bobsledding	3.95	.90	.80
1132	36¢ Volunteer Week	3.00	.65	.20
1133	36¢ Law Day	3.00	.65	.20
1134	36¢ Engineering Institute	3.00	.65	.20
1135-38	36¢ Canada Day, Communications, attd	3.25	2.75	2.50
1135-38	Set of 4 Singles	...	2.65	1.10
1139-40	36¢ Steamships, attd	3.15	1.35	1.10
1139-40	Set of 2 Singles	...	1.30	.55
1141-44	36¢ Underwater Archaeology, attd	3.25	2.75	2.50
1141-44	Set of 4 Singles	...	2.65	1.10

1987 Commemoratives (cont.)

1145 1148 1152-53

Scott's No.		Plate Block	F-VF NH	F-VF Used
1145	36¢ Air Canada 50th Anniv	3.00	.65	.20
1146	36¢ Francophone Int'l. Summit	3.00	.65	.20
1147	36¢ Commonwealth Heads of Gov't	3.00	.65	.20
1148	36¢ Christmas, Poinsettia	3.00	.65	.18
1149	42¢ Christmas, Holly Wreath	3.95	.90	.80
1150	72¢ Christmas, Mistletoe	6.75	1.50	1.10
1151	31¢ Christmas Gifts Bklt. Sgl	...	.75	.50
1151a	Christmas Bklt. Pane of 10	...	6.50	...
1152-53	36¢ Calgary Winter Olympics, attd	3.00	1.30	1.00
1152-53	Set of 2 Singles Skiing, Ski Jumping	...	1.25	.50
1154	36¢ Grey Cup 75th Anniv	3.00	.65	.20

1987-91 Regular Issues

1162 1165 1166 1173

1155-83	**Set of 30**	**...**	**33.95**	**10.85**
#1155-61, 1170-80 Mammals				
1155	1¢ Flying Squirrel, Pf. 13 x 13½ (1988)	.40	.20	.15
1155a	1¢ Perf 13 x 12½ (1991) (Blank)	14.75	3.50	1.95
1156	2¢ Porcupine (1988)	.40	.20	.15
1157	3¢ Muskrat (1988)	.50	.20	.15
1158	5¢ Hare (1988)	.60	.20	.15
1159	6¢ Red Fox (1988)	.70	.20	.15
1160	10¢ Skunk, Pf. 13 x 13½ (1988)	.85	.20	.15
1160a	10¢ Perf. 13 x 12½ (1991) (Blank)	24.50	5.25	.50
1161	25¢ Beaver (1988)	2.10	.45	.15
1162	37¢ Elizabeth II	3.50	.75	.15
1163	37¢ Parliament Perf. 13½ x 13	3.50	.75	.15
1163a	Booklet Pane of 10 (1163c) ('88)	...	7.50	...
1163b	Booklet Pane of 25 (1163c) ('88)	...	18.50	...
1163c	37¢ Bklt. sgl., Pf. 13½ x 14 ('88)	...	.90	.18
1164	38¢ QE II pf. 13 x 12½ ('88)	3.25	.70	.15
1164a	38¢ Bklt. sgl., pf. 13 x 13½ ('88)	...	1.25	.50
1164b	Bklt. Pane of 10 + 2 labels (1988)	...	8.25	...
1165	38¢ Parliament Clock Tower ('88)	3.25	.70	.15
1165a	Bklt. Pane of 10 + 2 labels (1988)	...	8.50	...
1165b	Bklt. Pane of 25 + 2 labels (1988)	...	21.50	...
1166	39¢ Flag & Clouds ('89)	3.50	.75	.15
1166a	Bklt. Pane of 10 (1989)	...	8.50	...
1166b	Bklt. Pane of 25 (1989)	...	21.75	...
1166c	39¢ Perf. 12½ x 13 ('90) (Blank)	49.50	11.00	.75
1167	39¢ Elizabeth II, Perf. 13 x 13½ ('90)	3.25	.70	.15
1167a	Bklt. Pane of 10 (1990)	...	10.50	...
1167b	39¢ Perf. 13 ('90) (Blank)	55.00	12.50	.50
1168	40¢ Elizabeth II ('90)	3.25	.70	.15
1168a	Bklt. Pane of 10 + 2 labels (1990)	...	8.75	...
1169	40¢ Flag & Mountains ('90)	3.25	.70	.15
1169a	Bklt. Pane of 25 + 2 labels	...	26.50	...
1169b	Bklt. Pane of 10 + 2 labels	...	8.75	...
1170	43¢ Lynx ('88)	4.95	1.00	.30
1171	44¢ Walrus Perf. 14½ x 14 ('89)	8.50	1.85	.22
1171a	44¢ Bklt. Sgl. Perf. 12½ x 13 (1989)	...	3.25	.60
1171b	Perf. 12½ x 13, Bklt. Pane of 5+label	...	13.95	...
1171c	44¢ Perf. 13½ x 13 ('89) (Blank)	1650.00	375.00	35.00
1172	45¢ Pronghorn ('90) Perf. 14½ x 14 ('90)	3.75	.85	.30
1172f	Bklt. Sgl. Perf. 12½ x 13 ('90)	...	3.25	.65
1172b	Bklt. Pane of 5 + label, Perf. 12½ x 13	...	13.75	.65
1172d	45¢ Perf. 13 ('90) (Blank)	95.00	19.75	.95
1172A	46¢ Wolverine, Perf. 13 ('90)	3.95	.85	.30
1172Ac	46¢ Wolverine,Bklt. Sgl. Perf. 12½ x 13 ('90)	...	1.60	.60
1172Ae	Bklt. pn. of 5 + label, Perf. 12½x13 ('91)	...	8.75	...
1172Ag	46¢ Wolverine, Perf. 14½ x 14 ('90)	15.00	3.00	.35
1173	57¢ Killer Whale ('88)	6.75	1.00	.30
1174	59¢ Musk-ox Perf. 14½ x 14 ('89)	5.75	1.25	.35
1174a	59¢ Perf. 13 ('89) (Blank)	45.00	10.75	4.75

1987-91 Regular Issues (cont.)

	1175	1183	1185

Scott's No.		Plate Block	F-VF NH	F-VF Used
1175	61¢ Timber Wolf Perf. 14½ x 14 ('90)	5.00	1.10	.40
1175a	61¢ Perf. 13 ('90)........................(Blank)	375.00	75.00	2.25
1176	63¢ Harbor Porpoise Perf. 14½ x 14 ('90)...	9.50	1.35	.40
1176a	63¢ Perf. 13 (1990).....................(Blank)	37.50	5.00	.50
1177	74¢ Wapiti ('88)	6.50	1.30	.40
1178	76¢ Grizzly Bear, Perf. 14½ x 14 ('89)	7.00	1.40	.40
1178a	76¢ Bklt sgl. perf. 12½ x 13 (1989)	...	2.75	1.25
1178b	Bklt. pane of 5 + label, Perf. 12½x13	...	18.50	...
1178c	Perf. 13 ....(Blank)	275.00	57.50	11.75
1179	78¢ Beluga ('90) Perf. 14½ x 14 ('90)	7.00	1.50	.55
1179a	Bklt. Pane of 5, Perf. 12½ x 13	...	13.50	...
1179b	78¢ Perf. 13 ('90)........................(Blank)	225.00	47.50	2.25
1179c	78¢ Blklt. Sgl. Perf. 12½ x 13 (1990)	...	2.95	.95
1180	80¢ Peary Caribou, Perf. 13 ('90)............	9.50	2.10	.70
1180a	80¢ Bklt. Sgl. Perf 12½ x 13 ('90)............	...	1.85	1.25
1180b	Bklt. Pane of 5+label, Perf. 12½x13 ('91) ...	...	19.50	...
1180c	80¢ Perf. 14½ x 14 ('91)	29.50	7.00	.90
1181	$1 Runnymede Library ('89)	7.75	1.75	.40
1182	$2 McAdam Train Station ('89)	15.50	3.50	.80
1183	$5 Bonsecours Market ('90)	38.50	8.50	1.95

1988-90 Booklet Singles and Panes

		Plate Block	F-VF NH	F-VF Used
1184-90	**Set of 7..............**		**4.95**	**1.70**
1184	1¢ Flag, Perf. 13½ x 14 (1990)		.20	.20
1184a	1¢ Perf. 12½ x 13 (1990)		16.50	9.75
1185	5¢ Flag, Perf. 13½ x 14 (1990)		.20	.20
1185a	5¢ Perf. 12½ x 13 (1990)		13.50	9.75
1186	6¢ Parliament (1988)		.85	.30
1187	37¢ Parl. Library ('88).............................		.85	.28
1187a	Bklt. Pane of 4 (#938,2 #942,#1187)		1.50	...
1188	38¢ Parliament Center, ('89)		.85	.30
1188a	Bklt. pane of 5 (3 #939a, 1186, 1188)		1.65	...
1189	39¢ Canadian Flag, ('90)		1.50	.35
1189a	Bklt. pn. of 4 (#1184,2 #1185,#1189)		1.80	...
1189b	39¢ Perf. 12½ x 13		23.50	19.50
1189c	Same, Bklt. pn. of 4 (#1184a,2 #1185a,#1189b)		62.50	...
1190	40¢ Canadian Flag ('90)		2.10	.90
1190a	Bklt. pane of 4 (2 #1184,1185,1190)		2.75	...

1193	1203	1204

1989-91 Self-Adhesive Stamps

			F-VF NH	F-VF Used
1191	38¢ National Flag, bklt. sgl.		1.00	.50
1191a	Booklet of 12		11.75	...
1192	39¢ Flag & Landscape, bklt. sgl. ('90)........		1.00	.50
1192a	Booklet of 12		11.75	...
1193	40¢ Flag & Seacoast, bklt. sgl. ('91)		1.00	.50
1193a	Booklet of 12		11.75	...

1988-90 Coil Stamps, Perf. 10 Horizontal

			F-VF NH	F-VF Used
1194-94c	**Set of 4.............**		**3.70**	**1.10**
1194	37¢ Parliament Library ('88)		.95	.30
1194A	38¢ Parliament Library ('89)		.95	.30
1194B	39¢ Canadian Flag (1990)		.95	.30
1194C	40¢ Canadian Flag (1990)		.95	.30

1988 Commemoratives

		Plate Block	F-VF NH	F-VF Used
1195-1228	**Set of 34 ....**	...	**26.75**	**10.65**
1195-96	37¢ Winter Olympics, attd...............	3.25	1.50	1.10
1195-96	Set of 2 Singles Alpine Skiing, Curling	...	1.35	.50
1197	43¢ Winter Olympics, Figure Skating	3.75	.80	.60
1198	74¢ Winter Olympics,Luge	6.25	1.40	.85
1199-1202	37¢ 18th Century Explorers, attd	2.95	3.00	2.25
1199-1202	Set of 4 Singles	...	2.90	1.20
1203	50¢ Canadian Art, The Young Reader	5.00	1.10	.95
1204-05	37¢ Wildlife Conservation., attd	3.15	1.40	.90
1204-05	Set of 2 Singles, Duck, Moose......................	...	1.35	.60

1988 Commemoratives (continued)

	1214	1215	1216

Scott's No.		Plate Block	F-VF NH	F-VF Used
1206-09	37¢ Science & Technology, attd	3.25	2.95	2.25
1206-09	Set of 4 Singles.....................................	...	2.90	1.20
1210-13	37¢ Butterflies, attd	4.50	3.95	2.25
1210-13	Set of 4 Singles.....................................	...	3.85	1.20
1214	37¢ St. John's Newfld. City Cent	3.00	.65	.20
1215	37¢ 4-H Clubs Anniversary......................	3.00	.65	.20
1216	37¢ Les Forges du Saint-Maurice..............	3.00	.65	.20
1217-20	37¢ Kennel Club Cent. (Dogs) attd	5.50	4.95	2.95
1217-20	Set of 4 Singles.....................................	...	4.85	1.40

1221	1223	1226	1228

		Plate Block	F-VF NH	F-VF Used
1221	37¢ Canadian Baseball Sesqui	3.25	.70	.20
#1222-25	Icons of the Eastern Church			
1222	37¢ Christmas, Conception	2.95	.65	.20
1223	43¢ Christmas, Virgin and Child	3.95	.85	.65
1224	74¢ Christmas, Virgin and Child	5.75	1.35	.95
1225	32¢ Christmas Nativity, bklt. single	...	.70	.50
1225a	Bklt. Pane of 10	...	6.75	...
1226	37¢ Bishop Charles Inglis	3.00	.65	.20
1227	37¢ Frances Ann Hopkins	3.00	.65	.20
1228	37¢ Angus Walters	3.00	.65	.20

1989 Commemoratives

1229	1241	1249

		Plate Block	F-VF NH	F-VF Used
1229-63	**Set of 34.............................**	...	**24.95**	**11.95**
1229-32	38¢ Small Craft Series, attd	3.35	3.00	2.25
1229-32	Set of 4 Singles, Canoes and Kayak	...	2.90	1.20
1233-36	38¢ Explorers/Canadian North, attd	3.35	3.00	2.25
1233-36	Set of 4 Singles.....................................	...	2.90	1.20
1237-40	38¢ Canada Day Photography, attd.............	3.35	3.00	2.25
1237-40	Set of 4 Singles.....................................	...	2.90	1.20
1241	50¢ Art, Ceremonial Frontlet	4.50	2.80	.85
1243-44	38¢ Poets, Frechette, Lampman attd	2.95	1.35	.75
1243-44	Set of 2 Singles.....................................	...	1.30	.50
1245-48	38¢ Mushrooms, attd	3.35	3.00	2.25
1245-48	Set of 4 Singles.....................................	...	2.90	1.20
1249-50	38¢ Canadian Infantry Regiments, attd........	*225.00	1.50	1.10
1249-50	Set of 2 Singles.....................................	...	1.45	.70

* Printing difficulties caused a severe shortage of inscription blocks.

1989 Commemoratives (cont.)

| | 1251 | 1252 | 1260 |

Scott's No.		Plate Block	F-VF NH	F-VF Used
1251	38¢ International Trade	2.95	.65	.20
1252-55	38¢ Performing Arts, attd.	3.35	3.00	2.25
1252-55	Set of 4 Singles	...	2.90	1.20
1256	38¢ Christmas Landscape, pf. 13 x 13½	3.00	.65	.20
1256a	Bklt. pane of 10, perf. 13 x 12½	...	37.50	...
1256b	38¢ Bklt. sgl., perf. 13 x 12½	...	3.75	2.75
1257	44¢ Christmas Landscape	3.75	.80	.75
1257a	Bklt. pane of 5 + label	...	22.50	...
1258	76¢ Christmas Landscape	6.50	1.40	1.15
1258a	Bklt. pane of 5 + label	...	29.50	...
1259	33¢ Christmas Landscape bklt. sgl	...	1.25	1.00
1259a	Bklt. Pane of 10	...	11.75	...
1260-63	38¢ WWII, 1939 Events, attd...................	4.25	3.50	2.75
1260-63	Set of 4 Singles	...	3.35	1.40

1990 Commemoratives

| | 1264 | 1270 | 1271 |

		Plate Block	F-VF NH	F-VF Used
1264-71,1274-1301 Set of 36		...	**29.75**	**14.95**
1264-65	39¢ Norman Bethune, attd	3.25	1.45	1.00
1264-65	Set of 2 Singles	...	1.40	.60
1266-69	39¢ Small Work Crafts, attd.	3.65	3.25	2.25
1266-69	Set of 4 Singles	...	3.15	1.20
1270	39¢ Multicultural Heritage of Canada........	3.25	.70	.25
1271	50¢ Canadian Art, The West Wind	4.75	1.00	.85

| | 1272-73 | 1278 |

1990 Regular Issue Prestige Booklet

1272-73	39¢ Postal Truck bklt. singles	...	1.70	.90
1273a	Bk. pn. of 8 (4 Eng. + 4 Fr. Inscriptions). ...	...	6.75	...
1273b	Bk. pn. of 9 (4 Eng. + 5 Fr. Inscriptions)....	...	9.75	...

1990 Commemoratives (continued)

1274-77	39¢ Dolls, attd	4.50	3.75	2.50
1274-77	Set of 4 Singles	...	3.65	1.20
1278	39¢ Canada Day, 25 Anniv. of Flag	3.25	.70	.25
1279-82	39¢ Prehistoric Life, attd.	4.50	3.75	2.50
1279-82	Set of 4 Singles	...	3.65	1.20
1283-86	39¢ Forests, World Congress, attd	4.25	3.60	2.25
1283-86	Set of 4 Singles	...	3.50	1.00
1283a-86b	Miniature sheets of 4 (Set of 4)	...	22.50	...

1990 Commemoratives (cont.)

| | 1287 | 1288 | 1293 | 1294 |

Scott's No.		Plate Block	F-VF NH	F-VF Used
1287	39¢ Weather Observations Sesqui..............	3.25	.70	.20
1288	39¢ International Literacy Year	3.25	.70	.20
1289-92	39¢ Canadian Lore and Legend, attd	4.65	4.00	2.75
1289-92	Set of 4 Singles, Perf. 12½ x 13	...	3.90	3.20
1289v-92v	39¢ Lore, Perf. 12½ x 12, attd.	...	27.50	15.00
1289v-92v	Set of 4 Singles, Perf. 12½ x 12	...	27.00	14.00
1293	39¢ Agnes Macphail, 1st Woman MP	3.25	.70	.20
1294	39¢ Christmas, Virgin Mary......................	3.25	.70	.20
1294a	Booklet Pane of 10................................	...	11.00	...
1295	45¢ Christmas, Mother & Child	5.25	1.20	.85
1295a	Booklet Pane of 5 + label	...	7.50	...
1296	78¢ Christmas, Children/Raven	8.50	1.85	1.20
1296a	Booklet Pane of 5 + label	...	11.75	...
1297	34¢ Christmas, Rebirth, bklt. sgl	...	.70	.50
1297a	Bklt. Pane of 10	...	7.00	...
1298-1301	39¢ World War II, 1940 Events, attd	4.65	4.00	3.75
1298-1301	Set of 4 Singles	...	3.90	3.40

1991 Commemoratives

| | 1302-05 | 1310 | 1316 |

		Plate Block	F-VF NH	F-VF Used
1302-43,1345-48 Set of 45...............................		...	**35.75**	**14.75**
1302-05	40¢ Physicians, attd	3.50	2.90	2.75
1302-05	Set of 4 Singles	...	2.90	1.20
1306-09	40¢ Prehistoric Life in Canada, attd	4.25	3.60	3.00
1306-09	Set of 4 Singles	...	3.50	1.20
1310	50¢ Canadian Art, Emily Carr....................	4.75	1.00	.85
1311-15	40¢ Public Gardens, bklt. sgls, strip of 5 ...	...	4.00	...
1311-15	Set of 5 Singles	...	3.90	1.65
1315b	Booklet Pane of 10................................	...	7.75	...
1316	40¢ Canada Day	3.75	.80	.20
1317-20	40¢ Small Craft, attd.	3.50	3.00	2.75
1317-20	Set of 4 Singles	...	2.90	1.20
1321-25	40¢ River Heritage, bklt. sgls, strip of 5 ...	...	4.00	3.25
1321-25	Set of 5 Singles	...	3.90	1.65
1325b	River Booklet Pane of 10	...	7.75	...
1326-29	40¢ Ukrainian Migration to Canada, attd....	3.50	3.00	2.75
1326-29	Set of 4 Singles	...	2.90	1.20
1330-33	40¢ Dangerous Public Service orgs,attd	3.50	3.00	2.75
1330-33	Set of 4 Singles	...	2.90	1.20
1334-37	40¢ Canadian Folktales, attd	3.50	3.00	2.75
1334-37	Set of 4 Singles	...	2.90	1.20

| | 1338 | 1339 | 1345 |

1338	40¢ Queen's University, bklt. single	...	.80	.25
1338a	Booklet Pane of 10................................	...	7.75	...
1339	40¢ Christmas, Santa at Fireplace	3.25	.75	.20
1339a	Booklet Pane of 10................................	...	7.50	...
1340	46¢ Christmas,Santa with Tree...................	3.75	.80	.70
1340a	Booklet Pane of 5..................................	...	5.75	...
1341	80¢ Christmas, Sinterklass & Girl	7.75	1.75	1.20
1341a	Booklet Pane of 5..................................	...	9.50	...
1342	35¢ Greet More, Santa Claus, bklt. sgl.......	...	.95	.28
1342a	Bklt. Pane of 10	...	6.95	...

1991 Commemoratives (continued)

Scott's No.		Plate Block	F-VF NH	F-VF Used
1343	40¢ Basketball Centennial	4.25	.95	.30
1344	40¢, 46¢, 80¢ Basketball S/S of 3	...	5.75	4.75
1345-48	40¢ World War II, 1941 Events, attd.	4.25	3.50	2.75
1345-48	Set of 4 Singles	...	3.35	1.40

1991-98 Regular Issues

1349 1358 1359 1361

Scott's No.		Plate Block	F-VF NH	F-VF Used
1349-78	**Set of 29**	**...**	**35.95**	**10.75**
#1349-55, 1361-74 Edible Berries				
1349	1¢ Blueberry (1992)	.40	.20	.15
1350	2¢ Strawberry (1992)	.40	.20	.15
1351	3¢ Crowberry (1992)	.50	.20	.15
1351v	3¢ Crowberry, reprint (1998)	.50	.20	...
1352	5¢ Rose Hip (1992)	.50	.20	.15
1353	6¢ Black Raspberry (1992)	.60	.20	.15
1354	10¢ Kinnikinnik (1992)	.80	.20	.15
1355	25¢ Saskatoon Berry (1992)	1.95	.45	.20
1358	42¢ Canadian Flag & Rolling Hills	3.25	.70	.15
1358a	Booklet Pane of 10	...	7.50	...
1358b	Booklet Pane of 50	...	95.00	...
1358c	Booklet Pane of 25	...	18.95	...
1359	42¢ QE II, Karsh Portrait	3.25	.70	.15
1359a	Booklet Pane of 10	...	7.50	...
1360	43¢ QE II Karsh Portrait (1992)	3.50	.75	.15
1360a	Booklet Pane of 10	...	7.50	...
1360B	43¢ Flag & Prairie, Perf. 13½ x 13 (1992)	3.50	.75	.15
1360Bc	Booklet Pane of 10, Perf. 13½ x 13	...	7.50	...
1360Bd	Booklet Pane of 25, Perf. 13½ x 13	...	20.95	...
1360Be	43¢ Flag & Prairie Perf. 14½ (1994)	5.50	1.10	.20
1360Bf	Booklet Pane of 10, Perf. 14½	...	8.95	...
1360Bg	Booklet Pane of 25, Perf. 14½	...	25.00	...
1360H	45¢ Elizabeth II ('95)	3.50	.75	.15
1360Hi	Booklet Pane of 10	...	8.50	...
1360J	45¢ Flag Perf. 14½ ('95)	3.50	.75	.15
1360Jk	Booklet Pane of 10, Perf 14½	...	8.50	...
1360Jl	Booklet Pane of 25, Perf 14½	...	25.00	...
1360Jm	45¢ Bklt. Single, Perf. 13½ x 13	...	.80	.20
1360Jn	Booklet Pane of 10, Perf 13½ x 13	...	8.50	...
1360Jo	Booklet Pane of 25, Perf 13½ x 13	...	21.50	...
1360P	45¢ Flag, smaller 16 x 20mm size, Perf. 13 x 13½ (1998)	...	.75	.20
1360Pq	Booklet Pane of 10, 13 x 13½	...	7.50	...
1360Pr	Booklet Pane of 30, 13 x 13½	...	21.95	...
1361	48¢ McIntosh Apple Tree, Perf. 13	4.25	.90	.20
1361a	48¢ Bklt. single, Perf. 14½x14 on 3 sides	...	1.10	.30
1361b	Booklet Pane of 5	...	5.50	...
1362	49¢ Delicious Apple, Perf. 13 (1992)	4.25	.90	.20
1362a	49¢ Perf. 14½ x 14	...	1.10	.30
1362b	Booklet Pane of 5, Perf. 14½ x 14	...	5.50	...
1362c	Booklet Pane of 5, Perf. 13	...	7.95	...
1363	50¢ Snow Apple, Perf. 13 (1994)	4.25	.90	.25
1363a	Booklet Pane of 5, Perf. 13	...	5.50	...
1363b	50¢ Bklt. Single Perf. 14½ x 14 (1995	...	1.90	.50
1363c	Booklet Pane of 5, Pf. 14½ x 14	...	9.75	...
1364	52¢ Gravenstein Apple Perf. 13 ('95)	9.50	1.85	.30
1364a	Booklet Pane of 5, Perf. 13	...	9.50	...
1364b	52¢ Bklt. Single, Perf. 14½ x 14	...	2.75	.70
1364c	Booklet Pane of 5, Perf 14½ x 14	...	12.50	...
1366	65¢ Black Walnut Tree	7.25	1.45	.50
1367	67¢ Beaked Hazlenut (1992)	7.00	1.40	.45
1368	69¢ Shagbark Hickory (1994)	5.95	1.30	.40
1369	71¢ American Chestnut ('95)	5.95	1.30	.45
1369a	71¢ Perf. 14½ x 14	18.75	3.75	.95
1371	84¢ Stanley Plum Tree, Perf. 13	9.50	1.90	.50
1371a	84¢ Bklt. single, Perf. 14½x14	...	2.40	.70
1371b	Booklet Pane of 5	...	12.00	...
1372	86¢ Bartlett Pear, Perf. 13 (1992)	9.95	2.25	.60
1372a	86¢ Bklt. Single, Perf. 14½ x 14	...	3.75	1.50
1372b	Booklet Pane of 5, Perf. 14½ x 14	...	14.50	...
1372c	Booklet Pane of 5, Perf. 13	...	18.50	...
1373	88¢ Westcot Apricot, Perf. 13(1994)	8.50	1.75	.50
1373a	Booklet Pane of 5, Perf. 13	...	9.00	...
1373b	88¢ Bklt. Single, Perf. 14½ x 14 (1995)	...	3.95	.85
1373c	Booklet Pane of 5, Pf. 14½ x 14	...	19.50	...
1374	90¢ Elberta Peach, Perf. 13 ('95)	7.95	2.35	.55
1374a	Booklet Pane of 5, Perf. 13	...	12.50	...
1374b	90¢ Bklt. Single, Perf 14½ x 14	...	3.75	.85
1374c	Booklet Pane of 5, Perf. 14½ x 14	...	14.75	...

1991-96 Regular Issues (continued)

1375 1388 1395

Scotts No.		Plate Block	F-VF NH	F-VF Used
1375	$1 Yorkton Court House Perf. 14½x 14 (1994)	7.75	1.70	.50
1375a	$1 Yorkton, Perf. 13½ x 13	8.25	1.80	.60
1376	$2 Truro Normal School (1994) Perf. 14½x 14	15.75	3.50	1.10
1376a	$2 Truro, Perf 13½ x 13	16.75	3.65	1.10
1378	$5 Victoria Public Library ('96)	40.75	8.75	3.50
1992 Self-Adhesive Stamps				
1388	42¢ Flag & Mountains, bklt.sgl.	...	.90	.50
1388a	Booklet of 12	...	10.50	...
1389	43¢ Flag & Seashore,bklt.sgl.	...	.90	.50
1389a	Booklet of 12	...	10.50	...
1991-95 Coil Stamps, Perf. 10 Horizontal				
1394	42¢ Canadian Flag & Rolling Hills	...	.80	.18
1395	43¢ Canadian Flag (1992)	...	.80	.18
1396	45¢ Canadian Flag (1995)	...	.80	.20

1992 Commemoratives

1407 1413 1419

1399-1407,1408-19,1432-55	**Set of 45**		**36.50**	**16.65**
1399-1403	42¢ Winter Olympics, strip of 5 bklt. stamps	4.75	3.50	
1399-1403	Set of 5 Singles	...	4.65	1.75
1403b	Olympics Bklt. Pane of 10	...	9.50	...
	#1404-7a Canada Day, Explorers			
1404-05	42¢ 350th Anniv. of Montreal, attd. pair	3.50	1.50	.80
1404-05	Set of 2 Singles	...	1.45	.60
1406	48¢ Jacques Cartier	3.95	.85	.80
1407	84¢ Christopher Columbus	6.95	1.50	.85
1407a	$2.16 Explorers S/S of 4, regular edition	...	4.00	4.00
1407a var	Same, special ed., w/Maisonneuve sig.	...	160.00	...
1408-12	42¢ Rivers, strip of 5 bklt. stamps	...	4.25	3.25
1408-12	Set of 5 Singles	...	4.15	1.75
1412b	Rivers Bklt. Pane of 10	...	8.25	...
1413	42¢ Alaska Highway	3.50	.75	.20
1414-18	42¢ Summer Olympics,strip of 5 bklt.stamps	4.75	3.75	
1414-18	Set of 5 Singles	...	4.65	1.75
1418b	Olympics Bklt. Pane of 10	...	9.50	...
1419	50¢ Art, Red Nasturtiums	4.50	.95	.85
1431a	42¢ Canada Day, min.sht.of 12 paintings	...	25.95	24.75
1420-31	Set of 12 Singles, Provincial Views	...	24.95	12.50

1436 1441-42

1432-35	42¢ Legendary Heroes, attd	3.50	3.00	2.25
1432-35	Set of 4 Singles	...	2.95	1.20
1436-40	42¢ Minerals, strip of 5 bklt. stamps	...	4.50	4.00
1436-40	Set of 5 Singles	...	4.35	1.75
1440b	Minerals Bklt. Pane of 10	...	8.75	...
1441-42	42¢ Space Exploration, Pair	3.95	1.80	1.50
1441-42	Set of 2 Singles	...	1.70	1.40

1445	1446-47	1453

Scott's No.		Plate Block	F-VF NH	F-VF Used
1443	42¢ Hockey, Early Years	...	.75	.25
1443a	Skates, sticks, bklt. pane of 8.............	...	5.95	...
1444	42¢ Hockey, Six-Team Years	...	.75	.25
1444a	Team emblems, bklt. pane of 8...........	...	5.95	...
1445	42¢ Hockey, Expansion Years	...	.75	.25
1445a	Goalie's mask, bklt. pane of 9............	...	7.50	...
1446-47	42¢ Order of Canada & R. Michener, pair	4.25	1.80	1.30
1446	42¢ Order of Canada.........................	...	.75	.25
1447	42¢ Roland Michener.........................	...	1.10	.35
1448-51	42¢ WWII, 1942 Events, attd.............	3.75	3.25	2.25
1448-51	Set of 4 Singles.................................	...	3.20	1.20
1452	42¢ Christmas, Jouluvana, perf. 12½...	3.50	.75	.15
1452a	42¢ Bklt. Single Perf. 13½................	...	.85	.20
1452b	Booklet Pane of 10, Perf. 13½...........	...	7.50	...
1453	48¢ Christmas, La Befana	4.00	.85	.75
1453a	Booklet Pane of 5..............................	...	5.25	...
1454	84¢ Christmas, Weihnachtsmann..........	7.25	1.50	.80
1454a	Booklet Pane of 5..............................	...	8.50	...
1455	37¢ Christmas, Santa Claus, Bklt. Sgl	...	.75	.50
1455a	Booklet Pane of 10............................	...	7.25	...

1460	1466	1484

1993 Commemoratives

Scott's No.		Plate Block	F-VF NH	F-VF Used
1456-71,1484-89,1491-1506 Set of 38		...	31.75	12.95
1456-59	43¢ Canadian Woman, attd................	3.75	3.25	2.25
1456-59	Set of 4 Singles.................................	...	3.20	1.20
1460	43¢ Stanley Cup Centennial	3.50	.75	.20
1461-65	43¢ Hand-crafted Textiles, strip of 5	...	4.00	3.00
1461-65	Set of 5 Singles.................................	...	3.90	1.75
1465b	Textiles, Booklet Pane of 10..............	...	7.75	...
1466	86¢ Art, Drawing for the Owl	7.00	1.50	1.00
1467-71	43¢ Historic Hotels, Strip of 5 bklt. sgls.......	...	4.00	3.00
1467-71	Set of 5 Singles.................................	...	3.90	1.75
1471b	Historic Hotels, Booklet Pane of 10...	...	7.75	...
1483a	43¢ Canada Day, Provincial & Territorial Parks, miniature sheet of 12...	...	17.95	14.95
1472-83	Set of 12 Singles...............................	...	16.95	7.50
1484	43¢ Founding of Toronto....................	3.50	.75	.20

1485-89	1491-94	1495-98

1485-89	43¢ Rivers, Strip of 5 bklt. sgls.	...	4.00	3.00
1485-89	Set of 5 Singles.................................	...	3.90	1.75
1489b	Rivers, Booklet Pane of 10................	...	7.75	...
1490	$3.56 Motor Vehicles, Souv. Sheet of 6	...	7.75	7.50
1490a-f	Set of 6 Singles, 2-43¢,2-49¢,2-86¢...	...	7.50	6.95
1491-94	43¢ Folk Songs, attd.........................	3.75	3.25	2.75
1491-94	Set of 4 Singles.................................	...	3.20	1.20
1495-98	43¢ Dinosaurs, attd...........................	4.00	3.50	3.00
1495-98	Set of 4 Singles.................................	...	3.40	1.20

Scott's No.		Plate Block	F-VF NH	F-VF Used
1499	43¢ Christmas, Swiety Mikolaj	3.50	.75	.15
1499a	Booklet Pane of 10............................	...	7.50	...
1500	49¢ Christmas, Ded Moroz	4.15	.90	.70
1500a	Booklet Pane of 5..............................	...	4.50	...
1501	86¢ Christmas, Father Christmas	7.50	1.60	.80
1501a	Booklet Pane of 5..............................	...	7.95	...
1502	38¢ Christmas, Santa Claus, bklt. sgl............	...	.75	.30
1502a	Booklet Pane of 10............................	...	7.35	...
1503-06	43¢ World War II, 1943 Events, attd.............	4.00	3.50	2.25
1503-06	Set of 4 Singles.................................	...	3.40	1.20

1509	1510	1511-15

1994 Regular Issues

1507-08	43¢ Greetings, Self-adhesive	...	2.00	1.00
1508a	Booklet Pane of 10 (5 each) w/stickers...........	...	9.95	...

1994 Commemoratives

1509-22,1525-26,1528-40 Set of 29		...	25.95	12.50
1509	43¢ Jeanne Sauve with Tab	...	.90	.30
1509	Block of 4 w/4 different tabs	4.25	3.75	2.25
1510	43¢ T. Eaton Company.......................	...	.85	.30
1510a	Prestige Booklet of 10........................	...	7.95	...
1511-15	43¢ Rivers, Strip of 5 bklt. sgls.	...	6.50	5.00
1511-15	Set of 5 Singles.................................	...	6.40	2.75
1515b	Rivers, Booklet Pane of 10................	...	12.50	...
1516	88¢ Canadian Art, Vera.....................	7.50	1.60	1.25

1522	1529-32

1517-22	43¢-88¢ Commonwealth Games(6)	15.00	4.95	1.95
1517-18	43¢ Lawn Bowl and Lacrosse, Pair	3.50	1.50	.90
1517-18	Set of 2 Singles.................................	...	1.45	.50
1519-20	43¢ High Jump and Wheelchair Marathon, Pair	3.50	1.50	.90
1519-20	Set of 2 Singles.................................	...	1.45	.50
1521	50¢ Diving	5.25	1.10	.80
1522	88¢ Cycling.....................................	7.50	1.60	.85
1523	43¢ Year of the Family, Souv. Sht. of 5........	...	5.25	4.50
1523a-e	Set of 5 Singles.................................	...	5.15	2.25
1524	43¢ Canada Day, Maple Trees, Miniature Sheet of 12	...	12.75	9.95
1524a-l	Set of 12 Singles...............................	...	12.50	6.50
1525-26	43¢ Billy Bishop and Mary Travers, Pair.......	3.50	1.50	.80
1525-26	Set of 2 Singles.................................	...	1.45	.60
1527	$3.62 Public Service Vehicles, Souvenir Sheet of 6	...	8.50	7.25
1527a-f	Set of 6 Singles, 2-43¢,2-50¢,2-88¢	...	8.35	5.75
1528	43¢ Civil Aviation, ICAO..................	3.50	.75	.20
1529-32	43¢ Prehistoric Life, attd.	3.50	3.00	2.25
1529-32	Set of 4 Singles.................................	...	2.95	1.20
1533	43¢ Christmas, Singing Carols	3.50	.75	.15
1533a	Booklet Pane of 10............................	...	7.50	...
1534	50¢ Christmas, Choir.........................	4.25	.90	.70
1534a	Booklet Pane of 5..............................	...	4.50	...
1535	88¢ Christmas, Caroling.....................	7.50	1.60	.90
1535a	Booklet Pane of 5..............................	...	7.75	...
1536	38¢ Christmas, Soloist, bklt. sgl.	...	.85	.30
1536a	Booklet Pane of 10............................	...	8.25	...
1537-40	43¢ World War II, 1944 Events, attd.	4.50	4.00	3.25
1537-40	Set of 4 Singles.................................	...	3.95	1.60

1995 Commemoratives

1552

Scott's No.		Plate Block	F-VF NH	F-VF Used
1541-51,1553-58,1562-66,1570-90 Set of 46		...	36.50	13.50
1541-44	43¢ World War II, 1995 Events, attd.	4.65	3.75	2.75
1541-44	Set of 4 Singles	...	3.65	1.60
1545	88¢ Art, "Floraison"	7.50	1.60	.85
1546	(43¢) Canada Flag 30th Anniv.	3.50	.75	.25
1547-51	(43¢) Fortress of Louisbourg, Strip of 5 Bklt. Singles	...	3.75	3.50
1547-51	Set of 5 singles	...	3.65	1.75
1551b	Louisbourg, Booklet Pane of 10	...	7.50	...
1552	$3.62 Farm and Frontier Vehicles, Souvenir Sheet of 6	...	8.50	6.95
1552a-f	Set of 6 Singles, 2-43¢,2-50¢,2-88¢	...	8.25	5.75
1553-57	43¢ Golf, Strip of 5 Bklt. Sgls.	...	3.75	3.25
1553-57	Set of 5 Singles	...	3.65	1.75
1557b	Golf, Booklet Pane of 10	...	7.50	...

1558	1536-66	1562

1558	43¢ Lunenburg Academy	3.50	.75	.25
1559-61	43¢ Canada Day, Set of 3 Souvenir Sheets bearing 10 different stamps	...	9.95	9.50
1559a-c,1560a-d,1561a-c	Set of 10 Singles	...	9.75	8.75
1562	43¢ Manitoba	3.50	.75	.25
1563-66	43¢ Migratory Wildlife,"Aune" Block of 4	5.50	4.75	2.25
1563-66	Set of 4 singles	...	4.50	1.20
1563/67	43¢ Migratory Wildlife revised Inscribed "Faune", Block of 4	5.50	4.75	2.50
1567	43¢ Belted Kingfisher Single "Faune"	...	1.50	1.10

1568-69

1995 Greetings Booklets

Scotts No.		Plate Block	F-VF NH	F-VF Used
1568-69	45¢ Greetings, Self-adhesive	...	2.10	.90
1569a	Booklet Pane of 10 (5 Each) w/ labels	...	9.75	...
1569c	Booklet Pane of 10 w/ "Canadian Memorial Chiropractic College", covers and labels	...	9.75	...

1579	1584	1585

1995 Commemoratives (continued)

1570-73	45¢ Bridges, Block of 4	3.75	3.25	2.25
1570-73	Set of 4 Singles	...	3.20	1.20
1574-78	45¢ Canadian Arctic, Strip of 5 Bklt.Sgls.	...	4.00	3.25
1574-78	Set of 5 Singles	...	3.90	1.60
1578b	Arctic, Booklet Pane of 10	...	7.75	...
1579-83	45 Comic Books, Strip of 5 Bklt. Singls.	...	4.00	3.25
1579-83	Set of 5 Singles	...	3.90	1.60
1583b	Comic Books, Booklet Pane of 10	...	7.75	...
1584	45¢ U.N. 50th Anniversary	3.95	.80	.25
1585	45¢ Christmas,The Nativity	3.95	.80	.20
1585a	Booklet Pane of 10	...	8.00	...
1586	52¢ Christmas,The Annunciation	4.75	1.00	.70
1586a	Booklet Pane of 10	...	4.75	...
1587	90¢ Christmas,Flight to Egypt	7.95	1.60	.70
1587a	Booklet Pane of 5	...	8.25	...
1588	40¢ Christmas,Holly, booklet single	...	.80	.50
1588a	Booklet Pane of 10	...	7.95	...
1589	45¢ La Francophonie	3.95	.80	.25
1590	45¢ End of Holocaust	3.95	.80	.25

1996 Commemoratives

1591-98,1602-3,1606-14,1617-21,1622-29 Set of 36		...	33.50	13.75
1591-94	45¢ Birds, Strip of 4	...	3.00	2.25
1591-94	Set of 4 singles	...	2.95	1.10
1591-94d	Diamond Pane of 12	...	11.95	...
1591-94r	Rectangular Pane of 12	...	15.95	...

1595-98

1595-98	45¢ High Technology Industries, Block of 4 Booklet singles	...	5.00	4.00
1595-98	Set of 4 singles	...	4.95	1.40
1598b	Technology, Booklet Pane of 12	...	14.75	...

1996 Greetings Booklets

1600-1	45¢ Greetings, Self-adhesive	...	2.25	1.10
1601a	Booklet Pane of 10 (5 each) with labels	...	9.95	...

NOTE: #1600-1 are slightly larger than #1568-69.

1996 Commemoratives (continued)

1602	90¢ Art "The Spirit of Haidi Gwali"	7.00	1.50	.90
1603	45¢ Aids Awareness	3.75	.75	.25
1604	$3.74 Industrial and Commercial Vehicles Souvenir Sheet of 6	...	7.75	7.50
1604a-f	Set of 6 singles, 2-45¢,2-52¢,2-90¢	...	7.50	5.75
1605	5¢ (10), 10¢ (4), 20¢ (10), 45¢ Canadian Vehicles Souvenir Pane of 25	...	9.75	...
1605a-y	Set of 25 Singles	...	9.65	7.75

NOTE: The above pane pictures all 24 stamps shown on the Vehicles series souvenir sheets of 6 plus one additional vehicle.

1996 Commemoratives (continued)

| | 1607 | 1613 | 1614 |

Scott's No.		Plate Block	F-VF NH	F-VF Used
1606	45¢ Yukon Gold Strip of 5	...	4.50	3.00
1606a-e	Yukon Set of 5 Singles	...	4.40	1.50
1606	Yukon Miniature Pane of 10	...	9.00	...
1607	45¢ Canada Day, Maple Leaf in stylized Quilt Design, self-adhesive	...	1.20	.40
1607a	Canada Day Pane of 12	...	13.50	...
1608-12	45¢ Canadian Olympic Gold Medalist, Strip of 5 Booklet Singles	...	5.65	3.75
1608-12	Set of 5 Singles	...	5.50	2.75
1612b	Olympics, Booklet Pane of 10	...	11.00	...
1613	45¢ British Columbia	3.50	.75	.25
1614	45¢ Canadian Heraldry	3.50	.75	.25
1615-16	45¢ 100 Years of Cinema, Self-adhesive Souvenir Sheets of 5 (2)	...	9.75	...
1615a-16a	Set of 10 Singles	...	9.65	7.50

| | 1617 | 1627 | 1630 |

1617	45¢ Edouard Montpetit	3.50	.75	.25
1618-21	45¢ Winnie the Pooh, Block of 4	...	7.00	6.50
1618-21	Set of 4 Singles	...	6.95	1.60
1618-21	Booklet of 16 (4 each design)	...	28.00	...
1621b	Winnie the Pooh, Souvenir Sheet of 4	7.00	6.50	...
1622-26	45¢ Authors, Booklet Strip of 5	...	3.75	2.25
1622-26	Set of 5 Singles	...	3.65	1.50
1626b	Authors, Booklet Pane of 10	...	7.50	...
1627	45¢ Christmas, Snowshoes, Sled	3.50	.75	.20
1627a	Booklet Pane of 10	...	7.50	...
1628	52¢ Christmas, Skiing	4.25	.90	.75
1628a	Booklet Pane of 5	...	4.50	...
1629	90¢ Christmas, Skating	6.95	1.50	1.25
1629a	Booklet Pane of 5	...	7.50	...

1997 Commemoratives

1630, 1631-36, 1637-38, 1639-48, 1649-60, 1661-69, 1670, 1671, 1672, Set of 43		...	33.50	22.95
1630	45¢ Chinese New Year, Year of the Ox	4.25	.90	.30
1630a	New Year Souvenir Sheet of 2	...	2.25	2.10
1630v	Hong Kong '97 Overprint SS of 2	...	7.95	...

| | 1631-34 | 1636 |

1997 Commemoratives (continued)

Scott's No.		Plate Block	F-VF NH	F-VF Used
1631-34	45¢ Birds, Block or Strip of 4	3.50	3.00	1.60
1631-34	Set of 4 Singles	...	2.90	1.10
1635	90¢ Art, "York Boat on Lake Winnipeg"	6.95	1.50	1.25
1636	45¢ Canadian Tire, 75th Anniversary	...	.75	.40
1636a	Tire, Booklet of 12	...	8.95	...

| | 1637 | 1638 | 1639 |

1637	45¢ Father Charles-Emile Gadbois	3.50	.75	.25
1638	45¢ Quebec Floral Festival, Blue Poppy	...	.75	.25
1638a	Blue Poppy, Booklet Pane of 12	...	8.95	...
1639	45¢ Victorian Order of Nurses	3.50	.75	.25

| | 1640 | 1641-44 |

1640	45¢ Law Society of Upper Canada	3.50	.75	.25
1641-44	45¢ Ocean Water Fish, Block of 4	3.50	3.00	1.85
1641-44	Fish, Set of 4 Singles	...	2.90	1.10
1645-46	45¢ Confederation Bridge, Pair	3.50	1.50	.95
1645-46	Bridge, Set of 2 Singles	...	1.45	.50

| | 1647 | 1649 | 1655 |

1647	45¢ Gilles Villeneuve	3.50	.75	.25
1648	90¢ Gilles Villeneuve	8.95	1.95	1.50
1648b	45¢-90¢ Gilles Villeneuve, S/S of 8	...	11.75	...
1649	45¢ John Cabot	3.50	.75	.25
1650-53	45¢ Scenic Highways, Block of 4	3.50	3.00	1.85
1650-53	Highways, Set of 4 Singles	...	2.90	1.10
1654	45¢ Canadian Industrial Designers	3.50	.75	.25
1654	45¢ Industrial, Sheet of 24 w/12 diff. labels	...	17.75	...
1655	45¢ Highland Games	3.50	.75	.25
1656	45¢ Knights of Columbus	3.50	.75	.25
1657	45¢ World Congress PTTI	3.50	.75	.25
1658	45¢ Year of Asia-Pacific	3.50	.75	.25
1659-60	45¢ Hockey Series of Century, bklt. single	...	1.50	.60
1660a	45¢ Hockey, Booklet Pane of 10 (5 ea.)	...	7.50	...
1661-64	45¢ Prominent Canadians, block or strip	3.50	3.00	1.85
1661-64	45¢ Prominent Canadians, set of 4 singles	...	2.90	1.10

1665-68

Scott's No.		Plate Block	F-VF NH	F-VF Used
1665-68	45¢ Supernatural, block of 4	3.50	3.00	1.85
1665-68	45¢ Supernatural, set of 4 singles	...	2.90	1.00
1665-68	45¢ Supernatural, sheetlet of 16	...	11.95	...

1669   1672

1669	45¢ Christmas, Stained Glass Windows	3.50	.75	.20
1669a	45¢ Christmas, Booklet Pane of 10	...	7.50	...
1670	52¢ Christmas, Stained Glass Windows	4.50	.90	.75
1670a	52¢ Christmas, Booklet Pane of 5	...	4.50	...
1671	90¢ Christmas, Stained Glass Windows	7.50	1.50	.95
1671a	90¢ Christmas, Booklet Pane of 5	...	7.50	...
1672	45¢ Royal Agricultural Winter Fair	3.50	.75	.25

1997-99 Regular Issues

1673   1682   1687   1692   1698

1700

1673	1¢ Bookbinding (1999)	.40	.20	.15
1674	2¢ Decorative Ironwork (1999)....................	.40	.20	.15
1675	3¢ Glass-blowing (1999).............................	.40	.20	.15
1676	4¢ Oyster Farming (1999)...........................	.45	.20	.15
1677	5¢ Weaving (1999).....................................	.45	.20	.15
1678	9¢ Quilting (1999)......................................	.70	.20	.15
1679	10¢ Artistic Woodworking (1999)................	.75	.20	.15
1680	25¢ Leatherworking (1999).........................	1.75	.40	.20
1682	46¢ Queen Elizabeth II (1998)	3.25	.70	.18
1687	46¢ Flag over Mountains (1998)	3.25	.70	.18
1687a	Flag, Booklet Pane of 10	...	6.95	...
1692	55¢ Maple Leaf, (1998)	3.85	.85	.70
1692a	Maple Leaf, Booklet Pane of 5	...	4.15	...
1694	73¢ Maple Leaf (1998)	4.85	1.10	.90
1696	95¢ Maple Leaf (1998)	6.65	1.45	1.25
1696a	Maple Leaf, Booklet Pane of 5	...	7.25	...
1697	$1 Loon (1998)..	6.95	1.55	1.20
1698	$2 Polar Bear (1998)...................................	12.95	3.00	1.95
1700	$8 Grizzly Bear, ...	62.50	13.50	9.95
1703	46¢ Canadian Flag Coil, Perf. 10 Horiz. (1998)	...	.70	.20
1705	46¢ Flag over Mountains, S.A. Booklet Single	...	.70	.22
1705a	Flag, Self-adhesive Booklet Pane of 30 (1998)	...	19.75	...
1706	46¢ Maple Leaf, Self-adhesive Booklet Single	...	.70	.22
1706a	Maple Leaf, S.A. Booklet Pane of 18 (1998)	...	12.50	...

1708   1710-13

Scott's No.		Plate Block	F-VF NH	F-VF Used
1708,1710-13, 1715-20, 1721-24, 1735-37, 1738-42, 1750-54, 1756-60, 1761-66 Set of 40		...	**32.75**	**14.50**
1708	45¢ Year of the Tiger	3.50	.75	.25
1708a	45¢ Year of the Tiger S/S of 2	...	1.50	1.40
1709	45¢ Provincial Prime Ministers Souvenir Sheet of 10	...	7.50	7.50
1709a-j	Set of 10 Singles..	...	7.50	5.50
1710-13	45¢ Birds, Strip or Block of 4.......................	3.50	3.00	2.95
1710-13	45¢ Birds, Set of 4 Singles	...	2.90	1.20

1714,14B   1721   1722   1735

1998 Self-Adhesive Stamps

1714	45¢ Maple Leaf, die-cut	...	2.25	1.35
1714a	Sheetlet of 18	...	29.50	...
1714B	45¢ Maple Leaf Coil, die-cut........................	...	.75	.25

1998 Commemoratives (continued)

1715-20	45¢ Fishing Flies, Strip of 6 Bklt. Stamps	...	7.00	4.25
1715-20	Flies, Set of 6 Singles	...	6.75	3.50
1720a	Flies, Bklt. Pane of 12	...	13.85	...
1721	45¢ Institute of Mining, Metallurgy and Petroleum	3.50	.75	.25
1722	45¢ Imperial Penny Postage Centennial	4.50	.95	.35
1722	45¢ Penny Postage, Pane of 14	...	12.95	...
1723-24	45¢ Sumo Wrestling, 2 designs.....................	3.50	1.50	1.25
1723-24	Sumo, Set of 2 Singles................................	...	1.50	.60
1724b	45¢ Sumo, Souvenir Sheet of 2	...	1.50	1.40
1734a	45¢ Canals, Booklet of 10 Stamps	...	11.75	...
1725-34	........................Canals, Set of 10 Singles	...	11.50	5.75
1735	45¢ Health Professionals	3.50	.75	.25

1737b

1736-37	45¢ Royal Canadian Mounted Police..............	3.50	1.50	1.40
1736-37	Mounties, Set of 2 Singles	...	1.50	.60
1737b	45¢ Mounties, Souvenir Sheet of 2	...	2.25	1.95
1737c	Same, "French" Overprint............................	...	3.50	3.50
1737d	Same, "Portugal" Overprint.........................	...	4.95	4.75
1737e	Same, "Italia, "98" Overprint	...	4.95	4.75

1738   1761

1750-53

Scott's No.		Plate Block	F-VF NH	F-VF Used
1738	45¢ William J. Roue, "Bluenose"	3.50	.75	.25
1738	Roue, Sheet of 25	...	18.50	...
1739-42	45¢ Scenic Highways, Block or Strip of 4	3.50	3.00	2.90
1739-42	Highways, Sheet of 20	...	14.75	...
1739-42	Highways, Set of 4 Singles	...	3.00	1.20
1743-49	45¢ Montreal Painters, Set of 7 Singles		5.15	3.95
1749a	45¢ Montreal Painters "The Automatistes Booklet of 7	...	5.25	...
1750-53	45¢ Legendary Canadians, Block/Strip of 4	3.50	3.00	2.90
1750-53	Canadians, Sheet of 20	...	14.75	...
1750-53	Canadians, Set of 4 Singles	...	3.00	1.20
1754	90¢ Canadian Art, "The Farmers Family"	7.00	1.50	1.25
1754	Art, Sheet of 16	...	23.50	...
1755	45¢ Housing in Canada, Sheetlet of 9	...	6.75	...
1755a-1	45¢ Housing, Set of 9 Singles	...	6.65	5.25
1756	45¢ University of Ottawa	3.50	.75	.25
1756	University, Sheet of 20	...	14.75	...
1757-60	45¢ Circus, Set of 4 Singles	...	3.90	1.50
1760a	45¢ Circus, Booklet of 12	...	11.50	...
1760b	45¢ Circus, Souvenir Sheet of 4	...	3.95	3.85
1761	45¢ John Humphrey	3.50	.75	.25
1761	Humphrey, Sheet of 20	...	14.75	...

1762-63

1762-63	45¢ Naval Vessels, attd.	3.50	1.50	1.40
1762-63	45¢ Naval Vessels, Sheet of 20	...	14.75	...
1762-63	45¢ Naval Vessels, set of 2 singles	...	1.45	.60
1764	45¢ Christmas Angel	3.50	.75	.20
1764a	45¢ Christmas Booklet Pane of 10	...	7.50	...
1765	52¢ Christmas Angel	4.50	.90	.75
1765a	52¢ Christmas Booklet Pane of 5	...	4.50	...
1766	90¢ Christmas Angel	7.50	1.50	.95
1766a	90¢ Christmas Booklet Pane of 5	...	7.50	...

1767   1769   1779

Scott's No.		Plate Block	F-VF NH	F-VF Used
1767	46¢ Year of the Rabbit	3.25	.70	.30
1767	Rabbit, Sheetlet of 25	...	17.00	...
1768	95¢ Year of the Rabbit Souvenir Sheet		1.40	...
1769	46¢ Theatre du Rideau Vert	3.25	.70	.30
1769	Theatre, Sheetlet of 16	...	10.95	...
1770-73	46¢ Birds of Canada, attd.	3.25	2.80	2.70
1770-73	Birds, Sheetlet of 20	...	13.95	...
1770-73	Birds, set of 4 singles	...	2.75	1.60
1774-77	46¢ Birds of Canada, Self-adhesive singles		2.80	2.00
1777a	Birds, Booklet Pane, 2-1774-5, 1-1776-7	...	4.25	...
1777b	Birds, Booklet Pane, 1-1774-5, 2-1776-7	...	4.25	...
1777v	Birds, Booklet of 12, Self-adhesive	...	8.35	...
1778	46¢ UBC Museum of Anthropology	3.25	.70	.30
1778	Museum, Sheetlet of 16	...	10.95	...
1779	46¢ "Marco Polo", 19th Century Ship	3.25	.70	.30
1779	Marco Polo, Sheetlet of 16	...	10.95	...
1779a	46¢"Marco Polo" on Souvenir Sheet with 85¢ Australian Joint Issue	...	1.85	1.85

1780-83

1780-83	46¢ Scenic Highways , 4 designs, attd.	3.25	2.80	2.70
1780-83	Highways, Sheetlet of 20	...	13.95	...
1780-83	Highways, set of 4 singles	...	2.75	1.60
1784	46¢ Nunavit	3.25	.70	.30
1784	Nunavit, Sheetlet of 20	...	13.95	...
1785	46¢ Year of Older Person	3.25	.70	.30
1785	Older Persons, Sheetlet of 16	...	10.95	...
1786	46¢ Sikh Canadians	3.25	.70	.30
1786	Sikh, Sheetlet of 16	...	10.95	...
1787-90	46¢ Orchids, 4 Booklet Singles	...	2.80	2.00
1790a	Orchids, Booklet of 12	...	8.35	...
...	46¢ Canadian Horses 4 designs , attd	3.25	2.80	2.00
...	Horses, Sheetlet of 20	...	13.95	...
...	Horses, Set of 4 singles	...	2.75	1.60
...	46¢ Barreau du Quebec	3.25	.70	.30
...	Barreau, Sheetlet of 16	...	10.95	...
...	95¢ Canadian Art. "Cog Licorne"	6.75	1.45	1.25
...	Art, Sheetlet of 16	...	22.75	...
...	46¢ Pan-American Games, attd	3.25	2.80	2.00
...	Games, Sheetlet of	...		...
...	Games, Set of 4 singles	...	2.75	1.60
...	46¢ World Rowing Championship	3.25	.70	.30
...	46¢ Universal Postal Union	3.25	.70	.30
...	46¢ Canadian Air Force	3.25	.70	.30
...	46¢ Canadian Air Show, attd	3.25	2.80	2.00
...	Air Show, Sheetlet of	...		...
...	Air Show, Set of 4 singles	...	2.75	1.60
...	46¢ NATO 50th Anniversary	3.25	.70	.30
...	46¢ Frontier College	3.25	.70	.30

MINT CANADA COMMEMORATIVE YEAR SETS
All Fine To Very Fine, Never Hinged

Year	Scott Nos.	Qty.	F-VF NH
1947-49	274-77,82-83	6	.90
1951-52	303-04,11-15,17-19	10	4.65
1953-54	322-24,35-36,49-50	7	1.35
1955	352-58	7	1.60
1956	359-61,64	4	.95
1957	365-74	10	3.95
1958	375-82	8	1.60
1959	383-88	6	1.10
1960-61	389-95	7	1.30
1962	396-400	5	.90
1963	410,12-13	3	.65
1964	416,431-35	6	1.15
1964-66	417-29A (Coats of Arms & Flowers)	14	2.75
1965	437-44	8	1.50
1966	445-52	8	1.50
1967	453,469-77	10	1.90
1968	478-89	12	3.95
1969	490-504	15	9.25
1970	505-18,531	15	11.50
1970	519-30 (Christmas)	12	4.35
1971	532-42,552-58	18	5.25
1972	559-61,582-85,606-10	12	8.95
1972-76	562-81 (Indians)	20	4.95
1973	611-28	18	5.15
1974	629-55	27	8.25
1975	656-80	25	14.75
1976	681-703	23	16.75

Scott Nos.		Qty.	F-VF NH
1977	704,732-51	21	5.95
1978	752-56,757-79	28	10.25
1979	780,813-20,833-46	23	7.85
1980	847-77	31	11.50
1981	878-906	29	9.50
1982	909-13,914-16,954,967-75	18	11.85
1983	976-82,993-1008	23	19.95
1984	1009-15,1028-39,1040-4444	24	14.95
1985	1045-49,1060-66,1067-70,1071-76	22	14.50
1986	1077-79,1090-1107,1108-15,1116b,1117-21	32	25.00
1987	1122-25,1126-54	33	23.85
1988	1195-1228	34	26.75
1989	1229-63	34	24.95
1990	1264-71,1274-1301	36	29.75
1991	1302-43,1345-48	45	35.75
1992	1399-1407,1408-19,1432-55	45	36.50
1993	1456-71,1484-89,1491-1506	38	31.75
1994	1509-22,1525-26,1528-40	29	25.95
1995	1541-51,1553-58,1562-67,1570-90	47	36.50
1996	1591-98,1602-3,1606-14,1617-21,1622-29	36	33.50
1997	1630, 1631-36, 1637-38, 1639-48, 1649-60 1661-69, 1670, 1671, 1672,	43	33.50
1998	1708, 1710-13, 1715-20, 1721-24, 1735-37, 1738-42, 1750-54, 1756-60, 1761-66	40	32.75

249

| B1 | B4 | B7 | B10 |

Scott's No.		Plate Block	F-VF NH	F-VF Used
B1-12	Montreal Olympics, Set of 12	...	5.50	5.50

1974 Olympic Games

B1	8¢+2¢ Olympic Emblem, Bronze	1.40	.30	.30
B2	10¢+5¢ Olympic Emblem, Silver	2.00	.45	.45
B3	15¢+5¢ Olympic Emblem, Gold	2.75	.60	.60

1975 Olympic Games - Water Sports

B4	8¢+2¢ Swimming	1.40	.30	.30
B5	10¢+5¢ Rowing	2.00	.45	.45
B6	15¢+5¢ Sailing	2.75	.60	.60

1975 Olympic Games - Combat Sports

B7	8¢+2¢ Fencing	1.40	.30	.30
B8	10¢+5¢ Boxing	2.00	.45	.45
B9	15¢+5¢ Judo	2.75	.60	.60

1976 Olympic Games - Team Sports

B10	8¢+2¢ Basketball	1.40	.30	.30
B11	10¢+5¢ Vaulting	2.00	.45	.45
B12	20¢+5¢ Soccer	3.50	.75	.75

1996 Literacy Issue

B13

B13	45¢ + 5¢ Literacy Singles	...	1.00	.75
B13a	Booklet Pane of 10	...	9.50	...

AIR MAIL STAMPS

| C1 | C2 | C5 |

1928-1932 Airmail Issues VF + 30% (B)

Scott's No.		NH VF	F-VF	Unused VF	F-VF	Used F-VF
C1	5¢ Allegory (1928)	13.75	10.00	9.00	6.75	2.50
C2	5¢ Globe, Brown (1930)	55.00	41.50	36.50	27.50	16.50
C3	6¢ on 5¢ Allegory (1932)	9.00	6.75	6.00	4.50	2.25
C4	6¢ on 5¢ Ottawa (1932)	23.75	16.75	16.00	11.75	8.50

| C6 | C7 | C9 |

1935-46 Airmail Issues VF + 25%

Scott's No.		Plate Blocks NH	Unused	F-VF NH	Unused	F-VF Used
C5-9	Set of 5	...	...	9.15	7.25	1.85
C5	6¢ Daedalus, Red Brown ....(6)	16.50	12.50	2.25	1.75	.75
C6	6¢ Steamer (1938)	14.50	10.75	2.95	2.25	.25
C7	6¢ Student Flyers (1942)	18.50	14.00	3.50	2.75	.75
C8	7¢ Student Flyers (1943)	3.50	2.75	.70	.55	.15
C9	7¢ Canada Geese (1946)	3.50	2.50	.70	.55	.15
C9a	7¢ Booklet Pane of 4	...	...	2.95	2.50	...

AIRMAIL SPECIAL DELIVERY 1942-1947 VF + 25%

| CE1 | E1 |

Scott's No.		Plate Blocks NH	Unused	F-VF NH	Unused	F-VF Used
CE1-4	Set of 4	...	...	12.95	9.50	9.15
CE1	16¢ Aerial View	14.00	10.75	1.90	1.40	1.35
CE2	17¢ Aerial Veiw (1943)	15.00	11.75	2.70	1.95	1.85
CE3	17¢ Plane, Original Die (1946)	23.00	18.00	4.50	3.25	3.15
CE4	17¢ Corrected Die (1947)	23.00	18.00	4.50	3.25	3.15

CE3 has circumflex (e) over second "E" of "EXPRESS". CE4 has an accent (e).

AIRMAIL OFFICIAL STAMPS 1949-1950 VF + 20%

CO1	7¢ Ovptd. "O.H.M.S." (C9)	47.50	35.00	10.75	7.95	3.85
CO2	7¢ Ovptd. "G" (#C9) (1950)	75.00	58.50	15.00	12.00	11.00

SPECIAL DELIVERY STAMPS 1898-1933
E1 VF Used + 50% (B) E2-5 VF Used + 30% (B)

| E2 | E3 | E4 |

Scott's No.		NH VF	F-VF	Unused VF	F-VF	Used F-VF
E1	10¢ Blue Green (1898)	125.00	75.00	57.50	37.50	6.25
E2	20¢ Carmine (1922)	100.00	65.00	55.00	37.50	5.50
E3	20¢ Mail Transport (1927)	19.50	14.50	11.75	8.50	7.50
E4	20¢ "TWENTY" (1930)	75.00	47.50	42.50	27.50	10.75
E5	20¢ "20 CENTS" (1933)	73.50	46.50	42.50	27.50	13.00

| E6 | E7 |

| E10 | E11 |

SPECIAL DELIVERY 1935-1946 VF + 25%

Scott's No.		Plate Blocks NH	Unused	F-VF NH	Unused	F-VF Used
E6-11	Set of 6	...	...	41.50	29.50	27.50
E6	20¢ Progress ....(6)	65.00	45.00	6.75	4.50	4.25
E7	10¢ Arms, Green (1939)	22.50	17.50	4.00	3.00	2.50
E8	20¢ Arms, Carm. (1938)	195.00	140.00	27.50	19.50	19.50
E9	10¢ on 20¢ (#E8) (1939)	33.50	24.00	4.50	3.25	3.25
E10	10¢ Arms & Flags (1942)	12.00	8.75	2.25	1.65	1.25
E11	10¢ Arms (1946)	8.75	6.50	1.50	1.15	.75

SPECIAL DELIVERY OFFICIAL STAMPS 1949-1950 VF + 20%

EO1	10¢ Ovptd. "O.H.M.S." (#E11)	75.00	55.00	13.00	9.50	9.50
EO2	10¢ Ovptd. "G" (#E11) (1950)	140.00	110.00	22.50	17.50	17.50

NOTE: PRICES THROUGHOUT THIS LIST ARE SUBJECT TO CHANGE WITHOUT NOTICE IF MARKET CONDITIONS REQUIRE. MINIMUM ORDER MUST TOTAL AT LEAST $20.00.

| | F1 | J1 | J6 | J11 |

REGISTRATION STAMPS 1875-1888 (OG + 20%) VF + 80% (C)

Scott's No.		NH Fine	Unused Fine	Unused Ave.	Used Fine	Used Ave.
F1	2¢ Orange, Perf. 12	120.00	50.00	30.00	2.25	1.40
F1a	2¢ Vermillion, Perf. 12	130.00	57.50	35.00	6.50	3.75
F1b	2¢ Rose Carmine, Perf. 12..........	325.00	150.00	90.00	75.00	42.50
F1d	5¢ Orange, Perf. 12 x 11½..........	...	250.00	150.00	75.00	42.50
F2	5¢ Dark Green, Perf. 12..............	175.00	80.00	45.00	2.50	1.50
F2a	5¢ Blue Green, Perf. 12..............	185.00	85.00	47.50	2.75	1.60
F2b	5¢ Yellow Green, Perf. 12...........	265.00	120.00	70.00	4.25	2.50
F2d	5¢ Green, Perf. 12 x 11½............	...	850.00	500.00	140.00	85.00
F3	8¢ Blue (1876)	...	250.00	150.00	200.00	125.00

POSTAGE DUE STAMPS
1906-1928 VF Used + 40% (B)

Scott's No.		NH VF	NH F-VF	Unused VF	Unused F-VF	Used F-VF
J1-5	Set of 5	170.00	117.50	97.50	69.50	26.75
J1	1¢ Violet	18.75	9.75	11.00	7.50	2.50
J1a	1¢ Thin Paper (1924)..................	25.00	18.59	15.00	10.75	5.00
J2	2¢ Violet	18.75	12.50	11.00	7.50	.60
J2a	2¢ Thin Paper (1924)..................	33.50	24.00	20.00	14.50	6.50
J3	4¢ Violet (1928)	75.00	55.00	45.00	32.50	13.50
J4	5¢ Violet	18.50	12.50	11.00	7.50	1.00
J4a	5¢ Thin Paper (1928)..................	14.00	9.50	8.25	5.75	4.75
J5	10¢ Violet (1928)	48.00	33.75	28.00	19.50	10.75

1930-1932 VF Used + 40% (B)

Scott's No.		NH VF	NH F-VF	Unused VF	Unused F-VF	Used F-VF
J6-10	Set of 5	153.50	107.50	92.50	66.75	15.65
J6	1¢ Dark Violet	12.00	8.50	7.00	5.00	2.40
J7	2¢ Dark Violet	8.75	6.25	5.25	3.75	.65
J8	4¢ Dark Violet	18.50	13.00	11.50	8.00	2.50
J9	5¢ Dark Violet (1931)	19.50	13.75	12.00	8.50	5.50
J10	10¢ Dark Violet (1932)	105.00	75.00	63.50	45.00	5.50

1933-1934 VF Used + 40% (B)

Scott's No.		NH VF	NH F-VF	Unused VF	Unused F-VF	Used F-VF
J11-14	Set of 4	55.00	38.75	33.75	23.75	11.50
J11	1¢ Dark Violet (1934)	13.75	9.75	8.50	6.00	3.95
J12	2¢ Dark Violet	5.65	4.00	3.50	2.50	.70
J13	4¢ Dark Violet	13.75	9.75	8.50	6.00	4.25
J14	10¢ Dark Violet..........................	25.00	18.00	15.00	10.75	3.50

| J15 | J23 | J28 | MR1 | MR3 |

POSTAGE DUE STAMPS
1935-1965 VF + 20%

Scott's No.		Plate Block	F-VF NH	F-VF Used
J15-20	Set of 7	...	4.75	3.15
J15	1¢ Dark Violet	1.75	.20	.15
J16	2¢ Dark Violet	1.75	.20	.15
J16B	3¢ Dark Violet ('65)...................	15.00	2.00	1.10
J17	4¢ Dark Violet	2.25	.25	.15
J18	5¢ Dark Violet ('48)	3.00	.40	.30
J19	6¢ Dark Violet ('57)...................	12.50	1.65	1.35
J20	10¢ Dark Violet..........................	2.75	.35	.15

1967 Centennial Issue Regular Size 20 x 17 mm., Perf. 12

Scott's No.		Plate Block	F-VF NH	F-VF Used
J21-27	Set of 7	...	3.10	3.10
J21	1¢ Carmine Rose.........................	7.00	.20	.20
J22	2¢ Carmine Rose.........................	1.40	.25	.25
J23	3¢ Carmine Rose.........................	1.50	.28	.28
J24	4¢ Carmine Rose.........................	2.75	.40	.40
J25	5¢ Carmine Rose.........................	8.75	1.40	1.40
J26	6¢ Carmine Rose.........................	2.75	.40	.40
J27	10¢ Carmine Rose.......................	2.50	.35	.35

POSTAGE DUE STAMPS (cont.)

Scott's No.		Plate Block	F-VF NH	F-VF Used
	1969-1974 Modular Size 20 x 15¾ mm., Perf. 12			
J28,J31,J32a,J34,J35,J36 Dextrose (Yellow) (6)		...	21.50	21.00
J28v,J29-30,J31v,J33,J34v,J35v,J36v,J37 White Gum(9)			2.30	2.15
J28	1¢ Dextrose (Yellow Gum) ('70)....................	2.75	.50	.45
J28v	1¢ Carmine Rose, White Gum ('74)	1.65	.35	.35
J29	2¢ Carmine Rose White Gum ('73)	1.50	.20	.20
J30	3¢ Carmine Rose White Gum ('74)................	1.65	.25	.20
J31	4¢ Dextrose (Yellow Gum) ('69)...................	2.25	.45	.40
J31v	4¢ Carmine Rose, White Gum ('74)	1.20	.25	.22
J32a	5¢ Dextrose (Yellow Gum) ('69)...................	95.00	19.50	19.50
J33	6¢ Carmine Rose White Gum('73)	1.20	.25	.22
J34	8¢ Dextrose (Yellow Gum)	2.10	.35	.30
J34v	8¢ Carmine Rose, White Gum ('74)	1.25	.25	.22
J35	10¢ Dextrose (Yellow Gum) ('69)	2.25	.50	.15
J35v	10¢ Carmine Rose, White Gum ('73)	1.25	.25	.22
J36	12¢ Dextrose (Yellow Gum) ('69)	3.95	.70	.60
J36v	12¢ Carmine Rose, White Gum ('73)	1.50	.25	.25
J37	16¢ Carmine Rose White Gum('74)	2.25	.40	.35
	1977-78 Modular Size 20 x 15¾mm., Perf. 12½ x 12			
J28a-40	Set of 9	...	4.15	3.50
J28a	1¢ Carmine Rose	.50	.20	.15
J31a	4¢ Carmine Rose	.60	.20	.18
J32	5¢ Carmine Rose	.75	.20	.18
J34a	8¢ Carmine Rose (1978)...............................	2.10	.35	.30
J35a	10¢ Carmine Rose	1.10	.22	.22
J36a	12¢ Carmine Rose	9.75	1.20	.85
J38	20¢ Carmine Rose	2.25	.45	.40
J39	24¢ Carmine Rose	2.75	.60	.55
J40	50¢ Carmine Rose	4.75	.95	.90

WAR TAX STAMPS 1915-1916 VF Used + 50% (B)

Scott's No.		NH VF	NH F-VF	Unused VF	Unused F-VF	Used F-VF
MR1	1¢ George V, Green	18.75	12.75	11.00	7.25	.20
MR2	2¢ Carmine	18.75	12.75	11.00	7.25	.25
MR3	2¢ + 1¢ Carm., T.1 ('16)	26.50	18.00	15.00	10.00	.15
MR3a	2¢ + 1¢ Carm., Type II	200.00	125.00	110.00	67.50	3.00
MR4	2¢ + 1¢ Brown, Type II	22.50	15.00	13.75	9.00	.15
MR4a	2¢ + 1¢ Brown, Type I	...	...	240.00	160.00	6.50
MR5	2¢ + 1¢ Carm., Perf. 12 x 8	55.00	37.50	30.00	20.00	17.50
MR6	2¢ + 1¢ Carm., P.8 Vert. Coil......	165.00	110.00	90.00	60.00	5.00
MR7	2¢ + 1¢ Br.,T.II P.8 Vt. Coil........	28.00	19.50	16.50	11.00	.70
MR7a	2¢ + 1¢ Br.,T.I P.8 Vt. Coil.........	200.00	135.00	115.00	75.00	5.25

OFFICIAL STAMPS (VF + 30%)

| O1 | O12 | O16 | 021 |

1949-50 Issues of 1942-46 Overprinted O.H.M.S. VF + 25%

Scott's No.		Plate Blocks NH	Unused	F-VF NH	F-VF Unused	F-VF Used
O1-10	Set of 9	...	...	225.00	165.00	137.50
O1	1¢ George VI, Green (249)..............	9.50	7.25	1.85	1.40	1.35
O2	2¢ George VI, Brown (250)...........	100.00	80.00	7.50	5.50	6.50
O3	3¢ George VI, Violet (252).............	9.75	7.25	1.85	1.40	1.00
O4	4¢ George VI, Carmine (254)	17.50	12.50	2.15	1.60	.55
O6	10¢ Great Bear Lake (269)..............	18.75	15.00	2.50	1.80	.50
O7	14¢ Hydroelectric Sta. (270)...........	26.75	21.75	3.35	2.50	1.85
O8	20¢ Reaper (271)..........................	75.00	55.00	10.00	7.50	2.50
O9	50¢ Lumbering (272).....................	950.00	700.00	160.00	115.00	100.00
O10	$1 Train Ferry (273)......................	395.00	295.00	42.50	31.50	32.50

1950 Issues of 1949-50 Overprinted O.H.M.S. VF + 25%

Scott's No.		Plate Blocks NH	Unused	F-VF NH	F-VF Unused	F-VF Used
O11	50¢ Development (294)	135.00	95.00	25.00	17.50	16.50
O12-15A	Set of 5.......................................	...	...	4.50	3.65	2.35
O12	1¢ George VI, Green (284).............	3.65	3.00	.30	.25	.25
O13	2¢ George VI, Sepia (285)..............	4.50	3.50	.95	.75	.55
O14	3¢ G. VI, Rose Violet (286)	5.75	4.50	1.00	.80	.45
O15	4¢ G. VI, Carmine (287).................	5.75	4.50	1.00	.80	.15
O15A	5¢ G. VI, Deep Blue (288)	10.75	8.00	1.65	1.25	1.10

NOTE: NUMBER IN ( ) INDICATES CATALOG NUMBER OF BASIC STAMP WHICH HAS NOT BEEN OVERPRINTED.

1950 Issues of 1948-50 Overprinted G VF + 25%

Scott's No.		Plate Blocks NH	Unused	F-VF NH	F-VF Unused	F-VF Used
O16-25	Set of 11	....	...	105.00	80.00	65.00
O16	1¢ George VI, Green (284)	2.50	2.00	.35	.25	.15
O17	2¢ George VI, Sepia (285)	5.00	4.00	1.20	.90	.70
O18	3¢ G. VI, Rose Violet (286)	6.25	5.00	1.20	.90	.18
O19	4¢ G. VI, Carmine (287)	6.25	5.00	1.20	.90	.15
O20	5¢ G. VI, Deep Blue (288)	13.00	10.75	1.40	1.10	.75
O21	10¢ Great Bear Lake (269)	12.50	10.00	2.00	1.60	.40
O22	14¢ Hydroelectric Sta. (270)	28.50	23.50	4.75	3.75	1.80
O23	20¢ Reaper (271)	87.50	65.00	11.75	9.00	.90
O24	50¢ Oil Development (294)	52.50	40.00	8.25	6.50	4.75
O25	$1 Train Ferry (273)	375.00	300.00	80.00	60.00	60.00
O26	10¢ Fur Trading (301)	5.95	4.75	1.00	.80	.20

1951-53 Issues of 1951-53 Overprinted G VF + 25%

028 033 040 046

O27	$1 Fisheries (302)	375.00	300.00	75.00	60.00	60.00
O28	2¢ G. VI, Olive Green (305)	2.40	1.95	.50	.40	.15
O29	4¢ George VI, Orange (306)	4.50	3.25	.80	.60	.15
O30	20¢ Forestry Products (316)	10.75	8.00	2.00	1.50	.18
O31	7¢ Canada Goose (320)	16.00	12.00	3.65	2.75	.95
O32	$1 Totem Pole (321)	85.00	65.00	16.50	12.00	9.50

1953-55 Issues of 1953-55 Overprinted G VF + 20%

Scott's No.		Plate Blocks NH	Unused	F-VF NH	F-VF Unused	F-VF Used
O33-37	Set of 5		...	1.70	1.35	.65
O33	1¢ Queen Elizabeth (325)	1.70	1.40	.30	.25	.15
O34	2¢ Queen Elizabeth (326)	1.70	1.40	.30	.25	.15
O35	3¢ Queen Elizabeth (327)	1.70	1.40	.30	.25	.15
O36	4¢ Queen Elizabeth (328)	2.40	1.95	.45	.35	.15
O37	5¢ Queen Elizabeth (329)	2.40	1.95	.45	.35	.15
O38	50¢ Textile (334)	24.00	19.50	4.25	3.25	1.00
O38a	50¢ Textile, Flying G (1961)	23.50	18.75	4.25	3.25	1.50
O39	10¢ Eskimo (351)	4.75	3.75	.85	.65	.15
O39a	10¢ Eskimo, Flying G (1962)	12.50	10.00	1.75	1.40	.85

1955-56 Issues of 1955-56 Overprinted G VF + 20%

O40-45	Set of 5		...	3.35	2.75	.80
O40	1¢ Queen Elizabeth (337)	1.50	1.30	.30	.25	.25
O41	2¢ Queen Elizabeth (338)	1.85	1.60	.30	.25	.15
O43	4¢ Queen Elizabeth (340)	4.50	3.75	.95	.80	.15
O44	5¢ Queen Elizabeth (341)	2.75	2.25	.55	.45	.15
O45	20¢ Paper Industry (362)	8.25	6.75	1.50	1.20	.18
O45a	20¢ Paper, Flying G (1962)	43.50	35.00	6.50	5.25	.45

1963 Issue of 1962-63 Overprinted G

Scott's No.		Plate Block	F-VF NH	F-VF Used
O46-49	Set of 4	...	2.75	2.75
O46	1¢ Queen Elizabeth (401)	(Blank)	.80	.80
O47	2¢ Queen Elizabeth (402)	(Blank)	.80	.80
O48	4¢ Queen Elizabeth (404)	(Blank)	.80	.80
O49	5¢ Queen Elizabeth (405)	(Blank)	.50	.50

CANADA "TAGGED" ISSUES

(A) = Wide Side Bars
(B) = Wide Bar in Middle
(C) = Bar at Left or Right
(D) = Narrow Bar in Middle
(E) = Narrow Side Bars - General

Scott's No.		F-VF NH
	1962-63 Elizabeth II	
337-41p	1¢-5¢, Set of 5	9.50
337p	1¢ Violet Brown (A)	1.20
338p	2¢ Green (A)	1.20
339p	3¢ Carmine Rose (A)	1.20
340p	4¢ Violet (B)	2.95
341p	5¢ Blue (A)	3.25
401-5p	1¢-5¢, Set of 5	1.90
401p	1¢ Brown (A)	.20
402p	2¢ Green (A)	.20
403p	3¢ Purple (A)	.25
404p	4¢ Carmine (C)	.90
404pa	4¢ Carmine (D)	.90
404pb	4¢ Carmine (B)	4.00
405p	5¢ Violet Blue (A)	.55
405q	5¢ Min. Pane of 20	49.50
	1964-67	
434p	3¢ Brown (A)	.65
434q	3¢ Min. Pane of 25	11.00
435p	5¢ 1964 Xmas (A)	1.00
443p	3¢ 1965 Xmas (A)	.25
443q	3¢ Min. Pane of 25	9.00
444p	5¢ 1965 Xmas (A)	.30
451p	3¢ 1966 Xmas (A)	.25
451q	3¢ Min. Pane of 25	4.95
452p	5¢ 1966 Xmas (A)	.45
453p	5¢ Flag over Globe (A)	.40

Scott's No.		F-VF NH
	1967-72 Definitives, Pf. 12	
454p	1¢ Brown (A)	.30
454pa	1¢ Brown (B)	.30
454pb	1¢ Brown (E)	.20
454ep	1¢ Booklet single, Perf. 12½ x 12 (E)	.60
455p	2¢ Green (A)	.25
455pa	2¢ Green (B)	.25
455pb	2¢ Green (E)	.20
456p	3¢ Purple (A)	.25
456pa	3¢ Purple (E) precan	.65
457p	4¢ Carmine (C)	.55
457pa	4¢ Carmine (A)	.50
457pb	4¢ Carmine (E)	.20
458p	5¢ Blue (A)	.60
458bp	5¢ Min. Pane of 20	62.50
458pa	5¢ Blue (B)	.45
459p	6¢ Orange, Pf. 10 (A)	.60
459bp	6¢ Orange, Perf. 12½ x 12 (A)	.60
460p	6¢ Black, Die I, Perf. 12½ x 12 (A)	.40
460cp	6¢ Black, Die II, Perf. 12½ x 12 (B)	.60
460cpa	6¢ Black, Bklt. Sgl., Die II (A)	4.50
460fp	6¢ Black, Die I (B)	.30
460fpa	6¢ Black, Die I (E)	.65
462p	10¢ Jack Pine (A)	1.00
462pa	10¢ Jack Pine (E)	.85
463p	15¢ Bylot Island (A)	.90
463pa	15¢ Bylot Island (E)	.90
464p	20¢ Ferry (A)	1.50

Scott's No.		F-VF NH
465p	25¢ Solemn Land (A)	2.75
	1967-69	
476p	3¢ 1967 Xmas (A)	.25
476q	3¢ Min. Pane of 25	4.95
477p	5¢ 1967 Xmas (A)	.28
488p	5¢ 1968 Xmas (A)	.25
488q	5¢ B. Pane of 10	3.75
489p	6¢ 1968 Xmas (A)	.30
502p	5¢ 1969 Xmas (B)	.22
502q	5¢ B. Pane of 10	3.50
503p	6¢ 1969 Xmas (A)	.28
	1970	
505p	6¢ Manitoba (A)	.35
508-11p	25¢ Expo '70 (A)	11.75
513p	10¢ UN (A)	.90
514p	15¢ UN (A)	1.50
519-30p	5¢-15¢ Set of 12 sngls	6.95
519-23p	5¢ Strip of 5 (B)	4.50
524-28p	5¢ Strip of 5 (B)	4.95
529p	10¢ Manager (B)	.55
530p	15¢ Snowmobile (B)	1.00
	1971-72	
541p	15¢ Radio Canada (A)	2.75
543p	7¢ Green (A)	.60
544p	8¢ Slate (A)	.35
544pa	8¢ Slate (E)	.30
544q	B.Pn.of 6 [#454pb (3), 460cpa (1),544p (2)]	2.25
544r	B.Pn.of 18 [#454pb (6), 460cpa (1),544pa (11)]	5.95

Scott's No.		F-VF NH
544s	B.Pn.of 10 [#454pb (4), 460cpa (1),544p (5)]	2.50
550p	8¢ Coil, Slate (E)	.30
554p	6¢ Snowflake (B)	.25
555p	7¢ Snowflake (A)	.35
556p	10¢ Snowflake (A)	.50
557p	15¢ Snowflake (A)	.95
560p	8¢ World Health (E)	.60
561p	8¢ Fronterac (E)	.65
562-63p	8¢ Indians (E)	1.10
564-65p	8¢ Indians (E)	1.10
582-85p	15¢ Sciences (E)	11.00
	1972 Pictorials	
594	10¢ Forests (E)	.25
594p	10¢ Forests (A)	1.10
595	15¢ Mountain Sheep (E)	.35
595p	15¢ Mountain Sheep (A)	1.20
596	20¢ Prairie Mosaic (E)	.40
596p	20¢ Prairie Mosaic (A)	1.75
597	25¢ Polar Bears (E)	.50
597p	25¢ Polar Bears (A)	1.85
	1972 Commemoratives	
606p	6¢ Christmas (E)	.25
606pa	6¢ Christmas (A)	.30
607p	8¢ Christmas (E)	.30
607pa	8¢ Christmas (A)	.35
608p	10¢ Christmas (E)	.60
608pa	10¢ Christmas (A)	.65
609p	15¢ Christmas (E)	1.20
609pa	15¢ Christmas (A)	1.25
610p	8¢ Krieghoff (E)	.35

CANADA HUNTING PERMIT STAMPS

AB 1

NS2

No.	Description	F-VF NH
	CANADA	
CN 1	'85 $4 Mallards Bklt	12.00
CN 2	'86 $4 Canvasbks Bklt	12.00
CN 2B	'86 Min. Sheet of 16	275.00
CN 3	'87 $6.50 Can. G'se Bklt	11.00
CN 3B	'87 Min. Sheet of 16	275.00
CN 4	'88 $6.50 Pintails Bklt	14.00
CN 4B	'88 Min. Sheet of 16	275.00
CN 5	'89 $7.50 Snow G'se Bklt	14.50
CN 5B	'89 Min. Sheet of 16	275.00
CN 6	'90 $7.50 Wood Duck Bklt	13.00
CN 6B	'90 Min. Sheet of 16	220.00
CN 7	'91 $8.50 Blk. Duck Bklt	13.00
CN 7B	'91 Min. Sheet of 16	220.00
CN 7J	'91 Joint Issue w/US	31.50
CN 7JI	'91 J'nt Issue w/US, Impf	72.50
CN 8	'92 $8.50 Cmn Elders Bklt	13.00
CN 8B	'92 Min. Sheet of 16	220.00
CN 9	'93 $8.50 Hd'd Mergans'r	13.00
CN 9B	'93 Min. Sheet of 16	220.00
CN 10	'94 $8.50 Ross' Geese	13.00
CN10B	'94f Min. Sheet of 16	220.00
CN 11	'95 $8.50 Redheads	13.00
CN11B	'95 Min. Sheet of 16	220.00
CN12	'96 $8.50 Goldeneyes	13.00
CN12B	'96 Min. Sheet of 16	220.00
CN13	'97 $8.50 Gadwalls	13.00
CN13B	'97 Min. sheet of 16	220.00
CN14	'98 $8.50 Ring Necked Duck	13.00
CN14B	'98 Mini Sheet of 16	195.00
	ALBERTA	
AB 1	'89 $6.00 Canada Geese	25.00
AB 2	'90 $7.00 Mallards	20.00
AB 3	'91 $7.71 Pintails	18.00
AB 4	'92 $7.90 Snow Geese	17.00
AB 5	'93 $7.90 Canvasbacks	15.00
AB 6	'94 $8.36 Redheads	13.00
AB 7	'95 $8.36 Wh. Fronted Geese	13.00
AB 8	'96 $8.36 Goldeneyes	13.00
AB 9	'97 $8.36 Harlequin	13.00
	ALBERTA HABITAT	
ABH 1	'96 $6.00 Big Horn Sheep	8.00
ABH 1B	'96 $6.00 Same-Booklet	10.00
ABH 1M	'96 $6.00 Same-Minisheet	34.00
ABH 2	'97 $6.00 Rocky Mnt. Goat	8.00
ABH 2B	'97 $6.00 Same-Booklet	10.00
ABH 2M	'97 $6.00 Same-Minisheet	34.00
ABH 3	'98 $6.00 Cougar	8.00
ABH 3B	'98 $6.00 Same, Booklet	10.00
ABH 3M	'98 $6.00 Mini Sheet	34.00
ABH 4	'99 $6.00 Elk	8.00
ABH 4B	'99 Same, Booklet	10.00
ABH 4M	'99 Same, Mini Sheet	34.00
	BRITISH COLUMBIA	
BC 1	'95 $6 Bighorn Sheep	8.00
BC 1B	'95 Same, Booklet	10.00
BC 1M	'95 Same, Mini Sheet	34.00
BC 2	'96 $6 Elk	8.00
BC 2B	'96 Same, Booklet	10.00
BC 2M	'96 Same, Mini Sheet	34.00
BC 3	'97 $6 Grizzly Bear	8.00
BC 3B	'97 Same, Booklet	10.00
BC 3M	'97 Same, Mini Sheet	34.00
BC 4	'98 $6 Tufted Puffins	8.00
BC 4B	'98 Same, Booklet	10.00
BC 4M	'98 Same, Mini Sheet	34.00
BC 5	'99 $6 Bald Eagle	8.00
BC 5B	'99 Same, Booklet	10.00
BC 5M	'99 Same, Mini Sheet	34.00
	MANITOBA	
	Winnipeg Duck Stamp	11.00
	Winnipeg Duck, Flourescent Paper	11.00
MAN 1	'94 $6 Polar Bear	8.00
MAN 1B	'94 Same, Booklet	10.00
MAN 1M	'94 Same, Mini Sheet 4	34.00
MAN 2	'95 $6 Whitetailed Deer	8.00
MAN 2B	'95 Same, Booklet	10.00
MAN 2M	'95 Same, Mini Sheet 4	34.00
MAN 3	'96 $6 Lynx	8.00
MAN 3B	'96 Same, Booklet	10.00
MAN 3M	'96 Same, Mini Sheet	34.00
MAN 4	'97 $6 Falcon	8.00
MAN 4B	'97 Same, Booklet	10.00
MAN 4M	'97 Same, Mini Sheet	34.00
MAN 5	'98 $6 Moose	8.00
MAN 5B	'98 Same, Booklet	10.00
MAN 5M	'98 Same, Minisheet	34.00
	NEW BRUNSWICK	
NB 1	'94 $6 White Tail Deer	8.00
NB 1B	'94 Same, Booklet	10.00
NB 1M	'94 Same, Mini Sheet of 4	34.00
NB 2	'95 $6 Cougar	8.00
NB 2B	'95 Same, Booklet	10.00
NB 2M	'95 Same, Mini Sheet of 4	34.00
NB 3	'96 $6 Moose	8.00
NB 3B	'96 Same, Booklet	10.00
NB 3M	'96 Same, Mini Sheet	34.00
NB 4	'97 $6 Pheasant	8.00
NB 4B	'97 Same, Booklet	10.00
NB 4M	'97 Same, Mini Sheet	34.00
NB 4	'98 $6 Rainbow Trout	8.00
NB 4B	'98 Same, Booklet	10.00
NB 4M	'98 Same, Mini Sheet	34.00
	NEWFOUNDLAND	
NEWF 1	'94 $6 Woodland Caribou	8.00
NEWF 1B	'94 Same, Booklet	10.00
NEWF 1M	'94 Same, Mini Sht. 4	34.00
NEWF 2	'95 $6 Goldeneyes	8.00
NEWF 2B	'95 Same, Booklet	10.00
NEWF 2M	'95 Same, Mini Sheet	34.00
NEWF 3	'96 $6 Moose	8.00
NEWF 3B	'96 Same, Booklet	10.00
NEWF 3M	'96 Same, Mini Sheet	34.00
NEWF 4	'97 $6 Harlequin Duck	8.00
NEWF 4B	'97 Same, Booklet	10.00
NEWF 4M	'97 Same, Mini Sheet	34.00
NEWF 5	'98 $6 Bear	8.00
NEWF 5B	'98 Same, Booklet	10.00
NEWF 5M	'98 Same, Mini Sheet	34.00
	NORTHWEST TERRITORIES	
NWT 1	'97 $6 Arctic Hare	8.00
NWT 1B	'97 Same, Booklet	10.00
NWT 1M	'97 Same, Mini Sheet	34.00
NWT 2	'98 $6 Snowy Owl	8.00
NWT 2B	'98 Same, Booklet	10.00
NWT 2M	'98 Same, Mini Sheet	34.00
	NOVA SCOTIA	
NS 1	'92 $6 Whitetail Deer	12.00
NS 1B	'92 $6 Wh'tail Deer Bklt	35.00
NS 1M	'92 $6 Mini Sheet of 4	50.00
NS 2	'93 $6 Summer Pheasant	10.00
NS 2B	'93 $6 Pheasant Bklt	12.50
NS 2M	'93 $6 Mini Sheet of 4	34.00
NS 3	'94 $6 Wood Duck	8.00
NS 3B	'94 Same, Booklet	10.00
NS 3M	'94 Same, Mini Sheet of 4	34.00
NS 4	'95 $6 Coyote	8.00
NS 4B	'95 Same, Booklet	10.00
NS 4M	'95 Same, Mini Sheet of 4	34.00
NS 5	'96 $6 Osprey	8.00
NS 5B	'96 Same, Booklet	10.00
NS 5M	'96 Same, Mini Sheet	34.00
NS 6	'97 $6 Woodpecker	8.00
NS 6B	'97 Same, Booklet	10.00
NS 6M	'97 Same, Mini Sheet	34.00
NS 7	'98 $6 Blue Winged Teal	8.00
NS 7B	'98 Same, Booklet	10.00
NS 7M	'98 Same, Mini Sheet	34.00
	NUNUVUT TERRITORY	
NT 1	'99 $6.00 Polar Bear	8.00
NT 1B	'99 Same, Booklet	10.00
NT 1M	'99 Same, Mini Sheet	34.00
	ONTARIO	
ON 1	'93 $6 Ruffled Grouse	11.00
ON 1B	'93 $6 Grouse Bklt	10.00
ON 1M	'93 $6 Mini Sheet of 4	34.00
ON 2	'94 $6 Deer	8.00
ON 2B	'94 Same, Booklet	10.00
ON 2M	'94 Same, Mini Sheet of 4	34.00
ON 3	'95 $6 Fish	8.00
ON 3B	'95 Same, Booklet	10.00
ON 3M	'95 Same, Mini Sheet/4	34.00
ON 4	'96 $6 Blue Wing Teal	8.00
ON 4B	'96 Same, Booklet	10.00
ON 4M	'96 Same, Mini Sheet	34.00
ON 5	'97 $6 Lesser Scamp	8.00
ON 5B	'97 Same, Booklet	10.00
ON 5M	'97 Same, Mini Sheet	34.00
ON 6	'98 $6 River Otter	8.00
ON 6B	'98 Same, Booklet	10.00
ON 6M	'98 Same, Mini Sheet	34.00
	PRINCE EDWARD ISLAND	
PEI 1	'95 $6 Canada Geese	8.00
PEI 1B	'95 Same, Booklet	10.00
PEI 1M	'95 Same, Mini Sheet of 4	34.00
PEI 2	'96 $6 Woodcock	8.00
PEI 2B	'96 Same, Booklet	10.00
PEI 2M	'96 Same, Mini Sheet	34.00
PEI 3	'97 $6 Red Fox	8.00
PEI 3B	'97 Same, Booklet	10.00
PEI 3M	'97 Same, Mini Sheet	34.00
PEI 4	'98 $6 Wigeon	8.00
PEI 4B	'98 Same, Booklet	10.00
PEI 4M	'98 Same, Mini Sheet	34.00
	QUEBEC	
QU 1	'88 $6 Ruffled Grouse	120.00
QU 1M	'88 $6 Mini Sheet of 4	225.00
QU 1MI	'88 Imperf. Sheet of 4	1100.00
QU 2	'89 $6 Black Ducks	37.50
QU 2M	'89 $6 Mini Sheet of 4	140.00
QU 2MI	'89 Imperf. Sheet of 4	350.00
QU 3	'90 $6 Common Loons	22.00
QU 3M	'90 $6 Mini Sheet of 4	135.00
QU 3MI	'90 Imperf. Sheet of 4	350.00
QU 4	'91 $6 Cmn Gldneyes	16.00
QU 4M	'91 $6 Mini Sheet of 4	83.40
QU 4MI	'91 Imperf. Sheet of 4	350.00
QU 5	'92 $6.50 Lynx	12.50
QU 5A	'92 $10 Lynx Surcharge	25.00
QU 5M	'92 $6 Mini Sheet of 4	90.00
QU 5MI	'92 Imperf. Sheet of 4	280.00
QU 6	'93 $6.50 Pergrn Falcon	12.50
QU 6M	'93 $6.50 Mini Sheet of 4	60.00
QU 6MI	'93 $6.50 Impf Sht. of 4	225.00
QU 7	'94 $7 Beluga Whale	13.00
QU 7M	'94 Same, Mini Sheet of 4.	45.00
QU 7MI	'94 Same, Imperf. Sht. 4	225.00
QU 8	'95 $7 Moose	12.00
QU 8M	'95 Same, Mini Sht of 4	45.00
QU 8MI	'95 Same, Imperf.Sht/4	225.00
QU 9	'96 $7 Blue Heron	12.00
QU 9A	'96 Same,Ovrprinted WWF	18.00
QU 9M	'96 Same, Mini Sheet of 4.	45.00
QU 9MI	'96 Same, Imperf. Sht. 4	225.00
QU 10	'97 $8.50 Snowy Owl	14.00
QU 10A	'97 Same,Ovrprinted WWF	18.00
QU 10M	'97 Same, Mini Sheet of 4.	45.00
QU 10MI	'97 Same, Imperf. Sht. 4	225.00
QU 11	'98 $10.00 Snow Goose	14.00
QU 11A	'98 Same, Overprinted WWF	18.00
QU 11M	'98 Same, Mini Sheet of 4.	55.00
QU 11MI	'98 Same, Imperf Sheet	225.00
QU 12	'99 $10.00 River Otter	14.00
QU 12A	'99 Same, Overprinted WWF	18.00
QU 12M	'99 Same, Mini Sheet of 4.	55.00
QU 12MI	'99 Same, Imperf Sheet of 4	150.00
	SASKATCHEWAN	
SK 1	'88 $5 American Widg'n	40.00
SK 2	'89 $5 Bull Moose	40.00
SK 3	'90 $5 Shp Tail'd Grouse	50.00
SK 4	'93 $6 Mallards	8.00
SK 4B	'93 $6 Mallards Bklt	10.00
SK 4M	'93 $6 Mini Sht. of 4	34.00
SK 5	'94 $6 Wood Ducks	8.00
SK 5B	'94 Same, Booklet	10.00
SK 5M	'94 Same, Mini Sheet/4	34.00
SK 6	'95 $6 Antelope	8.00
SK 6B	'95 Same, Booklet	10.00
SK 6M	'95 Same, Mini Sheet/4	34.00
SK 7	'96 $6 Ruddy Duck	8.00
SK 7B	'96 Same, Booklet	10.00
SK 7M	'96 Same, Mini Sheet	34.00
SK 8	'97 $6 Wigeon	8.00
SK 8B	'97 Same, Booklet	10.00
SK 8M	'97 Same, Mini Sheet	34.00
	YUKON TERRITORY	
YT 1	'96 $6 Bald Eagle	8.00
YT 1B	'96 Same, Booklet	10.00
YT 1M	'96 Same, Mini Sheet	34.00
YT 2	'97 $6 Moose	8.00
YT 2B	'97 Same, Booklet	10.00
YT 2M	'97 Same, Mini Sheet	34.00
YT 3	'98 $6 Polar Bear	8.00
YT 3B	'98 Same, Booklet	10.00
YT 3M	'98 Same, Mini Sheet	34.00
YT 4	'99 $6 Rocky Mnt Goat	8.00
YT 4B	'99 Same, Booklet	10.00
YT 4M	'99 Same, Mini Sheet	34.00

NEWFOUNDLAND

1,15A-16   3,11A   13,20   23

1857 Imperf. Thick Wove Paper, Mesh (OG + 50%) (C)

Scott's No.		Unused Fine	Ave.	Used Fine	Ave.
1	1p Crown & Flowers, Brn. Violet	60.00	35.00	100.00	65.00
3	3p Triangle, Green	250.00	160.00	300.00	200.00
5	5p Crown & Flowers, Vlt. Brown	150.00	90.00	250.00	165.00
8	8p Flowers, Scarlet Vermillion	160.00	95.00	225.00	150.00

1860 Imperf. Thin Wove Paper, No Mesh (OG + 50%) (C)

		Fine	Ave.	Fine	Ave.
11	2p Flowers, Orange	165.00	110.00	250.00	165.00
11A	3p Triangle, Green	45.00	29.50	75.00	50.00
12	4p Flowers, Orange	...	...	600.00	400.00
12A	5p Crown & Flowers, Vlt. Brown	45.00	25.00	100.00	65.00
13	6p Flowers, Orange	...	...	500.00	350.00

1861-62 Imperforate Thin Wove Paper (OG + 50%) (C)

		Fine	Ave.	Fine	Ave.
15A	1p Crown & Flowers, Vlt. Brown	100.00	60.00	160.00	110.00
17	2p Flowers, Rose	95.00	55.00	120.00	77.50
18	4p Flowers, Rose	23.75	14.50	47.50	27.50
19	5p Crown & Flowers, Red Brown	30.00	17.50	50.00	31.50
20	6p Flowers, Rose	12.50	7.00	38.50	24.50
21	6½ Flowers, Rose	50.00	27.50	170.00	100.00
22	8p Flowers, Rose	45.00	25.00	195.00	120.00
23	1sh Flowers, Rose	25.00	13.75	165.00	95.00

24   28-29   32-32A   35-36

1865-1894 Perf. 12 (OG + 40%, NH + 140%) (C)

24	2¢ Codfish, Green, White Paper	45.00	30.00	20.00	12.00
24a	2¢ Green, Yellow Paper	50.00	32.50	23.00	14.00
25	5¢ Harp Seal, Brown	350.00	225.00	225.00	150.00
26	5¢ Harp Seal, Black (1868)	170.00	110.00	85.00	55.00
27	10¢ Prince Albert, Black, White Paper ..	115.00	75.00	37.50	22.50
27a	10¢ Black, Yellow Paper	135.00	85.00	65.00	40.00
28	12¢ Victoria, Red Brown, Yel.Paper	27.50	15.00	27.50	15.00
28a	12¢ Red Brown, White Paper	275.00	150.00	110.00	15.00
29	12¢ Brown, Yellow Paper (1894)	24.50	14.00	24.50	70.00
30	13¢ Fishing Ship, Orange	75.00	45.00	55.00	33.50
31	24¢ Victoria, Blue	22.50	14.00	18.50	11.50

1868-1894 Perf. 12 (OG + 40%, NH + 130%) (C)

32	1¢ Prince of Wales, Violet	27.50	17.50	26.50	17.00
32A	1¢ Brown Lilac (1871)	35.00	35.00	35.00	21.00
33	3¢ Victoria, Vermillion (1870)	170.00	100.00	90.00	55.00
34	3¢ Blue (1873)	170.00	100.00	18.00	10.00
35	6¢ Victoria, Dull Rose (1870)	9.50	6.00	9.50	6.00
36	6¢ Carmine Lake (1894)	11.75	7.25	11.75	7.25

1876-1879 Rouletted (OG + 30%, NH + 110%) (C)

37	1¢ Prince of Wales, Brn. Lilac (1877) ...	55.00	32.50	22.50	13.00
38	2¢ Codfish, Green (1879)	75.00	45.00	22.50	15.75
39	3¢ Victoria, Blue (1877)	175.00	110.00	7.75	5.25
40	5¢ Harp Seal, Blue	110.00	70.00	7.75	5.25

1880-1896 Perf. 12 (OG + 20%) VF + 50% (C)

41-45   46-48   56-58   59

NEWFOUNDLAND
1880-1896 Perf. 12 (OG + 20%) VF + 50% (C)

Scott's No.		NH Fine	Unused Fine	Ave.	Used Fine	Ave.
41	1¢ Prince, Vlt. Brown....................27.50	14.00	9.50	6.50	3.25
42	1¢ Gray Brown..............................25.00	13.00	8.50	6.50	3.25
43	1¢ Brown (1896)............................50.00	25.00	14.00	23.00	14.00
44	1¢ Deep Green (1887)....................10.00	5.50	3.50	2.75	1.65
45	1¢ Green (1897)..............................10.00	5.50	3.50	2.75	1.65
46	2¢ Codfish, Yellow Green...............32.00	16.00	10.00	9.50	5.00
47	2¢ Green (1896)..............................47.50	25.00	15.00	14.00	8.50
48	2¢ Red Orange (1887)....................23.50	12.00	7.00	5.25	3.00
49	3¢ Victoria, Blue............................39.50	20.00	12.00	3.50	1.95
51	3¢ Umber Brown (1887)..................26.50	13.50	9.00	3.00	1.65
52	3¢ Violet Brown (1896)...................75.00	40.00	23.00	40.00	23.00
53	5¢ Harp Seal, Pale Blue................300.00	170.00	100.00	7.00	4.25
54	5¢ Dark Blue (1887).....................110.00	60.00	35.00	5.25	3.25
55	5¢ Bright Blue (1894)....................31.75	17.00	10.00	4.25	2.50

1887-1896 (OG + 20%) VF + 50% (C)

56	½¢ Dog, Rose Red...........................10.00	5.50	3.25	4.00	2.25
57	½¢ Orange Red (1896)....................65.00	35.00	21.50	27.00	16.00
58	½¢ Black (1894) 10.00	5.50	3.25	4.00	2.25
59	10¢ Schooner, Black.........................85.00	45.00	27.50	30.00	16.00

60   61   63   69   74

1890 Issue (OG + 20%) VF + 50% (C)

60	3¢ Victoria, Slate 15.00	8.25	4.75	1.35	.80

1897 John Cabot Issue VF Used + 30% (B)

Scott's No.		NH VF	F-VF	Unused VF	F-VF	Used F-VF
61-74	Set of 14 .... 380.00	280.00	190.00	140.00	99.50
61	1¢ Queen Victoria 3.25	2.40	1.60	1.20	1.20
62	2¢ Cabot 3.95	3.00	1.95	1.50	1.10
63	3¢ Cape Bonavista 6.00	4.50	2.95	2.25	1.00
64	4¢ Caribou Hunting 8.75	6.50	4.25	3.25	2.25
65	5¢ Mining 10.75	8.00	5.25	4.00	2.25
66	6¢ Logging 9.75	7.00	4.75	3.50	3.00
67	8¢ Fishing 21.50	15.00	10.50	7.50	4.50
68	10¢ Ship "Matthew" 27.50	20.00	13.50	10.00	3.95
69	12¢ Willow Ptarmigan 35.00	26.00	17.50	13.00	6.25
70	15¢ Seals 35.00	26.00	17.50	13.00	6.25
71	24¢ Salmon Fishing 32.50	23.00	16.00	11.50	7.00
72	30¢ Colony Seal 72.50	50.00	35.00	25.00	25.00
73	35¢ Iceberg 140.00	100.00	70.00	50.00	40.00
74	60¢ King Henry VII 19.00	14.00	9.00	6.75	6.00

1897 Surcharges VF Used + 50% (C)

75	1¢ on 3¢ Type a (#60)................. 70.00	47.50	35.00	23.50	15.00
76	1¢ on 3¢ Type b (#60)............... 300.00	200.00	150.00	100.00	110.00
77	1¢ on 3¢ Type c (#60)............. 1075.00	700.00	525.00	350.00	335.00

78   79-80   81-82   85   86

1897-1901 Royal Family Issue VF Used + 30% (B)

78-85	Set of 8 .... 135.00	100.00	72.50	55.00	14.75
78	½¢ Edward VII as Child................. 4.00	3.10	2.25	1.70	1.65
79	1¢ Victoria, Carm. Rose................. 6.75	4.75	3.75	2.65	2.65
80	1¢ Yellow Green (1898)................. 6.25	4.50	3.50	2.50	.18
81	2¢ Prince, Orange......................... 6.75	4.95	3.75	2.75	2.75
82	2¢ Vermillion (1898)................... 16.00	11.75	8.75	6.50	.45
83	3¢ Princess (1898)....................... 25.75	19.50	14.00	10.75	.45
84	4¢ Duchess (1901) 36.00	26.50	19.50	14.50	3.00
85	5¢ Duke of York (1899)............... 42.50	31.00	23.00	17.00	2.00

1908 Map Stamp VF Used + 30% (B)

86	12¢ Map of Newfoundland........... 47.50	35.00	26.50	19.00	1.00

NOTE: PRICES THROUGHOUT THIS LIST ARE SUBJECT TO CHANGE WITHOUT NOTICE IF MARKET CONDITIONS REQUIRE. MINIMUM ORDER MUST TOTAL AT LEAST $20.00.

1910 Guy Issue (Lithographed) Perf. 12 except as noted
VF Used + 30% (B)

	87	88	91	92-92A,98	96,102

Scott's No.		NH VF	NH F-VF	Unused VF	Unused F-VF	Used F-VF
87-97	Normal Set of 12	550.00	390.00	270.00	195.00	195.00
87	1¢ James I,Pf. 12 x 11	2.60	2.00	1.30	1.00	.80
87a	1¢ Perf. 12	5.50	4.00	2.95	2.25	1.50
87b	1¢ Perf. 12 x 14	4.50	3.25	2.25	1.75	1.40
88	2¢ Company Arms	10.00	7.75	5.25	4.00	.75
88a	2¢ Perf. 12 x 14	9.00	7.00	4.75	3.75	.65
88c	2¢ Perf. 12 x 11½	...	...	300.00	225.00	225.00
89	3¢ John Guy	17.50	13.00	9.00	6.75	7.00
90	4¢ The "Endeavor"	26.50	19.00	13.75	10.00	7.50
91	5¢ Cupids, Perf. 14 x 12	20.00	14.50	10.50	7.50	2.50
91a	5¢ Perf. 12	26.00	19.00	13.50	10.00	3.75
92	6¢ Lord Bacon Claret (Z Reversed)	120.00	87.50	60.00	45.00	37.50
92A	6¢ Claret (Z Normal)	39.50	29.00	20.00	15.00	15.00
93	8¢ Mosquito, Pale Brown	90.00	65.00	45.00	32.50	32.50
94	9¢ Logging, Ol. Green	90.00	65.00	45.00	32.50	32.50
95	10¢ Paper Mills, Black	90.00	65.00	45.00	32.50	32.50
96	12¢ Edward VII, L. Brown	90.00	65.00	45.00	32.50	32.50
97	15¢ George V, Gray Black	105.00	75.00	54.00	38.50	38.50

1911 Guy Issue (Engraved) Perf. 14 VF Used + 30% (B)

98-103	Set of 6	495.00	375.00	260.00	197.50	197.50
98	6¢ Lord Bacon Brown Violet	37.50	28.00	20.00	15.00	14.00
99	8¢ Mosquito, Bistre Brn	90.00	65.00	47.50	35.00	35.00
100	9¢ Logging, Ol. Grn	70.00	52.50	37.00	28.00	28.00
101	10¢ Paper Mills, Vi. Black	130.00	95.00	70.00	52.50	52.50
102	12¢ Edward VII, Red Brn	110.00	80.00	56.50	42.50	42.50
103	15¢ George V, Slate Gr	110.00	80.00	56.50	42.50	42.50

	104	105	107	115

1911 Royal Family Coronation Issue VF Used + 30% (B)

104-14	Set of 11	375.00	280.00	200.00	152.50	125.00
104	1¢ Queen Mary	3.50	2.50	1.80	1.35	.18
105	2¢ George V	3.35	2.50	1.80	1.35	.18
106	3¢ Prince of Wales	33.50	25.00	18.00	13.50	13.50
107	4¢ Prince Albert	29.00	22.00	16.00	12.00	10.00
108	5¢ Princess Mary	13.75	10.00	7.25	5.50	1.00
109	6¢ Prince Henry	31.50	23.50	17.50	13.00	13.00
110	8¢ George (color paper)	90.00	70.00	47.50	36.00	33.50
110a	8¢ White Paper	100.00	75.00	55.00	40.00	35.00
111	9¢ Prince John	36.00	27.00	19.50	14.50	13.50
112	10¢ Queen Alexandra	51.50	37.50	27.50	20.00	17.50
113	12¢ Duke of Connaught	47.50	35.00	25.00	18.50	17.50
114	15¢ Seal of Colony	47.50	35.00	25.00	18.50	17.50

1919 Trail of the Caribou Issue VF Used + 30% (B)

115-26	Set of 12	320.00	230.00	175.00	125.00	112.50
115	1¢ Suvla Bay	2.60	1.95	1.40	1.10	.20
116	2¢ Ubigue	2.95	2.20	1.60	1.20	.35
117	3¢ Gueudecourt	3.65	2.75	2.00	1.50	.20
118	4¢ Beaumont Hamel	7.00	5.25	3.75	2.95	.85
119	5¢ Ubigue	8.15	6.15	4.50	3.35	.85
120	6¢ Monchy	29.00	21.50	16.50	12.00	12.00
121	8¢ Ubigue	29.00	21.50	16.50	12.00	10.50
122	10¢ Steenbeck	15.00	11.50	8.25	6.25	2.50
123	12¢ Ubigue	80.00	60.00	45.00	32.50	27.50
124	15¢ Langemarck	50.00	36.00	27.50	20.00	22.50
125	24¢ Cambrai	60.00	43.50	32.50	24.00	24.00
126	36¢ Combles	49.00	37.00	26.50	20.00	20.00

1920 Stamps of 1897 Surcharged VF Used + 30% (B)

127	2¢ on 30¢ Seal (#72)	9.00	6.75	5.00	3.75	3.75
128	3¢ on 15¢ Bars 10½ mm	350.00	270.00	195.00	150.00	150.00
129	3¢ on 15¢ Bars 13½ mm	18.75	14.00	10.75	8.00	8.00
130	3¢ on 35¢ Iceberg (#73)	14.00	10.50	7.75	6.00	6.00

1923-1924 Pictorial Issue VF Used + 30% (B)

	131	132	133	139

Scott's No.		NH VF	NH F-VF	Unused VF	Unused F-VF	Used F-VF
131-44	Set of 14	182.50	140.00	105.00	79.50	72.50
131	1¢ Twin Hills, Tor's Cove	2.50	1.80	1.50	1.10	.20
132	2¢ South West Arm, Trinity	2.50	1.80	1.50	1.10	.18
133	3¢ War Memorial	2.75	2.00	1.60	1.20	.18
134	4¢ Humber River	3.35	2.50	1.95	1.50	1.40
135	5¢ Coast of Trinity	5.00	3.75	3.00	2.25	1.75
136	6¢ Upper Steadies, Humber R.	6.25	4.75	3.75	2.75	2.75
137	8¢ Quidi Vidi	5.00	3.75	3.00	2.25	2.15
138	9¢ Caribou Crossing Lake	41.50	30.00	25.00	18.00	18.00
139	10¢ Humber River Canyon	6.00	4.75	3.50	2.75	1.60
140	11¢ Shell Bird Island	10.00	7.75	6.00	4.50	4.50
141	12¢ Mt. Moriah	10.00	7.75	6.00	4.50	4.50
142	15¢ Humber River	11.50	8.50	6.75	5.00	4.50
143	20¢ Placentia (1924)	15.00	11.50	8.75	6.75	4.50
144	24¢ Topsail Falls (1924)	76.50	60.00	45.00	35.00	35.00

	145,163,172	146,164,173	148,166,175	155

1928 Publicity Issue - Unwatermarked - Thin Paper VF Used + 30% (B)

145-59	Set of 15	115.00	87.50	70.00	53.50	47.50
145	1¢ Map, Deep Green	1.85	1.40	1.15	.85	.50
146	2¢ "Caribou", Deep Carmine	2.60	2.00	1.60	1.25	.45
147	3¢ Mary & George V, Brown	2.95	2.25	1.80	1.35	.30
148	4¢ Prince, Lilac Rose	3.40	2.75	2.15	1.60	1.35
149	5¢ Train, Slate Green	7.25	5.50	4.50	3.25	2.50
150	6¢ Newfld. Hotel, Ultramarine	6.35	4.75	3.95	3.00	2.85
151	8¢ Heart's Content, Lt. Red Brn	8.00	6.00	5.00	3.75	3.50
152	9¢ Cabot Tower Myrtle Green	8.50	6.50	5.25	4.00	3.75
153	10¢ War Mem., Dark Violet	8.50	6.50	5.25	4.00	3.50
154	12¢ P.O., Brown Carmine	6.50	5.00	3.95	3.00	2.50
155	14¢ Cabot Tower, Red Brown	8.50	6.50	5.25	4.00	3.75
156	15¢ Nonstop Flight, Dark Blue	9.75	7.50	6.00	4.50	4.25
157	20¢ Colonial Bldg, Gray Blk	9.35	6.75	5.75	4.25	3.75
158	28¢ P.O., Gray Green	31.00	25.00	19.00	15.00	13.50
159	30¢ Grand Falls, Olive Brown	10.50	7.75	6.50	4.75	4.75

1929 Stamp of 1923 Surcharged VF Used + 30% (B)

160	3¢ on 6¢ Upper Steadies(#136)	4.95	3.75	2.95	2.25	2.25

1929-31 Publicity Issue Re-engraved -
Like Preceding but Thicker Paper VF Used + 30% (B)
(See your favorite Specialized catalog for details)

163-71	Set of 9	150.00	115.00	92.50	70.00	49.75
163	1¢ Green	2.25	1.80	1.40	1.10	.35
164	2¢ Deep Carmine	2.25	1.80	1.40	1.10	.18
165	3¢ Deep Red Brown	2.35	1.80	1.50	1.15	.18
166	4¢ Magenta	3.35	2.65	2.15	1.65	.75
167	5¢ Slate Green	4.75	3.65	2.95	2.25	.80
168	6¢ Ultramarine	15.75	12.00	9.75	7.50	7.00
169	10¢ Dark Violet	6.00	4.50	3.75	2.75	1.20
170	15¢ Deep Blue (1930)	53.50	40.00	33.00	25.00	23.50
171	20¢ Gray Black (1931)	68.50	52.50	42.50	32.50	19.50

1931 Publicity Issue - Re-engraved - Wmk. Arms VF Used + 30% (B)

172-82	Set of 11	247.50	190.00	153.50	115.00	85.00
172	1¢ Green	2.35	1.75	1.45	1.10	.70
173	2¢ Red	2.70	2.80	2.30	1.75	.85
174	3¢ Red Brown	3.70	2.80	2.30	1.75	.70
175	4¢ Rose	4.75	3.65	2.95	2.25	1.00
176	5¢ Greenish Gray	12.50	9.25	7.75	5.75	5.50
177	6¢ Ultramarine	24.00	18.50	15.00	11.50	11.00
178	8¢ Red Brown	24.00	18.50	15.00	11.50	11.00
179	10¢ Dark Violet	17.00	12.75	10.50	8.00	5.50
180	15¢ Deep Blue	53.50	42.50	32.50	25.00	21.50
181	20¢ Gray Black	68.50	52.50	42.50	32.50	8.75
182	30¢ Olive Brown	52.50	40.00	32.50	25.00	22.50

1932-1937 Pictorial Set, Perf. 13½ or 14 VF Used + 25%

183-84,253 190-91,257 199,266 210,264

Scott's No.		NH VF	NH F-VF	Unused VF	Unused F-VF	Used F-VF
183-99	Set of 17	83.75	67.50	60.75	47.75	32.95
183	1¢ Codfish, Green	1.85	1.50	1.35	1.10	.30
183a	1¢ Booklet Pane of 4	85.00	70.00	60.00	50.00	...
184	1¢ Gray Black	.40	.30	.27	.22	.15
184a	1¢ Bk. Pane of 4, Pf. 13½	65.00	52.50	45.00	37.50	...
184b	1¢ Bk. Pane of 4, Pf. 14	80.00	65.00	55.00	45.00	...
185	2¢ George V, Rose	1.85	1.50	1.35	1.10	.15
185a	2¢ Bk. Pane of 4	52.50	42.50	36.50	30.00	...
186	2¢ Green	1.50	1.15	1.10	.85	.15
186a	2¢ Bk. Pane of 4, Pf. 13½	26.00	21.50	20.00	16.50	...
186b	2¢ Bk. Pane of 4, Pf. 14	37.50	29.50	26.00	21.00	...
187	3¢ Queen Mary	1.50	1.15	1.10	.85	.18
187a	3¢ Bk. Pane of 4, Pf. 13½	70.00	55.00	47.50	37.00	...
187b	3¢ Bk. Pane of 4, Pf. 14	85.00	67.50	57.50	45.00	...
187c	3¢ Bk. Pane of 4, Pf. 13	85.00	70.00	60.00	50.00	...
188	4¢ Prince, Deep Violet	6.25	5.00	4.50	3.50	1.25
189	4¢ Rose Lake	.70	.55	.50	.40	.15
190	5¢ Caribou V. Brown (I)	6.25	5.00	4.50	3.50	.70
191	5¢ Deep Violet (II)	1.25	1.00	.90	.70	.15
191a	5¢ Deep Violet (I)	11.50	9.50	8.25	6.75	.75
192	6¢ Elizabeth, Dull Blue	11.50	9.00	8.00	6.50	6.50
193	10¢ Salmon, Olive Black	1.50	1.15	1.10	.85	.60
194	14¢ Dog, Intense Black	3.30	2.60	2.35	1.85	1.50
195	15¢ Seal Pup, Magenta	3.30	2.60	2.35	1.85	1.50
196	20¢ Cape Race, Gray Green	3.30	2.60	2.35	1.85	.65
197	25¢ Sealing Fleet, Gray	3.50	2.80	2.50	2.00	1.40
198	30¢ Fishing Fleet, Ultra	29.50	23.50	21.00	16.50	16.50
199	48¢ Fishing Fleet Red Brown (1937)	12.50	9.75	8.75	7.00	3.50

#191 Antler under "T" higher, #190,191a Antlers are even height.

1932 New Values VF Used + 25%

208	7¢ Duchess, Red Brown	1.50	1.20	1.10	.85	.85
209	8¢ Corner Brook, Or. Red	1.50	1.20	1.10	.85	.65
210	24¢ Bell Island, Light Blue	3.25	2.70	2.35	1.95	1.95

1933 "L & S Post" Overprinted on C9 VF + 20%

211	15¢ Dog Sled & Plane	8.75	7.00	6.75	5.50	5.50

1933 Sir Humphrey Gilbert Issue VF + 25%

212 213 216 222

212-25	Set of 14	185.00	150.00	122.50	96.50	90.00
212	1¢ Sir Humphrey Gilbert	1.25	1.00	.85	.70	.50
213	2¢ Compton Castle	1.60	1.25	1.10	.85	.50
214	3¢ Gilbert Coat of Arms	2.00	1.70	1.40	1.15	.45
215	4¢ Eton College	2.00	1.70	1.40	1.15	.45
216	5¢ Token from Queen	2.75	2.25	1.90	1.50	.85
217	7¢ Royal Patents	19.50	16.50	13.00	10.75	9.50
218	8¢ Leaving Plymouth	12.50	10.00	8.25	6.50	6.25
219	9¢ Arriving St. John's	13.50	11.00	9.00	7.25	7.00
220	10¢ Annexation	11.75	9.50	7.85	6.25	5.50
221	14¢ Coat of Arms	24.50	19.50	16.00	12.75	12.50
222	15¢ Deck of "Squirrel"	21.00	16.50	13.50	10.75	10.50
223	20¢ 1626 Map of Nwfld	16.50	13.50	11.00	8.75	8.25
224	24¢ Queen Elizabeth I	32.00	25.00	21.00	16.50	16.50
225	32¢ Gilbert Statue at Truro	34.00	26.50	22.50	17.50	17.00

1935 Silver Jubilee Issue VF + 20%

226 230 233

Scott's No.		NH F-VF	Unused F-VF	Used F-VF
226-29	Set of 4	12.00	8.50	7.25
226	4¢ George V, Bright Rose	1.10	.85	.50
227	5¢ Violet	1.10	.85	.65
228	7¢ Dark Blue	3.50	2.50	2.00
229	24¢ Olive Green	6.75	5.00	4.50

1937 Coronation Issue VF + 25%

230-32	Set of 3	3.20	2.10	1.30
230	2¢ Elizabeth & George VI Deep Green	.90	.65	.40
231	4¢ Carmine Rose	.90	.65	.30
232	5¢ Dark Violet	1.60	1.20	.70

1937 Coronation Issue (Long Set) VF + 30%

233-43	Set of 11	27.75	20.00	16.95
233	1¢ Codfish	.45	.35	.20
234	3¢ Map of Newfoundland (I), Fine	1.80	1.35	.70
234a	3¢ Map (II), Coarse	1.60	1.20	.70
235	7¢ Caribou	2.00	1.50	1.20
236	8¢ Corner Brook Paper Mills	2.00	1.50	1.20
237	10¢ Salmon	3.65	2.75	2.50
238	14¢ Newfoundland Dog	2.80	2.10	2.00
239	15¢ Harp Seal Pup	3.65	2.40	2.00
240	20¢ Cape Race	2.85	2.10	1.50
241	24¢ Loading Iron Ore	3.35	2.50	2.40
242	25¢ Sealing Fleet	3.65	2.70	2.25
243	48¢ Fishing Fleet	4.00	2.95	2.50

245 249 252

1938 Royal Family, Perf. 13½ VF + 25%

		NH F-VF	Unused F-VF	Used F-VF
245-48	Set of 4	6.15	4.70	1.30
245	2¢ George VI, Green	1.50	1.20	.15
246	3¢ Queen Elizabeth, Dark Carmine	1.50	1.20	.18
247	4¢ Princess Elizabeth, Light Blue	1.95	1.50	.15
248	7¢ Queen Mother, Ultramarine	1.40	1.10	.90

1939 Royal Visit VF + 20%

Scott's No.		Plate Blocks NH	Plate Blocks Unused	F-VF NH	F-VF Unused	F-VF Used
249	5¢ George VI - Elizabeth	8.00	6.50	.80	.65	.65

1939 Royal Visit Surcharge VF + 20%

250	2¢ on 5¢ (#249)	11.75	9.50	1.10	.85	.85
251	4¢ on 5¢ (#249)	10.50	8.50	.85	.65	.65

1941 Grenfell Issue VF + 20%

252	5¢ Wilfred Grenfell	2.75	2.25	.30	.25	.25

1941-1944 Pictorial Set, Perf. 12½ VF + 25%

		NH	Unused	Used
253-66	Set of 14	...	...	14.00 11.35 9.00
253	1¢ Codfish, Dark Gray	3.00	2.40	.30 .25 .15
254	2¢ George VI, Deep Green	3.00	2.40	.30 .25 .15
255	3¢ Elizabeth, Rose Carm	3.75	2.95	.30 .25 .15
256	4¢ Princess Elizabeth, Blue	5.25	4.25	.60 .50 .15
257	5¢ Caribou, Violet (I)	5.25	4.25	.60 .50 .15
258	7¢ Queen Mother (1942)	...	...	1.00 .80 .80
259	8¢ Corner Brook, Red	6.75	5.25	.75 .60 .60
260	10¢ Salmon, Brown Black	6.75	5.25	.75 .60 .50
261	14¢ Dog, Black	14.00	10.75	1.60 1.25 1.00
262	15¢ Seal Pup, Rose Violet	13.75	10.75	1.50 1.20 1.10
263	20¢ Cape Race, Green	12.50	9.75	1.25 1.00 1.00
264	24¢ Bell Island, Deep Blue	13.75	10.75	1.90 1.50 1.25
265	25¢ Sealing Fleet, Slate	12.50	9.75	1.75 1.35 1.25
266	48¢ Fishing, Red Br. (1944)	17.50	13.50	2.50 1.95 1.40

267 269 270

C13 C19 J3

1943 University Issue VF + 20%

Scott's No.		Plate Blocks NH	Plate Blocks Unused	F-VF NH	F-VF Unused	F-VF Used
267	30¢ Memorial University	8.00	6.50	1.25	1.00	.90

1946 Two Cent Provisional VF + 20%

268	2¢ on 30¢ (#267)	3.50	3.00	.30	.25	.25

1947 Issues VF + 20%

269	4¢ Princess Elizabeth	2.35	2.00	.30	.25	.15
270	5¢ Cabot in the "Matthew"	2.75	2.25	.30	.25	.20

AIRMAIL STAMPS

1919-21 Overprint Issues VF Used + 40% (B)

Scott's No.		NH VF	NH F-VF	Unused VF	Unused F-VF	Used F-VF
C2	$1 on 15¢ "Trans-Atlantic" AIRPOST, 1919. ONE DOLLAR (#70)	295..00	215.00	190.00	135.00	135.00
C2a	$1 on 15¢ Without Comma after "Post""	325.00	235.00	210.00	150.00	165.00
C3	35¢ "AIR MAIL to Halifax, N.S. 1921"(#73)..............................	215.00	150.00	135.00	95.00	100.00
C3a	35¢ Period after "1921".............	250.00	175.00	155.00	110.00	120.00

C7,C10 C6,C9 C8,C11

1931 Airs, Unwatermarked VF Used + 30% (B)

C6-8	Set of 3	115.00	90.00	75.00	57.50	57.50
C6	15¢ Dog Sled & Airplane..............	10.00	7.50	6.50	5.00	5.00
C7	50¢ Trans-Atlantic Plane..............	28.50	22.50	18.75	15.00	15.00
C8	$1 Flight Routes............................	80.00	62.50	52.50	40.00	40.00

1931 Airs, Watermarked "Coat of Arms" VF Used + 30% (B)

C9-11	Set of 3	175.00	120.00	110.00	80.00	77.50
C9	15¢ Dog Sled & Airplane..............	10.00	7.50	6.50	5.00	5.00
C10	50¢ Trans-Atlantic Plane..............	45.00	32.50	29.50	22.50	21.50
C11	$1 Flight Routes..........................	125.00	85.00	80.00	60.00	55.00

1932 DO-X Trans-Atlantic Surcharge VF Used + 30% (B)

Scott's No.		NH VF	NH F-VF	Unused VF	Unused F-VF	Used F-VF
C12	$1.50 on $1 Routes (#C11)............	385.00	300.00	250.00	195.00	195.00

1933 Labrador Issue VF Used + 25%

C13-17	Set of 5	200.00	155.00	130.00	105.00	115.00
C13	5¢ "Put to Flight"	14.75	11.50	9.75	7.75	7.75
C14	10¢ "Land of Heart's Delight"......	23.00	17.00	14.50	11.50	11.50
C15	30¢ "Spotting the Herd"..............	38.00	30.00	25.00	20.00	22.50
C16	60¢ "News from Home"	66.50	52.50	43.75	35.00	40.00
C17	75¢ "Labrador, Land of Gold"	66.50	52.50	43.75	35.00	40.00

1933 General Balbo Flight VF Used + 25%

C18	$4.50 on 75¢ (#C17)	450.00	350.00	295.00	235.00	235.00

1943 St. John's VF + 20%

Scott's No.		Plate Blocks NH	Plate Blocks Unused	F-VF NH	F-VF Unused	F-VF Used
C19	7¢ View of St. John's	3.00	2.50	.35	.30	.25

POSTAGE DUE STAMPS 1939-1949 VF + 25%
Unwatermarked, Perf. 10 x 10½ Unless Otherwise Noted

Scott's No.		F-VF NH	F-VF Unused	F-VF Used
J1-6	Set of 6..	32.75	24.00	22.50
J1	1¢ Yellow Green.................................	5.00	3.75	3.75
J1a	1¢ Perf. 11 (1949).............................	5.50	4.25	4.25
J2	2¢ Vermillion.....................................	6.25	4.75	4.00
J2a	2¢ Perf. 11 x 9 (1946).......................	6.25	4.75	4.25
J3	3¢ Ultramarine...................................	7.00	5.25	4.50
J3a	3¢ Perf. 11 x 9 (1949).......................	7.75	5.75	5.75
J4	4¢ Yellow Orange Perf. 11x9............	9.75	7.00	7.00
J4a	4¢ Perf. 10x10½ (1949).....................	12.75	9.50	9.50
J5	5¢ Pale Brown	3.75	2.75	2.75
J6	10¢ Dark Violet	3.75	2.75	2.75
J7	10¢ Watermarked, Perf. II..................	11.50	8.50	9.75

NOTE: PRICES THROUGHOUT THIS LIST ARE SUBJECT TO CHANGE WITHOUT NOTICE IF MARKET CONDITIONS REQUIRE. MINIMUM ORDER MUST TOTAL AT LEAST $20.00.

BRITISH COLUMBIA AND VANCOUVER ISLAND
1860 British Columbia & Vancouver I (C)

Scott's No.		Unused Fine	Ave.	Used Fine	Ave.
2	2½p Victoria, Dull Rose	225.00	110.00	140.00	70.00

1865 Vancouver Island (OG + 50%) (C)

4	10¢ Victoria, Blue, Imperf	1250.00	850.00	850.00	550.00
5	5¢ Victoria, Rose, Perf. 14	225.00	130.00	150.00	85.00
6	10¢ Victoria, Blue, Perf. 14	225.00	130.00	150.00	85.00

1865 British Columbia (OG + 50%) (C)

7	3p Seal, Blue, Perf. 14	80.00	50.00	80.00	50.00

1867-1869 Surcharges on #7 Design, Perf. 14 (OG + 40%) (C)

8	2¢ on 3p Brown (Black Surch)	100.00	60.00	100.00	60.00
9	5¢ on 3p Bright Red (Black)	170.00	100.00	170.00	100.00
10	10¢ on 3p Lilac Rose (Blue)	1250.00	750.00	...	...
11	25¢ on 3p Orange (Violet)	165.00	100.00	165.00	100.00
12	50¢ on 3p Violet (Red)	475.00	285.00	475.00	285.00
13	$1 on 3p Green (Green)	1100.00	600.00	...	...

1869 Surcharges on #7 Design, Perf. 12½ (OG + 40%) (C)

14	5¢ on 3p Bright Red (Black)	1000.00	600.00	1000.00	600.00
15	10¢ on 3p Lilac Rose (Blue)	825.00	500.00	825.00	500.00
16	25¢ on 3p Orange (Violet)	500.00	300.00	500.00	300.00
17	50¢ on 3p Green (Green)	675.00	400.00	675.00	400.00
18	$1 on 3p Green (Green)	1250.00	750.00	1250.00	750.00

NEW BRUNSWICK

Scott's No.		Unused Fine	Ave.	Used Fine	Ave.
	1851 Imperforate - Blue Paper - Unwatermarked (OG + 50%) (C)				
1	3p Crown & Flowers, Red	950.00	525.00	250.00	150.00
2	6p Olive Yellow	2500.00	1400.00	500.00	300.00
3	1sh Bright Red Violet	...	...	...	1400.00
4	1sh Dull Violet	...	...	...	1800.00

1860-1863 - Perf. 12 - White Paper (VF + 50%, OG + 30%, NH + 80%) (C)

| | 6 | 7 | 8 | 9 | 10 |

6	1¢ Locomotive, Red Lilac	17.50	10.00	17.00	9.75
6a	1¢ Brown Violet	27.50	16.00	25.00	15.00
7	2¢ Victoria, Orange (1863)	7.00	4.15	7.00	4.15
8	5¢ Victoria, Green	7.00	4.15	7.00	4.15
8b	5¢ Olive Green	70.00	42.50	15.00	9.50
9	10¢ Victoria, Vermillion	27.50	16.50	27.50	16.50
10	12½¢ Steam & Sailing Ship, Blue	35.00	21.50	35.00	21.50
11	17¢ Prince of Wales, Black	27.50	16.50	27.50	16.50

NOVA SCOTIA
1851-1853 - Imperforate - Blue Paper (OG + 50%) (C)

2,3

Scott's No.		Unused Fine	Ave.	Used Fine	Ave.
1	1p Victoria, Red Brown	1500.00	900.00	275.00	175.00
2	3p Crown & Flowers, Blue	435.00	250.00	110.00	70.00
3	3p Dark Blue	750.00	450.00	140.00	85.00
4	6p Crown & Flowers, Yellow Green	...	1500.00	350.00	210.00
5	6p Dark Green	...	3000.00	625.00	375.00
6	1sh Crown & Flowers, Reddish Violet	...	...	...	1500.00
7	1sh Dull Violet	...	...	...	2575.00

1860-1863 - Perforated 12 (VF + 50%, OG + 20%, NH + 60%)

| | 8 | 9 | 11 | 12 | 13 |

8	1¢ Victoria, Black, Yellow Paper	4.50	2.75	3.50	2.15
8a	1¢ White Paper	4.50	2.75	3.50	2.15
9	2¢ Lilac, White Paper	4.50	3.00	4.50	3.00
9a	2¢ Yellowish Paper	4.50	3.00	4.50	3.00
10	5¢ Blue, White Paper	210.00	130.00	5.00	3.25
10a	5¢ Yellowish Paper	210.00	130.00	5.00	3.25
11	8½¢ Green, Yellowish Paper	4.25	2.60	12.00	7.50
11a	8½¢ White Paper	4.25	2.60	9.00	5.50
12	10¢ Vermillion, White Paper	5.50	3.50	5.00	3.25
12a	10¢ Yellowish Paper	5.50	3.50	5.00	3.25
13	12½¢ Black, Yellowish Paper	18.50	11.00	17.50	11.00
13a	12½¢ White Paper	18.50	11.00	17.50	11.00

PRINCE EDWARD ISLAND

| | 1,5 | 2,6 | 9 | 10 |

1861 - Perf. 9 - Typographed (OG + 50%)

Scott's No.		Unused Fine	Ave.	Used Fine	Ave.
1	2p Victoria, Dull Rose	285.00	180.00	140.00	90.00
2	3p Blue	625.00	375.00	300.00	185.00
3	6p Yellow Green	1000.00	650.00	600.00	375.00

1862-1865 - Perf. 11,11½,12 and Compound - Typographed (VF + 50%, OG + 30%, NH + 80%)

4	1p Victoria, Yellow Orange	16.50	10.50	16.50	10.50
5	2p Rose, White Paper	4.00	2.50	4.00	2.50
5a	2p Yellowish Paper	4.25	2.65	4.25	2.65
6	3p Blue, White Paper	5.50	3.25	7.50	4.50
6a	3p Yellowish Paper	8.50	5.15	7.50	4.50
7	6p Yellow Green	52.50	31.50	52.50	31.50
8	9p Violet	42.50	25.00	42.50	25.00

1868-1870 Issues (VF + 50%, OG + 30%, NH + 80%)

9	4p Victoria, Black, White Paper	5.25	3.15	13.50	8.50
9a	4p Yellowish Paper	8.50	5.50	17.50	11.50
10	4½p Brown (1870)	35.00	22.50	37.50	24.50

1872 Issue, Perf. 12,12½ (VF + 50%, OG + 20%, NH + 60%)

| | 11 | 13 | 14 | 15 | 16 |

11	1¢ Victoria, Brown Orange	3.00	1.85	5.00	3.25
12	2¢ Ultramarine	9.00	5.75	17.50	11.00
13	3¢ Rose	13.50	8.00	13.50	8.00
14	4¢ Green	3.50	2.25	8.50	5.50
15	6¢ Black	3.50	2.25	8.50	5.00
16	12¢ Violet	3.50	2.25	14.50	8.50

WIN $2000 WORTH OF FREE COVERS and/or STAMPS

In honor of the 2000 Edition of the Brookman Price Guide we will be giving away $2000 in Stamps and/or Covers to the person who in 25 words or less best describes his or her choice for the BEST UNITED STATES stamp issued in the 20th Century. Five renowned Philatelic personalities have accepted the huge undertaking of judging.

Our Judges are:
Robert Lamb, A.P.S. Executive Director
Michael Laurance, Editor & Publisher–Linn's Stamp News
Joseph B. Savarese, Executive Vice-President, ASDA
Betsy Towle – Exec. Director – Postal History Foundation
Les Winick – Prolific Stamp Journalist

The winner will have the option of choosing stamps and/or covers featured on price lists from **2 MAJOR NATIONAL PHILATELIC COMPANIES..... DALE ENTERPRISES, INC.** of Emmaus, Pa. And **BROOKMAN/BARRETT & WORTHEN** of Bedford, NH.

 **BROOKMAN Barrett & Worthen**

All entries must be postmarked no later than
May 31, 2000 to be eligible to win.

STAMP OF THE 20th CENTURY ENTRY FORM

My choice for the best United States Postage Stamp issued in the 20th Century is:

Stamp Choice (Full Description) : _____

The reason I choose this stamp is (25 words or less) : _____
_____
_____

Please print all information clearly.

Name : _____

Address : _____

City, State, Zip : _____   Phone # : _____

If I Win I'll be interested in receiving   Stamps: _____   Covers: _____   Both: _____

No purchase necessary and no age restrictions, however, Judges, employees, and their families, of Brookman/Barrett & Worthen and Dale Enterprises, Inc. are not eligible to win. All entries must be postmarked no later than May 31, 2000 to be eligible to win.

Mail to: Brookman/Barrett & Worthen, 10 Chestnut Drive, Bedford, NH 03110

Looking For Those Missing Stamps, Covers & Supplies
And at Bargain Prices Too!!!
Do You Enjoy Great Articles from the Leading Philatelic Writers?
You'll Find the Answer in the

BROOKMAN TIMES

"The Brookman Times" is published 6 times a year and has ads from leading stamp dealers and articles from leading Philatelic writers, such as Les Winick, Marjory Sente, Barry Schreiber & George Griffenhagen. In addition we have added a classified advertisement section. There are bargains galore and of particular note is that only dealer's who advertise in the Brookman Price Guide can advertise in "The Brookman Times." We feel these dealers are the "cream of the crop" and heartily endorse them.

SOME OF THE LEADING DEALERS YOU WILL FIND IN "THE BROOKMAN TIMES:"

American Philatelic Society
American Topical Assoc.
Artmaster
Brooklyn Gallery
Brookman Barrett & Worthen
Brookman Stamp Co.
Champion Stamp Co., Inc.
Dale Enterprises
D & N Petro
Eric Jackson
Henry Gitner Philatelists, Inc.
Global Stamp News
Michael Jaffe Stamps, Inc.
Kenmore Stamp Co.

Krause Publications
Linn's Stamp News.
James T. McCusker, Inc.
Mekeel's Weekly Stamp News
Alan Miller Stamps
Miller's Stamp Shop
Plate Block Stamp Co.
Gary Posner, Inc.
Regency Stamp, Ltd.
Scott Publishing
Stamp Collector
Stamp Finder
United Nations
U.S. Stamp News
Vidiforms Co., Inc.

Now You Can Get This $9.95 Value FREE!!!

Everyone who purchases a Brookman Price Guide can *receive the Brookman Times FREE*. All you have to do is fill out the coupon below (or a copy of coupon). (If you purchased your copy directly from Brookman/Barrett & Worthen you will automatically receive the Brookman Times)

$5 THIS COUPON IS WORTH $5.00 **$5**
Towards any order over $55.00 from this
2000 Brookman Price Guide

ONE COUPON PER ORDER
Available from:

$5 Brookman/Barrett & Worthen
10 Chestnut Drive
Bedford, NH 03110 **$5**

$10 THIS COUPON IS WORTH $10.00 **$10**
Towards any order over $110.00 from this
2000 Brookman Price Guide

ONE COUPON PER ORDER

Available from:

$10 Brookman/Barrett & Worthen
10 Chestnut Drive
Bedford, NH 03110 **$10**

$10 THIS COUPON IS WORTH $10.00 **$10**
Towards any order over $110.00 from this
2000 Brookman Price Guide

ONE COUPON PER ORDER

Available from:

$10 Brookman/Barrett & Worthen
10 Chestnut Drive
Bedford, NH 03110 **$10**

$10 THIS COUPON IS WORTH $10.00 **$10**
Towards any order over $110 from this
2000 Brookman Price Guide

ONE COUPON PER ORDER

Available from:

$10 Brookman/Barrett & Worthen
10 Chestnut Drive
Bedford, NH 03110 **$10**

$25 THIS COUPON IS WORTH $25.00 **$25**
Towards any order over $275.00 from this
2000 Brookman Price Guide

ONE COUPON PER ORDER

Available from:

$25 Brookman/Barrett & Worthen
10 Chestnut Drive
Bedford, NH 03110 **$25**

$40 THIS COUPON IS WORTH $40.00 **$40**
Towards any order over $450.00 from this
2000 Brookman Price Guide

ONE COUPON PER ORDER

Available from:

$40 Brookman/Barrett & Worthen
10 Chestnut Drive
Bedford, NH 03110 **$40**

HOW TO WRITE YOUR ORDER—PLEASE USE THE ORDER BLANK

Please send the items listed below for which I enclose: $_____ Date: 9/1/98

SHIP TO:
Name: Brian Williams
Address: P.O. Box 4621

City: Louisville
State: KY   Zip: 40216
Phone: (999) 555-1234   Please charge my: Visa ✓ MasterCard_____   Check Enclosed.
Card#: 4620 999-888-777

CREDIT CARD BILLING ADDRESS:
1622 Meadow Lane

City: Louisville
State: KY   Zip: 40216
Expiration Date: 12/98

From Page#	Qty. Wanted	Country and items ordered: Specify Scott Numbers plus first day cover, souvenir card, plate block, mint sheet or other description	Quality Wanted	Unused	Used	Price Each	Leave Blank
4	1	# 229	FVFNH			400.00	
16	1	#740-49 P.B.Set	FVFNH			160.00	
122	1	# 681 FDC, Louisville, KY	Cacheted			35.00	
141	1	#1949 Truman Inaugural				60.00	
154	1	B23 Souvenir Card	Cancelled			50.00	

1. Fill out date, phone#.

2. Print name and address, information including ZIP CODE. Please make sure to include your credit card billing address.

3. Note Minimum order of $20.00.

4. If ordering by Visa or Mastercard, please indicate charge # and expiration date.

5. If paying by check, please make payments in U.S. Funds.

6. Example of how to write up your orders above.

PAY SHIPPING/INSURANCE AS FOLLOWS:		
Total this page	705	00
Total from reverse		
Shipping/Insurance (see chart at left)	8	00
SUBTOTAL	713	00
Sales Tax (if any)		
Less any discounts, refund checks, (coupons) etc.	< 40	00 >
TOTAL ENCLOSED	673	00

PAY SHIPPING/INSURANCE AS FOLLOWS:

Stamps only - $ 3.50

Other orders:

$20.00 to $49.99 - $ 3.50
$50.00 to $199.99 - $ 5.50
$200.00 & over - $ 8.00

SATISFACTION GUARANTEED
MINIMUM ORDER MUST TOTAL AT LEAST $20.00
On orders outside the U.S. additional postage will be billed if necessary

EASY ORDER FORM – 2000 EDITION

Please send the items listed below for which I enclose: $_____ **Date:**_____

SHIP TO: **CREDIT CARD BILLING ADDRESS:**

Name:_____   _____

Address:_____   _____

City:_____   **City:**_____

State:_____ **Zip:**_____   **State:**_____ _____ **Zip:**_____

Phone:_____   **Please charge my: Visa**_____ **MasterCard**_____ _____**Check Enclosed.**

Card#:_____   **Expiration Date:**_____

MINIMUM ORDER MUST BE $20.00

From Page#	Qty. Wanted	Country and items ordered: Specify Scott Numbers plus first day cover, souvenir card, plate block, mint sheet or other description	Qty. Wanted	Unused	Used	Price Each	Leave Blank

PAY SHIPPING/INSURANCE AS FOLLOWS:		
	Total this page	
	Total from reverse	
Stamps only - $ 3.50	Total from reverse	
Other orders:	Shipping/Insurance (see chart at left	
$20.00 to $49.99 - $ 3.50	**SUBTOTAL**	
$50.00 to $199.99 - $ 5.50	Sales Tax (if any)	
$200.00 & over - $ 8.00	Less any discounts, refund checks, coupons, etc.	
	TOTAL ENCLOSED	

SATISFACTION GUARANTEED
MINIMUM ORDER MUST TOTAL AT LEAST $20.00
On orders outside the U.S. additional postage will be billed if necessary

Easy Order Form (continued)							
From Page#	Qty. Wanted	Country and items ordered: Specify Scott Numbers plus first day cover, souvenir card, plate block, mint sheet or other description	Qty. Wanted	Unused	Used	Price Each	Leave Blank
		Total This Page					

EASY ORDER FORM – 2000 EDITION

Please send the items listed below for which I enclose: $_____ Date:_____

SHIP TO: **CREDIT CARD BILLING ADDRESS:**

Name: _____   _____

Address: _____   _____

City:_____   City:_____

State: _____ Zip:_____   State: _____ _____ Zip:_____

Phone:_____ Please charge my: Visa_____ MasterCard_____ _____Check Enclosed.

Card#:_____   Expiration Date:_____

MINIMUM ORDER MUST BE $20.00

From Page#	Qty. Wanted	Country and items ordered: Specify Scott Numbers plus first day cover, souvenir card, plate block, mint sheet or other description	Qty. Wanted	Unused	Used	Price Each	Leave Blank

PAY SHIPPING/INSURANCE AS FOLLOWS:

Stamps only - $ 3.50
Other orders:
$20.00 to $49.99 - $ 3.50
$50.00 to $199.99 - $ 5.50
$200.00 & over - $ 8.00

Total this page _____

Total from reverse _____

Total from reverse _____

Shipping/Insurance (see chart at left _____

SUBTOTAL _____

Sales Tax (if any) _____

Less any discounts, refund checks, coupons, etc. _____

TOTAL ENCLOSED

SATISFACTION GUARANTEED
MINIMUM ORDER MUST TOTAL AT LEAST $20.00
On orders outside the U.S. additional postage will be billed if necessary

From Page#	Qty. Wanted	Country and items ordered: Specify Scott Numbers plus first day cover, souvenir card, plate block, mint sheet or other description	Qty. Wanted	Unused	Used	Price Each	Leave Blank
			Total This Page				

EASY ORDER FORM – 2000 EDITION

Please send the items listed below for which I enclose: $_____ **Date:**_____

SHIP TO: **CREDIT CARD BILLING ADDRESS:**

Name: _____   _____

Address: _____   _____

City:_____   **City:**_____

State: _____ **Zip:**_____   **State:** _____ _____ **Zip:**_____

Phone: _____ **Please charge my: Visa**_____ **MasterCard**_____ _____**Check Enclosed.**

Card#: _____   **Expiration Date:**_____

MINIMUM ORDER MUST BE $20.00

From Page#	Qty. Wanted	Country and items ordered: Specify Scott Numbers plus first day cover, souvenir card, plate block, mint sheet or other description	Qty. Wanted	Unused	Used	Price Each	Leave Blank

PAY SHIPPING/INSURANCE AS FOLLOWS:

Stamps only - $ 3.50
Other orders:
$20.00 to $49.99 - $ 3.50
$50.00 to $199.99 - $ 5.50
$200.00 & over - $ 8.00

Total this page _____

Total from reverse _____

Total from reverse _____

Shipping/Insurance (see chart at left _____

SUBTOTAL _____

Sales Tax (if any) _____

Less any discounts, refund checks, coupons, etc. _____

TOTAL ENCLOSED

SATISFACTION GUARANTEED
MINIMUM ORDER MUST TOTAL AT LEAST $20.00
On orders outside the U.S. additional postage will be billed if necessary

From Page#	Qty. Wanted	Country and items ordered: Specify Scott Numbers plus first day cover, souvenir card, plate block, mint sheet or other description	Qty. Wanted	Unused	Used	Price Each	Leave Blank
				Total This Page			

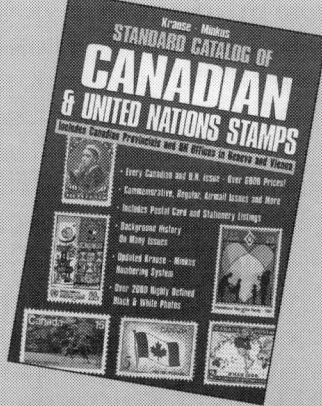

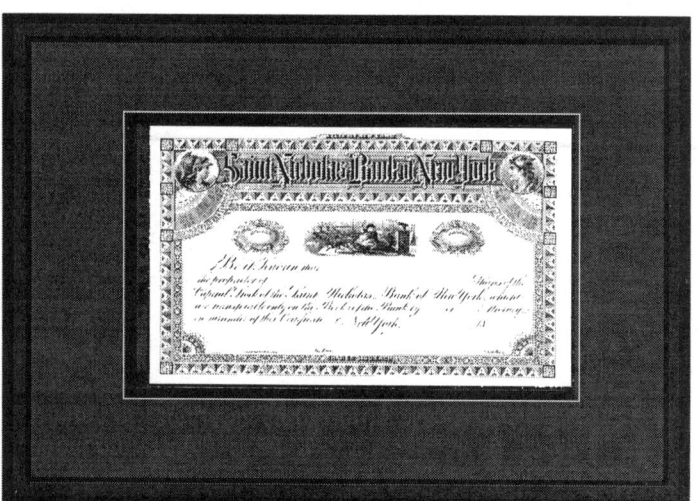

<u>24 HOURS A DAY...</u>

Over 400,000 Individual Stamps For Sale Now At Philately's Superstore OnThe Internet.

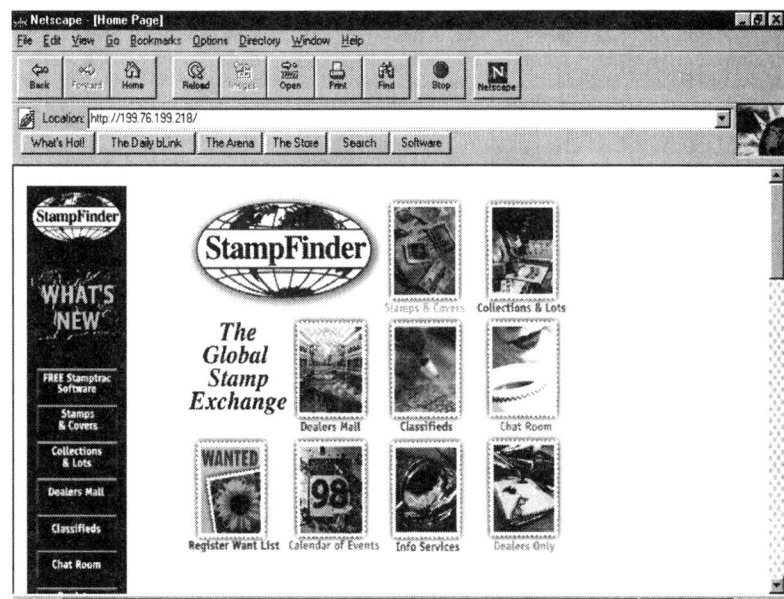

We just made stamp buying easier at our Newly-Updated Internet website—the stamp store of the 21st century.

• **Use our "shopping cart" system** and secure credit card transaction process to purchase the stamps you need.

• **View images in full color** from over 400,000 Stamps & Covers For Sale By Country Or Topic

• **WE CROSS-CODE ITEMS BY MICHEL AND YVERT AND BY TOPIC**—thus giving topical collectors an unlimited range of purchasing opportunities.

• **Want List Service.** Enter your wants with us while you're online. We'll e-mail you whenever items you need appear on our site!

• **FREE StampTRAC Inventory Software.** The world's most widely-used collector inventory application is yours to download **free** when you visit our site.

• **CLASSIFIED ADS.** Put your own offers to buy and sell into our classified ad section. It's the fastest-growing international marketplace for all collectors everywhere.

• **THE INTERNATIONAL PHILATELIC REGISTRY.** Register the most important items in your collection and place them into this international registry of philately's greatest collectibles.

• **THE CHAT ROOMS.** You and your club or specialty group are free to participate in your own live chats in this special section.

• **STAMPS.NET—Philately's Electronic Magazine.** Visit this unque (and free) online magazine for the stamp collector.

• **StampTRAC—Our Amazing FREE Inventory Software.** Get a free download of the world's easiest-to-use stamp collection inventory software application!

• **Our "BEST BUYS" GUIDES.** Purchase the most authoritative series of books ever published on selecting stamps for investment purposes.

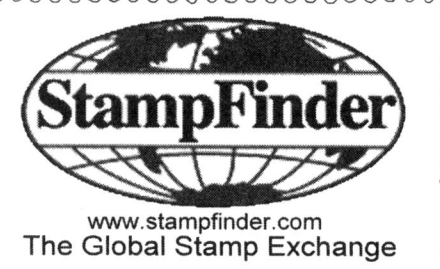

www.stampfinder.com
The Global Stamp Exchange

6175 NW 153rd St.
Suite 201
Miami Lakes FL 33014
(305) 557-1135
Fax: 557-1454
usid@stampfinder.com

Collect New Issues Or Stamps By Topic? Search our site for your favorite topical & thematic specialties—and buy from a wide range of brand NEW issues from around the world!

WITH THE DAWNING OF A NEW CENTURY
COMES THE OPPORTUNITY TO BROADEN YOUR HORIZONS
WITH THE STAMPS OF THE UNITED NATIONS

Only United Nations stamps can take you around the world
To places you might never have been
As these stamps tell the stories
Of the United Nations and its specialized agencies.

Travel to the four corners of the earth to marvel at World Heritage sites,
Support the protection of endangered species of flora and fauna,
Soar into space, wander through the rainforests or celebrate the oceans,
Protect human rights, strive for peace,
And create a better world for all.
These are the stories of United Nations stamps.

**UNITED NATIONS STAMPS
ARE YOUR WINDOW TO THE WORLD**

UNITED NATIONS   BROOK
POSTAL ADMINISTRATION
P.O. BOX 5900
GRAND CENTRAL STATION
NEW YORK, N.Y. 10163-9992

Please send information on how I can
collect United Nations stamps.

Name _____

Address _____

City _____

State _____ Zip _____

**UNITED NATIONS POSTAL ADMINISTRATION
UNITED NATIONS, NEW YORK, N.Y. 10017
http://www.un.org/Depts/unpa**

Brookman's Classifieds

Brookman's Classifieds

U.S. COVERS - Sports History

OWN A PIECE OF SPORTS HISTORY

The following 1999 covers are attractively illustrated and are sold with a money back GUARANTY.

ONLY 50 of each were serviced................ PRICE $20. Each

1 - Baseball All Star Game Boston, July 13th
2 - U.S. Women's Soccer World Cup Champs, Pasadena July 10th3
3 - Indianapolis 500 Auto Race, May 30th
4 - PGA U.S. Open Pinehurst NC, June 17th
5 - PGA The Masters Augusta GA, April 11th
6 - Joe Di Maggio Date of Death cover Hollywood, florida March 8th
7 - Kentucky Derby Louisville, May 1st

Herb Meisels Box 230143   New York, NY 10023

STAMP STORES

B.J.'s STAMPS

6342 West Bell Road
Glendale, Arizona 85308
Phone (623) 878-2080
Fax   (623) 412-3456

U.S. Want Lists Filled At 20% Off Brookman Better Foreign at 30% Off Scott. Top Prices paid for collections

 Same Location

Fireside Stamp Company
WORLDWIDE STAMPS FOR COLLECTORS
BID BOARD – SUPPLIES – COVERS
INSURANCE & ESTATE APPRAISALS
COLLECTIONS & ACCUMULATIONS
BOUGHT & SOLD
Mike Campbell – Owner
A.S.D.A. – A.P.S.
(Over 35 years exp.)
302 Town & Country Village
Sunnyvale, Ca. 94086
(408) 720-9779 Fax 720-9754

US STAMPS FOR SALE

FREE Price List Available
On mint & used singles, plate blocks, year sets, postal stationary & postal cards.
D&N Petro
Renaissance Building
933 Liberty Ave. Suite 402
Pittsburgh, Pa. 15222

We offer you "Premium Quality Service" At reasonable prices for the very best in early quality stamps. Call bob Prager to discuss your want list and we'll send you true-to-life color copies of in-stock items that meet your needs.
Gary Posner, Inc. P.O. Box 340362
Brooklyn, NY 11234

Unused

MINT SOUVENIR SHEETS AT LOW PRICES

CARLSON STAMPS
15 W. College St. - Dept. BG
Arlington Heights, IL 60004
Fax (847)255-1605

Send for **FREE PRICE LIST**

U.S. STAMPS FOR SALE

USED

Send for our catalog of Used U.S. Stamps.
(77¢ postage appreciated) Our extensive inventory includes stamps from 1-771, Airmails, Back of Book & Duck Stamps, all at low prices.
Alan Miller Stamps

PLATE BLOCKS

Send for our *PRICE LIST* from America's premier plate block dealer. Largest selection at very competitive prices, also with quick turnaround service.

PLATE BLOCK STAMP CO.
1-800-829-6777
P.O. Box 6417B, Leawood, Ks 66206
www.plateblockstamps.com

Revenues

ACCESSORIES

Your Ultimate Source for
Coin & Stamp Supplies,
Available with savings of
10-40% OFF Retail Prices.
Send for our catalog
Brooklyn Gallery
Coin & Stamps, Inc.
8725 – 4th Ave., Brooklyn, NY 11209
(718) 745-5701
www.brooklyngallery.com

ACCESSORIES

STAMP COLLECTORS

welcome

We have a nice sample for you.

Our product, the Showgard® mount, is the accepted standard in the hobby for truly protecting postage stamps. If you select Showgard mounts for your stamps early in your collection career it will save much remounting time later. The evidence is clear that collectors eventually switch to Showgard mounts.

Confirm this with any experienced collector. Or proceed directly to your neighborhood dealer who will advise and sell you that important first package of Showgard mounts-the stamp mounts that need no change.

The promised sample is available free, specify "Welcome Kit" and write:

VIDIFORMS COMPANY, INC.
Showgard House
115 No. Rte. 9W
Congers, NY 10920

STAMP SOCIETIES

Brookman's Classifieds

WANTED TO BUY	INTERNET RELATED	INTERNET RELATED
	Online Services	Online Services

SHOWGARD®

THE STAMP MOUNTING SPECIALISTS

Item Code	QTY	Description	Pcs. in Pkg.	Price $	Total
		Cut Style	40	2.75	
C 50/31		US Jumbo Singles-Horizontal	40	2.75	
CV31/50		Same - Vertical	40	2.75	
J 40/25		US Comm - Horizontal	40	2.75	
JV 25/40		Same - Vertical	40	2.75	
E 22/25		US Regular Issues	40	2.75	
EH25/22		Same Horizontal	40	2.75	
T 25/27		US Famous Americans	40	2.75	
U 33/27		UN and Germany	40	2.75	
N 40/27		United Nations	40	2.75	
AH41/31		US Semi-Jumbo, Gershwin, etc.	40	2.75	
DH 52/36		US Duck Stamps	30	2.75	
		Sets			
US 2		Cut Style with Tray	320	16.75	
US 3		Strip Style with Tray	75	24.95	
		Plate Blocks & Covers			
67/25		US Coil Strips of 3	40	4.75	
57/55		Regular Issue US	25	4.75	
106/55		US 3¢, 4¢ Commems	20	4.75	
105/57		US Giori Press, Modern	20	4.75	
127/70		US Jumbo Issues	10	4.75	
140/89		Postal Cards	10	4.75	
165/94		First Day Covers	10	4.75	
		Strips 215mm Long			
20		Mini Stamps US, etc.	22	5.95	
22		Narrow US, Airs	22	5.95	
24		GB and Canada, early US	22	5.95	
25		US Commem & Reg. Issue	22	5.95	
27		US Famous Americans & UN	22	5.95	
28		Switzerland & Liechtenstein	22	5.95	
30		US Jamestown, Foreign	22	5.95	
31		US Squares & Semi-Jumbos	22	5.95	
33		GB Issues, Misc. Foreign	22	5.95	
36		Duck Stamps, Misc. Foreign	15	5.95	
39		US Magsaysay, Misc. Foreign	15	5.95	
41		US Vertical Comm., Israel Tabs	15	5.95	
44		US Hatteras Quartet	15	5.95	
48		Canada Reg. Issue & Comm Blks.	15	5.95	
50		US Plain Blocks of 4	15	5.95	
52		France Paintings	15	5.95	
57		US Comm Plate Blocks (4)	15	5.95	
61		Souvenir Sheets, Tab Singles	15	5.95	
		Strips 240mm Long			
63		US Squares, Plain Blocks (4)	10	6.75	
66		Israel Plate Blocks, etc.	10	6.75	
68		Canadian Plate Blks, $1 Fundy, etc.	10	6.75	
74		UN Inscription Blocks (4)	10	6.75	
80		US Comm, Plain Blocks (4)	10	6.75	
82		UN Chagell SS, Canada, Plt Blks.	10	6.75	
84		Israel Tab Blocks, etc.	10	6.75	
89		UN Inscription Blocks (6)	10	6.75	
100		US Squares - Plate Blocks	7	6.75	
120		Miniature Sheets	7	6.75	
		Strips 264mm Long			
70		US Jumbo Plate Blocks	10	9.75	
91		GB Souvenir Sheets	10	9.75	

Item Code	QTY	Description	Pcs. in Pkg.	Price $	Total
105		GB Blocks, Covers, Cards	10	9.75	
107		US Plate No. Strip (20)	10	9.75	
111		US Floating Nos. Plate Strips (20)	10	11.25	
127		US UPU & LBJ Plate Blocks (16)	10	13.75	
137		GB Coronation, UN SS	10	14.50	
158		Souvenir Shts, Apollo Soyuz Plt. Blk.	10	15.25	
175		Special Issue Full Sheets	5	9.75	
188		US Miniature Sheets	5	10.75	
198		US Miniature Sheets	5	10.95	
		Miscellaneous			
MPK		Assortment No. 22 thru No. 41	12	4.75	
MPKII		Assortment No. 76 thru No. 171	15	19.25	
Group AB		US SS to 1975, Not W. Plains	11	5.25	
265/231		Full Sheets and Souvenir Cards	5	14.25	
		Blocks			
260/25		Plate # Coil Strips	25	8.25	
260/40		US Postal People Full Strip	10	6.50	
260/46		US Vending Booklets	10	6.95	
260/55		US 13¢ Eagle Full Strip	10	6.50	
260/59		US Double Press Reg. Issue Strip (20)	10	6.50	
111/91		Columbian Souvenir Sheets	6	2.95	
229/131		WW II Souvenir Sheets	5	6.95	
187/144		UN Flag Sheetlets	10	12.25	
204/153		US Bicentennial & W. Plains SS	5	6.95	
120/207		Ameripex Presidential Sheetlets	4	4.75	
		Accessories			
506		Desert Magic Drying Book 8½ x5¾	1	4.95	
507		Desert Magic II, Like 506, double height	1	6.95	
602		Guillotine "EXCAL" Mini	1	19.95	
604		Guillotine "ORTHOMATIC" Major	1	39.95	
790		"At Home" Organizer	1	13.95	
793		Modular Drawer Set	1	22.50	
894		FDC Album US size, Blk, Tan, Red	1	18.95	
894C		Closed End Slip Case for #894, Blk	1	9.50	
895		FDC Album GB & Canada size, Blk, Tan, Red	1	19.95	
896		FDC Album #10 Size, Blk, Tan, Red		20.95	
900		Large Leather Case for #902, #907, #908, #909	1	4.50	
901		Tongs, Point Tip	1	5.50	
902		Tongs, Point Tip, Professional	1	6.95	
907		Tongs, Angled Tip, Professional	1	6.95	
908		Tongs, Sharp Point, Professional	1	6.95	
909		Tongs, Spade Tip, Professional	1	6.95	

Showgard Dark Background - All Strips 264mm Long

$1.50 #76 #109 #115 #117 #121 #129 #131 #135 #143 #149

$1.75 Ea. #147 #151 #163 #167 #171 #201

Protect stamp values in Showgard!

AVAILABLE FROM DEALERS EVERYWHERE

Or
Vidiforms Co., Inc.
Showgard House
115 North Rt 9W
Congers, NY 10920
914-268-4005